Lecture Notes in Computer Science 3328

Commenced Publication in 1973
Founding and Former Series Editors:
Gerhard Goos, Juris Hartmanis, and Jan van Leeuwen

Kamal Lodaya   Meena Mahajan (Eds.)

FSTTCS 2004:
Foundations of
Software Technology
and Theoretical
Computer Science

24th International Conference
Chennai, India, December 16-18, 2004
Proceedings

 Springer

Volume Editors

Kamal Lodaya
Meena Mahajan
Institute of Mathematical Sciences
CIT Campus, Taramani, Chennai 600 113, India
E-mail: {kamal, meena}@imsc.res.in

Library of Congress Control Number: 2004116533

CR Subject Classification (1998): F.3, D.3, F.4, F.2, F.1, G.2

ISSN 0302-9743
ISBN 3-540-24058-6 Springer Berlin Heidelberg New York

Springer is a part of Springer Science+Business Media

springeronline.com

© Springer-Verlag Berlin Heidelberg 2004
Printed in Germany

Typesetting: Camera-ready by author, data conversion by Scientific Publishing Services, Chennai, India
Printed on acid-free paper   SPIN: 11365822   06/3142   5 4 3 2 1 0

Professor Rani Siromoney

Rani Siromoney is one of the foremost theoretical computer scientists in India and a leading authority on Formal Languages and Automata Theory. Over a period spanning four decades, she has made tremendous technical contributions to the field through her research. She has also inspired generations of students in Chennai with her teaching and has been responsible for building up a community of dedicated teachers and researchers in this part of India to carry forward her vision.

Prof. Siromoney has served on the Editorial Board of the journals *Theoretical Computer Science* and *International Journal of Foundations of Computer Science* and has headed several international collaborative research projects. She also served on the Programme Committee for the first 10 editions of FSTTCS.

She is currently Professor Emeritus at Madras Christian College, the illustrious institution where she has spent most of her professional life. She continues to play an active role in research and teaching as an Adjunct Professor at the Chennai Mathematical Institute.

Preface

The international conference on the Foundations of Software Technology and Theoretical Computer Science (FSTTCS) is the longest-running conference on computer science in India, and is organized under the aegis of the Indian Association for Research in Computing Science, IARCS. Since its inception in 1981, the conference (held annually in the month of December) has helped in nurturing and creating an environment for the exchange of ideas amongst the research community in the country, by attracting top scientists around the world to the conference. This volume contains the proceedings of the 24th FSTTCS conference held in December 2004.

A strong point of the FSTTCS programmes has been excellent invited talks by eminent computer scientists of international renown. Continuing this tradition, this FSTTCS featured invited talks by Javier Esparza, Piotr Indyk, Pavel A. Pevzner, John C. Reynolds, and Denis Thérien. We thank our invited speakers for readily agreeing to come to FSTTCS, and for providing write-ups for the proceedings.

It is our pleasure that IARCS chose to honor Prof. Rani Siromoney at this conference, on the occasion of her 75th birthday. The influence she has wielded (and the impact she has exerted) in Indian theoretical computer science is tremendous, and the tribute is fitting and richly deserved. We thank R.K. Shyamasundar for chairing the special session in her honor, and Kamala Krithivasan and K.G. Subramanian for speaking at the session.

The 24th FSTTCS conference attracted 176 submissions with authors from 35 countries. We thank the authors for their interest in the conference.

The Programme Committee (PC) decided that 21 submissions were out of scope. The authors were immediately informed that they could submit their work elsewhere. The remaining papers went through a rigorous refereeing process; 526 referee reports were produced, some by the 24 PC members themselves. The bulk of the reports were from 328 other referees from 23 countries.

A conference stands or falls on its refereeing. On behalf of the PC, we express our immense appreciation for the time and effort spent by the referees in assessing submissions and writing (often meticulous) reports.

Referees do not always agree on the merits of a paper. During August it was the job of the PC to arrive at a consensus and select papers for the conference. We thank our PC colleagues for their quality time and effort.

And of course our thanks go to the 85 authors (hailing from 12 countries) of the 38 contributed submissions that form most of this volume. We also thank them for ensuring that at least one author came to the conference to present the paper.

We thank Springer for agreeing to publish these proceedings in their prestigious Lecture Notes in Computer Science series, and for their professional management of the publication.

Satellite workshops/tutorials have by now become a standard feature at the FSTTCS conferences. This year, the conference had two satellite workshops: a Workshop on Algorithms for Dynamic Data, organized by Pankaj Agarwal and S. Muthukrishnan, and a Workshop on Logics for Dynamic Data, organized by Uday Reddy. We thank the workshop coordinators for putting together these very interesting workshops, and the workshop speakers for agreeing to give talks at the workshops.

We thank the Institute of Mathematical Sciences for readily agreeing to provide partial financial support for the conference. We are a rather small institution, but the administration here worked very hard to ensure that the organization was smooth. Our colleagues in the theoretical computer science group, along with colleagues at the Chennai Mathematical Institute, put in a lot of effort in coordinating all the work. Our graduate students cheerfully volunteered for any jobs which needed to be done, and did them well. We thank them all.

FSTTCS uses its own conference software, developed initially by V Vinay and modified in successive years. This year Jaikumar Radhakrishnan programmed the web-based submission, and the IMSc system administrators, G. Subramoniam and Raveendra Reddy, handled the installation. We thank them for being always at hand for help, and taking care of one request after another.

The silver jubilee conference in December 2005 will be held, for the first time in FSTTCS's history, in the city of Kolkata. We look forward to seeing you there!

December 2004   Kamal Lodaya and Meena Mahajan

Organization

The 24th FSTTCS Conference and associated workshops were held at the Institute of Mathematical Sciences, Chennai, India during December 13–18, 2004.

Programme Committee

S. Arun-Kumar *(IIT Delhi)*
Gérard Boudol *(INRIA Sophia)*
Gerth S. Brodal *(Univ. Aarhus)*
Harry Buhrman *(CWI)*
Chandra Chekuri *(Bell Labs MH)*
E. Allen Emerson *(UT Austin)*
Valentin Goranko *(RAU)*
Deepak Kapur *(UNM)*
Nils Klarlund *(Bell Labs MH)*
K. Narayan Kumar *(CMI)*
Kamal Lodaya *(IMSc)*, Co-chair
Meena Mahajan *(IMSc)*, Co-chair

S. Muthukrishnan *(Rutgers)*
S.P. Pal *(IIT Kharagpur)*
R. Ramanujam *(IMSc)*
Uday Reddy *(Univ. Birmingham)*
Ashok Sreenivas *(TRDDC Pune)*
Venkatesh Srinivasan *(Univ. Victoria)*
C.R. Subramanian *(IMSc)*
Amnon Ta-Shma *(TAU)*
K. Varadarajan *(Univ. Iowa)*
Sundar Vishwanathan *(IIT Bombay)*
Heribert Vollmer *(Univ. Hannover)*
Pascal Weil *(LaBRI)*

Referees

Dave Clarke	Alain Griffault	Rajeev Kumar
Ken Clarkson	Martin Grohe	Ravi Kumar
Loek Cleophas	Philippe de Groote	V.S. Anil Kumar
Thomas Colcombet	Roberto Grossi	Orna Kupferman
Don Coppersmith	Sumit Gulwani	Dietrich Kuske
Véronique Cortier	Gopal Gupta	Marcel Kyas
Bruno Courcelle	Dan Gutfreund	Jens Lagergren
Jean-Michel Couvreur	Stefan Haar	Jim Laird
Silvia Crafa	Ramesh Hariharan	Laks V.S. Lakshmanan
Nadia Creignou	John Havlicek	Klaus-Jörn Lange
Deepak D'Souza	Hugo Herbelin	Martin Lange
Wim van Dam	Kouichi Hirata	Troy Lee
Dennis Dams	Wiebe van der Hoek	Boaz Leskes
Sandip Das	Hardi Hungar	Paul Blain Levy
Jyotirmoy Deshmukh	S. Iyer	Cedric Lhoussaine
Tamal Dey	Riko Jacob	Sachin Lodha
Martin Dietzfelbinger	Lalita Jategaonkar	Satya Lokam
Catalin Dima	Jagadeesan	Zhang Louxin
A.A. Diwan	David Janin	Etienne Lozes
Irène Durand	T.S. Jayram	Olivier Ly
Rogier van Eijk	Emmanuel Jeandel	Anders Möller
John Ellis	Thierry Joly	P. Madhusudan
Javier Esparza	Mathai Joseph	Anil Maheshwari
Harald Fecher	Marcin Jurdziński	Rupak Majumdar
David Fink	Charanjit S. Jutla	Oded Maler
Riccardo Focardi	Johannes Köbler	P.K. Manivannan
Lance Fortnow	Ata Kaban	Shawn Manley
Gudmund S. Frandsen	Valentine Kabanets	Fabio Martinelli
Stephen Freund	Fairouz Kamareddine	Ralph Matthes
Carsten Fuhrmann	Michael Kaminski	Guy McCusker
Anna Gal	Bruce Kapron	Dieter van Melkebeek
Nicola Galesi	Sujatha Kashyap	Bernd Meyer
Didier Galmiche	Joost-Pieter Katoen	John-Jules Meyer
Paul Gastin	T. Kavitha	Pascal Michel
Simon J. Gay	Sanjeev Khanna	Sushmita Mitra
Konstantinos Georgatos	Victor Khomenko	Neeraj Mittal
Sasthi Charan Ghosh	Astrid Kiehn	Swarup Mohalik
Subir Ghosh	Gerwin Klein	Jonathan W. Moody
Sukumar Ghosh	Sven Kosub	Matthew Morgenstern
Jonathon Giffin	Michal Koucky	Gabriel Moruz
Christian Glaßer	Hugo Krawczyk	David Mount
Shantanu Godbole	S.N. Krishna	Madhavan Mukund
Rodolfo Gomez	Michael Krivelevich	Andrzej Murawski
Partha P. Goswami	Antonín Kučera	Neil V. Murray
Mohamed G. Gouda	Vinay Kulkarni	Anca Muscholl

Wendy Myrvold
Mayur Naik
Kedar Namjoshi
Subhas Chandra Nandy
Giri Narasimhan
N.S. Narayanaswamy
Vijay Natarajan
David Naumann
Ashwin Nayak
Mikhail Nesterenko
Rolf Niedermeier
Johan Nilsson
Tobias Nipkow
Hans de Nivelle
Gethin Norman
Peter O'Hearn
David von Oheimb
Hitoshi Ohsaki
Luke Ong
Alon Orlitsky
Martin Otto
Joel Ouaknine
Eric Pacuit
Jens Palsberg
Girish Keshav Palshikar
P.K. Pandya
Marc Pantel
Marc Pauly
Gheorghe Paun
Benjamin Pierce
Denis Poitrenaud
Emmanuel Polonovski
Sanjiva Prasad
Pavel Pudlak
David Pym
Jaikumar
  Radhakrishnan
C.R. Ramakrishnan
Rajiv Raman
Venkatesh Raman
S. Ramesh
Abhiram Ranade
M.R.K. Krishna Rao
S. Srinivasa Rao
B. Ravikumar
Rahul Ray
Sandip Ray

Ran Raz
Sreedhar Reddy
Kenneth W. Regan
Laurent Regnier
Horst Reichel
Jan Reimann
Steffen Reith
Greg Restall
Ingrid Rewitzky
Eike Ritter
Willem-Paul de Roever
Philipp Rohde
Shmuel (Mooly) Sagiv
Alex Samorodnitsky
Prahladavaradan
  Sampath
Sudeshna Sarkar
Jayalal Sarma
Saket Saurabh
Anuj Saxena
Uwe Schöning
Christian Scheideler
Rick Schlichting
Holger Schlingloff
Alan Schmitt
Philippe Schnoebelen
Roy Schwartz
Alper Sen
Pranab Sen
Sandeep Sen
Micaela Serra
Olivier Serre
Anil Seth
Natarajan Shankar
Priti Shankar
R.K. Shyamasundar
Sudhir Kumar Singh
Bhabani Prasad Sinha
Aravinda Sistla
D. Sivakumar
Steve Skiena
Milind Sohoni
Robert Spalek
Jeremy Sproston
Ulrike Stege
Colin Stirling
Mariëlle Stoelinga

Thomas Streicher
Srihari Sukumaran
S.P. Suresh
Grégoire Sutre
Sebastiaan Terwijn
Hendrik Tews
Prasannaa Thati
Denis Thérien
P.S. Thiagarajan
Hayo Thielecke
Wolfgang Thomas
Cesare Tinelli
Sophie Tison
Jacobo Toran
Leen Torenvliet
Csaba Toth
Tayssir Touili
Richard Trefler
Stavros Tripakis
John Tromp
Pascal Urso
Moshe Vardi
G. Venkatesh
R. Venkatesh
Nikolai Vereshchagin
S. Vijayakumar
Janis Voigtländer
Adnan Vora
Klaus Wagner
Thomas Wahl
Nico Wallmeier
Igor Walukiewicz
Peng-Jun Wan
Yusu Wang
John Watrous
Stephanie Wehner
Thomas Wilke
Stefan Wöhrle
Ronald de Wolf
Hongseok Yang
Greta Yorsh
Nobuko Yoshida
Wiesław Zielonka
Pascal Zimmer
Uri Zwick

Table of Contents

Invited Papers

Contributed Papers

Genome Halving Problem Revisited

Max A. Alekseyev and Pavel A. Pevzner

Department of Computer Science and Engineering,
University of California at San Diego,
La Jolla, CA 92093-0114, U.S.A.
{maxal, ppevzner}@cs.ucsd.edu

Abstract. The Genome Halving Problem is motivated by the whole genome duplication events in molecular evolution that double the gene content of a genome and result in a perfect duplicated genome that contains two identical copies of each chromosome. The genome then becomes a subject to rearrangements resulting in some rearranged duplicated genome. The Genome Halving Problem (first introduced and solved by Nadia El-Mabrouk and David Sankoff) is to reconstruct the ancestral pre-duplicated genome from the rearranged duplicated genome. The El-Mabrouk–Sankoff algorithm is rather complex and in this paper we present a simpler algorithm that is based on a generalization of the notion of the breakpoint graph to the case of duplicated genomes. This generalization makes the El-Mabrouk–Sankoff result more transparent and promises to be useful in future studies of genome duplications.

1 Introduction

The Genome Halving Problem is motivated by the *whole genome duplication* events in molecular evolution [13], [17], [15], [12], [5]. These dramatic evolutionary events double the gene content of a genome R and result in a *perfect duplicated genome* $R \oplus R$ that contains two identical copies of each chromosome. The genome then becomes a subject to rearrangements that shuffle the genes in $R \oplus R$ resulting in some *rearranged duplicated genome* P. The *Genome Halving Problem* is to reconstruct the ancestral *pre-duplicated genome* R from the rearranged duplicated genome P (Fig. 1a).

From the algorithmic perspective, the genome is a collection of chromosomes, and each chromosome is a sequence over a finite alphabet (depending on the scale, the alphabet may vary from *genes* to *synteny blocks*). DNA has two strands and genes on a chromosome have directionality that reflects the strand of the genes. We represent the order and directions of the genes on each chromosome as a sequence of *signed elements*, i.e., elements with signs "+" and "-".

For the sake of simplicity, we focus on the *unichromosomal* case, where the genomes consist of just one chromosome and assume that the genomes are *circular*. A unichromosomal genome where each gene appears in a single copy sometimes is referred to as *signed permutation*.

K. Lodaya and M. Mahajan (Eds.): FSTTCS 2004, LNCS 3328, pp. 1–15, 2004.

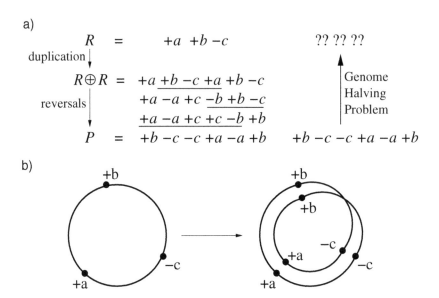

a)

$$R \quad = \quad +a \; +b \; -c \qquad\qquad ?? \; ?? \; ??$$

duplication $\downarrow$

$$R \oplus R = +a \; \underline{+b \; -c \; +a} \; +b \; -c$$
$$+a \; \underline{-a \; +c \; -b} \; +b \; -c$$
$$+a \; -a \; +c \; \underline{+c \; -b} \; +b$$
$$P \quad = \quad +b \; -c \; -c \; +a \; -a \; +b \qquad +b \; -c \; -c \; +a \; -a \; +b$$

reversals $\downarrow$

Genome Halving Problem $\uparrow$

b)

Fig. 1. a) Whole genome duplication of genome $R = +a+b-c$ into a perfect duplicated genome $R \oplus R = +a+b-c+a+b-c$ followed by three reversals. b) Whole genome duplication of a circular genome

For unichromosomal genomes the rearrangements are limited to *reversals*. The reversal (i, j) over genome $x_1 x_2 \ldots x_n$ "flips" genes $x_i \ldots x_j$ as follows:

$$\overrightarrow{x_1 \ldots x_{i-1} \quad x_i \quad x_{i+1} \ldots \quad x_j x_{j+1} \ldots x_n}$$
$$\downarrow$$
$$\overleftarrow{x_1 \ldots x_{i-1} \; -x_j \; - \; x_{j-1} \; \cdots \; - \; x_i} x_{j+1} \ldots x_n.$$

The *reversal distance* between two genomes is defined as the minimal number of reversals required to transform one genome into another.

The *whole genome duplication* is a concatenation of the genome R with itself resulting in a *perfect duplicated genome* $R \oplus R$ (Fig. 1b). The genome $R \oplus R$ becomes a subject to reversals that change the order and signs of the genes and transforms $R \oplus R$ into a *duplicated* genome P. The Genome Halving Problem is formulated as follows.

Genome Halving Problem. *Given a duplicated genome P, recover the ancestral pre-duplicated genome R minimizing the reversal distance from the perfect duplicated genome $R \oplus R$ to the duplicated genome P.*

The Genome Halving Problem was solved in a series of papers by El-Mabrouk and Sankoff [6], [7], [8] culminating in a rather complex algorithm in [9]. The El-Mabrouk-Sankoff algorithm is one of the most technically challenging results in bioinformatics and its proof spans almost 40 pages in [9] (covering

both unichromosomal and multichromosomal genomes). In this paper we revisit the El-Mabrouk–Sankoff work and present a simpler algorithm for the case
of unichromosomal genomes.[1]

The paper is organized as follows. Section 2 reviews the Hannenhalli-Pevzner
theory and formulates the duality theorem for genomes without duplicated genes.
Section 3 discusses the problem of finding rearrangement distance between duplicated genomes and extension of the Hannenhalli-Pevzner theory to this case.
Section 4 introduces the concept of the contracted breakpoint graph for duplicated genomes. In section 5 we study cycle decompositions of contracted breakpoint graphs in the case when one of the genomes is perfect duplicated. Finally,
in section 6 we present our new Genome Halving Algorithm.

2   Hannenhalli-Pevzner Theory

A duality theorem and a polynomial algorithm for computing reversal distance
between two signed permutations was first proposed by Hannenhalli and Pevzner
[10]. The algorithm was further simplified and improved in a series of papers
[3], [11], [1], [16] using the *breakpoint graph* construction introduced in [2]. Recently, Bergeron et al., [4] proposed yet another simplification of the Hannenhalli-
Pevzner proof that does not use the breakpoint graph construction.

Let P be a circular signed permutation. Bafna and Pevzner [2] described a
transformation of a signed permutation on n elements into an unsigned permutation on $2n$ elements by substituting every element x in the signed permutation
by two elements x^t and x^h in the unsigned permutation.[2] Each element $+x$ in the
permutation P is replaced with $x^t x^h$, and each element $-x$ is replaced with $x^h x^t$
resulting in an unsigned permutation P'. For example, a permutation $+a + b - c$
will be transformed into $a^t a^h b^t b^h c^h c^t$. Element x^t is called an *obverse* of element
x^h, and vice versa.

Let P and Q be two circular signed permutations on the same set of elements
$\mathcal{G}$, and P' and Q' be corresponding unsigned permutations. The breakpoint
graph[3] $G = G(P, Q)$ is defined on the set of vertices $V = \{x^t, x^h \mid x \in \mathcal{G}\}$ with
edges of three colors: "obverse", black, and gray (Fig. 3). Edges of each color
form a matching on V:

- pairs of obverse elements form an *obverse matching*;
- adjacent elements in P', other than obverse, form a *black matching*;
- adjacent elements in Q', other than obverse, form a *gray matching*.

Every pair of matchings forms a collection of *alternating* cycles in G, called
black-gray, *black-obverse*, and *gray-obverse* cycles respectively (a cycle is alternating if colors of its edges alternate). The permutation P' can be read along a

---

[1] A generalization of our results to *multichromosomal* and *linear* genomes will be
discussed elsewhere.

[2] Indices "t" and "h" stand for "tail" and "head" respectively.

[3] Our definition of the breakpoint graph is slightly different from the original definition
from [2] and is more suitable for analysis of duplicated genomes.

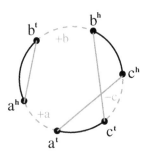

Fig. 2. The breakpoint graph $G(P,Q)$ for $P = +a + b - c$ and $Q = +a + b + c$

single black-obverse cycle while the permutation Q' can be read along a single gray-obverse cycle in G. The black-gray cycles in the breakpoint graph G play an important role in computing the reversal distance between the permutations P and Q. According to the Hannenhalli-Pevzner theory, the reversal distance between permutations P and Q is given by the formula:

$$d(P,Q) = b(G) - c(G) + h(G) \tag{1}$$

where $b(G)$ is the number of black edges in the breakpoint graph G, $c(G)$ is the number of black-gray cycles in the breakpoint graph G, and $h(G)$ is a small easily computable combinatorial parameter.

3   Reversal Distance Between Duplicated Genomes

While the Hannenhalli-Pevzner theory leads to a fast algorithm for computing reversal distance between two signed permutations, the problem of computing reversal distance between two genomes with duplicated genes remains unsolved.

Let P and Q be duplicated genomes on the same set of genes $\mathcal{G}$ (i.e., each gene appears in two copies). If one labels copies of each gene x as x_1 and x_2 then genomes P and Q become signed permutations and the Hannenhalli-Pevzner theory applies. As before we turn the labelled genomes P and Q into unsigned permutations P' and Q' by replacing each element x_i with a pair of obverses $x_i^t x_i^h$ in the order defined by the sign of x_i. Breakpoint graph $G(P,Q)$ of the labelled genomes P and Q has a vertex set $V = \{x_1^t, x_1^h, x_2^t, x_2^h \mid x \in \mathcal{G}\}$ and uniquely defines permutations P' and Q' (and, thus, the original genomes P and Q) as well as an inter-genome correspondence between gene copies.

We remark that different labellings may lead to different breakpoint graphs for the same genomes P and Q (Fig. 3a) and it is not clear how to choose a labelling that results in the minimum reversal distance between the labelled copies of P and Q.

Currently, the only known option for solving the reversal distance problem for duplicated genomes is to consider all possible labellings for each duplicated gene, to solve the reversal distance problem for each labelling, and to

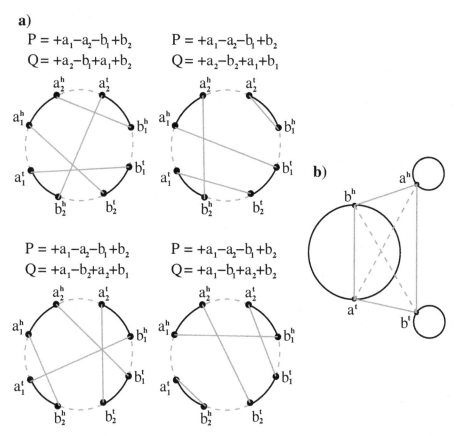

Fig. 3. a) The breakpoint graphs corresponding to four different labellings of $P = +a - a - b + b$ and $Q = +a - b + a + b$. b) The contracted breakpoint graph $G'(P,Q)$

choose the labelling with the minimal reversal distance. For genomes with n genes, each present in k copies, it leads to $(k!)^n$ invocations of the Hannenhalli-Pevzner algorithm rendering this approach impractical. In particular, for dupli-cated genomes with n genes (each gene present in 2 copies) it results in 2^n calls to the Hannenhalli-Pevzner algorithm. Moreover, the problem remains open if one of the genomes is perfectly duplicated (i.e., computing $d(P, R \oplus R)$). Sur-prisingly enough the problem of computing $\min_R d(P, R \oplus R)$ that we address in this paper is solvable in polynomial time.

Using the concept of the breakpoint graph and formula (1) the Genome Halv-ing Problem can be posed as follows. For a given duplicated genome P, find a perfect duplicated genome $R \oplus R$ and a labelling of gene copies such that the breakpoint graph $G(P, R \oplus R)$ of the labelled genomes P and $R \oplus R$ attains the minimum value of $b(G) - c(G) + h(G)$. Since $b(G)$ is constant and $h(G)$ is typically small, the value of $d(P,Q)$ mostly depends on $c(G)$. El-Mabrouk and

Sankoff [9] showed that the problems of maximizing $c(G)$ and minimizing $h(G)$ can be solved separately in a consecutive manner. In this paper we focus on the former, much harder, problem.

Weak Genome Halving Problem. *For a given duplicated genome P, find a perfect duplicated genome $R \oplus R$ and a labelling of gene copies that maximizes the number of black-gray cycles $c(G)$ in the breakpoint graph G of labelled genomes P and $R \oplus R$.*

4   Contracted Breakpoint Graph

Let P and Q be duplicated genomes on the same set of genes $\mathcal{G}$ and G be a breakpoint graph defined by some labelling of P and Q. For a vertex $u = x_i^j$ in G (where $x \in \mathcal{G}$, $i \in \{1, 2\}$, $j \in \{t, h\}$), we denote its *counterpart* by $\bar{u} = x_{3-i}^j$. Counterpart vertices form yet another matching in G.

A *contracted breakpoint graph* $G'(P, Q)$ is a result of contracting every pair of counterpart vertices in the breakpoint graph G into a single vertex (e.g., x_1^t and x_2^t are contracted into a single vertex x^t). So the contracted breakpoint graph $G' = G'(P, Q)$ is a graph on the set of vertices $V' = \{x^t, x^h \mid x \in \mathcal{G}\}$ with each vertex incident to two black, two gray, and a pair of parallel obverse edges (Fig. 3b). The contracted breakpoint graph $G'(P, Q)$ is uniquely defined by P and Q and does not depend on a particular labelling.[4] The following theorem gives a characterization of the contracted breakpoint graphs.

Theorem 1. *A graph H with black, gray, and obverse edges is a contracted breakpoint graph for some duplicated genomes if and only if*

- *each vertex in H is incident to two black edges, two gray edges, and a pair of parallel obverse edges;*
- *H is connected with respect to black and obverse edges (black-obverse connected);*
- *H is connected with respect to gray and obverse edges (gray-obverse connected).*

Proof. Suppose that graph H is a contracted breakpoint graph of the genomes P and Q. Consider the graph H as a contraction of a breakpoint graph $G(P, Q)$ for some labelling of the genomes P and Q. Since there is a single black-obverse cycle in G that cannot be split by contraction, the graph H is black-obverse connected. Similar reasoning implies that the graph H is gray-obverse connected.

---

[4] The contracted breakpoint graph is a natural generalization of the notion of breakpoint graph for genomes with duplicated genes. The conventional breakpoint graph (Bafna and Pevzner [2]) of signed permutations P and Q on n elements can be defined as gluing of n *pairs* of obverse edges in the corresponded unsigned permutations P' and Q' (assuming P' and Q' are represented as black-obverse and gray-obverse alternating cycles). The breakpoint graph of duplicated genomes P and Q on n elements is simply gluing of n *quartets* of obverse edges.

Consider a black-obverse and gray-obverse connected graph H and label endpoint of each obverse edge x by x^t and x^h. Since the graph H is black-obverse connected, there exists an alternating Eulerian black-obverse cycle traversing all the black edges in this graph. The order of vertices in this cycle defines some duplicated genome P. Similarly, since the graph H is gray-obverse connected, there exists an alternating Eulerian gray-obverse cycle traversing all gray edges that defines some duplicated genome Q. Then the graph H is a contracted breakpoint graph for the genomes P and Q.   □

In the case when Q is perfect duplicated genome (i.e., $Q = R \oplus R$) the gray edges in the contracted breakpoint graph $G'(P, Q)$ form pairs of parallel gray edges that we refer to as *double* gray edges. Similarly to the obverse edges, the double gray edges form a matching in the contracted breakpoint graph G'.

Let $G(P, Q)$ be a breakpoint graph for some labelling of P and Q. A set of black-gray cycles in $G(P, Q)$ is being contracted into a set of black-gray cycles in the contracted breakpoint graph $G'(P, Q)$ thus forming a black-gray cycle decomposition of $G'(P, Q)$. Therefore, each labelling induces a black-gray cycle decomposition of the contracted breakpoint graph. We are interested in a reverse problem: given a black-gray cycle decomposition of the contracted breakpoint graph $G'(P, Q)$, find labelling of P and Q that induces this cycle decomposition.

Theorem 2. *Any black-gray cycle decomposition of the contracted breakpoint graph $G'(P, R \oplus R)$ is induced by some labelling of P and $R \oplus R$.*

Proof. Consider a contracted breakpoint graph $G' = G'(P, R \oplus R)$ of the genomes P and $R \oplus R$ and suppose that labelling of P is fixed. We will show how a particular black-gray cycle decomposition C of the graph G' defines a labelling on $R \oplus R$ that induces this cycle decomposition.

We will label elements of $R \oplus R$ in one-by-one fashion. First we represent $R \oplus R$ as two copies of a linear sequence of unlabeled elements from $\mathcal{G}$ corresponding to R. We label the first element x in the copies of R by x_1 and x_2.

Suppose that first m elements are labelled in both copies of R. Let x be the m-th element in R. Without loss of generality we assume that x is labelled as x_1 in the first copy of R and as x_2 in the second copy. Let y be the $(m+1)$-th (yet unlabeled) element in R. Since x and y are adjacent elements in $R \oplus R$, there exists a double gray edge (x, y) in the graph G'. In the black-gray cycle decomposition this edge appears two times. Consider its adjacent black edges for each appearance. Let $(u, x), (x, y), (y, v)$ and $(z, x), (x, y), (y, t)$ be two triples of edges consecutively appearing in some black-gray cycles from C. For the black edges $(u, x), (y, v), (z, x), (y, t)$ we consider adjacencies in the labelled genome P that these edges originated from. Without loss of generality we assume that the originating adjacencies are $(u_i, x_1), (y_j, v_k), (z_l, x_2), (\bar{y}_j, t_m)$ for some indices $i, j, k, l, m \in \{1, 2\}$. We label the element y as y_j in the first copy of R and as $\bar{y}_j$ in the second copy so that elements x_1, y_j and $x_2, \bar{y}_j$ will be adjacent in the labelled genome $R \oplus R$. We continue labelling in a similar manner until the whole genome $R \oplus R$ is labelled.

Consider a breakpoint graph $G(P, R \oplus R)$ for the labelled genomes P and $R \oplus R$. The labelling procedure implies that any black edge and gray edge adjacent in the breakpoint graph $G(P, R \oplus R)$ are contracted into a pair of adjacent edges in the cycle decomposition C of the graph $G'(P, R \oplus R)$. Hence, the constructed labelling induces the cycle decomposition C.   □

Let $c_{max}(G')$ be the number of cycles in a maximal black-gray cycle decompositions of the contracted breakpoint graph $G' = G'(P, R \oplus R)$. Theorem 2 implies that the Weak Genome Halving Problem is equivalent to the following.

Cycle Decomposition Problem. *For a given duplicated genome P, find a perfect duplicated genome $R \oplus R$ maximizing $c_{max}(G'(P, R \oplus R))$.*

Black and gray edges of the contracted breakpoint graph $G'(P, R \oplus R)$ form a bi-colored graph that we study in the next section.

5   Cycle Decomposition of BG-Graphs

A *BG-graph* G is a graph with black and gray edges such that the black edges form *black cycles* and the gray edges form gray matching in G (Fig. 5a). We refer to gray edges in G as *double* gray edges and assume that every double gray edge is a pair of parallel gray edges. This assumption implies that every BG-graph can be decomposed into edge-disjoint black-gray alternating cycles.

Below we prove an upper bound on the maximal number of black-gray cycles $c_{max}(G)$ in cycle decomposition of the BG-graph G, and formulate necessary and sufficient conditions for achieving this bound.

A BG-graph is *connected* if it is connected with respect to both black and gray edges. A double gray edge in the BG-graph connecting vertices of distinct black cycles is called *interedge*. A double gray edge connecting vertices of the same black cycle is called *intraedge*. Note that a connected BG-graph with m black cycles has at least $m - 1$ interedges.

Let G be a BG-graph on $2n$ vertices with $m > 1$ black cycles, C be a black-gray cycle decomposition of G, and $e = (x, y)$ be an interedge in G. We define an *e-transformation* $(G, C) \xrightarrow{e} (G^\star, C^\star)$ of the graph G and its black-gray cycle decomposition C into a new BG-graph $G^\star$ on $2(n-1)$ vertices with $m - 1$ black cycles and a black-gray cycle decomposition $C^\star$ of $G^\star$ of the same size as C. In the cycle decomposition C there are two black-gray cycles c_1 and c_2 passing through edge e (it may happen that $c_1 = c_2$ when the same cycle passes through e two times). Suppose that c_1 traverses edges $(u, x), (x, y), (y, v)$ while c_2 traverses edges $(z, x), (x, y), (y, t)$. To obtain graph $G^\star$ from G we replace these edges with black edges (u, v) and (z, t) respectively and delete vertices x and y (Fig. 5). This operation transforms the cycles c_1 and c_2 in G into into cycles $c_1^\star$ and $c_2^\star$ in $G^\star$. We define the black-gray cycle decomposition $C^\star$ as cycles $c_1^\star, c_2^\star$ and all cycles from C, except c_1 and c_2.

Lemma 1. *Let C be a maximal black-gray cycle decomposition of a BG-graph G and $(G, C) \xrightarrow{e} (G^\star, C^\star)$ be the e-transformation for some interedge $e = (x, y)$ in G. Then $c_{max}(G) = c_{max}(G^\star)$.*

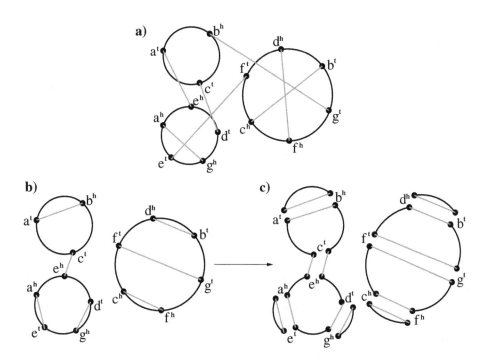

Fig. 4. For a genome $P = -a - b + g + d + f + g + e - a + c - f - c - b - d - e$, a) a BG-graph corresponding to the contracted breakpoint graph $G'(P, R \oplus R)$ for $R = +a - g - b - c + d - f + e$; b) a BG-graph corresponding to the contracted breakpoint graph $G'(P, R \oplus R)$ for $R = -a - b - d - g + f - c - e$; c) a maximal cycle decomposition of the BG-graph in b)

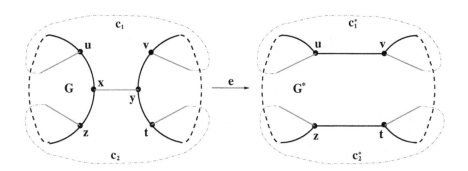

Fig. 5. e-transformation of a graph G into a graph G^*. Black-gray cycles c_1, c_2 in G passing through interedge $e = (x, y)$ are transformed into black-gray cycles c_1^*, c_2^* in G^*. The black cycles connected by e in G are merged into a single black cycle in G^*

Proof. By the definition of e-transformation, $c_{max}(G) = |C^\star| \leq c_{max}(G^\star)$. On the other hand, every black-gray cycle decomposition $D^\star$ of the graph $G^\star$ can be transformed into a black-gray cycle decomposition D of G of the same size (by simply substituting the black edges (u,v) and (z,t) in some black-gray cycles in $D^\star$ by black-gray-black triples $(u,x),(x,y),(y,v)$ and $(z,x),(x,y),(y,t)$). Therefore, $c_{max}(G^\star) \leq c_{max}(G)$.   □

Theorem 3. *If G is a connected BG-graph with $2n$ vertices and m black cycles, then*

$$c_{max}(G) \leq n + 2 - m.$$

Proof. Suppose that $c_{max}(G) = k$, i.e., a maximal cycle decomposition of G contains k black-gray cycles. Consider the BG-graph G as a result of contracting these k black-gray cycles by a series of n gluings of pairs of gray edges into double gray edges. Since one needs at least $k - 1$ such gluings to contract k disconnected black-gray cycles into a connected BG-graph, $k - 1 \leq n$. It implies the theorem for $m = 1$.

Assume $m > 1$. Since the BG-graph G is connected and contains m black cycles, there exists an interedge e in G. For a maximal cycle decomposition C of the BG-graph G, consider an e-transformation $(G, C) \overset{e}{\to} (G^\star, C^\star)$. Lemma 1 implies $c_{max}(G) = c_{max}(G^\star)$. Note that $G^\star$ is a connected BG-graph on $2(n-1)$ vertices with $m - 1$ black cycles. Iteratively applying similar e-transformations $m - 1$ times we will end up with a BG-graph G^+ of size $2(n - (m - 1))$ that contains a single black cycle. Hence, $c_{max}(G) = c_{max}(G^+) \leq n + 2 - m$.   □

Note that for a BG-graph G, $c_{max}(G)$ equals the sum of $c_{max}(H)$ over all connected components H of G. Since the total size of all connected components is $b(G)$, Theorem 3 implies

$$c_{max}(G) \leq b(G)/2 + 1 \cdot s_1 + 0 \cdot s_2 + (-1) \cdot s_3 + (-2) \cdot s_4 + \dots,$$

where s_m is the number of connected components with m black cycles. Let $b_e(G)$ be the number of even black cycles (i.e., black cycles of even size) in G. Since s_1 does not exceed $b_e(G)$,

$$c_{max}(G) \leq b(G)/2 + b_e(G). \qquad (2)$$

To achieve the upper bound (2), each connected component of G must contain either a single even black cycle (a *simple BG-graph*), or a pair of odd black cycles (a *paired BG-graph*). Fig. 5b shows a BG-graph containing an even black cycle forming a simple BG-graph, and a pair of odd black cycles forming a paired BG-graph.

We represent each black cycle of a BG-graph as points on a circle such that the arcs between adjacent points represent the black edges, and intraedges are drawn as straight chords within these circles. A BG-graph is *non-crossing* if its intraedges (as chords within each black circle) do not cross. A BG-graph in Fig. 5b is non-crossing while a BG-graph on in Fig. 5a is not.

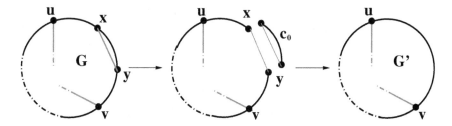

Fig. 6. Transformation of a BG-graph G into a BG-graph G' by splitting a black-gray cycle c_0 consisting of parallel black and gray edges (x, y)

Theorem 4. *For a simple BG-graph G on $2n$ vertices, $c_{max}(G) = n + 1$ if and only if G is non-crossing.*

Proof. We prove the theorem in both directions by induction on n. The statement is trivial for $n = 1$. Assume that the statement is true for any simple BG-graph of size $2(n-1)$ and prove it for a simple BG-graph G of size $2n$.

We first prove (reasoning depends on the proof direction) that there exists a double gray edge e in G parallel to a black edge (i.e., connecting two adjacent points on a black circle) forming a black-gray cycle c_0 of length 2.

If $c_{max}(G) = n + 1$, then a maximum cycle decomposition of the BG-graph G consists of $n + 1$ black-gray cycles. Since these cycles contain $2n$ gray edges in total, the pigeonhole principle implies that there exists a cycle c_0 with a single gray edge e.

If the BG-graph G is non-crossing, consider a double gray edge e with the minimal span. If e spanned more than one black edge then there would exist a double gray edge with endpoints within the span of e, i.e., an edge with an even smaller span, a contradiction.

For a found edge $e = (x, y)$, let u and v be vertices adjacent to x and y on the black cycle. Transform G into a simple BG-graph G' on $2(n-1)$ vertices by removing the vertices x and y and all the incident edges, and by adding the black edge (u, v) (Fig. 5). Note that $c_{max}(G') = c_{max}(G) - 1$ and G' is non-crossing if and only if G is non-crossing.

By induction the graph G' is non-crossing if and only if $c_{max}(G') = n$. Therefore, G is non-crossing if and only if $c_{max}(G') = n + 1$. □

Let G be a paired BG-graph G of size $2n$ (consisting of two odd black cycles) and e be an interedge in G. For a maximal black-gray cycle decomposition C of G, let $(G, C) \xrightarrow{e} (G^\star, C^\star)$ be an e-transformation of G. Note that the graph $G^\star$ is a simple BG-graph on $2(n-1)$ vertices. Lemmas 1 and 3 imply $c_{max}(G) = c_{max}(G^\star) \leq n$. Therefore, according to Theorem 4, $c_{max}(G) = n$ if and only if the BG-graph $G^\star$ is non-crossing. We are interested in a particular case of this statement.

Theorem 5. *For a paired BG-graph G of size $2n$ with a single interedge, $c_{max}(G) = n$ if and only if G is non-crossing.*

Proof. It is easy to see that for a single interedge e in a paired BG-graph G, the e-transformation turns G into a non-crossing BG-graph if and only if G is non-crossing.   □

We call a BG-graph *optimal* if its connected components are either simple BG-graphs, or paired BG-graphs with single interedges. Theorems 4 and 5 imply

Theorem 6. *For an optimal BG-graph G, $c_{max}(G) = b(G)/2 + b_e(G)$.*

An optimal BG-graph and its maximal cycle decomposition are shown at Fig. 5b,c.

6   Genome Halving Algorithm

In order to solve the Cycle Decomposition Problem for a genome P, we will construct a contracted breakpoint graph $G'(P, \cdot)$ which achieves the upper bound (2). The genome P alone defines a vertex set of the graph G', an obverse matching, and black cycles in G' so that G' is black-obverse connected.

A *BO-graph* is a connected graph with black and obverse edges such that the black edges form black cycles and the obverse edges form an obverse matching (every duplicated genome P corresponds to a BO-graph). A *BOG-graph* is a graph with black, obverse, and gray edges such that black and obverse edges form a BO-graph (a *BO-subgraph*), and black and gray edges form an optimal BG-graph (a *BG-subgraph*). Note that each black-gray connected component of a BOG-graph is a simple non-crossing BG-graph or a paired non-crossing BG-graph with a single interedge.

We now pose the Cycle Decomposition Problem for a genome P as follows. For a given BO-graph G (defined by the genome P), find a gray-obverse connected BOG-graph G' having G as a BO-subgraph. Theorems 1 and 6 imply that such a BOG-graph graph is a contracted breakpoint graph $G'(P, R \oplus R)$ for some genome R for which $c_{max}(G')$ achieves the upper bound (2).

We remark that gray-obverse connected components of a BOG-graph form gray-obverse cycles (alternating double gray and obverse edges). Hence, a BOG-graph is gray-obverse connected if and only if it has a single gray-obverse cycle.

Lemma 2. *For a BOG-graph with more than one gray-obverse cycle, there exists a black edge connecting two distinct gray-obverse cycles.*

Proof. Let H be a BOG-graph with more than one gray-obverse cycle. First we will show that there exists a black-gray connected component of the graph H containing two double gray edges from distinct gray-obverse cycles. Assume that all the double gray edges within each black-gray connected component belong to the same gray-obverse cycle. Then each gray-obverse cycle contains vertices of one or more black cycles. Let V_1 and V_2 be vertex sets of two distinct gray-obverse cycles. Since black and obverse edges connect vertices within the same set, the sets V_1 and V_2 are black-obverse disconnected, a contradiction to black-obverse connectivity of the graph H.

Let C be a black-gray connected component of the BOG-graph H containing two double gray edges from distinct gray-obverse cycles. We represent double gray edges of the component C as vertices of a graph E with edges induced by black edges of the component C. Black-gray connectivity of the component C implies that the graph E is connected. If every two double gray edges in C connected by a black edge belong to the same gray-obverse cycle in H, then connectivity of the graph E would imply that all the double gray edges in C belong to the same gray-obverse cycle. □

Theorem 7. *For a given BO-graph G, there exists a BOG-graph G' with a single gray-obverse cycle having G as a BO-subgraph.*

Proof. First we group odd black cycles in G into pairs (formed arbitrary), and introduce an arbitrary interedge connecting cycles in each pair. Then we complete each black cycle with an arbitrary non-crossing gray matching so that each vertex of G becomes incident to exactly one double gray edge. Denote the resulting graph by H. Note that H is a BOG-graph having G as a BO-subgraph.

If H has a single gray-obverse cycle, then the theorem holds for $G' = H$. Otherwise, we show how to modify the set of double gray edges in H to reduce the number of gray-obverse cycles.

Assume that there is more than one gray-obverse cycle in H. By Lemma 2 there is a black edge (x, y) connecting distinct gray-obverse cycles c_1 and c_2. Let (x, u) and (y, v) be double gray edges incident to the vertices x and y respectively. We replace the edges (x, u) and (y, v) in H with double gray edges (x, y) and (u, v) resulting in a graph H'. Fig. 6 illustrates two cases depending on whether the edge (y, v) is an interedge (since (x, u) and (y, v) belong to the same black-gray connected component, at most one of them can be an interedge).

We will show that the BG-subgraph of H' is optimal. There are two new double gray edges in the BG-subgraph of H' compared to H. Since the introduced double gray edge (x, y) is parallel to a black edge, it does not cross any other intraedge (as chords). The introduced double gray edge (u, v) is either an intraedge, or an interedge. In the former case any intraedge crossing the intraedge (u, v) would necessary cross (x, u) or (y, v) (as chords), a contradiction to the fact that H has a non-crossing BG-subgraph. Hence, the BG-subgraph of H' is non-crossing. On the other hand, it is easy to see that the transformation $H \to H'$ turns a simple black-gray connected component of the graph H into a simple black-gray connected component of H' (Fig. 6a), and a paired black-gray connected component with a single interedge into a paired black-gray connected component with a single interedge (Fig. 6b). Hence, the BG-subgraph of H' is optimal and H' is a BOG-graph.

Note that the BOG-graph H' has G as a BO-subgraph (since black and obverse edges were not affected by the transformation). The graph H' has the same gray-obverse cycles as H, except for the gray-obverse cycles c_1 and c_2 which are joined into a single cycle in H'. Hence, the number of gray-obverse cycles in H' is reduced as compared to H.

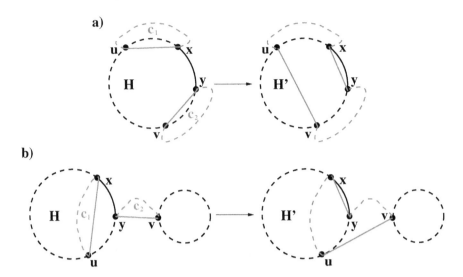

Fig. 7. Merging gray-obverse cycles c_1, c_2 connected by a black edge (x, y) passing through a) intraedges (x, u) and (y, v); b) an intraedge (x, u) and an interedge (y, v)

Iteratively reducing the number of gray-obverse cycles we will eventually come up with a BOG-graph G' having G as a BO-subgraph with a single gray-obverse cycle.   □

We outline the Genome Halving Algorithm for a duplicated genome P as follows.

1. Construct a BO-graph G defined by the genome P.
2. Find a BOG-graph G' with a single gray-obverse cycle having G as a BO-subgraph (Theorem 7).
3. Read a pre-duplicated genome R along the gray-obverse cycle in G'.

References

1. D.A.Bader, B.M.E.Moret, and M.Yan "A linear-time algorithm for computing inversion distances between signed permutations with an experimental study". *J. Comput. Biol.*, 8 (2001), pp.483-491.
2. V.Bafna and P.A.Pevzner "Genome rearrangement and sorting by reversals". *SIAM Journal on Computing*, 25 (1996), pp. 272-289.
3. A.Bergeron. "A very elementary presentation of the Hannenhalli-Pevzner theory". In *Proceedings of the 12th Annual Symposium on Combinatorial Pattern Matching, Lecture Notes in Computer Science*, 2089 (2001), pp. 106-117.
4. A. Bergeron, J. Mixtacki, and J. Stoye A. Bergeron, J. Mixtacki, and J. Stoye. "Reversal distance without hurdles and fortresses". In *Proceedings of the 15th Annual Symposium on Combinatorial Pattern Matching, Lecture Notes in Computer Science*, 3109 (2004), pp. 388-399

5. F.S.Dietrich et al. "The *Ashbya gossypii* Genome as a Tool for Mapping the Ancient *Saccharomyces cerevisiae* Genome". *Science*, 304 (2004), pp. 304-307.
6. N.El-Mabrouk, J.H.Nadeau, and D.Sankoff "Genome halving". In *Proceedings of the 9th Annual Symposium on Combinatorial Pattern Matching, Lecture Notes in Computer Science*, 1448 (1998), pp. 235-250.
7. N.El-Mabrouk and D.Sankoff "On the reconstruction of ancient doubled circular genomes using minimum reversal". *Genome Informatics*, 10 (1999), pp. 83-93.
8. N.El-Mabrouk, B.Bryant, and D.Sankoff "Reconstructing the pre-doubling genome". In *Proceedings of the Third Annual International Conference on Computational Molecular Biology (RECOMB)* (1999), pp. 154-163.
9. N.El-Mabrouk and D.Sankoff "The Reconstruction of Doubled Genomes". *SIAM Journal on Computing*, 32 (2003), pp. 754-792.
10. S.Hannenhalli and P.Pevzner "Transforming cabbage into turnip (polynomial algorithm for sorting signed permutations by reversals)". In *Proceedings of the Twenty-Seventh Annual ACM Symposium on Theory of Computing* (1995), pp. 178-189. *Journal of the ACM*, 46 (1999), pp. 1-27.
11. H.Kaplan, R.Shamir, and R.Tarjan. "Faster and simpler algorithm for sorting signed permutations by reversals". *SIAM Journal on Computing*, 29 (1999), pp. 880-892
12. M.Kellis et al. "Proof and evolutionary analysis of ancient genome duplication in the yeast *Saccharomyces cerevisiae*". *Nature*, 428 (2004), pp. 617-624.
13. S.Ohno, U.Wolf, and N.Atkin "Evolution from fish to mammals by gene duplication". *Hereditas*, 59 (1968), pp. 169-187.
14. P.Pevzner and G.Tesler "Genome Rearrangements in Mammalian Evolution: Lessons from Human and Mouse Genomes". *Genome Research*, 13 (2003), 37-45.
15. L.Skrabanek and K.H.Wolfe "Eukaryote genome duplication - where's the evidence?". *Curr. Opin. Genet. Devel.*, 8 (1998), pp. 694-700.
16. E. Tannier and M.-F. Sagot "Sorting by reversals in subquadratic time". In *Proceedings of the 15th Annual Symposium on Combinatorial Pattern Matching, Lecture Notes in Computer Science*, 3109 (2004).
17. K.H.Wolfe and D.C.Shields "Molecular evidence for an ancient duplication of the entire yeast genome". *Nature*, 387 (1997), pp. 708-713.

Verifying Probabilistic Procedural Programs

Javier Esparza[1] and Kousha Etessami[2]

[1] Institute for Formal Methods in Computer Science,
University of Stuttgart
[2] School of Informatics,
University of Edinburgh

Abstract. Monolithic finite-state probabilistic programs have been abstractly modeled by finite Markov chains, and the algorithmic verification problems for them have been investigated very extensively. In this paper we survey recent work conducted by the authors together with colleagues on the algorithmic verification of probabilistic procedural programs ([BKS, EKM04, EY04]). Probabilistic procedural programs can more naturally be modeled by *recursive Markov chains* ([EY04]), or equivalently, *probabilistic pushdown automata* ([EKM04]). A very rich theory emerges for these models. While our recent work solves a number of verification problems for these models, many intriguing questions remain open.

1 Introduction

The topic of this paper is the decidability and computational complexity of verification problems for models of probabilistic programs. Loosely speaking, a program is probabilistic if it can flip a coin in order to decide the next execution step. Probabilistic models of programs are of interest for at least two reasons. First, we may wish to model and analyze randomized algorithms, which are intrinsically probabilistic. Second, sometimes when we model a program's behavior we may wish to replace a deterministic branching choice by a probabilistic one in order to obtain information about the induced probability of certain behaviors, e.g., that the program terminates in a certain state. The probabilities chosen for the branches may either be subjective choices or be based, e.g., on statistics accumulated from profiling data.

As usual, in the area of automated software verification we assume that the variables of the program have a finite domain, either because the program was so designed, or because it is an abstraction of another program. The complexity of probabilistic verification has been extensively studied for finite-state *flat-programs*, where the program consists of one procedure containing no procedure calls, and the control mechanisms are only the basic **if-then-else** instructions and **while** loops.

In this case, the program has a finite number of states, and can be modeled abstractly by a finite Markov Chain. There is already an extensive literature on analysis of such models (see, e.g., [Var85, CY95, Kwi03]). Since last year, both

K. Lodaya and M. Mahajan (Eds.): FSTTCS 2004, LNCS 3328, pp. 16–31, 2004.

authors, together with colleagues, have initiated a study of verification problems for programs with multiple (possibly recursive) procedures, called *procedural programs* in this paper [EKM04, EY04]. Since the state of such a program must contain information about the stack of calls that have not yet been completed, the state space is potentially infinite, and so these programs are more naturally modeled by countably infinite Markov chains of a certain kind. As we will see, verification questions related to these models lead to very interesting algorithmic and mathematical problems.

In this paper we survey our published results and report on our work in progress [EKM04, EY04, BKS]. While a number of interesting algorithmic questions have been answered, many questions remain. We use this opportunity to emphasize the intuition behind the results and avoid the technicalities.

2   Models of Probabilistic Programs

The *state* of a running program, as usual, consists of the contents of memory together with the location of the program's control. This defines a *state transition system*, whose transitions are from a state s to a state t whenever the program can move in one step from s to t.

In the case of probabilistic programs we assume that transitions are labelled with a positive probability, i.e., a number in the interval $(0, 1]$, and that the sum of the probabilities attached to the transitions leaving a state is 1, or 0 if the state is a halting state. This transforms the state space into a *Markov chain*.

A state of a flat-program contains information about the current control point and the current values of the variables. If we assume that variables have a finite domain, as we always do in this paper, the state space of the program is finite, and so probabilistic flat-programs can be modelled as finite Markov chains.

Let us now discuss formal models for probabilistic programs with procedures. When a procedure or function Q is called from another procedure or function P, with parameter values v passed from P to Q,

(1) the return address (i.e. the point of P to control has to return after completion of the call) and the current values of the local variables of P are stored as an *activation record* on the *call stack*;
(2) control is transferred to an initial control point of Q, and the passed parameter values v can be treated as a value of a local variable of Q.
(3) upon completion of the call, control is transferred to the return address, and the values of the local variables of P are restored according to the top activation record on the call stack, and if the procedure Q returned a value r, the value r is passed back to P in a local variable.

Thus, the state of a program with procedures contains information about the current control point, the current values of the variables, and the current contents of the call stack. We may represent a state by a triple (g, l, r), where g represents the current values of the global variables, l the control point and values of the local variables of the current procedure (which may include parameters passed to it, or values returned to it), and r is a sequence of activation records, with the top of the stack as first element of the sequence. Since the stack size is not bounded a priori, the program may have an infinite state space, and the Markov chain associated with a program with procedures may be infinite.

As in the case of finite flat-programs, we assume that transitions are labelled with a positive probability. We also assume that the probability of a transition $(q_1, l_1, r_1) \rightarrow (g_2, l_2, r_2)$ depends only on g_1, l_1 and g_2, l_2. Intuitively, this means that the probability of executing a particular instruction of the program code only depends on the current program control point and the current values of the program variables, and not on the contexts of the call stack. There are some special situations in which one might like to weaken this condition (for instance, some methods of the Java Development Kit inspect the stack of activation records [BJMT01]), but even in this case, using coding tricks, one can construct equivalent Markov chains satisfying it.

When the number of control points and the domains of program variables are finite, such probabilistic procedural programs induce a particular family of infinite Markov chains. We can not work directly with infinite Markov chains, but need to work with finite representations of them. We consider two equivalent finitely presented models of these Markov chains: *Probabilistic Pushdown Automata* (PPDAs) (studied in [EKM04]) and *Recursive Markov Chains* (RMCs) (studied in [EY04]). These models have non-probabilistic counterparts which have been studied extensively in recent research on verification and program analysis: for *Pushdown Systems* (PDAs) see, e.g., [BEM97, EHRS00], and for *Recursive State Machines* (RSMs) see [AEY01, BGR01].

2.1   Recursive Markov Chains

A *recursive Markov chain* is a tuple $(A_1, \ldots, A_k)$, where each A_i is a *component*. Each component models a procedure of the program and consists of:

- A set of *nodes*, with two distinguished subsets of *entry* and *exit* nodes.
- A set of *boxes*. A box b is labelled with an integer $Y(b) \in \{1, .., k\}$, and has a *call port*, or just a *call* (en, b) for each entry node en of $A_{Y(b)}$, and a *return port*, or just a *return* (ex, b) for each exit node ex of $A_{Y(b)}$.
- A set of transitions $u \xrightarrow{x} v$ where
  - u is either a non-exit node or a call port,
  - v is either non-entry node, or a return port, and
  - x is a positive probability, with the condition that the sum of the probabilities of all the transitions having source u is 1 or 0, if the vertex u is an exit node or call port, which has no outgoing edges in A_i.

Recursive Markov chains reflect the structure of a program with procedures. Each procedure is modelled by a component. A node corresponds to a local state of the procedure, i.e., to one of its control points and a valuation of its local variables, plus the values of the global variables, if any. Entry nodes correspond to the possible initial states of the procedures, which also reflect the parameter values passed to it, and exit nodes correspond to local states from which control is returned to the caller and the returned value. A transition to a call port (en, b)

of a box b labeled by $Y(b) = i$ models a call with particular parameter values reflected by the node en, to the procedure modelled by A_i. Similarly, a transition from a return port corresponds to a return, with particular return values.

A RMC $A = (A_1, \ldots, A_k)$ defines a (possibly infinite) Markov chain M_A as follows. Let a *vertex* be either a node, a call, or a return. The states of M_A, which we call *global states*, are pairs $\langle u, B \rangle$, where u is a vertex and $B = b_1 \ldots b_n$ is a sequence of boxes. M has the following transitions:

- a transition $\langle u, B \rangle \xrightarrow{x} \langle u', B \rangle$ for every transition $u \xrightarrow{x} u'$ and every sequence of boxes B;
- a transition $\langle (en, b), B \rangle \xrightarrow{1} \langle en, bB \rangle$ for every call port (b, en), and every sequence of boxes B; and
- a transition $\langle ex, bB \rangle \xrightarrow{1} \langle (ex, b), B \rangle$ for every return port (ex, b), and every sequence of boxes B.

RMCs can be depicted visually in a natural way. An example RMC is in Figure 1. This RMC has only one component, $A1$. It contains two nodes: entry en and exit ex, and two boxes, $b1$, and $b2$, both of which are labeled by the same component, $A1$, i.e., $Y(b1) = Y(b2) = 1$. Each box bi has a call port (en, bi), and a return port (ex, bi). (In this example, it so happens that the probability of reaching the state $\langle ex, \epsilon \rangle$ from $\langle en, \epsilon \rangle$ is $1/2$. We will see why this is the case later.)

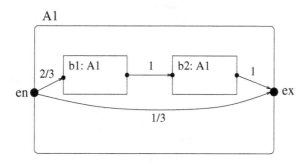

Fig. 1. An example RMC, A

2.2 Probabilistic Pushdown Automata

A probabilistic pushdown automaton (pPDA) consists of
- a finite set of *control states*,
- a finite *stack alphabet*, and
- a finite set of *rules* of the form $pX \xrightarrow{x} q\alpha$, where p and q are control states, X is a stack symbol, α is a word of stack symbols, and x is a positive probability. The left hand side pX of a rule is the rule's *head*, or just a head, for short.

A pPDA defines a Markov chain M: the states of M are pairs $\langle p, S \rangle$, where p is a control state and S is a sequence of stack symbols. M has a transition $\langle p, X\beta \rangle \xrightarrow{x} \langle q, \alpha\beta \rangle$ for every rule $pX \xrightarrow{x} q\alpha$ and sequence of stack symbols β.

We can easily transform a RMC into a pPDA. It suffices to take the set of vertices as control states, boxes as stack symbols, and the following set of rules:

- a rule $ub \xrightarrow{x} u'$ for every transition $u \xrightarrow{x} u'$ and every box b,
- a rule $(en, b)b' \xrightarrow{1} en\ bb'$ for every call port (b, en) and every box b', and
- a rule $ex\ b \xrightarrow{1} (ex, b)$ for every exit node ex and every box b.

In this paper we assume that pPDA are in the following *normal form*:

- for every rule $pX \xrightarrow{x} q\alpha$, α has length at most 2, and
- for every p and every X at least one rule has pX as left hand side.

Note that the pPDAs obtained from RMCs by the translation above are in normal form. Normal form pPDAs can also be transformed to RMCs of the same size, by mimicking a translation of PDAs to RSMs given in [AEY01]. Thus RMCs have a tight correspondence to normal form pPDAs.[1] Every pPDA can also be put in normal form in linear time while preserving all properties of interest.

3   Reachability

Given two states s_0, s_f of a probabilistic sequential program, let $[s_0, s_f]$ denote the probability of eventually reaching s_f starting from s_0. We wish to answer the following questions:

(1) The *qualitative* reachability problem: Is $[s_0, s_f] = 1$?
(2) The *quantitative* reachability problem: Given $\rho \in (0, 1]$, is $[s_0, s_f] \geq \rho$?
    We may also wish to compute or approximate the probability $[s_0, s_f]$.

3.1   Flat Programs

In the case of flat-programs, s_0 and s_f are states of a finite Markov chain M. The answers to (1) and (2) are well-known, but we quickly recall them in order to compare them with the answers in the procedural case.

In a finite Markov chain $[s_0, s_f] = 1$ holds if and only if either (a) there is a single Bottom Strongly Connected Component (BSCC) of M that is reachable from s_0 and s_f belongs to that component, or (b) s_f belongs to every path from s_0 to any BSCC, i.e., removing s_f makes all BSCC's unreachable from s_0. These properties can be checked in linear time using standard graph algorithms. Observe that whether $[s_0, s_f] = 1$ or not depends only on the topology of the Markov chain, and not on the probabilities labelling the transitions.

Let us consider now the quantitative problem. Assume that the transitions leaving s_0 are $s_0 \xrightarrow{p_1} s_1, \ldots, s_0 \xrightarrow{p_k} s_k$. We have the following equation:

$$[s_0, s_f] = p_1 \cdot [s_1, s_f] + \ldots + p_k[s_k, s_f]$$

If we write down the same equation for every pair s, s', and look at the terms $[s, s']$ as unknowns, we obtain a linear system of equations $\mathbf{x} = L(\mathbf{x})$,

---

[1] There is a minor loss of information of the structure of the RMC when going from an RMC to a pPDA (see [AEY01]).

in m unknowns $\mathbf{x} = (x_1, \ldots, x_m)$, where each variable x_i corresponds to some unknown probability $[s, s']$. It can be show that the probabilities we wish to compute are given by the least non-negative solution for this system, by which we mean a vector $q = (q_1, \ldots, q_m) \in \mathbb{R}^m_{\geq 0}$, such that $q = L(q)$, and such that if $v \in \mathbb{R}^m_{\geq 0}$ is another solution then $q_i \leq v_i$ for all i, $1 \leq i \leq m$. We will see a generalization of this when we study RMCs and pPDAs.

There are a number of ways to compute this least solution. Since the system is linear, the least solution is rational, and one could use, e.g., linear programming methods to compute it. More efficiently, it turns out the system can be transformed into another one such that the least solution of the old system is the *unique* solution of the new system. The new system can then be solved using, e.g., Gaussian elimination, or its solution can be approximated efficiently using iterative numerical procedures like Jacobi or Gauss-Seidel, etc.

3.2   Procedural Programs

When we try to generalize the answers for probabilistic flat programs to the procedural case, we quickly encounter a number of obstacles. To begin with, the answer to the qualitative problem is no longer independent of the values of the probabilities, as shown by the following example. Consider the pPDA given by the rules.

$$pX \xrightarrow{\ x\ } pXX$$
$$pX \xrightarrow{\ 1-x\ } p\epsilon$$

(We could also take the RMC A depicted in Figure 1, with the probabilities 2/3 and 1/3 replaced by x and $1-x$, respectively.) The infinite Markov chain defined by this pPDA corresponds to a 'truncated' Bernoulli walk, depicted in Figure 2, and a standard result states that $[pX, p\epsilon] = 1$ if and only if $x \leq 1/2$. So the answer to the qualitative problem "is $[pX, p\epsilon] = 1$?" depends not only on the topology of the RMC, but also on the value of x.

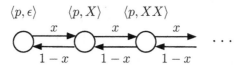

Fig. 2. The Markov chain of a pPDA

For computing these probabilities we can not simply proceed as in the finite case to write down one linear equation for each probability $[s, s']$, for every pair s, s', because the Markov chain is in general infinite and this would lead us to an infinite system of linear equations in infinitely many variables.

For the moment, let us consider a simpler problem: given a vertex u and an exit node ex of the same component A_i, what is the probability of starting at the global state $\langle u, \epsilon \rangle$, eventually reaching the state $\langle ex, \epsilon \rangle$? Let us denote this probability by $[u, ex]$. Although we do not expand on it in this survey, computing(or approximating) these probabilities is sufficient to allow us to compute (approximate) reachability probabilities between other pairs of states s, s'.

Consider three cases of what $[u, ex]$ might be, based on the vertex u:

- $u = ex$. Then $[u, ex] = 1$.
- If u is a node or a return port, and the transitions leaving u are $u \xrightarrow{p_1} v_1, \ldots, v \xrightarrow{p_n} v_n$. Then, as in the case of a finite Markov chain,

$$[u, ex] = p_1 \cdot [v_1, ex] + \ldots + p_n \cdot [v_n, ex]$$

- $u = (b, en)$ is a call port of a box b corresponding to a component A_j. Then, in order to reach $\langle ex, \epsilon \rangle$ from $\langle (b, en), \epsilon \rangle$, we must follow a path of the form

$$\langle (en, b), \epsilon \rangle \xrightarrow{1} \langle en, b \rangle \cdots \langle ex', b \rangle \xrightarrow{1} \langle (ex', b), \epsilon \rangle$$

If the exit nodes of the component A_j are $ex'_1, \ldots, ex'_n$, then, since the probability of eventually reaching $\langle ex', b \rangle$ from $\langle en, b \rangle$ is equal to the probability of eventually reaching $\langle ex', \epsilon \rangle$ from $\langle en, \epsilon \rangle$, we get

$$[(en, b), ex] = [en, ex'_1] \cdot [(ex'_1, b), ex] + \ldots + [en, ex'_n] \cdot [(ex'_n, b), ex]$$

We thus have a finite system of <u>non-linear</u> multi-variate polynomial equations for the unknowns $[u, ex]$, ranging over every pair u, ex, where u is a vertex of the RMC and ex is an exit node of the same component. Lets associate each unknown probability $[u, ex]$ with a corresponding variable $x_{[u,ex]}$. For convenience we index these variables $x_1, \ldots, x_m$, obtaining a vector $\mathbf{x}$, and we have m multi-variate polynomial equations, $x_j = P_j(\mathbf{x})$, which we write together as

$$\mathbf{x} = P(\mathbf{x}) \tag{1}$$

Consider the partial order on m-vectors given by $\mathbf{x} \preceq \mathbf{y}$ if and only if $x_i \leq y_i$ for all i, $1 \leq i \leq m$. The mapping $P : \mathbb{R}^m \mapsto \mathbb{R}^m$ defines a <u>monotone</u> operator on a compact and downward-closed (with respect to $\preceq$) subspace D of $[0, 1]^m$. Let $P^r(x)$ denote $P(\mathbf{x})$ if $r = 1$, and $P(P^{r-1}(\mathbf{x}))$, for $r > 1$. It is clear, by the non-negativity of coefficients of $P(\cdot)$, that $P^r(0) \preceq P^{r+1}(0)$, for $r \geq 1$.

Theorem 1. *(see [EY04] and see [EKM04] for an equivalent result for pPDAs)* $\mathbf{x} = P(\mathbf{x})$ *has a (unique)* <u>*Least Fixed Point*</u> *(LFP) solution* $q \in [0, 1]^m$*, given by* $q = \lim_{r \to \infty} P^r(\mathbf{0})$*. I.e.,* $q = P(q)$*, and* $q \preceq v$ *for any solution* v*. Moreover the vector* q *gives precisely the probabilities* $[u, ex]$*, i.e.:* $[u, ex] = q_{[u,ex]}$*.*

Now, how do we compute this LFP? Well, we can't compute it exactly, and there are several other nasty features to the systems $\mathbf{x} = P(\mathbf{x})$ that distinguish them from the linear systems for finite Markov chains:

Theorem 2. *([EY04])*

1. *Irrational probabilities: There is an RMC for which the probability [en,ex] is* <u>*irrational, and in fact not "solvable by radicals"*</u>*.*

2. *Slow convergence:* There is an RMC for which $|[en, ex] - P^{2^i}_{[en,ex]}(0)| \geq \frac{1}{2^i}$.
   In other words, we need 2^i applications of the operator P to get within i bits
   of precision of the LFP.
3. *Very small & large probabilities:* There is a family of *hierarchical* (i.e., no
   recursion) RMCs, $A(n)$, parameterized by their size cn, for which $[en, ex] = \frac{1}{2^{2^n}}$ in $A(n)$. And a family, $A'(n)$, of size cn, for which $[en, ex] = 1 - \frac{1}{2^{2^n}}$.

We can still ask whether a probability is exactly 1, or at least ρ for some
rational number ρ, and we can still try to efficiently <u>approximate</u> the probabilities
to within a desired number of bits of precision.

RMCs and the Existential Theory of Reals. Given a system $x = P(x)$ associated with an RMC, and a vector $q \in [0, 1]^n$, consider the following existential
first-order sentence in the theory of reals:

$$\varphi \equiv \exists x_1, \ldots, x_m \bigwedge_{i=1}^{m} P_i(x_1, \ldots, x_m) = x_i \wedge \bigwedge_{i=1}^{m} 0 \leq x_i \wedge \bigwedge_{i=1}^{m} x_i \leq q_i$$

φ holds true precisely when there is some solution $0 \preceq z \preceq q$, with $z = P(z)$.
Thus, if we had a way to decide the truth of this sentence, we would be
able to tell whether $[u, ex] \leq q_i$, for some rational q_i, by using the vector
$q = (1, 1, \ldots, q_i, 1, \ldots, 1)$. Now consider the sentence ψ, obtained from φ by
replacing $\bigwedge_{i=1}^{m} x_i \leq q_i$ with $\bigvee_{i=1}^{m} x_i < q_i$. ψ is false precisely when there is no
solution $z \succeq 0$, such that $q \not\preceq z$. Thus, to decide whether q is the LFP, we need to
check the truth of φ and the falsehood of ψ. Furthermore, by a straightforward
"binary search", we could use j "queries" to the existential theory of reals to
obtain a probability $[u, ex]$ to within j bits of precision (see [EY04]).

Happily, beginning with Tarski, the decidability and complexity of the first-
order theory of real and its fragments has been deeply investigated. The current
state of the art (see e.g. [Can88, Ren92, BPR96]) provides a PSPACE algorithm
that decides whether an existential sentence with rational coefficients is true for
the real numbers. The algorithm's running time is exponential only in the number
of variables of the sentence. Using these results one can obtain the following:

Theorem 3. *([EY04]) Given RMC A and rational value ρ, there is a PSPACE
algorithm to decide whether $[u, ex] \leq \rho$, with running time $O(|A|^{O(1)} \cdot 2^{O(m)})$
where m is the number of variables in the system $x = P(x)$ for A. Moreover
$[u, ex]$ can be approximated to within j bits of precision within PSPACE and
with running time at most j times the above.*

Single-Exit RMCs and Stochastic Context-Free Grammars. Stochastic
Context-Free Grammars (SCFGs) have rules $N \xrightarrow{x} \alpha$, labeled with a probability
x, where N is a non-terminal, and α a string of terminals and nonterminals. The
probabilities of the rules associated with each non-terminal N must sum to 1.

It can be shown that SCFGs are "equivalent" in a precise sense to *single-
exit RMCs* where each component can have only a single exit (see [EY04]). In
particular, the probability $[u, ex]$ of the RMC is the same as the probability

of termination starting at the corresponding non-terminal $N_{[u,ex]}$ in the corresponding SCFG. They are also equivalent to pPDAs with a single control state, also known as pBPAs: just write $pN \xrightarrow{x} p\alpha$ instead of $N \xrightarrow{x} \alpha$.

SCFGs have been studied extensively since the 1970s in connection with Natural Language Processing (see, e.g., [MS99]), and their theory is intimately connected with that of *multi-type Branching Processes*. Based on results on branching processes (see, e.g., [Har63]), one can "characterize" questions of almost sure termination for SCFGs based on eigenvalues of certain matrices associated with the SCFG (see, e.g., [BT73]). These characterizations unfortunately often omit special uncovered cases, or, worse, contain errors (e.g., the often cited [BT73] contains errors). In [EY04], a detailed treatment of these characterizations is given together with their algorithmic implications, establishing the following:

Theorem 4. *([EY04]) There is polynomial-time algorithm that for a 1-exit RMC A, and every vertex u and exit ex, determines which of the following three cases hold: (1) $[u, ex] = 0$, (2) $[u, ex] = 1$, or (3) $0 < [u, ex] < 1$.*

RMCs and Newton's Method. Although we can not compute the probabilities associated with an RMC exactly, because as we saw they can be irrational, we can nevertheless aim to efficiently approximate the probabilities numerically within a desired number of bits of precision. Given that the LFP for equation system $\mathbf{x} = P(\mathbf{x})$ is given by $\lim_{r \to \infty} P^r(\mathbf{0})$, and $P^r(0)$ grows monotonically with r, one way to try to do this would be to calculate $P^r(\mathbf{0})$ for a "large enough" r. Unfortunately, as we saw in Theorem 2, there are RMCs for which this approach fails terribly, requiring 2^i iterations to obtain i bits of precision.

A powerful numerical method for obtaining roots of equations is *Newton's method*. In its n-dimensional version (see, e.g., [SB93]), given a suitably differentiable map $F : \mathbb{R}^n \mapsto \mathbb{R}^n$ we wish to find a solution to the system $F(\mathbf{x}) = \mathbf{0}$. Starting at some $\mathbf{x_0} \in \mathbb{R}^n$, the method works by iterating

$$\mathbf{x}_{k+1} := \mathbf{x}_k - (F'(\mathbf{x}_k))^{-1} F(\mathbf{x}_k)$$

where $F'(\mathbf{x})$ is the *Jacobian matrix* of partial derivatives given by

$$F'(\mathbf{x}) = \begin{bmatrix} \frac{\partial f_1}{\partial x_1} & \cdots & \frac{\partial f_1}{\partial x_n} \\ \vdots & \vdots & \vdots \\ \frac{\partial f_n}{\partial x_1} & \cdots & \frac{\partial f_n}{\partial x_n} \end{bmatrix}$$

The method is not even defined if for some iterate $\mathbf{x_k}$ the matrix $F'(\mathbf{x_k})$ is not invertible, and when defined it may not converge. In practice, however, if it converges then it typically converges very fast. Remarkably, in [EY04] it is shown that for a decomposed version of the monotone non-linear systems $\mathbf{x} = P(\mathbf{x})$ arising from an RMC, Newton's method started at $\mathbf{x_0} = \mathbf{0}$ not only converges to the LFP, but does so monotonically:

Theorem 5. *([EY04]) Starting at $\mathbf{x_0} = 0$, Newton's method converges monotonically to the LFP, q, of the system $\mathbf{x} = P(\mathbf{x})$ (appropriately decomposed) of an RMC. In other words, $\lim_{k\to\infty} \mathbf{x}_k = q$, and $\mathbf{x}_k \preceq \mathbf{x}_{k+1}$, for all $k \geq 0$.*

Moreover, from the proof it follows that, for all $k \geq 0$, $\mathbf{x}_k \geq P^k(0)$, and that Newton's method corresponds to a clever "acceleration" of the standard iteration $P^k(\cdot)$ which will typically be much faster than iterating $P^k(\cdot)$. In particular, on the examples known to require exponentially many iterations of $P(\cdot)$ to achieve a given number of bits of precision, Newton's method converging in only a linear number of iterations (see [EY04] for an expanded explanation of these remarks).

Lower Bounds for Reachability. We have seen that basic questions about reachability probabilities can be answered in PSPACE by using the existential theory of reals, and that for the special case of single-exit RMCs (SCFGs), the qualitative reachability problem, whether $[u, ex] = 1$, can be answered in polynomial time. Can we provide any lower bounds for the remaining questions? Hardness for standard complexity classes, such as NP or PSPACE, remains open. However, we have the following strong evidence of "difficulty". The *square-root sum problem* is the following decision problem: given $(d_1, \ldots, d_n) \in \mathbb{N}^n$ and $k \in \mathbb{N}$, decide whether $\sum_{i=1}^n \sqrt{d_i} \leq k$. It is known to be solvable in PSPACE, but it has been a major open problem in the complexity of numerical computation since the 1970's (see, e.g., [GGJ76, Tiw92]) whether it is solvable even in NP, with important consequences in subjects like computational geometry.

Theorem 6. *([EY04]) The square-root sum problem is polynomial-time reducible to the problem of determining, given a single-exit RMC, a vertex u and exit ex, and a rational value r, whether $[u, ex] \geq r$.*

A simple modification of this reduction shows that the square-root sum problem is polynomial-time reducible to problem of determining, given a 2-exit RMC, a vertex u and exit ex, whether $[u, ex] = 1$.

4   Repeated Reachability

Let a *run* of a Markov chain be either an infinite path or a finite path ending at a halting state without successors. Given an initial state s_0 and a set of states S, we are interested in the probability that the runs starting at s_0 *repeatedly visit* states of S, i.e., that they visit S infinitely often. (For a formal definition of this probability and a proof that it exists, see for instance [Var85, EKM04].) If the case of flat-programs, both the qualitative and the quantitative repeated reachability problems can be solved by slight modifications of the algorithms for the reachability problems, with the same complexity. Let us now consider procedural programs. For convenience, we model the program as a pushdown automaton with an initial configuration $c_0 = \langle p_0, X_0 \rangle$. To simplify the presentation we assume that the set of configurations that should be repeatedly visited, denoted by C_r, is the set of configurations with head $p_r X_r$ for some control state p_r and some stack symbol X_r (see [EKM04] for a more general case).

We define a new *finite* Markov chain MH such that the repeated reachability problem for c_0 and C_r can be reduced to a repeated reachability problem for MH, which we already know how to solve. The key notion we need are the *minima* of an infinite run, defined inductively as follows. The first minimum of an infinite run $c_0 \xrightarrow{x_1} c_1 \xrightarrow{x_2} \ldots$, where $c_i = \langle p_i, \alpha_i \rangle$, is the smallest index j such that $|\alpha_k| \geq |\alpha_j|$ for every $k \geq j$. For every $i > 1$, if j is the i-th minimum of the run, then the $(i+1)$-th minimum is the first minimum of the suffix $c_{j+1} \xrightarrow{x_{j+2}} c_{j+2} \ldots$. In words, the first minimum is the index of the first configuration having minimal stack length and the $(i+1)$-th minimum is obtained by chopping off the prefix of the run up to the i-minimum, and taking the first minimum of the rest. Now, what is the probability that the $(i+1)$-th minimum has head qY, if the i-th minimum has head pX? It is proved in [EKM04] that this probability depends only on pX and qY. Intuitively, if $\langle p, X\alpha \rangle$ is the configuration at the i-th minimum, all its successor configurations in the run have α at the bottom of the stack. So α plays no rôle in determining the head of the next minimum, because from $\langle p, X\alpha \rangle$ onward all stack operations "happen above α".

This result allows us to define a Markov chain whose states are the heads of the pPDA plus two special states *Init* and *Ter*, and whose transitions are as follows, where $PMin(pX, qY)$ denotes the probability that a minimum has head pY assuming that the previous minimum has head pX:

- *Init* $\xrightarrow{x}$ *Ter*, where x is the probability that a run starting at c_0 terminates, i.e., reaches a configuration of the form $\langle p, \epsilon \rangle$;
- *Ter* $\xrightarrow{1}$ *Ter*;
- *Init* $\xrightarrow{x}$ pX for every head pX such that $x = PMin(p_0X_0, pX) > 0$; and
- $pX \xrightarrow{x} qY$ for every two heads pX and qY such that $x = PMin(pX, qY) > 0$.

How can we decide if $PMin(pX, qY) > 0$? Using the results of the previous section, we can compute for every p, q, X the probability $[pXq]$ of reaching $\langle q, \epsilon \rangle$ from $\langle p, X \rangle$ (these are essentially the probabilities $[u, ex]$ of the previous section), and the probability $[pX]\!\uparrow$ of never emptying the stack from $\langle p, X \rangle$ (i.e., of never reaching a configuration of the form $\langle q, \epsilon \rangle$ for any control state q). Consider now a run starting at $\langle p, X \rangle$. In order to reach the next minimum at $\langle q, Y\beta \rangle$ for some β, the pPDA has the following possibilities:

- Apply the rule $pX \xrightarrow{x} qY$, if it exists, and then, from $\langle q, Y \rangle$, never empty the stack.
- Apply a rule $pX \xrightarrow{x} qYZ$ for some Z, and then keep Z forever at the bottom of the stack.
- Apply a rule $pX \xrightarrow{x} rZY$ for some r, Z, from $\langle r, ZY \rangle$ reach the configuration $\langle q, Y \rangle$, and then never empty the stack.

It is easy to compute the probability of each case. Adding them we obtain:

$$PMin(pX, qY) = \sum_{pX \xrightarrow{x} qY} x \cdot [qY]\!\uparrow + \sum_{pX \xrightarrow{x} qYZ} x \cdot [qY]\!\uparrow + \sum_{pX \xrightarrow{x} rZY} x \cdot [rZq] \cdot [qY]\!\uparrow$$

Since $[pX]\uparrow + \sum_{q \in Q}[pXq] = 1$, where Q is the set of control states of the pPDA, deciding if $PMin(pX, qY) > 0$ reduces to deciding if $[qY]\uparrow > 0$ for each head qY. By the results of the previous section, this can be done in PSPACE, and in PTIME for pBPAs or 1-exit RMCs.

Using this finite chain we can decide if a run repeatedly visits configurations of C_r *at minima* with probability 1 (at least ρ). But, what happens if the configurations of C_r occur *between* minima? To solve this problem, we split each state pX into $(pX, 0)$ and $(pX, 1)$, and assign transition probabilities as follows. For a transition $(pX, f) \xrightarrow{x_1} (qY, 1)$, where $f \in \{0, 1\}$, we set x_1 to the probability that a run starting at $\langle p, X \rangle$ hits the second minimum ($\langle p, X \rangle$ itself is the first) at a configuration with head qY *and visits some configuration of C_r in-between*. For a transition $(pX, f) \xrightarrow{x_0} (qY, 0)$ we set $x_0 = PMin(pX, qY) - x_1$. The Markov chain MH mentioned at the beginning of the section is the result of performing this modification. A run of the pPDA repeatedly visits configurations of C_r if and only if it corresponds to a run of MH that repeatedly visits states of the form $(pX, 1)$. In order to solve the qualitative repeated reachability problem, we construct MH and then apply the algorithm for the finite state case. Notice, however, that we do not need the exact values of the transition probabilities of MH, we only have to decide if they are positive. This yields a PSPACE-algorithm for the qualitative repeated reachability problem, and a PTIME-algorithm for pBPA or 1-exit RMC, the same status as for reachability. A lower bound for the general case is open, but the remarks in section 3 on lower bounds for reachability apply also to repeated reachability.

For the quantitative repeated reachability problem we need to solve a linear system of equations whose coefficients are the probabilities of the transitions of MH. Complexity questions have not been studied in detail yet.

5   Model Checking PCTL

The syntax of PCTL, the probabilistic extension of CTL proposed in [HJ94] is given by:

$$\varphi ::= \mathtt{tt} \mid A \mid \neg\varphi \mid \varphi_1 \wedge \varphi_2 \mid \mathcal{X}^{\geq \rho}\varphi \mid \varphi_1 \mathcal{U}^{\geq \rho}\varphi_2$$

where A is an atomic proposition, ρ is a probability, and $\mathcal{X}$ and $\mathcal{U}$ are the next and until operators of LTL. Formulas with operators $\leq, =, <, >$ can be 'simulated' by boolean combinations. A state of a Markov chain satisfies $\mathcal{X}^{\geq \rho}\varphi$ or $\varphi_1 \mathcal{U}^{\geq \rho}\varphi_2$ if the probability that a run starting at it satisfies $\mathcal{X}\varphi$ or $\varphi_1 \mathcal{U} \varphi_2$, respectively, is at least ρ. The *qualitative fragment* of PCTL is obtained by requiring $\rho \in \{0, 1\}$.

Given a Markov chain M and a PCTL formula φ, let $[\![\varphi]\!]$ denote the set of states of M satisfying φ. As in the case of CTL, the key to a model-checking algorithm for PCTL consists of, given $[\![\varphi_1]\!], [\![\varphi_2]\!]$, computing $[\![\varphi_1 \mathcal{U}^{\geq \rho}\varphi_2]\!]$. In the case of flat-programs, $[\![\phi]\!]$ is computed bottom-up, i.e., computing first $[\![\phi']\!]$ for all subformulas ϕ' of ϕ. This can be done using well-known graph algorithms if $\rho \in \{0, 1\}$, and solving linear systems of equations otherwise [HJ94].

In the procedural case, we face an obstacle: Since the Markov chain is infinite, the set $[\![\, \varphi \,]\!]$ may be infinite, and cannot be computed by explicit enumeration of its elements. Let us see the implications of this.

A valuation is *regular* if $[\![\, A \,]\!]$ is a regular set for every atomic proposition A, where 'regular' is used in the language-theoretic sense: A configuration $\langle p, \alpha \rangle$ is seen as the word $p\alpha$. It is shown in [EKM04] that if a valuation is effectively regular, then $[\![\, \varphi \,]\!]$ is effectively regular for every PCTL formula φ. This provides a solution to the infinity problem: Compute a finite automaton recognizing $[\![\, \varphi \,]\!]$.

We sketch the proof of this regularity result for a particular case. We show that $[\![\, \varphi_1 \mathcal{U}^{\geq 1} \varphi_2 \,]\!]$ is regular if $[\![\, \varphi_1 \,]\!]$ is the set of all configurations, and $[\![\, \varphi_2 \,]\!] = \{\langle q, \epsilon \rangle\}$ for some given control state q. Let a head pX be *almost surely terminating* (a.s.t.) if a run starting at $\langle p, X \rangle$ empties the stack with probability 1. Given an a.s.t. pX, let $Emp(pX)$ be the set of states r such that the probability of reaching $\langle r, \epsilon \rangle$ from $\langle p, X \rangle$ is non-zero. Then $[\![\, \varphi_1 \mathcal{U}^{\geq 1} \varphi_2 \,]\!]$ is the least set C containing $\langle q, \epsilon \rangle$ and satisfying: If pX is a.s.t. and $\langle r, \alpha \rangle \in C$ for every $r \in Emp(pX)$, then $\langle p, X\alpha \rangle \in C$. Consider now the automaton having the set of stack symbols as alphabet, all subsets of control states as states, all singletons $\{p\}$ as initial states, the set $\{q\}$ as final state, and a transition $P_1 \xrightarrow{X} P_2$ if and only if the head pX is a.s.t. for every $p \in P_1$, and $P_2 = \bigcup_{p \in P_1} Emp(pX)$. This automaton accepts $\alpha \in \Gamma^*$ from the state p if and only if $\langle p, \alpha \rangle \in C$, and so $[\![\, \varphi_1 \mathcal{U}^{\geq 1} \varphi_2 \,]\!]$ is regular.

The exact complexity of the model checking problem for pPDAs and the qualitative fragment of PCTL with regular valuations is still open. Using results of [Wal00] it is easy to show that the problem is EXPTIME-hard, even for pPBAs or 1-exit RMCs [May04]. We also know that the problem can be solved in triple exponential time [Kuč04].

If φ does not belong to the qualitative fragment, the set $[\![\, \varphi \,]\!]$ may not be regular, even for a regular valuation. Consider the pPDA

$$
\begin{array}{ccccc}
pX \xrightarrow{1/2} qX & qX \xrightarrow{1/2} q\epsilon & rX \xrightarrow{1} re & sX \xrightarrow{1} sX \\
pX \xrightarrow{1/2} rX & qX \xrightarrow{1/2} sX & rY \xrightarrow{1/2} re & sY \xrightarrow{1} sY \\
 & qY \xrightarrow{1} q\epsilon & rY \xrightarrow{1/2} qY &
\end{array}
$$

and atomic propositions A_1, A_2 together with the regular valuation in which $[\![\, A_1 \,]\!]$ is the set of all configurations, and $[\![\, A_2 \,]\!] = \{\langle q, \epsilon \rangle\}$. It is easy to see that

$$\{\langle p, X^n Y^m \rangle \mid n, m > 0\} \cap [\![\, A_1 \mathcal{U}^{=1/2} A_2 \,]\!] = \{\langle p, X^n Y^n \rangle \mid n > 0\}$$

which, since $\{\langle p, X^n Y^m \rangle \mid n, m \geq 0\}$ is regular and $\{\langle p, X^n Y^n \rangle \mid n \geq 0\}$ is not, implies that $[\![\, A_1 \mathcal{U}^{=1/2} A_2 \,]\!]$ is not regular. In [BKS], the pPDA above is used as a building block in a reduction from the halting problem for 2-counter machines to the model checking problem for pPDA's and PCTL, which shows that the latter is undecidable.

6   Model Checking Büchi Automata Specifications

Let M be a Markov chain modelling a program. We formalize the specification as a Büchi automaton $\mathcal{B}$. A word accepted by $\mathcal{B}$ is seen as a 'good behaviour' of the program. (Recall that $\mathcal{B}$ accepts a word $a_1 a_2 \ldots$ if it has a run $q_0 \xrightarrow{a_1} q_1 \xrightarrow{a_2} \ldots$ and an accepting state q that the run visits infinitely often.) The verification problem is to decide if a run of M is accepted by $\mathcal{B}$ (i.e., is 'a good behaviour') with probability 1, or with probability at least ρ for a given $\rho \in [0,1]$.

For flat-programs, the alphabet of $\mathcal{B}$ is the set of states of M, which is finite. For procedural programs, we take as alphabet the set of heads of $\mathcal{P}$. This means that specifications can refer to the control points and variables of the program, but not to the stack of activation records (see [BKS] for a generalization).

The verification problem for flat-programs is solved (in two ways) in [Var85, CY95]. For the procedural case, assume first that $\mathcal{B}$ is deterministic, as done in [EKM04]. We construct the pPDA $\mathcal{P} \times \mathcal{B}$ having pairs (p,b) as states, where p is a control state of $\mathcal{P}$ and b is a state of $\mathcal{B}$, and rules $(p,b)X \xrightarrow{x} (p',b')\alpha$, where $pX \xrightarrow{x} p'\alpha$ is a rule of $\mathcal{P}$ and $q \xrightarrow{pX} q'$ is a transition of $\mathcal{B}$. We construct the Markov chain MH having states of the form $((p,b)X, f)$, where $f = 1$ denotes that some configuration $\langle (q,b'), \alpha \rangle$ with b' accepting has been visited since the last minimum. A run of $\mathcal{P}$ is accepted by $\mathcal{B}$ with probability 1 (at least ρ) if and only if a run of MH repeatedly visits states satisfying $f = 1$ with probability 1 (at least ρ). So the verification problem reduces to the repeated reachability problem.

The nondeterministic case was left open in [EKM04]. The following solution is from [BKS]. In a first step, $\mathcal{B}$ is transformed into a *deterministic Muller automaton* $\mathcal{B}'$ with acceptance sets $Q_1, \ldots, Q_n$. (Recall that $\mathcal{B}'$ accepts a word $a_1 a_2 \ldots$ if it has a run $q_0 \xrightarrow{a_1} q_1 \xrightarrow{a_2} \ldots$ and an acceptance set Q_i such that the set of states visited by the run infinitely often is exactly Q_i.) The product $\mathcal{P} \times \mathcal{B}'$ is defined as above. However, we redefine the states of the Markov chain MH so that they not only reflect whether some accepting state was visited since the last minimum, but also *which states* of $\mathcal{B}'$ were visited. More formally, we replace the boolean f by a set of states of $\mathcal{B}'$, and in a transition $((p_1,b_1)X_1, S_1) \xrightarrow{x} ((p_2,b_2)X_2, S_2)$ we set x to the probability of, starting at $\langle (p_1,b_1), X_1 \rangle$, hitting the next minimum at a configuration with head $(p_2,b_2)X_2$, and visiting exactly the states of S_2 in-between. With this definition of MH, the runs of $\mathcal{P}$ are accepted by $\mathcal{B}'$ with probability 1 if and only if every bottom strongly connected component of MH satisfies the following property: if the states of the component are $((p_1,b_1)X_1, S_1), \ldots ((p_n,b_n)X_n, S_n)$, then $S_1 \cup \ldots \cup S_n$ is an acceptance set of $\mathcal{B}'$. While this shows that the problem of checking Büchi automata specifications is decidable, the exact complexity of the problem is open.

Acknowledgments. This survey is based on joint work by the first author together with Tomáš Brázdil, Antonín Kučera, Richard Mayr and Oldřich Stražovský [BKS, EKM04], and on joint work by the second author together with Mihalis Yannakakis [EY04]. We would both like to acknowledge and thank our collaborators.

References

[AEY01]   R. Alur, K. Etessami, and M. Yannakakis. Analysis of recursive state machines. In *Proceedings of CAV'01*, volume 2102 of *LNCS*, pages 304–313, 2001.

[BEM97]   A. Bouajjani, J. Esparza, and O. Maler. Reachability analysis of pushdown automata: Applications to model checking. In *Proceedings of CONCUR'97*, volume 1243 of *LNCS*, pages 135–150, 1997.

[BGR01]   M. Benedikt, P. Godefroid, and T. Reps. Model checking of unrestricted hierarchical state machines. In *Proceedings of ICALP'01*, volume 2076 of *LNCS*, pages 652–666, 2001.

[BJMT01] F. Besson, T. Jensen, D.L. Métayer, and T. Thorn. Model checking security properties of control flow graphs. *Journal of Computer Security*, 9:217–250, 2001.

[BKS]   T. Brázdil, A. Kučera, and O. Stražovský. Decidability of temporal properties of probabilistic pushdown automata. Technical report. In preparation.

[BPR96]   S. Basu, R. Pollack, and M. F. Roy. On the combinatorial and algebraic complexity of quantifier elimination. *Journal of the ACM*, 43(6):1002–1045, 1996.

[BT73]   T. L. Booth and R. A. Thompson. Applying probability measures to abstract languages. *IEEE Transactions on Computers*, 22(5):442–450, 1973.

[Can88]   J. Canny. Some algebraic and geometric computations in pspace. In *Proceedings of 20th ACM STOC*, pages 460–467, 1988.

[CY95]   C. Courcoubetis and M. Yannakakis. The complexity of probabilistic verification. *Journal of the ACM*, 42(4):857–907, 1995.

[EHRS00] J. Esparza, D. Hansel, P. Rossmanith, and S. Schwoon. Efficient algorithms for model checking pushdown systems. In *Proceedings of CAV'00*, volume 1855 of *LNCS*, pages 232–247, 2000.

[EKM04]   J. Esparza, A. Kučera, and R. Mayr. Model checking probabilistic pushdown automata. In *Proceedings of LICS'04*, pages 12–21. IEEE Computer Society, 2004. Full version: Tech. report FIMU-RS-2004-03, Masaryk University, Brno, available online at http://www.fmi.uni-stuttgart.de/szs/publications/info/esparza.EKM04rep.shtml.

[EY04]   K. Etessami and M. Yannakakis. Recursive markov chains, stochastic grammars, and monotone systems of non-linear equations. Technical report, 2004. School of Informatics, University of Edinburgh.

[GGJ76]   M. R. Garey, R. L. Graham, and D. S. Johnson. Some NP-complete geometric problems. In *Proceedings of 8th ACM STOC*, pages 10–22, 1976.

[Har63]   T. E. Harris. *The Theory of Branching Processes*. Springer-Verlag, 1963.

[HJ94]   H. Hansson and B. Jonsson. A logic for reasoning about time and reliability. *Formal Aspects of Computing*, 6:512–535, 1994.

[Kuč04]   A. Kučera. Private communication, 2004.

[Kwi03]   M. Kwiatkowska. Model checking for probability and time: From theory to practice. In *Proceedings of LICS'03*, pages 351–360. IEEE Computer Society Press, 2003.

[May04]   R. Mayr. Private communication, 2004.

[MS99]   C. Manning and H. Schütze. *Foundations of Statistical Natural Language Processing*. MIT Press, 1999.

[Ren92]   J. Renegar. On the computational complexity and geometry of the first-order theory of the reals. Parts I,II, III. *Journal of Symbolic Computation*, pages 255–352, 1992.

[SB93]   J. Stoer and R. Bulirsch. *Introduction to Numerical Analysis.* Springer-Verlag, 1993.

[Tiw92]   P. Tiwari. A problem that is easier to solve on the unit-cost algebraic RAM. *Journal of Complexity*, pages 393–397, 1992.

[Var85]   M. Vardi. Automatic verification of probabilistic concurrent finite-state programs. In *Proceedings of FOCS'85*, pages 327–338. IEEE Computer Society Press, 1985.

[Wal00]   I. Walukiewicz. Model checking CTL properties of pushdown systems. In *Proceedings of FST&TCS'00*, volume 1974 of *Lecture Notes in Computer Science*, pages 127–138. Springer, 2000.

Streaming Algorithms for Geometric Problems

Piotr Indyk

Computer Science and Artificial Intelligence Lab, MIT

1 Introduction

Computing over data streams is a recent phenomenon that is of growing interest in many areas of computer science, including databases, computer networks and theory of algorithms. In this scenario, it is assumed that the algorithm sees the elements of the input one-by-one in arbitrary order, and needs to compute a certain function of the input. However, it does not have enough memory to store the whole input. Therefore, it must maintain a "sketch" of the data. Designing a sketching method for a given problem is a novel and exciting challenge for algorithm design.

The initial research in streaming algorithms has focused on computing simple numerical statistics of the input, like median [MP80], number of distinct elements [FM85] or frequency moments [AMS96]. More recently, the researchers showed that one can use those algorithms as subroutines to solve more complex problems; see the survey [Mut03] for detailed description of the past and recent developments. Still, the scope of algorithmic problems for which stream algorithms exist is not well understood. It is therefore of importance to identify new classes of problems that can be solved in this restricted settings.

Recently, several authors proposed streaming algorithms for geometric problems [AHP01, FKZ02, TGIK02, Ind03, CM03, MS03, HS04, BCEG04, Cha04, STZ04], [Ind04, HPM04, FIS04][1]. Most of the algorithms appear to follow one of the two approaches:

1. **Merge and Reduce.** The main component of this approach is an (off-line) algorithm which, given a set of points P, constructs a subset of P which is small but nevertheless 'well-approximates' P. The algorithm is then applied in a divide-and-conquer manner to the whole data stream. Because of the tree-structured computation, the algorithm can be simulated using small memory.

   This very general approach goes back to [MP80], and has been first adapted to the geometric setting in [AHP01, AHPV], using the notion of a *core-set*. However, it does not (appear to) work in the dynamic setting, where the points can be *deleted* as well as inserted.

---

[1] Several other algorithms were proposed for the more general metric space setting [CCFM97, GMMO01, Mey01, COP03].

K. Lodaya and M. Mahajan (Eds.): FSTTCS 2004, LNCS 3328, pp. 32–34, 2004.

2. **Randomized Embeddings.** This approach relies on approximate embeddings of the set of points represented by a stream into a low-dimensional space (see [Ind01] for more information on embeddings). Specifically, the set of points is mapped to a low-dimensional vector, typically using a random linear map or its variants. The vector is then used to estimate the desired statistics of the data, such as the cost of the minimum tree spanning the set of points.

In the context of streaming algorithms, this approach goes back to [AMS96] or even [FM85]. The use of linear mappings enables to perform point deletions as well as insertions. However, the resulting algorithms have typically higher complexity than their insertions-only counterparts.

In this talk I will present an overview of the known results, and describe the aforementioned methods. I will also present a list of open problems in the area. The slides for the talk are available at

http://theory.csail.mit.edu/~indyk/GEOSTREAM/geostream.html

References

[AHP01]   P. Agarwal and S. Har-Peled. Maintaining approximate extent measures of moving points. *Proceedings of the ACM-SIAM Symposium on Discrete Algorithms*, 2001.

[AHPV]   P. K. Agarwal, S. Har-Peled, and K. R. Varadarajan. Approximating extent measure of points. *Journal of the ACM*.

[AMS96]   N. Alon, Y. Matias, and M. Szegedy. The space complexity of approximating the frequency moments. *Proceedings of the Symposium on Theory of Computing*, pages 20–29, 1996.

[BCEG04]   A. Bagchi, A. Chaudhary, D. Eppstein, and M. T. Goodrich. Deterministic sampling and range counting in geometric data streams. *Proceedings of the ACM Symposium on Computational Geometry*, 2004.

[CCFM97]   M. Charikar, C. Chekuri, T. Feder, and R. Motwani. Incremental clustering and dynamic information retrieval. *Proceedings of the Symposium on Theory of Computing*, 1997.

[Cha04]   T. Chan. Faster core-set constructions and data stream algorithms in fixed dimensions. *Proceedings of the ACM Symposium on Computational Geometry*, 2004.

[CM03]   G. Cormode and S. Muthukrishnan. Radial histograms for spatial streams. *DIMACS Tech Report*, 2003.

[COP03]   M. Charikar, L. O'Callaghan, and R. Panigrahy. Better streaming algorithms for clustering problems. *Proceedings of the Symposium on Theory of Computing*, pages 30–39, 2003.

[FIS04]   G. Frahling, P. Indyk, and C. Sohler. Estimating the weight of euclidean minimum spanning trees in data streams. *Manuscript*, 2004.

[FKZ02]   Joan Feigenbaum, Sampath Kannan, and Jian Zhang. Computing diameter in the streaming and sliding-window models. *Yale University Technical Report YALEU/DCS/TR-1245*, 2002.

[FM85]   P. Flajolet and G. Martin. Probabilistic counting algorithms for data base applications. *Journal of Computer and System Sciences*, 31:182–209, 1985.

[GMMO01] S. Guha, N. Mishra, R. Motwani, and L. O'Callaghan. Clustering data streams. *Proceedings of the Symposium on Theory of Computing*, 2001.

[HPM04]   S. Har-Peled and S. Mazumdar. Coresets for k-means and k-medians and their applications. *Proceedings of the Symposium on Theory of Computing*, 2004.

[HS04]   J. Hershberger and S. Suri. Adaptive sampling for geometric problems over data streams. *Proceedings of the ACM Symposium on Principles of Database Systems*, 2004.

[Ind01]   P. Indyk. Tutorial: Algorithmic applications of low-distortion geometric embeddings. *Proceedings of the Symposium on Foundations of Computer Science*, 2001.

[Ind03]   P. Indyk. Better algorithms for high-dimensional proximity problems via asymmetric embeddings. *Proceedings of the ACM-SIAM Symposium on Discrete Algorithms*, 2003.

[Ind04]   P. Indyk. Algorithms for dynamic geometric problems over data streams. *Proceedings of the Symposium on Theory of Computing*, 2004.

[Mey01]   Adam Meyerson. Online facility location. *Proceedings of the Symposium on Foundations of Computer Science*, pages 426–431, 2001.

[MP80]   J. I. Munro and M. S. Paterson. Selection and sorting with limited storage. *TCS*, 12, 1980.

[MS03]   S. Muthukrishnan and M. Strauss. Maintenance of multidimensional histograms. *Proceedings of the FSTTCS*, 2003.

[Mut03]   S. Muthukrishnan. Data streams: Algorithms and applications (invited talk at soda'03). *Available at http://athos.rutgers.edu/~muthu/stream-1-1.ps*, 2003.

[STZ04]   S. Suri, C. Toth, and Y. Zhou. Range counting over multidimensional data streams. *Proceedings of the ACM Symposium on Computational Geometry*, 2004.

[TGIK02]   N. Thaper, S. Guha, P. Indyk, and N. Koudas. Dynamic multidimensional histograms. *Proceedings of the ACM SIGMOD International Conference on Management of Data (SIGMOD)*, 2002.

Toward a Grainless Semantics for Shared-Variable Concurrency*

John C. Reynolds

Carnegie Mellon University and Edinburgh University
john.reynolds@cs.cmu.edu

Abstract. Conventional semantics for shared-variable concurrency suffers from the "grain of time" problem, i.e., the necessity of specifying a default level of atomicity. We propose a semantics that avoids any such choice by regarding all interference that is not controlled by explicit critical regions as catastrophic. It is based on three principles:

- Operations have duration and can overlap one another during execution.
- If two overlapping operations touch the same location, the meaning of the program execution is "wrong".
- If, from a given starting state, execution of a program can give "wrong", then no other possibilities need be considered.

1 Introduction

Ever since the early 1970's, when researchers began to propose programming languages in which concurrent processes interact via shared variables, the problem of default atomicity, which Dijkstra called the "grain of time" phenomenon, has plagued the design and definition of such languages. Basically, if two concurrent processes access the same variable, without any explicit description of atomicity or mutual exclusion, the variety of outcomes will depend on a default choice of the level of atomicity, increasing as the atomicity becomes more fine-grained.

For example, consider the concurrent execution of two assignments to the same variable:

$$\mathsf{x} := \mathsf{x} \times \mathsf{x} \parallel \mathsf{x} := \mathsf{x} + 1 \,.$$

1. If each of these assignment commands is an atomic action, then there are two possible interleavings of the actions, which lead to two distinct possible outcomes.
2. If the evaluation of expressions and the storing of a value in a variable are atomic, then there are more interleavings and more possible outcomes.

---

* Research was partially supported by National Science Foundation Grant CCR-0204242, by an EPSRC Visiting Fellowship at Edinburgh University, and by the Basic Research in Computer Science (http://www.brics.dk/) Centre of the Danish National Research Foundation. A more preliminary version of this material was presented at POPL 2004 [1].

K. Lodaya and M. Mahajan (Eds.): FSTTCS 2004, LNCS 3328, pp. 35–48, 2004.

3. If each load and store of a variable is atomic, there are still more interleavings and outcomes.
4. In the extreme case, say if x is a double-precision floating-point number, the atomic actions might be loads and stores of parts of the number representation, so that the possible outcomes would depend upon details of the machine representation of numbers.

In practice, at most the first of these interpretations would be useful to a programmer, while efficient implementation would be possible only at levels 3 or 4, where hardware-implemented mutual exclusion of memory references would suffice to guarantee atomicity.

The fact that there is no default level of atomicity that is natural for both user and implementor led researchers such as Hoare [2] and Brinch-Hansen [3] to propose that interfering concurrent commands such as $x := x \times x \parallel x := x + 1$ should be prohibited syntactically, so that, whenever interference is possible, the programmer must indicate atomicity explicitly by means of critical regions, e.g.,

$$\textbf{with lock do } x := x \times x \parallel \textbf{with lock do } x := x + 1 \,.$$

Unfortunately, this proposal floundered when applied to languages that permit a flexible usage of pointers (which is why, for instance, the approach was not followed in ADA, even though it was mandated in the early requirements specifications of that language). For example, consider the concurrent composition of two indirect assignments:

$$[x] := [x] \times [x] \parallel [y] := [y] + 1$$

(where $[x]$ denotes the contents of the pointer that is the value of x). This command should be prohibited just when $x = y$ — but in general this kind of condition cannot be determined by a compiler.

Our answer to this dilemma is that, when $x = y$, the semantics of the above program is simply "**wrong**". To provide any further information would make no sense at any level of abstraction above the machine-language implementation, and would unnecessarily restrict the ways in which the program could be implemented.

More precisely, we propose a compositional semantics of shared-variable concurrency that avoids the "grain of time" phenomenon by employing three principles:

– All operations, except locking and unlocking, have duration, and can overlap one another during execution.
– If two overlapping operations lookup or set the same location, which may be either a variable or a pointer, then the meaning of program execution is **wrong**.
– If, from a given starting state, execution of a program can give **wrong**, then no other possibilities need be considered.

It must be emphasized that there is no intention of implementing **wrong** as a run-time error stop, which would be extremely inefficient and, in view of the nondeterminacy of concurrent computation, of little use. Instead, when the semantics of a program execution is **wrong**, there are no constraints on how it may be implemented.

Thus it is the programmer's obligation to make a convincing argument that his program will not go wrong. We can define what that means, and we should be able to provide a logic in which such arguments can be made rigorous. But the development of programming languages over the past thirty years makes it clear that this concept of wrongness cannot be decided automatically without restricting the programming language in ways that are unacceptable for many applications.

Our hope of providing an appropriate logic lies in the development of separation logic [4], and, more particularly, in its extension to shared-variable concurrency [5]. The soundness of this extension is very delicate, however, and thus must be demonstrated rigorously with respect to a compelling semantics of the concurrent programming language. Although we will not discuss separation logic further in this paper, we believe that the work described herein can provide such a semantics.

Recently, Steve Brookes proposed a novel semantics for shared-variable concurrency and used it to establish the soundness of separation logic [6]. There are considerable similarities between this work and ours: The starting point of both is a form of transition-trace semantics developed earlier by Brookes [7] (and based on still earlier ideas of Park [8]), in which traces are sequences of start-finish pairs of states. In Brookes's current semantics, these pairs are replaced by "actions", the actions of concurrent processes are interleaved, and uncontrolled interference is mirrored by interference between adjacent actions.

In contrast, our semantics captures duration directly by regarding start and finish as separate actions, between which the actions of other processes may intervene. (Although these two approaches are conceptually quite distinct, each has had significant influence on the other.)

2 Some Examples

The meaning of a command is a set of traces, each of which is a finite or infinite sequence of actions. Except for critical regions, the relevant actions are states labelled "**start**" or "**fin**".

For example, the meaning of the operation $x := x \times x$, which we write $[\![x := x \times x]\!]$ is the set of traces of the form

$$\mathbf{start}[\, x \colon n \,] \, \mathbf{fin}[\, x \colon n \times n \,] \, ,$$

for all integers n. Notice that the states in the start and finish actions have the same domain, which is the *footprint* of the operation, i.e., the exact set of locations that are examined or set by the operation.

If $x := x \times x$ runs by itself, without other processes running concurrently, its behavior is determined by *executing* the traces in its meaning. For example, starting in the state $[\, x \colon 3 \mid t \colon 22 \,]$, the trace $\mathbf{start}[\, x \colon 3 \,] \, \mathbf{fin}[\, x \colon 9 \,]$ has the execution

$$[\,\mathsf{x}\!:3\mid\mathsf{t}\!:22\,]$$
$$\downarrow \qquad\qquad \mathbf{start}[\,\mathsf{x}\!:3\,]$$
$$[\,\mathsf{t}\!:22\,]$$
$$\downarrow \qquad\qquad \mathbf{fin}[\,\mathsf{x}\!:9\,]$$
$$[\,\mathsf{x}\!:9\mid\mathsf{t}\!:22\,]\,.$$

In essence, the effect of the start action is to check that $\mathsf{x}=3$ and then mark x "busy" by removing $[\,\mathsf{x}\!:3\,]$ from the current state. Then the effect of the finish action is to return x to the current state with a new value.

On the other hand, when started in a state with a different value of x, the trace $\mathbf{start}[\,\mathsf{x}\!:3\,]\,\mathbf{fin}[\,\mathsf{x}\!:9\,]$ is irrelevant and has no execution. But an execution will be provided by another trace, such as $\mathbf{start}[\,\mathsf{x}\!:4\,]\,\mathbf{fin}[\,\mathsf{x}\!:16\,]$, in $[\![\,\mathsf{x}:=\mathsf{x}\times\mathsf{x}\,]\!]$.

A third possibility arises when x does not occur in the domain of the starting state. In this case the execution goes wrong:

$$[\,\mathsf{t}\!:22\,]$$
$$\downarrow \qquad \mathbf{start}[\,\mathsf{x}\!:3\,]$$
$$\mathbf{wrong}\,.$$

When a command assigns indirectly to a pointer, its footprint is more complex. For example, the meaning $[\![\,[\mathsf{x}]:=[\mathsf{x}]\times[\mathsf{x}]\,]\!]$ is the set of traces

$$\mathbf{start}[\,\mathsf{x}\!:n_1\mid n_1\!:n_2\,]\,\mathbf{fin}[\,\mathsf{x}\!:n_1\mid n_1\!:n_2\times n_2\,]\,,$$

for all integers n_1 and n_2. Here the footprint contains both x and its value n_1, which is a pointer. (We regard pointers as integers, in order to permit unrestricted pointer arithmetic.) Similarly, the meaning $[\![\,[\mathsf{y}]:=[\mathsf{y}]+1\,]\!]$ is the set of traces

$$\mathbf{start}[\,\mathsf{y}\!:n_3\mid n_3\!:n_4\,]\,\mathbf{fin}[\,\mathsf{y}\!:n_3\mid n_3\!:n_4+1\,]\,,$$

for all integers n_3 and n_4.

Now consider the concurrent execution of these two indirect assignments. The meaning

$$[\![\,[\mathsf{x}]:=[\mathsf{x}]\times[\mathsf{x}]\parallel[\mathsf{y}]:=[\mathsf{y}]+1\,]\!]$$

is the set of interleavings of the traces of each subcommand. This set includes traces of the form

$$\mathbf{start}[\,\mathsf{x}\!:n_1\mid n_1\!:n_2\,]\,\mathbf{start}[\,\mathsf{y}\!:n_3\mid n_3\!:n_4\,]$$
$$\mathbf{fin}[\,\mathsf{y}\!:n_3\mid n_3\!:n_4+1\,]\,\mathbf{fin}[\,\mathsf{x}\!:n_1\mid n_1\!:n_2\times n_2\,]\,,$$

in which the two assignment operations overlap.

When $n_1 \neq n_3$, such a trace executes without interference:

$$[\,x\colon n_1 \mid n_1\colon n_2 \mid y\colon n_3 \mid n_3\colon n_4\,]$$
$$\downarrow \qquad\qquad\qquad \mathbf{start}[\,x\colon n_1 \mid n_1\colon n_2\,]$$
$$[\,y\colon n_3 \mid n_3\colon n_4\,]$$
$$\downarrow \qquad\qquad\qquad \mathbf{start}[\,y\colon n_3 \mid n_3\colon n_4\,]$$
$$[\,]$$
$$\downarrow \qquad\qquad\qquad \mathbf{fin}[\,y\colon n_3 \mid n_3\colon n_4 + 1\,]$$
$$[\,y\colon n_3 \mid n_3\colon n_4 + 1\,]$$
$$\downarrow \qquad\qquad\qquad \mathbf{fin}[\,x\colon n_1 \mid n_1\colon n_2 \times n_2\,]$$
$$[\,y\colon n_3 \mid n_3\colon n_4 + 1 \mid x\colon n_1 \mid n_1\colon n_2 \times n_2\,]\,.$$

On the other hand, when $n_1 = n_3$ and $n_2 = n_4$, the two assignments interfere:

$$[\,x\colon n_1 \mid n_1\colon n_2 \mid y\colon n_1\,]$$
$$\downarrow \qquad\qquad\qquad \mathbf{start}[\,x\colon n_1 \mid n_1\colon n_2\,]$$
$$[\,y\colon n_1\,]$$
$$\downarrow \qquad\qquad\qquad \mathbf{start}[\,y\colon n_1 \mid n_1\colon n_2\,]$$
$$\mathbf{wrong}\,.$$

Our treatment of critical regions follows the recent work of Brookes [6]. Three actions are involved, each of which names a *lock* or semaphore:

$\mathbf{try}(k)$: Try to acquire k, but find it is already locked.

$\mathbf{acq}(k)$: Succeed in acquiring k, and lock it.

$\mathbf{rel}(k)$: Unlock k (or signal "impossible" if it is already unlocked).

For example, the meaning of the critical region **with k do** x := x × x is the set of traces (for all integers n):

$$\mathbf{acq}(k)\,\mathbf{start}[\,x\colon n\,]\,\mathbf{fin}[\,x\colon n \times n\,]\,\mathbf{rel}(k),$$
$$\mathbf{try}(k)\,\mathbf{acq}(k)\,\mathbf{start}[\,x\colon n\,]\,\mathbf{fin}[\,x\colon n \times n\,]\,\mathbf{rel}(k),$$
$$\mathbf{try}(k)\,\mathbf{try}(k)\,\mathbf{acq}(k)\,\mathbf{start}[\,x\colon n\,]\,\mathbf{fin}[\,x\colon n \times n\,]\,\mathbf{rel}(k),$$
$$\vdots$$
$$\mathbf{try}(k)\,\mathbf{try}(k)\,\mathbf{try}(k)\,\cdots\,.$$

To execute these new actions, we augment the current state of the computation with a set κ of "closed" locks. When $k \notin \kappa$ (and n is 3), a trace of the first form has an execution:

$$\kappa, [\,x\colon 3 \mid t\colon 22\,]$$
$$\downarrow \qquad\qquad\qquad \mathbf{acq}(k)$$
$$\kappa \cup \{k\}, [\,x\colon 3 \mid t\colon 22\,]$$
$$\downarrow \qquad\qquad\qquad \mathbf{start}[\,x\colon 3\,]$$
$$\kappa \cup \{k\}, [\,t\colon 22\,]$$
$$\downarrow \qquad\qquad\qquad \mathbf{fin}[\,x\colon 9\,]$$
$$\kappa \cup \{k\}, [\,x\colon 9 \mid t\colon 22\,]$$
$$\downarrow \qquad\qquad\qquad \mathbf{rel}(k)$$
$$\kappa, [\,x\colon 9 \mid t\colon 22\,]\,.$$

On the other hand, when $k \in \kappa$, the last trace has a nonterminating execution that represents deadlock:

$$\kappa, [\, x\!:3 \mid t\!:22 \,]$$
$$\downarrow \qquad \mathbf{try}(k)$$
$$\kappa, [\, x\!:3 \mid t\!:22 \,]$$
$$\downarrow \qquad \mathbf{try}(k)$$
$$\vdots$$

The remaining traces in $[\![\mathbf{with\ k\ do}\ x := x \times x]\!]$ can only execute successfully after being interleaved with other traces that affect the same lock. For example, one possible interleaving of

$$\mathbf{try}(k)\ \mathbf{try}(k)\ \mathbf{acq}(k)\ \mathbf{start}[\,x\!:3\,]\ \mathbf{fin}[\,x\!:9\,]\ \mathbf{rel}(k)$$

with

$$\mathbf{acq}(k)\ \mathbf{start}[\,x\!:2\,]\ \mathbf{fin}[\,x\!:3\,]\ \mathbf{rel}(k)$$

(which is a trace in the meaning of $\mathbf{with\ k\ do}\ x := x + 1$) is

$$\mathbf{acq}(k)\ \mathbf{start}[\,x\!:2\,]\ \mathbf{try}(k)\ \mathbf{fin}[\,x\!:3\,]\ \mathbf{try}(k)$$
$$\mathbf{rel}(k)\ \mathbf{acq}(k)\ \mathbf{start}[\,x\!:3\,]\ \mathbf{fin}[\,x\!:9\,]\ \mathbf{rel}(k)\ ,$$

which executes as follows when $k \notin \kappa$:

$$\kappa, [\, x\!:2 \,]$$
$$\downarrow \qquad \mathbf{acq}(k)$$
$$\kappa \cup \{k\}, [\, x\!:2 \,]$$
$$\downarrow \qquad \mathbf{start}[\,x\!:2\,]$$
$$\kappa \cup \{k\}, [\,]$$
$$\downarrow \qquad \mathbf{try}(k)$$
$$\kappa \cup \{k\}, [\,]$$
$$\downarrow \qquad \mathbf{fin}[\,x\!:3\,]$$
$$\kappa \cup \{k\}, [\, x\!:3 \,]$$
$$\downarrow \qquad \mathbf{try}(k)$$
$$\vdots$$

$$\kappa \cup \{k\}, [\, x\!:3 \,]$$
$$\downarrow \qquad \mathbf{rel}(k)$$
$$\kappa, [\, x\!:3 \,]$$
$$\downarrow \qquad \mathbf{acq}(k)$$
$$\kappa \cup \{k\}, [\, x\!:3 \,]$$
$$\downarrow \qquad \mathbf{start}[\,x\!:3\,]$$
$$\kappa \cup \{k\}, [\,]$$
$$\downarrow \qquad \mathbf{fin}[\,x\!:9\,]$$
$$\kappa \cup \{k\}, [\, x\!:9 \,]$$
$$\downarrow \qquad \mathbf{rel}(k)$$
$$\kappa, [\, x\!:9 \,]\ .$$

3 Syntax, States, and the Semantics of Expressions

The programing language we will use throughout this paper is an extension of the simple imperative language:

$$\langle exp \rangle ::= \langle var \rangle \mid \langle constant \rangle \mid \langle exp \rangle + \langle exp \rangle \mid \cdots$$

$$\langle boolexp \rangle ::= \langle exp \rangle = \langle exp \rangle \mid \cdots \mid \langle boolexp \rangle \wedge \langle boolexp \rangle \mid \cdots$$

$$\langle comm \rangle ::= \langle var \rangle := \langle exp \rangle \mid \mathbf{skip} \mid \langle comm \rangle\ ;\ \langle comm \rangle$$
$$\mid\ \mathbf{if}\ \langle boolexp \rangle\ \mathbf{then}\ \langle comm \rangle\ \mathbf{else}\ \langle comm \rangle$$
$$\mid\ \mathbf{while}\ \langle boolexp \rangle\ \mathbf{do}\ \langle comm \rangle$$

with operations for looking up and mutating the contents of addresses:

$$\langle exp \rangle ::= [\langle exp \rangle]$$

$$\langle comm \rangle ::= [\langle exp \rangle] := \langle exp \rangle$$

concurrent composition:

$$\langle comm \rangle ::= \langle comm \rangle \parallel \langle comm \rangle$$

and critical regions:

$$\langle comm \rangle ::= \textbf{with } \langle lock \rangle \textbf{ do } \langle comm \rangle \mid \textbf{with } \langle lock \rangle \textbf{ when } \langle boolexp \rangle \textbf{ do } \langle comm \rangle$$

(In fact, the unconditional critical region **with** k **do** c can be regarded as an abbreviation for the conditional critical region **with** k **when true do** c. We treat it as a separate form for expository reasons.)

We assume that constants are integers, and that variables and locks are unstructured syntactic names (which are not integers). We also identify addresses with integers. Then we define a location to be either a variable or an address, and a state to be a mapping from a finite set of locations to integers:

$$\text{Addresses} = \text{Integers}$$

$$\text{Locations} = \langle var \rangle \uplus \text{Addresses}$$

$$\text{States} = \bigcup \{ \delta \to \text{Integers} \mid \delta \overset{\text{fin}}{\subseteq} \text{Locations} \} \, .$$

We will use the following metavariables (with occasional decorations) to range over specific sets:

$v : \langle var \rangle$ (Variables) $\qquad\qquad$ δ : Finite Sets of Locations
$e : \langle exp \rangle$ (Expressions) $\qquad\qquad$ σ : States
$b : \langle boolexp \rangle$ (Boolean Expressions) $\qquad$ $k : \langle lock \rangle$ (Locks)
$c : \langle comm \rangle$ (Commands) $\qquad\qquad$ κ : Finite Sets of Locks
n : Integers $\qquad\qquad\qquad\qquad\qquad$ τ : Traces
t : Truth Values $\qquad\qquad\qquad\qquad$ T : Sets of Traces
ℓ : Locations $\qquad\qquad\qquad\qquad\qquad$ Φ : Configurations

(Traces and configurations will be defined later.)

We will also need some concepts and notations for states. We say that σ and σ' are *compatible*, written $\sigma \smile \sigma'$, iff $\sigma \cup \sigma'$ is a function, or equivalently, σ and σ' agree on the intersection of their domains. We also write $\delta \perp \delta'$ when the sets δ and δ' are disjoint, and $\sigma \perp \sigma'$ when $\text{dom}\,\sigma \perp \text{dom}\,\sigma'$.

When $\ell_1, \ldots, \ell_m$ are distinct, we write $[\ell_1 : n_1 \mid \ldots \mid \ell_m : n_m]$ for the state with domain $\{\ell_1, \ldots, \ell_m\}$ that maps each ℓ_i into n_i. We also write $[\sigma \mid \ell : n]$ for the state such that

$$\text{dom}[\sigma \mid \ell : n] = \text{dom}\,\sigma \cup \{\ell\}$$

$$[\sigma \mid \ell : n](\ell) = n$$

$$[\sigma \mid \ell : n](\ell') = \sigma(\ell') \text{ when } \ell \neq \ell' \, .$$

(Note that $[\sigma \mid \ell{:}n]$ may either be an extension of σ or a possibly altered function with the same domain as σ.)

The meaning $[\![e]\!]$ of an expression (or boolean expression) e is a set of pairs $\langle \sigma, n \rangle$ in which n is the value obtained by evaluating e in any state that is an extension of σ, and in which the domain of σ is the *footprint* of the evaluation, i.e., the set of locations that are actually examined during the evaluation.

For example,

$$[\![x - x]\!] = \{\, \langle [\,x{:}m\,], 0 \rangle \mid m \in \text{Integers} \,\}$$

$$[\![x + [y]]\!] = \{\, \langle [\,x{:}m \mid y{:}n \mid n{:}n'\,], m + n' \rangle \mid m, n, m' \in \text{Integers} \,\}\,.$$

The relevant semantics equations are

$$[\![\langle \exp \rangle]\!] \subseteq \text{States} \times \text{Integers}$$

$$[\![n]\!] = \{\langle [\,], n \rangle\}$$

$$[\![v]\!] = \{\, \langle [\,v{:}n\,], n \rangle \mid n \in \text{Integers} \,\}$$

$$[\![e + e']\!] = \{\, \langle \sigma \cup \sigma', n + n' \rangle \mid \langle \sigma, n \rangle \in [\![e]\!], \langle \sigma', n' \rangle \in [\![e']\!], \text{ and } \sigma \smile \sigma' \,\}$$

$$[\![[e]]\!] = \{\, \langle \sigma \cup [\,n{:}n'\,], n' \rangle \mid \langle \sigma, n \rangle \in [\![e]\!], n' \in \text{Integers}, \text{ and } \sigma \smile [\,n{:}n'\,] \,\}$$

$$[\![\langle \text{boolexp} \rangle]\!] \subseteq \text{States} \times \text{Bool}$$

$$[\![e = e']\!] = \{\, \langle \sigma \cup \sigma', n = n' \rangle \mid \langle \sigma, n \rangle \in [\![e]\!], \langle \sigma', n' \rangle \in [\![e']\!], \text{ and } \sigma \smile \sigma' \,\}$$

$$[\![b \wedge b']\!] = \{\, \langle \sigma, \mathbf{false} \rangle \mid \langle \sigma, \mathbf{false} \rangle \in [\![b]\!] \,\}$$
$$\cup \{\, \langle \sigma \cup \sigma', t' \rangle \mid \langle \sigma, \mathbf{true} \rangle \in [\![b]\!], \langle \sigma', t' \rangle \in [\![b']\!], \text{ and } \sigma \smile \sigma' \,\}\,.$$

(Note that the final equation describes short-circuit evaluation of conjunction.)

Since expression evaluation in our programming language happens to be deterministic (though this is not required by the nature of our semantics), the meaning of an expression will be a function, but because its domain contains only states whose domains are footprints, this function will be a restriction of the meaning in a conventional denotational semantics.

Nevertheless, one can show an appropriate property of *totality*: For all e and σ, there are σ' and n such that $\sigma \smile \sigma'$ and $\langle \sigma', n \rangle \in [\![e]\!]$. A similar property holds for boolean expressions.

4   Traces and the Semantics of Commands

Actions can be defined grammatically:

$$\langle \text{action} \rangle ::= \mathbf{start}(\langle \text{state} \rangle) \mid \mathbf{fin}(\langle \text{state} \rangle) \mid \mathbf{try}(\langle \text{lock} \rangle) \mid \mathbf{acq}(\langle \text{lock} \rangle) \mid \mathbf{rel}(\langle \text{lock} \rangle)$$

Then a *trace* is a finite or infinite sequence of actions, or a finite sequence of actions followed by either **wrong** or $\bot$.

We use ";" to denote the following concatenation of traces:

$$\tau_1 \,;\, \tau_2 = \begin{cases} \tau_1 & \text{if } \tau_1 \text{ is infinite, or ends in } \textbf{wrong} \text{ or } \bot, \\ \tau_1\,\tau_2 & \text{otherwise.} \end{cases}$$

Then we can define the concatenation and exponentiation of trace sets in a standard way:

$$T\,;\,T' = \{\,\tau\,;\,\tau' \mid \tau \in T, \tau' \in T'\,\}$$

$$T^0 = \{\epsilon\}$$

$$T^{n+1} = T\,;\,T^n$$

$$T^* = \bigcup_{n=0}^{\infty} T^n$$

$$T^\omega = \{\,\tau_0\,;\,\tau_1\,;\,\cdots \mid \forall i \geq 0.\ \tau_i \in T\,\}\,.$$

We will also need the concept of a *filter* to describe the use of boolean expressions to determine control flow:

$$\text{filter}(\langle\text{boolexp}\rangle) \subseteq \text{Traces}$$

$$\text{filter}(b) = \{\,\textbf{start}(\sigma)\,\textbf{fin}(\sigma) \mid \langle\sigma, \textbf{true}\rangle \in [\![b]\!]\,\}\,.$$

From the totality property of boolean expressions, one can obtain a totality condition for filters: For all b and σ, there is a σ' such that $\sigma \smile \sigma'$ and

$$\textbf{start}(\sigma')\,\textbf{fin}(\sigma') \in \text{filter}(b) \cup \text{filter}(\neg b)\,.$$

With these preliminaries, we can give semantic equations that determine the sets of traces that are meanings of sequential commands:

$$[\![\langle\text{comm}\rangle]\!] \subseteq \text{Traces}$$

$$[\![v := e]\!] = \{\,\textbf{start}(\sigma \cup [v{:}\,n_{\text{old}}])\,\textbf{fin}([\,\sigma \mid v{:}\,n\,]) \mid$$
$$\langle\sigma, n\rangle \in [\![e]\!], \sigma \smile [v{:}\,n_{\text{old}}]\,\}$$

$$[\![[e] := e']\!] = \{\,\textbf{start}(\sigma \cup \sigma' \cup [n{:}\,n_{\text{old}}])\,\textbf{fin}([\,\sigma \cup \sigma' \mid n{:}\,n'\,]) \mid$$
$$\langle\sigma, n\rangle \in [\![e]\!], \langle\sigma', n'\rangle \in [\![e']\!], \sigma \smile \sigma', (\sigma \cup \sigma') \smile [n{:}\,n_{\text{old}}]\,\}$$

$$[\![\textbf{skip}]\!] = \{\textbf{start}[\,]\,\textbf{fin}[\,]\}$$

$$[\![c_1\,;\,c_2]\!] = [\![c_1]\!]\,;\,[\![c_2]\!]$$

$$[\![\textbf{if } b \textbf{ then } c_1 \textbf{ else } c_2]\!] = (\text{filter}(b)\,;\,[\![c_1]\!]) \cup (\text{filter}(\neg b)\,;\,[\![c_2]\!])$$

$$[\![\textbf{while } b \textbf{ do } c]\!] = ((\text{filter}(b)\,;\,[\![c]\!])^*\,;\,\text{filter}(\neg b)) \cup (\text{filter}(b)\,;\,[\![c]\!])^\omega\,.$$

For example

$$[\![x := [y] + 1]\!] =$$
$$\{\, \mathbf{start}[x\colon m \mid m\colon m' \mid y\colon n \mid n\colon n'\,] \mathbf{fin}[x\colon m \mid m\colon n' + 1 \mid y\colon n \mid n\colon n'\,]$$
$$\mid m, m', n, n' \in \text{Integers and } m \neq n\,\}$$
$$\cup \{\, \mathbf{start}[x\colon n \mid y\colon n \mid n\colon n'\,] \mathbf{fin}[x\colon n \mid y\colon n \mid n\colon n' + 1\,] \mid n, n' \in \text{Integers}\,\}\,.$$

To define concurrent composition, we must first introduce the concept of a *fair merge* of the traces τ_1 and τ_2, which is an merge (or interleaving) that contains every occurrence of actions in τ_1 and τ_2 (even when τ_1 or τ_2 is infinite).

To make this concept precise, we regard a trace as a function whose domain is the finite or infinite set of nonnegative numbers less than the length of the trace. Then τ is a *fair merge* of τ_1 and τ_2 iff there are functions ϕ_1 and ϕ_2 such that

$$\operatorname{dom}\phi_1 = \operatorname{dom}\tau_1 \text{ and } \operatorname{dom}\phi_2 = \operatorname{dom}\tau_2.$$

ϕ_1 and ϕ_2 are strictly monotone.

The ranges of ϕ_1 and ϕ_2 are a partition of $\operatorname{dom}\tau$.

For all $i \in \operatorname{dom}\tau_1$, $\tau_1(i) = \tau(\phi_1(i))$.

For all $i \in \operatorname{dom}\tau_2$, $\tau_2(i) = \tau(\phi_2(i))$.

Next, we define

$$\tau_1 \parallel \tau_2 = \{\, \text{truncate}(\tau) \mid \tau \text{ is a fair merge of } \tau_1 \text{ and } \tau_2 \,\}\,,$$

where truncate is a function that captures the fact that **wrong** and $\bot$ always terminate traces: When τ does not contain **wrong** or $\bot$,

$$\text{truncate}(\tau) = \tau$$
$$\text{truncate}(\tau\, \mathbf{wrong}\, \tau') = \tau\, \mathbf{wrong}$$
$$\text{truncate}(\tau \bot \tau') = \tau \bot\,.$$

Finally, the meaning of the concurrent composition $c_1 \parallel c_2$ is the set of truncated fair merges of traces in the meaning of c_1 with traces in the meaning of c_2:

$$[\![c_1 \parallel c_2]\!] = \bigcup \{\, \tau_1 \parallel \tau_2 \mid \tau_1 \in [\![c_1]\!], \tau_2 \in [\![c_2]\!]\,\}\,.$$

Our semantics of critical regions follows closely that of Brookes [6]:

$$[\![\mathbf{with}\ k\ \mathbf{do}\ c]\!] = \bigl(\{\mathbf{try}(k)\}^* \,;\, \{\mathbf{acq}(k)\} \,;\, [\![c]\!] \,;\, \{\mathbf{rel}(k)\}\bigr) \cup \{\mathbf{try}(k)\}^\omega$$

$$[\![\mathbf{with}\ k\ \mathbf{when}\ b\ \mathbf{do}\ c]\!] =$$
$$\bigl(\text{wait}^* \,;\, \{\mathbf{try}(k)\}^* \,;\, \{\mathbf{acq}(k)\} \,;\, \text{filter}(b) \,;\, [\![c]\!] \,;\, \{\mathbf{rel}(k)\}\bigr) \cup \text{wait}^\omega\,,$$

where

$$\text{wait} = \bigl(\{\mathbf{try}(k)\}^* \,;\, \{\mathbf{acq}(k)\} \,;\, \text{filter}(\neg b) \,;\, \{\mathbf{rel}(k)\}\bigr) \cup \{\mathbf{try}(k)\}^\omega\,.$$

Notice that **with** k **when** b **do** c will fail to terminate if either it fails to ever acquire the lock k, or if it acquires k, but never when b is true.

There is a concept of totality that is appropriate to sets of traces: A set T of traces is said to be *total* whenever, if

$$\tau\, \mathbf{start}(\sigma_0)\, \tau' \in T\,,$$

holds for some state σ_0, then for every state σ there is a trace

$$\tau\, \mathbf{start}(\sigma')\, \tau'' \in T\,,$$

such that $\sigma \smile \sigma'$.

There is also a somewhat analogous concept related to locks: A set T of traces is *lock-total* whenever, if

$$\tau\, \mathbf{acq}(k)\, \tau' \in T\,,$$

then there is a trace

$$\tau\, \mathbf{try}(k)\, \tau'' \in T\,.$$

It can be shown that, for all commands c, $[\![c]\!]$ is total and lock-total.

5   Executing Traces

The execution of traces is described by a small-step operational semantics. A configuration Φ consists of a trace to be executed, coupled with the currently available state and a finite set of closed locks, or it is one of three special configurations that indicate abnormal termination or explicit nontermination:

Configurations =

Finite Sets of Locks × States × Traces ∪ {wrong, impossible, ⊥} .

A configuration is *nonterminal* if it contains a nonempty trace; otherwise it is *terminal*. (For readability, we omit empty traces from terminal configuations.)

Informally, the special terminal configurations have the following meanings:

- "wrong" indicates that a **start** operation has tried to access a location that is not in the domain of the currently available state.
- "impossible" indicates that a **fin** operation has tried to extend the current state at a location that is already in its domain, or that a **rel** has tried to open a lock that is not closed.
- ⊥ indicates that the trace will execute forever without performing further actions.

Transitions go from nonterminal configurations to configurations that are either nonterminal or terminal. They are described by the relation

$$\rightarrow\ \subseteq \text{Nonterminal Configurations} \times \text{Configurations}$$

that is the least relation satisfying:

$$\kappa, \sigma, \mathbf{start}(\sigma')\,\tau \rightarrow \begin{cases} \kappa, \sigma - \sigma', \tau & \text{if } \sigma' \subseteq \sigma \\ \mathbf{wrong} & \text{if } \sigma \smile \sigma' \text{ and } \sigma' \nsubseteq \sigma \\ \mathbf{no\ transition} & \text{if } \sigma \not\smile \sigma' \end{cases}$$

$$\kappa, \sigma, \mathbf{fin}(\sigma')\,\tau \rightarrow \begin{cases} \kappa, \sigma \cup \sigma', \tau & \text{if } \sigma' \perp \sigma \\ \mathbf{impossible} & \text{otherwise} \end{cases}$$

$$\kappa, \sigma, \mathbf{try}(k)\,\tau \rightarrow \begin{cases} \kappa, \sigma, \tau & \text{if } k \in \kappa \\ \mathbf{no\ transition} & \text{if } k \notin \kappa \end{cases}$$

$$\kappa, \sigma, \mathbf{acq}(k)\,\tau \rightarrow \begin{cases} \kappa \cup \{k\}, \sigma, \tau & \text{if } k \notin \kappa \\ \mathbf{no\ transition} & \text{if } k \in \kappa \end{cases}$$

$$\kappa, \sigma, \mathbf{rel}(k)\,\tau \rightarrow \begin{cases} \kappa - \{k\}, \sigma, \tau & \text{if } k \in \kappa \\ \mathbf{impossible} & \text{if } k \notin \kappa \end{cases}$$

$$\kappa, \sigma, \mathbf{wrong} \rightarrow \quad \mathbf{wrong}$$

$$\kappa, \sigma, \perp \rightarrow \quad \perp .$$

It is easy to see that $\rightarrow$ is a partial, but not total function.

A sequence of configurations that begins with the nonterminal $\Phi = \kappa, \sigma, \tau$, and in which each configuration is related to the next, is called an *execution of* τ *in* κ, σ. If there is such an execution that is finite and ends with Φ', we write $\Phi \rightarrow^* \Phi'$; if there is such an execution that is infinite, we say that Φ diverges.

Since $\rightarrow$ is a partial function, if Φ diverges, then there is no terminal Φ' such that $\Phi \rightarrow^* \Phi'$, while if Φ does not diverge, then there is at most one Φ' such that $\Phi \rightarrow^* \Phi'$. In other words, the execution of a trace is always determinate.

On the other hand, since $\rightarrow$ is not a total function, there are nonterminal $\Phi = \kappa, \sigma, \tau$ such that Φ does not diverge and there is no terminal Φ' such that $\Phi \rightarrow^* \Phi'$. In this case, there is no execution of τ in κ, σ, and we say that τ is *irrelevant* to κ, σ.

Another property of trace execution stems from from the fact that in any trace of any command in our programming language, the actions **acq** and **rel**, and also **start** and **fin**, are balanced, in much the same sense as with parentheses. Specifically, in any prefix of any trace of any command, the number of occurrences of $\mathbf{rel}(k)$ for a particular lock k will never exceed the number of occurrences of $\mathbf{acq}(k)$ for the same lock, and the number of occurrences of $\mathbf{fin}(\sigma)$ for which a particular variable occurs in $\mathrm{dom}\,\sigma$ will never exceed the number of occurrences of $\mathbf{start}(\sigma')$ for which the same variable occurs in $\mathrm{dom}\,\sigma'$.

Because of this property (which might not hold for a lower-level programming language), one can show that the abnormal termination "impossible" never arises: For all commands c, traces $\tau \in [\![c]\!]$, lock sets κ, and states σ:

$$\kappa, \sigma, \tau \not\to^* \text{ impossible}.$$

Finally, we define the execution of a set of traces T, in κ, σ:

$$\text{Exec}(\kappa, \sigma, T) = \{ \langle \kappa', \sigma' \rangle \mid \exists \tau \in T.\ \kappa, \sigma, \tau \to^* \kappa', \sigma' \}$$

$$\cup \text{ if } \kappa, \sigma, \tau \to^* \text{wrong then Wrong else } \{\}$$

$$\cup \text{ if } \kappa, \sigma, \tau \text{ diverges then } \{\bot\} \text{ else } \{\},$$

where Wrong is the set of all terminal configurations, including "wrong". Since

$$\text{Wrong} \cup S = \text{Wrong},$$

for all sets S of terminal configurations, this captures the principle that Wrong overrides other possible outcomes. It also captures the notion that Wrong can be implemented arbitrarily.

In contrast to the execution of a particular trace, the execution of a trace set that is the meaning of a command can be nondeterminate. On the other hand, since command meanings are total and lock-total, $\text{Exec}(\kappa, \sigma, [\![c]\!])$ contains at least one terminal configuration for every command c, state σ, and finite lock set κ.

6   Future Directions

Our trace semantics leads to a broader notion of observational equivalence than the conventional semantics of shared-variable concurrency. For example, in a conventional semantics the commands

$$\mathsf{x} := \mathsf{x} + 1 \,;\, \mathsf{x} := \mathsf{x} + 2 \qquad \text{and} \qquad \mathsf{x} := \mathsf{x} + 3$$

are distinguishable when run concurrently with, say, $\mathsf{x} := 1$. But in our semantics, these commands are observationally equivalent: They would both go wrong if run concurrently with any command that assigns to or evaluates x; otherwise they would both increase x by three.

As suggested by this example, the broader notion of observational equivalence should provide greater scope for the development of code optimization. Unfortunately, however, our trace semantics is far from fully abstract; for example, the above commands denote distinct trace sets.

We intend to study equivalences on trace sets that at least approach observational equivalence. For example, we conjecture that every command without critical regions has a meaning that is equivalent to a set of traces whose members each have one of the forms:

$$\mathbf{start}(\sigma) \; \mathbf{fin}(\sigma') \text{ where } \operatorname{dom} \sigma = \operatorname{dom} \sigma'$$

$$\mathbf{start}(\sigma) \perp$$

$$\mathbf{start}(\sigma) \; \mathbf{wrong}.$$

I hope to report more on this topic in my talk.

We also hope to extend the programming language described by our semantics to include declarations of variables and locks. This should be a straightforward adaptation of the approach used by Brookes for transition traces [7]. It would also be useful to introduce operations for storage allocation and deallocation, perhaps similar to the **cons** and **dispose** operations of separation logic.

Another important direction would be permit passivity, i.e., to relax the assumption that overlapping operations on the same location go wrong, in order to allow the overlapping of read-only operations.

Finally, we hope to use our grainless semantics to model concurrent separation logic [5], and to relate the semantics to Brookes's model [6].

Acknowledgement

The author wishes to thank Stephen D. Brookes for numerous helpful discussions.

References

1. Reynolds, J.C.: Towards a grainless semantics for shared variable concurrency (abstract only). In: Conference Record of POPL 2004: The 31st ACM SIGPLAN-SIGACT Symposium on Principles of Programming Languages, New York, ACM Press (2004)
2. Hoare, C.A.R.: Towards a theory of parallel programming. In Hoare, C.A.R., Perrott, R.H., eds.: Operating Systems Techniques. Volume 9 of A.P.I.C. Studies in Data Processing, London, Academic Press (1972) 61–71
3. Brinch Hansen, P.: Structured multiprogramming. Communications of the ACM **15** (1972) 574–578
4. Reynolds, J.C.: Separation logic: A logic for shared mutable data structures. In: Proceedings Seventeenth Annual IEEE Symposium on Logic in Computer Science, Los Alamitos, California, IEEE Computer Society (2002) 55–74
5. O'Hearn, P.W.: Resources, concurrency and local reasoning. In: CONCUR 2004 — Concurrency Theory, Proceedings of the 15th International Conference. Volume 3170 of Lecture Notes in Computer Science, Berlin, Springer-Verlag (2004) 49–67
6. Brookes, S.D.: A semantics for concurrent separation logic. In: CONCUR 2004 — Concurrency Theory, Proceedings of the 15th International Conference. Volume 3170 of Lecture Notes in Computer Science, Berlin, Springer-Verlag (2004) 16–34
7. Brookes, S.D.: Full abstraction for a shared-variable parallel language. Information and Computation **127** (1996) 145–163
8. Park, D.M.R.: On the semantics of fair parallelism. In Bjørner, D., ed.: Abstract Software Specifications. Volume 86 of Lecture Notes in Computer Science, Berlin, Springer-Verlag (1980) 504–526

Regular Languages, Unambiguous Concatenation and Computational Complexity

Denis Thérien

School of Computer Science, McGill University
denis@cs.mcgill.ca

Abstract. Regular languages are central objects of study in computer science. Although they are quite "easy" in the traditional space-time framework of sequential computations, the situation is different when other models are considered. In this paper we consider the subclass of regular languages that can be defined via unambiguous concatenation. We show remarkable algorithmic properties of this class in the context of boolean circuits and in that of computational learning.

1 Introduction

This paper will discuss various computational complexity issues that can be related to regular languages. Our interest is two-fold.

First, the class of regular languages plays a central role in all of computer science; it possibly constitutes the computational notion with the widest range of real world applications and it thus appears quite meaningful to investigate the class in details. The interest of the concept becomes even more apparent in the light of the many equivalent characterizations arising from several, a priori unrelated, points of view: for example, in terms of machines (finite-state automata), in terms of algebra (finite monoids) or in terms of logic (second-order monadic formulas).

Secondly, it has been realized over the years that regular languages can be used to analyze some computational complexity questions that are of interest in theoretical computer science. In the classical sequential model of space-time complexity, regular languages appear as a most simple class as they are precisely the languages that are recognizable in constant space and linear time, which seems to leave little to add. In models that have appeared later, e.g. boolean circuits or communication complexity, the situation is quite different: the class of regular languages provide "hard" examples for these models, and it becomes interesting to understand natural parametrizations of the class in terms of computational difficulty in the given framework. It is a pleasing situation that standard classification on the language side corresponds often to computational parametrization of interest. This is true in the two models mentioned above ([3] for boolean circuits, [24] for communcation complexity), but in several other contexts as well: constraint satisfaction problems ([13]), linear temporal logic ([26]), quantum automata ([1]), computational learning ([10]).

K. Lodaya and M. Mahajan (Eds.): FSTTCS 2004, LNCS 3328, pp. 49–57, 2004.

In this paper, we will argue for our paradigm by presenting two examples in which it is possible to investigate computational issues in terms of regular languages: boolean circuits and computational learning. As a running theme we will focus attention on the subclass of so-called *unambiguous* languages, those that are definable using disjoint union and unambiguous concatenation. In both our examples, it will be seen that this restricted class corresponds to the existence of efficient algorithms within the model being considered. A first survey of this class has appeared in [23]; we here add some more recent results. The paper is organized as follows: a first section will summarize the definitions on regular languages that will be needed for our discussion. Our two examples are then discussed in turn.

2   Regular Languages

The class of regular languages is well-known. We sketch here the small portion of the framework that we will need; a more detailed treatment is found e.g. in [15]. For each alphabet A, the class of regular languages over A consists of the smallest family of subsets of A^* that contains the finite sets, and that is closed under union, concatenation and star. Regular languages arise naturally when studying computations: in particular the famous theorem of Kleene asserts that a language is regular iff it can be recognized by a deterministic finite automaton. This immediately implies that the complement of a regular language is also regular.

A slight variant of Kleene's theorem paves the way to a very powerful algebraic treatment to understand regular languages. A monoid is a set equipped with a binary operation that is associative and that admits a two-sided identity element. A language $L \subseteq A^*$ is recognized by a monoid M iff there exists a morphism $\phi : A^* \to M$ such that $L = \phi^{-1}(\phi(L))$. Kleene's result can be restated as follows: a language is regular iff it can be recognized by a finite monoid. Actually, to each regular language L can be associated in a canonical way a unique minimal monoid that will recognize it; it is called the syntactic monoid of L and denoted $M(L)$. This algebraic object can be effectively computed, e.g. from any regular expression for L, and this often plays a key role in decidability issues in this theory. Intuitively, one would believe that combinatorial characteristics of a language L can be related to algebraic properties of its syntactic recognizer. This intuition is validated beyond all hopes and the two theories, finite monoids and regular languages, are now deeply intertwined [9]. There also exists an elegant relationship between regular languages and logic. Indeed, once the formalism is properly set up, regular languages are exactly those arising in the monadic second-order theory of successor. We refer the reader to [22] for a treatment of regular languages from that point of view.

The notion of regular language is thus ubiquitous, a good sign of mathematical relevance. Moreover, because this class describes the computations of finite-state devices, one is not surprised to see it showing up in a wide range of real-world applications. Our interest in this article will be to present some computational complexity results about a remarkable subclass of regular languages, those that can be defined via unambiguous concatenation.

2.1   Unambiguous Languages

Although Rabin and Scott [16] had early on discussed some specific subfamilies of the regular laguages, the first really significant subclass was investigated by Schützenberger in [17]. The class of star-free languages over an alphabet A is the smallest family containing the finite subsets of A^*, and closed under boolean operations and concatenation. Note that closure under complement is required explicitly. Schützenberger proved the difficult theorem that a language is star-free iff its syntactic monoid contains no non-trivial groups; this implies that one can decide if a given language is star-free. This class is also meaningful from a logical point of view; it is not too hard to show that star-freeness corresponds to definability in first-order logic with $<$ being used as a numerical predicate.

Our attention will be focussed on yet a smaller class than the star-free sets. Let us say that a concatenation of languages $L_1 \cdots L_k$ is *unambiguous* iff any word belonging to this product admits a unique factorization $w = w_1 \cdots w_k$, with each w_i in L_i. The class of *unambiguous* languages is defined by taking disjoint unions of unambiguous concatenations of the form $A_0^* a_1 A_1^* \cdots a_k A_k^*$, where each a_i is a letter and each A_i is a subset of A. The a_i's will be refered to as bookmarks. Note that each unambiguous language is star-free, since, for every $B \subseteq A$, $B^* = \cap_{a \notin B} \overline{\overline{\emptyset} a \overline{\emptyset}}$.

It is not apparent at all that the class of unambiguous languages is closed under complement. This follows from another difficult theorem of Schützenberger [18]. Let **DA** be the class of finite monoids M satisfying the condition that for all $e = e^2$ and for all s in M, $MeM \subseteq MsM$ implies $ese = e$.

Theorem 1. *A language is unambiguous iff its syntactic monoid is in* **DA**.

It is thus decidable if a language is unambiguous and the class is closed under complement, because L and $\overline{L}$ always have the same syntactic monoid. Unambiguity of concatenation is essential here, i.e. not all products of the form $A_0^* a_1 A_1^* \ldots a_s A_s^*$ have the property that their complement can be written in the same form; for example the language $A^* aa A^* \subseteq \{a, b\}^*$ cannot be written as a disjoint union of unambiguous products (proof: its syntactic monoid can be shown to be outside of **DA**) and its complement cannot be written as a union of products of the same form, a result whose proof requires the deep theory of partially ordered monoids introduced in [14]. The algebraic description of unambiguous languages given by the theorem above once again has a logical counterpart [25]; they correspond to languages which are definable by first-order sentences using two variables only, and they also are those for which both a Σ_2 and a Π_2 sentence can be constructed.

Two further characterizations of unambiguous languages (or **DA**) will be useful in our discussion. The first one is folklore.

Theorem 2. *A group-free monoid is in* **DA** *iff it cannot recognize the language* $A^* aa A^*$ *nor the language* $(ab)^*$.

The second one is proved in [19].

Theorem 3. *A language is unambiguous iff it can be recognized by a partially ordered two-way finite automaton.*

We will use the following model which is equivalent to partially ordered finite two-way automaton. A turtle program is given by $T = (d_1, a_1) \cdots (d_k, a_k)$, where each d_i is either R or L, each a_i is a letter. The program executes as follows on input w of length n; if $d_1 = R$ then the initial position of the head is 0, otherwise the initial position is $n + 1$; Each instruction (d, a) is then executed in turn, moving the head from its current position to the next on the right (if $d = R$) or on the left (if $d = L$) that contains the letter a. If no such position exists, the instruction fails, and the language accepted by T is the set of words for which no instruction fails. It can be shown that a language is unambiguous iff it is a boolean combination of languages that can be recognized by turtle programs.

3   Boolean Circuits

An important result of Barrington [2] asserts that every language in NC^1, i.e. recognizable by a circuit of logarithmic depth constructed with binary gates, reduces to a regular language via a polynomial-length projection. This theorem is refined in [3] where, for example, it is shown that languages reducible to star-free languages are exactly those in AC^0, i.e. recognizable by constant-depth, polynomial-size circuits constructed with unbounded AND and OR gates.

We will now consider at a finer level what is the difficulty of recognizing star-free languages with boolean circuits. The result of [3] together with the theorem of Sipser [21] stating that circuits of depth k can do strictly more than circuits of depth $k - 1$, implies that there is no fixed constant-depth in which we can do all star-free languages in polynomial size. We are interested here in the number of wires. Surprisingly, for every star-free language L, for every unbounded primitive recursive function g, there is a constant-depth circuit recognizing L with $O(ng^{-1}(n))$ wires [7]. That is every star-free language can be recognized by a constant-depth circuit with a number of wires that is just above linear. For general languages in AC^0, no such claim can be made.

Theorem 4. *For every fixed k, there is a language in AC^0 which cannot be decided in constant-depth with $O(n^k)$ wires.*

Proof. We prove the result in terms of gates, which is equivalent. The argument here is due to Harry Buhrman [6]. For large enough n, the number of circuits with $O(n^k)$ gates is less than $2^{n^{2k} \log n}$. We diagonalize as follows: order the strings of length n arbitrarily, and consider the first $n^{2k} \log n$ of them. Declare the first one to be in the language iff the majority of circuits with n^k gates reject that string. Declare the second string to be in the language iff the majority of the remaining circuits reject that string. Continuing in this way for our $n^{2k} \log n$ strings, and declaring all other strings to be rejected, we create a language which cannot be recognized by any circuit of the required size, although it clearly can be done in polynomial-size depth 2 using DNF.

Subsequent to the work of [7], the question can be asked as to which star-free languages can be done with $O(n)$ wires. This has recently been resolved in [12]. For technical reasons, we consider in this section only regular languages that contain a *neutral letter*, i.e. a letter e such that for any word $uv \in L$ iff $uev \in L$. For example, the language $(ab)^*$ is trivial from a circuit point of view since for any n it contains at most one word of that length; adding a neutral letter to the language makes it much more interesting.

Theorem 5. *A star-free language with a neutral letter can be recognized by an AC^0 circuit with a linear number of wires iff this language is unambiguous.*

Proof. For the upper bound, it suffices to construct an efficient circuit for a language recognized by a unique turtle program $T = (d_1, a_1) \cdots (d_k, a_k)$. Let us assume that $d_1 = R$, the other case is similar. We compute the value of $k + 1$ variables $B_0, \ldots, B_k$ where B_i indicates if the program has failed or not after i instructions. In particular, $B_0 = 1$ and B_k is the output gate of the required circuit. For $i = 1, \ldots, k$ we also compute a vector $b_{i1} \ldots b_{in} = 0^j 1^{n-j}$ to indicate that the reading head is in position j after i instructions (if $B_i = 0$ then this vector is arbitrary). We have $B_1 = \bigvee_j ((x_j = a_1))$ and $b_{11} \ldots b_{1n} = $ PREFIX-OR$_j((x_j = a_1))$. Here, the function PREFIX-OR $(y_1, \ldots, y_n)$ returns n boolean values $z_1, \ldots, z_n$ with $z_i = OR(y_1, \ldots, y_i)$. It is known by [4] that this function can be computed with linear number of wires. In general, let the ith instruction be (R, a); we set $B_i = B_{i-1} \wedge \bigvee_j (b_{i-1j} \wedge (x_j = a))$, and $b_{i1} \ldots b_{in} = $ PREFIX-OR$_j((b_{i-1j} \wedge (x_j = a)))$. If the ith instruction is (L, a), we rather set $B_i = B_{i-1} \wedge \bigvee_j (\overline{b_{i-1j}} \wedge \overline{b_{i-1j+1}} \wedge (x_j = a))$, and $b_{i1} \ldots b_{in} = $ SUFFIX-OR$_j(\overline{b_{i-1j}} \wedge \overline{b_{i-1j+1}} \wedge (x_j = a))$. This clearly implies our claim.

The lower bound builds upon previous arguments dealing with superconcentrators. We refer to [12] for that proof.

4   Computational Learning

We will here consider Angluin's model of exact learning, adapted to the framework we are looking at. In a first variant, we are interested in functions $f : (A^*)^n \to \{0, 1\}$ that can be expressed as follows: there is a fixed language L and the function is given by an expression $f(X_1, \ldots, X_n) = u_0 X_{i_1} u_1 \ldots X_{i_s} u_s$ which evaluates to 1 on a given n-tuple $w = (v_1, \ldots, v_n)$ iff the corresponding word belongs to L. A learning algorithm must identify an unknown function of this form by asking queries to a Teacher who knows f. In general, the model allows Evaluation queries, where the algorithm sends a tuple w in $(A^*)^n$ and receives $f(w)$, and Equivalence queries, where the algorithm sends an hypothesis g and either succeeds or else is given a counterexample w where $f(w) \neq g(w)$. We now show that unambiguity once again corresponds to a natural border in computational complexity within this model.

Theorem 6. *If a language is unambiguous then any expression over it can be identified with a polynomial number of Evaluation queries.*

Proof. Let L be an unambiguous language and let t be a constant such that every language recognized by the syntactic monoid of L can be written as a disjoint union of terms of the form $A_0^* a_1 A_1^* \cdots a_s A_s^*$, where the product is unambiguous and $s \leq t$. The learning algorithm asks the polynomially many Evaluation queries for all tuples $w \in (A^*)^n$ where the sum of the lengths of the components of w is at most $2t$. We argue that this defines the function uniquely for all tuples. Suppose on the contrary that there are two distinct functions f and g consistent with all the values returned by the teacher, and let w be a tuple on which they differ. In particular $f(w)$ and $g(w)$ map to different elements in the syntactic monoid and thus belongs to different unambiguous products, each having at most t bookmarks. Let z be the tuple obtained from w by erasing all letters that do not contribute any bookmark in neither $f(w)$ nor $g(w)$. Thus the sum of the lengths of the components of z is at most $2t$. We have $f(w) = f(z)$ and $g(w) = g(z)$, since e.g. $f(z)$ is obtained from $f(w)$ by deleting letters which are not bookmarks; because of consistency we also have $f(z) = g(z)$, hence $f(w) = g(w)$, a contradiction.

We next show that the two minimal star-free languages which are not unambiguous cannot be identified efficiently.

Theorem 7. *Let $L = (ab)^*$. Then expressions over L cannot be identified with a subexponential number of Evaluation queries.*

Proof. Consider expressions of the form $T_1 \ldots T_n$ where each T_i is either abX_ib or aX_iab; there are thus 2^n expressions of that form. Such an expression will evaluate to a word in L for a given input $(v_1, \ldots, v_n)$ iff for each i $v_i \in La*$ if $T_i = abX_ib$ and $v_i \in bL$ if $T_i = aX_iab$. A standard adversary argument shows that $2^n - 1$ Evaluation queries are needed to identify the expression.

Theorem 8. *Let $L = A^* aa A^*$. Then expressions over L cannot be identified with a subexponential number of Evaluation queries.*

Proof. Consider a monotone DNF formula $T_1 \vee \ldots \vee T_k$; form the expression $aT_1a \ldots aT_kaP(X_1) \ldots P(X_n)$, where $P(X) = bXaXba$. If any variable X_i is replaced by a word in L or by a word that begins or ends with the letter a, the expression necessarily evaluates to a word in the language since it contains the factor $P(X_i)$ which is in L. The only interesting queries are thus for tuples where each component is either the empty word (corresponding to the original boolean variable being set to True) or to a word in $bA^*b - L$ (corresponding to the original boolean variable being set to False). On a given tuple the expression then evaluates to a word in the language L iff the original DNF is satisfied by the corresponding boolean assignment. Being able to identify expressions over L thus implies being able to identify monotone DNF functions; this is known to require an exponential number of Evaluation queries by [5].

In a second variant that has been studied, one looks at boolean functions that can be reduced to regular languages via projections of polynomial length. That is there is a fixed regular language $L \subseteq A^*$ and a reduction $f : \{0,1\}^n \to A^{n^k}$ having the property that for every j between 1 and n^k, there exists i_j between 1 and n such that the jth bit of $f(w)$ depends only on the i_j^{th} bit of w. The boolean function F being defined is $F(w) = \text{True}$ iff $f(w) \in L$. As in the case of boolean circuits, it is necessary here to consider languages which have a neutral letter.

A theorem proved in [11] asserts that a boolean function can thus be computed by a projection to an unambiguous language iff it can be computed by a decision tree of bounded rank. These are known [20] to be learnable with a polynomial number of Equivalence queries. The status of functions computed by a projection to the language $A^* ac^* aA^*$ is unknown as learning these corresponds to learning functions given by DNF, which is the major open question in computational learning theory. A result of [8] implies that functions computed by projections to $(c^* ac^* bc^*)^*$ can also be learned with polynomially many Equivalence queries. An important difference with the case of unambiguous languages though is that the polynomial in this second case is in n and also in the length of the projection; on the contrary it can be shown that every projection to an umambiguous language can be realized in polynomial length, hence the number of queries in this case is a polynomial in n only.

5   Conclusion

Computer science students are most often introduced to theoretical ideas of the discipline via regular languages and finite automata. These concepts are then heavily used in formalizing several types of applications. The point that we are making in this paper is that regular languages provide a good vehicle to study issues arising in computations, in more general models than finite-state machines. It is often the case that the natural combinatorial parametrizations known for regular languages imply corresponding algorithmic parametrizations in various models.

We have given two examples in favour of this paradigm, boolean circuits and computational learning. In both cases we have shown that the well-known class of unambiguous languages enjoyed remarkable algorithmic properties. In the case of boolean circuits, it corresponds to those star-free languages which can be recognized by constant-depth circuits with linear number of wires. It is an interesting question to verify if the same statement holds when we count gates instead of wires; we conjecture that the answer is affirmative and thus that, for star-free languages, $O(n)$ wires and $O(n)$ gates have the same computational power. In computational learning, unambiguity corresponds to certain type of functions which can be identified with a polynomial number of Evaluation queries; in case of boolean functions realized by projections to regular languages, the situation is not completely resolved, but there again, unambiguity seems to be playing a role.

References

1. A. Ambainis, M. Beaudry, M. Golovkins, A. Kikusts, M. Mercer, and D. Thérien. Algebraic results on quantum automata. In *STACS*, pages 93–104, 2004.
2. D. Barrington. Bounded-width polynomial-size branching programs recognize exactly those languages in NC^1. In *STOC*, pages 1–5, 1986.
3. D. Barrington and D. Thérien. Finite monoids and the fine structure of NC^1. *J. ACM*, 35(4):941–952, 1988.
4. G. Bilardi and F. Preparata. Characterization of associative operations with prefix circuits of constant depth and linear size. *SIAM J.Computing*, 19(2):246–255, April 1990.
5. N. Bshouty, R. Cleve, R. Gavaldà, S. Kannan, and C. Tamon. Oracles and queries that are sufficient for exact learning. *Journal of Computer and System Sciences*, 52:421–433, 1996.
6. H. Buhrman. Private communication. 2004.
7. A. Chandra, S. Fortune, and R. Lipton. Unbounded fan-in circuits and associative functions. *JCSS*, 30:222–234, 1985.
8. Z. Chen and S. Homer. On learning counting functions with queries. In *COLT*, pages 218–227. ACM press, 1994.
9. S. Eilenberg. *Automata, Languages and Machines*, volume B. Academic Press, New York, 1976.
10. R. Gavaldà and D. Thérien. Learning expressions over monoids. In *STACS*, pages 283–293, 2001.
11. R. Gavaldà and D. Thérien. Algebraic characterizations of small classes of boolean functions. In *STACS*, pages 331–342, 2003.
12. M. Koucký, P. Pudlák, and D. Thérien. Star-free languages needing linear number of wires. In preparation.
13. C. Moore, P. Tesson, and D. Thérien. Satisfiability of systems of equations over finite monoids. In *MFCS*, pages 537–547, 2001.
14. J. Pin and P. Weil. Polynomial closure and unambiguous product. In *22nd ICALP*, volume 944 of *Lecture Notes in Computer Science*, pages 348–359, Berlin, 1995. Springer-Verlag.
15. J. E. Pin. *Varieties of Formal Languages*. Plenum, London, 1986.
16. M. O. Rabin and D. Scott. Finite automata and their decision problems. *IBM J. Res. Dev.*, 3:114–125, 1959.
17. M. Schützenberger. On finite monoids having only trivial subgroups. *Inform. and Control*, 8:190–194, 1965.
18. M. Schützenberger. Sur le produit de concatenation non ambigu. *Semigroup Forum*, 13:47–75, 1976.
19. T. Schwentick, D. Thérien, and H. Vollmer. Partially-ordered two-way automata : A new characterization of DA. In *Developments in Language Theory*, pages 239–250, 2001.
20. H. Simon. Learning decision lists and trees with equivalence-queries. In *EuroCOLT*, pages 322–336, 1995.
21. M. Sipser. Borel sets and circuit complexity. In *STOC*, pages 61–69, 1983.
22. H. Straubing. *Finite Automata, Formal Logic and Circuit Complexity*. Birkhäuser, 1994.
23. P. Tesson and D. Thérien. Diamonds are forever: the variety DA. In G. Gomez, P. Silva, and J. Pin, editors, *Semigroups, Algorithms, Automata and Languages*. WSP, 2002.

24. P. Tesson and D. Thérien. Complete classifications of the communication complexity of regular languages. In *STACS*, pages 62–73, 2003.
25. D. Thérien and T. Wilke. Over words, two variables are as powerful as one quantifier alternation. In *STOC*, pages 234–240, 1998.
26. D. Thérien and T. Wilke. Nesting until and since in linear temporal logic. *Theory of Computing Systems*, 37(1):111–131, 2004.

Decidability of Zenoness, Syntactic Boundedness and Token-Liveness for Dense-Timed Petri Nets

Parosh Abdulla[1], Pritha Mahata[1], and Richard Mayr[2]

[1] Uppsala University, Sweden
[2] North Carolina State University, Raleigh NC, USA
{parosh, pritha}@it.uu.se, mayr@csc.ncsu.edu

Abstract. We consider *Timed Petri Nets (TPNs)*: extensions of Petri nets in which each token is equipped with a real-valued clock. We consider the following three verification problems for TPNs.

(i) *Zenoness:* whether there is an infinite computation from a given marking which takes only a finite amount of time. We show decidability of zenoness for TPNs, thus solving an open problem from [dFERA00].

(ii) *Token Liveness:* whether a token is *alive* in a marking, i.e., whether there is a computation from the marking which eventually consumes the token. We show decidability of the problem by reducing it to the *coverability problem*, which is decidable for TPNs.

(iii) *Boundedness:* whether the size of the reachable markings is bounded. We consider two versions of the problem; namely *semantic boundedness* where only live tokens are taken into consideration in the markings, and *syntactic boundedness* where also dead tokens are considered. We show undecidability of semantic boundedness, while we prove that syntactic boundedness is decidable through an extension of the Karp-Miller algorithm.

1   Introduction

Petri nets are one of the most widely used models for analysis and verification of concurrent systems. *Timed Petri nets (TPNs)* are extensions of Petri nets in the sense that each token has an "age" which is represented by a real valued clock (see [Bow96] for a survey). TPNs are computationally more powerful than timed automata [AD90], since they operate on a potentially unbounded number of clocks. This implies that TPNs can, among other things, model parameterized timed systems (systems consisting of an unbounded number of timed processes) [AN01]. Recently, several verification problems have been studied for TPNs (see e.g. [RGdFE99, dFERA00, AN01, AN02]). These problems are both extensions of classical problems previously studied for standard (untimed) Petri nets, and problems which are related to the timed behavior of TPNs. In this paper, we consider three verification problems for TPNs.

Zenoness. A fundamental progress property for timed systems is that it should be possible for time to *diverge* [Tri99]. This requirement is justified by the fact that timed processes cannot be infinitely fast. Computations violating this property are called *zeno*. Given a TPN and a marking M, we check whether M is a *zeno-marking*, i.e., whether there is an infinite computation from M with a finite duration. The zenoness problem is solved in [Alu91] for timed automata using the region graph construction. Since region

K. Lodaya and M. Mahajan (Eds.): FSTTCS 2004, LNCS 3328, pp. 58–70, 2004.
© Springer-Verlag Berlin Heidelberg 2004

graphs only deal with a finite number of clocks, the algorithm of [Alu91] cannot be extended to check zenoness for TPNs. The zenoness problem was left open in [dFERA00] both for dense TPNs (the model we consider in this paper) and for discrete TPNs (where behavior is interpreted over the discrete time domain).

We show that even for dense-timed Petri nets, a decidable symbolic representation of all zeno-markings can be effectively constructed. The construction can easily be modified (in fact simplified) to deal with the discrete-time case.

Token Liveness. Markings in TPNs may contain tokens which cannot be used by any future computations of the TPN. Such tokens do not affect the behavior of the TPN and are therefore called *dead tokens*. We give an algorithm to check, given a token and a marking, whether the token is dead (or alive). We do this by reducing the problem to the problem of *coverability* in TPNs. An algorithm to solve the coverability problem is given in [AN01]. Token liveness for dense TPNs was left open in [dFERA00].

Boundedness. We consider the *boundedness problem* for TPNs: given a TPN and an initial marking, check whether the size of reachable markings is bounded. The decidability of this problem depends on whether we take dead tokens into consideration. In *syntactic boundedness* one considers dead tokens as part of the (size of the) marking, while in *semantic boundedness* we disregard dead tokens; that is we check whether we can reach markings with unboundedly many live tokens. Using techniques similar to [RGdFE99] it can be shown that semantic boundedness is undecidable. On the other hand we show decidability of syntactic boundedness. This is achieved through an extension of the Karp-Miller algorithm where each node represents a region (rather than a single marking). The underlying ordering on the nodes (regions) inside the Karp-Miller tree is a *well quasi-ordering* [Hig52]. This guarantees termination of the procedure.

Decidability of syntactic boundedness was shown for the simpler discrete-time case in [dFERA00], while the problem was left open for the dense-time case.

2   Definitions

Timed Petri Nets. We consider *Timed Petri Nets* (*TPNs*) where each token is equipped with a real-valued clock representing the "age" of the token. The firing conditions of a transition include the usual ones for Petri nets. Additionally, each arc between a place and a transition is labeled with a subinterval of natural numbers. When firing a transition, tokens which are removed (added) from (to) places should have their ages lying in the intervals of corresponding arcs.

We use $\mathcal{N}, \mathcal{R}^{\geq 0}$ to denote the sets of natural numbers and nonnegative reals, respectively. For a natural number k, we let $\mathcal{N}^k$ and $\mathcal{N}_\omega^k$ denote the set of vectors of dimension k over $\mathcal{N}$ and $\mathcal{N} \cup \{\omega\}$, respectively.

We use a set *Intrv* of intervals. An open interval is written as $(w : z)$ where $w \in \mathcal{N}$ and $z \in \mathcal{N} \cup \{\infty\}$. Intervals can also be closed in one or both directions, e.g. $[w : z]$ is closed in both directions and $[w : z)$ is closed to the left and open to the right.

For a set A, we use A^* and $A^\odot$ to denote the set of finite words and finite multisets over A, respectively. We view a multiset over A as a mapping from A to $\mathcal{N}$. Sometimes, we write multisets as lists, so $b = [2.4 , 5.1 , 5.1 , 2.4 , 2.4]$ represents a multiset b

over $\mathcal{R}^{\geq 0}$ where $b(2.4) = 3$, $b(5.1) = 2$ and $b(x) = 0$ for $x \neq 2.4, 5.1$. For multisets b_1 and b_2 over $\mathcal{N}$, we say that $b_1 \leq b_2$ if $b_1(a) \leq b_2(a)$ for each $a \in A$. We define $b_1 + b_2$ to be the multiset b where $b(a) = b_1(a) + b_2(a)$, and (assuming $b_1 \leq b_2$) we define $b_2 - b_1$ to be the multiset b where $b(a) = b_2(a) - b_1(a)$, for each $a \in A$. We write $|b|$ for the number of elements in b. We use $\emptyset$ to denote the empty multiset and ϵ to denote the empty word.

Given a set A with an ordering $\preceq$ and a subset $B \subseteq A$, B is said to be *upward closed* if $a_1 \in B, a_2 \in A$ and $a_1 \preceq a_2$ implies $a_2 \in B$. Given a set $B \subseteq A$, we define the *upward closure* $B \uparrow$ to be the set $\{a \in A| \exists a' \in B : a' \preceq a\}$. A *downward closed* set B and the *downward closure* $B \downarrow$ are defined in a similar manner. We also use $a \uparrow, a \downarrow$, a instead of $\{a\} \uparrow, \{a\} \downarrow, \{a\}$, respectively.

Definition 1. *[AN01] A* Timed Petri Net (TPN) *is a tuple* $N = (P, T, In, Out)$ *where P is a finite set of places, T is a finite set of transitions and In, Out are partial functions from $T \times P$ to $Intrv$.*

If $In(t, p)$ (resp. $Out(t, p)$) is defined, then p is an *input (resp. output) place* of t. We let max denote the maximum integer appearing on the arcs of TPN. A *marking* M of N is a multiset over $P \times \mathcal{R}^{\geq 0}$. The marking M defines the numbers and ages of tokens in each place in the net. We identify a token in a marking M by the pair (p, x) representing its place and age in M. Then, $M((p, x))$ defines the number of tokens with age x in place p. Abusing notation again, we define, for each place p, a multiset $M(p)$ over $\mathcal{R}^{\geq 0}$, where $M(p)(x) = M((p, x))$. For a set M of markings, we define $|\mathsf{M}| = max(|M| : M \in \mathsf{M})$. For a marking M of the form $[(p_1, x_1), \ldots, (p_n, x_n)]$ and $x \in \mathcal{R}^{\geq 0}$, we use M^{+x} to denote the marking $[(p_1, x_1 + x), \ldots, (p_n, x_n + x)]$.

Transitions: We define two transition relations on the set of markings : timed transition and discrete transition. A *timed transition* increases the age of each token by the same real number. Formally, for $x \in \mathcal{R}^{\geq 0}$, $M_1 \longrightarrow_x M_2$ if $M_2 = M_1^{+x}$. We use $M_1 \longrightarrow_\delta M_2$ to denote that $M_1 \longrightarrow_x M_2$ for some $x \in \mathcal{R}^{\geq 0}$.

We define the set of *discrete transitions* $\longrightarrow_D$ as $\bigcup_{t \in T} \longrightarrow_t$, where $\longrightarrow_t$ represents the effect of *firing* the discrete transition t. More precisely, $M_1 \longrightarrow_t M_2$ if the set of input arcs $\{(p, \mathcal{I})| In(t, p) = \mathcal{I}\}$ is of the form $\{(p_1, \mathcal{I}_1), \ldots, (p_k, \mathcal{I}_k)\}$, the set of output arcs $\{(p, \mathcal{I})| Out(t, p) = \mathcal{I}\}$ is of the form $\{(q_1, \mathcal{J}_1), \ldots, (q_\ell, \mathcal{J}_\ell)\}$, and there are multisets $b_1 = [(p_1, x_1), \ldots, (p_k, x_k)]$ and $b_2 = [(q_1, y_1), \ldots, (q_\ell, y_\ell)]$ over $P \times \mathcal{R}^{\geq 0}$ such that the following holds: $b_1 \leq M_1, x_i \in \mathcal{I}_i$, for $i : 1 \leq i \leq k$, $y_i \in \mathcal{J}_i$, for $i : 1 \leq i \leq \ell$, $M_2 = (M_1 - b_1) + b_2$. We say that t is *enabled* in M if there is a b_1 such that the first two conditions are satisfied. A transition t may be fired only if for each incoming arc, there is a token with the "right" age in the corresponding input place. These tokens will be removed when the transition is fired. The newly produced tokens may only have ages which belong to the relevant intervals.

We write $\longrightarrow = \longrightarrow_\delta \cup \longrightarrow_D$ to denote all transitions and use $\overset{*}{\longrightarrow}$ to denote the reflexive transitive closure of $\longrightarrow$. It is easy to extend $\overset{*}{\longrightarrow}$ for sets of markings. We define $Reach(M) := \{M' | M \overset{*}{\longrightarrow} M'\}$ as the set of markings reachable from M.

A *M-computation* π from a marking M is a sequence $M_0, M_1, \ldots$ of markings s.t $M_0 = M$ and $M_i \longrightarrow M_{i+1}$ for $i \geq 0$.

For a computation π from M, the *delay* $\Delta(\pi)$ of the computation is defined as follows.

– $\Delta(M_0) = 0$.
– $\Delta(M_0, \ldots, M_{i+1}) = \Delta(M_0, \ldots, M_i)$ if $M_i \longrightarrow_D M_{i+1}$.
– $\Delta(M_0, \ldots, M_{i+1}) = \Delta(M_0, \ldots, M_i) + x$ if $M_i \longrightarrow_x M_{i+1}$.

Intuitively, the delay is the total amount of time passed in all timed transitions in the sequence. Notice that untimed Petri nets are a special case in our model where all intervals are of the form $[0 : \infty)$. Next, we recall a constraint system called *regions* defined for *Timed automata* [AD90].

Regions. A *region* defines the integral parts of clock values up to max (the exact age of a token is irrelevant if it is greater than max), and also the ordering of the fractional parts. For TPNs, we need to use a variant which also defines the place in which each token (clock) resides. Following Godskesen [God94] we represent a region in the following manner.

Definition 2. *A region is a triple* (b_0, w, b_{max}) *where*

– $b_0 \in (P \times \{0, \ldots, max\})^{\odot}$. b_0 *is a multiset of pairs. A pair of the form* (p, n) *represents a token with age exactly n in place p.*
– $w \in \left((P \times \{0, \ldots, max - 1\})^{\odot} \right)^*$. w *is a word over the set*

   $(P \times \{0, \ldots, max - 1\})^{\odot}$, *i.e., w is a word where each element in the word is a multiset over $P \times \{0, \ldots, max - 1\}$. Pair (p, n) represents a token in place p with age x such that $x \in (n : n + 1)$. Pairs in the same multiset represent tokens whose ages have equal fractional parts. The order of the multisets in w corresponds to the order of the fractional parts.*
– $b_{max} \in P^{\odot}$. b_{max} *is a multiset over P representing tokens with ages strictly greater than max. Since the actual ages of these tokens are irrelevant, the information about their ages is omitted in the representation.*

Formally, each region characterizes an infinite set of markings as follows. Assume a marking $M = [(p_1, x_1), \ldots, (p_n, x_n)]$ and a region $R = (b_0, b_1 b_2 \cdots b_m, b_{m+1})$. Let b_j be of the form $[(q_{j1}, y_{j1}), \ldots, (q_{j\ell_j}, y_{j\ell_j})]$ for $j : 0 \le j \le m$ and b_{m+1} is of the form $[q_{m+1\ 1}, \ldots, q_{m+1\ l_{m+1}}]$. We say that M *satisfies* R, written $M \in R$, if there is a bijection h from the set $\{1, \ldots, n\}$ to the set of pairs

   $\{(j, k) \mid (0 \le j \le m + 1) \wedge (1 \le k \le \ell_j)\}$ such that the following conditions hold:

– $p_i = q_{h(i)}$. Each token should have the same place as that required by the corresponding element in R.
– If $h(i) = (j, k)$ then $j = m + 1$ iff $x_i > max$. Tokens older than max should correspond to elements in multiset b_{m+1}. The actual ages of these tokens are not relevant.
– If $x_i \le max$ and $h(i) = (j, k)$ then $\lfloor x_i \rfloor = y_{j\ k}$. The integral part of the age of tokens should agree with the natural number specified by the corresponding elements in w.

– If $x_i \leq max$ and $h(i) = (j, k)$ then $frac(x_i) = 0$ iff $j = 0$. Tokens with zero fractional parts correspond to elements in multiset b_0.
– If $x_{i_1}, x_{i_2} < max$, $h(i_1) = (j_1, k_1)$ and $h(i_2) = (j_2, k_2)$ then $frac(x_{i_1}) \leq frac(x_{i_2})$ iff $j_1 \leq j_2$. Tokens with equal fractional parts correspond to elements in the same multiset (unless they belong to b_{m+1}). The ordering among multisets inside R reflects the ordering among fractional parts in clock values.

Notice that given a marking M, it is easy to compute the unique region R_M satisfied by M. We let $[\![R]\!] = \{M| \ M \in R\}$. Given a marking M and a set $\mathbf{R}$ of regions, we say that $M \in \mathbf{R}$ if there is a region $R \in \mathbf{R}$ such that $M \in R$. We also let $[\![\mathbf{R}]\!] = \{M| \ \exists R \in \mathbf{R}. \ M \in R\}$. The region construction defines an equivalence relation $\equiv$ on the set of markings such that $M_1 \equiv M_2$ if, for each region R, it is the case that $M_1 \in [\![R]\!]$ iff $M_2 \in [\![R]\!]$. It is easy to show (similar to [AD90]) that $\equiv$ is a congruence on the set of markings. In other words, if $M_1 \longrightarrow M_2$ and $M_1 \equiv M_3$ then there is an M_4 such that $M_2 \equiv M_4$ and $M_3 \longrightarrow M_4$.

Ordering. We define an ordering $\preceq$ on the set of markings s.t. $M_1 \preceq M_2$ if there is an M_2' with $M_1 \equiv M_2'$ and $M_2' \leq M_2$. In other words, $M_1 \preceq M_2$ if we can delete a number of tokens from M_2 and as a result obtain a new marking equivalent to M_1. We let $M_1 \prec M_2$ denote that $M_1 \preceq M_2$ and $M_1 \not\equiv M_2$. Notice that $\longrightarrow$ is *monotonic* with respect to the ordering $\preceq$, i.e, if $M_1 \longrightarrow M_2$ and $M_1 \preceq M_3$ then there is an M_4 such that $M_2 \preceq M_4$ and $M_3 \longrightarrow M_4$. We identify a region R with the language $[\![R]\!]$ it represents (we write R instead of $[\![R]\!]$). Next we show how to compute the language entailment of two regions. We lift $\preceq$ on the set of markings to the set of regions.

Definition 3. *Let $R = (b_0, b_1 \ldots b_m, b_{m+1})$ and $R' = (c_0, c_1 \ldots c_l, c_{l+1})$ be regions. Then, $R \preceq R'$ iff there is a strict monotone injection $g : \{0, \ldots, m+1\} \rightarrow \{0, \ldots, l+1\}$ with $g(0) = 0$ and $g(m+1) = l+1$ and $b_i \leq c_{g(i)}$ for each $i : 0 \leq i \leq m+1$.*

For regions R and R', if $R \preceq R'$ then for each $M \in [\![R]\!], M' \in [\![R']\!]$, we have $M \preceq M'$. We let $R \prec R'$ denote that $R \preceq R'$ and $R \neq R'$.

Lemma 4. *Union and intersection of (sets of) regions are computable as finite sets of regions.*

We define a function *Post* such that for a region R, $Post(R)$ is a finite set of regions where a marking M' satisfies a region in $Post(R)$ iff there is a marking $M \in [\![R]\!]$ such that $M \longrightarrow M'$. Thus $Post(R)$ characterizes the set of markings we can reach from a marking satisfying R by a single transition.

Lemma 5. *The set $Post(R)$ is effectively constructible.*

For a set $\mathbf{R}_1$ of regions, we define $Pre(\mathbf{R}_1) := \{R| \ \exists M_1 \in \mathbf{R}_1, M \in R. \ M \longrightarrow M_1\}$. We use min to denote a function which, given a set $\mathbf{R}_1$ of regions, returns the minimal elements of $\mathbf{R}_1$. We use $minpre([\![R]\!] \uparrow)$ to denote the set $\min(Pre(\{R\} \uparrow))$. We define Pre^* to be the reflexive, transitive closure of $minpre$.

Lemma 6. *Given a region R, the set $Pre^*([\![R]\!] \uparrow)$ is effectively constructible as a finite set of regions [AN01].*

3   Zenoness

A zeno-run of a timed Petri net is an infinite run that takes only finite time.

Definition 7. *Let $N = (P, T, In, Out)$ be a TPN. A marking M is called a zeno-marking iff there exists an infinite M-computation π and a finite number m s.t. $\Delta(\pi) < m$. Let ZENO denote the set of all zeno-markings.*

The computability of the zenoness-problem for timed Petri nets (i.e., the problem if $M \in ZENO$ for a given marking M, or, more generally, constructing $ZENO$) was mentioned in [dFERA00] as an open problem for discrete-time Petri nets. Here we solve this problem even for the more general class of dense-time Petri nets. We show that, for any TPN, a decidable symbolic representation of the set $ZENO$ can be effectively computed. This implies the computability of $ZENO$ also for discrete-time Petri nets, since they can be encoded into dense-time ones. An alternative solution for discrete-time Petri nets is discussed in Remark 23.

The following brief outline explains the main steps of our proof.

1. We translate the original timed Petri net N into an untimed simultaneous-disjoint-transfer net N'. Simultaneous-disjoint-transfer nets are a subclass of transfer nets where all transfers happen at the same time and don't affect each other. The computations of N' represent, in a symbolic way, the computations of N that can be done in time $< 1 - \delta$ for some predefined $\delta > 0$.
2. Consider the set INF of markings of N' where infinite computations start. Since INF is upward-closed, it is characterized by its finitely many minimal elements; let INF_{min} be this set of minimal elements. While INF_{min} is not computable for general transfer nets [DJS99, May03], it is computable for simultaneous-disjoint-transfer nets, as shown in Lemma 21.
3. We re-interpret the set INF (resp. INF_{min}) of N' markings in the context of the timed Petri net N and construct from it $ZENO$ as a finite set of regions.

Definition 8. A simultaneous-disjoint-transfer net (short SD-TN) N is described by a tuple $(P, T, Input, Output, Trans)$ where P is a set of places, T is a set of ordinary transitions, $Input, Output : T \to 2^P$ are functions that describe the input and output places of every transition, respectively. *Trans* describes the simultaneous and disjoint transfer transition. We have $Trans = (I, O, S)$ where $I \subseteq P$, $O \subseteq P$, and $S \subseteq P \times P$. I and O describe the normal input and output places of the transfer transition and the pairs in S describe the source and target place of the transfer. The following restrictions on *Trans* must be satisfied: If $(s, t), (s', t') \in S$ then s, s', t, t' are all different and $\{s, t\} \cap (I \cup O) = \emptyset$. Let $M : P \to \mathcal{N}$ be a marking of N. The firing of normal transitions $t \in T$ is defined just as for ordinary Petri nets. The transfer transition *Trans* is enabled at M iff $\forall p \in I. M(p) \geq 1$. Firing *Trans* yields the new marking M' where

$$
\begin{array}{llll}
M'(p) = M(p) & \text{if } p \in I \cap O & M'(p) = M(p) - 1 & \text{if } p \in I - O \\
M'(p) = M(p) + 1 & \text{if } p \in O - I & M'(p) = 0 & \text{if } \exists p'. (p, p') \in S \\
M'(p) = M(p) + M(p') & \text{if } (p', p) \in S & M'(p) = M(p) & \text{otherwise}
\end{array}
$$

(The restrictions above ensure that these cases are disjoint.)

Definition 9. For a given TPN $N = (P, T, In, Out)$ we now construct a SD-TN $N' = (P', T', Input, Output, Trans)$. The rough intuition is that N' simulates symbolically all computations of N which can happen in time $< 1 - \delta$ for some predefined $\delta > 0$.

Let max be the maximal finite constant that appears in the arcs of the TPN. We define a finite set of symbols $Sym := \{k \mid k \in \mathcal{N}, 0 \leq k \leq \max\} \cup \{k+ \mid k \in \mathcal{N}, 0 \leq k \leq \max\} \cup \{k- \mid k \in \mathcal{N}, 1 \leq k \leq \max\}$ and a total order on Sym by $k < k+ < (k+1)- < (k+1)$ for every k.

For every place $p \in P$ of N we have several corresponding places $p(s)$ for all $s \in Sym$ in P' of the SD-TN N'. Thus $P' = \{p(s) \mid p \in P, s \in Sym\}$. The intuition is as follows. A token on place $p(k)$ encodes a token of age exactly k on place p. A token on $p(k+)$ encodes a token on place p of an age a which satisfies $k < a \leq k + \delta$ for some a-priori defined $\delta > 0$. This means that the age of this token cannot reach $k + 1$ in any run taking time $< 1 - \delta$. A token on $p(k-)$ encodes a token on p whose age a satisfies $k - 1 + \delta < a < k$ and which may or may not reach age k during a run taking time $1 - \delta$. The SD-TN tokens $p(k), p(k+)$ and $p(k-)$ are called *symbolic encodings* of the corresponding TPN token (p, a).

In particular, the age of such a $p(k-)$ token could be chosen arbitrarily close to k, such that its age could reach (or even exceed) k in runs taking an arbitrarily small time. For example, consider a run taking time $\epsilon > 0$ and a transition with an outgoing arc labeled with the interval $[0 : 1)$. This transition could produce a token with age $1 - \epsilon/2$ which could reach age 1 or even $1 + \epsilon/2$ later.

We define a function $enc : Intrv \rightarrow 2^{Sym}$ as follows.

$$enc([x : y]) := \{s \in Sym \mid x \leq s \leq y\} \qquad enc((x : y]) := \{s \in Sym \mid x < s \leq y\}$$
$$enc([x : y)) := \{s \in Sym \mid x \leq s < y\} \qquad enc((x : y)) := \{s \in Sym \mid x < s < y\}$$

For every transition $t \in T$ in the TPN N we have a set $T'(t)$ of new transitions in N'. The intuition is that the transitions in $T'(t)$ encode all possibilities of the age intervals of input and output tokens. For example, a discrete transition t with an input arc from place p labeled $[0 : 1]$ would yield 4 different transitions in $T'(t)$ with input arcs from places $p(0), p(0+), p(1-)$ and $p(1)$, respectively.

We denote the transitions with their sets of input and output places A and B by $t'(A, B)$, i.e., $Input(t'(A, B)) = A$ and $Output(t'(A, B)) = B$. For every $t \in T$ we define $A(t) \subseteq 2^{P'}$ as follows.

$$A(t) := \{A \subseteq P' \mid In(t, p) \neq \bot \Leftrightarrow \exists_1 s \in enc(In(t, p)). p(s) \in A\}$$

For every $t \in T$ we define $B(t) \subseteq 2^{P'}$ as follows.

$$B(t) := \{B \subseteq P' \mid Out(t, p) \neq \bot \Leftrightarrow \exists_1 s \in enc(Out(t, p)). p(s) \in B\}$$

We use $\exists_1$ to mean there exists 'exactly one' in the above.

We define $T'(t) := \{t'(A, B) \mid A \in A(t), B \in B(t)\}$ and finally $T' := \bigcup_{t \in T} T'(t)$. Note that in transition $t'(A, B)$ of N', the set of input places A contains only one input place $p(s)$ for each non-empty interval $In(t, p)$ s.t. $s \in enc(In(t, p))$. A similar remark holds for the set of output places B.

So far, the transitions in T' only encode the discrete transitions of N. The transfer arc will be used to encode the passing of time. However, since we need to keep discreet transitions and time-passing separate, we must first modify the net to obtain alternating discrete phases and time-passing phases.

First we add two extra places p_{disc} and p_{time} to P' which act as control-states for the different phases. Then we modify all transitions $t \in T'$ by adding p_{disc} to $Input(t)$ and $Output(t)$. Thus normal transitions can fire iff p_{disc} is marked.

The transitions which encode the passing of time include both the transfer transition and several normal transitions. After an arbitrarily small amount of time < 1 passes, all tokens of age k have an age $> k$. This is encoded by the simultaneous-disjoint transfer arc, which moves all tokens from places $p(k)$ to places $p(k+)$. Formally, $Trans := (I, O, S)$ where $I := \{p_{disc}\}$, $O := \{p_{time}\}$, and $S := \{(p(k), p(k+)) \mid 0 \le k \le \max\}$. Note that $Trans$ starts the time-passing phase and switches the control-state from p_{disc} to p_{time}. Now we add a new set of transitions which encode what happens to tokens of age $k-$ when (a small amount of) time passes. Their age might either stay below k, reach k or exceed k. For every $k \in \{1, \ldots, \max\}$ we have a transition with input places p_{time} and $p(k-)$ and output places p_{time} and $p(k)$. Furthermore, for every $k \in \{1, \ldots, \max\}$ we have a transition with input places p_{time} and $p(k-)$ and output places p_{time} and $p(k+)$. Finally, we add an extra transition t_{switch} with input place p_{time} and output place p_{disc}, which switches the net back to normal discrete mode. Note that after a time-passing phase the only tokens on places $p(k)$ are those which came from $p(k-)$, because all tokens on $p(k)$ were first transferred to $p(k+)$ by the transfer transition.

Definition 10. *Let N be a TPN and N' the corresponding SD-TN, defined as in Def. 9. We say that a marking M' of N' is a* standard marking *if $M'(p_{disc}) = 1$ and $M'(p_{time}) = 0$. We denote by INF the set of all markings of N' from which infinite computations start. Since INF is upward-closed it can be characterized by its finitely many minimal elements. Let INF_{min} be the finite set of these minimal elements. Let INF' and INF'_{min} be the restriction to standard markings of INF and INF_{min}, respectively.*

The following definitions establish the connection between the markings of the timed Petri net N and the markings of the SD-TN N'.

Definition 11. *For every δ with $0 < \delta < 1$ we define a function $int_\delta : (P \times \mathcal{R}^{\ge 0})^{\odot} \to (P' \to \mathcal{N})$ that maps a marking M of N to its corresponding marking M' in N'. $M' := int_\delta(M)$ is defined as follows. For any k we have*

$$
\begin{aligned}
M'(p(k)) &:= M((p, k)) & M'(p_{disc}) &:= 1 \\
M'(p(k+)) &:= \textstyle\sum_{k < x \le k+\delta} M((p, x)) & M'(p_{time}) &:= 0 \\
M'(p((k+1)-)) &:= \textstyle\sum_{k+\delta < x < k+1} M((p, x))
\end{aligned}
$$

Note that $M' = int_\delta(M)$ is a standard marking by Def. 10.

The intuition is as follows. In an infinite computation π starting at M with $\Delta(\pi) < 1 - \delta$, no token (p, x) with $k < x \le k + \delta$ can reach age $k + 1$ by aging. This is reflected in N' by the fact that $p(k+)$ tokens stay $p(k+)$ tokens during the symbolic time-passing phase. On the other hand, tokens (p, x) with $k + \delta < x < k + 1$ can reach an age $\ge k + 1$ by aging. This is reflected in N' by the fact that $p((k+1)-)$ tokens can become $p(k+1)$ or $p((k+1)+)$ tokens during the symbolic time-passing phase.

Lemma 12. *Given a TPN N with marking M_0, the corresponding SD-TN N' from Def. 9 and $0 < \delta < 1$. If there exists an infinite M_0-computation π s.t. $\Delta(\pi) < 1 - \delta$ then in N' there exists an infinite $int_\delta(M_0)$-computation π', i.e., $int_\delta(M_0) \in INF'$.*

The reverse implication of Lemma 12 does not generally hold. The fact that $int_\delta(M) \in INF'$ for some marking M of a TPN N does not imply that $M \in ZENO$. The infinite $int_\delta(M)$-run in N' depends on the fact that the $p(k-)$ tokens do (or don't) become $p(k)$ or $p(k+)$ tokens at the right step in the computation.

To establish a reverse correspondence between markings of N' and markings of N we need the following definitions.

Definition 13. *Let N' be a SD-TN with places $P' = \{p(s) \mid p \in P, s \in Sym\} \cup \{p_{disc}, p_{time}\}$ and a standard marking $M' : P' \to \mathcal{N}$. Let $M'^- := M'_{|\{p(k-) \mid k-\in Sym\}}$ and $M'^+ := M'_{|\{p(k+) \mid k+\in Sym\}}$ be the sub-markings of M, restricted to $p(k-)$ and $p(k+)$ tokens, respectively. We define $perm(M'^-)$ as the set of all words $w = b_1 \ldots b_n \in \left((P \times \{0, \ldots, max - 1\})^{\odot} \right)^*$ s.t. for all p and $k < max$ we have that $\left(\bigcup_{1 \le i \le n} b_i \right) ((p, k)) = M'^- (p((k+1)-))$. Similarly, let $perm(M'^+)$ be the set of all words $w = b_1 \ldots b_n \in \left((P \times \{0, \ldots, max - 1\})^{\odot} \right)^*$ s.t. for all p and $k < max$ we have $\left(\bigcup_{1 \le i \le n} b_i \right) ((p, k)) = M'^+ (p(k+))$.*

Intuitively, $perm(M'^-)$ describes all possible permutations of the fractional parts of tokens in a TPN marking M which are symbolically encoded as $p(k-)$ tokens in the corresponding SD-TN standard marking M'. Every symbolic marking M' of the SD-TN defines a set of TPN markings, depending on which permutation of the $p(k-)$ tokens and $p(k+)$ tokens is chosen.

Definition 14. *Let N' be a SD-TN. Every standard marking $M' : P' \to \mathcal{N}$ induces a set of regions $R(M', x, y)$ given by $R(M', x, y) = (b_0, xy, b_{max})$, where $b_0((p, k)) = M'(p(k))$ for all p and all $k \le max$, $x \in perm(M'^+)$, $y \in perm(M'^-)$ and $b_{max}(p) = M'(p(max+))$ for all p.*

Lemma 15. *Let N be a TPN with corresponding SD-TN N' and $M' \in INF'$.*

$$\exists y \in perm(M'^-). \forall x \in perm(M'^+). [\![R(M', x, y)]\!] \uparrow \subseteq ZENO$$

Definition 16. *Let N be a TPN with corresponding SD-TN N'.*

$$Z := \bigcup_{M' \in INF'_{min}} \bigcup_{x \in perm(M'^+)} \bigcap_{y \in perm(M'^-)} Pre^*([\![R(M', x, y)]\!] \uparrow)$$

Now we show that the set $ZENO$ is effectively constructible.

Lemma 17. $ZENO = [\![Z]\!] \uparrow$.

Now we show that, for any SD-TN, the set INF'_{min} is effectively constructible. For this we use a result by Valk and Jantzen.

Theorem 18. *[VJ85] A finite basis of an upward-closed set $K \subseteq \mathcal{N}^k$ is effectively computable iff for any vector $u \in \mathcal{N}_\omega^k$, the predicate $u \!\downarrow\, \cap K \neq \emptyset$ is decidable.*

Lemma 19. *For any SD-TN N with initial marking M_0 the coverability graph can be effectively constructed.*

Note that Lemma 19 implies that place-boundedness is decidable for simultaneous-disjoint transfer nets, while it is undecidable for general transfer nets [DJS99, May03].

Lemma 20. *Given an SD-TN N with k places and an ω-marking $M_0 \in \mathcal{N}_\omega^k$, it is decidable if $M_0 \!\downarrow\, \cap INF \neq \emptyset$.*

Lemma 21. *For any SD-TN N' the set INF'_{min} can be effectively constructed.*

Proof. Since INF is upward-closed, we can, by Lemma 20 and Theorem 18, construct a finite basis of INF, i.e., the set INF_{min}. We obtain INF'_{min} by the restriction of INF_{min} to standard markings. □

Theorem 22. *Let N be a TPN. The set $ZENO$ is effectively constructible.*

Proof. We first construct the SD-TN N' corresponding to N, according to Def. 9. Then we consider the set Z from Def. 16. We have $ZENO = [\![Z]\!]\uparrow$ by Lemma 17. The set Z is effectively constructible by Lemma 21, Definition 16 and Lemmas 6 and 4. □

Remark 23. To compute $ZENO$ for discrete-time Petri nets (left open in [dFERA00]), one can simply remove the transfer-transition from the net N' in Def. 9. This modified construction would yield $ZENO$ for the discrete-time case, because (unlike in the dense-time case) every infinite zeno-run in a discrete-time net has an infinite suffix taking no time at all.

4 Token Liveness

First, we define the *liveness* of a token in a marking. Let M be a marking in a TPN $N = (P, T, In, Out)$. A token in M is called *syntactically k-dead* if its age is $\geq k$. It is trivial to decide whether a token is k-dead from a marking. A token is called *semantically live* from a marking M, if we can fire a sequence of transitions starting from M which eventually consumes the token. Formally, given a token (p, x) and a marking M, we say that (p, x) can be *consumed* in M if there is a transition t satisfying the following properties: (a) t is enabled in M, (b) $In(t, p)$ is defined and $x \in In(t, p)$.

Definition 24. *A token (p, x) in M is semantically live if there is a finite M-computation $\pi = MM_1 \cdots M_r$ such that $(p, x + \Delta(\pi))$ can be consumed in M_r.*

For a marking M, we let $L(M)$ be the multiset of live tokens in M.

<small>SEMANTIC LIVENESS OF TOKENS IN TPN</small>

Instance: A timed Petri net N with marking M and a token $(p, x) \in M$.
Question: Is (p, x) live, i.e., $(p, x) \in L(M)$?

We show decidability of the semantic token liveness problem by reducing it to the *coverability problem* for TPNs.

Instance: A TPN N, a finite set of initial markings M_{init} of N, and an upward closed set $\mathsf{M}_{fin} \uparrow$ of markings of N, where M_{fin} is finite.

Question: $\mathsf{M}_{init} \xrightarrow{*} \mathsf{M}_{fin} \uparrow$?

Theorem 25. *The coverability problem is decidable for TPN [AN01].*

Suppose that we are given a TPN $N = (P, T, In, Out)$ with marking M and a token $(p, x) \in M$. We shall translate the question of whether $(p, x) \in L(M)$ into (several instances of) the coverability problem. To do that, we construct a new TPN N' by adding a new place p^* to the set P. The new place is not input or output of any transition. Now there are 2 cases. Either there is no transition in N which has p as its input place. Then it is trivial that $(p, x) \notin L(M)$. Otherwise, we consider all instances of the coverability problem defined on N' such that

- M_{init} contains a single marking $M - (p, x) + (p^*, x)$.
- M_{fin} is the set of markings of the form $[(p_1, x_1), \ldots, (p_n, x_n), (p^*, x')]$ such that there is a transition t and
  - the set of input places of t is given by $\{p, p_1, \ldots, p_n\}$.
  - $x' \in In(t, p)$ and $x_i \in In(t, p_i)$ for each $i : 1 \leq i \leq n$.

In the construction above, we replace a token (p, x) in the initial marking by a token (p^*, x); we also replace a token (p, x') in the final marking with $x' \in In(t, p)$, by a token (p^*, x'). The fact that the token in the question is not consumed in any predecessor of a marking in M_{fin}, is simulated by moving the token into the place p^* (in both the initial and final markings), since $p^* \notin P$ and not an input or output place in N'. Therefore, the token is live in M of N iff the answer to the coverability problem is 'yes'. From Theorem 25, we get the following.

Theorem 26. *The token liveness problem is decidable.*

5   Boundedness

Instance: A timed Petri net N with initial marking M_0.

Question: Is $|Reach(M_0)|$ bounded ?

We give an algorithm similar to the Karp-Miller algorithm [KM69] for solving the syntactic boundedness problem for TPNs. The algorithm builds a tree, where each node is labeled with a region. We build the tree successively, starting from the root, which is labeled with R_{M_0}: the unique region satisfied by M_0 (it is easy to compute this region). At each step we pick a leaf with label R and perform one of the following operations:

1. If $post(R)$ is empty we declare the current node *unsuccessful* and close the node.
2. If there is another (already generated) node which is labeled with R then declare the current node *duplicate* and close the node.

3. If there is a predecessor of the current node labeled with $R' \prec R$ then declare $|Reach(M_0)|$ unbounded (the TPN is unbounded), and terminate the procedure.

4. Otherwise, declare the current node as an *interior* node, add a set of successors to it, each labeled with an element in $Post(R)$. This step is possible due to Lemma 5.

If the condition of step 3 is never satisfied during the construction of the tree, declare $|Reach(M_0)|$ bounded (the TPN is bounded).

The proof of correctness of the above algorithm is similar to that of original Karp-Miller construction [KM69]. The termination of the algorithm is guaranteed due to the fact that the ordering $\preceq$ on the set of regions is a well-quasi-ordering (follows from [Hig52]).

Theorem 27. *Syntactic boundedness is decidable for TPNs.*

It follows that termination is also decidable for TPNs. Since dead tokens cannot influence the behavior of a TPN, one would like to abstract from them. Let N be a TPN with marking M. Then we define the live part of TPN markings as $Reach^l(M) := \{L(M') \mid M' \xrightarrow{*} M'\}$, i.e, the set of reachable markings without dead tokens.

SEMANTIC BOUNDEDNESS OF TPN

Instance: A timed Petri net N with initial marking M_0.

Question: Is $|Reach^l(M_0)|$ bounded ?

Using slightly modified constructions of [RGdFE99] or [AN02], we can easily derive the undecidability of semantic boundedness even for dense-timed Petri nets.

6   Conclusions

We have shown decidability of zenoness, token-liveness and syntactic boundedness for dense-time *timed Petri nets (TPNs)* in which each token has an age represented by a real number, and where the transitions are constrained by the ages of the tokens. This class is closely related to the class of parameterized systems of timed processes where each process is restricted to a single clock [AJ03]. We have considered TPNs with just one real-valued clock per token. For all the problems studied so far, the decidability results coincide for dense-time and discrete time (although the proofs for dense-time are harder). However, if we consider TPNs with *two* clocks per token, there is a decidability gap between the dense-time and the discrete time domain. The coverability problem becomes undecidable for dense-time TPNs with only *two* clocks per token, while it remains decidable for discrete TPNs with any finite number of clocks per token [ADM04]. The class of TPNs with multiple clocks per token is related to parameterized systems of timed processes, with multiple clocks per process [ADM04]. It is therefore worth investigating whether this more general class induces a similar gap for the problems we have considered in this paper.

References

[AD90]   R. Alur and D. Dill. Automata for modelling real-time systems. In *Proc. ICALP '90*, volume 443 of *Lecture Notes in Computer Science*, pages 322–335, 1990.

[ADM04]   P. A. Abdulla, J. Deneux, and P. Mahata. Multi-clock timed networks. In *Proc. LICS '04*, pages 345–354. IEEE Computer Society Press, 2004.

[AJ03]   P. A. Abdulla and B. Jonsson. Model checking of systems with many identical timed processes. *Theoretical Computer Science*, 290(1):241–264, 2003.

[Alu91]   R. Alur. *Techniques for Automatic Verification of Real-Time Systems*. PhD thesis, Dept. of Computer Sciences, Stanford University, 1991.

[AN01]   P. A. Abdulla and A. Nylén. Timed Petri nets and BQOs. In *Proc. ICATPN'2001: 22nd Int. Conf. on application and theory of Petri nets*, volume 2075 of *Lecture Notes in Computer Science*, pages 53 –70, 2001.

[AN02]   P. A. Abdulla and A. Nylén. Undecidability of ltl for timed petri nets. In *INFINITY 2002, 4th International Workshop on Verification of Infinite-State Systems*, 2002.

[Bow96]   F. D. J. Bowden. Modelling time in Petri nets. In *Proc. Second Australian-Japan Workshop on Stochastic Models*, 1996.

[dFERA00] D. de Frutos Escrig, V. Valero Ruiz, and O. Marroquín Alonso. Decidability of properties of timed-arc Petri nets. In *ICATPN 2000*, number 1825 in Lecture Notes in Computer Science, pages 187–206, 2000.

[DJS99]   C. Dufourd, P. Jančar, and Ph. Schnoebelen. Boundedness of Reset P/T Nets. In *Proc. of ICALP'99*, volume 1644 of *LNCS*. Springer Verlag, 1999.

[God94]   J.C. Godskesen. *Timed Modal Specifications*. PhD thesis, Aalborg University, 1994.

[Hig52]   G. Higman. Ordering by divisibility in abstract algebras. *Proc. London Math. Soc.*, 2:326–336, 1952.

[KM69]   R.M. Karp and R.E. Miller. Parallel program schemata. *Journal of Computer and Systems Sciences*, 3(2):147–195, May 1969.

[May03]   R. Mayr. Undecidable problems in unreliable computations. *TCS*, 297(1-3):337–354, 2003.

[RGdFE99] V. Valero Ruiz, F. Cuartero Gomez, and D. de Frutos Escrig. On non-decidability of reachability for timed-arc Petri nets. In *Proc. 8th International Workshop on Petri Nets and Performance Models*, pages 188–196, 1999.

[Tri99]   S. Tripakis. Verifying progress in times systems. In *Proc. ARTS '99*, pages 299–314, 1999.

[VJ85]   R. Valk and M. Jantzen. The Residue of Vector Sets with Applications to Decidability Problems in Petri Nets. *Acta Informatica*, 21:643–674, 1985.

On the Urgency Expressiveness

Michaël Adélaïde and Claire Pagetti

Labri (UMR 5800), Domaine Universitaire,
351, cours de la Libï£¡ation 33405 Talence Cedex, France
{adelaide, pagetti}@labri.fr

Abstract. We present an algorithm for finding the minimal number of clocks of a given timed automaton recognizing the language described by a so-called *bounded timed regular expression w*. This algorithm is based on the partition of the timed projection of w into so-called *delay cells*. Using this decomposition, we give a method to compute practically this number for w. We then apply this technique to prove that for some n-clock timed automaton we need an additional clock to encode *urgency*.

Keywords: Timed automaton, timed regular expression, minimal number of clocks, n-clock timed language, urgency.

1 Introduction

Timed automata have been introduced by R. ALUR and D. DILL in [2]. Practically, a timed automaton is a finite automaton extended with positive real-valued variables called *clocks*. A linear behavior of such a model is an alternation of discrete steps and continuous elapses of time. As with classical (without timing constraints) finite automata, we can associate an equivalent *timed regular language* [2] which coincides with the language recognized by a timed automaton. Like untimed languages, we can express this language with a *timed regular expression* [6] and actually compute this expression from the timed automaton [9].

Urgency. For modeling huge systems, it is interesting to use high level hierarchical modeling languages such as AltaRica [5] or Charon [3] for instance. Such languages contain modeling operators which allow an easiest specification of particular complex behavior. A classical operator is the *urgency* [8, 7] operator. If a transition labeled by an urgent event is enabled in a location, some discrete transition must occur immediately. It is equivalent to use *time invariants* [15] or urgency. Using urgency or time invariants does not change the expressiveness of timed automata and a procedure to turn a timed automaton with urgency into a classical timed automaton with time invariants is given in [18, 13, 10]. This procedure always adds a new clock.

Problem to Solve. The starting point of our work is the following question: "Is it possible to make the urgency encoding with no addititional clock?". [13] gives a negative answer for $n = 2$ and conjectures that $\forall n \in \mathbb{N}$, there exists a n-clock timed automaton with urgency which can only be translated into a $n + 1$-clock timed automaton.

K. Lodaya and M. Mahajan (Eds.): FSTTCS 2004, LNCS 3328, pp. 71–83, 2004.

Contribution. For $n \geq 1$, we find a n-clock timed automaton with urgency which can only be translated into a $n + 1$-clock timed automaton. This answers positively to the conjecture. From the theoretical point of view, it gives a limit for anyone who wants to better the algorithm [18, 13, 10].

In our proof, we compute the minimal number of clocks of a bounded timed regular expression. One must note that the general problem is not computable [20, 19]. We introduce a representation for timing part of disjunction-free finite timed languages, which is independent of the number of clocks, namely the *convex delay polyhedra*. A convex delay polyhedron is a conjunction of timed inequalities [17]. A timed inequality $\sum_{i=j}^{k} \delta_i$ measures the time elapsed from the entrance in the jth node to the leaving of the kth.

The representation consists in taking all the timed inequalities. Thus, we show there exists a canonical representant for each convex delay polyhedron. Our canonization is for timed inequalities what Difference Bound Matrices [14] are for clocks constraints. Then, delay polyhedra are the dual of clocks constraints and our delay-cells are the dual of zones. It means that two dates in the same delay-cell cannot be distinguished by any clock-constraint. In other words, you can add any clocks you want and any clock-constraints you want, you cannot differentiate the two dates.

Related Works. One of the first results [4, 20] on minimizing the number of clocks claims that for every n there exists an n-clock timed automaton for which the accepting timed regular language cannot be recognized by any $n - 1$-clock timed automaton. [20, 19] have yet shown that minimizing the number of clocks in timed automata is known to be a non-computable problem. Consequently, the authors in [12] use heuristics to turn a timed automaton into a timed system (not necessarily a timed automaton) which have less clocks. In the other works on minimization, the authors try to limit the explosion of the constraints. In [16], the authors combine the symbolic computation with DBM and partial order techniques to reduce the explosion of the size of the constraints that appear when calculating reachable states. In [14], the authors replace the DBMs by shorter representation included in the original DBMs.

Outline. The document is organized as follows. Section 2 is devoted to the definition of the notions we will need thereafter, timed automata and timed languages. In section 3, we detail the practical method to compute the minimal number of clocks for a bounded expression. Finally, in section 4, we apply this technique to prove the Labroue's conjecture with the Theorem 2.

2   Timed Systems

In this section, after reminding some notations, we recall the definitions [2] of finite timed regular expression.

Notations. A clock is a positive real-valued variable following an evolution law. We consider a finite set of clocks X. A *clock valuation* [2] on X is a map $v : X \to \mathbb{R}_{\geq 0}$ which assigns a positive real value to each clock of X. We denote by $\mathbb{R}_{\geq 0}^X$

the set of all clock valuations. For $t \in \mathbb{R}_{\geq 0}$, the clock valuation $v + t$ is defined by $\forall x \in X, (v + t)(x) = v(x) + t$.

The set of *convex clock constraints* $\mathcal{C}_c(X)$ on X is inductively defined by:

$$g := x \smile r \mid x - y \smile r \mid g \wedge g$$

with $x, y \in X, \smile \in \{<, \leq, >, \geq, =\}$, $r \in \mathbb{N}$.

We denote by $\mathcal{I}(\mathbb{N})$ the set of intervals $I \subset \mathbb{R}_{\geq 0}$ with bounds in $\mathbb{N} \cup \{\infty\}$.

2.1 Timed Automata

Practically a timed automaton [2] is a finite state machine constrained by timing requirements handled by formulas on clocks.

Definition 1 (Timed Automaton [2]). *A timed automaton is tuple* $\mathcal{A} = (Q, E, X, q_0, F, \rightarrow)$ *such that:* Q *is a finite set of locations,* E *is a finite set of actions,* X *is a finite set of clocks,* $q_o \in Q$ *is the initial location,* $F \subseteq Q$ *are the accepted locations and* $\rightarrow \subseteq Q \times (\mathcal{C}_c(X) \times E \times 2^X) \times Q$ *is the transition relation.*

Definition 2 (Timed Automaton Semantics [2]). *The semantics of the timed automaton* $\mathcal{A}$ *is given by the transition system* $(S, E \cup \mathbb{R}, s_0, F_S, \rightarrow_S)$ *with:*

1. $S = Q \times \mathbb{R}_{\geq 0}^X$ *is the set of states;*
2. $s_0 = (q_0, \nu_0)$ *such that* $\forall x \in X, \nu_0(x) = 0$ *is the set of initial states;*
3. $F_S = F \times \mathbb{R}_{\geq 0}^X$ *is the set of final states;*
4. $\rightarrow_S \subseteq S \times (E \cup \mathbb{R}) \times S$ *is the transition relation, it is defined by* $((q, \nu), e, (q', \nu')) \in \rightarrow_S$ *iff*

$$\begin{cases} either\ e \in E \wedge \exists (q, g, e, R, q') \in \rightarrow\ such\ that\ g(\nu) = tt\ \wedge \\ \quad \nu'(x) = \begin{cases} 0\ if\ x \in R \\ \nu(x)\ otherwise \end{cases} \\ or\ e = \delta \in \mathbb{R} \wedge q' = q \wedge \nu' = \nu + \delta \end{cases}$$

For all $d \in \mathbb{R} \cup E$, $s, s' \in S$ *such that* $(s, d, s') \in \rightarrow$, *we write* $s \rightarrow^d s'$.

Definition 3 (Particular Classes). *We define the class* $LTA(n)$ *for* $n \in \mathbb{N}$ *of* line timed automata *as the set of timed automata of the form* $(Q = \{q_1, \cdots, q_n\}, E, X, q_1, q_n, \rightarrow)$ *and* $\rightarrow = \{(q_i, g_i, e_i, R_i, q_{i+1}) | i = 1, \cdots, n - 1\}$. *Graphically, such automaton is a line.*

We define the class $Star(n)$ *for* $n \in \mathbb{N}$ *of* star timed automata *as the set of timed automata of the form* $\mathcal{A} = \cup_{k \in K} \mathcal{A}_k$ *is a finite union of* $\mathcal{A}_k = (Q_k, E, X, q_0, q_{n_k}^k, \rightarrow_k) \in LTA(n_k)$ *with* $n_k \leq n$ *and* $\forall i \neq j, Q_i \cap Q_j = \{q_1\}$. *We notice that an* $LTA(n)$ *automaton is a particular* $Star(n)$ *automaton.*

Example 1. We consider the Star timed automaton $\mathcal{A}$ represented in the Figure 1. It is the union of two LTA automata.

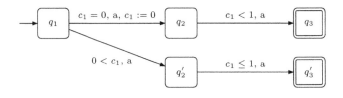

Fig. 1.

2.2　Finite Regular Timed Expressions

It is also possible to give the semantics of a timed automaton by means of a *timed language* [2]. Like in the untimed case, we compute the language recognized by a finite automaton. It is equivalent to express a timed language by a *timed regular expression* [6,9]. We restrict ourselves to finite timed regular expressions. Moreover, we will assume the alphabet $E = \{a\}$. This will not matter on our results.

Definition 4 (Finite (Bounded) Timed Regular Expression). *A finite timed regular expression (FTRE for short) over an alphabet E is defined by the following grammar:*

$$w ::= \emptyset \mid \epsilon \mid a \mid < w >_I \mid w.w' \mid w \vee w' \mid w \wedge w'$$

with $a \in E$, $I \in \mathcal{I}(\mathbb{N})$ (integer-bounded interval).

A timed regular expression w is bounded (BTRE for short) if it is finite and its time projection is bounded, i.e. there exists a bounded interval $I \in \mathcal{I}(\mathbb{N})$ such that $w =< w >_I$.

The semantics of these regular expressions associates to each expression a timed language with:

1. $[\![\emptyset]\!] = \emptyset$, $[\![\epsilon]\!] = \{\epsilon\}$, $[\![a]\!] = \mathbb{R} \times a$,
2. $[\![< w >_I]\!] = \{(l_1, a_1)(l_2, a_2) \cdots \in [\![w]\!] \mid \Sigma l_i \in I\}$,
3. $[\![w.w']\!] = [\![w]\!].[\![w']\!]$, $[\![w \vee w']\!] = [\![w]\!] \cup [\![w']\!]$, $[\![w \wedge w']\!] = [\![w]\!] \cap [\![w']\!]$.

Example 2. We can express the timed language of the timed automaton in the Figure 1 by $L(\mathcal{A}) =< a >_0 < a >_{[0,1[} \vee << a >_{]0,\infty[} a >_{[0,1]}$.

3　Computing the Number of Clocks Practically

3.1　For Bounded Timed Regular Expressions

We are going to illustrate on an example how the following theorem, extracted from [1] can be proved.

Theorem 1. *The minimal number of clocks of a BTRE is computable.*

We proceed as follows. Let w be a disjunction-free FTRE w, the general case is straightforward since a BTRE is a finite union of disjunction-free FTREs . We first note that any timed automaton A that recognizes w can be transformed into a Star automaton with the same number of clocks (as w is finite, it is sufficient to transform A into a tree, which can be turned into a Star). It means that it is sufficient to make the minimization on Star.

The general idea in [1] is to find a canonical representation of convex FTREs and to describe a general FTRE as a union of indivisible convex FTREs .

Delay Polyhedra. We represent the timing part of a FTRE w by a particular polyhedron, namely *delay polyhedron*. We introduce the family of delay polyhedra for representing the constraints satisfied by the durations x_i in the locations q_i.

Definition 5 (Delay Polyhedron). *Let $n \in \mathbb{N}$ and $\mathcal{T}_n = \{(i,j) \mid (i,\ j) \in \mathbb{N}^2 \land 1 \leq i \leq j \leq n\}$, a convex delay polyhedron of $\mathbb{R}^n$ is a tuple $S = (J, I_J)$ with $J \subseteq \mathcal{T}_n$ and $\forall (i,j) \in J$, $I_{i,j} \in \mathcal{I}(\mathbb{N})$. This tuple induces the linear system of inequalities on the variables $(x_1, \cdots, x_n)$:*

$$\left(\bigwedge_{(i,j) \in J} \Sigma_{k=i}^{j} x_k \in I_{i,j} \right) \land \left(\bigwedge_{i=1}^{n} x_i \geq 0 \right)$$

We denote by $Sol(S) \subseteq \mathbb{R}^n_{\geq 0}$ the set of solutions of the linear system and in the sequel we will indifferently refer to a convex delay polyhedron Π under its 3 forms: tuple, linear system or the set of solutions. We denote by $\mathcal{P}$ the set of convex delay polyhedra and by $\mathcal{P}^*$ the subset of $\mathcal{P}$ of non empty systems. We denote by $s_{i,j}(x) = \Sigma_{k=i}^{j} x_k$. We write $S \sim S'$ for $(S, S') \in \mathcal{P}^2$ iff $Sol(S) = Sol(S')$. A delay polyhedron of $\mathbb{R}^n$ is a finite union of convex delay polyhedra of $\mathbb{R}^n$.

We notice that any disjunction-free FTRE w will induce a convex delay polyhedron.

Example 3. Let us consider the timed regular expression $w = < a < a >_{[0,1[} >_{[0,1]}$. The timing part of w can be expressed by the convex delay polyhedron $\Pi_w = (0 \leq x_1 + x_2 \leq 1) \land (0 \leq x_1) \land (0 \leq x_2 < 1)$. Thus $\Pi_w = (\mathcal{T}_2, \{I_{1,1} = \mathbb{R}_{\geq 0}, I_{1,2} = [0,1], I_{2,2} = [0,1[\})$.

The LTA automaton given in the Figure 2, page 75 recognizes w.

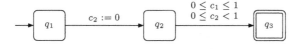

Fig. 2.

The Star automaton given in the Figure 1, page 74 recognizes also w. It illustrates the link between Star-automata and union of convex delay polyhedra.

We can write the same polyhedron in many different ways. We need a canonical representation for the convex delay polyhedra to get rid of the multiple ways for writing the same set.

Definition 6 (Canonical Representation in $\mathcal{P}$). *We define the mapping* canon $: \mathcal{P}^* \rightarrow \mathcal{P}^*$ *which associates to each non-empty $\mathcal{P}$-system $S = (I, b_I)$ an equivalent system $S' = (\mathcal{T}_n, b'_{\mathcal{T}_n})$ with $b'_{i,j}$ given by:*

$$y \in b'_{i,j} \iff \exists x_1 \ldots x_n \in \mathbb{R}^n . y = s_{i,j}(x) \wedge \bigwedge_{(l,p) \in I} s_{l,p}(x) \in b_{l,p} \wedge \bigwedge_{i=1}^{n} x_i \geq 0$$

In the sequel, for a subset of indices $J \subseteq \mathcal{T}_n$, we denote by $canon(S)_J$ the subset of intervals of $canon(S)$ indexed by J, i.e. b'_J.

Here, the $b'_{i,j}$ are the least intervals containing $\sum_{k=i}^{j} x_k$ when $x \in Sol(I, b_I)$. The variable elimination can be realized by a Fourier-Motzkin elimination [11] for instance, which ensures that $b'_{i,j} \in \mathcal{I}(\mathbb{N})$.

Example 4. Let us consider again the convex delay polyhedron Π defined in Example 3. As the timed language is $w = < a < a >_{[0,1[} >_{[0,1]}$, we have $\Pi = (\mathcal{T}_2, (I_{1,1} = \mathbb{R}_{\geq 0}, I_{1,2} = [0,1], I_{2,2} = [0,1[))$. Its canonical representation is $(\mathcal{T}_n, b'_{\mathcal{T}_n})$ with:

$$\begin{pmatrix} b_{1,1} & b_{1,2} \\ & b_{2,2} \end{pmatrix} = \begin{pmatrix} [0,1] & [0,1] \\ & [0,1[\end{pmatrix}$$

This matricial representation is a shorthand for representing some convex delay polyhedron.

This representation is canonical in the sense that any convex delay polyhedron and its canonical representation have the same set of solutions and testing the equality of two convex delay polyhedra can be performed by testing the equality on their canonical representations [1].

From now on, the hypothesis of boundedness plays a role. Let us assume that any interval in the canonical representation $canon(w)$ of w is bounded by a constant M.

Delay-Cells and Delay-Blocks. We will partition the region $\{x \in \mathbb{R}_{\geq 0}^n \mid \sum_{k=1}^{n} x_k \leq M\}$ into a finite number of *cells*. The *blocks* will be unions of cells.

Definition 7 (Canonical Delay-Cells and Delay-Blocks). *Let $n, M \in \mathbb{N}$. We define the set of intervals $\mathcal{I}_M \subseteq \mathcal{I}(\mathbb{N})$ composed by:*

1. *The singletons $\{k\}$ for all $k \leq M$;*
2. *The open intervals $]k, k+1[$ for $k \in \mathbb{N}, 0 \leq k < M$.*

A M-bounded-delay-cell of $\mathbb{R}^n$ is given by the following predicate :

$$\bigwedge_{(i,j) \in \mathcal{T}_n} \sum_{k=i}^{j} x_k \in I_{i,j}$$

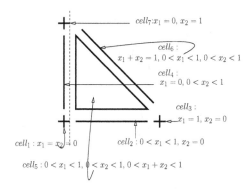

$cell_7 : x_1 = 0, x_2 = 1$

$cell_6 :$
$x_1 + x_2 = 1, 0 < x_1 < 1, 0 < x_2 < 1$

$cell_4 :$
$x_1 = 0, 0 < x_2 < 1$

$cell_3 :$
$x_1 = 1, x_2 = 0$

$cell_1 : x_1 = x_2 = 0$ $cell_2 : 0 < x_1 < 1, x_2 = 0$

$cell_5 : 0 < x_1 < 1, 0 < x_2 < 1, 0 < x_1 + x_2 < 1$

Fig. 3. Delay-cells for $\{(x, y) \mid x \leq 1 \wedge y \leq 1 \wedge x + y \leq 1\}$

where $I_{i,j} \in \mathcal{I}_M$. We denote by $\mathcal{C}_M$ be the set of non-empty M-bounded-delay-cells.

A M-bounded-delay-block *is a finite union of non-empty M-bounded-delay-cells. We denote by* $\mathcal{B}_M$ *the set of M-bounded-delay-blocks.*

We can prove now that the cells of $\mathcal{C}_M$ makes a finite partition of $\{x \in \mathbb{R}^n_{\geq 0} \mid \sum_{k=1}^{n} x_k \leq M\}$.

Property 1 (Dividing the Space into Delay-Cells). Let $M \in \mathbb{N}$. Then the following holds:

1. Let *cell* and *cell'* be two delay-cells, then either $cell = cell'$ or $cell \cap cell' = \emptyset$;
2. For any $x \in \mathbb{R}^n_{\geq 0}$ such that $\sum_{k=1}^{n} x_i \leq M$, there exists $cell \in \mathcal{C}_M$ such that $x \in cell$. In the sequel, we denote by $cell(x)$ such a cell;
3. The sets $\mathcal{C}_M$ and $\mathcal{B}_M$ are finite.

Example 5. For $n = 2$ and $M = 1$, the space $\{(x, y) \mid x \leq 1 \wedge y \leq 1 \wedge x + y \leq 1\}$ is the union of the 7 delay-cells as it is shown in Figure 3, page 77.

If w is a BTRE , we show that $Sol(w)$ is a M-bounded-delay-block. We characterize the sub expressions w' of w and we prove that they also verify $Sol(w') \in \mathcal{B}_M$.

Property 2 (Expressions as Delay Blocks). Let w be a BTRE , let M be the greatest integer in $canon(w)$. Suppose that w is not equivalent to the empty expression. We have:

1. $Sol(w)$ is a delay polyhedron and it is either a delay-block, i.e. $Sol(w)$ belongs to $\mathcal{B}_M$;
2. Let w' be a disjunction-free FTRE such that $Sol(w') \subseteq Sol(w)$, if M' is the greatest integer in $canon(w')$, then $M' \leq M$. Moreover, $Sol(w')$ belongs to $\mathcal{B}_{M'}$.

As the number of delay-blocks of $\mathcal{B}_M$ are finite, there exists a finite number of possibilities for writing $Sol(w)$ as a disjunction of convex delay-blocks. If we write $Sol(w) = \cup Sol(\Pi_i)$ where the Π_i are convex delay polyhedra, all we have to do is to find for every Π_i, an LTA automaton that recognizes it with a minimal number of clocks. Then, we introduce another representation of LTA automata.

Definition 8 (LTA Representation). *We can now represent an LTA timed automaton $\mathcal{A} = (\{q_1, \cdots, q_{n+1}\}, E, \{a\}, q_1, q_{n+1}, \rightarrow)$ by a tuple (n, I, b_I, p, h) where:*

1. *$(I, b_I) \in \mathcal{P}$ is a delay polyhedron such that $Sol(I, b_I) = proj_{\mathbb{R}^n}(L(\mathcal{A}))$,*
2. *p is the number of clocks of $\mathcal{A}$,*
3. *$h : I \rightarrow \{1, ..., p\}$ maps for each temporal condition $\sum_{k=i}^{j} x_k \in b_{i,j}$ the index of the clock which manages it. The mapping h is called a clock mapping. It means that:*
   (a) *$p = 0$ is equivalent to $I = \emptyset$;*
   (b) *if $I \neq \emptyset$ and $h : I \rightarrow \{1, ..., p\}$, then $h(i, k) = h(j, l)$ implies that $[i, k] \cap [j, l] = \emptyset$ or $i = j$.*

Example 6. For instance, the automaton of Figure 2, page 75 can be represented by the tuple

$$\left(2, \{(1, 2), (2, 2)\}, \begin{pmatrix} [0, 1] \\ [0, 1[\end{pmatrix}, 2, \begin{cases} h(1, 2) = 1 \\ h(2, 2) = 2 \end{cases} \right).$$

It means that there are 2 non-final nodes, $(1, 2)$ and $(2, 2)$ are the indices of the *useful constraints*, the canonical-representation restricted on these indices is $\begin{pmatrix} [0, 1] & [0, 1] \\ & [0, 1[\end{pmatrix}$, there are 2 clocks, and the clock mapping $\begin{cases} h(1, 2) = 1 \\ h(2, 2) = 2 \end{cases}$ maps each clock constraint to the index of clock used for measuring it.

It becomes clear that for a given convex delay-polyhedron of dimension n, there exists a finite set of possibility for the clock mappings (with less than n clocks).

3.2   Finding a Lower Bound for the Number of Clocks

We only want to find a lower bound on the number of clocks. We explain here the principle of the method and illustrate it on a short example. Let w be a disjunction-free FTRE and Π the delay polyhedron associated to w, we find some "extreme point" x in the sense that the x belongs to Π and some cells around $cell(x)$ which are disjoint from Π give some information of the possible writings of Π.

Definition 9 (Neighbor Cells). *We say that two delay-cells cell and cell' are neighbor cells if there exist $x \in$ cell and $x' \in$ cell' such that the segment $[x, x']$ is contained in cell $\cup$ cell'.*

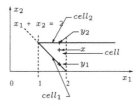

Fig. 4. Example of Neighbor Cells

Example 7. Let us consider the following cells of the plane:

1. $cell = 1 < x_1 < 2 \wedge 0 < x_2 < 1 \wedge 2 < x_1 + x_2 < 3$
2. $cell_1 = Sol\big((1 < x_1 < 2) \wedge (0 < x_2 < 1) \wedge x_1 + x_2 = 2)\big);$
3. $cell_2 = Sol\big((1 < x_1 < 2) \wedge (x_2 = 1) \wedge 2 < x_1 + x_2 < 3)\big),$

drawn in the Figure 4, page 79. Then, *cell* and $cell_1$ are neighbor cells; *cell* and $cell_2$ are neighbor cells.

Definition 10 (Difference Set). *Given two neighbor cells* $cell = \bigwedge_{(i,j) \in \mathcal{T}_n}$ $\sum_{k=i}^{j} x_k \in b_{i,j}$ *and* $cell' = \bigwedge_{(i,j) \in \mathcal{T}_n} \sum_{k=i}^{j} x_k \in b'_{i,j}$, $\mathcal{T}_n$ *can be divided into two disjoint subsets:*

1. *The first one contains the common constraints,* $Com(cell, cell') = \{(i, j) \mid b_{i,j} = b'_{i,j}\};$
2. *The second one, called the difference set, contains the distinct constraints, i.e.* $Diff(cell, cell') = \{(i, j) \mid b_{i,j} \neq b'_{i,j}\}.$

To compute $Diff(cell, cell')$ for two neighbor cells, it is sufficient to take an element of each cell.

Example 8. In the example given in the Figure 4, we consider $x = \left(\frac{7}{4}, \frac{3}{4}\right)$ in *cell*, $y^1 = \left(\frac{7}{4}, \frac{1}{4}\right)$ in $cell_1$ and $y^2 = \left(\frac{7}{4}, 1\right)$ in $cell_2$.
  We have $x_1, y_1^1, y_1^2 \in]1, 2[$, $x_2, y_2^1 \in]0, 1[$ and $x_1 + x_2, y_1^2 + y_2^2 \in]2, 3[$. Thus, we have $Diff(cell, cell_1) = \{(1, 2)\}$ and $Diff(cell, cell_2) = \{(2, 2)\}$.

This is the core of the method: if two neighbor cells differ on a unique index and if one belongs to a delay polyhedron but no the other, then we are sure that the index is necessary to depict the delay polyhedron.

Property 3 (of Neighbor Cells). If two neighbor cells *cell* and *cell'* differ on a single index, i.e. $Diff(cell, cell') = \{(i_1, j_1)\}$, and if a convex delay polyhedron (I, b''_I) is such that:

1. $cell \subseteq Sol(I, b''_I)$ and
2. $cell' \cap Sol(I, b''_I) = \emptyset,$

then $(i_1, j_1) \in I$.

The main idea is the following: one can transform any timed automaton A that recognizes a disjunction-free BTRE w into a Star automaton A' without changing the number of clocks. Let x be an "extreme point" and *cell* the delay-cell that contains x. There exists an LTA automaton LA which is a branch of A' such that *cell* belongs to the timed projection of the word recognized by LA. Then, minimizing the number of clocks of LA gives a lower bound on the number of clocks of A', which in turn gives the result for A.

Example 9. Let $w = <\ a\ <\ a\ >_{]0,1[}>_{]2+\infty[}$ and $\Pi = (x_2 \in]0,1[)\ \wedge\ (x_1 + x_2 \in]2, +\infty[)$. Let $x = (\frac{7}{4}, \frac{3}{4})$, then, $cell(x) = cell$ defined in the Figure 4. We have $cell \subseteq Sol(\Pi)$, $cell_1 \not\subseteq Sol(\Pi)$ and $cell_2 \not\subseteq Sol(\Pi)$. Then for all representation (I, b_I) of Π, necessarily $\{(1,2), (2,2)\} \subseteq I$. It means that there must be some clocks verifying some constraints on $\{(1,2), (2,2)\}$. We conclude any Star automaton that recognizes w has at least 2 clocks.

4   Application: Encoding Urgency

In this section, we show a first application of the previous result. We introduce the modeling notion of *urgency* [18, 8, 7]. We show how to encode urgency in an LTA automaton. Thus, we construct an n-clock timed automaton, we add some urgency on it and we prove we require an additional clock to encode urgency, so that we generate a $n + 1$-clock timed automaton.

4.1   Different Aspects of Urgency

Semantical Effect of Urgency Let $\mathcal{A} = (Q, E, X, q_0, F, \rightarrow)$ be a timed automaton such that $E = \{a, a_u\}$ and a_u is an urgent event. The urgency reduces the relation transition since it forbids some delay transitions in some state.

Let $(S, E \cup \mathbb{R}, s_0, F_S, \rightarrow_S) = [\![\mathcal{A}]\!]$, then the semantics of $\mathcal{A}$ taking in account the urgency is the transition system $[\![\mathcal{A}]\!] \restriction_{urg} = (S, E \cup \mathbb{R}, s_0, F_S, \rightarrow'_S)$ with: $((q, \nu), \delta, (q, \nu + \delta)) \in \rightarrow'_S \Longleftrightarrow \forall \delta' \leq \delta, ((q, \nu + \delta'), a_u, (q', \nu')) \notin \rightarrow_S$. It is also possible to encode syntactically urgency [18, 13, 10].

Effect of Urgency on a Finite Timed Regular Expressions. The aspect of urgency we are interested in consists in defining the effect of the urgency on the recognized language.

Let $\mathcal{A} = (n, \rightarrow, E, I, b_I, p, h)$ be an LTA automaton with $E = \{a, a_u\}$ and a_u is an urgent event. Assume that there is only one transition labeled a_u: $(q_i, g, a_u, r, q_{i+1})$. Suppose also that g is left closed, i.e. for all $l \leq i$, $inf(b_{l,i}) \in b_{l,i}$.

The action a_u must be fired as soon as all the $b_{l,i}$ are satisfied, this means that at least one of the $b_{l,i}$ has just become true. Thus the finite timed regular expression recognized by $\mathcal{A}$ with urgency is $\omega_u = \bigvee_{1 \leq l \leq i} \left(\omega\ \wedge\ a \cdots < a \cdots a_u >_{inf(b_{l,i})} \cdots a \right)$.

We first remark this procedure transforms an LTA automaton into a Star automaton. We also notice that if the urgent transition is guarded by *true* then the effect is straightforward. Indeed, for all $l \leq i$, $inf(b_{l,i}) = 0$ and we have $\omega_u = \omega \wedge a \cdots < a_u >_0 \cdots a$.

4.2   An Answer to the Labroue's Conjecture

We know precisely the effect of urgency on the recognized language, the second question is the effect on the number of clocks. The author of [13] conjectures that $\forall n \in \mathbb{N}$, there exists a n-clock timed automaton with urgency which can only be translated into a $n + 1$-clock timed automaton.

Let us consider the timed regular expressions W_n, defined by the following induction:

$$\begin{cases} W_1 =< aaa >_{]0,1[} \\ W_{n+1} =< aW_n a >_{]0,2n+1[} \end{cases}$$

Assume that the transition $q_{n+1} \xrightarrow{a} q_{n+2}$ of $\mathcal{A}_n$ is a urgent transition. Since the transition is guarded by *true*, the timed regular expression W_n is turned into W_n^u as follows:

$$\begin{cases} W_1^u =< a < a >_0 a >_{]0,1[} \\ W_{n+1}^u =< aW_n^u a >_{]0,2n+1[} \end{cases}$$

We can now conclude the conjecture given in [13] is a theorem.

Theorem 2 (Requiring a Fresh Clock in the Syntactical Encoding of Urgency). *$\forall n \in \mathbb{N}$, there exists a n-clock timed automaton with urgency which can only be translated into a $n + 1$-clock timed automaton.*

The timed regular expressions W_n and W_n^u give a positive answer to the conjecture since any timed automaton that recognizes W_n has got at least n clocks and any timed automaton that recognizes W_n^u has got at least $n+1$ clocks. The proof is given in [1]. We only give here the choice of the extreme point and of the neighbors. In both cases, we use the same point $x = (x_1, \cdots, x_{2n+1})$ defined as follows:

$$\begin{cases} x_k & = 1 + \varepsilon - c \text{ for } 1 \leq k \leq n - 1 \\ x_{n+1+k} & = 1 - \varepsilon \quad\;\; \text{ for } 1 \leq k \leq n \\ x_n & = \varepsilon - c \\ x_{n+1} & = 0 \end{cases}$$

where $0 < n^4 c < n^2 \varepsilon < 1$. For the neighbor cells, let us take the points y^p:

$$\begin{cases} y^0 = x + b\, e_{n+1} \\ y^p = x + pc\, e_{n+1-p} \text{ for } 1 \leq p \leq n \end{cases}$$

where the e_i are the ith unit vector of the canonical base of $\mathbb{R}^{2n+1}$ and $0 < n^2 b < c$. Finally, we can show that:

1. $cell(x)$ and $cell(y^p)$ are neighbor cells;
2. $Diff(cell(x), cell(y^p)) = \{(n + 1 - p, n + 1 + p)\}$.

5   Conclusion

In order to answer to the question of the urgency encoding, we have been brougth to consider finite bounded timed regular expressions. We have given a procedure based on enumeration for the computation of the minimal number of clocks required for the recognition of a finite bounded timed regular expression. And we have given an answer about the urgency encoding.

A great number of questions arises from these results:

1. is the assumption of boundedness necessary?
2. is it possible to carry over the computation of the minimal number of clocks in case of infinite timed regular expressions with particular patterns. For instance if w is a bounded timed regular expression, then can we deduce the minimal number of clocks for $w^\star$?

References

1. M. Adélaïde and C. Pagetti. When the minimal number of clocks is computable. Technical Report 1329-04, Labri/CNRS, Bordeaux, 2004. http://www.labri.fr/Labri/Publications/Rapports-internes/Publications.htm.
2. R. Alur and D. Dill. A theory of timed automata. *Theoretical Computer Science B*, 126:183–235, 1994.
3. R. Alur, R. Grosu, Y. Hur, V. Kumar, and I. Lee. Modular specification of hybrid systems in CHARON. In *HSCC*, pages 6–19, 2000.
4. R. Alur and T. A. Henzinger. Back to the future: Towards a theory of timed regular languages. In *IEEE Symposium on Foundations of Computer Science*, pages 177–186, 1992.
5. A. Arnold, A. Griffault, G. Point, and A. Rauzy. The AltaRica formalism for describing concurrent systems. *Fundamenta Informaticae*, 40:109–124, 2000.
6. E. Asarin, P. Caspi, and O. Maler. Timed regular expressions. *Journal of the ACM*, 49(2):172–206, 2002.
7. S. Bornot and J. Sifakis. An algebraic framework for urgency. *Information and Computation*, 163(1):172–202, 2000.
8. S. Bornot, J. Sifakis, and S. Tripakis. Modeling urgency in timed systems. *Lecture Notes in Computer Science*, 1536:103–129, 1998.
9. P. Bouyer and A. Petit. A Kleene/Bchi-like theorem for clock languages. *Journal of Automata, Languages and Combinatorics*, 7:167–186, 2001.
10. F. Cassez, C. Pagetti, and O. Roux. A timed extension for AltaRica, 2004. To appear in Fundamenta Informaticae.
11. V. Chandru and M.R. Rao. 175 years of Linear Programming, part 1. The French Connection. *The Journal of Science Education*, 1998.
12. C. Daws and S. Yovine. Reducing the number of clock variables of timed automata. In *7th IEEE Real Time Systems Symposium, RTSS'96*, pages 73–81, Washington, DC, USA, 1996. IEEE Computer Society Press.
13. A. Labroue. Conditions de vivacité dans les automates temporisés. Technical Report LSV-98-7, Lab. Specification and Verification, ENS de Cachan, 1998.
14. K. Larsen, F Larsson, and P. Pettersson. Efficient verification of real-time systems: Compact data structure and state-space reduction. *Real-Time Systems — The International*, 25:255–275, 2003.

15. K. G. Larsen, P. Pettersson, and W. Yi. Compositional and Symbolic Model-Checking of Real-Time Systems. In *Proc. of the 16th IEEE Real-Time Systems Symposium*, pages 76–87. IEEE Computer Society Press, December 1995.
16. D. Lugiez, P. Niebert, and S. Zennou. A Partial Order Semantics Approach to the Clock Explosion Problem of Timed Automata. In *TACAS*, pages 296 – 311, Barcelona, Spain, 2004.
17. O. Maler and A. Pnueli. On Recognizable Timed Languages. In *FOSSACS*, 2004.
18. J. Sifakis and S. Yovine. Compositional specification of timed systems. In *13th Annual Symp. on Theoretical Aspects of Computer Science, STACS'96*, volume 1046, pages 347–359. Lecture Notes in Computer Science, Springer-Verlag, 1996. Invited paper.
19. S. Tripakis. Folk Theorems on the Determinization and Minimization of Timed Automata. In *FORMATS*, 2003.
20. T. Wilke. *Automaten und Logiken zur Beschreibung zeitabhängiger Systeme*. PhD thesis, Inst. f. Informatik u. Prakt. Math., CAU Kiel, 1994.

Asynchronous Automata-Theoretic Characterization of Aperiodic Trace Languages

Bharat Adsul[1] and Milind Sohoni[2]

[1] Chennai Mathematical Institute, 92 G. N. Chetty Road,
Chennai 600 017, India
abharat@cmi.ac.in
[2] Department of Computer Sc and Engg, Indian Institute of Technology,
Mumbai 400 076, India
sohoni@cse.iitb.ac.in

Abstract. We characterize aperiodic distributed behaviours, modelled as Mazurkiewicz traces in terms of a very natural cascade product of the *gossip* automaton with a counter-free asynchronous automaton. The characterization strengthens the fundamental results of Schutzenberger and, McNaughton and Papert and implies that star-free, equivalently, first-order-definable trace languages admit counter-free asynchronous acceptors modulo the gossip automaton.

1 Introduction

We focus on a special class of behaviours of distributed systems modelled as Mazurkiewicz traces [DR, Maz, Tho]–the class of aperiodic distributed behaviours. These behaviours are non-trivial generalizations of aperiodic (or equivalently, counter-free) sequential behaviours. A fundamental result of Schutzenberger [Sch] characterizes aperiodic sequential behaviours in terms of word languages admitting star-free regular expressions or simply star-free word languages. Aperiodic sequential behaviours also coincide with languages expressible in the popular specification formalism of the first-order logic, by a result of McNaughton and Papert [McNP]. In the context of traces, aperiodic behaviours also coincide with appropriate star-free and first-order definable trace languages [GRS, EM, DK].

Undoubtedly, aperiodic behaviours are an important and interesting subclass of regular behaviours. Automata are natural machine models for sequential systems and precisely generate regular word languages. In a similar vein, regular trace languages are generated by asynchronous automata which are natural and robust machine models of distributed systems [Zie].

Our result concerns an asynchronous automaton-based characterization of aperiodic trace languages. Towards this, we introduce the notion of cascade product of two asynchronous automata. A similar construct has proved to be extremely useful in the context of sequential automata [Arb]. The new characterization crucially uses the gossip automaton [MS2]—an asynchronous automaton

K. Lodaya and M. Mahajan (Eds.): FSTTCS 2004, LNCS 3328, pp. 84–96, 2004.

which allows to keep track of the latest information that the processes in a distributed system have about each other. Finally, we characterize aperiodic trace languages in terms of a very natural cascade product of the gossip automaton with a counter-free asynchronous automaton.

In the next section we develop notations for traces and setup the framework of asynchronous automata. In Section 3, we present the gossip automaton and use it in Section 4 to give an event calculus also called residue calculus which is implicit in the work [MS1]. We present the important notion of cascade product in Section 5 and use it to construct an asynchronous automaton for a regular trace language. In Section 6, a novel analysis of this construction is carried out which leads to the main result.

2 Preliminaries

Traces. Let $\mathcal{P} = \{1, 2, \ldots, K\}$ be a set of processes. A distributed alphabet over $\mathcal{P}$ is a family $\widetilde{\Sigma} = (\Sigma_i)_{i \in \mathcal{P}}$. Let $\Sigma = \bigcup_{i \in \mathcal{P}} \Sigma_i$. For $a \in \Sigma$, we set $\mathrm{loc}(a) = \{i \in \mathcal{P} \mid a \in \Sigma_i\}$. By (Σ, I) we denote the corresponding trace alphabet, i.e., I is the independence relation $I = \{(a, b) \in \Sigma^2 \mid \mathrm{loc}(a) \cap \mathrm{loc}(b) = \emptyset\}$ induced by $\widetilde{\Sigma}$. The corresponding dependence relation $\Sigma^2 \setminus I$ is denoted by D.

A Σ-labelled poset is a structure $F = (E, \leq, \lambda)$, where E is a set, $\leq$ is a partial order on E and $\lambda : E \to \Sigma$ is a labelling function. For $e, e' \in E$, define $e \lessdot e'$ iff $e < e'$ and for each e'' with $e \leq e'' \leq e'$ either $e = e''$ or $e' = e''$. For $X \subseteq E$, let $\downarrow X = \{y \in E \mid y \leq x \text{ for some } x \in X\}$. For $e \in E$, we set $\downarrow e = \downarrow\{e\}$. A trace over $\widetilde{\Sigma}$ is a *finite* Σ-labelled poset $F = (E, \leq, \lambda)$ such that

- If $e, e' \in E$ with $e \lessdot e'$ then $(\lambda(e), \lambda(e')) \in D$.
- If $e, e' \in E$ with $(\lambda(e), \lambda(e')) \in D$ then $e \leq e'$ or $e' \leq e$.

Let $TR(\widetilde{\Sigma})$ (or simply TR) denote the set of traces over $\widetilde{\Sigma}$. Henceforth, a trace means a trace over $\widetilde{\Sigma}$ unless specified otherwise. Let $F = (E, \leq, \lambda) \in TR$. Then $c \subseteq E$ is a configuration iff $\downarrow c = c$. We let $\mathcal{C}_F$ denote the set of configurations of F. Notice that the empty set and E are configurations. The event based transition relation $\Rightarrow_F \subseteq \mathcal{C}_F \times E \times \mathcal{C}_F$ is defined as $c \overset{e}{\Longrightarrow}_F c'$ iff $e \notin c$ and $c \cup \{e\} = c'$. The action-based transition relation $\to_F \subseteq \mathcal{C}_F \times \Sigma \times \mathcal{C}_F$ is defined as $c \overset{a}{\longrightarrow}_F c'$ iff there exists $e \in E$ such that $\lambda(e) = a$ and $c \overset{e}{\Longrightarrow}_F c'$.

Trace Languages. Let $F = (E, \leq, \lambda) \in TR$ and $F' = (E', \leq', \lambda') \in TR$. We define $FF' \in TR$ to be a trace $(E'', \leq'', \lambda'')$ where

- $E'' = E \sqcup E'$,
- $\leq''$ is the transitive closure of $\leq \cup \leq' \cup \{(e, e') \in E \times E' \mid (\lambda(e), \lambda'(e')) \in D\}$,
- $\lambda'' : E'' \to \Sigma$ where $\lambda''(e) = \lambda(e)$ if $e \in E$; otherwise, $\lambda''(e) = \lambda'(e)$.

This operation, henceforth referred to as trace concatenation, is a generalization of the concatenation operation on words and gives TR a monoid structure.

Let $\eta : TR \to M$ be a morphism to a monoid M. A trace language $L \subseteq TR$ is said to be *recognized* by η if $\eta^{-1}(\eta(L)) = L$. A trace language L is said to be regular if it is recognized by a morphism into a finite monoid. Similarly, a trace language L is said to be aperiodic if it is recognized by a morphism into an aperiodic finite monoid. Recall that a monoid M is aperiodic if for some positive integer n and for all $m \in M$, $m^n = m^{n+1}$.

Asynchronous Automata. Each process $i \in \mathcal{P}$ is equipped with a non-empty finite set of local i-states, denoted S_i. We set $S = \bigcup_{i \in \mathcal{P}} S_i$ and call S the set of local states. We let P, Q range over non-empty subsets of $\mathcal{P}$ and i, j range over $\mathcal{P}$. A Q-state is a map $s : Q \to S$ such that $s(j) \in S_j$ for every $j \in Q$. We let S_Q denote the set of Q-states. We call $S_\mathcal{P}$ the set of global states. If $Q' \subseteq Q$ and $s \in S_Q$ then $s_{Q'}$ is s restricted to Q'. We abbreviate loc(a) by a when talking about states. Thus an a-state is a loc(a)-state and S_a denotes the set of loc(a)-states.

A (deterministic) asynchronous automaton over $\widetilde{\Sigma}$ is presented as a structure $\mathcal{A} = (\{S_i\}_{i \in \mathcal{P}}, \{\to_a\}_{a \in \Sigma}, s_{in}, S_{fin})$ where

- S_i is a finite non-empty set of i-states for each process i.
- For $a \in \Sigma$, $\to_a \subseteq S_a \times S_a$ is a transition function on a-states.
- $s_{in} \in S_\mathcal{P}$ is an initial global state.
- $S_{fin} \subseteq S_\mathcal{P}$ is a set of final global states.

The global transition function $\to_\mathcal{A} \subseteq S_\mathcal{P} \times \Sigma \times S_\mathcal{P}$ is defined as: $s \xrightarrow{a}_\mathcal{A} s'$ iff $(s_a, s'_a) \in \to_a$ and $s_{\mathcal{P}-\text{loc}(a)} = s'_{\mathcal{P}-\text{loc}(a)}$.

A run of $\mathcal{A}$ over $F \in TR$ is a map $\rho : \mathcal{C}_F \to S_\mathcal{P}$ such that $\rho(\emptyset) = s_{in}$ and for every $(c, a, c') \in \to_F$, $\rho(c) \xrightarrow{a}_\mathcal{A} \rho(c')$. The run ρ is accepting if $\rho(E) \in S_{fin}$. As $\mathcal{A}$ is deterministic, each trace F gives rise to a unique run. The trace language accepted by $\mathcal{A}$ is the set $L(\mathcal{A}) = \{F \in TR \mid \text{the run of } \mathcal{A} \text{ over } F \text{ is accepting}\}$.

3   Local Views and Gossip Automaton

We develop some notation to introduce the important notion of a local view. Let $F = (E, \leq, \lambda) \in TR$. Then E is the set of events in F and for an event e in F, loc(e) abbreviates loc$(\lambda(e))$. Further, let $i \in \mathcal{P}$. The set of i-events in F is $E_i = \{e \in E \mid i \in \text{loc}(e)\}$. This is the set of events in which process i participates. It is clear that E_i is totally ordered with respect to $\leq$.

Let $c \in \mathcal{C}_F$ and $i \in \mathcal{P}$. Then $\downarrow^i(c)$ is the i-view of c and it is defined as: $\downarrow^i(c) = \downarrow(c \cap E_i)$. We note that $\downarrow^i(c)$ is also a configuration. It is the "best" configuration that the process i is aware of at c. Indeed, at c, process i is oblivious to the occurrence of any event outside its local view $\downarrow^i(c)$. It is easy to see that if $\downarrow^i(c) \neq \emptyset$ then there exists $e \in E_i$ with $\downarrow^i(c) = \downarrow e$. For $Q \subseteq \mathcal{P}$ and $c \in \mathcal{C}_F$, we let $\downarrow^Q(c)$ denote the set $\bigcup_{i \in Q} \downarrow^i(c)$. Again, $\downarrow^Q(c)$ is a configuration. It represents the collective knowledge of the processes in Q about the configuration c.

Now we develop more notation to describe the latest information of a process about other processes at a given configuration.

Latest Information. Fix $F = (E, \leq, \lambda) \in TR$ and $c \in \mathcal{C}_F$. Let $i, j, k \in \mathcal{P}$. We define $\mathsf{latest}_{i \to j}(c) = e$ where e is the maximum j-event in $\downarrow^i(c)$. If e does not exist then $\mathsf{latest}_{i \to j}(c)$ is undefined. Further, we define $\mathsf{latest}_{i \to j \to k}(c)$ to be the maximum k-event in $\downarrow \mathsf{latest}_{i \to j}(c)$. We often write $\mathsf{latest}_{i \to j}(F)$ and $\mathsf{latest}_{i \to j \to k}(F)$ for $\mathsf{latest}_{i \to j}(E)$ and $\mathsf{latest}_{i \to j \to k}(E)$ respectively.

Let $i \in \mathcal{P}$. We set $\mathsf{primary}_i(c) = \cup_{j \in \mathcal{P}} \{\mathsf{latest}_{i \to j}(c)\}$. Further, we also set $\mathsf{secondary}_i(c) = \cup_{j,k \in \mathcal{P}} \{\mathsf{latest}_{i \to j \to k}(c)\}$. Note, as $\mathsf{latest}_{i \to j}(c) = \mathsf{latest}_{i \to j \to j}(c)$, $\mathsf{primary}_i(c) \subseteq \mathsf{secondary}_i(c)$. We denote $\mathsf{primary}_i(E)$ and $\mathsf{secondary}_i(E)$ also by $\mathsf{primary}_i(F)$ and $\mathsf{secondary}_i(F)$ respectively.

The key ingredient in our analysis is an asynchronous automaton called as the gossip automaton [MS1, MS2] which solves the gossip problem: whenever processes i and j meet at configuration c, they have to decide among themselves whether $\mathsf{latest}_{i \to k}(c) \leq \mathsf{latest}_{j \to k}(c)$ or $\mathsf{latest}_{i \to k}(c) \geq \mathsf{latest}_{j \to k}(c)$, for each process k in the system. The gossip automaton may be thought of as computing the ordering information among primary events.

Now we present another automaton which maintains the ordering information among secondary events as well. We start with encoding this information in the form of a labelled directed graph. Fix $F = (E, \leq, \lambda) \in TR$ and $c \in \mathcal{C}_F$. Further, let $P \subseteq \mathcal{P}$ and let i, j, k, i', j', k' range over $\mathcal{P}$. By $\mathsf{SG}_{F,P}(c)$, we denote a finite labelled directed graph whose labelled vertices correspond to the events in $\bigcup_{i \in P} \mathsf{secondary}_i(c)$. The vertex corresponding to $\mathsf{latest}_{i \to j \to k}(c)$ is labelled (i, j, k). As it is possible to have $\mathsf{latest}_{i \to j \to k}(c) = \mathsf{latest}_{i' \to j' \to k'}(c)$, a vertex may receive multiple labels. The directed edges of $\mathsf{SG}_{F,P}(c)$ record the ordering information between the events corresponding to vertices. We will refer to the graph $\mathsf{SG}_{F,P}(c)$ as the gossip of F at c among the processes in P or simply the gossip graph. As usual, for $F = (E, \leq, \lambda) \in TR$, $\mathsf{SG}_P(F)$ abbreviates $\mathsf{SG}_{F,P}(E)$. Let $\mathcal{G} = \{\mathsf{SG}_{F,P}(c) \mid F \in TR, c \in \mathcal{C}_F, P \subseteq \mathcal{P}\}$ be the set of all possible gossips.

Theorem 1 ([MS1]). *There exists a deterministic asynchronous automaton $\mathcal{A}$ of the form $\mathcal{A} = (\{\Gamma_i\}, \{\Rightarrow_a\}, \gamma_{in})$ and, for each $P = \{i_1, i_2, \ldots, i_n\}$, a function $\mathsf{gossip}_P : \Gamma_P \to \mathcal{G}$ with the following property. Let $F \in TR$ and $c \in \mathcal{C}_F$. Further, let ρ_F be the unique run of $\mathcal{A}$ over F with $\rho_F(c) = \gamma$. Then $\mathsf{SG}_{F,P}(c) = \mathsf{gossip}_P(\gamma(i_1), \ldots, \gamma(i_n))$.*

Any automaton that meets the requirements in Theorem 1 is called a gossip automaton/implementation. Note that all gossip implementations compute the same abstract gossip graphs.

4 Residue Calculus

We introduce residues and study their dynamics using the gossip information.

Let $F = (E, \leq, \lambda) \in TR$ and $P \subseteq \mathcal{P}$. We also let i, j, k range over $\mathcal{P}$. By F_P we denote the trace $F_P = (\downarrow^P(E), \leq', \lambda') \in TR$ where $\leq'$ and λ' are $\leq$ and λ restricted to $\downarrow^P(E)$ respectively. With $P = \{i\}$, we abbreviate F_P by F_i.

Fix $F \in TR$. Let $i \in \mathcal{P}$ and $P \subseteq \mathcal{P}$. We start with the definition of a simple residue $\mathcal{R}(F, i, P)$. We set $\mathcal{R}(F, i, P)$ to be another trace $F' = (E', \leq', \lambda') \in TR$

where $E' = (\downarrow^i(E) - \downarrow^P(\downarrow^i(E))) \subseteq E$ and $\leq'$, λ' are restrictions of $\leq$, λ to E' respectively. The residue $\mathcal{R}(F, i, P)$ represents the information that process i knows and as far as i knows, no process in P knows.

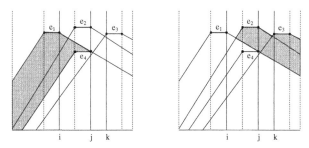

Fig. 1. Simple and General Residue

Now we introduce general residues. Let $P, Q \subseteq \mathcal{P}$. We set $\mathcal{R}(F, P, Q)$ to be the trace $F' = (E', \leq', \lambda')$ where $E' = (\downarrow^P(E) - \downarrow^Q(\downarrow^P(E)))$ and $\leq'$ and λ' are the same $\leq$ and λ restricted to E'. Clearly $\mathcal{R}(F, P, Q)$ represents the information that processes in P collectively know and, as far as processes in P know, no process in Q knows. We abuse the notation to denote the final configuration E' of $\mathcal{R}(F, P, Q)$ by $\mathcal{R}(E, P, Q)$. Clearly, $\mathcal{R}(F, i, P) = \mathcal{R}(F, \{i\}, P)$. Also, $\mathcal{R}(F, P, \emptyset) = F_P$.

Figure 1 visualizes a simple residue and a general residue in a trace F. The picture highlights the four key events e_1, e_2, e_3 and e_4. As shown there, e_1, e_2 and e_3 are the last i-event, j-event and k-event in F respectively. Further, we have $\text{latest}_{i \to j}(\downarrow e_1) = e_4$. The views $\downarrow e_1, \downarrow e_2, \downarrow e_3$ and $\downarrow e_4$ are visualized as inverted cones starting at the horizontal line-segments corresponding to e_1, e_2, e_3 and e_4 respectively. The shaded portion in the left part visualizes $\mathcal{R}(F, i, \{j\})$. Similarly, the shaded portion in the right part visualizes $\mathcal{R}(F, \{i, j, k\}, \{i\})$.

We now show that general residues can be expressed as concatenation of simple residues using the gossip information in an appropriate gossip graph. Recall that $\mathsf{SG}_P(F)$ abbreviates $\mathsf{SG}_{F,P}(E)$ which is a gossip graph recording the gossip of the processes in P at the final configuration E of F.

Lemma 1. *Let* $F \in TR, P, Q \subseteq \mathcal{P}$. *Further, let* $P = \{i_1, i_2, \ldots, i_n\}$ *with a fixed order* $i_1, i_2, \ldots, i_n$. *Then there exist subsets* $Q_1, Q_2, \ldots, Q_n \subseteq \mathcal{P}$ *such that* $\mathcal{R}(F, P, Q)$ *is a trace concatenation of* $\mathcal{R}(F, i_1, Q_1), \mathcal{R}(F, i_2, Q_2), \ldots, \mathcal{R}(F, i_n, Q_n)$ *in that order. Moreover, the sets* $Q_1, Q_2, \ldots, Q_n$ *are determined by* $\mathsf{SG}_P(F)$.

5   Asynchronous Implementation

In this section, we use residue calculus to design an asynchronous implementation of a morphism from the trace monoid to a finite monoid.

Cascade Product. In order to define a cascade of two asynchronous automata, we develop some more notation. We associate, to an arbitrary finite set X, the distributed alphabet $\widetilde{\Sigma^X} = (\Sigma_i^X)_{i \in \mathcal{P}}$ where, for each i, $\Sigma_i^X = \Sigma_i \times X$ and $\Sigma^X = \cup_{i \in \mathcal{P}} \Sigma_i^X = \Sigma \times X$. The induced location function loc^X is: $\mathrm{loc}^X((a,x)) = \{i \in \mathcal{P} \mid (a,x) \in \Sigma_i^X\}$ and I^X is the induced independence relation. Recall that loc is the induced location function and I is the induced independence relation for the distributed alphabet $\widetilde{\Sigma}$. An easy computation shows that, for $a, b \in \Sigma$ and $x, x' \in X$, $(a, b) \in I$ iff $((a, x), (b, x')) \in I^X$. We abuse the notation and write loc and I also for loc^X and I^X respectively.

Let $\mathcal{A} = (\{S_i\}, \{\delta_a\}, \{s_{in}\})$ be an asynchronous automaton. Fix a set of values V and further, let v, v' range over V. A valuation v on $\mathcal{A}$ is a map $\mathsf{v} : \cup_{a \in \Sigma}(\{a\} \times S_a) \to \Sigma \times V$ which acts as identity on the first component. More precisely, for $(a, s_a) \in \{a\} \times S_a$, $\mathsf{v}((a, s_a)) = (a, v)$ for some $v \in V$. Thus a valuation simply records observations of a-states of $\mathcal{A}$ through V.

Definition 1 (Asynchronous Transducer). *Let* $\theta_{\mathsf{v}}^{\mathcal{A}} : TR \to TR(\widetilde{\Sigma^V})$ *be defined as follows. Fix* $F = (E, \leq, \lambda) \in TR$ *and let* ρ_F *be the unique run of $\mathcal{A}$ over F. We set* $\theta_{\mathsf{v}}^{\mathcal{A}}(F) = H$ *where* $H = (E, \leq, \mu) \in TR(\widetilde{\Sigma^V})$ *with the labelling* $\mu : E \to \Sigma \times V$ *defined as:*

$$\text{for } e \in E, \mu(e) = \mathsf{v}((a, s_a)) \text{ where } a = \lambda(e) \text{ and } s = \rho_F(\downarrow e - e)$$

We call $\theta_{\mathsf{v}}^{\mathcal{A}}$ *the asynchronous transducer of $\mathcal{A}$.*

Now we are ready to define the important operation of cascade product of two asynchronous automata. Towards this, let $\mathcal{B} = (\{Q_i\}, \{\delta_{(a,v)}\}, \{q_{in}\})$ be an asynchronous automaton over $\widetilde{\Sigma^V}$. Note that, for each $(a, v) \in \Sigma \times V$, as $\mathrm{loc}((a, v)) = \mathrm{loc}(a)$, $\delta_{(a,v)}$ is a function from Q_a to Q_a.

We define the cascade product of $\mathcal{A}$ and $\mathcal{B}$ to be an asynchronous automaton $\mathcal{A} \circ_{\mathsf{v}} \mathcal{B}$ over $\widetilde{\Sigma}$. We set $\mathcal{A} \circ_{\mathsf{v}} \mathcal{B} = (\{S_i \times Q_i\}, \{\Delta_a\}, \{(s_{in}, q_{in})\})$ where, for $a \in \Sigma, s_a \in S_a$ and $q_a \in Q_a$, $\Delta_a((s_a, q_a)) = (\delta_a(s_a), \delta_{\mathsf{v}((a,s_a))}(q_a))$.

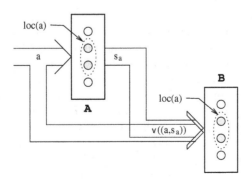

Fig. 2. Cascade Product

We call $\mathcal{A}$ and $\mathcal{B}$ as the first and second component of $\mathcal{A} \circ_v \mathcal{B}$ respectively. We write a global state of $\mathcal{A} \circ_v \mathcal{B}$ as (s, q) where s and q are global states of $\mathcal{A}$ and $\mathcal{B}$, and refer to s and q as the first and second component respectively. We also follow the same convention when dealing with a-states of $\mathcal{A} \circ_v \mathcal{B}$.

The functionality of $\mathcal{A} \circ_v \mathcal{B}$ may be described as follows (see Figure 2). While in operation, the first component $\mathcal{A}$ runs independently and at the same time drives the second component $\mathcal{B}$. On an action a, in $\mathcal{A}$, processes in $\mathrm{loc}(a)$ record the valuation v on their collective a-state and jointly update their local states. In $\mathcal{B}$, processes in $\mathrm{loc}(a)$ use the input action a as well as the feedback v from $\mathcal{A}$ to jointly update their local states. In fact, a run of $\mathcal{A} \circ_v \mathcal{B}$ over a trace F may be viewed as a run of $\mathcal{A}$ over F alongwith a run of $\mathcal{B}$ over $\theta_v^{\mathcal{A}}$.

Cascade Construction. Now we describe the asynchronous implementation of a morphism $\eta : TR \to M$ from the trace monoid to the finite monoid M.

It turns out that the asynchronous implementation can be realized in the form of a cascade $\mathcal{A} \circ_v \mathcal{B}$ of two appropriately defined asynchronous automata $\mathcal{A}$ and $\mathcal{B}$. We take $\mathcal{A}$ to be the gossip automaton (cf. Theorem 1). That is, $\mathcal{A} = (\{S_i\}, \{\delta_a\}, \{s_{in}\}) = (\{\Gamma_i\}, \{\Rightarrow_a\}, \gamma_{in})$. We set V to be the set $\mathcal{G}$ of gossips and the valuation $\mathsf{v} : \cup_{a \in \Sigma}(\{a\} \times \Gamma_a) \to \Sigma \times V$ is defined as follows. For $a \in \Sigma$ and $\gamma_a \in \Gamma_a$, we set $\mathsf{v}((a, \gamma_a)) = (a, \mathsf{gossip}_{\mathrm{loc}(a)}(\gamma_a))$.

Now we define the component $\mathcal{B} = (\{Q_i\}, \{\delta_{(a,v)}\}, \{q_{in}\})$ of the cascade. Recall that $|\mathcal{P}| = K$. For $i \in \mathcal{P}$, we let $Q_i = M \times M \times \cdots \times M$ (2^K times). It will turn out that the reachable i-states of $\mathcal{B}$ correspond to sequences of the form $(\eta(\mathcal{R}(F, i, P)))_{P \subseteq \mathcal{P}}$ for some $F \in TR$. Moreover, the reachable global states are of the form $\left((\eta(\mathcal{R}(F, i, P)))_{P \subseteq \mathcal{P}} \right)_{i \in \mathcal{P}}$ for some $F \in TR$.

Note that an i-state q_i consists of a sequence $(m_P)_{P \subseteq \mathcal{P}}$ of elements of monoid M, one for each subset $P \subseteq \mathcal{P}$. The transition functions are defined so that the following invariant is maintained: the monoid element m_P records $\eta(\mathcal{R}(F, i, P))$ for a trace $F \in TR$ which takes the cascade automaton to the i-state q_i (starting at the global initial state q_{in}). We set the global initial state $q_{in} = ((id)_{P \subseteq \mathcal{P}})_{i \in \mathcal{P}}$ where id is the identity element of M. Now we define the transition functions $\{\delta_{(a,v)}\}_{(a,v) \in \Sigma \times V}$. We define them only on reachable states. Also, $\delta_{(a,v)}$ is defined only for those v which correspond to gossips among processes in $\mathrm{loc}(a)$.

Fix $a \in \Sigma$ with $\mathrm{loc}(a) = \{i_1, i_2, \ldots, i_n\}$ and let $v \in \mathcal{G}$ be a gossip graph corresponding to a gossip among processes in $\mathrm{loc}(a)$. Let $q_a \in Q_a$ be a reachable a-state with $q_a(i) = (m_{i,P})_{P \subseteq \mathcal{P}}$ for each $i \in \mathrm{loc}(a)$. Let $\delta_{(a,v)}(q_a) = q'_a$ with $q'_a(i) = (m'_{i,P})_{P \subseteq \mathcal{P}}$ for each $i \in \mathrm{loc}(a)$ where $(m'_{i,P})_{P \subseteq \mathcal{P}, i \in \mathrm{loc}(a)}$ is computed as follows. Fix $i \in \mathrm{loc}(a)$ and $P \subseteq \mathcal{P}$. If $\mathrm{loc}(a) \cap P \neq \emptyset$ then we set $m'_{i,P} = id$. Otherwise, we use the gossip graph v to determine sets $Q_1, Q_2, \ldots Q_n$ as in Lemma 1 and set $m'_{i,P} = m_{i_1, Q_1} m_{i_2, Q_2} \cdots m_{i_n, Q_n} \eta(a)$.

Now we verify that the invariant is preserved by the above definition of the transition function. Let $F \in TR$ be a trace which takes the cascade automaton to the a-state q_a. Then, for $i \in \mathrm{loc}(a)$ and $P \subseteq \mathcal{P}$, $m_{i,P} = \eta(\mathcal{R}(F, i, P))$. It follows from the definition of the gossip automaton and the asynchronous transducer that $v = \mathsf{SG}_{\mathrm{loc}(a)}(F)$. Clearly, with $F' = Fa$, in order to maintain the invariant, we want $m'_{i,P} = \eta(\mathcal{R}(F', i, P))$. Now if $\text{loc}(a) \cap P \neq \emptyset$ then $\mathcal{R}(F', i, P)$ is the empty trace and hence $m'_{i,P} = id$. Otherwise, observe that $\mathcal{R}(F', i, P) = \mathcal{R}(F, \text{loc}(a), P)a$ and hence $m'_{i,P} = \eta(\mathcal{R}(F, \text{loc}(a), P))\eta(a)$. Thus it suffices to compute $\eta(\mathcal{R}(F, \text{loc}(a), P))$. From Lemma 1, $\mathcal{R}(F, \text{loc}(a), P)$ is a concatenation of $\mathcal{R}(F, i_1, Q_1), \mathcal{R}(F, i_2, Q_2), \ldots, \mathcal{R}(F, i_n, Q_n)$. Therefore

$$
\begin{aligned}
m'_{i,P} &= \eta(\mathcal{R}(F, \text{loc}(a), P))\eta(a) \\
&= \eta(\mathcal{R}(F, i_1, Q_1))\eta(\mathcal{R}(F, i_2, Q_2)) \cdots \eta(\mathcal{R}(F, i_n, Q_n))\eta(a) \\
&= m_{i_1,Q_1} m_{i_2,Q_2} \cdots m_{i_n,Q_n} \eta(a)
\end{aligned}
$$

This shows that the invariant is indeed maintained and immediately leads to the next proposition.

Proposition 1. *Let $F = (E, \leq, \lambda) \in TR$ and ρ_F be the unique run of $\mathcal{A} \circ_{\mathsf{v}} \mathcal{B}$ over F. Further, let $\rho_F(E) = (s, q) \in S_{\mathcal{P}} \times Q_{\mathcal{P}}$ and $q(i) = (m_{i,P})_{P \subseteq \mathcal{P}}$ for each $i \in \mathcal{P}$. Then $m_{i,P} = \eta((\mathcal{R}(F, i, P))$ for every $P \subseteq \mathcal{P}$.*

We define a map $\phi : S_{\mathcal{P}} \times Q_{\mathcal{P}} \to M$ as follows. Let $(s, q) \in S_{\mathcal{P}} \times Q_{\mathcal{P}}$. Further, let v be the global gossip graph $\mathsf{gossip}_{\mathcal{P}}(s)$ and $q(i) = (m_{i,P})_{P \subseteq \mathcal{P}}$ for every $i \in \mathcal{P}$. We compute subsets $Q_1, Q_2, \ldots, Q_K$ as in Lemma 1 (with $P = \{1, 2, \ldots, K\}$) from the gossip graph v. Now we set $\phi((s, q)) = m_{1,Q_1} m_{2,Q_2} \cdots m_{K,Q_K}$. Note that the function $\phi((s, q))$ depends only on $\mathsf{gossip}_{\mathcal{P}}(s)$ and q. That is, for (s, q), $(s', q) \in S_{\mathcal{P}} \times Q_{\mathcal{P}}$ with $\mathsf{gossip}_{\mathcal{P}}(s) = \mathsf{gossip}_{\mathcal{P}}(s')$, we have $\phi((s, q)) = \phi((s', q))$.

The next proposition says that the map ϕ computes the monoid morphism η. It follows from the previous proposition, the above discussion and Lemma 1.

Proposition 2. *Let $F = (E, \leq, \lambda) \in TR$ and ρ_F be the unique run of $\mathcal{A} \circ_{\mathsf{v}} \mathcal{B}$ over F with $\rho_F(E) = (s, q) \in S_{\mathcal{P}} \times Q_{\mathcal{P}}$. Then $\phi((s, q)) = \eta(F)$.*

Let $L \subseteq TR$ be a trace language recognized by the morphism η. We set $N = \eta(L)$. Clearly, for $F \in TR$, $F \in L$ iff $\eta(F) \in N$. It is immediate from the above proposition that with $\phi^{-1}(N)$ as the set of final global states, L is accepted by $\mathcal{A} \circ_{\mathsf{v}} \mathcal{B}$. This shows that every regular trace language is accepted by an asynchronous automaton and hence proves Zielonka's theorem.

6   Counter-Free Automata

The main result of this section is about an asynchronous automata-theoretic characterization of aperiodic trace languages.

We first recall the notion of counter-free sequential automata. Let Π be an alphabet and $\mathcal{C} = (S, \{\delta_\pi\}_{\pi \in \Pi}, s_0)$ be a sequential transition system where

- S is a finite non-empty set of states with $s_0 \in S$.
- For $\pi \in \Pi$, $\delta_\pi : S \to S$ is a transition function.

For $u \in \Pi^*$, let $\delta_u : S \to S$ denote the naturally induced transition function. We say $\mathcal{C}$ is counter-free if for every word $u \in \Pi^*$ and for every $S' \subseteq S$ such that size of S' is atleast two, δ_u does not induce a non-trivial permutation on S'. It is not very difficult to see that $\mathcal{C}$ is counter-free iff the corresponding transition monoid $\{\delta_u \mid u \in \Pi^*\}$ is aperiodic [McNP]. In other words, $\mathcal{C}$ is counter-free iff there exists a constant n such that, for $u \in \Pi^*$ and $s \in S$, $\delta_{u^n}(s)$ stabilizes, that is, $\delta_{u^{n+1}}(s) = \delta_{u^n}(s)$.

Let $s \in S$ be reachable from the initial state s_0. Then there exists a word $w \in \Pi^*$ such that $\delta_w(s_0) = s$. In that case, the condition $\delta_{u^{n+1}}(s) = \delta_{u^n}(s)$ is clearly equivalent to the condition $\delta_{wu^{n+1}}(s_0) = \delta_{wu^n}(s_0)$. We use this variant as the definition of counter-free-ness. More precisely, the automaton $\mathcal{C}$ is said to be counter-free iff there exists a constant n such that, for every $u, w \in \Pi^*$, $\delta_{wu^n}(s_0)$ stabilizes, that is, $\delta_{wu^{n+1}}(s_0) = \delta_{wu^n}(s_0)$.

An asynchronous automaton is said to be counter-free iff the corresponding global sequential automaton is counter-free. It is easy to see that this is equivalent to the condition that there exists a constant n such that, for $F, H \in TR$, starting at the initial global state, the global states reached at the end of FH^n and FH^{n+1} are the same.

We now turn our attention to the main result of this section (Theorem 2). Let L be an aperiodic trace language and $\eta : TR \to M$ be a morphism to an aperiodic monoid M recognizing L. We use the notation from the previous section and fix an asynchronous implementation $\mathcal{A} \circ_v \mathcal{B}$ of η. Recall that $\mathcal{A}$ is the gossip implementation fixed in Theorem 1. Moreover, L is accepted by $\mathcal{A} \circ_v \mathcal{B}$.

A basic observation regarding $\mathcal{A} \circ_v \mathcal{B}$ is that the component $\mathcal{B}$ of the cascade product does not depend on the particular gossip implementation $\mathcal{A}$. In other words, we can take $\mathcal{A}$ to be any gossip implementation.

Residue Stabilization. Below we show that the second component $\mathcal{B}$ of $\mathcal{A} \circ_v \mathcal{B}$ is always counter-free. Recall that $\mathcal{B}$ is an asynchronous automaton over $\widetilde{\Sigma^V}$. We have to show that, there exists a constant n such that, for $F', H' \in TR(\widetilde{\Sigma^V})$, starting at the initial global state of $\mathcal{B}$, the global states reached at the end of $F'H'^n$ and $F'H'^{n+1}$ are the same. We verify this condition only when $F'H'^n$ and $F'H'^{n+1}$ are generated by the transducer $\theta_v^{\mathcal{A}}$, that is, we assume that $F'H'^n, F'H'^{n+1} \in \theta_v^{\mathcal{A}}(TR)$.

In fact, we will show that, for an appropriate n and for $F, H \in TR$, $\theta_v^{\mathcal{A}}(FH^n)$ and $\theta_v^{\mathcal{A}}(FH^{n+1})$ lead to the same global state in $\mathcal{B}$. It is easy to see that this implies the earlier condition. From the definition of the cascade product, it is clear that this amounts to showing that the second components of the global states of $\mathcal{A} \circ_v \mathcal{B}$ remain the same when FH^n and FH^{n+1} are processed using the cascade $\mathcal{A} \circ_v \mathcal{B}$. By Proposition 1, the second components of the respective global states are $\left(\eta(\mathcal{R}(FH^n, i, P))_{P \subseteq \mathcal{P}}\right)_{i \in \mathcal{P}}$ and $\left(\eta(\mathcal{R}(FH^{n+1}, i, P))_{P \subseteq \mathcal{P}}\right)_{i \in \mathcal{P}}$.

Proposition 3. *There exists a constant n such that the following holds. Let $F, H \in TR, i \in \mathcal{P}$ and $P \subseteq \mathcal{P}$. Then $\eta(\mathcal{R}(FH^n, i, P)) = \eta(\mathcal{R}(FH^{n+1}, i, P))$.*

Proof. We examine $\mathcal{R}(FH^k, i, \emptyset)$ for large values of k. For $m \geq 1$, let $Q_m \subseteq \mathcal{P}$ be such that $Q_m = \{j \in \mathcal{P} \mid \mathsf{latest}_{i \to j}(H^m) \text{ is defined}\}$. It is clear that $Q_m \subseteq Q_{m+1}$. Therefore there exists $l \geq 1$ such that for all $m \geq l$, $Q_m = Q_l$. In fact, we can take $l = K$. We call this Q_l as Q. Observe that, for $k \geq l$,

$$\mathcal{R}(FH^k, i, \emptyset) = F_Q \underbrace{H_Q H_Q \ldots H_Q}_{k-l \text{ times}} H_{Q_{l-1}} H_{Q_{l-2}} \cdots H_{Q_1} H_i$$

Clearly $\eta(\mathcal{R}(FH^k, i, \emptyset)) = \eta(F_Q)\eta(H_Q)^{k-l}\eta(H_{Q_{l-1}})\eta(H_{Q_{l-2}})\ldots\eta(H_{Q_1})\eta(H_i)$. Recall that M is aperiodic and hence, for large k, $\eta(H_Q)^{k-l} = \eta(H_Q)^{k+1-l}$. It follows that there exists n such that $\eta(\mathcal{R}(FH^n, i, \emptyset)) = \eta(\mathcal{R}(FH^{n+1}, i, \emptyset))$. Also, note that n depends only on $K = |\mathcal{P}|$ and the monoid M.

Now we turn our attention to $\mathcal{R}(FH^k, i, P)$ for $P \subseteq \mathcal{P}$. We define, for each $m \geq 1$, a pair of subsets (Q_m, R_m) with $Q_m \subseteq Q_{m+1}$ and $R_m \subseteq R_{m+1}$ as follows:

$$Q_m = \{k \in \mathcal{P} \mid \mathsf{latest}_{i \to k}(H^m) \text{ is defined}\}$$
$$R_m = \{k \in \mathcal{P} \mid \exists j \in P \text{ such that } \mathsf{latest}_{i \to j \to k}(H^m) \text{ is defined}\}$$

With these definitions, we have

$$\mathcal{R}(H^k, i, P) = \mathcal{R}(H, Q_{k-1}, R_{k-1})\mathcal{R}(H, Q_{k-2}, R_{k-2})\ldots\mathcal{R}(H, Q_1, R_1)\mathcal{R}(H, i, P)$$

Clearly there exists $l \geq 1$ such that for all $m \geq l$, $Q_m = Q_l$ and $R_m = R_l$. We can take this l to be K^2. We call this Q_l as Q and R_l as R. Then, for $k \geq l$,

$$\mathcal{R}(FH^k, i, P) = \mathcal{R}(F, Q, R) \underbrace{\mathcal{R}(H, Q, R)\mathcal{R}(H, Q, R)\ldots\mathcal{R}(H, Q, R)}_{k-l \text{ times}} H'$$

where $H' = \mathcal{R}(H, Q_{l-1}, R_{l-1})\mathcal{R}(H, Q_{l-2}, R_{l-2})\ldots\mathcal{R}(H, Q_1, R_1)\mathcal{R}(H, i, P)$. From the above expression for $\mathcal{R}(FH^k, i, P)$ and the aperiodicity of M, it is clear that there exists a constant n such that $\eta(\mathcal{R}(FH^n, i, P)) = \eta(\mathcal{R}(FH^{n+1}, i, P))$.   □

We can conclude from the above analysis that the second component $\mathcal{B}$ is counter-free. This implies one direction of our main result (Theorem 2).

Proposition 4. *Let $L \subseteq TR$ be aperiodic. Then L is accepted by a cascade $\mathcal{A} \circ_v \mathcal{B}$ of a gossip implementation $\mathcal{A}$ over $\widetilde{\Sigma}$ and a counter-free asynchronous automaton $\mathcal{B}$ over $\widetilde{\Sigma^V}$.*

Gossip Stabilization. Now we examine the first component $\mathcal{A}$ of the cascade $\mathcal{A} \circ_v \mathcal{B}$. Recall that $\mathcal{A}$ is the gossip implementation from Theorem 1. As noted earlier, we can take $\mathcal{A}$ to be any gossip implementation.

The following example shows that no gossip implementation is counter-free.

Example 1. Let $\widetilde{\Pi} = (\Pi_1, \Pi_2, \Pi_3)$ with $\Pi_1 = \{a, c\}, \Pi_2 = \{b, c\}$ and $\Pi_3 = \{a, b\}$ be a distributed alphabet. Observe that, with $\Pi = \{a, b, c\}$, $TR(\widetilde{\Pi}) = \Pi^*$. Keeping this in mind, we sometimes write a trace over $\widetilde{\Pi}$ as a word over Π.

Let $\mathcal{CG} = (\{S_1, S_2, S_3\}, \{\delta_a, \delta_b, \delta_c\}, s_{in} \in S_1 \times S_2 \times S_3)$ be a deterministic asynchronous automaton which computes the gossip among processes 1 and 2 about process 3. That is, there is a function $\mathbf{g}_{1,2} : S_1 \times S_2 \to \{1, 2\}$ such that: if $F = (E, \leq, \lambda) \in TR(\widetilde{\Pi})$ and ρ_F is the unique run of $\mathcal{CG}$ over F with $\rho_F(E) = (s_1, s_2, s_3)$, then $\mathbf{g}_{1,2}((s_1, s_2)) = 1$ iff $\mathsf{latest}_{1 \to 3}(F) \geq \mathsf{latest}_{2 \to 3}(F)$.

We show that $\mathcal{CG}$ is not counter-free. On the contrary suppose that $\mathcal{CG}$ is counter-free. Then there exists n such that, starting at the initial global state s_{in}, the traces $(ab)^n$ and $(ab)^{n+1}$ lead to the same global state, say s with $s = (s_1, s_2, s_3)$. It follows that the trace ab fixes the state s. In other words, $\delta_{ab}(s) = \delta_b(\delta_a((s_1, s_2, s_3))) = (s_1, s_2, s_3)$.

Recall that δ_a does not change the 2-state and δ_b does not change the 1-state. This implies that $\delta_a((s_1, s_2, s_3)) = (s_1, s_2, s_3')$ for some $s_3' \in S_3$. Hence both $(ab)^n$ and $(ab)^n a$ lead to global states with the same local states for processes 1 and 2. Clearly the gossip function $\mathbf{g}_{1,2}$ fails to distinguish between $(ab)^n$ and $(ab)^n a$. But $\mathsf{latest}_{1 \to 3}((ab)^n) < \mathsf{latest}_{2 \to 3}((ab)^n)$ and $\mathsf{latest}_{1 \to 3}((ab)^n a) > \mathsf{latest}_{2 \to 3}((ab)^n a)$. This gives a contradiction.

Although no gossip implementation $\mathcal{A}$ is counter-free, the related valuation v turns out to be counter-free. Recall that the valuation is given in terms of the family $\{\mathsf{gossip}_P\}_{P \subseteq \mathcal{P}}$ of functions which compute the gossip graphs. The next proposition shows that these gossip graphs eventually stabilize.

Proposition 5. *There exists a constant n such that the following holds. Let $F, H \in TR$ and $P \subseteq \mathcal{P}$. Then, for $m \geq n$, $\mathsf{SG}_P(FH^m) = \mathsf{SG}_P(FH^{m+1})$.*

A simple observation regarding secondary graphs is recorded in the next proposition. See [MS1] for a proof.

Proposition 6. *Let $F, H \in TR$ with $\mathsf{SG}_{\mathcal{P}}(F) = \mathsf{SG}_{\mathcal{P}}(H)$. Then, for $a \in \Sigma$ and $P \subseteq \mathcal{P}$, $\mathsf{SG}_P(Fa) = \mathsf{SG}_P(Ha)$.*

Main Result. Now we are ready to state the partial converse to Proposition 4.

Let L be accepted by a cascade $\mathcal{A} \circ_{\mathsf{v}} \mathcal{B}$ where $\mathcal{A}$ is any gossip implementation over $\widetilde{\Sigma}$ and $\mathcal{B}$ is an arbitrary counter-free asynchronous automaton over $\widetilde{\Sigma^V}$. Moreover, the final global states accepting L satisfy the following property: for $(s, q), (s', q) \in S_{\mathcal{P}} \times Q_{\mathcal{P}}$ with $\mathsf{gossip}_{\mathcal{P}}(s) = \mathsf{gossip}_{\mathcal{P}}(s')$, (s, q) is a final global state iff (s', q) is so. We abbreviate this by writing that L is accepted modulo the gossip implementation. The partial converse to Proposition 4 claims that L is aperiodic.

We show the following strong pumping property for L which implies that L is aperiodic (see [McNP]). We will demonstrate existence of a constant k such that, for $F_1, F_2, F_3 \in TR$, $F_1 F_2^k F_3 \in L$ iff $F_1 F_2^{k+1} F_3 \in L$. In other words, we have to show that the unique run of $\mathcal{A} \circ_{\mathsf{v}} \mathcal{B}$ over $F_1 F_2^k F_3$ is accepting iff the unique run of $\mathcal{A} \circ_{\mathsf{v}} \mathcal{B}$ over $F_1 F_2^{k+1} F_3$ is accepting.

Towards this, let $F_1, F_2, F_3 \in TR$. It follows from Proposition 5 and Proposition 6 that, for large m, $\mathsf{SG}_{\mathcal{P}}(F_1 F_2^m F_3) = \mathsf{SG}_{\mathcal{P}}(F_1 F_2^{m+1} F_3)$. Let s and s' be the global states reached at the end of the runs of $\mathcal{A}$ over $F_1 F_2^m F_3$ and $F_1 F_2^{m+1} F_3$ respectively. Then clearly we have $\mathsf{gossip}_{\mathcal{P}}(s) = \mathsf{gossip}_{\mathcal{P}}(s')$.

Now by the definition of $\mathcal{A} \circ_{\mathsf{v}} \mathcal{B}$, the second component of the global state reached at the end of the run of $\mathcal{A} \circ_{\mathsf{v}} \mathcal{B}$ over $F_1 F_2^m F_3$ is same as the global state reached at the end of the run of $\mathcal{B}$ over $\theta_v^{\mathcal{A}}(F_1 F_2^m F_3)$. By Proposition 5, we know that there exists a constant n such that, for $m \geq n$ and $P \subseteq \mathcal{P}$, $\mathsf{SG}_P(F_1 F_2^m) = \mathsf{SG}_P(F_1 F_2^{m+1})$.

Let $F_1' = \theta_v^{\mathcal{A}}(F_1 F_2^n) \in TR(\widetilde{\Sigma^V})$ and $F_2' \in TR(\widetilde{\Sigma^V})$ be such that, we have $F_1' F_2' = \theta_v^{\mathcal{A}}(F_1 F_2^{n+1})$. Then Proposition 5 and Proposition 6 imply that, for large m, $\theta_v^{\mathcal{A}}(F_1 F_2^m) = F_1' F_2'^{m-n}$. Again, it follows from Proposition 6 that there exists $F_3' \in TR(\widetilde{\Sigma^V})$ such that, for large m, $\theta_v^{\mathcal{A}}(F_1 F_2^m F_3) = F_1' F_2'^{m-n} F_3'$. Recall that $\mathcal{B}$ is counter-free. Hence there exists a constant l such that the global states reached at the end of the runs of $\mathcal{B}$ over $F_1' F_2'^l F_3'$ and $F_1' F_2'^{l+1} F_3'$ are the same.

The above discussion implies existence of a constant, namely $n + l$, with the following property. Let $(s, q), (s', q') \in S_{\mathcal{P}} \times Q_{\mathcal{P}}$ be the global states reached at the end of the runs of $\mathcal{A} \circ_v \mathcal{B}$ over $F_1 F_2^{n+l} F_3$ and $F_1 F_2^{n+l+1} F_3$ respectively. Then $\mathsf{gossip}_{\mathcal{P}}(s) = \mathsf{gossip}_{\mathcal{P}}(s')$ and $q = q'$. Finally recall that L is accepted by $\mathcal{A} \circ_v \mathcal{B}$ modulo the gossip implementation. This implies that $F_1 F_2^{n+l} F_3 \in L$ iff $F_1 F_2^{n+l+1} F_3 \in L$. This completes the proof that L is aperiodic.

Theorem 2. *Let $L \subseteq TR$. Then L is aperiodic iff L is accepted by a cascade $\mathcal{A} \circ_v \mathcal{B}$ of a gossip implementation $\mathcal{A}$ over Σ and a counter-free asynchronous automaton $\mathcal{B}$ over $\widetilde{\Sigma^V}$, modulo the gossip implementation.*

7 Discussion

Stated differently, our main result characterizes aperiodic, first-order-definable or equivalently star-free trace languages by counter-free asynchronous acceptors modulo the gossip automaton. We do not know if counter-free asynchronous automata alone suffice in the above characterization. Nevertheless, we have shown that no gossip implementation (*asynchronous computation* of latest information of processes about each other) can be counter-free.

Aperiodic sequential behaviours also coincide with properties expressible in the popular and powerful specification formalism of propositional linear-time temporal logic (LTL). The logic LTL is as expressive as the first-order logic and has an elementary decision procedure for satisfiability. Designing "LTL-like" trace logics has turned out to be a challenging problem (see [Ads] and references therein). In this context, the main result suggests a decomposition of "global" aperiodic behaviours into "local" aperiodic behaviours and highlights the importance of the gossip information (see [Ads] for more details). Simultaneously, it gives a counter-free asynchronous implementation upto the gossip information.

References

[Ads] B. ADSUL: Complete Local Logics for Reasoning about Traces, *Ph.D. Thesis*, Indian Institute of Technology – Bombay, Mumbai, India (2004).

[Arb] M.A. ARBIB (Ed.): *Algebraic Theory of Machines, Languages and Semigroups*, Academic Press, New York (1968).

[DK]   M. DROSTE AND D. KUSKE: Languages and Logical Definability in Concurrency Monoids, *Proc. CSL '95, LNCS* **1092** (1996) 233–251.

[DR]   V. DIEKERT AND G. ROZENBERG (Eds.): *The Book of Traces*, World Scientific, Singapore (1995).

[EM]   W. EBINGER AND A. MUSCHOLL: Logical Definability on Infinite Traces, *Proc. ICALP '93, LNCS* **700** (1993) 335–346.

[GRS]   G. GUAIANA, A. RESTIVO AND S. SALEMI: Star-free Trace Languages, *Theoretical Computer Science* **97** (1992) 301–311.

[Maz]   A. MAZURKIEWICZ: Concurrent Program Schemes and Their Interpretations, *Report DAIMI-PB-78*, Comp Sci Dept, Aarhus University, Denmark (1978).

[McNP]   R. MCNAUGHTON AND S. PAPERT: *Counter-free Automata*, MIT Press, Cambridge (1971).

[MS1]   M. MUKUND AND M. SOHONI: Gossiping, Asynchronous Automata and Zielonka's Theorem, *Report TCS-94-2*, Chennai Mathematical Institute, Chennai, India (1994).

[MS2]   M. MUKUND AND M. SOHONI: Keeping Track of the Latest Gossip in a Distributed System, *Distributed Computing* **10** (3) (1997) 137–148.

[Sch]   M.P. SCHUTZENBERGER: On Finite Monoids Having Only Trivial Subgroups, *Information and Control* **48** (1965) 190–194.

[Tho]   W. THOMAS: Languages, Automata and Logic, in: *Handbook of Formal Languages Vol. 3*, Springer-Verlag, New York (1997) 389–456.

[Zie]   W. ZIELONKA: Notes on Finite Asynchronous Automata, *RAIRO Inform. Théor. Appl.* **21** (1987) 99–135.

A Decidable Fragment of Separation Logic

Josh Berdine[1], Cristiano Calcagno[2], and Peter W. O'Hearn[1]

[1] Queen Mary, University of London
{berdine, ohearn}@dcs.qmul.ac.uk
[2] Imperial College, London
ccris@doc.ic.ac.uk

Abstract. We present a fragment of separation logic oriented to linked lists, and study decision procedures for validity of entailments. The restrictions in the fragment are motivated by the stylized form of reasoning done in example program proofs. The fragment includes a predicate for describing linked list segments (a kind of reachability or transitive closure). Decidability is first proved by semantic means: by showing a small model property that bounds the size of potential countermodels that must be checked. We then provide a complete proof system for the fragment, the termination of which furnishes a second decision procedure.

1 Introduction

Separation logic is a new approach to reasoning about programs that manipulate pointer structures [1]. The main advantage of the logic is the way it supports reasoning about different portions of heap which can be combined in a modular way using the separating conjunction operation. In this paper we present a fragment of separation logic and study decision procedures for validity of entailments.

These results are part of a bigger project that aims to provide algorithms and tools to transfer the simplicity of handwritten proofs with separation logic to an automatic setting. To make the task of automatic verification more feasible, we restrict our attention to structural integrity properties (like not following dangling pointers, preserving noncircularity of linked lists, not leaking memory), rather than full correctness. Moreover, we restrict the language by disallowing pointer arithmetic.

Even with these restrictions, the decidability questions are nontrivial. In particular, one of the most treacherous passes in pointer verification and analysis is *reachability*. To describe common loop invariants, and even some pre- and post-conditions, one needs to be able to assert that there is a path in the heap from one value to another; a fragment that cannot account for reachability in some way will be of very limited use. When we inquire about decidability we are then square up against the bugbear of transitive closure (reachability is the transitive closure of points-to); there are various decidable fragments of, say, the first-order logic of graphs, but for many of these decidability breaks if transitive closure is added.

K. Lodaya and M. Mahajan (Eds.): FSTTCS 2004, LNCS 3328, pp. 97–109, 2004.

So, a main technical challenge is to take on a form of reachability, in a way that fits with the separating conjunction (and the possibility of dangling pointers). We begin simply, with linked list structures only, instead of general heap structures with arbitrary sharing. Our analysis can be adapted to certain kinds of tree structure, but we do not yet have a general picture of the kinds of inductive definitions that are amenable to the style of analysis presented here.

Our approach started by observing the stylized reasoning that was done in typical manual proofs using separation logic (e.g., [2–4]). For instance, we would often say "I have a list here, and another there occupying separate storage", but never would we assert the negation of such a statement. Generally, in many examples that have been given, the assertions include a heap-independent, or pure, boolean condition, and a number of heap-dependent (or "spatial") assertions separately conjoined. So, we consider a restricted fragment where the formulæ are of the form $\Pi \mid \Sigma$, where Π is a conjunction of equalities and inequalities and Σ is a separating conjunction of points-to facts and list segment remarks. We show the decidability of entailment between formulæ of this form.

In fact, two decision procedures are given. The first, a semantic procedure, is based on a "small model property". In essence, we have designed the fragment so that formulæ do not admit any "unspecified" sharing, and then exploited separation logic's local reasoning to capitalize on the absence of interference by avoiding case analysis on the possible interaction patterns between formulæ. The essential result, which fails for separation logic as a whole, is that when considering the possible models of our list segment predicate, no case analysis on the possible interference patterns is necessary, instead considering either the length zero or length two model immediately suffices. So decidability is achieved not through some brute force interference analysis, but by leveraging locality.

The second is a proof-theoretic procedure. It has the advantage of not generating the exponentially-many potential countermodels in every case, as the semantic procedure does. Also, this is the first complete proof theory that has been given for (a fragment of) separation logic. It is a candidate for extension to richer fragments (where we might not insist on decidability).

It is worth remarking on what is left out of the fragment. Although we are asking about the validity of entailments, entailment is not itself internalized with an implication connective; the additive and multiplicative implications ($\rightarrow$ and $-\!\ast$) from BI are omitted. A hint of the computational significance of these omissions can be seen in the (easier) problem of model checking assertions (checking satisfaction). In earlier work it was shown that a fragment with points-to and nesting of $-\!\ast$ and $\rightarrow$, but no list segment predicate, has model checking complexity PSpace-Complete [5]. Even just wrapping negations around the separating conjunction leads to PSpace-Complete model checking. In contrast, the model checking problem for the fragment of this paper, which goes further in that it considers list segments, is linear.

The fragment of this paper has been used in a prototype tool that checks properties of pointer programs. Typically in tools of this kind, the assertion language is closed under taking weakest preconditions of atomic commands. This is not the case for our fragment. However, it is possible to reduce entailments arising from weakest preconditions to entailments in our fragment, by way of a form of symbolic execution. Here we confine ourselves to the question of decidability for the fragment, and leave a description of the symbolic execution phase to a future paper.

2   Fragment of Separation Logic

The fragment of separation logic we are concerned with is specified by restricting the assertion language to that generated by the following grammar:

$$x, y, \ldots \in \text{Variables} \qquad \text{variables}$$
$$E ::= \text{nil} \mid x \qquad \text{Expressions}$$
$$P ::= E{=}E \mid \neg P \qquad \text{simple Pure formulæ}$$
$$\Pi ::= \text{true} \mid \Pi \wedge P \qquad \text{Pure formulæ}$$
$$S ::= E{\mapsto}E \mid \text{ls}(E, E) \qquad \text{simple Spatial formulæ}$$
$$\Sigma ::= \text{emp} \mid S * \Sigma \qquad \text{Spatial formulæ}$$
$$A ::= P \mid \Pi \mid S \mid \Sigma \mid \Pi \mid \Sigma \qquad \text{formulæ}$$

Note that we abbreviate $\neg(E_1{=}E_2)$ as $E_1{\neq}E_2$, and use $\equiv$ to denote "syntactic" equality of formulæ, which are considered up to symmetry of $=$ and permutations across $\wedge$ and $*$, e.g., $\Pi \wedge P \wedge P' \equiv \Pi \wedge P' \wedge P$. We use notation treating formulæ as sets of simple formulæ, e.g., writing $P \in \Pi$ for $\Pi \equiv P \wedge \Pi'$ for some Π'.

Formulæ are interpreted as predicates on program States with a forcing relation, while expressions denote Values and depend only on the stack:[1]

$$s, h \vDash A \qquad\qquad \llbracket E \rrbracket \in \text{Stacks} \to \text{Values}$$
$$\text{Stacks} \stackrel{\text{def}}{=} \text{Variables} \to \text{Values} \qquad \text{R-values} \stackrel{\text{def}}{=} \text{Values}$$
$$\text{Heaps} \stackrel{\text{def}}{=} \text{L-values} \stackrel{\text{fin}}{\to} \text{R-values} \qquad \text{L-values} \stackrel{\text{def}}{\subset} \text{Values}$$
$$\text{States} \stackrel{\text{def}}{=} \text{Stacks} \times \text{Heaps} \qquad\qquad nil \stackrel{\text{def}}{\in} \text{Values} \backslash \text{L-values}$$

The semantics of the assertion language is shown in Table 1, where $fv(E)$ simply denotes the variables occurring in E. Below we try to give some intuitive feel for the assertions and what sorts of properties are expressible with a few examples.

As always, a formula $S * \Sigma$ is true in states where the heap can be split into two separate parts (with disjoint domains) such that S is true in one part and Σ is true in the other. The unit of this conjunction is emp, which is true only in the empty heap. The only primitive spatial predicate is $\mapsto$, which describes individual L-values in the heap. So $10{\mapsto}42$ is true in the heap in which L-value 10

---

[1] For a concrete instance of this model, take Values $= \mathbb{Z}$, L-values $= \mathbb{N}\backslash\{0\}$, $nil = 0$.

Table 1. Semantics of Assertion Language

$$[\![x]\!]s \stackrel{\mathrm{def}}{=} s(x) \qquad\qquad [\![\mathsf{nil}]\!]s \stackrel{\mathrm{def}}{=} nil$$

$s,h \vDash E_1{=}E_2$ $\quad$ $\stackrel{\mathrm{def}}{\text{iff}}$ $[\![E_1]\!]s = [\![E_2]\!]s$

$s,h \vDash \neg P$ $\quad$ $\stackrel{\mathrm{def}}{\text{iff}}$ $s,h \nvDash P$

$s,h \vDash \mathsf{true}$ $\quad$ always

$s,h \vDash \Pi \wedge P$ $\quad$ $\stackrel{\mathrm{def}}{\text{iff}}$ $s,h \vDash \Pi$ and $s,h \vDash P$

$s,h \vDash E_1{\mapsto}E_2$ $\quad$ $\stackrel{\mathrm{def}}{\text{iff}}$ $h = [\emptyset \mid [\![E_1]\!]s{\rightarrow}[\![E_2]\!]s]$

$s,h \vDash \mathsf{ls}(E_1,E_2)$ $\quad$ $\stackrel{\mathrm{def}}{\text{iff}}$ there exists $n.\, s,h \vDash \mathsf{ls}^n(E_1,E_2)$

$s,h \vDash \mathsf{ls}^0(E_1,E_2)$ $\quad$ $\stackrel{\mathrm{def}}{\text{iff}}$ $[\![E_1]\!]s = [\![E_2]\!]s$ and $h = \emptyset$

$s,h \vDash \mathsf{ls}^{n+1}(E_1,E_2)$ $\stackrel{\mathrm{def}}{\text{iff}}$ $[\![E_1]\!]s \neq [\![E_2]\!]s$ and

$\qquad\qquad$ there exists $v \in \mathrm{Values}.\,[s \mid x{\rightarrow}v]\,,h \vDash E_1{\mapsto}x * \mathsf{ls}^n(x,E_2)$

$\qquad\qquad$ for $x \notin \mathit{fv}(E_1,E_2)$

$s,h \vDash \mathsf{emp}$ $\quad$ $\stackrel{\mathrm{def}}{\text{iff}}$ $h = \emptyset$

$s,h \vDash S * \Sigma$ $\quad$ $\stackrel{\mathrm{def}}{\text{iff}}$ there exists $h_1 \perp h_2.\, h = h_1{*}h_2$ and $s,h_1 \vDash S$ and $s,h_2 \vDash \Sigma$

$s,h \vDash \Pi \mathbin{|} \Sigma$ $\quad$ $\stackrel{\mathrm{def}}{\text{iff}}$ $s,h \vDash \Pi$ and $s,h \vDash \Sigma$

contains 42, and nothing else—the domain is the singleton $\{10\}$. Similarly, $x{\mapsto}42$ asserts that whichever L-value the stack maps x to contains 42. In addition to the spatial (heap-dependent) part, formulæ also have a pure (heap-independent) part. So extending the last example, with $x{=}y \mathbin{|} x{\mapsto}42$ we also assert that the stack maps x and y to equal R-values. Since the conjuncts of a $*$ formula must be true in disjoint heaps, $x{=}y \mathbin{|} x{\mapsto}\mathsf{nil} * y{\mapsto}\mathsf{nil}$ is unsatisfiable.

The ls predicate describes segments of linked list structures in the heap: $\mathsf{ls}(x,y)$ describes a list segment starting at the L-value denoted by x whose last link contains the value of y, which is a dangling pointer. That y is dangling is significant, as it precludes cycles. So $\mathsf{ls}(x,x)$ describes the empty list segment, and is equivalent to emp. Were the endpoint not required to be dangling, then $\mathsf{ls}(x,x)$ could describe cyclic lists containing x. Instead, a cyclic list is described for instance with $x{\mapsto}y * \mathsf{ls}(y,x)$. For some further examples, $\mathsf{ls}(x,\mathsf{nil})$ describes "complete" lists, rather than segments. A list with an intermediate link can be expressed with $\mathsf{ls}(x,y){*}\mathsf{ls}(y,\mathsf{nil})$, two non-overlapping lists with $\mathsf{ls}(x,\mathsf{nil}){*}\mathsf{ls}(y,\mathsf{nil})$, and two lists with a shared tail with $\mathsf{ls}(x,z) * \mathsf{ls}(y,z) * \mathsf{ls}(z,\mathsf{nil})$.

Our restriction to unary heap cells, and hence lists with links containing nothing but a pointer to the next link, is not significant and need not cause alarm: our development extends straightforwardly, all the formulæ just get longer.[2]

---

[2] While with binary heap cells, unrolling a ls involves generating a fresh variable, this is unproblematic for decidability in part due to Definition 10.

3   Decidability, Model-Theoretically

As mentioned earlier, our primary concern in this paper is deciding *validity* of entailments between formulæ in the fragment. That is, for entailments of the form $\Pi \mid \Sigma \vdash \Pi' \mid \Sigma'$, we wish to check if for all s, h. $s, h \models \Pi \mid \Sigma$ implies $s, h \models \Pi' \mid \Sigma'$. Before getting stuck into decidability, we try to develop some intuition with a few examples.

First trivially, anything entails itself, up to equalities: $x{=}y \wedge E{=}F \mid x{\mapsto}E \vdash y{\mapsto}F$. As *nil* $\notin$ L-values, $x{\mapsto}E \vdash x{\neq}nil \mid x{\mapsto}E$. Also, since $*$ guarantees separation, spatial formulæ have implicit non-alias consequences: $x{\mapsto}E * y{\mapsto}F \vdash x{\neq}y \mid x{\mapsto}E * y{\mapsto}F$. Explicit descriptions of list segments entail the inductive descriptions: $x{=}y \mid \mathsf{emp} \vdash \mathsf{ls}(x, y)$ for length 0, $x{\neq}y \mid x{\mapsto}y \vdash \mathsf{ls}(x, y)$ for length 1, $x{\neq}y \wedge z{\neq}y \mid x{\mapsto}z * z{\mapsto}y \vdash \mathsf{ls}(x, y)$ for length 2, and $x{\neq}y \mid x{\mapsto}z * \mathsf{ls}(z, y) \vdash \mathsf{ls}(x, y)$ for length "$n + 1$". All the inequalities in these examples are actually necessary: Since the ls predicate prohibits cycles in the consequent, there must be enough inequalities in the antecedent to guarantee acyclicity. Crucially, there are valid entailments which generally require induction to prove, such as appending a list segment and a list: $\mathsf{ls}(x, z) * \mathsf{ls}(z, \mathsf{nil}) \vdash \mathsf{ls}(x, \mathsf{nil})$.

Before attacking entailment validity, we must consider formula satisfaction:

Lemma 1 (Satisfaction Decidable).   *For given $s, h, \Pi \mid \Sigma$, checking the satisfaction $s, h \models \Pi \mid \Sigma$ is decidable.*

In fact, satisfaction checking is linear in the combined size of the model and the formula. For a given stack and heap, first we check the pure part of the formula against the stack in the obvious way. Then, to check the spatial part we start from the left and proceed as follows. If the first formula is a points-to, we remove the evident singleton from the heap (if present) and continue; if the sigleton is not present we report "no". If the formula is a ls we simply try to traverse through the heap from the putative start until we get to the putative end (deleting cells as we go). If the traversal fails we report "no", otherwise we continue on with the rest of the spatial part. When we get to the empty spatial formula we just check to see if we have the empty heap.

Informally, checking validity of entailments of the form $\Pi \mid \Sigma \vdash \Pi' \mid \Sigma'$ is decidable because it suffices to consider finitely-many potential models of the antecedent. This small model property is captured primarily by:

Proposition 2.   *The following rule is sound:*

UNROLLCOLLAPSE
$$\frac{\Pi \wedge E_1{=}E_2 \mid \Sigma \vdash \Pi' \mid \Sigma' \qquad \Pi \wedge E_1{\neq}E_2 \wedge x{\neq}E_2 \mid E_1{\mapsto}x * x{\mapsto}E_2 * \Sigma \vdash \Pi' \mid \Sigma'}{\Pi \mid \mathsf{ls}(E_1, E_2) * \Sigma \vdash \Pi' \mid \Sigma'} \quad x \notin fv(\Pi, E_1, E_2, \Sigma, \Pi', \Sigma')$$

This rule says that to prove that a ls entails a formula, it suffices to check if the lss of lengths zero and two[3] entail the formula. That is, it eliminates ls from the form of antecedents, and allows the conclusion of an inductive property from finitely-many non-inductive premises. From a different perspective, this rule expresses a form of heap abstraction in that, as far as entailment is concerned, each of all the possible models of the ls is equivalent to either the empty one or the length two one. Pushing this further, we see that the case analysis UNROLLCOLLAPSE performs when read bottom-up effects a sort of symbolic state space exploration.

Before presenting the proof, we show how this result yields decidability.

Lemma 3. *For fixed $\Pi, \Sigma, \Pi', \Sigma'$ such that no subformula of Σ is of form* $\mathsf{ls}(E_1, E_2)$*, checking $\Pi \mid \Sigma \vdash \Pi' \mid \Sigma'$ is decidable.*

Proof (Sketch). Because the antecedent's spatial part is a list of points-to facts, any potential model must have a heap whose domain is exactly the size of the antecedent. Furthermore, there is an evident notion of isomorphism, where two states are isomorphic just if one is obtained from the other by L-value renaming. The fragment is closed (semantically) under isomorphism and, up to isomorphism, there are only finitely-many states of any given size. So, we check the antecedent on finitely-many canonical representatives of these equivalence classes, and when the antecedent holds we check the conclusion.   □

Corollary 4 (Validity Decidable). *For fixed $\Pi, \Sigma, \Pi', \Sigma'$, checking $\Pi \mid \Sigma \vdash$ $\Pi' \mid \Sigma'$ is decidable.*

Proof. Applying UNROLLCOLLAPSE repeatedly yields a set of entailments whose antecedents do not contain ls, and so can each be decided due to Lemma 3.   □

The semantic decision procedure gotten from the small model property shows that validity is in coNP; to show invalidity we can guess one of exponentially-many models of a suitably bounded size, and then satisfaction of both antecedent and consequent can easily be checked in polynomial time. We are not sure about hardness. On one side, the absence of negation from the fragment may suggest a polynomial complexity. However, a subtle form of negation is implicit in formulæ like $y \neq z \mid \mathsf{ls}(x, y) * \mathsf{ls}(x, z)$, which implies that either ls is empty, but not both. Preliminary attempts to exploit these implicit disjunctions to reduce one of the standard coNP-complete problems to validity of entailment have failed.

3.1   Soundness of UNROLLCOLLAPSE

Note that while we are only investigating a fragment, the metatheory uses the whole of separation logic. The full logic is used in particular to state the following properties of the ls predicate, upon which soundness of UNROLLCOLLAPSE depends:

---

[3] There is no need to consider length one because if the right-hand side accepts a list of length two then it also accepts a list of length one. The converse does not hold because of $\mapsto$.

- The end of a ls dangles:

$$\mathsf{ls}(-, E_2) \rightarrow (E_2 \not\hookrightarrow -) \tag{1}$$

- Each L-value reachable in a ls, except the end, does not dangle:

$$(E_1 \neq E_2 \wedge \mathsf{ls}(-, E_2) \wedge - \hookrightarrow E_1) \rightarrow (E_1 \hookrightarrow -) \tag{2}$$

- Models of subls can be changed provided cycles are not introduced:

$$\begin{aligned} &\mathsf{ls}(E_1, E_4) \wedge (\mathsf{ls}(E_2, E_3) * \mathsf{true}) \\ &\leftrightarrow (\mathsf{ls}(E_2, E_3) \wedge E_4 \not\hookrightarrow -) * ((\mathsf{ls}(E_2, E_3) \wedge E_4 \not\hookrightarrow -) \mathbin{-\!\!*} \mathsf{ls}(E_1, E_4)) \end{aligned} \tag{3}$$

These can be understood simply as particular properties of ls, but there are more elucidating readings. That is, (1) and (2) provide a non-inductive characterization of what L-values are, and are not, in heaps modeling a ls. In other words, they characterize the points-to facts about models of lss.

Property (3) states that heaps containing segments from E_1 to E_4 ($\mathsf{ls}(E_1, E_4)$) via a segment from E_2 to E_3 ($\wedge(\mathsf{ls}(E_2, E_3) * \mathsf{true})$) can be split into a heap containing the subsegment ($\mathsf{ls}(E_2, E_3)$) which, due to acyclicity, must not contain the endpoint ($\wedge E_4 \not\hookrightarrow -$), and (*) a heap which when augmented with *any* heap containing a segment from E_2 to E_3 without E_4 ($\mathsf{ls}(E_2, E_3) \wedge E_4 \not\hookrightarrow -$) yields ($\mathbin{-\!\!*}$) a segment from E_1 to E_4 ($\mathsf{ls}(E_1, E_4)$). That is, while the semantics in Table 1 specifies how models of a ls are related to models of the inductive occurrence, (3) characterizes how models of a ls are related to *any* submodel which is a ls (which, summarizing the above, is simply that the submodels do not contain the endpoint). In other words, (3) characterizes the ls facts about models of lss.

The soundness argument for UNROLLCOLLAPSE is largely concerned with analyzing the impact on validity of entailment which changing from one model of a ls to another has. For atomic formulæ, (1)–(3) give us a handle on this impact. For compound formulæ, the local reasoning supported by *, and precision of every predicate is essentially all we need. A predicate is *precise* [6] just when for any given stack and heap, there is at most one subheap that satisfies it; and so every predicate cuts out an unambiguous area of storage.

The general property we need is expressed in the following key lemma:

Lemma 5.

$$\text{If} \qquad \Pi \mid \mathsf{ls}^2(E_2, E_3) * \Sigma \vdash \Pi' \mid \Sigma' \tag{4}$$

$$\text{and} \quad s, h \vDash \Pi \wedge E_2 \neq E_3 \wedge E_2 \not\hookrightarrow - \wedge \Sigma \tag{5}$$

$$\text{then} \quad s, h \vDash \Pi' \wedge (\mathsf{ls}(E_2, E_3) \mathbin{-\!\!*} \Sigma')$$

This expresses that the ls predicate is, in some sense, "abstract"; stating, basically, that if a length two ls validates an entailment, then the entailment's consequent is insensitive to the particular model of the ls. The proof of this lemma is omitted for space reasons. But it may be useful to note some formulæ that, were they allowed, would cause this result to fail. First are imprecise predicates. Nearly everything breaks in their presence, but in particular, for imprecise A, B such that $s, h \vDash A * B$, not all subheaps of h which model A need leave or take enough heap for the remainder to model B, and so changing models of A can easily falsify B. Another problematic addition would be existentials in consequents, which would allow consequents to, e.g., impose minimum lengths with formulæ such as $\exists x, y. E_1 \mapsto x * x \mapsto y * \mathsf{ls}(y, E_2)$, which changing models of antecedents could violate. Finally, allowing "unspecified" sharing with formulæ such as $\mathsf{ls}(x, y) \wedge \Sigma$ gives two views of the same heap, one of which may be invalidated when replacing the heap with a different model of the other. Banning unspecified sharing forces the program annotations to explicate sharing; a restriction whose impact is presently unclear.

Once we know that consequents are insensitive to particular models of lss, we can replace any model with one of either length 0 or 2, depending on whether or not the pure part of the antecedent forces the endpoints to be equal, making proving soundness of UNROLLCOLLAPSE straightforward:

Proof (Proposition 2). Suppose the premisses are valid:

$$\Pi \wedge E_1{=}E_2 \mid \Sigma \vdash \Pi' \mid \Sigma' \tag{6}$$

$$\Pi \wedge E_1{\neq}E_2 \wedge x{\neq}E_2 \mid E_1 \mapsto x * x \mapsto E_2 * \Sigma \vdash \Pi' \mid \Sigma' \tag{7}$$

for $x \notin fv(\Pi, E_1, E_2, \Sigma, \Pi', \Sigma')$. Fix s, h and assume the antecedent of the conclusion: $s, h \vDash \Pi \mid \mathsf{ls}(E_1, E_2) * \Sigma$. Proceed by cases:

$[\llbracket E_1 \rrbracket s = \llbracket E_2 \rrbracket s]$: Hence $s, h \vDash \Pi \wedge E_1{=}E_2 \mid \Sigma$, and so by (6), $s, h \vDash \Pi' \mid \Sigma'$.

$[\llbracket E_1 \rrbracket s \neq \llbracket E_2 \rrbracket s]$: Hence $h = h_{12} * h_\Sigma$ and there exists l. $s', h_{12} \vDash E_1 \mapsto x * \mathsf{ls}(x, E_2)$ and $s', h_\Sigma \vDash \Pi \wedge E_1{\neq}E_2 \mid \Sigma$ where $s' = [s \mid x \to l]$ for x fresh. Therefore by (7), Lemma 5 ensures $s', h_\Sigma \vDash \Pi' \mid (\mathsf{ls}(E_1, E_2) \rightarrow\!\!\!* \ \Sigma')$, and hence $s, h \vDash \Pi' \mid \Sigma'$.

$\square$

4   Proof Theory

In the previous section we saw how UNROLLCOLLAPSE yields decidability of the fragment model-theoretically. We now see that it also forms the basis of a sound and complete proof theory, and a decision procedure based on proof-search.

The rules of the proof system are shown in Table 2. Since there is no CUT rule, the rules have a rather odd form. What we have, essentially, is a collection of axioms for the semantic properties of the assertion language, each of which has been CUT with an arbitrary formula. A noteworthy point is that the rules generally have only one premiss, so proof-search is largely simply rewriting.

Proposition 6 (Soundness). *Every derivable entailment is valid.*

Proof. The result follows from validity of each axiom's conclusion, and validity of each rule's premisses implies validity of its conclusion. The UNROLLCOLLAPSE case is Proposition 2, and the others are straightforward calculations. $\square$

Table 2. Proof System

AXIOM

$$\overline{\Pi \mathbin{\vert} \mathsf{emp} \vdash \mathsf{true} \mathbin{\vert} \mathsf{emp}}$$

INCONSISTENT

$$\overline{\Pi \wedge E{\neq}E \mathbin{\vert} \Sigma \vdash \Pi' \mathbin{\vert} \Sigma'}$$

SUBSTITUTION

$$\frac{\Pi[E/x] \mathbin{\vert} \Sigma[E/x] \vdash \Pi'[E/x] \mathbin{\vert} \Sigma'[E/x]}{\Pi \wedge x{=}E \mathbin{\vert} \Sigma \vdash \Pi' \mathbin{\vert} \Sigma'}$$

=REFLEXIVEL

$$\frac{\Pi \mathbin{\vert} \Sigma \vdash \Pi' \mathbin{\vert} \Sigma'}{\Pi \wedge E{=}E \mathbin{\vert} \Sigma \vdash \Pi' \mathbin{\vert} \Sigma'}$$

nilNOTLVAL

$$\frac{\Pi \wedge E_1{\neq}\mathsf{nil} \mathbin{\vert} E_1{\mapsto}E_2 * \Sigma \vdash \Pi' \mathbin{\vert} \Sigma'}{\Pi \mathbin{\vert} E_1{\mapsto}E_2 * \Sigma \vdash \Pi' \mathbin{\vert} \Sigma'}$$

*PARTIAL

$$\frac{\Pi \wedge E_1{\neq}E_3 \mathbin{\vert} E_1{\mapsto}E_2 * E_3{\mapsto}E_4 * \Sigma \vdash \Pi' \mathbin{\vert} \Sigma'}{\Pi \mathbin{\vert} E_1{\mapsto}E_2 * E_3{\mapsto}E_4 * \Sigma \vdash \Pi' \mathbin{\vert} \Sigma'}$$

UNROLLCOLLAPSE

$$\frac{\begin{array}{c}\Pi \wedge E_1{=}E_2 \mathbin{\vert} \Sigma \vdash \Pi' \mathbin{\vert} \Sigma' \\ \Pi \wedge E_1{\neq}E_2 \wedge x{\neq}E_2 \mathbin{\vert} E_1{\mapsto}x * x{\mapsto}E_2 * \Sigma \vdash \Pi' \mathbin{\vert} \Sigma'\end{array}}{\Pi \mathbin{\vert} \mathsf{ls}(E_1,E_2) * \Sigma \vdash \Pi' \mathbin{\vert} \Sigma'} \quad x \notin fv(\Pi, E_1, E_2, \Sigma, \Pi', \Sigma')$$

=REFLEXIVER

$$\frac{\Pi \mathbin{\vert} \Sigma \vdash \Pi' \mathbin{\vert} \Sigma'}{\Pi \mathbin{\vert} \Sigma \vdash \Pi' \wedge E{=}E \mathbin{\vert} \Sigma'}$$

HYPOTHESIS

$$\frac{\Pi \wedge P \mathbin{\vert} \Sigma \vdash \Pi' \mathbin{\vert} \Sigma'}{\Pi \wedge P \mathbin{\vert} \Sigma \vdash \Pi' \wedge P \mathbin{\vert} \Sigma'}$$

EMPTYls

$$\frac{\Pi \mathbin{\vert} \Sigma \vdash \Pi' \mathbin{\vert} \Sigma'}{\Pi \mathbin{\vert} \Sigma \vdash \Pi' \mathbin{\vert} \mathsf{ls}(E,E) * \Sigma'}$$

FRAME

$$\frac{\Pi \mathbin{\vert} \Sigma \vdash \Pi' \mathbin{\vert} \Sigma'}{\Pi \mathbin{\vert} S * \Sigma \vdash \Pi' \mathbin{\vert} S * \Sigma'}$$

NONEMPTYls

$$\frac{\Pi \wedge E_1{\neq}E_3 \mathbin{\vert} \Sigma \vdash \Pi' \mathbin{\vert} \mathsf{ls}(E_2,E_3) * \Sigma'}{\Pi \wedge E_1{\neq}E_3 \mathbin{\vert} E_1{\mapsto}E_2 * \Sigma \vdash \Pi' \mathbin{\vert} \mathsf{ls}(E_1,E_3) * \Sigma'}$$

4.1   Decidability and Completeness

The proof-search algorithm makes use of a class of formulæ which are "maximally explicit". The primary characteristic of these formulæ, discussed later, is that the FRAME rule is complete for entailments with such formulæ as antecedents.

Definition 7 (Normal Form). *A formula $\Pi \mathbin{\vert} \Sigma$ is in* normal form *if*

$$\Pi \mathbin{\vert} \Sigma \equiv (x_i{\neq}x_j)_{1 \leq i \neq j \leq n} \wedge (x_i{\neq}\mathsf{nil})_{1 \leq i \leq n} \wedge (E_i{\neq}E_i')_{1 \leq i \leq m} \wedge \mathsf{true}$$
$$\mathbin{\vert} x_1{\mapsto}E_1'' * \cdots * x_n{\mapsto}E_n'' * \mathsf{emp}$$

for some n, m and where $x_i \not\equiv x_j$ for $i \neq j$ and $E_i \not\equiv E_i'$.

We will be concerned with the following proof-search algorithm:

Algorithm 8. *For goal entailment g,* PS(g) *either fails or returns a proof of g:*

PS(g) = nondeterministically select a rule r such that:

> g unifies with the conclusion of r, via some substitution s
> and if r is nilNOTLVAL, then $E_1{\neq}\mathsf{nil} \notin \Pi$ (8)
> and if r is *PARTIAL, then $E_1{\neq}E_3 \notin \Pi$ (9)

and if r is FRAME or NonEmptyls,

then the antecedent of g is in normal form   (10)

if no such rule exists, then fail

else if r is an axiom, then return r

else let $p_0, \ldots, p_n$ for some n be the premisses of r after applying s

in return $r(\text{PS}(p_0), \ldots, \text{PS}(p_n))$

Here we consider axioms in the proof system to be proof constants, and rules to be functions from proofs of their premises to proofs of their conclusions.

A point to note about this algorithm is that as long as the additional sideconditions (8)–(10) are met, the order in which the rules are applied is inconsequential. The first step toward showing that PS is a decision procedure is termination:

Lemma 9 (Termination). *For any goal entailment,* PS *terminates.*

Proof. Termination of PS is established by observing that, with additional sideconditions (8) and (9), applying any rule makes progress: the size of each premiss of any rule application is lexicographically less than the size of the conclusion, where size is defined by:

Definition 10 (Size). *The* size *of an entailment* $\Pi \mid \Sigma \vdash \Pi' \mid \Sigma'$ *is a triple of:*

1. *The number of* lss *occurring in* $\Pi \mid \Sigma \vdash \Pi' \mid \Sigma'$,
2. *The number of inequalities missing from* Π, *that is,* $|\{E_0 \neq E_1 \mid E_0, E_1 \in fv(\Pi \mid \Sigma, \Pi' \mid \Sigma') \cup \{\text{nil}\}\} \setminus \Pi|$,
3. *The length of* $\Pi \mid \Sigma \vdash \Pi' \mid \Sigma'$, *where length is defined in the obvious way taking all simple formulæ to have length 1.*

$\square$

When PS fails, the short story is that it has found a disproof of the goal. We begin explaining this by analyzing entailments with antecedents in normal form.

Observation 11. *The antecedent of every entailment to which no rule applies, except possibly* FRAME *and* NonEmptyls, *is in normal form.*

For a more intuitive characterization of normal form, note that formulæ $\Pi \mid \Sigma$ in normal form satisfy the following properties:

1. No equalities $E=E'$ (other than reflexive $E=E$) are guaranteed to hold.
2. The only inequalities $E \neq E'$ guaranteed to hold appear explicitly in Π.
3. The only expressions E guaranteed to be in the domain of the heap appear explicitly as $E \mapsto E'$ in Σ.

A key property of normal forms is satisfiability. Later we will make use of two different types of model of such formulæ:

Definition 12 (Bad Model). *For* $\Pi \mid \Sigma$ *in normal form:*

1. *A bad model of* $\Pi \mid \Sigma$ *is a state* $s, h \models \Pi \mid \Sigma$ *where nil* $\notin$ *range(s) and s is one-one on* $fv(\Pi \mid \Sigma)$, *and h is uniquely determined by s.*

2. *A bad model of $\Pi \mid \Sigma$ with $x{=}E$ is a state s, $h \vDash \Pi{\wedge}x{=}E \mid \Sigma$ where, for s', h' a bad model of $\Pi \mid \Sigma$, $s = [s' \mid x{\rightarrow}\llbracket E\rrbracket s']$, and h is uniquely determined by s.*

Lemma 13. *For any formula $\Pi \mid \Sigma$ in normal form:*

1. *There exists a bad model of $\Pi \mid \Sigma$.*
2. *For any $x{\neq}E \notin \Pi$, there exists a bad model of $\Pi \mid \Sigma$ with $x{=}E$.*

Now for the crux of correctness of PS in the failure case, and completeness of the proof system: when PS reaches a stuck entailment, it is invalid, and invalidity is preserved throughout the path of rule applications PS made from the goal to the stuck entailment.[4]

Lemma 14 (Stuck Invalidity). *Every entailment stuck for PS is invalid.*

Proof (Sketch). Consider a stuck entailment $\Pi \mid \Sigma \vdash \Pi' \mid \Sigma'$, whose antecedent, by Observation 11, is in normal form. Proceed by cases:

$[\Sigma' \equiv \mathsf{emp}$ and $\Pi' \equiv \Pi'' \wedge E{=}E']$: Note $E \not\equiv E'$ since $\Pi \mid \Sigma \vdash \Pi' \mid \Sigma'$ is stuck. Therefore a bad model of $\Pi \mid \Sigma$ is a countermodel.

$[\Sigma' \equiv \mathsf{emp}$ and $\Pi' \equiv \Pi'' \wedge E{\neq}E']$: Note $E{\neq}E' \notin \Pi$ since $\Pi \mid \Sigma \vdash \Pi' \mid \Sigma'$ is stuck. Therefore a bad model of $\Pi \mid \Sigma$ with $E{=}E'$ is a countermodel.

$[\Sigma' \equiv E{\mapsto}E' * \Sigma'']$: Therefore since $\Pi \mid \Sigma \vdash \Pi' \mid \Sigma'$ is stuck, $E{\mapsto}E' \notin \Sigma$. Hence, s, h a bad model of $\Pi \mid \Sigma$ is a countermodel, since either $\llbracket E\rrbracket s \notin dom(h)$ or $h(\llbracket E\rrbracket s) \neq \llbracket E'\rrbracket s$.

$[\Sigma' \equiv \mathsf{ls}(\mathsf{nil}, E) * \Sigma'']$: Therefore s, h a bad model of $\Pi \mid \Sigma$ is a countermodel, since $nil \neq \llbracket E\rrbracket s$.

$[\Sigma' \equiv \mathsf{ls}(x, E) * \Sigma''$ and for all $E'. x{\mapsto}E' \notin \Sigma]$: Therefore s, h a bad model of $\Pi \mid \Sigma$ is a countermodel, since $\llbracket x\rrbracket s \neq \llbracket E\rrbracket s$ and $\llbracket x\rrbracket s \notin dom(h)$.

$[\Sigma \equiv x{\mapsto}E * \Sigma_0$ and $\Sigma' \equiv \mathsf{ls}(x, E') * \Sigma_1]$: Note that Σ_1 contains only lss, since the other cases have already been covered. Let s, h be a bad model of $\Pi \mid \Sigma$ with $x{=}E'$ ($x{\neq}E' \notin \Pi$ since $\Pi \mid \Sigma \vdash \Pi' \mid \Sigma'$ is stuck). Therefore s, $h \vDash \Pi \mid x{\mapsto}x * \Sigma_0$ and s, $h \nvDash \Pi' \mid \mathsf{ls}(x, E') * \Sigma_1$, since no ls contains a nonempty cycle. Therefore s, h is a countermodel. $\qquad\square$

Lemma 15 (Invalidity Preservation). *For all rule applications satisfying sidecondition (10) of Algorithm 8, invalidity of any of the rule's premises implies invalidity of the rule's conclusion.*

Proposition 16 (Decidability). *Validity of entailment is decidable, in particular, PS is a decision procedure.*

Proof. Lemma 9 establishes termination. For correctness, in case PS returns normally with a proof, correctness is immediate from Proposition 6. Otherwise PS

---

[4] Furthermore, countermodels of stuck entailments could be computed, and countermodels of a rule's conclusion could be computed from a countermodel of one the rule's premises. So PS could be defined so as to either return a proof or a countermodel of the goal.

has failed after reaching a stuck entailment. We argue that this implies invalidity of the goal entailment, and hence correctness, by noting that each stuck entailment is itself invalid, due to Lemma 14, and that each rule application in the path from the goal preserves invalidity, due to Lemma 15. Transitively, all the entailments down to the goal are invalid.   □

Corollary 17 (Completeness). *Every underivable entailment is invalid.*

5   Conclusions

In this paper we have proven a decidability result for a logic for just one kind of pointer data structure: linked lists. And it was not easy work. There have been other results as well in this territory (e.g., [7–10]) but, frankly, we are not sure if it is possible to obtain a canonical decidable fragment that covers a large variety of structures. For example, decidability of monadic second-order logic with a unary function symbol [7] implies decidability of our fragment. However, that result is only applicable because we used unary heap cells, while our techniques generalize to n-ary heap cells (necessary for binary trees for example).

Although the main focus in this paper was decidability, the fragment appears to be of some interest in itself. Crucially, its proof theory is extremely deterministic. In particular, there is no need to attempt many different splittings of a context as is usually the case in proof-search for substructural logics. This is a reflection of a semantic property enjoyed by the fragment: every assertion is precise. This then implies that there can be at most one heap splitting used to satisfy a * formula. The absence of (general) disjunction in the fragment is crucial for precision. It is, however, possible to incorporate restricted, disjoint, forms of disjunction, corresponding to if-then-else, without sacrificing precision. These forms are useful in playing the role of guards for inductive definitions, and one of them is implicitly present in the ls predicate.

In future work we plan to add a mechanism for inductive definitions to the fragment. At present we can see how some definitions (e.g., trees) preserve decidability, but we are not sure how far we can go in this direction. Even if decidability cannot be maintained, the computational nature of the proof theory of precise predicates should give a way to selectively consider how deep to go in inductions in a way that gives strong control over proof-search.

Acknowledgements. We are grateful to the anonymous referees for helpful comments. During Berdine's stay at Carnegie Mellon University, this research was sponsored in part by National Science Foundation Grant CCR-0204242. All three authors were supported by the EPSRC.

References

1. Reynolds, J.C.: Separation logic: a logic for shared mutable data structures. In: LICS, IEEE (2002) 55–74

2. Reynolds, J.C.: Intuitionistic reasoning about shared mutable data structure. In Davies, J., Roscoe, B., Woodcock, J., eds.: Millennial Perspectives in Computer Science, Houndsmill, Hampshire, Palgrave (2000) 303–321
3. Isthiaq, S., O'Hearn, P.: BI as an assertion language for mutable data structures. In: POPL, London (2001) 39–46
4. O'Hearn, P., Reynolds, J., Yang, H.: Local reasoning about programs that alter data structures. In: CSL. Volume 2142 of LNCS., Springer (2001) 1–19
5. Calcagno, C., Yang, H., O'Hearn, P.: Computability and complexity results for a spatial assertion language for data structures. In: FSTTCS. Volume 2245 of LNCS., Springer (2001) 108–119
6. O'Hearn, P.W., Yang, H., Reynolds, J.C.: Separation and information hiding. In: POPL, Venice (2004) 268–280
7. Rabin, M.O.: Decidability of secon-order theories and automata on infinite trees. Trans. of American Math. Society **141** (1969) 1–35
8. Jenson, J., Jorgensen, M., Klarkund, N., Schwartzback, M.: Automatic verification of pointer programs using monadic second-order logic. In: PLDI. (1997) 225–236 SIGPLAN Notices 32(5).
9. Benedikt, M., Reps, T., Sagiv, M.: A decidable logic for describing linked data structures. In: ESOP. Volume 1576 of LNCS., Springer (1999) 2–19
10. Immerman, N., Rabinovich, A., Reps, T., Sagiv, M., Yorsh, G.: Verification via structure simulation. In: CAV. Volume 3114 of LNCS. (2004)

Approximate Range Searching Using Binary Space Partitions

Mark de Berg [*] and Micha Streppel[**]

Department of Computer Science,
TU Eindhoven, P.O.Box 513,
5600 MB Eindhoven,
The Netherlands

Abstract. We show how any BSP tree $\mathcal{T}_P$ for the endpoints of a set of n disjoint segments in the plane can be used to obtain a BSP tree of size $O(n \cdot \text{depth}(\mathcal{T}_P))$ for the segments themselves, such that the range-searching efficiency remains almost the same. We apply this technique to obtain a BSP tree of size $O(n \log n)$ such that ε-approximate range searching queries with any constant-complexity convex query range can be answered in $O(\min_{\varepsilon>0}\{(1/\varepsilon)+k_\varepsilon\} \log n)$ time, where k_ε is the number of segments intersecting the ε-extended range. The same result can be obtained for disjoint constant-complexity curves, if we allow the BSP to use splitting curves along the given curves.

We also describe how to construct a linear-size BSP tree for low-density scenes consisting of n objects in $\mathbb{R}^d$ such that ε-approximate range searching with any constant-complexity convex query range can be done in $O(\log n + \min_{\varepsilon>0}\{(1/\varepsilon^{d-1}) + k_\varepsilon\})$ time.

1 Introduction

Multi-functional data structures and BSP trees. In computational geometry, efficient data structures have been developed for a variety of geometric query problems: range searching, point location, nearest-neighbor searching, etc. The theoretical performance of these structures is often close to the theoretical lower bounds. In order to achieve close to optimal performance, most structures are dedicated to very specific settings; for instance, a structure for range searching with rectangular ranges in a set of line segments will not work for range searching with circular ranges in a set of line segments or for range searching with rectangular ranges in a set of circles. It would be preferable, however, to have a single *multi-functional geometric data structure*: a data structure that can store different types of data and answer various types of queries. Indeed, this is what is often done in practice.

---

[*] MdB is supported by the Netherlands Organisation for Scientific Research (N.W.O.) under project no. 639.023.301.

[**] MS is supported by the Netherlands Organisation for Scientific Research (N.W.O.) under project no. 612.065.203.

K. Lodaya and M. Mahajan (Eds.): FSTTCS 2004, LNCS 3328, pp. 110–121, 2004.

Another potential problem with the structures developed in computational geometry is that they are sometimes rather involved, and that it is unclear how large the constant factors in the query time and storage costs are. Moreover, they may fail to take advantage of the cases where the input objects and/or the query have some nice properties. Hence, the ideal would be to have a multi-functional data structure that is simple and takes advantage of any favorable properties of the input and/or query.

The existing multi-functional data structures can be roughly categorized into *bounding-volume hierarchies (BVHs)* and *space-partitioning structures (SPSs)*. A BVH on a set S of objects is a tree structure whose leaves are in a one-to-one correspondence with the objects in S and where each node ν stores some bounding volume—usually the bounding box—of the objects corresponding to the leaves in the subtree of ν. Note that the size of a BVH is linear in the number of objects stored in it. An SPS is based on a partitioning of the space into cells. With each cell, (pointers to) all objects intersecting that cell are stored. Moreover, there is some search structure that makes it possible to quickly find the cells in the partitioning intersecting a query range. Often the partitioning is done in a hierarchical fashion, and the search structure is a tree whose leaves are in one-to-one correspondence with the cells in the partitioning. Because objects can potentially intersect many cells, the size of an SPS is not necessarily linear. Both BVHs and SPSs can in principle store any type of input object, they can be used to perform range searching with any type of query range—this implies they can also be used for point location—and they can be used to do nearest neighbor searching. The main challenge is to construct the BVH or SPS in such a way that queries are answered efficiently and, for SPSs, that their size is small. In this paper we study this problem for SPSs or, more precisely, for binary space partition trees.

A *binary space partition tree*, or *BSP tree*, is an SPS where the subdivision of the underlying space is done in a hierarchical fashion using hyperplanes (that is, lines in case the space is 2D, planes in 3D, etc.) The hierarchical subdivision process usually continues until each cell contains at most one (or maybe a small number of) input object(s). BSP trees are used for many purposes. For example, they are used for range searching [2], for hidden surface removal with the painter's algorithm [15], for shadow generation [12], for set operations on polyhedra [18, 26], for visibility preprocessing for interactive walkthroughs [23], for cell decomposition methods in motion planning [7], and for surface approximation [5].

In some applications—hidden-surface removal is a typical example—the efficiency is determined by the size of the BSP tree, as the application needs to traverse the whole tree. Hence, several researchers have proposed algorithms to construct small BSP trees in various different settings [3, 4, 9, 10, 20, 21, 25]. For instance, Paterson and Yao [20] proved that any set of n disjoint line segments in the plane admits a BSP tree of size $O(n \log n)$. Recently Tóth [24] showed that this is close to optimal by exhibiting a set of n segments for which any BSP tree must have size $\Omega(n \log n / \log \log n)$. Paterson and Yao also proved that there are sets of n disjoint triangles in $\mathbb{R}^3$ for which any BSP tree must have quadratic size, and they gave a construction algorithm that achieves this bound. Since a quadratic-size BSP tree is useless in most practical applications, de Berg [9] studied BSP trees for so-called uncluttered scenes. He proved that uncluttered scenes admit a BSP tree of linear size, in any fixed dimension. Unfortunately, his BSP tree can have linear depth, so it is not efficient for range searching or point location. However, by constructing additional data structures that help to speed up the search in the BSP tree, he showed it is possible to perform point location in $O(\log n)$ time in uncluttered scenes. Range searching in low-density scenes can be done as well in $O(\log n)$ time—again using some additional structures—but only if the diameter of the query range is about the same as the diameter of the smallest object in the scene. Surprisingly, we do not know of any papers that investigate the efficiency of BSP trees, without any additional data structures as in [9], for range searching on non-point objects.

Approximate Range Searching. Developing a multi-functional geometric datastructure—one that can store any type of object and can do range searching with any type of query range—that provably has good performance seems quite hard, if not impossible. As it turns out, however, such results can be achieved if one is willing to settle for ε-*approximate range searching*, as introduced by Arya and Mount [6]. Here one considers, for a parameter $\varepsilon > 0$, the ε-extended query range Q_ε, which is the set of points lying at distance at most $\varepsilon \cdot \mathrm{diam}(Q)$ from Q, where $\mathrm{diam}(Q)$ is the diameter of Q. Objects intersecting Q must be reported, while objects intersecting Q_ε (but not Q) may or may not be reported; objects outside Q_ε are not allowed to be reported. In practice, one would expect that for small values of ε, not too many extra objects are reported.

Arya and Mount [6] showed that approximate range searching can be done very efficiently when the input is a set of n points in $\mathbb{R}^d$. Their BBD-tree can answer range queries with any constant-complexity convex[1] query range in $O(\log n + (1/\varepsilon)^{d-1} + k_\varepsilon)$ time, where k_ε is the number of points inside Q_ε. Later Duncan *et al.* [13, 14] achieved the same results using so-called BAR-trees, which are a special type of BSP trees that use splitting hyperplanes with only a fixed number of orientations. In fact, as observed by Haverkort *et al.* [17], the parameter ε is only needed in the analysis and not in the query algorithm, which can simply report only the objects intersecting Q. This means that a query can be answered in time $O(\log n + \min_{\varepsilon > 0}\{(1/\varepsilon)^{d-1} + k_\varepsilon\})$.

Our main objective is to obtain similar results for more general input objects than points, thus providing a truly multi-functional geometric data structure. Some results in this direction have been obtained recently by Agarwal *et al.* [1] and Haverkort *et al.* [17]. Agarwal *et al.* showed how to construct a boxtree—that is, a BVH that uses axis-aligned bounding boxes as bounding volumes—for any set S of n input boxes in $\mathbb{R}^d$, such that a range query with a box as query

---

[1] For non-convex ranges, one needs to replace the factor $1/\varepsilon^{d-1}$ by $1/\varepsilon^d$. This holds for all results mentioned below, including ours, so we do not mention this extension in the sequel.

can be answered in time $\Theta(n^{1-1/d} + k)$, where k is the number of input boxes intersecting the query box. They also showed that this is optimal in the worst case, even if the input boxes are disjoint. Unfortunately, this result is rather limited: even though a boxtree can store any type of object and query with any range, there is only a performance guarantee for a very specific setting: orthogonal range searching in a set of boxes. Moreover, the bound is fairly high. Haverkort et al. therefore studied approximate range searching. They presented a BVH that can answer range queries on a set of boxes in $\mathbb{R}^3$, for any constant-complexity query range, in time $O((\lambda/\epsilon) \log^4 n + k_\epsilon)$, where λ is the *density* of the scene.[2] The density of a set of objects is defined as the smallest number λ such that any ball B intersects at most λ objects whose minimal enclosing ball has radius at least $radius(B)$ [11]. When the input objects are disjoint and fat, the density λ is a constant (depending on the fatness). This result is more general than the result of Agarwal et al. [1], as it holds for any range, but still there is no performance guarantee for input objects other than boxes. Indeed, even for disjoint fat objects, the query time can be linear for a point location query, because the bounding boxes of the input boxes may all contain a common point.

Our Results. In this paper we show that it is possible to construct BSP trees for sets of disjoint segments in the plane, and for low-density scenes in any dimension, whose query time for approximate range searching is as good, or almost as good, as the best known bounds for point data. More precisely, our results are as follows.

In Section 3 we study BSP trees for a set of n disjoint line segments in the plane. We give a general technique to convert a BSP tree $\mathcal{T}_P$ for a set of points to a BSP tree for a set of disjoint line segments, such that the size of the BSP tree is $O(n \cdot \text{depth}(\mathcal{T}_P))$, and the time for range searching remains almost the same. By combining this result with the BAR-tree of Duncan et al. [14], we obtain a BSP tree that can answer range queries with any convex constant-complexity query range in time $O(\min_{\varepsilon > 0}(1/\varepsilon + k_\varepsilon) \log n)$, where k_ε is the number of segments intersecting the ε-extended query range. This is the first result on approximate range searching for disjoint segments in the plane. This result can be extended to disjoint constant-complexity curves in the plane, if we allow the BSP to use splitting curves (which will be along the input curves) in the partitioning.

In Section 4 we consider low-density scenes. We prove that any scene of constant density in $\mathbb{R}^d$ admits a BSP of linear size, such that range-searching queries with arbitrary convex ranges can be answered in time $O(\log n + \min_{\varepsilon > 0}\{(1/\varepsilon^{d-1}) + k_\varepsilon\})$. (The dependency on the density λ is linear.) This result is more general than the result of Haverkort et al. [17], as they only have a performance guarantee for boxes as input. Moreover, our time bound is better by several logarithmic factors, and our result holds in any dimension.

---

[2] In fact, the result is more general: the bound holds if the so-called slicing number of the scene is λ.

2   Preliminaries

In this section we briefly introduce some terminology and notation that we will use throughout the paper.

A BSP tree for a set S of n objects in $\mathbb{R}^d$ is a binary tree $\mathcal{T}$ with the following properties.

- Every (internal or leaf) node ν corresponds to a subset region(ν) of $\mathbb{R}^d$, which we call the *region* of ν. These regions are not stored with the nodes. When ν is a leaf node, we sometimes refer to region(ν) as a *cell*. The root node root($\mathcal{T}$) corresponds to $\mathbb{R}^d$.
- Every internal node ν stores a hyperplane $h(\nu)$, which we call the *splitting hyperplane* (*splitting line* when $d = 2$) of ν. The left child of ν then corresponds to region(ν) $\cap\, h(\nu)^-$, where $h(\nu)^-$ denotes the half-space below $h(\nu)$, and the right child corresponds to region(ν) $\cap\, h(\nu)^+$, where $h(\nu)^+$ is the half-space above $h(\nu)$.
  A node ν stores, besides the splitting hyperplane $h(\nu)$, a list $\mathcal{L}(\nu)$ with all objects contained in $h(\nu)$ that intersect region(ν). Observe that this list will always be empty when the objects in S are d-dimensional.
- Every leaf node μ stores a list $\mathcal{L}(\mu)$ of all objects in S intersecting the interior of region(μ).

Note that we do not place a bound on the number of objects stored with a leaf. In the BSP trees discussed in this paper, however, this number will be constant.

The *size* of a BSP tree is defined as the total number of nodes plus the total size of the lists $\mathcal{L}(\nu)$ over all (internal and leaf) nodes ν in $\mathcal{T}$. For a node ν in a tree $\mathcal{T}$, we use $\mathcal{T}(\nu)$ to denote the subtree of $\mathcal{T}$ rooted at ν, and we use depth($\mathcal{T}$) to denote the depth of $\mathcal{T}$.

We assume that all our input objects, as well as the query range have constant complexity. This means that we can compute the intersection of an object with a line or with the query range in $O(1)$ time.

3   BSPs for Segments in the Plane

Let S be a set of n disjoint line segments in the plane. In this section we describe a general technique to construct a BSP for S, based on a BSP on the endpoints of S. The technique uses a segment-tree like approach similar to, but more general than, the deterministic BSP construction of Paterson and Yao [20]. The range-searching structure of Overmars *et al.* [19] also uses similar ideas, except that they store so-called long segments—see below—in an associated structure, so they do not construct a BSP for the segments. The main extra complication we face compared to these previous approaches is that we must ensure that we only work with the relevant portions of the given tree during the recursive construction, and prune away irrelevant portions. The pruning has to be done carefully, however, because too much pruning can have a negative effect on the query time.

More specifically the construction of the BSP for S is as follows. Let P be the set of $2n$ endpoints of the segments in S, and let $\mathcal{T}_P$ be a BSP tree for P. We assume that $\mathcal{T}_P$ has size $O(n)$, and that the leaves of $\mathcal{T}_P$ store at most one point from P. Below we describe the global construction of the BSP tree for S. Some details of the construction will be omitted here.

The BSP tree $\mathcal{T}_S$ for S is constructed recursively from $\mathcal{T}_P$, as follows. Let ν be a node in $\mathcal{T}_P$. We call a segment $s \in S$ *short* at ν if region(ν) contains an endpoint of s. A segment s is called *long* at ν if (i) s intersects the interior of region(ν), and (ii) s is short at parent(ν) but not at ν. In a recursive call there are two parameters: a node $\nu \in \mathcal{T}_P$ and a subset $S^* \subset S$, clipped to lie within region(ν). The recursive call will construct a BSP tree $\mathcal{T}_{S^*}$ for S^* based on $\mathcal{T}_P(\nu)$. Initially, $\nu = \text{root}(\mathcal{T}_P)$ and $S^* = S$. The recursion stops when S^* is empty, in which case $\mathcal{T}_{S^*}$ is a single leaf.

We will make sure that during the recursive calls we know for each segment (or rather, fragment) in S^* which of its endpoints lie on the boundary of region(ν), if any. This means we also know for each segment whether it is long or short. This information can be maintained during the recursive calls without asymptotic overhead.

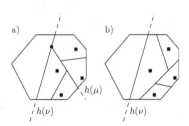

Fig. 1. Illustration of the pruning strategy. The black squares indicate endpoints of input segments. a) There is a T-junction on $h(\nu)$: a splitting line in the subtree $h(\mu)$ ends on $h(\nu)$. Pruning $h(\nu)$ would partition the empty part of the region, which might have a negative effect on the query time. b) There is no T-junction on $h(\nu)$, so we can prune $h(\nu)$

Let $L \subset S^*$ be the set of segments from S^* that are long at ν. The recursive call is handled as follows.

Case 1: L is empty.

We first compute $S_l = S^* \cap h(\nu)^-$ and $S_r = S^* \cap h(\nu)^+$. If both S_l and S_r are non-empty, we create a root node for $\mathcal{T}_{S^*}$ which stores $h(\nu)$ as its splitting line. We then recurse on the left child of ν with S_l to construct the left subtree of the root, and on the right child of ν with S_r to construct the right subtree of the root.

If one of S_l and S_r is empty, it seems the splitting line $h(\nu)$ is useless in $\mathcal{T}_{S^*}$ and can therefore be omitted in $\mathcal{T}_{S^*}$. We have to be careful, however, that we do not increase the query time: the removal of $h(\nu)$ can cause other splitting lines, which used to end on $h(\nu)$, to extend further. Hence, we proceed as follows. Define a *T-junction*, see Fig. 1, to be a vertex of the original BSP subdivision induced by $\mathcal{T}_P$; in other words, the T-junctions are the endpoints of the segments $h(\mu) \cap \text{region}(\mu)$, for nodes μ in $\mathcal{T}_P$. To decide whether or not to use $h(\nu)$, we check if $h(\nu) \cap R$ contains a T-junction in its interior, where R is the region that corresponds to the root of $\mathcal{T}_{S^*}$. If this is the case, we do not prune: the root node of $\mathcal{T}_{S^*}$ will store the splitting line $h(\nu)$, one of its subtrees will be empty, and the other subtree will be constructed recursively on the non-empty subset. If $h(\nu) \cap R$ does not contain a T-junction, however, we prune: the tree $\mathcal{T}_{S^*}$ will be the tree we get when we recurse on the non-empty subset, and there will be no node in $\mathcal{T}_{S^*}$ that stores $h(\nu)$.

Case 2: L is not empty.

Now the long segments partition R into $m := |L| + 1$ regions, $R_1, \ldots, R_m$. We take the following steps.

(i) We split $S^* \setminus L$ into m subsets $S_1^*, \ldots, S_m^*$, where S_i^* contains the segments from S^* lying inside R_i.

(ii) We construct a binary tree $\mathcal{T}$ with $m-1$ internal nodes whose splitting lines are the lines containing the long segments. We call these *free splits* because they do not cause any fragmentation. The leaves of $\mathcal{T}$ correspond to the regions R_i, and will become the roots of the subtrees to be created for the sets S_i^*. To keep the overall depth of the tree bounded by $O(\text{depth}(\mathcal{T}_P))$, we make $\mathcal{T}$ weight-balanced, where the weights correspond to the sizes of the sets S_i^*, as in the trapezoid method for point location [22]. The tree $\mathcal{T}$ is constructed as follows. Let $\ell_i \in L$ separate the regions R_i and R_{i+1}. If $\sum_{i=1}^{r-1} |S_i^*| = 0$ simply build a binary tree on the long segments, otherwise determine the integer r such that $\sum_{i=1}^{r-1} |S_i^*| < |S^* \setminus L|/2$ and $\sum_{i=1}^{r} |S_i^*| \geq |S^* \setminus L|/2$. The line ℓ_{r-1} is then stored at ν, the root of $\mathcal{T}$, and ℓ_r is stored at the root of the right child μ. The left child of ν, denoted τ_1, and the right child of μ, denoted τ_2 are constructed recursively. Note that both region(τ_1) and region(τ_2) contain each less than $|S^* \setminus L|/2$ short segments. The tree $\mathcal{T}_{S^*}$ then consists of the tree $\mathcal{T}$, with, for every $1 \leq i \leq m$, the leaf of $\mathcal{T}$ corresponding to R_i replaced by a subtree for S_i^*. More precisely, each subtree T_i is constructed using a recursive call with node ν and S_i^* as parameters.

The following theorem states bounds on the tree $\mathcal{T}_S$ created by the previous algorithm.

Theorem 1. *Let $\mathcal{R}$ be a family of constant-complexity query ranges in $\mathbb{R}^2$. Suppose that for any set P of n points in $\mathbb{R}^2$, there is a BSP tree $\mathcal{T}_P$ of linear size, where each leaf stores at most one point from P, with the following property: any query Q with a range from $\mathcal{R}$ intersects at most $v(\mathcal{T}_P, Q)$ cells in the BSP subdivision. Then for any set S of n disjoint segments in $\mathbb{R}^2$, there is a BSP tree $\mathcal{T}_S$ which can be constructed in $O(n \cdot \text{depth}(\mathcal{T}_P))$ time such that*

(i) the depth of $\mathcal{T}_S$ is $O(\text{depth}(\mathcal{T}_P))$
(ii) the size of $\mathcal{T}_S$ is $O(n \cdot \text{depth}(\mathcal{T}_P))$

(iii) any query Q with a range from $\mathcal{R}$ visits at most $O((v(\mathcal{T}_P, Q) + k) \cdot \text{depth}(\mathcal{T}_P))$
nodes from $\mathcal{T}_S$, where k is the number of segments intersecting the range.

Proof. In this extended abstract we only prove the bound on the number of nodes visited with a query Q.

We distinguish two categories of visited nodes: nodes ν such that region(ν) is intersected by ∂Q (the boundary of Q), and nodes ν such that region(ν) $\subset Q$.

We first bound the number of leaves of the first category, that is, the number of cells intersected by ∂Q. This number is bounded by the number of intersections of ∂Q and cell boundaries (except for the trivial case where Q lies completely inside a single region). A cell boundary is composed of pieces of splitting lines that were already present in $\mathcal{T}_P$ and fragments of segments in S. Because we made sure that the pruning step in our construction did not cause splitting 'lines' to be extended, the number of pieces of splitting lines in $\mathcal{T}_S$ intersected by ∂Q is not more than the number of cells of the subdivision induced by $\mathcal{T}_P$ that are intersected by ∂Q. Furthermore, the number of segments in S intersected by ∂Q is $O(k)$. Hence, the total number of leaf cells intersected by ∂Q is $O(v(\mathcal{T}_P, Q) + k)$. Because the depth of $\mathcal{T}_S$ is $O(\text{depth}(\mathcal{T}_P))$, the total number of nodes in the first category is $O((v(\mathcal{T}_P, Q) + k) \cdot \text{depth}(\mathcal{T}_P))$.

Nodes in the second category are organized in subtrees rooted at nodes ν such that region(ν) $\subset Q$ but region(parent(ν)) $\not\subset Q$. Let $N(Q)$ be the collection of these roots. Note that the regions of the nodes in $N(Q)$ are disjoint. For a node $\nu \in N(Q)$, let $k_s(\nu)$ denote the number of segments that are short at ν, and $k_l(\nu)$ the number of segments that are long at ν. Then the size of the subtree $\mathcal{T}_S(\nu)$ is $O(k_l(\nu) + k_s(\nu) \cdot \text{depth}(\mathcal{T}_S(\nu)))$. Hence, the total number of nodes in the subtrees $\mathcal{T}_S(\nu)$ rooted at the nodes $\nu \in N(Q)$ is bounded by

$$\sum_\nu O(k_l(\nu) + k_s(\nu) \cdot \text{depth}(\mathcal{T}_S(\nu))) = O(\sum_\nu k_l(\nu)) + O(\text{depth}(\mathcal{T}_P) \cdot \sum_\nu k_s(\nu)).$$

The first term is bounded by $O(k \cdot \text{depth}(\mathcal{T}_P))$, because a segment is long at $O(\text{depth}(\mathcal{T}_P))$ nodes. The second term is bounded by $O(k \cdot \text{depth}(\mathcal{T}_P))$, because the regions of the nodes in $N(Q)$ are disjoint which implies that a segment will be short at at most two such nodes (one for each endpoint).

Adding up the bounds for the first and the second category, we get the desired bound. $\qquad\square$

A bound on the number of visited nodes does not directly give a bound on the query time, because at a node ν we have to test whether Q intersects the regions associated with the children of ν. These regions are not stored at the nodes and, moreover, they need not have constant complexity.

In the application we consider in this paper, however, all regions have constant complexity. In this case one can simply maintain the regions region(ν) of the visited nodes, and so for constant-complexity query ranges the query time will be linear in the number of visited nodes.

3.1   Application to Approximate Range Searching

Several of the known data structures for range searching in point sets are actually BSP trees. For example, if we use the partition tree of Haussler en Welzl [16] as underlying structure we can get a BSP on a set of n disjoint line segments whose query time is $O(n^{2/3+\varepsilon} + k \log n)$. Here we focus on the application using BAR-trees [14], as it gives good bounds for approximate range searching for line segments in the plane. The BAR-tree is a BSP tree, where all splitting lines have orientations that come from a fixed set of predefined possibilities. In the plane for a corner-cut BAR-tree e.g., the orientations that are used are horizontal, vertical, and the two diagonal directions ($45°$ and $135°$). Hence, the regions in a BAR-tree have constant complexity. This also holds for the regions we get when we transform a BAR-tree on the endpoints of a set of segments to a BSP tree for the segments; such regions can only be twice as complex as the regions in a BAR-tree.

The main strength of a BAR-tree is that it produces regions with bounded aspect ratio: the smallest enclosing circle of a region is only a constant times larger than the largest inscribed circle. This makes that a BAR-tree has excellent query time for approximate range queries—see Duncan's thesis [13] for details. In the plane one can construct BAR-trees with logarithmic depth, such that the number of leaves visited by a query with a convex query range Q is bounded by $O((1/\varepsilon) + k_\varepsilon)$.

By applying Theorem 1, we can thus obtain a BSP for segments with a query time of $O((\varepsilon^{-1} + k_\varepsilon) \log n)$. We can even extend this result to disjoint constant-complexity curves in the plane, if we allow the BSP to use splitting curves in the partitioning. For the construction algorithm to work we have to ensure that any splitting line can intersect a curve only once. We do this by cutting the curve at every point where the orientation of its tangent is one of the possible orientations of the splitting lines. These pieces are then used in the construction of $\mathcal{T}_S$. Since the curves have constant-complexity and BAR-tree splitting lines have only four possible orientations, a curve is cut at most into a constant number of pieces.

Corollary 1. *Let S be a set of n disjoint constant-complexity curves in $\mathbb{R}^2$. In $O(n \log n)$ time one can construct a BSP tree for S of size $O(n \log n)$ and depth $O(\log n)$ such that a range query with a constant-complexity convex range can be answered in time $O(\min_{\varepsilon>0}\{(1/\varepsilon) \log n + k_\varepsilon \log n\})$, where k_ε is the number of curves intersecting the extended query range Q_ε.*

4   BSPs for Low-Density Scenes

Let S be a set of n objects in $\mathbb{R}^d$. For an object o, we use $\rho(o)$ to denote the radius of the smallest enclosing ball of o. Recall from the introduction that the *density* of a set S is the smallest number λ such that the following holds: any ball B is intersected by at most λ objects $o \in S$ with $\rho(o) \geqslant \rho(B)$ [11]. If S has density λ, we call S a λ-low-density scene. In this section we show how to construct a BSP tree for S that has linear size and very good performance for approximate range searching if the density of S is constant. Our method combines ideas from de Berg [9] with the BAR-tree of Duncan *et al.* [14]. We will call this BSP an *object BAR-tree*, or oBAR-tree for short.

Our overall strategy, also used by de Berg [9], is to compute a suitable set of points that will guide the construction of the BSP tree. Unlike in [9], however, we cannot use the bounding-box vertices of the objects in S for this, because that does not work in combination with a BAR-tree. What we need is a set G of points with the following property: any cell in a BAR-tree that does not contain a point from G in its interior is intersected by at most κ objects from S, for some constant κ. We call such a set G a κ-*guarding set* [8] against BAR-tree cells, and we call the points in G *guards*.

The algorithm is as follows.

1. Construct a κ-guarding set G for S, as explained below. The construction of the guarding set is done by generating $O(1)$ guards for each object $o \in S$, so that the guards created for any subset of the objects will form a κ-guarding set for that subset. We will use object(g) to denote the object for which a guard $g \in G$ was created.
2. Create a BAR-tree $\mathcal{T}$ on the set G using the algorithm of Duncan *et al.* [14], with the following adaptation: whenever a recursive call is made with a subset $G^* \subset G$ in a region R, we delete all guards g from G^* for which object(g) does not intersect R. This pruning step, which was not needed in [9], is essential to guarantee a bound on the query time.
3. Search with each object $o \in S$ in $\mathcal{T}$ to determine which leaf cells are intersected by o. Store with each leaf the set of all intersected objects. Let $\mathcal{T}_S$ be the resulting BSP tree.

Constructing the Guarding Set. De Berg *et al.* [8] proved that any set S that has a small guarding set against hypercubes also has a small guarding set against arbitrary fat ranges. Since the bounding-box vertices of a λ-low-density scene form a λ-guarding set against hypercubes, this implies that low-density scenes admit linear-size guarding sets against fat ranges, as stated more precisely in the following lemma.

Lemma 1. [8] *Let S be a λ-low-density scene consisting of n objects in $\mathbb{R}^d$. Then there is an $O(\lambda)$-guarding set for S of size $O(n/\beta)$ against β-fat ranges.*

Since BAR-tree cells are fat, this implies there exists a guarding set for λ-low-density scenes such that any BAR-tree cell without guards in its interior intersects at most $\kappa = O(\lambda)$ objects. Unfortunately the constants in the construction are large: $\kappa = 14^d \lambda$, and the dependency on d in the size is more than $2^{3d(d-1)}$. In the full version of the paper we show that in the plane we can construct a much smaller guarding set against BAR-tree cells.

The following theorem summarizes the properties of the oBAR-tree.

Theorem 2. *Let S be a λ-low-density scene consisting of n objects in $\mathbb{R}^d$. A BSP tree $\mathcal{T}_S$ of size $O(\lambda n)$ and depth $O(\log n)$ for S can be constructed in $O(\lambda n \log n)$ time such that a query range with a convex range Q takes*

$O(\log n + \lambda \cdot \min_{\varepsilon>0}\{(1/\varepsilon) + k_\varepsilon\})$ *time, where k_ε is the number of objects intersecting the extended query range Q_ε.*

Proof. The bound on the size, depth and construction time follow almost immediately from the bounds on the BAR-tree. The proof of the query time is similar to the proof of Theorem 1. The complete proof is given in the full version of this paper.

5   Conclusions

We have presented a general method to convert a BSP $\mathcal{T}$ on the endpoints of a set of line segment into a BSP on the segments themselves, in such a way that the time for range searching queries remains almost the same and the size of the BSP is $O(n \cdot \text{depth}(\mathcal{T}))$. We used this to obtain a BSP of size $O(n \log n)$ with $O(\min_{\varepsilon>0}\{(1/\varepsilon) + k_\varepsilon\} \log n)$ query time for approximate range searching with arbitrary ranges and showed how to generalize this to curves.

We also presented a linear-size BSP for approximate range searching in low-density scenes in any dimension. Its query time is $O(\log n + \min_{\varepsilon>0}\{(1/\varepsilon^{d-1}) + k_\varepsilon\})$. Thus we obtain the same bounds as for point data, but for much more general objects. This improves the previously best known bounds for approximate range searching in $\mathbb{R}^3$ [17] by several logarithmic factors, and generalizes the results to higher dimensions as well.

Our structures are the first pure BSP structures with guarantees on the query time. This is attractive because of the simplicity of such structures, and the fact that they are quite versatile. E.g., they can easily be used for (approximate) nearest-neighbor searching, and one can readily insert new objects into the structure (although then the query time may deteriorate). Moreover, the query times for approximate range searching are quite good, and our methods are surprisingly simple. Unfortunately, some of the constants (especially in the BSP for low-density scenes) can be fairly large in theory. We expect that this bad behavior will not show up in real applications, and that our structures will be quite competitive in practice, but this still needs to be verified experimentally.

References

1. P.K. Agarwal, M. de Berg, J. Gudmundsson, M. Hammar, H.J. Haverkort, Box-trees and R-trees with near-optimal query time, Discrete Comput. Geom. 28 (2002) 291–312.
2. P.K. Agarwal and J. Erickson. Geometric range searching and its relatives. In: B. Chazelle, J. Goodman, and R. Pollack (Eds.), *Advances in Discrete and Computational Geometry*, Vol. 223 of *Contemporary Mathematics*, pages 1–56, American Mathematical Society, 1998.
3. P.K. Agarwal, E. Grove, T.M. Murali and J.S. Vitter. Binary space partitions for fat rectangles. *SIAM J. Comput.* 29:1422-1448, 2000.
4. P.K. Agarwal, T.M. Murali and J.S. Vitter. Practical techniques for constructing binary space partition for orthogonal rectangles. In *Proc. 13th ACM Symp. of Comput. Geom.*, pages 382–384, 1997.

5. P.K. Agarwal and S. Suri. Surface Approximation and Geometric Partitions. *SIAM J. Comput.* 19: 1016-1035, 1998.
6. A. Arya, D. Mount, Approximate range searching, Comput. Geom. Theory Appl. 17 (2000) 135–152.
7. C. Ballieux. Motion planning using binary space partitions. Technical Report Inf/src/93-25, Utrecht University, 1993.
8. M. de Berg, H. David, M. J. Katz, M. Overmars, A. F. van der Stappen, and J. Vleugels. Guarding scenes against invasive hypercubes. *Comput. Geom.*, 26:99–117, 2003.
9. M. de Berg. Linear size binary space partitions for uncluttered scenes. *Algorithmica* 28:353–366, 2000.
10. M. de Berg, M. de Groot, and M. Overmars. New results on binary space partitions in the plane. In *Proc. 4th Scand. Workshop Algorithm Theory*, volume 824 of *Lecture Notes Comput. Sci.*, pages 61–72. Springer-Verlag, 1994.
11. M. de Berg, M.J. Katz, A. F. van der Stappen, and J. Vleugels. Realistic input models for geometric algorithms. In *Proc. 13th Annu. ACM Sympos. Comput. Geom.*, pages 294–303, 1997.
12. N. Chin and S. Feiner. Near real time shadow generation using bsp trees. In *Proc. SIGGRAPH'89*, pages 99–106, 1989.
13. C.A. Duncan, Balanced Aspect Ratio Trees, Ph.D. Thesis, John Hopkins University, 1999.
14. C.A. Duncan, M.T. Goodrich, S.G. Kobourov, Balanced aspect ratio trees: Combining the advantages of k-d trees and octrees, In *Proc. 10th Ann. ACM-SIAM Sympos. Discrete Algorithms*, pages 300–309, 1999.
15. H. Fuchs, Z. M. Kedem, and B. Naylor. On visible surface generation by a priori tree structures. *Comput. Graph.*, 14(3):124–133, 1980. Proc. SIGGRAPH '80.
16. D. Haussler, and E. Welzl Epsilon-nets and simplex range queries *Discrete Comput. Geom.*, 2:127–151, 1987.
17. H.J. Haverkort, M. de Berg, and J. Gudmundsson. Box-Trees for Collision Checking in Industrial Installations. In *Proc. 18th ACM Symp. on Computational Geometry*, pages 53–62, 2002
18. B. Naylor, J. A. Amanatides, and W. Thibault. Merging BSP trees yields polyhedral set operations. *Comput. Graph.*, 24(4):115–124, August 1990. Proc. SIGGRAPH '90.
19. M.H. Overmars, H. Schipper, and M. Sharir. Storing line segments in partition trees. *BIT*, 30:385–403, 1990
20. M. S. Paterson and F. F. Yao. Efficient binary space partitions for hidden-surface removal and solid modeling. *Discrete Comput. Geom.*, 5:485–503, 1990.
21. M. S. Paterson and F. F. Yao. Optimal binary space partitions for orthogonal objects. *J. Algorithms*, 13:99–113, 1992.
22. F.P. Preparata and M.I. Shamos. *Computational Geometry: An Introduction.* Springer-Verlag, 1985.
23. S. J. Teller and C. H. Séquin. Visibility preprocessing for interactive walkthroughs. *Comput. Graph.*, 25(4):61–69, July 1991. Proc. SIGGRAPH '91.
24. C.D. Tóth. A Note on Binary Plane Partitions. *Discrete Comput. Geom.* 20:3–16, 2003.
25. C.D. Tóth. Binary Space Partitions for Line Segments with a Limited Number of Directions. *SIAM J. Comput.* 32:307–325, 2003.
26. W. C. Thibault and B. F. Naylor. Set operations on polyhedra using binary space partitioning trees. *Comput. Graph.*, 21(4):153–162, 1987. Proc. SIGGRAPH '87.

Representable Disjoint NP-Pairs

Olaf Beyersdorff

Institut für Informatik,
Humboldt-Universität zu Berlin,
D-10099 Berlin, Germany
beyersdo@informatik.hu-berlin.de

Abstract. We investigate the class of disjoint NP-pairs under different reductions. The structure of this class is intimately linked to the simulation order of propositional proof systems, and we make use of the relationship between propositional proof systems and theories of bounded arithmetic as the main tool of our analysis. Specifically we exhibit a pair which is complete under strong reductions for all disjoint NP-pairs representable in a theory. We use these pairs to explain the simulation order of NP-pairs under these reductions. As corollaries we also get simplified proofs of results obtained earlier in [3] and [5].

1 Introduction

Disjoint NP-pairs (DNPP) naturally occur in cryptography (cf. [4]). The investigation of disjoint NP-pairs in connection with propositional proof systems was initiated by Razborov [12] and further developed by Pudlák [11] and Köbler et al. [5]. These applications attracted more complexity theoretic research on the structure of the class of disjoint NP-pairs (cf. [2, 3, 5]). Various reductions between NP-pairs were introduced by Grollmann and Selman [4]. For the most usual form of a many-one-reduction between DNPP a polynomial time computable function is required to map the components of the two pairs to each other. We denote this reduction here by $\leq_p$. Later Köbler et al. defined in [5] a strong reduction (denoted by $\leq_s$), where additionally to $\leq_p$ the reduction function has to map the complements of the pairs to each other.

One of the most prominent questions regarding disjoint NP-pairs is whether there exist complete pairs for the class of all DNPP under these reductions. These problems remain open and various oracle results from [2] indicate that these are indeed difficult questions. Under the assumption that there is an optimal proof system, however, Razborov showed the existence of a $\leq_p$-complete pair. This was improved by Köbler et al. in [5] to the existence of a complete pair for $\leq_s$.

Razborov associates to a proof system a canonical disjoint NP-pair and uses the relationship between theories of bounded arithmetic and propositional proof systems for his investigation. In this paper we define another canonical pair for a proof system which plays the same role for the stronger $\leq_s$-reduction as Razborov's pair for $\leq_p$. We show that these canonical pairs are quite typical for the class of all DNPP in the sense that every DNPP is $\leq_s$-reducible to such a

K. Lodaya and M. Mahajan (Eds.): FSTTCS 2004, LNCS 3328, pp. 122–134, 2004.

canonical pair, and if there exists a $\leq_s$-complete pair then it is equivalent to a canonical pair. As one consequence we obtain that, while $\leq_p$ and $\leq_s$ are generally different, the existence of a $\leq_p$-complete pair already implies the existence of a $\leq_s$-complete pair. This was also observed by Glaßer et al. in [3] using direct arguments where no reference to proof systems is made.

In this paper, however, we aim to explain some facts about the structure of disjoint NP-pairs by using the close relationship between NP-pairs, proof systems and bounded arithmetic. This also considerably simplifies proofs of earlier results in [3] and [5] which were originally shown by more involved simulation techniques.

Pursuing the afore mentioned goal we start in Sect. 2 by reviewing relevant facts about the connection between propositional proof systems and bounded arithmetic. We only give a very brief presentation tailored to our applications in later sections and refer the reader to [6] or [10] for a detailed account of this rich relationship.

In Sect. 3 we define and separate the afore mentioned reductions between NP-pairs.

In Sect. 4 we start to explain the relationship between disjoint NP-pairs and propositional proof systems by restricting the class of all DNPP to the DNPP representable in some theory T of bounded arithmetic, where a DNPP is called representable in T if the disjointness of the pair is provable in the theory T. We present a $\leq_s$-complete pair for all DNPP representable in sufficiently strong theories. To make the paper self contained we also reprove some known results.

In Sect. 5 we show that if $\leq_s$-complete pairs exist then these are equivalent to a canonical pair from Sect. 4 and derive some consequences on the relationship between the simulation order of proof systems and the class of DNPP.

In Sect. 6 we discuss separators and Turing reductions. We show that our pairs from Sect. 4 are candidates for NP-pairs which can not be separated by sets from P, and that the class of all DNPP representable in some theory T is closed under smart Turing-reductions implying that even the existence of smart Turing-complete pairs suffices for the existence of $\leq_s$-complete DNPP which is also shown in [3].

2   Preliminaries

Propositional proof systems were defined in a very general way by Cook and Reckhow in [1] as polynomial time functions P which have as its range the set of all tautologies. A string π with $P(\pi) = \varphi$ is called a P-proof of the tautology φ. By $P \vdash_{\leq m} \varphi$ we indicate that there is a P-proof of φ of length $\leq m$. If φ_n is a sequence of propositional formulas we write $P \vdash_* \varphi_n$ if there is a polynomial p such that $P \vdash_{\leq p(|\varphi_n|)} \varphi_n$.

Given two proof systems P and S we say that S simulates P (denoted by $P \leq S$) if there exists a polynomial p such that for all tautologies φ and P-proofs π of φ there is a S-proof π' of φ with $|\pi'| \leq p(|\pi|)$. If such a proof π' can even be computed from π in polynomial time we say that S p-simulates P and denote this by $P \leq_p S$. A proof system is called (p-)optimal if it (p-)simulates all proof systems.

In this paper we are only concerned with sufficiently strong proof systems simulating the extended Frege proof system EF, where EF is a usual textbook proof system based on axioms and rules and augmented by the possibility to abbreviate complex formulas by propositional variables to reduce the proof size (see e.g. [6]). For simplicity we call proof systems simulating EF strong. A method how to actually construct strong proof systems was recently described in [7].

We now review the relationship between theories of arithmetic and proof systems. Let L be the language of arithmetic (cf. [6]). Bounded L-formulas are formulas in the language of L where only quantifiers of the form $(\forall x \leq t(y))$ and $(\exists x \leq s(y))$ occur with L-terms t and s. In the following we are particularly interested in Π_1^b and Σ_1^b-formulas where only bounded universal and bounded existential quantifiers are allowed, respectively.

To explain the connection to propositional proof systems we have to translate L-formulas into propositional formulas. Let $\varphi(x)$ be a Π_1^b-formula. We can assume that φ is of the form $(\forall y) |y| \leq |x|^k \to \psi(x, y)$ with some polynomial time computable predicate ψ. Hence we can compute $\psi(x, y)$ by polynomial size boolean circuits C_n for numbers x of length n. From C_n we build a propositional formula $\|\varphi\|^n$ with atoms $p_1, \ldots, p_n$ for the bits of x, atoms $q_1, \ldots, q_{n^k}$ for the bits of y and auxiliary atoms $r_1, \ldots, r_{n^{O(1)}}$ for the inner nodes of C_n. The formula $\|\varphi\|^n$ describes that if the values for $\bar{r}$ are correctly computed from $\bar{p}$ and $\bar{q}$ then the output of the computation of C_n is 1. Thus we get a sequence of propositional formulas $\|\varphi\|^n$ of polynomial size in n and $\|\varphi\|^n$ is a tautology iff $\varphi(x)$ holds for all natural numbers of length $\leq n$.

Encoding propositional formulas as numbers in some straightforward way we can in a theory T speak of propositional formulas, assignments and proofs. Let $\text{Prf}_P(\pi, \varphi)$ be a L-formula describing that π is the encoding of a correct P-proof of the propositional formula encoded by φ. Similarly, let $\text{Taut}(\varphi)$ be a L-formula asserting that all assignments satisfy the formula φ. Because P is computable in polynomial time Prf_P is definable by a Σ_1^b-formula whereas Taut is in Π_1^b.

The reflection principle for a propositional proof system P is the L-formula

$$\text{RFN}(P) = (\forall \pi)(\forall \varphi)\text{Prf}_P(\pi, \varphi) \to \text{Taut}(\varphi)$$

and states a strong form of the consistency of the proof system P. From the last remark it follows that $\text{RFN}(P)$ is a $\forall \Pi_1^b$-formula.

In [8] a general correspondence between L-theories T and propositional proof systems P is introduced. Pairs (T, P) from this correspondence possess in particular the following two properties:

1. For all $\varphi(x) \in \Pi_1^b$ with $T \vdash (\forall x)\varphi(x)$ we have polynomially long P-proofs of the tautologies $\|\varphi(x)\|^n$.
2. T proves the correctness of P, i.e. $T \vdash \text{RFN}(P)$. Furthermore P is the strongest proof system for which T proves the correctness, i.e. $T \vdash \text{RFN}(S)$ for a proof system S implies $S \leq_p P$.

The most prominent example for this correspondence is the pair (S_2^1, EF) where S_2^1 is a L-theory with induction for Σ_1^b-formulas. This in particular allows the formalization of polynomial time computations and the provability of its basic properties (see e.g. [6] Chapter 6).

To every L-theory $T \supseteq S_2^1$ with a polynomial time set of axioms we can associate a proof system P which is unique up to $\leq_p$-equivalence by property 2 above. Conversely every strong proof system has a corresponding theory, but here according to property 1 only the $\forall \Pi_1^b$-consequences of T are determined by P.

As the correspondence only works for sufficiently strong proof systems we will restrict ourselves to proof systems $P \geq EF$ and theories $T \supseteq S_2^1$.

By $\mathcal{N}$ we denote the standard model of arithmetic which is in particular a submodel of all models of theories T considered here.

3   Reductions Between NP-Pairs

A pair (A, B) is called a disjoint NP-pair (DNPP), if $A, B \in$ NP and $A \cap B = \emptyset$. To exclude trivial cases we additionally require $A \neq \emptyset$ and $B \neq \emptyset$. We consider the following reductions between disjoint NP-pairs.

Definition 1. *Let (A, B) and (C, D) be DNPP.*

1. *(A, B) is polynomially reducible to (C, D) ($(A, B) \leq_p (C, D)$), if there exists a function $f \in FP$ such that $f(A) \subseteq C$ and $f(B) \subseteq D$.*
2. *(A, B) is strongly reducible to (C, D) ($(A, B) \leq_s (C, D)$), if there exists a function $f \in FP$ such that $f^{-1}(C) = A$ and $f^{-1}(D) = B$.*
3. *As usual we write $(A, B) \equiv_p (C, D)$ for $(A, B) \leq_p (C, D)$ and $(C, D) \leq_p (A, B)$. $\equiv_s$ is defined in the same way.*

$(A, B) \leq_p (C, D)$ does not in general imply that A and B are reducible to C and D, respectively, but if f realizes a $\leq_s$-reduction from (A, B) to (C, D), then f is simultaneously a many-one-reduction between A and C as well as between B and D. Equivalently we can also view $\leq_s$ as a reduction between triples. In addition to the two conditions $f(A) \subseteq C$ and $f(B) \subseteq D$ for $\leq_p$ we also require $f(\overline{A \cup B}) \subseteq \overline{C \cup D}$.

Obviously $\leq_s$ is a refinement of $\leq_p$. Under the assumption P $\neq$ NP this is indeed a proper refinement. The reason for this lies in the following proposition:

Proposition 2. *For every DNPP (A, B) there exists a DNPP (A', B') such that $(A, B) \equiv_p (A', B')$ and A', B' are NP-complete.*

Proof. Choose $A' = A \times$ SAT and $B' = B \times$ SAT. Then we have $(A, B) \leq_p (A', B')$ via $x \mapsto (x, \varphi_0)$ with a fixed formula $\varphi_0 \in$ SAT, and $(A', B') \leq_p (A, B)$ via the projection $(x, \varphi) \mapsto x$. $\square$

With this proposition we can easily separate the reductions $\leq_p$ and $\leq_s$ under the assumption P $\neq$ NP. Namely, let A and B be nonempty sets in P such that $\overline{A \cup B}$ is also nonempty. Choose A' and B' as in the last proposition. Then $(A, B) \equiv_p (A', B')$ but $(A, B) \not\equiv_s (A', B')$ because $(A', B') \leq_s (A, B)$ would imply in particular $A' \leq_m^p A$ and hence P=NP. On the other hand if P=NP then all DNPP (A, B) where all three components $A, B, \overline{A \cup B}$ are nonempty would be $\leq_s$-equivalent. This equivalence of P $\neq$ NP and the separation of $\leq_p$ from $\leq_s$ for DNPP with all three components nonempty (or equivalently for DNPP with all three components infinite) is also observed in [3].

4   Representable NP-Pairs

In the following we investigate the relationship between disjoint NP-pairs and propositional proof systems. We will use the correspondence between proof systems and arithmetical theories as explained in Sect. 2. For this section let P be a strong proof system and T be a corresponding theory.

Following Razborov we call a Σ_1^b-formula φ a representation of an NP-set A, if for all natural numbers a

$$\mathcal{N} \models \varphi(a) \iff a \in A .$$

A DNPP (A, B) is representable in T, if there are Σ_1^b-formulas φ and ψ representing A and B, respectively, such that

$$T \vdash (\forall x)(\neg\varphi(x) \vee \neg\psi(x)) .$$

For the last line we also use the abbreviation $T \vdash A \cap B = \emptyset$. Since $A \cap B = \emptyset$ is a $\forall \Pi_1^b$-formula we can also express the disjointness of A and B propositionally by the sequence of tautologies $\|\neg\varphi(x) \vee \neg\psi(x)\|^n$, which we again shortly denote by $\|A \cap B = \emptyset\|^n$.

The DNPP representable in T can also be characterized via the corresponding proof system P in the following way:

Proposition 3. *A DNPP (A, B) is representable in T if and only if*

$$P \vdash_* \|A \cap B = \emptyset\|^n$$

for suitable representations of A and B.

Proof. Let φ and ψ be representations for A and B, respectively, such that

$$T \vdash (\forall x)(\neg\varphi(x) \vee \neg\psi(x)) .$$

Because this is a $\forall \Pi_1^b$-formula, we have $P \vdash_* \|\neg\varphi(x) \vee \neg\psi(x)\|^n$, which we write by definition as $P \vdash_* \|A \cap B = \emptyset\|^n$.

For the other direction let φ and ψ be representations of A and B, such that for some natural number k we have $P \vdash_{\leq n^k} \|\neg\varphi(x) \vee \neg\psi(x)\|^n$. Consider the formula

$$\psi'(x) = \psi(x) \wedge (\exists \pi)|\pi| \leq |x|^k \wedge \mathrm{Prf}_P(\pi, \|\neg\varphi(y) \vee \neg\psi(y)\|^{|x|}) .$$

We have $\psi' \in \Sigma_1^b$ and furthermore $\mathcal{N} \models (\forall x)\psi'(x) \leftrightarrow \psi(x)$, i.e. ψ' is also a representation of B. From $T \vdash \text{RFN}(P)$ it follows that $T \vdash (\forall x)(\neg\varphi(x) \vee \neg\psi'(x))$, hence (A, B) is representable in T. $\square$

The next lemma shows that all pairs representable in a theory form a reasonable complexity class.

Lemma 4 (Razborov [12]). *The set of all DNPP representable in T is closed under $\leq_p$-reductions.*

Proof. Let (A, B) and (C, D) be DNPP such that $f : (A, B) \leq_p (C, D)$ and $T \vdash C \cap D = \emptyset$. Consider the NP-sets

$$A' = \{x \mid x \in A \text{ and } f(x) \in C\}$$
$$B' = \{x \mid x \in B \text{ and } f(x) \in D\} .$$

Obviously $A = A'$ and $B = B'$. From $T \supseteq S_2^1$ and $f \in FP$ we get $T \vdash (\forall x)(\exists! y) f(x) = y$. Hence

$$T \vdash (\forall x)(x \in A' \cap B' \rightarrow f(x) \in C \cap D)$$

and with $T \vdash C \cap D = \emptyset$ we conclude $T \vdash A' \cap B' = \emptyset$. $\square$

Following Razborov [12] we associate a disjoint NP-pair $(\text{Ref}(P), \text{SAT}^*)$ with a proof system P with

$$\text{Ref}(P) = \{(\varphi, 1^m) \mid P \vdash_{\leq m} \varphi\}$$
$$\text{SAT}^* = \{(\varphi, 1^m) \mid \neg\varphi \in \text{SAT}\} .$$

$(\text{Ref}(P), \text{SAT}^*)$ is called the canonical pair of P.

Lemma 5 (Razborov [12]). *The canonical pair of P is representable in T.*

Proof. We argue in T. Let $(\varphi, 1^m) \in \text{Ref}(P)$. Then there is a P-proof π of φ. Since $\text{RFN}(P)$ is available in T we conclude from $\text{Prf}_P(\pi, \varphi)$ the formula $\text{Taut}(\varphi)$, hence $\neg\varphi \notin \text{SAT}$ and therefore $(\varphi, 1^m) \notin \text{SAT}^*$. $\square$

Now we associate a second disjoint NP-pair with a proof system P. For a propositional formula φ let $\text{Var}(\varphi)$ be the set of propositional variables occurring in φ. Let

$$U_1(P) = \{(\varphi, \psi, 1^m) \mid \text{Var}(\varphi) \cap \text{Var}(\psi) = \emptyset, \ \neg\varphi \in \text{SAT and } P \vdash_{\leq m} \varphi \vee \psi\}$$
$$U_2 = \{(\varphi, \psi, 1^m) \mid \text{Var}(\varphi) \cap \text{Var}(\psi) = \emptyset \text{ and } \neg\psi \in \text{SAT}\} .$$

As for the canonical pair we get:

Lemma 6. *The pair $(U_1(P), U_2)$ is representable in T.*

Proof. Let $(\varphi, \psi, 1^m) \in U_1(P)$ and π be a P-proof of $\varphi \vee \psi$ of length $\leq m$. Because $\neg\varphi \in \text{SAT}$ we have an assignment α with $\varphi(\alpha) = 0$. If we substitute the variables of φ by 0 or 1 according to α, we get from the proof π a proof π' of ψ. Hence we have $T \vdash (\exists \pi') \text{Prf}_P(\pi', \psi)$. Because T proves the correctness of P, we get $T \vdash \text{Taut}(\psi)$ and thus $T \vdash (\varphi, \psi, 1^m) \notin U_2$. $\square$

Now we come to the main theorem of this section which states the completeness of $(U_1(P), U_2)$ for all DNPP representable in T under $\leq_s$-reductions.

Theorem 7. *A DNPP (A, B) is representable in T if and only if $(A, B) \leq_s (U_1(P), U_2)$.*

Proof. Let (A, B) be a DNPP such that $T \vdash A \cap B = \emptyset$. Let the NP-sets A and B be of the form

$$A = \{x \mid (\exists y)|y| \leq |x|^{O(1)} \wedge (x, y) \in C\}$$
$$B = \{x \mid (\exists z)|z| \leq |x|^{O(1)} \wedge (x, z) \in D\}$$

with polynomial time predicates C and D. Because of the correspondence between T and P there is a polynomial p for the $\forall \Pi_1^b$-formula $A \cap B = \emptyset$ such that

$$P \vdash_{\leq p(n)} \|A \cap B = \emptyset\|^n .$$

Here the formula $\|A \cap B = \emptyset\|^n$ is more explicitly $\|(x, y) \notin C \vee (x, z) \notin D\|^n$ and has propositional variables for x, y and z and auxiliary variables for the computation of boolean circuits for C and D. We can plug into this formula natural numbers a of length n for x by substituting the propositional variables corresponding to x by the bits of a. We indicate this by the suffix (x/a).

Now we claim that the function

$$f(a) = (\|(x, y) \notin C\|^{|a|}(x/a), \|(x, z) \notin D\|^{|a|}(x/a), 1^{p(|a|)})$$

realizes a $\leq_s$-reduction from (A, B) to $(U_1(P), U_2)$.

If we choose different auxiliary variables for the computation of C and D and also disjoint variables for y and z, then the formulas $\|(x, y) \notin C\|^{|a|}(x/a)$ and $\|(x, z) \notin D\|^{|a|}(x/a)$ have no common variables. Furthermore for every natural number a the formulas

$$\|(x, y) \notin C\|^{|a|}(x/a) \vee \|(x, z) \notin D\|^{|a|}(x/a) =$$
$$\|(x, y) \notin C \vee (x, z) \notin D\|^{|a|}(x/a) \quad =$$
$$\|A \cap B = \emptyset\|^{|a|}(x/a)$$

have P-proofs of length $\leq p(|a|)$, which we get from the P-proofs of $\|A \cap B = \emptyset\|^{|a|}$ by substituting the variables for x by the bits of a.

The last thing to check is that the formula

$$\neg\|(x, y) \notin C\|^{|a|} = \|(x, y) \in C\|^{|a|},$$

expressing, that there is a correct accepting computation of C with input (x, y), is satisfiable if and only if the variables of x are substituted by the bits of a number $a \in A$.

Similarly, $\neg\|(x, z) \notin D\|^{|a|}(x/a)$ is satisfiable if and only if $a \in B$.

The backward implication follows from Lemma 6 and the fact, that the DNPP representable in T are closed under $\leq_p$ and hence also under $\leq_s$ according to Lemma 4. $\square$

The pair $(U_1(P), U_2)$ strongly resembles the interpolation pair defined by Pudlák in [11]:

$$I_P^0 = \{(\varphi, \psi, \pi) \mid P(\pi) = \varphi \vee \psi, \, \mathrm{Var}(\varphi) \cap \mathrm{Var}(\psi) = \emptyset \text{ and } \neg\varphi \in \mathrm{SAT}\}$$
$$I_P^1 = \{(\varphi, \psi, \pi) \mid P(\pi) = \varphi \vee \psi, \, \mathrm{Var}(\varphi) \cap \mathrm{Var}(\psi) = \emptyset \text{ and } \neg\psi \in \mathrm{SAT}\} \ .$$

This pair is p-separable, if and only if the proof system P has the efficient interpolation property. For $\|.\|$-translations of $\forall\Pi_1^b$-formulas provable in T we can efficiently construct polynomially long P-proofs (i.e. with functions from FP). Hence the proof of the last theorem also shows the $\leq_s$-completeness of (I_P^0, I_P^1) for all DNPP representable in T.

In [11] Pudlák defined a DNPP (A, B) to be symmetric if $(B, A) \leq (A, B)$. With Lemma 6 also the pair $(U_2, U_1(P))$ is representable in T, hence by the last theorem $(U_1(P), U_2)$ is symmetric even with respect to the stronger $\leq_s$-reduction.

As a corollary of Theorem 7 we obtain the $\leq_p$-completeness of the canonical pair for all DNPP representable in T, which was shown by Razborov:

Theorem 8 (Razborov [12]). *A DNPP (A, B) is representable in T if and only if $(A, B) \leq_p (\mathrm{Ref}(P), \mathrm{SAT}^*)$.*

Proof. For the forward implication we reduce $(U_1(P), U_2)$ to $(\mathrm{Ref}(P), \mathrm{SAT}^*)$ via the projection

$$(\varphi, \psi, 1^m) \mapsto (\psi, 1^{m+p(|\varphi|)})$$

with a suitable polynomial p.

Let $(\varphi, \psi, 1^m) \in U_1(P)$. Then there is a P-proof π of length $\leq m$ of $\varphi(\bar{x}) \vee \psi(\bar{y})$. The formula $\neg\varphi(\bar{x})$ is satisfiable, so by substituting a satisfying assignment $\bar{a}$ into the proof π we get a proof π' with $|\pi'| \leq m$ for $\varphi(\bar{a}) \vee \psi(\bar{y})$. Since $\varphi(\bar{a})$ is a false formula without free variables we can evaluate it in polynomially long P-proofs to $\bot$. Let p be a corresponding polynomial. Thus we get a P-proof of length $\leq m + p(|\varphi|)$ for ψ.

If $(\varphi, \psi, 1^m) \in U_2$, then $\neg\psi$ is satisfiable and hence $(\psi, 1^{m+p(|\varphi|)}) \in \mathrm{SAT}^*$.

This $\leq_p$-reduction from $(U_1(P), U_2)$ to $(\mathrm{Ref}(P), \mathrm{SAT}^*)$ yields together with the last theorem the $\leq_p$-completeness of $(\mathrm{Ref}(P), \mathrm{SAT}^*)$ for all DNPP representable in T.

The backward implication follows from Lemma 4 and Lemma 5.   □

Thus the pairs $(\mathrm{Ref}(P), \mathrm{SAT}^*)$ and $(U_1(P), U_2)$ are complete for all DNPP representable in T under $\leq_p$- and $\leq_s$-reductions, respectively.

5   NP-Pairs and the Simulation Order of Proof Systems

Now we use the results of the last section to make some observations about the connection between the simulation order of proof systems and disjoint NP-pairs.

In Sect. 3 it was shown that the reductions $\leq_p$ and $\leq_s$ are different under the assumption P $\neq$ NP. Still we have:

Proposition 9. *For all strong proof systems P and DNPP (A, B) it holds*

$$(A, B) \leq_p (U_1(P), U_2) \iff (A, B) \leq_s (U_1(P), U_2) .$$

Proof. Let $(A, B) \leq_p (U_1(P), U_2)$. $(U_1(P), U_2)$ is representable in T. Hence with Lemma 4 also (A, B) is representable in T, from which we conclude with Theorem 7 $(A, B) \leq_s (U_1(P), U_2)$.

The opposite implication follows by definition. ☐

Corollary 10. *Let P and S be strong proof systems. Then we have:*

$$(\mathrm{Ref}(P), \mathrm{SAT}^*) \leq_p (\mathrm{Ref}(S), \mathrm{SAT}^*) \iff (U_1(P), U_2) \leq_s (U_1(S), U_2) .$$

Proof. For the first direction we get from

$$(U_1(P), U_2) \leq_p (\mathrm{Ref}(P), \mathrm{SAT}^*) \leq_p (\mathrm{Ref}(S), \mathrm{SAT}^*) \leq_p (U_1(S), U_2)$$

together with the last proposition $(U_1(P), U_2) \leq_s (U_1(S), U_2)$.

The other implication follows from

$$(\mathrm{Ref}(P), \mathrm{SAT}^*) \leq_p (U_1(P), U_2) \leq_p (U_1(S), U_2) \leq_p (\mathrm{Ref}(S), \mathrm{SAT}^*) .$$

☐

The following proposition is well known (see e.g. [11]):

Proposition 11. *If P and S are proof systems with $P \leq S$, then we have*

$$(\mathrm{Ref}(P), \mathrm{SAT}^*) \leq_p (\mathrm{Ref}(S), \mathrm{SAT}^*) .$$

Proof. By assumption there is a polynomial p, such that for all formulas φ and P-proofs π of φ there is a S-proof π' of length $\leq p(|\pi|)$. Therefore the mapping

$$(\varphi, 1^m) \mapsto (\varphi, 1^{p(m)})$$

is a $\leq_p$-reduction from $(\mathrm{Ref}(P), \mathrm{SAT}^*)$ to $(\mathrm{Ref}(S), \mathrm{SAT}^*)$. ☐

Proposition 11 and Corollary 10 yield:

Corollary 12. *If P and S are strong proof systems with $P \leq S$, then we have*

$$(U_1(P), U_2) \leq_s (U_1(S), U_2) .$$

Köbler, Messner and Torán proved in [5] that the existence of an optimal proof system implies the existence of $\leq_s$-complete NP-pairs. This result also follows from the last corollary. Additionally we can exhibit a complete DNPP in this case:

Corollary 13. *If P is an optimal proof system, then $(U_1(P), U_2)$ is $\leq_s$-complete for the class of all DNPP.*

Proof. Let P be an optimal proof system and (A, B) a DNPP. The sequence of tautologies $\|A \cap B = \emptyset\|^n$ can be constructed in polynomial time. Hence there is a proof system S with polynomially long proofs of these tautologies (for example just add these tautologies as axioms to the extended Frege system). Using Proposition 3 and Theorem 7 we get $(A, B) \leq_s (U_1(S), U_2)$. By assumption we have $S \leq P$. Together with the previous corollary this yields $(U_1(S), U_2) \leq_s (U_1(P), U_2)$, and hence $(A, B) \leq_s (U_1(P), U_2)$.

Therefore the pair $(U_1(P), U_2)$ is $\leq_s$-complete for all DNPP.   □

Proposition 14. *Let (A, B) be $\leq_p$-complete for the class of all DNPP. Then we have $(A, B) \equiv_p (\mathrm{Ref}(P), \mathrm{SAT}^*)$ for some proof system P.*

Proof. As in the last proof let P be a proof system with $P \vdash_* \|A \cap B = \emptyset\|^n$. Then $(A, B) \leq_p (\mathrm{Ref}(P), \mathrm{SAT}^*)$ and by assumption $(\mathrm{Ref}(P), \mathrm{SAT}^*) \leq_p (A, B)$.   □

In the same way we get:

Proposition 15. *Let (A, B) be $\leq_s$-complete for the class of all DNPP. Then we have $(A, B) \equiv_s (U_1(P), U_2)$ for some proof system P.*

The following proposition is also observed in [3]:

Proposition 16. *The class of all DNPP contains a $\leq_p$-complete DNPP if and only if it contains a $\leq_s$-complete DNPP.*

Proof. For the first direction we can assume with Proposition 14 that the $\leq_p$-complete DNPP has the form $(\mathrm{Ref}(P), \mathrm{SAT}^*)$ for some proof system P. Then by Theorem 7 and Theorem 8 all DNPP are $\leq_s$-reducible to $(U_1(P), U_2)$.

The other direction holds by definition.   □

6   Separators and Turing Reductions

For disjoint NP-pairs we can also study Turing reductions as defined by Grollmann and Selman in [4]. For this we need the notion of a separator.

Definition 17. *A set S is a separator for the DNPP (A, B) if $A \subseteq S$ and $B \subseteq \overline{S}$.*

Of central interest is the case where a given DNPP has a separator belonging to P. Such a pair is called p-separable. The set of all p-separable DNPP form the lowest degree with respect to the $\leq_p$-reduction. For the stronger $\leq_s$-reduction this minimal degree shrinks to the set of all p-separable pairs with empty complement, i.e. sets of the form $(A, \overline{A})$ with $A \in$ P. But also the set of all p-separable pairs with nonempty complement splits into different $\equiv_s$-degrees. Namely, if (A, B) is a p-separable DNPP then the pair $(A \times \mathrm{SAT}, B \times \mathrm{SAT})$ is also p-separable and both of its components are NP-complete, hence we have:

Proposition 18. $P \neq NP$ *iff there exist p-separable pairs* (A, B) *and* (C, D), *such that* $\overline{A \cup B}$ *and* $\overline{C \cup D}$ *are nonempty and* $(A, B) \not\equiv_s (C, D)$.

The question whether p-inseparable pairs exist is open. Candidates for p-inseparable pairs come from cryptography (cf. [4]) and proof systems. Namely, Krajíček and Pudlák demonstrate in [9] that a pair (A_0, A_1) associated with the RSA-cryptosystem is representable in the theory S_2^1 corresponding to EF. By the results from Sect. 4 this means that $(A_0, A_1) \leq_p (\mathrm{Ref}(EF), \mathrm{SAT}^*)$ and $(A_0, A_1) \leq_s (U_1(EF), U_2)$. Assuming the security of RSA the pair (A_0, A_1) is not p-separable, hence under this assumption neither $(\mathrm{Ref}(P), \mathrm{SAT}^*)$ nor $(U_1(P), U_2)$ is p-separable for any $P \geq EF$.

If we look at the property of symmetry of pairs under $\leq_s$ it is clear that a DNPP (A, B) can not be symmetric if we choose A from P and B NP-complete. In other words:

Proposition 19. $P \neq NP$ *iff there exist non-symmetric pairs with respect to* $\leq_s$.

A similar result for $\leq_p$ is not known as $\leq_p$-non-symmetric pairs are p-inseparable and it is not clear how to derive the existence of p-inseparable pairs from the assumption $P \neq NP$.

We now come to the definition of Turing-reductions between DNPP from [4]:

Definition 20. *Let* (A, B) *and* (C, D) *be DNPP.* (A, B) *is Turing reducible to* (C, D) $((A, B) \leq_T (C, D))$, *if there exists a polynomial time oracle Turing machine* M *such that for every separator* T *of* (C, D) $L(M^T)$ *separates* (A, B).

If for inputs from $A \cup B$ *the machine* M *makes only queries to* $C \cup D$ *we call the reduction performed by* M *a smart Turing reduction.*

In [3] Glaßer et al. prove that the existence of a complete DNPP under smart Turing reductions already implies the existence of a $\leq_p$-complete DNPP (and hence by Proposition 16 also of a $\leq_s$-complete pair). We can easily reprove their result in our framework by noticing:

Lemma 21. *The set of all DNPP representable in a theory* T *is closed under smart Turing reductions.*

Proof. Let the pair (A, B) be smartly Turing reducible to (C, D) via the deterministic oracle Turing machine M, and let (C, D) be representable in T. Consider the NP-sets

$$A' = \{x \mid x \in A \text{ and } M(x) \text{ accepts}\}$$
$$B' = \{x \mid x \in B \text{ and } M(x) \text{ rejects}\} \ .$$

By "$M(x)$ accepts" we mean that M accepts the input x by a computation where all oracle queries that are positively answered are verified by a computation of a nondeterministic machine for C and all negative answers are verified by D. Since the reduction is smart we have $A = A'$ and $B = B'$. For $T \vdash A' \cap B' = \emptyset$

it suffices to show in T the uniqueness of the computation of M at inputs x from $A \cup B$. T can prove the uniqueness of computations of the deterministic machine M, and the possibility to answer an oracle query both positively and negatively is excluded by $T \vdash C \cap D = \emptyset$. □

From this we conclude:

Proposition 22. *Suppose* (A, B) *is a smart* $\leq_T$*-complete pair. Then for any theory* T *such that* $T \vdash A \cap B = \emptyset$ *the pair* $(U_1(P), U_2)$ *is* $\leq_s$*-complete for all DNPP where* P *is the proof system corresponding to* T.

Proof. Choose a theory T with $T \vdash A \cap B = \emptyset$. Then by the last lemma all DNPP are representable in T and hence by Theorem 7 the pair $(U_1(P), U_2)$ is $\leq_s$-complete. □

It is not clear whether the class of pairs representable in some theory T is also closed under $\leq_T$-reductions. This corresponds to the open problem from [3] whether the existence of a $\leq_T$-complete pair implies the existence of a $\leq_p$-complete DNPP.

Acknowledgments. For helpful conversations and suggestions on this work I am very grateful to Johannes Köbler, Jan Krajíček, and Pavel Pudlák.

References

1. S. Cook and R. Reckhow. The relative efficiency of propositional proof systems. *Journal of Symbolic Logic* **44**:36-50, 1979.
2. C. Glaßer, A. Selman, S. Sengupta, and L. Zhang. Disjoint NP-pairs. In *Proceedings 18th Annual IEEE Conference on Computational Complexity*, pages 313-332, 2003.
3. C. Glaßer, A. Selman, and S. Sengupta. Reductions between disjoint NP-pairs. In *Proceedings 19th Annual IEEE Conference on Computational Complexity*, 2004.
4. J. Grollmann and A. Selman. Complexity measures for public-key cryptosystems. *SIAM Journal on Computing* **17(2)**:309-335, 1988.
5. J. Köbler, J. Messner, and J. Torán. Optimal proof systems imply complete sets for promise classes. *Information and Computation* **184**:71-92, 2003.
6. J. Krajíček. *Bounded Arithmetic, Propositional Logic, and Complexity Theory.* Encyclopedia of Mathematics and Its Applications, volume **60**, Cambridge University Press, Cambridge, 1995.
7. J. Krajíček. Implicit proofs. *Journal of Symbolic Logic* **69(2)**:387-397, 2004.
8. J. Krajíček and P. Pudlák. Quantified propositional calculi and fragments of bounded arithmetic. *Zeitschr. f. math. Logik und Grundlagen d. Math.* **36**:29-46, 1990.
9. J. Krajíček and P. Pudlák. Some consequences of cryptographical conjectures for S_2^1 and EF. *Information and Computation* **140(1)**:82-94, 1998.
10. P. Pudlák. The lengths of proofs. In *Handbook of Proof Theory*, S. R. Buss ed., pages 547-637, Elsevier, Amsterdam, 1998.

11. P. Pudlák. On reducibility and symmetry of disjoint NP-pairs. In *Proceedings 26th International Symposium on Mathematical Foundations of Computer Science*, volume 2136 of *Lecture Notes in Computer Science*, pages 621-632. Springer-Verlag, Berlin, 2001.
12. A. A. Razborov. On provably disjoint NP-pairs. Technical Report TR94-006, Electronic Colloquium on Computational Complexity, 1994.

Symbolic Reachability Analysis of Higher-Order Context-Free Processes

Ahmed Bouajjani and Antoine Meyer

LIAFA, Univ. of Paris 7, Case 7014, 2 place Jussieu 75251,
Paris Cedex 5, France
{abou, ameyer}@liafa.jussieu.fr

Abstract. We consider the problem of symbolic reachability analysis of higher-order context-free processes. These models are generalizations of the context-free processes (also called BPA processes) where each process manipulates a data structure which can be seen as a nested stack of stacks. Our main result is that, for any higher-order context-free process, the set of all predecessors of a given regular set of configurations is regular and effectively constructible. This result generalizes the analogous result which is known for level 1 context-free processes. We show that this result holds also in the case of backward reachability analysis under a regular constraint on configurations. As a corollary, we obtain a symbolic model checking algorithm for the temporal logic $E(U, X)$ with regular atomic predicates, i.e., the fragment of CTL restricted to the EU and EX modalities.

1 Introduction

Pushdown systems and their related decision and algorithmic analysis problems (reachability analysis, model checking, games solving and control synthesis, etc) have been widely investigated in the last few years [11, 7, 22, 5, 15, 8, 2]. This recent intensive research effort is mainly motivated by the fact that pushdown systems are quite natural models for sequential programs with recursive procedure calls (see e.g., [16, 14]), and therefore they are particularly relevant for software verification and design.

Higher-order pushdown systems [13] (HPDS) are generalizations of these models in which the elements appearing in a pushdown stack are no longer single letters but stacks themselves. We call this kind of nested stack structures *higher-order stores*. Stores of level 1 are sequences of symbols in some finite alphabet (those are standard pushdown stacks), and stores of level $n + 1$ are sequences of stores of level n, for any $n > 1$. The operations allowed on these structures are (1) the usual *push* and *pop* operations on the top-most level 1 store, (2) higher-order *push* and *pop* operations allowing to *duplicate* or *erase* the top-most level k store of any given level $k \leq n$.

K. Lodaya and M. Mahajan (Eds.): FSTTCS 2004, LNCS 3328, pp. 135–147, 2004.

This general model is quite powerful and has nice structural characterizations [12, 10]. It has been in particular proved in [19] that HPDS are equivalent to (safe) higher-order recursive program schemes. Interestingly, it has also been proved that the monadic second-order theory of an infinite tree generated by a HPDS is decidable [19, 11], which generalizes the analogous result for pushdown systems proved by Muller and Schupp [20]. Also, it has been proved that parity games can be solved for HPDS [9], which generalizes the result of Walukiewicz for pushdown systems [22]. These results actually show that model checking is decidable for HPDS. However, they only allow to check that a property holds in a *single* initial configuration and they do not provide a procedure for computing a representation of the set of configurations which satisfy some given property (the satisfiability set of the property).

The basic step toward defining an algorithm which effectively computes the satisfiability sets of properties is to provide a procedure for computing the set of backward reachable configurations from a given set of configurations, i.e. their set of predecessors. In fact, the computation of forward- or backward-reachable sets is a fundamental problem in program analysis and in verification.

Since HPDS are infinite-state systems, to solve this problem we need to consider *symbolic representation structures* which (1) provide finite representations of potentially infinite sets of configurations, and (2) enjoy closure properties and decidability properties which are necessary for their use in verification. Minimal requirements in this regard are closure under union and intersection, and decidability of the emptiness and inclusion problems.

A natural class of symbolic representations for infinite-state systems is the class of finite-state automata. Recently, many works (including several papers on the so-called *regular model-checking*) have shown that finite-state automata are suitably generic representation structures, which allow to uniformly handle a wide variety of systems including pushdown systems, FIFO-channel systems, parameterized networks of processes, counter systems, etc. [5, 3, 18, 1, 23, 6, 4, 17].

In particular, for the class of pushdown systems, automata-based symbolic reachability analysis techniques have been developed and successfully applied in the context of program analysis [5, 15, 21]. Our aim in this paper is to extend this approach to a subclass of HPDS called *higher-order context-free processes* (HCFP for short). This class corresponds to the higher order extension of the well-known context-free processes (also called BPA processes). HCFP can actually be seen as HPDS with a single control state, similarly to level 1 CFP which are equivalent to level 1 PDS with a single control state. The contributions of our paper can be summarized as follows.

First, we observe that, due to the duplication operation, the set of immediate successors (i.e. the *post* image) of a given regular set of configurations is in general *not* regular, but it is always a context-sensitive set.

Then, we prove that, and this is our main result, for every HCFP of any level, the set of all predecessors (i.e. the *pre** image) of any given regular set of configurations is a regular set and effectively constructible. As a corollary of this result, we obtain a symbolic model checking algorithm (an algorithm which computes the set of all configurations satisfying a formula) for the temporal logic $E(F, X)$ with regular atomic predicates, i.e., the fragment of CTL with the modalities EF (there exist path where a property eventually holds) and EX (there exist an immediate successor satisfying some property).

Furthermore, we extend our construction of the pre^* images by showing that the set of predecessors under a regular constraint (i.e., the set of all predecessors reachable by computations which stay in some given regular set of configurations) is also regular and effectively constructible. For that, we use representation structures which can be seen as alternating finite-state automata. This result allows us to provide a symbolic model checking algorithm for the logic $E(U, X)$ with regular atomic predicates, i.e., the fragment of CTL with the operators EU (exists until) and EX (exists next).

The structure of this paper is the following. In the next two sections, we introduce higher-order stores and the model of higher-order context-free processes. We also provide a symbolic representation for (infinite) *regular* sets of stores using a certain type of finite automata. Then, for the sake of readability, we first present our algorithm for computing the unconstrained *pre* and *pre** sets of a regular set of stores (Section 4), before extending it to the case of *pre** sets constrained by a regular set C (Section 5). Due to lack of space, additional definitions and detailed proofs can be found in the full version of this paper[1].

2   Higher-Order Context-Free Processes

We introduce a class of models we call *higher-order context-free processes*, which generalize context-free processes (CFP) and are a subclass of higher-order pushdown systems (HPDS). They manipulate data structures called *higher-order stores*.

Definition 2.1 (Higher-Order Store). *The set $\mathcal{S}_1$ of* level 1 stores *(or 1-stores) over store alphabet Γ is the set of all sequences $[a_1 \ldots a_l] \in [\Gamma^*]$. For $n \geq 2$, the set $\mathcal{S}_n$ of* level n stores *(or n-stores) over Γ is the set of all sequences $[s_1 \ldots s_l] \in [\mathcal{S}_{n-1}^+]$.*

The following operations are defined on 1-stores:

$$push_1^w([a_1 \ldots a_l]) = [wa_2 \ldots a_l] \qquad \text{for all } w \in \Gamma^*,$$
$$top_1([a_1 \ldots a_l]) = a_1.$$

We will sometimes abbreviate $push_1^\varepsilon$ as pop_1. The following operations are defined on n-stores $(n > 1)$:

$$push_1^w([s_1 \ldots s_l]) = [push_1^w(s_1) \ldots s_l]$$
$$push_k([s_1 \ldots s_l]) = [push_k(s_1) \ldots s_l] \qquad \text{if } k \in [2, n[,$$

---

[1] Available at http://www.liafa.jussieu.fr/~ameyer/

$$push_n([s_1 \ldots s_l]) = [s_1 s_1 \ldots s_l]$$
$$pop_k([s_1 \ldots s_l]) = [pop_k(s_1) \ldots s_l] \text{ if } k \in [2, n[,$$
$$pop_n([s_1 \ldots s_l]) = [s_2 \ldots s_l] \qquad \text{if } l > 1, \text{ else undefined,}$$
$$top_k([s_1 \ldots s_l]) = top_k(s_1) \qquad \text{if } k \in [1, n[,$$
$$top_n([s_1 \ldots s_l]) = s_1.$$

We denote by O_n the set of operations consisting of:

$$\{ push_k, pop_k \mid k \in [2, n] \} \cup \{ push_1^w \mid w \in \Gamma^* \}.$$

We say that operation o is of level n, written $l(o) = n$, if o is either $push_n$ or pop_n, or $push_1^w$ if $n = 1$. We can now define the model studied in this paper.

Definition 2.2. *A higher-order context-free process of level n (or n-HCFP) is a pair $\mathcal{H} = (\Gamma, \Delta)$, where Γ is a finite alphabet and $\Delta \in \Gamma \times O_n$ is a finite set of transitions. A configuration of $\mathcal{H}$ is a n-store over Γ. $\mathcal{H}$ defines a transition relation $\hookrightarrow_{\mathcal{H}}$ between n-stores (or $\hookrightarrow$ when $\mathcal{H}$ is clear from the context), where*

$$s \hookrightarrow_{\mathcal{H}} s' \iff \exists (a, o) \in \Delta \text{ such that } top_1(s) = a \text{ and } s' = o(s).$$

The level $l(d)$ of a transition $d = (a, o)$ is simply the level of o. Let us give a few more notations concerning HCFP computations. Let $H = (\Gamma, \Delta)$ be a n-HCFP. A *run* of $\mathcal{H}$ starting from some store s_0 is a sequence $s_0 s_1 s_2 \ldots$ such that for all $i \geq 0$, $s_i \hookrightarrow s_{i+1}$. The reflexive and transitive closure of $\hookrightarrow$ is written $\overset{*}{\hookrightarrow}$ and called the *reachability* relation. For a given set C of n-stores, we also define the *constrained transition* relation $\hookrightarrow_C = \hookrightarrow \cap (C \times C)$, and its reflexive and transitive closure $\overset{*}{\hookrightarrow}_C$. Now for any set of n-stores S, we consider the sets:

$$post_{\mathcal{H}}[C](S) = \{ s \mid \exists s' \in S, \ s' \hookrightarrow_C s \},$$
$$post_{\mathcal{H}}^*[C](S) = \{ s \mid \exists s' \in S, \ s' \overset{*}{\hookrightarrow}_C s \},$$
$$pre_{\mathcal{H}}[C](S) = \{ s \mid \exists s' \in S, \ s \hookrightarrow_C s' \},$$
$$pre_{\mathcal{H}}^*[C](S) = \{ s \mid \exists s' \in S, \ s \overset{*}{\hookrightarrow}_C s' \}.$$

When C is the set S_n of all n-stores, we omit it in notations and simply write for instance $pre_{\mathcal{H}}(S)$ instead of $pre_{\mathcal{H}}[C](S)$. We will also omit $\mathcal{H}$ when it is clear from the context. When $\mathcal{H}$ consists of a single transition d, we may write $pre_d(S)$ instead of $pre_{\mathcal{H}}(S)$.

3 Sets of Stores and Symbolic Representation

To be able to design symbolic verification techniques over higher-order context-free processes, we need a way to finitely represent infinite sets (or languages) of configurations. In this section we present the sets of configurations (i.e. sets of stores) we consider, as well as the family of automata which recognize them.

A n-store $s = [s_1 \ldots s_l]$ over Γ is associated to a word $w(s) = [w(s_1) \ldots w(s_l)]$, in which store letters in Γ only appear at nesting depth n. A set of stores over Γ is called *regular* if its set of associated words is accepted by a finite automaton over $\Gamma' = \Gamma \cup \{[,]\}$, which in this case we call a *store automaton*. We will often make no distinction between a store s and its associated word $w(s)$. Due to the nested structure of pushdown stores, it will sometimes be more convenient to characterize sets of stores using *nested store automata*.

Definition 3.1. *A level 1 nested store automaton is a finite automaton whose transitions have labels in Γ. A nested store automaton of level $n \geq 2$ is a finite automaton whose transitions are labelled by level $n-1$ nested automata over Γ.*

The existence of a transition labelled by $\mathcal{B}$ between two control states p and q in a finite automaton $\mathcal{A}$ is written $p \xrightarrow[\mathcal{A}]{\mathcal{B}} q$, or simply $p \xrightarrow{\mathcal{B}} q$ when $\mathcal{A}$ is clear from the context. Let $\mathcal{A} = (Q, \Gamma, \delta, q_0, q_f)$ be a level n nested automaton[2] with $n \geq 2$. The level k language of $\mathcal{A}$ for $k \in [1, n]$ is defined recursively as:

$$L_k(\mathcal{A}) = \{ [L_k(\mathcal{A}_1) \ldots L_k(\mathcal{A}_l)] \mid [\mathcal{A}_1 \ldots \mathcal{A}_l] \in L_n(\mathcal{A}) \} \qquad \text{if } k < n,$$

$$L_k(\mathcal{A}) = \{ [\mathcal{A}_1 \ldots \mathcal{A}_l] \mid q_0 \xrightarrow[\mathcal{A}]{\mathcal{A}_1} \cdots \xrightarrow[\mathcal{A}]{\mathcal{A}_l} q_f \} \qquad \text{if } k = n.$$

For simplicity, we often abbreviate $L_1(\mathcal{A})$ as $L(\mathcal{A})$. We say a nested automaton $\mathcal{B}$ occurs in $\mathcal{A}$ if $\mathcal{B}$ labels a transition of $\mathcal{A}$, or occurs in the label of one. Level n automata are well suited to representing sets of n-stores, but have the same expressive power as standard level 1 store automata.

Proposition 3.2. *The store languages accepted by nested store automata are the regular store languages.*

Moreover, regular n-store languages are closed under union, intersection and complement in $\mathcal{S}_n$. We define for later use the set of automata $\{ \mathcal{A}_a^n \mid a \in \Gamma,\ n \in \mathbb{N} \}$ such that for all a and n, $L(\mathcal{A}_a^n) = \{ s \in \mathcal{S}_n \mid top_1(s) = a \}$. We also write $\mathcal{A} \times \mathcal{B}$ the product operation over automata such that $L(\mathcal{A} \times \mathcal{B}) = L(\mathcal{A}) \cap L(\mathcal{B})$.

4   Symbolic Reachability Analysis

Our goal in this section is to investigate effective techniques to compute the sets $pre(S)$, $post(S)$, $pre^*(S)$ and $post^*(S)$ for a given n-HCFP $\mathcal{H}$, in the case where S is a regular set of stores. For level 1 pushdown systems, it is a well-known result that both $pre^*_{\mathcal{H}}(S)$ and $post^*_{\mathcal{H}}(S)$ are regular. We will see that this is still the case for $pre(S)$ and $pre^*(S)$ in the higher-order case, but not for $post(S)$ (hence not for $post^*(S)$ either).

---

[2] Note that we only consider automata with a single final state.

4.1   Forward Reachability

Proposition 4.1. *Given a n-HCFP $\mathcal{H}$ and a regular set of n-stores S, the set $post(S)$ is in general not regular. This set is a context-sensitive language.*

Proof. Let $post_{(a,o)}(S)$ denote the set $\{\, s' \mid \exists s \in S,\ top_1(s) = a \,\wedge\, s' = o(s) \,\}$. Suppose S is a regular set of n-stores, then if $d = (a, push_1^w)$ or $d = (a, pop_k)$, it is not difficult to see that $post_{(a,o)}(S)$ is regular. However, if $d = (a, push_k)$ with $k > 1$, then $post_{(a,o)}(S)$ is the set $\{\, \lceil^{n-k+1}t\,t\,w \mid \lceil^{n-k+1}t\,w \in S \,\}$. It can be shown using the usual pumping arguments that this set is not regular, because of the duplication of t. However, one can straightforwardly build a linearly bounded Turing machine recognizing this set.   □

4.2   Backward Reachability

We first propose a transformation on automata which corresponds to the *pre* operation on their language. In a second time, we extend this construction to deal with the more difficult computation of pre^* sets.

Proposition 4.2. *Given a n-HCFP $\mathcal{H}$ and a regular set of n-stores S, the set $pre(S)$ is regular and effectively computable.*

We introduce a construction which, for a given HCFP transition d and a given regular set of n-stores S recognized by a level n nested automaton $\mathcal{A}$, allows us to compute a nested automaton $\mathcal{A}'_d$ recognizing the set $pre(S)$ of direct predecessors of S by d. This construction is a transformation over nested automata, which we call T_d. We define $\mathcal{A}'_d = T_d(\mathcal{A}) = (Q', \Gamma, \delta', q'_0, q_f)$ as follows.

If $l(d) < n$, we propagate the transformation to the first level $n-1$ automaton encountered along each path. We thus have $Q' = Q$, $q'_0 = q_0$ and

$$\delta' = \{\, q_0 \xrightarrow{T_d(\mathcal{A}_1)} q_1 \mid q_0 \xrightarrow[\mathcal{A}]{\mathcal{A}_1} q_1 \,\} \cup \{\, q \xrightarrow{B} q' \mid q \xrightarrow[\mathcal{A}]{B} q' \wedge q \neq q_0 \,\}.$$

If $l(d) = n$, we distinguish three cases according to the nature of d:

1. If $d = (a, push_1^w)$, then $Q' = Q \cup \{q'_0\}$ and $\delta' = \delta \cup \{\, q'_0 \xrightarrow{a} q_1 \mid q_0 \xrightarrow[\mathcal{A}]{w} q_1 \,\}$.
2. If $d = (a, push_n)$ and $n > 1$, then $Q' = Q \cup \{q'_0\}$ and
   $\delta' = \delta \cup \{\, q'_0 \xrightarrow{B} q_2 \mid \exists q_1,\ q_0 \xrightarrow[\mathcal{A}]{\mathcal{A}_1} q_1 \xrightarrow[\mathcal{A}]{\mathcal{A}_2} q_2 \,\}$ where $B = \mathcal{A}_1 \times \mathcal{A}_2 \times \mathcal{A}_a^{(n-1)}$.
3. If $d = (a, pop_n)$, then $Q' = Q \cup \{q'_0\}$ and $\delta' = \delta \cup \{\, q'_0 \xrightarrow{\mathcal{A}_a^{(n-1)}} q_0 \,\}$.

It is not difficult to prove that $L(\mathcal{A}'_d) = pre_d(L(\mathcal{A}))$. Hence, if Δ is the set of transitions of $\mathcal{H}$, then we have $pre(S) = pre(L(\mathcal{A})) = \bigcup_{d \in \Delta} L(\mathcal{A}'_d)$.

This technique can be extended to compute the set $pre^*(S)$ of all predecessors of a regular set of stores S.

Theorem 4.3. *Given a n-HCFP $\mathcal{H}$ and a regular set of n-stores S, the set $pre^*(S)$ is regular and effectively computable.*

To compute $pre^*(S)$, we have to deal with the problem of termination. A simple iteration of our previous construction will in general not terminate, as each step would add control states to the automaton. As a matter of fact, even the sequence $(pre^i(S))_{i\geq 0}$, defined as $pre^0(S) = S$ and for all $n \geq 1$ $pre^n(S) = pre^{n-1}(S) \cup pre(pre^{n-1}(S))$, does not reach a fix-point in general. For instance, if $d = (a, pop_1)$, then for all n, $pre^n([a]) = \{ [a^i] \mid i \leq n \} \neq pre^{n+1}([a])$.

To build $pre^*(S)$ for some regular S, we modify the previous construction in order to keep constant the number of states in the nested automaton we manipulate. The idea, instead of creating new control states, is to add edges to the automaton until saturation, eventually creating loops to represent at once multiple applications of a HCFP transition. Then, we prove that this new algorithm terminates and is correct.

Let us first define operation T_d for any n-HCFP transition d (see Figure 1 for an illustration). Let $\mathcal{A} = (Q, \Gamma, \delta, q_0, q_f)$ and $\mathcal{A}' = (Q, \Gamma, \delta', q_0, q_f)$ be nested n-store automata over $\Gamma' = \Gamma \cup \{ [,] \}$, and d a n-HCFP transition. We define $\mathcal{A}' = T_d(\mathcal{A})$ as follows.

If the level of d is less than n, then we simply propagate the transformation to the first level $n - 1$ automaton encountered along each path:

$$\delta' = \{ q_0 \xrightarrow{T_d(\mathcal{A}_1)} q_1 \mid q_0 \xrightarrow[\mathcal{A}]{\mathcal{A}_1} q_1 \} \cup \{ q \xrightarrow{B} q' \mid q \xrightarrow[\mathcal{A}]{B} q' \wedge q \neq q_0 \}.$$

If $l(d) = n$ then as previously we distinguish three cases according to d:

1. If $n = 1$ and $d = (a, push_1^w)$, then $\delta' = \delta \cup \{ q_0 \xrightarrow{a} q_1 \mid q_0 \xrightarrow[\mathcal{A}]{w} q_1 \}$.

2. If $d = (a, push_n)$ for some $n > 1$, then
   $$\delta' = \delta \cup \{ q_0 \xrightarrow{B} q_2 \mid \exists q_1, q_0 \xrightarrow[\mathcal{A}]{\mathcal{A}_1} q_1 \xrightarrow[\mathcal{A}]{\mathcal{A}_2} q_2 \} \text{ where } B = \mathcal{A}_1 \times \mathcal{A}_2 \times \mathcal{A}_a^{(n-1)}.$$

3. If $d = (a, pop_n)$, then $\delta' = \delta \cup \{ q_0 \xrightarrow{\mathcal{A}_a^{(n-1)}} q_0 \}$

Suppose $H = (\Gamma, \Delta)$ with $\Delta = \{ d_0, \ldots, d_{l-1} \}$. Given an automaton $\mathcal{A}$ such that $S = L(\mathcal{A})$, consider the sequence $(\mathcal{A}_i)_{i\geq 0}$ defined as $\mathcal{A}_0 = \mathcal{A}$ and for all $i \geq 0$ and $j = i \bmod l$, $\mathcal{A}_{i+1} = T_{d_j}(\mathcal{A}_i)$. In order to obtain the result, we have to prove that this sequence always reaches a fix-point (Lemma 4.4) and this fix-point is an automaton actually recognizing $pre^*(S)$ (Lemmas 4.5 and 4.6).

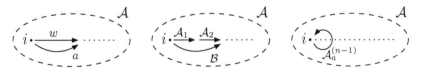

Fig. 1. Transformation $T_d(\mathcal{A})$ for $d = (a, push_1^w)$, $(a, push_k)$ and (a, pop_k)

Lemma 4.4 (Termination). *For all nested n-store automaton $\mathcal{A}$ and n-HCFP $\mathcal{H} = (\Gamma, \Delta)$, the sequence $(\mathcal{A}_i)_{i\geq 0}$ defined with respect to $\mathcal{A}$ eventually stabilizes: $\exists k \geq 0, \forall k' \in \Delta, \mathcal{A}_{k'} = \mathcal{A}_k$, which implies $L(\mathcal{A}_k) = \bigcup_{i\geq 0} L(\mathcal{A}_i)$.*

Proof. First, notice that for all d, T_d does not change the set of control states of any automaton occurring in $\mathcal{A}$, and only adds transitions. This means $(\mathcal{A}_i)_{i\geq 0}$ is monotonous in the size of each $\mathcal{A}_i$.

To establish the termination of the conctruction, we prove that the number of transitions which can be added to $\mathcal{A}_0$ is finite. Note that by definition of T_d, the number of states of each $\mathcal{A}_i$ is constant. Moreover, each new transition originates from the initial state of the automaton it is added to. Hence, the total number of transitions which can be added to a given automaton is equal to $|V_n| \cdot |Q|$, where V_n is the level n vocabulary and Q its set of states. Since $|Q|$ does not change, we only have to prove that V_n is finite for all n. If $n = 1$, $V_1 = \Gamma$, and the property holds. Now suppose $n > 1$ and the property holds up to level $n - 1$. By induction hypothesis, V_{n-1} is finite. With this set of labels, one can build a finite number N of different level $n - 1$ automata which is exponential in $|V_{n-1}| \cdot K$, where K depends on the number of level $n - 1$ automata in $\mathcal{A}_0$ and of their sets of control states. As each transition of a level n automaton is labelled by a product of level $n - 1$ automata, then $|V_n|$ is itself exponential in N, and thus doubly exponential in $|V_{n-1}|$. Remark that, as a consequence, the number of steps of the construction is non-elementary in n.   □

Lemma 4.5 (Soundness). $\bigcup_{i\geq 0} L(\mathcal{A}_i) \subseteq pre_{\mathcal{H}}^*(S)$.

Proof (Sketch). We prove by induction on i the equivalent result that $\forall i$, $L(\mathcal{A}_i) \subseteq pre_{\mathcal{H}}^*(S)$. The base case is trivial since by definition $\mathcal{A}_0 = \mathcal{A}$ and $L(\mathcal{A}) = S \subseteq pre_{\mathcal{H}}^*(S)$. For the inductive step, we consider a store s accepted by a run in $\mathcal{A}_{i+1}$ and reason by induction on the number m of new level k transitions used in this run, where k is the level of the operation d such that $\mathcal{A}_{i+1} = T_d(\mathcal{A}_i)$. The idea is to decompose each run containing m new transitions into a first part with less than m new transitions, one new transition, and a second part also containing less than m new transitions. Then, by induction hypothesis on m and i, one can re-compose a path in $\mathcal{A}_i$ recognizing some store s' such that $s' \in pre_{\mathcal{H}}^*(S)$ and $s \in pre_{\mathcal{H}}^*(s')$.   □

Lemma 4.6 (Completeness). $pre_{\mathcal{H}}^*(S) \subseteq \bigcup_{i\geq 0} L(\mathcal{A}_i)$.

Proof (Sketch). We prove the sufficient property that for all nested store automaton $\mathcal{A}$ and HCFP transition d, $pre_d(L(\mathcal{A})) \subseteq L(T_d(\mathcal{A}))$. We consider automata $\mathcal{A}$ and $\mathcal{A}'$ such that $\mathcal{A}' = T_d(\mathcal{A})$, and any pair of stores $s \in L(\mathcal{A})$ and $s' \in pre_{d_j}(s)$. It suffices to isolate a run in $\mathcal{A}$ recognizing s and enumerate the possible forms of s' with respect to s and d to be able to exhibit a possible run in $\mathcal{A}'$ accepting s', by definition of T_d. This establishes the fact that T_d adds to the language L of its argument *at least* the set of direct predecessors of stores of L by d.   □

As a direct consequence of Proposition 4.2 and Theorem 4.3, we obtain a symbolic model checking algorithm for the logic $\mathsf{E}(\mathsf{F}, \mathsf{X})$ with regular store languages as atomic predicates, i.e. the fragment of the temporal logic CTL for the modal operators EF (there exists a path where eventually a property holds) and EX (there exist an immediate successor satisfying a property).

Theorem 4.7. *For every HCFP $\mathcal{H}$ and formula φ of $\mathsf{E}(\mathsf{F}, \mathsf{X})$, the set of configurations (stores) satisfying φ is regular and effectively computable.*

5 Constraining Reachability

In this section we address the more general problem of computing a finite automaton recognizing $pre^*_{\mathcal{H}}[C](S)$ for any HCFP H and pair of regular store languages C and S. We provide an extension of the construction of Proposition 4.3 allowing us to ensure that we only consider runs of H whose configurations all belong to C. Again, from a given automaton $\mathcal{A}$, we construct a sequence of automata whose limit recognizes exactly $pre^*_{\mathcal{H}}[C](L(\mathcal{A}))$. The main (and only) difference with the previous case is that we need to compute language intersections at each iteration without invalidating our termination arguments (i.e. without adding any new states to the original automaton). For this reason, we use a class of *alternating* automata, which we call *constrained* nested automata.

Definition 5.1 (Constrained Nested Automata). *Let $\mathcal{B}$ be a non-nested m-store automaton[3] (with $m \geq n$). A level n $\mathcal{B}$-constrained nested automaton $\mathcal{A}$ is a nested automaton $(Q_{\mathcal{A}}, \Gamma, \delta_{\mathcal{A}}, i_{\mathcal{A}}, f_{\mathcal{A}})$ with special transitions of the form $p \xrightarrow[\mathcal{A}]{\mathcal{C}} (q, r)$ where $p, q \in Q_{\mathcal{A}}$, r is a control state of $\mathcal{B}$ and $\mathcal{C}$ is a level $n - 1$ $\mathcal{B}$-constrained nested automaton.*

For lack of space, we are not able to provide here the complete semantics of these automata. However, the intuitive idea is quite simple. Suppose $\mathcal{A}$ is a $\mathcal{B}$-constrained nested n-store automaton, and $\mathcal{B}$ also recognizes n-stores. First, we require all the words accepted by $\mathcal{A}$ to be also accepted by $\mathcal{B}$: $L(\mathcal{A}) \subseteq L(\mathcal{B})$. Then, in any run of $\mathcal{A}$ where a transition of the form $p \xrightarrow{\mathcal{D}} (q, r)$ occurs, the remaining part of the input word should be accepted both by $\mathcal{A}$ when resuming from state q and by $\mathcal{B}$ when starting from state r. Of course, when expanding $\mathcal{D}$ into a word of its language, it may require additional checks in $\mathcal{B}$. As a matter of fact, constrained nested automata can be transformed into equivalent level 1 alternating automata. As such, the languages they accept are all regular.

Proposition 5.2. *Constrained nested automata accept regular languages.*

The construction we want to provide needs to refer to whole sets of paths in a level 1 store automaton recognizing the constraint language. To do this, we need to introduce a couple of additional definitions and notations.

Definition 5.3. *Let $\mathcal{A}$ be a finite store automaton over $\Gamma' = \Gamma \cup \{\, [\, , \,]\, \}$. A state p of $\mathcal{A}$ is of level 0 if it has no successor by $[$ and no predecessor by $]$. It is of level k if all its successors by $[$ and predecessors by $]$ are of level $k - 1$. The level of p is written $l(p)$.*

---

[3] i.e. a standard, level 1 finite state automaton.

We can show that any automaton recognizing only n-stores is equivalent to an automaton whose control states all have a well-defined level. A notion of level can also be defined for paths. A *level n path* in a store automaton is a path $p_1 \ldots p_k$ with $l(p_1) = l(p_k) = n$ and $\forall i \in [2, k-1]$, $l(p_i) < n$. All such paths are labelled by n-stores. Now, to concisely refer to the whole set of level n paths between two level n control states, we introduce the following notation. Let

$$Q = \{ q \in Q_{\mathcal{A}} \mid l(q) < n \wedge p_1 \xrightarrow[\mathcal{A}]{+} q \xrightarrow[\mathcal{A}]{+} p_2 \}$$

be the set of all states of $\mathcal{A}$ occurring on a level n path between p_1 and p_2. If Q is not empty, we write $p_1 \overset{\mathcal{B}}{\underset{\mathcal{A}}{\rightsquigarrow}} p_2$, where $\mathcal{B}$ is defined as:

$$\mathcal{B} = \big(Q_{\mathcal{B}} = Q \cup \{p_1, p_2\}, \ \Gamma', \ \delta_{\mathcal{B}} = \delta_{\mathcal{A}} \cap (Q_{\mathcal{B}} \times \Gamma' \times Q_{\mathcal{B}}), \ p_1, \ p_2 \big).$$

Thanks to these few notions, we can state our result:

Theorem 5.4. *Given a n-HCFP $\mathcal{H}$ and regular sets of n-stores S and C, the set $pre^*_{\mathcal{H}}[C](S)$ is regular and effectively computable.*

To address this problem, we propose a modified version of the construction of the previous section, which uses constrained nested automata. Let $d = (a, o)$ be a HCFP transition rule, $\mathcal{A} = (Q_{\mathcal{A}}, \Gamma, \delta, i, f)$ and $\mathcal{A}' = (Q_{\mathcal{A}}, \Gamma, \delta', i, f)$ two nested k-store automata constrained by a level 1 n-store automaton $\mathcal{B} = (Q_{\mathcal{B}}, \Gamma', \delta_{\mathcal{B}}, i_{\mathcal{B}}, f_{\mathcal{B}})$ accepting C (with $n \geq k$). We define a transformation $T^{\mathcal{B}}_d(\mathcal{A})$, which is very similar to T_{d_j}, except that we need to add alternating transitions to ensure that no new store is accepted by $\mathcal{A}'$ unless it is the transformation of a store previously accepted by $\mathcal{B}$ (Cf. Figure 2). If $l(d) < k$, we propagate the transformation to the first level $k-1$ automaton along each path:

$$\delta' = \{ i \xrightarrow{T^{\mathcal{B}}_d(\mathcal{C})} (p, q) \mid i \xrightarrow[\mathcal{A}]{\mathcal{C}} (p, q) \} \cup \{ p \xrightarrow{\mathcal{C}} (p', q') \in \delta \mid p \neq i \}.$$

If $l(d) = n$, we distinguish three cases according to the nature of d:

1. If $d = (a, push^w_1)$, then

$$\delta' = \delta \cup \big\{ i \xrightarrow{a} (p, q) \mid i \xrightarrow[\mathcal{A}_i]{w} (p, q') \quad \wedge \quad \exists q_1, q \in Q_{\mathcal{B}},$$

$$l(q_1) = l(q) = 0, \ i_{\mathcal{B}} \xrightarrow[\mathcal{B}]{[^n} q_1 \xrightarrow[\mathcal{B}]{w} q \big\}.$$

2. If $d = (a, push_k)$, then for $m = n - k + 1$ and $\mathcal{C} = (\mathcal{C}_1 \times \mathcal{C}_2) \times (\mathcal{B}_1 \times \mathcal{B}_2) \times \mathcal{A}^{(k-1)}_a$,

$$\delta' = \delta \cup \big\{ i \xrightarrow{\mathcal{C}} (p, q) \mid i \xrightarrow[\mathcal{A}_i]{\mathcal{C}_1} \xrightarrow[\mathcal{A}_i]{\mathcal{C}_2} (p, q') \quad \wedge \quad \exists q_1, q_2, q \in Q_{\mathcal{B}},$$

$$l(q_1) = l(q_2) = l(q) = k-1, \ i_{\mathcal{B}} \xrightarrow[\mathcal{B}]{[^m} q_1 \overset{\mathcal{B}_1}{\underset{\mathcal{B}}{\rightsquigarrow}} q_2 \overset{\mathcal{B}_2}{\underset{\mathcal{B}}{\rightsquigarrow}} q \big\}.$$

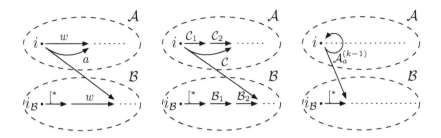

Fig. 2. transformation $T_d^{\mathcal{B}}(\mathcal{A})$ for $d = (a, push_1^w)$, $(a, push_k)$ and (a, pop_k)

3. If $d = (a, pop_k)$, then for $m = n - k + 1$,

$$\delta' = \delta \cup \big\{ i \xrightarrow{A_a^{(k-1)}} (i,q) \mid \exists q \in Q_{\mathcal{B}},\ l(q) = k-1,\ i_{\mathcal{B}} \xrightarrow[\mathcal{B}_1]{l^m} q \big\}.$$

Suppose $H = (\Gamma, \Delta)$ with $\Delta = \{ d_0, \dots, d_{l-1} \}$. Given an automaton $\mathcal{A}$ such that $S = L(\mathcal{A})$, consider the sequence $(\mathcal{A}_i)_{i \geq 0}$ defined as $\mathcal{A}_0 = \mathcal{A}^{\mathcal{B}}$ (the $\mathcal{B}$-constrained automaton with the same set of states and transitions as $\mathcal{A}$, whose language is $L(\mathcal{A}) \cap L(\mathcal{B})$) and for all $i \geq 0$ and $j = i \mod l$, $\mathcal{A}_{i+1} = T_{d_j}^{\mathcal{B}}(\mathcal{A}_i)$. By definition of $T_d^{\mathcal{B}}$, the number of states in each $\mathcal{A}_i$ does not vary, and since the number of control states of $\mathcal{B}$ is finite the same termination arguments as in Lemma 4.4 still hold. It is then quite straightforward to extend the proofs of Lemma 4.5 and Lemma 4.6 to the constrained case.

This more general construction also allows us to extend Theorem 4.7 to the larger fragment $E(U, X)$ of CTL, where formulas can now contain the modal operator EU (there exists a path along which a first property continuously holds until a second property eventually holds) instead of just EF.

Theorem 5.5. *Given a HCFP $\mathcal{H}$ and formula φ of $E(U, X)$, the set of configurations (stores) satisfying φ is regular and effectively computable.*

6 Conclusion

We have provided an automata-based symbolic technique for backward reachability analysis of higher-order context-free processes. This technique can be used to check temporal properties expressed in the logic $E(U, X)$. In this respect, our results provide a first step toward developing symbolic techniques for the model-checking of higher-order context-free or pushdown processes.

Several important questions remain open and are left for future investigation. In particular, it would be interesting to extend our approach to the more general case of higher-order pushdown systems, i.e. by taking into account a set of control states. This does not seem to be technically trivial, and naive extensions of our construction lead to procedures which are not guaranteed to terminate.

Another interesting issue is to generalize our symbolic approach to more general properties than reachability and/or safety, including liveness properties.

Finally, it would also be very interesting to extend our symbolic techniques in order to solve games (such as safety and parity games) and to compute representations of the sets of all winning configurations for these games.

References

1. P. Abdulla, A. Bouajjani, and B. Jonsson. On-the-fly analysis of systems with unbounded, lossy fifo channels. In *10th CAV*, volume 1427 of *LNCS*, pages 305–318, 1998.
2. R. Alur, K. Etessami, and P. Madhusudan. A temporal logic of nested calls and returns. In *10th TACAS*, volume 2988 of *LNCS*, pages 467–481, 2004.
3. B. Boigelot, P. Godefroid, B. Willems, and P. Wolper. The power of qdds. In *4th SAS*, volume 1302 of *LNCS*, pages 172–186, 1997.
4. A. Bouajjani. Languages, rewriting systems, and verification of infinite-state systems. In *28th ICALP*, volume 2076 of *LNCS*, pages 24–39, 2001.
5. A. Bouajjani, J. Esparza, and O. Maler. Reachability analysis of pushdown automata: Application to model-checking. In *8th CONCUR*, volume 1243 of *LNCS*, pages 135–150, 1997.
6. A. Bouajjani, B. Jonsson, M. Nilsson, and T. Touili. Regular model checking. In *12th CAV*, volume 1855 of *LNCS*, pages 403–418, 2000.
7. O. Burkart, D. Caucal, and B. Steffen. Bisimulation collapse and the process taxonomy. In *7th CONCUR*, volume 1119 of *LNCS*, pages 247–262, 1996.
8. T. Cachat. Symbolic strategy synthesis for games on pushdown graphs. In *29th ICALP*, volume 2380 of *LNCS*, pages 704–715, 2002.
9. T. Cachat. Higher order pushdown automata, the caucal hierarchy of graphs and parity games. In *30th ICALP*, volume 2719 of *LNCS*, pages 556–569, 2003.
10. A. Carayol and S. Wöhrle. The caucal hierarchy of infinite graphs in terms of logic and higher-order pushdown automata. In *23rd FSTTCS*, volume 2914 of *LNCS*, pages 112–123, 2003.
11. D. Caucal. On the regular structure of prefix rewriting. *TCS*, 106:61–86, 1992.
12. D. Caucal. On infinite terms having a decidable monadic theory. In *27th MFCS*, volume 2420 of *LNCS*, pages 165–176, 2002.
13. J. Engelfriet. Iterated pushdown automata and complexity classes. In *15th STOC*, pages 365–373, 1983.
14. J. Esparza. Grammars as processes. In *Formal and Natural Computing*, volume 2300 of *LNCS*, pages 232–247, 2002.
15. J. Esparza, D. Hansel, P. Rossmanith, and S. Schwoon. Efficient algorithm for model checking pushdown systems. In *12th CAV*, volume 1885 of *LNCS*, pages 232–247, 2000.
16. J. Esparza and J. Knoop. An automata-theoretic approach to interprocedural data-flow analysis. In *FoSSaCS*, volume 1578 of *LNCS*, pages 14–30, 1999.
17. J. Henriksen, J. Jensen, M. Jørgensen, N. Klarlund, R. Paige, T. Rauhe, and A. Sandholm. Mona: Monadic second-order logic in practice. In *1st TACAS*, volume 1019 of *LNCS*, pages 89–110, 1995.
18. Y. Kesten, O. Maler, M. Marcus, A. Pnueli, and E. Shahar. Symbolic model checking with rich assertional languages. In *9th CAV*, volume 1254 of *LNCS*, pages 424–435, 1997.
19. T. Knapik, D. Niwinski, and P. Urzyczyn. Higher-order pushdown trees are easy. In *5th FoSSaCS*, volume 2303 of *LNCS*, pages 205–222, 2002.

20. D. Muller and P. Schupp. The theory of ends, pushdown automata, and second-order logic. *TCS*, 37:51–75, 1985.
21. Stefan Schwoon. *Model-Checking Pushdown Systems*. PhD thesis, Technische Universität München, 2002.
22. I. Walukiewicz. Pushdown processes: Games and model checking. In *8th CAV*, volume 1102 of *LNCS*, pages 62–74, 1996.
23. P. Wolper and B. Boigelot. Verifying systems with infinite but regular state spaces. In *10th CAV*, volume 1427 of *LNCS*, pages 88–97, 1998.

Optimal Strategies in Priced Timed Game Automata

Patricia Bouyer[1,*], Franck Cassez[2,*], Emmanuel Fleury[3], and Kim G. Larsen[3]

[1] LSV, UMR 8643, CNRS & ENS de Cachan, France
`bouyer@lsv.ens-cachan.fr`
[2] IRCCyN, UMR 6597, CNRS, France
`cassez@irccyn.ec-nantes.fr`
[3] Computer Science Department, BRICS[**], Aalborg University, Denmark
`{fleury,kgl}@cs.auc.dk`

Abstract. Priced timed (game) automata extend timed (game) automata with costs on both locations and transitions. In this paper we focus on reachability priced timed game automata and prove that the optimal cost for winning such a game is computable under conditions concerning the non-zenoness of cost. Under stronger conditions (strictness of constraints) we prove that in case an optimal strategy exists, we can compute a state-based winning optimal strategy.

1   Introduction

Optimal Scheduling in Timed Systems. In recent years the application of model-checking techniques to scheduling problems has become an established line of research. Static scheduling problems with timing constraints may often be formulated as reachability problems on timed automata, viz. as the possibility of reaching a given goal state. Real-time model checking tools such as KRONOS and UPPAAL have been applied on a number of industrial and benchmark scheduling problems [13, 15].

Often the scheduling strategy needs to take into account uncertainty with respect to the behavior of an environmental context. In such situations the scheduling problem becomes a dynamic (timed) game between the controller and the environment, where the objective for the controller is to find a *dynamic* strategy that will guarantee the game to end in a goal state [5, 11, 17].

Optimality of schedules may be obtained within the framework of timed automata by associating with each run a performance measure. Thus it is possible to compare runs and search for the optimal run from an initial configuration to a final (goal) target. The most obvious performance measure for timed automata is clearly that of time itself. Time-optimality for timed automata was first considered in [10] and proved computable in [18]. The related problem of synthesizing time-optimal winning strategies for timed game automata was shown computable in [4].

---

* Work partially supported by ACI Cortos, a program of the French government. Visits to Aalborg supported by CISS, Aalborg University, Denmark.
** Basic Research in Computer Science (`www.brics.dk`).

K. Lodaya and M. Mahajan (Eds.): FSTTCS 2004, LNCS 3328, pp. 148–160, 2004.

More recently, the ability to consider more general performance measures has been given. Priced extensions of timed automata have been introduced where a cost c is associated with each location ℓ giving the cost of a unit of time spent in ℓ. In [2] cost-bound reachability has been shown decidable. [6] and [3] independently solve the cost-optimal reachability problem for priced timed automata. Efficient incorporation in UPPAAL is provided by use of so-called priced zones as a main data structure [16]. More recently in [9], the problem of computing optimal *infinite* schedules (in terms of minimal limit-ratios) is solved for the model of priced timed automata.

The Optimal Control Problem for Timed Games. In this paper we combine the notions of game and price and solve the problem of cost-optimal winning strategies for priced timed game automata. The problem we consider is: "Given a priced timed game automaton A, a goal location Goal, what is the optimal cost we can achieve to reach Goal in A?". We refer to this problem as the Optimal Control Problem (OCP). Consider the example of a priced timed game automaton given in Fig. 1. Here the cost-rates (cost per time unit) in locations ℓ_0, ℓ_2 and ℓ_3 are 5, 10 and 1 respectively. In ℓ_1 the environment may choose to move to either ℓ_2 or ℓ_3 (dashed arrows are uncontrollable). However, due to the invariant $y = 0$ this choice must be made instantaneous. Obviously, once ℓ_2 or ℓ_3 has been reached the optimal strategy for the controller is to move to Goal immediately (however there is a discrete cost (resp. 1 and 7) on each discrete transition). The crucial (and only remaining) question is how long the controller should wait in ℓ_0 before taking the transition to ℓ_1. Obviously, in order for the controller to win this duration must be no more than two time units. However, what is the optimal choice for the duration in the sense that the overall cost of reaching Goal is minimal? Denote by t the chosen delay in ℓ_0. Then $5t + 10(2 - t) + 1$ is the minimal cost through ℓ_2 and $5t + (2 - t) + 7$ is the minimal cost through ℓ_3. As the environment chooses between these two transitions the best choice for the controller is to delay $t \leq 2$ such that $\max(21 - 5t, 9 + 4t)$ is minimum, which is $t = \frac{4}{3}$ giving a minimal cost of $14\frac{1}{3}$.

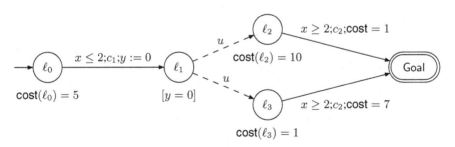

Fig. 1. A Reachability Priced Time Game Automaton A

Related Work. Acyclic priced (or weighted) timed games have been studied in [14] and the more general case of non-acyclic games have been recently considered in [1]. In [1], the problem they consider is "compute the optimal cost within k steps": we refer to this bounded problem as the k-OCP. This is a weaker version than the one we consider (OCP) and roughly corresponds to unfolding the game k times and to reducing the problem to solving an acyclic game. In [1], the authors focus on the complexity of the k-OCP rather than on the decidability of the OCP and give a clever (exponential) bound on the number of regions that appear after unfolding the game k times. In the conclusion the authors also indicate that under some non-Zenoness assumption (similar to the one we use in theorem 6) the number of iterations required to compute the optimal cost (OCP) is finite and thus that, under this assumption, any game can be reduced to an "optimal game in finite number of steps". However both our work and [1] fail in solving the general OCP without any (non-Zenoness) assumption.

In this work (following our research report [7]) that was done simultaneously and independently from [1], we don't provide any complexity bound for (k-)OCP, but rather focus on the synthesis of winning strategies and their structural properties. The method we use is radically different from the one proposed in [14, 1] and our main contributions (which extend previous works) are then the following:

– in both above-mentioned papers, the definition of the optimal cost is based on a recursive definition of a function (like the O function given in definition 11, page 155) that can be very complex (e.g. in [1]); we propose a new run-based definition (definition 9) of the optimal cost that is more natural and enables us to obtain new results. For instance the definition of the optimal cost in [14, 1] is based on an infimum-supremum computation: if the optimal cost is c the algorithm does not give any hint whether c is actually realized (there is a strategy of cost c) or if c is the limit of the optimal cost (there is a family of strategies of cost $c+\varepsilon$ for all $\varepsilon > 0$). In our settings, we can compute the optimal cost and answer the question whether an optimal strategy exists or not (corollaries 1 and 2). Moreover we provide a proof that non-Zenoness implies termination of our algorithm (theorem 6).

– in addition to the previous new results on optimal cost computation that extend the ones in [14, 1] we also tackle the problem of strategy synthesis. In particular we study the properties of the strategies (memoryless, cost-dependence) needed to achieve the optimal cost which is a natural question that arises in game theory. For example, in [1] setting, it could be the case that in two instances of the unfolding of the game, the values of a strategy for a given state are different. In this paper we prove that if an optimal strategy exists then one can effectively construct an optimal strategy which only depends on the current state and on the accumulated cost since the beginning of the play. We also prove that under some assumptions, if an optimal strategy exists then a state-based cost-independent strategy exists and can be effectively computed (theorem 7).

– finally the algorithms we obtain can be implemented [8] in HYTECH.

Proofs are omitted but can be found in [7].

2   Reachability Timed Games (RTG)

In this paper we focus on *reachability games*, where the control objective is to enforce that the system eventually evolves into a particular state. It is classical in the literature to define *reachability timed games (RTG)* [5, 11, 17] to model control problems. In this section we recall some known general results about RTG.

Timed Transition Systems and Games

Definition 1 (Timed Transition Systems (TTS)). *A* timed transition system *is a tuple* $S = (Q, Q_0, \mathsf{Act}, \longrightarrow)$ *where* Q *is a set of states,* $Q_0 \subseteq Q$ *is the set of initial states,* Act *is a finite set of actions, disjoint from* $\mathbb{R}_{\geq 0}$, $\longrightarrow \subseteq Q \times \Sigma \times Q$ *is a set of edges. We let* $\Sigma = \mathsf{Act} \cup \mathbb{R}_{\geq 0}$. *If* $(q, e, q') \in \longrightarrow$, *we also write* $q \xrightarrow{e} q'$.

We make the following common assumptions about TTSs:

- 0-DELAY: $q \xrightarrow{0} q'$ if and only if $q = q'$,
- ADDITIVITY: if $q \xrightarrow{d} q'$ and $q' \xrightarrow{d'} q''$ with $d, d' \in \mathbb{R}_{\geq 0}$, then $q \xrightarrow{d+d'} q''$,
- CONTINUITY: if $q \xrightarrow{d} q'$, then for every d' and d'' in $\mathbb{R}_{\geq 0}$ such that $d = d' + d''$, there exists q'' such that $q \xrightarrow{d'} q'' \xrightarrow{d''} q'$,
- DETERMINISM: if $q \xrightarrow{e} q'$ and $q \xrightarrow{e} q''$ with $e \in \Sigma$, then $q' = q''$.

A *run* $\rho = q_0 \xrightarrow{t_0} q_0' \xrightarrow{e_0} q_1 \xrightarrow{t_1} q_1' \xrightarrow{e_1} \cdots q_n \xrightarrow{t_n} q_n' \xrightarrow{e_n} q_{n+1} \cdots$ in S is a finite or infinite sequence of alternating time ($t_i \in \mathbb{R}_{\geq 0}$) and discrete ($e_i \in \mathsf{Act}$) steps. States$(\rho) = \{q_0, q_0', , q_1, q_1', \ldots, q_n, q_n', \ldots\}$ is the set of states encountered on ρ. We denote by $first(\rho) = q_0$ and if ρ is finite and has n alternating time and discrete steps $last(\rho) = q_n$. Runs(q, S) is the set of (finite and infinite) runs in S starting from q. The set of runs of S is Runs$(S) = \bigcup_{q \in Q}$ Runs(q, S). We use $q \xrightarrow{e}$ as a shorthand for "$\exists q'$ s.t. $q \xrightarrow{e} q'$" and extends this notation to finite runs $\rho \xrightarrow{e}$ whenever $last(\rho) \xrightarrow{e}$.

Definition 2 (Timed Games (TG)). *A* timed game *$G = (Q, Q_0, \mathsf{Act}, \longrightarrow)$ is a TTS such that* Act *is partitioned into* controllable *actions* Act_c *and* uncontrollable *actions* Act_u.

Strategies, Reachability Games. A strategy [17] is a function that during the cause of the game constantly gives information as to what the controller should do in order to win the game. In a given situation the strategy could suggest the controller to either i) "do a particular controllable action" or ii) "do nothing at this point in time, just wait" which will be denoted by the special symbol λ. For instance if one wants to delay until some clock value x reaches $\frac{4}{3}$ (as would be a good strategy in the location ℓ_0 of Fig. 1) then the strategy would be: for $x < \frac{4}{3}$ do λ and for $x = \frac{4}{3}$ do the control action from ℓ_0 to ℓ_1.

Definition 3 (Strategy). *Let* $G = (Q, Q_0, \mathsf{Act}, \longrightarrow)$ *be a TG. A* strategy *f over G is a partial function from* Runs(G) *to* $\mathsf{Act}_c \cup \{\lambda\}$.

We denote Strat(G) the set of strategies over G. A strategy f is *state-based* whenever $\forall \rho, \rho' \in$ Runs$(G), last(\rho) = last(\rho')$ implies that $f(\rho) = f(\rho')$. State-based strategies are also called *memoryless* strategies in game theory [11, 19]. The possible runs that may be realized when the controller follows a particular strategy is defined by the following notion of outcome (see e.g. [11]):

Definition 4 (Outcome). *Let* $G = (Q, Q_0, \mathsf{Act}, \longrightarrow)$ *be a TG and f a strategy over G. The* outcome Outcome(q, f) *of f from q in G is the subset of* Runs(q, G) *defined inductively by:*

- $q \in \mathsf{Outcome}(q, f)$,
- if $\rho \in \mathsf{Outcome}(q, f)$ then $\rho' = \rho \xrightarrow{e} q' \in \mathsf{Outcome}(q, f)$ if $\rho' \in \mathsf{Runs}(q, G)$ and
  one of the following three conditions hold:
  1. $e \in \mathsf{Act}_u$,
  2. $e \in \mathsf{Act}_c$ and $e = f(\rho)$,
  3. $e \in \mathbb{R}_{>0}$ and $\forall 0 \le e' < e, \exists q'' \in Q$ s.t. $last(\rho) \xrightarrow{e'} q'' \wedge f(\rho \xrightarrow{e'} q'') = \lambda$.
- for an infinite run ρ, $\rho \in \mathsf{Outcome}(q, f)$ if all the finite prefixes of ρ are in
  $\mathsf{Outcome}(q, f)$.

Note that some strategies may block the evolution at some point for instance if condition 3 above is not satisfied. One has to be careful when synthesizing strategies to ensure condition 3 and this is not trivial (see [7], theorem 2 for details).

Definition 5 (Reachability Timed Games (RTG)). *A reachability timed game* $G = (Q, Q_0, \mathsf{Goal}, \mathsf{Act}, \longrightarrow)$ *is a timed game* $(Q, Q_0, \mathsf{Act}, \longrightarrow)$ *with a distinguished set of goal states* $\mathsf{Goal} \subseteq Q$ *such that for all* $q \in \mathsf{Goal}$, $q \xrightarrow{e} q'$ *implies* $q' \in \mathsf{Goal}$.

If G is a RTG, a run ρ is a *winning run* if $\mathsf{States}(\rho) \cap \mathsf{Goal} \neq \emptyset$. The set of winning runs in G from q is denoted $\mathsf{WinRuns}(q, G)$.

For reachability games one has to choose a semantics for uncontrollable actions: either i) they can only spoil the game and it is up to the controller to do some controllable action to win ([5, 17, 14]) or ii) if at some state s only an uncontrollable action is enabled but forced to happen and leads to a winning state then s is winning. The choice we make is to follow the framework used by La Torre *et al* in [14, 1] where uncontrollable actions cannot help to win. This choice is made for the sake of simplicity (mainly for the proof of theorem 3). However, we can handle any reasonable semantics like ii) above but the proofs are more involved (see [7]).

We now formalize the previous notions. A *maximal run* ρ is either an infinite run (supposing strict alternation of delays and actions) or a finite run ρ that satisfies either (i) $last(\rho) \in \mathsf{Goal}$ or ii) $\forall t \ge 0$, if $\rho \xrightarrow{t} q' \xrightarrow{a}$ then $a \in \mathsf{Act}_u$ (i.e. the only possible next discrete actions from $last(\rho)$, if any, are uncontrollable actions). A strategy f is *winning* from q if all maximal runs in $\mathsf{Outcome}(q, f)$ are in $\mathsf{WinRuns}(q, G)$. A state q in a RTG G is *winning* if there exists a winning strategy f from q in G. We denote by $\mathcal{W}(G)$ the set of winning states in G and $\mathsf{WinStrat}(q, G)$ the set of winning strategies from q over G.

Control of Linear Hybrid Games. In the remainder of this section we summarize previous results [11, 17, 20] obtained for particular classes of RTG: Linear Hybrid Games (LHG).

Let X be a finite set of real-valued variables. We denote $Lin(X)$ the set of linear constraints over the variables in X. $Lin_c(X)$ is the subset of convex linear constraints over X. A *valuation* of the variables in X is a mapping from X to $\mathbb{R}$ (thus an element of $\mathbb{R}^X$). For a valuation v and a *linear assignment*[1] α we denote $v[\alpha]$ the valuation defined by $v[\alpha](x) = \alpha(x)(v)$. $Assign(X)$ is the set of linear assignments over X. For $r : X \longrightarrow \mathbb{Q}$ and $\delta \in \mathbb{R}_{\ge 0}$ we denote $v + r \cdot \delta$ the valuation s.t. for all $x \in X$, $(v + r \cdot \delta)(x) = v(x) + r(x) \cdot \delta$.

---

[1] A linear assignment assigns to each variable a linear expression.

Definition 6 (LHG [12]). *A* Linear Hybrid Game $H = (L, \ell_0, \mathsf{Act}, X, E, \mathsf{inv}, Rate)$ *is a tuple where L is a finite set of* locations, *$\ell_0 \in L$ is the* initial *location,* $\mathsf{Act} = \mathsf{Act}_c \cup \mathsf{Act}_u$ *is the set of* actions *(controllable and uncontrollable actions), X is a finite set of* real-valued variables, *$E \subseteq L \times Lin(X) \times \mathsf{Act} \times Assign(X) \times L$ is a finite set of* transitions, $\mathsf{inv} : L \longrightarrow Lin_c(X)$ *associates to each location its* invariant, *$Rate : L \longrightarrow (X \longrightarrow \mathbb{Q})$ associates to each location and variable an* evolution rate. *A reachability LHG is a LHG with a distinguished set of locations* Goal $\subseteq L$ *(with no outgoing edges). It defines the set of goal states* Goal $\times \mathbb{R}^X$.

The semantics of a LHG $H = (L, \ell_0, \mathsf{Act}, X, E, \mathsf{inv}, Rate)$ is a TTS $S_H = ((L \times \mathbb{R}^X, (\ell_0, 0), \mathsf{Act}, \longrightarrow))$ where $\longrightarrow$ consists of: i) *discrete steps:* $(\ell, v) \xrightarrow{e} (\ell', v')$ if there exists $(\ell, g, e, \alpha, \ell') \in E$ s.t. $v \models g$ and $v' = v[\alpha]$; ii) *time steps:* $(\ell, v) \xrightarrow{\delta} (\ell, v')$ if $\delta \in \mathbb{R}_{\geq 0}$, $v' = v + Rate(\ell) \cdot \delta$ and $v, v' \in \mathsf{inv}(\ell)$.

For reachability LHG, the computation of the winning states is based on the definition of a *controllable predecessors* operator [11, 17]. Let $Q = L \times \mathbb{R}^X$. For a subset $X \subseteq Q$ and $a \in \mathsf{Act}$ we define $\mathsf{Pred}^a(X) = \{q \in Q \mid q \xrightarrow{a} q', q' \in X\}$. The controllable and uncontrollable discrete predecessors of X are defined by $\mathsf{cPred}(X) = \bigcup_{c \in \mathsf{Act}_c} \mathsf{Pred}^c(X)$ and $\mathsf{uPred}(X) = \bigcup_{u \in \mathsf{Act}_u} \mathsf{Pred}^u(X)$. A notion of *safe* timed predecessors of a set X w.r.t. a set Y is also needed. Intuitively a state q is in $\mathsf{Pred}_t(X, Y)$ if from q we can reach $q' \in X$ by time elapsing and along the path from q to q' we avoid Y. Formally this is defined by:

$$\mathsf{Pred}_t(X, Y) = \{q \in Q \mid \exists \delta \in \mathbb{R}_{\geq 0} \text{ s.t. } q \xrightarrow{\delta} q', \ q' \in X \text{ and } Post_{[0,\delta]}(q) \subseteq \overline{Y}\}$$

where $Post_{[0,\delta]}(q) = \{q' \in Q \mid \exists t \in [0, \delta] \text{ s.t. } q \xrightarrow{t} q'\}$. Now we are able to define the *controllable predecessors* operator π as follows:

$$\pi(X) = \mathsf{Pred}_t\left(X \cup \mathsf{cPred}(X), \mathsf{uPred}(\overline{X})\right) \qquad (1)$$

Note that this definition of π captures the choice that uncontrollable actions cannot be used to win. A symbolic version of the π operator can be defined on LHG [11, 17]. Hence there is a semi-algorithm CompWin which computes the least fixed point of $\lambda X.\{\mathsf{Goal}\} \cup \pi(X)$ as the limit of an increasing sequence of sets of states (starting with the initial state Goal). If H is a reachability LHG, the result of the computation $\mu X.\{\mathsf{Goal}\} \cup \pi(X)$ is denoted $\mathsf{CompWin}(H)$.

Theorem 1 (Symbolic Algorithm for LHG [11]). $\mathcal{W}(S_H) = \mathsf{CompWin}(H)$ *for a reachability LHG H and hence* CompWin *is a symbolic semi-algorithm for computing the winning states of a reachability LHG.*

As for controller synthesis the previous algorithm allows us to compute the winning states of a game but the extraction of strategies is not made particularly explicit. The proof of the following theorem (given in [7]) provides a symbolic algorithm (assuming time determinism) that synthesizes winning.

Theorem 2 (Synthesis of Winning Strategies [7]). *Let H be a LHG. If the semi-algorithm* CompWin *terminates for H, then we can compute a polyhedral[2] strategy which is winning in each state of* $\mathsf{CompWin}(H)$ *and state-based.*

---

[2] A strategy f is polyhedral if for all $a \in \mathsf{Act}_c \cup \{\lambda\}$, $f^{-1}(a)$ is a finite union of convex polyhedra for each location of the LHG.

3   Priced Timed Games (PTG)

In this section we define *Priced Timed Games (PTG)*. We focus on *reachability PTG (RPTG)* where the aim is to reach a particular state of the game at the *lowest* possible cost. We give a new run-based definition of the *optimal cost*. We then relate our definition with the one given in [14] (note that the definition of [1] seems close to the one in [14] but it is not clear enough for us how close they are) and prove both definitions are indeed equivalent.

Priced Timed Games

Definition 7 (Priced Timed Transition Systems (PTTS)). *A priced timed transition system is a pair (S, Cost) where $S = (Q, Q_0, \mathsf{Act}, \longrightarrow)$ is a TTS and Cost is a cost function i.e. a mapping from $\longrightarrow$ to $\mathbb{R}_{\geq 0}$ that satisfies:*

- PRICE ADDITIVITY: *if $q \xrightarrow{d} q'$ and $q' \xrightarrow{d'} q''$ with $d, d' \in \mathbb{R}_{\geq 0}$, then the following holds: $\mathsf{Cost}(q \xrightarrow{d+d'} q'') = \mathsf{Cost}(q \xrightarrow{d} q') + \mathsf{Cost}(q' \xrightarrow{d'} q'')$.*
- BOUNDED COST RATE: *there exists $K \in \mathbb{N}$ such that for every $q \xrightarrow{d} q'$ where $d \in \mathbb{R}_{\geq 0}$, $\mathsf{Cost}(q \xrightarrow{d} q') \leq d.K$*

For a transition $q \xrightarrow{e} q'$, $\mathsf{Cost}(q \xrightarrow{e} q')$ is the cost *of the transition and we note $q \xrightarrow{e,p} q'$ if $p = \mathsf{Cost}(q \xrightarrow{e} q')$.*

All notions concerning runs on TTS extend straightforwardly to PTTS. Let S be a PTTS and $\rho = q_0 \xrightarrow{e_1} q_1 \xrightarrow{e_2} \ldots \xrightarrow{e_n} q_n$ a finite run[3] of S. The *cost* of ρ is defined by $\mathsf{Cost}(\rho) = \sum_{i=0}^{n-1} \mathsf{Cost}(q_i \xrightarrow{e_{i+1}} q_{i+1})$.

Definition 8 (Priced Timed Games). *A priced timed game (PTG) (resp. Reachability PTG) is a pair $G = (S, \mathsf{Cost})$ such that S is a TG (resp. RTG) and Cost is a cost function.*

All the notions like strategies, outcomes, winning states are already defined for (R)TG and carry over in a natural way to (R)PTG. The *cost* $\mathsf{Cost}(q, f)$ of a winning strategy $f \in \mathsf{WinStrat}(q, G)$ is defined by: $\mathsf{Cost}(q, f) = \sup \{\mathsf{Cost}(\rho) \mid \rho \in \mathsf{Outcome}(q, f)\}$.

Definition 9 (Optimal Cost for a RPTG). *Let G be a RPTG and q be a state in G. The* reachable costs set $\mathsf{Cost}(q)$ *from q in G is defined by:*

$$\mathsf{Cost}(q) = \{\mathsf{Cost}(q, f) \mid f \in \mathsf{WinStrat}(q, G)\}$$

The optimal cost from q in G is $\mathsf{OptCost}(q) = \inf \mathsf{Cost}(q)$. *The optimal cost in G is $\sup_{q \in Q_0} \mathsf{OptCost}(q)$ where Q_0 denotes the set of initial states.*

---

[3] We are not interested in defining the cost of an infinite run as we will only use costs of winning runs which must be finite in the games we play.

Definition 10 (Optimal Strategies for a RPTG). *Let G be a RPTG and q a state in G. A winning strategy $f \in$ WinStrat(q, G) is said to be* optimal *whenever* Cost$(q, f) =$ OptCost(q).

Optimal winning strategies do not always exist, even for RPTGs deriving from timed automata (see [7]). A family of winning strategies (f_ε) which get arbitrarily close to the optimal cost may be rather determined. Our aim is many-fold. We want to 1) compute the optimal cost of winning, 2) decide whether there is an optimal strategy, and 3) in case there is an optimal strategy compute one such strategy. Before giving a solution to the previous problems we relate our definition of cost optimality to the one given in [14, 1].

Recursive Definition of the Optimal Cost. In [14, 1] a method for computing the optimal cost in priced timed games is introduced: it is defined as the optimal cost one can expect from a state by a function satisfying a set of recursive equations, and not using a run-based definition as we did in the last subsection. We give hereafter the definition of the function used in [14] and prove that it does correspond to our run-based definition of optimal cost. In [1], a similar but more involved definition is proposed, we do not detail this last definition here.

Definition 11 (The O Function (Adapted from [14])). *Let G be a RPTG. Let O be the function from Q to $\mathbb{R}_{\geq 0} \cup \{+\infty\}$ that is the least fixed point[4] of the following functional:*

$$
O(q) = \inf_{\substack{q \xrightarrow{t,p} q' \\ t \in \mathbb{R}_{\geq 0}}} \max
\begin{cases}
\min \left(\left(\min_{\substack{q' \xrightarrow{c,p'} q'' \\ c \in \mathsf{Act}_c}} p + p' + O(q'') \right), p + O(q') \right) & (1) \\[4ex]
\sup_{\substack{q \xrightarrow{t',p'} q'' \\ t' \leq t}} \max_{\substack{q'' \xrightarrow{u,p''} q''' \\ u \in \mathsf{Act}_u}} p' + p'' + O(q''') & (2)
\end{cases}
\qquad (\diamondsuit)
$$

The following theorem relates the two definitions:

Theorem 3. *Let $G = (S, \mathsf{Cost})$ be a RPTG induced by a LHG and Q its set of states. Then $O(q) = $ OptCost(q) for all $q \in Q$.[5]*

4   Reducing Priced Timed Games to Timed Games

In this section we show that computing the optimal cost to win a priced timed game amounts to solving a control problem (without cost).

---

[4] The righthand-sides of the equations for $O(q)$ defines a functional $\mathcal{F}$ on $(Q \longrightarrow \mathbb{R}_{\geq 0} \cup \{+\infty\})$. $(Q \longrightarrow \mathbb{R}_{\geq 0} \cup \{+\infty\})$ equipped with the natural lifting of $\leq$ on $\mathbb{R}_{\geq 0} \cup \{+\infty\}$ constitutes a complete lattice. Also $\mathcal{F}$ can be quite easily seen to be a monotonic functional on this lattice. It follows from Tarski's fixed point theory that the least fix point of $\mathcal{F}$ exists.

[5] Note that if a state $q \in Q$ is not winning, both $O(q)$ and OptCost(q) are $+\infty$.

Priced Timed Game Automata. Let X be a finite set of real-valued variables called clocks. We denote $\mathcal{B}(X)$ the set of constraints φ generated by the grammar: $\varphi ::= x \sim k \mid \varphi \wedge \varphi$ where $k \in \mathbb{Z}$, $x, y \in X$ and $\sim \in \{<, \leq, =, >, \geq\}$. A *valuation* of the variables in X is a mapping from X to $\mathbb{R}_{\geq 0}$ (thus an element of $\mathbb{R}_{\geq 0}^X$). For a valuation v and a set $R \subseteq X$ we denote $v[R]$ the valuation that agrees with v on $X \setminus R$ and is zero on R. We denote $v + \delta$ for $\delta \in \mathbb{R}_{\geq 0}$ the valuation s.t. for all $x \in X$, $(v + \delta)(x) = v(x) + \delta$.

Definition 12 (PTGA). *A Priced Timed Game Automaton A is a tuple $(L, \ell_0, \mathsf{Act}, X, E, \mathsf{inv}, f)$ where L is a finite set of locations, $\ell_0 \in L$ is the initial location, $\mathsf{Act} = \mathsf{Act}_c \cup \mathsf{Act}_u$ is the set of actions (partitioned into controllable and uncontrollable actions), X is a finite set of real-valued clocks, $E \subseteq L \times \mathcal{B}(X) \times \mathsf{Act} \times 2^X \times L$ is a finite set of transitions, $\mathsf{inv} : L \longrightarrow \mathcal{B}(X)$ associates to each location its invariant, $f : L \cup E \longrightarrow \mathbb{N}$ associates to each location a cost rate and to each discrete transition a cost. A reachability PTGA (RPTGA) is a PTGA with a distinguished set of locations $\mathsf{Goal} \subseteq L$ (with no outgoing edges). It defines the set of goal states $\mathsf{Goal} \times \mathbb{R}_{\geq 0}^X$.*

The semantics of the PTGA is a PTTS $S_A = ((L \times \mathbb{R}_{\geq 0}^X, (\ell_0, \mathbf{0}), \mathsf{Act}, \longrightarrow), \mathsf{Cost})$ where $\longrightarrow$ consists of: i) *discrete steps:* $(\ell, v) \xrightarrow{e} (\ell', v')$ if there exists $(\ell, g, e, R, \ell') \in E$ s.t. $v \models g$ and $v' = v[R]$; $\mathsf{Cost}((\ell, v) \xrightarrow{e} (\ell', v')) = f(\ell, g, e, R, \ell')$; ii) *time steps:* $(\ell, v) \xrightarrow{\delta} (\ell, v')$ if $\delta \in \mathbb{R}_{\geq 0}$, $v' = v + \delta$ and $v, v' \in \mathsf{inv}(\ell)$; and $\mathsf{Cost}((\ell, v) \xrightarrow{\delta} (\ell, v')) = \delta \cdot f(\ell)$. Note that this definition of Cost gives a cost function as defined in Def. 7.

From Optimal Reachability Game to Reachability Game. Assume we want to compute the optimal cost to win a reachability priced timed game automaton A. We define a (usual and unpriced) LHG H as follows: we use a variable *cost* in the LHG to stand for the cost value. We build H with the same discrete structure as A and specify a rate for *cost* in each location: if the cost increases with a rate of $+k$ per unit of time in A, then we set the derivative of *cost* to be $-k$ in H; if the cost of a discrete transition is $+k$ in A, then we update *cost* by $cost := cost - k$ in H. To each state q in (the semantics of) A there are many corresponding states (q, c) in H, where c is the value of the *cost* variable. For such a state (q, c) we denote $\exists cost.(q, c)$ the state q. If X is a set of states in (the semantics of) H then $\exists cost.X = \{q \mid \exists c \geq 0 \mid (q, c) \in X\}$. From the PTGA of Fig. 1 we obtain the LHG of Fig. 2.

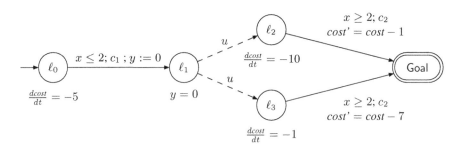

Fig. 2. The Linear Hybrid Game H

Now we solve the following control problem on the LHG: "can we win in H with the goal states Goal $\land cost \geq 0$?" Intuitively speaking we are asking the question: "what is the minimal amount of resource ($cost$) needed to win the control game H?" For a PTGA A we can compute the winning states of H with the semi-algorithm CompWin (defined at the end of section 2) and if it terminates the wining set of states $W_H = \text{CompWin}(H)$ is a union of zones of the form $(\ell, R \land cost \succ h)$ where ℓ is a location, $R \subseteq \mathbb{R}^X_{\geq 0}$, h is a piece-wise affine function on R and $\succ \in \{>, \geq\}$ (because π preserves this kind of sets). Hence we have the answer to the optimal reachability game: we intersect the set of initial states with the set of winning states W_H, and in case it is not empty, the projection on the $cost$ axis yields a constraint on the cost like $cost \succ k$ with $k \in \mathbb{Q}_{\geq 0}$ and $\succ \in \{>, \geq\}$. By definition of winning set of states in reachability games, *i.e.* this is the largest set from which we can win, no cost lower than or equal to k is winning and we can deduce that k is the optimal cost. Also we can decide whether there is an optimal strategy or not: if $\succ$ is equal to $>$ there is no optimal strategy and if $\succ$ is $\geq$ there is one.

Note that with our reduction of optimal control of PTGA to control of LHG, the cost information becomes part of the state and that the runs in A and H are closely related. The correctness of the reduction is then given by the next theorem.

Theorem 4. *Let A be a RPTGA and H its corresponding LHG (as defined above). If the semi-algorithm CompWin terminates for H and if $W_H = \text{CompWin}(H)$, then: 1)* CompWin *terminates for A and $W_A \stackrel{def}{=} \text{CompWin}(A) = \exists cost.W_H$; and 2) $(q, c) \in W_H \iff$ there exists $f \in \text{WinStrat}(q, W_A)$ with $\text{Cost}(q, f) \leq c$.*

Computation of the Optimal Cost and Strategy. Let $X \subseteq \mathbb{R}^n_{\geq 0}$. The *upward closure* of X, denoted $\uparrow X$ is the set $\uparrow X = \{x' \mid \exists x \in X \text{ s.t. } x' \geq x\}$.

Theorem 5. *Let A be a RPTGA and H its corresponding LHG. If the semi-algorithm CompWin terminates for H then for $q \in W_A$, $\uparrow \text{Cost}(q) = \{c \mid (q, c) \in W_H\}$.*

Corollary 1 (Optimal Cost). *Let A be a RPTGA and H its corresponding LHG. If the semi-algorithm CompWin terminates for H then $\uparrow \text{Cost}(\ell_0, \mathbf{0})$ is computable and is of the form $cost \geq k$ (left-closed) or $cost > k$ (left-open) with $k \in \mathbb{Q}_{\geq 0}$. In addition we get that $\text{OptCost}(l_0, \mathbf{0}) = k$.*

Corollary 2 (Existence of an Optimal Strategy). *Let A be a RPTGA. If $\uparrow \text{Cost}(\ell_0, \mathbf{0})$ is left-open then there is no optimal strategy. Otherwise we can compute a winning and optimal strategy.*

Termination Criterion and Optimal Strategies

Theorem 6. *Let A be a RPTGA satisfying the following hypotheses: 1) A is bounded, i.e. all clocks in A are bounded ; 2) the cost function of A is strictly non-zeno, i.e. there exists some $\kappa > 0$ such that the accumulated cost of every cycle in the region automaton associated with A is at least κ. Then the semi-algorithm CompWin terminates for H, where H is the LHG associated with A.*

Note that the strategy built in corollary 2 is state-based for H but is *a priori* no more state-based for A: indeed the strategy for H depends on the current value of the cost (which is part of the state in H). The strategy for A is thus dependent on the run and not memoryless. More precisely it depends on the last state (ℓ, v) of the run and on the accumulated cost along the run.

Nevertheless, we now give a sufficient condition for the existence of optimal cost-independent strategies and exhibit a restricted class of automata for which this conditions holds.

Theorem 7. *Let A be a RPTGA and H the associated LHG. If* CompWin *terminates for H and W_H is a union of sets of the form $(\ell, R, cost \geq h)$ then there exists a state-based strategy f defined over $W_A = \exists cost.W_H$ s.t. for each $q \in W_A$, $f \in$ WinStrat(q, W_A) and* Cost$(q, f) =$ OptCost(q).

Note that under the previous conditions we build a strategy f which is *uniformly optimal i.e.* optimal for all states of W_A. A syntactical criterion to enforce the condition of theorem 7 is that the constraints (guards) on controllable actions are non-strict and constraints on uncontrollable actions are strict.

Remarks on the Hypotheses in Theorems 6 and 7. The hypothesis on A being bounded is not restrictive because all priced timed automata can be transformed into bounded priced timed automata having the same behaviours (see for example [16]). The strict non-zenoness of the cost function can be checked on priced timed game automata: indeed it is sufficient to check whether there is a cycle whose price is 0 in the so-called "corner-point abstraction" (see [6, 9]) ; then, if there is no cycle with cost 0, it means that the cost is strictly non-zeno, otherwise, it is not strictly non-zeno.

5   Conclusion

In this paper we have given a new run-based definition of cost optimality for priced timed games. This definition enables us to prove the following results: the optimal cost can be computed for the class of priced timed game automata with a strictly non-zeno cost. Moreover we can decide whether there exists an optimal strategy which could not be done in previous works [14, 1]. In case an optimal strategy exists we can compute a witness. Finally we give some additional results concerning the type of information needed by the optimal strategy and exhibit a class of priced timed game automata for which optimal state-based (no need to keep track of the cost information) can be synthetized. Our strategy extraction algorithm has been implemented using the tool HYTECH [8].

Our future work will be on extending the class of systems for which termination is ensured. Our claim is that there is no need for the strict non-zenoness hypothesis for termination. Another direction will consist in extending our work to optimal safety games where we want to minimize for example the cost per time unit along infinite schedules whatever the environment does, which would naturally extends both this current work and [9].

References

1. R. Alur, M. Bernadsky, and P. Madhusudan. Optimal reachability in weighted timed games. In *Proc. 31st Int. Coll. Automata, Languages and Programming (ICALP'04), LNCS 3142*, pp. 122–133. Springer, 2004.
2. R. Alur, C. Courcoubetis, and T. Henzinger. Computing accumulated delays in real-time systems. In *Proc. 5th Int. Conf. Computer Aided Verification (CAV'93), LNCS 697*, pp. 181–193. Springer, 1993.
3. R. Alur, S. La Torre, and G. Pappas. Optimal paths in weighted timed automata. In *Proc. 4th Int. Work. Hybrid Systems: Computation and Control (HSCC'01), LNCS 2034*, pp. 49–62. Springer, 2001.
4. E. Asarin and O. Maler. As soon as possible: Time optimal control for timed automata. In *Proc. 2nd Int. Work. Hybrid Systems: Computation and Control (HSCC'99), LNCS 1569*, pp. 19–30. Springer, 1999.
5. E. Asarin, O. Maler, A. Pnueli, and J. Sifakis. Controller synthesis for timed automata. In *Proc. IFAC Symp. System Structure and Control*, pp. 469–474. Elsevier Science, 1998.
6. G. Behrmann, A. Fehnker, T. Hune, K. Larsen, P. Pettersson, J. Romijn, and F. Vaandrager. Minimum-cost reachability for priced timed automata. In *Proc. 4th Int. Work. Hybrid Systems: Computation and Control (HSCC'01), LNCS 2034*, pp. 147–161. Springer, 2001.
7. P. Bouyer, F. Cassez, E. Fleury and K. Larsen. Optimal Strategies on Priced Timed Game Automata. BRICS Report Series, February 2004.
8. P. Bouyer, F. Cassez, E. Fleury and K. Larsen. Synthesis of Optimal Strategies Using HyTech. In Proc. Games in Design and Verification (GDV'04), ENTCS. Elsevier, 2004. To appear.
9. P. Bouyer, E. Brinksma, and K. Larsen. Staying alive as cheaply as possible. In *Proc. 7th Int. Work. Hybrid Systems: Computation and Control (HSCC'04), LNCS 2993*, pp. 203–218. Springer, 2004.
10. C. Courcoubetis and M. Yannakakis. Minimum and maximum delay problems in real-time systems. *Formal Methods in System Design*, 1(4):385–415, 1992.
11. L. De Alfaro, T. Henzinger, and R. Majumdar. Symbolic algorithms for infinite-state games. In *Proc. 12th Int. Conf. Concurrency Theory (CONCUR'01), LNCS 2154*, pp. 536–550. Springer, 2001.
12. T. Henzinger. The theory of hybrid automata. In *Proc. 11th IEEE Annual Symp. Logic in Computer Science (LICS'96)*, pp. 278–292. IEEE Computer Society Press, 1996.
13. T. Hune, K. Larsen, and P. Pettersson. Guided synthesis of control programs using UPPAAL. In *Proc. IEEE ICDS Int. Work. Distributed Systems Verification and Validation*, pp. E15–E22. IEEE Computer Society Press, 2000.
14. S. La Torre, S. Mukhopadhyay, and A. Murano. Optimal-reachability and control for acyclic weighted timed automata. In *Proc. 2nd IFIP Int. Conf. Theoretical Computer Science (TCS 2002), IFIP Proceedings 223*, pp. 485–497. Kluwer, 2002.
15. K. Larsen. Resource-efficient scheduling for real time systems. In *Proc. 3rd Int. Conf. Embedded Software (EMSOFT'03), LNCS 2855*, pp. 16–19. Springer, 2003. Invited talk.
16. K. Larsen, G. Behrmann, E. Brinksma, A. Fehnker, T. Hune, P. Pettersson, and J. Romijn. As cheap as possible: Efficient cost-optimal reachability for priced timed automata. In *Proc. 13th Int. Conf. Computer Aided Verification (CAV'01), LNCS 2102*, pp. 493–505. Springer, 2001.
17. O. Maler, A. Pnueli, and J. Sifakis. On the synthesis of discrete controllers for timed systems. In *Proc. 12th Annual Symp. Theoretical Aspects of Computer Science (STACS'95), LNCS 900*, pp. 229–242. Springer, 1995.

18. P. Niebert, S. Tripakis, and S. Yovine. Minimum-time reachability for timed automata. In *Proc. 8th IEEE Mediterranean Conf. Control and Automation*, 2000.
19. W. Thomas. On the synthesis of strategies in infinite games. In *Proc. 12th Annual Symp. Theoretical Aspects of Computer Science (STACS'95), LNCS 900*, pp. 1–13. Springer, 1995. Invited talk.
20. H. Wong-Toi. The synthesis of controllers for linear hybrid automata. In *Proc. 36th IEEE Conf. Decision and Control*, pp. 4607–4612. IEEE Computer Society Press, 1997.

A Calculus for Trust Management

Marco Carbone[1], Mogens Nielsen[1], and Vladimiro Sassone[2]

[1] BRICS*, University of Aarhus
[2] Dept. of Informatics, University of Sussex

Abstract. We introduce ctm, a process calculus which embodies a notion of trust for global computing systems. In ctm each principal (location) is equipped with a policy, which determines its legal behaviour, and with a protocol, which allows interactions between principals and the flow of information from principals to policies. We elect to formalise policies using a Datalog-like logic, and to express protocols in the process algebra style. This yields an expressive calculus very suitable for the global computing scenarios, and provides a formalisation of notions such as trust evolution. For ctm we define barbed equivalences and study their possible applications.

1 Introduction

In the last few years Global Computing (GC) has emerged as an important part of computer science. A GC system is composed of entities which are autonomous, decentralised, mobile, dynamically configurable, and capable of operating under partial information. Such systems, e.g. the Internet, become easily very complex, and bring forward the need to guarantee security properties. Traditional security mechanisms, however, have severe limitations in this setting, as they often are either too weak to safeguard against actual risks, or too stringent, imposing unacceptable burdens on the effectiveness and flexibility of the infrastructure. Trust management systems, in which safety critical decision are made based on trust policies and their deployment in the presence of partial knowledge, have been proposed as an alternative attempting to deal with those limitations.

Building on the experience of our previous work on trust [8] we introduce a process calculus for modelling trust management systems (ctm). Many models for trust based system have appeared in the literature, and most of them feature some sort of logic to describe trust policies. However, lacking a notion of protocol,

Marco Carbone and Mogens Nielsen supported by '**SECURE**: Secure Environments for Collaboration among Ubiquitous Roaming Entities', EU FET-GC IST-2001-32486. Marco Carbone supported by '**DisCo**: Semantic Foundations of Distributed Computation', EU IHP 'Marie Curie' HPMT-CT-2001-00290. Vladimiro Sassone supported by '**MyThS**: Models and Types for Security in Mobile Distributed Systems', EU FET-GC IST-2001-32617. *Basic Research In Computer Science funded by the Danish National Research Foundation.

K. Lodaya and M. Mahajan (Eds.): FSTTCS 2004, LNCS 3328, pp. 161–173, 2004.

such approaches typically fall short to describe the exact behaviour of systems, which is a fundamental property when security concerns are present. Consider for instance a server whose policy is to grant access only to a certain class of users, but whose (flawed) protocol of communication always allows access to a particular resource. Even though the policy may be correct, the whole system is not. A second aspect of paramount importance here is to allow principals' interactions to feedback to the security mechanisms and influence future policies. For instance, access rights can change for a principal in response to its behaviour, and how precisely this behaviour should be observed and the variation should take place ought to be part of the model.

The aim of this work is to develop a coherent framework centred on these two aspects, and establish its basic theory. In ctm, a principal is specified by a pair, a policy α and a protocol P, which interact in precise ways, as described below. The policy α informs the protocol P as to what actions are allowed at any given time, and works on the basis of evidence and observations collected from past interactions. Dually, P interacts with a network of other principals, and in doing so it produces the observations gathered in α. The protocol P will consult α when making a decision, e.g. whether or not to grant a specific service to a specific principal. Schematically, we can represent the situation as in the informal picture below.

$$(\text{Policy} \iff \text{Protocol}) \quad \| \quad \text{Network}$$

We model the "policy" side of the drawing with a decidable logic. The choice is a Datalog-like logic: a principal's policy will be represented as a set of formulas depending on a set of past observations. On the "protocol" side, our model is based on a process calculus in the style of the π-calculus [14]. More precisely, ctm is a calculus with locations linked by channel names. Each location (uniquely) identifies a principal, and the diagram above would be represented as $a\{\ P\ \}_\alpha \mid N$, where a is a principal with protocol P and policy α, in parallel with the rest of the network N. In ctm we associate the action of sending a message to another principal as granting a particular resource (viz. the service represented by the channel name). Outputs will then be guarded by a formula ϕ from the logic, as for instance $\phi :: b \cdot \ell\langle \tilde{m}\rangle$, which according to the truth value of ϕ allows the protocol to send $\tilde{m}$ to b on channel (or method) ℓ. As a concrete example, a protocol like $Access(b, R) :: b \cdot l\langle n\rangle$ would stand for "if my policy grants b '$Access$' to R, then send n along l to b." Symmetrically, inputs represent requests of services, and form the observable basis mentioned above. For instance, if executing an input action $b \cdot \mathtt{print}(y) \cdot P$, we receive a message 'junk' for y from b, we observe and record that b has attempted to print a corrupted file. As mentioned above, multiple channels at a single location allows to distinguish among different services provided by a principal. We assume in ctm that the identity of communicating principals cannot be corrupted (i.e. we assume implicitly that authenticity etc. is guaranteed by lower level protocols).

In order to allow principals to offer services to generic (as opposed to named) clients, ctm features a new form of input capability, which allows to abstract from the communicating principal. For instance, in order to offer a printing service for all, we would write $x \cdot \mathtt{print}(y) \cdot P$, where x is a variable, which at the time of interaction will be bound to the name of the principal requesting the service. We call this operation *global input*.

The calculus $\mathtt{ctm}$ seems a powerful tool for expressing several examples of trust-based systems for GC. Casting these ingredients in the world of process algebras provides many interesting theoretical notions, and in particular behavioural equivalences. The natural separation of principals in pairs of components, viz. policies and protocols, induces new notions of equivalences. In particular, besides studying equivalences of principals and networks, one can focus on protocols as well as policies. Technically, the main contribution of this paper is to introduce a theory of observational equivalence for trust-based systems, which captures in a single, homogeneous framework with equivalence of protocols, policies, and principals.

Related Work. To the best of our knowledge, the notion of trust has never been fully treated in process calculi. In $D\pi$ [3, 10] policies are statically specified, not allowing dynamic updates; [9] considers a formalism for cryptographic protocols, similar to ours: communications are guarded by logical formulas meant for proving correctness, whereas protocols are expressed with strand-spaces. Concerning policies for access control, there are many works on logics, where a trust engine is responsible for constructing [6, 11, 12] or checking [4] a proof that a desired request is valid. In [13] and [5] authors provide a decidable logic for policies, proposing variants of Datalog. In particular, *Cassandra*, provides a formalism for expressing policies in a GC scenario, where, as in our case, each principal has its own policy. They also allow references to other principals' polices and delegation, using fixed-point computations as in [8].

Plan of the Paper. Section 2 defines the calculus: logic for policies, syntax and semantics of networks and protocols. In Section 3 we study barbed equivalences on protocols, policies and principals, while Section 4 is about the expressiveness of global input.

2   The Calculus

Let Val be a denumerable set of values ranged over by l, m and partitioned into sets P and N, respectively the set of principals (ranged over by a, b, c) and the set of names (ranged over by n). Moreover Var (ranged over by x, y, z) is a set of variables such that $\mathsf{Var} \cap \mathsf{Val} = \emptyset$. In the sequel we assume u, v in $\mathsf{Var} \cup \mathsf{Val}$ and p in $\mathsf{Var} \cup \mathsf{P}$. As usual a tilde over a letter indicates the extension to vectors.

A Small Logic for Policies. As explained in the introduction, each principal acts on a body of knowledge built on the past interactions with other principals. We represent such information using the notion of interaction datatype. Messages in our calculus have form $a \cdot \tilde{l} \triangleright \tilde{m}$ representing a message $\tilde{m}$ from principal a on channel $\tilde{l}$.

Definition 1 (Interaction Datatype). An interaction datatype $\mathcal{M}$ over Val is a triple $(\mathcal{S}, \mathcal{R}, \mathsf{upd})$ where $\mathcal{S}$ is a generic set of so-called interaction values, $\mathcal{R}$ is a set of decidable subset of $\mathcal{S} \times \mathsf{Val}^k$, and upd is a function which given $s \in \mathcal{S}$ and a message $a \cdot \tilde{l} \triangleright \tilde{m}$ returns an element of $\mathcal{S}$.

According to the above definition, the set $\mathcal{S}$ is a generic set: the idea is to build elements of $\mathcal{S}$ as representation of abstract information about past interactions with other principals. The set $\mathcal{R}$ defines the basic predicates binding together interaction values and elements of Val, and upd defines the effect in $\mathcal{S}$ by receiving a message.

Example 1 (Lists and Multisets). Let $\mathcal{S}$ be the set of lists with elements $a \cdot \tilde{l} \triangleright \tilde{m}$, i.e. $\mathcal{S} = \{[a_1 \cdot \tilde{l}_1 \triangleright \tilde{m}_1, \ldots, a_k \cdot \tilde{l}_k \triangleright \tilde{m}_k] \mid k \geq 0\}$ and upd the operation of list concatenation. The set $\mathcal{R}$ could contain the relation $\mathsf{last}_{\tilde{m}}$ which holds true of lists whose last element carries the message $\tilde{m}$, and the relation $\mathsf{from}{\geq}5(a)$, satisfied whenever the number of messages in the list from a is larger than 5. Another interesting example is when $\mathcal{S}$ is the set of multisets over elements $a \cdot \tilde{l} \triangleright \tilde{m}$ with multiset union as upd. Predicates can express the number of message occurrences, e.g. predicate $x \cdot - \triangleright y < k$ is satisfied by all elements of $\mathcal{S}$ such that the number of occurrences of elements $x \cdot z \triangleright y$ is less than k.

Principals use policies to make decisions based on the information contained in an element $s \in \mathcal{S}$ of a given interaction datatype $\mathcal{M}$.

Definition 2 (Policy). Let $\mathcal{M} = (\mathcal{S}, \mathcal{R}, \mathsf{upd})$ be an interaction datatype, let $\mathcal{P}$ and $\mathcal{P}_{\mathcal{M}}$ be disjoint signatures of predicates symbols, with $\mathcal{P}_{\mathcal{M}}$ in one-to-one correspondence with $\mathcal{R}$. A policy π is defined as a set of rules of type $L(\tilde{u}) \leftarrow L_1(\tilde{u}_1), \ldots L_k(\tilde{u}_k)$ such that $L \in \mathcal{P}$ and $L_i \in \mathcal{P} \cup \mathcal{P}_{\mathcal{M}}$.

π is interpreted as a Datalog program [2] relative to an element $s \in \mathcal{S}$. More precisely, each rule in π is interpreted as Datalog implication, where predicate symbols in $\mathcal{P}_{\mathcal{R}}$ take as an implicit first argument the interaction value s. Given a pair (π, s) and a predicate $A(\tilde{l})$ we write $(\pi, s) \vdash A(\tilde{l})$ meaning that $A(\tilde{l})$ is entailed by the Datalog program π relative to s. In the sequel, letters α, β will denote pairs (π, s).

Syntax for the Calculus. Let $\mathcal{M}$ be a interaction datatype, $\mathcal{P}$ a signature. The syntax of $\mathtt{ctm}$ is then featured by two main syntactic categories: *networks* (N) and *protocols* (P, Q).

$N, M ::=$	ϵ	(empty)	$P, Q ::=$	$\mathbf{0}$	(null)
	$\mid N \mid N$	(net-par)		$\mid Z$	(sub)
	$\mid a\{\, P \,\}_\alpha$	(principal)		$\mid P \mid P$	(par)
	$\mid (\nu n)\, N$	(new-net)		$\mid (\nu n)\, P$	(new)
				$\mid\, !P$	(bang)

$Z ::=$	$p \cdot \tilde{u}(\tilde{v}) . P$	(input)			
	$\mid \phi :: p \cdot \tilde{u}\langle \tilde{v}\rangle . P$	(output)	$\phi ::=$	$L(\tilde{l}) \quad L \in \mathcal{P}$	(null)
	$\mid Z + Z$	(sum)		$\phi \wedge \phi$	(and)

A network N is composed of principals running in parallel. Each principal is equipped with a protocol P and a policy α. From now on we assume to work only with networks N where principals names are unique, i.e. for each $a \in \mathsf{P}$ there is at most one subterm of N of the kind $a\{\ P\ \}_\alpha$.

A protocol P is given in the style of π-calculus [14]. The protocol $\mathbf{0}$ represents the inactive process. Terms (input) and (output) represent the main actions, and both can be part of the standard sum operator (guarded choice). As remarked in the introduction, the input capability can either refer to a specific principal, or be global. The output action sends a message on a channel and is guarded by a predicate ϕ in the signature $\mathcal{P}$. For generality, we allow composite channel names as in [7]. The (bang) and (par) operators are standard. The rest of the paper will omit trailing inactive processes.

The set of free names fn (resp. bound names bn) and free variables fv (resp. bound variables bv) are defined as usual on networks and protocols. Closed and open terms are defined as usual (with respect to variables). The symbol σ denotes a substitution from variables to names. Applying a substitution σ to a network N (or a protocol P) will be denoted by $N\sigma$ ($P\sigma$). The global input variable is a strong binder, e.g. in $x \cdot l(y).x \cdot l(y)$ the first x binds the second, instead the first y does not bind the second y. We omit trivial guards from outputs, i.e. $\mathtt{tt} :: b \cdot \tilde{l}\langle \tilde{m} \rangle$ will be written as $b \cdot \tilde{l}\langle \tilde{m} \rangle$ where $\mathtt{tt}$ denotes the "always" true predicate.

Reduction Semantics. In this section we give the formal semantics of the calculus in terms of reduction semantics. The structural congruence relation $\equiv$ is the least congruence relation on N such that $|$ and $+$ are commutative monoids on protocols, $|$ is a commutative monoid on networks, and such that it satisfies alpha-conversion and the rules

$$(Struct_1) \qquad a\{\ !P\ |\ Q\ \}_\alpha \equiv a\{\ P\ |\ !P\ |\ Q\ \}_\alpha$$

$$(Struct_2) \qquad (\nu n)\ (\nu n')\ W \equiv (\nu n')\ (\nu n)\ W \text{ for } W \in \{P, N\}$$

$$(Struct_3) \qquad a\{\ (\nu n)\ P\ |\ Q\ \}_\alpha \equiv a\{\ (\nu n)\ (P\ |\ Q)\ \}_\alpha \quad \text{if } n \notin fn(Q)$$

$$(Struct_4) \qquad (\nu n)\ N\ |\ M \equiv (\nu n)\ (N\ |\ M) \quad \text{if } n \notin fn(M)$$

$$(Struct_5) \qquad a\{\ (\nu n)\ P\ \}_\alpha \equiv (\nu n)\ a\{\ P\ \}_\alpha$$

We define $\rightarrow$ as the least binary relation on N satisfying the rules given in Table 1. Rule (RCom) defines communication between two principals. For $\alpha = \langle \pi, s \rangle$, the operator $\alpha \oplus [b \cdot \tilde{l} \rhd \tilde{m}]$ returns a new $\alpha' = \langle \pi, s' \rangle$ such that $s' = \mathsf{upd}(s, b \cdot \tilde{l} \rhd \tilde{m})$. The operator $\odot$ is defined on tuples, as the most general unifier returning a substitution σ, whose application in the semantics is conditioned by successful unification. The rule (RInt) describes internal communication and is similar to (RCom). Rules (RStruct) and (RPar) are standard. As usual we define $\rightarrow^*$ as the reflexive and transitive closure of $\rightarrow$.

Example 2. Suppose a printer a has two functions: black-and-white and colour printing. The latter service is more expensive and therefore "harder" to get access to. The system is trust-based, meaning that according to its behaviour a principal may not be allowed to use a printer. In ctm this corresponds to writing

Table 1. Reduction Rules

$$\text{(RCom)} \ \frac{\beta \vdash \phi \quad \alpha' = \alpha \oplus [b \cdot \tilde{l} \rhd \tilde{m}] \quad b : \tilde{m} \odot p : \tilde{x} = \sigma}{a\{p \cdot \tilde{l}(\tilde{x}) . P + P' \mid P''\}_\alpha \mid b\{\phi :: a \cdot \tilde{l}\langle \tilde{m}\rangle . Q + Q' \mid Q''\}_\beta \to a\{P\sigma \mid P''\}_{\alpha'} \mid b\{Q \mid Q''\}_\beta}$$

$$\text{(RInt)} \ \frac{\alpha \vdash \phi \quad \alpha' = \alpha \oplus [a \cdot \tilde{l} \rhd \tilde{m}] \quad a : \tilde{m} \odot p : \tilde{x} = \sigma}{a\{p \cdot \tilde{l}(\tilde{x}) . P + P' \mid \phi :: a \cdot \tilde{l}\langle \tilde{m}\rangle . Q + Q' \mid Q''\}_\alpha \to a\{P\sigma \mid Q \mid Q''\}_{\alpha'}}$$

$$\text{(RRes)} \ \frac{N \to N'}{(\nu n) \ N \to (\nu n) \ N'}$$

$$\text{(RStruct)} \frac{N \equiv N' \quad N' \to M' \quad M' \equiv M}{N \to M} \qquad \text{(RPar)} \frac{N \to M}{N \mid N' \to M \mid N'}$$

principal $a\{ P \}_\alpha$ where the policy and the protocol are defined as follows. Let message j represent the reception of a 'junk document' and $\mathcal{M}$ be the interaction datatype of lists, where the predicate $a \cdot - \rhd \text{j} < k$ checks that messages in the list of type $a \cdot \tilde{l} \rhd \text{j}$ occur less than k times. We then define the policy π as $\{ Access(x, Colour) \leftarrow x \cdot - \rhd \text{j} < 3; \ Access(x, BW) \leftarrow x \cdot - \rhd \text{j} < 6\}$ where $Access(x, y)$ is a predicate meaning that x can access y. Moreover we assume that upd() keeps only lists of length at most n deleting the oldest messages and judging if a message is junk. Finally protocol P is defined as

$$P = !x \cdot \texttt{printC}(y) . Access(x, Colour) :: printer \cdot \texttt{printC}\langle y\rangle \mid$$
$$!x \cdot \texttt{printBW}(y) . Access(x, BW) :: printer \cdot \texttt{printBW}\langle y\rangle$$

In this example the action of granting access to the printer is modelled by sending a message to *printer*. A user could then be modelled as principal b running the protocol

$$Q = a \cdot \texttt{printC}\langle\texttt{spam}\rangle . a \cdot \texttt{printBW}\langle\texttt{spam}\rangle . a \cdot \texttt{printC}\langle\texttt{spam}\rangle \mid a \cdot \texttt{printC}\langle\texttt{doc}\rangle$$

Suppose that upd() will store spam as j and consider the network $N = a\{ P \}_{(\pi, \emptyset)} \mid b\{ Q \}_\alpha$ where $\emptyset$ is the empty list. If $a \cdot \texttt{printC}\langle\texttt{doc}\rangle$ is executed first, b will get the authorisation to use the printer. But if the left component is all executed then b will no longer be able to colour-print as he has printed too much junk. Note that as we chose the function upd() to keep lists of length at most n, any principal can behave well for n times and regain trust.

3   Barbed Equivalences

We now move to study the semantic theory of ctm. We first discuss the notion of observation formalised in terms of the actions offered to the environment. Formally we write $N \downarrow a \cdot b$ whenever one of the following conditions is satisfied:

- $N \downarrow a \cdot b$ if $N \equiv (\boldsymbol{\nu}\tilde{n})\, a\{\ \phi :: b \cdot \tilde{l}\langle \tilde{m}\rangle . P + P' \mid Q\ \}_\alpha \mid N'$ and $\alpha \vdash \phi, b \notin$
  $\mathsf{P}(N')$;
- $N \downarrow a \cdot b$ if $N \equiv (\boldsymbol{\nu}\tilde{n})\, a\{\ p \cdot \tilde{l}(\tilde{x}) . P + P' \mid Q\ \}_\alpha \mid N'$ and $b \notin \mathsf{P}(N')$.

where $\mathsf{P}(N')$ is the set of principals contained in N', $\tilde{l} \cap \tilde{n} = \emptyset$ and if $p \notin \mathsf{Var}$ then $p = a$. This definition excludes observing internal and restricted actions. Moreover we write $N \Downarrow a \cdot b$ whenever there exists M such that $N \to^* M$ and $M \downarrow a \cdot b$.

In the following we assume to work with closed protocols and networks.

Definition 3. A network barbed bisimulation is a symmetric relation $\mathcal{R}$ on networks such that whenever $N \mathcal{R} M$

- $N \downarrow a \cdot b$ implies $M \downarrow a \cdot b$;
- $N \to N'$ implies $M \to M'$ and $N' \mathcal{R} M'$.

Two networks are barbed bisimilar ($\overset{\bullet}{\simeq}$) if related by a network barbed bisimulation. Moreover we define $\approx$ as above where $\downarrow$ and $\to$ after the two "implies" are substituted resp. by $\Downarrow$ and $\to^*$.

3.1   Barbed Equivalences for Principals

We now define three different barbed equivalences for principals: one on protocols, one on policies and one on principals.

Protocol Congruence. Protocol barbed congruence compares only protocols. Contexts are, as usual, terms with a hole. We write $C_a[P]$ for the insertion of protocol P in the hole of context C, when the hole is placed in principal a.

Definition 4 (Protocol Barbed Congruence). Given a principal a, we say that P and Q are a-barbed congruent, written $P \simeq_a Q$, if $C_a[P] \overset{\bullet}{\simeq} C_a[Q]$ for all contexts $C_a[-]$.

Intuitively two protocols are congruent whenever they are able to observe the same events, input the same data and granting access in the same way, i.e. guards are such that there is no policy able to distinguish them. For instance, $\phi :: b \cdot l\langle m \rangle$ and $\phi' :: b \cdot l\langle m \rangle$ are equated only if ϕ and ϕ' hold true for exactly the same set of policies α.

Policy Equivalence. Varying the kind of contexts we use, we can use bisimulation to assess policies with respect to a fixed protocol P. The idea is that, given P, two policies are going to be equivalent whenever they "control" P's behaviour in the same way.

Definition 5 (Policy Equivalence). Given a principal a, we say that π and π' are a-barbed equivalent wrt P, written $\pi \simeq_a^P \pi'$, if for all contexts $C_a^P[\cdot] = a\{\ P\ \}_{(-,s)} \mid N$, we have $C_a^P[\pi] \overset{\bullet}{\simeq} C_a^P[\pi']$.

This notion allows, e.g., to remove formulas which P would never use.

Definition 6. We write

- $P \downarrow \phi$ if $P \equiv (\boldsymbol{\nu}\tilde{n}) \, (\phi :: b \cdot \tilde{l}\langle \tilde{m} \rangle . P + P' \mid P'')$ for $\tilde{n} \cap \tilde{l} = \emptyset$;
- $P \Downarrow \phi$ if there exists N and α such that $a\{ \, P \, \}_\alpha \mid N \rightarrow^* a\{ \, P' \, \}_{\alpha'} \mid N'$ and $P' \downarrow \phi$;
- $P \Downarrow H$ if $H = \{\phi \mid P \Downarrow \phi\}$.

We can now state the following.

Theorem 1. *Suppose that $P \Downarrow H$ and for all $\phi \in H$ and $s \in \mathcal{S}$ we have that $(\pi, s) \vdash \phi$ if and only if $(\pi', s) \vdash \phi$. Then $\pi \simeq^P_a \pi'$.*

The opposite is of course not true. Consider the protocol $P = \phi :: b \cdot l\langle m \rangle \mid \phi' :: b \cdot l\langle m \rangle$ and policies π and π' such that $(\pi, s) \vdash \phi$, $(\pi, s) \nvdash \phi'$, $(\pi', s) \vdash \phi'$ and $(\pi', s) \nvdash \phi$ for all s. In this case we have that $\pi \simeq^P_a \pi'$ but the policies entail different formulas wrt s.

Corollary 1. *Suppose that for all ϕ and s we have $(\pi, s) \vdash \phi$ if and only if $(\pi', s) \vdash \phi$. Then, $\pi \simeq^P_a \pi'$, for all P.*

In the following we write $\pi \vdash H$ whenever $H = \{\phi \mid (\pi, s) \vdash \phi \text{ for some } s\}$.

Theorem 2. *Suppose that $\pi \vdash H$ and $\pi' \vdash H'$. If $\pi \simeq^P_a \pi'$ for all P, then H and H' are equivalent, i.e. equal up to logical equivalence of the formulas they contain.*

Principal Equivalence. We now introduce the last of our equivalences which is the most general one.

Definition 7 (Principal Barbed Equivalence). Given a principal a, we say that (π, P) and (π', Q) are a-barbed equivalent, written $(\pi, P) \simeq^s_a (\pi', Q)$, if $C^s_a[\pi, P] \stackrel{\bullet}{\simeq} C^s_a[\pi', Q]$ for any context $C^s_a[-_1, -_2] = a\{ \, -_2 \, \}_{(-_1, s)} \mid N$.

It is possible to define the previous two equivalences in terms of barbed principal equivalence. We are now able to state the following.

Proposition 1. *$P \simeq_a Q$ if and only if for all s, π and protocols R we have that $(\pi, P \mid R) \simeq^s_a (\pi, Q \mid R)$.*

Proposition 2. *$\pi \simeq^P_a \pi'$ if and only if for all s we have that $(\pi, P) \simeq^s_a (\pi', P)$.*

Example 3 (Implication). We consider a variation of the printer access control example and apply principal barbed equivalence. Suppose that a server a manages two printers both offering colour and b/w printing as before. The only difference between them is that Printer 1 does not distinguish colour from b/w printing, while Printer 2 does, e.g., by granting access only for b/w printing. For $z \in \{1, 2\}$ we define the following protocol for a print server.

$$
\begin{aligned}
P(z) = &(\boldsymbol{\nu}n) \, (a \cdot n() \mid !a \cdot n\langle\rangle . x \cdot z(y) . Access(z, x) :: x \cdot z\langle OK \rangle . \\
&(x \cdot z \cdot col() . Col(z, x) :: x \cdot z \cdot col\langle OK \rangle . a \cdot n() + \\
&x \cdot z \cdot bw() . BW(z.x) :: x \cdot z \cdot bw\langle OK \rangle . a \cdot n()))
\end{aligned}
$$

Note that the protocol first checks if it can give access to any type of printing, then verifies which one. The bang is used for writing a recursive protocol: after finishing dealing with a principal, the protocol will be ready once again to provide the service for printer z. The final server protocol is $P(1) \mid P(2)$; its policy is as below, where j and doc represents respectively a junk and a proper document.

$$\pi = \{Access(1,x) \leftarrow x \cdot 1 \rhd \mathsf{j} \leq x \cdot 1 \rhd doc;\ Col(1,x) \leftarrow Access(1,x);$$
$$Col(2,x) \leftarrow x \cdot 2 \rhd \mathsf{j} = 0;\ BW(1,x) \leftarrow Access(1,x);\ BW(2,x) \leftarrow Access(2,x);$$
$$Access(2,x) \leftarrow x \cdot 2 \rhd \mathsf{j} \leq 5\}$$

Then the principal would be represented by the pair $(\pi, P(1) \mid P(2))$. Using the equivalence $\simeq_a^s$ we can rewrite the principal as $(\pi, Q \mid P(2))$ where

$$Q = (\nu n)\ (a \cdot n() \mid !a \cdot n\langle\rangle \cdot x \cdot 1(y) \cdot Access(1,x) :: x \cdot 1\langle OK\rangle \cdot$$
$$(x \cdot 1 \cdot col() \cdot x \cdot 1 \cdot col\langle OK\rangle \cdot a \cdot n() + x \cdot 1 \cdot bw() \cdot x \cdot 1 \cdot bw\langle OK\rangle \cdot a \cdot n()))$$

In fact $(\pi, P(1) \mid P(2)) \simeq_a^s (\pi, Q \mid P(2))$ for any s and this can be explained by the following argument. In protocol $P(1) \mid P(2)$ the output $x \cdot 1 \cdot Col\langle OK\rangle$ is guarded by $Col(1,x)$ instead in $Q \mid P(2)$ it is unguarded. We need to show that $Col(1,x)$ is always true at that point of the computation. In fact in π the predicate $Access(1,x)$ implies $Col(1,x)$ and the action $x{\cdot}1{\cdot}bw$ does not change the value of $Access(1,x)$ (Q and $P(z)$ are sequential) as well as the inputs executed by the branch $P(2)$.

We can also use our previous results: by Theorem 1 we have that $\pi \simeq_a^{Q|P(2)} \pi'$ where

$$\pi' = \{\ Access(1,x) \leftarrow x \cdot 1 \rhd \mathsf{j} \leq x \cdot 1 \rhd doc;\ Col(2,x) \leftarrow x \cdot 2 \rhd \mathsf{j} = 0;$$
$$Access(2,x) \leftarrow x \cdot 2 \rhd \mathsf{j} \leq 5\}.$$

Now by Proposition 2 we then have that $(\pi, P(1) \mid P(2)) \simeq_a^s (\pi', Q \mid P(2))$ for all s.

3.2   A Barbed Congruence for Networks

Above we have analysed equivalences for manipulating single principals. But clearly we also need techniques to reason about networks forming webs of trust. For this purpose, we now introduce a barbed congruence for networks.

Definition 8 (Network Barbed Congruence). We say that two networks N and M are barbed congruent, written $N \approx M$, if for any context $C[-]$ $C[N] \overset{\bullet}{\approx} C[M]$.

The above definition defines a congruence which is well known as weak barbed congruence. We now show an interesting application of such a congruence in an example where recommendations are taken into account.

Example 4 (Recommendations and Trust Security). Trusting someone may be a consequence of observed good behaviour, but it may also be a consequence of good recommendations from a trusted third party. In this example we show how to describe in ctm a system where principals' trust is based both on observations and recommendations. We consider a European network of banks where each bank issues mortgages for customers according to a policy. The policy grants a mortgage whenever the customer has always paid back previous mortgages and, additionally, other banks' opinions about the customer are positive. In ctm, granting the mortgage is equivalent to proving a predicate $G(x)$ from the following policy

$$\pi_1(Y) = \{G(x) \leftarrow Y \cdot - \rhd (x, \text{Bad}) = 0, \ M(x); \ \text{Good}(x) \leftarrow M(x), \ \text{Bad}(x) \leftarrow \text{NoM}(x)\}.$$

The interaction datatype is multiset. The predicates Good and Bad (which will be used for recommendations) depend on the predicate M and NoM only (local observations), instead the predicate G depends also on the recommendations received from Y. The predicate $M(x)$ is assumed to check whether every mortgage granted to x is matched by a full repayment: in order to get a mortgage, there must be no outstanding mortgages. This is expressed by identifying messages with a fresh name w. We can then define the following template for banks.

$$\begin{aligned}
P_1(X, Y) = \ & !x \cdot \text{mg}(w) . (\nu k) \ (Y \cdot \text{rec}\langle k, x \rangle . Y \cdot k(x, z) . G(x) :: X \cdot \text{gr}\langle x, w \rangle) \\
& | \ !X \cdot \text{gr}(x, w) . x \cdot w \langle \rangle . x \cdot w() \\
& | \ !Y \cdot \text{rec}(k, x) . (\text{Good}(x) :: Y \cdot k\langle x, \text{Good} \rangle + \text{Bad}(x) :: Y \cdot k\langle x, \text{Bad} \rangle)
\end{aligned}$$

Bank X has three components: one for granting mortgages, one for accounting, and one for giving recommendations to another bank Y. When receiving a request from a on channel mg a fresh name w reserved for the particular transaction is received. Then X will send a request of recommendation to bank Y. At this point, if the predicate G is provable from the policy, the protocol will transfer the request to the accounting component (on channel gr), which will send an authorisation message to a, and will finally be waiting for a repayment. In case G is not provable, the request will be pending. As pointed out before, the policy will take care of denying further authorisations until repayment. The third component, which gives recommendations to bank Y, just checks whether the predicate Good or Bad are provable, and sends a message accordingly. Suppose now that B_F and B_I are respectively French and Italian banks. We can define a network of banks as follows.

$$N_1 = B_F\{ \ P_1(B_F, B_I) \ \}_{(\pi_1(B_I), \emptyset)} \ | \ B_I\{ \ P_1(B_I, B_F) \ \}_{(\pi_1(B_F), \emptyset)}$$

Suppose now that a customer a has just moved from Italy to France, and she is asking the French bank B_F for a mortgage, e.g. with the protocol $(\nu w) \ B_F \cdot \text{mg}\langle w \rangle . B_F \cdot w() . B_F \cdot w\langle \rangle$. Let us now define a different network of banks using a third party (O) which is going to deal with all the requests. The following policy is used by principal O.

$$\pi_2(X, Y) = \{G(X, x) \leftarrow M(Y, x), M(X, x)\}$$

All the operations previously performed by the banks will now be performed by this policy, and we no longer need recommendations. The following is part of the protocol for principal O.

$$F(W) = W(x, w) \cdot \mathtt{G}(W, x) :: O \cdot W \cdot \mathtt{gr}\langle x, w \rangle \mid !O \cdot W \cdot \mathtt{gr}(x, w) \cdot W \cdot w \langle \rangle \cdot W \cdot w()$$

The banks will only forward messages from the principals to O and vice-versa.

$$P_2 = !x \cdot \mathtt{mg}(w) \cdot O\langle x, w \rangle \cdot O \cdot w() \cdot x \cdot w \langle \rangle \cdot x \cdot w() \cdot O \cdot w \langle \rangle$$

The entire new network will be

$$N_2 = O\{ !(F(B_F) + F(B_I)) \}_{(\pi_2(B_F, B_I) \cup \pi_2(B_I, B_F), \emptyset)} \mid B_F \{ P_2 \}_{(\emptyset, \emptyset)} \mid B_I \{ P_2 \}_{(\emptyset, \emptyset)}$$

We then have that $N_1 \approx N_2$ accordingly to the definition of $\approx$.

In this example, O works as a "headquarter" which collects information from the banks. This is a further step from our previous work [8] where we computed principal trust policies as the least fixed point of a global function. Such a thing, plainly unfeasible in a distributed scenario, can be implemented in $\mathtt{ctm}$. For instance, the global trust function can be expressed as the policy of a principal, e.g. O, and the fixed point as a computation. Then, using the network equivalence, one may be able to simplify the network and avoid the use of "headquarters," like in this example. This is generic technique for stating (and proving) the correctness of a "web of trust", whith a specification in the form of a centralised "headquarter".

4   On the Expressive Power of Global Input

Our calculus uses a new input construct: global input. In this section we prove that such a construct adds expressiveness to the language. Let $\mathtt{ctm}^{-\phi}$ be the fragment of $\mathtt{ctm}$ where all inputs are guarded by $\mathtt{tt}$ and let $\mathtt{ctm}^{-x;\phi}$ be the fragment of $\mathtt{ctm}^{-\phi}$ without global input. Moreover let S be a list of observations $a_1 \cdot b_1; \ldots a_k \cdot b_k; \ldots$ and $N \Downarrow S$ if and only if $N \rightarrow^* N_1 \rightarrow^* \ldots N_k \rightarrow^*$ and $N_1 \downarrow a_1 \cdot b_1, \ldots, N_k \downarrow a_k \cdot b_k, \ldots$ In the following, with abuse of notation, we will use $[\![-]\!]$ for both networks and protocols.

Definition 9. *An encoding* $[\![-]\!] : \mathtt{ctm}^{-\phi} \longrightarrow \mathtt{ctm}^{-x;\phi}$ *is sensible whenever for all protocols P, Q and networks N, M*

- $[\![P \mid Q]\!] = [\![P]\!] \mid [\![Q]\!]$
- $[\![N \mid M]\!] = [\![N]\!] \mid [\![M]\!]$
- $[\![a\{ P \}_\alpha]\!] = a\{ [\![P]\!] \}_\alpha$
- *for any N, $a\{ P \}_\alpha \mid N \Downarrow S$ if and only if $[\![a\{ P \}_\alpha \mid N]\!] \Downarrow S$*

The first three rules represent the notion of uniform encoding, while the last one corresponds to the notion of reasonable encoding according to [15].

Theorem 3. *There is no sensible encoding $[\![-]\!]$ from $\mathtt{ctm}_P^{-\phi}$ into $\mathtt{ctm}_P^{-x;\phi}$.*

Proof. [Sketch] Suppose there exists such an encoding and consider $a\{ x \cdot l(y) \}_\alpha$. Principal a is such that $a\{ x \cdot l(y) \}_\alpha \downarrow a \cdot b$ for any b. Now we have that

$a\{ [\![x \cdot l(y)]\!] \}_\alpha \not\Downarrow a \cdot b$ for all b. In fact we can prove by induction on the protocols of $\mathtt{ctm}_P^{-x;\phi}$ that such a protocol does not exists.   □

5   Conclusion

We have introduced $\mathtt{ctm}$, a calculus for trust management. The calculus enjoys many new features which fit in global computing scenarios making use of the notion of trust.

Principals in $\mathtt{ctm}$ have two components: the policy and the protocol. The policy consists of an immutable part, α, and a variable s. The former expresses the logic of the policy, i.e. the rules following which decisions are taken, on the basis of past experiences. The latter records the observations which make up such experiences, as a function of the messages exchanged in interactions between principals.

It may be objected that this yields a generic concurrent calculus of stateful entities, and not a calculus specifically designed to represent trust-based systems. This is actually not the case. The key to the matter is that, while s is definitely a kind of store, principals have absolutely no control as to what it stores, or when it stores it: s is updated uniquely and exactly to reflect the outcome of interactions. These include feedback on untrusted clients and advice from trusted principals. In particular, a principal cannot store arbitrary values to s, or retrieve them from it. In other words, the calculus represents faithfully a distributed set of principals interacting with each other according to trust policies and risk assessment based on computational histories. Similarly it is not possible to compare $\mathtt{ctm}$ to an extension to locations of the applied π-calculus [1] as the latter does not model the notion of collecting observations even though function guards can represent policies.

We remark also that our use of guards works quite effectively with the choice of synchronous communications, to abstract the sequence of actions service request, risk assessment, response to client, and record observation, in a single, atomic step where trust-based decisions are localised.

The equivalences for $\mathtt{ctm}$ are interesting but still lack efficient proof methods. In order to accomplish this we aim at defining a labelled transition system for characterising all the equivalences studied. It would also be interesting to treat static analysis for the calculus, e.g. a type system, and study its relationship with what shown in this paper.

Acknowledgements. We thank J. Almansa, S. Agarwal, B. Klin, K. Krukow and P. Oliva for useful comments. Thanks also goes to the anonymous referees for their helpful suggestions.

References

1. M. Abadi and C. Fournet. Mobile values, new names, and secure communication. In *Proc. of the 28th symposium on Principles of Programming Languages (POPL'01)*, pages 104–115. ACM Press, 2001.

2. S. Abiteboul, R. Hull, and V. Vianu. *Foundations of databases*. Addison-Wesley, 1995.
3. R. Amadio, G. Boudol, and C. Lhoussaine. The receptive distributed pi-calculus. In *Proc. of the 19th Conference on Foundations of Software Technology and Theoretical Computer Science (FSTTCS '99)*, volume 1738 of *LNCS*, pages 304–315. Springer-Verlag, 1999.
4. A. W. Appel and E. W. Felten. Proof-carrying authentication. In *Proc. of 6th ACM Conference on Computer and Communications Security (CCS '99)*, 1999.
5. M. Y. Becker and P. Sewell. Cassandra: Flexible trust management, applied to electronic health records. In *Proc. of the 17th IEEE Computer Security Foundations Workshop (CSFW '04)*. IEEE Computer Society Press, 2004.
6. M. Burrows, M. Abadi, B. W. Lampson, and G. Plotkin. A calculus for access control in distributed systems. In *Proc. of 11th Annual International Cryptology Conference Advances in Cryptology (CRYPTO '91)*, volume 576, pages 1–23, 1991.
7. M. Carbone and S. Maffies. On the expressive power of polyadic synchronisation in π-calculus. *Nordic Journal of Computing (NJC)*, 10(2), September 2003.
8. M. Carbone, M. Nielsen, and V. Sassone. A formal model for trust in dynamic networks. In *Proc. of International Conference on Software Engineering and Formal Methods (SEFM'03)*, pages 54–61. IEEE Computer Society Press, 2003.
9. J. Guttman, J. Thayer, J. Carlson, J. Herzog, J. Ramsdell, and B. Sniffen. Trust management in strand spaces: A rely-guarantee method. In *Proc. of the European Symposium on Programming (ESOP '04)*, LNCS, pages 325–339. Springer-Verlag, 2004.
10. M. Hennessy and J. Riely. Resource access control in systems of mobile agents. *Information and Computation*, 173(1):82–120, 2002.
11. S. Jajodia, P. Samarati, and V. S. Subrahmanian. A logical language for expressing authorizations. In *Proc. of the IEEE Symposium on Security and Privacy*, pages 31–42. IEEE Computer Society Press, 1997.
12. A. J. I. Jones and B. S. Firozabadi. On the characterisation of a trusting agent. In *Workshop on Deception, Trust and Fraud in Agent Societies*, 2000.
13. N. Li, J. C. Mitchell, and W. H. Winsborough. Design of a role-based trust management framework. In *Proc. of the IEEE Symposium on Security and Privacy*, pages 114–130. IEEE Computer Society Press, 2002.
14. R. Milner, J. Parrow, and D. Walker. A calculus of mobile processes, I and II. *Information and Computation*, 100(1):1–40,41–77, September 1992.
15. C. Palamidessi. Comparing the expressive power of the synchronous and the asynchronous π-calculus. In *Proc. of the 24th symposium on Principles of Programming Languages (POPL'97)*, pages 256–265. ACM Press, 1997.

Short-Cuts on Star, Source and Planar Unfoldings

Vijay Chandru, Ramesh Hariharan, and Narasimha M. Krishnakumar

Dept. of Computer Science and Automation, Indian Institute of Science,
Bangalore, India

Abstract. When studying a 3D convex polyhedron, it is often easier to cut it open and flatten in on the plane. There are several ways to perform this unfolding. Standard unfoldings which have been used in literature include *Star* Unfoldings, *Source* Unfoldings, and *Planar* Unfoldings, each differing only in the cuts that are made. Note that every unfolding has the property that a straight line between two points on this unfolding need not be contained completely within the body of this unfolding. This could potentially lead to situations where the above straight line is shorter than the shortest path between the corresponding end points on the convex polyhedron. We call such straight lines *short-cuts*. The presence of short-cuts is an obstacle to the use of unfoldings for designing algorithms which compute shortest paths on polyhedra. We study various properties of Star, Source and Planar Unfoldings which could play a role in circumventing this obstacle and facilitating the use of these unfoldings for shortest path algorithms.

We begin by showing that Star and Source Unfoldings do not have short-cuts. We also describe a new structure called the *Extended Source* Unfolding which exhibits a similar property. In contrast, it is known that Planar unfoldings can indeed have short-cuts. Using our results on Star, Source and Extended Source Unfoldings above and using an additional structure called the *Compacted Source* Unfolding, we provide a necessary condition for a pair of points on a Planar Unfolding to form a short-cut. We believe that this condition could be useful in enumerating all Shortest Path Edge Sequences on a convex polyhedron in an output-sensitive way, using the Planar Unfolding.

1   Introduction

Star Unfoldings have proved useful tools in arguing about shortest paths on the surface of a 3D convex polyhedron $\mathcal{P}$ (see Fig. 1(a)). A Star Unfolding is obtained by cutting a 3D convex polyhedron along shortest paths emanating from a reference point x and going to each of the vertices of $\mathcal{P}$; the resulting structure is then flattened on the plane. We denote the Star Unfolding with respect to the reference point x by $star(x)$. The idea of such an unfolding is due to Aleksandrov [1], who uses it to show that $\mathcal{P}$ can be triangulated. Aronov and O'Rourke [10] showed that this unfolding does not self-overlap (in fact they show

K. Lodaya and M. Mahajan (Eds.): FSTTCS 2004, LNCS 3328, pp. 174–185, 2004.
© Springer-Verlag Berlin Heidelberg 2004

a stronger property, which we shall describe shortly). Subsequently, Agarwal, Aronov, O'Rourke and Schevon [12] showed how the Star Unfolding can be used for enumerating Shortest Path Edge Sequences on a convex polyhedron and for finding the geodesic diameter of a convex polyhedron. Chen and Han [11], independently, used Star Unfoldings for computing shortest path information from a single fixed point on the surface of a convex polyhedron.

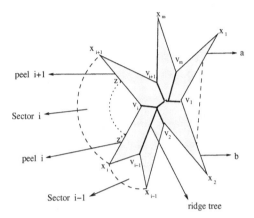

Fig. 1. Star Unfolding

The *Source Unfolding* of a 3D convex polyhedron $\mathcal{P}$ is obtained by transforming the Star Unfolding as follows. The Star Unfolding $star(x)$ (with respect to the reference point x) has a *ridge tree* [7] comprising all points which have two or more distinct shortest paths from the reference point x. The leaves of this ridge tree are the vertices of $\mathcal{P}$ (x aside) and internal ridge nodes are those points on $\mathcal{P}$ which have 3 or more shortest paths to x. Cutting along each of the ridge tree edges and the shortest paths to the vertices from x breaks the Star Unfolding into several convex polygons, called *peels*. The Source Unfolding is obtained by rearranging these peels around x. We denote the Source Unfolding with respect to the reference point x by $source(x)$. In Fig. 2(a) and (b), we have shown the Source Unfolding of $\mathcal{P}$ with respect to x for the cases when x is not a vertex on $\mathcal{P}$ and when x is a vertex of $\mathcal{P}$, respectively. This unfolding was defined in [3]. Note that in case 1, x is completely surrounded by the body of the unfolding while in the other case, there is an empty angular region incident on x due to the positive curvature of the convex polyhedron at x.

We define *Planar Unfoldings* as follows. Consider any sequence of distinct faces $f_1 \ldots f_k$ on the surface of $\mathcal{P}$ such that f_i and f_{i+1} share an edge e_i, for all i, $1 \leq i \leq k-1$. Consider cutting out $f_1 \ldots f_k$ from $\mathcal{P}$ by cutting along each edge that is on the boundary of some f_i, with the exception of the edges $e_1 \ldots e_{k-1}$. Note that by virtue of $f_1 \ldots f_k$ being distinct, cuts are made along all but exactly two of the boundary edges for each f_i, $2 \leq i \leq k-1$, (the exceptions being e_{i-1}, e_i for f_i). Further, for f_1 and f_k, cuts are made along all but exactly one of the boundary edges (the exceptions being e_2, e_{k-1}). With

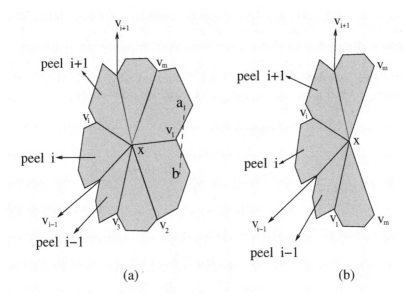

Fig. 2. Source Unfolding

these properties, it is easy to see that the resulting structure can be flattened out on a plane (because, after cutting out, f_i and f_{i+1} are attached to each other by exactly one edge, around which we can rotate to get f_i and f_{i+1} on one plane). We call this structure the Planar Unfolding with respect to the edge sequence $e_1 \ldots e_{k-1}$.

Our Results. Our contribution is four-fold, all using only elementary geometry.

1. Aronov and O'Rourke [10] showed that the Star Unfolding does not self-overlap. Further, they showed a stronger property: the circular sectors between adjacent peels (see Fig.1(a)) are also disjoint. As a corollary of this property, they show that there are no short-cuts in the Star Unfolding with one endpoint being the reference point x. In other words, a straight line between any instance of x in the Star Unfolding and any other point a in the Star Unfolding is no shorter than the shortest path between x and a on $\mathcal{P}$. We extend this result to all pairs of points on the Star Unfolding. So, for any pair of points a and b on the Star Unfolding, we show that the straight line joining these two points is no shorter than the shortest path between a and b on $\mathcal{P}$.
2. Using the above result that the Star Unfolding has no short-cuts, we show that the Source Unfolding also does not have short-cuts. The proof uses a stepwise transformation of the Star Unfolding into the Source Unfolding.
3. Next, using the above result for Source Unfoldings, we show that the extension (with respect to any point y) of the Source Unfolding does not have short-cuts, i.e., for any point a on the extended line xy in the Extended Source Unfolding and any other point b on the Source Unfolding, the straight line joining a and

b is no shorter than the shortest path between a and b on $\mathcal{P}$. This notion of *Extended Source* Unfoldings will be defined later.

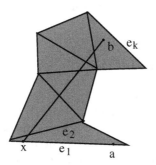

Fig. 3. Planar Unfolding

4. It is known [5] that, unlike Star and Source Unfoldings, Planar Unfoldings could have short-cuts, i.e., the distance between a pair of points x and y on a Planar Unfolding can be shorter than the distance between the same pair of points on the convex polyhedron. However, the above result on Extended Source Unfoldings gives the following necessary condition for a pair of points to form a short-cut on a Planar Unfolding.

A Necessary Condition for a Short-Cut on Planar Unfoldings: Consider three points x, a, b on some Planar Unfolding of $\mathcal{P}$ (see Fig.3) such that xa and xb are images of geodesics completely within this unfolding. For ab to be a short-cut in this Planar Unfolding, neither xa nor xb must be a shortest path on $\mathcal{P}$.

In the above process, we also define a new structure called the *Compacted Source Unfolding* by re-folding the Source Unfolding in a certain way, and then use this structure to show properties of shortest paths which are then used to prove the above claims on Star, Source, Extended Source and Planar Unfoldings.

Applications and Further Work. Our motivation for studying short-cuts was to obtain an output-sensitive algorithm for enumerating SPES's (i.e., shortest path edge sequences, sequences of edges which are crossed by at least one shortest path) on the convex polyhedron P. Unlike previous work [12, 7] which uses the Star Unfolding as its main tool, our approach was to use the Planar Unfolding, where a particular edge sequence is considered if and only if all its prefixes are SPES's; this would lead naturally to output-sensitivity, as only SPES's are considered for further extension using a Dijkstra like scheme. The first hurdle encountered in this process is that of short-Cuts. While we haven't yet obtained a complete output-sensitive algorithm for enumerating SPES's, we believe that the properties of short-cuts listed above could be useful in obtaining such an algorithm.

Road Map. Section 2 lays out some preliminaries. Section 3 defines *Compacted Source Unfoldings* and proves some properties needed in later sections. Sections

4, 5 and 6 prove that there are no short-cuts on Star, Source and Extended Source Unfoldings, respectively. Section 7 shows our necessary condition for a pair of points on a Planar Unfolding to form a short-cut. For want of space, proofs do not appear in this abstract. They will appear in the full version of the paper.

2   Definitions and Preliminaries

Let $\mathcal{P}$ denote a 3D convex polyhedron. We use the term *vertex* of $\mathcal{P}$ to denote one of the corners of $\mathcal{P}$. For any two points a, b on $\mathcal{P}$, let $SP(a, b)$ denote the shortest path between a and b on $\mathcal{P}$. For any two points a, b on the plane, let ab denote both the straight line segment connecting a, b and the length of this straight line segment as well (for convenience). Let $C(a, ab)$ denote the circle with center a and radius ab.

Definitions. For any two points a, b on the Star Unfolding, let $star(a, b)$ be the length of the straight line ab. $source(a, b)$ and $planar(a, b)$ are defined analogously.

Aronov and O'Rourke [10] showed that the Star Unfolding can be embedded in the plane without overlap. The resulting structure is a simple polygon (see Fig.1(a)) whose vertices in cyclic order are denoted by $x_1, v_1, x_2, v_2, \ldots, x_m, v_m$, where $x_1 \ldots x_m$ are images of the source point x and $v_1 \ldots v_m$ are the vertices of $\mathcal{P}$ (excluding x, if it is a vertex). Note that for each i, $1 \leq i \leq m$, $x_i v_i = v_i x_{i+1}$ (here, and in what follows, $i + 1$ is taken modulo m, implicitly). Aronov and O'Rourke actually showed the following stronger fact in Lemma 1, for which we need the following definition. Let $Sector(i)$ denote the sector of the circle $C(v_i, x_i v_i)$ which lies between the lines $x_i v_i$ and $x_{i+1} v_i$ (see Fig.1).

Lemma 1. *[10] The various sectors $Sector(1) \ldots Sector(m)$ are mutually pairwise disjoint; further these sectors lie completely outside the Star Unfolding. It follows that the Star Unfolding does not self-overlap and is a simple polygon.*

Lemma 1 yields the following lemma on peels (recall, peels were defined in the introduction).

Lemma 2. *For any point y on $star(x)$, the Star Unfolding with respect to x, there exists an x_i, $1 \leq i \leq m$, such that the straight line $x_i y$ is contained completely within the peel containing x_i; further, $star(x_i, y) = SP(xy)$.*

Fact 1. *Consider two points a, b on either a Star, Source or Planar Unfolding such that the straight line joining them lies completely inside the unfolding. Then, this straight line is an image of a geodesic on the surface of $\mathcal{P}$ and therefore, has length at least $SP(a, b)$.*

Triangulating $star(x)$ and Triangle Images. Note that if we triangulate the peels in $star(x)$ using triangles whose one endpoint is always the copy of x on the same peel, then each such triangle has a congruent *image triangle* on some other peel; this is illustrated in the picture below where t'_j is the image of t_j and t'_i is the image of t_i. This is because, such a triangle will have one of the ridge edges in the boundary of the peel as its base; since ridge edge is the locus a point that has more than one shortest path from x on the polyhedron, the triangles are mirror images of each other. This notion of image of a triangle will be used in defining Compacted Source Unfoldings in the next section. Note that the image pairing of triangles has a nesting property, namely that the various angular stretches between triangles and their respective images are either mutually disjoint or one stretch contains the other.

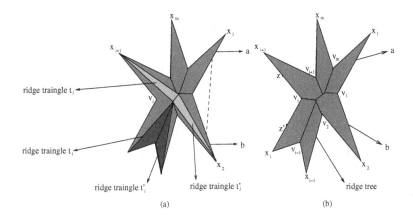

(a)   (b)

Fig. 4. Star Unfolding: Triangle Images

3   The Compacted Source Unfolding

In this section we define a new structure called the *Compacted Source* Unfolding which is obtained by folding the Source Unfolding as follows. Consider *source*(a), the Source Unfolding with respect to a and suppose one is given any two points u and v on the ridge tree. Then the line segments $SP(au)$ and $SP(av)$ are maximal shortest paths in *source*(a). Consider the region of *source*(a_{uv}) which lies clockwise from $SP(au)$ to $SP(av)$ and consider the triangles into which peels in this region are triangulated. Some of these triangles will have their images within this region as well, while others will not. Fold *source*(a_{uv}) in such a way that each triangle which has its image in this region gets pasted to its image, back to back (this is possible because of the nesting property described above). The resulting structure will have a *backbone*, (Fig.5) comprising those triangles which do not have images in this region, and *ribs* comprising triangles which indeed have images in this region, with the images pasted back to back; this is the *Compacted Source* unfolding with respect to a and u, v.

We can show the following properties on this Compacted Source Unfolding. Theorem 1 and its corollary below follow from the fact that a path which goes

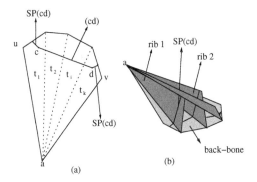

Fig. 5. The Compacted Source Unfolding: Backbones and Ribs

through the ribs can be shortened to one that stays on the backbone but has the same source and destination. Theorem 2 is the key non-trivial claim that we prove.

Lemma 3. *The back-bone of source($a_{(uv)}$) is a convex polygon.*

Theorem 1. *Every pair of points on a peel is joined by a unique shortest path on the convex polyhedron thats lies entirely on that peel.*

Corollary 1. *The intersection of a shortest path with a peel is connected.*

Theorem 2. *Consider a portion source($a_{(uv)}$) of source(a), where u and v are any pair of ridge points such that the angle $\angle vau < \pi$ (Fig.6(a)). Let (uv) denote the line segment that joins u and v on the plane that contains source(a) and suppose that $SP(av) \geq SP(au)$. If (uv) lies completely outside the Source Unfolding (except for its endpoints), then there exists another shortest path $SP(au)$ in source($a_{(uv)}$).*

4   Star Unfoldings

We prove the following theorem in this section.

Theorem 3. *Consider any two points a, b on the Star Unfolding with respect to point x on $\mathcal{P}$. Then star(ab) $\geq SP(ab)$.*

The proof outline is as follows: By Fact 1., this is true if the line segment ab is completely inside $star(x)$. It now suffices to consider the case when ab is completely outside $star(x)$, for the only remaining case can be handled by splitting ab into internal and external segments and arguing on each segment. For the case when ab is completely outside as shown in Fig.7, using Lemma 1, one can show that the path a to x_i and then x_j to b on the convex polyhedron $\mathcal{P}$ is shorter than ab, as required.

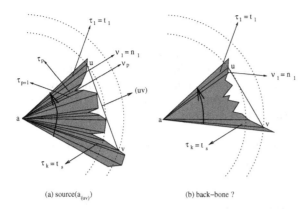

(a) source($a_{(uv)}$)   (b) back–bone ?

Fig. 6. $Source(a_{(uv)})$ and its back-bone

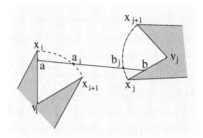

Fig. 7. a, b completely outside

5   Source Unfoldings

Theorem 4. *Consider any two points a, b on the Source Unfolding with respect to point x on $\mathcal{P}$. Then $source(ab) \geq SP(ab)$.*

Note that as in the case of $star(x)$, we need only consider the case when the line segment ab is completely outside $source(x)$. The proof proceeds by induction on the number of peels (call this the *peel distance*) in $source(x_{ab})$. If this is one or two, then the argument is easily made by rotating peels from the source configuration to the star configuration while showing that distance ab only decreases in this process; this along with Theorem 3 finishes the proof. If the peel distance is more than two, then Theorem 2 gives us a tool to perform induction. Without loss of generality, we assume that the angle at x in $source(x_{ab})$ is $< \pi$ and that $xb \leq xa$ on $source(x)$. Then, by Theorem 2, there exists another copy b' of b in $source(x_{ab})$. We then argue inductively on ab' instead of ab, as the former has a provably smaller peel distance.

6   Extended Source Unfoldings

We define the *Extended Source Unfolding* of *source*(*x*) constructively as the structure obtained from the Source Unfolding by taking a shortest path *xy* on *source*(*x*) (which also corresponds to a shortest path on the convex polyhedron $\mathcal{P}$) and then extending it as a geodesic for a finite stretch or until it reaches a vertex of $\mathcal{P}$. We prove the following theorem in this section.

Theorem 5. *Consider the Source Unfolding source*(*x*) *with respect to x. Let xb and xy be any pair of shortest paths. Let a be any point that lies on a geodesic that is a finite extension of the shortest path xy. Then source*(*ab*) $\geq$ *SP*(*ab*).

Proof. Let us assume that *xa* in the Extended Source Unfolding is along the x-axis (in a Cartesian coordinate system). Then we have *x*, *y* and *a* in that order from left to right along x-axis as shown in Fig.8. We have the following two cases to consider.

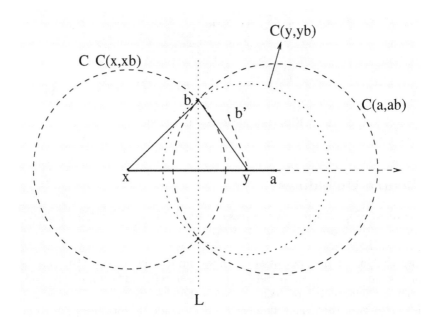

Fig. 8. *source*(*ab*) $\geq$ *SP*(*ab*) in extended source unfolding: Case 1

Case 1: The portion *ya* of *xa* is a shortest path in *source*(*y*): Let *source*(*x*), *source*(*y*) and *source*(*a*) denote the Source Unfoldings of the convex polyhedron with respect to *x*, *y* and *a* respectively. Let us superimpose *source*(*y*) and *source*(*a*) on the line segment *xa* in the Extended Source Unfolding of *source*(*x*) such that the following conditions are satisfied.

- The portions xy (a shortest path) and ya (a shortest path) of xa in the Extended Source Unfolding coincide with the shortest paths xy and ya in $source(y)$. This is always possible for the following reason. Since xa is an extension of the shortest path xy in the Extended Source Unfolding, y cannot be a polyhedral vertex (according to the definition of the Extended Source Unfolding). Hence, a small neighborhood of y in the Extended Source Unfolding is identical to a small neighborhood of y in $source(y)$. Thus, the angle between the shortest paths ya and yx in each of the Extended Source Unfolding and $source(y)$ is equal to π.
- The portion ya (a shortest path) of xa coincides with the shortest path ya in $source(a)$.

Let b' denote the position of b in $source(y)$. That is, a shortest path from y to b in $source(y)$ is denoted by yb'. Consider the three discs $C(x, xb), C(y, yb)$ and $C(a, ab)$ (we define the disc $C(x, xb)$ as the set of points p such that $xp \leq xb$, other discs are defined similarly). Since xy and xb are shortest paths, according to Theorem 4, $yb \geq SP(yb)$. Thus, the shortest path from y to b, that is yb', in $source(y)$ is shorter than yb. Thus, b' lies on the disc $C(y, yb)$ (Fig.8). Since yx and yb' are shortest paths in $source(y)$, $xb' \geq SP(xb') = SP(xb)$. Hence, b' does not lie inside the disc $C(x, xb)$ (because the radius of this disc is a shortest path). Thus we have b' on the portion of the disc $C(y, yb)$ that is not inside $C(x, xb)$. Hence, b' cannot lie to the left of the line segment L through b that is normal to the x-axis. But this portion of the disc $C(y, yb)$ (that contains b') is on the disc $C(a, ab)$ because a is to the right of y. Thus, we have b' on or inside $C(a, ab)$, that is, $ab \geq ab'$.

Consider the two shortest paths ya and yb' in $source(y)$. Since, we have assumed that the portion ya of xa is a shortest path, according to Theorem 4, $ab' \geq SP(ab') = SP(ab)$. Thus, we have $ab \geq ab' \geq SP(ab)$, and the theorem holds for this case.

Case 2: ya is not a shortest path in $source(y)$: Let us partition xa into a sequence of shortest paths (Fig.9) $a_0a_1, a_1a_2, a_2a_3, ..., a_{m-1}a_m$ (where $a_0 = x$, $a_1 = y$ and $a_m = a$) such that, each partition a_ia_{i+1} is the portion of ya that lies on a single peel. Each of these partitions satisfies the following two properties.

- Each partition is a shortest path (we will be showing in Theorem 1 that any geodesic that lies inside a peel is a shortest path).
- We will show that the number of peels crossed by any finite geodesic is countable. Hence, the number of partitions in xa is also countable.

The number of peels crossed by any finite geodesic xa is countable for the following reason. Since xa is a geodesic, there is no polyhedral vertex in the interior of xa. Thus, the intersection of a peel with xa is either null or of non-zero length. Hence, we can order the peels that intersect xa in the direction from x to a. Thus, the set of peels that have a non-empty intersection with xa is countable.

Let b_i denote the image of b in $source(a_i)$ for each $i, 0 \leq m$. Consider the three points a_i, a_{i+1}, a_{i+2} for any $i, 0 \leq i \leq m - 2$. We have already mentioned that

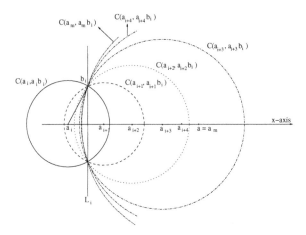

Fig. 9. $source(ab) \geq SP(ab)$ in extended source unfolding: Case 2

b_i, b_{i+1} and b_{i+2} denotes the images of the point b in the $source(a_i)$ $source(a_{i+1})$ and $source(a_{i+2})$, respectively. We have the following analogy to Case 1. We can view the four points a_i, a_{i+1}, a_{i+2} and b_i as x, y, a and b in Case 1, respectively. An argument on lines similar to that of Case 1 shows the following (see Fig.9).

Since $a_i b_i$ and $a_i a_{i+1}$ are shortest paths in $source(a_i)$, $a_{i+1} b_i \geq SP(a_{i+1} b_i) = SP(a_{i+1} b_{i+1}) = SP(a_{i+1} b)$. Thus, b_{i+1} lies on the disc $C(a_{i+1}, a_{i+1} b_i)$.

Since $a_{i+1} a_i$ and $a_{i+1} b_{i+1}$ are shortest paths in $source(a_{i+1})$, $a_i b_{i+1} \geq a_i b_i = SP(a_i b_i)$. Hence, b_{i+1} does not lie inside the disc $C(a_i, a_i b_i)$.

Thus, b_{i+1} lies on the disc $C(a_{i+1}, a_{i+1} b_i)$ but not inside the disc $C(a_i, a_i b_i)$. That is, b_{i+1} lies on the portion of the disc $C(a_{i+1}, a_{i+1} b_i)$ that is on or to the right of L_i where L_i is the normal from b_i to the x-axis.

Since, for each $j \geq i+2$, the point a_j lies to the right of a_{i+1}, the above mentioned portion of the disc $C(a_{i+1}, a_{i+1} b_i)$ lies inside $C(a_j, a_j b_i)$. Thus we have $a_j b_i \geq a_j b_{i+1}$ for each $j \geq i+2$. In particular we have $a_m b_i \geq a_m b_{i+1}$.

Since the above claims are true for each $i, 0 \leq i \leq m-2$, we get

$$a_m b_0 \geq a_m b_1 \geq a_m b_2 \geq a_m b_3 \geq \ldots \geq a_m b_{m-1}.$$

Since $a_{m-1} a_m$ and $a_{m-1} b_{m-1}$ are shortest paths in the Source Unfolding $source(a_{m-1})$, we have $a_m b_{m-1} \geq SP(a_m b)$. Thus we have $source(ab) = a_m b_0 \geq SP(a_m b) = SP(ab)$ (recall $a_m = a$), and we have proved the theorem for case 2.
$\square$

7   A Necessary Condition for Short-Cuts in a Planar Unfolding

Our result on Extended Source Unfoldings above provides a necessary condition for ab to be a short-cut on a Planar Unfolding, i.e., for $planar(ab) \geq SP(ab)$.

Theorem 6. *Consider three points x, a, b on some Planar Unfolding such that xa and xb are images of geodesics completely within this unfolding, and further, the xa geodesic is actually a shortest path on $\mathcal{P}$. Then $planar(ab) \geq SP(ab)$, and therefore ab cannot be a short-cut.*

Proof. Since the local neighborhoods of x in the Source and the Planar Unfoldings are identical, the angle between xa and xb in these two unfoldings are the same. Hence, we have $planar(ab) = source(ab)$. However, according Theorem 5, we have $source(ab) \geq SP(ab)$. Hence, we have $planar(ab) = source(ab) \geq SP(ab)$. $\qquad\square$

In particular note that if a lies on an edge of $\mathcal{P}$ and we take x to be on the same edge, if xa is a geodesic then ab cannot be a short-cut. Since geodesics are locally verifiable in contrast to shortest paths, this is a non-trivial condition. A simple further corollary is that any planar unfolding between edges e_0 and e_k with a geodesic from e_0 to e_k which lies completely inside this planar unfolding cannot have shortcuts which cross this geodesic.

References

1. A. D. Aleksandrov and V. A. Zalgaller, *Intrinsic Geometry of Surfaces*, American Mathematical Society, Providence, RI, 1967.
2. H. Buseman, *Convex Surfaces*, Interscience Publishers, 1958.
3. M. Sharir and A. Schorr, *On shortest paths in polyhedral spaces*, SIAM J. Comput.,15(1986), pp.193-215.
4. C. Schevon and J. O'Rourke, *The number of maximal edge sequences on a convex polytope*, In Proc. 26th Allerton Conf. Commun. Control Comput., pages 49–57, October 1988.
5. C. Schevon, Algorithms for geodesics on polytopes, PhD thesis, Johns Hopkins University, 1989.
6. J. Mitchell, D. M. Mount, and C. H. Papadimitriou, *The discrete geodesic problem*, SIAM Journal on Computing, 16(4):647-668, August 1987.
7. M. Sharir, *On shortest paths amidst convex polyhedra*, SIAM Journal on Computing, 16(3):561-572, June 1987.
8. D. M. Mount, *The number of shortest paths on the surface of a polyhedron*, SIAM Journal on Computing, 19(4):593-611, August 1990.
9. P.K. Agarwal, B. Aronov, J. O'Rourke and C. Schevon, *Star Unfolding of a polytope with applications*, in Proc. of 2nd Annual Scandinavian Workshop on Algorithm Theory, Lecture Notes in Computer Science,447, Springer-Verlag,Berlin,1990,pp.251-263.
10. B. Aronov and J. O'Rourke, *Non-overlap of the Star Unfolding*, Discrete Comput. Geom.,8(1992).pp. 219-250.
11. J. Chen and Y. Han, *Shortest paths on a polyhedron*, in Proc. 6th Annual ACM Sympos. Comput. Geom., ACM,New York, 1990, pp.360-369.
12. P. K. Agarwal, B. Aronov, J. O'Rourke, Catherine A. Schevon, *Star Unfolding of a Polytope with Applications*, SIAM J. Comput. 26(6): 1689-1713 (1997).
13. V. Chandru, N. Krishnakumar, R. Hariharan, *Properties of Planar Unfoldings*, Manuscript under preparation.
14. N. Krishnakumar *Properties of Short-Cuts*, PhD Thesis, IISc, 2003.

Subdividing Alpha Complex

Ho-lun Cheng and Tony Tan

School of Computing, National University of Singapore
{hcheng, tantony}@comp.nus.edu.sg

Abstract. Given two simplicial complexes $\mathcal{C}_1$ and $\mathcal{C}_2$ embedded in Euclidean space $\mathbb{R}^d$, $\mathcal{C}_1$ *subdivides* $\mathcal{C}_2$ if (i) $\mathcal{C}_1$ and $\mathcal{C}_2$ have the same underlying space, and (ii) every simplex in $\mathcal{C}_1$ is contained in a simplex in $\mathcal{C}_2$. In this paper we present a method to compute a set of weighted points whose alpha complex subdivides a given simplicial complex.

Following this, we also show a simple method to approximate a given polygonal object with a set of balls via computing the subdividing alpha complex of the boundary of the object. The approximation is robust and is able to achieve a union of balls whose Hausdorff distance to the object is less than a given positive real number ϵ.

1   Introduction

The notion of alpha complexes is defined by Edelsbrunner [6, 10] and since then it has been widely applied in various fields such as computer graphics, solid modeling, computational biology, computational geometry and topology [7, 8]. In this paper, we propose a simple algorithm to compute the alpha complex that subdivides a given simplicial complex. This can be considered as representing the complex with a finite set of weighted points. See Figure 1 as an example. Moreover, we also present a method to approximate an object with a union of balls via its subdividing alpha complex.

1.1   Motivation and Related Works

The motivation of this paper can be classified into two categories: the skin approximation and the conforming Delaunay complex.

Skin approximation. Our eventual goal is to approximate a given simplicial complex with the *skin surface*, which is a smooth surface based on a finite set of balls [7]. Amenta et. al. [1] have actually raised this question and the purpose was to perform deformation between polygonal objects. As noted in some previous works [2, 7], deformation can be performed robustly and efficiently with the skin surface. Our work here can be viewed as a stepping stone to our main goal.

As mentioned by Kruithof and Vegter [13], one of the first steps to approximate an object with a skin surface is to have a set of balls that approximate the object. For this purpose, we produce a set of balls whose alpha shape is the same as the object. It is well known that such union of balls is homotopy equivalent

K. Lodaya and M. Mahajan (Eds.): FSTTCS 2004, LNCS 3328, pp. 186–197, 2004.

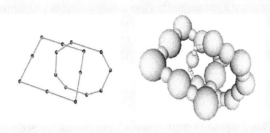

Fig. 1. An example of a subdividing alpha complex of a *link* embedded in $\mathbb{R}^3$. The right hand side of the figure shows a union of balls whose alpha complex resemble the input *link*, shown in the left hand side

to the object [6]. At the same time, we are able to produce a union of balls that approximate the object.

Approximating an object by a union of balls itself has applications in deformation. In such representation, shapes can be interpolated [15]. Some shape matching algorithms also use the union of balls representation [18]. We believe such approximation can also be useful for collision detection and coarse approximation [12].

Conforming Delaunay Complex(CDC). The work on conforming Delaunay complex(CDC) are done mainly for the unweighted point set in two and three dimensional cases [3, 4, 5, 11, 14]. As far as our knowledge is concerned, there is no published work yet on the construction of CDC for any given simplicial complex in arbitrary dimension. The relation of CDC to our work here should be obvious, that is, we compute CDC of weighted points in arbitrary dimension.

1.2   Assumptions and Approach

The assumption of our algorithm is a constrained triangulation of a simplicial complex $\mathcal{C}$ is given, that is, a triangulation of the convex hull of $\mathcal{C}$ that contains $\mathcal{C}$ itself. An example of this is the constrained Delaunay triangulation of $\mathcal{C}$ [19, 20].

Our approach is to construct the subdividing alpha complex of the l-skeleton of $\mathcal{C}$ before its $(l+1)$-skeleton. For each simplex in the l-skeleton, we add weighted points until it is subdivided by the alpha complex. In the process, we maintain the invariant that the alpha shape is a subset of the underlying space of $\mathcal{C}$. This is done by avoiding two weighted points intersecting each other when their centers are not in the same simplex. For this purpose, we introduce the *protecting cells*.

The main issue in this approach is that we do not add infinitely many points, that is, our algorithm is able to terminate. To establish this, we guarantee that, for each simplex, there is a positive lower bound for the weight of the added point. This fact, together with the compactness of each simplex, ensures that only finitely many points are added into the simplex. We will formalize this fact in Section 5.

For our object approximation method, our main idea is to compute the subdividing alpha complex of the object by assigning very small weights to the points inserted in the boundary of the object. In this way, the weighted points in the interior will have relatively big weights and they make a good approximation for the object. Further clarification is in Section 6.

1.3   Outline

We start by describing some definitions and notations in Section 2. Then, in Section 3 we outline some properties which our algorithm aims at. Section 4 introduces the notion of *protecting cells*. Finally, we present our algorithm and method of object approximation in Sections 5 and 6, respectively. We conclude with certain remarks in Section 7.

2   Definitions and Notations

We briefly review some definitions and notations on simplicial and alpha complexes that we use in this paper.

Simplicial Complexes. The convex hull of a set of points, $S \subseteq \mathbb{R}^d$, is denoted by $\mathrm{conv}(S)$. It is a *k-simplex* if $|S| = k + 1$ and S is affinely independent. Let $\sigma = \mathrm{conv}(S)$ be a k-simplex, its *dimension* is denoted as $\dim(\sigma) = k$. For any $T \subset S$, $\tau = \mathrm{conv}(T)$ is also a simplex and it is called a *face* of σ, denoted by $\tau \prec \sigma$. We consider σ is not a face of itself. If $\dim(\tau) = l$, then τ is called an l-face of σ. Note that the faces of a simplex σ constitutes the boundary of σ, whereas, the interior of σ is σ minus all its faces. A *simplicial complex*, $\mathcal{C}$, is a set of simplices with the following properties.

1. If $\sigma \in \mathcal{C}$ and $\tau \prec \sigma$ then $\tau \in \mathcal{C}$, and,
2. If $\sigma_1, \sigma_2 \in \mathcal{C}$ then $\sigma_1 \cap \sigma_2$ is a face of both σ_1, σ_2.

The *underlying space* of $\mathcal{C}$ is the space occupied by $\mathcal{C}$, namely, $|\mathcal{C}| = \bigcup_{\sigma \in \mathcal{C}} \sigma$. We denote $\mathrm{vert}(\mathcal{C})$ to be the set of vertices in $\mathcal{C}$.

For a set of simplices $\mathcal{J} \subseteq \mathcal{C}$, the *closure* of $\mathcal{J}$, denoted by $\mathrm{cl}(\mathcal{J})$, is the minimal simplicial complex that contains $\mathcal{J}$. For $\sigma \in \mathcal{C}$, the *star* of σ, denoted by $\mathrm{star}(\sigma)$, is the set of simplices in $\mathcal{C}$ that contains σ.

A *constrained triangulation* T_c of a simplicial complex $\mathcal{C}$ is a triangulation of the convex hull of $|\mathcal{C}|$ in which $\mathcal{C} \subseteq T_c$. Note that not all simplicial complexes can be triangulated without additional vertices, e.g. the Schönhardt polyhedron [16].

Alpha Complexes. A *ball* $b = (z, w) \in \mathbb{R}^d \times \mathbb{R}$, is the set of points whose distance to z is less than or equal to $\sqrt{w}$. We also call this a *weighted point* with center z and weight w. The *weighted distance* of a point $p \in \mathbb{R}^d$ to a ball $b = (z, w)$ is defined as $\pi_b(p) = \|pz\|^2 - w$. $\bigcup X$ is to denote the union of a set of balls X and $\bigcap X$ is to denote the common intersection of X.

Let B be a finite set of balls in $\mathbb{R}^d$. The *Voronoi cell* of a ball $b \in B$, ν_b, is the set of points in $\mathbb{R}^d$ whose weighted distance to b is less than or equal to any other ball in B. For $X \subseteq B$, the *Voronoi cell* of X is $\nu_X = \bigcap_{b \in X} \nu_b$. The *Voronoi complex* of B is $V_B = \{\nu_X \mid X \subseteq B \text{ and } \nu_X \neq \emptyset\}$.

For a ball b and a set of balls X, we denote $z(b)$ to be the center of b and $z(X)$ to be the ball centers of X. The Delaunay complex of B is the collection of simplices,

$$D_B = \{\delta_X = \text{conv}(z(X)) \mid \nu_X \in V_B\}.$$

The *alpha complex* of B is a subset of the Delaunay complex D_B which is defined as follow [6],

$$\mathcal{K}_B = \{\delta_X \mid \bigcup X \cap \nu_X \neq \emptyset, \nu_X \in V_B\}.$$

The *alpha shape* of B is the underlying space of $\mathcal{K}_B$, namely, $|\mathcal{K}_B|$. Remark that if $\delta_X \in \mathcal{K}_B$ then $\bigcap X \neq \emptyset$.

3   Conditions for Subdividing Alpha Complex

The alpha complex of a set of balls, B, is said to *subdivide* a simplicial complex, $\mathcal{C}$, if (i) $|\mathcal{K}_B| = |\mathcal{C}|$, and (ii) every simplex in $\mathcal{K}_B$ is contained in a simplex in $\mathcal{C}$. We have the following main theorem that is used to construct the subdividing alpha complex.

Theorem 1. *Let B be a set of balls and $\mathcal{C}$ be a simplicial complex. If B satisfies the following Conditions C1 and C2:*

C1. *for a subset $X \subseteq B$, if $\bigcap X \neq \emptyset$ then $z(X) \subseteq \sigma$ for some $\sigma \in \mathcal{C}$, and,*
C2. *for each $\sigma \in \mathcal{C}$, define $B(\sigma) = \{b \in B \mid b \cap \sigma \neq \emptyset\}$.*
     Then we have: $z(B(\sigma)) \subseteq \sigma \subseteq \bigcup B(\sigma)$,

then $\mathcal{K}_B$ subdivides $\mathcal{C}$.

The proof is fairly tedious and it is presented in the next subsection.

Condition C1 states that for a set of balls whose common intersection is not empty, their centers must be in the same simplex in $\mathcal{C}$. This also implies that the center of each ball must be in $\mathcal{C}$. In Condition C2, we require that if a ball intersects with a simplex then its center must be in the simplex. Furthermore, the simplex is covered by a set of balls whose centers are in the simplex.

To construct a set of balls that satisfies Condition C1, we introduce the notion of *protecting cell* for each simplex in $\mathcal{C}$, which is defined by the barycentric subdivision. We use the protecting cell in order to control the weight of each point. This will be discussed in Section 4. We show how to achieve Condition C2 in Section 5. Figure 1 on the front page illustrates an example of a subdividing alpha complex satisfying Conditions C1 and C2.

3.1   Proof of Theorem 1

It is obvious that the following two properties are equivalent to the criteria for subdividing alpha complex:

P1. Every simplex in $\mathcal{K}_B$ is contained in a simplex in $\mathcal{C}$.
P2. Every simplex in $\mathcal{C}$ is a union of some simplices in $\mathcal{K}_B$.

We divide the theorem into two lemmas. Lemma 1 states that Condition C1 implies property P1, while Lemma 2 states that Condition C2 implies property P2.

Lemma 1. *If B satisfies Condition C1, then every simplex in $\mathcal{K}_B$ is contained in a simplex in $\mathcal{C}$, that is, property P1.*

Proof. It is immediate that every vertex in $\mathcal{K}_B$ is inside a simplex in $\mathcal{C}$. Let δ_X be a simplex in $\mathcal{K}_B$. By the remark in the definition of alpha complex, $\bigcap X \neq \emptyset$. Then, by Condition C1, all their centers are in the same simplex $\sigma \in \mathcal{C}$. Therefore, $\delta_X = \mathrm{conv}(z(X)) \subseteq \sigma$. □

Lemma 2. *If B satisfies Condition C2, then every simplex in $\mathcal{C}$ is a union of some simplices in $\mathcal{K}_B$, that is, property P2.*

Proof. Let $\sigma \in \mathcal{C}$, recall that $B(\sigma) \subseteq B$ is the set of balls which intersect with σ and each of their centers are inside σ. We consider $D_{B(\sigma)}$, the Delaunay complex of the balls $B(\sigma)$. To prove σ is a union of simplices in $\mathcal{K}_B$, we prove the following claims:

A. σ is a union of simplices in $D_{B(\sigma)}$, and,
B. every simplex in $D_{B(\sigma)}$ is a simplex in $\mathcal{K}_B$.

These two claims establish Lemma 2.

The proof of Claim A is as follow. For any vertex of σ, there exists a ball $b \in B(\sigma)$ centered on σ. Furthermore, the centers of balls of $B(\sigma)$ are inside σ. Thus, σ is the convex hull of $z(B(\sigma))$. It is a fact that the convex hull of a set of points is the union of its Delaunay simplices. Therefore, σ is a union of simplices in $D_{B(\sigma)}$.

For Claim B, we first show that *if $\delta_X \in D_{B(\sigma)}$ then $\nu_X \cap \sigma \neq \emptyset$*, where $\nu_X \in V_{B(\sigma)}$. The intuitive meaning is that every Voronoi cell in $V_{B(\sigma)}$ always intersects σ. We prove it by induction on $\dim(\sigma)$.

The base case is $\dim(\sigma) = 0$. It is true by Condition C2. Assume the statement is true for every $k-1$-simplex in $\mathcal{C}$.

Let $\dim(\sigma) = k$ and δ_X be a simplex in $D_{B(\sigma)}$. There are two cases:

1. $X \subseteq B(\tau)$, where $\tau \prec \sigma$.
   Consider the Voronoi cell $\nu'_X \in V_{B(\tau)}$ and the Voronoi cell $\nu_X \in V_{B(\sigma)}$. Under Condition C2, each point in τ has negative distance to some ball in $B(\tau)$ and positive distance to every ball in $B(\sigma) - B(\tau)$. This means the Voronoi cell ν'_X is not effected by the additional balls $B(\sigma) - B(\tau)$, that is, $\nu_X \cap \tau = \nu'_X \cap \tau$. Applying the induction hypothesis, $\nu_X \cap \tau = \nu'_X \cap \tau \neq \emptyset$. In particular, since $\tau \prec \sigma$, we have $\nu_X \cap \sigma \neq \emptyset$.
2. $X \not\subseteq B(\tau)$, for any $\tau \prec \sigma$.
   This means X contain some balls which do not belong to $B(\tau)$, for any $\tau \prec \sigma$. Let b be such a ball, that is, $b \in X - \{b' \mid b' \in B(\tau), \tau \prec \sigma\}$.

By Condition C2, each point in τ has negative distance to some balls in $B(\tau)$ and positive distance to b. Since Voronoi cell ν_b is convex and $\nu_b \neq \emptyset$, we have the Voronoi cell of a ball $b \in B(\sigma)$ lies entirely in the interior of σ. In particular, the Voronoi cell ν_x is inside the interior of σ. Therefore, $\nu_x \cap \sigma \neq \emptyset$.

Thus, this proves that for every $\delta_x \in D_{B(\sigma)}$, $\nu_x \cap \sigma \neq \emptyset$ where $\nu_x \in V_{B(\sigma)}$.

Back to Claim B, we prove that if a simplex δ_x belongs to $D_{B(\sigma)}$, then $\delta_x \in \mathcal{K}_B$. Note that by result above, if $\delta_x \in D_{B(\sigma)}$ then $\nu_x \cap \sigma \neq \emptyset$ where $\nu_x \in V_{B(\sigma)}$. Under Condition C2, σ is covered $\bigcup B(\sigma)$. Thus, for every point $p \in \nu_x \cap \sigma$, p has negative distance to some balls in $B(\sigma)$, in particular, p has negative distance to all balls in X. Therefore, $\bigcup X \cap \nu_x \neq \emptyset$. Moreover, by Condition C2, p has positive distance to every ball which does not belong to $B(\sigma)$. This implies that p still belongs to the Voronoi cell of X in V_B, thus, δ_x is also a simplex in D_B. This proves that $\delta_x \in \mathcal{K}_B$. $\square$

4   Achieving Condition C1

We divide this section into two subsections. In Subsection 4.1 we give a formal but brief construction of barycentric subdivision of a simplicial complex. In Subsection 4.2 we define our notion of protecting cells. For some discussions of barycentric subdivision, we refer the reader to [17].

4.1   Barycentric Subdivision

Let σ be a k-simplex with vertices $S = \{s_1, \ldots, s_{k+1}\}$. The barycenter of σ is denoted by $\overline{\sigma}$, or $\overline{S} = \frac{1}{k+1} \sum_{i=1}^{k+1} s_i$.

Definition 1. *Let $\sigma = \mathrm{conv}(S)$ be a simplex and $T \subseteq S$. For any $t \in T$, denote $\sigma_T(t) = \mathrm{conv}(S \cup \{\overline{T}\} - \{t\})$. The subdivision of σ by the barycenter of $\mathrm{conv}(T)$ is the set of simplices: $\mathrm{subdiv}(\sigma, T) = \{\sigma_T(t) \mid t \in T\}$.*

Let $\mathcal{C}$ be a simplicial complex embedded in $\mathbb{R}^d$. We have a sequence of complexes $\mathcal{C}^0, \mathcal{C}^1, \ldots, \mathcal{C}^d$ which is defined inductively as follows:

Definition 2. *Let $\mathcal{C}^0$ be a constrained triangulation of $\mathcal{C}$. The simplicial complex $\mathcal{C}^j = \mathrm{cl}(\{\mathrm{subdiv}(\sigma, T) \mid \sigma \in \mathcal{C}^{j-1}\})$ where*

1. *$\sigma = \mathrm{conv}(S)$ is of dimension d, and,*
2. *$T = S \cap \mathrm{vert}(\mathcal{C}^0)$.*

The simplicial complex $\mathcal{C}^d$ is called *the barycentric subdivision* of $\mathcal{C}^0$. We have the following fact concerning $\mathcal{C}^0$ and $\mathcal{C}^d$.

Fact 1. *There is a 1-1 correspondence between simplices in $\mathcal{C}^0$ and vertices in $\mathcal{C}^d$. More precisely, each simplex in $\mathcal{C}^0$ corresponds to its barycenter in $\mathcal{C}^d$.*

4.2   Protecting Cells

Given a simplicial complex $\mathcal{C}$ in $\mathbb{R}^d$, let $\mathcal{C}^d$ be the barycentric subdivision of T_c, a constrained triangulation of $\mathcal{C}$. We use Fact 1 to define the protecting cells of simplices in $\mathcal{C}$.

Definition 3. *Let $\sigma \in \mathcal{C}$. The* protecting cell *of σ, denoted by ψ_σ, is defined as the closure of the star of the barycenter of σ in $\mathcal{C}^d$, namely,*

$$\psi_\sigma = \mathrm{cl}(\mathrm{star}(\overline{\sigma})),$$

where $\overline{\sigma}$ is a vertex in $\mathcal{C}^d$.

Figure 2 illustrates parts of protecting cells of various simplices in $\mathbb{R}^2$.

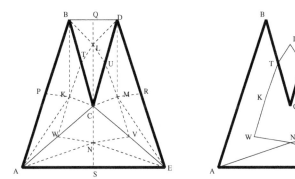

Fig. 2. Suppose we have the polygon $ABCDE$ as simplicial complex $\mathcal{C}$ embedded in $\mathbb{R}^2$. The left figure illustrates the barycentric subdivision of T_c. Vertices P, Q, R, S, T, U, V, W are barycenters of the edges in T_c. Vertices K, L, M, N are barycenters of the triangles in T_c. The right figure shows the protecting cells of the vertex C and the edge AE, respectively. ψ_C is the polygon $KTLUMVNW$, while ψ_{AE} is the triangle AEN

Let p be a point in the interior of σ. Consider the *link* of the centroid of σ, $\overline{\sigma}$, in $\mathcal{C}^d$, that is, $\mathrm{cl}(\mathrm{star}(\sigma)) - \mathrm{star}(\sigma)$. This link uniquely defines the maximal ball with the center on p and not intersecting any simplex which is not in ψ_σ. We denote the weight of such maximal ball by $\mathrm{MaxWeight}(p)$. We call $\mathrm{MaxWeight}(p)$ the *maximum weight* of p. The value $\mathrm{MaxWeight}(p)$ can be computed by finding the distance from p to the nearest bounding $(d-1)$-simplices.

Proposition 1. *Let $p_1, p_2 \in |\mathcal{C}|$. Suppose p_1 is in the interior of $\sigma_1 \in \mathcal{C}$ and p_2 is in the interior of $\sigma_2 \in \mathcal{C}$. If σ_1 and σ_2 are not faces of each other then the two balls $(p_1, \gamma \cdot \mathrm{MaxWeight}(p_1))$ and $(p_2, \gamma \cdot \mathrm{MaxWeight}(p_2))$ do not intersect for any $\gamma < 1$.*

Proof. We observe that if σ_1 and σ_2 are not faces of each other then their protecting cells can only intersect in their boundary. Thus, the proposition follows.

Therefore, Condition C1 can be achieved if all balls in B have their weight strictly less than the maximum weight of their centers.

5 Algorithm

The input is a simplicial complex C embedded in $\mathbb{R}^d$, together with its triangulation T_C. As stated in Subsection 1.2, our algorithm will subdivide the l-skeleton of C, starting from $l = 0$ up to $l = d$. For each simplex σ in C, we will construct the set of balls $B(\sigma)$ by executing the procedure ConstructBalls(σ). (Recall the definition of $B(\sigma)$ as stated in Theorem 1.)

Before we proceed to describe the details of ConstructBalls(σ) in the next subsection, we need the following concept of restricted Voronoi complex.

For a set of balls $B \subset \mathbb{R}^d \times \mathbb{R}$, consider the restriction of V_B on a k-simplex $\sigma \in C$. The *restricted Voronoi cell* of $X \subseteq B$ is $\nu_X(\sigma) = \nu_X \cap \sigma$. Similarly, the *restricted Voronoi complex* $V_B(\sigma)$ is the collection of the restricted Voronoi cells. For convenience, we also include the intersection of $\nu_X(\sigma)$ with faces of σ into $V_B(\sigma)$. That is, $V_B(\sigma) = \{\nu_X(\tau) \mid \tau \in \mathrm{cl}(\sigma)\}$.

Let $\sigma \in C$ be an k-simplex. For a set of balls X, consider its restricted Voronoi complex on σ, $V_X(\sigma)$. We define the following terms that will be used in this subsection. A Voronoi vertex v in $V_X(\sigma)$ is called a *negative, zero* or *positive* vertex, if $\pi_b(v) < 0$, $\pi_b(v) = 0$, or $\pi_b(v) > 0$, respectively, where v is the Voronoi vertex in the Voronoi cell of $b \in X$, i.e. $v \in \nu_b(\sigma)$. Note that if a vertex is positive then it is outside every ball in X.

5.1 Procedure ConstructBalls(σ)

Procedure 1 describes the details of ConstructBalls() . In the procedure, we denote γ by a real constant where $0 < \gamma < 1$. Recall also that a ball centered at a point u with weight w is written as (u, w).

Procedure 1 ConstructBalls(σ)

1: **if** dim $\sigma = 0$ **then**
2:    $B(\sigma) := (\sigma, \gamma \cdot \mathrm{MaxWeight}(\sigma))$
3: **else**
4:    Let $l := $ dim σ
5:    Let $\tau_1, \ldots, \tau_{l+1}$ be the $(l-1)$-faces of σ.
6:    $X := B(\tau_1) \cup \cdots \cup B(\tau_{l+1})$
7:    **while** $\exists$ a positive vertex u in $V_X(\sigma)$ **do**
8:       $w := \gamma \cdot \mathrm{MaxWeight}(u)$
9:       $X := X \cup \{(u, w)\}$
10:    **end while**
11:    $B(\sigma) := X$
12: **end if**

It is obvious that the whole algorithm produces a correct set of balls B provided that the procedure ConstructBalls(σ) produces the correct balls $B(\sigma)$ for each $\sigma \in C$. Since the weights of constructed balls are all strictly less than the maximum weights of the centers, Condition C1 is achieved by Proposition 1. The following Proposition 2 ensures that Condition C2 is achieved provided that the procedure ConstructBalls() terminates. We establish the termination of our algorithm in Theorem 2.

Proposition 2. *Let X be a set of balls. Suppose $z(X) \subseteq \sigma$. Then $\sigma \subseteq \bigcup X$ if and only if there is no positive vertex in $V_X(\sigma)$.*

Proof. ($\Rightarrow$) Suppose X covers σ. Let v be an arbitrary Voronoi vertex of $\nu_b(\sigma)$ for some ball $b \in X$. If $\pi_b(v) > 0$ then for any $b' \in X$, $\pi_{b'}(v) \geq \pi_b(v) > 0$, thus, contradicts our assumption that $\sigma \subseteq \bigcup X$. Therefore, every voronoi vertex is not a positive vertex.

($\Leftarrow$) Suppose there is no positive Voronoi vertex in $V_X(\sigma)$. We claim that $\nu_b(\sigma) \subseteq b$ for all $b \in X$. This claim follows from the fact that $\nu_b(\sigma)$ is bounded and is indeed the convex hull of its Voronoi vertices. So, by our assumption that the Voronoi vertices are not positive, it is immediate that $\nu_b(\sigma) \subseteq b$ for any $b \in X$. Since σ is partitioned into $\nu_b(\sigma)$ for all $b \in X$, it follows that $\sigma \subseteq \bigcup X$.

Theorem 2. *The procedure ConstructBalls(σ) terminates for any $\sigma \in C$ and each weighted point in $B(\sigma)$ has positive weight.*

5.2 Proof of Theorem 2

The proof of Theorem 2 is based on the following proposition and the fact that each simplex is compact.

Proposition 3. *Let Λ be a subset of σ whose boundary lies entirely in the interior of σ. Then there exists a constant $c > 0$ such that for all $p \in \Lambda$, MaxWeight(p) > c.*

Proof. For a point p in the interior of a simplex $\sigma \in C$, MaxWeight(p) > 0, since it has nonzero distance to all other faces of d-simplex in ψ_σ. Let $p_1, p_2, \ldots$ be a convergent sequence of points in σ. Suppose $\{p_i\}$ converges to p. MaxWeight($\cdot$) is a continuous function. So, $\lim_{i \to \infty}$ MaxWeight(p_i) = MaxWeight($\lim_{i \to \infty} p_i$) = MaxWeight(p) = 0 if and only if p is in the boundary of σ. Since the boundary of Λ lies entirely inside the interior of σ, the infimum of the set MaxWeight(Λ) > 0. Thus, our proposition follows.

The fact that each simplex $\sigma \in C$ is compact can be rephrased as follow: For every sequence of points $p_1, p_2, \ldots, p_n, \ldots$, where each $p_i \in \sigma$, there exists a Cauchy subsequence that converges to a point $p \in \sigma$. For the detail discussion we refer the reader to [17].

We prove Theorem 2 by induction on dim(σ). The base case is dim(σ) = 0. It is immediate that the procedure terminates and its weight is greater than zero. Assume that for any simplex of dimension $k - 1$ Theorem 2 holds.

Let $\dim(\sigma) = k$. We apply the induction hypothesis on the $(k-1)$-faces of σ. Let $\{\tau_1, \ldots, \tau_{k+1}\}$ be the $(k-1)$-faces of σ. By induction hypothesis, the procedure $\texttt{ConstructBalls}(\tau_i)$ terminates for each τ_i and balls in $B(\tau_i)$ have weights greater than zero. Consider the space $\Lambda = \sigma - \bigcup_{1 \leq i \leq k+1} B(\tau_i)$. Since all balls in each $B(\tau_i)$ have weights greater than zero, the boundary of Λ lies entirely inside interior of σ. By Proposition 3, there exists a constant $c > 0$ such that MaxWeight of each point in this space is greater than c.

Assume the contrary that $\texttt{ConstructBalls}(\sigma)$ does not terminate. Thus, it inserts infinitely many balls into X, (u_i, w_i) for $i = 0, 1, 2, \ldots$ with (u_i, w_i) is inserted first before (u_{i-1}, w_{i-1}). According to the procedure, the balls are inserted at a positive vertex, thus, each u_i is not inside the ball (u_j, w_j) with $i > j$.

Since σ is compact there exists a Cauchy subsequence of centers of the balls $u_{k_1}, \ldots, u_{k_n}, \ldots$ with $k_i \geq i$. We apply the Cauchy sequence criteria with some $\epsilon < \gamma \cdot c$. Thus, there exists N such that $|u_{k_i} u_{k_j}| < \epsilon < c$ for any $i, j > N$. Assume $k_i < k_j$, this means u_{k_j} is inside the ball (u_{k_j}, w_{k_j}) since $w_{k_j} > c$. This contradicts that u_{k_j} is a positive vertex. Therefore, the procedure $\texttt{ConstructBalls}(\sigma)$ terminates.

6   Object Approximation

Let $\mathcal{O}$ be a simplicial complex representing an object in $\mathbb{R}^3$ and $\mathcal{C}$ be its boundary such that $|\mathcal{C}|$ is a piecewise linear 2-manifold. For a given real positive number ϵ, we can construct a subdividing alpha complex of $\mathcal{C}$ such that the weighted points produced have weights less than ϵ. We achieve this by the following modification. Replace line 8 in procedure $\texttt{ConstructBalls}(\sigma)$ with the instruction below:

if $(\gamma \cdot \text{MaxWeight}(u) > \epsilon)$ **then** $w := \epsilon$ **else** $w := \gamma \cdot \text{MaxWeight}(u)$

It should be obvious that our algorithm is still correct and able to terminate.

Let $\Delta = \{\delta_X \in D_B \mid D_X \subseteq |\mathcal{O}|\}$, that is, all the Delaunay tetrahedra that are inside $\mathcal{O}$. Each Delaunay tetrahedron determines a sphere which is orthogonal to all the four weighted points. We consider the collection of all such balls B' and observe that $\bigcup B'$ makes a good approximation of $\mathcal{O}$. We make the following observations:

1. All balls in B' have positive weights and does not intersect with $\mathcal{C}$.
2. The space $\mathcal{O} - \bigcup B$ is fully covered by the balls in B'.
3. The boundary of $\bigcup B'$ is homeomorphic to $|\mathcal{C}|$.
4. The Hausdorff distance from $\mathcal{O}$ to $\bigcup_{b \in B'} b'$ is less than ϵ.

7   Concluding Remarks

In this paper we propose an algorithm to compute an alpha complex that subdivides a simplicial complex. We also show how via subdividing alpha complex we can approximate a closed polygonal object. It should be obvious that the approximation method can be generalized fairly easily to arbitrary dimension.

Discussion. The subdividing alpha complex discussed here is the weighted alpha complex. Figure 3 shows that a simple example where unweighted subdividing alpha complex is not always possible.

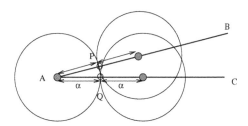

Fig. 3. The unweighted subdividing alpha cannot exist when $\angle A < 2\arcsin(\frac{1}{4})$. There must exist a ball centered on A. Also, there must be some balls centered on the segments $\overline{AP}$ and $\overline{AQ}$. Those balls will inevitably intersect and create an extra edge in the alpha complex

One point worth mentioning here is that the number of balls needed for subdividing alpha complex does not depend on the combinatorial properties of the given $\mathcal{C}$. Figure 4 illustrates a relatively simple simplicial complex which requires huge number of balls for its subdividing alpha complex.

Fig. 4. The simplicial complex consists of only four vertices and two parallel edges. The number of weighted points needed for subdividing alpha complex will be greater than $\frac{2 \times l}{w}$. So if l is much bigger than w then the number of weighted points needed can be huge too

References

1. N. Amenta, S. Choi and R. Kolluri. The power crust, union of balls, and the medial axis transform. *Comput. Geom. Theory Appl.*, **19**:(2-3), 127-153, 2001.
2. H.-L. Cheng, H. Edelsbrunner and P. Fu. Shape space from deformation. *Comput. Geom. Theory Appl.* **19**, 191-204, 2001.
3. S.-W. Cheng, T. K. Dey, E. A. Ramos and T. Ray. Quality meshing for polyhedra with small angles. *Proc. 20th Sympos. Comput. Geom.*, 290-299, ACM-SIAM, 2004.

4. S.-W. Cheng and S.-H. Poon. Graded conforming Delaunay tetrahedralization with bounded radius-edge ratio. *Proc. 14th Sympos. Discrete Alg.*, 295-304, ACM-SIAM, 2003.

5. D. Cohen-Steiner, E. Colin de Verdière and M. Yvinec. Conforming Delaunay triangulations in 3D. *Proc. 18th Sympos. Comput. Geom.*, 199-208, ACM-SIAM, 2002.

6. H. Edelsbrunner. *Weighted alpha shape*. Report UIUCDCS-R-92-1760, Dept. Comput. Sci., Univ. Illinois, Urbana, Illinois, USA, 1992.

7. H. Edelsbrunner. Deformable smooth surface design. *Discrete Computational Geometry.* **21**, 87-115, 1999.

8. H. Edelsbrunner, M. A. Facello and J. Liang. On the Definition and the Construction of Pockets in Macromolecules. *Discrete Appl. Math.*, **88**, 83-102, 1998.

9. H. Edelsbrunner, D. Letscher and A. Zomorodian. Topological Persistence and Simplification. *Discrete Comput. Geom.*, **28** (2002), 511-533.

10. H. Edelsbrunner and E. P. Mucke. Three-dimensional alpha shapes. *ACM Trans. Graphics*, 13, 43-72, 1994.

11. H. Edelsbrunner and T. S. Tan. An upper bound for conforming Delaunay triangulation. *Discrete and Computational Geometry*, **10**:2, 197-213, 1991.

12. P. M. Hubbard. Approximating polyhedra with spheres for time-critical collision detection. *ACM Transactions on Graphics*, **15**: 3, 179-210, 1996.

13. N. Kruithof and G. Vegter. Approximation by skin surfaces. *Proc. 8th Sympos. Solid Modeling and Applications*, 86-95, ACM-SIAM,2003.

14. M. Murphy, D. M. Mount and C. W. Gable. A point-placement strategy for conforming Delaunay tetrahedralization. *Proc. 11th Sympos. Discrete Alg.*, 67-74, ACM-SIAM, 2000.

15. V. Ranjan and A. Fournier. Matching and interpolation of shapes using unions of circles. *Computer Graphics Forum*, **15**: 3, 129-142, 1996.

16. E. Schönhardt. Überdie Zerlegung von Dreieckspolyedern in Tetraeder. *Mathematische Annalen*, **98**, 309-312, 1928.

17. H. Schubert. *Topologie*. English edition, translated by S. Moran, London, 1968.

18. A. Sharf and A. Shamir. Feature-Sensitive 3D Shape Matching. *Computer Graphics International*, 596-599, 2004.

19. J. R. Shewchuk. Sweep algorithms for constructing higher-dimensional constrained Delaunay triangulations. *Proc. 16th Sympos. Comput. Geom.*, 350-359, ACM-SIAM, 2000.

20. J. R. Shewchuk. Updating and Constructing Constrained Delaunay and Constrained Regular Triangulations by Flips. *Proc. 19th Sympos. Comput. Geom.*, 181-190, ACM-SIAM, 2003.

Real-Counter Automata and Their Decision Problems* (Extended Abstract)

Zhe Dang[1,**], Oscar H. Ibarra[2], Pierluigi San Pietro[3], and Gaoyan Xie[1]

[1] School of Electrical Engineering and Computer Science,
Washington State University, Pullman, WA 99164, USA
[2] Department of Computer Science, University of California, Santa Barbara, CA 93106, USA
[3] Dipartimento di Elettronica e Informazione, Politecnico di Milano, Italia

Abstract. We introduce real-counter automata, which are two-way finite automata augmented with counters that take real values. In contrast to traditional word automata that accept sequences of symbols, real-counter automata accept real words that are bounded and closed real intervals delimited by a finite number of markers. We study the membership and emptiness problems for one-way/two-way real-counter automata as well as those automata further augmented with other unbounded storage devices such as integer-counters and pushdown stacks.

1 Introduction

An automaton is a finite-state language acceptor, that is possibly augmented with other unbounded storage devices like counters, stacks, and queues. Decision problems like membership and emptiness have been extensively studied in automata theory in the past 50 years. The membership problem is to decide whether a given word is accepted by an automaton, while the emptiness problem is to decide whether the language accepted by an automaton is empty. Studies on the decision problems have been one of the focuses in automata theory and have already benefited almost every area in computer science, including model-checking [7, 26] that seeks (semi-) automatic procedures to check whether a system design satisfies its requirements. Algorithmic solutions to decision problems like emptiness for various classes of automata (e.g., finite automata, Buchi automata, tree automata, pushdown automata, etc.) have become part of the theoretical foundation of model-checking finite-state/infinite-state systems. For instance, it is known that various model-checking problems such as LTL model-checking over finite-state transition systems and reachability for some infinite-state transition systems can be reduced to various emptiness problems (e.g., [26, 10]). Still, practitioners in formal specification/verification keep challenging automata theorists with new models emerging from verification applications. Some of the models, however, have not been

---

* The research of Zhe Dang and Gaoyan Xie was supported in part by NSF Grant CCF-0430531. The research of Oscar H. Ibarra has been supported in part by by NSF Grants IIS-0101134, CCR-0208595, and CCF-0430945. The research of Pierluigi San Pietro has been supported in part by MIUR grants FIRB RBAU01MCAC, COFIN 2003012437-004.
** Corresponding author (zdang@eecs.wsu.edu).

K. Lodaya and M. Mahajan (Eds.): FSTTCS 2004, LNCS 3328, pp. 198–210, 2004.

well-studied in traditional automata theory. A typical example concerns the theory and fundamental verification techniques for analyzing hybrid transition systems containing both real variables (e.g., to model time, water level, etc.) and other unbounded discrete data structures (e.g., to model the number of times a request is sent, the call stack of a recursive process, etc.). To this end, in this paper, we study real-counter automata which contain counters that take real values.

In contrast to a traditional word automaton, a two-way real-counter automaton works on a real word provided on the input tape. A real word is a bounded and closed real interval (like [0,10]), in which the two end points and a finite number of other given (intermediate) points are called markers. Each marker as well as each segment between two consecutive markers is labeled with a color drawn from a finite color set. The automaton scans through the input real word in a two-way fashion, and can distinguish whether the current read head is over a marker or within a segment. The automaton can also recognize the color of the corresponding marker/segment. During the scan, each real-counter stays unchanged or is incremented/decremented (according to the instruction that is being executed) for an amount equal to the "distance" the head moves. The automaton can also test a real-counter against 0.

In this paper, we focus on membership and emptiness problems for two-way real-counter automata (R-2NCMs), In general, these problems are undecidable, since R-2NCMs automata have Turing computing power. Therefore, we study some restrictions that can be applied to the model to obtain decidable membership/emptiness problems. For instance, we show decidability for R-2NFAs (i.e., R-2NCMs that do not have real-counters). Another restriction is reversal-boundedness: a real-counter is *reversal-bounded* (r.b. for short) if the counter changes modes between nondecreasing and nonincreasing for at most a fixed number of times during any computation. We use r.b. R-2NCMs to denote R-2NCMs where each real-counter is reversal-bounded. We show that the membership problem for r.b. R-2NCMs is decidable, while the emptiness problem is undecidable. The latter undecidability remains even when the input real-words have only k markers, for a fixed k. We also study the decision problems for various versions of one-way real-counter automata. In particular, we study one-way/two-way real-counter automata that are further augmented with other unbounded discrete storages like integer-counters and/or a pushdown stack. Some of our decidability results make use of mixed linear constraints over both integer variables and real variables and the concept of mixed semilinearity over a language of real words. The concept generalizes the traditional notion of semilinearity [23] over a language of words. This makes it convenient for us to study various classes of one-way/two-way real-counter automata that have a mixed accepting condition which is a Boolean combination of mixed linear constraints over real-counters and integer-counters.

The rest of the paper is organized as follows. Section 2 defines basic notations and introduces some known results on integer-counter automata. Section 3 studies the membership and emptiness problems for two-way real-counter automata. Section 4 presents decidability results on one-way real-counter automata, also further augmented with integer-counters and a pushdown stack. Section 5 is a brief conclusion, also outlining possible applications of the real counter model to the verification of classes of hybrid systems.

2   Preliminaries

Let m and n be nonnegative integers. Consider formula $\Sigma_{1 \leq i \leq m} a_i x_i + \Sigma_{1 \leq j \leq n} b_j y_j \sim c$, where each x_i is a real variable, each y_j is an integer variable, each a_i, each b_j and c are integers, $1 \leq i \leq m, 1 \leq j \leq n$, and $\sim$ is $=, >$, or $\equiv_d$ for some integer $d > 0$. The formula is a *mixed linear constraint* if $\sim$ is $=$ or $>$. The formula is called a *real linear constraint* if $\sim$ is $=$ or $>$ and each $b_j = 0, 1 \leq j \leq n$. The formula is called a *discrete linear constraint* if $\sim$ is $>$ and each $a_i = 0, 1 \leq i \leq m$. The formula is called a *discrete mod constraint*, if each $a_i = 0, 1 \leq i \leq m$, and $\sim$ is $\equiv_d$ for some integer $d > 0$.

A formula is a *mixed* (resp. *real, Presburger*) formula if it is the result of applying quantification ($\exists$) and Boolean operations ($\neg$ and $\wedge$) over mixed (resp. real, discrete) linear constraints. It is decidable whether the formula is satisfiable. It is well-known that a Presburger formula can be written (i.e., Skolemized) as a disjunctive normal form of discrete linear constraints and discrete mod constraints. It is also known that a real formula can be written as a disjunctive normal form of real linear constraints. >From the results in [27], a mixed formula can also be written as a disjunctive normal form of real linear constraints, discrete linear constraints, and discrete mod constraints, when a real variable is separated into an integral part and a fractional part. We use $\mathbf{N}$ (resp. $\mathbf{R}$) to denote the set of nonnegative integers (resp. nonnegative reals). A subset S of $\mathbf{R}^m \times \mathbf{N}^n$ (resp. $\mathbf{R}^m, \mathbf{N}^n$) is definable by a mixed (resp. real, Presburger) formula P if S is exactly the solution set of the formula (i.e., $P(v)$ iff $v \in S$, for all v).

It is well-known that a finite automaton augmented with two integer-counters (each integer-counter can store a nonnegative integer and can independently be incremented or decremented by 1 and tested against 0), called a two-counter machine, is equivalent to a Turing machine [20]. Therefore, in order to obtain some decidable results, we need to restrict the behavior of an integer-counter. One such restriction is to make an integer-counter *reversal-bounded* [17]: there is a nonnegative integer r such that in any computation, each integer-counter can change mode between nondecreasing and nonincreasing for at most r times.

We will use the following notations: a DFA (resp. NFA) is a deterministic (resp. nondeterministic) finite automaton with a one-way input tape; a DCM (resp. NCM) is a DFA (resp. NFA) augmented with multiple integer-counters; DPDA (resp. NPDA) is a deterministic (resp. nondeterministic) pushdown automaton with a one-way input tape; DPCM (resp. NPCM) is a DPDA (resp. NPDA) augmented with multiple integer-counters. 2DFA, 2NFA, 2NCM, 2NPCM, ... will denote the variants with a two-way input tape. A two-way model is *finite-crossing* if there is a nonnegative integer k such that in any computation, the read head crosses the boundary between any two adjacent cells of the input tape no more than k times.

We use reversal-bounded NCM (resp. NPCM, 2NCM, 2NPCM, etc) to denote an NCM (resp. NPCM, 2NCM, 2NPCM, etc) where the integer-counters are reversal-bounded. Many classes of machines with reversal-bounded integer-counters have nice decidable properties (see, e.g., [17, 18, 13]), and the languages accepted by some of the one-way variants have the so-called *semilinear* property, which have been useful in showing that various verification problems concerning infinite-state systems are decidable [10, 9, 11, 14, 12, 24].

Recall the definition of semilinear sets. A set $S \subseteq \mathbf{N}^n$ is a *linear set* if there exist vectors $v_0, v_1, \ldots, v_t$ in $\mathbf{N}^n$ such that $S = \{v \mid v = v_0 + a_1 v_1 + \cdots + a_t v_t, a_i \in \mathbf{N}\}$. A set $S \subseteq \mathbf{N}^n$ is *semilinear* if it is a finite union of linear sets. It is known that S is a semilinear set if and only if it is definable by a Presburger formula. Therefore, the emptiness, containment, and equivalence problems for semilinear sets are decidable.

Let $\Sigma = \{a_1, a_2, \ldots, a_n\}$ be an alphabet. For each word w in Σ^*, define the *Parikh map* of w to be $\psi(w) = (\#_{a_1}(w), \ldots, \#_{a_n}(w))$, where each $\#_{a_i}(x)$ is the number of occurrences of a_i in w. For a language $L \subseteq \Sigma^*$, the *Parikh map* of L is $\psi(L) = \{\psi(w) \mid w \in L\}$. We say that a class $\mathcal{L}$ of languages over Σ is *semilinear* (or have the semilinear property) if for every language L in $\mathcal{L}$, $\psi(L)$ is a semilinear set. Many classes of languages are known to be semilinear; e.g., regular languages, context-free languages, etc. The following theorem summarizes what is known about language acceptors with reversal-bounded integer-counters.

Theorem 1

1. *Languages accepted by r.b. NCMs, r.b. NPCMs, and r.b. finite crossing 2NCMs are effectively semilinear [17]. Hence, their emptiness problem is decidable.*
2. *The emptiness problem for r.b. 2DCMs is undecidable, even when there are only two reversal-bounded integer-counters and the input comes from a bounded language (i.e., from $a_1^* \ldots a_n^*$ for some fixed n and distinct symbols $a_1, \ldots, a_n$) [17].*
3. *The emptiness problem for r.b. 2DCMs with only one reversal-bounded integer-counter is decidable [18].*
4. *The emptiness problem for r.b. 2NCMs with only one reversal-bounded integer-counter and with the input coming from a bounded language is decidable [13]. (The case when the input is unrestricted is open.)*

The language acceptors mentioned so far work on words (i.e., sequences of symbols). In this paper, we will study language acceptors that work on real words, where each "symbol" is a real line segment.

3   Two-Way Real-Counter Automata

Let $A_0, \cdots, A_k$ be $k + 1$ real numbers with $0 = A_0 < \cdots < A_k$ for some k. We use

$$W = \langle A_0, \cdots, A_k \rangle \tag{1}$$

to denote the real line between A_0 and A_k (i.e., the set $\{x : A_0 \leq x \leq A_k\}$) associated with *markers* $A_0, \cdots, A_k$. In W, A_0 (resp. A_k) is called the left (resp. right) *end marker*, and each A_i $(1 \leq i < k)$ is called an *internal marker*. Each open interval $S_i = (A_i, A_{i+1})$, $0 \leq i < k$, is called a *segment* with *length* $A_{i+1} - A_i$. Let $C = \{c_1, \cdots, c_m\}$ be a nonempty and finite set of *colors*. W is a *real word* if each segment and each marker is associated with a color in C, written

$$\langle A_0, c^0 \rangle \langle S_0, d^0 \rangle \cdots \langle A_{k-1}, c^{k-1} \rangle \langle S_{k-1}, d^{k-1} \rangle \langle A_k, c^k \rangle, \tag{2}$$

where each c^i $(0 \leq i \leq k)$ is the color of marker A_i, and each d^i $(0 \leq i < k)$ is the color of segment S_i. We use $\mathrm{color}(W) \in C^*$ to denote the sequence $c^0 d^0 \cdots c^{k-1} d^{k-1} c^k$ of colors in W. For the real word W and a color c,

- $\mathrm{marker}_c(W)$ is the number of markers in W with color c;
- $\mathrm{seg}_c(W)$ is the number of segments in W with color c;
- $\mathrm{len}_c(W)$ is the total length of segments in W with color c.

The *Parikh map* of W is the following vector $Parikh(W)$ in $\mathbf{N}^m \times \mathbf{N}^m \times \mathbf{R}^m$:

$$(\mathrm{marker}_{c_1}(W), \cdots, \mathrm{marker}_{c_m}(W), \mathrm{seg}_{c_1}(W), \cdots, \mathrm{seg}_{c_m}(W), \mathrm{len}_{c_1}(W), \cdots, \mathrm{len}_{c_m}(W))$$

A *real language* L is a set of real words. The Parikh map of L is defined to be $Parikh(L) = \{Parikh(W) : W \in L\}$. We say that L is a *mixed semilinear language* if $Parikh(L)$ is definable by a mixed formula.

Before we proceed further, some more definitions are needed. We use $\mathrm{color}(L)$ to denote the set $\{\mathrm{color}(W) : W \in L\}$. Let $\mathcal{L}$ be a family of languages, e.g., regular, context-free (accepted by NPDA), context-sensitive, 2NPDA languages, etc. L is an $\mathcal{L}$ real language if $\mathrm{color}(L)$ is an $\mathcal{L}$ language over alphabet C and, for any real word W, only $\mathrm{color}(W)$ decides the membership of W in L (the length of each segment in W does not matter); i.e., $W \in L$ iff $\mathrm{color}(W) \in \mathrm{color}(L)$. A *homomorphism* h is a pair of mappings $h_{\mathrm{marker}}, h_{\mathrm{seg}} : C \to C$. We use $h(W)$ to denote the real word obtained from W by modifying the color c of each marker (resp. segment) into $h_{\mathrm{marker}}(c)$ (resp. $h_{\mathrm{seg}}(c)$). We use $h(L)$ to denote the set $\{h(W) : W \in L\}$. L is *commutative* if, for any W, only $Parikh(W)$ decides the membership of W in L; i.e., $W \in L$ iff $Parikh(W) \in Parikh(L)$. A real word W is *uniform* if segments sharing the same color have the same length. We use $\mathrm{uniform}(L)$ to denote all uniform $W \in L$. The following results can be shown easily.

Theorem 2. *(1). Let $\mathcal{L}$ be a family of semilinear languages (e.g., regular, context-free, languages accepted by NFAs augmented with reversal-bounded integer-counters, etc.). Then $\mathcal{L}$ real languages are mixed semilinear languages. (2). Let h be a homomorphism. If L is a mixed semilinear language, then so is $h(L)$. (3). Let L_1 and L_2 be two mixed semilinear languages. If L_2 is commutative, then $L_1 \cap L_2$ is also a mixed semilinear language. (4). If L is a commutative and mixed semilinear language, then so is $\mathrm{uniform}(L)$. In fact, both of them share the same Parikh map.*

A two-way *nondeterministic finite automaton over real words* (**R**-2NFA), $\mathcal{M}$, consists of a finite number of states, a two-way read head, and an input tape that stores a real word in (1). When $\mathcal{M}$ is about to make a move, it "knows" the current state. Additionally, even though $\mathcal{M}$ does not know the exact position of the head, it knows whether the head is right over a marker or is located within a segment, as well as the color of the corresponding marker or segment. A move makes use of what $\mathcal{M}$ knows and switches $\mathcal{M}$'s state, moves the head to the right or to the left (depending on the instruction of the move) for some distance and stops at a neighboring marker or within the current segment. Formally, an **R**-2NFA $\mathcal{M}$ is defined as a tuple $\langle C, Q, q_0, F, T \rangle$, where C is the color set mentioned earlier, Q is the set of *states* in $\mathcal{M}$, q_0 is the *initial* state, and F is the set of accepting states. The finite set T specifies the *transitions* or *instructions* in $\mathcal{M}$, where each transition is in the form $\langle q, a, c, m, q' \rangle$, where:

- $q, q' \in Q$ indicates that, after firing the transition, the state is switched from q to q';

- $a \in \{\texttt{Marker}, \texttt{Segment}\}$ indicates whether the current position of the head is right over a marker or within a segment;
- $c \in C$ indicates the color of the corresponding marker or segment;
- $m \in \{\texttt{Left\_Marker}, \texttt{Right\_Marker}, \texttt{Left\_Segment}, \texttt{Right\_Segment}, \texttt{Stay}\}$ indicates how the head is going to move after firing the transition:
  - when $m = \texttt{Stay}$, the head does not move;
  - when $a = \texttt{Marker}$ and $m = \texttt{Left\_Segment}$ (resp. $m = \texttt{Right\_Segment}$), the head moves into the closest segment to the left (resp. to the right);
  - when $a = \texttt{Segment}$ and $m = \texttt{Left\_Segment}$ (resp. $m = \texttt{Right\_Segment}$), the head moves within the current segment to the left (resp. to the right);
  - when $a = \texttt{Segment}$ and $m = \texttt{Left\_Marker}$ (resp. $m = \texttt{Right\_Marker}$), the head moves right over the closest marker to the left (resp. to the right).

At any moment when $\mathcal{M}$ is running, if $\mathcal{M}$ tries to move beyond the left end marker or beyond the right end marker, $\mathcal{M}$ crashes.

The semantics of $\mathcal{M}$ is defined as follows. A *configuration* is a triple (W, q, x) consisting of an (input) real word W, a state q, and a nonnegative real x indicating the position of the head (i.e., the distance between the left end marker of W and the head). Clearly, when the configuration is given, one can figure out, from the values of internal markers given in W, whether the head is over a marker or located within a segment, as well as the color (also given in W) of the corresponding marker or segment. Let $t = \langle q, a, c, m, q' \rangle$ be a transition in T. The *one-step* transition relation $\xrightarrow{t}$ of t is defined as follows: $(W, q, x) \xrightarrow{t} (W, \hat{q}, \hat{x})$ iff all of the following conditions are satisfied:

- $\hat{q} = q'$;
- Suppose that W is in the form of (1) for some k. One of the following two items is true:
  - for some $0 \leq i \leq k$, $x = A_i$ (i.e., the current head is over the marker A_i). Then $a = \texttt{Marker}$ and c is exactly the color of the marker. Additionally, one of the following is true:
    * $m = \texttt{Stay}$ and $\hat{x} = x$ (i.e., the head does not move);
    * $m = \texttt{Left\_Segment}$. In this case, $i > 0$, and $A_{i-1} < \hat{x} < A_i$. That is, the current marker is not the left end marker and the new position of the head is within the segment (A_{i-1}, A_i);
    * $m = \texttt{Right\_Segment}$. In this case, $i < k$, and $A_i < \hat{x} < A_{i+1}$. That is, the new position of the head is within the segment (A_i, A_{i+1});
  - for some $0 \leq i < k$, $A_i < x < A_{i+1}$ (i.e., the current head is within segment (A_i, A_{i+1})). Then $a = \texttt{Segment}$ and c is exactly the color of the segment. Additionally, one of the following is true:
    * $m = \texttt{Stay}$ and $\hat{x} = x$ (i.e., the head does not move);
    * $m = \texttt{Left\_Segment}$. In this case, $A_i < \hat{x} < A_{i+1}$ and $\hat{x} < x$. That is, the head moves to the left but still within the same segment;
    * $m = \texttt{Right\_Segment}$. In this case, $A_i < \hat{x} < A_{i+1}$ and $\hat{x} > x$. That is, the head moves to the right but still within the same segment;
    * $m = \texttt{Left\_Marker}$. In this case, $\hat{x} = A_i$. That is, the head moves to the left marker of the segment;

    * $m = $ Right_Marker. In this case, $\hat{x} = A_{i+1}$. That is, the head moves to
    the right marker of the segment.

A *run* τ on input real word W is a sequence of one-step transitions, for some n,

$$(W, q^1, x^1) \xrightarrow{t^1} (W, q^2, x^2) \xrightarrow{t^2} \cdots \xrightarrow{t^{n-1}} (W, q^n, x^n).$$

The run is an *accepting run* if (W, q^1, x^1) is the initial configuration (i.e., $q^1 = q_0$ and $x^1 = A_0 = 0$) and (W, q^n, x^n) is an accepting configuration (i.e, $q^n \in F$ and the head position x^n is over the right end marker of W). W is *accepted* by $\mathcal{M}$ if $\mathcal{M}$ has an accepting run on input W. We use $L(\mathcal{M})$ to denote all the real words accepted by $\mathcal{M}$. $\mathcal{M}$ is an **R**-NFA if the input tape is one-way; i.e., $\mathcal{M}$ does not move to the left during any run. One can show,

Theorem 3. *$\mathbf{R}$-2NFAs as well as $\mathbf{R}$-NFAs accept exactly regular real languages.*

Similarly, one can generalize **R**-2NFAs and **R**-NFAs to **R**-2NPDAs and **R**-NPDAs (where a pushdown stack is operated along the moves in **R**-2NFAs and **R**-NFAs).

Corollary 1. *$\mathbf{R}$-2NPDAs accept exactly 2NPDA real languages, and $\mathbf{R}$-NPDAs accept exactly context-free real languages.*

Remark 1. Completely in parallel to NFAs, one can show that decision problems like membership, emptiness, containment, complement, equivalence, universe, are all decidable for **R**-2NFAs as well as **R**-NFAs. Similarly, membership and emptiness are decidable for **R**-NPDAs.

A (free) real-counter is a nonnegative real variable that can be incremented, decremented by some real amount and can be tested against zero. The counter is *reversal-bounded* if it changes mode between nondecreasing and nonincreasing for a bounded number of times. A two-way nondeterministic real-counter automaton with real input (**R**-2NCM) $\mathcal{M}$ is an **R**-2NFA augmented with a number of real-counters. That is, each instruction in the **R**-2NFA is augmented with an enabling condition and a flow. The enabling condition compares real-counters to 0; e.g., $x_1 > 0 \wedge x_2 = 0$. The flow specifies whether a real-counter is incremented, decremented, or staying unchanged. The increment/decrement amount for each real-counter is exactly the same as the head position change after running the instruction in the **R**-2NFA. $\mathcal{M}$ crashes whenever a real-counter becomes negative. Without loss of generality, we assume that when $\mathcal{M}$ accepts on an accepting state, the read head is at the right end marker and all the real-counters are zero. One can show that,

Theorem 4. *The membership problem as well as the emptiness problem for $\mathbf{R}$-2NCMs is undecidable. The undecidability remains even when the $\mathbf{R}$-2NCMs contain 2 real-counters and work on input real words with only one segment.*

Remark 2. It is open whether the membership/emptiness problems become decidable when the **R**-2NCMs contain only one real-counter. This is in contrast to the fact that the membership problem for 2NCMs containing only one integer-counter is decidable while the emptiness problem is undecidable.

From Theorem 4 and Remark 2, it is necessary for us to restrict the behavior of an R-2NCM $\mathcal{M}$ in order to obtain some decidable decision problems. One such restriction is to consider r.b. R-2NCMs by making each real-counter in $\mathcal{M}$ reversal-bounded. We say that the input real words are *k-bounded* if they contain at most k segments. One can show,

Theorem 5. *The emptiness problem for r.b. R-2NCMs is undecidable. The undecidability remains even when the R-2NCMs work on k-bounded input real words for some fixed k.*

It is open whether the emptiness problem for r.b. R-2NCMs becomes decidable when the R-2NCMs contain only one reversal-bounded real-counter. However, we can show that the emptiness problem is decidable when the r.b. real-counter makes only one reversal.

Theorem 6. *The emptiness problem for r.b. R-2NCMs is decidable when the R-2NCMs contain only one reversal-bounded real-counter that makes only one reversal.*

Let L be a real language consisting of all the reals words with exactly two segments such that: the length of the first segment divided by the length of the second segment results in an integer. Clearly, L is not a mixed semilinear language. However, one can easily construct an automaton in Theorem 6 accepting L. Therefore, the automata in the theorem can accept languages that are not mixed semilinear.

Membership for R-2NCM is decidable, while emptiness is not. We say that a r.b. R-2NCM is with *mixed accepting condition* if at the end of an accepting run, the r.b. real-counters satisfy a given mixed formula (instead of returning to 0).

Theorem 7. *The membership problem for r.b. R-2NCMs is decidable, even for r.b. R-2NCMs with a mixed accepting condition.*

While by Theorem 5, emptiness is in general undecidable for r.b. R-2NCMs, using Theorem 7, one can show that the emptiness problem for r.b. R-2NCMs is decidable when the R-2NCMs work on input real words with only one segment.

Theorem 8. *The emptiness problem for r.b. R-2NCMs is decidable when the R-2NCMs work on input real words with only one segment.*

Remark 3. According to Remark 2, we do not know whether Theorem 7 still holds when the r.b. R-2NCMs are further augmented with a free real-counter that is not necessarily reversal-bounded.

4   One-Way Real-Counter Automata

The real-counter automata discussed in Section 3 are equipped with a two-way input tape. Studies in classic automata theory have shown that many decision problems become decidable when a one-way (instead of two-way) input tape is considered. In this section, we use R-NCM to denote an R-2NCM $\mathcal{M}$ that does not move to the left during any computation (i.e., the input tape is one-way). We first show that in general the membership/emptiness problems for R-NCMs are undecidable.

Theorem 9. *The membership problem as well as the emptiness problem for* R*-NCMs is undecidable. The undecidability remains even when the* R*-NCMs contain four real-counters and work on input real words with only one segment.*

From Theorem 9, it is necessary to consider whether the emptiness problem becomes decidable when the real-counters in the R-NCMs are reversal-bounded.

Theorem 10. *Languages accepted by r.b.* R*-NCMs augmented with a free real-counter are mixed semilinear. Hence, the emptiness problem for the* R*-NCMs is decidable. The decidability remains even when the* R*-NCMs are with a mixed accepting condition.*

A R-2NCM $\mathcal{M}$ is *finite-crossing* if there is a fixed constant k such that during any run of $\mathcal{M}$ on any input, the read head never crosses a point within the input real word for more than k times.

Theorem 11. *Languages accepted by finite-crossing r.b.* R*-2NCMs are mixed semilinear. Hence, the emptiness problem for finite-crossing r.b.* R*-2NCMs is decidable. The decidability remains even when the* R*-NCMs are with a mixed accepting condition.*

Remark 4. We do not know whether Theorem 11 still holds when the R-2NCMs are further augmented with a free real-counter. Additionally, the results in Theorems 10 and 11 become undecidable when the input real words are uniform (segments with the same color share the same length). The proof can be easily obtained following the proof of Theorem 5.

A real-counter automaton can be further augmented with unbounded discrete storage devices such as integer-counters, a pushdown stack, etc. In such an augmented automaton, instructions can be added, each of which performs a state transition and an integer-counter/stack operation while keeping other real-counters and the read head unchanged. However, decidable results are hard to obtain for two-way automata equipped with integer-counters.

Theorem 12. *(1). The emptiness problem for* R*-2NFAs augmented with one integer-counter is undecidable. The undecidability therefore remains if one replaces the integer-counter with a pushdown stack. (2). The emptiness problem for* R*-2NFAs augmented with two reversal-bounded integer-counters is undecidable.*

By restricting the input real word to the R-2NFAs to be bounded, we can show:

Theorem 13. *The emptiness problem for* R*-2NFAs augmented with a pushdown stack and a number of reversal-bounded integer-counters is decidable when the* R*-2NFAs operate on a bounded language.*

Currently, we do not know whether the decidability remains in Theorem 13 when the R-2NFAs are further augmented with a (reversal-bounded) real-counter. Turning to the case of one-way input, we can generalize Theorem 10 as follows.

Theorem 14. *(1). Languages accepted by r.b.* R*-NCMs augmented with r.b. integer-counters are mixed semilinear. Hence, the emptiness problem for* R*-NCMs is decidable. The decidability remains when the* R*-NCMs are with a mixed accepting condition over*

Table 1. Main decidability results (U=undecidable, D = decidable, Emp. = Emptiness, Mem.= Membership)

	r.b.**R**-2NCM	r.b.**R**-NCM	**R**-2NFA	**R**-2NCM	**R**-NCM
Emp.	U (also with bounded input words). D with one-segment words or with finite-crossing or with only 1 rb counter making at most one reversal	D (also with one free real counter and a mixed accepting condition)	D. U with one free integer-counter or with 2 rb integer counters, but D on bounded languages also with a stack and rb integer counters	U (already with 2 free counters and one-segment words)	U (already with 4 free counters and one-segment words)
Mem.	D (also with a mixed accepting condition)	D also with r.b. integer counters and one pushdown stack	D		

the real-counters and the integer-counters. (2). The membership problem for r.b. **R-***2NCMs augmented with reversal-bounded integer-counters and a pushdown stack is decidable. The decidability remains when the* **R***-2NCMs are with a mixed accepting condition over the real-counters and the integer-counters. (3). The emptiness problem for r.b.* **R***-NCMs augmented with a free real-counter, reversal-bounded integer-counters and a pushdown stack is decidable.*

Remark 5. Theorem 14(1) can be generalized to finite-crossing **R**-2NCMs. Also, as in Remark 4, the results in Theorem 14 become undecidable when the input real words are uniform. The proof can also be easily followed from the proof of Theorem 5.

Theorem 14 (2) is interesting, since it entails the decidability of emptiness for **R**-NFAs augmented with a free real-counter and a free integer-counter. This is in contrast to the undecidability result when the real-counter is replaced with an integer-counter.

5   Conclusions

In this paper, we introduced real-counter automata, which are two-way finite automata augmented with counters that take real values. In contrast to traditional word automata that accept sequences of symbols, real-counter automata accept real words that are bounded and closed real intervals delimited by a finite number of markers. We studied the membership and emptiness problems for one-way/two-way real-counter automata as well as those automata further augmented with other unbounded storage devices such as integer-counters and pushdown stacks. The main results are summarized in the following table.

Results obtained in the previous sections can be useful in the area of formal verification, in particular for hybrid systems that contain operations on both continuous variables and discrete variables. The model itself may not be suitable for directly modeling hybrid systems. However, a different approach may be followed, by using the real counter model to study properties of hybrid systems.

Our results on real-counter automata may be used to investigate reachability problems for a class of finite-state programs augmented with real-counters. Such a program is capable of incrementing/decrementing the real-counters synchronously (for the same amount that is nondeterministically chosen) and comparing a real-counter with an integer constant. For instance, let P be a finite-state program containing a real-counter x and an integer-counter y. An instruction in P, besides its state transition, can increment/decrement x by some (nondeterministically chosen) amount. An instruction can also increment/decrement y by 1. Additionally, both x and y can be tested against a given integer constant. This program may model a discrete controller regulating one continuous, bounded physical variable (such as the water level in a reservoir) monitored only at discrete steps and measured with finite precision. The exact law governing the real variable may not be known. The difference between the measured value and the actual value may be considered as a noise, potentially disrupting system behavior.

The following reachability problem may be shown to be decidable: starting from a given state in P with both counters are 0, can P reach a designated state during which x is always bounded between two constants (e.g., 0 and 10), and when the designated state is reached, a linear constraint such as $2x - 3y + 4z > 5 \wedge 3x + y > 6z$ is satisfied? Here z denotes the total amount of increments made to the real-counter x. The decidability derives immediately from one of the results in the paper, namely the decidability of the membership problem for r.b. **R**-2NCMs, with a mixed linear accepting condition, augmented with additional reversal-bounded integer-counters and a pushdown stack.

Our model of real-counter automata and the decidability results are new and are related to but disjoint with the existing results on hybrid automata. The above decidability result cannot be obtained from existing results on computing transitive closures for a restricted class of hybrid systems (e.g., [25, 5, 15, 8]). The decidability does not follow from decidable models of hybrid automata [1, 16] either. For instance, some decidable results exist for restricted hybrid automata (see, e.g., timed automata [2], some multirate automata [1, 21], initialized rectangular automata [22], etc.). However, modeling the amount z in the above reachability problem (recall that the z stands for the total amount of increments made to the real-counter x) would require a stop-watch like variable. But even under a simple set-up, it is known that timed automata augmented with one stopwatch [22] is already undecidable. The decidable reachability cannot be derived from our recent results [28] on a different model, called dense-counter machines, of real-counter programs. In a dense-counter machine, each counter can be incremented/decremented by 1 or some amount between 0 and 1. Additionally, the counter can be tested against 0. The main result in [28] shows a decidable case of a dense-counter machine, which is not strong enough to show the decidable reachability in the above mentioned example: the real-counter x in the example can be compared to an integer constant (while in a dense-counter machine, only comparisons to 0 are possible), and moreover the integer-counter y is not allowed in a dense-counter machine.

Future work will be devoted to better understanding the applicability of real-counter automata, and their relation with more established timed models, such as the timed languages of [4] (also in the two-way version of [3]) and the data languages of [6], and with decidable classes of hybrid systems, such as the Integration Graphs of [19].

References

1. R. Alur, C. Courcoubetis, T. A. Henzinger, and P. Ho. Hybrid automata: An algorithmic approach to the specification and verification of hybrid systems. In *Hybrid Systems*, volume 736 of *Lecture Notes in Computer Science*, pages 209–229. Springer, 1992.
2. R. Alur and D. L. Dill. A theory of timed automata. *Theoretical Computer Science*, 126(2):183–235, April 1994.
3. R. Alur and T. A. Henzinger. Back to the future: Towards a theory of timed regular languages. In *Proceedings of FOCS'92*. IEEE press.
4. E. Asarin, P. Caspi, and O. Maler. Timed regular expressions. *Journal of the ACM*, 49(2):172–206,.
5. B. Boigelot and P. Wolper. Symbolic verification with periodic sets. In *Proceedings of the 6th International Conference on Computer Aided Verification*, volume 818 of *Lecture Notes in Computer Science*, pages 55–67. Springer-Verlag, 1994.
6. P. Bouyer, A. Petit, and D. Therien. An algebraic characterization of data and timed languages. In *CONCUR'01*, volume 2154 of *Lecture Notes in Computer Science*, pages 248–261. Springer-Verlag, 2001.
7. E. M. Clarke, E. A. Emerson, and A. P. Sistla. Automatic verification of finite-state concurrent systems using temporal logic specifications. *ACM Transactions on Programming Languages and Systems*, 8(2):244–263, April 1986.
8. H. Comon and Y. Jurski. Multiple counters automata, safety analysis and Presburger arithmetic. In *CAV'98*, volume 1427 of *Lecture Notes in Computer Science*, pages 268–279. Springer, 1998.
9. Z. Dang. Pushdown time automata: a binary reachability characterization and safety verification. *Theoretical Computer Science*, 302:93–121, 2003.
10. Z. Dang, O. H. Ibarra, T. Bultan, R. A. Kemmerer, and J. Su. Binary reachability analysis of discrete pushdown timed automata. In *Proceedings of the International Conference on Computer Aided Verification (CAV 2000)*, volume 1855 of *Lecture Notes in Computer Science*, pages 69–84. Springer, 2000.
11. Z. Dang, O. H. Ibarra, and R. A. Kemmerer. Generalized discrete timed automata: decidable approximations for safety verification. *Theoretical Computer Science*, 296:59–74, 2003.
12. Z. Dang, O. H. Ibarra, and P. San Pietro. Liveness Verification of Reversal-bounded Multicounter Machines with a Free Counter. In *Proceedings of the 20th International Conference on Foundations of Software Technology and Theoretical Computer Science (FSTTCS 2001)*, volume 2245 of *Lecture Notes in Computer Science*, pages 132–143. Springer, 2001.
13. Z. Dang, O. H. Ibarra, and Z. Sun. On the emptiness problems for two-way nondeterministic finite automata with one reversal-bounded counter. In *Proceedings of the 13th International Symposium on Algorithms and Computation (ISAAC 2002)*, volume 2518 of *Lecture Notes in Computer Science*, pages 103–114. Springer, 2002.
14. Z. Dang, P. San Pietro, and R. A. Kemmerer. Presburger liveness verification for discrete timed automata. *Theoretical Computer Science*, 299:413–438, 2003.
15. L. Fribourg and H. Olsen. A decompositional approach for computing least fixed-points of Datalog programs with Z-counters. *Constraints*, 2(3/4):305–335, 1997.
16. T. A. Henzinger, P.-H. Ho, and H. Wong-Toi. HyTech: A Model Checker for Hybrid Systems. In O. Grumberg, editor, *Proceedings of the 9th International Conference on Computer Aided Verification*, volume 1254 of *Lecture Notes in Computer Science*, pages 460–463. Springer-Verlag, 1997.
17. O. H. Ibarra. Reversal-bounded multicounter machines and their decision problems. *Journal of the ACM*, 25(1):116–133, January 1978.

18. O. H. Ibarra, T. Jiang, N. Tran, and H. Wang. New decidability results concerning two-way counter machines. *SIAM J. Comput.*, 24:123–137, 1995.

19. Y. Keste, A. Pnueli, J. Sifakis, and S. Yovine. Integration graphs: A class of decidable hybrid systems. In *Workshop on Theory of Hybrid Systems*, volume 736 of *Lecture Notes in Computer Science*, pages 179–208. Springer-Verlag, 1992.

20. M. Minsky. Recursive unsolvability of Post's problem of Tag and other topics in the theory of Turing machines. *Ann. of Math.*, 74:437–455, 1961.

21. X. Nicollin, A. Olivero, J. Sifakis, and S. Yovine. An approach to the description and analysis of hybrid systems. In *Hybrid Systems*, volume 736 of *Lecture Notes in Computer Science*, pages 149–178. Springer, 1992.

22. A. Puri P. Kopke, T. Henzinger and P. Varaiya. What's decidable about hybrid automata? *27th Annual ACM Symposium on Theory of Computing (STOC'95)*, pages 372–382, 1995.

23. R. Parikh. On context-free languages. *Journal of the ACM*, 13:570–581, 1966.

24. P. San Pietro and Z. Dang. Automatic verification of multi-queue discrete timed automata. In *Proceedings of the 9th Annual International Computing and Combinatorics Conference (COCOON 2003)*, volume 2697 of *Lecture Notes in Computer Science*, pages 159–171. Springer, 2003.

25. P. Z. Revesz. A closed form for datalog queries with integer order. volume 470 of *Lecture Notes in Computer Science*, pages 187–201. Springer, 1990.

26. M. Y. Vardi and P. Wolper. An automata-theoretic approach to automatic program verification (preliminary report). In *Proceedings 1st Annual IEEE Symp. on Logic in Computer Science, LICS'86, Cambridge, MA, USA, 16–18 June 1986*, pages 332–344, Washington, DC, 1986. IEEE Computer Society Press.

27. V. Weispfenning. Mixed real-integer linear quantifier elimination. *Proc. Intl. Symp. on Symbolic and Algebraic Computation*, pages 129–136, Vancouver, B.C., Canada, July 29-31, 1999.

28. G. Xie, Z. Dang, O. H. Ibarra, and P. San Pietro. Dense counter machines and verification problems. In *Proceedings of the 15th International Conference on Computer Aided Verification (CAV 2003)*, volume 2759 of *Lecture Notes in Computer Science*, pages 163–175. Springer, 2003.

Adjunct Elimination Through Games in Static Ambient Logic (Extended Abstract) *

Anuj Dawar[1], Philippa Gardner[2], and Giorgio Ghelli[3]

[1]Cambridge University
[2]Imperial College, London
[3]Pisa University

Abstract. Spatial logics are used to reason locally about disjoint data structures. They consist of standard first-order logic constructs, spatial (structural) connectives and their corresponding adjuncts. Lozes has shown that the adjuncts add no expressive power to a spatial logic for analysing tree structures, a surprising and important result. He also showed that a related logic does not have this adjunct elimination property. His proofs yield little information on the generality of adjunct elimination. We present a new proof of these results based on model-comparison games, and strengthen Lozes' results. Our proof is directed by the intuition that adjuncts can be eliminated when the corresponding moves are not useful in winning the game. The proof is modular with respect to the operators of the logic, providing a general technique for determining which combinations of operators admit adjunct elimination.

1 Introduction

Spatial logics have been introduced to provide local reasoning about disjoint data structures: O'Hearn and Reynolds have developed a new program logic (the separation logic) for low-level programs that manipulate RAM data structures, based on the bunched logic of O'Hearn and Pym [1]; Cardelli, Gardner and Ghelli have developed techniques for analysing and manipulating tree structures (such as XML), based on the ambient logic of Cardelli and Gordon [2–4]. These logics extend first-order logic with "spatial" connectives and their corresponding adjuncts. The spatial connectives allow us to reason locally about disjoint substructures. The adjuncts are used to obtain weakest pre-conditions for a Hoare logic for updating heaps [5], an elegant proof of the Schorr-Waite algorithm [6], and specifications of security properties of ambients [4].

We study adjunct elimination results for spatial logics. Lozes has recently proved that adjuncts add no expressive power to the ambient logic for specifying properties about trees with hidden names [7]. This result is fascinating as, for

---

* A preliminary version of this work was presented at the LICS'04 workshop LRPP.

K. Lodaya and M. Mahajan (Eds.): FSTTCS 2004, LNCS 3328, pp. 211–223, 2004.

the logic without adjuncts, validity is undecidable while model-checking is in PSPACE, while for the logic with adjuncts, validity can be reduced to model-checking, suggesting that adjuncts are powerful. However, Lozes proof is not modular with respect to the operators of the logic. This means that the proof is not particularly illuminating and it is difficult to determine which variants of the logic enjoy the adjunct-elimination property.

We take a different approach. We provide a natural adaptation of Ehrenfeucht-Fraïssé games to the ambient logic, and use these games to provide a modular proof and an intuitive explanation of Lozes' results. Ehrenfeucht-Fraïssé games are two-players games, played on a pair of structures (in our case trees) T_1 and T_2, where one player Spoiler aims to show that the two structures are different while the other player Duplicator aims to show that they are similar. The number of moves in the game is determined by a fixed rank. Each move corresponds to an operator in the logic. At each move, Spoiler selects one of the trees and makes a move to which Duplicator must respond in the other tree. Spoiler wins if Duplicator has no reply. Duplicator wins if Spoiler runs out of moves without having forced a win. A winning strategy for Duplicator implies that the two trees cannot be distinguished by any sentence of the corresponding rank. Such games have previously been used for proving inexpressivity results for a variety of logics (see, for instance [8]). Here, we use them as tool for establishing a translation.

Our adaptation of the game to spatial logics is natural, reinforcing our view that spatial logics are themselves natural. For example, the standard composition operators $A \mid B$ or $A * B$ declare that the data structure can be split into two parts, one part satisfying A and the other B. The corresponding game move is: Spoiler chooses one of the two structures (here called *boards*) and splits it into two disjoint boards; Duplicator answers by splitting the other board into two corresponding boards; Spoiler then chooses on which pair to continue playing the game. The standard adjoint operators $A \triangleright B$ and $A -* B$ declare that whenever the data structure is put into a composition context that satisfies A then the result satisfies B. The corresponding game move is based on choosing a context to add to each board and going on either with the contexts or with the extended boards. Our proof is based on the intuition that adjuncts can be eliminated if extending a tree does not help Spoiler win, as Duplicator can respond by extending the other tree identically.

We prove soundness and completeness results for our games: that is, Spoiler has a winning strategy with rank r if and only if there is a logical sentence of rank r that can distinguish between the two trees. One feature of the games we define is that the rank (of a formula or a game) is more refined than just a number. This helps us to extend Lozes' result, by showing that any sentence admits an adjunct-less equivalent of *the same rank*. This preservation of rank is intriguing, as model-checking for the logic without adjuncts is decidable while that for the logic with adjuncts is undecidable. This implies that the translation from a formula with adjuncts to an equivalent one without adjuncts is not computable. However, the preservation of rank implies that the uncomputability is not due to an unbounded increase in size of the formula.

Our elimination results focus on a spatial logic for analysing tree structures with private names (using the hiding quantification and appears construct). A natural question is whether the result holds in the analogous logic with existential quantification. We prove adjunct non-elimination in the presence of existential quantification, regardless of the additional logical operators present. In contrast, Lozes simply provides a specific counterexample for a logic with existential quantification and *appears* operator, and, moreover, the counterexample relies on the absence of equality. Indeed, our game approach provides an intuitive insight into the interaction of existential and hiding quantifiers with adjuncts.

2   Tree Model and Logic

2.1   Trees

We give a simple algebra to describe unordered, edge-labelled trees, where the labels may be free (public) or hidden (private). These trees have been used to form the basic structure of ambients [9] for describing public or private firewalls, and web data [3] (similar to XML) for describing public or private information.

We assume a set $\mathcal{N}$ of names, ranged over by $n, m, \dots$. The set of trees, denoted $\mathcal{T}$, is defined by the grammar

$$
\begin{array}{lll}
T ::= & \mathbf{0} & \text{the tree consisting of a single root node} \\
& n[T] & \text{the tree with a single edge from root,} \\
& & \text{labelled with free name } n, \text{ leading to } T \\
& T \,|\, T & \text{the root-merge of two trees (commutative and associative)} \\
& (\nu n)T & \text{the tree } T \text{ where label } n \text{ is hidden.}
\end{array}
$$

The set of free names of a term is given by $\mathrm{fn}(T)$: for example, $\mathrm{fn}(n[T]) = \{n\} \cup \mathrm{fn}(T)$ and $\mathrm{fn}((\nu n)T) = \mathrm{fn}(T) \setminus \{n\}$. The congruence on trees, analogous to that given for π-processes, is an equivalence relation generated by the axioms in Table 2.1 and closed with respect to the tree constructors. It says that edges are unordered, and that the actual name of a private name is irrelevant, provided that its difference with other names (private and public) is preserved.

Table 2.1. Congruence

$T \,|\, U \equiv U \,|\, T$	$(T \,|\, U) \,|\, V \equiv T \,|\, (U \,|\, V)$	$T \,|\, \mathbf{0} \equiv T$
$m \notin \mathrm{fn}(T) \Rightarrow (\nu n)T \equiv (\nu m)T\{n \leftarrow m\}$		$(\nu n_1)(\nu n_2)T \equiv (\nu n_2)(\nu n_1)T$
$n \notin \mathrm{fn}(T) \Rightarrow T \,|\, (\nu n)U \equiv (\nu n)(T \,|\, U)$		$(\nu n)\mathbf{0} \equiv \mathbf{0}$
$n_1 \neq n_2 \Rightarrow n_1[(\nu n_2)T] \equiv (\nu n_2)n_1[T]$		

The following decomposition properties are standard.

Lemma 1 (Decomposition)

1. *If $T \,|\, U \equiv n[V]$ then either $T \equiv n[V]$ and $U \equiv \mathbf{0}$, or $U \equiv n[V]$ and $T \equiv \mathbf{0}$.*
2. *If $T \,|\, U \equiv V_1 \,|\, V_2$, then $\exists T_1, T_2, U_1, U_2.\; T_1 \,|\, T_2 \equiv T$, $U_1 \,|\, U_2 \equiv U$, $T_1 \,|\, U_1 \equiv V_1$, $T_2 \,|\, U_2 \equiv V_2$.*

2.2   Logic

We describe the (static) ambient logic for specifying properties about trees with hidden names, which we denote in this paper by $\mathcal{L}$. It has been used to analyse security properties for ambients [4], and to declare typing properties in a pattern-matching language for manipulating web data [3]. It consists of the Boolean connectives, additional spatial (structural) connectives and their corresponding adjuncts from the propositional ambient logic, and the less familiar hiding quantifier $\mathsf{H}x.\,\_$ for analysing private names and *appears* operator $\copyright n$ declaring that n occurs free [10].

Definition 1. *The set $\mathcal{A}$ of the formulae of $\mathcal{L}$ is defined by the following grammar, where pebble η stands for either a name $n \in \mathcal{N}$ or a name variable $x \in \mathcal{X}$:*

$$A, B ::= \mathbf{0} \mid \eta[A] \mid A\,|\,B \mid A \wedge B \mid \neg A \mid \mathsf{T} \mid A@\eta \mid A \triangleright B \mid \mathsf{H}x.\,A \mid \copyright\eta$$

The satisfaction relation $T \vDash A$ between trees in $\mathcal{T}$ and closed formulae in $\mathcal{L}$ is defined in Table 2.2. The relation $T \vDash A\,|\,B$ specifies that T can be split into two trees satisfying A and B respectively. For example, the formula $n[\mathsf{T}]\,|\,\neg\mathbf{0}$ means that a tree can be split into an edge n with an unspecified subtree satisfying the true formula T, and a non-empty tree satisfying the formula $\neg\mathbf{0}$. The order of edges is irrelevant, since satisfaction is closed with respect to tree isomorphism.

The location adjunct $A@n$ states that property A holds when the tree is put under edge n. The composition adjunct $A \triangleright B$ specifies that whenever we compose a tree satisfying A to the tree being analysed, then the result satisfies B. For example, if formula $\mathsf{attacker}$ specifies what an attacker can do, then $T \vDash \mathsf{attacker} \triangleright A$ states that, for any attacker O described by $\mathsf{attacker}$, the system $O\,|\,T$ must satisfy A (for example, secret names are not communicated).

A tree T satisfies $\mathsf{H}x.\,A$ if $T \equiv (\nu n)T'$ and $T'\{n \leftarrow m\} \vDash A\{x \leftarrow m\}$, for some fresh m. Hence, $\mathsf{H}x.\,\_$ quantifies x over the private names in T. However, m may be also bound to a private name that is not in fact used in T, since $T \equiv (\nu n)T$ when $n \notin \mathrm{fn}(T)$. The appears construct $\copyright n$ can be used to prevent this possibility. In particular, $T \vDash \mathsf{H}x.\,(\copyright x \wedge A)$ states that $T \equiv (\nu m)T'$, $T'\{n \leftarrow m\} \vDash A\{x \leftarrow m\}$, and $n \in \mathrm{fn}(T')$. Thus, the private name structure can be fully analysed by the logic.

The definition of free variables is standard: variable x is free in $x[A]$, $\copyright x$, $A@x$, and the hiding quantification $\mathsf{H}x.\,A$ binds x in A. A *sentence* is a formula where no variable is free. We use $\mathrm{fv}(A)$ to denote all the free variables in A, and $\mathrm{fn}(A)$ to denote all the free names in A. Notice that, while name occurrences can be bound in a term by $(\nu n)\_$, only variables can be bound in formulae.

Table 2.2. Satisfaction

$T \vDash \mathbf{0}$	$\overset{\text{def}}{\Leftrightarrow}$	$T \equiv \mathbf{0}$
$T \vDash n[A]$	$\overset{\text{def}}{\Leftrightarrow}$	$\exists U \in \mathcal{T}.\, T \equiv n[U] \;\wedge\; U \vDash A$
$T \vDash A \mid B$	$\overset{\text{def}}{\Leftrightarrow}$	$\exists T_1, T_2 \in \mathcal{T}.\, T \equiv T_1 \mid T_2 \;\wedge\; T_1 \vDash A \;\wedge\; T_2 \vDash B$
$T \vDash A \wedge B$	$\overset{\text{def}}{\Leftrightarrow}$	$T \vDash A \;\wedge\; T \vDash B$
$T \vDash \neg A$	$\overset{\text{def}}{\Leftrightarrow}$	$T \nvDash A$
$T \vDash \mathsf{T}$	always	
$T \vDash A@n$	$\overset{\text{def}}{\Leftrightarrow}$	$n[T] \vDash A$
$T \vDash A \triangleright B$	$\overset{\text{def}}{\Leftrightarrow}$	$\forall U \in \mathcal{T}.\, U \vDash A \;\Rightarrow\; T \mid U \vDash B$
$T \vDash \mathsf{H}x.\, A$	$\overset{\text{def}}{\Leftrightarrow}$	$\exists n \in (\mathcal{N} \setminus \mathrm{fn}(A)), U \in \mathcal{T}.\, T \equiv (\nu n)U \wedge U \vDash A\{x \leftarrow n\}$
$T \vDash \copyright n$	$\overset{\text{def}}{\Leftrightarrow}$	$n \in \mathrm{fn}(T)$

Lemma 2 (Basic Properties)

1. *Satisfaction relation is closed wrt congruence:* $T \vDash A \wedge T \equiv U \Rightarrow U \vDash A$.
2. *Logical equivalence $\equiv_L$ equals structural congruence:* $T \equiv_L T' \Leftrightarrow T \equiv T'$.

With the interpretation of hiding quantification $\mathsf{H}x.\, A$, it is intuitively clear the property $A\{x \leftarrow m\}$ holds regardless of which fresh m is chosen. This universal property is formally stated in the following lemma, mimicking a previous result in Gabbay and Pitts' seminal work on abstract syntax with binders [11].

Lemma 3 (Universal Characterization of H)

$$T \vDash \mathsf{H}x.\, A \;\Leftrightarrow\; \forall n \in \mathcal{N} \setminus (\mathit{fn}(A) \cup \mathit{fn}(T)).\, \exists U \in \mathcal{T}.\, T \equiv (\nu n)U \;\wedge\; U \vDash A\{x \leftarrow n\}$$

The hiding quantifier $\mathsf{H}x.\, A$ and $\copyright\eta$ are taken here as primitive in the original spirit of [12]. Lozes focuses on the alternative formulation [10, 13], using freshness quantification $\mathsf{N}x.\, A$ and revelation $\eta \circledR A$ introduced in [4]. The two pairs can be mutually encoded, as we prove in the full paper [14]. Throughout the paper, we comment on how our results adapt to the case with revelation. In particular, revelation $\circledR$ has an accompanying adjunct $A \oslash \eta$. As part of our adjunct-elimination results, we show that the revelation adjunct is also eliminable (Corollary 2). We report here the definition of $\mathsf{N}x.\, A$, $n \circledR A$, and $A \oslash n$. The interdefinability of $\mathsf{N}x.\, A$, $n \circledR A$ and $\mathsf{H}x.\, A$ and $\copyright\eta$ is described in the full paper.

Definition 2 (Alternative Operators)

$$T \vDash \mathsf{N}x.\, A \;\overset{\text{def}}{\Leftrightarrow}\; \exists n \in (\mathcal{N} \setminus (\mathit{fn}(T) \cup \mathit{fn}(A))).\, T \vDash A\{x \leftarrow n\}$$

$$T \vDash n \circledR A \;\overset{\text{def}}{\Leftrightarrow}\; \exists U \in \mathcal{T}.\, T \equiv (\nu n)U \text{ and } U \vDash A$$

$$T \vDash A \oslash n \;\overset{\text{def}}{\Leftrightarrow}\; (\nu n)T \vDash A$$

3   Games

We define an Ehrenfeucht-Fraïssé style game for $\mathcal{L}$. We prove that the game is sound and complete: that is, Spoiler has a winning strategy for a game on (T_1, T_2) with rank r if and only if there is a sentence of rank r that distinguishes T_1 from T_2. Each move in the game is associated with a specific operator from the logic. Our results are modular with respect to these moves, which means that they automatically extend to sublogics of $\mathcal{L}$ (as long as $\wedge$, $\neg$ and T are present).

3.1   Ranks, Valuation, and Discrimination

The rank of a formula A is a function $|A|$ that maps each operator (other than $\wedge$, $\neg$, T) to the depth of nesting of that operator in A. For example, the rank $|n[\mathsf{T}] \triangleright (n[\mathsf{T}] \triangleright \mathbf{0})|$ is the tuple $\{\mathbf{0} \mapsto 1; \_[] \mapsto 1; \triangleright \mapsto 2; else \mapsto 0\}$. The operators $\wedge$, $\neg$, and T are not in the rank domain, since there are no associated game moves. The leaf operators $\mathbf{0}$ and $\copyright$ may only be mapped to 0 or 1, since they do not nest.

We write $r + r'$, $r - r'$, $r \sqcup r'$, $r \geq r'$ to denote pointwise sum, subtraction, lub, and comparison between ranks r and r'. We write $\delta(Op)$ for the Kronecker delta function: $\delta(Op)$ is the tuple $\{Op \mapsto 1; else \mapsto 0\}$. Hence, a rank $\{\triangleright \mapsto 2; n \mapsto 1; else \mapsto 0\}$ can be written $2\delta(\triangleright) + \delta(n)$.

Table 3.3. Examples of Ranks

$$
\begin{array}{rcl}
|n[\mathbf{0}] \,|\, (n[\mathbf{0}] \,|\, n[\mathbf{0}])| & = & 2\delta(\,|\,) + \delta(\_[]) + \delta(\mathbf{0}) \\
|\mathsf{H}x.\, \neg\mathbf{0} \wedge m[x[\mathbf{0}]]| & = & \delta(\mathsf{H}) + \delta(\mathbf{0}) + 2\delta(\_[])
\end{array}
$$

For rank r, $Ops(r) \stackrel{\text{def}}{=} \{Op \,:\, r(Op) > 0\}$. For rank r, set of names N, and set of variables $\mathcal{Y}$, $\mathcal{L}(r, N, \mathcal{Y})$ are the formulae of rank r which only use names and variables in N and $\mathcal{Y}$, i.e. $\mathcal{L}(r, N, \mathcal{Y}) \stackrel{\text{def}}{=} \{A \,:\, |A| \leq r,\ \mathrm{fn}(A) \subseteq N,\ \mathrm{fv}(A) \subseteq \mathcal{Y}\}$.

We say that a tree T is distinguished from U by a sentence A when $T \vDash A$ and $U \nvDash A$. A sentence identifies a set of trees (those that satisfy it). We therefore say that two trees are distinguished by a set P if one is in the set and the other is not. To deal with open formulae, we define a *valuation* to be a finite partial function f from $\mathcal{N} \cup \mathcal{X}$ into $\mathcal{N}$, such that, for every $n \in \mathcal{N}$, either $f(n) = n$ or $f(n)$ is undefined. (This extension of valuations to names as well as variables is used in Section 3.2.) For any valuation $f : \mathcal{N} \cup \mathcal{X} \to \mathcal{N}$, let $A\{f\}$ denote the result of substituting x with $f(x)$ in A for every $x \in \mathrm{fv}(A)$ for which f is defined. We use $dom(f)$ and $ran(f)$ to denote the domain and range of f.

Definition 3. *For any valuation f, T is f-discriminated from U by a formula A with $\mathrm{fv}(A) \subseteq dom(f)$ iff $T \vDash A\{f\}$ and $U \nvDash A\{f\}$.*

The next lemma is standard, but crucial.

Lemma 4. *For each rank r, finite set of names N, and finite set of variables $\mathcal{Y}$, a finite subset $\mathcal{A}_{r,N,\mathcal{Y}}$ of $\mathcal{L}(r,N,\mathcal{Y})$ exists such that any formula in $\mathcal{L}(r,N,\mathcal{Y})$ is equivalent to some formula in $\mathcal{A}_{r,N,\mathcal{Y}}$.*

For $f : \mathcal{N} \cup \mathcal{X} \to \mathcal{N}$, the formula $D_T^{r,N,f} = \bigwedge\{A \in \mathcal{A}_{r,N,dom(f)} \,:\, T \vDash A\{f\}\}$ is itself a formula of rank r and has the property that if $U \vDash D_T^{r,N,f}\{f\}$ then U and T cannot be f-discriminated by a formula of rank r (Lemma 5). Hence, $D_T^{r,N,f}$ describes T as seen at rank r.

Lemma 5. *For any T, U, f, r, N:*

$$(\forall A \in \mathcal{L}(r,N,dom(f)).\ T \vDash A\{f\} \Leftrightarrow U \vDash A\{f\}) \ \Leftrightarrow \ U \vDash D_T^{r,N,f}\{f\}$$

Before proceeding to define the games, we present a final lemma, which will be crucial in the proof of Adjunct Elimination (Corollary 2).

Lemma 6. *Let P be a set of trees such that, for any P-discriminated pair (T,U), there is a sentence $A_{T,U} \in \mathcal{L}(r,N,\emptyset)$ that discriminates T from U. Then, P is defined by a sentence $A \in \mathcal{L}(r,N,\emptyset)$.*

Proof Hint. The disjunction of the descriptors $D_U^{r,N}$ of the trees U in P defines P: $A \stackrel{\text{def}}{=} \bigvee\{B \in \mathcal{A}_{r,N,\emptyset} \mid \exists U \in P.\ B \Leftrightarrow D_U^{r,N}\}$.

3.2   Games

We define a game parametrised by a finite rank r. The game is played by two players, Spoiler and Duplicator. At any stage of the game, the position consists of a quadruple (T_1, T_2, f, r) where T_1 and T_2 are trees, f is an injective valuation, and r is a rank. Initially, for some set of names N, f coincides with f_N, the function that sends every $n \in N$ to itself and is undefined otherwise. While a complete game position is given by (T_1, T_2, f, r), we will just write (T_1, T_2, f) or (T_1, T_2) when the rest is clear, or irrelevant.

At each turn, Spoiler makes a move and Duplicator responds. Spoiler can choose any move Op such that $r(Op) > 0$, provided that the move preconditions are met. Either the Op move terminates the game, as described below, or the game goes on with the T_i's and f updated as prescribed by the move and with $r(Op)$ decreased by one. Spoiler wins if it plays a move which Duplicator cannot answer ($\mathbf{0}$, ⓒ, and sometimes $\_[]$). Duplicator wins when Spoiler has no move left to play, because r has become zero on every Op which can be played.

In the description below, most moves begin with Spoiler choosing a tree T between T_1 and T_2; in these cases, U is used for the other tree.

0 move Spoiler chooses T so that $T \equiv \mathbf{0}$ and $U \not\equiv \mathbf{0}$, and wins.

$\_[]$ **move** Spoiler chooses a tree T and a pebble η such that $T \equiv f(\eta)[T']$. If $U \equiv f(\eta)[U']$, the game continues with (T', U'); otherwise, Spoiler wins.

$\mid$ **move** Spoiler chooses T, and two trees T' and T'' such that $T \equiv T' \mid T''$. Duplicator chooses U' and U'' such that $U \equiv U' \mid U''$. Spoiler decides whether the game will continue with (T', U'), or with (T'', U'').

▷ **move** Spoiler chooses T and new tree T'; Duplicator chooses new tree U'. Spoiler decides whether the game will continue with $(T \mid T', U \mid U')$ or (T', U').

@ **move** Spoiler chooses a pebble η, and replaces T with $f(\eta)[T]$ and U with $f(\eta)[U]$.

H **move** Spoiler chooses T, a name n not in $fn(T) \cup fn(U) \cup ran(f)$, a variable $x \notin dom(f)$, and a tree T' such that $(\nu n)T' \equiv T$. Duplicator chooses a tree U' such that $(\nu n)U' \equiv U$. The game continues with $(T', U', (f; x \mapsto n))$.

ⓒ **move** Spoiler chooses T and η so that $f(\eta)$ is in T but not in U, and wins.

The definition is easily extended to the operators for freshness, revelation and the revelation adjunct (see [14]).

We may classify the moves according to their effect on the state of the game:

- _[], **0**, ⓒ may end the game;
- H may extend f and change h-names to names;
- |, _[] reduce the size of the board; @ and ▷ may increase the board.

Indeed, one begins to see why adjunct moves may be useless. Spoiler is trying to show that the two boards are different, while Duplicator aims to show that they are similar enough. In a challenging game, Spoiler plays with a small rank over two large boards with a small difference buried somewhere. A typical strategy for Spoiler is "zooming in": splitting the boards, removing edges, until the small difference is exposed. In this setting, adjunct moves are quite useless: ▷ and @ blur the difference between the two boards by extending both with isomorphic trees (in a ▷ move, Duplicator will typically choose a U' isomorphic to the T' chosen by Spoiler). This is the intuition that we are going to exploit in our adjunct-elimination proof.

3.3   Soundness and Completeness

We state soundness and completeness results for our game. The proofs are in the full paper [14]. The proofs are completely "modular"; for each move, they only depend on the properties of the corresponding operator in the logic. This means that the result holds for any sublogic of $\mathcal{L}$, provided that it includes all the operators that appear in r. Similarly, our results easily extend to the logic with operators N, ⓡ and Ⓢ

Lemma 7 (Game Soundness). *If a sentence $A \in \mathcal{L}(r, N, \emptyset)$ exists such that $T \vDash A \ \wedge \ U \nvDash A$, then Spoiler has a winning strategy for the game (T, U, f_N, r).*

Lemma 8 (Game Completeness). *If Spoiler has a winning strategy for the game (T, U, f_N, r), then there exists $A \in \mathcal{L}(r, N, \emptyset)$ such that $T \vDash A \ \wedge \ U \nvDash A$.*

4   Adjunct Elimination

We prove that any sentence can be transformed to an equivalent adjunct-free sentence of the same rank, hence extending Lozes result which does not express rank preservation. The basic idea is that, when Spoiler adds a context around one board, Duplicator can answer by adding the same context around the other board; whatever Spoiler does on the new context, Duplicator can mimic on the other copy. Our result requires that $r(\mathbf{0})$ is non-zero. This condition is not surprising, since, for example, the formula $n[\mathsf{T}] \triangleright n[\mathsf{T}]$ is logically equivalent to $\mathbf{0}$, and cannot be expressed without adjuncts and without $\mathbf{0}$ itself. Recall that we focus on the logic $\mathcal{L}$ with hiding and appears. Since our proofs are modular, the results also hold for the logic without these constructs. We include hiding and appears to link more closely to Lozes' original work, and to make the comparison with the non-eliminability of adjuncts in the presence of existential quantification (Section 5). Our results simply extend to the logic $\mathcal{L}$ with the additional revelation adjunct $\oslash$ [14]. We use DW (and SW) to denote the sets of game positions such that Duplicator (and Spoiler) has a winning strategy.

Lemma 9.   If $(T, U, f, r) \in DW$ and $r(\mathbf{0}) > 0$, then $T \equiv \mathbf{0} \Leftrightarrow U \equiv \mathbf{0}$.

Theorem 1.   If $(T, U, f, r) \in DW$ and $(T', U', f, r) \in DW$ for $\{\mathbf{0}\} \subseteq Ops(r)$ and $\eta \in dom(f)$, then:

$$(f(\eta)[T], f(\eta)[U], f, r) \in DW \quad (1)$$
$$(T \mid T', U \mid U', f, r) \in DW \quad (2)$$

Proof. (Sketch). The proof is by induction on r, and by cases on the possible moves of Spoiler. We analyse each move Op that Spoiler may make on the bigger board, and show that he cannot win under the hypothesis that he could not win on the original boards. We only show here the cases $Op = \mid$ and $Op = \triangleright$, assuming that Spoiler chooses T; the complete proof is in the full paper. When we analyse a move Op, we write r^- for $r - \delta(Op)$.

$\mid$, property (1): Spoiler splits $f(\eta)[T]$ into two trees, which must be congruent to $f(\eta)[T]$ and $\mathbf{0}$ by Lemma 1(1). Duplicator splits $f(\eta)[U]$ into $f(\eta)[U]$ and $\mathbf{0}$. The game $(\mathbf{0}, \mathbf{0}, f, r^-)$ is in DW by game completeness (Lemma 8) ($\mathbf{0}$ is logically equivalent to $\mathbf{0}$). $(T, U, f, r) \in DW$ implies that $(T, U, f, r^-) \in DW$, hence $(f(\eta)[T], f(\eta)[U], f, r^-) \in DW$ by induction.

$\mid$, (2): Spoiler splits $T \mid T'$ into two trees T_1 and T_2 which, by Lemma 1(2), can be written expressed as $T_1 \equiv T_1' \mid T_1''$ and $T_2 \equiv T_2' \mid T_2''$ such that $T_1' \mid T_2' \equiv T$ and $T_1'' \mid T_2'' \equiv T'$. Since $(T, U, f, r) \in DW$ and $(T', U', f, r) \in DW$, Duplicator has a response to a move by Spoiler in the game (T, U, f, r) where Spoiler splits T into T_1' and T_2' and similarly for the game (T', U', f, r). Suppose the moves for Duplicator in these two games involve splitting U into $U_1' \mid U_2'$ (respectively U' into $U_1'' \mid U_2''$), then by hypothesis Duplicator wins each of the four games (T_1', U_1', f, r^-), (T_2', U_2', f, r^-), (T_1'', U_1'', f, r^-) and (T_2'', U_2'', f, r^-). By induction hypothesis, this means that $(T_1' \mid T_1'', U_1' \mid U_1'', f, r^-) \in DW$ and $(T_2' \mid T_2'', U_2' \mid U_2'', f, r^-) \in DW$. Thus, splitting the tree $U \mid U'$ as $(U_1' \mid U_1'') \mid (U_2' \mid U_2'')$ is a winning move for Duplicator as required.

$\triangleright$ (1,2): Let $C\{T\}$ be either $T \mid T'$, or $f(\eta)[T]$ and $C\{U\}$ denote $U \mid U'$, or $f(\eta)[U]$, respectively. Spoiler chooses a tree V to compose with $C\{T\}$. Duplicator responds by adding the same tree to $C\{U\}$. If Spoiler chooses to proceed with

(V, V), then Duplicator wins by game completeness (Lemma 8). Assume that Spoiler chooses to proceed with $(C\{T\} \,|\, V,\, C'\{U\} \,|\, V, f, r^-)$. $(T, U, f, r) \in DW$ and $(T', U', f, r) \in DW$ imply that $(T, U, f, r^-) \in DW$ and $(T', U', f, r^-) \in DW$, hence $(C\{T\},\, C'\{U\}, f, r^-) \in DW$ follows by induction, and hence $(C\{T\} \,|\, V,\, C'\{U\} \,|\, V, f, r^-) \in DW$ also follows by induction.

Corollary 1 (Move Elimination). *If* $(T, U, f, r) \in DW$, $r^{\sqcup} \stackrel{\text{def}}{=} r \sqcup \delta(\mathbf{0})$, *and* $\{\triangleright, @\} \supseteq Ops(r^{adj})$, *then:*

$$(T, U, f, r^{\sqcup}) \in DW \;\Rightarrow\; (T, U, f, r + r^{adj}) \in DW$$
$$(T, U, f, r + r^{adj}) \in SW \;\Rightarrow\; (T, U, f, r^{\sqcup}) \in SW$$

We can finally show that adjuncts do not add expressive power to the logic. Not only that but, for each sentence containing adjuncts, there is an equivalent adjunct-less sentence of a related rank. There are only a finite number of inequivalent sentences for each rank (Lemma 4), but it remains an undecidable problem to determine which one is equivalent to a given sentence with adjuncts.

Corollary 2 (Adjunct Elimination). *Any property that can be expressed by a sentence in* $\mathcal{L}(r + r^{adj}, N, \emptyset)$, *where* $\{\triangleright, @\} \supseteq Ops(r^{adj})$, *can be expressed by a sentence in* $\mathcal{L}(r \sqcup \delta(\mathbf{0}), N, \emptyset)$.

Proof. Let P be defined by a sentence A in $\mathcal{L}(r + r^{adj}, N, \emptyset)$. For each $T \in P$ and $U \notin P$, by Game Soundness (Lemma 7), $(T, U, f_N, r + r^{adj}) \in SW$. By Corollary 1, $(T, U, f_N, r \sqcup \delta(\mathbf{0})) \in SW$. By Game Completeness (Lemma 8), this implies that, for each P-discriminated pair T, U, there is a sentence B_{TU} in $\mathcal{L}(r \sqcup \delta(\mathbf{0}), N, \emptyset)$ that discriminates T from U. By Lemma 6, there is a sentence B in $\mathcal{L}(r \sqcup \delta(\mathbf{0}), N, \emptyset)$ that defines P.

In the full paper we use the same technique to prove adjunct elimination for the logic extended with revelation adjunct. Revelation adjunct allows $\copyright n$ to be expressed as $(n[0] \triangleright ((\neg(\neg \mathbf{0} \,|\, \neg \mathbf{0})) \oslash n)) @ m$ (for any $m \neq n$). For this reason, in the revelation-adjunct version of Theorem 1 the hypothesis $\{\mathbf{0}\} \subseteq Ops(r)$ must be strengthened to $\{\mathbf{0}, \copyright\} \subseteq Ops(r)$, and $\delta(\copyright)$ appears in the statement of the adjunct elimination result, as follows.

Theorem 2 (Adjunct Elimination with). *Any property that can be expressed by a sentence in* $\mathcal{L}(r + r^{adj}, N, \emptyset)$, *where* $\{\triangleright, @, \oslash\} \supseteq Ops(r^{adj})$, *can be expressed by a sentence in* $\mathcal{L}(r \sqcup \delta(\copyright) \sqcup \delta(\mathbf{0}), N, \emptyset)$.

5   Adjunct Non-eliminability for $\exists$

The hiding quantifier H is similar to existential quantification $\exists$. A natural question is whether a similar adjunct elimination result holds for the logic with existential quantification. In [7], Lozes gives a counterexample to show that adjuncts cannot be eliminated in a logic with both existential quantification *and*

ⓒ. This result, although interesting, is weak since existential quantification is not usually associated with ⓒ and, moreover, the counterexample relies on the absence of primitive equality from the logic. Here we complete the analysis, by proving that adjuncts cannot be eliminated in a logic with $\exists$ and without ⓒ, regardless of the presence of equality.

Let $\mathcal{L}_{\exists,\triangleright}$ denote the (static) ambient logic with existential quantification and the composition adjunct, and let $\mathcal{L}_{\exists,=}$ denote the corresponding logic without the composition adjunct and with equality. We have shown that the parity of trees is not definable in $\mathcal{L}_{\exists,=}$ (and, hence, neither in $\mathcal{L}_{\exists}$), using a standard game inexpressivity argument which we give in the full paper (Theorem 3). It is however definable in $\mathcal{L}_{\exists,\triangleright}$, a result due to Hongseok Yang and reported here (Theorem 4).

Theorem 3 (No Parity in $\mathcal{L}_{\exists,=}$). *No sentence A in $\mathcal{L}_{\exists,=}$ expresses the property that T is flat,[1] differently-labelled, and has an even number of edges.*

The $\mathcal{L}_{\exists,\triangleright}$ sentence used in Theorem 4 to describe parity in $\mathcal{L}_{\exists,\triangleright}$ is based on the following sentences:

$$EachEdge(A) \stackrel{\text{def}}{=} \neg(((\exists y.\, y[\mathsf{T}]) \wedge \neg A) \mid \mathsf{T})$$
$$Flat \stackrel{\text{def}}{=} EachEdge(\exists x.\, x[\mathbf{0}])$$
$$Diff \stackrel{\text{def}}{=} \neg(\exists x.\, x[\mathbf{0}] \mid x[\mathbf{0}] \mid \mathsf{T})$$
$$Pairs \stackrel{\text{def}}{=} EachEdge(\exists x, y.\, c[x[\mathbf{0}] \mid y[\mathbf{0}]])$$
$$DiffP \stackrel{\text{def}}{=} \neg\exists x.\, (c[x[\mathbf{0}] \mid x[\mathbf{0}]] \mid \mathsf{T}) \vee (c[x[\mathbf{0}] \mid \mathsf{T}] \mid c[x[\mathbf{0}] \mid \mathsf{T}] \mid \mathsf{T})$$
$$A \propto B \stackrel{\text{def}}{=} \neg(A \triangleright \neg B)$$

$T \vDash EachEdge(A)$ denotes that every top-level edge of T satisfies A. Hence, $T \vDash Flat$ states that T is a flat-tree, and $Flat \wedge Diff$ means that its edges have different labels. Similarly, $T \vDash Pairs$ means that T is composed of $c[n[\mathbf{0}] \mid m[\mathbf{0}]]$ edges, while $Pairs \wedge DiffP$ means that all second-level labels are mutually different. Finally, $T \vDash A \propto B$ iff there exists U such that $U \vDash A$ and $T \mid U \vDash B$.

Theorem 4 (Yang: Parity in $\mathcal{L}_{\exists,\triangleright}$). *The sentence*

$$Even \stackrel{\text{def}}{=} (Flat \wedge Diff) \ \wedge \ ((Pairs \wedge DiffP) \propto (\forall x.\, x[\mathbf{0}] \mid \mathsf{T} \ \Leftrightarrow \ c[x[\mathbf{0}] \mid \mathsf{T}]))$$

defines the set of flat, differently-labelled trees with an even number of edges.

Proof. $T \vDash Even$ iff T is a flat tree where all the labels are different (expressed formally by $T \vDash Flat \wedge Diff$), and there exists U such that $U \vDash Pairs \wedge DiffP$ and $T \mid U \vDash \forall x.\, x[\mathbf{0}] \mid \mathsf{T} \ \Leftrightarrow \ c[x[\mathbf{0}] \mid \mathsf{T}]$. Hence, U has a shape

$$c[n_1[\mathbf{0}] \mid n_2[\mathbf{0}]] \mid \ldots \mid c[n_{2k-1}[\mathbf{0}] \mid n_{2k}[\mathbf{0}]],$$

all the n_i's are different, and U contains an even number of them. Finally, $T \mid U \vDash \forall x.\, x[\mathbf{0}] \mid \mathsf{T} \ \Leftrightarrow \ c[x[\mathbf{0}] \mid \mathsf{T}]$ says that the labels of T are exactly the same as the second-level labels of U, hence T has an even number of edges.

---

[1] A 'flat' tree looks like $n_1[] \mid \ldots \mid n_j[]$; 'differently labelled' means $n_i \neq n_j$ for $i \neq j$.

Games offer an explanation why $\mathcal{L}_{\exists,\triangleright}$ is more expressive than $\mathcal{L}_{\exists,=}$. Consider a $\mathcal{L}_{\exists,\triangleright}$ strategy that corresponds to Yang's sentence. Spoiler must distinguish between even board $T = n_1[] \mid \ldots \mid n_{2k}[]$ and odd board $U = m_1[] \mid \ldots \mid m_{2k+1}[]$. Spoiler adds the context $V = c[n_1[\mathbf{0}] \mid n_2[\mathbf{0}]] \mid \ldots \mid c[n_{2k-1}[\mathbf{0}] \mid n_{2k}[\mathbf{0}]]$ to the even board. Now Duplicator is lost. He may add $c[m_1[\mathbf{0}] \mid m_2[\mathbf{0}]] \mid \ldots \mid c[m_{2k-1}[\mathbf{0}] \mid m_{2k}[\mathbf{0}]]$ to the other board, but in this case there will be a name m_{2k+1} which appears once in $U \mid V$, while every name (but c) appears exactly twice in $T \mid V$. Now Spoiler can use $\exists$ to pebble that name and win.

In a game for $\mathcal{L}$ (with hiding and appears), such a strategy is not available to Spoiler because only hidden names can be pebbled in that game, and no hidden name can be shared between T and V above. Indeed, the key is that a counterpart to Theorem 1(2) does not hold for $\mathcal{L}_{\exists,\triangleright}$ games. It is possible for Duplicator to have a winning strategy on each of (T, U) and (T', U') while Spoiler wins on $(T \mid T', U \mid U')$ because of names shared between T and T'.

6   Conclusions

We have investigated adjunct elimination results for spatial logics, by introducing game techniques for such logics. Our work provides a modular proof of adjunct elimination which helps our understanding of why some combinations of operators admit adjunct elimination while others do not. In particular, we show the adjunct elimination results hold for a logic with hiding quantification and appears (for reasoning about private and public names), and do not hold for the analogous logic with existential quantification (for analysing shared names). Another consequence of our proof is a rank preservation result that shows that the elimination of adjuncts does not increase the rank of a sentence, which is surprising as adjuncts cannot be computably eliminated.

References

1. O'Hearn, P., Pym, D.: The logic of bunched implications. Bulletin of Symbolic Logic **5** (1999) 215–244
2. Cardelli, L., Ghelli, G.: TQL: A query language for semistructured data based on the ambient logic. Mathematical Structures in Comp. Sci. **14** (2004) 285–327
3. Cardelli, L., Gardner, P., Ghelli, G.: Manipulating trees with hidden labels. In: Proc. of FOSSACS'03, Warsaw, Poland. (2003) 216–232
4. Cardelli, L., Gordon, A.: Anytime, anywhere: modal logics for mobile ambients. In: Proc. of POPL'00. (2000) 365–377
5. Ishtiaq, S., O'Hearn, P.: BI as an assertion language for mutable data structures. In: Proc. of POPL'01. (2001) 14–26
6. Yang, H.: An example of local reasoning in BI pointer logic: the Schorr-Waite graph marking algorithm. In: Proc. of SPACE'01 Workshop, London. (2001)
7. Lozes, E.: Adjuncts elimination in the static ambient logic. In: Proc. of Express'03, Marseille. (2003)
8. Ebbinghaus, H.D., Flum, J.: Finite Model Theory. 2 edn. Springer (1999)

9. Cardelli, L., Gordon, A.: Mobile ambients. In: Proc. of FOSSACS'98, Springer-Verlag (1998) 140–155

10. Cardelli, L., Gordon, A.D.: Logical properties of name restriction. In: Proc. of TCLA'01, Krakow, Poland. Volume 2044 of LNCS., Springer (2001) 46–60

11. Gabbay, M.J., Pitts, A.M.: A new approach to abstract syntax with variable binding. Formal Aspects of Computing (2002)

12. Caires, L.: A specification logic for mobility. Technical Report 4/2000, DI/FCT/UNL (2000)

13. Caires, L., Cardelli, L.: A spatial logic for concurrency (Part I). In: Proc. of TACS'01. Volume 2215 of LNCS. (2001) 1–37

14. Dawar, A., Ghelli, G., Gardner, P.: Adjunct elimination through games. (unpublished)

On the Bisimulation Invariant Fragment of Monadic Σ_1 in the Finite

Anuj Dawar[1] and David Janin[2]

[1] University of Cambridge Computer Laboratory, Cambridge CB3 0FD, UK
anuj.dawar@cl.cam.ac.uk
[2] LaBRI, Université Bordeaux I, 33405 Talence, France
janin@labri.fr

Abstract. We investigate the expressive power of existential monadic second-order logic (monadic Σ_1) on finite transition systems. In particular, we look at its power to express properties that are invariant under forms of bisimulation and compare these to properties expressible in corresponding fixed-point modal calculi. We show that on finite unary transition systems the bisimulation invariant fragment of monadic Σ_1 is equivalent to bisimulation-invariant monadic second order logic itself or, equivalently, the mu-calculus. These results contrast with the situation on infinite structures. Although we show that these results do not extend directly to the case of arbitrary finite transition systems, we are still able to show that the situation there contrasts sharply with the case of arbitrary structures. In particular, we establish a partial expressiveness result by means of tree-like tiling systems that does not hold on infinite structures.

1 Introduction

The second author and Walukiewicz [5] showed in 1996 that any sentence of monadic second-order logic (MSO) whose models are invariant under bisimulation is equivalent to a sentence of Kozen's modal μ-calculus (L_μ).

The importance of the theorem lies, on the one hand, in the fact that monadic second-order logic is seen as a natural upper limit on the reasonable expressive power of languages for the specification of behaviours of concurrent systems. Indeed, almost all logics used in practice, such as LTL and CTL* are fragments of this logic. On the other hand, bisimulation is a natural relation describing the behavioral equivalence of processes. In speaking of behavioral specifications expressed in MSO, it seems natural to restrict oneself to those that are invariant under bisimulation. The theorem of Janin and Walukiewicz provides a syntactic characterization of the properties that are bisimulation invariant. Looked at from the other side, the theorem is also seen as an expressive completeness result for the μ-calculus.

The methodology used in the proof of this theorem is based on automata on infinite trees. Every transition system is equivalent by bisimulation to a tree

K. Lodaya and M. Mahajan (Eds.): FSTTCS 2004, LNCS 3328, pp. 224–236, 2004.

and, on trees, the evaluation of MSO formulas can be expressed as the evaluation of alternating tree automata. By considering trees that are, in a precise sense, *saturated* one can transform automata to show that these formulas are equivalent to formulas of the μ-calculus. This essential methodology has proved productive in establishing variants of the original result. It is known, for instance, that sentences of MSO that are invariant under *counting bisimulation* are equivalent to C_μ—the modal fixed-point calculus with counting modalities [12, 4]. It has also been shown that the existential fragment of MSO (which we denote monadic Σ_1) is, for bisimulation invariant properties, expressively equivalent to N_1—the fragment of the μ-calculus with only greatest fixed points [4].

However, it remains an open question whether a version of this expressive completeness result is true if we restrict ourselves to finite structures. That is, is it the case that every sentence of MSO that is bisimulation-invariant *on finite structures* is equivalent, *again on finite structures* to a sentence of L_μ?

This statement has a weaker hypothesis and conclusion than the original theorem and is therefore not a consequence of it. It has been the subject of much recent investigation. The corresponding finite versions of the equivalence between monadic Σ_1 and N_1 for bisimulation invariant properties and of MSO and C_μ for counting bisimulation also remain open. One related result that is known to carry over into the finite is the theorem of van Benthem (see [11]) that any first-order definable property that is invariant under bisimulation is definable in propositional modal logic. It has been shown by Rosen [8] that this statement is still true when we restrict ourselves to finite structures.

One reason why the question of the equivalence of these logics is so different in the finite is that, once we restrict ourselves to finite structures, we no longer have a tree model property. That is, it is no longer the case that every structure is equivalent by bisimulation to a tree. In the general case, it is possible to take the collection of all (saturated) infinite trees as a canonical class of models that intersects every bisimulation equivalence class. Thus, as one is considering formulae invariant under bisimulation, one can restrict oneself to this class and on this class there are well-behaved automata models for the logics we consider. Unfortunately, there is no class of finite structures that fulfills these conditions.

Main Results

In this paper, we are mainly concerned with the study of the bisimulation invariant fragment of monadic Σ_1 in the finite.

We show that restricting ourselves to finite structures that are *unary*. i.e. in which each node has a single successor, this fragment is as expressive as (the bisimulation invariant fragment of) full monadic second order logic. In other words, we obtain a complete characterization of the expressive power of the bisimulation invariant fragment of MSO on such structures. As a corollary, the correspondence between monadic Σ_1 and N_1 that holds on arbitrary (finite and infinite) unary structures just fails in the finite.

On finite structures that are not necessarily unary, however, the situation is less clearcut. We obtain a counterexample to the equivalence of monadic Σ_1 with NC_1 (the first level of the C_μ hierarchy) on finite structures, demonstrating that this situation is distinct from the case of arbitrary (finite and infinite) systems. We also show that monadic Σ_1 is not as expressive as bisimulation-invariant MSO, so the situation also differs from the unary case.

These two negative results leads us to consider tiling systems [10], which are known to capture monadic Σ_1 on finite structures. We show that when the properties concerned are bisimulation invariant, simple tiling systems suffice. More precisely, we show that if a sentence φ of monadic Σ_1 is invariant under bisimulation then there is a class of structures, including representatives of all bisimulation classes, on which φ is characterized by a *tree-like* tiling system of *radius one* (these terms are made precise below). One might expect that this normal form could be further refined so that the tiles are what we call *forward looking*. This would establish that bisimulation invariant properties of monadic Σ_1 can be expressed in N_1. However, such a methodology would also yield the result for the counting case, which is refuted by the counterexample obtained on unary structures.

2   Background and Definitions

Models and Standard Logics

The logics we consider are interpreted in *transition systems*, also called Kripke structures, or simply labeled directed graphs (in the sequel, when we use the term *graph*, we mean a labeled directed graph). Fix a set A of actions and a set *Prop* of atomic propositions. A transition system for A and *Prop* is a structure

$$\mathcal{K} = \langle V, r, \{E_a\}_{a \in A}, \{p^{\mathcal{K}}\}_{p \in Prop}\rangle$$

with universe V (whose elements are called states), a distinguished element called the *root* $r \in V$, binary relations $E_a \subseteq V \times V$ for each $a \in A$ and unary relations $p^{\mathcal{K}} \subseteq V$ for each atomic proposition $p \in Prop$. For the sake of clarity, we confine ourselves in this paper to vocabularies where A consists of a single action. We then drop the subscript a on the binary relation E. All of our results apply equally well to the more general case.

Such transition systems are usually used to interpret modal logics, which we consider below. We also interpret standard predicate logics, in particular first-order logic (FO) and monadic second-order logic (MSO) in transition systems. In the sequel, we shall write $\varphi(x_1, \cdots, x_n)$ or simply $\varphi(\bar{x})$ for an FO or MSO formula with free first-order variables among $\bar{x} = (x_1, \cdots, x_n)$ *regardless* of the free monadic predicate (or set) variables occurring in φ. More precisely, given the set $\{X_1, \cdots, X_n\}$ of all set variables occurring free in φ, we shall implicitly and whenever required interpret the formula φ on transition systems with the set of atomic proposition $Prop' = Prop \cup \{X_1, \cdots, X_n\}$.

Bisimulation and Counting Bisimulation

A *directed (resp. undirected) path* in a transition system $\mathcal{K}$ is a (finite or infinite) sequence of vertices such that for any two consecutive vertices v_1 and v_2 in the sequence one has $(v_1, v_2) \in E$ (resp. (v_1, v_2) or $(v_2, v_1) \in E$). The directed (resp. undirected) distance $d_d(v_1, v_2)$ (resp. $d(v_1, v_2)$) between two vertices v_1 and v_2 is the length of the shortest directed (resp. undirected) path from v_1 to v_2.

A directed (resp. undirected) cycle in $\mathcal{K}$ is a periodic infinite directed (resp. undirected) path. Given an integer k, we say that a graph $\mathcal{K}$ is k-*acyclic* if any *undirected* cyclic path in $\mathcal{K}$ contains at least $k + 1$ distinct vertices. Given two transition systems $\mathcal{K} = \langle V, r, E, \{p^{\mathcal{K}}\}_{p \in Prop} \rangle$ and $\mathcal{K}' = \langle V', r', E', \{p^{\mathcal{K}'}\}_{p \in Prop} \rangle$, a *bisimulation* between $\mathcal{K}$ and $\mathcal{K}'$ is a relation $B \subseteq V \times V'$ such that, if $(v, v') \in B$ then:

- for each $p \in Prop$, $v \in p^{\mathcal{K}} \iff v' \in p^{\mathcal{K}'}$;
- for each w with $(v, w) \in E$ there is a w' with $(v', w') \in E'$ and $(w, w') \in B$; and
- for each w' with $(v', w') \in E'$ there is a w with $(v, w) \in E$ and $(w, w') \in B$.

A *counting bisimulation* between $\mathcal{K}$ and $\mathcal{K}'$ is a relation $B \subseteq V \times V'$ such that, if $(v, v') \in B$ then:

- for each $p \in Prop$, $v \in p^{\mathcal{K}} \iff v' \in p^{\mathcal{K}'}$;
- B contains a bijection between the sets $\{w : (v, w) \in E\}$ and $\{w' : (v', w') \in E'\}$.

Observe that any counting bisimulation is a bisimulation.

We say that $\mathcal{K}$ and $\mathcal{K}'$ are (counting) bisimilar if there is a (counting) bisimulation B between them with $(r, r') \in B$. More generally, we say that two states $v \in \mathcal{K}$ and $v' \in \mathcal{K}'$ (where $\mathcal{K}$ and $\mathcal{K}'$ are not necessarily distinct) are (counting) bisimilar if there is a (counting) bisimulation B between the two structures with $(v, v') \in B$.

Given a class $\mathcal{C}$ of transition systems, we say that an FO or MSO sentence φ is (counting) bisimulation invariant on $\mathcal{C}$ when, for any two (counting) bisimilar models $\mathcal{K}$ and $\mathcal{K}' \in \mathcal{C}$ one has $\mathcal{K} \models \varphi$ if, and only if, $\mathcal{K}' \models \varphi$. Accordingly, we say that φ is bisimulation invariant *in the finite* when it is bisimulation invariant on the class of finite structures.

Modal Logic and the Mu-calculus

The *modal propositional logic* (ML) consists of formulas built up from the propositions in *Prop* and the propositional constants *true* and *false* using the Boolean connectives and the modalities $\Box$ and $\Diamond$: i.e., for a formula α, $\Box\alpha$ and $\Diamond\alpha$ are also formulas. For the semantics, we just note that $\mathcal{K}, v \models \Diamond\alpha$ if, and only if, there is a v' with $(v, v') \in E$ such that $\mathcal{K}, v' \models \alpha$ (and dually for $\Box\alpha$).

The *modal depth* of a modal formula is defined to be the maximal depth of nesting of modalities in α, i.e. the modal depth of a modality free formula is defined to be zero; if α is of modal depth k then the modal depth of $\Diamond\alpha$ or

$\Box\alpha$ is $k+1$; and the modal depth of a Boolean combination of formulas is the maximum modal depth of any one of the formulas.

The *modal μ-calculus L_μ* is obtained by extending ML with a countable collection of propositional variables X so that a variable by itself is a formula and, if α is a formula and X a variable which occurs only positively (i.e., only within the scope of an even number of negation signs) in α then $\mu X.\alpha$ and $\nu X.\alpha$ are also formulas in which the variable X is bound. For the semantics, given a structure $\mathcal{K}$ and an interpretation in $\mathcal{K}$ for all the free variables of α, we say that $\mathcal{K}, v \models \mu X.\alpha$ if v is in the least set $X \subseteq V$ such that $X \iff \alpha$. Similarly $\mathcal{K}, v \models \nu X.\alpha$ if v is in the *greatest fixed point* defined by α.

A key feature of the modal logics ML and L_μ is that the properties they express are bisimulation invariant. That is, if $\mathcal{K}$ and $\mathcal{K}'$ are bisimilar then for any formula α, $\mathcal{K} \models \alpha$ if, and only if, $\mathcal{K}' \models \alpha$.

There is a standard translation of formulas of ML into the first-order logic of transition systems. That is, for each formula α of ML, there is a formula $\varphi_\alpha(x)$ of first-order logic with one free first-order variable x (in the vocabulary with a binary relation symbol E and unary relation symbols for each $p \in Prop$) that defines in each $\mathcal{K}$ exactly the set of states in which α is true. Similarly, there is a straightforward translation from L_μ to monadic second-order logic.

By results of van Benthem [11] and Janin and Walukiewicz [5] we know that there are converses for these translations. That is, every property of transition systems that is expressible in FO and is invariant under bisimulation is expressible in ML and any bisimulation-invariant property that is definable in MSO is also definable in L_μ.

Using the equivalences $\Box\alpha \iff \neg\Diamond\neg\alpha$, $\nu X.\alpha \iff \neg\mu X.\neg\alpha[\neg X/X]$ and De Morgan's laws, it is possible to transform any formula of L_μ into negation normal form, where negation signs only appear before propositional atoms. We write N_1 for the collection of formulas in negation normal form in which no instance of the operator μ appears. Similarly, M_1 is the collection of formulas without ν. These are the bottom two levels of an alternation hierarchy which is known to give strictly increasing expressive power (see [2]).

It is easily seen that when we translate L_μ to MSO, formulas of N_1 yield *existential* MSO formulas (i.e., in prenex normal form, all second-order quantifiers are existential) while formulas of M_1 yield *universal* MSO formulas. By a result of Janin and Lenzi [4] we get a converse of these statements for bisimulation-invariant properties. That is, any bisimulation-invariant property definable in existential MSO (also written as monadic Σ_1) is definable in N_1.

The *counting modal logic* and the *counting μ-calculus C_μ* are defined similarly to ML and L_μ except the rules for $\Box$ and $\Diamond$ are replaced by: for each $i \in \mathbb{N}$, if α is a formula then so are $\Box_i\alpha$ and $\Diamond_i\alpha$. For the semantics, we say that $\mathcal{K}, v \models \Diamond_i\alpha$ if there are at least i distinct v' such that $(v, v') \in E$ and $\mathcal{K}, v' \models \alpha$. We write NC_1 (by analogy with N_1) for the fragment of C_μ without least fixed-points.

In the sequel, we also use *backward modalities* $\Diamond^{-1}$ and $\Box^{-1}$, and *backward counting modalities* $\Diamond_i^{-1}$ and $\Box_i^{-1}$ that are defined like the ordinary modalities but with respect to the inverse edge relation E^{-1} in place of E. In the presence of backward modalities, the standard modalities are referred to as *forward modalities*.

3 Monadic Σ_1 on Finite Unary Graphs

In this section, we study the expressive power of monadic Σ_1 on unary graphs. We first review the straightforward relationship between (bisimulation classes of) finite unary graphs and ultimately periodic infinite words. We establish that monadic Σ_1 in the finite is expressive enough to define all ω-regular languages. Then we prove that, on finite unary graphs, the bisimulation (or counting bisimulation) invariant fragment of monadic Σ_1 is the same as the bisimulation invariant fragment of full MSO. These results contrast with the case of arbitrary (finite or infinite) unary graphs where monadic Σ_1 can only express topologically closed regular languages.

A graph $\mathcal{K}$ is a *unary graph* if every vertex in $\mathcal{K}$ has a unique successor under the relation E. Of course, the bisimulation class of a unary graph is completely characterized by the infinite word (in the alphabet $\Sigma = P(\textit{Prop})$) that is described by the path emanating from the root. Thus, we can see any bisimulation-invariant property of unary finite graphs as described by a language of eventually periodic ω-words. So, given such a language $L \subseteq \Sigma^\omega$, and a class of finite unary graphs C, we say that C is equivalent to L in the finite if:

- for any graph $\mathcal{K} \in C$, there is a word $w_\mathcal{K} \in L$ such that $w_\mathcal{K}$ is the Σ-word defined by the unique infinite path starting at the root of $\mathcal{K}$.
- for any ultimately periodic word $w \in L$ there is a graph $\mathcal{K}_w \in C$ such that w is the Σ-word defined by the infinite path starting at the root of $\mathcal{K}$.

By extension, we say that an MSO sentence φ is equivalent to L when the class C_φ of finite unary graphs it defines is equivalent to L. Note that if this is the case then φ is invariant under counting bisimulation. Note further that on the class of finite unary graphs, counting bisimulation coincides with bisimulation.

Theorem 1. *For any regular ω-language $L \subseteq \Sigma^\omega$ there is a (counting bisimulation-invariant) monadic Σ_1 formula φ_L equivalent to L in the finite.*

Proof. Let L be an ω-regular language. First, one can show that that there is a nondeterministic finite Büchi automaton $\mathcal{A}_L = \langle Q, Q_0, \delta, F \rangle$ with set of states Q, set of initial states Q_0, transition function $\delta : Q \times \Sigma \to P(Q)$ and accepting states F, that recognizes L and such that, for any infinite word of L of the form $u.v^\omega$, there is an initial state $q_0 \in Q_0$ and an accepting state $q \in F$ such that, there is a path in $\mathcal{A}_L$ from state q_0 to state q reading u (with $q_0 = q$ when $u = \epsilon$), and a cycle in $\mathcal{A}_L$ from q to q reading v.

The formula φ_L can now be defined as follows: there is a collection of disjoint sets X_q ($q \in Q$), such that: (i) $r \in X_{q_0}$ for some $q_0 \in Q_0$; (ii) for each $q \in Q$ and $x \in X_q$, x has a single successor y and there is a state $q' \in \delta(q, \lambda(x))$ such that $y \in X_{q'}$, where $\lambda(x) = \{p \in \textit{Prop} : p(x) \text{ holds}\}$; and (iii) any element with two predecessors in $\bigcup_{q \in Q} X_q$ (and the root if it has one predecessor in $\bigcup_{q \in Q} X_q$) must belong to some X_q with $q \in F$.

One can check that φ_L defined in such a way (i) is counting bisimulation invariant, (ii) does enforce that there is a unique path from the root and, (iii) the word described by this path is accepted by the automaton $\mathcal{A}_L$.   □

Since only topologically closed regular languages are definable in the level N_1 of the mu-calculus hierarchy, this first theorem already shows that:

Corollary 2. *There is a bisimulation invariant class of unary finite models definable in monadic Σ_1 that is not definable in N_1.*

One might expect a converse to Theorem 1 to hold. Indeed, we even prove a stronger result.

Theorem 3. *For any MSO formula φ, counting-bisimulation invariant on finite graphs and true only on unary graphs, there is a regular language $L_\varphi \subseteq \Sigma^\omega$ equivalent to φ in the finite.*

The remainder of this section is dedicated to the proof of this theorem.

A unary graph $\mathcal{K}$ is called a *lasso* if the root of $\mathcal{K}$ has no predecessor and all other vertices except one (called the *knot*) have exactly one predecessor while the knot has exactly two predecessors.

Any lasso $\mathcal{K}$ is completely characterized by the two non empty finite words u and v (in the alphabet Σ) that are described respectively by the (acyclic) path from the root to the knot of $\mathcal{K}$ (excluding the knot) and the cyclic path from the knot to itself (excluding the second occurrence of the knot). In the sequel, we write $\mathcal{K}_{u,v}$ for such a lasso.

Observe that any finite unary graph is counting bisimilar to a lasso. More precisely, it is counting bisimilar to the subgraph induced by the set of vertices reachable from the root that forms (possibly after duplicating the root so that it is distinct from the knot) a lasso.

We are now ready to start the proof of Theorem 3. Let φ be an MSO formula as in Theorem 3.

Proposition 4. *There is a finite set of pairs of regular languages $(U_i, V_i)_{i \in I}$ such that, for any two words u and $v \in \Sigma^+$, $\mathcal{K}_{u,v} \models \varphi$ if, and only if, there is some $i \in I$ such that $u \in U_i$ and $v \in V_i$.*

Proof. The mapping that maps any pair of non empty finite words $(u, v) \in \Sigma^+ \times \Sigma^+$ to the lasso $\mathcal{K}_{u,v}$ is a FO-definable transduction. It follows, by an extension of Shelah's decomposition theorem [6–Theorem 11] that there is a finite set of pairs of MSO formulas $\{(\varphi_i, \psi_i)\}_{i \in I}$ over finite Σ-words such that for any two words u and $v \in \Sigma^+$, $\mathcal{K}_{u,v} \models \varphi$ if and only if there is some $i \in I$ such that $u \models \varphi_i$ and $v \models \psi_i$. By Büchi's theorem, for all $i \in I$, the MSO-formulas φ_i and ψ_i define the regular languages U_i and V_i we are looking for.   □

Remark. One might think that Proposition 4 concludes the proof of the theorem. Indeed, if $\mathcal{K}_{u,v} \models \varphi$, then $u.v^\omega$ belongs to some $U_i.V_i^\omega$ so one might think that φ

is equivalent to the language $\bigcup_{i \in I} U_i.V_i^\omega$. However, this idea fails since, a priori, nothing ensures that when an ultimately periodic word w belongs to some $U_i.V_i^\omega$ then it is of the form $u.v^\omega$ with $u \in U_i$ and $v \in V_i$ so that $K_{u,v} \models \varphi$.

So far, we have not used the fact that φ is counting bisimulation invariant on finite graphs.

Proposition 5. *For any $i \in I$ and any $(u, v) \in U_i \times V_i$, there is a triple $t = (j, r, s) \in I \times \Sigma^+ \times \Sigma^+$ such that:*

1. *$r.s^\omega = u.v^\omega$ (hence $K_{u,v}$ and $K_{r,s}$ are counting bisimilar),*
2. *for all $n > 0$, $r.s^n \in U_j$ and $s^n \in V_j$.*

Proof. Let i, u and v be as above, so $K_{u,v} \models \varphi$. By invariance of φ, for each $k > 0$, we also have $K_{u.v^k,v^k} \models \varphi$. Hence, by Proposition 4 for each $k > 0$ there is some $i_k \in I$ such that $(u.v^k, v^k) \in U_{i_k} \times V_{i_k}$. Since I is finite, there is some $j \in I$ such that $j = i_k$ for infinitely many k. Now, since both U_j and V_j are regular languages and there are infinitely many k such that $u.v^k \in U_j$ and $v^k \in V_j$ there must be some $p > 0$ such that $u.v^{pn} \in U_j$ and $v^{pn} \in V_j$ for all $n > 0$. Taking $r = u.v^p$ and $s = v^p$ gives us the desired triple t. $\square$

A triple $t = (j, r, s)$ as in Proposition 5 is called *special*. Write $\mathcal{S}$ for the set of all special triples.

To continue the proof of Theorem 3, we need some standard definitions from formal language theory. Recall that the *left congruence class* $[w]_L^l$ and the *right congruence class* $[w]_L^r$ of a finite word $w \in \Sigma^+$ with respect to a language $L \subseteq \Sigma^+$ are defined as the sets of words

$$[w]_L^l = \{w' \in \Sigma^+ : \forall u \in \Sigma^*, u.w \in L \Leftrightarrow u.w' \in L\}$$

and

$$[w]_L^r = \{w' \in \Sigma^+ : \forall v \in \Sigma^*, w.v \in L \Leftrightarrow w'.v \in L\}$$

We know that if L is regular there are only finitely many distinct sets $[w]_L^l$ and $[w]_L^r$ for $w \in \Sigma^*$ and each one is a regular language.

For any special triple $t = (j, r, s)$ we define the languages

$$D_t = [r]_{U_j}^r.([s]_{U_j}^l \cap [s]_{V_j}^r) \quad and \quad E_t = ([s]_{U_j}^l \cap [s]_{V_j}^r)$$

By construction, both languages D_t and E_t are regular. Moreover:

Proposition 6. *For any special triple $t = (j, r, s)$, $D_t \subseteq U_j$, $E_t \subseteq V_j$, $D_t.E_t^+ \subseteq D_t$ and $E_t^+ \subseteq E_t$ and, for any u and $v \in \Sigma^+$, if $u \in D_t$ and $v \in E_t$ then $K_{u,v} \models \varphi$.*

Proof. Immediate consequence of the constructions, Proposition 5 and Proposition 4. $\square$

We now conclude the proof of Theorem 3 by proving the following proposition:

Proposition 7. *The ω-regular language $L = \bigcup_{t \in \mathcal{S}} D_t.(E_t)^\omega$ is equivalent to φ.*

Proof. Assume that $\mathcal{K} \models \varphi$ for some finite model $\mathcal{K}$. By assumption, $\mathcal{K}$ is unary and counting bisimilar to some lasso $\mathcal{K}_{u,v}$. We show that $u.v^\omega$ belongs to L by applying Proposition 5. Indeed, this guarantees that there is a special triple $t = (j, s, r)$ such that $u.v^\omega = r.s^\omega$ and, by construction, $r.s^\omega \in D_t.E_t^\omega$.

For the converse, let w be an ultimately periodic word in L. By definition of L, this means that there is a special triple $t = (j, r, s)$ such that $w \in D_t.(E_t)^\omega$. In other words, $w = u_1.w_1$ with $u_1 \in U_t$ and $w_1 \in V_t^\omega$.

Now, since w is ultimately periodic so is w_1 and thus, because V_t is regular, w_1 is of the form $v_1.v_2 \ldots v_n.(v_{n+1} \ldots v_{n+m})^\omega$ for some $v_1, \ldots, v_{n+m} \in V_t$.

Defining $u = u_1.v_1 \ldots v_n$ and $v = v_{n+1} \ldots v_{n+m}$, we have $w = u.v^\omega$ by construction. Hence $\mathcal{K}_w$ is counting bisimilar to $\mathcal{K}_{u,v}$. We also have $u \in D_t$ and $v \in E_t$ (applying Proposition 6) hence $\mathcal{K}_{u,v} \models \varphi$ and thus $\mathcal{K}_w \models \varphi$.   □

Putting Theorems 1 and 3 together gives the following corollary.

Corollary 8. *Any MSO formula counting bisimulation-invariant on finite unary graphs is equivalent to a monadic Σ_1 formula.*

Moreover, restricted to the class of unary graphs, the (counting or modal) mu-calculus can define exactly the classes corresponding to ω-regular languages. This gives us the following.

Corollary 9. *The counting bisimulation-invariant fragment of monadic Σ_1 on finite unary graphs is equivalent to L_μ.*

4   Monadic Σ_1 on Arbitrary Finite Graphs

In this section, we aim at a characterization of the bisimulation invariant fragment of monadic Σ_1 on finite graphs. We establish two negative results that demonstrate how this case differs from both the more restricted class of finite unary graphs and the wider class of arbitrary (finite or infinite) graphs. Nonetheless, by means of a translation to tiling systems [10], we obtain a partial characterization of this fragment.

Theorem 10. *There is monadic Σ_1 counting bisimulation invariant formula φ that is not equivalent to a formula of the level NC_1 of the counting mu-calculus.*

Proof. The monadic Σ_1 formula φ_L of Theorem 1 is counting bisimulation invariant on *all* finite graphs, not just unary ones. Since any formula of NC_1 defining a regular language must define a topologically closed regular language, it suffices to take for L a language that is not closed, e.g. $L = (a + b)^*.b^\omega$.   □

Theorem 11. *There is a bisimulation invariant MSO formula that is not equivalent (on finite graphs) to a bisimulation invariant monadic Σ_1 formula.*

Proof. We know [1] that directed reachability, though definable in monadic Π_1 in the finite, is not definable in monadic Σ_1. Consider now the μ-calculus formula $p \wedge \mu X.(q \vee \Diamond X)$ that defines the set of vertices satisfying p from which there is a (directed) path to a vertex satisfying q. If there were an equivalent monadic Σ_1 formula we would be able to define in monadic Σ_1 the class of graphs in which a distinguished target t is reachable from a source s. We would get this by replacing p and q by formulas that define s and t respectively.   □

We are now left with a direct attempt to characterize the expressive power of the bisimulation invariant fragment of monadic Σ_1 in the finite.

It is known (see, for instance, [9]) that monadic Σ_1 formulas can only define *local* properties. Indeed, such formulas can be characterised by *tiling systems* [10], which are a generalization of automata operating on graphs rather than strings or trees.

Given a positive integer k, we say an FO-formula φ is *k-local* around a first-order variable x if it is equivalent to the formula obtained from φ by restricting all quantifiers in φ to the k-neighborhood of x, i.e. replacing any subformula of the form $\forall y\psi$ (resp. $\exists y\psi$) in φ by one of the form $\forall y(d(x,y) \leq k) \to \psi$ (resp. $\exists y(d(x,y) \leq k) \wedge \psi$). A *local* formula is one that is k-local for some k.

Note for any modal (or counting modal) formula α of modal depth k, the FO translation $\varphi_\alpha(x)$ is k-local around x. Indeed, it is k-local and *forward-looking*, in that we can restrict the quantifiers to the *directed* k-neighborhood by replacing $\forall y\psi$ by $\forall y(d_d(x,y) \leq k) \to \psi$, etc.

Furthermore, when a sentence is (counting) bisimulation invariant, its truth in a model only depends on the submodels induced by the vertices reachable from the root. The following proposition is a consequence.

Proposition 12. *Any (counting) bisimulation invariant sentence φ of monadic Σ_1 is equivalent, on the class of finite structures, to one of the form*

$$\exists X_1 \ldots \exists X_l \forall x \varphi$$

where φ is local.

Proof. Immediate consequence of Theorem 3.4 in [9].   □

Adapting the terminology of Thomas [10], we call a monadic Σ_1 formula of this form a *tiling system*. The local formula φ in such a tiling system is called a *tiling constraint*. When the tiling constraint is k-local, we say that k is the *radius* of the tiling system. When the tiling constraint is equivalent to a modal formula (with forward and backward modalities), we say that the tiling system is *tree-like*. One can check that when no backward modalities occur in the tiling constraint, a tiling system is just a closed (modal counting) alternating tree automaton (see [4] for a precise definition).

Now, our aim is to push the construction that transforms a (counting) bisimulation invariant tiling system into a tree automaton as far as it can go on finite structures. We show that any such tiling system is equivalent to a tree-like tiling system of radius 1 on a sufficiently rich class of graphs.

We say that a graph is *k-acyclic* when it contains no undirected cycle of length less than $k + 1$. We first show that for any structure $\mathcal{K}$ and positive integer k, we can find a k-acyclic structure that is counting bisimilar to $\mathcal{K}$ but contains no undirected cycles of length smaller than k. The construction is similar to that of acyclic covers in [7].

Definition 13 (Powergraph). *For a finite graph* $\mathcal{K} = \langle V, r, E, \{p^{\mathcal{K}}\}_{p \in Prop} \rangle$ *define its powergraph* $2^{\mathcal{K}}$ *to be the graph* $2^{\mathcal{K}} = \langle V', r', E', \{p^{\mathcal{K}'}\}_{p \in Prop} \rangle$ *defined by* $V' = V \times 2^V$ *(where* 2^V *denotes the set of maps* $V \to \{0, 1\}$*),* $r' = (r, \bar{0})$*, there is an edge* E' *from a vertex* (v, f) *to a vertex* (w, g) *whenever* $(v, w) \in E$ *and* g *equals the function defined from* f *by taking, for each* $u \in V$*,* $g(u) = f(u)$ *when* $u \neq w$ *and* $g(w) = 1 - f(w)$*, and with, for each* $p \in Prop$*,* $p^{\mathcal{K}'} = \{(v, \bar{b}) \in V' : v \in p^{\mathcal{K}'}\}$*.*

Proposition 14. *Graphs* $\mathcal{K}$ *and* $2^{\mathcal{K}}$ *are counting bisimilar and, if* $\mathcal{K}$ *is* k*-acyclic for some* k *then* $2^{\mathcal{K}}$ *is* $2k$*-acyclic.*

Proof. (sketch) The mapping $h : V' \to V$ that maps each vertex (v, f) in $2^{\mathcal{K}}$ to the vertex $h(v, f) = v$ in $\mathcal{K}$ induces a counting bisimulation. Now, consider an undirected cycle in the graph $2^{\mathcal{K}}$. Along any edge from (v, f) to (w, g), f and g must differ in exactly one bit. Thus, for the cycle to return to its starting point, all bits that are changed must flip at least twice. This then maps via h to a cyclic path in $\mathcal{K}$ where all vertices occur at least twice. □

Corollary 15. *For each positive integer* k *and every graph* $\mathcal{K}$*, there is a* k*-acyclic graph* $\mathcal{K}'$ *counting bisimilar to* $\mathcal{K}$*.*

Proof. By iterating the powergraph construction. □

Let φ be a counting bisimulation invariant monadic Σ_1 formula. By applying Proposition 12, we may assume that φ is a tiling system of the form $\varphi \equiv \exists X_1 \ldots \exists X_l \forall x \psi$ with ψ k-local. The following proposition is straightforward from definitions:

Proposition 16. *Let* ψ_a *be the* k*-local FO formula asserting that the* k*-neighbourhood of* x *is acyclic. The formula* φ *is equivalent, over* k*-acyclic graphs, to the formula,* $\varphi' \equiv \exists X_1 \ldots \exists X_l \forall x (\psi \wedge \psi_a)$

Now, we obtain the following

Theorem 17. *Formula* φ *is equivalent on* k*-acyclic graphs to a formula* φ'' *of the form* $\varphi'' \equiv \exists Y_1 \ldots \exists Y_m \forall x \psi'$ *with* ψ' *a* 1*-local tree-like constraint.*

Proof. (Sketch) The proof is based on the observation that the Hintikka type (see [3]) of a tree centered on a node c is completely determined by the atomic propositions that are true at c and the Hintikka types of the subtrees rooted at the neighbours of c. Thus, by introducing a fresh set of second-order quantifiers (logarithmic in the number of Hintikka types), it is not difficult to build the formula φ''. □

As the constraint ψ' is tree-like of radius 1, it can be described by a counting modal formula with forward and backward modalities.

Remark. If this formula were equivalent to one without backward modalities, then one could show that we can obtain a formula θ of NC_1 that is equivalent to φ on k-acyclic graphs. As φ is invariant under counting bisimulation on finite structures by hypothesis and θ by definition and since the class of k-acyclic graphs contains representatives of all bisimulation classes on finite structures, it follows that θ and φ are equivalent on the class of all finite structures. Thus, we would have proved that every formula of monadic Σ_1 invariant under counting bisimulation is equivalent to a formula of NC_1, contradicting Theorem 10.

5 Conclusions

On finite unary graphs, we provide a precise characterization of bisimulation-invariant MSO. In this case, the structure of unary graphs is simple enough so that standard techniques from mathematical logic and language theory apply. Since unary graphs are closed under counting bisimulation, this also allows us to show that on finite graphs in general, monadic Σ_1 can express more counting-bisimulation invariant properties than C_μ with only greatest fixed points.

In the general case the question of whether bisimulation-invariant MSO is equivalent on finite structures to L_μ remains a challenging open problem. By investigating this question at the first level of the monadic hierarchy we have shown that the the problem is radically different to its counterpart on infinite structures, while also being different to the restriction to unary structures.

We provide a translation of bisimulation-invariant monadic Σ_1 formulas to tree-like tiling systems on a sufficiently rich class of structures. However, it seems that the use of backward modalities in such tiling systems cannot be eliminated without passing to infinite structures. The relationship between these tiling systems and the μ-calculus needs to be investigated further out.

References

1. M. Ajtai and R. Fagin. Reachability is harder for directed rather than undirected finite graphs. *Journal of Symbolic Logic*, 55:113–150, 1990.
2. J. Bradfield. The modal mu-calculus alternation hierarchy is strict. *Theoretical Computer Science*, 195:133–153, 1998.
3. H-D. Ebbinghaus and J. Flum. *Finite Model Theory*. Springer, 2 edition, 1999.
4. D. Janin and G. Lenzi. On the logical definability of topologically closed recognizable languages of infinite trees. *Computing and Informatics*, 21:185–203, 2002.
5. D. Janin and I. Walukiewicz. On the expressive completeness of the modal mu-calculus with respect to monadic second order logic. In *Conf. on Concurrency Theory (CONCUR'96)*, pages 263–277. LNCS 1119, 1996.
6. J.A. Makowski and E. Ravve. Incremental model checking for decomposable strutures. In J. Wiedermann and P. Hajek, editors, *Mathematical Foundation of Comp.Sci (MFCS'95)*, LNCS 969, pages 540–551, 1995.
7. M. Otto. Modal and guarded characterisation theorems over finite transition systems. In *Proc. of the 17th IEEE Symp. on Logic in Computer Science (LICS)*, pages 371–380, 2002.

8. E. Rosen. Modal logic over finite structures. *Journal of Logic, Language and Information*, 6:427–439, 1997.

9. T. Schwentick and K. Barthelmann. Local normal forms for first-order logic with applications to games and automata. *Discrete Mathematics and Theoretical Computer Science*, 3:109–124, 1999.

10. W. Thomas. Automata theory on trees and partial orders. In M. Dauchet M. Bidoit, editor, *TAPSOFT'97*, pages 20–38. LNCS 1214, Springer-Verlag, 1997.

11. J. van Benthem. *Modal Logic and Classical Logic*. Bibliopolis, 1983.

12. I. Walukiewicz. Monadic second order logic on tree-like structures. In *Symp. on Theoretical Aspects of Computer Science*, 1996. LNCS 1046. Full version in *Information and Computation* 164 (2001) pp. 234-263,.

On the Complexity of Hilbert's 17th Problem

Nikhil R. Devanur, Richard J. Lipton, and Nisheeth K. Vishnoi

College of Computing, Georgia Institute of Technology,
Atlanta GA 30332

Abstract. Hilbert posed the following problem as the 17th in the list of 23 problems in his famous 1900 lecture:

Given a multivariate polynomial that takes only non-negative values over the reals, can it be represented as a sum of squares of rational functions?

In 1927, E. Artin gave an affirmative answer to this question. His result guaranteed the existence of such a finite representation and raised the following important question:

*What is the **minimum number** of rational functions needed to represent any non-negative n-variate, degree d polynomial?*

In 1967, Pfister proved that any n-variate non-negative polynomial over the reals can be written as sum of squares of at most 2^n rational functions. In spite of a considerable effort by mathematicians for over 75 years, it is *not* known whether $n + 2$ rational functions are sufficient!

In lieu of the lack of progress towards the resolution of this question, we initiate the study of Hilbert's 17th problem from the point of view of Computational Complexity. In this setting, the following question is a natural relaxation:

*What is the **descriptive complexity** of the sum of squares representation (as rational functions) of a non-negative, n-variate, degree d polynomial?*

We consider *arithmetic circuits* as a natural representation of rational functions. We are able to show, assuming a standard conjecture in complexity theory, that it is impossible that every non-negative, n-variate, degree four polynomial can be represented as a sum of squares of a *small* (polynomial in n) number of rational functions, each of which has a *small* size arithmetic circuit (over the rationals) computing it.

1 Introduction

Hilbert proposed 23 problems in 1900, in which he tried *to lift the veil behind which the future lies hidden*[1]. His description of the 17th problem is (see [7]):

---

[1] A quote taken from [29].

K. Lodaya and M. Mahajan (Eds.): FSTTCS 2004, LNCS 3328, pp. 237–249, 2004.

A rational integral function or form in any number of variables with real coefficient such that it becomes negative for no real values of these variables, is said to be definite. The system of all definite forms is invariant with respect to the operations of addition and multiplication, but the quotient of two definite forms in case it should be an integral function of the variables is also a definite form. The square of any form is evidently always a definite form. But since, as I have shown [12], not every definite form can be compounded by addition from squares of forms, the question arises which I have answered affirmatively for ternary forms [13] whether every definite form may not be expressed as a quotient of sums of squares of forms. At the same time it is desirable, for certain questions as to the possibility of certain geometrical constructions, to know whether the coefficients of the forms to be used in the expression may always be taken from the realm of rationality given by the coefficients of the form represented.

An affirmative answer to this problem was given by Emil Artin in 1927 [3]:

> For every non-negative polynomial $f \in \mathbb{R}[x_1, \ldots, x_n]$, there exist rational functions $g_1, \ldots, g_s \in \mathbb{R}(x_1, \ldots, x_n)$, such that $f = g_1^2 + \cdots + g_s^2$.

Motzkin's example (see [26]) of $P(x, y, z) = z^6 + x^4 z^2 + x^2 y^4 - 3x^2 y^2 z^2$ illustrates that the rational functions in Artin's result cannot, in general, be replaced by polynomials. $P(x, y, z)$ is non-negative everywhere over the reals, and yet, cannot be written as sum of squares of polynomials over the reals. Notice that Artin's result shows that every non-negative polynomial can be written as sum of squares of *finitely* many rational functions. This raised the following important question about the *size* of such a representation:

> What is the smallest number (denoted as $\nu(n, d)$), such that every n-variate, degree d, non-negative polynomial can be written as sum of squares of $\nu(n, d)$ rational functions over the reals?

In 1967, Pfister [21] proved that $\nu(n, d) \leq 2^n$. However, this upper bound holds when one is allowed rational functions over a *real closed field* [2]. Remarkably enough, his bound does not depend on the degree of the polynomial. The best lower bound on $\nu(n, 3)$ is $n + 2$. Over 75 years of effort by various mathematicians, these are still the best known bounds in general. We remark that the function $\nu(n, 2)$ is quite well understood from the time of Hilbert (see [12, 14, 15]).

In lieu of the lack of progress towards the determination of $\nu(n, d)$, we initiate the study of Hilbert's 17th problem from the point of view of Computational Complexity. In this setting, the following question is a natural relaxation:

> What is the **descriptive complexity** of the sum of squares representation (as rational functions) of a non-negative, n-variate, degree d polynomial?

---

[2] See [5, 23] for a definition.

We consider *arithmetic circuits* as a natural representation of rational functions. We are able to show, assuming a standard conjecture in complexity theory, that it is impossible that every non-negative, n-variate, degree four polynomial can be represented as a sum of squares of a *small* (polynomial in n) number of rational functions, each of which has a *small* size arithmetic circuit (over the rationals) computing it.

1.1   Related Work

Like all of Hilbert's problems, the 17th has received a lot of attention from the mathematical community and beyond. For an extensive survey of the development and impact of Hilbert's 17th problem on Mathematics, the reader is referred to excellent surveys by [10, 24, 26, 27]. The books [5, 23] also provide good accounts of this and related problems.

Apart from what can be found in the references above, we are aware of some recent work on various quantitative aspects of Hilbert's 17th problem. For instance, in [4], it has been proved that if the degree is fixed and the number of variables are allowed to increase, then there are significantly many more non-negative polynomials than those that can be written as sum of squares of polynomials. Further, in [25], it is shown that in general, one cannot obtain a sum of squares representation in which each rational function has the *same* denominator.

To the best of our knowledge the problem raised by this work, about the representational complexity of non-negative polynomials in the computational setting, is new.

2   Overview of Our Result

Notations. For $k = \mathbb{R}, \mathbb{Q}$ or $\mathbb{Z}$, $k[x_1, \ldots, x_n]$ denotes the ring of polynomials over k and $k(x_1, \ldots, x_n)$ denotes the corresponding field of fractions. The following notation about polynomials is used throughout this paper: A polynomial is written as $f = \sum_\alpha c_\alpha \mathbf{x}^\alpha$. Here $\mathbf{x}^\alpha = x_1^{\alpha_1} \cdots x_n^{\alpha_n}$. $\deg(f)$ denotes the maximum *total degree* of f. $H(f) := \max_\alpha |c_\alpha|$.

Arithmetic Circuits. An *arithmetic circuit* C over k [3] is a directed acyclic graph. Each vertex has in-degree 0 or 2 and is labeled either by addition, multiplication, one of the input variables: $\{x_1, \ldots, x_n\}$, or scalars from k. If the vertex is labeled by a scalar or an input variable, then its in-degree must be 0. If the vertex has in-degree 2, then it must be labeled either by $+$ or by $\times$. There is exactly one vertex with no outgoing edge, which naturally corresponds to the polynomial (over $k[x_1, \ldots, x_n]$) computed by C. The size of C is the number of gates along with description size of all the constants used. As observed, C

---

[3] In general k could be a commutative ring, but here k will be either the fields $\mathbb{R}$ and $\mathbb{Q}$, or the ring of integers $\mathbb{Z}$.

computes a polynomial $f(x_1, \ldots, x_n) \in k[x_1, \ldots, x_n]$. The size of the smallest arithmetic circuit that computes $f \in k[x_1, \ldots, x_n]$ is denoted by $\mathcal{L}_k(f)$. We will drop the subscript wherever k is clear from the context. By allowing divisions as well, the definition of $\mathcal{L}_k(f)$ can be extended to all $f \in k(x_1, \ldots, x_n)$.

2.1   Computational Complexity Preliminaries

The aim of this section is to present the definitions and notions in Computational Complexity Theory. [4] The reader is referred to the book by Papadimitriou [20] for a comprehensive treatment of this subject.

Some Complexity Classes. A *language* is a subset of $\{0,1\}^*$. For a language L, $\bar{L} := \{0,1\}^* \backslash L$. A p-ary *relation* is a language over the following p-ary product: $\{0,1\}^* \times \cdots \times \{0,1\}^*$.[5] The complexity class $\mathsf{DTIME}(f(n))$ is the set of all languages for which membership can be tested in time $f(n)$, by a deterministic Turing machine, in time $f(n)$. $\mathsf{P} := \cup_{t \geq 0} \mathsf{DTIME}(n^t)$. NP is the collection of all languages L, such that there is a 2-ary relation $R_L \in \mathsf{P}$ (called a *polynomially decidable relation*) and a polynomial $p(\cdot)$, such that $x \in L$ if and only if there is a $y \in \{0,1\}^*$, with $|y| = O(p(|x|))$, and $(x,y) \in R_L$. The class $\mathsf{co\text{-}NP}$ is defined as $\cup_{L \in \mathsf{NP}} \bar{L}$. It follows that a language L is in $\mathsf{co\text{-}NP}$ if and only if there is a polynomially decidable 2-ary relation R_L and a polynomial $p(\cdot)$, such that $x \in L$ if and only if and for all $y \in \{0,1\}^*$, with $|y| = O(p(|x|))$, $(x,y) \in R_L$. It is natural to define complexity classes based on compositions of these *existential* and *universal* quantifiers. Starting with $\Sigma_1 = \mathsf{NP}$ and $\Pi_1 = \mathsf{co\text{-}NP}$, one can define Σ_i and Π_i as follows. For $i \geq 2$, Σ_i is the collection of all languages L such that there is a i-ary relation $R_L \in \Pi_{i-1}$, and a polynomial $p(\cdot)$, such that $x \in L$ if and only if there exists a $y \in \{0,1\}^*$, with $|y| = O(p(|x|))$, $(x,y) \in R_L$. Π_i is defined similarly as $\mathsf{co\text{-}}\Sigma_i$. Further, define $\Delta_i := \Sigma_i \cap \Pi_i$. One often thinks of $\Delta_0 = \Sigma_0 = \Pi_0 = \mathsf{P}$ and $\Delta_1 = \mathsf{NP} \cap \mathsf{co\text{-}NP}$. *Polynomial Hierarchy* (PH) is defined to be the collection of classes Δ_i, Σ_i and Π_i, for all $i \geq 0$. It follows from definitions that if $\mathsf{NP} = \mathsf{co\text{-}NP}$ then $\Sigma_i = \Delta_i$ for all $i \geq 1$.

Completeness. A language L is said to be *hard* for a a complexity class $\mathcal{C}$, for all $L' \in \mathcal{C}$, there is a polynomial $p(\cdot)$ and a Turing machine $M_{L,L'} : \{0,1\}^* \to \{0,1\}^*$, such that $x \in L$ if and only if $M_{L,L'}(x) \in L'$. Moreover, for the complexity classes we will be interested in, we assume that $M_{L,L'}$ runs in time $O(p(|x|))$. If $L \in \mathcal{C}$ and L is hard for $\mathcal{C}$, then L is said to be *complete* for $\mathcal{C}$. Complete problems for a complexity class can be thought of as the hardest problems in their class and can be thought of as characterizing the complexity class.

Next we define a problem which is known to be NP-complete. Consider a boolean function $\phi : \{0,1\}^n \mapsto \{0,1\}$ in the conjunctive normal form (3-CNF),

---

[4] The reason we do so is it to broaden the scope of this paper to mathematicians who may not be familiar with these notions, but are interested in understanding our results on Hilbert's 17th problem.

[5] A 1-ary relation is just a language.

that is $\phi(x_1, \ldots, x_n) = \bigwedge_{i=1}^m C_i$, where each C_i is a boolean OR of at most 3 literals from $\{x_1, \overline{x}_1, \ldots, x_n, \overline{x}_n\}$. ϕ is said to be *satisfiable* if there is a *satisfying assignment* $a_1, \ldots, a_n \in \{0,1\}$, such that $\phi(a_1, \ldots, a_n) = 1$. The set of such boolean functions, in 3-CNF form, that have a satisfying assignment is denoted 3SAT. One of the earliest and most important results in complexity Theory (see [9, 18, 19]) was establishing that 3SAT is NP-complete. The corresponding co-NP problem is UN3SAT, i.e. the set of boolean functions in 3-CNF that have no satisfying assignment. It follows that UN3SAT is complete for co-NP. Generalizing these results, it is known that there is a complete problem for Σ_i (and hence for each Π_i), for all $i \geq 1$. This is precisely the reason why it is widely believed that for all $i \geq 1$, $\Sigma_i \neq \Pi_i$. This implies that PH $\neq \Sigma_2$, a conjecture on which our result will be based on.

Probabilistic Complexity Classes. Randomized complexity classes are defined with respect to Turing machines which have access to an additional tape which contains an infinite number of uniform and independent random bits. For this paper, we are just concerned with *probabilistic polynomial time* Turing machines which always halt (independently of the random tape) after a polynomial number of steps (in the length of the input). Naturally, for an input x to such a randomized machine M, one associates probabilities to the computation $M(x)$. The class RP is the class of all languages L, such that there is a probabilistic polynomial time Turing machine M_L, such that for all $x \in L$, $\Pr[M_L(x) \text{ accepts}] = 1$ and for all $x \notin L$, $\Pr[M_L(x) \text{ accepts}] \leq 1/2$. The probabilistic complexity classes important for this paper will be RP and co-RP. Finally, we define the class $\mathsf{NP}^{\mathsf{co-RP}}$ as the collections of languages L, for which there is a probabilistic polynomial time machine M_L, and a polynomial $p(\cdot)$, such that if $x \in L$ there is a $y \in \{0,1\}^*$, with $|y| = O(p(|x|))$, $\Pr[M_L(x,y) \text{ accepts}] \leq 1/2$, and if $x \notin L$, then for all $y \in \{0,1\}^*$, with $|y| = O(p(|x|))$, $\Pr[M_L(x,y) \text{ accepts}] = 1$.

Unsatisfiability. Consider a boolean function $\phi : \{0,1\}^n \mapsto \{0,1\}$ in the conjunctive normal form (3-CNF), that is $\phi(x_1, \ldots, x_n) = \bigwedge_{i=1}^m C_i$, where each C_i is a boolean OR of at most 3 literals from $\{x_1, \overline{x}_1, \ldots, x_n, \overline{x}_n\}$. ϕ is said to be *satisfiable* if there is a *satisfying assignment* $a_1, \ldots, a_n \in \{0,1\}$, such that $\phi(a_1, \ldots, a_n) = 1$. The set of such boolean functions, in 3-CNF form, that have a satisfying assignment is denoted 3SAT. It is well known that 3SAT is NP-complete. The corresponding co-NP problem is UN3SAT, i.e. the set of boolean functions in 3-CNF that have no satisfying assignment. It follows that UN3SAT is complete for co-NP.

Now we give the key definition and the main result of this paper.

Definition 1

$$\mathsf{H}^{\mathbb{Z}}(n, d, h) := \{f \in \mathbb{Z}[x_1, \ldots, x_n] : \deg(f) \leq d, H(f) = O(h),$$
$$\forall (x_1, \ldots, x_n) \in \mathbb{R}^n \; f \geq 0\}.$$

Further, let $\mathsf{H}^{\mathbb{Z}}(d, h) := \cup_{n \geq 0} \mathsf{H}^{\mathbb{Z}}(n, d, h)$.

Remark 1. Note that we are implicitly viewing $H^{\mathbb{Z}}(d, h)$ as a language. Fixing a unique representation of polynomials (say the smallest arithmetic circuit over $\mathbb{Q}$), we can view polynomials in this set as binary strings, thus, justifying our viewpoint. Hence, the length of the input is related to the description of the polynomial and **not** n. But we concern ourselves only with the case when the smallest arithmetic circuit computing an n-variate polynomial f is of size at most a fixed polynomial in n, say n^6. [6]

2.2 Main Theorems

Theorem 1. *Assuming* $\mathsf{PH} \neq \Sigma_2$, *for all* $n \geq 1$, *there exists a polynomial* $f \in H^{\mathbb{Z}}(n, 6, 1)$ *such that no representation of* f *as sum of squares of rational functions over* $\mathbb{Q}$, $f = \sum_{i=1}^{s} g_i^2$, $g_i \in \mathbb{Q}(x_1, \ldots, x_n)$, *satisfies both of the following:*

1. $s = \mathrm{poly}\,(\mathcal{L}(f))$.
2. *For all* $i = 1, 2, \ldots, s$, $\mathcal{L}(g_i) = \mathrm{poly}\,(\mathcal{L}(f))$.

Thus, unless the polynomial hierarchy collapses to the second level, not every non-negative polynomial has a *succinct* sum of squares representation. It is a standard hypothesis in complexity theory that $\mathsf{PH} \neq \Sigma_2$. In fact this theorem says that even if the polynomial has degree 6 and all coefficients are integers and bounded by a constant, there is no such representation. As remarked earlier, the degree 2 case is well understood. We strengthen the previous result by bringing the degree down to 4, at the cost of blowing up the size of the coefficients. It is an interesting open problem if such a statement can be obtained for degree 3.

Theorem 2. *Assuming* $\mathsf{PH} \neq \Sigma_2$, *for all* $n \geq 1$, *there exists a polynomial* $f \in H^{\mathbb{Z}}(n, 4, \mathrm{poly}(n))$ *such that no representation of* f *as sum of squares of rational functions over the rationals,* $f = \sum_{i=1}^{s} g_i^2$, $g_i \in \mathbb{Q}(x_1, \ldots, x_n)$, *satisfies both of the following:*

1. $s = \mathrm{poly}\,(\mathcal{L}(f))$.
2. *For all* $i = 1, 2, \ldots, s$, $\mathcal{L}(g_i) = \mathrm{poly}\,(\mathcal{L}(f))$.

A Remark About the Representation Field. Although we state our theorems for $\mathbb{Q}$, one can replace it by a finite real algebraic extension of $\mathbb{Q}$. The details are easy and we omit the details for the ease of presentation. It is important to note though, that Artin's result does not, in general, imply existence of a sum of squares representation, where each rational function is over $\mathbb{Q}$. The *hard to represent* polynomials guaranteed by our results have a further property that these have small arithmetic circuits over the integers. It is conceivable that for such polynomials, a succinct representation (in our sense) exists if and only if a succinct representation exists over the reals. This is an interesting question for which we do not know an answer.

---

[6] For a non-negative, n-variate polynomial with arithmetic circuit complexity not bounded by any polynomial in n, one cannot hope to write an efficient (polynomial in n) sum of square representation by rational functions. Hence it makes sense only to consider polynomials which are efficiently computable by small circuits.

Outline of the Proofs. As the first step in the proof of Theorems 1 and 2, we reduce an instance ϕ of UN3SAT to a polynomial F_ϕ which is non-negative if and only if ϕ is unsatisfiable. This is a variant of an often used trick, which allows one to use algebraic considerations to study a boolean formula. We give two such reductions, corresponding to the two theorems: for Theorem 1 we give a reduction such that F_ϕ is an instance of $\mathsf{H}^\mathbb{Z}(6,1)$ and for Theorem 2, F_ϕ is an instance of $\mathsf{H}^\mathbb{Z}(4,\mathrm{poly}(\cdot))$. These results establish the co-NP hardness of the languages $\mathsf{H}^\mathbb{Z}(6,1)$ and $\mathsf{H}^\mathbb{Z}(4,\mathrm{poly}(\cdot))$. Artin's Theorem guarantees a sum of squares representation of F_ϕ over the reals. If there is some such representation which is *succinct* (describable by a polynomial number of polynomial size arithmetic circuits), in NP we can guess it and in co-RP, check if the guessed representation is the same as F_ϕ. (This last step is done by invoking polynomial identity testing.) Formally we prove the following theorem:

Theorem 3. *For all $n, d, h \geq 1$, if for all $f \in \mathsf{H}^\mathbb{Z}(n,d,h)$, there exist $g_1, g_2, \ldots, g_s \in \mathbb{Q}(x_1, \ldots, x_n)$, such that $f = \sum_{i=1}^s g_i^2$, $s = \mathrm{poly}\,(\mathcal{L}(f))$, and for all $i = 1, 2, \ldots, s$, $\mathcal{L}(g_i) = \mathrm{poly}\,(\mathcal{L}(f))$, then $\mathsf{H}^\mathbb{Z}(d,h) \in \mathsf{NP}^{\mathsf{co-RP}}$.*

To derive the desired contradiction, in the end we invoke a result of Boppana, Hastad and Zachos [6], which states that co-NP$\not\subseteq$ NP$^{\mathsf{co-RP}}$, unless PH=Σ_2.

Organization. Section 3 contains the arithmetizations of SAT needed to prove Theorems 1 and 2. The main results, viz proofs of Theorems 1, 2, 3, are proved in Section 4.

3   Arithmetization of SAT

In this section we give two different arithmetizations of instances of UN3SAT, each of which will be used in proving one of Theorems 1, 2.

Given an instance $\phi = \wedge_{i=1}^m C_i$ of a UN3SAT problem: Call a literal $z \in \{z_1, \bar{z}_1, \ldots, z_n, \bar{z}_n\}$ *positive*, if $z \in \{z_1, \ldots, z_n\}$. Else, call it *negative*. For a clause $C = C_+ \vee C_-$ (C_+ consists of positive literals while C_- consists of negative literals), define

$$\mathcal{A}(C) := \left(\prod_{z \in C_+} (1 - z) \right) \cdot \left(\prod_{z \in C_-} z \right).$$

For instance, if $C = x_1 \vee \bar{x}_2 \vee x_3$, then $\mathcal{A}(C) = (1 - x_1)x_2(1 - x_3)$. Further for $a_1, a_2, a_3 \in \{0,1\}$, $\mathcal{A}(C)(a_1, a_2, a_3) = 0$ if and only if $C(a_1, a_2, a_3) = 1$, (or C is satisfiable). Now define

$$F_\phi(z_1, \ldots, z_n) := 300 \left(\sum_{i=1}^n z_i^2(1 - z_i)^2 + \sum_{j=1}^m (\mathcal{A}(C_j))^2 \right) - 1. \qquad (1)$$

Thus for all ϕ, $F_\phi \in \mathbb{Z}[z_1, \ldots, z_n]$. It is convenient to let $f_\phi := F_\phi/300$. The problem remains the same though, as the sign of f_ϕ is the same as that of F_ϕ. Let $\epsilon = \frac{1}{300}$.

Lemma 1. ϕ *is not satisfiable if and only if $f_\phi \geq 0$ over the reals.*

Proof. If ϕ is satisfiable, let $a = (a_1, \ldots, a_n) \in \{0,1\}^n \subset \mathbb{R}^n$ be a satisfying assignment. Then by definition $f_\phi(a) = -\epsilon < 0$. To prove the converse, consider the case when ϕ is unsatisfiable. We need to show that $f_\phi \geq 0$ over the reals. Let $\delta = 1/4$. We consider two cases:

1. Case 1: Let $(s_1, \ldots, s_n) \in \mathbb{R}^n$ be a point such that there is an $1 \leq i \leq n$ such that s_i does not lie in either of the two intervals: $[-\delta, \delta], [1 - \delta, 1 + \delta]$. In this case $s_i^2(1 - s_i)^2 > \delta^4$. Since $\epsilon \leq \delta^4$, $f_\phi(s_1, \ldots, s_n) > 0$.
2. Case 2: Hence, we may assume that for a point $(s_1, \ldots, s_n)$, all s_i are in one of the intervals: $[-\delta, \delta], [1 - \delta, 1 + \delta]$. From this we construct a point $a = (a_1, \ldots, a_n) \in \{0,1\}^n$ as follows:
   - If $s_i \in [-\delta, \delta]$ then let $a_i = 0$.
   - If $s_i \in [1 - \delta, 1 + \delta]$ then let $a_i = 1$.

   Since ϕ is unsatisfiable, there is a clause, say C, which is not satisfied by a. Let $\mathcal{A}(C) = \left(\prod_{z \in C_+}(1 - z)\right) \cdot \left(\prod_{z \in C_-} z\right)$. If $z_i \in C_+$, since C is not satisfied by a, it must be that $a_i = 0$, and hence $s_i \in [-\delta, \delta]$, or equivalently $(1 - s_i) \in [1 - \delta, 1 + \delta]$. Similarly, if $\bar{z}_i \in C_-$, $a_i = 1$, and hence $s_i \in [1 - \delta, 1 + \delta]$. This implies that at the point $(s_1, \ldots, s_n)$, $f_\phi \geq \mathcal{A}^2(C) \geq (1 - \delta)^6 > \epsilon$.

Thus, if ϕ is unsatisfiable, $f_\phi > 0$ over the reals. This completes the proof.

The above arithmetization reduces UN3SAT to $\mathsf{H}^{\mathbb{Z}}(6,1)$. Thus, the following proposition follows from Lemma 1 and co-NP hardness of UN3SAT.

Proposition 1. $\mathsf{H}^{\mathbb{Z}}(6,1)$ *is* co-NP *hard.*

Next we show how to obtain a quantitatively better result, if we allow the coefficients to grow with the input size. First, we need a new reduction. As before, let ϕ be a boolean function given in 3-CNF form on n variables and m clauses.

$$f'_\phi(z_1, \ldots, z_n) := \sum_{i=1}^{n} \frac{(3^3 + 1)m}{\delta(m)^4} z_i^2(1 - z_i)^2 + \sum_{j=1}^{m}(\mathcal{A}(C_j)) - \epsilon(m). \qquad (2)$$

Here δ and ϵ are positive functions (but less than 1) of m such that $\epsilon < (1-\delta)^3 - m\delta(1+\delta)^2$. Note that one can choose such a δ and an ϵ since $(1-\delta)^3 \to 1$ and $m\delta(1 + \delta)^2 \to 0$ as $\delta \to 0$. As in the previous case, we can always multiply f'_ϕ suitably to obtain a polynomial F'_ϕ over the integers.

Lemma 2. ϕ *is not satisfiable if and only if $f'_\phi \geq 0$ over the reals.*

Proof. If ϕ is satisfiable, let $a = (a_1, \ldots, a_n) \in \{0,1\}^n \subset \mathbb{R}^n$ be a satisfying assignment. Then by definition $f'_\phi(a) = -\epsilon < 0$. To prove the converse, consider the case when ϕ is unsatisfiable. We need to show that $f'_\phi \geq 0$ over the reals. We consider two cases:

Case 1: Suppose that for a point $s := (s_1, \ldots, s_n)$, all s_i are in one of the intervals: $[-\delta, \delta], [1 - \delta, 1 + \delta]$. From this we construct a point $a = (a_1, \ldots, a_n) \in \{0, 1\}^n$ as follows:

- If $s_i \in [-\delta, \delta]$ then let $a_i = 0$.
- If $s_i \in [1 - \delta, 1 + \delta]$ then let $a_i = 1$.

Since ϕ is unsatisfiable, there is a clause, say C, which is not satisfied by a. Let $\mathcal{A}(C) = \left(\prod_{z \in C_+} (1 - z) \right) \cdot \left(\prod_{z \in C_-} z \right)$. If $z_i \in C_+$, since C is not satisfied by a, $s_i \in [-\delta, \delta]$, or equivalently $(1 - s_i) \in [1 - \delta, 1 + \delta]$. Similarly, if $\overline{z}_i \in C_-$, $a_i = 1$ and hence $s_i \in [1 - \delta, 1 + \delta]$. This means that at the point s, $\mathcal{A}(C) \geq (1 - \delta)^3$.

Now consider a clause C' satisfied by a. Writing $C' = C'_+ \vee C'_-$, we see that either some variable in C'_+ is set to 1, or some variable in C'_- is set to 0 in the assignment a. Without loss of generality, assume that $z_i \in C'_+$ is set to 1 ($a_i = 1$). Thus, $s_i \in [1 - \delta, 1 + \delta]$, or $(1 - s_i) \in [-\delta, \delta]$. Thus

$$\mathcal{A}(C') = \left(\prod_{z \in C'_+} (1 - z) \right) \cdot \left(\prod_{z \in C'_-} z \right) \geq -\delta(1 + \delta)^2.$$

Adding the inequalities for unsatisfied and satisfied clauses, one gets that

$$\sum_{j=1}^{m} \mathcal{A}(C_j) \geq (1 - \delta)^3 - m\delta(1 + \delta)^2.$$

By the choice of ϵ and δ, we have $\epsilon < (1 - \delta)^3 - m\delta(1 + \delta)^2$, and therefore $f'_\phi(s) > 0$.

Case 2: Now consider a point $s = (s_1, \ldots, s_n)$ such that, there is an $1 \leq i \leq n$, such that s_i does not lie in either of the two intervals: $[-\delta, \delta], [1 - \delta, 1 + \delta]$. For a clause C, define

$$\Delta_C := \max \{\{|1 - s_i| : z_i \in C_+\} \cup \{|s_j| : \overline{z}_j \in C_-\}\}.$$

It follows that $\mathcal{A}(C)(s) \geq -\Delta_C^3$. Now consider the following 2 cases:

Case 2a. $\Delta_C > 3$

Let s_{j*} be such that either $|s_{j*}|$ or $|1 - s_{j*}|$ is equal to Δ_C. Then $(s_{j*})^2 (1 - s_{j*})^2 \geq \Delta_C^2 (\Delta_C - 1)^2 > \Delta_C^3 + 1$. This implies that $\mathcal{A}(C)(s) + \frac{3^3 + 1}{\delta^4} (s_{j*})^2 (1 - s_{j*})^2 > -\Delta_C^3 + \frac{3^3 + 1}{\delta^4} (\Delta_C^3 + 1) > 1$. The last inequality follows by noticing that $\delta < 1$.

Case 2b. $\Delta_C \leq 3$

From the definition of case 2, $\exists s_{j*}$ such that $(s_{j*})^2 (1 - s_{j*})^2 \geq \delta^4$. Hence, $\frac{3^3 + 1}{\delta^4} (s_{j*})^2 (1 - s_{j*})^2 > 3^3 + 1$. By definition of Δ_C, $\mathcal{A}(C)(s) \geq -3^3$. Combining these inequalities, we get $\mathcal{A}(C)(s) + \frac{3^3 + 1}{\delta^4} (s_{j*})^2 (1 - s_{j*})^2 > 1$.

Now summing over all clauses, we get, $\sum_{j=1}^{m} \mathcal{A}(C_j)(s) + \sum_{i=1}^{n} \frac{(3^3 + 1)m}{\delta^4} s_i^2 (1 - s_i)^2 > m$. This is exactly what we set out to prove: $f_\phi(s) > 0$.

Thus, if ϕ is unsatisfiable, $f'_\phi > 0$ over the reals. This completes the proof.

This leads to the following:

Proposition 2. $H^{\mathbb{Z}}(4, \text{poly}(\cdot))$ *is* co-NP *hard.*

Amplifying Positivity. Using the PCP Theorem of [1,2], one can transform the given formula so that, if it is unsatisfiable, then a large fraction (say $c, 0 < c < 1$) of clauses are unsatisfiable. This gives rise to an arithmetization such that $f_\phi > cm - 1$ if and only if ϕ is unsatisfiable. This shows that even if one is given that whenever $f > 0$, $f > cm - 1$, it is still co-NP hard to decide the positivity of f.

Circuit Complexity of the Arithmetized Polynomials. It is important to note that for any 3CNF formula ϕ, there is an arithmetic circuit over $\mathbb{Z}$ which computes F_ϕ and F'_ϕ, whose sizes are at most n^6. [7] In fact, the explicit arithmetizations written down earlier can be converted into such circuits.

4   Main Results

Testing Identities. The *Identity Testing* problem for arithmetic circuits is to decide if two given arithmetic circuits evaluate the same polynomial. More formally, given two arithmetic circuits C_1, C_2 over $\mathbb{Z}$, let $f, g \in \mathbb{Z}[x_1, \ldots, x_n]$ be the polynomials computed by them respectively. The problem is to decide efficiently if $f - g$ is identically zero over the integers. Here, efficiency is measured in terms of the input size, which in this case, is the sum of the sizes of C_1 and C_2. The following result by Ibarra and Moran [16] establishes that, in the presence of randomness, there is an efficient solution to this problem. Formally, there is an efficient randomized algorithm which takes as input two circuits and decides if they compute the same polynomial. The algorithm is always correct when it says NO, but there is a small chance that is is wrong when it says YES. This simple but important result will play a crucial role in the proof of the main results which we describe next.

Lemma 3. *([16]) The Identity Testing problem for arithmetic circuits over $\mathbb{Z}$ is in* co-RP.

The fact that non-negative polynomials can be represented as sum of squares suggests the following algorithm for checking if $f \in H^{\mathbb{Z}}(n, d, \cdot)$. Suppose it is true that $f = g_1^2 + \cdots + g_s^2$, and that this representation is *succinct*, that is $s = \text{poly}(n)$ and for all $1 \leq i \leq s$, $\mathcal{L}(g_i) \leq \text{poly}(n)$. But we know [28,17] that $\mathcal{L}(p), \mathcal{L}(q) = O\left(d^2 \mathcal{L}(p/q)\right)$, for any integer polynomials p and q, where d is the degree of pq. If d is a constant, then up to a constant factor, the most efficient way to represent a rational polynomial is to represent the numerator and the denominator separately. Hence we may assume that each $g_i = \frac{\alpha_i}{\beta_i}$, α_i and β_i are polynomials over the integers, and $\beta_i \neq 0$, and for all $1 \leq i \leq s$,

---

[7] Since ϕ is in 3CNF, $m \leq (2n)^3$.

$\mathcal{L}(\alpha_i), \mathcal{L}(\beta_i) \leq \text{poly}(n)$. Then in NP, we can *guess* these polynomials α_i, β_i, as the total bits one has to guess is a polynomial in n. Once we have guessed the representation, one checks the following identity:

$$f \prod_{j=1}^{s} \beta_j^2 - \sum_{i=1}^{s} \left(\alpha_i \prod_{j \neq i} \beta_j \right)^2 \equiv 0 \tag{3}$$

Since f itself has an arithmetic circuit over the integers of size at most n^6, the polynomial on the LHS of the above identity has a polynomial size circuit. Hence using the identity testing algorithm for arithmetic circuits over the integers, one can verify the above identity in co-RP. Thus checking the validity of the guessed representation.

This is formalized in the following proof:

Proof (of Theorem 3). Using NP, guess each $g_i = \frac{\alpha_i}{\beta_i}$ where α_i and β_i are polynomials over $\mathbb{Q}$. By hypothesis, we know that $f \prod_{j=1}^{s} \beta_j^2$ and $\sum_{i=1}^{s} \left(\alpha_i \prod_{j \neq i} \beta_j \right)^2$ are arithmetic circuits with length a polynomial in n. Hence by Lemma 3, checking whether they are equal is in co-RP. The time required to evaluate the g_i's is also a polynomial in n. Hence we get $\mathsf{H}^{\mathbb{Z}}(d, h) \in \mathsf{NP}^{\text{co-RP}}$, for any constant d.[8]

Finally, we need the following result of Bopanna, *et al* [6].

Theorem 4. *[6]* co-NP $\subseteq \mathsf{NP}^{\text{co-RP}} \Rightarrow \mathsf{PH} = \Sigma_2$.

Now we are ready to prove Theorem 1.

Proof (of Theorem 1). Assume on the contrary. From Theorem 3, $\mathsf{H}^{\mathbb{Z}}(6, 1) \in \mathsf{NP}^{\text{co-RP}}$. But $\mathsf{H}^{\mathbb{Z}}(6, 1)$ is co-NP-Hard by Proposition 1. Now by Theorem 4, $\mathsf{PH} = \Sigma_2$, a contradiction is achieved.

Using Proposition 2 instead of Proposition 1 in the above proof, one obtains a proof of Theorem 2.

Acknowledgments

We are grateful to Marie-Françoise Roy for valuable comments on an earlier draft of this paper. We also thank Bruce Reznick for pointing us to references [4, 8]. We would also like to thank Peter Bürgisser for his encouragement.

---

[8] In fact, if polynomial identity testing could be done deterministically, then we obtain the stronger result that $\mathsf{H}^{\mathbb{Z}}(d, h) \in \mathsf{NP}$, implying co-NP $\subseteq \mathsf{NP}$.

References

1. S. Arora, C. Lund, R. Motwani, M. Sudan, M. Szegedy. Probabilistic checking of proofs: a new characterization of NP. *Journal of the ACM*, 45(1) (1998), 70–122.
2. S. Arora, S. Safra. Probabilistic Checking of Proofs. *Proceedings of the 33rd Annual Symposium on Foundations of Computer Science*, 2–13, 1992.
3. E. Artin. Über die Zerlegung definiter Funktionen in Quadrate. *Abh. Math. Sem. Univ. Hamburg*, 5 (1927), 100–115.
4. G. Blekherman. There are significantly more non-negative polynomials than sums of squares. *Preprint*.
5. H. Bochnak, M. Coste, M.-F. Roy. **Real algebraic geometry**. Springer, 1998.
6. R. Boppana, J. Hastad, and S. Zachos. Does Co-NP Have Short Interactive Proofs? *Information Processing Letters*, 25 (1987), 127–132.
7. Felix Browder (ed.) Mathematical developments arising from Hilbert's Problems. *Proc. Symp. Pure Math.*, 28 (1976), Amer. Math. Soc.
8. M. D. Choi, Z. D. Dai, T. Y. Lam, B. Reznick: The pythagoras number of some affine algebras and local algebras, *J. Reine Angew. Math.*, 336 (1982), 45-82.
9. S.A. Cook. The complexity of theorem-proving procedures. *Proceedings of the Third ACM Symposium on the Theory of Computing*, 151–158, 1971.
10. D. W. Dubois. Note on of Hilbert's 17th problem. *Bull. Amer. Math. Soc.*, 73 (1967), 540–541.
11. M. R. Garey, D. S. Johnson. **Computers and Intractability: A Guide to the Theory of NP-Completeness**. Freeman, 1979.
12. D. Hilbert. Über die Darstellung definiter Formen als Summen von Formenquadraten. *Math. Ann.*, 32 (1888), 342–350.
13. D. Hilbert. Über ternäre definite Formen. *Acta Math.*, 17 (1893), 169–198.
14. D. Hilbert. **Grundlagen der Geometrie**. Leipzig, Chap. 7, 1899.
15. D. Hilbert. Darstellung definiter Formen durch Quadrate. *Akad. Wiss. Göttingen* (1900), 284–285.
16. Oscar H. Ibarra, Shlomo Moran. Probabilistic Algorithms for Deciding Equivalence of Straight-Line Programs. *JACM* , 30(1) (1983), 217–228.
17. E. Kaltofen. Greatest common divisors of polynomials given by straight-line programs. *JACM*, 35(1) (1988), 231–264.
18. R.M. Karp. Reducibility among combinatorial problems. *Complexity of Computer Computations*, (R.E. Miller and J.M. Thatcher, eds.), 85–103, Plenum Press 1972.
19. Leonid A. Levin. Universal'nye perebornye zadachi (Universal search problems : in Russian). *Problemy Peredachi Informatsii*, 9(3) (1973), 265–266.
20. C. Papadimitriou. **Computational Complexity**. Addison-Wesley, 1994.
21. A. Pfister. Zur Darstellung definiter Funktionen als Summe von Quadraten. *Invent. Math.* 4 (1967), 229–237.
22. V. Powers, B. Reznick. A new bound for Po'lya's Theorem with applications to polynomials positive on polyhedra, J. Pure Appl. Alg. 164 (2001) 221–229.
23. A. Prestel, C.N. Delzell. **Positive Polynomials: From Hilbert's 17th Problem to Real Algebra**. Springer Monographs in Mathematics, 2001.
24. B. Reznick. Some concrete aspects of Hilbert's 17th Problem. *Publ. Math. Univ. Paris VII*, No. 56, Jan. 1996.
25. B. Reznick. On the absence of uniform denominators in Hilbert's Seventeenth Problem. *Preprint*.

26. Marie-Francoise Roy. The role of Hilbert's problems in real algebraic geometry. *Proceedings of the ninth EWM Meeting*, Loccum, Germany 1999.
27. G. Stengle. A Nullstellensatz and a Positivstellensatz in semialgebraic geometry. *Math. Ann.*, 207 (1974), 87–97.
28. V. Strassen. Vermiedung von Divisionen. *J. Reine Angew. Math*, 264 (1973), 184–202.
29. R. Thiele. Hilbert's Twenty-Fourth Problem. *American Math. Monthly*, 110(1) (2003), 1–23.

Who is Pointing When to Whom?

On the Automated Verification of Linked List Structures

Dino Distefano*, Joost-Pieter Katoen, and Arend Rensink

Department of Computer Science, University of Twente,
P.O. Box 217, 7500 AE Enschede, The Netherlands

Abstract. This paper introduces an extension of linear temporal logic
that allows to express properties about systems that are composed of
entities (like objects) that can refer to each other via pointers. Our logic
is focused on specifying properties about the dynamic evolution (such
as creation, adaptation, and removal) of such pointer structures. The
semantics is based on automata on infinite words, extended with appropriate means to model evolving pointer structures in an abstract manner.
A tableau-based model-checking algorithm is proposed to automatically
verify these automata against formulae in our logic.

1 Introduction

Pointers are references to memory cells. Programming with pointers is an error-
prone activity with potential pitfalls such as dereferencing null pointers and the
creation of memory leaks. Unwanted side-effects may occur due to aliasing where
apparently unaffected variables are modified by changing a shared memory cell –
the so-called "complexity of pointer swing". The analysis of pointer programs has
been a topic of continuous research interest since the early seventies [3, 7]. The
purpose of this research is twofold: to assess the correctness of pointer programs,
and to identify the potential values of pointers at compile time to allow more
efficient memory management strategies and code optimization.

Properties of Pointer Programs. Alias analysis, i.e., checking whether pairs of
pointers can be aliases, has received much attention initially (see, e.g., [6, 14]).
[8] introduced and provided algorithms to check the class of so-called position-
dependent alias properties, such as "the n-th cell of v's list is aliased to the m-th
cell of list w". Recently, extensions of predicate calculus to reason about pointer
programs have become *en vogue*: e.g., BI [12], separation logic [20], pointer assertion logic (PAL) [13], alias logic [2], local shape logic [19] and extensions of
spatial logic [4]. These approaches are almost all focused on verifying pre- and
postconditions in a Hoare-style manner.

Since our interest is in concurrent (object-oriented) programs and in expressing properties over dynamically evolving pointer structures, we use first-order

---

* Currently at Dept. of Computer Science, Queen Mary, University of London, UK.

K. Lodaya and M. Mahajan (Eds.): FSTTCS 2004, LNCS 3328, pp. 250–262, 2004.
© Springer-Verlag Berlin Heidelberg 2004

linear-time *temporal logic* (LTL) as a basis and extend it with *pointer assertions* on single-reference structures, such as aliasing, as well as predicates to reason about the *birth* and *death* of cells (which provide a model for object references). The expressiveness of the resulting logic, called NTL (Navigation Temporal Logic), is similar to that of the recent Evolution Temporal Logic (ETL) [23]. Whereas ETL uses 3-valued logical structures as semantic models, we follow an automata-based approach: models of NTL are infinite runs that are accepted by Büchi automata where states are equipped with a representation of the heap. PAL contains similar pointer assertions as NTL (and goes beyond lists), but has neither primitives for the birth and death of entities nor temporal operators. Evolving heaps have been lately used to model mobile computations. In that view NTL combines both spatial and temporal features similar to the ambient logic introduced in [5].

Heap Abstraction. A major issue in analyzing pointer programs is the choice of an appropriate representation of the heap. As the number of memory cells for a program is not known a priori and in general is unpredictable, a concrete representation is inadequate. Analysis techniques for pointer programs therefore typically use abstract representations of heaps such as, e.g., location sets [22] (that only distinguish between single and multiple cells), k-limiting paths [14] (allowing up to k distinct cells for some fixed k), or summary nodes [21] in shape graphs. This paper uses an abstract representation of heaps that is tailored to *unbounded* linked list structures. The novelty of our abstraction is its *parameterization* in the pointer program as well as in the formula. Cells that represent up to M elements, where M is a formula-dependent constant, are exact whereas unbounded cells (akin to summary nodes) represent longer lists. The crux of our abstraction is that it guarantees each unbounded cell to be preceded by a chain of at least L exact cells, where L is a program-dependent constant. Parameters L and M depend on the longest pointer dereferencing in the program and formula, respectively. In contrast with the k-limiting approach, where an adequate general recipe to determine k is lacking, (minimal bounds on) the parameters L and M can be easily determined by a static analysis.

Pointer Program Analysis. Standard type-checking systems are not expressive enough to establish properties of pointers such as memory leaks and dereferencing null pointers. Instead, techniques for analyzing pointer programs are more powerful and include abstract interpretation [8], deduction techniques [2,12,13,20], design by derivation à la Dijkstra [16], and shape analysis [21], or combinations of these techniques.

As our aim is to obtain a fully automated verification technique the approach in this paper is based on *model checking*. Our model-checking algorithm is a nontrivial extension of the tableau-based algorithm for LTL [15]. For given NTL-formula Φ, this algorithm is able to check whether the automaton-model of the concurrent pointer program at hand satisfies Φ. The algorithm, like the ETL approach [23], suffers from false negatives, i.e., a verification may wrongly conclude that the program refutes a formula. In such case, however, diagnostic information can be provided (unlike ETL, and as for PAL [13]) that may be used for further analysis. Besides, by incrementing the parameters M and L, a more concrete model is obtained that is *guaranteed* to be a correct refinement of the (too coarse) abstract representation. This contrasts with the ETL approach where manually-provided instrumentation predicates are needed. Compared to the PAL approach which is fully automated for loop-free (sequential) programs, our technique is fully automated for concurrent pointer programs that may include loops.

Main Contributions. Summarizing, the main contributions of this paper are: *(i)* A first-order temporal logic that both contains pointer assertions as well as predicates referring to the birth or death of memory cells; *(ii)* An automaton-based model for pointer programs where states are abstract heap structures and transitions represent the dynamic evolvement of these heaps; the model deals finitely with unbounded allocations. *(iii)* A way of parameterizing the degree of "correctness" of abstract heap structures, on the basis of a straightforward static analysis of the program and formula at hand. On incrementing these parameters, refined heap structures are automatically obtained. *(iv)* A model-checking algorithm to check abstract representations of pointer programs against formulae in our logic.

The main advantage of our approach is that it is completely automated: given a program and a temporal logic property, the abstract automaton as well as the verification result for the property are determined completely algorithmically. Moreover, to our knowledge, this paper is the first to develop model-checking techniques for (possibly) unbounded evolving heaps of the kind described above[1].

Our current approach restricts to single outgoing pointers. This still allows us to consider many interesting structures such as acyclic, cyclic and unbounded lists (as in [16] and [8]), as well as hierarchies (by backpointers). Besides, several "resource managers" such as memory managers only work with lists [18]. Our abstract heap structures can also model mobile ambients (see [9]).

Details of the model checking algorithm and all proofs can be found in [10].

2   A Logic for Dynamic References

Syntax. Let LV be a countable set of logical variables ranged over by x, y, z, and Ent be a countable set of entities ranged over by e, e', e_1 etc. $\perp \notin Ent$ is used to represent "undefined"; we denote $E^{\perp} = E \cup \{\perp\}$ for arbitrary $E \subseteq Ent$. Navigation Temporal Logic (*NTL*) is a linear temporal logic with quantification of logical variables that range over entities, or may be undefined. The syntax of navigation expressions is defined by the grammar:

$$\alpha ::= nil \mid x \mid \alpha\!\uparrow$$

---

[1] In this respect, the recent paper [1] only introduces a symbolic representation for heaps intended for checking safety properties (but not liveness), and does not consider model checking algorithms.

where *nil* denotes the null reference, x denotes the entity (or nil) that is the value of x, and $\alpha\uparrow$ denotes the entity referred to by (the entity denoted by) α (if any). Let $x\uparrow^0 = x$ and $x\uparrow^{n+1} = (x\uparrow^n)\uparrow$ for natural n. The syntax of *NTL* is:

$$\varPhi ::= \alpha = \alpha \mid \alpha\ \text{new} \mid \alpha \rightsquigarrow \alpha \mid \varPhi \wedge \varPhi \mid \neg \varPhi \mid \exists x.\varPhi \mid \mathsf{X}\varPhi \mid \varPhi\,\mathsf{U}\,\varPhi\ .$$

The basic proposition α new states that the entity (referred to by) α is fresh, $\alpha = \beta$ states that α and β are aliases, and $\alpha \rightsquigarrow \beta$ expresses that (the entity denoted by) β is reachable from (the entity denoted by) α. The boolean connectives, quantification, and the linear temporal connectives X (next) and U (until) have the usual interpretation. We denote $\alpha \neq \beta$ for $\neg(\alpha = \beta)$, α dead for $\alpha = nil$, α alive for $\neg(\alpha\ \text{dead})$, $\alpha \not\rightsquigarrow \beta$ for $\neg(\alpha \rightsquigarrow \beta)$ and $\forall x.\varPhi$ for $\neg(\exists x.\ \neg\varPhi)$. The other boolean connectives and temporal operators $\Diamond$ (eventually) and $\Box$ (always) are standard. For example, $\Diamond(\exists x.x \neq v \wedge x \rightsquigarrow v \wedge v \rightsquigarrow x)$ expresses that eventually v will point to a non-empty cycle.

Semantics. Logical formulae are interpreted over infinite sequences of sets of entities that are equipped with information concerning the linking structure between these entities. Formally, an *allocation sequence* σ is an infinite sequence of pairs $(E_0,\mu_0)(E_1,\mu_1)(E_2,\mu_2)\ldots$ where for all $i \geqslant 0$, $E_i \subseteq Ent$ and $\mu_i : E_i^\perp \to E_i^\perp$ such that $\mu_i(\perp) = \perp$; μ_i encodes the pointer structure of E_i. Let $\theta : LV \to Ent^\perp$ be a partial valuation of logical variables. The semantics of navigation expression α is given by:

$$[\![\,nil\,]\!]_{\mu,\theta} = \perp$$
$$[\![\,x\,]\!]_{\mu,\theta} = \theta(x)\ \text{if}\ \theta(x) \neq \perp,\ \text{and}\ \perp\ \text{otherwise}$$
$$[\![\,\alpha\uparrow\,]\!]_{\mu,\theta} = \mu([\![\,\alpha\,]\!]_{\mu,\theta})$$

For a given allocation sequence σ, E_i^σ and μ_i^σ denote the set of entities, respectively the pointer structure, in the i-th state of σ. The semantics of *NTL*-formulae is defined by satisfaction relation $\sigma, N, \theta \models \varPhi$ where σ is an allocation sequence, $N \subseteq E_0^\sigma$ is the set of entities that are initially new, and θ is a valuation of the free variables in $\varPhi$. Let N_i^σ denote the set of new entities in state i, i.e., $N_0^\sigma = N$ and $N_{i+1}^\sigma = E_{i+1}^\sigma \backslash E_i^\sigma$, and let θ_i^σ denote the valuation at state i, where $\theta_i^\sigma(x) = \theta(x)$ if $\theta(x) \in E_k^\sigma$ for all $k \leqslant i$, and is $\perp$ otherwise. The latter condition prevents that contradictions like $\exists x.\mathsf{X}(x\ dead \Rightarrow \mathsf{X}x\ alive)$ are satisfiable. Note that once a logical variable is mapped to an entity, this association remains valid along σ until the entity is deallocated. The satisfaction relation $\models$ is defined as follows:

$$\sigma, N, \theta \models \alpha\ \text{new} \quad \text{iff} \quad [\![\,\alpha\,]\!]_{\mu_0^\sigma,\theta} \in N$$
$$\sigma, N, \theta \models \alpha = \beta \quad \text{iff} \quad [\![\,\alpha\,]\!]_{\mu_0^\sigma,\theta} = [\![\,\beta\,]\!]_{\mu_0^\sigma,\theta}$$
$$\sigma, N, \theta \models \alpha \rightsquigarrow \beta \quad \text{iff} \quad \exists k \geqslant 0.\,[\![\,\alpha\uparrow^k\,]\!]_{\mu_0^\sigma,\theta} = [\![\,\beta\,]\!]_{\mu_0^\sigma,\theta}$$
$$\sigma, N, \theta \models \exists x.\varPhi \quad \text{iff} \quad \exists e \in E_0^\sigma : \sigma, N, \theta\{e/x\} \models \varPhi$$
$$\sigma, N, \theta \models \neg\varPhi \quad \text{iff} \quad \sigma, N, \theta \not\models \varPhi$$
$$\sigma, N, \theta \models \varPhi \vee \varPsi \quad \text{iff} \quad \text{either}\ \sigma, N, \theta \models \varPhi\ \text{or}\ \sigma, N, \theta \models \varPsi$$
$$\sigma, N, \theta \models \mathsf{X}\phi \quad \text{iff} \quad \sigma^1, N_1^\sigma, \theta_1^\sigma \models \varPhi$$
$$\sigma, N, \theta \models \varPhi\,\mathsf{U}\,\varPsi \quad \text{iff} \quad \exists i.\,(\sigma^i, N_i^\sigma, \theta_i^\sigma \models \varPsi\ \text{and}\ \forall j < i.\,\sigma^j, N_j^\sigma, \theta_j^\sigma \models \varPhi).$$

Here, $\theta\{e/x\}$ is defined as usual, i.e., $\theta\{e/x\}(x) = e$ and $\theta\{e/x\}(y) = \theta(y)$ for $y \neq x$. Note that the proposition $\alpha \rightsquigarrow \beta$ is satisfied if $[\![\beta]\!] = \bot$ and $[\![\alpha]\!]$ can reach some entity with an undefined outgoing reference.

Program Variables. To enable the specification of properties over entities pointed to by program variables (rather than just logical ones), we introduce for each program variable v_i a logical variable x_{v_i}. This variable always points to a distinguished entity e_{v_i} which exists in every state. For convenience in *NTL*-formulae let v_i denote $x_{v_i}\!\uparrow$ and let $\exists x.\,\Phi$ abbreviate $\exists x.\,(x \neq x_{v_1} \wedge \ldots \wedge x \neq x_{v_n}) \Rightarrow \Phi$.

Example 1. Consider the following list-reversal program (see, e.g., [2, 20, 21]):

decl v, w, t : $w := nil$; while $(v \neq nil)$ do $t := w; w := v; v := v\!\uparrow; w\!\uparrow := t$ od

Properties of interest of this program include, for instance: "v and w always point to distinct lists (heap non-interference)": $\Box(\forall x.\, v \rightsquigarrow x \Rightarrow w \not\rightsquigarrow x)$. "$v$'s list will be (and remains to be) reversed" [2]: $\forall x.\forall y.\,\big((v \rightsquigarrow x \wedge x\!\uparrow = y) \Rightarrow \Diamond\Box(y\!\uparrow = x)\big)$. "None of the elements in v's list will ever be deleted": $\forall x.\,(v \rightsquigarrow x \Rightarrow \Box x \text{ alive})$.

Example 2. The following program consists of two processes that concurrently produce and add entities to the tail tl of a buffer, respectively remove and consume them from the head hd of that buffer:

decl hd, tl, t : $\big(\text{new}(tl); hd := tl; \text{while } (true) \text{ do } \text{new}(tl\!\uparrow); tl := tl\!\uparrow$ od
         $\|$ while $(true)$ do if $(hd \neq tl)$ then $t := hd; hd := hd\!\uparrow; \text{del}(t)$ fi od$\big)$

For navigation expression α, new(α) creates (i.e., allocates) a new entity that will be referred to by the expression α. The old value of α is lost. Thus, if α is the only pointer to entity e, say, then after the execution of new(α), e is automatically garbage collected together with the entities that are only reachable from e. del(α) destroys (i.e., deallocates) the entity associated to α, so that α and every pointer referring to it becomes undefined. Some example properties: "Every element in the buffer is eventually consumed": $\Box(hd \neq tl \Rightarrow \exists x.\,(x = hd \wedge \Diamond x \text{ dead}))$. "The tail is never deleted or disconnected from the head": $\Box(tl \text{ alive} \wedge hd \rightsquigarrow tl)$.

3   Abstracting Linked List Structures

The most obvious way to model pointer structures is to represent each entity and each pointer individually. For most programs, like, e.g., the producer/consumer program, this will give rise to infinite representations. To obtain more abstract (and compact) views of pointer structures, in this paper chains of entities will be aggregated and represented by one (or more) entities. We consider the abstraction of *pure chains* (and not of arbitrary graphs) in order to be able to keep the "topology" of pointer structures invariant in a more straightforward manner.

---

[2] If one is interested in only checking whether v's list is reversed at the end of the program, program locations can be added and referred to in the standard way.

Pure Chains. Let $\prec$ be the binary relation on entities (excluding $\perp$) representing μ, i.e., $e \prec e'$ iff $\mu(e) = e'$. A sequence $e_1, \ldots, e_k$ is a chain (of length k) if $e_i \prec e_{i+1}$, for $0 < i < k$. The non-empty set E of entities is a chain of length $|E|$ iff there exists a bijection $f : \{1, \ldots, k\} \to E$ such that $f(1), \ldots, f(k)$ is a chain; let $first(E) = f(1)$ and $last(E) = f(k)$. E is a *pure chain* if $|\{e' \mid e' \prec e\}| = 1$ for all $e \in f(2), f(3), \ldots, f(k)$ and f is unique (which may fail to be the case if the chain is a cycle). Note that chains consisting of a single element are trivially pure.

Abstracting Pure Chains. An abstract entity may represent a pure chain of "concrete" entities. The concrete representation of abstract entity e is indicated by its *cardinality* $\mathcal{C}(e) \in \mathbb{M} = \{1, \ldots, M\} \cup \{*\}$, for some fixed constant $M > 0$. Entity e for which $\mathcal{C}(e) = m \leqslant M$ represents a chain of m "concrete" entities; if $\mathcal{C}(e) = *$, e represents a chain that is longer than M. In the latter case, the entity is called *unbounded.* (Such entities are similar to summary nodes [21], with the specific property that they always abstract from pure chains.) The special cardinality function $\mathbf{1}$ yields one for each entity. The precision of the abstraction is improved on increasing M.

Configurations and Morphisms. States in our automata are triples $(E, \mu, \mathcal{C})$, called *configurations.* Configurations representing pure chains at different abstraction levels are related by morphisms, defined as follows. Let *Cnf* denote the set of all configurations ranged over by c and c', and $\mathcal{C}(\{e_1, \ldots, e_n\}) = \mathcal{C}(e_1) \oplus \ldots \oplus \mathcal{C}(e_n)$ where $n \oplus m = n+m$ if $n+m \leqslant M$ and $*$ otherwise.

Definition 1. *For $c, c' \in Cnf$, surjective function $h : E \to E'$ is a morphism if:*

1. *for all $e \in E'$, $h^{-1}(e)$ is a pure chain and $\mathcal{C}'(e) = \mathcal{C}(h^{-1}(e))$*
2. *$e \prec' e' \Rightarrow last(h^{-1}(e)) \prec first(h^{-1}(e'))$*
3. *$e \prec e' \Rightarrow h(e) \preceq' h(e')$ where $\preceq'$ denotes the reflexive closure of $\prec'$.*

According to the first condition only pure chains may be abstracted by a single entity while keeping the cardinalities invariant. The last two conditions enforce the preservation of the pointer structure under h. Intuitively speaking, by means of a morphism the abstract shape of the pointer dependencies represented by the two related configurations is maintained. The identity function *id* is a morphism and morphisms are closed under composition. Configurations c and c' are isomorphic, denoted $c \cong c'$, iff there exist morphisms from c to c' and from c' to c such that their composition is *id*.

4   An Automaton-Based Model for Pointer Evolution

Evolving Pointer Structures. Morphisms relate configurations that model the pointer structure at distinct abstraction levels. They do not model the dynamic evolution of such linking structures. To reflect the execution of pointer-manipulating statements, such as either the creation or deletion of entities (e.g., **new** in Java and **delete** in C++), or the change of pointers by assignments (e.g., $x = x{\uparrow}{\uparrow}$), we use *reallocations.*

Definition 2. *For $c, c' \in Cnf$, $\lambda : (E^\perp \times E'^\perp) \to \mathbb{M}$ is a reallocation if:*

1. *(a) $\mathcal{C}(e) = \bigoplus \lambda(e, e')$ and (b) $\mathcal{C}'(e') = \bigoplus \lambda(e, e')$*
2. *(a) for all $e \in E$, $|\{e' \mid \lambda(e, e') = *\}| \leqslant 1$ and (b) $\{e' \mid \lambda(\perp, e') = *\} = \varnothing$*
3. *(a) for all $e \in E$, $\{e' \mid \lambda(e, e') \neq 0\}$ and (b) for all $e' \in E'$, $\{e \mid \lambda(e, e') \neq 0\}$ are chains.*

We write $c \overset{\lambda}{\leadsto} c'$ if there is a reallocation (named λ) from c to c'.

The special entity $\perp$ is used to model birth and death: $\lambda(\perp, e) \neq 0$ denotes the birth of (some instances of) e whereas $\lambda(e, \perp) \neq 0$ denotes the death of (some instances of) e. Intuitively speaking, reallocation λ redistributes cardinalities on E to E' such that (1a) the total cardinality allocated by λ to $e \in E$ equals $\mathcal{C}(e)$ and (1b) the total cardinality assigned to $e' \in E'$ equals $\mathcal{C}'(e')$. Moreover, (2a) for each entity e unbounded cardinalities (i.e., equal to $*$) are assigned only once (according to (1b) to an unbounded entity in E'), and (2b) no unbounded entities can be born. The last condition is self-explanatory. Note that the identity function id is a reallocation. The concept of reallocation can be considered as a generalisation of the idea of identity change as, for instance, present in history-dependent automata [17]: besides the possible change of the abstract identity of concrete entities, it allows for the evolution of pointer structures. Reallocations allow "extraction" of concrete entities from abstract entities by a redistribution of cardinalities between entities. Extraction is analogous to *materialisation* [21]. Reallocations ensure that entities that are born cannot be reallocated from any other entity. Moreover, entities that die can only be reallocated to $\perp$.

Relating Abstract and Concrete Evolutions. As a next step we relate transitions between abstract representations of pointer structures to transitions between their corresponding concrete representations. To that end, "abstract" reallocations are related to "concrete" ones. These are called *concretions*.

Definition 3. *Let $c \overset{\lambda}{\leadsto} c'$ and $\widehat{c} \overset{\widehat{\lambda}}{\leadsto} \widehat{c}'$ with $\mathcal{C}_{\widehat{c}} = \mathcal{C}_{\widehat{c}'} = 1$. $\widehat{\lambda}$ is a concretion of λ, denoted $\widehat{\lambda} \triangleright \lambda$, iff there exist h and h' such that:*

1. *h is a morphism between $\widehat{c}$ and c, and h' is a morphism between $\widehat{c}'$ and c'*
2. *$\lambda(e, e') = \bigoplus\{\widehat{\lambda}(\widehat{e}, \widehat{e}') \mid (h(\widehat{e}), h'(\widehat{e}')) = (e, e')\}$*
3. *$h(e) = h(e') \vee (h' \circ \widehat{\lambda})(e) = (h' \circ \widehat{\lambda})(e')$ implies $e \prec_{\widehat{c}} e' \Leftrightarrow \widehat{\lambda}(e) \prec_{\widehat{c}'} \widehat{\lambda}(e')$*
4. *$(\mathcal{C}_{\widehat{c}} \circ h')(e) = * \Rightarrow e \in cod(\widehat{\lambda})$, the co-domain of $\widehat{\lambda}$.*

The first condition states that the concrete source-configuration $\widehat{c}$ and its abstract source c are related by a morphism, and the same applies to their target configurations $\widehat{c}'$ and c'. (Stated differently, reallocations and morphisms commute in this case.) The second condition requires the multiplicity of λ and $\widehat{\lambda}$ to correspond, while the third condition forbids the change of order (according to $\prec$) between concrete entities and their abstract counterparts (unlike reallocations). Hence, the order of entities in a chain should remain identical. The last condition says that entities that are mapped onto unbounded ones in the target states are not fresh. Due to the third condition all concrete entities represented by an abstract entity enjoy a common fate: either all of them "survive" the reallocation or all die.

Automaton-Based Model. In order to model the dynamic evolution of programs manipulating (abstract) linked lists, we use a generalisation of Büchi automata (extending [11]) where each state is a configuration and transitions exist between states iff these states can be related by means of a reallocation reflecting the possible change in the pointer structure.

Definition 4. *A* high-level allocation Büchi automaton *(HABA) H is a tuple* $\langle X, C, \rightarrow, I, \mathcal{F} \rangle$ *with:*

- $X \subseteq LV$, *a finite set of logical variables;*
- $C \subseteq Cnf$, *a set of configurations (also called* states*);*
- $\rightarrow \; \subseteq C \times (Ent \times Ent \times \mathbb{M}) \times C$, *a transition relation, s.t.* $c \rightarrow_\lambda c' \; \Rightarrow \; c \overset{\lambda}{\rightsquigarrow} c'$;
- $I : C \rightarrow 2^{Ent} \times (X \rightharpoonup Ent)$, *an initialisation* function *such that for all c with* $I(c) = (N, \theta)$ *we have* $N \subseteq E$ *and* $\theta : X \rightharpoonup E$.
- $\mathcal{F} \subseteq 2^C$ *a set of sets of* accept *states.*

Note that initial new entities cannot be unbounded. HABA can be used to model the behaviour of pointer-manipulating programs at different levels of abstraction. In particular, when all entities in any state are concrete (i.e., $\mathcal{C}(e) = 1$ for all e), and states are related by the identity reallocation, a concrete automaton is obtained that is very close to the actual program behaviour.

Automata for Pointer-Manipulating Programs. As a start, we determine by means of a static analysis of the program p, the "longest" navigation expression that occurs in it and fix constant L such that $L > \max\{ n \mid (v\uparrow)^n \text{ occurs in } p \}$. Besides the formula-dependent constant M, the program-dependent constant L can be used to tune the precision of the symbolic representation, i.e., by increasing L the model becomes less abstract. Unbounded entities (i.e., those with cardinality $*$) will be exploited in the semantics to keep the model finite. The basic intuition of our symbolic semantics is that unbounded entities should always be preceded by a chain of at least L concrete entities. This principle allows us to precisely determine the concrete entity that is referred to by any assignment, new and del-statement. As assignments may yield unsafe configurations (due to program variables that are "shifted" too close to an unbounded entity), these statements require some special treatment (see [10]).

Folded Allocation Sequences. In *NTL*-formulae, entities can only be addressed through logical variables, and logical variables can only be compared in the same state. These observations allow a mapping of entities from one state in an allocation sequence onto entities in its next state, as long as this preserves the conditions of being a reallocation. A *folded allocation sequence* is an infinite alternating sequence $(E_0, \mu_0, \mathbf{1}_0)\lambda_0(E_1, \mu_1, \mathbf{1}_1)\lambda_1 \cdots$, where λ_i is a reallocation from $(E_i, \mu_i, \mathbf{1}_i)$ to $(E_{i+1}, \mu_{i+1}, \mathbf{1}_{i+1})$ for $i \geqslant 0$. Due to the unitary cardinality functions, λ_i associates at most one entity in E_{i+1} to an entity in E_i. We write λ_i^σ for the reallocation function of σ in state i, and we define $N_0^\sigma = N$, and $N_{i+1}^\sigma = E_{i+1}^\sigma \setminus cod(\lambda_i^\sigma)$. Similarly, $\theta_0^\sigma = \theta$ and $\theta_{i+1}^\sigma = \lambda_i^\sigma \circ \theta_i^\sigma$ where $\lambda \circ \theta_i(x)$ equals e if $\theta_i(x) \neq \perp$ and $\lambda(\theta_i(x), e) = 1$, and $\perp$ otherwise. Using these adapted definitions of N and θ, a semantics of *NTL* can be defined in terms of folded allocation sequences that is equivalent to $\models$ (see [10]). Runs of our symbolic HABA automata "generate" folded allocation sequences in the following way:

Definition 5. *HABA-run* $q_0\lambda_0 q_1\lambda_1\cdots$ *generates an allocation triple* (σ, N, θ) *where* $\sigma = c_0^{\sigma}\lambda_0^{\sigma}c_1^{\sigma}\lambda_1^{\sigma}\cdots$ *is a folded allocation sequence, if there exists a family of morphisms* h_i *(called a generator) from* c_i^{σ} *to* c_{q_i} *such that, for all* $i \geqslant 0$:

$$\lambda_i^{\sigma} \rhd \lambda_i \text{ (via } h_i \text{ and } h_{i+1}), \text{ and } I(q_0) = (N', h_0 \circ \theta) \text{ where } N = h_0^{-1}(N').$$

We adopt the generalised Büchi acceptance condition, i.e, $c_0 c_1 c_2 \cdots$ is a *run* of HABA H if $c_i \to c_{i+1}$ for all $i \geqslant 0$ and $|\{\, i \mid c_i \in F \,\}| = \omega$ for all $F \in \mathcal{F}$. Let *runs*(H) denote the set of runs of H. Then $\mathcal{L}(H) = \{\, (\sigma, N, \theta) \mid \exists \rho \in runs(H).\, \rho \text{ generates } (\sigma, N, \theta)\,\}$.

Relating the Concrete and Symbolic Model. A given HABA abstracts a *set* of concrete automata. We formally define this by first defining an implementation relation over HABA and then using the correspondence of concrete automata to a certain class of HABA. We say that a given HABA abstracts another one if there exists a so-called simulation relation (denoted $\lesssim$) between their state sets.

Definition 6. *Let* H *and* H' *be two HABAs such that* $\mathcal{C}(e) = 1$ *for all* e *in* H. H' *abstracts* H, *denoted* $H \sqsubseteq H'$, *iff there exists a simulation relation* $\lesssim \subseteq C \times (Ent \to Ent) \times C'$ *between their state sets such that:*

1. $c_1 \lesssim_h c_1'$ *implies that* h *is a morphism between* c_1 *and* c_1';
2. $c_1 \lesssim_h c_1'$ *with* $c_1 \to_\lambda c_2$ *implies* $c_1' \to_{\lambda'} c_2'$ *for some* λ' *and* c_2' *such that* $c_2 \lesssim_{h'} c_2'$ *and* $\lambda \rhd \lambda'$ *via* h *and* h';
3. $c \in dom(I)$ *implies* $I'(c') = (N, h \circ \theta)$ *for some* $c' \in C'$ *and* h *such that* $c \lesssim_h c'$ *and* $I(c) = (h^{-1}(N), \theta)$;
4. *there exists a bijection* $\psi : \mathcal{F} \to \mathcal{F}'$ *such that for all* $F \in \mathcal{F}$ *and* $c \in F$, $c \lesssim_h c'$ *for some* $c' \in \psi(F)$ *and* h.

$c \lesssim_h c'$ denotes that c' simulates c, according to a given morphism h. This implies (*1*) that c' is an abstraction of the pointer structure in c (due to the morphism h), and (*2*) that every λ-transition of c is mimicked by a λ'-transition of c' such that $\lambda' \rhd \lambda$ and the resulting target states are again in the simulation relation. H is abstracted by H' if there is a simulation relation between their states such that (*3*) initial states and (*4*) accept conditions correspond.

Let $H \models \Phi$ if for all $(\sigma, N, \theta) \in \mathcal{L}(H)$ we have $\sigma, N, \theta \models \Phi$, where $\models$ is the satisfaction relation for NTL defined on folded allocation sequences.

Theorem 1. *For* $H \sqsubseteq H'$: $\mathcal{L}(H) \subseteq \mathcal{L}(H')$ *and* $(H' \models \Phi \Rightarrow H \models \Phi)$.

From this result it follows that all positive verification results on the (typically finite) abstraction H' carry over to the (mostly infinite) concrete automaton H.

Note that false negatives may occur as the refutation of a formula by H' does not necessarily has to imply that H refutes it as well[3].

Example 3. Consider the following NTL-formulae: *tl alive* $\Rightarrow$ $\Box$(*tl alive*) and $\Box$(*hd alive* $\Rightarrow$ *hd* $\leadsto$ *tl*). It turns out that both formulae are valid in the abstract HABA ($L = M = 1$) modelling the producer/consumer program. By Theorem 1 we conclude that they are valid also on the infinite corresponding concrete model.

5   Model Checking

The Parameters M and L. The precision of automaton H is ruled by two parameters: L, which controls the distance between entities before they are collected into unbounded entities, and M, which controls the information we have about unbounded entities. L is used in the generation of models from programs; it is no longer of importance in the model checking stage. M is a formula-dependent constant exceeding $\sum_{x \in \Phi} \max\{ i \mid (x\uparrow)^i$ occurs in $\Phi \}$ *for the formula Φ to check.* This may mean that the model H at hand is not (yet) suitable for checking a given formula Φ, namely if M for that model does not meet this lower bound. In that case we have to *stretch* the model. Fortunately, we can stretch a given model without loss of information (but with loss of compactness, and hence increase of complexity of the model checking). In fact, in [10] we define an operation $H \Uparrow \widehat{M}$, which stretches H so that in the resulting model the corresponding constant is $\widehat{M}$, and we have the following:

Theorem 2. *For all HABA H such that $\mathcal{C}(H) < \widehat{M}$: $\mathcal{L}(H) = \mathcal{L}(H \Uparrow \widehat{M})$.*

Here, $\mathcal{C}(H)$ is the maximal cardinality of some entity in H. The automaton $H \Uparrow \widehat{M}$ is a factor $\widehat{M} - M$ times as large as H.

The Tableau Graph. The next step is to construct a *tableau graph* $G_H(\Phi)$ for Φ from a given model H, assuming that stretching has been done, so M satisfies the given lower bound for Φ. $G_H(\Phi)$ enriches H, for each of its states q, with information about the collections of formulae relevant to the validity of Φ that possibly hold in q. These "relevant formulae" are essentially sub-formulae of Φ and their negations; they are collected into the so-called *closure* of Φ [15]. The states of $G_H(\Phi)$ are now so-called *atoms* (q, D) where q is a state of H and D a consistent and complete set of valuations of formulae from the closure of Φ on (the entities of) q. Consistency and completeness approximately mean that, for instance, if Ψ_1 is in the closure then exactly one of Ψ_1 and $\neg\Psi_1$ is "included in" D (i.e., D contains a valuation for it), and if $\Psi_1 \vee \Psi_2$ is in the closure then it

---

[3] In [11] where we only considered the birth and death of entities we obtained a stronger relationship between (a somewhat simpler variant of) the concrete and symbolic model. Here, the abstraction is less precise and permits the abstracted model to exhibit spurious behaviours that do not occur in the concrete model.

is "in" D iff Ψ_1 or Ψ_2 is "in" D, etc. For any q, the number of atoms on q is exponential in the size of the closure and in the number of entities in q.

A transition from (q, D) to (q', D') exists in the tableau graph $G_H(\Phi)$ if $q \to_\lambda q'$ in H and, moreover, to the valuation of each sub-formula $\mathsf{X}\Psi$ in D there exists a corresponding valuation of Ψ in D' — where the correspondence is defined modulo the reallocation λ. A *fulfilling path* in $G_H(\Phi)$ is then an infinite sequence of transitions, starting from an initial state, that also satisfies all the "until" sub-formulae $\Psi_1 \cup \Psi_2$ in the atoms, in the sense that if a valuation of $\Psi_1 \cup \Psi_2$ is in a given atom in the sequence, then a corresponding valuation of Ψ_2 (modulo a sequence of reallocations) occurs in a later atom.

Proposition 1. $H \models \Phi$ *iff there does not exist a fulfilling path in* $G_H(\neg\Phi)$.

Unfortunately, in contrast to the case of propositional logic (in [15]) and our own earlier results in the absence of pointers (in [11]), in the setting of this paper we have not found a decision procedure for the existence of a fulfilling path. In fact, the existence of a *self-fulfilling strongly connected sub-component* (SCS) of the tableau graph, which is the technique used in these other papers, gives only a necessary criterion for the existence of a fulfilling path. To be precise, if we use $Inf(\pi)$ to denote the set of atoms that occur infinitely often in an (arbitrary) infinite path π in $G_H(\Phi)$, then we have:

Proposition 2. $Inf(\pi)$ *is not a self-fulfilling SCS* $\Rightarrow$ π *is not a fulfilling path.*

Since the number of SCSs of any finite tableau graph is finite, and the property of self-fulfillment is decidable, this gives rise to a mechanical procedure for verifying the satisfiability of formulae.

Theorem 3. $H \models \Phi$ *can be verified mechanically for any finite HABA H.*

This, combined with Th. 1, implies that, for any concrete automaton A of which H is an abstraction, it is also possible to verify mechanically whether $A \models \Phi$. Note that this theorem leaves the possibility of *false negatives*, as usual in model checking in the presence of abstraction. This means that if the algorithm fails to show $H \models \Phi$ then it cannot be concluded that Φ is *not* satisfiable (by some run of H). However, since such a failure is always accompanied by a "prospective" fulfilling path of Φ, further analysis or testing may be used to come to a more precise conclusion.

6   Conclusions

Although our heap structures are less general than those used in shape analysis, our abstractions are less non-deterministic, and therefore, are potentially more exact. Experimental research is needed to validate this claim. Although *NTL* is essentially a first-order logic, it contains two second-order features: the reachability predicate $\alpha \rightsquigarrow \beta$ (which computes the transitive closure of pointers), and the freshness predicate $\alpha\,\mathsf{new}$. The latter is second-order because it essentially expresses that the entity denoted by α did not occur in the *set* of entities existing in the directly preceding state. In fact it would be very useful to extend the latter to freshness with respect to an arbitrary previous state, for instance by introducing formulae $\sigma X.\Phi$ which bind X to the set of entities existing in the current state, and predicates $\alpha \in X$ which express that the entity denoted by α is in the set X. We conjecture that the results of this paper can be lifted to such an extension without essential changes.

References

1. S. Bardin, A. Finkel, and D. Nowak. Towards symbolic verification of programs handling pointers. In: *AVIS 2004*. ENTCS 2004 to appear.
2. M. Bozga, R. Iosif, and Y. Lakhnech. Storeless semantics and alias logic. In: *PEPM*, pp. 55–65. ACM Press, 2003.
3. R. Burstall. Some techniques for proving correctness of programs which alter data structures. *Machine Intelligence* **6**: 23–50, 1971.
4. L. Cardelli, P. Gardner, and G. Ghelli. A spatial logic for querying graphs. In: *ICALP*, LNCS 2380, pp. 597–610. Springer, 2002.
5. L. Cardelli and A.D. Gordon. Anytime, anywhere: modal logics for mobile ambients. In: *POPL*, pp. 365–377. ACM Press, 2000.
6. D.R. Chase, M. Wegman and F. Zadeck. Analysis of pointers and structures. In *PLDI*, pp. 296–310. ACM Press, 1990.
7. S.A. Cook and D. Oppen. An assertion language for data structures. In: *POPL*, pp. 160–166. ACM Press, 1975.
8. A. Deutsch. Interprocedural may-alias analysis for pointers: beyond k-limiting. In: *PLDI*, pp. 230–241. ACM Press, 1994.
9. D. Distefano. On model checking the dynamics of object-based software: a foundational approach. PhD. Thesis, Univ. of Twente, 2003.
10. D. Distefano, A. Rensink and J.-P. Katoen. Who is pointing when to whom? CTIT Tech. Rep. 03-12, 2003.
11. D. Distefano, A. Rensink, and J.-P. Katoen. Model checking birth and death. In: *TCS*, pp. 435–447. Kluwer, 2002.
12. S. Ishtiaq and P.W. O'Hearn. BI as an assertion language for mutable data structures. In *POPL*, pp. 14–26, ACM Press, 2001.
13. J. Jensen, M. Jørgensen, M. Schwartzbach and N. Klarlund. Automatic verification of pointer programs using monadic second-order logic. In: *PLDI*, pp. 226–236. ACM Press, 1997.
14. N.D. Jones and S.S. Muchnick. Flow analysis and optimization of Lisp-like structures. In S.S. Muchnick and N.D. Jones, editors, *Program Flow Analysis: Theory and Applications*, Chapter 4, pp. 102-131, Prentice-Hall, 1981.
15. O. Lichtenstein and A. Pnueli. Checking that finite state concurrent programs satisfy their linear specification. In: *POPL*, pp. 97–107. ACM Press, 1985.
16. G. Nelson. Verifying reachability invariants of linked structures. In: *POPL*, pp. 38–47. ACM Press, 1983.
17. U. Montanari and M. Pistore. An introduction to history-dependent automata. *ENTCS* **10**, 1998.
18. P.W. O'Hearn, H. Yang, and J.C. Reynolds. Separation and information hiding. In: *POPL*, pp. 268–280. ACM Press, 2004.

19. A. Rensink. Canonical graph shapes. In: *ESOP*, LNCS 2986, pp. 401–415. Springer,2004.
20. J.C. Reynolds. Separation logic: A logic for shared mutable data structures. In *LICS*, pp. 55–74. IEEE CS Press, 2002.
21. M. Sagiv, T. Reps, and R. Wilhelm. Solving shape-analysis problems in languages with destructive updating. *ACM TOPLAS*, **20**(1): 1–50, 1998.
22. L. Séméria, K. Sato and G. de Micheli. Resolution of dynamic memory allocation and pointers for the behavioural synthesis from C. In *DATE*, pp. 312–319. ACM Press, 2000.
23. E. Yahav, T. Reps, M. Sagiv, and R. Wilhelm. Verifying temporal heap properties specified via evolution logic. In: *ESOP*, LNCS 2618, pp. 204–222. Springer, 2003.

An Almost Linear Time Approximation Algorithm for the Permanent of a Random (0-1) Matrix

Martin Fürer[*] and Shiva Prasad Kasiviswanathan

Computer Science and Engineering, Pennsylvania State University,
University Park, PA 16802
{furer, kasivisw}@cse.psu.edu

Abstract. We present a simple randomized algorithm for approximating permanents. The algorithm with inputs A, $\epsilon > 0$ produces an output X_A with $(1-\epsilon)\mathrm{per}(A) \leq X_A \leq (1+\epsilon)\mathrm{per}(A)$ for almost all (0-1) matrices A. For any positive constant $\epsilon > 0$, and almost all (0-1) matrices the algorithm runs in time $O(n^2\omega)$, i.e., almost linear in the size of the matrix, where $\omega = \omega(n)$ is any function satisfying $\omega(n) \to \infty$ as $n \to \infty$. This improves the previous bound of $O(n^3\omega)$ for such matrices. The estimator can also be used to estimate the size of a backtrack tree.

1   Introduction

The permanent of an $n \times n$ matrix A is defined as

$$\mathrm{per}(A) = \sum_\pi \prod_i a(i, \pi(i)),$$

where the sum is over all permutations π of $\{1, 2, \ldots, n\}$. The permanent function was first introduced in the memoirs of Cauchy and Binet in 1812 (see [11] for a comprehensive history). The (0-1) permanent also has a simple combinatorial interpretation, $\mathrm{per}(A)$ counts the perfect matchings in the $(n + n)$-vertex bipartite graph whose adjacency matrix is A. The permanent has important applications in physical sciences and plays a central role in many linear algebra and combinatorial enumeration problems.

Despite its syntactic similarity to the determinant, no efficient method for computing the permanent could be found for almost two centuries. This apparent paradox was solved by Valiant [16] who showed in his celebrated paper that $\mathrm{per}(A)$ is #P-complete. The class #P is defined as $\{f : \exists$ a non deterministic polynomial time Turing Machine M such that on input x, M has exactly $f(x)$ accepting leaves$\}$. Thus, it comes as no surprise that there is no polynomial time deterministic algorithm for calculating the permanent exactly. The best known deterministic algorithm has a running time of $O(n2^n)$ [14]. Therefore,

---

[*] Research supported in part by NSF Grant CCR-0209099.

K. Lodaya and M. Mahajan (Eds.): FSTTCS 2004, LNCS 3328, pp. 263–274, 2004.

the more recent research has focussed on efficient approximation algorithms for the permanent with desired performance guarantees. In this paper, we describe a simple estimator for the permanent and prove that it has an overall running time of $O(n^2\omega)$ for random (0-1) matrices from $G(n, 1/2)$, where $\omega = \omega(n)$ is any function satisfying $\omega(n) \to \infty$ as $n \to \infty$. We then generalize our technique to obtain a running time which is polynomial in the size of the input matrix for the case of $G(n, p)$. We also show how the same estimator when applied to another problem, that of estimating the size of a tree, could result in better running times for some kinds of random trees. The estimator is a randomized approximation scheme.

2   Definitions

Let Q be some function from Σ^* to the natural numbers. A fully-polynomial randomized approximation scheme (a.k.a. fpras) for Q is a randomized algorithm that accepts an input $x \in \sum^*$ together with an accuracy parameter $\epsilon \in (0, 1]$, outputs a number X (a random variable depending on the coin tosses of the algorithm) such that

$$\Pr[(1 - \epsilon)Q(x) \leq X \leq (1 + \epsilon)Q(x)] \geq \frac{3}{4}$$

and runs in time polynomial in $|x|$ and ϵ^{-1}. The probability of $\frac{3}{4}$ can be boosted to $1 - \delta$ for any $0 < \delta < 1$ by outputting the median of $O(\log \delta^{-1})$ independent trials [7].

Suppose we would like to estimate Q and have a probabilistic algorithm running in time polynomial in $|x|$, whose output is a random variable X such that $E[X] = Q(x)$ and $E[X^2]$ is finite. Suppose further that we can repeat this experiment as many times as we wish, and the outcomes of the successive trials are independent and identically distributed. Let X_i be the outcome of the ith trial. A straightforward application of Chebychev's inequality shows that, if we conduct $O(\frac{E[X^2]}{E[X]^2}\epsilon^{-2})$ trials and take the mean, we have an fpras for Q. Together, the complexity of performing the stochastic experiment, and the ratio of $\frac{E[X^2]}{E[X]^2}$ (a.k.a. critical ratio) will determine the efficiency of the algorithm.

3   Related Work

Current research in the area of permanents has been divided into four major categories [2]. They are: elementary recursive algorithms; reductions to determinants; iterative balancing; and Markov chain Monte-Carlo methods. One of the simplest estimators of the permanent using elementary recursive algorithms was proposed by Rasmussen [13]. This estimator has a running time of $O(n^3\omega)$ for almost all (0-1) matrices. We will extend Rasmussen's idea to get a running time of $O(n^2\omega)$ for almost all (0-1) matrices. The more famous K^2L^3 [8] estimator uses reductions to determinants. This estimator, which is based on the

Godsil/Gutman estimator [4], has a running time of poly$(n)2^{n/2}$ for all (0-1) matrices. In 1995, Frieze and Jerrum [3] proved that the K^2L^3 estimator runs in time $O(nM(n)\omega)$ for almost all non-negative matrices, where $M(n)$ is the time required to perform matrix multiplications. Recently, an fpras for computing the permanent of an arbitrary matrix with non-negative entries was proposed by Jerrum, Sinclair, Vigoda [6]. This is based on the Markov chain Monte-Carlo approach. However, due to their high exponent in the running time, i.e. $\tilde{O}(n^{10})$, the algorithm is unlikely to be practical [2]. For this reason, it is still worth investigating alternative approaches. The following table summarizes the running times of various estimators of the permanent of a random (0-1) matrix.

Authors	Year	Running Time
Jerrum and Sinclair [5]	1989	$O(n^{O(1)})$
K^2L^3 [8], Frieze and Jerrum [3]	1993, 1995	$O(nM(n)\omega)$
Rasmussen [13]	1994	$O(n^3\omega)$
Ours	2004	$O(n^2\omega)$

Fig. 1. Performance of Various Estimators for Random (0-1) matrices of $G(n, 1/2)$

4   The Rasmussen Estimator

The Rasmussen [13] estimator is inspired by Laplace's expansion formula for the permanent:

$$\text{per}(A) = \sum_{j=1}^{n} a_{1j}\text{per}(A_{1j}),$$

where A_{1j} denotes the submatrix obtained from A by removing the 1st row and the jth column, and the permanent of the empty matrix is set to 1. The idea is similar to that of Knuth's estimator [9] for estimating the size of a backtrack tree. Let $W=\{j : a_{1j} = 1\}$ (the set of columns with 1 in the current row). The estimator X_A is defined as the product of the number of 1's in the current row with the estimator $X_{A_{1j}}$ for the remaining submatrix. The column j is chosen uniformly at random from W. The estimator is clearly unbiased ($E[X] =$ per(A) and $E[X^2]$ is finite) and one run of the algorithm can be implemented in $O(n^2)$. The benefits of such an estimator are its simplicity and wide range of applicability.

5   A Better Estimator

A closer look at the above estimator tells us that this estimator makes most of its mistakes towards the end when the matrix becomes small. This motivates us to increase the frequency of runs as we go down (here run stands for a single application of the estimator algorithm over the remaining submatrix). At every

Random Approximator of the Permanent:

```
RAP(A,n,s,r)
if n = 0 then
      X_A = 1
else
            W = {j : a_1j = 1}
            if W = ∅ then
                  X_A = 0
            else
                  if n = s^i for some i ≥ 1 then
                        K = r
                  else
                        K = 1
                  for ℓ = 1 to K do
                        choose J(ℓ) u.a.r. from W
                        compute X_{A_{1J(ℓ)}} using RAP (A_1j, n − 1, s, r)
                  X_A = |W|(1/K ∑_{ℓ=1}^{K} X_{A_{1J(ℓ)}})
```

Fig. 2. The Algorithm

level with height $s^i (i \geq 1)$ (= branching points), we do r (= branching factor) runs on the submatrix, rather than the usual one. At height 1, we have only one element. The estimator X_A of a (0-1) $n \times n$ matrix $A=(a_{ij})(1 \leq i, j \leq n)$ is computed as in Figure 2. We call our algorithm RAP. This idea is similar to one used by Karger and Stein [15] to obtain a faster algorithm for Min-Cut. The computation has a tree structure (Figure 3). Each path from the root to a leaf represents one run of the Rasmussen estimator. We do a bottom-up evaluation. At each branching level, we find the estimator by taking the product of the number of 1's in that row with the mean over the estimators of the previous level. This gives an unbiased estimator for permanent of any (0-1) matrix.

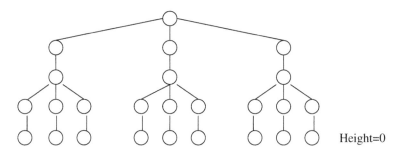

Height=0

Fig. 3. Run of the Algorithm RAP(A,4,2,3)

6   The Permanent of a Random Matrix

The two most frequently used models of random graphs are $G(n, p)$ and $G(n, m)$. $G(n, p)$ includes each possible edge with independent probability p and $G(n, m)$ assigns equal probability to all graphs with m edges (see [1] for an extensive treatment). Following [13] we use $\mathcal{A}(n)$ to represent the set of all $n \times n$ (0-1) matrices, $\mathcal{A}(n, m)$ to represent the set of all $n \times n$ (0-1) matrices with exactly m 1's, E_σ to represent the mean over the coin-tosses of the estimator, $E_{\mathcal{A}}$ to represent the mean over $\mathcal{A}(n)$, and $E_{\mathcal{A}(n,m)}$ to represent the mean over $\mathcal{A}(n, m)$. In this section we deal with the more widely used random graph model $G(n, 1/2)$. Here at every level with height $2^i (i \geq 1)$ $(s = 2)$, we do $r = 3$ runs on the submatrix.

Theorem 1. *The running time of the algorithm* $\mathrm{RAP}(A, n, 2, 3)$ *is* $O(n^2)$.

Proof. Let $2^{i-1} < n \leq 2^i$. Then the running time: Between top and 1st branching level is $< n^2 \leq 2^{2i}$. Between 1st and 2nd branching level is $< 3(2^{i-1})^2$. Between 2nd and 3rd branching level is $< 9(2^{i-2})^2$. As this forms a geometric series, the total running time is $O(n^2)$.   □

Our result rests on the following results of Frieze and Jerrum [3], Rasmussen [13], which we state here without proof.

Lemma 1 *(**Frieze and Jerrum [3]**). Suppose $m = m(n)$ satisfies $\frac{m^2}{n^3} \to \infty$ as $n \to \infty$, and choose A from $\mathcal{A}(n, m)$ (set of all (0-1) matrices with exactly m 1's). Then*

$$E[\mathrm{per}(A)^2] = (n!)^2 (\frac{m}{n^2})^{2n} \exp(-\frac{n^2}{m} + 1 + O(\frac{n^3}{m^2}))$$

and

$$\frac{E[\mathrm{per}(A)^2]}{E[\mathrm{per}(A)]^2} = 1 + O(\frac{n^3}{m^2})$$

Lemma 2 *(**Rasmussen [13]**). Let $\omega = \omega(n)$ be any function satisfying $\omega \to \infty$ as $n \to \infty$. Let $\mu(n) = E_{\mathcal{A}(n)}[\mathrm{per}(A)]$ denote the mean of the permanent of a random matrix. Then for almost all (0-1) matrices A, and any unbiased estimator X_A of the permanent,*

$$\mathrm{per}(A) \geq \frac{\mu(n)}{\omega} \quad and \quad \frac{E_\sigma[X_A^2]}{E_\sigma[X_A]^2} \leq \omega \frac{E_{\mathcal{A}}[E_\sigma[X_A^2]]}{E_{\mathcal{A}}[E_\sigma[X_A]]^2}$$

For Rasmussen's algorithm the critical factor $\frac{E_\sigma[X_A^2]}{E_\sigma[X_A]^2}$ is $O(n\omega)$. The idea of repeated runs allows us to achieve an asymptotically lower bound on the critical ratio.

Our algorithm RAP (Figure 2) differs from Rasmussen's algorithm on what it does only at branching points. $\widehat{\mathrm{RAP}}$ is an auxiliary random approximator of the permanent. It's only difference from RAP is that K=1 at the start, i.e., there is no branching in the root of the computation tree even if $n = 2^j$. The random variables $\hat{X}$ and X are the outputs of $\widehat{RAP}$ and RAP respectively. To model the quality of $\widehat{RAP}$ and RAP, we introduce two terms $\hat{R}(h)$ and $R(h)$. $\hat{R}(h)$ models the ratio of means of the auxiliary approximator $\widehat{RAP}$, while $R(h)$ models the ratio of means of RAP until height h.

$$\hat{R}(h) = \frac{E_A[E_\sigma[\hat{X}_h^2]]}{E_A[E_\sigma[\hat{X}_h]]^2} \quad \text{and} \quad R(h) = \frac{E_A[E_\sigma[X_h^2]]}{E_A[E_\sigma[X_h]]^2}$$

The proofs are organized as follows: We establish the recursive relationship between $R(h)$ and $\hat{R}(h)$ in Theorems 2 and 3. With Theorems 4 and 5, we establish the claimed performance bounds. The following Theorem shows how $\hat{R}(h)$ varies as a function of $R(2^{\lfloor \lg(h-1) \rfloor})$, i.e. R at the previous branching point.

Theorem 2. *Let A_n denote a random matrix from the set $\mathcal{A}(n)$, and let $R(h)$ and $\hat{R}(h)$ be the functions defined as above. Then*

$$\hat{R}(h) = \begin{cases} 2 & \text{for } h = 1 \\ \frac{h+1}{2^{\lfloor \lg(h-1) \rfloor}+1} R(2^{\lfloor \lg(h-1) \rfloor}) & \text{for } h > 1 \end{cases}$$

Proof. The numerator of $\hat{R}(h)$ is

$$E_A[E_\sigma[\hat{X}_h^2]] = \sum_{m=0}^{h} E_A[E_\sigma[\hat{X}_h^2]|M_h = m] \Pr[M_h = m]$$

$$= \sum_{m=0}^{h} E_A[m^2 E_\sigma[(X_{h-1})^2]] \Pr[M_h = m]$$

$$= E_A[M_h^2] E_A[M_{h-1}^2] \dots E_A[M_{(2^{\lfloor \lg(h-1) \rfloor}+1)}^2] E_A[E_\sigma[(X_{2^{\lfloor \lg(h-1) \rfloor}})^2]]$$

where M_i denotes a binomial variable with parameters i and $p = \frac{1}{2}$ and thus $\sum_{m=0}^{h} m^2 \Pr[M_h = m]$ is equal to $E_A[M_h^2]$. The denominator of $\hat{R}(h)$ is

$$E_A[E_\sigma[\hat{X}_h]]^2 = E[\text{per}(A_h)]^2 = \left(\frac{h!}{2^h}\right)^2 = \prod_{i=1}^{h} E[M_i]^2$$

$$\hat{R}(h) = \frac{E[M_h^2]}{E[M_h]^2} \frac{E[M_{h-1}^2]}{E[M_{h-1}]^2} \cdots \frac{E[M_{(2^{\lfloor \lg(h-1) \rfloor}+1)}^2]}{E[M_{(2^{\lfloor \lg(h-1) \rfloor}+1)}]^2} \frac{E_A[E_\sigma[(X_{2^{\lfloor \lg(h-1) \rfloor}})^2]]}{E_A[E_\sigma[X_{2^{\lfloor \lg(h-1) \rfloor}}]]^2}$$

$$= \frac{4h(h+1)}{4h^2} \cdots \frac{4(2^{\lfloor \lg(h-1) \rfloor}+1)(2^{\lfloor \lg(h-1) \rfloor}+2)}{4(2^{\lfloor \lg(h-1) \rfloor}+1)^2} \frac{E_A[E_\sigma[(X_{2^{\lfloor \lg(h-1) \rfloor}})^2]]}{E_A[E_\sigma[X_{2^{\lfloor \lg(h-1) \rfloor}}]]^2}$$

$$= \frac{h+1}{2^{\lfloor \lg(h-1) \rfloor}+1} R(2^{\lfloor \lg(h-1) \rfloor}) \qquad \square$$

Before venturing into showing the dependence of $R(h)$ on $\hat{R}(h)$ we establish a few important lemmas. The following lemma estimates a bound of higher moment of the binomial distribution. A lot of similar results have appeared in literature (see [10] for more details).

Lemma 3. *For $n \geq 0$ we have*

$$\frac{1}{2^{n^2}} \sum_{j=0}^{n^2} \binom{n^2}{j} j^{2n} = O\left(\left(\frac{n^2}{2}\right)^{2n}\right)$$

Proof. The term $\binom{n^2}{j} j^{2n}$ has its maximum value around $j = \frac{n^2}{2} + n$. The idea is to split the summation into three parts around this point and to bound each part. □

In the following lemma we try to establish a relationship which is similar to the one established in Lemma 1. Note that Lemma 1 holds for the random graph model $G(n, m)$, but we are interested in the more commonly used $G(n, p)$ model.

Lemma 4. *Let A_n be a matrix from the set $\mathcal{A}(n)$. Then for some constant c independent of n*

$$\frac{\mathrm{E}[(\mathrm{per}(A_n))^2]}{\mathrm{E}[\mathrm{per}(A_n)]^2} \leq c$$

Proof. We can split the numerator by conditioning it on the number of 1's (M) in the matrix as

$$\Pr[M < \frac{n^2}{4}]\mathrm{E}[(\mathrm{per}(A_n))^2|M < \frac{n^2}{4}] + \Pr[M \geq \frac{n^2}{4}]\mathrm{E}[(\mathrm{per}(A_n))^2|M \geq \frac{n^2}{4}]$$

By Chernoff's Bound, we have $\Pr[M < \frac{n^2}{4}] < \exp(\frac{-n^2}{16})$. So for the numerator we have

$$\Pr[M < \frac{n^2}{4}] < \Pr[M \geq \frac{n^2}{4}] \text{ and } \mathrm{E}[(\mathrm{per}(A_n))^2|M < \frac{n^2}{4}] \leq \mathrm{E}[(\mathrm{per}(A_n))^2|M \geq \frac{n^2}{4}]$$

The second inequality follows as adding more 1's can't reduce the value of the permanent. This implies

$$\mathrm{E}[\mathrm{per}(A_n)^2] < 2\Pr[M \geq \frac{n^2}{4}]\mathrm{E}[(\mathrm{per}(A_n))^2|M \geq \frac{n^2}{4}]$$

$$\leq 2\mathrm{E}[(\mathrm{per}(A_n))^2|M \geq \frac{n^2}{4}] = 2 \sum_{j=\frac{n^2}{4}}^{n^2} \mathrm{E}[(\mathrm{per}(A_n))^2|M = j]\Pr[M = j]$$

Substituting for the probability of having j 1's and using Lemma 1 for the value of $\mathrm{E}[(\mathrm{per}(A_n))^2]$, we obtain

$$\frac{\mathrm{E}[(\mathrm{per}(A_n))^2]}{\mathrm{E}[\mathrm{per}(A_n)]^2} \leq \frac{(2^{2n+1})}{(n!)^2} \sum_{j=\frac{n^2}{4}}^{n^2} (n!)^2 (\frac{j}{n^2})^{2n} \underbrace{\exp\left(-\frac{n^2}{j} + 1 + O(\frac{n^3}{j^2})\right)}_{\leq c'} \binom{n^2}{j} \left(\frac{1}{2}\right)^{n^2}$$

$$< \frac{2^{2n+1}\exp(c')}{n^{4n}} \sum_{j=0}^{n^2} j^{2n} \binom{n^2}{j} 2^{-n^2}$$

However from Lemma 3, we know that $\sum_{j=0}^{n^2} j^{2n} \binom{n^2}{j} = O(\left(\frac{n^2}{2}\right)^{2n} 2^{n^2})$. Substituting this result we finish the proof of the Lemma 4.   □

We are now prepared to establish the dependence of $R(h)$ on $\hat{R}(h)$. As mentioned earlier $R(h)$ and $\hat{R}(h)$ vary only at the branching points.

Theorem 3. *Let $R(h)$ and $\hat{R}(h)$ be the functions defined as above. Then*

$$R(h) \leq \begin{cases} \frac{\hat{R}(h)}{K} + \frac{(K-1)c}{K} & \text{if } h \text{ is a branching point} \\ \hat{R}(h) & \text{otherwise} \end{cases}$$

where c is an upper bound on $\frac{E_A[\text{per}(A)^2]}{E_A[\text{per}(A)]^2}$.

Proof. At all levels other than the branching levels, we have $K = 1$ implying $R(h)=\hat{R}(h)$. However, at the branching levels we have:

$$R(h) = \frac{E_A[E_\sigma[X_h^2]]}{E_A[E_\sigma[X_h]]^2} = \frac{E_A[E_\sigma[(\frac{1}{K}\sum_{i=1}^{K}\hat{X}_h^{(i)})^2]]}{E_A[E_\sigma[\frac{1}{K}\sum_{i=1}^{K}\hat{X}_h^{(i)}]]^2}.$$

Furthermore since the outcomes of the successive trials $\hat{X}_h^{(i)}$ are independent and identically distributed

$$E_\sigma[(\frac{1}{K}\sum_{i=1}^{K}\hat{X}_h^{(i)})^2] = \frac{E_\sigma[\hat{X}_h^2] + (K-1)E_\sigma[\hat{X}_h]^2}{K}$$

$$R(h) = \frac{E_A[E_\sigma[\hat{X}_h^2]]}{KE_A[E_\sigma[\hat{X}_h]]^2} + \frac{(K-1)E_A[E_\sigma[\hat{X}_h]^2]}{KE_A[E_\sigma[\hat{X}_h]]^2} = \frac{\hat{R}(h)}{K} + \frac{(K-1)E_A(\text{per}(A_h)^2]}{KE_A[\text{per}(A_h)]^2}$$

Using Lemma 4 we complete the proof.   □

Substituting $K = 3$, we get $R(h) = \frac{\hat{R}(h)+2O(1)}{3}$ at the branching points. In the following two Theorems we show that both $R(h)$ and $\hat{R}(h)$ are bound by a constant implying that the critical ratio is $O(\omega)$ from Lemma 2.

Theorem 4. *Let $\hat{R}(h)$ and $R(h)$ be the functions defined as above. Then for all $h \leq n$ and for c from Theorem 3*

$$\hat{R}(h) \leq \frac{2c(h+1)}{2^{\lfloor\lg(h-1)\rfloor}+1} \quad \text{and} \quad R(h) \leq \begin{cases} 2c & h = \text{branching point} \\ \frac{2c(h+1)}{2^{\lfloor\lg(h-1)\rfloor}+1} & \text{otherwise} \end{cases}$$

Proof. We use induction over h. We know that $c \geq 1$. For $h = 1$, $\hat{R}(1) = 2 \leq 2c$ and $R(1) = 2 \leq 2c$. Assuming the statement is true for h, we prove it for $h + 1$. There are two cases:

Case 1: $h + 1$ is a branching point. From Theorem 2 we get

$$\hat{R}(h+1) = \frac{h+2}{2^{\lfloor\lg(h)\rfloor}+1} R(2^{\lfloor\lg(h)\rfloor}) \leq \frac{2c(h+2)}{2^{\lfloor\lg(h)\rfloor}+1}$$

(where $R(2^{\lfloor \lg(h) \rfloor}) \leq 2c$ is by induction hypothesis). From Theorem 3, we also get $R(h+1) \leq 2c$.

Case 2: $h+1$ is not a branching point.

$$\hat{R}(h+1) = R(2^{\lfloor \lg(h) \rfloor}) \frac{h+2}{2^{\lfloor \lg(h) \rfloor} + 1} = \frac{2c(h+2)}{2^{\lfloor \lg(h) \rfloor} + 1}$$

From Theorem 3, $R(h+1) = \hat{R}(h+1)$.   □

Theorem 5. *Let $\omega = \omega(n)$ be any function satisfying $\omega \to \infty$ as $n \to \infty$. Then for almost all (0-1) matrices A, we have,*

$$\frac{E_\sigma[X_A^2]}{E_\sigma[X_A]^2} = O(\omega)$$

Proof. The factor of $\frac{2h}{2^{\lfloor \lg(h-1) \rfloor + 1} + 1}$ is less than 2. Hence, both $R(h)$ and $\hat{R}(h)$ are $O(1)$ (Theorem 4). Using Lemma 2, we bound the critical factor by $O(\omega)$.   □

Each run of the estimator presented here can be performed using $O(n^2)$ operations, and the number of times we need to repeat the experiment to obtain an fpras is $O(\omega)$. Thus, we obtain a total running time of $O(n^2\omega)$ for almost all (0-1) matrices.

7   Arbitrary Probabilities

Till now we have been dealing with the interesting random graph model $G(n, \frac{1}{2})$. In this section we investigate the performance of the proposed estimator for the case $G(n,p)$ for arbitrary edge probability p. We propose three different choices of the branching point parameter s (Figure 4) to RAP depending on p. We always branch by a factor of 2 at powers of s (branching point) rounded up to the next integer. One can pretend the powers of s are integers because

1. With rounding up, one gets a result that is not worse (compared to rounding down).
2. The extra cost (of rounding up compared to rounding down) is negligible. It can trivially be bound by a factor of 2.

As before, together the complexity of performing the stochastic experiment, and the ratio of $\frac{E[X^2]}{E[X]^2}$ will determine the efficiency of the algorithm. Results are summarized in Figure 4.

Probability	B.P. Selector s	Single Run	Critical Ratio	Total Running Time
$p > \frac{1}{3}$	$\sqrt{2} < s < 2^{\frac{1}{(p^{-1}-1)}}$	$O(n^2)$	$O(\omega(n))$	$O(n^2\omega(n))$
$p = \frac{1}{3}$	$\sqrt{2}$	$O(n^2 \lg n)$	$O(\lg(n)\omega(n))$	$O(n^2 \lg^2(n)\omega(n))$
$p < \frac{1}{3}$	$2^{\frac{1}{(p^{-1}-1)}} < s < \sqrt{2}$	$O(n^{\frac{1}{\lg s}})$	$O(n^{\frac{1}{p}-1-\frac{1}{\lg s}}\omega(n))$	$O(n^{\frac{1}{p}-1}\omega(n))$

Fig. 4. Performance of the Estimator for different Probabilities

7.1   Probability p > $\frac{1}{3}$

Here, the major contribution to the complexity is from the work we do at the top of the computation tree, handling the first $n/2$ rows costs $O(n^2)$. In the remaining part, the time spent between two consecutive branching levels decrease as geometric series, giving us total running time of $O(n^2)$. Also as in Section 6, we can show that $R(n) = O(1)$.

7.2   Probability p = $\frac{1}{3}$

Here we do $O(n^2)$ work between any two branching points, since we have $O(\lg n)$ such branching levels, the complexity of a single run of the experiment is $O(n^2 \lg n)$.

Theorem 6. *Let $h = s^k$ and $h' = s^{k+1}$ be two consecutive branching points. Let 2 be the branching factor. Then*

$$R(h') = \frac{R(h)s^{(\frac{1}{p}-1)} + c}{2}$$

where c is the constant from Theorem 3

Proof. In this probability space where each entry is chosen to be 1 with probability p

$$\frac{E[M_h^2]}{E[M_h]^2} = \left(1 + \frac{1-p}{hp}\right)$$

Hence, between h and h' the ratio $\hat{R}$ grows by

$$\prod_{j=s^k+1}^{s^{k+1}} \left(1 + \frac{1-p}{jp}\right) = \exp\left(\ln \prod_{j=s^k+1}^{s^{k+1}} \left(1 + \frac{1-p}{jp}\right)\right) \le \exp\left(\sum_{j=s^k+1}^{s^{k+1}} \frac{1-p}{jp}\right)$$

$$\le \exp\left(\frac{1-p}{p} \int_{s^k}^{s^{k+1}} \frac{dx}{x}\right) = s^{(\frac{1}{p}-1)}$$

As in Theorem 2, we can show for this probability space $\hat{R}(h') = s^{(\frac{1}{p}-1)}R(h)$. By using these values in Theorem 3 we complete the proof.   □

From Theorem 6, we can see that for $p = 1/3$ the $R(h)$ increases by $\frac{c}{2}$ between two consecutive branching points. Since there are $O(\lg n)$ such branching points, $R(n) = O(\lg n)$.

7.3   Probability p < $\frac{1}{3}$

Here the major contribution to the complexity of the experiment is from the work we do at the leaves which is of order $O(2^{\frac{\lg n}{\lg s}}) = O(n^{\frac{1}{\lg s}})$. Again by application of Theorem 6, we can show $R(n)$ is $O\left(n^{\frac{1}{p}-1-\lg s}\right)$.

8   Permanent of Matrices with Arbitrary Entries

Let $S = \{e_1, e_2, \ldots, e_n\}$ be a large set, with element e_i having weight w_i. One could again use the idea (Figure 5) of randomized selection to obtain an estimate of the weight $W = \sum_{i=1}^{n} w_i$ of S. The estimator can easily be shown to be unbiased. This idea can be used to extend our algorithm to deal with an arbitrary matrix A with non-negative entries. When working with some row r containing some vector v of entries. Choose entry a_{rj} with probability $p_v(j)$ and output $a_{rj}/p_v(j)$, where one reasonable choice of probabilities is $p_v(j) = (\sum_i a_{ri})^{-1} a_{rj}$

Algorithm to Estimate the Weight W **of** S: Assume $\sum_{i=1}^{n} p_i \leq 1$
Let $q_i = \sum_{j=1}^{i} p_j$
Select y uniformly at random from $[0, 1)$. If $q_{i-1} \leq y < q_i$ then pick e_i and output $X = \frac{w_i}{p_i}$, else $(q_n \leq y < 1)$ don't pick anything and output $X = 0$.

Fig. 5. Estimator of the weight of S

9   Estimating the Size of Tree

One of the chief difficulties involved with the backtracking technique for combinatorial problems has been the inability to predict efficiency of the algorithm. Knuth [9] was the first to present a reasonable estimator for this problem and it was later enhanced by Purdom [12]. Knuth's idea is to estimate the size of a backtrack tree by repeatedly following random paths from the root. We could also apply our method to construct an unbiased estimator for determining the size of backtrack trees.

We conjecture that for certain classes of trees our estimator performs better than Knuth's estimator. One example where we perform better is a random tree model where for every node at depth d we toss $h - d$ coins to generate at most $h - d$ children. This results in height bounded random tree with degree of nodes strictly decreasing as we go down. One could easily see that such a restricted random tree model is essentially what we encounter with permanents, and in previous sections we have shown that our estimator outperforms Knuth's estimator (Knuth's estimator works similar to Rasmussen's estimator).

10   Concluding Remarks

We have presented a very simple, randomized algorithm for approximating the permanent. We have also shown that for almost all matrices the estimator runs in time almost linear in the number of entries. This is the fastest known algorithm for approximating permanents of random (0-1) matrices. To do better than $O(n^2)$, one could think of an estimator that inspects only a fraction of elements in a given row. Indeed, such unbiased estimators can easily be constructed by estimating the number of ones in a row by sampling. However, on the flip side, such a sublinear estimator may have a much higher variance.

We envisage such a scheme to be part of larger general framework which can be used to solve similar combinatorial problems. We already know that a similar schema gives a good algorithm for finding a Min-Cut [15]. Also in the mean time the same schema has been successfully extended to count matchings in general graphs by the authors.

Acknowledgements

The authors would like to thank the referees for pointing out similarity of our method with [15] and for providing valuable comments on the results.

References

1. B. Bollobás. *Random Graphs.* Academic Press, London, England, 1985.
2. S. Chien, L. Rasmussen, and A. Sinclair. Clifford algebras and approximating the permanent. *Proceedings of the 34th ACM Symposium on Theory of Computing*, pages 222–231, 2002.
3. A. Frieze and M. Jerrum. An analysis of a Monte-Carlo algorithm for approximating the permanent. *Combinatorica*, pages 67–83, 1995.
4. C. Godsil and I. Gutman. On the matching polynomial of a graph. *Algebraic Methods in Graph Theory*, pages 241–249, 1981.
5. M. Jerrum and A. Sinclair. Approximating the permanent. *SIAM Journal of Computing*, 18:1149–1178, 1989.
6. M. Jerrum, A. Sinclair, and E. Vigoda. A polynomial time approximation algorithm for the permanent of a matrix with non-negative entries. *Journal of the ACM*, 51(4), 2004.
7. M. Jerrum, L. Valiant, and V. Vazirani. Random generation of combinatorial structures from a uniform distribution. *Theoretical Computer Science*, 43:169–188, 1986.
8. N. Karmarkar, R. Karp, R. Lipton, L. Lovsáz, and M. Luby. A Monte-Carlo algorithm for estimating the permanent. *SIAM Journal of Computing*, 22:284–293, 1993.
9. D. E. Knuth. Estimating the efficiency of backtrack programs. *Mathematics of Computation*, 29:121–136, 1974.
10. V. D. la Pena and E. Giné. *Decoupling, from Dependence to Independence.* Springer Verlag, New York, 1999.
11. H. Minc. *Permanents, Encyclopedia of Mathematics and its Applications.* Addison-Wesley Publishing Company, 1982.
12. P. W. Purdom. Tree size by partial backtracking. *SIAM Journal on Computing*, 7(4):481–491, 1978.
13. L. Rasmussen. Approximating the permanent:A simple approach. *Random Structures and Algorithms*, 5:349–361, 1994.
14. H. Ryser. *Combinatorial Mathematics, The Carus Mathematical Monographs.* The Mathematical Association of America, Washington DC, 1963.
15. C. Stein and D. R. Karger. A new approach to the minimum cut problem. *Journal of the ACM*, 43(4):601–640, 1996.
16. L. Valiant. The complexity of computing the permanent. *Theoretical Computer Science*, 8:189–201, 1979.

Distributed Games with Causal Memory Are Decidable for Series-Parallel Systems*

Paul Gastin, Benjamin Lerman, and Marc Zeitoun

LIAFA, Université Paris 7 & CNRS,
2, pl. Jussieu, case 7014, F-75251 Paris cedex 05, France
{Paul.Gastin, Benjamin.Lerman, Marc.Zeitoun}@liafa.jussieu.fr

Abstract. This paper deals with distributed control problems by means of distributed games played on Mazurkiewicz traces. The main difference with other notions of distributed games recently introduced is that, instead of having a *local* view, strategies and controllers are able to use a more accurate memory, based on their *causal* view. Our main result states that using the causal view makes the control synthesis problem decidable for series-parallel systems for *all* recognizable winning conditions on finite behaviors, while this problem with local view was proved undecidable even for reachability conditions.

1   Introduction

This paper addresses a distributed control problem. We are given a *distributed open system* interacting with its environment. While actions of the environment cannot be controlled, actions performed by the system are controllable. We are also given a *specification* and the problem is to find, for each local process, a finite-state *local* controller such that synchronizing each local process with its local controller makes an overall system satisfying the specification.

Sequential versions of control problems have been studied for a long time [2, 16, 14] and have usually decidable answers. What makes the *distributed* control problem more difficult is that a given process and its associated local controller only have a partial view of what happened so far. For instance, a controller cannot take a decision depending on what occurred on a concurrent process, unless such information is forwarded to it (via another process or via the environment).

The problem can be modeled by a game with incomplete information. Each process is a player of the controller team and the environment is the other team. Finding a distributed controller is then equivalent to computing a distributed winning strategy for the controller team. The general situation for multiplayer games with incomplete information is undecidable [13, 12] and in this light, it is not really surprising that the distributed control problem is undecidable even for simple specifications [15, 7, 8, 10]. The aim of the present paper is to open

---

* Work partly supported by the European research project HPRN-CT-2002-00283 GAMES and by the ACI Sécurité Informatique 2003-22 (VERSYDIS).

K. Lodaya and M. Mahajan (Eds.): FSTTCS 2004, LNCS 3328, pp. 275–286, 2004.

a breach in the list of undecidable results for distributed systems. Obtaining efficient and broadly applicable algorithms is a long term issue, out of the scope of the paper.

We believe that there are two main reasons for undecidability results obtained in previous works and that they are both related to the fact that interleavings were used to model distributed behaviors. First, specifications were often given as regular conditions on *linearizations* and were not necessarily closed under commutations of independent actions. This is a well-known cause of undecidability, already addressed in [10]. The second reason has to do with the memory that local controllers are allowed to use. This memory is an abstraction of the part of the behavior that the controller is able to see. Previous works used a *local view*: a process can only see its own previous actions. However, the distributed control problem remains undecidable using this local view even when specification are both regular and closed under commutations [10]. For distributed games defined in [11], even reachability specifications are undecidable [1].

In our work, the local memory is based on the *causal view* of a process (a notion which already yielded positive decidability results for branching-time specifications [9]). This causal view is more accurate than the local one and includes all actions that are *causally* in the past of the current local action. Importantly, this causal memory can be implemented for reasonable communication architectures by forwarding additional informations along with usual messages. The main contribution of this paper is that, if we use causal memory, the distributed control problem becomes decidable for series-parallel systems and for *controlled reachability* conditions, encompassing specifications such as recognizability on finite behaviors, and reachability and safety conditions (on finite or infinite behaviors). Further, one can effectively compute a distributed controller when it exists. This result contrasts deeply with previous work since the problem is undecidable with local memory. Our proof is based on a structural induction that is possible for series-parallel systems.

The causal view was also considered in [6]. It was shown that distributed games with causal memory are undecidable for rational winning conditions on linearizations even for cograph dependence alphabets. This explains why we consider only recognizable winning conditions in this paper.

The distributed control problem remains open for classical conditions on infinite traces such as Büchi, liveness, parity conditions, . . . We conjecture that these problems are still decidable. Another important issue is to exhibit a more direct construction of the winning strategies. Finally, the distributed control problem is still open, even for finite behaviors, on non-cograph alphabets.

Due to lack of space, most proofs had to be omitted.

2   Definitions and Notation

Mazurkiewicz Traces. We briefly recall definitions for our models of distributed behaviors, see [4] for details.

If $(V, \leq)$ is a poset and $S \subseteq V$, the past of S is $\downarrow S = \{x \in V \mid \exists s \in S, x \leq s\}$. If $x \in V$, we write $\downarrow x$ for $\downarrow\{x\}$ and we let $\Downarrow x = \downarrow x \setminus \{x\}$ be the strict past of x. The successor relation associated with the partial order $<$ is $\lessdot = < \setminus <^2$.

A *dependence alphabet* is a pair (Σ, D) where Σ is a finite alphabet and D is a reflexive, symmetric binary relation over Σ, called the *dependence relation*. For $A \subseteq \Sigma$, we let $D(A)$ be the set of letters that depend on some letters in A.

A *(Mazurkiewicz) trace* over (Σ, D) is an isomorphism class $[V, \leq, \ell]$ of a pomset such that for all $x, y \in V$: (1) $\ell(x) D \ell(y) \Rightarrow x \leq y$ or $y \leq x$, (2) $x \lessdot y \Rightarrow \ell(x) D \ell(y)$ and (3) $\downarrow x$ is finite. We denote by $\mathbb{R}(\Sigma, D)$ (resp. by $\mathbb{M}(\Sigma, D)$) the set of traces (resp. of finite traces) over (Σ, D).

If $t = [V, \leq, \ell]$ is a trace, we denote by $\max(t)$ (resp. by $\min(t)$) the set of maximal (resp. minimal) elements of t. The *alphabet* of t is $\mathrm{alph}(t) = \ell(V)$. A *prefix* of t is a trace $s = [U, \leq, \ell]$, where $U \subseteq V$ satisfies $\downarrow U = U$. We write $s \leq t$ if s is a prefix of t. In this case, we let $s^{-1}t = [V \setminus U, \leq, \ell]$. The empty trace is denoted by ε.

Distributed Games. The distributed systems we want to control are based on asynchronous automata [18]. We are given a finite set of processes communicating asynchronously via shared memory variables. Each process stores a value in a register. When executing, an action reads registers of some processes, and then writes some other registers through a test-and-set instruction. Some actions are controllable. The other ones, representing the environment's actions, are uncontrollable.

We model these systems by distributed games [6] over a given *architecture* $(\Sigma, \mathcal{P}, R, W)$. Here, $\mathcal{P}$ is a finite set of *processes*, $\Sigma = \Sigma_0 \uplus \Sigma_1$ is a finite set of *players* (or *actions*), where Σ_0 is the set of players of team 0 (the controller) and Σ_1 the set of players of team 1 (the environment). Player $a \in \Sigma$ can atomically read states of processes in $R(a) \subseteq \mathcal{P}$ and write new states on processes in $W(a) \subseteq \mathcal{P}$. We require two natural restrictions also considered in [18].

$$
\begin{aligned}
\forall a \in \Sigma, \quad & \emptyset \neq W(a) \subseteq R(a) \\
\forall a, b \in \Sigma, \quad & R(a) \cap W(b) = \emptyset \iff R(b) \cap W(a) = \emptyset
\end{aligned}
\tag{$\mathcal{S}$}
$$

These conditions encompass in particular all purely asynchronous architectures (*i.e.*, such that $R = W$) and all cellular architectures (*i.e.*, such that $|W(a)| = 1$ for all $a \in \Sigma$). In contrast, we do not treat here "one way" communication architectures, as the one depicted opposite, where circles represent processes read by the corresponding player, and squares represent processes which are both read and written. That is, $R(a) = \{q_1, q_2\}$, $W(a) = \{q_2\}$, $R(b) = \{q_2, q_3\}$, $W(b) = \{q_3\}$, which obviously violates $(\mathcal{S})$.

A *distributed game* over the architecture $(\Sigma, \mathcal{P}, R, W)$ is given by a tuple $G = (\Sigma_0, \Sigma_1, (Q_i)_{i\in\mathcal{P}}, (T_a)_{a\in\Sigma}, q^0, \mathcal{W})$, where Q_i is the set of local states (register values) of process i. Given $I \subseteq \mathcal{P}$, we let $Q_I = \prod_{i\in I} Q_i$, and if $q = (q_i)_{i\in\mathcal{P}} \in Q_{\mathcal{P}}$, we let $q_I = (q_i)_{i\in I}$. A global state of the game is then a tuple $q \in Q_{\mathcal{P}}$. Player a has a table of legal moves $T_a \subseteq Q_{R(a)} \times Q_{W(a)}$. A (sequential) play is a sequence of moves starting in the global state $q^0 \in Q_{\mathcal{P}}$, the *initial position of the game*. There is an a-move from $p \in Q_{\mathcal{P}}$ to $q \in Q_{\mathcal{P}}$ if $(p_{R(a)}, q_{W(a)}) \in T_a$ and $q_{\mathcal{P}\setminus W(a)} = p_{\mathcal{P}\setminus W(a)}$. The winning condition $\mathcal{W}$ describes a set of desired plays and will be discussed later on.

Note that, if $R(a) \cap W(b) = \emptyset = R(b) \cap W(a)$ then in any global state p the two moves a and b can be executed simultaneously or in any order without affecting the resulting global state q: they are *independent*. Therefore, a (distributed) play of a distributed game is more accurately defined by an equivalence class of sequential plays, or equivalently, by a Mazurkiewicz trace over a suitable dependence alphabet.

Distributed plays will be defined as traces with doubly labeled vertices: the first label is the player's name, and the second one is a vector of local states representing what was written by the player. Formally, we consider a new symbol $\# \notin \Sigma$, with $R(\#) = W(\#) = \mathcal{P}$. Let then $\Sigma' = \{(a, p) \mid a \in \Sigma \uplus \{\#\}$ and $p \in Q_{W(a)}\}$. We define the dependence relation D over $\Sigma \uplus \{\#\}$ by $a \, D \, b \Leftrightarrow R(a) \cap W(b) \neq \emptyset \Leftrightarrow R(b) \cap W(a) \neq \emptyset$ and D' over Σ' by $(a, p) \, D' \, (b, q) \Leftrightarrow a \, D \, b$. We write a trace of $\mathbb{R}(\Sigma', D')$ as $[V, \leq, \ell, \sigma]$, where $\ell : V \to \Sigma \uplus \{\#\}$ and $\sigma : V \to \bigcup_{a \in \Sigma \uplus \{\perp\}} Q_{W(a)}$ together define the labeling: a vertex x is labeled by $(\ell(x), \sigma(x))$. A trace $t = [V, \leq, \ell, \sigma] \in \mathbb{R}(\Sigma', D')$ is *rooted* if $\ell^{-1}(\#) = \{x_\#\}$ is a singleton and $x_\# \leq y$ for all $y \in V$. The global state reached on a finite rooted trace $t \in \mathbb{M}(\Sigma', D')$ is $\bar{q}(t) = (\bar{q}_i(t))_{i \in \mathcal{P}} \in Q_{\mathcal{P}}$ where:

$$\bar{q}_i(t) = (\sigma(y))_i \text{ with } y = \max\{x \in V \mid i \in W(\ell(x))\}.$$

In other words, we retain the last write action performed on each process.

A (distributed) *play* is a rooted trace $t = [V, \leq, \ell, \sigma] \in \mathbb{R}(\Sigma', D')$ which obeys the rules given by $(T_a)_{a \in \Sigma}$, i.e., $\sigma(x_\#) = q^0$ and

$$\forall x \in V, \quad \ell(x) = a \neq \# \implies (\bar{q}(\Downarrow x)_{R(a)}, \sigma(x)) \in T_a$$

Note that after the beginning of a play, several moves may be enabled, concurrently or not, from Σ_0 or from Σ_1. Thus, we do not see a distributed play as turn-based. The winning condition $\mathcal{W}$ can then formally be defined as a subset of $\mathbb{R}(\Sigma', D')$. Team 0 wins the play t if $t \in \mathcal{W}$.

Example. Romeo and Juliet are in two separate houses and they want to set up an appointment. There are four communication lines of which exactly one is broken. At any time, Romeo (or Juliet) may look at the status of the communication lines to see which one is broken and then chooses to connect to one line (the whole operation is atomic). The environment tries to prevent the communication. For this, at any time, it might look at which line Romeo and Juliet are connected, and then decide to change the broken line (again this operation is atomic). The actions of Romeo and Juliet are independent but they both depend on the action of the environment. The

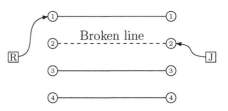

$$Q_1 \quad Q_2 \quad Q_3$$

Fig. 1. A simple cograph architecture

problem is to find two strategies, one for Romeo and one for Juliet, so that they
end up communicating whatever the environment does. If there is no restriction
on the environment then it might monopolize the system by constantly changing the broken line, thus preventing any action by Romeo or Juliet due to the
dependence of actions. Therefore we restrict the environment so that it cannot
act twice consecutively.

We formalize this system using three processes with states $Q_1 = Q_2 = Q_3 =$
$\{1, 2, 3, 4\} \times \{0, 1\}$ and three players r, e, j whose read and write domains are
depicted in Figure 1, where circles represent processes read by the corresponding
player, and squares represent processes which are both read and written. State
$(1, 0)$ for process 1 means that Romeo is connected to the first line and has played
an even number of times. The situation is similar for process 3 and Juliet. State
$(2, 1)$ for process 2 means that line number 2 is broken and the environment
has played an odd number of times. The environment is allowed to play only if
the total number of moves is odd. A process based picture and a Hasse diagram
representation of a distributed play are given below. Between moves (whose reads
are • and read-writes are ■), we draw local states which get modified by the test-
and-set legal moves. For instance, the first e reads (3,1), (1,0), (4,0) on processes
1, 2 and 3 and writes (3,1) on process 2. The global state reached at the end is
(1,0), (4,0), (1,1) which is winning for Romeo and Juliet. The interested reader
might check that Romeo and Juliet have memoryless strategies to win this game.

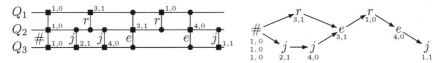

Strategies and Memory. Intuitively, player a of team 0 can restrict its set of
potential moves depending on its own history of the play. In the distributed
setting, it would not make sense to define this history on *sequential* plays. Indeed,
the strategy of player a should not depend on the ordering of independent moves
that are in its past and it should not depend either on concurrent moves that
happen to occur before it in some linearization.

A first solution is to define the history of some move a as the sequence of
moves that have written on process $W(a)$ (assuming $W(a)$ is a singleton). This
is the minimal reasonable amount of information we want to provide to players.
This defines strategies with *local memory* [11, 8, 10]. Unfortunately, even games
with reachability conditions on the simple architecture given in Figure 1 are
undecidable with the local view [1].

The representation of plays by traces provides another natural solution. In order to choose which move to take, player a may look at all the causal past (in the partial order) of the last write-events on the processes in $R(a)$. This is intuitively the *maximal* amount of information we can provide to players. This is technically a bit more complicated since this memory information has to be computed in a distributed way via states. The idea is that any player a can compute, in addition to the values $q_{W(a)}$, a memory value that he also writes in all locations of $W(a)$.

Let $t = [V, \leq, \ell, \sigma] \in \mathbb{R}(\Sigma', D')$ be a rooted trace. For $A \subseteq \Sigma$, the trace $\partial_A t$ is the smallest prefix of t containing all vertices labeled in A under ℓ. For $I \subseteq \mathcal{P}$, the trace $\partial_I t$ is the smallest prefix of t containing all vertices x such that $W(\ell(x)) \cap I \neq \emptyset$.

An asynchronous mapping [3] is a function $\mu : \mathbb{M}(\Sigma', D') \to M$ such that $\mu(\partial_{A \cup B} t)$ only depends on $\mu(\partial_A t)$ and $\mu(\partial_B t)$, and $\mu(\partial_{D(a)} t.a)$ only depends on $\mu(\partial_{D(a)} t)$ and a. Asynchronous mappings can be computed in a distributed way [3]. A *distributed memory* is a computable abstraction of an asynchronous mapping. Formally, $\mu : \mathbb{M}(\Sigma', D') \to M$ is a *distributed memory* if there is a computable asynchronous mapping $\nu : \mathbb{M}(\Sigma', D') \to N$ and a computable function $\pi : N \to M$ such that $\pi \circ \nu = \mu$. The function μ is the information actually needed for a strategy, and the asynchronous mapping ν represents an asynchronous implementation of this memory. Property $(\mathcal{S})$ makes it possible to *implement* causal memory. Indeed, if $x \lessdot y$ in a trace, then by definition $\ell(x) D \ell(y)$ and therefore, by $(\mathcal{S})$, there is at least one process where x writes and y reads. Hence, information computed by player $\ell(x)$ can be forwarded to player $\ell(y)$. Observe that the environment's team participates to the computation of the causal view. This is not unrealistic: one cannot know when an environment's action will occur, but some systems may be designed so that events of the environment forward the necessary information to compute the needed abstraction of the causal view.

Intuitively, a given memory will be used by players of team 0 as an abstraction (computed in M) of their past in a play. (This is why we call these memories *causal*.) For instance, $\mu(t) = t$ is the largest possible memory and would provide for each player a full view of its past.

The distributed memory $\mu : \mathbb{M}(\Sigma', D') \to M$ is said to be *finite* if it is realized by a finite asynchronous mapping $\nu : \mathbb{M}(\Sigma', D') \to N$. In this case, its *size* is defined as the number of elements of a minimal such N.

A *distributed strategy with memory* $\mu : \mathbb{M}(\Sigma', D') \to M$ for team 0 is a function $f : \bigcup_{a \in \Sigma_0} Q_{R(a)} \times M \times \{a\} \to Q_{W(a)} \cup \{\text{stop}\}$ such that if $f(p, m, a) = q \neq \text{stop}$, then $(p, q) \in T_a$. Intuitively, if $f(p, m, a) = q \neq \text{stop}$, then the strategy f dictates an a-move to $q \in Q_{W(a)}$ on any distributed play $t \in \mathbb{R}(\Sigma', D')$ such that $\partial_{R(a)} t$ is finite, $p = \overline{q}(\partial_{R(a)} t)_{R(a)}$ and $m = \mu(\partial_{R(a)} t)$. If $f(p, m, a) = \text{stop}$, the a-move is disabled by the strategy. Note that several players of team 0 may be simultaneously enabled by f during a play. A distributed play $t = [V, \leq, \ell, \sigma] \in \mathbb{R}(\Sigma', D')$ is an f-*play* if for all $x \in V$ with $\ell(x) \in \Sigma_0$, we have $\sigma(x) = f(\overline{q}(\Downarrow x)_{R(a)}, \mu(\Downarrow x), a)$.

A play t is f-*maximal* if $f(\overline{q}(\partial_{R(a)}t)_{R(a)}, \mu(\partial_{R(a)}t), a) = \text{stop}$ for all $a \in \Sigma_0$ such that $\partial_{R(a)}t$ is finite. The *maximality* condition is natural: if the distributed strategy of team 0 dictates some a-moves at some f-play t, then the f-play t is not over. This applies also if t is infinite and corresponds to some fairness condition: along an infinite f-play, a move of team 0 cannot be ultimately continuously enabled by f without being taken. Note that any f-play t is the prefix of some f-maximal f-play. If each f-maximal f-play is in $\mathcal{W}$ then f is a *winning distributed strategy* (WDS) for team 0.

3   Controlled Reachability Games

In this section, we introduce controlled reachability games and we prove their decidability on cograph dependence alphabets.

Define the set of global states seen along a rooted (possibly infinite) trace t as

$$\overline{P}(t) = \{\overline{q}(s) \mid s \text{ finite and } \varepsilon < s < t\}$$

Observe that $\overline{q}(t)$ is not necessarily in the set $\overline{P}(t)$.

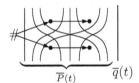

$$\underbrace{\hspace{4cm}}_{\overline{P}(t)} \quad \overline{q}(t)$$

Define $(\overline{P}, \overline{q})(t) = (\overline{P}(t), \overline{q}(t))$ with $\overline{q}(t) = \infty$ if t is infinite.

Let $G = (\Sigma_0, \Sigma_1, (Q_i)_{i \in \mathcal{P}}, (T_a)_{a \in \Sigma}, q^0, \mathcal{W})$ be a distributed game. Say that G is a *controlled reachability game* if there is a set $\mathcal{F} \subseteq 2^{Q_\mathcal{P}} \times (Q_\mathcal{P} \uplus \{\infty\})$ such that a play t is winning for team 0 iff $(\overline{P}, \overline{q})(t) \in \mathcal{F}$. One will then write $G = (\Sigma_0, \Sigma_1, (Q_i)_{i \in \mathcal{P}}, (T_a)_{a \in \Sigma}, q^0, \mathcal{F})$. Note that we get classical reachability or safety conditions as special cases of controlled reachability conditions.

An undirected graph is a *cograph* if it belongs to the smallest class of graphs containing singletons and closed under parallel product and complementation. Therefore, if (A, D_A) and (B, D_B) are cographs with $A \cap B = \emptyset$, then so are $(A \cup B, D_A \cup D_B)$ and $(A \cup B, D_A \cup D_B \cup A \times B \cup B \times A)$ and vice versa, every cograph can be decomposed using these two operations. All Mazurkiewicz traces on a cograph alphabet are *series-parallel*, that is, they can be described by an expression using only single-vertex traces, and parallel and sequential product of directed graphs. It is well-known that cographs are undirected graphs with no P_4, i.e., no induced subgraph of the form $a - b - c - d$. We can now state the main result of the paper.

Theorem 1. *Given a controlled reachability game on a cograph alphabet, one can decide if team 0 has a WDS on this game. One can effectively compute such a strategy if it exists.*

We would like to stress that this theorem might be applied to more general settings than series-parallel systems by adding dependencies (communication channels) and thus turning an arbitrary dependence alphabet into a cograph.

Any recognizable winning condition on finite traces can be reduced to a (controlled) reachability condition by building a product of the game with an asynchronous automaton on the same architecture for this recognizable winning condition.

Corollary 1. *Given a distributed game on a cograph alphabet, with a recognizable set of finite traces as winning condition, one can decide if team 0 has a WDS on this game. One can effectively compute such a strategy if it exists.*

To prove Theorem 1, we will build from an arbitrary WDS f with memory μ another WDS f' whose memory is bounded by an effectively computable function depending only on $|\Sigma|$ and $|Q_\mathcal{P}|$. By [6], given a distributed memory μ, one can then effectively transform a distributed game G into a new game G^μ such that team 0 has a winning distributed strategy with memory μ in G iff it has a memoryless strategy in G^μ, which is decidable, again by [6].

We build f' from f by induction on the cograph alphabet. For technical reasons, one proves in the induction the following additional property on f'.

Definition 1. *Let f, f' be two distributed strategies. Then f' is f-compatible if for all finite f'-play t', there exists an f-play t such that $(\overline{P}, \overline{q})(t) = (\overline{P}, \overline{q})(t')$.*

Obviously, the compatibility relation is transitive. The following result we shall prove is more accurate than Theorem 1.

Theorem 2. *Let G be a controlled reachability game. There exists a computable function $M : \mathbb{N}^2 \to \mathbb{N}$, such that, for any WDS f over G, there exists a WDS f' which is f-compatible and whose memory is bounded by $M(|\Sigma|, |Q_\mathcal{P}|)$.*

We start with an intuitive sketch of the proof of Theorem 2. We build the f-compatible WDS f' using strategies obtained by induction over smaller alphabets. The parallel case is easy: the game defines two subgames, one on each alphabet of the parallel product, and f induces WDS's on these subgames. The induction provides compatible WDS's with bounded memory, which we recombine into a new strategy on the parallel product.

The sequential case is more complex. To simplify notation, we write $\max(r) \subseteq A$ instead of $\ell(\max(r)) \subseteq A$ and we use similar a notation for min. We also write $\mathrm{alph}(t)$ instead of $\ell(t)$. On $\Sigma = A \uplus B$, where $A \times B \subseteq D$ (with A, B cographs), f-plays have the form $(\#, q^0)s_1 s_2 \cdots$ where $\mathrm{alph}(s_i) \subseteq A$ iff $\mathrm{alph}(s_{i+1}) \subseteq B$. Each block s_i can be seen as a play $(\#, q^{i-1})s_i$ over A or B where $q^i = \overline{q}((\#, q^0)s_1 \cdots s_i)$. From f, one derives restricted strategies over A or B to go from q^{i-1} to q^i, visiting the same set of states. We then replace, using the induction, these restricted strategies by strategies with bounded memory. This is where controlled reachability is used: the induction hypothesis ensures that states visited by the new strategies are the same as for original strategies. We need this information to ensure we won't reach new states from which team 1 could escape in the other alphabet. By simplifying the strategy f (removing unwanted loops from all f-plays), this makes it possible to recombine the strategies over the smaller alphabets to obtain the desired strategy f'. We also have to prove that players of team 0 can detect with a distributed memory if they are minimal in some block s_i, to know which restricted strategy they have to play. The rest of this section is devoted to the formal proof of Theorem 2.

Induction Basis: $|\Sigma| = 1$
In this case, G is a 1-player sequential game. If we do not insist on getting an f-compatible strategy for f' it would be enough to observe that the winning condition is recognizable (alphabetic condition on states seen along the play and reachability on the possible last state) and computable by an automaton of size $2^{|Q_\mathcal{P}|}$. The existence of a winning strategy is therefore equivalent to the existence of a winning strategy with memory less than $2^{|Q_\mathcal{P}|}$. However, the strategy f' we have to build must be f-compatible, and we cannot use directly this result. For our proof, we distinguishes two cases.

1. $\Sigma = \{a\} = \Sigma_1$. Then, the set of plays does not depend on the strategy of team 0, since team 0 has no choice. Hence, if team 0 has a winning strategy, this winning strategy is memoryless.
2. $\Sigma = \{a\} = \Sigma_0$. Then, if player a has a winning strategy f, there exists a unique f-maximal f-play r and this play is winning. It is possible to show that one can build from r a new play t satisfying the following three conditions:

$$\forall s, s' \leq t, \quad (\overline{P}, \overline{q})(s) = (\overline{P}, \overline{q})(s') \Rightarrow s^{-1}t = s'^{-1}t \tag{1}$$

$$(\overline{P}, \overline{q})(t) = (\overline{P}, \overline{q})(r) \tag{2}$$

$$\forall t' \leq t, \exists r' \leq r, \quad (\overline{P}, \overline{q})(t') = (\overline{P}, \overline{q})(r') \tag{3}$$

Observe that property (1) guarantees that t is played according to a strategy f' with memory $\mu : s \rightarrow (\overline{P}, \overline{q})(s)$ which is indeed distributed since Σ is a singleton. Property (2) ensures that f' is winning, while (3) implies that f' is f-compatible. It follows that $M(1, |Q_\mathcal{P}|) \leq |Q_\mathcal{P}| \cdot 2^{|Q_\mathcal{P}|}$.

Induction, First Case: $\Sigma = A \uplus B$ with $(A \times B) \cap D = \emptyset$
Without loss of generality, we may assume that $\mathcal{P} = R(A) \cup R(B)$ and that $R(A) \cap R(B) = \emptyset$. Indeed, since $R(A) \cap W(B) = R(B) \cap W(A) = \emptyset$, we have $i \notin W(A) \cup W(B)$ if $i \in R(A) \cap R(B)$. In other terms, such a component i remains constant along a run, and does not play any role during the moves.

Abusing notation we write q_A instead of $q_{R(A)}$ for $q \in Q_\mathcal{P}$. Let $q_A \in Q_{R(A)}$ and $q_B \in Q_{R(B)}$. One defines $q = q_A \| q_B$ by $q_i = (q_A)_i$ if $i \in R(A)$ and $q_i = (q_B)_i$ if $i \in R(B)$. Further, $\infty \| q_B = q_A \| \infty = \infty \| \infty = \infty$. One extends this definition to pairs of $2^{Q_\mathcal{P}} \times (Q_\mathcal{P} \uplus \{\infty\})$ by

$$(P, q) \| (P', q') = \big((((P \cup \{q\} \setminus \{\infty\}) \| P') \cup (P \| (P' \cup \{q'\} \setminus \{\infty\}))), q \| q'\big).$$

Let $A' = \{(a, p) \in \Sigma' \mid a \in A\} \cup (\{\#\} \times Q_{R(A)})$, and B' be defined similarly. Let $r_A = (\#, q_A^0) \cdot s_A$ be a rooted trace over A' and $r_B = (\#, q_B^0) \cdot s_B$ a rooted trace over B'. Define $r_A \| r_B = (\#, q_A^0 \| q_B^0) \cdot s_A \cdot s_B = (\#, q_A^0 \| q_B^0) \cdot s_B \cdot s_A$.

Lemma 1. *Let r_A and r_B be two rooted traces on the alphabets A' and B' respectively. Then $(\overline{P}, \overline{q})(r_A \| r_B) = (\overline{P}, \overline{q})(r_A) \| (\overline{P}, \overline{q})(r_B)$.*

A rooted trace t over Σ' can be uniquely factorized as $t = t_A \parallel t_B$ where t_A and t_B are rooted traces over alphabets A' and B' respectively.

If $r = r_A \parallel r_B$ and $s = s_A \parallel s_B$ are f-plays on G then $r_A \parallel s_B$ is again an f-play of G. Indeed, since $A \times B \cap D = \emptyset$, the strict past of a vertex of $r_A \parallel s_B$ is either $(\#, q^0)$, or the same as that of the corresponding vertex in r or in s (depending on whether $\ell(x) \in A$ or $\ell(x) \in B$). If r and s are f-maximal, then $r_A \parallel s_B$ is also f-maximal since, if $c \in A$ for instance, $\partial_{R(c)}(r_A \parallel s_B) = \partial_{R(c)}(r_A \parallel (\#, q_B^0)) = \partial_{R(c)}(r)$.

The set S of f-maximal f-plays is therefore of the form $S = S_A \parallel S_B$. Let $\mathcal{F}_A = (\overline{P}, \overline{q})(S_A)$ and $\mathcal{F}_B = (\overline{P}, \overline{q})(S_B)$. Let us show that $\mathcal{F}_A \parallel \mathcal{F}_B \subseteq \mathcal{F}$. Let $r_A \in S_A$ and $s_B \in S_B$. By definition, there exists r_B and s_A such that $r = r_A \parallel r_B \in S$ and $s = s_A \parallel s_B \in S$. We have seen that this implies $t = r_A \parallel s_B \in S$. Using Lemma 1, one gets $(\overline{P}, \overline{q})(r_A) \parallel (\overline{P}, \overline{q})(s_B) = (\overline{P}, \overline{q})(t) \in \mathcal{F}$, since the strategy f is winning and $t \in S$.

Let $G_A = (\Sigma_0 \cap A, \Sigma_1 \cap A, (Q_i)_{i \in R(A)}, (T_a)_{a \in A}, q_A^0, \mathcal{F}_A)$ on the architecture $(A, R(A), R_{|A}, W_{|A})$. This is again a distributed game. Define G_B symmetrically.

Define $f_A(\overline{q}(r_A), \mu(r_A), a) = f(\overline{q}(r_A \parallel (\#, q_B^0)), \mu(r_A \parallel (\#, q_B^0)), a)$. Let us show that f_A is a WDS for G_A. First, f_A is a distributed strategy with memory μ in G_A, since one can associate to any play r_A of G_A the play $r_A \parallel (\#, q_B^0)$ of G. It remains to show that f_A is winning. Consider an f_A-maximal f_A-play r_A and let r_B be an f_B-maximal f_B-play of G_B. Then, $r_A \parallel r_B$ is an f-maximal f-play. Hence, $(\overline{P}, \overline{q})(r_A) \in \mathcal{F}_A$, and r_A is a winning play of G_A.

By induction, there exists an f_A-compatible winning strategy f_A' for team $\Sigma_0 \cap A$ in G_A with memory μ_A of size less that $M(|A|, |Q_\mathcal{P}|)$, and dually for B. We define the memory μ on $\mathbb{M}(\Sigma', D')$ by $\mu(t) = (\mu_A(t_A), \mu_B(t_B))$ for $t = t_A \parallel t_B$. We build from f_A' and f_B' an f-compatible winning strategy f' for Σ_0 in G as follows. For $a \in A$ and $q_{R(a)} \in Q_{R(a)}$, we define $f'(q_{R(a)}, (m_A, m_B), a) = f_A'(q_{R(a)}, m_A, a)$ and similarly, we let $f'(q_{R(b)}, (m_A, m_B), b) = f_B'(q_{R(b)}, m_B, b)$ for $b \in B$ and $q_{R(b)} \in Q_{R(b)}$.

Using the next statement, one can bound the memory of f' by a function depending only on $M(|A|, |Q_\mathcal{P}|)$ and $M(|B|, |Q_\mathcal{P}|)$, which finishes the induction for the parallel case.

Lemma 2. *The strategy f' is an f-compatible WDS for team 0 on G.*

Induction, Second Case: $\Sigma = A \uplus B$ with $(A \times B) \subseteq D$
We define the product $r \cdot_A s$ by $r \cdot_A s = rs$ if $\max(r) \not\subseteq A$ and $\min(s) \subseteq A$. The product is undefined otherwise. Let f be a WDS for team 0 on G and let S the set of all f-plays. If t is a finite f-play, we let $t^{-1}S = \{t^{-1}S \mid t \leq s \text{ and } s \in S\}$ and $\mathrm{From}_A(t) = t^{-1}S \cap (\min \subseteq A)$. We also define

$$\mathrm{Cut}_{A,P,q} = \{t \in S \mid t \text{ is finite}, \max(t) \not\subseteq A \text{ and } (\overline{P}, \overline{q})(t) = (P, q)\}.$$

A distributed strategy f is (A, P, q)-*uniform* if for all $r_1, r_2 \in \mathrm{Cut}_{A,P,q}$, we have $\mathrm{From}_A(r_1) = \mathrm{From}_A(r_2)$. Say that f is *uniform* if it is (A, P, q)-*uniform* and (B, P, q)-*uniform* for all $(P, q) \in 2^{Q_\mathcal{P}} \times Q_\mathcal{P}$.

Lemma 3. *For any winning distributed strategy f on G, there exists a winning f-compatible distributed strategy on G, which in addition is uniform.*

Thanks to Lemma 3 and using the transitivity of the compatibility relation, we may assume that f is uniform for the rest of the proof of Theorem 2. Let then

$$\text{Next}_A(t) = \text{From}_A(t) \cap (\text{alph} \subseteq A)$$

A play r is (f, A)-maximal if for all $a \in A \cap \Sigma_0$, $f(\overline{q}(r)_{R(a)}, \mu(r), a) = \{\text{stop}\}$. If $\text{Cut}_{A,P,q} \neq \emptyset$, we choose $r \in \text{Cut}_{A,P,q}$ and define a winning condition $\mathcal{F}_{A,P,q}$:

$$\mathcal{F}_{A,P,q} = \{(\overline{P},\overline{q})((\#,q)s) \mid s \in \text{Next}_A(r) \text{ and } rs \text{ is } (f, A)\text{-maximal}\}$$

Since f is uniform, $\text{From}_A(r)$ and $\text{Next}_A(r)$ do not depend on r. One shows that if rs is (f, A)-maximal, then for all $r' \in \text{Cut}_{A,P,q}$, $r's$ is also f_A-maximal. One deduces that $\mathcal{F}_{A,P,q}$ does not depend on the choice of r.

If $\text{Cut}_{A,P,q} \neq \emptyset$, define $G_{A,P,q} = (\Sigma_0 \cap A, \Sigma_1 \cap A, (Q_i)_{i \in \mathcal{P}}, (T_a)_{a \in A}, q, \mathcal{F}_{A,P,q})$. From f, one can derive a distributed strategy for the distributed game $G_{A,P,q}$:

$$f_{A,P,q}(\overline{q}((\#,q)s), \mu((\#,q)s), a) = f(\overline{q}(rs), \mu(rs), a) \text{ where } r \in \text{Cut}_{A,P,q}$$

Since f is uniform, $f_{A,P,q}$ does not depend on r, and by construction of $f_{A,P,q}$, the set of $f_{A,P,q}$-plays is exactly $(\#,q)\text{Next}_A(r)$. By construction of $G_{A,P,q}$ and $\mathcal{F}_{A,P,q}$, all $f_{A,P,q}$-maximal $f_{A,P,q}$-plays are winning in G_A, so $f_{A,P,q}$ is winning.

Moreover, $G_{A,P,q}$ is a controlled reachability game on the alphabet A, smaller than Σ. By induction, there exists a winning strategy $f'_{A,P,q}$ on $G_{A,P,q}$ which is $f_{A,P,q}$-compatible and whose memory is of size at most $M(|A|, |Q_{\mathcal{P}}|)$. One easily transforms $f'_{A,P,q}$ to ensure that if $(\emptyset, q) \in \mathcal{F}_{A,P,q}$, then $f'_{A,P,q}((\#,q), a) = \{\text{stop}\}$ for all $a \in \Sigma_0 \cap A$. This modification does not change the amount of memory necessary for $f'_{A,P,q}$. Further, $f'_{A,P,q}$ is still $f_{A,P,q}$-compatible and winning.

We now have WDS on smaller games $G_{A,P,q}, G_{B,P,q}$ whose memories have a controlled size. It remains to glue them suitably to reconstruct the f-compatible WDS f'. For this, we need to know on which subgame (A, P, q) or (B, P, q) to play. To this aim, we have to compute necessary information with a distributed memory: The *lb-factorization* (for last-block factorization) of a rooted trace $t \neq (\#, q^0)$ is defined (in a unique way) as the factorization $t = rs$ such that

$$t = \begin{cases} r \cdot_A s \text{ with } \emptyset \neq \text{alph}(s) \subseteq A \\ r \cdot_B s \text{ with } \emptyset \neq \text{alph}(s) \subseteq B. \end{cases}$$

One can write an $\text{MSO}_{\Sigma'}(\leq)$-formula $\text{Lastcut}_{P,q}$ which is satisfied by a trace t if and only if $(\overline{P}, \overline{q})(r) = (P, q)$ where $t = rs$ is the lb-factorization of t. Now, an $\text{MSO}_{\Sigma'}(\leq)$-definable trace language can be accepted by an asynchronous mapping [17, 5, 3]. Hence, the mapping $t \mapsto (\overline{P}, \overline{q})(r)$ where $t = rs$ is the lb-factorization of t is a distributed memory. Similarly, one can show that a mapping indicating to a player if its move (if played) would change the alphabet from A to B or from B to A, is also a distributed memory. These informations give exactly the needed information to players of team 0 to know in which game they are playing. Hence, they make it possible to glue strategies $f'_{A,P,q}, f'_{B,P,q}$ to obtain the desired f-compatible WDS f'. For lack of space, we cannot provide details for this construction. Since we have bounded the sizes of the memories used by the small strategies, this gives us a bound for the memory needed for f'.

Acknowledgements. The authors wish to thank the anonymous referees for their careful reading of the submitted version of the paper, which helped us improve its presentation. We also thank J. Bernet, D. Janin and I. Walukiewicz for fruitful discussions.

References

1. J. Bernet, D. Janin, and I. Walukiewicz. Private communication. 2004.
2. J. R. Büchi and L. H. Landweber. Solving sequential conditions by finite-state strategies. *Trans. Amer. Math. Soc.*, 138:295–311, 1969.
3. R. Cori, Y. Métivier, and W. Zielonka. Asynchronous mappings and asynchronous cellular automata. *Inform. and Comput.*, 106:159–202, 1993.
4. V. Diekert and G. Rozenberg, editors. *The Book of Traces.* World Scientific, 1995.
5. W. Ebinger and A. Muscholl. Logical definability on infinite traces. *Theoret. Comput. Sci.*, 154(1):67–84, 1996. Conference version in ICALP '93.
6. P. Gastin, B. Lerman, and M. Zeitoun. Distributed games and distributed control for asynchronous systems. In *LATIN04*, volume 2976 of *LNCS*, pages 455–465. Springer, 2004.
7. O. Kupferman and M. Y. Vardi. Synthesizing distributed systems. In *LICS '01*, pages 389–398. Computer Society Press, 2001.
8. P. Madhusudan and P. S. Thiagarajan. Distributed controller synthesis for local specifications. In *ICALP '01*, volume 2076 of *LNCS*. Springer, 2001.
9. P. Madhusudan and P. S. Thiagarajan. Branching time controllers for discrete event systems. *Theor. Comput. Sci.*, 274(1-2):117–149, 2002.
10. P. Madhusudan and P. S. Thiagarajan. A decidable class of asynchronous distributed controllers. In *CONCUR '02*, volume 2421 of *LNCS*. Springer, 2002.
11. S. Mohalik and I. Walukiewicz. Distributed games. In *FSTTCS '03*, volume 2914 of *LNCS*, pages 338–351. Springer, 2003.
12. G. Peterson, J. Reif, and S. Azhar. Lower bounds for multiplayer noncooperative games of incomplete information. *Comput. Math. Appl.*, 41(7-8):957–992, 2001.
13. G. L. Peterson and J. H. Reif. Multiple-person alternation. In *20th Annual Symposium on Foundations of Computer Science (San Juan, Puerto Rico, 1979)*, pages 348–363. IEEE, New York, 1979.
14. A. Pnueli and R. Rosner. On the synthesis of an asynchronous reactive module. In *ICALP '89*, volume 372 of *LNCS*, pages 652–671. Springer, 1989.
15. A. Pnueli and R. Rosner. Distributed reactive systems are hard to synthetize. In *31th IEEE Symp. FOCS*, pages 746–757, 1990.
16. P. Ramadge and W. Wonham. The control of discrete event systems. In *IEEE*, volume 77, pages 81–98, 1989.
17. W. Thomas. On logical definability of traces languages. In *workshop of ESPRIT BRA 3166, ASMICS*, pages 172–182, Kochel am See, 1990.
18. W. Zielonka. Asynchronous automata. In G. Rozenberg and V. Diekert, editors, *Book of Traces*, pages 175–217. World Scientific, Singapore, 1995.

Expand, Enlarge, and Check: New Algorithms for the Coverability Problem of WSTS*

Gilles Geeraerts, Jean-François Raskin, and Laurent Van Begin**

DI, Université Libre de Bruxelles

Abstract. In this paper, we present a general algorithmic schema called "Expand, Enlarge and Check" from which new efficient algorithms for the coverability problem of WSTS can be constructed. We show here that our schema allows us to define forward algorithms that decide the coverability problem for several classes of systems for which the Karp and Miller procedure cannot be generalized, and for which no complete forward algorithms were known. Our results have important applications for the verification of parameterized systems and communication protocols.

1 Introduction

Model-checking is nowadays widely accepted as a powerful technique for the automatic verification of reactive systems that have natural finite state abstractions. However, many reactive systems are only naturally modelled as infinite-state systems. Consequently, a large (and successful) research effort has recently focused on the application of model-checking techniques to infinite-state models such as FIFO channel systems [2], Petri nets [15], broadcast protocols [7], etc.

One of the positive results is the decidability of the *coverability problem* for *well-structured transition systems* (WSTS for short). WSTS enjoy an infinite set of states that is well-quasi ordered by $\leq$ and their transition relation is monotonic w.r.t $\leq$. Examples of such systems are Petri nets and their monotonic extensions [5, 15], broadcast protocols [8], lossy channel systems [2]. The *coverability problem* asks, given two states c_1 and c_2, whether there is $c_3 \geq c_2$ (c_3 covers c_2) that is reachable from c_1.

A general algorithm (i.e. a procedure that always terminates) is known to solve the coverability problem for WSTS [1,10]. It symbolically manipulates upward-closed sets of states, obtained by unrolling the transition relation in a *backward* fashion. Unfortunately, backward search is seldom efficient in practise [12], and the only complete forward approach known so far is the Karp-Miller algorithm that can only be applied to a small subclass of WSTS: Petri nets.

The Karp and Miller procedure computes, through a combination of a forward exploration strategy and a simple acceleration technique, the so-called *covering*

---

* This research has been partially supported by the FRFC grant 2.4530.02.
** Supported by a "First Europe" grant EPH3310300R0012 of the Walloon Region.

K. Lodaya and M. Mahajan (Eds.): FSTTCS 2004, LNCS 3328, pp. 287–298, 2004.

set of the net, which is known to be well-suited to decide the coverability problem. After several attempts to generalize this procedure to WSTS (which have all produced incomplete approaches [8, 9]), it has been shown in [6] that Petri nets form the sole class (among the examples cited above) for which the covering set is constructible in general. However, this set always exists and is usually finitely representable. Our *main contribution* is to make the best of this fact and devise a forward technique that is complete to decide the coverability problem for a large class of WSTS. This class includes, among others, all the monotonic extensions of Petri nets defined in the literature, as well as lossy channel systems.

We present a new schema of algorithm: "Expand, Enlarge and Check" that works by iteratively constructing more and more precise abstractions of the system. These abstractions (made up of reachable states and limit elements) are guaranteed to become precise enough to decide the coverability problem after a finite number of steps. We show how to apply the schema on two classes of WSTS of practical interest: monotonic extensions of Petri nets (that are useful to model parameterized systems [11, 15]) and lossy channels systems (that are useful to model communication protocols [2]).

Due to lack of space, most of the proofs have been omitted. A complete version of the paper can be found at:
http://www.ulb.ac.be/di/ssd/cfv/TechReps/TechRep_CFV_2004_25.pdf

2   Preliminaries

In this section, we recall some fundamental results about *well-quasi orderings* and *well-structured transition systems* (the systems we analyze here). We show how to *finitely* represent upward- and downward-closed sets of states (which will allow us to devise *symbolic* algorithms), and discuss And-Or graphs (useful to represent abstractions of systems).

Well Quasi-Orderings and Adequate Domains of Limits. A *well quasi ordering* $\leq$ on the elements of a set C (wqo for short) is a *reflexive* and *transitive* relation such that for any infinite sequence $c_0 c_1 \ldots c_n \ldots$ of elements in C, there exist two indices i and j, such that $i < j$ and $c_i \leq c_j$. In the following, we note $c_i < c_j$ if $c_i \leq c_j$ but $c_j \not\leq c_i$.

Let $\langle C, \leq \rangle$ be a well-quasi ordered set. A $\leq$-*upward closed set* $U \subseteq C$ is such that for any $c \in U$, for any $c' \in C$ such that $c \leq c'$, $c' \in U$. A $\leq$-*downward closed set* $D \subseteq C$ is such that for any $c \in D$, for any $c' \in C$ such that $c' \leq c$, $c' \in D$. It is well-known that any $\leq$-upward closed set $U \subseteq C$ is uniquely determined by its finite sets of minimal elements. Formally, the set of $\leq$-*minimal* elements $\mathsf{Min}(U)$ of a set $U \subseteq C$ is a minimal set such that $\mathsf{Min}(U) \subseteq U$ and $\forall s' \in U : \exists s \in \mathsf{Min}(U) : s \leq s'$. The next proposition is a consequence of wqo:

Proposition 1. *Let $\langle C, \leq \rangle$ be a wqo set and $U \subseteq C$ be an $\leq$-upward closed set, then:* $\mathsf{Min}(U)$ *is finite and* $U = \{c \mid \exists c' \in \mathsf{Min}(U) : c' \leq c\}$.

Thus, any $\leq$-upward closed set can be *effectively represented* by its finite set of minimal elements. To obtain a finite representation of downward-closed sets, we must use well-chosen limit elements $\ell \notin C$ to represent downward closures of infinite increasing chains of elements. Thus, we introduce the notion of *adequate domain of limits*.

Definition 1. Let $\langle C, \leq \rangle$ be a well-quasi ordered set and L be a set of elements disjoint from C, the tuple $\langle L, \sqsubseteq, \gamma \rangle$ is called an *adequate domain of limits* for $\langle C, \leq \rangle$ if the following conditions are satisfied: (L_1: representation mapping) $\gamma :$ $L \cup C \rightarrow 2^C$ associates to each element in $L \cup C$ a $\leq$-downward closed set $D \subseteq C$, furthermore, for any $c \in C$, we impose that $\gamma(c) = \{c' \mid c' \leq c\}$. In the following, γ is extended to sets $\mathcal{S} \subseteq L \cup C$ in the natural way: $\gamma(\mathcal{S}) = \cup_{c \in \mathcal{S}} \gamma(c)$; ($L_2$: top element) There exists a special element $\top \in L$ such that $\gamma(\top) = C$; (L_3: precision order) The elements of $C \cup L$ are ordered by the complete quasi order $\sqsubseteq$, defined as follows: $d_1 \sqsubseteq d_2$ if and only if $\gamma(d_1) \subseteq \gamma(d_2)$; ($L_4$: completeness) for any downward closed set $D \subseteq C$, there exists a finite set $D' \subseteq C \cup L$ with $\gamma(D') = D$.

Well-Structured Transition Systems and Coverability Problem. A *transition system* is a tuple $S = \langle C, c_0, \rightarrow \rangle$ where C is a (possibly infinite) set of states, $c_0 \in C$ is the initial state, $\rightarrow \subseteq C \times C$ is a transition relation. In the following, $c \rightarrow c'$ will denote that $\langle c, c' \rangle \in \rightarrow$. For any state c, $\mathsf{Post}(c)$ denotes the set of one-step successors of c, i.e. $\mathsf{Post}(c) = \{c' \mid c \rightarrow c'\}$. We require $\mathsf{Post}(c) \neq \emptyset$ for any $c \in C$[1]. This operator is extended to sets of states $C' \subseteq C$ as follows: $\mathsf{Post}(C') = \{c \mid \exists c' \in C' : c' \rightarrow c\}$. A *path* of S is a sequence of states $c_1, c_2, \ldots, c_k$ such that $c_1 \rightarrow c_2 \rightarrow \cdots \rightarrow c_k$. A state c' is reachable from a state c, noted $c \rightarrow^* c'$, if we have a path $c_1, c_2, \ldots c_k$ in S with $c_1 = c$ and $c_k = c'$. Given a transition system $S = \langle C, c_0, \rightarrow \rangle$, $\mathsf{Reach}(S)$ denotes the set $\{c \in C \mid c_0 \rightarrow^* c\}$.

Definition 2. A transition system $S = \langle C, c_0, \rightarrow \rangle$ is a *well-structured transition system* for the quasi order $\leq \subseteq C \times C$ if the two following properties hold: (W_1: well-ordering) $\leq$ is a well-quasi ordering and (W_2: monotonicity) for all $c_1, c_2, c_3 \in C$ such that $c_1 \leq c_2$ and $c_1 \rightarrow c_3$, there exists $c_4 \in C$ such that $c_3 \leq c_4$ and $c_2 \rightarrow c_4$.

From now on, $S = \langle C, c_0, \rightarrow, \leq \rangle$ will denote the well-structured transition system $\langle C, c_0, \rightarrow \rangle$ for $\leq$. In the sequel, we need to manipulate WSTS and adequate domain of limits. In particular, we need the following effectiveness properties:

Definition 3. A WSTS $S = \langle C, c_0, \rightarrow, \leq \rangle$ and an adequate domain of limits $\langle L, \sqsubseteq, \gamma \rangle$ are *effective* if the following conditions are satisfied: (E_1) C and L are recursively enumerable; (E_2) for any $c_1, c_2 \in C$, we can decide whether $c_1 \rightarrow c_2$; (E_3) for any two finite subsets $C' \subseteq C$ and $L' \subseteq L$, for any $d \in C' \cup L'$ and any finite subset $D \subseteq C' \cup L'$, we can decide whether $\mathsf{Post}(\gamma(d)) \subseteq \gamma(D)$; ($E_4$) For any finite subsets $D_1, D_2 \subseteq C \cup L$, we can decide whether $\gamma(D_1) \subseteq \gamma(D_2)$.

Problem 1. The *coverability problem for well-structured transition systems* is defined as follows: "Given a well-structured transition system S and the $\leq$-upward closed set $U \subseteq C$, determine whether $\mathsf{Reach}(S) \cap U \neq \emptyset$?"

---

[1] Note that this condition is not restrictive since we can always add a transition to a dummy state.

To solve the coverability problem, we use covering sets, defined as follows:

Definition 4. Let $S = \langle C, c_0, \rightarrow, \leq \rangle$ be a WSTS. The *covering set* of S, noted Cover(S), is the (unique) smallest subset of C which (CS$_1$) is $\leq$-downward closed and (CS$_2$) contains Reach(S).

Property. For any WSTS $S = \langle C, c_0, \rightarrow, \leq \rangle$ with an adequate domain of limits $\langle L, \sqsubseteq, \gamma \rangle$ for $\langle C, \leq \rangle$, by property L$_4$ of Definition 1, there exists a finite subset CS$(S) \subseteq L \cup C$ such that $\gamma(\text{CS}(S)) = \text{Cover}(S)$. In the following, CS$(S)$ is called a *coverability set* of the covering set Cover(S) and finitely represents that set.

Proposition 2. *For any* WSTS $S = \langle C, c_0, \rightarrow, \leq \rangle$, *the covering set of S is such that for any $\leq$-upward closed set $U \subseteq C$:* Reach$(S) \cap U = \emptyset$ *iff* Cover$(S) \cap U = \emptyset$.

And-Or Graph and its Avoidability Problem. An *And-Or graph* is a tuple $G = \langle V_A, V_O, v_i, \Rightarrow \rangle$ where $V = V_A \cup V_O$ is the set of nodes (V_A is the set of "And" nodes and V_O is the set of "Or" nodes), $V_A \cap V_O = \emptyset$, $v_i \in V_O$ is the initial node, and $\Rightarrow \subseteq (V_A \times V_O) \cup (V_O \times V_A)$ is the transition relation such that for any $v \in V_A \cup V_O$, there exists $v' \in V_A \cup V_O$ such that $(v, v') \in \Rightarrow$.

Definition 5. A *compatible unfolding* of an And-Or graph $G = \langle V_A, V_O, v_i, \Rightarrow \rangle$ is an infinite labelled tree $T_G = \langle N, root, B, \Lambda \rangle$ where: (i) N is the set of nodes of T_G, (ii) $root \in N$ is the root of T_G, (iii) $B \subseteq N \times N$ is the transition relation of T_G, (iv) $\Lambda : N \rightarrow V_A \cup V_0$ is the labelling function of the nodes of T_G by nodes of G that respects the three following compatibility conditions (Λ is extended to sets of nodes in the usual way): (C$_1$)$\Lambda(root) = v_i$; (C$_2$) for all $n \in N$ such that $\Lambda(n) \in V_A$, we have that (a) for all nodes $v' \in V_O$ such that $\Lambda(n) \Rightarrow v'$, there exists one and only one $n' \in N$ such that $B(n, n')$ and $\Lambda(n') = v'$, and conversely (b) for all nodes $n' \in N$ such that $B(n, n')$, there exists $v' \in V_O$ such that $\Lambda(n) \Rightarrow v'$ and $\Lambda(n') = v'$. (C$_3$) for all $n \in N$ such that $\Lambda(n) \in V_O$, we have that: there exists one and only one $n' \in N$ such that $B(n, n')$, and $\Lambda(n) \Rightarrow \Lambda(n')$.

Problem 2. The *And-Or Graph Avoidability Problem* is defined as follows: "Given an And-Or graph $G = \langle V_A, V_O, v_i, \Rightarrow \rangle$ and a set $E \subseteq V_A \cup V_O$, does there exist $T = \langle N, root, \Lambda, B \rangle$, a compatible unfolding of G, such that $\Lambda(N) \cap E = \emptyset$?". When the answer is positive, we say that E is *avoidable* in G.

It is well-known that this problem is complete for *PTIME*.

3   A New Schema of Algorithms

In this section, we introduce our new schema of algorithms to decide the coverability problem for WSTS. We first explain, in subsection 3.1, how to build an *abstraction* of a given WSTS, w.r.t. a given finite set of reachable states $C' \subseteq C$ and a given finite set of limit elements $L' \subseteq L$. These abstractions are *And-Or graphs* whose nodes are annotated by downward-closed sets of states of a WSTS. We show in subsection 3.2 that any unfolding of this And-Or graph is able to *simulate* the behaviours of its associated WSTS (Proposition 3). Moreover, if the downward-closed sets that are used to annotate the And-Or graph are *precise enough* (in a sense that we make clear in Theorem 2), then the And-Or graph can be used to decide *negative instances* of the coverability problem. Based on those results, we propose a new algorithmic schema to decide the coverability problem of WSTS. It works by iteratively constructing abstractions of the WSTS which become more and more precise. In parallel, it also explores, in a breadth-first fashion, the set of reachable states of the system (to be able to decide the *positive instances* of the problem). Thus, after a finite number of steps either a concrete trace to a *covering state* will be found, or *precise enough abstraction* will be computed to prove that no covering state can ever be reached.

3.1   The And-Or Graph $\mathsf{Abs}(S, C', L')$

Definition 6. Given a WSTS $S = \langle C, c_0, \rightarrow, \leq \rangle$, an adequate domain of limits $\langle L, \sqsubseteq, \gamma \rangle$ for $\langle C, \leq \rangle$, a finite subset $C' \subseteq C$ with $c_0 \in C'$, and a finite subset $L' \subseteq L$ with $\top \in L'$, the And-Or graph $G = \langle V_A, V_O, v_i, \Rightarrow \rangle$, noted $\mathsf{Abs}(S, C', L')$, is defined as follows: $(\mathsf{A_1})$ $V_O = C' \cup L'$; $(\mathsf{A_2})$ $V_A = \{S \in 2^{L' \cup C'} \setminus \{\emptyset\} \mid \nexists d_1 \neq d_2 \in S : d_1 \sqsubseteq d_2\}$; $(\mathsf{A_3})$ $v_i = c_0$; $(\mathsf{A_{4.1}})$ $(n_1, n_2) \in \Rightarrow$ with $n_1 \in V_A, n_2 \in V_O$ if and only if $n_2 \in n_1$; $(\mathsf{A_{4.2}})$ for any $n_1 \in V_O, n_2 \in V_A : (n_1, n_2) \in \Rightarrow$ if and only if (i) *successor covering:* $\mathsf{Post}(\gamma(n_1)) \subseteq \gamma(n_2)$, (ii) *preciseness:* $\nexists n \in V_A : \mathsf{Post}(\gamma(n_1)) \subseteq \gamma(n) \subset \gamma(n_2)$.

The following lemma states that the And-Or graph can be constructed for any WSTS and adequate domain of limits that are effective.

Lemma 1. *Given a WSTS $S = \langle C, c_0, \rightarrow, \leq \rangle$ and an adequate domain of limits $\langle L, \sqsubseteq, \gamma \rangle$ for $\langle C, \leq \rangle$ that are effective, a finite subset $C' \subseteq C$ with $c_0 \in C'$, and a finite subset $L' \subseteq L$ with $\top \in L'$, $\mathsf{Abs}(S, C', L')$ is effectively constructible.*

Notice that in $\mathsf{Abs}(S, C', L')$ all the nodes have at least one successor. Indeed, for all $n \in V_A$, since $n \neq \emptyset$ (following point $\mathsf{A_{4.1}}$ and point $\mathsf{A_2}$ of Definition 6), n has at least one successor. Since And-nodes are subsets of limits that may contain the $\top$ element, with $\gamma(\top) = C$ (following point $\mathsf{L_2}$ of Definition 1), we can always approximate for any $n \in V_O$ the (non-empty) set of successors of $\gamma(n)$, hence we are guaranteed to have at least one successor of n (point $\mathsf{A_{4.2}}$ of Definition 6).

Given a WSTS $S = \langle C, c_0, \rightarrow, \leq \rangle$, an associated And-Or graph $\mathsf{Abs}(S, L', C') = \langle V_A, V_O, v_i, \Rightarrow \rangle$, and an $\leq$-upward-closed set of states $U \subseteq C$, we note $\mathsf{Abs}(U)$ the set of nodes $v \in V_A \cup V_O$ such that $\gamma(v) \cap U \neq \emptyset$, that is, the set of nodes whose associated downward-closed set of states intersects with U. It is easy to show that this subset of nodes can be effectively computed for any effective WSTS with adequate domain of limits.

Degenerated Case. If an And-Or graph is such that any Or-node has exactly one successor, the And-Or graph is said to be *degenerated*. In that case, the avoidability problem is equivalent to the (un)reachability problem in a plain graph. From the definition of $\mathsf{Abs}(S, C', L')$, we remark that the And-Or graph will be degenerated if for any $d \in C' \cup L'$, there exists a *unique* minimal set $\gamma(D)$ such that $D \in V_A$ and $\mathsf{Succ}(\gamma(d)) \subseteq \gamma(D)$. This motivates the next definition:

Definition 7. Given a WSTS $S = \langle C, c_0, \rightarrow, \leq \rangle$ and an adequate domain of limits $\langle L, \sqsubseteq, \gamma \rangle$ for $\langle C, \leq \rangle$, we say that a pair $\langle C', L' \rangle$, where $C' \subseteq C$ with $c_0 \in C$ and $L' \subseteq L$ with $\top \in L'$, is *perfect* if for any $d \in C' \cup L'$, there exists a unique minimal set $D \subseteq C' \cup L'$ such that (*i*) $\mathsf{Post}(\gamma(d)) \subseteq \gamma(D)$ and (*ii*) there is no $D' \subseteq C' \cup L'$ with $\mathsf{Post}(\gamma(d)) \subseteq \gamma(D') \subset \gamma(D)$.

Lemma 2. *Given a WSTS* $S = \langle C, c_0, \rightarrow, \leq \rangle$, *an adequate domain of limits* $\langle L, \sqsubseteq, \gamma \rangle$ *for* $\langle C, \leq \rangle$, *a finite subset* $C' \subseteq C$ *with* $c_0 \in C'$, *and a finite subset* $L' \subseteq L$ *with* $\top \in L'$ *such that* $\langle C', L' \rangle$ *is perfect, then* $\mathsf{Abs}(S, C', L')$ *is a degenerated And-Or graph.*

3.2   Properties of $\mathsf{Abs}(S, C', L')$

In this section, we prove important properties of $\mathsf{Abs}(S, C', L')$. Roughly speaking, we prove now that the abstraction we have defined above is *adequate* for any pair $\langle C', L' \rangle$ such that $c_0 \in C'$ and $\top \in L'$ (Theorem 1) and *complete* (Theorem 2) for some pair $\langle C', L' \rangle$. To establish those results, we first show that $\mathsf{Abs}(S, C', L')$ can simulate for any $\langle C', L' \rangle$ such that $c_0 \in C'$ and $\top \in L'$ its underlying WSTS.

Proposition 3 (Simulation). *Given a WSTS* $S = \langle C, c_0, \rightarrow, \leq \rangle$ *with an adequate domain of limits* $\langle L, \sqsubseteq, \gamma \rangle$ *for* $\langle C, \leq \rangle$, *the following holds for any* $C' \subseteq C$ *with* $c_0 \in C'$ *and* $L' \subseteq L$ *with* $\top \in L'$: *for any path* $c_0 c_1 \ldots c_k$ *of* S *and any unfolding* $T = \langle N, root, B, \Lambda \rangle$ *of* $\mathsf{Abs}(S, C', L')$ *there exists a path* $n_0 n_1 \ldots n_{2k}$ *of* T *with* $n_0 = root$ *and such that* $c_i \in \gamma(\Lambda(n_{2i}))$ *for* $0 \leq i \leq k$.

Since any unfolding of $\mathsf{Abs}(S, C', L')$ can simulate $S = \langle C, c_0, \rightarrow, \leq \rangle$ for any C', L' with $c_0 \in C'$ and $\top \in L'$, for any upward-closed set $U \subseteq C$ we know that if $\mathsf{Abs}(U)$ is avoidable in $\mathsf{Abs}(S, C', L')$ then U does not intersect with $\mathsf{Reach}(S)$. That is formally stated by the next theorem.

Theorem 1 (Adequacy). *Given a WSTS* $S = \langle C, c_0, \rightarrow, \leq \rangle$, *an adequate domain of limits* $\langle L, \sqsubseteq, \gamma \rangle$ *for* $\langle C, \leq \rangle$, *and an upward-closed set* $U \subseteq C$, *the following holds for any* $C' \subseteq C$ *with* $c_0 \in C'$ *and* $L' \subseteq L$ *with* $\top \in L'$: *if* $\mathsf{Abs}(U)$ *is avoidable in* $\mathsf{Abs}(S, C', L')$, *then* $\mathsf{Reach}(S) \cap U = \emptyset$.

Finally, we prove the *completeness* of our approach. Intuitively, the next theorem puts forward that, when the pair $\langle C', L' \rangle$ is *precise enough*, $\mathsf{Abs}(S, C', L')$ allows us to decide *negative instances* of the coverability problem.

Theorem 2 (Completeness). *Given a WSTS* $S = \langle C, c_0, \rightarrow, \leq \rangle$, *an adequate domain of limits* $\langle L, \sqsubseteq, \gamma \rangle$ *for* $\langle C, \leq \rangle$ *and an upward closed set* $U \subseteq C$, *the following holds for any* $C' \subseteq C$ *with* $c_0 \in C'$ *and* $L' \subseteq L$ *with* $\top \in L'$ *such that* $\mathsf{CS}(S) \subseteq C' \cup L'$: *if* $\mathsf{Reach}(S) \cap U = \emptyset$ *then* $\mathsf{Abs}(U)$ *is avoidable in* $\mathsf{Abs}(S, C', L')$.

$i := 0$;
while (**true**) **do**
  "Expand" Compute S_i;
  "Enlarge" Compute L_i;
  "Check" **if** $\exists c_1, \ldots, c_k : c_0 \to \ldots \to c_k$ *with* $c_j \in S_i$ *for all* $0 \le j \le k$ *and* $c_k \in U$ **then return** "Reachable";
  else if $\mathsf{Abs}(U)$ *is avoidable in* $\mathsf{Abs}(S, S_i, L_i)$ **then return** "Unreachable";

Fig. 1. Abstract algorithm Its inputs are an effective representation of a WSTS $S = \langle C, c_0, \to, \le \rangle$ with the adequate limit domain $\langle L, \sqsubseteq, \gamma \rangle$ for $\langle C, \le \rangle$ and a finite representation of the upward-closed set of states $U \subseteq C$

3.3   The New Algorithmic Schema

Let $S_0, S_1, \ldots, S_n \ldots$ be an infinite sequence of finite sets of reachable states of S such that (i) $\forall i \ge 0 : S_i \subseteq S_{i+1}$, (ii) $\forall c \in \mathsf{Reach}(S) : \exists i \ge 0 : c \in S_i$, and (iii) $c_0 \in S_0$. Let $L_0, L_1, \ldots, L_n, \ldots$ be a infinite sequence of finite sets of limits such that (i) $\forall i \ge 0 : L_i \subseteq L_{i+1}$, (ii) $\forall \ell \in L : \exists i \ge 0 : \ell \in L_i$ and (iii) $\top \in L_0$. A schema of algorithm is given at Figure 1 and its correctness is stated in Theorem 3.

Theorem 3. *For any* WSTS *S with adequate domain of limits $\langle L, \sqsubseteq, \gamma \rangle$ that are effective, for any upward-closed set U represented by* $\mathsf{Min}(U)$, *Algorithm at Fig. 1 terminates after a finite amount of time and returns "Reachable" if* $\mathsf{Reach}(S) \cap U \ne \emptyset$, *"Unreachable" otherwise.*

Proof. (Sketch) If $\mathsf{Reach}(S) \cap U \ne \emptyset$, we have from Theorem 1 that $\mathsf{Abs}(U)$ is not avoidable in $\mathsf{Abs}(S, S_i, L_i)$ for all $i \ge 0$. Moreover, since for all $c \in \mathsf{Reach}(S)$ there exists j such that $c \in S_{j'}$ for all $j' \ge j$, there exists $i \ge 0$ such that we have $c_0 \to \ldots \to c_k$ with $c_j \in S_i$ for all j such that $0 \le j \le k$ and $c_k \in U$. We conclude that the algorithm at Fig. 1 returns "Reachable" if $\mathsf{Reach}(S) \cap U \ne \emptyset$.

If $\mathsf{Reach}(S) \cap U = \emptyset$, we know that there exists $i \ge 0$ and a finite coverability set $\mathsf{CS}(S)$ such that $\mathsf{CS}(S) \subseteq S_i \cup L_i$. Hence, from Theorem 2 we have that $\mathsf{Abs}(U)$ is avoidable in $\mathsf{Abs}(S, S_i, L_i)$ and we conclude that the algorithm at Fig. 1 returns "Unreachable" if $\mathsf{Reach}(S) \cap U = \emptyset$. $\square$

Remark 1. Note that Theorem 3, that states the adequation and completeness of our algorithmic schema for the coverability problem of effective WSTS, is not in contradiction with the result of [6] which establishes that there does not exist a procedure that always terminates and returns a coverability set for a large class of WSTS, including ours. Indeed, to establish the correctness of our algorithm, we only need to ensure that a coverability set will be included at some point in the sequence of S_i's and L_i's. Nevertheless, given a pair $\langle S_i, L_i \rangle$, it is not possible to establish algorithmically that this pair contains a coverability set. Also, given a particular upward-closed set U, our algorithm may terminate before reaching a pair $\langle S_i, L_i \rangle$ that contains a coverability set, because the set U is reachable or because the abstraction constructed from a pair $\langle S_j, L_j \rangle$, with $j < i$, is sufficiently precise to prove that U is not reachable.

Remark 2. Note that the constraints on the sequence of L_i's computed by the algorithm of Fig. 1 may be relaxed. Indeed, those constraints ensure that the algorithm eventually considers a set of limits which allows to construct a graph that is precise enough to decide negative instances of the coverability problem. However, following Theorem 2, it is sufficient to ensure that there exists $i \geq 0$ such that $S_i \cup L_i$ contains a coverability set. Hence, only the limits of a coverability set must appear in the sequence of L_i's.

4   Application to Self-Modifying Petri Nets

Let us show how to apply the approach proposed in the previous section to solve the coverability problem for a large subclass of *Self-modifying Petri nets* [14] (SMPN). SMPN are a general extension of Petri nets that includes almost all the monotonic extensions of Petri nets defined in the literature and for which, so far, there was no complete forward procedure.

4.1   Self-Modifying Petri Nets

A *Self-Modifying Petri net* [14], SMPN for short, is a tuple $\langle P, T, D^-, D^+, \mathbf{m}_0 \rangle$. $P = \{p_1, \ldots, p_{k_P}\}$ is a finite (non-empty) set of places. A *marking* is a function $\mathbf{m} : P \to \mathbb{N}$ that assigns a natural value to each place. In the following, markings are also seen as tuples in $\mathbb{N}^{k_P}$ where the ith dimension is the value assigned to place p_i. $T = \{t_1, \ldots, t_{k_T}\}$ is a finite (non-empty) set of transitions. For any $1 \leq i \leq k_T$ and any $1 \leq j \leq k_P$, $D_{ij}^- : \mathbb{N}^{k_P} \to \mathbb{N}$ and $D_{ij}^+ : \mathbb{N}^{k_P} \to \mathbb{N}$ describe respectively the input and output effect of transition t_i on place p_j. Namely, D_{ij}^- and D_{ij}^+ are functions of the marking $\mathbf{m}$ restricted to the form $\alpha + \sum_{k=1..k_P} \beta_k \cdot \mathbf{m}(p_k)$ where $\alpha \in \mathbb{N}$ and $\beta_k \in \mathbb{N}$ for all $1 \leq k \leq k_P$. $\mathbf{m}_0$ is the initial marking of the SMPN.

We define the quasi order $\preccurlyeq \subseteq \mathbb{N}^{k_P} \times \mathbb{N}^{k_P}$ on markings such that $\langle m_1, \ldots, m_{k_P} \rangle \preccurlyeq \langle m_1', \ldots, m_{k_P}' \rangle$ if $m_i \leq m_i'$ for all $1 \leq i \leq k_P$. It is well-known that $\preccurlyeq$ is a wqo.

A transition t_i is firable from a marking $\mathbf{m}$ if $\mathbf{m}(p_j) \geq D_{ij}^-(\mathbf{m})$ for all $p_j \in P$. Firing t_i from $\mathbf{m}$ leads to a marking $\mathbf{m}' \in \mathbb{N}^{k_P}$, noted $\mathbf{m} \to_{t_i} \mathbf{m}'$, such that, for any $p_j \in P : \mathbf{m}'(p_j) = \mathbf{m}(p_j) + D_{ij}^+(\mathbf{m}) - D_{ij}^-(\mathbf{m})$. Given a set S of markings and a transition t_i, $\mathsf{Post}(S, t_i) = \{\mathbf{m}' \mid \exists \mathbf{m} \in S : \mathbf{m} \to_{t_i} \mathbf{m}'\}$.

A SMPN $\mathcal{P}$ defines a transition system $\mathcal{T}_\mathcal{P} = \langle \mathbb{N}^{k_P}, \mathbf{m}_0, \to \rangle$ where $\to \subseteq \mathbb{N}^{k_P} \times \mathbb{N}^{k_P}$ is a transition relation and is such that we have $\langle \mathbf{m}, \mathbf{m}' \rangle \in \to$, noted $\mathbf{m} \to \mathbf{m}'$, if and only if there exists $t_i \in T$ such that t_i is firable from $\mathbf{m}$ and $\mathbf{m} \to_{t_i} \mathbf{m}'$.

A SMPN $\mathcal{P}$ is $\preccurlyeq$-*monotonic* when the underlying transition system $\mathcal{T}_\mathcal{P}$ satisfies the monotonicity property for $\preccurlyeq$. A SMPN $\mathcal{P}$ is *strongly monotonic* when for every transition t_i and markings $\mathbf{m}_1, \mathbf{m}_2$ and $\mathbf{m}_3$, the following holds: if $\mathbf{m}_1 \to_{t_i} \mathbf{m}_3$ and $\mathbf{m}_1 \preccurlyeq \mathbf{m}_2$, there exists $\mathbf{m}_4$ such that $\mathbf{m}_2 \to_{t_i} \mathbf{m}_4$ and $\mathbf{m}_3 \preccurlyeq \mathbf{m}_4$. Obviously, all the strongly monotonic SMPN are $\preccurlyeq$-monotonic.

We say that a transition t is *unfirable*, whenever there exists no marking $\mathbf{m}$ such that t is enabled in $\mathbf{m}$. In the following, we assume that the SMPN's we consider do not contain unfirable transitions. The following lemma defines the syntactical subclass of SMPN's that are strongly monotonic.

Lemma 3. *Given a* SMPN $\mathcal{P} = \langle P, T, D^-, D^+, \mathbf{m}_0 \rangle$ *without unfirable transitions,* $\mathcal{P}$ *is strongly monotonic if and only if for all* $t_i \in T, p_j \in P : D_{ij}^- = \alpha$ *with* $\alpha \in \mathbb{N}$ *or* $D_{ij}^- = \mathbf{m}(p_j)$.

Although strongly monotonic SMPN is a sub-class of SMPN, it remains a general class of monotonic systems. Indeed, almost all the monotonic extensions of Petri nets studied in the literature are syntactical sub-classes of strongly monotonic SMPN, i.e. sub-classes defined by imposing constraints on the linear expressions defining the effect of transitions. Examples of such extensions are Petri nets with transfers [5], with reset [3] and Post self-modifying Petri nets [14]. On the other hand, the other monotonic extensions of Petri nets are not syntactical sub-classes of strongly monotonic SMPN, but we can construct (in polynomial time) a strongly monotonic SMPN with the same set of places that is equivalent to the original net with respect to the coverability problem. Examples of such extensions are Petri nets with non-blocking arcs [13] and Lossy Petri nets [4]. So the algorithm that we propose in the next section is a forward algorithm that decides the coverability problem for all monotonic extensions of Petri nets proposed in the literature.

In the following, we define the adequate domain of limits we consider, state its effectiveness and show how to construct the sequences of S_i's and L_i's. Finally, we show that we always obtain degenerated And-Or graph.

4.2   A Forward Algorithm to Decide the Coverability Problem for Strongly Monotonic SMPN

Domain of Limits. We will consider the domain of limits $\langle \mathcal{L}, \preccurlyeq_e, \gamma(.) \rangle$ where $\mathcal{L} = (\mathbb{N} \cup \{+\infty\})^k \setminus \mathbb{N}^k$, $\preccurlyeq_e \subseteq (\mathbb{N} \cup \{+\infty\})^k \times (\mathbb{N} \cup \{+\infty\})^k$ is such that $\langle m_1, \ldots, m_k \rangle \preccurlyeq_e \langle m_1', \ldots, m_k' \rangle$ if and only if $\forall 1 \leq i \leq k : m_i \leq m_i'$ where $c < +\infty$ for all $c \in \mathbb{N}$ ($\leq$ is the natural order over $\mathbb{N} \cup \{+\infty\}$). $\gamma(.)$ is defined as: $\gamma(\mathbf{m}) = \{\mathbf{m}' \in \mathbb{N}^k \mid \mathbf{m}' \preccurlyeq_e \mathbf{m}\}$. In the following, tuples in $\mathcal{L}$ are called extended markings. It is well-known, see for instance [15], that the following lemma holds.

Lemma 4. $\langle \mathcal{L}, \preccurlyeq_e, \gamma(.) \rangle$ *is an adequate domain of limits for* $\langle \mathbb{N}^k, \preccurlyeq \rangle$.

Notice that in this case the $\top$ element such that $\gamma(\top) = \mathbb{N}^k$ is the marking that assigns $+\infty$ to all the places.

Given a strongly monotonic SMPN $\mathcal{P}$, we extend the underlying transition relation from markings to extended markings by assuming that $+\infty + +\infty = +\infty$, $+\infty \cdot c = +\infty$ for all $c \in \mathbb{N} \setminus \{0\}$, $0 \cdot +\infty = 0$, $+\infty + c = +\infty$ for all $c \in \mathbb{Z}$.

Since our algorithm requires the WSTS and its associated domain of limits to be effective (Definition 3), we state the following lemma :

Lemma 5. *Any strongly monotonic* SMPN $\mathcal{P}$ *with the adequate domain of limits* $\langle \mathcal{L}, \preccurlyeq_e, \gamma(.) \rangle$ *are effective.*

$i \leftarrow 1;$
while (**true**) **do**
  | **if** $\exists \mathbf{m} \in \mathsf{Reach}_{\mathsf{exact}}(\mathsf{Abs}(\mathcal{P}, i)), \mathbf{m}' \in G_U : \mathbf{m} \preccurlyeq \mathbf{m}'$ **then return** *Reachable*;
  | **else**
  | | **if** $\not\exists \mathbf{m} \in \mathsf{Reach}(\mathsf{Abs}(\mathcal{P}, i)), \mathbf{m}' \in G_U : \mathbf{m} \preccurlyeq_e \mathbf{m}'$ **then return** *Unreachable*;
  | | **else** $i \leftarrow i + 1$;

Fig. 2. A forward algorithm for SMPN Its inputs are $\mathcal{P}$, a strongly monotonic SMPN and G_U, the set of minimal elements of the $\preccurlyeq$-upward closed set U

The following definition explains how we construct the S_i's and L_i's. Following Definition 6, this is sufficient to define the And-Or graphs built by our verification algorithm.

Definition 8. *The sequences of S_i's and L_i's are defined as follows:* (D_1) $S_i = \{0, \ldots, i\}^k \cup \{\mathbf{m}_0\}$, *i.e. S_i is the set of markings where each place is bounded by i (plus the initial marking);* (D_2) $L_i = \{\mathbf{m} \in \{0, \ldots i, +\infty\}^k \mid \mathbf{m} \notin \mathbb{N}^k\}$.

It is easy to see that the S_i's and L_i's are finite sets and (i) for all $i \geq 0$: $S_i \subset S_{i+1}$ and $L_i \subset L_{i+1}$, (ii) for any $\mathbf{m} \in \mathbb{N}^k$, there exists $i \in \mathbb{N}$ such that for all $j \geq i : \mathbf{m} \in S_j$, (iii) for any $\mathbf{m} \in \mathcal{L}$, there exists $i \in \mathbb{N}$ such that for all $j \geq i : \mathbf{m} \in L_j$, and (iv) $\mathbf{m}_0 \in S_0$ and $\top \in L_0$.

Degenerated And-Or Graph. Let us show that in the present case, one obtains a *degenerated* And-Or graph. For this purpose, we prove, following Lemma 2, that the pairs $\langle S_i, L_i \rangle$ are *perfect* pairs.

Lemma 6. *Given a* SMPN *$\mathcal{P} = \langle P, T, D^-, D^+ \rangle$ with the adequate domain of limits $\langle \mathcal{L}, \preccurlyeq_e, \gamma(.) \rangle$ any pair $\langle S_i, L_i \rangle$, with $S_i \subseteq \mathbb{N}^{k_P}$ and $L_i \subseteq \mathcal{L}$ constructed following Definition 8, is a perfect pair.*

Corollary 1. *Given a strongly monotonic* SMPN *net $\mathcal{P}$ with the adequate domain of limits $\langle \mathcal{L}, \preccurlyeq_e, \gamma(.) \rangle$ and the sets $S_i \subseteq \mathbb{N}^{k_P}$ and $L_i \subseteq \mathcal{L}$ constructed following Definition 8,* $\mathsf{Abs}(\mathcal{P}, S_i, L_i)$ *is a degenerated And-Or graph.*

Algorithm for the Coverability Problem. Let $\mathsf{Abs}(\mathcal{P}, i)$ be the graph (degenerated And-Or graph) $\mathsf{Abs}(\mathcal{P}, S_i, L_i)$ constructed from $\mathcal{P}$, S_i and L_i. We note $\Rightarrow$ its transition relation. We define $\mathsf{Reach}_{\mathsf{exact}}(\mathsf{Abs}(\mathcal{P}, i))$ as the set $\{\mathbf{m} \mid \mathbf{m}_0 \Rightarrow \mathbf{m}_1 \Rightarrow \ldots \Rightarrow \mathbf{m}_n$ with $\forall 1 \leq j \leq n : \mathbf{m}_j \in S_i, \mathbf{m}_n = \mathbf{m}\}$ and $\mathsf{Reach}(\mathsf{Abs}(\mathcal{P}, i))$ as the set $\{\mathbf{m} \mid \mathbf{m}_0 \Rightarrow \mathbf{m}_1 \Rightarrow \ldots \Rightarrow \mathbf{m}_n$ with $\forall 1 \leq j \leq n : \mathbf{m}_j \in S_i \cup L_i, \mathbf{m}_n = \mathbf{m}\}$. By applying the schema presented in Section 3 to strongly monotonic self-modifying Petri nets, we obtain the algorithm at Fig. 2. Remark that this algorithm is *incremental*: one can compute $\mathsf{Reach}_{\mathsf{exact}}(\mathsf{Abs}(\mathcal{P}, i+1))$ by extending $\mathsf{Reach}_{\mathsf{exact}}(\mathsf{Abs}(\mathcal{P}, i))$ for all $i \geq 0$. Similarly, one can construct $\mathsf{Reach}(\mathsf{Abs}(\mathcal{P}, i))$ from $\mathsf{Reach}_{\mathsf{exact}}(\mathsf{Abs}(\mathcal{P}, i))$.

Theorem 4. *For any strongly monotonic* SMPN, *the algorithm of Fig. 2 returns "Reachable" if* $\mathsf{Reach}(\mathcal{C}) \cap U \neq \emptyset$, *"Unreachable" otherwise.*

5   Application to Lossy Channel Systems

To show the generality of our new approach, we apply our schema of algorithm to *lossy channel systems*, which are systems made up of automata extended with FIFO channels that may lose messages. We recall the model, define an adequate domain of limits and show how to construct the sets S_i's and L_i's.

A *Lossy Channel System*, LCS for short, is a tuple $\mathcal{C} = \langle Q, q_i, F, \Sigma, T \rangle$ where Q is a finite set of locations, $q_i \in Q$ is the initial location, F is a finite set of channels, Σ is a finite alphabet, $T \subseteq Q \times Op \times Q$ where $Op : F \mapsto \bigcup_{a \in \Sigma}\{?a, !a\} \cup \{\text{nop}\}$. A *state* is a pair $\langle q, W \rangle$ where $q \in Q$, $W : F \mapsto \Sigma^*$. In the following, $\mathcal{S}_\mathcal{C}$ will denote the 3B set of states of the LCS $\mathcal{C}$. We define the order $\precsim$ on states in $\mathcal{S}_\mathcal{C}$ such that for any $s = \langle q, W \rangle, s' = \langle q', W' \rangle : s \precsim s'$ if and only if $q = q'$ and $W(c)$ is a (not necessarily contiguous) subword of $W'(c)$ for all $c \in F$, i.e $W(c)$ is obtained from $W'(c)$ by deleting characters. It is well-known that $\precsim$ is a well-quasi order (see for instance [1]). A LCS $\langle Q, q_i, F, \Sigma, T \rangle$ defines a transition system $\langle \mathcal{S}_\mathcal{C}, s_0, \to \rangle$ where (i) $s_0 = \langle q_i, W_i \rangle$ with $W_i(c) = \varepsilon$ for each $c \in F$ and (ii) $(\langle q, W \rangle, \langle q', W' \rangle) \in \to$ if and only if there exists $t = \langle q_1, Op, q_2 \rangle \in T$ and $\langle q, W'' \rangle$ with $W'' \precsim W$ such that $q = q_1$, $q' = q_2$ and for all $c \in F : Op(c) = ?a$ implies $W''(c) = a \cdot W'(c)$. Furthermore, $W'(c) = W''(c) \cdot a$ if $Op(c) = !a$ and $W'(c) = W''(c)$ if $Op(c) = \text{nop}$. In the following, we always consider a LCS $\mathcal{C} = \langle Q, q_i, F, \Sigma, T \rangle$.

Domain of Limits. Let $L(\Sigma)$ be the set of downward closed regular expressions (dc-re) $\{(a_1 + \ldots + a_n)^* \mid \forall 1 \leq i \leq n : a_i \in \Sigma, \forall a_i, a_j : i \neq j$ implies that $a_i \neq a_j\} \cup \{(a + \varepsilon) \mid a \in \Sigma\} \cup \{\varepsilon\}$. A simple regular expression (sre) is either a dc-re or an expression $a_1 \cdot \ldots \cdot a_n$ where $\forall 1 \leq i \leq n : a_i$ is a dc-re. The size of a sre is the number of dc-re that compose it. The set of limits is $\mathcal{L}(\Sigma, Q) = \{\langle q, E \rangle \mid q \in Q, E : F \mapsto L(\Sigma)^*$ assigns a sre to each channel[2]$\} \cup \{\top\}$. For $\langle q, E \rangle \in \mathcal{L}(\Sigma, Q) \setminus \{\varepsilon\}$: $[\![\langle q, E \rangle]\!]$ denotes the set of pairs $\langle q, W \rangle \in \mathcal{S}_\mathcal{C}$ such that $W(c)$ is a word in the language generated by the regular expression $E(c)$ for all $c \in F$. We define the function $\gamma : \mathcal{S}_\mathcal{C} \cup \mathcal{L}(\Sigma, Q) \to 2^{\mathcal{S}_\mathcal{C}}$ such that (i) for all $\langle q, W \rangle \in \mathcal{S}_\mathcal{C} : \gamma(\langle q, W \rangle) = \{\langle q, W' \rangle \mid \langle q, W' \rangle \precsim \langle q, W \rangle\}$, (ii) $\gamma(\top) = \{\langle q, W \rangle \mid q \in Q, W(c) \in \Sigma^*$ for all $c \in F\}$ and (iii) for all $\langle q, E \rangle \in \mathcal{L}(\Sigma, Q) \setminus \{\top\}$: $\gamma(\langle q, E \rangle) = [\![\langle q, E \rangle]\!]$. We define $\sqsubseteq : (\mathcal{S}_\mathcal{C} \cup \mathcal{L}(\Sigma, Q)) \times (\mathcal{S}_\mathcal{C} \cup \mathcal{L}(\Sigma, Q))$ as follows : $c_1 \sqsubseteq c_2$ if and only if $\gamma(c_1) \subseteq \gamma(c_2)$.

It is easy to see that $(\mathcal{L}(\Sigma, Q), \sqsubseteq, \gamma)$ is an adequate domain of limits for $(\mathcal{S}_\mathcal{C}, \precsim)$ and that any LCS $\mathcal{C}$ with this domain of limits is effective.

Construction of the S_i's and the L_i's. We construct the sequences of the S_i's and L_i's as follows. $S_i = \{\langle q, W \rangle \in \mathcal{S}_\mathcal{C} \mid q \in Q, \forall c \in F : W(c) = \varepsilon$ or $W(c) = a_1 \cdot \ldots \cdot a_n$ with $n \leq i$ and $\forall 1 \leq j \leq n : a_j \in \Sigma\}$, i.e. S_i is the set of states where the contents of the channels are words of size at most i. Similarly, $L_i = \{\langle q, E \rangle \in \mathcal{L}(\Sigma, Q) \mid \forall c \in F : E(c) = \varepsilon$ or $E(c) = e_1 \cdot \ldots \cdot e_n$ with $n \leq i$ and $\forall 1 \leq j \leq n : e_j \in L(\Sigma)\} \cup \{\top\}$, i.e. L_i is the set of limits that assign sre of size at most i to the channels (plus the $\top$ element).

---

[2] We also require that E does not assign ε to all the channels because we require in Definition 1 that the set of limits be disjoint from $\mathcal{S}_\mathcal{C}$.

It is not difficult to see that the sequences of S_i's and L_i's satisfy the hypothesis of the algorithm of Fig. 1.

6   Conclusion

In this paper, we have defined a new approach to solve the coverability problem of WSTS, which we call "Expand, Enlarge and Check". When applied to a large class of monotonic counter systems (the strong monotonic Self-modifying Petri nets), our approach produces an algorithm that uses forward analysis to decide the coverability problem. Up to now, such a forward approach was known only for Petri nets (the Karp and Miller algorithm), a restricted subclass of strong monotonic SMPN. We have demonstrated the generality of our approach by showing how to apply the algorithmic schema to lossy channel systems.

References

1. P. A. Abdulla, K. Cerans, B. Jonsson, and Y.-K. Tsay. General Decidability Theorems for Infinite-state Systems. In *Proc. LICS'96*, pages 313–321. IEEE, 1996.
2. P.A. Abdulla and B. Jonsson. Verifying Programs with Unreliable Channels. In *Proc. LICS'93*, pages 160–170. IEEE, 1993.
3. T. Araki and T. Kasami. Some decision problems related to the reachability problem for petri nets. *Theoretical Computer Science*, 3(1):85–104, 1977.
4. A. Bouajjani and R. Mayr. Model Checking Lossy Vector Addition Systems. In *Proc. STACS'99*, LNCS 1563, pages 323–333. Springer, 1999.
5. G. Ciardo. Petri nets with marking-dependent arc multiplicity: properties and analysis. In *Proc. ICATPN 94*, LNCS 815, pages 179–198. Springer, 1994.
6. C. Dufourd, A. Finkel, and Ph. Schnoebelen. Reset Nets Between Decidability and Undecidability. In *In Proc. ICALP'98*, LNCS 1443, pages 103–115. Springer, 1998.
7. J. Esparza, A. Finkel, and R. Mayr. On the Verification of Broadcast Protocols. In *Proc. LICS'99*, pages 352–359. IEEE, 1999.
8. E. A. Emerson and K. S. Namjoshi. On Model Checking for Non-deterministic Infinite-state Systems. In *Proc. LICS '98*, pages 70–80. IEEE, 1998.
9. A. Finkel, J.-F. Raskin, M. Samuelides, and L. Van Begin. Monotonic Extensions of Petri Nets : Forward and Backward Search Revisited. In *Proc. INFINITY'02*, *ENTCS* 68(6). Elsevier, 2002.
10. A. Finkel and P. Schnoebelen. Well-structured transition systems everywhere! *Theoretical Computer Science*, 256(1-2):63–92, 2001.
11. S.M. German and A.P. Sistla. Reasoning about systems with many processes. JACM 39(3): 675–735, 1992.
12. T. A. Henzinger, O. Kupferman, and S. Qadeer. From *pre*historic to *post*modern symbolic model checking. *Formal Methods in System Design*, 23(3):303–327, 2003.
13. J.-F. Raskin and L. Van Begin. Petri Nets with Non-blocking Arcs are Difficult to Analyse. In *Proc. INFINITY'03*, *ENTCS* 96. Elsevier, 2003.
14. R. Valk. On the computational power of extended petri nets. In *Proc. MFCS'78*, LNCS 64, pages 527–535. Springer, 1978.
15. L. Van Begin. *Efficient Verification of Counting Abstractions for Parametric systems*. PhD thesis, Université Libre de Bruxelles, Belgium, 2003.

Minimum Weight Pseudo-Triangulations (Extended Abstract)

Joachim Gudmundsson[1],[*] and Christos Levcopoulos[2]

[1] Department of Mathematics and Computing Science, TU Eindhoven, 5600 MB, Eindhoven, the Netherlands
h.j.gudmundsson@tue.nl
[2] Department of Computer Science, Lund University, Box 118, 221 00 Lund, Sweden
christos@cs.lth.se

Abstract. We consider the problem of computing a minimum weight pseudo-triangulation of a set S of n points in the plane. We first present an $\mathcal{O}(n \log n)$-time algorithm that produces a pseudo-triangulation of weight $\mathcal{O}(wt(\mathcal{M}(S)) \cdot \log n)$ which is shown to be asymptotically worst-case optimal, i.e., there exists a point set S for which every pseudo-triangulation has weight $\Omega(\log n \cdot wt(\mathcal{M}(S)))$, where $wt(\mathcal{M}(S))$ is the weight of a minimum spanning tree of S. We also present a constant factor approximation algorithm running in cubic time. In the process we give an algorithm that produces a minimum weight pseudo-triangulation of a simple polygon.

1 Introduction

Pseudo-triangulations are planar partitions that recently received considerable attention [1, 2] mainly due to their applications in visibility [13, 14], ray-shooting [4, 8], kinetic collision detection [3, 9], rigidity [17], and guarding [16].

A pseudo-triangle is a planar polygon with exactly three convex vertices, called corners. A pseudo-triangulation of a set S of n points in the plane is a partition of the convex hull of S into pseudo-triangles whose vertex set is exactly S. A related problem is the problem of triangulating a point set. Minimizing the total length has been one of the main optimality criteria for triangulations and other kinds of partition. Indeed the minimum weight triangulation (MWT), i.e., minimizing the sum of the edge lengths, has frequently been referred to as the "optimal triangulation". This triangulation has some good properties [5] and is e.g. useful in numerical approximation of bivariate data [18]. The complexity of computing a minimum weight triangulation is one of the most longstanding open problems in computational geometry and it is included in Garey and Johnson's [6] list of problems from 1979 that neither are known to be NP-complete, nor known to be solvable in polynomial time. As a result approximation algorithms

---

[*] Supported by the Netherlands Organisation for Scientific Research (NWO).

K. Lodaya and M. Mahajan (Eds.): FSTTCS 2004, LNCS 3328, pp. 299–310, 2004.

for the MWT-problem have been considered. The best known approximation is a constant factor approximation algorithm by Levcopoulos and Krznaric [11].

We consider the problem of computing a pseudo-triangulation of minimum weight (MWPT) which was posed as an open problem by Rote et al. in [15]. An interesting observation that makes the pseudo-triangulation very favorable compared to a standard triangulation is the fact that there exist point sets where any triangulation, and also any convex partition (without Steiner points), has weight $\Omega(n \cdot wt(\mathcal{M}(\mathcal{S})))$, while there always exists a pseudo-triangulation of weight $\mathcal{O}(\log n \cdot wt(\mathcal{M}(\mathcal{S})))$, where $wt(\mathcal{M}(\mathcal{S}))$ is the weight of a minimum spanning tree of the point set. We also present an approximation algorithm that produces a pseudo-triangulation whose weight is within a factor 15 times the weight of the MWPT. In comparison, the best constant approximation factor for the MWT-problem which is proved to be achievable by a polynomial-time algorithm [11] is so much larger that it has not been explicitly calculated.

This paper is organized as follows. First we compare the worst-case weight of a triangulation with the worst-case weight of a pseudo-triangulation. We give an algorithm that produces a pseudo-triangulation that asymptotically meets this bound running in time $\mathcal{O}(n \log n)$. Even though this is asymptotically worst-case optimal it can be far from the optimal solution for many point sets. In sections 3 and 4 we show a constant factor approximation algorithm for the MWPT-problem. As a subroutine we use an algorithm that we believe is of independent interest since it computes an optimal solution of a simple polygon in cubic time.

An edge/segment with endpoints in two points u and v of $\mathcal{S}$ will be denoted by (u, v) and its length $|uv|$ is equal to the Euclidean distance between u and v. Given a graph $\mathcal{T}$ on $\mathcal{S}$ we denote by $wt(\mathcal{T})$ the sum of all the edge lengths of $\mathcal{T}$. The minimum spanning tree of $\mathcal{S}$ and the convex hull of $\mathcal{S}$, denoted $\mathcal{M}(\mathcal{S})$ and $\mathcal{CH}(\mathcal{S})$ respectively, will be used frequently throughout the paper. Both structures can be computed in $\mathcal{O}(n \log n)$ time.

The proofs omitted in this extended abstract can be found in the full version.

2   A Fast Approximation Algorithm

As mentioned in the introduction there exist point sets $\mathcal{S}$ where any triangulation will have weight $\Omega(n \cdot wt(\mathcal{M}(\mathcal{S})))$, an example is given in Fig. 1a. A natural question is whether there exist similar worst-case bounds for pseudo-triangulations. In this section we show that one can always construct a pseudo-triangulation of weight $\mathcal{O}(\log n \cdot wt(\mathcal{M}(\mathcal{S})))$, and this is asymptotically tight, i.e., there exists a point set $\mathcal{S}$ for which every pseudo-triangulation has weight $\Omega(\log n \cdot wt(\mathcal{M}(\mathcal{S})))$. We start with the lower bound.

Observation 1. *There exists a point set $\mathcal{S}$ in the plane such that any pseudo-triangulation has weight $\Omega(wt(\mathcal{M}(\mathcal{S})) \cdot \log n)$.*

Proof. The proof can be found in the full version. An illustration of the proof is shown in Fig. 1b.   □

(a) 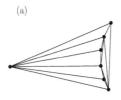   (b)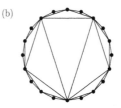

Fig. 1. (a) An example where any triangulation will have weight $\Omega(n \cdot wt(\mathcal{M}(\mathcal{S})))$. (b) An example where any pseudo-triangulation will have weight $\Omega(\log n \cdot wt(\mathcal{M}(\mathcal{S})))$

Next we present an algorithm that produces a pseudo-triangulation whose weight asymptotically meets the lower bound, that is:

Theorem 1. *Given a set $\mathcal{S}$ of n points in the plane one can in time $\mathcal{O}(n \log n)$ produce a pseudo-triangulation of $\mathcal{S}$ of weight $\mathcal{O}(\log n \cdot wt(\mathcal{M}(\mathcal{S})))$.*

The algorithm performs two main steps: a partition of $\mathcal{CH}(\mathcal{S})$ into simple polygons $P_1, \ldots, P_m$ followed by a pseudo-triangulation of each polygon.

We first show how a visibility polygon P can be pseudo-triangulated in time $\mathcal{O}(n \log n)$ using edges of total weight $\mathcal{O}(wt(P) \cdot \log n)$. In the same section we also show how to pseudo-triangulate a special polygon, called an hourglass polygon. Then, in section 2.2, we show how we can construct a spanning graph of $\mathcal{S}$ that partitions the convex hull of $\mathcal{S}$ into subpolygons that either are visibility polygons, or hourglass polygons by using segments of small total weight. Combining these results gives us Theorem 1.

2.1   Pseudo-Triangulating a Visibility Polygon

We start with some basic definitions. Two points p and q within a polygon P are said to *see* each other if there exists a straight-line segment within P with endpoints at p and q. A polygon P is said to be a *visibility polygon* with respect to a vertex q of P if every point within P can be seen from q. A polygon P is said to be a *weak visibility polygon* with respect to an edge (q_1, q_2) if every point within P can see at least one point on (q_1, q_2). The edge (q_1, q_2) is called the *visibility edge* of P. Finally, a (weakly) visibility polygon $P(q)$ of P is said to be maximal if $P(q)$ contains every point of P that can be seen from q, where q can be either a vertex or an edge.

Next we show that a weak visibility polygon whose visibility edge has two convex vertices easily can be pseudo-triangulated using segments of small total length. This result will be used in the algorithm that pseudo-triangulates a visibility polygon. We start with a simple observation.

Observation 2. *The geodesic shortest path between any pair of points p and q in a weak visibility polygon P is a concave chain.*

Proof. The observation follows since there exists a path containing three edges within P from p to q, via the "visibility" edge of P. This path may self-intersect but in that case the path can be shortened to two edges.   □

Observation 3. *A weak visibility polygon P whose visibility edge (p_1, p_2) has two interior convex vertices can be pseudo-triangulated in time $\mathcal{O}(n \log n)$ using edges of total weight $\mathcal{O}(wt(P) \cdot \log n)$.*

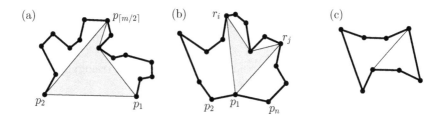

Fig. 2. (a) A pseudo-triangle can be found in a weak visibility polygon whose visibility edge has two convex vertices. (b) A pseudo-triangle partitions a visibility polygon into weak visibility polygons whose visibility edges has convex vertices. (c) An hourglass polygon P can be pseudo-triangulated by adding one edge of weight at most $1/2 \cdot wt(P)$

Now we are ready to extend the results to visibility polygons. Assume that we are given a visibility polygon P with respect to q with n vertices $p_1, \ldots, p_n$ ordered clockwise around the perimeter of P starting with q. Let $r_1, \ldots, r_m$ be the convex vertices of P. Since P is a weak visibility polygon we may use Observation 2, which implies that we can partition P into one pseudo-triangle and a set of weak-visibility polygons by adding the pseudo-triangle with corners at p_1, r_i and r_j, where $1 < i < j$. The two convex vertices r_i and r_j are chosen in such a way that the two angles $\angle p_2, p_1, r_i$ and $\angle p_n, p_1, r_j$ are less than π, as illustrated in Fig. 2b. Note also that p_2 and p_n are convex vertices since P is a visibility polygon. The pseudo-triangle will consist of the edges in the concave chain between r_i and r_j plus the edges (p_1, r_i) and (p_1, r_j). The resulting subpolygons outside the pseudo-triangle are weak visibility polygons whose visibility edges have convex vertices. According to Observation 3 each of these subpolygons can be pseudo-triangulated in $\mathcal{O}(n \log n)$ time using edges of total weight $\mathcal{O}(wt(P) \cdot \log n)$. Hence we have shown the following lemma.

Lemma 1. *The algorithm produces a pseudo-triangulation $\mathcal{T}$ of a visibility polygon P in $\mathcal{O}(n \log n)$ time whose weight is $\mathcal{O}(wt(P) \cdot \log n)$.*

Pseudo-Triangulating an Hourglass Polygon. We end this section by considering the pseudo-triangulation of an hourglass polygon. A polygon P is said to be an hourglass polygon if P consists of two concave chains connected by two edges, as illustrated in Fig. 2c.

We will later need the following straight-forward observation:

Observation 4. *An hourglass polygon P can be pseudo-triangulated in linear time by adding one edge e such that $wt(e) \leqslant 1/2 \cdot wt(P)$.*

2.2   Partition a Point Set into Simple Polygons

As input we are given a set $\mathcal{S}$ of n points in the plane, and as output we will produce a set of polygons that are either hourglass polygons or visibility polygons. The partition is done in two main steps.

Step 1: Construct the convex hull and the minimum spanning tree of $\mathcal{S}$. This is done in $\mathcal{O}(n \log n)$ time and it partitions $\mathcal{CH}(\mathcal{S})$ into simple (maybe degenerate) polygons, denoted $P_1, \ldots, P_m$.

Step 2: Each polygon P_i is processed independently. The task at hand is to partition P_i into a set of hourglass polygons and "restricted" visibility polygons, which can be pseudo-triangulated as described in the previous section.

A *restricted* visibility polygon $rvp(P, q)$ of a polygon P with respect to a vertex q is a visibility polygon of P with respect to q such that every vertex of $P(q)$ also is a vertex of P. A restricted visibility polygon can be obtained from a visibility polygon by short-cutting the part of the perimeter going through vertices in the visibility polygon that are not vertices of P.

Definition 1. *Every edge $e = (u, v)$ of a restricted visibility polygon $R(q)$ that short cuts exactly three edges of the maximal visibility polygon $P(q)$ is said to be a split edge, as illustrated in Fig. 3a.*

Note that this definition implies that any ray from q that intersects e will hit an edge $f = (u', v')$ of P where neither u' nor v' is seen from q.

Now, let $v_1, \ldots, v_n$ be the vertices of P in clockwise order, starting at $q = v_1$. It remains to show how we can partition P into visibility polygons and hourglass polygons in $\mathcal{O}(n \log n)$ time. The idea is to recursively partition P into restricted visibility polygons and hourglass polygons. Consider one level of the recursion. If P is not a restricted visibility polygon with respect to q, or an hourglass polygon then the following two steps are performed:

1. Build a restricted visibility polygon $rvp(P, q)$ of P.
2. For each split edge e in $rvp(P, q)$ construct an hourglass polygon H such that $H \cap R(q) = e$.

A simplified description of the partition is as follows. An arbitrary point q of P is chosen as start point. The restricted visibility polygon $rvp(P, q)$ of P is constructed. Assume that there are l split edges in $rvp(P, q)$. For each split edge $e = (u, v)$ consider the edge $f = (u', v')$ hit by a ray from q through (u, v). Add the edges in a geodesic shortest path from u to u' and, from v to v'. This process partitions P into $l + 1$ subpolygons of which one is a restricted visibility polygon and l are hourglass polygons, as shown in Fig. 3b. The process continues recursively on the remaining subpolygons, $P_1, \ldots, P_m$ (the subpolygons that are not restricted visibility polygons or hourglass polygons). Note that each

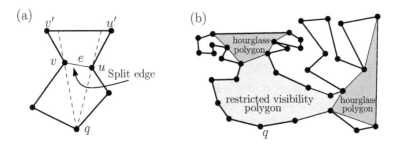

Fig. 3. (a) Illustrating a split edge (u, v) with respect to q, i.e., an edge that short cuts exactly three edges of the maximal visibility polygon $P(q)$. The shortest path within P from v to v' and from u to u' is the boundary of an hourglass polygon. (b) The first level in the recursion partitions P into a restricted visibility polygon, hourglass polygons and a set of subpolygons that are processed recursively

remaining subpolygon P_j has exactly one edge $e_j = (u_j, v_j)$ that is not an edge of P. For each of the subpolygons, either u_j or v_j is chosen as a visibility point. When all subpolygons either are restricted visibility polygons or hourglass polygons the recursion stops. A more precise description on how this can be performed in time $\mathcal{O}(n \log n)$ can be found in the full paper.

Lemma 2. *A simple polygon P with n vertices can be partitioned into restricted visibility polygons and hourglass polygons in $\mathcal{O}(n \log n)$ time.*

Proof. Recall that P is pre-processed in linear time to allow us to answer ray-shooting queries and geodesic shortest path queries in $\mathcal{O}(\log n)$ time. The total complexity of the partition is $\mathcal{O}(n)$, and since every edge requires at most one ray-shooting query and one shortest-path query the time-complexity of PARTITIONPOLYGON is $\mathcal{O}(n \log n)$ □

Lemma 3. *Algorithm PARTITIONPOLYGON produces a partition of P by adding edges of total length at most $5 \cdot wt(P)$.*

Theorem 1 follows by putting together Lemmas 1-3 and Observation 4.

3   A MWPT of a Simple Polygon

Even though the above algorithm is asymptotically worst-case optimal with respect to the weight of the minimum spanning tree it can be very far from the optimal solution. For example, often an optimal solution will have weight which is within a constant factor times the weight of a minimum weight spanning tree, which implies that the above algorithm will produce a solution which is a factor $\Theta(\log n)$ of the optimal. In the rest of this paper we will focus on developing a constant factor approximation algorithm for the MWPT-problem. As a subroutine we will also develop an algorithm that finds an optimal pseudo-triangulation of a simple polygon.

Theorem 2. *Given a simple polygon P one can compute the minimum weight pseudo-triangulation of P in $\mathcal{O}(n^3)$ time using $\mathcal{O}(n^2)$ space.*

We will use a similar dynamic programming method as proposed by Gilbert [7] and Klincsek [10] for finding a minimum weight triangulation of a simple polygon. The basic observation used is that once some (pseudo-)triangle of the (pseudo-)triangulation has been fixed the problem splits into subproblems whose solutions can be found recursively, hence avoiding recomputation of common subproblems.

Let $p_1, \ldots, p_n$ be the vertices of P in clockwise order. Let $\delta(p_i, p_j)$ be the shortest geodesic path between p_i and p_j. Define the *order* of a pair of points p_i, p_j to be the value $((i - j - 1) \mod n)$, i.e., the number of vertices on the path from p_i to p_j along the perimeter of P in clockwise order. Sort the pairs with respect on their order, ties are broken arbitrarily. Note that every pair of points p_i and p_j will occur twice; once as (p_i, p_j) and once as (p_j, p_i). Process each pair in sorted order as follows.

Assume we are about to process (p_i, p_{i+j}) and that the path $\delta(p_i, p_{i+j})$ goes through the vertices $p_i = p_{i+a_0}, p_{i+a_1}, \ldots, p_{i+a_k} = p_{i+j}$. Note that the path partitions P into $k+1$ (possibly empty) subpolygons, see Fig. 4(a). Let $L[i, i+j]$ be the total edge length of an optimal pseudo-triangulation for the subpolygon (or subpolygons) containing the chain $p_i, p_{i+1}, \ldots, p_{i+j}$ of the perimeter of P. Compute $L[i, i+j]$ recursively as follows. If (p_i, p_{i+j}) is not a convex or concave chain then we set $L[i, i+j] = \infty$. In the case when the path is a concave or convex chain we obtain one polygon P' bounded by the path $\delta(p_i, p_{i+j})$ and the path between p_i and p_{i+j}, and k polygons $P_1, \ldots, P_k$ where each P_l is bounded by the edge $(p_{i+a_l}, p_{i+a_{l-1}})$ and the edges from $p_{i+a_{l-1}}$ to p_{i+a_l} along the perimeter of P.

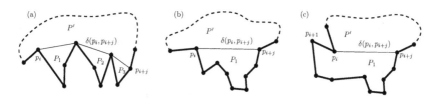

Fig. 4. Illustrating a concave shortest geodesic path between two points p_i and p_{i+j}

If the path is a concave or convex chain then we will have three cases. The three cases are shown in Fig. 4.

- If $\delta(p_i, p_{i+j})$ contains more than one edge then we know that $L[*, *]$ already has been computed for every edge along $\delta(p_i, p_{i+j})$, hence we only have to add up the values of $L[*, *]$ which can be done in linear time, i.e., calculating $\sum_{\alpha=0}^{k-1} L[p_{i+a_\alpha}, p_{i+a_{\alpha+1}}]$.
- If $\delta(p_i, p_{i+j})$ contains exactly one edge (p_i, p_{i+j}) then an optimal pseudo-triangulation of P_1 can be obtained in linear time as follows. We will have two cases; either p_i and p_{i+j} are corners of the pseudo-triangle in P_1 containing (p_i, p_{i+j}) or not.

In the case when both p_i and p_{i+j} are convex vertices within P_1 then an optimal pseudo-triangulation of P_1 can be obtained in linear time as follows. Any optimal pseudo-triangulation of P_1 that contains the edge (p_i, p_{i+j}) must have p_i and p_{i+j} as corners thus we can try all possible vertices p_m, $i < m < i + j$ as the third corner. Testing a pseudo-triangle with corners at p_i, p_{i+j} and p_m takes constant time since the $L[*, *]$-value of the paths between p_i and p_m, and p_m and p_{i+j} have already been computed.

– Otherwise, if one or both of the points are not convex interior corners of P, then it holds that there must be a pair of points p_x and p_y along the perimeter of P between p_i and p_{i+j} whose shortest geodesic path between them contains the edge (p_i, p_{i+j}). Hence, in this case the optimal solution has already been computed for P_1 and can be found in linear time.

There are $\mathcal{O}(n^2)$ pairs of points and each pair takes $\mathcal{O}(n)$ time to process. The space bound follows from the fact that for every pair of points p_i and p_j we store $L[p_i, p_j]$. When all the $L[*, *]$ have been computed we can easily test every possible pseudo-triangle in constant time, thus Lemma 2 follows.

Note that the minimum weight *pointed* (minimum number of edges) pseudo-triangulation can be computed using the same algorithm.

4 A Constant Factor Approximation Algorithm

In this section we will give an approximation algorithm for the MWPT-problem. It is similar to the approximation algorithm presented in Section 2 in the sense that the two main steps are the same; first a partition of the convex hull of the point set into simple polygons followed by a pseudo-triangulation of each polygon. In the pseudo-triangulation step we will use the optimal algorithm presented in the previous section. As input we are given a set $\mathcal{S}$ of n points in the plane, and as output we will produce a pseudo-triangulation $\mathcal{T}$ of $\mathcal{S}$.

Algorithm PSEUDOTRIANGULATE($\mathcal{S}$)

1. Construct the convex hull and the minimum spanning tree of $\mathcal{S}$. This partitions $\mathcal{CH}(\mathcal{S})$ into simple (maybe degenerate) polygons denoted $Q_1, \ldots, Q_k$.
2. Apply Theorem 2 to each of the k polygons. The pseudo-triangulation obtained together with the convex hull and the minimum spanning tree of $\mathcal{S}$ is reported.

The aim of this section is to prove the following theorem.

Theorem 3. *Given a point set $\mathcal{S}$ algorithm PSEUDOTRIANGULATE computes a pseudo-triangulation $\mathcal{T}$ of $\mathcal{S}$ in time $\mathcal{O}(n^3)$ using $\mathcal{O}(n^2)$ space such that $wt(\mathcal{T}) = 15 \cdot wt(\mathcal{T}_{opt})$, where $\mathcal{T}_{opt}$ is a minimum weight pseudo-triangulation of $\mathcal{S}$.*

The running time of the algorithm is $\mathcal{O}(n^3)$ since the time-complexity is dominated by computing the MWPT of each polygon. Note that the algorithm produces the minimum weight pseudo-triangulation that includes $\mathcal{M}(\mathcal{S})$, thus it suffices to prove that there exists a pseudo-triangulation of S that includes the edges in a minimum spanning tree of S and whose weight is $15 \cdot wt(\mathcal{T}_{opt})$.

4.1   The Weight of a Pseudo-Triangulation That Includes a Minimum Spanning Tree

In this section we will prove the following lemma, which completes the proof of Theorem 3.

Lemma 4. *Let S be a set of n points in the plane and let $\mathcal{T}_{opt}$ denote a minimum weight pseudo-triangulation of S. There exists a pseudo-triangulation $\mathcal{T}$ of S that includes the edges of $\mathcal{M}(S)$ and whose weight is at most $15 \cdot wt(\mathcal{T}_{opt})$).*

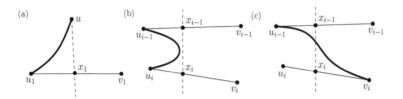

Fig. 5. Three of the cases that may occur when the partial minimum spanning tree edges (dashed) is replaced by a chain (fat).

Before we continue we need the following generalization of a pseudo-triangle.

Definition 2. *A simple polygon P is said to be a* pseudo-k-gon *if P includes exactly k convex vertices.*

The proof of Lemma 4 is performed in two steps. First it will be shown that one can construct a graph $\mathcal{G}$ of the vertices of P such that no edge of $\mathcal{G}$ intersects an edge of $\mathcal{M}(S)$, every face of $\mathcal{G}$ is a pseudo-k-gon for $3 \leqslant k \leqslant 6$, and the weight of $\mathcal{G}$ is bounded by $5 \cdot wt(\mathcal{T}_{opt})$. The second step, Observation 6, shows how a pseudo-k-gon P, $4 \leqslant k \leqslant 6$, can be partitioned into pseudo-triangles by adding $k - 3$ edges to P of length at most $wt(P)$. Since every edge can belong to at most two polygons the final bound is $15 \cdot wt(\mathcal{T}_{opt})$.

Constructing $\mathcal{G}$. Initially $\mathcal{G}$ contains the edges in $\mathcal{M}(S)$. Process every edge $e = (u, v)$ in $\mathcal{T}_{opt}$ as follows. If e does not intersect any edge of $\mathcal{M}(S)$ then add e to $\mathcal{G}$. Otherwise assume for simplicity that e is vertical and that u lies above v. Let $f_1 = (u_1, v_1), \ldots, f_m = (u_m, v_m)$ be the edges of $\mathcal{M}(S)$ that intersect e ordered with respect to their intersection with e from top to bottom, and let x_i denote the intersection point between e and f_i. The following edges are now added to $\mathcal{G}$, as illustrated in Fig. 5.

(1) If $|u_1 x_1| < |v_1 x_1|$ then the concave path $\delta(u, u_1)$ between u and u_1 for which the region bounded by (u, v), $\delta(u, u_1)$ and f_1 is empty is added to $\mathcal{G}$. Otherwise, if $|v_1 x_1| \leqslant |u_1 x_1|$, the corresponding path between u and v_1 is added to $\mathcal{G}$, as shown in Fig. 5a.

(2) If $|u_m x_m| < |v_m x_m|$ then the concave path $\delta(v, u_m)$ between v and u_m for which the region bounded by (u, v), $\delta(v, u_m)$ and f_m is empty is added to $\mathcal{G}$. Otherwise, if $|v_m x_m| \leqslant |u_m x_m|$, the corresponding path between v and v_m is added to $\mathcal{G}$.

(3) If $m \geqslant 1$ then for each $1 < i < m$ we will have four cases. Note that case (b) and (d) are symmetric to (a) and (c) respectively. Let a_{i-1} be the endpoint of (u_{i-1}, v_{i-1}) closest to x_{i-1}, and let a_i be the endpoint of (u_i, v_i) closest to x_i.

   a. If $a_{i-1} = u_{i-1}$ and $a_i = u_i$ then the concave path $\delta(u_{i-1}, u_i)$ between u_{i-1} and u_i for which the region bounded by (u, v), $\delta(u_{i-1}, u_i)$, f_{i-1} and f_i is empty is added to $\mathcal{G}$, as illustrated in Fig. 5b.

   b. If $a_{i-1} = v_{i-1}$ and $a_i = v_i$ then the concave path $\delta(v_{i-1}, v_i)$ between v_{i-1} and v_i for which the region bounded by (u, v), $\delta(v_{i-1}, v_i)$, f_{i-1} and f_i is empty is added to $\mathcal{G}$.

   c. If $a_{i-1} = u_{i-1}$ and $a_i = v_i$ then the shortest path $\delta(u_{i-1}, v_i)$ between u_{i-1} and v_i for which it holds that the two regions bounded by (u, v), $\delta(u_{i-1}, v_i)$, f_{i-1} and f_i are empty is added to $\mathcal{G}$, see Fig. 5c.

   d. If $a_{i-1} = v_{i-1}$ and $a_i = u_i$ then the shortest path $\delta(v_{i-1}, u_i)$ between v_{i-1} and u_i for which it holds that the two regions bounded by (u, v), $\delta(v_{i-1}, u_i)$, f_{i-1} and f_i is empty is added to $\mathcal{G}$.

Properties of $\mathcal{G}$. It remains to prove that $\mathcal{G}$ has two important properties to complete the proof of Lemma 4.

Observation 5. $\mathcal{G}$ *is a planar spanning graph of $\mathcal{S}$ and each face of $\mathcal{G}$ is a pseudo-k-gon, for $3 \leqslant k \leqslant 6$.*

Lemma 5. $wt(\mathcal{G}) \leqslant 5 \cdot wt(\mathcal{T}_{opt})$.

Proof. Consider an edge $e = (u, v)$. If e does not intersect any edges of $\mathcal{M}(\mathcal{S})$ then we are done, otherwise consider the edges added to $\mathcal{G}$ when e is processed in the construction of $\mathcal{G}$. Using the same notations as in the construction algorithm, it holds that the path added between u and v can be seen as $m + 1$ subpaths, $P_1, \ldots, P_{m+1}$, where P_1 connects u to an edge of $\mathcal{M}(\mathcal{S})$, P_{m+1} connects v to an edge of $\mathcal{M}(\mathcal{S})$, and each the subpaths P_i, $1 < i \leqslant m$ connects two edges of $\mathcal{M}(\mathcal{S})$, as shown in Fig. 5.

Let e_i denote the part of e that is replaced by P_i. It will be shown that P_1 and P_{m+1} can be charged to e_1 and e_{m+1} respectively, and that P_i, $1 < i \leqslant m$, can be charged to e_i.

Consider an edge (x, y) of $\mathcal{M}(\mathcal{S})$, and let $\mathcal{D}(x, |xy|)$ and $\mathcal{D}(y, |xy|)$ be the discs with radius $|xy|$ and with center at x and y respectively. From the properties of an edge of $\mathcal{M}(\mathcal{S})$ it holds that the intersection of $\mathcal{D}(x, |xy|)$ and $\mathcal{D}(y, |xy|)$ must be empty of points. From this it follows that $|u, x_1| > \min(|x_1 u_1|, |x_1 v_1|)$ and that $|v, x_m| > \min(|x_m, u_m|, |x_m, v_m|)$, thus the length of P_1 is bounded by $2|e_1|$ and the length of P_{m+1} is bounded by $2|e_{m+1}|$. Since the part of a path P_i on one side of e_i is concave it holds that the length of $P_2, \ldots, P_m$ is bounded by

$|e| - (|e_1| + |e_{m+1}|) + 2 \sum_{1 \leqslant i < m} (\min\{|u_i x_i|, |v_i x_i|\} + \min\{|u_{i+1} x_{i+1}|, |v_{i+1} x_{i+1}|\})$.
Using the same emptiness property as discussed in the previous paragraph, gives
that $\sum_{1 \leqslant i < m} (\min\{|u_i x_i|, |v_i x_i|\} + \min\{|u_{i+1} x_{i+1}|, |v_{i+1} x_{i+1}|\}) \leqslant 2 \cdot |e|$ and since
$wt(\mathcal{M}(\mathcal{S})) < wt(\mathcal{T}_{opt})$ the lemma follows.   □

It remains to show how the resulting pseudo-k-gons, $3 < k \leqslant 6$, can be
pseudo-triangulated. Note that the pseudo-k-gons in $\mathcal{G}$ are very special in the
sense that $k - 3$ of the convex chains are straight-line segments and they are
connected to concave chains that may or may not be straight-line segments, we
call these *restricted* pseudo-k-gons, see Fig. 6. To complete the proof of Lemma 4
we end this section with the following observation, which also completes the proof
of Theorem 3.

Observation 6. *For any $3 < k \leqslant 6$ it holds that a restricted pseudo-k-gon P
can be pseudo-triangulated in $\mathcal{O}(n)$ time by adding $k - 3$ edges of total weight at
most $wt(P)$.*

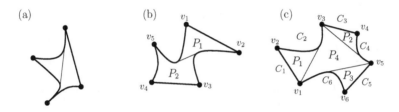

Fig. 6. For any $3 < k \leqslant 6$ it holds that a pseudo-k-gon can be pseudo-triangulated by
adding $k - 3$ edges of total weight $wt(P)$

5   Open Problems and Acknowledgement

An obvious question is whether the minimum weight pseudo-triangulation problem is NP-hard. Is it as hard as finding the minimum weight triangulation?
Computing the minimum weight triangulation is one of the few open problems
listed in Garey and Johnson's 1979 book on NP-completeness [6] that remain
open today.
    A second open problem concerning the weight of a pseudo-triangulation is
if there exists a minimum pseudo-triangulation of low weight. It was shown by
Streinu [17] that every point set allows a minimum planar pseudo-triangulation
that has $2n - 3$ edges. Neither of the two algorithms presented in this paper
produces minimum pseudo-triangulations, although the dynamic programming
algorithm for simple polygons can be modified to compute a minimum weight
minimum pseudo-triangulation.
    The authors would like to thank Mattias Andersson, Mark de Berg and Bet-
tina Speckmann for valuable discussions during the work of this paper.

References

1. O. Aichholzer, D. Orden, F. Santos, and B. Speckmann. On the Number of Pseudo-Triangulations of Certain Point Sets. Proc. 15th Canadian Conference on Computational Geometry, pp. 141-144, 2003.
2. O. Aichholzer, G. Rote, B. Speckmann, and I. Streinu. The Zigzag Path of a Pseudo-Triangulation Proc. 8th International Workshop on Algorithms and Data Structures, pp. 377-388, Lecture Notes in Computer Science 2748, Springer Verlag, 2003.
3. J. Basch, L. J. Guibas, J. Hershberger, and L. Zhang. Deformable free space tiling for kinetic collision detection. Proc. 4th Workshop on Algorithmic Foundations of Robotics, 2000.
4. B. Chazelle, H. Edelsbrunner, M. Grigni, L. J. Guibas, J. Hershberger, M. Sharir, and J. Snoeyink. Ray shooting in polygons using geodesic triangulations. Algorithmica, 12:54–68, 1994.
5. G. Das and D. Joseph. Which triangulations approximate the complete graph? In Proc. International Symposium on Optimal Algorithms, pp. 168–192, Lecture Notes in Computer Science 401, Springer Verlag, 1989.
6. M. Garey and D. Johnson. Computers and Intractability. W. H. Freeman and Company, 1979.
7. P. D. Gilbert. New results in planar triangulations. Report R–850, Univ. Illinois Coordinated Science Lab, 1979.
8. M. T. Goodrich and R. Tamassia. Dynamic Ray Shooting and Shortest Paths in Planar Subdivisions via Balanced Geodesic Triangulations. Journal of Algorithms, 23(1):51–73, 1997.
9. D. Kirkpatrick and B. Speckmann. Kinetic Maintenance of Context-Sensitive Hierarchical Representations for Disjoint Simple Polygons. Proc. 18th ACM Symposium on Computational Geometry, pp. 179–188, 2002.
10. G. Klincsek. Minimal triangulations of polygonal domains. Annals of Discrete Math., 9:121-123, 1980.
11. D. Krznaric and C. Levcopoulos. Quasi-greedy triangulations approximating the minimum weight triangulation. Journal of Algorithms 27(2): 303-338. 1998.
12. D. A. Plaisted and J. Hong. A heuristic triangulation algorithm. J. of Algorithms 8:405-437, 1987.
13. M. Pocchiola and G. Vegter. Pseudo-triangulations: Theory and applications. In Proc. 12th ACM Symposium on Computational Geometry, pp. 291–300, 1996.
14. M. Pocchiola and G. Vegter. Topologically sweeping visibility complexes via pseudo-triangulations. Discrete Computational Geometry, 16(4):419–453, 1996.
15. G. Rote, C. A. Wang, L. Wang, and Y. Xu. On constrained minimum pseudotriangulations. Proc. 9th Symposium on Computing an Combinatorics, pp. 445–454, Lecture Notes in Computer Science 2697 Springer Verlag, 2003.
16. B. Speckmann and C. D. Tóth. Allocating Vertex pi-guards in Simple Polygons via Pseudo-Triangulations. Proc. 14th ACM-SIAM Symposium on Discrete Algorithms, pp. 109–118,2003.
17. I. Streinu. A Combinatorial Approach to Planar Non-Colliding Robot Arm Motion Planning. Proc. 41st ACM Annual Symposium on Foundations of Computer Science, pp. 443–453, 2000.
18. P. Yoeli. Compilation of data for computer-assisted relief cartography. In J. Davis, and M. McCullagh, eds., Display and Analysis of Spatial Data. John Wiley & Sons, New York, 1975.

Join Algorithms for the Theory of Uninterpreted Functions*

Sumit Gulwani[1], Ashish Tiwari[2], and George C. Necula[1]

[1] University of California, Berkeley, CA 94720
{gulwani, necula}@cs.berkeley.edu
[2] SRI International, Menlo Park, CA 94025
tiwari@csl.sri.com

Abstract. The join of two sets of facts, E_1 and E_2, is defined as the set of all facts that are implied independently by both E_1 and E_2. Congruence closure is a widely used representation for sets of equational facts in the theory of uninterpreted function symbols (UFS). We present an optimal join algorithm for special classes of the theory of UFS using the abstract congruence closure framework. Several known join algorithms, which work on a strict subclass, can be cast as specific instantiations of our generic procedure. We demonstrate the limitations of any approach for computing joins that is based on the use of congruence closure. We also mention some interesting open problems in this area.

1 Introduction

Computational logic is used extensively in formal modeling and analysis of systems, particularly in areas such as verification of hardware and software systems, and program analysis. A wide variety of logical theories are used for this purpose. However, even for the simplest of theories, reasoning on formulas in the presence of the conjunction $\wedge$ and disjunction $\vee$ connectives is computationally hard. Unsurprisingly, therefore, almost all practical uses of logical computation have come in the form of decision procedures that work on facts stored as *conjunctions of atomic formulas*. What happens when the application requires the computation of the logical disjunction of two such facts? *Join* algorithms provide an approximate solution by constructing a conjunction of atomic formulas that is implied by the original disjunction.

Join algorithms were first studied in the context of program analysis. Abstract interpretation [5] is a well-known static program analysis technique that can be used to automatically generate program invariants, and to verify program assertions, even in the absence of loop invariants. The program is evaluated over

* Research of the first and third authors was supported in part by NSF grants CCR-0081588, CCR-0085949, and CCR-0326577, and gifts from Microsoft Research. Research of the second author was supported in part by NSF grant CCR-0326540 and NASA Contract NAS1-20334.

K. Lodaya and M. Mahajan (Eds.): FSTTCS 2004, LNCS 3328, pp. 311–323, 2004.

a lattice of abstract states, each one representing one or more concrete execution states. The lattice join operation ($\sqcup$) is used to compute the abstract state following a merge in a control-flow graph, from the abstract states before the merge point. The join operation can be viewed as computing the intersection of the facts (or union of the models) before the merge point. The lack of a suitable join algorithm restricts the utility of several interesting theories for abstract interpretation. Nevertheless, join algorithms are known for some important theories such as linear arithmetic [10], linear inequalities [6, 3], polynomial equations [17], and the initial term algebra [8, 18].

A join algorithm for a theory Th takes as input two sets of atomic facts and produces the strongest set of facts that is implied independently by both the input sets of facts in Th. For example, the join of the sets $\{a = 2, b = 3\}$ and $\{a = 1, b = 4\}$ in the theory of linear arithmetic can be represented by $\{a + b = 5\}$. The join of $\{a = x, b = f(x)\}$ and $\{a = y, b = f(y)\}$ in the theory of uninterpreted function symbols (UFS) can be represented by $\{b = f(a)\}$.

It is interesting to point out that though decision procedures for satisfiability of a conjunction of atomic formulas are well studied for a wide class of logical theories, the same is not true for join algorithms. Join algorithms appear to be much harder than the decision procedures for the same theory. While there are efficient congruence closure based decision procedures for the theory of UFS, join algorithms for this theory have been studied in this paper and independently in [19]. In the special case of the theory of initial term algebra, several join algorithms have been proposed [1, 18, 8]. All of these algorithms primarily use EDAG/value graph like data structures [15, 12].

This paper has two main technical contributions. In Section 3, we present an abstract congruence closure based algorithm that generalizes all the known join algorithms for subclasses of UFS and can compute the join for a strictly bigger subclass of the theory of UFS than these algorithms. We show that the existing algorithms are a special case of our algorithm.

In Section 4 we present some results concerning the limitations of any congruence closure based approach for obtaining join algorithms for the general theory of UFS. We show that the join of two finite sets of ground equations cannot be finitely represented (using ground equations). In special cases when it can be finitely represented, the presentation can become exponential. This partially explains the lack of any known complete join algorithms for even special classes of the UFS theory.

2   Notation

A set Σ of function symbols and constants is called a *signature*. Function symbols in Σ are denoted by f, g and constants by a, b. In the context of program analysis, these constants arise from program variables, and henceforth we refer to them as (program) variables. We use $\mathcal{T}(\Sigma)$ to refer to the set of ground terms over Σ, which are constructed using symbols only from Σ. We use the notation

$ft_1 \ldots t_k$ to refer to the term $f(t_1, \ldots, t_k)$. We also use the notation $f^i t$ to denote i applications of the unary function f on term t.

Definition 1 (Join). *Let Th be some (first-order) theory over a signature Σ. Let E_1 and E_2 be two sets of ground equations over Σ. The* join *of E_1 and E_2 in theory Th is denoted by $E_1 \sqcup_{Th} E_2$, and is defined to be (any presentation for) the set $\{s = t \mid s, t \in \mathcal{T}(\Sigma), Th \models E_1 \Rightarrow s = t, Th \models E_2 \Rightarrow s = t\}$.*

We ignore the subscript *Th* from $\sqcup_{Th}$ whenever it is clear from the context. In this paper, we mainly concern ourselves with the theory of UFS. If E is a set of equations (interpreted as a binary relation over terms, not necessarily symmetric), the notation $\rightarrow_E$ denotes the closure of E under the congruence axiom. If $\rightarrow$ is a binary relation, we use the notation $\rightarrow^*$ and $\leftrightarrow^*$ to denote the reflexive-transitive and reflexive-symmetric-transitive closure of $\rightarrow$. Note that $\leftrightarrow_E^*$ is the equational theory induced by E.

The theory of *uninterpreted function symbols* (UFS) is just the pure theory of equality, that is, there are no additional equational axioms. Treating the constants in Σ as variables, we define the theory of *initial term algebra* as the extension of UFS with the axioms (a) if $f s_1 \ldots s_m = g t_1 \ldots t_n$ for $m, n \geq 1$, then $f = g$, $m = n$, and $s_i = t_i$ for all i, and (b) $C[a] \neq a$ for any nontrivial context $C[\_]$ and variable a.

3   Join Algorithms for Uninterpreted Functions

We represent (the equational theory induced by) finite sets of ground equations using an "abstract congruence closure" [9,2], which is closely related to a bottom-up tree automaton where the automaton specifies an *equivalence* on a set of terms, rather than specifying a set of accepted terms. Abstract congruence closure is reviewed in Section 3.1. The join of two abstract congruence closures is closely related to their product, which we describe in Section 3.2.

3.1   Abstract Congruence Closure

An abstract congruence closure provides a rewrite rules (tree-automata) based representation for a finite set of ground equations [2]. An *abstract congruence closure* R is a convergent set of ground rewrite rules of the form $f c_1 \ldots c_k \rightarrow c_0$ or $c_1 \rightarrow c_2$, where $f \in \Sigma$ is a k-ary function symbol ($k \geq 0$) and c_i's are all special constants from a set K disjoint from Σ. If E is a set of ground equations over Σ, then R is said to be an abstract congruence closure *for* E if for all $s, t \in \mathcal{T}(\Sigma)$, $s \leftrightarrow_E^* t$ iff there exists a term $u \in \mathcal{T}(\Sigma \cup K)$ such that $s \rightarrow_R^* u$ and $t \rightarrow_R^* u$. We will assume that R is fully-reduced, that is, if $f c_1 \ldots c_k \rightarrow c_0 \in R$, then there is no rule in R such that $c_i \rightarrow_R d$ for any $i = 0, 1, \ldots$ and any d. R is fully-reduced implies that R is convergent.

If $s \rightarrow_R^* c$, then we say that c *represents* s (via R). Given an abstract congruence closure R, it is not the case that every term $s \in \mathcal{T}(\Sigma)$ is represented by

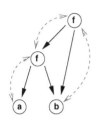

Consider the set $E = \{fab = a, f(fab)b = b\}$. An EDAG representing the set E is shown in Figure 1. An EDAG consists of a term graph (dark directed edges) and a set of congruence closed equality (dotted) edges. A corresponding abstract congruence closure representation is $\{a \rightarrow c_0, b \rightarrow c_1, fc_0c_1 \rightarrow c_2, fc_2c_1 \rightarrow c_3, c_1 \rightarrow c_0, c_2 \rightarrow c_0, c_3 \rightarrow c_0\}$. A fully-reduced abstract congruence closure for E is $R = \{a \rightarrow c_0, b \rightarrow c_0, fc_0c_0 \rightarrow c_0\}$. The rewrite system R can be seen as a specification of a tree-automaton over the set $K = \{c_0\}$ of *states*.

Fig. 1. EDAG and abstract congruence closure for $E = \{fab = a, f(fab)b = b\}$

a constant. Note that an abstract congruence closure provides a formal way for reasoning about EDAG data-structure [15], as illustrated in Figure 1.

3.2 Join of Two Congruence Closures

We use congruence closures to represent sets of equations. If R_1 and R_2 are abstract congruence closures over signatures $\Sigma \cup K_1$ and $\Sigma \cup K_2$ respectively, then we want to construct an abstract congruence closure R_3 such that for all terms $s, t \in T(\Sigma)$, it is the case that $s \leftrightarrow^*_{R_1} t$ and $s \leftrightarrow^*_{R_2} t$, if and only if, $s \leftrightarrow^*_{R_3} t$. The solution involves the construction of the *product* congruence closure.

Definition 2. *Let R_1 and R_2 be abstract congruence closures over signatures $\Sigma \cup K_1$ and $\Sigma \cup K_2$. We define the* product *congruence closure R_3 over the signature $\Sigma \cup (K_1 \times K_2)$ as follows:*

$$R_3 = \{f(\langle c_1, d_1 \rangle, \langle c_2, d_2 \rangle, \dots, \langle c_k, d_k \rangle) \rightarrow \langle c, d \rangle :$$
$$f \in \Sigma, \; fc_1c_2 \dots c_k \rightarrow c \in R_1, \; fd_1d_2 \dots d_k \rightarrow d \in R_2\}$$

Example 1. Let $E_1 = \{f^2a = a\}$ and $E_2 = \{f^3a = a\}$. A fully-reduced abstract congruence closure for E_1 is $R_1 = \{a \rightarrow c_0, \; fc_0 \rightarrow c_1, \; fc_1 \rightarrow c_0\}$, and that for E_2 is $R_2 = \{a \rightarrow d_0, \; fd_0 \rightarrow d_1, \; fd_1 \rightarrow d_2, \; fd_2 \rightarrow d_0\}$.

A fully reduced abstract congruence closure for the join $E_1 \sqcup E_2$ is given over the signature $\{a, f\} \cup \{\langle c_i, d_j \rangle : i \in \{0,1\}, j \in \{0,1,2\}\}$ as $R_3 = \{a \rightarrow \langle c_0, d_0 \rangle, f\langle c_0, d_0 \rangle \rightarrow \langle c_1, d_1 \rangle, f\langle c_1, d_1 \rangle \rightarrow \langle c_0, d_2 \rangle, f\langle c_0, d_2 \rangle \rightarrow \langle c_1, d_0 \rangle, f\langle c_1, d_0 \rangle \rightarrow \langle c_0, d_1 \rangle, f\langle c_0, d_1 \rangle \rightarrow \langle c_1, d_2 \rangle, f\langle c_1, d_2 \rangle \rightarrow \langle c_0, d_0 \rangle\}$. Here R_3 is just the product of R_1 and R_2.

The following lemma shows that product construction is sound (i.e., it represents only true equivalences), but complete (i.e., it represents all true equivalences) only on terms represented explicitly by constants in R_1 and R_2.

Lemma 1. *Let R_1 and R_2 be fully reduced abstract congruence closures over signatures $\Sigma \cup K_1$ and $\Sigma \cup K_2$. Let R_3 be the product congruence closure. Then, for all terms $s, t \in T(\Sigma)$, it is the case that $s \rightarrow^*_{R_1} c \leftarrow^*_{R_1} t$ and $s \rightarrow^*_{R_2} d \leftarrow^*_{R_2} t$ for some constants $c \in K_1$ and $d \in K_2$, if and only if, $s \rightarrow^*_{R_3} \langle c, d \rangle \leftarrow^*_{R_3} t$.*

Proof. By induction on the structure of the term s, we can prove that it is the case that $s \to^*_{R_1} c$ and $s \to^*_{R_2} d$, iff $s \to^*_{R_3} \langle c, d \rangle$. The lemma follows immediately.

3.3   Special Cases for Which the Join Algorithm Is Complete

In this section, we show that for certain special cases, the product captures the exact join.

Injective Functions. An important special case, from the point of view of program analysis, is the theory of injective functions. In this case, all function symbols $f \in \Sigma$ are assumed to be injective, that is, whenever $f s_1 \ldots s_k = f t_1 \ldots t_k$, then $s_i = t_i$ for all i.

Uninterpreted functions are a commonly used abstraction for modeling program operators for the purpose of program analysis. If the conditionals of a program are abstracted as non-deterministic, and all program assignments are of the form $a := e$ (where a is a program variable and e is some uninterpreted function term), then it can be shown that if $f s_1 \ldots s_k = f t_1 \ldots t_k$ holds at some program point, then $s_i = t_i$ for all i must also be true at that program point [8]. Hence, the analysis of such programs can use the theory of injective functions. Furthermore, injective functions can be used to model fields of tree-like data structures in programs.

As a consequence of injectivity, there cannot be two *distinct* rules $f \ldots \to c$ and $f \ldots \to c$ in any fully-reduced abstract congruence closure.

Theorem 1. *Let R_1 and R_2 be fully reduced abstract congruence closures over signatures $\Sigma \cup K_1$ and $\Sigma \cup K_2$ that satisfy the injectivity assumption described above. Let R_3 be the product congruence closure. Then, the relation $\leftrightarrow^*_{R_3}$ is equal to $\leftrightarrow^*_{R_1} \cap \leftrightarrow^*_{R_2}$ over $\mathcal{T}(\Sigma)$.*

Proof. Suppose $s, t \in \mathcal{T}(\Sigma)$ such that $s \leftrightarrow^*_{R_1} t$ and $s \leftrightarrow^*_{R_2} t$. Consider the cases:
(1) *there are constants $c \in K_1$ and $d \in K_2$ equivalent to s modulo R_1 and R_2 respectively.* Since R_1 and R_2 are fully-reduced, it follows that $s \to^*_{R_1} c' \leftarrow^*_{R_1} t$ and $s \to^*_{R_2} d' \leftarrow^*_{R_2} t$ for some constants c', d'. It follows from Lemma 1 that $s \leftrightarrow^*_{R_3} t$.
(2) *there is no constant in the equivalence class of s modulo R_1:* Then $s = f s_1 \ldots s_m$ and $t = f t_1 \ldots t_m$ for some $f \in \Sigma$ and $s_i \leftrightarrow^*_{R_1} t_i$ for all i. Since s and t are also equivalent modulo R_2, by injectivity it follows that for all i, s_i and t_i are equivalent modulo R_2. By induction on the depth of s and t, we conclude that $s_i \leftrightarrow^*_{R_3} t_i$, and consequently, $s \leftrightarrow^*_{R_3} t$.
(3) *there is no constant in the equivalence class of s modulo R_2:* This case is analogous to the second case above.

Finite Number of Congruence Classes. As a second specialization, consider the case when only a finite number of distinct congruence classes are induced by both R_1 and R_2. In this case, the product of R_1 and R_2 represents the complete join of R_1 and R_2.

Theorem 2. *Let R_1 and R_2 be fully reduced abstract congruence closures over signatures $\Sigma \cup K_1$ and $\Sigma \cup K_2$. Let R_3 be the product congruence closure. If the congruence relation $\leftrightarrow^*_{R_1}$ defined by R_1 over $\mathcal{T}(\Sigma)$ induces only finitely many congruence classes, and the same is true for R_2, then the relation $\leftrightarrow^*_{R_3}$ is equal to $\leftrightarrow^*_{R_1} \cap \leftrightarrow^*_{R_2}$ over $\mathcal{T}(\Sigma)$.*

Proof. If $\mathcal{T}(\Sigma)$ is partitioned into a finite number of congruence classes modulo R_1, then we claim that every term $s \in \mathcal{T}(\Sigma)$ is equivalent to some constant modulo R_1. Thereafter the proof is identical to case (1) of the proof of Theorem 1. To prove the claim, note that if s is not equivalent to a constant, then all the infinite terms $C[s]$, where C is an arbitrary context, are in distinct equivalence classes, thus contradicting the assumption.

3.4   Complexity and Optimizations

If the size of R_1 and R_2 is n_1 and n_2 respectively, then the product R_3 of R_1 and R_2 can be constructed in $O(n_1 n_2)$ time and the size of R_3 is $O(n_1 n_2)$. Example 1 generalizes to show that in the case of finitely many equivalence classes, the abstract congruence closure representation of the (complete) join can be quadratic in size of the inputs, and hence product construction is optimal in this case. Surprisingly, the same is also true for the theory of injective functions and the special subclass of initial term algebra, as the following example demonstrates.

Example 2. Let $\Sigma = \{a_i, b_i, a'_i, b'_i \mid i \in I = \{1, \ldots, n\}\}$ be a set of $4n$ variables. It is easy to see that the join of $\{a_1 = \cdots = a_n = b_1 = \cdots = b_n = fb'_1\} \cup \{fb'_{i+1} = b_i, fa_i = a_{i+1} \mid i \in I\}$ and $\{a'_1 = \cdots = a'_n = b'_1 = \cdots = b'_n = fb_1\} \cup \{fb_{i+1} = b_i, fa_i = a_{i+1} \mid i \in I\}$ is $\{a'_i = f^i b_i, a_i = f^i b'_i \mid i \in I\}$, which can only be represented by a congruence closure of quadratic size.

In the context of program analysis, abstract interpretation of a program with n conditionals (in sequence) requires computing n successive joins. A quadratic blowup in each step can lead to a double exponential complexity. In practice, however, we would not expect the join to be quadratic in each step. Product construction can be optimized using some heuristics. First we can delete *unreachable constants*, that is, a constant $\langle c, d \rangle$ that does not represent any term over the original signature Σ. Rules that contain unreachable constants can also be deleted. This optimization can be enforced at the product construction phase by only creating constants that are guaranteed to be reachable. Second note that any node that is not pointed to by any subterm edge or any equational edge can also be recursively deleted. In other words, if $\langle c, d \rangle$ occurs exactly once, then the rule containing $\langle c, d \rangle$ can be deleted, cf. [11].

3.5   Related Work

We recently discovered that Vagvolgyi [19] has shown that it is decidable if the join of two congruence closures is finitely generated, and has described an algorithm for computing the join that is based on tree-automata techniques. Our work has focused on identifying classes of UFS for which joins are *guaranteed to* be finitely generated in *polynomial* time using product construction of abstract congruence closures.

Join algorithms for the theory of initial term algebra have been studied in the context of the global value numbering problem [4, 8]. We show here that these algorithms are specific instantiations of our generic join algorithm. The global value numbering problem seeks to discover equivalences of program expressions by treating all program operators as uninterpreted, all conditionals as non-deterministic, while all assignments are of the form $a := e$ (where a is a program variable and e is some uninterpreted function term). In this special case, a congruence closure R is, in fact, a *unification closure*, i.e. whenever s and t are equivalent modulo R, then (a) either s or t is a constant, or (b) $s = f s_1 \ldots s_m$, $t = f s_1 \ldots t_m$, and s_i and t_i are equivalent modulo R. The three different algorithms proposed for computing joins in the initial term algebra [1, 18, 8] can be viewed as essentially computing the product congruence closure. However, since there is a potential of computing n successive joins and getting an exponential blowup [8], these algorithms use heuristics to optimize computation of n joins.

The popular partition refinement algorithm proposed by Alpern, Wegman, and Zadeck (AWZ) [1] is efficient, however at the price of implementing an incomplete join. The novel idea in AWZ algorithm is to represent the values of variables after a join using a fresh *selection* function ϕ, similar to the functions used in the static single assignment form [7]. The ϕ functions are an abstraction of the if-then-else operator wherein the conditional in the if-then-else expression is abstracted away, but the two possible values of the if-then-else expression are retained. However, the AWZ algorithm treats the ϕ functions as new uninterpreted functions. It then performs congruence partitioning and finally eliminates the ϕ functions. For example, the join of $\{x = a, y = f(a), z = a\}$ and $\{x = b, y = f(b), z = b\}$ is represented as $\{x = \phi(a, b), y = \phi(f(a), f(b)), z = \phi(a, b)\}$ and computed to be $\{x = z\}$. Note that the equality $y = f(x)$ is missing in the join. The AWZ algorithm is incomplete because it treats ϕ functions as uninterpreted. In an attempt to remedy this problem, Rüthing, Knoop and Steffen have proposed a polynomial-time algorithm (RKS) [18] that alternately applies the AWZ algorithm and some rewrite rules for normalization of terms involving ϕ functions (namely $\phi(a, a) \rightarrow a$ and $\phi(f(a), f(b)) \rightarrow f(\phi(a, b))$), until the congruence classes reach a fixed point. Their algorithm discovers more equivalences than the AWZ algorithm. Recently, Gulwani and Necula [8] gave a join algorithm (GN) for the initial term algebra that takes as input a parameter s and discovers all equivalences among terms of size at most s.

The GN Algorithm. In our framework, the basic strategy of the GN algorithm [8] for computing the join of two congruence closures R_1 and R_2 can be described by the recursive function *match*:

```
match(c, d) =
    if ∃a : a → c ∈ R₁, a → d ∈ R₂ create a → ⟨c, d⟩; return;
    else if ∃fc₁ ... cₖ → c ∈ R₁ and ∃fd₁ ... dₖ → d ∈ R₂
        create f⟨c₁, d₁⟩ ... ⟨cₖ, dₖ⟩ → ⟨c, d⟩; match(c₁, d₁); ...; match(cₖ, dₖ);
    else delete all rules created until now;
```

For each variable $a \in \Sigma$ such that $a \rightarrow c \in R_1$ and $a \rightarrow d \in R_2$, the function $match(c, d)$ is invoked once. Note that rules are deleted if they contain unreachable nodes. If $R_1 = \{a \rightarrow c_1, fc_2 \rightarrow c_1, b \rightarrow c_2\}$ and $R_2 = \{a \rightarrow d_1, fd_2 \rightarrow d_1, b \rightarrow d_2\}$, then the GN algorithm creates the rules $\{a \rightarrow \langle c_1, d_1 \rangle, f\langle c_2, d_2 \rangle \rightarrow \langle c_1, d_1 \rangle, b \rightarrow \langle c_2, d_2 \rangle\}$ in that order.

The RKS Algorithm. This algorithm [18] uses the special ϕ function to represent the join problem. The binary ϕ function corresponds to the pairing operator $\langle \_, \_ \rangle : K_1 \times K_2 \mapsto K_3$, but extended to terms $\langle \_, \_ \rangle : T(\Sigma \cup K_1) \times T(\Sigma \cup K_2) \mapsto T(\Sigma \cup K_3)$. The process of creating the rewrite rule $f\langle c_1, d_1 \rangle \ldots \langle c_k, d_k \rangle \rightarrow \langle c, d \rangle$ from the two initial rewrite rules $fc_1 \ldots c_k \rightarrow c \in R_1$ and $fd_1 \ldots d_k \rightarrow d \in R_2$ is achieved by first explicitly representing the rewrite rule $\langle fc_1 \ldots c_k, fd_1 \ldots d_k \rangle \rightarrow \langle c, d \rangle$, and then commuting the ϕ function with the f symbol to get $f\langle c_1, d_1 \rangle \ldots \langle c_k, d_k \rangle \rightarrow \langle c, d \rangle$. Finally, in the base case, when we get $\langle a, a \rangle \rightarrow \langle c, d \rangle$, the second property of ϕ functions is used to simplify the left-hand side to a.

The AWZ Algorithm. The AWZ algorithm [1] also uses the special ϕ function, but does not use any of the two properties of it (as described above). Consequently, it only computes a few rewrite rules of the product congruence closure and not all of them.

4   Limits of Congruence Closure Based Approaches

The congruence closure representation is inherently limited in its expressiveness. It can only represent sets of equations that have a finite presentation. However, the join of two finite sets of ground equations may not have a finite presentation. For example, consider the following sets of equations E_1 and E_2.

$$E_1 = \{a = b\} \qquad E_2 = \{fa = a, fb = b, ga = gb\}$$
$$E_1 \sqcup E_2 = \{gf^n a = gf^n b \mid n \geq 0\}$$

We prove that $E_1 \sqcup E_2$ cannot be represented by a finite number of ground equations below. We first define signature of a term.

Definition 3. *Let $\equiv$ be a congruence on the set of all ground terms. Let K denote the set of all congruence classes induced by $\equiv$. The signature $Sig(t)$ of a term $t = f(t_1, \ldots, t_k)$ with respect to $\equiv$ is the term $f([t_1], \ldots, [t_k])$ over $\Sigma \cup K$, where $[t_i]$ denotes the congruence class of t_i modulo $\equiv$ and symbols in K are treated as constants.*

The following theorem gives a complete characterization of equational theories that admit finite presentations using ground equations, see also [11].

Theorem 3. *A congruence relation $\equiv$ on the set of ground terms (over Σ) can be represented by a finite set of ground equations iff there are only finitely many congruence classes that contain terms with different signatures, and each such congruence class contains terms with only finitely many different signatures.*

We will only use the forward ($\Rightarrow$) implication of this theorem, which follows immediately using either an abstract congruence closure construction of the finite set of ground equations, or analyzing the equational proofs.

Note that the two terms $gf^n a$ and $gf^n b$, for a fixed $n \geq 0$, are equal in $E_3 = E_1 \sqcup E_2$, but their arguments are not (because $E_2 \not\models a = b$.) Thus, $E_1 \sqcup E_2$ contains infinitely many congruence classes with two distinct signatures. Hence it follows from Theorem 3 that E_3 does not admit a finite presentation using ground equations. We conclude that *the congruence closure based approach cannot be used to obtain a complete join algorithm for the full theory of UFS.* In fact, this example shows that this is true for even the special class of *unary* UFS.

A set E of ground equations is said to be *cyclic* if there exists a term that is equivalent to a proper subterm of itself modulo E, otherwise it is *acyclic*. The acyclic subclass of UFS is closed under joins and guaranteed to have finite presentations. Unfortunately, the (complete) join of two sets of acyclic ground equations can be exponential in the size of the inputs. For example, consider the following sets of equations E_1 and E_2.

$$E_1 = \{a = b\}$$
$$E_2 = \{g(b', a) = g(b', b), b' = f(a_1, \ldots, a_n), a_1 = a'_1, \ldots, a_n = a'_n\}$$
$$E_1 \sqcup E_2 = \{g(s, a) = g(s, b) \mid s \in f(t_1, \ldots, t_n), t_i \in \{a_i, a'_i\}\} \cup \{g(b', a) = g(b', b)\}$$

The set $E_1 \sqcup E_2$ requires an exponential number of ground equations for representation. We conclude that *the congruence closure based approach cannot be used to get a polynomial time complete join algorithm for the acyclic subclass of UFS.* This remains true even when the signature is restricted to unary symbols, as the following example shows.

$$E_1 = \{x_0 = y_0\}$$
$$E_2 = \{fx_0 = x_1, \ldots, fx_{n-1} = x_n, gx_0 = x_1, \ldots, gx_{n-1} = x_n,$$
$$fy_0 = y_1, \ldots, fy_{n-1} = y_n, gy_0 = y_1, \ldots, gy_{n-1} = y_n, x_n = y_n\}$$
$$E_1 \sqcup E_2 = \{sx_0 = sy_0 \mid s \in (f|g)^n\}$$

Note that the set $E_1 \sqcup E_2$ contains 2^n equations. The smallest set of ground equations representing $E_1 \sqcup E_2$ is exponentially large.

4.1   Relatively Complete Join Algorithm

We cannot hope to get a complete join algorithm using the congruence closure, or EDAG, data-structure. We can, however, get an algorithm that is complete on a given set I of *important* terms.

Definition 4 (Relatively Complete Join Algorithm). *A relatively complete join algorithm for a theory Th over a signature Σ takes as input two sets of ground equations E_1 and E_2, and a set I of terms over Σ and returns E_3 such that $Th \models (E_1 \sqcup E_2) \Rightarrow E_3$ and $Th \models E_3 \Rightarrow (E_1 \sqcup E_2)|_I$, where $(E_1 \sqcup E_2)|_I = \{s = t \mid s \text{ and } t \text{ occur as sub-terms in } I, (s = t) \in E_1 \sqcup E_2\}$.*

Lemma 1 shows that the product construction method will detect exactly those equivalences which involve terms that are explicitly represented (via constants) in the two congruence closures. Hence, we can obtain relatively complete join algorithms by first representing the set I of important terms in R_1 and R_2. Define the function $addTerm(K, R, s)$, which takes as input a set K of constants, an abstract congruence closure R over $\Sigma \cup K$, and a term s, and returns a tuple $\langle K', R', c \rangle$ as follows:

$$addTerm(K, R, c) = \langle K, R, c \rangle, \text{ if } c \in K$$
$$addTerm(K, R, fc_1 \ldots c_k) = \langle K, R, c \rangle, \text{ if } fc_1 \ldots c_k \rightarrow c \in R$$
$$addTerm(K, R, fc_1 \ldots c_k) = \langle K \cup \{c\}, R \cup \{fc_1 \ldots c_k \rightarrow c\}, c \rangle, \text{ if } c_i \in K, c \notin K$$
$$addTerm(K, R, f \ldots s_i \ldots) = addTerm(K_1, R_1, f \ldots c \ldots),$$
$$\text{if } \langle K_1, R_1, c \rangle = addTerm(K, R, s_i)$$

The function $addTerm(K, R, s)$ adds new rules to R, if necessary, so that the term s is explicitly represented (by a constant) in R. We extend this function to add a set I of terms by successively calling the function $addTerm(K, R, s)$ for each $s \in I$. The relatively complete join algorithm $relJoin$ for UFS involves adding the new terms and then computing the product.

$relJoin(R_1, R_2, I)$ =
$\quad \langle K_1, R_1 \rangle := addTerm(K_1, R_1, I);$
$\quad \langle K_2, R_2 \rangle := addTerm(K_2, R_2, I);$
$\quad R_3 := product(R_1, R_2); \text{ return } R_3;$

For example, consider the congruence closures $R_1 = \{a \rightarrow c, b \rightarrow c\}$ and $R_2 = \{a \rightarrow d_1, b \rightarrow d_2, fd_1 \rightarrow d_3, fd_2 \rightarrow d_3, gd_1 \rightarrow d_4, gd_2 \rightarrow d_4\}$ for $\{a = b\}$ and $\{fa = fb, ga = gb\}$ respectively. The product of R_1 and R_2 will be a congruence closure for the empty set $\{\}$ of equations since fa, fb, ga and gb are not represented in R_1. If $I = \{fa\}$, then we will add, say, the rule $fc \rightarrow c'$ to R_1, and the product now represents $\{fa = fb\}$. It will still miss the equality $ga = gb$.

The correctness of the relatively complete join algorithm outlined above follows immediately from Lemma 1 and noting that $addTerm$ returns a fully reduced congruence closure if the input congruence closure is fully reduced [2]. As a post-processing step, we can only keep those rules in R_3 that are used in the proof of $s \rightarrow^*_{R_3} c$ for some $s \in I$. This way the size of the output can be forced to be linear in the size of the input I.

5   Interesting Future Extensions

Join Algorithms for Other Theories: Join algorithms for the theory of commutative UFS can be used to reason about program operators like bitwise operators and floating-point arithmetic operators. However, the join algorithm for commutative UFS (*cufs*) may be more challenging than the one for UFS. For example, consider the following sets of equations E_1 and E_2.

$$E_1 = \{a = a', b = b'\} \qquad E_2 = \{a = b', b = a'\}$$
$$E_1 \sqcup_{ufs} E_2 = \emptyset$$
$$E_1 \sqcup_{cufs} E_2 \supset \{f(C[a], C[b]) = f(C[a'], C[b']) \mid C \text{ is any context }\}$$

Here f is a binary symbol assumed commutative in the *cufs* theory. Note that $E_1 \sqcup_{cufs} E_2$ contains equalities like $f(a, b) = f(a', b')$ and is not finitely representable using ground equations even though $E_1 \sqcup_{ufs} E_2$ is finite.

Context-Sensitive Join Algorithm: Precise inter-procedural program analysis requires computing "context-sensitive procedure summaries", that is, invariants parameterized by the inputs so that given an instantiation for the inputs, the invariant can be instantiated to the most precise result for that input. Reps, Horwitz, and Sagiv described a general way to accomplish this for a simple class of data-flow analyses [16] . It is not clear how to do this in general for any abstract interpretation. The real challenge is in building an appropriate data-structure and a join algorithm for it that is context sensitive. For example, consider the following sets of equations E_1 and E_2.

$$E_1 = \{a = a', b = F(a')\} \qquad E_2 = \{a = b', b = F(b')\}$$
$$E_1 \sqcup E_2 = \{b = F(a)\}$$
$$E_1[a' = b'] \sqcup E_2[a' = b'] = \{a = a', b = F(a)\}$$
$$(E_1 \sqcup E_2)[a' = b'] = \{b = F(a)\}$$

This example illustrates that our join algorithm is not context-sensitive since it represents $E_1 \sqcup E_2$ as $\{b = F(a)\}$ which when instantiated in the context $a' = b'$ does not yield the most precise result. This suggests that a different data structure is required to obtain a context-sensitive join algorithm. Recently, Olm and Seidl have described a context-sensitive join algorithm for the theory of linear arithmetic with equality [13]. Their data structure is very different from the one used in Karr's join algorithm [10], which is not context-sensitive.

Combining Join Algorithms: Combining the join algorithm for UFS with the one for linear arithmetic (la) will give a join algorithm for the combined theory (la_ufs), which can be used to analyze programs with arrays and pointers. There are some nice results in the literature for combining decision procedures for different theories [14], but none for combining join algorithms. Consider, for example, the following sets of equations E_1 and E_2.

$$E_1 = \{a = a', b = b'\} \qquad E_2 = \{a = b', b = a'\}$$
$$E_1 \sqcup_{la} E_2 = \{a + b = a' + b'\} \qquad E_1 \sqcup_{ufs} E_2 = \emptyset$$
$$E_1 \sqcup_{la\_ufs} \subset \{\forall i \geq 0, f^i a + f^i b = f^i a' + f^i b'\}$$

Here f is uninterpreted. Note that $E_1 \sqcup_{la\_ufs} E_2$ does not even admit finite presentation using ground equations. However, it may be possible to obtain a relatively complete join algorithm for the combined abstraction.

6   Conclusion

This paper explores the closure properties of congruence closure under the join operation. We show that the congruence closure representation is neither expressive enough nor compact enough to be able to represent the result of a join in the theory of UFS. The product of two congruence closures is related to the join and we show that it indeed provides a complete algorithm for certain special cases. This generalizes the known specific case of unification closures.

References

1. B. Alpern, M. N. Wegman, and F. K. Zadeck. Detecting equality of variables in programs. In *15th Annual ACM Symposium on POPL*, pages 1–11. ACM, 1988.
2. L. Bachmair, A. Tiwari, and L. Vigneron. Abstract congruence closure. *J. of Automated Reasoning*, 31(2):129–168, 2003.
3. B. Blanchet, P. Cousot, R. Cousot, J. Feret, L. Mauborgne, A. Miné, D. Monniaux, and X. Rival. A static analyzer for large safety-critical software. In *ACM PLDI '03*, pages 196–207, 2003.
4. P. Briggs, K. D. Cooper, and L. T. Simpson. Value numbering. *Software Practice and Experience*, 27(6):701–724, June 1997.
5. P. Cousot and R. Cousot. Abstract interpretation: A unified lattice model for static analysis of programs by construction or approximation of fixpoints. In *4th Annual ACM Symposium on Principles of Programming Languages*, pages 234–252, 1977.
6. P. Cousot and N. Halbwachs. Automatic discovery of linear restraints among variables of a program. In *Fifth ACM Symposium on POPL*, pages 84–96, 1978.
7. R. Cytron, J. Ferrante, B. K. Rosen, M. N. Wegman, and F. K. Zadeck. Efficiently computing static single assignment form and the control dependence graph. *ACM Transactions on Programming Languages and Systems*, 13(4):451–490, Oct. 1990.
8. S. Gulwani and G. C. Necula. A polynomial-time algorithm for global value numbering. In *11th Static Analysis Symposium*, volume 3148 of *Lecture Notes in Computer Science*, pages 212–227. Springer, 2004.
9. D. Kapur. Shostak's congruence closure as completion. In *Rewriting Techniques and Applications, RTA 1997*, pages 23–37. Springer-Verlag, 1997. LNCS 1103.
10. M. Karr. Affine relationships among variables of a program. In *Acta Informatica*, pages 133–151. Springer, 1976.
11. D. Kozen. Partial automata and finitely generated congruences: an extension of Nerode's theorem. In R. Shore, editor, *Proc. Conf. Logical Methods in Math. and Comp. Sci.*, 1992. Also Tech. Rep. PB-400, Comp. Sci. Dept., Aarhus Univ., 1992.
12. S. S. Muchnick. *Advanced Compiler Design and Implementation*. Morgan Kaufmann, San Francisco, 2000.
13. M. Müller-Olm and H. Seidl. Precise interprocedural analysis through linear algebra. In *31st ACM Symposium on POPL*, pages 330–341. ACM, Jan. 2004.
14. G. Nelson and D. Oppen. Simplification by cooperating decision procedures. *ACM Transactions on Programming Languages and Systems*, 1(2):245–257, Oct. 1979.
15. G. Nelson and D. Oppen. Fast decision procedures based on congruence closure. *Journal of the Association for Computing Machinery*, 27(2):356–364, Apr. 1980.
16. T. Reps, S. Horwitz, and M. Sagiv. Precise interprocedural dataflow analysis via graph reachability. In *22nd ACM Symposium on POPL*, pages 49–61. ACM, 1995.

17. E. Rodriguez-Carbonell and D. Kapur. An abstract interpretation approach for automatic generation of polynomial invariants. In *11th Static Analysis Symposium*, volume 3148 of *Lecture Notes in Computer Science*. Springer, 2004.

18. O. Rüthing, J. Knoop, and B. Steffen. Detecting equalities of variables: Combining efficiency with precision. In *SAS*, volume 1694 of *LNCS*, pages 232–247, 1999.

19. S. Vagvolgyi. Intersection of finitely generated congruences over term algebra. *Theoretical Computer Science*, 300:209–234, 2003.

No, Coreset, No Cry[*]

Sariel Har-Peled[**]

Department of Computer Science,
University of Illinois,
201 N. Goodwin Avenue,
Urbana, IL, 61801, USA

Abstract. We show that coresets do not exist for the problem of 2-slabs in $\mathbb{R}^3$, thus demonstrating that the natural approach for solving approximately this problem efficiently is infeasible. On the positive side, for a point set P in $\mathbb{R}^3$, we describe a near linear time algorithm for computing a $(1 + \varepsilon)$-approximation to the minimum width 2-slab cover of P. This is a first step in providing an efficient approximation algorithm for the problem of covering a point set with k-slabs.

1 Introduction

Geometric optimization in low dimensions is an important problem in computational geometry [1]. One of the central problems is to compute the shape best fitting a given point set, where the shape is restricted to belong to a certain family of shapes parameterized by a few parameters, while minimizing a certain quantity of the shape. For example, covering a point set P with minimum width slab, where a *slab* is the region enclosed between two parallel hyperplanes and the width of the slab is the distance between the two hyperplanes (i.e., this is equivalent to computing the width of P). Problems falling under this framework include computing the width and diameter of the point set, covering a point set with minimum volume bounding box, covering with minimum volume ellipsoid, covering with minimum width annulus, and a lot of other problems.

While some of those problems have exact fast solution, at least in low dimension, most of them can be solved only with algorithms that have running time exponential in the number of parameters defining the shape. For example, the fastest algorithm for computing the minimum width slab that covers a point set in $\mathbb{R}^d$ runs in $n^{O(d)}$ time.

It is thus natural to look for an efficient approximation algorithms for those problems. Here, one specifies an approximation parameter $\varepsilon > 0$, and one wish to find a shape which is $(1 + \varepsilon)$-approximation to the optimal shape, see [2]. For the 1-slab width problem, we wish to find a slab $\mathcal{S}$ that covers a point set P,

---

[*] The full version of this paper is available from http://www.uiuc.edu/~sariel/ papers/02/http://www.uiuc.edu/ sariel/papers/02/2slab/ 2slab/.

[**] Work on this paper was partially supported by a NSF CAREER award CCR-0132901.

K. Lodaya and M. Mahajan (Eds.): FSTTCS 2004, LNCS 3328, pp. 324–335, 2004.

such that $\text{width}(\mathcal{S}) \leq (1+\varepsilon)\text{width}_{opt}(P,1)$, where $\text{width}_{opt}(P,1)$ is the minimum width of a slab covering P.

In recent years, there was a lot research done on those and similar problems (see [3, 4, 5, 6, 7, 8, 9, 10, 11, 12, 13, 14, 15, 16, 17, 18, 19] and references therein) and currently most of them can be solved in $O(n + 1/\varepsilon^c)$ time [20], where c is a constant that depends on the problem at hand.

The problem becomes notably harder when one wish to perform clustering of the point set. Namely, cover the point set by k shapes (k is an integer constant larger than one), while simultaneously minimizing a global parameter of those shapes. For example, the k-slab problem ask to cover the point set by k slabs $(\mathcal{S}_1, \ldots, \mathcal{S}_k)$ of minimum width, where the width of $(\mathcal{S}_1, \ldots, \mathcal{S}_k)$ is $\max_{i=1}^{k} \text{width}(\mathcal{S}_i)$. Problems falling under this category with efficient approximation algorithms include the k-center problem [21, 22], and the k-cylinder problem [23] (here we want to cover the point set with k cylinders of minimum radius).

It is known that in high dimensions, the exact problem is NP-Complete [24] even for covering the point set by a single cylinder, and there is no FPTAS for this problem [25]. For the problem of covering the point set with k cylinders of minimum maximum radius, it is known that the problem is NP-Complete even in three dimensions if k is part of the input [26], and it can not be approximated in polynomial time unless $P = NP$. The currently fastest approximation algorithm known in high dimensions [27, 28], runs in $d \cdot n^{O(\text{poly}(k,1/\varepsilon))}$ time, where $\text{poly}(\cdot)$ is a polynomial of constant degree independent of the dimension. On the other hand, if we are interested in finding a single minimum radius m-flat covering the given point set, this can be ε-approximated in $O(nd)$ time [25] (here the constant in the O depends exponentially on $1/\varepsilon$), where an m-flat is a m-dimensional affine subspace.

In the k-*slab problem*, we wish to cover the point set with k slabs of minimum width (i.e., we wish to find k affine subspaces each of dimension $d-1$, such that the maximum distance of any point of the input to its closest subspace is minimized). At first, this problem might look somewhat artificial. However, it is related to projective clustering in high dimensions. In the projective clustering problem, we are looking for a cover of the points by k m-flats that have small radius. Such a projective clustering implies that the point set can be indexed as k point sets each of them being only m-dimensional. This is a considerable saving when the dimension is very large, as most efficient indexing structures have exponential dependency on the dimension. Thus, finding such a cover might result in a substantial performance improvements for various database applications. Furthermore, a lot of other clustering problems, that currently it is unknown how to solve them efficiently, can be reduced to this problem or its dual. In particular, problems of covering a point set with: (i) k rings with minimum max width, (ii) k bounding boxes of minimum maximum volume, (iii) k cylindrical shells of minimum maximum radius, and others all fall into this framework (see [20] for the details of the reduction of those problems into this problem).

This and the more general problem of finding efficient approximation algorithm for the minimum radius k m-flat problem are still relatively open (both in low and high dimensions). The most natural approach to attack this problem is to try and use coresets. Those are small subsets of the input, such that if we solve the problem on those subsets, this yield an efficient solution for the original problem. Coresets had recently proved to be very useful in solving several clustering problems, both in low dimensions [20, 23], and high dimensions [29, 27, 30, 25]. The surprising facts known about coresets is that their size is sometime dimension independent [29], and they are small even in the presence of outliers [31]. (Note however, that the notion of coresets in high-dimensions is slightly weaker.) Interestingly, in low-dimensions, the existence of coresets immediately implies an efficient approximation algorithm for the problem at hand [23].

Surprisingly, we show in Section 2, that there is no such coresets for the 2-slab problem, in the worst case. Namely, any subset of the input that provides a good estimate of the width of the coverage of the points by two slabs, for all possible 2-slabs, must contain (almost) the whole point set. Thus, showing that solving this problem efficiently would require a different approach.

On the positive size, in Section 3, we make a first step in the direction of finding an efficient algorithm for this problem, and solve a special case which still has no efficient approximation algorithm and does not have a coreset; namely, the 2-slab problem in three dimensions. Formally, given a set P of n points in three dimensions, and a parameter $\varepsilon > 0$, the algorithm compute, in near linear time, a cover of P by two slabs, where the width of the solution is at most $(1+\varepsilon)\text{width}_{opt}(P, 2)$, where $\text{width}_{opt}(P, 2)$ denotes the width of the optimal (i.e., minimum) cover of P by two slabs.

A natural application of our algorithm is for edge detection in surface reconstruction. Indeed, given a set of points in $\mathbb{R}^3$ sampled from a region of a model that corresponds to an edge, the edge can be detected by best fitting the given points with two planes, that corresponds to the two faces adjacent to the edge. One need to slightly modify our algorithm to deploy it for this case.

The paper is organized as follows: In Section 2 we precisely define the notion of additive and multiplicative coresets, and prove that no small coresets exists for the 2-slab problem. As an additional result, we show that there exists a multiplicative coreset for the k-center problem. In Section 3, we present a a near linear time approximation algorithm for the 2-slab problem in three dimensions. Concluding remarks are given in Section 4.

2   When Coresets Do Not Exist

2.1   Definitions

Definition 1. Given a set P of n objects (usually points) in $\mathbb{R}^d$, we are interested in the shape fitting problem, of finding the best shape that belongs to a certain family of shapes $\mathcal{F}$ that matches P. For example, the smallest ball that encloses the points of P. The *price function* radius(P), which returns the radius of the smallest ball enclosing P, measures the quality of this fitting.

In the clustering problem, we are provided with an additional parameter k, and we are interested in finding the best clustering of P into k clusters.

Namely, we would like to partition P into k sets, such that the overall price of the clustering is minimized. Formally, we are interested in minimizing

$$\mathrm{rd}_k(P) = \min_{(P_1,\ldots,P_k)\in\mathcal{PW}(P,k)} \max_i \mathrm{radius}(P_i),$$

where $\mathcal{PW}(P,k) = \left\{ (P_1,\ldots,P_k) \,\middle|\, \cup_i P_i = P, P_i \cap P_j = \emptyset, \text{ for } i \neq j \right\}$ is the set of all partitions of P into k sets.

For example, we would like to cover P by k balls, such that the radius of maximum radius ball is minimized. This is known as the *k-center clustering* problem (or just *k-center*). The *price function*, in this case, $\mathrm{rd}_k(P)$ is the radius of the maximum radius ball in the optimal solution.

Definition 2. Let P be a point set in $\mathbb{R}^d$, $1/2 > \varepsilon > 0$ a parameter.

For a cluster c, let $c(\delta)$ denote the cluster resulting form expanding c by δ. Thus, if c is a ball of radius r, then $c(\delta)$ is a ball of radius $r + \delta$. For a set $\mathcal{C}$ of clusters, let

$$\mathcal{C}(\delta) = \left\{ c(\delta) \,\middle|\, c \in \mathcal{C} \right\},$$

be the *additive expansion operator*; that is, $\mathcal{C}(\delta)$ is a set of clusters resulting form expanding each cluster of $\mathcal{C}$ by δ.

Similarly,

$$(1+\varepsilon)\mathcal{C} = \left\{ (1+\varepsilon)c \,\middle|\, c \in \mathcal{C} \right\},$$

is the *multiplicative expansion operator*, where $(1 + \varepsilon)c$ is the cluster resulting from expanding c by a factor of $(1+\varepsilon)$. Namely, if $\mathcal{C}$ is a set of balls, then $(1+\varepsilon)\mathcal{C}$ is a set of balls, where a ball $c \in \mathcal{C}$, corresponds to a ball radius $(1 + \varepsilon)\,\mathrm{radius}(c)$ in $(1 + \varepsilon)\mathcal{C}$.

A set $Q \subseteq P$ is an (additive) ε-*coreset* of P, in relation to a price function radius, if for any clustering $\mathcal{C}$ of Q, we have that P is covered by $\mathcal{C}\,(\varepsilon\,\mathrm{radius}(\mathcal{C}))$, where $\mathrm{radius}(\mathcal{C}) = \max_{c\in\mathcal{C}} \mathrm{radius}(c)$. Namely, we expand every cluster in the clustering by an ε-fraction of the size of the *largest* cluster in the clustering. Thus, if $\mathcal{C}$ is a set of k balls, then $\mathcal{C}(\varepsilon f(\mathcal{C}))$ is just the set of balls resulting from expanding each ball by εr, where r is the radius of the largest ball.

A set $Q \subseteq P$ is a *multiplicative ε-coreset* of P, if for any clustering $\mathcal{C}$ of Q, we have that P is covered by $(1 + \varepsilon)\mathcal{C}$.

Note, that ε-multiplicative coresets are by definition also ε-additive coresets.

Remark 1. Let $\mathcal{C}$ be a given clustering, and apply to it a constant length sequence of δ-expansion operations, either additive or multiplicative. Let $\mathcal{C}'$ be the resulting clustering. It is easy to verify that there exists a constant c, such that the clustering $\mathcal{D}$ resulting from $c\delta$-additive expansion of $\mathcal{C}$, is larger than $\mathcal{C}'$. Namely, all the clusters of $\mathcal{C}'$ are contained inside the corresponding clusters of $\mathcal{D}$.

Thus, we can simulate any sequence of expansion operations, by a single additive expansion.

2.2   On Multiplicative Coresets

Coresets for k-Center Clustering. The k-center problem, is NP-Complete, and can be approximated up to a factor of two in linear time [32]. For a set P of n points in $\mathbb{R}^d$, let $rd(P, k)$ denote the radius of the optimal clustering. This is the minimum over all covering of P by k balls, of the largest ball in the covering set.

Lemma 1. *Let P be a set of n points in $\mathbb{R}^d$, and $\varepsilon > 0$ a parameter. There exists an additive ε-coreset for the k-center problem, and this coreset has $O(k/\varepsilon^d)$ points.*

Proof. Let $\mathcal{C}$ denote the optimal clustering of P. Cover each ball of $\mathcal{C}$ by a grid of side length $\varepsilon r_{opt}/d$, where r_{opt} is the radius of the optimal k-center clustering of P. From each such grid cell, pick one points of P. Clearly, the resulting point set Q is of size $O(k/\varepsilon^d)$ and it is an additive coreset of P.

The following is a minor extension of an argument used in [23].

Lemma 2. *Let P be a set of n points in $\mathbb{R}^d$, and $\varepsilon > 0$ a parameter. There exists a multiplicative ε-coreset for the k-center problem, and this coreset has $O\left(k!/\varepsilon^{dk}\right)$ points.*

Proof. For $k = 1$, the additive coreset of P is also a multiplicative coreset, and it is of size $O(1/\varepsilon^d)$.

As in the proof of Lemma 1, we cover the point set by a grid of radius $\varepsilon r_{opt}/(5d)$, let SQ the set of cells (i.e., cubes) of this grid which contains points of P. Clearly, $|SQ| = O(k/\varepsilon^d)$.

Let Q be the additive ε-coreset of P. Let $\mathcal{C}$ be any k-center clustering of Q, and let Δ be any cell of SQ.

If Δ intersects all the k balls of $\mathcal{C}$, then one of them must be of radius at least $(1 - \varepsilon/2)rd(P, k)$. Let c be this ball. Clearly, when we expand c by a factor of $(1 + \varepsilon)$ it would completely cover Δ, and as such it would also cover all the points of $\Delta \cap P$.

Thus, we can assume that Δ intersects at most $k - 1$ balls of $\mathcal{C}$. As such, we can inductively compute an ε-multiplicative coreset of $P \cap \Delta$, for $k - 1$ balls. Let Q_Δ be this set, and let $\mathcal{Q} = Q \cup \bigcup_{\Delta \in SQ} Q_\Delta$.

Note that $|\mathcal{Q}| = T(k, \varepsilon) = O(k/\varepsilon^d)T(k - 1, \varepsilon) + O(k/\varepsilon^d) = O\left(k!/\varepsilon^{dk}\right)$. The set $\mathcal{Q}$ is the required multiplicative coreset by the above argumentation.

When Multiplicative Coresets Do Not Exist. Recently, Agarwal *et al.* [23] proved that an additive ε-coreset exists for the problem of covering a point set by k-cylinders. We next show that there is no small *multiplicative* coreset for this problem. Note, that for a strip c, the set $c(\delta)$ is the strip with the same center line as c, and of width $w + 2\delta$, where w is the width of c, and similarly, $(1 + \varepsilon)c$ is the strip of width $(1 + \varepsilon)w$ with the same center line as c.

Lemma 3. *There exists a point set P in $\mathbb{R}^2$, such that any multiplicative $(1/2)$-coreset of P, must be of size at least $|P| - 2$. Here the coreset is for the problem of covering the point set with 2 strips, such that the width of the wider strip is minimized.*

Proof. Consider the point set $P(m) = \left\{ (1/2^j, 2^j) \,\middle|\, j = 1, \ldots, m \right\}$, where m is an arbitrary parameter. Let Q be a $(1/2)$-coreset of $P = P(n)$.

Let $Q_i^- = Q \cap P(i)$ and $Q_i^+ = Q \setminus Q_i^-$.

If the set Q does not contain the point $p(i) = (1/2^i, 2^i)$, then Q_i^- can be covered by a horizontal strip h^- of width $\leq 2^{i-1}$ that has the x-axis as its lower boundary, and clearly if we expand h^- by a factor of $3/2$, the new $(3/2)h^-$ still will not cover $p(i)$. Similarly, we can cover Q_i^+ by a vertical strip h^+ of width $1/2^{i+1}$ that has the y-axis as its left boundary. Again, if we expand h^+ by a factor of $3/2$, the new strip $(3/2)h^+$ will not cover $p(i)$. We conclude, that any multiplicative $(1/2)$-coreset for P must include all the points $p(2), p(3), \ldots, p(n-1)$.

Thus, no small multiplicative coreset exists for the problem of covering a point set by strips.

When Small Additive Coresets Do Not Exist

Definition 3. A *slab* S in $\mathbb{R}^3$ is the close region enclosed between two parallel planes. The *width* of S is the distance between those two parallel planes. The plane parallel to the two boundary planes and with equal distance to both of them, is the *center* of S.

Definition 4. Given a tuple $\Delta = (S_1, \ldots, S_k)$ of k slabs in three dimensions, the width of Δ; denoted by $\mathrm{width}(\Delta) = \mathrm{width}(S_1, \ldots, S_k) = \max_{i=1}^k \mathrm{width}(S_i)$. The *$k$-slab width* of a point set P in $\mathbb{R}^3$, is the width of the set of k slabs that covers P and minimizes the k-slab width. We denote the this minimum width by $\mathrm{width}_{opt}(P, k)$.

In the following, let P be a set of points in $\mathbb{R}^3$, which we want to cover by k-slabs of minimum width.

Lemma 4. *There exists a point set P in $\mathbb{R}^3$, such that any additive $(1/2)$-coreset of P, for the 2-slab problem, must be of size at least $|P| - 2$.*

Proof. Let P' be the two-dimensional point set used in Lemma 3. Let P be the three-dimensional point set resulting from interpreting any point of P' as a point lying on the plane $z = 0$. Let $\delta = 1/2$.

Let C be an additive δ-coreset C of P, for the 2-slab problem, and let C' be the corresponding subset of P'. We claim that C' is a multiplicative δ-coreset of P' for the problem of 2-strips cover.

Indeed, let S_1, S_2 be any two strips that covers C', and assume that S_1 is wider than S_2. And let T_1, T_2 be two slabs in three dimensions, *of the same width*, such that $S_1 = T_1 \cap h$, and $S_2 = T_2 \cap h$, where h is the plane $z = 0$. The existence of such two slabs of equal width can be easily proved, by starting from two slabs T_1', T_2 which are perpendicular to h, and their intersection with h form S_1 and S_2, respectively. Next, rotate the wider slab, T_1', such that its width go down, while keeping its intersection with h fixed. We stop as soon as the modified T_1' has equal width to T_2.

Now, additively expanding T_1 and T_2 corresponds to multiplicatively expanding them, since both of them have the same width. By assumption, the δ-expanded slabs cover P, and as such, they cover P'. Let V_1, V_2 be the intersection of the expanded slabs with h. Clearly, V_1 and V_2 are just the multiplicative expansion of S_1 and S_2, respectively, by a factor of $(1+\delta)$. Furthermore, V_1 and V_2 covers the points of P'. We conclude, that $\mathcal{C}'$ is a δ-multiplicative coreset of P', for the 2-strip problem.

However, since $\delta = 1/2$, and by Lemma 3, it follows that $|\mathcal{C}| = |\mathcal{C}'| \geq |P| - 2$.

Note, that Lemma 4 implies that there is no hope of solving the k-slab problem using coreset techniques. Furthermore, it is easy to verify that the above lemma implies (in the dual) that one can not use coresets for the "dual" (and more useful) problem of stabbing hyperplanes with segments.

Problem 1 (k-extent). Given a set $\mathcal{H}$ of n hyperplanes in $\mathbb{R}^d$, and a parameter k, find a set of k vertical segments that stabs all the hyperplanes of $\mathcal{H}$, and the length of the longest segment is minimized.

Lemma 5. *There exists a set $\mathcal{H}$ of planes in $\mathbb{R}^3$, such that any additive $(1/2)$-coreset of $\mathcal{H}$, for the 2-extent problem, must be of size at least $|P| - 2$.*

3   Algorithm for the 2-Slab in 3D

Our algorithm works, by deploying a decision procedure that decides (approximately) whether or not the point set can be covered by two slabs of width r. This is done by performing the decision when two points are specified which lie on the center plane of one of the slabs (Lemma 8). Then, we extend this algorithm, for the decision problem when two points are given, which are "faraway" and lie in the same slab in the optimal solution (Lemma 9). This yields the required decision procedure, by enumerating a small number of pairs, one of them guaranteed to be in the same slab in the optimal solution, and to be a long pair (see Lemma 10).

Having this decision procedure, we can now solve the problem using a binary search over the possible widths. Naively, this leads to a weakly polynomial algorithm. To improve this, we first show that if we know a pair of points that lie on the center plane of one of the slabs, then we can compute a constant factor approximation in near linear time (Lemma 11). Now, we again generate a small set of candidate pairs, and check for each one of them what solution it yields. This results in a constant factor approximation (Lemma 12). Combining this constant factor approximation, together with the binary search using the decision procedure, results in the required approximation algorithm (Theorem 7).

In describing the algorithm, we use binary search and random sampling to replace parametric search, since it is simpler to describe. Minor improvements in running time are probably possible by using parametric search, and a more careful implementation of the algorithm.

3.1 Preliminaries

Lemma 6 ([20]). *Given a set P of n points in $\mathbb{R}^3$, and a parameter $\varepsilon > 0$, one can compute a subset $S \subseteq P$, such that $\text{width}_{opt}(S, 1) \geq (1 - \varepsilon)\text{width}_{opt}(P, 1)$, and $|S| = O(1/\varepsilon^2)$. Furthermore, S can be computed in $O(n + 1/\varepsilon^2)$ time.*

Lemma 7 ([20]). *Given a set P of n points in $\mathbb{R}^3$, one can maintain an ε-approximate minimum width slab that contains P in $O((\log^3 n)/\varepsilon^2 + 1/\varepsilon^6)$ time per insertion/deletion. After each insertion/deletion the data-structure outputs a slab covering P which is wider by at most a factor of $(1 + \varepsilon)$ than the optimal slab that covers P.*

Fact 5. Given a set P of n points in $\mathbb{R}^3$, one can compute the width of P in $O(n^{3/2+\varepsilon})$ expected time [4]. To simplify the exposition, we would use the slower quadratic time algorithm of [33].

3.2 Decision Problem

We are given a set P of n points in $\mathbb{R}^3$, a candidate width r, and a parameter $\varepsilon > 0$. In this section, we describe an algorithm that decides whether one can cover P by two slabs of width at most r. More precisely, we describe an approximate decision procedure for this problem. Namely, if there is a cover of width $\leq r$, it outputs a cover of width at most $\leq (1 + \varepsilon)r$. If P can not be covered by two slabs of width $(1 + \varepsilon)r$, it outputs that no such cover exists. Otherwise (in this case the point set can not be covered with slabs of width r, but it can be covered by slabs of width $(1 + \varepsilon)r$), it output either of those two answers.

Lemma 8. *Given r, ε prescribed parameters, a set P of n points in $\mathbb{R}^3$, and a pair $p, q \in P$. Then one can compute a cover $(\mathcal{S}, \mathcal{S}')$ of P by two slabs, such that p, q lie on the center (plane) of $\mathcal{S}$, the width of $\mathcal{S}$ is r, and the width of $\mathcal{S}'$ is $\leq (1 + \varepsilon)\rho$, where ρ is the minimum width of $\mathcal{S}'$ under those constraints. The running time of the algorithm is $O\left(n(\log^3 n/\varepsilon^2 + 1/\varepsilon^6)\right)$.*

Proof. We assume that p, q lie on the x-axis. Let $\mathcal{S}(\alpha)$ be the slab of width r with its center plane passing through p, q and this plane has an angle α with the positive direction of the z-axis. Let $P_{in}(\alpha) = \mathcal{S}(\alpha) \cap P$ denote the points of P covered by $\mathcal{S}(\alpha)$, and let $P_{out}(\alpha) = P \backslash P_{in}(\alpha)$ denote the points not covered by it.

Using standard sweeping techniques, we can maintain the sets $P_{in}(\alpha), P_{out}(\alpha)$, for $0 \leq \alpha \leq \pi$. This would require $O(n)$ insertion/deletion operations, and would take $O(n \log n)$ time. Thus, to find the required cover, we need to compute the minimum width cover of $P_{out}(\alpha)$, for $0 \leq \alpha \leq \pi$, as the set $P_{in}(\alpha)$ is always covered by a slab of width r (i.e., $\mathcal{S}(\alpha)$). Using Lemma 7, this can be done approximately in $O\left(n(\log^3 n/\varepsilon^2 + 1/\varepsilon^6)\right)$ time. Indeed, let $\mathcal{S}_{out}(\alpha)$ denote the minimum width slab that covers $P_{out}(\alpha)$, and $\rho = \min_\alpha \text{width}(\mathcal{S}_{out}(\alpha))$. Overall, the algorithm computes an α^*, such that $\text{width}(\mathcal{S}_{out}(\alpha^*)) \leq (1 + \varepsilon)\rho$.

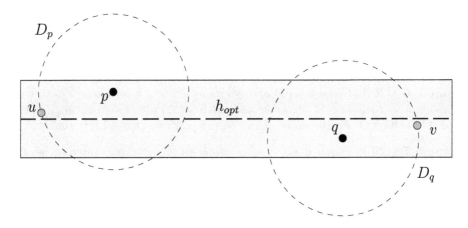

Fig. 1. Demonstration of the proof of Lemma 9

Corollary 1. *Given* r, ε *prescribed parameters, and a pair of points* $p, q \in P$ *such that* $\|pq\| \geq \mathrm{diam}(P)/10$. *Let* $(\mathcal{S}, \mathcal{S}')$ *be a 2-cover of* P, *such that* $\mathrm{width}(\mathcal{S}, \mathcal{S}') = r$ *and* p, q *lie on the center of* $\mathcal{S}$. *Then, one can compute a 2-cover of* P *of width at most* $(1 + \varepsilon)r$. *The running time of the algorithm is* $O\left(n\left(\log^3 n/\varepsilon^2 + 1/\varepsilon^6\right)\right)$.

Definition 6. *Given a sphere* $\varPhi$ *in* $\mathbb{R}^d$ *of radius* r, *a* δ-net *of* $\varPhi$, *is a subset* U *of* $\varPhi$, *such that for any* $x \in \varPhi$, *there exists a point* $u \in U$ *such that* $\|xu\| \leq \delta$.

   Given $\varPhi$ *and* δ, *one can compute a* δ-net *for* $\varPhi$ *of cardinality* $O\left((r/\delta)^{d-1}\right)$, *in linear time in the size of the* δ-net.

Lemma 9. *Given* r, ε *prescribed parameters, a point set* P *in* $\mathbb{R}^3$, *and two points* $p, q \in P$ *such that* $\mathrm{width}_{opt}(P, 2) \leq r$, $\|pq\| \geq \mathrm{diam}(P)/10$ *and* p, q *lie in the same slab in the optimal 2-slab cover of* P. *Then, one can compute a cover of* P *by two slabs of width* $\leq (1 + \varepsilon)r$ *in* $O\left(n\left(\log^3 n/\varepsilon^6 + 1/\varepsilon^{10}\right)\right)$ *time.*

Proof. Omitted. Will appear in the full-version.

Lemma 10. *Given* r, ε *prescribed parameters, and a set* P *of* n *points in* $\mathbb{R}^3$, *such that* $\mathrm{width}_{opt}(P, 2) \leq r$, *then one can compute a cover of* P *by two slabs of width* $\leq (1 + \varepsilon)r$ *in* $O\left(n\left(\log^3 n/\varepsilon^8 + 1/\varepsilon^{12}\right)\right)$ *time.*

Proof. Omitted. Will appear in the full-version.

3.3 A Strongly Polynomial Algorithm

The algorithm of Lemma 10 provides immediately a weakly polynomial algorithm that works by performing a binary search for the optimal width on the range $[0, \mathrm{diam}(P)]$. The resulting algorithm would execute the algorithm of Lemma 10 $O\left(\log\left(\mathrm{diam}(P)/(\mathrm{width}_{opt}(P, 2)\varepsilon)\right)\right)$ times. In practice, this might be quite acceptable, although it is only weakly polynomial.

In this section, we present a *strongly* polynomial algorithm for approximating the 2-slab width. We observe, that it is enough to compute a c-approximation w to the 2-slab cover to P, where $c > 1$ is a constant. Indeed, once we have such an approximation, one can compute a better approximation using a binary search over the range $[w/c, w]$.

Lemma 11. *Let p, q be a pair of points of P. One can compute in $O\left(n \log^4 n\right)$ a 2-slab cover $(\mathcal{S}, \mathcal{S}')$ of P of width w, such that p, q lie on the center of $\mathcal{S}$, and w is constant factor approximation to the optimal 2-slab cover under this condition.*

Proof. Omitted. Will appear in the full-version.

Lemma 12. *Given a set P of n points in $\mathbb{R}^3$, one can compute a cover of P by two slabs of width $O(\text{width}_{opt}(P, 2))$ in $O\left(n \log^4 n\right)$ time.*

Proof. Omitted. Will appear in the full-version.

Now, once we have a constant factor approximation, an $(1+\varepsilon)$-approximation can be easily performed by doing a binary search, and using the decision procedure (Lemma 10). This would require $O(\log 1/\varepsilon)$ calls to the decision procedure. We conclude:

Theorem 7. *Given a set P of n points in $\mathbb{R}^3$, one can compute a cover of P by two slabs of width $\leq (1 + \varepsilon)\text{width}_{opt}(P, 2)$ in $O\left(n \log^4 n + n(\log^3 n/\varepsilon^8 + 1/\varepsilon^{12})\right) \log 1/\varepsilon)$ time.*

4   Conclusions

In this paper, we showed that coresets do no exists for the problem of 2-slabs in three dimensions. The author find this fact to be quite bewildering, considering the fact that such coresets exists for balls and cylinders. This implies that solving the k-slab problem efficiently in low dimensions (i.e., in near linear time) would require developing new techniques and algorithms. We took a small and tentative step in this direction, providing a near linear time algorithm for approximating the min-width 2-slab cover of a point set in $\mathbb{R}^3$.

The main open question for further research, is to develop an efficient approximation algorithms for the k-slab problem in three and higher dimensions, for $k > 2$. Currently, the author is unaware of any efficient constant factor approximation algorithm for this problem.

Finally, there seems to be a connection between solving the problem of k-slabs in $\mathbb{R}^d$ in the presence of outliers, and solving the problem of $k + 1$ slabs in $\mathbb{R}^{d+1}$. (Intuitively and imprecisely, thats what our 2-slab algorithm in $\mathbb{R}^3$ is doing: It reduces the problem into the problem of covering a point set in $\mathbb{R}^2$ with a single slab, while making sure that the points that are not covered can be ignored.) Understanding this connection might be a key in understanding why the k-slab problem seems to be harder than one might expect.

Acknowledgments

The author wishes to thank Vladlen Koltun, Magda Procopiuc, Edgar Ramos, and Kasturi Varadarajan for useful discussions on the problems studied in this paper. The author would also thank the anonymous referees for their insightful comments.

References

1. Agarwal, P.K., Sharir, M.: Efficient algorithms for geometric optimization. ACM Comput. Surv. **30** (1998) 412–458
2. Bern, M., Eppstein, D.: Approximation algorithms for geometric problems. In Hochbaum, D.S., ed.: Approximationg algorithms for NP-Hard problems. PWS Publishing Company (1997) 296–345
3. Agarwal, P.K., Aronov, B., Sharir, M.: Computing envelopes in four dimensions with applications. SIAM J. Comput. **26** (1997) 1714–1732
4. Agarwal, P.K., Sharir, M.: Efficient randomized algorithms for some geometric optimization problems. Discrete Comput. Geom. **16** (1996) 317–337
5. Agarwal, P.K., Sharir, M., Toledo, S.: Applications of parametric searching in geometric optimization. J. Algorithms **17** (1994) 292–318
6. Ebara, H., Fukuyama, N., Nakano, H., Nakanishi, Y.: Roundness algorithms using the Voronoi diagrams. In: Proc. 1rd Canad. Conf. Comput. Geom. (1989) 41
7. Edelsbrunner, H., Guibas, L.J., Stolfi, J.: Optimal point location in a monotone subdivision. SIAM J. Comput. **15** (1986) 317–340
8. García-Lopez, J., Ramos, P., Snoeyink, J.: Fitting a set of points by a circle. Discrete Comput. Geom. **20** (1998) 389–402
9. Le, V.B., Lee, D.T.: Out-of-roundness problem revisited. IEEE Trans. Pattern Anal. Mach. Intell. **PAMI-13** (1991) 217–223
10. Mehlhorn, K., Shermer, T.C., Yap, C.K.: A complete roundness classification procedure. In: Proc. 13th Annu. ACM Sympos. Comput. Geom. (1997) 129–138
11. Preparata, F.P., Shamos, M.I.: Computational Geometry: An Introduction. Springer-Verlag, New York, NY (1985)
12. Rivlin, T.J.: Approximating by circles. Computing **21** (1979) 93–104
13. Roy, U., Liu, C.R., Woo, T.C.: Review of dimensioning and tolerancing: Representation and processing. Comput. Aided Design **23** (1991) 466–483
14. Roy, U., Zhang, X.: Establishment of a pair of concentric circles with the minimum radial separation for assessing roundness error. Comput. Aided Design **24** (1992) 161–168
15. Shermer, T.C., Yap, C.K.: Probing for near centers and relative roundness. In: Proc. ASME Workshop on Tolerancing and Metrology. (1995)
16. Smid, M., Janardan, R.: On the width and roundness of a set of points in the plane. Internat. J. Comput. Geom. Appl. **9** (1999) 97–108
17. Yap, C.K., Chang, E.C.: Issues in the metrology of geometric tolerancing. In Laumond, J.P., Overmars, M.H., eds.: Robotics Motion and Manipulation. A. K. Peters (1997) 393–400
18. Chan, T.M.: Approximating the diameter, width, smallest enclosing cylinder and minimum-width annulus. Internat. J. Comput. Geom. Appl. **12** (2002) 67–85
19. Agarwal, P.K., Aronov, B., Har-Peled, S., Sharir, M.: Approximation and exact algorithms for minimum-width annuli and shells. Discrete Comput. Geom. **24** (2000) 687–705

20. Agarwal, P.K., Har-Peled, S., Varadarajan, K.R.: Approximating extent measures of points. J. ACM **51** (2004) 606–635
21. Gonzalez, T.: Clustering to minimize the maximum intercluster distance. Theoret. Comput. Sci. **38** (1985) 293–306
22. Agarwal, P.K., Procopiuc, C.M.: Exact and approximation algorithms for clustering. Algorithmica **33** (2002) 201–226
23. Agarwal, P.K., Procopiuc, C.M., Varadarajan, K.R.: Approximation algorithms for k-line center. In: Proc. 10th Annu. European Sympos. Algorithms. (2002) 54–63
24. Megiddo, N.: On the complexity of some geometric problems in unbounded dimension. J. Symb. Comput. **10** (1990) 327–334
25. Har-Peled, S., Varadarajan, K.R.: High-dimensional shape fitting in linear time. Discrete Comput. Geom. **32** (2004) 269–288
26. Megiddo, N., Tamir, A.: On the complexity of locating linear facilities in the plane. Oper. Res. Lett. **1** (1982) 194–197
27. Bădoiu, M., Clarkson, K.L.: Optimal core-sets for balls. In: Proc. 14th ACM-SIAM Sympos. Discrete Algorithms. (2003) 801–802
28. Har-Peled, S., Varadarajan, K.R.: Projective clustering in high dimensions using core-sets. In: Proc. 18th Annu. ACM Sympos. Comput. Geom. (2002) 312–318
29. Bădoiu, M., Har-Peled, S., Indyk, P.: Approximate clustering via core-sets. In: Proc. 34th Annu. ACM Sympos. Theory Comput. (2002) 250–257
30. Kumar, P., Mitchell, J.S.B., Yildirim, E.A.: Fast smallest enclosing hypersphere computation. In: Proc. 5th Workshop Algorithm Eng. Exper. (2003) to appear
31. Har-Peled, S., Wang, Y.: Shape fitting with outliers. SIAM J. Comput. **33** (2004) 269–285
32. Har-Peled, S.: Clustering motion. Discrete Comput. Geom. **31** (2004) 545–565
33. Houle, M.E., Toussaint, G.T.: Computing the width of a set. IEEE Trans. Pattern Anal. Mach. Intell. **PAMI-10** (1988) 761–765

Hardness Hypotheses, Derandomization, and Circuit Complexity

John M. Hitchcock[1] and A. Pavan[2,*]

[1] Department of Computer Science, University of Wyoming
jhitchco@cs.uwyo.edu
[2] Department of Computer Science, Iowa State University,
pavan@cs.iastate.edu

Abstract. We consider three complexity-theoretic hypotheses that have been studied in different contexts and shown to have many plausible consequences.

- The *Measure Hypothesis*: NP does not have p-measure 0.
- The *pseudo*-NP *Hypothesis*: there is an NP Language L such that any $\mathrm{DTIME}(2^{n^\epsilon})$ Language L' can be distinguished from L by an NP refuter.
- The NP-*Machine Hypothesis*: there is an NP machine accepting 0^* for which no 2^{n^ϵ}-time machine can find infinitely many accepting computations.

We show that the NP-machine hypothesis is implied by each of the first two. Previously, no relationships were known among these three hypotheses. Moreover, we unify previous work by showing that several derandomization and circuit-size lower bounds that are known to follow from the first two hypotheses also follow from the NP-machine hypothesis. We also consider UP versions of the above hypotheses as well as related immunity and scaled dimension hypotheses.

1 Introduction

Unconditional results are very rare in complexity theory. Many results have been proved using traditional hypotheses such as "P $\neq$ NP," "NP $\neq$ co-NP," or "the polynomial-time hierarchy is infinite." It is often the case that these hypotheses lack explanatory power to answer some questions we are interested in. Thus researchers propose new reasonable hypotheses and study the relations among complexity classes. For example, we do not know if the derandomization of BPP follows from P $\neq$ NP. However, BPP has been shown to be equal to P under the hypothesis "EXP has high circuit complexity" [14]. Often these hypotheses are introduced with a specific subarea in mind, and at first glance it is not clear

---

* This research was supported in part by National Science Foundation grants CCR-0344187 and CCF-0430807.

K. Lodaya and M. Mahajan (Eds.): FSTTCS 2004, LNCS 3328, pp. 336–347, 2004.

whether the hypotheses that arise in different contexts are related. We study relationships among such hypotheses in this paper.

The principle hypotheses that we consider are "the measure hypothesis," "the pseudo-NP hypothesis," and the "NP-machine hypothesis."

- **Measure Hypothesis.** Lutz while developing resource-bounded measure theory introduced "the measure hypothesis" which states that NP does not have p-measure 0. This hypothesis has been extensively studied in the literature. Several remarkable consequences that are not known to be obtainable from traditional hypotheses have been shown under the measure hypothesis. For example, this hypothesis implies that Turing completeness for NP is different from many-one completeness [25], NP-complete languages are dense [24], BPP $\subseteq \Delta_2^P$ [2], and BPP$^{\Sigma_k^P}$ = P$^{\Sigma_k^P}$ for all $k \geq 1$ [22]. More recently, Impagliazzo and Moser [13] showed that if the p-measure of NP is not zero, then AM = NP.

- **Pseudo-NP Hypothesis.** Kabanets [15] introduced "pseudo" classes and the easy-witness method to show an unconditional derandomization result for RP in a uniform setting. Later, Lu [20] extended this to AM. He considered what we call the "pseudo-NP hypothesis". Informally, this says that there is a language L in NP such that if L' is in any language in DTIME(2^{n^ϵ}), then there is a nondeterministic refuter that outputs a string in $L \Delta L'$. Lu showed that the pseudo-NP hypothesis implies AM = NP.

- **NP-Machine Hypothesis.** The "NP-machine hypothesis" states that there is a NP machine M that accepts 0^* for which no 2^{n^ϵ} time-bounded machine can correctly compute infinitely many accepting computations of M. Pavan and Selman [27] showed that the NP-machine hypothesis implies that Turing completeness for NP is different from many-one completeness. Also, several variants of this hypothesis have been previously studied in the literature. Hemaspaandra, Rothe, and Wechsung [8] studied the question of whether there is a NP machine that accepts a language in P whose accepting computations cannot be computed by a polynomial-time-bounded machine. They showed that this question is related to several questions regarding printability and immunity. Fenner, Fortnow, Naik, and Rogers [6] showed that this question is equivalent to the question of whether there exists an NP machine that accepts Σ^* whose accepting computations cannot be computed by polynomial-time-bounded machines. They obtained several equivalent characterizations of this question, for example, they showed that such NP machines exist if and only if there exist honest, onto partial functions that are one-way. Recently, Glaßer et al. [7] showed that the UP version of this hypothesis implies the existence of disjoint Turing complete languages for NP whose union is not Turing complete.

Previously, no relationships among these three hypotheses are known. In this paper we show that the NP-machine hypothesis is implied by both the pseudo-NP hypothesis and the measure hypothesis. We show that this weaker NP-machine hypothesis also implies NP = AM, thereby unifying the results of Impagliazzo and Moser [13] and Lu [20] mentioned above.

In addition, we show a number of other consequences of the NP-machine hypothesis. For example, we show that this hypothesis implies E^{NP} does not have circuits of size $2^{\epsilon n}$, for some $\epsilon > 0$, and $NEXP \not\subseteq P/poly$. It is known that the NP-machine hypothesis is implied by the hypothesis "NP$\cap$co-NP has a DTIME($2^{n^{\epsilon}}$)-bi-immune language" [27]. Thus, if $NP \cap co\text{-}NP$ has a $2^{n^{\epsilon}}$-bi-immune language, then the above mentioned circuit lower bounds for E^{NP} and NEXP follow. This is particularly interesting, because concepts such as bi-immunity and circuit complexity have been studied for a long time under different contexts. Our results show an underlying relationships among these concepts. We also consider the UP version of the hypothesis and show several consequences.

Finally, we consider the hypothesis "the -3rd-order scaled dimension of NP is positive." Under this hypothesis, we achieve a partial derandomization of AM and show that $AM \subseteq NP/n^{\epsilon}$ for every $\epsilon > 0$. This hypothesis seems to be incomparable with the above mentioned hypothesis. We show that this hypothesis also implies $NEXP \not\subseteq P/poly$.

2   Preliminaries

Given a language L, L^n denotes the set $\{x \mid |x| = n, x \in L\}$. Given a string $L(x) = 1$ if $x \in L$, and $L(x) = 0$, if $x \notin L$. Given n, let $s_1, s_2, \cdots s_{2^n}$ be the strings of length n in lexicographic order. Then $L|n = L(s_1) \cdots L(s_{2^n})$. Given a complexity class $\mathcal{C}$, the class io-$\mathcal{C}$ is

$$\{L \mid (\exists A \in \mathcal{C})(\exists^{\infty} n)L^n = A^n\}.$$

An oracle circuit is a circuit that has special gates called *oracle gates*, in addition to the normal AND, OR, and NOT gates. Given an oracle A, an A-*oracle circuit* is an oracle circuit that has A as an oracle, i.e, if x is the input of an oracle gate, then the output is $A(x)$. Given a boolean function $f : \Sigma^n \to \{0, 1\}$, and an oracle A, the A-*oracle circuit complexity* of f is the size of the smallest A-oracle circuit that computes f. Given A, SIZE$^A(f(n))$, is the class of languages whose A-oracle circuit complexity is at most $f(n)$.

An infinite language is *immune* to a complexity class $\mathcal{C}$ or is $\mathcal{C}$-immune, if no infinite subset of L belongs to $\mathcal{C}$. An infinite language is $\mathcal{C}$-*bi-immune* if both L and $\overline{L}$ are $\mathcal{C}$-immune. Balcázar and Schöning [4] observed that a language L is DTIME($T(n)$)-bi-immune if and only if every machine that correctly decides L takes more than $T(n)$ time on all but finitely many strings. A set S is $t(n)$-printable, if there exists a $t(n)$-time bounded algorithm that on input 0^n outputs all elements of S^n.

Lutz [21] developed resource-bounded measure theory, analogous to classical Lebesgue measure, to study the quantitative structure of complexity classes. Here we briefly give the definitions; the reader is referred to the survey papers [23, 3] for more detail.

A *martingale* is a function $d : \Sigma^* \to [0, \infty)$ with the property that, for all $w \in \Sigma^*$, $2d(w) = d(w0) + d(w1)$. A martingale d *succeeds* on a language $A \subseteq \Sigma^*$ if

$$\limsup_{n \to \infty} d(A \restriction n) = \infty,$$

where $A \upharpoonright n$ is the length n prefix of A's characteristic sequence. A class X of languages has *p-measure zero*, written $\mu_p(X) = 0$, if there exists a polynomial-time computable martingale that succeeds on every language in X.

Kabanets [15] defined pseudo classes and refuters. Let A and B any two languages and R be a nondeterministic polynomial-time machine. We assume that R prints an output along every accepting path. We can view R as a machine that computes a multi-valued function. We say R *distinguishes* A *from* B, if for infinitely many n, every output of $R(0^n)$ is in $(A \Delta B) \cap \Sigma^n$. Such R is called a *refuter*.

Given a class $\mathcal{C}$, [pseudo$_{\text{NP}}$]-$\mathcal{C}$ is the class of all languages L such that there exists a language L' in $\mathcal{C}$ and every NP machine R, R does not distinguish L from L'. We similarly define the class [pseudo$_{\text{UP}}$]-$\mathcal{C}$ where we only insist that no UP machine distinguishes L from L'.

Next we briefly review definitions of pseudo-random generators. We refer the reader to the recent surveys of Miltersen [26] and Kabanets [16] for more details.

Let $G_n : \{0,1\}^{r \log n} \to \{0,1\}^n$ be a family of functions, and let $C = \{C_n\}_n$ the class of $\text{SIZE}(n)$-circuits. Then we say G *is a pseudo-random generator* if

$$\forall n, \left| \Pr_{x \in \Sigma^{r \log n}}[C_n(G_n(x))] - \Pr_{x \in \Sigma^n}[C(x)] \right| \leq \frac{1}{n}.$$

The celebrated result of Impagliazzo and Wigderson [14] states that pseudo-random generators can be constructed from any Boolean function with high circuit complexity. Klivans and van Melkebeek [18] observed that, the construction of Impagliazzo and Wigderson relativizes, i.e, for any A, given a Boolean function with high A-oracle circuit complexity, one can construct a pseudorandom generator that is secure against A-oracle circuits. More precisely,

Theorem 2.1. (Klivans and van Melkebeek [18]) *Let A be any language. There is a polynomial-time computable function $F : \Sigma^* \times \Sigma^* \to \Sigma^*$, with the following properties. For every $\epsilon > 0$, there exists $a, b \in \mathbb{N}$ such that*

$$F : \Sigma^{n^a} \times \Sigma^{b \log n} \to \Sigma^n,$$

and if r is the truth table of a $a \log n$-variable Boolean function whose A-oracle circuit complexity is bigger than $n^{a\epsilon}$, then $G_r(s) = F(r, s)$, $r \in \Sigma^{n^a}$, $s \in \Sigma^{b \log n}$, is a pseudo-random generator that is secure against $\text{SIZE}^A(n)$ circuits. If $A = SAT$, then this pseudo-random generator can be used to derandomize AM to NP and BPP^{NP} to P^{NP}.

3   Comparison of Hypotheses

We now formally state our principle hypotheses.

Measure Hypothesis. NP does not have p-measure 0.

Pseudo-NP Hypothesis. There exists $\epsilon > 0$ such that

$$\text{NP} \not\subseteq [\text{io-pseudo}_{\text{NP}}]\text{-DTIME}(2^{n^\epsilon}),$$

i.e., there exists a language L in NP such that for every language L' in DTIME (2^{n^ϵ}), there exists a NP refuter R such that for almost every n, $R(0^n)$ has an output, and if $R(0^n)$ outputs a string x on some path, then $|x| = n$, $x \in L\Delta L'$.

NP-Machine Hypothesis. There exists an NP machine M and $\epsilon > 0$ such that M accepts 0^* and no 2^{n^ϵ}-time-bounded Turing machine correctly computes infinitely many accepting computations of M.

UP-Machine Hypothesis. There exists a UP machine M and $\epsilon > 0$, such that M accepts 0^* and no 2^{n^ϵ}-time-bounded Turing machine correctly computes infinitely many accepting computations of M.

First, we show that NP-machine hypothesis is weaker than the measure hypothesis.

Theorem 3.1. *The measure hypothesis implies the NP-machine hypothesis.*

Theorem 3.1 follows immediately from Lemma 3.2 and Theorem 3.3 below.

Definition. A language L *does not have superpolynomial gaps* if there is a polynomial $p(n)$ such that for all n, there is some string x in L with $n \le |x| \le p(n)$.

Lemma 3.2. *The measure hypothesis implies that* NP *contains a* DTIME(2^{n^ϵ})-*bi-immune language that does not have superpolynomial gaps.*

Theorem 3.3. *If* NP *contains a* DTIME(2^{n^ϵ})-*immune language that does not have superpolynomial gaps, then the NP-machine hypothesis holds.*

In addition to Theorem 3.3, the following is also known regarding immunity and the NP-machine hypothesis.

Theorem 3.4. (Pavan and Selman [27]) *If* NP$\cap$co-NP *contains a* DTIME(2^{n^ϵ})-*bi-immune language, then the NP-machine hypothesis holds.*

Next we use a Kolmogorov-complexity argument to show that the NP-machine hypothesis is also weaker than the pseudo-NP hypothesis.

Theorem 3.5. *The pseudo-NP hypothesis implies the NP-machine hypothesis.*

Proof. Let L be a language NP that is not in [io-pseudo$_{\text{NP}}$]-DTIME(2^{n^ϵ}). Let $\epsilon' > 0$ be any constant that is less than ϵ. Consider the following machine N: Let x an input of length n. N considers every string w whose $2^{n^{\epsilon'}}$ time-bounded Kolmogorov complexity is less than $2\log n$, i.e, N considers a program p whose length is less than $2\log n$ and runs the universal machine on p for $2^{n^{\epsilon'}}$ steps to produce w. If w is a witness of x, then it accepts x, if no such w is found then it rejects x. It is clear that M is 2^{n^ϵ} time bounded. Let L' be the language defined by M. Since M is 2^{n^ϵ} time-bounded, L' is in DTIME(2^{n^ϵ}). Since L is not in [io-pseudo$_{\text{NP}}$]-DTIME(2^{n^ϵ}), there exists a NP refuter R such that for all but finitely many n, every accepting computation of $R(0^n)$ outputs a string of length n that is in $L \Delta L'$. Observe that if x is not in L, then N rejects x, i.e, N is always correct on strings that do not belong to L. Thus every output of $R(0^n)$ is in L but does not belong to L'. Also note that if $R(0^n)$ outputs x on some path, then it must be the case that every witness w of x has $2^{n^{\epsilon'}}$ time-bounded Kolmogorov complexity bigger than $2 \log n$.

We now define a NP machine M that accepts 0^*. M on input 0^n runs $R(0^n)$. If an accepting computation of $R(0^n)$ outputs x, then M guesses a string w, along that path, and accepts if and only if w is a witness of x. Recall that, for every n, $R(0^n)$ outputs at least one string and for every string x that is an output of $R(0^n)$, $x \in L$. Thus M accepts 0^*. Assume there exist a 2^{n^δ}-time-bounded machine P that outputs infinitely many accepting computations of M, where $\delta = \epsilon'/2$. Note that every accepting computation of $M(0^n)$ is of the form $x_n w_n$, where x_n is an output of $R(0^n)$, $|x_n| = n$, $x_n \in L$, and w_n is a witness of x_n. Recall that if x_n is an output of $R(0^n)$, then every witness w_n of x_n has $2^{n^{\epsilon'}}$ time-bounded Kolmogorov complexity bigger than $2 \log n$. However, by our assumption, $P(0^n)$ outputs $x_n w_n$ for infinitely many n. Consider the universal machine that given n as advice, simulates $P(0^n)$ and outputs w. Since $P(0^n)$ halts in 2^{n^δ} time, the universal machine halts in time $2^{n^{\epsilon'}}$. Thus there exists a constant $c > 0$ such that for infinitely many n, $K^{2^{n^{\epsilon'}}}(w_n) \leq \log n + c$. This is a contradiction. Thus no 2^{n^δ} time-bounded machine can compute infinitely many accepting computations of M. Thus the NP-machine hypothesis is true.   □

We can analogously define "the pseudo-UP hypothesis" and use a similar argument to prove the following.

Theorem 3.6. *The pseudo-UP hypothesis implies the* UP-*machine hypothesis.*

4   Consequences

In this section we show that several interesting consequences of the NP-machine and UP-machine hypotheses. We first show the following useful lemma using the easy witness method [15]. Given a string x of length m, we view it as a boolean function $f_x : \{0,1\}^{\log m} \to \{0,1\}$.

Lemma 4.1. *Let M be a* NP *machine that accepts 0^* such that, for some $\epsilon > 0$, no 2^{n^ϵ} time-bounded machine can compute infinitely many accepting computations of M. Without loss of generality assume that every accepting computation of $M(0^n)$ is of length n^k. Let $\delta = \epsilon/3$. Let w_n be any accepting computation of $M(0^n)$. Then, for every language $A \in E$, for all but finitely many n, the A-oracle circuit complexity of f_{w_n} is at least n^δ.*

Proof. Consider the following machine N that attempts to find accepting computations of M. On input 0^n, N considers every A-oracle circuit C, over $k \log n$ inputs, of size n^δ and computes the string $w = C(x_1)C(x_2) \cdots C(x_{n^k})$, where

$x_1, x_2, \cdots x_{n^k}$ are all strings of length $k \log n$. If w is an accepting computation of $M(0^n)$, then N outputs w.

An A-oracle n^δ size circuit, can make at most n^δ queries each of size at most n^δ. Since A can be decided in time 2^{cn}, each oracle query can be answered in time 2^{cn^δ} time. Thus the total time taken to evaluate the value of the circuit on all inputs is $O(2^{2cn^\delta})$. A circuit of size of size n^δ can be encoded as a string of length $n^\delta \delta \log n$. Thus the machine N considers at most $2^{n^{2\delta}}$ circuits. Thus the total time taken by N is $O(2^{2n^{2\delta}})$ which is less than 2^{n^ϵ}. Since no 2^{n^ϵ} time-bounded machine can compute infinitely many accepting computations of M, the above machine N fails to output accepting computations of $M(0^n)$ for all but finitely many n. Thus for all but finitely many n, for every accepting computation w_n of $M(0^n)$, the A-oracle circuit complexity of f_{w_n} is bigger than n^δ.   □

The following theorem states several consequences of the NP-machine hypothesis.

Theorem 4.2. *The* NP-*machine hypothesis implies the following.*

(1) AM $=$ NP.
(2) *There exists* $\epsilon > 0$ *such that for every* $A \in$ E, $\text{E}^{\text{NP}} \not\subseteq$ io-SIZE$^A(2^{\epsilon n})$.
(3) BPP$^{\text{NP}} =$ P^{NP}.
(4) NEXP $\not\subseteq$ P/poly.
(5) *For every constant* $k > 0$, P$^{\text{NP}} \not\subseteq$ io-SIZE(n^k).
(6) *There exist* $\epsilon > 0$, $\delta > 0$ *such that* NP $\not\subseteq$ io-DTIME$(2^{n^\delta})/n^\epsilon$.

Proof. Since the NP machine hypothesis is true, there exist a NP machine M and $\epsilon > 0$ such that no 2^{n^ϵ} time-bounded machine can compute infinitely many accepting computations of M. Without loss of generality assume that the length of every accepting computation of $M(0^n)$ is is n^k. Let $\delta = \epsilon/3$.

(1) Let L be any language in AM. Let the randomness of Arthur is bounded by n^{rk}. Let $\epsilon' = \delta/k$. Let a and b be the constants from Theorem 2.1. The following NP machine accepts L. Given an input x of length n guess an accepting computation w of $M(0^{n^{ra}})$. Let $m = n^{kr}$. Note that $|w| = n^{kra}$ and it can be viewed as a boolean function over $a \log m$ variables. By Lemma 4.1, any accepting computation w gives a boolean function over $a \log m$ variables whose SAT-oracle circuit complexity at least $(n^{ra})^\delta = m^{a\epsilon'}$. By Theorem 2.1, from this hard boolean function a pseudo random that maps $b \log m$ bits to $m = n^{kr}$ bits, can be constructed, and this pseudorandom generator derandomizes the AM protocol.

(2) Let A be any language in E. Let a_n denote the maximum accepting computation of $M(0^n)$. Thus $|a_n| = n^k$. By Lemma 4.1, f_{a_n} has A-oracle circuit complexity bigger than n^δ. We now define a language L as follows: Let $L|m$ denote the characteristic sequence of L on strings of length m. Given m, let m' be the largest integer such that $m' < m$ and m' is divisible by k. Let $n = 2^{m'/k}$. We set $L|m = a_n 0^l$, where $l = 2^m - 2^{m'}$.

We claim that L is in E^{NP}. Given a string x of length m, we can compute m' and now the goal is to compute the maximum accepting computation of

$M(0^{2^{m'/k}})$ which gives $L|m$. Note that the length of maximum accepting computation of $M(0^{2^{m'/k}}) = 2^{m'} \leq 2^m$. Thus we can extract the maximum accepting computation of $M(0^{2^{m'/k}})$ in linear exponential time using an NP oracle.

Let $\delta' = \delta/2k$. Assume that $L \in$ io-SIZE$^A(2^{\delta'm})$. Thus for infinitely many m there exists a A-oracle circuit that accepts L^m. This implies that the A-oracle circuit complexity of $f_{L|m}$ is at most $2^{\delta'm}$. Recall that $L|m = a_n 0^l$, where $n = 2^{m'/k}$ and $l = 2^m - 2^{m'}$. Thus the A-oracle circuit complexity of f_{a_n} is at most $2^{\delta'm}$. However $n^\delta = 2^{m'\delta/k} > 2^{\delta'm}$ for large enough m. Thus if $L \in$ io-SIZE$^A(2^{\delta'm})$, then for infinitely many n the A-oracle circuit complexity of a_n is less than n^δ. This is a contradiction.

(3) This immediately follows from (2) and Theorem 2.1.

(4) Impagliazzo, Kabanets, and Wigderson [12] showed that if NEXP $\subseteq$ P/poly, then NEXP = MA. By item (1), the NP-machine hypothesis implies AM = NP. Thus NEXP = NP which is a contradiction. Thus NEXP $\not\subseteq$ P/poly.

(5) By the results of Kannan [17], Bshouty et al. [5], and Kobler and Watanabe [19], ZPP$^{NP} \not\subseteq$ io-SIZE(n^k) for any $k > 0$. Since the NP-machine hypothesis implies BPP^{NP} = P^{NP}, P$^{NP} \not\subseteq$ io-SIZE(n^k) for every $k > 0$.

(6) Let $\epsilon' = \epsilon/3$ and $\delta' = \epsilon/6k$. Suppose NP $\subseteq$ io-DTIME$(2^{n^{\delta'}})/n^{\epsilon'}$. Consider the following language in NP.

$$L = \left\{ \langle 0^n, y \rangle \,\middle|\, \begin{array}{l} |y| \leq n^k, \text{ there exists } w \text{ such that } yw \\ \text{is an accepting computation of } M \text{ on } 0^n \end{array} \right\}.$$

We can use a pairing function $\langle \cdot, \cdot \rangle$ that encodes all tuples of the form $\langle 0^n, y \rangle, |y| \leq n^k$, at the same length. Note that if there is an oracle that gives the membership of $\langle 0^n, y \rangle, |y| \leq n^k$, we can compute an accepting computation of $M(0^n)$. Since NP $\subseteq$ io-DTIME$(2^{n^{\delta'}})/n^{\epsilon'}$, there is a L' in DTIME$(2^{n^{\delta'}})$ and an advice h_n such that, $|h_n| \leq n^{\epsilon'}$,

$$\exists^\infty n, \forall x \in \{0,1\}^n, x \in L \Leftrightarrow \langle x, h_n \rangle \in L'.$$

Consider the following algorithm that computes infinitely many accepting computations of M. On input 0^n, it considers all advices of size up to $n^{\epsilon'}$ and with each advice it does a prefix search for a witness by querying L'. This algorithm outputs infinitely many accepting computations of M and it can be verified that the algorithm is 2^{n^ϵ}-time bounded. This is a contradiction. $\square$

Fenner, Fortnow, Naik, and Rogers [6] asked the following question Q: Can we find the accepting computations of every NP machine that accept Σ^* in polynomial time? The following is trivial.

Proposition 4.3. *If the NP-machine hypothesis is true, then the answer to Q is "No."*

It is shown in [6] that Q has several equivalent characterizations, so we obtain from there a number of consequences of the NP-machine hypothesis. For example, while we do not know if the NP-machine hypothesis implies that P $\neq$ NP $\cap$ co-NP, we have the following.

Corollary 4.4. *The* NP-*machine hypothesis implies that* $P \neq NP \cap$ co-NP *or there is an* NP *multi-valued total function that does not have a* NP *single-valued refinement.*

From Theorem 3.4, we know that if NP∩co-NP has 2^{n^ϵ}-bi-immune sets, then the NP-machine hypothesis is true. This gives the following corollary.

Corollary 4.5. *If* NP∩co-NP *has* 2^{n^ϵ}-*bi-immune sets, then all the consequences in Theorem 4.2 follow.*

By Theorem 3.3, if NP has a 2^{n^ϵ}-bi-immune language that does not have superpolynomial gaps, then the NP-machine hypothesis is true. Thus all the consequences of Theorem 4.2 follow if NP has a DTIME(2^{n^ϵ})-bi-immune language that does not have superpolynomial gaps. We now consider the hypothesis "NP has a DTIME(2^{n^ϵ})-bi-immune language". This is weaker than both the hypotheses "NP ∩ co-NP has a 2^{n^ϵ}-bi-immune set," and "NP contains a DTIME(2^{n^ϵ})-bi-immune language that does not have superpolynomial gaps." Let L be any 2^{n^ϵ}-bi-immune language in NP, then for infinitely many n, 0^n belongs to L. By using similar arguments as in Lemma 4.1, we can show that for infinitely many n, every witness of 0^n has high circuit complexity. This gives io-versions of consequences in Theorem 4.2. For example:

Theorem 4.6. *If* NP *has a* 2^{n^ϵ}-*bi-immune language, then the following hold.*

(1) AM ⊆ io-NP.
(2) *There exists* $\epsilon > 0$ *such that for every* A *in* E, $E^{NP} \not\subseteq SIZE^A(2^{\epsilon n})$.
(3) NEXP ⊄ P/poly.

Now we turn our attention to the UP-machine hypothesis. It is obvious that all the consequences of the NP-machine hypothesis follow from the UP-machine hypothesis. In addition, we obtain the following consequences.

Theorem 4.7. *The* UP-*machine hypothesis implies the following.*

(1) $\exists \epsilon > 0, \forall A \in E$, UE ∩ co-UE $\not\subseteq$ io-SIZE$^A(2^{\epsilon n})$.
(2) PH ⊆ SPP.
(3) $\exists \epsilon > 0, \delta > 0$ UP ∩ co-UP $\not\subseteq$ io-DTIME(2^{n^δ})/n^ϵ.
(4) $\forall k > 0$, SPP $\not\subseteq$ SIZE(n^k).
(5) BPP ⊆ UP.
(6) *There exists a language in* NP *for which search does not reduce to decision.*

5   Scaled Dimension

In addition to the measure hypothesis on NP, hypotheses on the resource-bounded dimension of NP can also be considered (see [10] for example). While dimension hypotheses are easily seen to be weaker than the measure hypothesis, they seem incomparable with the other hypotheses considered in this paper. In

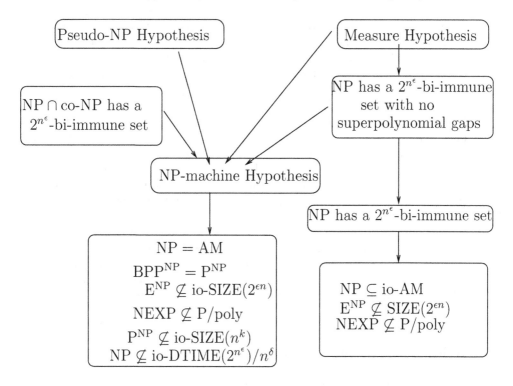

this section we consider a hypothesis on the *scaled dimension* of NP and its consequences for derandomization of NP and circuit-complexity lower bounds for NEXP. For background on scaled dimension, we refer to [11, 9].

In the following, we consider $\dim_p^{(-3)}(NP)$, the -3rd-order scaled polynomial-time dimension of NP. If $\mu_p(NP) \neq 0$, then $\dim_p^{(-3)}(NP) > 0$. We now show that this seemingly much weaker consequence of the measure hypothesis still implies a derandomization of AM, albeit with a small amount of nonuniform advice. This derandomization should be compared with the unconditional fact that $AM \subseteq NP/poly$.

Theorem 5.1. *If* $\dim_p^{(-3)}(NP) > 0$, *then* $AM \subseteq NP/n^\epsilon$ *for every* $\epsilon > 0$.

Using arguments of Impagliazzo, Kabanets, and Wigderson [12], the same hypothesis implies that NEXP does not have polynomial-size circuits.

Theorem 5.2. *If* $\dim_p^{(-3)}(NP) > 0$, *then* $NEXP \not\subseteq P/poly$.

6   Conclusion

The following figure captures relations among various hypotheses and known consequences. It is interesting to note that the UP-machine hypothesis implies $P \neq UP \cap co\text{-}UP$, whereas a similar consequence is not known to follow from the

NP-machine hypothesis. Theorem 3.1 partly explains this. Since the measure hypothesis implies the NP-machine hypothesis, if the NP-machine hypothesis implies P $\neq$ NP $\cap$ co-NP, then the measure hypothesis also implies P $\neq$ NP $\cap$ co-NP. However, it seems that the measure hypothesis does not say much about NP $\cap$ co-NP.

There are several unanswered questions. For example: "Does the NP-machine hypothesis imply NEXP $\not\subseteq$ io-P/poly?" Though the NP-machine hypothesis implies derandomization of AM and BPP^{NP}, we do not know whether we can derandomize BPP. Note that relative to any oracle where ZPP = EXP, the NP-machine hypothesis holds and BPP = EXP. Perhaps we can derandomize BPP using the UP-machine hypothesis. Another interesting question is the relation between the existence of cryptographic one-way functions and the measure hypothesis.

An anonymous referee pointed the possible relations between this paper and the work of Allender [1]. In that paper Allender introduced the notion of Kt-complexity and exhibited several relations among Kolmogorov complexity and derandomization. One of the hypotheses considered by Allender is similar to the NP-machine hypothesis. In the full version of this paper we will discuss this in more detail.

Acknowledgments

We thank an anonymous referee for pointing to the work of Allender [1]. We also thank N. V. Vinodchandran for interesting discussions.

References

1. E. Allender. When the worlds collide: derandomization, lower bounds and kolmogorov complexity. In *Foundations of Software Technology and Theoretical Computer Science*, pages 1–15. Springer-Verlag, 2001.
2. E. Allender and M. Strauss. Measure on small complexity classes with applications for BPP. In *Proceedings of the 35th Annual Symposium on Foundations of Computer Science*, pages 807–818. IEEE Computer Society, 1994.
3. K. Ambos-Spies and E. Mayordomo. Resource-bounded measure and randomness. In A. Sorbi, editor, *Complexity, Logic and Recursion Theory*, Lecture Notes in Pure and Applied Mathematics, pages 1–47. Marcel Dekker, New York, N.Y., 1997.
4. J. Balcázar and U. Schöning. Bi-immune sets for complexity classes. *Mathematical Systems Theory*, 18(1):1–18, 1985.
5. N. Bshouty, R. Cleve, S. Kannan, R. Gavalda, and C. Tamon. Oracles and queries that are sufficient for exact learning. *Journal of Computer and System Sciences*, 52:421–433, 1996.
6. S. Fenner, L. Fortnow, A. Naik, and J. Rogers. Inverting onto functions. *Information and Computation*, 186(1):90–103, 2003.
7. C. Glaßer, A. Pavan, A. L. Selman, and S. Sengupta. Properties of NP-complete sets. In *Proceedings of the 19th IEEE Conference on Computational Complexity*, pages 184–197. IEEE Computer Society, 2004.

8. L. A. Hemaspaandra, J. Rothe, and G. Wechsung. Easy sets and hard certificate schemes. *Acta Informatica*, 34(11):859–879, 1997.
9. J. M. Hitchcock. Small spans in scaled dimension. *SIAM Journal on Computing*. To appear.
10. J. M. Hitchcock. MAX3SAT is exponentially hard to approximate if NP has positive dimension. *Theoretical Computer Science*, 289(1):861–869, 2002.
11. J. M. Hitchcock, J. H. Lutz, and E. Mayordomo. Scaled dimension and nonuniform complexity. *Journal of Computer and System Sciences*, 69(2):97–122, 2004.
12. R. Impagliazzo, V. Kabanets, and A. Wigderson. In search of an easy witness: Exponential time vs. probabilistic polynomial time. *Journal of Computer and System Sciences*, 65:672–694, 2002.
13. R. Impagliazzo and P. Moser. A zero-one law for RP. In *Proceedings of the 18th IEEE Conference on Computational Complexity*, pages 43–47. IEEE Computer Society, 2003.
14. R. Impagliazzo and A. Wigderson. P = BPP if E requires exponential circuits: Derandomizing the XOR lemma. In *Proceedings of the 29th ACM Symposium on Theory of Computing*, pages 220–229, 1997.
15. V. Kabanets. Easiness assumptions and hardness tests: Trading time for zero error. *Journal of Computer and System Sciences*, 63:236–252, 2001.
16. V. Kabanets. Derandomization: A brief overview. *Bulletin of the EATCS*, 76:88–103, 2002.
17. R. Kannan. Circuit-size lower bounds and non-reducibility to sparse sets. *Information and Control*, 55:40–56, 1982.
18. A. Klivans and D. van Melkebeek. Graph nonisomorphism has subexponential size proofs unless the polynomial-time hierarchy collapses. *SIAM Journal on Computing*, 31:1501–1526, 2002.
19. J. Köbler and O. Watanabe. New collapse consequences of NP having small circuits. *SIAM Journal on Computing*, 28(1):311–324, 1998.
20. C.-J. Lu. Derandomizing Arthur-Merlin games under uniform assumptions. *Computational Complexity*, 10(3):247–259, 2001.
21. J. H. Lutz. Almost everywhere high nonuniform complexity. *Journal of Computer and System Sciences*, 44(2):220–258, 1992.
22. J. H. Lutz. Observations on measure and lowness for Δ_2^P. *Theory of Computing Systems*, 30(4):429–442, 1997.
23. J. H. Lutz. The quantitative structure of exponential time. In L. A. Hemaspaandra and A. L. Selman, editors, *Complexity Theory Retrospective II*, pages 225–260. Springer-Verlag, New York, 1997.
24. J. H. Lutz and E. Mayordomo. Measure, stochasticity, and the density of hard languages. *SIAM Journal on Computing*, 23(4):762–779, 1994.
25. J. H. Lutz and E. Mayordomo. Cook versus Karp-Levin: Separating completeness notions if NP is not small. *Theoretical Computer Science*, 164:141–163, 1996.
26. P. B. Miltersen. Derandomizing complexity classes. In *Handbook of Randomized Computing, volume II*, pages 843–934. Kluwer, 2001.
27. A. Pavan and A. L. Selman. Separation of NP-completeness notions. *SIAM Journal on Computing*, 31(3):906–918, 2002.

Improved Approximation Algorithms for Maximum Graph Partitioning Problems Extended Abstract

Gerold Jäger and Anand Srivastav

Mathematisches Seminar,
Christian-Albrechts-Universität Kiel,
Christian-Albrechts-Platz 4, D-24118 Kiel, Germany
{gej, asr}@numerik.uni-kiel.de

Abstract. In this paper we improve the analysis of approximation algorithms based on semidefinite programming for the maximum graph partitioning problems MAX-k-CUT, MAX-k-UNCUT, MAX-k-DIRECTED-CUT, MAX-k-DIRECTED-UNCUT, MAX-k-DENSE-SUBGRAPH, and MAX-k-VERTEX-COVER. It was observed by Han, Ye, Zhang (2002) and Halperin, Zwick (2002) that a parameter-driven random hyperplane can lead to better approximation factors than obtained by Goemans and Williamson (1994). Halperin and Zwick could describe the approximation factors by a mathematical optimization problem for the above problems for $k = \frac{n}{2}$ and found a choice of parameters in a heuristic way. The innovation of this paper is twofold. First, we generalize the algorithm of Halperin and Zwick to cover all cases of k, adding some algorithmic features. The hard work is to show that this leads to a mathematical optimization problem for an optimal choice of parameters. Secondly, as a key-step of this paper we prove that a sub-optimal set of parameters is determined by a *linear program*. Its optimal solution computed by CPLEX leads to the desired improvements. In this fashion a more systematic analysis of the semidefinite relaxation scheme is obtained which leaves room for further improvements.

1 Introduction

For a directed graph $G = (V, E)$ with $|V| = n$ and a non-negative weight $\omega_{i,j}$ on each edge $(i, j) \in E$, such that $\omega_{i,j}$ is not identically zero on all edges, and for $0 < \sigma := \frac{k}{n} < 1$ we consider the following problems:

a) MAX-k-CUT: determine a subset $S \subseteq V$ of k vertices such that the total weight ω^* of the edges connecting S and $V \setminus S$ or connecting $V \setminus S$ and S is maximized[1].

---

[1] In some literature MAX-k-CUT denotes the problem of partitioning the set of vertices into subsets $S_1, \cdots, S_k$, so that the total weight of the edges connecting S_i and S_j for $1 \leq i \neq j \leq k$ is maximized.

K. Lodaya and M. Mahajan (Eds.): FSTTCS 2004, LNCS 3328, pp. 348–359, 2004.

b) MAX-k-UNCUT: determine a subset $S \subseteq V$ of k vertices such that the total weight ω^* of the edges of the subgraphs induced by S and induced by $V \setminus S$ is maximized.

c) MAX-k-DIRECTED-CUT: determine a subset $S \subseteq V$ of k vertices such that the total weight ω^* of the edges connecting S and $V \setminus S$ is maximized.

d) MAX-k-DIRECTED-UNCUT: determine a subset $S \subseteq V$ of k vertices such that the total weight ω^* of the edges of the subgraphs induced by S and induced by $V \setminus S$ plus the edge weights connecting $V \setminus S$ and S is maximized.

e) MAX-k-DENSE-SUBGRAPH: determine a subset $S \subseteq V$ of k vertices such that the total weight ω^* of the edges of the subgraph induced by S is maximized.

f) MAX-k-VERTEX-COVER: determine a subset $S \subseteq V$ of k vertices such that the total weight ω^* of the edges touching S is maximized.

As all these problems are NP-hard, we are interested in approximating the optimal solution to these problems within a factor of $0 \leq \varrho \leq 1$. Goemans and Williamson [10] showed in their pioneer paper that via the semidefinite programming (SDP) relaxation an approximation factor of 0.878 can be proved for the MAX-CUT problem. Stimulated by their work, many authors have considered only one or two of the six problems above (see [2] for MAX-k-CUT, [9] and [15] for MAX-$\frac{n}{2}$-CUT, [1] for MAX-k-DIRECTED-CUT, [16] for MAX-$\frac{n}{2}$-UNCUT and MAX-$\frac{n}{2}$-DENSE-SUBGRAPH, [3], [7], [8] and [14] for MAX-k-DENSE-SUBGRAPH and [2] for MAX-k-VERTEX-COVER). Feige and Langberg [5] improved on known special and global approximation factors for the four undirected problems with some new techniques based on semidefinite programming. Their paper contains also a nice summary of known results. Han, Ye and Zhang [12] also applied semidefinite programming to these four problems and in most cases they managed to obtain better approximation factors than previously known. Halperin and Zwick [11] used more general methods for the balanced version ($\sigma = \frac{1}{2}$) and in this case achieved substantially improved approximation factors for all six problems above.

In this paper we give an algorithm for the problems a) - f), generalizing the approach of Halperin and Zwick, resp. of Han, Ye and Zhang by introducing new parameters which enlarge the region of the semidefinite programming relaxation. This gives a new version of the semidefinite relaxation scheme (Algorithm *Graph Partitioning*, section 2, page 351). In Theorem 1, we show that the expectation of the approximation factors depend on a set of parameters, which are used in the algorithm. The key observation is that a sub-optimal choice of these parameters can be determined by a finite *linear program* (section 4). By discretizing the other parameters, we finally obtain a choice leading to improvements over known approximation guarantees. Here are some examples for which the improvement is significant (comprehensive tables can be found in section 5).

Problem	σ	Prev.	Our Method
MAX-k-CUT	0.3	0.527	0.567
MAX-k-UNCUT	0.4	0.5258	0.5973
MAX-k-DIRECTED-CUT	0.5	0.644	0.6507
MAX-k-DIRECTED-UNCUT	0.5	0.811	0.8164
MAX-k-DENSE-SUBGRAPH	0.2	0.2008	0.2664
MAX-k-VERTEX-COVER	0.6	0.8453	0.8784

In summary, we see that our technique of combining the analysis of the random hyperplane with mathematical programming leads to improvements over many previously known approximation factors for the maximization problems considered in this paper. This shows that a more systematic analysis of the semidefinite relaxation scheme gives better approximation guarantees and opens room for further improvements, if better methods for choosing an optimal parameter set can be designed.

2   The Algorithm

For $S \subseteq V$ the set of edges E can be divided by $E = S_1 \cup S_2 \cup S_3 \cup S_4$, where $S_1 = \{(i,j) \mid i,j \in S\}, S_2 = \{(i,j) \mid i \in S, j \in V \setminus S\}, S_3 = \{(i,j) \mid i \in V \setminus S, j \in S\}, S_4 = \{(i,j) \mid i,j \in V \setminus S\}$. As we will see, we distinguish the six problems MAX-k-CUT, MAX-k-UNCUT, MAX-k-DIRECTED-CUT, MAX-k-DIRECTED-UNCUT, MAX-k-DENSE- SUBGRAPH, MAX-k-VERTEX-CO-VER by four $\{0,1\}$ parameters a_1, a_2, a_3, a_4. All these problems maximize some of the four edge classes S_1, S_2, S_3, S_4.

For $i = 1, 2, 3, 4$ we define a_i as 1, if the problem maximizes the edge weights of S_i, and 0 otherwise. The following values a_1, a_2, a_3, a_4 lead to the specific problems:

Problem	a_1	a_2	a_3	a_4
MAX-k-CUT	0	1	1	0
MAX-k-UNCUT	1	0	0	1
MAX-k-DIRECTED-CUT	0	1	0	0
MAX-k-DIRECTED-UNCUT	1	0	1	1
MAX-k-DENSE-SUBGRAPH	1	0	0	0
MAX-k-VERTEX-COVER	1	1	1	0

For $F \subseteq E$ we define $\omega(F) = \sum_{(i,j) \in F} \omega_{ij}$ and for $S \subseteq V$:

$$\omega_{a_1,a_2,a_3,a_4}(S) := a_1\omega(S_1) + a_2\omega(S_2) + a_3\omega(S_3) + a_4\omega(S_4).$$

The optimization problem considered in this paper is the following.

General Maximization Problem

$$\max_{S \subseteq V, |S| = k} \omega_{a_1, a_2, a_3, a_4}(S) \tag{1}$$

Let $\text{OPT}(a_1, a_2, a_3, a_4, \sigma)$ be the value of an optimal solution of (1). Our aim is to design a randomized polynomial-time algorithm which returns a solution of value at least $\varrho \cdot \text{OPT}(a_1, a_2, a_3, a_4, \sigma)$, where $\varrho = \varrho(a_1, a_2, a_3, a_4, \sigma)$ is the so-called approximation factor with $0 \le \varrho \le 1$. In fact, we will show that the expected value of ϱ is large.

In the algorithm we give a formulation of the general maximization problem (1) as a semidefinite program, generalizing Halperin and Zwick [11].

Algorithm *Graph Partitioning*
Input: A weighted directed graph $G = (V, E)$ with $|V| = n$, $0 < \sigma < 1$ and parameters $0 \le \theta, \vartheta, \nu \le 1$ and $-1 \le \kappa \le 1$, a maximum graph partitioning problem with parameters a_1, a_2, a_3, a_4.
Output: A set S of k vertices with large $\omega_{a_1, a_2, a_3, a_4}(S)$.

1. *Relaxation* We solve the following semidefinite program:
   Maximize $\sum_{1 \le i \ne j \le n} \frac{1}{4} w_{ij} \big[(a_1 + a_2 + a_3 + a_4) + (a_1 + a_2 - a_3 - a_4) X_{i0}$
   $+ (a_1 - a_2 + a_3 - a_4) X_{j0} + (a_1 - a_2 - a_3 + a_4) X_{ij} \big]$
   with the optimal value w^* subject to the constraints
   (a) $\sum_{i=1}^{n} X_{i0} = 2k - n$
   (b) $\sum_{1 \le i, j \le n} X_{ij} = (2k - n)^2$
   (c) $X_{ii} = 1$ for $i = 0, 1, \cdots, n$
   (d) $X \in \mathbb{R}^{n+1, n+1}$ is positive semidefinite and symmetric
   (e) $X_{ij} + X_{il} + X_{jl} \ge -1$ for $0 \le i, j, l \le n$
   (f) $X_{ij} - X_{il} - X_{jl} \ge -1$ for $0 \le i, j, l \le n$
   From b), c) and d) it follows:
   (g) $\sum_{1 \le i < j \le n} X_{ij} = \frac{1}{2} \big((2k - n)^2 - n \big)$
   (This is the same semidefinite program like in [11] with new constraint (a) and generalized constraint (b).)

   We repeat the following four steps polynomially often and output the best subset.
2. *Randomized Rounding*
   - Choose parameters $0 \le \theta, \vartheta \le 1$ and $-1 \le \kappa \le 1$ (note that for every problem and for each σ we choose different parameters).
   - Choose a positive semidefinite symmetric matrix $Y = Z^T Z \in \mathbb{R}^{n+1, n+1}$, depending on $\theta, \vartheta, \kappa$ as follows:
     Put $Y := \theta L + (1 - \theta) P$, where we define $L = (l_{ij})_{0 \le i, j \le n}$ and $P = (p_{ij})_{0 \le i, j \le n}$ by

$$(l_{ij})_{0 \le i, j \le n} = \begin{cases} 1 & \text{for } i = j \\ \vartheta X_{0i} & \text{for } i \ne 0, j = 0 \\ \vartheta X_{0j} & \text{for } i = 0, j \ne 0 \\ \vartheta X_{ij} \text{ or } X_{ij} \text{ or } \vartheta^2 X_{ij} & \text{for } 1 \le i \ne j \le n \end{cases}$$

$$(p_{ij})_{0 \le i,j \le n} = \begin{cases} 1 & \text{for } i = j \\ \kappa & \text{for } i = 0, j \ne 0 \vee i \ne 0, j = 0 \\ \kappa, \text{ if } \kappa \ge 0 \quad \text{or} \quad 1 \quad \text{or} \quad \kappa^2 \text{ for } 1 \le i \ne j \le n \end{cases}$$

We can write the non diagonal elements of Y for $0 \le i \ne j \le n$ as

$$Y_{ij} = \begin{cases} d_1 X_{ij} + e_1, & \text{if } i = 0 \vee j = 0 \\ d_2 X_{ij} + e_2, & \text{otherwise} \end{cases}$$

with $d_1 = \theta\vartheta$; $e_1 = (1 - \theta)\kappa$; $d_2 = \theta\vartheta, \theta, \theta\vartheta^2$; $e_2 = (1 - \theta)\kappa$, (if $\kappa \ge 0$),
$1 - \theta, (1 - \theta)\kappa^2$. Hence: $-1 \le e_1 \le 1$; $0 \le d_1, d_2, e_2 \le 1$.
(It is easy to show that Y is a positive semidefinite symmetric matrix.)
- We choose $\bar{u}$ with $\bar{u}_i \in N(0,1)$ for $i = 0, 1, \cdots, n$ and let $u = Z\bar{u}$.
- For $i = 1, \cdots, n$ let $\hat{x}_i = 1$, if $u_i \ge 0$ and -1 otherwise and let $S = \{i \ge 1 \mid \hat{x}_i = 1\}$ (see [4]).
  (As special cases we get previously used positive semidefinite matrices: $\vartheta = 1$ and case 3 for P in [12]; $\theta = 1$ and case 1 for L in [11], which is called *outward rotation*.)

3. *Linear Randomized Rounding*
   - Choose a parameter $0 \le \nu \le 1$ (again for every problem and for each σ we choose a different parameter).
   - With probability $0 \le \nu \le 1$ we overrule the choice of S made above, and for each $i \in V$, put i into S, independently, with probability $(1 + X_{i0})/2$ and into $V \setminus S$ otherwise.

4. *Size Adjusting*
   a) If the problem is symmetric (MAX-k-CUT or MAX-k-UNCUT):
   - If $k \le |S| < \frac{n}{2}$, we remove uniformly at random $|S| - k$ vertices from S.
   - If $|S| < k$, we add uniformly at random $k - |S|$ vertices to S.
   - If $\frac{n}{2} \le |S| < n - k$, we add uniformly at random $n - k - |S|$ vertices to S.
   - If $|S| \ge n - k$, we remove uniformly at random $|S| - n + k$ vertices from S.
   b) If the problem is not symmetric:
   - If $|S| \ge k$, we remove uniformly at random $|S| - k$ vertices from S.
   - If $|S| < k$, we add uniformly at random $k - |S|$ vertices to S.

5. *Flipping* (only for MAX-$\frac{n}{2}$-DIRECTED-CUT, MAX-$\frac{n}{2}$-DIRECTED-UN-CUT, MAX-$\frac{n}{2}$-DENSE-SUBGRAPH, and MAX-$\frac{n}{2}$-VERTEX-COVER)
   If $\omega_{a_1,a_2,a_3,a_4}(V \setminus S) > \omega_{a_1,a_2,a_3,a_4}(S)$, we output $V \setminus S$, otherwise S.

3   Computation of the Approximation Factors

3.1   Main Result

The main results are shown in the tables containing the approximation factors for the different problems. Nevertheless, let us state them also in a formal way:

Theorem 1 (Main Theorem). *The expected ratio* $\omega_{a_1,a_2,a_3,a_4}(S)/OPT$ *of the approximation factors for the problems MAX-k-CUT, MAX-k-UNCUT, MAX-k-DIRECTED-CUT, MAX-k-DIRECTED-UNCUT, MAX-k-DENSE-SUBGRAPH and MAX-k-VERTEX-COVER is bounded from below by the minimum of the solutions of some linear programs. Solving these linear programs lead to the approximation factors shown in the tables of section 5.*

We denote the sets S after the steps 2,3,4,5 by $S', S'', S''', S''''(= S)$ and define $\delta := \frac{|S''|}{n}$. We want to compute $\rho := \frac{\omega_{a_1,a_2,a_3,a_4}(S)}{\omega^*}$. For $x_1 \in \mathbb{R}$, $x_2 \in \mathbb{R}_0^+$ we consider the function of Han, Ye, Zhang [12]:

$$y(x_1, x_2) = \frac{\omega_{a_1,a_2,a_3,a_4}(S'')}{\omega^*} + x_1 \frac{|S''|}{n} + x_2 \frac{|S''|(n - |S''|)}{n^2}$$

(Halperin, Zwick [11] consider this function only for $x_1 \in \mathbb{R}_0^-$. The case $x_2 < 0$ could also be considered, but as it does not lead to any progress, we omit it.)

The first term $\frac{\omega_{a_1,a_2,a_3,a_4}(S'')}{\omega^*}$ gives the value of the partition S'' after step 3 in relation to the optimal value, $\frac{|S''|}{n}$ and $\frac{|S''|(n-|S''|)}{n^2}$ measure the closeness of the partition to the required size. x_1, x_2 are parameters which depend on the specific problem and σ. They are chosen so that the analysis leads to good approximation factors. For analyzing this function, we have to estimate the expected values of the three terms. This is done in the main lemma. Its proof is given in the full paper.

Lemma 1 (Main Lemma). *For $n \to \infty$ there are constants $\alpha, \beta^+, \beta^-, \gamma$ with:*

a) $E\left[\frac{\omega_{a_1,a_2,a_3,a_4}(S'')}{\omega^*}\right] \geq \alpha(\theta, \vartheta, \kappa, \nu)$

b) $E\left[\frac{|S''|}{n}\right] \geq \beta^+(\sigma, \theta, \vartheta, \kappa, \nu)$

c) $E\left[\frac{|S''|}{n}\right] \leq \beta^-(\sigma, \theta, \vartheta, \kappa, \nu)$

d) $E\left[\frac{|S''|(n-|S''|)}{n^2}\right] \geq \gamma(\sigma, \theta, \vartheta, \kappa, \nu)$

3.2   Proof of Theorem 1

For $x_1 \geq 0$ define $\beta(\sigma, \theta, \vartheta, \kappa, \nu)$ as $\beta^+(\sigma, \theta, \vartheta, \kappa, \nu)$ and otherwise as $\beta^-(\sigma, \theta, \vartheta, \kappa, \nu)$. As we repeat the steps 2 and 3 of the algorithm polynomially often, the function $z(x_1, x_2)$ is its expectation value, up to a factor of $1 - \epsilon$, which can be neglected. By Lemma 1 we get:

$$\frac{\omega_{a_1,a_2,a_3,a_4}(S'')}{\omega^*} + x_1 \frac{|S''|}{n} + x_2 \frac{|S''|(n - |S''|)}{n^2}$$

$$\geq E\left[\frac{\omega_{a_1,a_2,a_3,a_4}(S'')}{\omega^*}\right] + E\left[x_1 \frac{|S''|}{n}\right] + E\left[x_2 \frac{|S''|(n - |S''|)}{n^2}\right]$$

$$\geq \alpha(\theta, \vartheta, \kappa, \nu) + x_1 \beta(\sigma, \theta, \vartheta, \kappa, \nu) + x_2 \gamma(\sigma, \theta, \vartheta, \kappa, \nu)$$

and so

$$\frac{\omega_{a_1,a_2,a_3,a_4}(S'')}{\omega^*}$$

$$\geq \alpha(\theta, \vartheta, \kappa, \nu) + x_1(\beta(\sigma, \theta, \vartheta, \kappa, \nu) - \delta) + x_2(\gamma(\sigma, \theta, \vartheta, \kappa, \nu) - \delta(1 - \delta))$$

$$=: h(\delta, \sigma, \theta, \vartheta, \kappa, \nu, x_1, x_2) \tag{2}$$

With $\lambda_i := \frac{\omega(S_i'')}{\omega^*}$ for $i = 1, 2, 3, 4$ it is not difficult to show:

$$a_1\lambda_1 + a_2\lambda_2 + a_3\lambda_3 + a_4\lambda_4 \geq h(\delta, \sigma, \theta, \vartheta, \kappa, \nu, x_1, x_2)$$

$$\lambda_1 + \lambda_2 + \lambda_3 + \lambda_4 \geq 1$$

Define $M_1(p) := \begin{pmatrix} p^2 & 0 & 0 & 0 \\ p(1-p) & p & 0 & 0 \\ p(1-p) & 0 & p & 0 \\ (1-p)^2 & 1-p & 1-p & 1 \end{pmatrix}$, $M_2(q) := \begin{pmatrix} 1 & 1-q & 1-q & (1-q)^2 \\ 0 & q & 0 & q(1-q) \\ 0 & 0 & q & q(1-q) \\ 0 & 0 & 0 & q^2 \end{pmatrix}$.

Furthermore $M(\delta, \sigma) := \begin{cases} M_1\left(\frac{\sigma}{\delta}\right), & \text{if } \sigma \leq \delta < \frac{1}{2} \\ M_2\left(\frac{1-\sigma}{1-\delta}\right), & \text{if } 0 \leq \delta < \sigma \\ M_2\left(\frac{\sigma}{1-\delta}\right), & \text{if } \frac{1}{2} \leq \delta < 1-\sigma \\ M_1\left(\frac{1-\sigma}{\delta}\right), & \text{if } 1-\sigma \leq \delta \leq 1 \end{cases}$ in the symmetric case and

$$M(\delta, \sigma) := \begin{cases} M_1\left(\frac{\sigma}{\delta}\right), & \text{if } \sigma \leq \delta \leq 1 \\ M_2\left(\frac{1-\sigma}{1-\delta}\right), & \text{if } 0 \leq \delta < \sigma \end{cases} \quad \text{in the asymmetric case.}$$

Then it is straightforward to show:

$$z := E\left[\frac{\omega_{a_1,a_2,a_3,a_4}(S''')}{\omega^*}\right]$$

$$= (a_1 \ a_2 \ a_3 \ a_4) \cdot M(\delta, \sigma) \cdot (\lambda_1 \ \lambda_2 \ \lambda_3 \ \lambda_4)^T \tag{3}$$

$$=: f_{a_1,a_2,a_3,a_4}(\delta, \sigma, \lambda_1, \lambda_2, \lambda_3, \lambda_4) \tag{4}$$

The expected approximation factor of Algorithm *Graph Partitioning* thus is:

$$\min_{0\leq\delta\leq1} \left[\begin{array}{c} \min \quad z \\ \text{s.t.} \\ a_1\lambda_1 + a_2\lambda_2 + a_3\lambda_3 + a_4\lambda_4 \geq h(\delta, \sigma, \theta, \vartheta, \kappa, \nu, x_1, x_2) \\ \lambda_1 + \lambda_2 + \lambda_3 + \lambda_4 \geq 1 \\ 0 \leq \lambda_1, \lambda_2, \lambda_3, \lambda_4 \\ z \geq f_{a_1,a_2,a_3,a_4}(\delta, \sigma, \lambda_1, \lambda_2, \lambda_3, \lambda_4) \\ [\text{for MAX-}\frac{n}{2}\text{-DC, MAX-}\frac{n}{2}\text{-DU, MAX-}\frac{n}{2}\text{-DS, MAX-}\frac{n}{2}\text{-VC:} \\ z \geq f_{a_4,a_3,a_2,a_1}(\delta, \sigma, \lambda_1, \lambda_2, \lambda_3, \lambda_4)] \end{array} \right] \tag{5}$$

Note that for fixed δ, σ and constants $\theta, \vartheta, \kappa, \nu, x_1, x_2$ the last inner minimization problem is a linear program in the variables $z, \lambda_1, \lambda_2, \lambda_3, \lambda_4$.

4   The Optimization Algorithm

By Theorem 1 and (5), the expected approximation factor for the general maximization problem (1) is z, where $z = z(\delta, \sigma, \theta, \vartheta, \kappa, \nu, x_1, x_2)$ is a function depending on the parameters $\delta \in [0, 1], \sigma \in (0, 1), \theta, \vartheta, \nu \in [0, 1], \kappa \in [-1, 1], x_1 \in \mathbb{R}, x_2 \in \mathbb{R}_0^+$ in a complicated way. A polynomial-time algorithm for an optimal choice of all parameters in (5) is not known. Thus we choose a hierarchical approach.

For this we need the following theorem which shows that we can solve (5) by hand for arbitrary, but fixed $\delta, \sigma, \theta, \vartheta, \kappa, \nu$. Note that for a previous approximation factor ϱ and a candidate z for a new approximation factor, we would like to show $z \geq \varrho$ for a suitable set of parameters.

Theorem 1. Let $f_{a_1, a_2, a_3, a_4}(\lambda_1, \lambda_2, \lambda_3, \lambda_4) = b_1\lambda_1 + b_2\lambda_2 + b_3\lambda_3 + b_4\lambda_4$ with suitable b_1, b_2, b_3, b_4 (note that according to (3) and (4), (b_1, b_2, b_3, b_4) is given by the vector $(a_1, a_2, a_3, a_4) \cdot M(\delta, \sigma)$). Furthermore let $v := \min_{l \in \{1,2,3,4\}} \{b_l\}, w := \min_{l \in \{i \in I \,|\, a_i = 1\}} \{b_l\}$.

Then for all maximization problems except MAX-$\frac{n}{2}$-DIRECTED-CUT, MAX-$\frac{n}{2}$-DIRECTED-UNCUT,   MAX-$\frac{n}{2}$-DENSE-SUBGRAPH,   MAX-$\frac{n}{2}$-VERTEX-CO-VER it holds:

a) (5) has the solution

$$z = \begin{cases} w \cdot h, & \text{if } h \geq 1 \\ v \cdot (1 - h) + w \cdot h, & \text{if } 0 \leq h < 1 \\ v, & \text{if } h < 0 \end{cases}$$

b) For $v = w$, the condition $z \geq \varrho$ is equivalent to

$$h \geq \max\left\{\frac{\varrho}{w}, 1\right\} \tag{6}$$

c) For $v \neq w$, the condition $z \geq \varrho$ equivalent to

$$h \geq \min\left\{\frac{\varrho}{w}, \frac{\varrho - v}{w - v}\right\} \tag{7}$$

For the proof of Theorem 1 we refer to the full paper.

Remark 1. We can derive similar expressions for z for the four remaining maximization problems leading to inequalities for h. Again we refer to the full paper.

An Algorithm for Parameter Setting
Our approach consists of three main steps. Let us consider σ as fixed.

1. Fixing the right-hand side. Let ϱ_0 be the previously known best approximation factor for the problem in the literature [11], [12], [5], and put $\varrho :=$

$\varrho_0 + k \cdot 0.0001$ for $k = 0, 1, \cdots$. We would like to prove $z \geq \varrho$ for a k as large as possible.

2. The linear program $LP(\Delta)$. For the moment let us fix the parameters $\theta, \vartheta, \kappa, \nu$ and consider them as constants. Let $h = h(\delta, \sigma, \theta, \vartheta, \kappa, \nu, x_1, x_2)$ be the function defined in (2). Since h is a linear function in x_1 and x_2 due to (2), we may write $h(x_1, x_2) = f_1(\delta)x_1 + f_2(\delta)x_2 + f_3$, suppressing the dependence of h on $\theta, \vartheta, \kappa, \nu$, writing $h(x_1, x_2)$ instead of $h(\delta, \sigma, \theta, \vartheta, \kappa, \nu, x_1, x_2)$, and putting the dependence of h on δ into the coefficients $f_1(\delta)$ and $f_2(\delta)$.

Since by Theorem 1 a), z is only piecewise linear in h, $z \geq \varrho$ is not a linear inequality in h. But by Theorem 1 b), c) $z \geq \varrho$ is equivalent to a linear inequality in x_1 and x_2.

Still, the dependence on δ is an obstacle. We choose a discretization of $[0, 1]$ for the δ's, i.e. we define $\Delta := \left\{ k \cdot \frac{1}{10^l}, k = 0, 1, \cdots, 10^l \right\}$ for a sufficiently large $l \in \mathbb{N}$. The inequalities in (6) and (7), respectively for all $\delta \in \Delta$ form a finite linear program in the variables x_1 and x_2 which we denote by $LP(\Delta)$.

3. Discretization of the other parameters. Whether $LP(\Delta)$ is solvable or not depends on the choice of the parameters $\theta, \vartheta, \kappa, \nu$. We discretize the ranges of these parameters in finitely many points. For $\theta, \vartheta, \nu \in [0, 1], \kappa \in [-1, 1]$ we take the discretization of both intervals with step size $\frac{1}{10}$ (for some cases we try even the finer discretization with step size $\frac{1}{100}$). We consider all possible values of $(\theta, \vartheta, \kappa, \nu)$ in this discretization and denote it by the parameter set $\mathcal{P}$. We test about 250,000 possibilities of tuples $(\theta, \vartheta, \kappa, \nu)$.

The algorithm for finding the parameters $\theta, \vartheta, \kappa, \nu, x_1, x_2$ and a good approximation factor ϱ is the following.

Algorithm *Parameter Set*

1. Choose ϱ as the best previously known approximation factor ϱ_0.
2. Choose $(\theta, \vartheta, \kappa, \nu)$ from the parameter set $\mathcal{P}$.
3. Given ϱ, solve $LP(\Delta)$ in the variables x_1 and x_2 by the simplex algorithm using CPLEX.
4. a) If $LP(\Delta)$ is solvable, increase ϱ by 0.0001 and goto 3.
   b) If $LP(\Delta)$ is not solvable and if not all parameters are tested, goto 2.
5. Output ϱ.

Remark 2. Note that x_1, x_2 live in a large range, i.e. $x_1 \in \mathbb{R}$ and $x_2 \in \mathbb{R}_0^+$, while $\theta, \vartheta, \nu, \kappa$ are only in the relatively small ranges $[-1, 1]$ and $[0, 1]$, so that we have optimized the two most difficult parameters.

5   The Final Approximation Factors

We state the results in the following tables.

	MAX-k-C		MAX-k-UC		MAX-k-DC		MAX-k-DU	
σ	Prev.	Our Meth.	Prev.	Our Meth.	Prev.	Our Meth.	Prev.	Our Meth.
0.02	0.5	0.5	0.9608	0.9608	0.5	0.1439	–	0.9804
0.04	0.5	0.5	0.9232	0.9232	0.5	0.18	–	0.9616
0.06	0.5	0.5	0.8872	0.8872	0.5	0.2211	–	0.9436
0.08	0.5	0.5	0.8528	0.8528	0.5	0.258	–	0.9264
0.1	0.5	0.5	0.82	0.82	0.5	0.2916	–	0.91
0.12	0.5	0.5	0.7888	0.7888	0.5	0.3223	–	0.8944
0.14	0.5	0.5	0.7592	0.7592	0.5	0.351	–	0.8796
0.16	0.5	0.5	0.7312	0.7312	0.5	0.3791	–	0.8656
0.18	0.5	0.5	0.7048	0.7048	0.5	0.4062	–	0.8524
0.2	0.5	0.5	0.68	0.68	0.5	0.4321	–	0.84
0.22	0.5	0.5	0.6568	0.6568	0.5	0.456	–	0.8284
0.24	0.5	0.5026	0.6352	0.6352	0.5	0.4779	–	0.8176
0.26	0.5	0.5252	0.6152	0.6152	0.5	0.498	–	0.8076
0.28	0.5	0.5467	0.5968	0.5968	0.5	0.5165	–	0.7984
0.3	0.527	0.567	0.58	0.58	0.5	0.5335	–	0.79
0.32	0.562	0.5864	0.5648	0.5648	0.5	0.5493	–	0.7824
0.34	0.593	0.6045	0.5512	0.5512	0.5	0.5644	–	0.7756
0.36	0.616	0.6218	0.5392	0.5644	0.5	0.5786	–	0.7696
0.38	0.642	0.6451	0.5288	0.5787	0.5	0.5914	–	0.7644
0.4	0.671	0.6727	0.5258	0.5973	0.5	0.603	–	0.7705
0.42	0.698	0.6994	0.5587	0.6238	0.5	0.6134	–	0.7776
0.44	0.721	0.7216	0.6013	0.6483	0.5	0.6227	–	0.785
0.46	0.734	0.7351	0.6353	0.668	0.5	0.6305	–	0.7919
0.48	0.725	0.7257	0.6451	0.6737	0.5	0.6371	–	0.798
0.5	0.7027	0.7016	0.6414	0.6415	0.644	0.6507	0.811	0.8164

	MAX-k-DS		MAX-k-VC			MAX-k-DS		MAX-k-VC	
σ	Prev.	Our Meth.	Prev.	Our Meth.	σ	Prev.	Our Meth.	Prev.	Our Meth.
0.02	0.02	0.0193	0.75	0.75	0.52	0.6022	0.6339	0.822	0.843
0.04	0.04	0.0407	0.75	0.75	0.54	0.6161	0.6471	0.8307	0.8532
0.06	0.06	0.0604	0.75	0.75	0.56	0.6287	0.6585	0.8377	0.8625
0.08	0.08	0.084	0.75	0.75	0.58	0.6402	0.6667	0.8425	0.8707
0.1	0.1	0.1123	0.75	0.75	0.6	0.6488	0.6753	0.8453	0.8784
0.12	0.12	0.1421	0.75	0.75	0.62	0.6539	0.6807	0.8556	0.886
0.14	0.14	0.1726	0.75	0.75	0.64	0.6563	0.685	0.8704	0.8934
0.16	0.16	0.2027	0.75	0.75	0.66	0.66	0.6888	0.8844	0.9008
0.18	0.18	0.2335	0.75	0.75	0.68	0.68	0.6927	0.8976	0.9081
0.2	0.2008	0.2644	0.75	0.75	0.7	0.7	0.6976	0.91	0.916
0.22	0.232	0.295	0.75	0.75	0.72	0.72	0.7024	0.9216	0.9241
0.24	0.2631	0.3248	0.75	0.75	0.74	0.74	0.7068	0.9324	0.9328
0.26	0.2942	0.3548	0.75	0.75	0.76	0.76	0.7266	0.9424	0.9424
0.28	0.3245	0.3833	0.75	0.75	0.78	0.78	0.7491	0.9516	0.9516
0.3	0.3541	0.4102	0.75	0.75	0.8	0.8	0.7714	0.96	0.96
0.32	0.3827	0.4359	0.75	0.75	0.82	0.82	0.7934	0.9676	0.9676
0.34	0.4105	0.4619	0.75	0.75	0.84	0.84	0.8152	0.9744	0.9744
0.36	0.4372	0.4864	0.75	0.75	0.86	0.86	0.8367	0.9804	0.9804
0.38	0.4626	0.5092	0.75	0.7538	0.88	0.88	0.858	0.9856	0.9856
0.4	0.4867	0.5305	0.75	0.7684	0.9	0.9	0.8806	0.99	0.99
0.42	0.5095	0.5505	0.7518	0.7819	0.92	0.92	0.9048	0.9936	0.9936
0.44	0.531	0.5688	0.7687	0.7947	0.94	0.94	0.9288	0.9964	0.9964
0.46	0.5511	0.5861	0.7844	0.8082	0.96	0.96	0.9527	0.9984	0.9984
0.48	0.5697	0.6031	0.7987	0.8209	0.98	0.98	0.9764	0.9996	0.9996
0.5	0.6221	0.6223	0.8452	0.8454					

Comparison with Previous Results

For all six problems we compute approximation factors derived from our algorithm and compare it with the best approximation factors previously known. We

consider $\sigma = 0.02, 0.04, \cdots, 0.98$ for MAX k-DENSE-SUBGRAPH and MAX k-VERTEX-COVER and $\sigma = 0.02, 0.04, \cdots 0.5$ otherwise, because in these cases the approximation factors for σ are the same as for $1 - \sigma$.

We implemented the computation of the approximation factors in C++, using the program package CPLEX to solve the linear programs.

MAX-k-CUT. The previously best factors are due to Ageev and Sviridenko [2] for $\sigma = 0.02, \cdots 0.28$ and due to Han, Ye, Zhang [12] for $\sigma = 0.3, \cdots 0.48$. We have an improvement for $\sigma = 0.24, \cdots 0.48$. For the case $\sigma = 0.5$ we get the same approximation factor 0.7016 as Halperin and Zwick. Feige and Langberg [6] improved this factor to 0.7027, using the RPR^2 rounding technique, which additionally analyzes the correction step of changing the sides of so-called misplaced vertices.

MAX-k-UNCUT. For $\sigma = 0.02, \cdots 0.38$ the previously best factors were received by Feige and Langberg [5] and for $\sigma = 0.4, \cdots 0.48$ by Han, Ye, Zhang [12]. We improve these factors for $\sigma = 0.36, \cdots 0.48$. For $\sigma = 0.5$ the approximation factor of 0.6414^2 can be improved by our algorithm to 0.6415.

MAX-k-DIRECTED-CUT. Ageev and Sviridenko [1] showed an approximation factor of 0.5 for arbitrary σ. For $\sigma = 0.28, \cdots 0.48$, we substantially improve this factor. For the case $\sigma = 0.5$ we also improve the approximation factor of 0.644 of Halperin and Zwick to 0.6507.

MAX-k-DIRECTED-UNCUT. For $\sigma = 0.02, \cdots 0.48$, the approximation factors have not been considered until now. For $\sigma = 0.5$ the approximation factor of 0.811^3 can be improved by our algorithm to 0.8164.

MAX-k-DENSE-SUBGRAPH. For $\sigma = 0.2, \cdots 0.48$ and $\sigma = 0.52, \cdots 0.64$, the previously best approximation factors were given by Han, Ye and Zhang, for $\sigma = 0.5$ by Halperin and Zwick and in the other cases by Feige and Langberg [5]. Our improvement is for $\sigma = 0.04, \cdots 0.68$.

MAX-k-VERTEX-COVER. For $\sigma = 0.02, \cdots 0.4$, Ageev and Sviridenko [2] found the previously best approximation factors. For $\sigma = 0.42, \cdots 0.48$ and $\sigma = 0.52, \cdots 0.6$ they were found by Han, Ye and Zhang and for $\sigma = 0.5$ by Halperin and Zwick. For $\sigma = 0.62, \cdots 0.98$ Feige, Langberg [5] found the previously best factors. Our improvement is for $\sigma = 0.38, \cdots 0.74$.

---

[2] The approximation factor of 0.6436 of Halperin and Zwick seems to be incorrect. On page 16 [11], Halperin and Zwick claim that $\min_{x \in [-\frac{1}{3}, 0]} \{4 \arccos(d_2 x) - 3 \arccos\left(d_2 \frac{4x-1}{3}\right) - \arccos(d_2)\} \geq 0$ holds for all $d_2 \geq 0$. But for $d_2 = 0.81$ (their parameter for MAX-k-UNCUT) and $x = -\frac{1}{3}$ we have: $4 \arccos(-\frac{1}{3} \cdot 0.81) - 3 \arccos(-\frac{7}{9} \cdot 0.81) - \arccos(0.81) < 0$. Using $d_2 = 0.81$, we get an approximation factor of 0.6414.

[3] Again the approximation factor of 0.8118 of Halperin and Zwick seems to be incorrect, as for $d_2 = 0.74$ and $x = -\frac{1}{3}$ we have: $4 \arccos(-\frac{1}{3} \cdot 0.74) - 3 \arccos(-\frac{7}{9} \cdot 0.74) - \arccos(0.74) < 0$. Their approximation factor becomes 0.811.

Acknowledgement

We would like to thank Jiawei Zhang for some helpful discussions.

References

1. A. Ageev, R. Hassin, M. Sviridenko, *A 0.5–Approximation Algorithm for MAX DICUT with Given Sizes of Parts*, SIAM Journal on Discrete Mathematics 14 (2), p. 246-255, 2001.
2. A. Ageev, M. Sviridenko, *Approximation Algorithms for Maximum Coverage and Max Cut with Given Size of Parts*, IPCO '99, p. 17-30, 1999.
3. Y. Asahiro, K. Iwama, H. Tamaki, T. Tokuyama, *Greedily Finding a Dense Subgraph*, Journal of Algorithms 34, p. 203-221, 2000.
4. D. Bertsimas, Y. Ye, *Semidefinite Relaxations, Multivariate Normal Distributions, and Order Statistics*, Handbook of Combinatorial Optimization (Vol. 3), Kluwer Academic Publishers, p. 1-19, 1998.
5. U. Feige, M. Langberg, *Approximation Algorithms for Maximization Problems arising in Graph Partitioning*, Journal of Algorithms 41, p. 174-211, 2001.
6. U. Feige, M. Langberg, *The RPR^2 rounding technique for semidefinite programs*, Proceedings of the 33th Annual ACM Symposium on Theory of Computing, Crete, Greece, p. 213–224, 2001.
7. U. Feige, G. Kortsarz, D. Peleg, *The Dense k-Subgraph Problem*, Algorithmica 29, p. 410–421, 2001.
8. U. Feige, M. Seltser, *On the densest k-subgraph problem*, Technical report, Department of Applied Mathematics and Computer Science, The Weizmann Institute, Rehovot, September 1997.
9. A. Frieze, M. Jerrum, *Improved Approximation Algorithms for MAX k-CUT and MAX BISECTION*, Algorithmica 18, p. 67-81, 1997.
10. M.X. Goemans, D.P. Williamson, *Improved Approximation Algorithms for Maximum Cut and Satisfiability Problems Using Semidefinite Programming*, Journal of the ACM, 42, p. 1115–1145, 1995.
11. E. Halperin, U. Zwick, *A unified framework for obtaining improved approximation algorithms for maximum graph bisection problems*, Random Structures and Algorithms 20 (3), p. 382-402, 2002.
12. Q. Han, Y. Ye, J. Zhang, *An Improved Rounding Method and Semidefinite Programming Relaxation for Graph Partition*, Mathematical Programming 92 (3), p. 509–535, 2002.
13. S. Mahajan, H. Ramesh, *Derandomizing approximation algorithms based on semidefinite programming*, SIAM Journal on Computing 28, p. 1641–1663, 1999.
14. A. Srivastav, K. Wolf, *Finding Dense Subgraphs with Semidefinite Programming*, Approximation Algorithms for Combinatorial Optimization '98, p. 181–191, 1998. (Erratum, Mathematisches Seminar, Universität zu Kiel, 1999.)
15. Y. Ye, *A .699–approximation algorithm for MAX-Bisection*, Mathematical Programming 90 (1), p. 101–111, 2001.
16. Y. Ye, J. Zhang, *Approximation of Dense-$\frac{n}{2}$-Subgraph and the complement of Min-Bisection*, Unpublished Manuscript, 1999.

Learning Languages from Positive Data and a Finite Number of Queries

Sanjay Jain[1,*] and Efim Kinber[2]

[1] School of Computing, National University of Singapore, Singapore 117543
sanjay@comp.nus.edu.sg
[2] Department of Computer Science, Sacred Heart University, Fairfield, CT
06432-1000 U.S.A.
kinbere@sacredheart.edu

Abstract. A computational model for learning languages in the limit from full positive data and a bounded number of queries to the teacher (oracle) is introduced and explored. Equivalence, superset, and subset queries are considered. If the answer is negative, the teacher may provide a counterexample. We consider several types of counterexamples: arbitrary, least counterexamples, and no counterexamples. A number of hierarchies based on the number of queries (answers) and types of answers/counterexamples is established. Capabilities of learning with different types of queries are compared. In most cases, one or two queries of one type can sometimes do more than any bounded number of queries of another type. Still, surprisingly, a finite number of subset queries is sufficient to simulate the same number of equivalence queries when *behaviourally correct* learners do not receive counterexamples and may have unbounded number of errors in almost all conjectures.

1 Introduction

Finding an adequate computational model for learning languages has been an important objective for last four decades. In 1967, M. Gold [Gol67] introduced a classical model of learning languages in the limit from full positive data (that is, all correct statements in the target language). Under the Gold's paradigm, the learner stabilizes to a correct grammar of the target language (**Ex**-style learning). Based on the same idea of learning in the limit, J. Case and C. Lynes [CL82] and D. Osherson and S. Weinstein [OW82] (see also [Bär74] and [CS83]) introduced a more powerful *behaviorally correct* type of learning languages, when a learner almost always outputs correct (but not necessarily the same) grammars for the target language (**Bc**-style learning). In both cases, the authors also considered a much stronger (and less realistic) model of learning languages in the presence of full positive and *negative* data. In [BCJ95] the authors considered an intermediate model, where a learner gets full positive data and a finite number of negative examples. However, negative data in the latter paper is preselected, and, thus, dramatically affects learning capabilities.

---

* Supported in part by NUS grant number R252-000-127-112.

K. Lodaya and M. Mahajan (Eds.): FSTTCS 2004, LNCS 3328, pp. 360–371, 2004.

In the paper [Ang88], D. Angluin introduced another important learning paradigm, i.e. learning from queries to a teacher (oracle). Among others, D. Angluin introduced three types of queries: equivalence queries - when a learner asks if the current conjecture generates the target language; subset and superset queries - when a learner asks if the current conjecture generates a subset or a superset of the target language, respectively. If the answer is negative, the teacher may provide a *counterexample* showing where the current conjecture errs. This learning paradigm of testing conjectures against the target concept (and some other related types of queries) has been explored, primarily in the context of learning finite concepts and regular languages, in several papers, for example, [Ang01, NL00, Ang87, AHK93, Kin92, SHA03, IJ88]. In [LNZ02], the authors applied this paradigm to explore learning (potentially infinite) languages without knowing any data in advance (neither positive, nor negative) (see also [LZ04b, LZ04a]).

In this paper, we combine learning languages from positive data and learning language from queries into one model. The first attempt of this kind was made in [JK04a], where learning from positive data and negative counterexamples to conjectures was considered. In this model, a learner essentially asks a subset query about every conjecture. Thus, a learner, being provided with full positive data, is concerned with "overgeneralizing", that is, including into conjectures data not belonging to the target language. If the current conjecture is not a subset, the teacher may provide a negative counterexample. In the current paper, we concentrate on the case when a learner can query the teacher only a bounded (finite) number of times - thus, limiting the amount of help from the teacher. As avoiding overgeneralization is probably the main challenge a language learner can face (see, for example, [OSW86, ZL95]), exploring help from subset queries is our primary objective in this paper. In addition to subset queries, we also consider learning with equivalence and superset queries. Using the latter type of queries in the presence of full positive data may seem problematic, as "counterexamples" in this case are positive, and the learner gets them eventually anyway. However, sometimes, a teacher may have difficulty providing negative counterexamples. Moreover, as we have shown, positive counterexamples can help learning language that cannot be learned otherwise - even when full positive data is eventually available!

As the number of queries in our learning model is always uniformly bounded, it can naturally be considered as a measure of complexity of learning languages (number of queries as a measure of complexity of solving hard computational problems has been extensively explored, see, for example [GM98]).

Following [JK04a], in addition to the case when counterexamples provided by the teacher are arbitrary (our basic learning model), we consider two further variants of this basic model:

- the learner always gets the least counterexample (Ibarra et al. [IJ88] explored this type of learning using equivalence queries for finite deterministic automata);
- the learner gets only answers "yes" or "no", but no counterexamples (queries of this type are known as *restricted*).

In this paper we explore effects of different types of queries on learning capabilities. In particular, we explore:

- how the number of queries can affect learning capabilities (hierarchies based on the number of queries);
- relationships between learning capabilities based on different types of queries;
- how three different variants of the basic model (described above) using different types of counterexamples given affect learning capabilities;

The paper is organized as follows. Section 2 is devoted to notation and some basic definitions (in particular, definitions of **Ex** and **Bc** types of learning). In section 3 we define learning from positive data via subset, equivalence, and superset queries, as well as three abovementioned variants of the basic learning model.

In Section 4 general hierarchies based on the number of queries are exhibited. Our results here (Theorem 1 and Theorem 2) show that, for all three types of queries, learning with $(n + 1)$ queries is stronger than with n queries. Moreover, classes of languages witnessing hierarchies in question can be **Ex**-learned using $(n + 1)$ restricted queries (providing only answers "yes" or "no"), but cannot be learned by **Bc**-type learners getting the least counterexamples.

In Section 5 we establish hierarchies based on the differences between different variants of the basic learning model: using least counterexamples versus arbitrary counterexamples, and arbitrary counterexamples versus no counterexamples. First, we show that, for all three types of queries, when only one query is permitted, getting the least counterexample helps no better than getting no counterexample (Theorem 3). On the other hand, (again for all three types of queries) **Ex**-learners making just two queries and receiving the least counterexamples can do better than **Bc**-learners making n queries, making a finite number of errors in almost all conjectures, and receiving arbitrary counterexamples to queries (Theorem 4 and Theorem 5). In the rest of the section we demonstrate that **Ex**-learners making just two queries and getting arbitrary counterexamples can learn classes not **Bc**-learnable via any n queries with no counterexamples, even when a finite number of errors is allowed in almost all conjectures (Theorems 6 and 7).

In Section 6 we explore the relationship between various different kind of queries. We show that there are classes of languages **Ex**-learnable with one restricted subset query but not **Bc**-learnable with any finite number of equivalence queries, even when always getting least counterexamples and allowing any finite number of errors in almost all conjectures (Theorem 8). On the other hand, we show that **Ex**-learners using just one restricted equivalence (or superset) query can learn a class not learnable by **Bc**-learners which are allowed to ask finite number of subset queries, and make a bounded number of errors in almost all their conjectures (Theorem 9). We also disovered a subtle difference with the above result in the case when **Bc**-learners can make any unbounded finite number of errors in almost all conjectures: in this case, **Bc**-learners using n restricted equivalence queries cannot learn more than **Bc**-learners using the same number of restricted subset queries (Theorem 10). Still, if the teacher provides counterexamples, **Ex**-learners making just two equivalence queries can do better than **Bc**-

learners making any finite (unbounded) number of subset queries, getting least counterexamples and making any finite (unbounded) number of errors in almost all conjectures (Theorem 11). We then show that **Ex**-learners making just one restricted superset query can sometimes do better than **Bc**-learners making n equivalence queries, getting least counterexamples, and making finite (bounded) number of errors in almost all conjectures (Theorem 13). On the other hand one can show that finite number of superset queries do not help when **Bc**-learners are allowed unbounded finite number of errors in almost all its conjectures (Theorem 12). Thus, as a corollary we show that there exist classes which are learnable using one restricted subset or equivalence query, which cannot be learned using unbounded, but finite number of superset queries (Corollary 1).

We can show Theorems 2, 5, 7, 9 and 13 with **Ex*** inplace of **Bc**^{t} in the RHS. Furthermore, anomaly hierarchy for the criteria of learning with queries can also be shown (details omitted due to space constraints).

We also considered the case when the size of counterexamples is bounded by the size of positive data seen so far (thus, addressing complexity issues). We have shown, however, that counterexamples of this kind do not enhance learning capabilities. We also explored a variant of learning via positive data and negative counterexamples to conjectures (see [JK04a]) mentioned above, where we restrict the learner to receive only a bounded number of (negative) counterexamples. On the surface, learners of this kind seem to be at least as capable as learners using bounded number of subset queries. However, we have shown that one "clever" subset query can sometimes do more than testing every conjecture and getting up to any n counterexamples. We also discovered that for this criteria of learning, learners getting $(2n-1)$ negative answers (and no counterexamples to the conjectures) can simulate learners getting n least counterexamples, and this bound is tight. These topics and most of the proofs are not included in the current version due to size constraints. Interested readers may find the proofs and further results in [JK04b].

2   Notation and Preliminaries

Any unexplained recursion theoretic notation is from [Rog67]. The symbol N denotes the set of natural numbers, $\{0, 1, 2, 3, \ldots\}$. Cardinality of a set S is denoted by $\mathrm{card}(S)$. The maximum and minimum of a set are denoted by $\max(\cdot), \min(\cdot)$, respectively, where $\max(\emptyset) = 0$ and $\min(\emptyset) = \infty$. $L_1 \mathbf{\Delta} L_2$ denotes the symmetric difference of L_1 and L_2, that is $L_1 \mathbf{\Delta} L_2 = (L_1 - L_2) \cup (L_2 - L_1)$. For a natural number a, we say that $L_1 =^a L_2$, iff $\mathrm{card}(L_1 \mathbf{\Delta} L_2) \leq a$. We say that $L_1 =^* L_2$, iff $\mathrm{card}(L_1 \mathbf{\Delta} L_2) < \infty$. Thus, we take $n < * < \infty$, for all $n \in N$. If $L_1 =^a L_2$, then we say that L_1 is an a-variant of L_2.

We let $\{W_i\}_{i \in N}$ denote an acceptable numbering of all r.e. sets. Symbol $\mathcal{E}$ will denote the set of all r.e. languages. Symbol L, with or without decorations, ranges over $\mathcal{E}$. By $\overline{L}$, we denote the complement of L, that is $N - L$. Symbol $\mathcal{L}$, with or without decorations, ranges over subsets of $\mathcal{E}$. By $W_{i,s}$ we denote the set W_i enumerated within s steps, in some standard method of enumerating W_i.

We now present concepts from language learning theory. A *text* T is a mapping from N into $(N \cup \{\#\})$. Intuitively, #'s represent pauses in the presentation of data. $T(i)$ represents the $(i + 1)$-th element in the text. $T[n]$ denotes the finite initial sequence of T with length n. SEQ denotes the set of all finite initial sequences, $\{T[n] \mid T \text{ is a text}\}$. We let σ, τ, and γ, with or without decorations, range over finite sequences. The empty sequence is denoted by Λ.

The *content* of a text T, denoted by $\text{content}(T)$, is the set of natural numbers in the range of T. A text T is for a language L iff $\text{content}(T) = L$. One can define $\text{content}(\sigma)$, for $\sigma \in \text{SEQ}$ similarly. The *length* of σ, denoted by $|\sigma|$, is the number of elements in σ. For $n \le |\sigma|$, the initial sequence of σ of length n is denoted by $\sigma[n]$.

We denote the sequence formed by the concatenation of τ at the end of σ by $\sigma\tau$. Sometimes we abuse the notation and use σx to denote the concatenation of sequence σ and the sequence of length 1 which contains the element x.

A *language learning machine* [Gol67] is an algorithmic device which computes a mapping from SEQ into N. We let $\mathbf{M}$, with or without decorations, range over learning machines. $\mathbf{M}(T[n])$ is interpreted as the grammar (index for an accepting program) conjectured by the learning machine $\mathbf{M}$ on the initial sequence $T[n]$. We say that $\mathbf{M}$ converges on T to i, (written: $\mathbf{M}(T){\downarrow} = i$) iff $(\forall^\infty n)[\mathbf{M}(T[n]) = i]$.

There are several criteria for a learning machine to be successful on a language. Below we define some of them. All of the criteria defined below are variants of the **Ex**-style and **Bc**-style learning described in the Introduction; in addition, they allow a finite number of errors in almost all conjectures (uniformly bounded, or arbitrary).

Definition 1. [Gol67, CL82] Suppose $a \in N \cup \{*\}$
(a) $\mathbf{M}$ **TxtEx**^{a}*-identifies an r.e. language* L (written: $L \in \mathbf{TxtEx}^a(\mathbf{M})$) iff for all texts T for L, $(\exists i \mid W_i =^a L)(\forall^\infty n)[\mathbf{M}(T[n]) = i]$.
(b) $\mathbf{M}$ **TxtEx**^{a}*-identifies a class* $\mathcal{L}$ of r.e. languages (written: $\mathcal{L} \subseteq \mathbf{TxtEx}^a(\mathbf{M})$) just in case $\mathbf{M}$ **TxtEx**^{a}-identifies each language from $\mathcal{L}$.
(c) $\mathbf{TxtEx}^a = \{\mathcal{L} \subseteq \mathcal{E} \mid (\exists \mathbf{M})[\mathcal{L} \subseteq \mathbf{TxtEx}^a(\mathbf{M})]\}$.

Definition 2. [CL82] Suppose $a \in N \cup \{*\}$
(a) $\mathbf{M}$ **TxtBc**^{a}*-identifies an r.e. language* L (written: $L \in \mathbf{TxtBc}^a(\mathbf{M})$) iff for all texts T for L, $(\forall^\infty n)[W_{\mathbf{M}(T[n])} =^a L]$.
(b) $\mathbf{M}$ **TxtBc**^{a}*-identifies a class* $\mathcal{L}$ of r.e. languages (written: $\mathcal{L} \subseteq \mathbf{TxtBc}^a(\mathbf{M})$) just in case $\mathbf{M}$ **TxtBc**^{a}-identifies each language from $\mathcal{L}$.
(c) $\mathbf{TxtBc}^a = \{\mathcal{L} \subseteq \mathcal{E} \mid (\exists \mathbf{M})[\mathcal{L} \subseteq \mathbf{TxtBc}^a(\mathbf{M})]\}$.

For $a = 0$, we often write **TxtEx** and **TxtBc**, instead of **TxtEx**^{0} and **TxtBc**^{0}, respectively.

3   Learning with Queries

In this section we define learning with queries. The kind of queries considered are

(i) subset queries, i.e., for a queried language Q, "is $Q \subseteq L$?", where L is the language being learned;

(ii) equivalence queries, i.e., for a queried language Q, "is $Q = L$?", where L is the language being learned;

(iii) superset queries, i.e., for a queried language Q, "is $Q \supseteq L$?", where L is the language being learned.

In the model of learning, the learner is allowed to ask queries such as above during its computation. If the answer to query is "no", we additionally can have the following possibilities:

(a) Learner is given an arbitrary counterexample (for subset query, counterexample is a member of $Q - L$; for equivalence query the counterexample is a member of $L \Delta Q$; for superset query the counterexample is a member of $L - Q$);

(b) Learner is given the least counterexample;

(c) Learner is just given the answer 'no', without any counterexample.

We would often also consider bounds on the number of queries. We first formalize the definition of a learner which uses queries.

Definition 3. A learner using queries, can ask a query of form "$W_j \subseteq L$?" ("$W_j = L$?", "$W_j \supseteq L$?") on any input σ. Answer to the query is "yes" or "no" (along with a possible counterexample). Then, based on input σ and answers received for queries made on prefixes of σ, **M** outputs a conjecture (from N).

We assume without loss of generality that on any particular input σ, **M** asks at most one query. Also note that the queries we allow are for recursively enumerable languages, which are posed to the teacher using a grammar (index) for the language. Many of our diagonalization results (though not all) would still stand even if one uses arbitrary type of query language. However simulation results crucially use the queries being made only via grammars for the queried languages. We now formalize learning via subset queries.

Definition 4. Suppose $a \in N \cup \{*\}$

(a) **M SubQ^{a}Ex**-*identifies* a language L (written: $L \in$ **SubQ^{a}Ex(M)**) iff for any text T for L, it behaves as follows:

(i) The number of queries that **M** asks on prefixes of T is bounded by a (if $a = *$, then the number of such queries is finite). Furthermore, all the queries are of the form "$W_j \subseteq L$?"

(ii) Suppose the answers to the queries are made as follows. For a query "$W_j \subseteq L$?", the answer is "yes" if $W_j \subseteq L$, and the answer is "no" if $W_j - L \neq \emptyset$. For "no" answers, **M** is also provided with a counterexample, $x \in W_j - L$. Then, for some k such that $W_k = L$, for all but finitely many n, **M**$(T[n])$ outputs the grammar k.

(b) **M SubQ^{a}Ex**-*identifies* a class $\mathcal{L}$ of languages (written: $\mathcal{L} \subseteq$ **SubQ^{a}Ex(M)**) iff it **SubQ^{a}Ex**-identifies each $L \in \mathcal{L}$.

(c) $\mathbf{SubQ}^a\mathbf{Ex} = \{\mathcal{L} \mid (\exists \mathbf{M})[\mathcal{L} \subseteq \mathbf{SubQ}^a\mathbf{Ex}(\mathbf{M})]\}$

LSubQ^{a}Ex-identification and **ResSubQ^{a}Ex**-identification can be defined similarly, where for **LSubQ^{a}Ex**-identification the learner gets the least counterexample for "no" answers, and for **ResSubQ^{a}Ex**-identification, the learner does not get any counterexample along with the "no" answers.

For $a, b \in N \cup \{*\}$, for $\mathbf{I} \in \{\mathbf{Ex}^b, \mathbf{Bc}^b\}$, one can similarly define **SubQ^{a}I**, **SupQ^{a}I**, **EquQ^{a}I**, **LSubQ^{a}I**, **LSupQ^{a}I**, **LEquQ^{a}I**, **ResSubQ^{a}I**, **ResSupQ^{a}I**, **ResEquQ^{a}I**.

For identification with queries, where there is a bound n on the number of queries asked, we will assume without loss of generality that the learner never asks more than n queries, irrespective of whether the input language belongs to the class being learned, or whether the answers given to earlier queries are correct.

4   Hierarchies Based on the Number of Queries

Our first two results establish general hierarchies of learning capabilities with respect to the number of queries for all three types of queries.

Theorem 1. *Suppose $n \in N$. Then, there exists a class $\mathcal{L}$ such that following hold.*
(a) $\mathcal{L} \in \mathbf{ResSubQ}^{n+1}\mathbf{Ex} \cap \mathbf{ResEquQ}^{n+1}\mathbf{Ex}$.
(b) $\mathcal{L} \notin \mathbf{LSubQ}^n\mathbf{Bc}^* \cup \mathbf{LEquQ}^n\mathbf{Bc}^*$.

We now turn our attention to the hierarchy based on the number of superset queries. As $\mathbf{LSupQ}^*\mathbf{Bc}^* \subseteq \mathbf{TxtBc}^*$ (see Theorem 12), the hierarchy for superset queries takes a slightly weaker form than hierarchies for other types of queries.

Theorem 2. *Suppose $n, t \in N$. $\mathbf{ResSupQ}^{n+1}\mathbf{Ex} - \mathbf{LSupQ}^n\mathbf{Bc}^t \neq \emptyset$.*

5   Hierarchies Based on Type of Counterexamples

Before turning our attention to hierarchies based on the type of counterexamples, we first show that, when unbounded but finite number of queries is used, or only a single query is used, different types of counterexamples do not make a difference.

Proposition 1. *Suppose $a \in N \cup \{*\}$, $\mathbf{I} \in \{\mathbf{Ex}^a, \mathbf{Bc}^a\}$*
(a) $\mathbf{ResSubQ}^*\mathbf{I} = \mathbf{SubQ}^*\mathbf{I} = \mathbf{LSubQ}^*\mathbf{I}$.
(b) $\mathbf{ResSupQ}^*\mathbf{I} = \mathbf{SupQ}^*\mathbf{I} = \mathbf{LSupQ}^*\mathbf{I}$.
(c) $\mathbf{ResEquQ}^*\mathbf{I} = \mathbf{EquQ}^*\mathbf{I} = \mathbf{LEquQ}^*\mathbf{I}$.

Theorem 3. *Suppose $a \in N \cup \{*\}$, $n \in N$, $\mathbf{I} \in \{\mathbf{Ex}^a, \mathbf{Bc}^a\}$*
(a) $\mathbf{ResSubQ}^1\mathbf{I} = \mathbf{SubQ}^1\mathbf{I} = \mathbf{LSubQ}^1\mathbf{I}$.
(b) $\mathbf{ResEquQ}^1\mathbf{I} = \mathbf{EquQ}^1\mathbf{I} = \mathbf{LEquQ}^1\mathbf{I}$.
(c) $\mathbf{ResSupQ}^1\mathbf{I} = \mathbf{SupQ}^1\mathbf{I} = \mathbf{LSupQ}^1\mathbf{I}$.

The above theorem thus restricts us to consider at least two queries when showing differences between various types of counterexamples. We will now explore advantages of having least counterexamples.

We first consider equivalence and subset queries. Our result shows that **Ex**-learners using just two subset or equivalence queries and receiving the least counterexamples can sometimes do better than any **Bc***-learner making any n queries of either type and receiving arbitrary counterexamples.

Theorem 4. *For all* $n \in N$,
$$\mathbf{LSubQ}^2\mathbf{Ex} \cap \mathbf{LEquQ}^2\mathbf{Ex} - (\mathbf{SubQ}^n\mathbf{Bc}^* \cup \mathbf{EquQ}^n\mathbf{Bc}^*) \neq \emptyset.$$

The following theorem shows that **Ex**-learners using just two superset queries and getting least counterexamples can sometimes do better than any **Bc**^{t}-learner ($t \in N$) using superset queries and getting any n arbitrary counterexamples. Note, though, that this theorem cannot be generalized for diagonalization against **SupQ**^{n}**Bc*** (as **LSupQ*****Bc**$^* \subseteq$ **TxtBc***, see Theorem 12) or against **SupQ*****Ex** (as **LSupQ*****I** = **SupQ*****I** = **ResSupQ*****I**, see Proposition 1).

Theorem 5. *For* $n, t \in N$, $\mathbf{LSupQ}^2\mathbf{Ex} - \mathbf{SupQ}^n\mathbf{Bc}^t \neq \emptyset$.

We now consider the advantage of having arbitrary counterexamples versus being just told that there exists a counterexample. Again we separate the result for superset queries from the others.

First, we show that there exists a class of languages that can be **Ex**-learned using just two subset or equivalence queries returning arbitrary counterexamples, but cannot be learned by any **Bc***-learner via any m restricted queries of either type.

Theorem 6. *Suppose* $n \in N$. *Then,*
$$(\mathbf{EquQ}^2\mathbf{Ex} \cap \mathbf{SubQ}^2\mathbf{Ex}) - (\mathbf{ResEquQ}^n\mathbf{Bc}^* \cup \mathbf{ResSubQ}^n\mathbf{Bc}^*) \neq \emptyset.$$

Our next theorem shows that **Ex**-learners using just two superset queries and getting arbitrary counterexamples can sometimes do better than any **Bc**^{t}-learner ($t \in N$) using any n number of restricted superset queries. Note that this result cannot be generalized for diagonalization against **ResSupQ**^{n}**Bc*** (as **SupQ*****Bc**$^* \subseteq$ **TxtBc***, see Theorem 12) or against **ResSupQ*****Ex** (as **LSupQ*****I** = **SupQ*****I** = **ResSupQ*****I**, see Proposition 1).

Theorem 7. *For all* $n, t \in N$, $\mathbf{SupQ}^2\mathbf{Ex} - \mathbf{ResSupQ}^n\mathbf{Bc}^t \neq \emptyset$.

6   Separations Among Different Types of Queries

We first show that using $*$-number of equivalence queries, one can learn the class of all recursively enumerable sets. Thus, diagonalization against equivalence queries can only be done for bounded number of equivalence queries.

Proposition 2. $\mathcal{E} \in \mathbf{ResEquQ^*Ex}$.

We next consider relationship between subset and equivalence queries. The following theorem demonstrates that sometimes **Ex**-learners using just one restricted subset query can do better than any **Bc***-learner, asking at most n equivalence queries and receiving least counterexamples.

Theorem 8. $\mathbf{ResSubQ^1Ex} - \mathbf{LEquQ}^n\mathbf{Bc^*} \neq \emptyset$.

We now consider the advantages of having equivalence queries versus subset queries. The following theorem demonstrates that just one restricted equivalence (or superset query) made by an **Ex**-learner can sometimes do better than any **Bc**^{m}-learner asking finite (unbounded) number of subset queries and receiving least counterexamples.

Theorem 9. *For all* $t \in N$, $(\mathbf{ResEquQ^1Ex} \cap \mathbf{ResSupQ^1Ex}) - \mathbf{LSubQ^*Bc}^t \neq \emptyset$.

In contrast, our next theorem shows that n restricted equivalence queries made by **Bc***-learners can be simulated by n subset queries. Here, lack of the power of equivalence queries is compensated by possibility of unbounded number of errors in the correct conjectures.

Theorem 10. *For all* $n \in N$. $\mathbf{ResEquQ}^n\mathbf{Bc^*} \subseteq \mathbf{ResSubQ}^n\mathbf{Bc^*}$.

Proof. Suppose **M** $\mathbf{ResEquQ}^n\mathbf{Bc^*}$-identifies a class $\mathcal{L}$. Let **M**$'$ be defined as follows. On $T[m]$, **M**$'$ simulates **M**, asking the same queries as **M** does on prefixes of $T[m]$. In the simulation, the answers given to the queries by **M** is always no. Suppose the queried languages are (in order of query being made) $W_{j_0}, W_{j_1}, \ldots, W_{j_k}$, where $k < n$. Let p_m denote the final conjecture by **M** based on above simulation. Let,

$$x_m^i = \begin{cases} -1, & \text{if answer to subset query for } W_{j_i} \text{ was no.} \\ \min(\text{content}(T[m]) - W_{j_i,m}), & \text{if answer to subset query for } W_{j_i} \text{ was yes.} \end{cases}$$

For the following, we take $-1 \notin W_{j_i}$ (this is for ease of presentation). Then, **M**$'$ on $T[m]$, outputs a program for the following language:

$$L_m = \bigcup_{s \in N, (\forall i \leq k)[x_m^i \notin W_{j_i,s}]} [W_{p_m,s}] \cup \bigcup_{s \in N, r = \min(\{i \mid x_m^i \in W_{j_i,s}\})} [W_{j_r,s}]$$

Now suppose T is a text for $L \in \mathcal{L}$. Consider the following cases.
Case 1: For all $r \leq k$, $W_{j_r} \neq L$.

Let

$$y_m^i = \begin{cases} -1, & \text{if answer to subset query for } W_{j_i} \text{ was no.} \\ \min(\text{content}(T) - W_{j_i}), & \text{if answer to subset query for } W_{j_i} \text{ was yes.} \end{cases}$$

Note that, for all but finitely many m, $x_m^i = y_m^i$. Thus, for all but finitely many m, the language L_m defined above is W_{p_m}. Hence, **M**$'$ $\mathbf{ResSubQ}^n\mathbf{Bc^*}$-identifies L on text T.

Case 2: $W_{j_r} = L$, for some $r \leq k$.

Then choose the minimal such r. For $i < r$, define

$$y_m^i = \begin{cases} -1, & \text{if answer to subset query for } W_{j_i} \text{ was no.} \\ \min(\text{content}(T) - W_{j_i}), & \text{if answer to subset query for } W_{j_i} \text{ was yes.} \end{cases}$$

Now, for $i < r$, for all but finitely many m, $y_m^i = x_m^i$. Moreover, $x_m^r \neq -1$, and $x_m^r \in \text{content}(T) = W_{j_r}$ for all m. Thus, for all but finitely many m, for all but finitely many s, $(\forall i \leq k)[x_m^i \notin W_{j_i,s}]$, does not hold. Moreover, for all but finitely many m, for all but finitely many s, $\min(\{i \mid x_m^i \in W_{j_i,s}\})$ would be r. Thus, for all but finitely many m, $L_m =^* W_{j_r}$ (as L_m would contain W_{j_r} and some finite sets due to "finitely many s" for which $(\forall i \leq k)[x_m^i \notin W_{j_i,s}]$, holds, or $\min(\{i \mid x_m^i \in W_{j_i,s}\}) \neq r$ holds). Hence, $\mathbf{M'}$ $\mathbf{ResSubQ}^n\mathbf{Bc}^*$-identifies L on text T.

Theorem follows from above analysis.   ∎

Thus, for diagonalization against $\mathbf{Bc}^*$ learners asking subset queries, we need to consider at least two unrestricted equivalence queries. In the theorem below we show that $\mathbf{Ex}$-learners making just two equivalence queries can sometimes do better than any $\mathbf{Bc}^*$-learner making unbounded finite number of subset queries receiving least counterexamples.

Theorem 11. $\mathbf{EquQ}^2\mathbf{Ex} - \mathbf{LSubQ}^*\mathbf{Bc}^* \neq \emptyset$.

We now turn our attention to superset queries. First we show that, if unbounded finite number of errors in almost all conjectures is allowed for $\mathbf{Bc}$-learners, then no finite number of superset queries (even unbounded) receiving least counterexamples helps to learn more than what just regular $\mathbf{Bc}^*$-learners can do. In particular, this result will limit our search of separations of types of learning using bounded number of superset queries from other types of learning only to the cases when the latter types do not allow unbounded number of errors in the correct conjectures.

Theorem 12. $\mathbf{LSupQ}^*\mathbf{Bc}^* \subseteq \mathbf{TxtBc}^*$.

The above result is used to derive the following corollary, demonstrating that $\mathbf{Ex}$-learners making just one subset or equivalence query can sometimes do better than any $\mathbf{Bc}^*$-learner using any finite (unbounded) number of superset queries and receiving least counterexamples.

Corollary 1. $\mathbf{SubQ}^1\mathbf{Ex} \cap \mathbf{EquQ}^1\mathbf{Ex} - \mathbf{LSupQ}^*\mathbf{Bc}^* \neq \emptyset$.

Theorem 9 above already established the diagonalization from superset queries to subset queries. The following result establishes the separation of superset queries from equivalence queries. Note that $\mathbf{ResSupQ}^1\mathbf{Ex} - \mathbf{LEquQ}^n\mathbf{Bc}^t \neq \emptyset$ cannot be improved to having $\mathbf{Bc}^*$ on the RHS (as $\mathbf{LSupQ}^*\mathbf{Bc}^* \subseteq \mathbf{TxtBc}^*$, Theorem 12) or to having $*$-number of equivalence queries (as $\mathcal{E} \in \mathbf{ResEquQ}^*\mathbf{Ex}$, Proposition 2).

Theorem 13. *For* $n, t \in N$, $\mathbf{ResSupQ}^1\mathbf{Ex} - \mathbf{LEquQ}^n\mathbf{Bc}^t \neq \emptyset$.

7   Conclusion

In this paper we explored learning classes of recursively enumerable languages from full positive data and bounded number of subset, superset and equivalence queries. We compared capabilities of learning models using different types of queries and counterexamples and obtained hierarchies based on the number and types of counterexamples. We have not discussed yet another popular and natural type of queries considered in literature - membership queries, as a bounded number of such queries trivially does not help in the presence of full positive data. On the other hand, learning languages from full positive data and infinitely many membership queries is equivalent to learning from full positive and negative data (so-called informants) thoroughly explored in literature (see for example, [JORS99]). One can also show that infinite number of (superset, subset or equivalence) queries together with full positive data makes it possible to learn any recursively enumerable language.

In our research, we concentrated on learning classes of recursively enumerable languages. One might also consider learning from positive data and bounded number of queries for indexed classes of recursive languages (they include such important classes as regular languages and pattern languages [Ang80]). Some of our results are applicable to indexed classes of recursive languages. Still, further research in this direction might be promising.

References

[AHK93]   D. Angluin, L. Hellerstein, and M. Karpinski. Learning read-once formulas with queries. *Journal of the ACM*, 40(1):185–210, 1993.

[Ang80]   D. Angluin. Finding patterns common to a set of strings. *Journal of Computer and System Sciences*, 21:46–62, 1980.

[Ang87]   D. Angluin. Learning regular sets from queries and counter-examples. *Information and Computation*, 75:87–106, 1987.

[Ang88]   D. Angluin. Queries and concept learning. *Machine Learning*, 2:319–342, 1988.

[Ang01]   D. Angluin. Queries revisited. In *Algorithmic Learning Theory: Twelfth International Conference (ALT' 2001)*, volume 2225 of *Lecture Notes in Artificial Intelligence*, pages 12–31. Springer-Verlag, 2001.

[Bār74]   J. Bārzdiņš. Two theorems on the limiting synthesis of functions. In *Theory of Algorithms and Programs, vol. 1*, pages 82–88. Latvian State University, 1974. In Russian.

[BCJ95]   G. Baliga, J. Case, and S. Jain. Language learning with some negative information. *Journal of Computer and System Sciences*, 51(5):273–285, 1995.

[CL82]   J. Case and C. Lynes. Machine inductive inference and language identification. In M. Nielsen and E. M. Schmidt, editors, *Proceedings of the 9th International Colloquium on Automata, Languages and Programming*, volume 140 of *Lecture Notes in Computer Science*, pages 107–115. Springer-Verlag, 1982.

[CS83]   J. Case and C. Smith. Comparison of identification criteria for machine inductive inference. *Theoretical Computer Science*, 25:193–220, 1983.

[GM98]   W. Gasarch and G. Martin. *Bounded Queries in Recursion Theory*. Birkhauser, 1998.

[Gol67]   E. M. Gold. Language identification in the limit. *Information and Control*, 10:447–474, 1967.

[IJ88]   O. Ibarra and T. Jiang. Learning regular languages from counterexamples. In *Proceedings of the Workshop on Computational Learning Theory*, pages 337–351. Morgan Kaufmann, 1988.

[JK04a]   S. Jain and E. Kinber. Learning language from positive data and negative counterexamples. In *Algorithmic Learning Theory: Fifteenth International Conference (ALT' 2004)*. Springer-Verlag, 2004. To appear.

[JK04b]   S. Jain and E. Kinber. Learning languages from positive data and finite number of queries. Technical Report TRC4/04, School of Computing, National University of Singapore, 2004.

[JORS99]   S. Jain, D. Osherson, J. Royer, and A. Sharma. *Systems that Learn: An Introduction to Learning Theory*. MIT Press, Cambridge, Mass., second edition, 1999.

[Kin92]   E. Kinber. Learning a class of regular expressions via restricted subset queries. In K. Jantke, editor, *Analogical and Inductive Inference, Proceedings of the Third International Workshop*, volume 642 of *Lecture Notes in Artificial Intelligence*, pages 232–243. Springer-Verlag, 1992.

[LNZ02]   S. Lange, J. Nessel, and S. Zilles. Learning languages with queries. In *Proceedings of Treffen der GI-Fachgruppe Maschinelles Lernen (FGML), Learning Lab Lower Saxony, Hannover, Germany*, pages 92–99, 2002.

[LZ04a]   S. Lange and S. Zilles. Comparison of query learning and gold-style learning in dependence of the hypothesis space. In *Algorithmic Learning Theory: Fifteenth International Conference (ALT' 2004)*, Lecture Notes in Artificial Intelligence. Springer-Verlag, 2004. To appear.

[LZ04b]   S. Lange and S. Zilles. Replacing limit learners with equally powerful one-shot query learners. In John Shawe-Taylor and Yoram Singer, editors, *Proceedings of the Seventeenth Annual Conference on Computational Learning Theory*, volume 3120 of *Lecture Notes in Artificial Intelligence*, pages 155–169. Springer-Verlag, 2004.

[NL00]   J. Nessel and S. Lange. Learning erasing pattern languages with queries. In *Algorithmic Learning Theory: Eleventh International Conference (ALT' 2000)*, volume 1968 of *Lecture Notes in Artificial Intelligence*, pages 86–100. Springer-Verlag, 2000.

[OSW86]   D. Osherson, M. Stob, and S. Weinstein. *Systems that Learn: An Introduction to Learning Theory for Cognitive and Computer Scientists*. MIT Press, 1986.

[OW82]   D. Osherson and S. Weinstein. Criteria of language learning. *Information and Control*, 52:123–138, 1982.

[Rog67]   H. Rogers. *Theory of Recursive Functions and Effective Computability*. McGraw-Hill, 1967. Reprinted by MIT Press in 1987.

[SHA03]   H. Sakamoto, K. Hirata, and H. Arimura. Learning elementary formal systems with queries. *Theoretical Computer Science A*, 298:21–50, 2003.

[ZL95]   T. Zeugmann and S. Lange. A guided tour across the boundaries of learning recursive languages. In K. Jantke and S. Lange, editors, *Algorithmic Learning for Knowledge-Based Systems*, volume 961 of *Lecture Notes in Artificial Intelligence*, pages 190–258. Springer-Verlag, 1995.

The Complexity of the Local Hamiltonian Problem

Julia Kempe[1], Alexei Kitaev[2], and Oded Regev[3]

[1] CNRS & LRI, Université de Paris-Sud, 91405 Orsay, France, and UC Berkeley, Berkeley, CA94720
[2] Departments of Physics and Computer Science, California Institute of Technology, Pasadena, CA 91125
[3] Dept. of Computer Science, Tel-Aviv University, Tel-Aviv, 69978, Israel

Abstract. The k-LOCAL HAMILTONIAN problem is a natural complete problem for the complexity class QMA, the quantum analog of NP. It is similar in spirit to MAX-k-SAT, which is NP-complete for $k \geq 2$. It was known that the problem is QMA-complete for any $k \geq 3$. On the other hand 1-LOCAL HAMILTONIAN is in P, and hence not believed to be QMA-complete. The complexity of the 2-LOCAL HAMILTONIAN problem has long been outstanding. Here we settle the question and show that it is QMA-complete. We provide two independent proofs; our first proof uses a powerful technique for analyzing the sum of two Hamiltonians; this technique is based on perturbation theory and we believe that it might prove useful elsewhere. The second proof uses elementary linear algebra only. Using our techniques we also show that adiabatic computation with two-local interactions on qubits is equivalent to standard quantum computation.

1 Introduction

Quantum complexity theory has emerged alongside the first efficient quantum algorithms in an attempt to formalize the notion of an *efficient* algorithm. In analogy to classical complexity theory, several new quantum complexity classes have appeared. A major challenge today consists in understanding their structure and the interrelation between classical and quantum classes.

One of the most important classical complexity classes is NP - nondeterministic polynomial time. This class comprises languages that can be *verified* in polynomial time by a deterministic verifier. The celebrated Cook-Levin theorem (see, e.g., [1]) shows that this class has *complete* problems. More formally, it states that SAT is NP-complete, i.e., it is in NP and any other language in NP can be reduced to it with polynomial overhead. In SAT we are given a set of clauses (disjunctions) over n variables and asked whether there is an assignment that satisfies all clauses. One can consider the restriction of SAT in which each clause consists of exactly k literals. This is known as the k-SAT problem. It is known that 3-SAT is still NP-complete while 2-SAT is in P, i.e., has a polynomial time solution. We can also consider the MAX-k-SAT problem: here, given

K. Lodaya and M. Mahajan (Eds.): FSTTCS 2004, LNCS 3328, pp. 372–383, 2004.

a k-SAT formula and a number m we are asked whether there exists an assignment that satisfies at least m clauses. It turns out that MAX-2-SAT is already NP-complete; MAX-1-SAT is clearly in P.

The class QMA is the quantum analogue of NP in a probabilistic setting, i.e., the class of all languages that can be verified by a quantum verifier in polynomial time probabilistically (the name is derived from the classical class MA, which is the randomized analogue of NP). This class, which is also called BQNP, was first studied in [2, 3]; the name QMA was given to it by Watrous [4]. Several problems in QMA have been identified [4, 3, 5]. For a good introduction to the class QMA, see the book by Kitaev et al. [3] and the paper by Watrous [4].

Kitaev, inspired by ideas due to Feynman, defined the quantum analogue of the classical SAT problem, the LOCAL HAMILTONIAN problem [3].[1] An instance of k-LOCAL HAMILTONIAN can be viewed as a set of local constraints on n qubits, each involving at most k of them. We are asked whether there is a state of the n qubits such that the expected number of violated constraints is either below a certain threshold or above another threshold, with a promise that one of the two cases holds and both thresholds are at least a constant apart. More formally, we are to determine whether the *groundstate* energy of the Hamiltonian is below one threshold or above another.

Kitaev proved [3] that the 5-LOCAL HAMILTONIAN problem is QMA-complete. Later, Kempe and Regev showed that already 3-LOCAL HAMILTONIAN is complete for QMA [7]. In addition, it is easy to see that 1-LOCAL HAMILTONIAN is in P. The complexity of the 2-LOCAL HAMILTONIAN problem was left as an open question in [6, 8, 7, 9]. It is not hard to see that the k-LOCAL HAMILTONIAN problem contains the MAX-k-SAT problem.[2] Using the known NP-completeness of MAX-2-SAT, we obtain that 2-LOCAL HAMILTONIAN is NP-hard, i.e., any problem in NP can be reduced to it with polynomial overhead. But is it also QMA-complete? or perhaps it lies in some intermediate class between NP and QMA? Some special cases of the problem were considered by Bravyi and Vyalyi [9]; however, the question still remained open.

In this paper we settle the question of the complexity of 2-LOCAL HAMILTONIAN and show

Theorem 1. *The 2-LOCAL HAMILTONIAN problem is* QMA-*complete.*

In [3] it was shown that the k-LOCAL HAMILTONIAN problem is in QMA for any constant k (and in fact even for $k = O(\log n)$ where n is the total number of qubits). Hence, our task in this paper is to show that any problem in QMA can be reduced to the 2-LOCAL HAMILTONIAN problem with a polynomial overhead. We give two self contained proofs for this.

---

[1] For a good survey of the LOCAL HAMILTONIAN problem see [6].

[2] The idea is to represent the n variables by n qubits and represent each clause by a Hamiltonian. Each Hamiltonian is diagonal and acts on the k variables that appear in its clause. It 'penalizes' the assignment which violates the clause by increasing its eigenvalue. Therefore, the lowest eigenvalue of the sum of the Hamiltonians corresponds to the maximum number of clauses that can be satisfied simultaneously.

Our first proof is based on a careful selection of gates in a quantum circuit and several applications of a lemma called the *projection lemma*. The proof is quite involved; however, it only uses elementary linear algebra and hence might appeal to some readers.

Our second proof is based on perturbation theory – a collection of techniques that are used to analyze sums of Hamiltonians. This proof is more mathematically involved. Nevertheless, it might give more intuition as to why the 2-LOCAL HAMILTONIAN problem is QMA-complete. Unlike the first proof that shows how to represent any QMA circuit by a 2-local Hamiltonian, the second proof shows a reduction from the 3-LOCAL HAMILTONIAN problem (which is already known to be QMA-complete [7]) to the 2-LOCAL HAMILTONIAN problem. To the best of our knowledge, this is the first reduction *inside* QMA (i.e., not from the circuit problem). This proof involves what is known as *third order* perturbation theory (interestingly, the projection lemma used in our first proof can be viewed as an instance of *first order* perturbation theory). We are not aware of any similar application of perturbation theory in the literature and we hope that our techniques will be useful elsewhere.

Adiabatic Computation: It has been shown in [10] that the model of adiabatic computation with 3-local interactions is equivalent to the standard model of quantum computation (i.e., the quantum circuit model).[3] We strengthen this result by showing that 2-local Hamiltonians suffice.[4] Namely, the model of adiabatic computation with 2-local interactions is equivalent to the standard model of quantum computation. We obtain this result by applying the technique of perturbation theory, which we develop in the second proof of the main theorem. This gives another application of the powerful perturbation theory techniques developed in this paper.

Comparison with Previous Work: For readers familiar with [7], let us mention the main differences between their 3-local construction and the 2-local construction we use in our first proof (our second proof is very different from all previous proofs). We will describe these differences in more detail later. The main problem is in handling two-qubit gates. We would like to check a correct propagation by using only two-local terms. In other words, we are supposed to construct a Hamiltonian that penalizes bad propagations and does not penalize a correct propagation. It can be seen that the techniques [7] are not enough to implement such a Hamiltonian. We therefore need some new ideas. The first idea is to multiply the Hamiltonian that checks the one-qubit propagation by a large factor. This allows us to *assume* that the propagation according to one-qubit gates is correct. Hence, we only have to worry about the propagation according

---

[3] Interestingly, their proof uses ideas from the proof of QMA-completeness of the LOCAL HAMILTONIAN problem.

[4] The main result of [10] is that 2-local adiabatic computation on *six-dimensional particles* is equivalent to standard quantum computation. There, however, the particles were set on a two-dimensional grid and all two-local interactions were between closest neighbors; hence, the two results are incomparable.

to two-qubit gates. The main idea here is to pad each two-qubit gate with four Z gates, two before and two after. Since we know that the one-qubit propagation is correct we can *use* these additional gates in constructing our Hamiltonian. One of the crucial terms in our Hamiltonian is a term that connects time t and time $t + 2$. Essentially, it compares how the state of the system changes after two qubits have been changed. We can perform such a comparison thanks to the extra one-qubit gates and to the strong one-qubit propagation Hamiltonian.

Structure: We start with describing our notation and some basics in Section 2. Our first proof is omitted. In Section 3 we give the second proof of our main theorem. This proof does not require the projection lemma and is in fact independent of the first proof. We also omit the results relating to adiabatic computation. Some open questions are mentioned in Section 4.

2   Preliminaries

QMA is naturally defined as a class of promise problems: A promise problem L is a pair (L_{yes}, L_{no}) of disjoint sets of strings corresponding to YES and NO instances of the problem. The problem is to determine, given a string $x \in L_{yes} \cup L_{no}$, whether $x \in L_{yes}$ or $x \in L_{no}$. Let $\mathcal{B}$ be the Hilbert space of a qubit.

Definition 1 (QMA). *Fix $\varepsilon = \varepsilon(|x|)$ such that $\varepsilon = 2^{-\Omega(|x|)}$. Then, a promise problem $L \in$ QMA if there exists a quantum polynomial time verifier V and a polynomial p such that:*

- $\forall x \in L_{yes}$ $\exists |\xi\rangle \in \mathcal{B}^{\otimes p(|x|)}$ $\Pr\left(V(|x\rangle, |\xi\rangle) = 1\right) \geq 1 - \varepsilon$
- $\forall x \in L_{no}$ $\forall |\xi\rangle \in \mathcal{B}^{\otimes p(|x|)}$ $\Pr\left(V(|x\rangle, |\xi\rangle) = 1\right) \leq \varepsilon$

where $\Pr\left(V(|x\rangle, |\xi\rangle) = 1\right)$ denotes the probability that V outputs 1 given $|x\rangle$ and $|\xi\rangle$.

We note that in the original definition ε was defined to be $2^{-\Omega(|x|)} \leq \varepsilon \leq 1/3$. By using amplification methods, it was shown in [3] that for any choice of ε in the this range the resulting classes are equivalent. Hence our definition is equivalent to the original one. In a related result, Marriott and Watrous [11] showed that exponentially small ε can be achieved without amplification with a polynomial overhead in the verifier's computation.

A natural choice for the quantum analogue of SAT is the LOCAL HAMILTONIAN problem. As we will see later, this problem is indeed a complete problem for QMA:

Definition 2. *We say that an operator $H : \mathcal{B}^{\otimes n} \longrightarrow \mathcal{B}^{\otimes n}$ on n qubits is a k-local Hamiltonian if H is expressible as $H = \sum_{j=1}^{r} H_j$ where each term is a Hermitian operator acting on at most k qubits.*

Definition 3. *The (promise) problem k-LOCAL HAMILTONIAN is defined as follows: A k-local Hamiltonian on n-qubits $H = \sum_{j=1}^{r} H_j$ with $r = \text{poly}(n)$. Each*

H_j has a bounded operator norm $\|H_j\| \leq \text{poly}(n)$ and its entries are specified by $\text{poly}(n)$ bits. In addition, we are given two constants a and b with $a < b$. In YES instances, the smallest eigenvalue of H is at most a. In NO instances, it is larger than b. We should decide which one is the case.

An important notion that will be used in this paper is that of a restriction of a Hamiltonian.

Definition 4. *Let H be a Hamiltonian and let Π be a projection on some subspace S. Then we say that the Hamiltonian $\Pi H \Pi$ on S is the restriction of H to S. We denote this restriction by $H|_S$.*

3   Perturbation Theory Proof

In this section we give the second proof of our main theorem. The methods and techniques we use are different from the first proof and might constitute a useful tool for other Hamiltonian constructions. To this end, we keep the proof as general as possible.

The underlying idea is similar to the previous proof in that we add two Hamiltonians and analyze the spectrum of their sum. As before, we think of one of the Hamiltonians as having a large spectral gap (the *unperturbed* Hamiltonian H) and the other one (the *perturbation* Hamiltonian V) as having a small norm compared to the spectral gap of H. However, this time we will introduce the notion of an *effective* Hamiltonian, which describes the effect of the perturbation V *inside* the relevant (low-eigenvalue) subspace. More precisely, we will prove that adding a perturbation to H gives a Hamiltonian that has almost the same spectrum as the effective Hamiltonian H_{eff}. This will allow us to create an effective 3-local Hamiltonian from 2-local terms.

3.1   Perturbation Theory

For two Hermitian operators H and V, let $\widetilde{H} = H + V$. We refer to H as the *unperturbed Hamiltonian* and to V as the *perturbation Hamiltonian*. Let λ_j, $|\psi_j\rangle$ be the eigenvalues and eigenvectors of H, whereas the eigenvalues and eigenvectors of $\widetilde{H}$ are denoted by $\widetilde{\lambda}_j$, $|\widetilde{\psi}_j\rangle$. In case of multiplicities, some eigenvalues might appear more than once. We order the eigenvalues in a non-decreasing order

$$\lambda_1 \leq \lambda_2 \leq \cdots \leq \lambda_{\dim \mathcal{H}}, \qquad \widetilde{\lambda}_1 \leq \widetilde{\lambda}_2 \leq \cdots \leq \widetilde{\lambda}_{\dim \mathcal{H}}.$$

In general, everything related to the perturbed Hamiltonian is marked with a tilde.

Our goal in this section is to study the spectrum of $\widetilde{H}$. We start with a lemma that gives a rough approximation for this spectrum. This approximation will be greatly refined later.

Lemma 1. *For all j, $|\widetilde{\lambda}_j - \lambda_j| \leq \|V\|$.*

Proof. Omitted. □

Corollary 1. *Spec* $\widetilde{H}$ *is contained in the* $\|V\|$*-neighborhood of* Spec H.

The goal of perturbation theory is to find a more accurate approximation for $\widetilde{\lambda}_j$, assuming that $\|V\|$ is small. One important setting was described in the projection lemma. Specifically, let H have a zero eigenvalue with the associated eigenspace $\mathcal{S}$, whereas the other eigenvalues are greater than $\Delta \gg \|V\|$. The projection lemma shows that in this case, the lower part of Spec $\widetilde{H}$ is close to the spectrum of $V|_{\mathcal{S}}$. In this section we find a better approximation to Spec $\widetilde{H}$ by considering certain correction terms that involve higher powers of V. For the applications considered below, we need to carry out the calculation up to the third order in V. We remark that the projection lemma (in a slightly stronger form) can be obtained by following the development done in this section up to the first order.

In order to capture the lower part of the spectrum, one does not actually project the operator $\widetilde{H}$ itself, but rather the *resolvent* of $\widetilde{H}$:

$$\widetilde{G}(z) = \left(zI - \widetilde{H}\right)^{-1} = \sum_j (zI - \widetilde{\lambda}_j)^{-1} |\widetilde{\psi}_j\rangle\langle\widetilde{\psi}_j|. \tag{1}$$

It is a meromorphic[5] operator-valued function of the complex variable z with poles at $z = \widetilde{\lambda}_j$. In fact, for our purposes, it is sufficient to consider real z. The resolvent is the main tool in abstract spectral theory [12]; in physics, it is known as the *Green's function*.[6] Its usefulness comes from the fact that its poles can be preserved under certain projections (while eigenvalues are usually lost).

By analogy with $\widetilde{G}(z)$, one can define the unperturbed Green's function $G(z) = (zI - H)^{-1}$. The former can be expressed in terms of the latter (where we omit the variable z):[7]

$$\widetilde{G} = \left(G^{-1} - V\right)^{-1} = G(I - VG)^{-1} = G + GVG + GVGVG + GVGVGVG + \cdots .$$

We remark that from this expansion, one can obtain an alternative proof of Corollary 1. Indeed, let r be an arbitrary constant greater than $\|V\|$. For any z be of distance at least r to Spec H, we have that $\|G\|$ is at most $1/r$. Hence, for such z, the right hand side converges uniformly in the operator norm. It follows that all the poles of $\widetilde{G}$ (and hence Spec $\widetilde{H}$) lie within a $\|V\|$-neighborhood of Spec H.

To define the subspace over which we want to analyze $\widetilde{H}$, let $\lambda_* \in \mathbb{R}$ be some cutoff on the spectrum of H.

---

[5] A meromorphic function is analytic in all but a discrete subset of $\mathbb{C}$, and these singularities must be poles and not essential singularities.

[6] Physicists actually use slightly different Green's functions that are suited for specific problems.

[7] This expansion of $\widetilde{G}$ in powers of V may be represented by Feynman diagrams [13].

Definition 5. Let $\mathcal{H} = \mathcal{L}_+ \oplus \mathcal{L}_-$, where $\mathcal{L}_+$ is the space spanned by eigenvectors of H with eigenvalues $\lambda \geq \lambda_*$ and $\mathcal{L}_-$ is spanned by eigenvectors of H of eigenvalue $\lambda < \lambda_*$. Let $\Pi_\pm$ be the corresponding projection onto $\mathcal{L}_\pm$. For an operator X on $\mathcal{H}$ define the operator $X_{++} = X|_{\mathcal{L}_+} = \Pi_+ X \Pi_+$ on $\mathcal{L}_+$ and similarly $X_{--} = X|_{\mathcal{L}_-}$. We also define $X_{+-} = \Pi_+ X \Pi_-$ as an operator from $\mathcal{L}_-$ to $\mathcal{L}_+$, and similarly X_{-+}.

With these definitions, in a representation of $\mathcal{H} = \mathcal{L}_+ \oplus \mathcal{L}_-$ both H and G are block diagonal and we will omit one index for their blocks, i.e., $H_+ \overset{def}{=} H_{++}$, $G_+ \overset{def}{=} G_{++}$ and so on. Note that $G_\pm^{-1} = zI_\pm - H_\pm$. To summarize, we have:

$$\widetilde{H} = \begin{pmatrix} \widetilde{H}_{++} & \widetilde{H}_{+-} \\ \widetilde{H}_{-+} & \widetilde{H}_{--} \end{pmatrix} \quad V = \begin{pmatrix} V_{++} & V_{+-} \\ V_{-+} & V_{--} \end{pmatrix} \quad H = \begin{pmatrix} H_+ & 0 \\ 0 & H_- \end{pmatrix}$$

$$\widetilde{G} = \begin{pmatrix} \widetilde{G}_{++} & \widetilde{G}_{+-} \\ \widetilde{G}_{-+} & \widetilde{G}_{--} \end{pmatrix} \quad G = \begin{pmatrix} G_+ & 0 \\ 0 & G_- \end{pmatrix}$$

We write $\mathcal{H} = \widetilde{\mathcal{L}}_+ \oplus \widetilde{\mathcal{L}}_-$ according to the spectrum of $\widetilde{H}$ and the cutoff λ_*. Then in the following, we analyze $\mathrm{Spec}\, \widetilde{H}|_{\widetilde{\mathcal{L}}_-}$, the lower part of the spectrum of $\widetilde{H}$. To this end, we will study the poles of the projected resolvent $\widetilde{G}_{--}$ in the range $(-\infty, \lambda_*)$ and show that if H has a spectral gap around λ_* then these poles correspond exactly to the eigenvalues of $\widetilde{H}|_{\widetilde{\mathcal{L}}_-}$ (Lemma 2). We define

$$\Sigma_-(z) = zI_- - \widetilde{G}_{--}^{-1}(z)$$

so that we can write

$$\widetilde{G}_{--}(z) = \left(zI_- - \Sigma_-(z) \right)^{-1}$$

as in Eq. (1).

The operator-valued function $\Sigma_-(z)$ is called *self-energy*.[8] We will relate $\mathrm{Spec}\, \widetilde{H}|_{\widetilde{\mathcal{L}}_-}$ to $\mathrm{Spec}\, \Sigma_-(z)$ by showing that the poles of $\widetilde{G}_{--}$ in $(-\infty, \lambda_*)$ are all z such that z is an eigenvalue of $\Sigma_-(z)$ (Lemma 3).

For certain choices of H and V, it turns out that $\Sigma_-(z)$ is nearly constant in a certain range. In such a case, we can approximate it by a z-independent Hamiltonian H_{eff} to which we refer to as the *effective Hamiltonian*. The main theorem of this section shows that in this case the lower part of the spectrum of $\widetilde{H}$ is close to the spectrum of H_{eff}.

In order to find H_{eff}, we represent $\Sigma_-(z)$ using a series expansion in terms of G_+ and the four blocks of V. We start by expressing $\widetilde{G}$ in terms of G as

$$\widetilde{G} = (G^{-1} - V)^{-1} = \begin{pmatrix} G_+^{-1} - V_{++} & -V_{+-} \\ -V_{-+} & G_-^{-1} - V_{--} \end{pmatrix}^{-1}.$$

---

[8] The term H_- is not usually considered part of self-energy, but we have included it for notational convenience.

Then, using the block matrix identity

$$\begin{pmatrix} A & B \\ C & D \end{pmatrix}^{-1} = \begin{pmatrix} (A - BD^{-1}C)^{-1} & -A^{-1}B(D - CA^{-1}B)^{-1} \\ -D^{-1}C(A - BD^{-1}C)^{-1} & (D - CA^{-1}B)^{-1} \end{pmatrix}$$

we conclude that

$$\widetilde{G}_{--} = \left(G_-^{-1} - V_{--} - V_{-+}(G_+^{-1} - V_{++})^{-1} V_{+-} \right)^{-1}.$$

Finally, we can represent $\Sigma_-(z)$ using the series expansion $(I - X)^{-1} = I + X + X^2 + \dots$,

$$\begin{aligned} \Sigma_-(z) &= H_- + V_{--} + V_{-+}(G_+^{-1} - V_{++})^{-1} V_{+-} \\ &= H_- + V_{--} + V_{-+}G_+(I - V_{++}G_+)^{-1} V_{+-} \\ &= H_- + V_{--} + V_{-+}G_+V_{+-} + V_{-+}G_+V_{++}G_+V_{+-} + \\ &\quad V_{-+}G_+V_{++}G_+V_{++}G_+V_{+-} + \cdots . \end{aligned} \tag{2}$$

With these intuitions in place we now state and prove the main theorem of this section. It essentially says that if H and V are such that $\Sigma_-(z)$ can be closely approximated by a constant operator H_{eff} (independent of z), then the spectrum of $\widetilde{H}|_{\widetilde{\mathcal{L}}_-}$ can be closely approximated by the spectrum of H_{eff}.

Theorem 2. *Assume H has a spectral gap Δ around the cutoff λ_*, i.e., all its eigenvalues are in $(-\infty, \lambda_-] \cup [\lambda_+, +\infty)$, where $\lambda_+ = \lambda_* + \Delta/2$ and $\lambda_- = \lambda_* - \Delta/2$. Assume moreover that $\|V\| < \Delta/2$. Let $\varepsilon > 0$ be arbitrary. Assume there exists an operator H_{eff} such that $\operatorname{Spec} H_{\mathrm{eff}} \subseteq [a, b]$ for some $a < b < \lambda_* - \varepsilon$ and moreover, the inequality*

$$\|\Sigma_-(z) - H_{\mathrm{eff}}\| \le \varepsilon$$

holds for all $z \in [a - \varepsilon, b + \varepsilon]$. Then each eigenvalue $\widetilde{\lambda}_j$ of $\widetilde{H}|_{\widetilde{\mathcal{L}}_-}$ is ε-close to the jth eigenvalue of H_{eff}.

Proof. Our first lemma asserts that the poles of $\widetilde{G}_{--}$ in the range $(-\infty, \lambda_*)$ are in one to one correspondence with the eigenvalues of $\widetilde{H}|_{\widetilde{\mathcal{L}}_-}$. Hence we can recover the eigenvalues of $\widetilde{H}|_{\widetilde{\mathcal{L}}_-}$ from the poles of $\widetilde{G}_{--}$.

Lemma 2. *Let $\widetilde{\lambda}$ be in $(-\infty, \lambda_*)$ and let $m \ge 0$ be its multiplicity as an eigenvalue of $\widetilde{H}|_{\widetilde{\mathcal{L}}_-}$. Then around $\widetilde{\lambda}$, $\widetilde{G}_{--}$ is of the form $(z - \widetilde{\lambda})^{-1}A + O(1)$ where A is a rank m operator.*

Proof. Omitted. □

The next lemma relates the spectrum of $\widetilde{H}|_{\widetilde{\mathcal{L}}_-}$ to the operator $\Sigma_-(z)$.

Lemma 3. *For any $z < \lambda_*$, the multiplicity of z as an eigenvalue of $\widetilde{H}|_{\widetilde{\mathcal{L}}_-}$ is equal to the multiplicity of z as an eigenvalue of $\Sigma_-(z)$.*

Proof. Omitted.   □

We observe that the function $\Sigma_-(z)$ is monotone decreasing in the operator sense (i.e., if $z_1 \leq z_2$ then $\Sigma_-(z_1) - \Sigma_-(z_2)$ is positive semidefinite):

$$\frac{d\Sigma_-(z)}{dz} = \frac{d}{dz}\left(V_{--} + V_{-+}(zI_+ - H_+ - V_{++})^{-1}V_{+-}\right) =$$
$$-V_{-+}(zI_+ - H_+ - V_{++})^{-2}V_{+-} \leq 0.$$

Lemma 4. *Let $\tilde\lambda_j$ be the jth eigenvalue of $\tilde H|_{\tilde{\mathcal{L}}_-}$. Then it is also the jth eigenvalue of $\Sigma_-(\tilde\lambda_j)$.*

Proof. Omitted.   □

We can now complete the proof of the theorem. By Corollary 1 and our assumption on H_{eff}, we have that for any $z \in [a - \varepsilon, b + \varepsilon]$, Spec $\Sigma_-(z)$ is contained in $[a - \varepsilon, b + \varepsilon]$. From this and the monotonicity of Σ_-, we obtain that there is no $z \in (b + \varepsilon, \lambda_*]$ that is an eigenvalue of $\Sigma_-(z)$. Similarly, there is no $z < a - \varepsilon$ that is an eigenvalue of $\Sigma_-(z)$. Hence, using Lemma 3 we see that Spec $\tilde H|_{\tilde{\mathcal{L}}_-}$ is contained in $[a - \varepsilon, b + \varepsilon]$. Now let $\tilde\lambda_j \in [a - \varepsilon, b + \varepsilon]$ be the jth eigenvalue of $\tilde H|_{\tilde{\mathcal{L}}_-}$. By Lemma 4 it is also the jth eigenvalue of $\Sigma_-(\tilde\lambda_j)$. By Lemma 1 it is ε-close to the jth eigenvalue of H_{eff}.   □

3.2   The Three-Qubit Gadget

In this section we demonstrate how Theorem 2 can be used to transform a 3-local Hamiltonian into a 2-local one. The complete reduction will be shown in the next section. From now we try to keep the discussion more specialized to our QMA problem rather than presenting it in full generality as was done in Section 3.1.

Let Y be some arbitrary 2-local Hamiltonian acting on a space $\mathcal{M}$ of N qubits. Also, let B_1, B_2, B_3 be positive semidefinite Hamiltonians each acting on a different qubit (so they commute). We think of these four operators as having constant norm. Assume we have the 3-local Hamiltonian

$$Y - 6B_1B_2B_3. \tag{3}$$

The factor 6 is added for convenience. Recall that in the LOCAL HAMILTONIAN problem we are interested in the lowest eigenvalue of a Hamiltonian. Hence, our goal is to find a 2-local Hamiltonian whose lowest eigenvalue is very close to the lowest eigenvalue of (3).

We start by adding three qubits to our system. For $j = 1, 2, 3$, we denote the Pauli operators acting on the jth qubit by σ_j^α. Let $\delta > 0$ be a sufficiently small constant. Our 2-local Hamiltonian is $\tilde H = H + V$, where

$$H = -\frac{\delta^{-3}}{4}I \otimes \left(\sigma_1^z\sigma_2^z + \sigma_1^z\sigma_3^z + \sigma_2^z\sigma_3^z - 3I\right)$$
$$V = X \otimes I - \delta^{-2}\left(B_1 \otimes \sigma_1^x + B_2 \otimes \sigma_2^x + B_3 \otimes \sigma_3^x\right)$$
$$X = Y + \delta^{-1}(B_1^2 + B_2^2 + B_3^2)$$

The unperturbed Hamiltonian H has eigenvalues 0 and $\Delta \overset{def}{=} \delta^{-3}$. Associated with the zero eigenvalue is the subspace

$$\mathcal{L}_- = \mathcal{M} \otimes \mathcal{C}, \qquad \text{where} \quad \mathcal{C} = \big(|000\rangle, |111\rangle \big).$$

In the orthogonal subspace $\mathcal{C}^\perp$ we have the states $|001\rangle, |010\rangle$, etc. We may think of the subspace $\mathcal{C}$ as an effective qubit (as opposed to the three physical qubits); the corresponding Pauli operators are denoted by $\sigma_{\text{eff}}^\alpha$.

We now compute the self-energy $\Sigma_-(z)$ using the power expansion (2) up to the third order. There is no zeroth order term, i.e., $H_- = 0$. For the remaining terms, notice that $G_+ = (z - \Delta)^{-1} I_{\mathcal{L}_+}$. Hence, we have

$$\Sigma_-(z) = V_{--} + (z - \Delta)^{-1} V_{-+} V_{+-} + (z - \Delta)^{-2} V_{-+} V_{++} V_{+-} +$$
$$(z - \Delta)^{-3} V_{-+} V_{++} V_{++} V_{+-} + \ldots$$

The first term is $V_{--} = X \otimes I_{\mathcal{C}}$ because a σ^x term takes any state in $\mathcal{C}$ to $\mathcal{C}^\perp$. The expressions in the following terms are of the form

$$V_{-+} = -\delta^{-2}\Big(B_1 \otimes |000\rangle\langle 100| + B_2 \otimes |000\rangle\langle 010| + B_3 \otimes |000\rangle\langle 001|$$
$$+ B_1 \otimes |111\rangle\langle 011| + B_2 \otimes |111\rangle\langle 101| + B_3 \otimes |111\rangle\langle 110| \Big)$$
$$V_{++} = X \otimes I_{\mathcal{C}^\perp} - \delta^{-2}\Big(B_1 \otimes \big(|001\rangle\langle 101| + |010\rangle\langle 110| + |101\rangle\langle 001| +$$
$$|110\rangle\langle 010| \big) + B_2 \otimes (\ldots) + B_3 \otimes (\ldots) \Big),$$

where the dots denote similar terms for B_2 and B_3. Now, in the second term of $\Sigma_-(z)$, V_{+-} flips one of the physical qubits, and V_{-+} must return it to its original state in order to return to the space $\mathcal{C}$. Hence we have $V_{-+} V_{+-} = \delta^{-4}(B_1^2 + B_2^2 + B_3^2) \otimes I_{\mathcal{C}}$. The third term is slightly more involved. Here we have two possible processes. Indeed, we may act by the operator $X \otimes I_{\mathcal{C}^\perp}$ (first part of V_{++}) after one of the qubits is flipped. Alternatively, V_{-+}, V_{++}, and V_{+-} may correspond to flipping all three qubits in succession. Thus,

$$\begin{aligned}
\Sigma_-(z) = {}& X \otimes I_{\mathcal{C}} + (z - \Delta)^{-1}\delta^{-4}(B_1^2 + B_2^2 + B_3^2) \otimes I_{\mathcal{C}} \\
& + (z - \Delta)^{-2}\delta^{-4}(B_1 X B_1 + B_2 X B_2 + B_3 X B_3) \otimes I_{\mathcal{C}} \\
& - (z - \Delta)^{-2}\delta^{-6}\big(B_3 B_2 B_1 + B_2 B_3 B_1 + B_3 B_1 B_2 + \\
& B_2 B_1 B_3 + B_1 B_2 B_3 \big) \otimes \sigma_{\text{eff}}^x + O\big(\|V\|^4/\Delta^3 \big).
\end{aligned} \tag{4}$$

The asymptotic expression for the error term holds since we take $z = O(1) \ll \Delta$ and hence

$$(z - \Delta)^{-1} = -\frac{1}{\Delta}\Big(1 - \frac{z}{\Delta}\Big)^{-1} = -\frac{1}{\Delta} + O(z/\Delta^2) = -\delta^3 + O(\delta^6).$$

Simplifying the above, we obtain

$$\Sigma_-(z) = \underbrace{Y \otimes I_{\mathcal{C}} - 6 B_1 B_2 B_3 \otimes \sigma_{\text{eff}}^x}_{H_{\text{eff}}} + O(\delta).$$

Notice that $\|H_{\mathrm{eff}}\| = O(1)$ and hence we obtain that for all z in, say, $[-2\|H_{\mathrm{eff}}\|, 2\|H_{\mathrm{eff}}\|]$ we have

$$\|\Sigma_-(z) - H_{\mathrm{eff}}\| = O(\delta).$$

We may now apply Theorem 2 with $a = -\|H_{\mathrm{eff}}\|$, $b = \|H_{\mathrm{eff}}\|$, and $\lambda_* = \Delta/2$ to obtain the following result: Each eigenvalue $\tilde{\lambda}_j$ from the lower part of Spec $\tilde{H}$ is $O(\delta)$-close to the j-th eigenvalue of H_{eff}. In fact, for our purposes, it is enough that the lowest eigenvalue of $\tilde{H}$ is $O(\delta)$-close to the lowest eigenvalue of H_{eff}. It remains to notice that the spectrum of H_{eff} consists of two parts that correspond to the effective spin states $|+\rangle = \frac{1}{\sqrt{2}}(|0\rangle + |1\rangle)$ and $|-\rangle = \frac{1}{\sqrt{2}}(|0\rangle - |1\rangle)$. Since B_1, B_2, B_3 are positive semidefinite, the smallest eigenvalue is associated with $|+\rangle$. Hence, the lowest eigenvalue of $\tilde{H}$ is equal to the lowest eigenvalue of (3), as required.

3.3   Reduction from 3-LOCAL HAMILTONIAN to 2-LOCAL HAMILTONIAN

In this section we reduce the 3-LOCAL HAMILTONIAN problem to the 2-LOCAL HAMILTONIAN problem. By the QMA-completeness of the 3-LOCAL HAMILTONIAN problem [7], this establishes Theorem 1. The proof is based on the three-qubit gadget and is omitted.

4   Conclusion

Some interesting open questions remain. First, perturbation theory has allowed us to perform the first reduction *inside* QMA. What other problems can be solved using this technique? Second, there exists an intriguing class between NP (in fact, MA) and QMA known as QCMA. It is the class of problems that can be verified by a quantum verifier with a *classical* proof. Can one show a separation between QCMA and QMA? or perhaps show they are equal? Third, Kitaev's original 5-local proof has the following desirable property. For any YES instance produced by the reduction there exists a state such that each individual 5-local term is very close to its groundstate. Note that this is a stronger property than the one required in the LOCAL HAMILTONIAN problem. Using a slight modification of Kitaev's original construction, one can show a reduction to the 4-LOCAL HAMILTONIAN problem that has the same property. However, we do not know if this property can be achieved for the 3-local (or even 2-local) problem.

Acknowledgments

Discussions with Sergey Bravyi and Frank Verstraete are gratefully acknowledged. JK is supported by ACI Sécurité Informatique, 2003-n24, projet "Réseaux Quantiques", ACI-CR 2002-40 and EU 5th framework program RESQ IST-2001-37559, and by DARPA and Air Force Laboratory, Air Force Materiel Command,

USAF, under agreement number F30602-01-2-0524, and by DARPA and the Office of Naval Research under grant number FDN-00014-01-1-0826 and during a visit supported in part by the National Science Foundation under grant EIA-0086038 through the Institute for Quantum Information at the California Institute of Technology. AK is supported in part by the National Science Foundation under grant EIA-0086038. OR is supported by an Alon Fellowship and the Army Research Office grant DAAD19-03-1-0082. Part of this work was carried out during a visit of OR at LRI, Université de Paris-Sud and he thanks his hosts for their hospitality and acknowledges partial support by ACI Sécurité Informatique, 2003-n24, projet "Réseaux Quantiques".

References

1. Papadimitriou, C.: Computational Complexity. Addison Wesley, Reading, Massachusetts (1994)
2. Knill, E.: Quantum randomness and nondeterminism (1996) `quant-ph/9610012`.
3. Kitaev, A.Y., Shen, A.H., Vyalyi, M.N.: Classical and quantum computation. Volume 47 of Graduate Studies in Mathematics. AMS, Providence, RI (2002)
4. Watrous, J.: Succinct quantum proofs for properties of finite groups. In: Proc. 41st FOCS. (2000) 537–546
5. Janzing, D., Wocjan, P., Beth, T.: Identity check is QMA-complete (2003) `quant-ph/0305050`.
6. Aharonov, D., Naveh, T.: Quantum NP - a survey (2002) `quant-ph/0210077`.
7. Kempe, J., Regev, O.: 3-local Hamiltonian is QMA-complete. Quantum Inf. Comput. **3** (2003) 258–264
8. Wocjan, P., Beth, T.: The 2-local Hamiltonian problem encompasses NP. International J. of Quantum Info. **1** (2003) 349–357
9. Bravyi, S., Vyalyi, M.: Commutative version of the k-local Hamiltonian problem and non-triviality check for quantum codes (2003) `quant-ph/0308021`.
10. Aharonov, D., van Dam, W., Kempe, J., Landau, Z., Lloyd, S., Regev, O.: Adiabatic quantum computation is equivalent to standard quantum computation. In: Proc. 45th FOCS. (2004) `quant-ph/0405098`.
11. Marriott, C., Watrous, J.: Quantum Arthur-Merlin games. In: Proc. of 19th IEEE Annual Conference on Computational Complexity (CCC). (2004)
12. Rudin, W.: Functional analysis. Second edn. International Series in Pure and Applied Mathematics. McGraw-Hill Inc., New York (1991)
13. Abrikosov, A.A., Gorkov, L.P., Dzyaloshinski, I.E.: Methods of quantum field theory in statistical physics. Dover Publications Inc., New York (1975)

Quantum and Classical Communication-Space Tradeoffs from Rectangle Bounds (Extended Abstract)[*]

Hartmut Klauck[**]

Institut für Informatik,
Goethe-Universität Frankfurt,
60054 Frankfurt am Main, Germany
klauck@thi.informatik.uni-frankfurt.de

Abstract. We derive lower bounds for tradeoffs between the communication C and space S for communicating circuits. The first such bound applies to quantum circuits. If for any problem $f : X \times Y \to Z$ the multicolor discrepancy of the communication matrix of f is $1/2^d$, then any bounded error quantum protocol with space S, in which Alice receives some l inputs, Bob r inputs, and they compute $f(x_i, y_j)$ for the $l \cdot r$ pairs of inputs (x_i, y_j) needs communication $C = \Omega(lrd \log |Z|/S)$. In particular, $n \times n$-matrix multiplication over a finite field F requires $C = \Theta(n^3 \log^2 |F|/S)$, matrix-vector multiplication $C = \Theta(n^2 \log^2 |F|/S)$. We then turn to randomized bounded error protocols, and, utilizing a new direct product result for the one-sided rectangle lower bound on randomized communication complexity, derive the bounds $C = \Omega(n^3/S^2)$ for Boolean matrix multiplication and $C = \Omega(n^2/S^2)$ for Boolean matrix-vector multiplication. These results imply a separation between quantum and randomized protocols when compared to quantum bounds in [KSW04] and partially answer a question by Beame et al. [BTY94].

1 Introduction

1.1 Quantum Tradeoffs

Computational tradeoff results show how spending of one resource must be increased when availability of another resource is limited in solving computational problems. Results of this type have first been established by Cobham [Cob66], and have been found to describe nicely the joint behavior of computational resources in many cases. Among the most important such results are time-space tradeoffs, given the prominence of these two resources. It can be shown that e.g. (classically) sorting n numbers requires that the product of time and space is $\Omega(n^2)$ [Bea91], and time $O(n^2/S)$ can also be achieved in a reasonable model of computation for all $\log n \le S \le n/\log n$ [PR98].

---

[*] The complete version of this paper can be found on the quant-ph archive.
[**] Supported by DFG grant KL 1470/1. Work partially done at Department of Computer Science, University of Calgary, supported by Canada's NSERC and MITACS.

K. Lodaya and M. Mahajan (Eds.): FSTTCS 2004, LNCS 3328, pp. 384–395, 2004.

The importance of such results lies in the fact that they capture the joint behavior of important resources for many interesting problems as well as in the possibility to prove superlinear lower bounds for tradeoffs, while superlinear lower bounds for single computational resources can usually not be obtained with current techniques.

Quantum computing is an active research area offering interesting possibilities to obtain improved solutions to information processing tasks by employing computing devices based on quantum physics, see e.g. [NC00] for a nice introduction into the field. Since the number of known quantum algorithms is rather small, it is interesting to see which problems might be candidates for quantum speedups. Naturally we may also consider tradeoffs between resources in the quantum case. It is known that e.g. quantum time-space tradeoffs for sorting are quite different from the classical tradeoffs, namely $T^2 S = \widetilde{\Theta}(n^3)$ [KSW04] (for an earlier result see [A04]). This shorthand notation is meant as follows: the lower bound says that for all S any algorithm with space S needs time $\widetilde{\Omega}(n^{3/2}/\sqrt{S})$, while the upper bound says that for all $\log^3 n \le S \le n$ there is a space S algorithm with time $\widetilde{O}(n^{3/2}/\sqrt{S})$.

Communication-space tradeoffs can be viewed as a generalization of time-space tradeoffs. Study of these has been initiated in a restricted model by Lam et al. [LTT92], and several tight results in a general model have been given by Beame et al. [BTY94]. In the model they consider two players only restricted by limited workspace communicate to compute a function together. Note that whereas communication-space tradeoffs always imply time-space tradeoffs, the converse is not true: e.g. if players Alice and Bob receive a list of n numbers with $O(\log n)$ bits each, then computing the sorted list of these can be done deterministically with communication $O(n \log n)$ and space $O(\log n)$.

Most of the results in this paper are related to the complexity of matrix multiplication. The foremost question of this kind is of course whether quantum algorithms can break the current barrier of $O(n^{2.376})$ for the time-complexity of matrix multiplication [CW90] (it has recently been shown that *checking* matrix multiplication is actually easier in the quantum case than in the classical case, and can be done in time $O(n^{5/3})$ [BS04]). In this paper we investigate the communication-space tradeoff complexity of matrix multiplication and matrix-vector multiplication. Communication-space tradeoffs in the quantum setting have recently been established [KSW04] for *Boolean* matrix-vector product and matrix multiplication. In the former problem there are an $n \times n$ matrix A and a vector b of dimension n (given to Alice resp. to Bob), and the goal is to compute the vector $c = Ab$, where $c_i = \vee_{j=1}^n (A[i,j] \wedge b_j)$. In the latter problem of Boolean matrix multiplication two matrices have to be multiplied with the same type of Boolean product. The paper [KSW04] gives tight lower and upper bounds for these problems, namely $C^2 S = \widetilde{\Theta}(n^5)$ for Boolean matrix multiplication and $C^2 S = \widetilde{\Theta}(n^3)$ for Boolean matrix-vector multiplication.

Here we first study these problems in the case when the matrix product is not defined by for the Boolean operations $\wedge$ and $\vee$ (which form a semiring with $\{0, 1\}$), but over finite fields, and again for quantum circuits. Later we go back to the Boolean product and study the classical complexities of these problems, in order to get a quantum/classical separation for the Boolean case. All these results are collected in the following table.

	Fields F Matrix Mult.	Fields F Matrix-Vector	Boolean Matrix Mult.	Boolean Matrix-Vect.
Quantum upper bound	$O(n^3 \log^2 |F|/S)$ obvious	$O(n^2 \log^2 |F|/S)$ obvious	$\widetilde{O}(n^{5/2}/\sqrt{S})$ [KSW04]	$\widetilde{O}(n^{3/2}/\sqrt{S})$ [KSW04]
Quantum lower bound	$\Omega(n^3 \log^2 |F|/S)$ this paper	$\Omega(n^2 \log^2 |F|/S)$ this paper	$\Omega(n^{5/2}/\sqrt{S})$ [KSW04]	$\Omega(n^{3/2}/\sqrt{S})$ [KSW04]
Deterministic upper bound	$O(n^3 \log^2 |F|/S)$ obvious	$O(n^2 \log^2 |F|/S)$ obvious	$O(n^3/S)$ obvious	$O(n^2/S)$ obvious
Random. lower bound	$\Omega(n^3 \log^2 |F|/S)$ [BTY94]	$\Omega(n^2 \log^2 |F|/S)$ [BTY94]	$\Omega(n^3/S^2)$ this paper	$\Omega(n^2/S^2)$ this paper

Note that in the above table all upper bounds hold for $\log n \le S \le n$, and that the results from [BTY94] are actually shown in a slightly different model (branching programs that communicate field elements at unit cost) and hence stated with a factor of $\log |F|$ less there.

1.2   Direct Product Results

As in [KSW04] we use direct product type results to obtain quantum communication-space tradeoff lower bounds for functions with many outputs. In this approach (as in previous proofs concerning such tradeoffs) a space bounded circuit computing a function is decomposed into slices containing a certain amount of communication. Such a circuit slice starts with a (possibly complicated) initial state computed by the gates in previous slices, but this state can be replaced by the totally mixed state at the cost of reducing the success probability by a factor of $1/2^S$, where S is the space bound. If we manage to show that a circuit with the given resources (but with no initial information) can compute k output bits of the function only with success probability exponentially small in k, then $k = O(S)$, and we can prove a tradeoff result by concluding that the number of circuit slices times $O(S)$ must be larger than the number of output bits.

A direct product result says that when solving k instances of a problem simultaneously the success probability will go down exponentially in k. There are two different types of direct product results. In a *strong* direct product result we try to solve k instances with k times the resources that allow us to solve the problem on one instance with probability $2/3$. In a *weak* direct product theorem we have only the same amount of resources as for one instance.

Our approach is to show direct product type results for lower bound techniques that work for quantum resp. randomized communication complexity of functions f. We focus on lower bound methods defined in terms of the properties of rectangles in the communication matrix of f. There are several techniques available now for proving lower bounds on the quantum communication complexity (see [Ra03, Kla01]). The earliest such technique was the discrepancy bound first applied to quantum communication by Kremer [Kre95]. This bound is also related to the majority nondeterministic communication complexity [Kla01].

Definition 1. *Let ν be a distribution on $X \times Y$ and f be any function f : $X \times Y \rightarrow \{0,1\}$. Then let $disc_\nu(f) = \max_R |\nu(R \cap f^{-1}(0)) - \nu(R \cap f^{-1}(1))|$, where R runs over all rectangles in the communication matrix of f (see Section 2.2).*

In the rest of the paper μ will always denote the uniform distribution on some domain. $disc(f)$ will be a shorthand for $disc_\mu(f)$. We will also refer to the term maximized above as the discrepancy of a particular rectangle. Since we are dealing with multiple output problems, also a notion of *multicolor* discrepancy we are going to define later will be useful. $- \log(disc(f))$ gives a lower bound on the quantum communication complexity [Kre95].

As Shaltiel [Sha01] has pointed out, in many cases strong direct product theorems do not hold. He however gives a strong direct product theorem for the discrepancy bound, or rather a XOR-lemma: he shows that

$$disc(\oplus_{i=1,\ldots,k} f(x_i)) \leq disc(f(x))^{\Omega(k)}.$$

Previously Parnafes et al. [PRW97] showed a general direct product theorem for classical communication complexity, but in their result the success probability is only shown to go down exponentially in k/c, where c is the communication complexity of the problem on one instance, so this result cannot be used for deriving good tradeoff bounds. Klauck et al. [KSW04] have recently given a strong direct product theorem for computing k instances of the Disjointness problem in quantum communication complexity.

Instead of the usual direct product formulation (k independent instances of a problem have to be solved) we first focus on the following setup (a generalized form of matrix multiplication): Alice receives l inputs, Bob receives r inputs, and they want to compute $f(x_i, y_j)$ for all lr pairs of inputs for some function f. We denote this problem by $f_{l,r}$. We will show that when the communication in a quantum protocol is smaller than the discrepancy bound (for one instance) then the success probability of computing some k of the outputs of $f_{l,r}$ goes down exponentially in k (for all k smaller than the discrepancy bound), and refer to such a result as a *bipartite product result*. This differs from Shaltiel's direct product result for discrepancy [Sha01] in three ways: first, it only holds when the communication is smaller than the discrepancy bound for one instance (a weak direct product result), secondly, it deals with correlated input instances (in the described bipartite way). Furthermore it does not speak about discrepancy of the XOR of the outputs for k instances, but rather the multicolor discrepancy.

1.3   Our Results

The first lower bound result of this paper is the following:

Theorem 1. *Let* $f : X \times Y \to \{0,1\}$ *with* $disc(f) \le 1/2^d$. *Then any quantum protocol using space* S *that computes* $f_{l,r}$ *needs communication* $\Omega(dlr/S)$.

A completely analogous statement can be made for functions $f : X \times Y \to Z$ for some set Z of size larger than two and multicolor discrepancy, where the lower bound is larger by a factor of $\log |Z|$.

The inner product function over a field F is $IP^F(x,y) = \sum_{i=1}^{n} x_i \cdot y_i$ with operations over F. $IP^{GF(2)}$ has been considered frequently in communication complexity theory. It is known that its quantum communication complexity is $\Theta(n)$ (the lower bound can be proved using discrepancy [Kre95]). Note that $IP^F_{n,n}$ corresponds to the multiplication of two $n \times n$ matrices over F, while $IP^F_{n,1}$ is the matrix-vector product. It is well known that $disc(IP^{GF(2)}) \le 2^{-n/2}$ (see [KN97]). A generalization of this result given by Mansour et al. [MNT93] implies similar bounds on the multicolor discrepancy of inner products over larger fields. Together with a trivial deterministic algorithm in the model of communicating circuits we get the following corollary.

Corollary 1. *Assume* $\log n \le S \le n \log |F|$.

$IP^F_{n,n}$ *can be computed by a deterministic protocol with space* S *and communication* $O(n^3 \log^2(|F|)/S)$, *and any bounded error quantum protocol with space* S *needs communication* $\Omega(n^3 \log^2(|F|)/S)$ *for this problem.*

$IP^F_{n,1}$ *can be computed by a deterministic protocol with space* S *and communication* $O(n^2 \log^2(|F|)/S)$, *and any bounded error quantum protocol with space* S *needs communication* $\Omega(n^2 \log^2(|F|)/S)$ *for this problem.*

Using a lemma from [MNT93] (also employed in [BTY94]) we are also able to give a lower bound for pairwise universal hash functions.

Definition 2. *A pairwise universal family* Y *of hash functions from a set* X *to a set* Z *has the following properties when* $h \in Y$ *is chosen uniformly at random:*

1. *For any* $x \in X$: $h(X)$ *is uniformly distributed in* Z.
2. *For any* $x, x' \in X$ *with* $x \ne x'$, *and any* $z, z' \in Z$, *the events* $h(x) = z$ *and* $h(x') = z'$ *are independent.*

In the problem of evaluating a hash function by a protocol Alice gets $x \in X$, *Bob gets a function* $h \in Y$, *and they compute* $h(x)$.

Corollary 2. *Any bounded error quantum protocol that evaluates a pairwise universal family of hash functions using space* S *needs communication at least* $\Omega(\min\{\log(|X|) \cdot \log(|Z|)/S, \log^2(|Z|)/S\})$.

Beame et al. [BTY94] have established the first term in the above expression as a lower bound for randomized communicating circuits. Hence our quantum lower bound is weaker for hash functions that map to a small domain.

There are many examples of pairwise universal hash function, see [MNT93]. Let us just mention the function $f : GF(r) \times GF(r)^2 \to GF(r)$ defined by

$f(x, (a, b)) = a \cdot x + b$. If $n = \lceil \log r \rceil$ then this function has a quantum communication tradeoff $CS = \Omega(n^2)$. Also there are universal hash functions that can be reduced to matrix-multiplication and matrix-vector multiplication over finite fields, and we could have deduced the result about matrix-vector multiplication in Corollary 1 from the above result. The result about matrix multiplication would not follow, since the standard reduction from convolution (see [MNT93], matrix multiplication itself is not a hash function) has the problem that for convolution the $\log^2 |Z|$ term is much smaller than the $\log |X| \cdot \log |Z|$ term, and we would not get a good lower bound. Also not every function $f_{l,r}$, where f has small discrepancy, is a universal hash function.

We then turn to classical communication-space tradeoffs for Boolean matrix and Boolean matrix-vector multiplication. We show a weak direct product theorem for the one-sided rectangle bound on randomized communication complexity, which allows us to deduce a weak direct product theorem for the classical complexity of the Disjointness problem. Using this we can show a communication-space tradeoff lower bound for Boolean matrix multiplication, a problem posed by Beame et al. [BTY94].

In the Disjointness problem Alice has an n-bit input x and Bob has an n-bit input y. These x and y represent sets, and $DISJ(x, y) = 1$ iff those sets are disjoint. Note that $DISJ$ is $NOR(x \wedge y)$, where $x \wedge y$ is the n-bit string obtained by bitwise AND-ing x and y. The communication complexity of $DISJ$ has been well studied: it takes $\Theta(n)$ communication in the classical (randomized) world [KS92, Ra92] and $\Theta(\sqrt{n})$ in the quantum world [BCW98, HW02, AA03, Ra03]. A strong direct product theorem for the *quantum* complexity of Disjointness has been established in [KSW04], but the randomized case was left open. $DISJ_{n,n}$ is (the bitwise negation of) the Boolean matrix product.

Theorem 2. *There are constants $\epsilon, \gamma > 0$ such that when Alice and Bob have $k \leq \epsilon n$ instances of the Disjointness problem on n bits each, and they perform a classical protocol with communication ϵn, then the success probability of computing all these instances simultaneously correct is at most $2^{-\gamma k}$.*

An application of this gives a classical communication-space tradeoff.

Theorem 3. *For the problem $DISJ_{n,n}$ (Boolean matrix multiplication) every randomized space S protocol with bounded error needs communication $\Omega(n^3/S^2)$.*

For the problem $DISJ_{n,1}$ (Boolean matrix-vector multiplication) every randomized space S protocol with bounded error needs communication $\Omega(n^2/S^2)$.

The obvious upper bounds are $O(n^3/S)$ resp. $O(n^2/S)$ for all $\log n \leq S \leq n$. No lower bound was known prior to the recent quantum bounds in [KSW04]. Note that the known quantum bounds for these problems are tight as mentioned above. For small S we still get near-optimal separation results, e.g. for polylogarithmic space quantum protocols for Boolean matrix multiplication need communication $\widetilde{\Theta}(n^{2.5})$, classical protocols $\widetilde{\Theta}(n^3)$. The reason we are able to analyze the quantum situation more satisfactorily is the connection between quantum protocols and polynomials exhibited by Razborov [Ra03], allowing algebraic instead of combinatorial arguments.

2   Definitions and Preliminaries

2.1   Communicating Quantum Circuits

In the model of quantum communication complexity, two players Alice and Bob compute a function f on distributed inputs x and y. The complexity measure of interest in this setting is the amount of communication. The players follow some predefined protocol that consists of local unitary operations, and the exchange of qubits. The communication cost of a protocol is the maximal number of qubits exchanged for any input. In the standard model of communication complexity Alice and Bob are computationally unbounded entities, but we are also interested in what happens if they have bounded memory, i.e., they work with a bounded number of qubits. To this end we model Alice and Bob as communicating quantum circuits, following Yao [Yao93].

A pair of communicating quantum circuits is actually a single quantum circuit partitioned into two parts. The allowed operations are local unitary operations and access to the inputs that are given by oracles. Alice's part of the circuit may use oracle gates to read single bits from her input, and Bob's part of the circuit may do so for his input. The communication C between the two parties is simply the number of wires carrying qubits that cross between the two parts of the circuit. A pair of communicating quantum circuits uses space S, if the whole circuit works on S qubits.

In the problems we consider, the number of outputs is much larger than the memory of the players. Therefore we use the following output convention. The player who computes the value of an output sends this value to the other player at a predetermined point in the protocol, who is then allowed to forget the output. In order to make the model as general as possible, we allow the players to do local measurements, and to throw qubits away as well as pick up some fresh qubits. The space requirement only demands that at any given time no more than S qubits are in use in the whole circuit.

For more quantum background we refer to [NC00].

2.2   The Discrepancy Lower Bound and Other Rectangle Bounds

Definition 3. *The communication matrix M_f a function $f : X \times Y \to Z$ with rows and columns corresponding to X, Y is defined by $M_f(x, y) = f(x, y)$.*

A rectangle is a product set in $X \times Y$. Rectangles are usually labelled, an ℓ-rectangle being labelled with $\ell \in Z$. $\ell(R)$ gives the label of R.

The discrepancy bound has been defined above. The application of the discrepancy bound to communication complexity is as follows (see [Kre95]):

Fact 1. *A quantum protocol which computes a function $f : X \times Y \to \{0, 1\}$ correctly with probability $1/2 + \epsilon$ over a distribution ν on the inputs (and over its measurements) needs at least $\Omega(\log(\epsilon/disc_\nu(f)))$ communication.*

We will use the following generalization of discrepancy to matrices whose entries have more than two different values.

Definition 4. *For a matrix M with $M(x,y) \in Z$ for some finite set Z we denote its multicolor discrepancy as $mdisc(M) = \max_R \max_{z \in Z} |(\mu(R \cap f^{-1}(z)) - \mu(R)/|Z|)|$, where the maximization is over all rectangles R in M.*

The above definition corresponds to the notion of *strong* multicolor discrepancy used previously in communication complexity theory by Babai et al. [BHK01]. A matrix with high multicolor discrepancy has rectangles whose measure of one color is very different from the average $\mu(R)/|Z|$. Note that we have defined this only for the uniform distribution μ here, and that only functions for which all outputs have almost equal probabilities are good candidates for small multicolor discrepancy (e.g. the inner product over finite fields).

We next define the one-sided rectangle bound on randomized communication complexity, see Example 3.22 in [KN97] and also [Kla03b].

Definition 5. *Let ν be a distribution on $X \times Y$. Then ν is (strictly) balanced for $f : X \times Y \to \{0,1\}$, if $\nu(f^{-1}(1)) = 1/2 = \nu(f^{-1}(0))$.*

Definition 6. *Let $err(R, \nu, \ell) = \nu(f^{-1}(1 - \ell)|R)$ denote the error of an ℓ-rectangle R. Denote $size(\nu, \epsilon, f, \ell) = \max\{\nu(R) : err(R, \nu, \ell) \le \epsilon\}$, where R runs over all rectangles in M_f.*

$bound_\epsilon^{(1)}(f) = \max_\nu \log(1/size(\nu, \epsilon, f, 1))$, where ν runs over all balanced distributions on $X \times Y$. Then let $bound(f) = \max\{bound_{1/4}^{(1)}(f), bound_{1/4}^{(1)}(\neg f)\}$.

The application to classical communication is as follows.

Fact 2. *For any function $f : X \times Y \to \{0,1\}$, its (public coin) randomized communication complexity with error $1/4$ is lower bounded by $bound(f)$.*

3   Proving Quantum Communication-Space Tradeoffs

Suppose we are given a communicating quantum circuit that computes $f_{l,r}$, i.e., the Alice circuit gets l inputs from X, the Bob circuit gets r inputs from Y, and they compute all outputs $f(x_i, y_j)$. Furthermore we assume that the output for pair (i, j) is produced at a fixed gate in the circuit.

Our approach to prove the lower bound is by slicing the circuit. Let $mdisc(f) = 1/2^d$. Then we partition the circuit in the following way. The first slice starts at the beginning, and ends when $d/100$ qubits have been communicated, i.e., after $d/100$ qubit wires have crossed between the Alice and Bob circuits. The next slice starts afterwards and also contains $d/100$ qubits communication and so forth. Note that there are $O(C/d)$ slices, and lr outputs, so an average slice has to make about lrd/C outputs. We will show that every such slice can produce only $O(S)$ output bits. This implies the desired lower bound.

So we consider what happens at a slice. A slice starts in some state on S qubits that has been computed by the previous part of the computation. Then the two circuits run a protocol with $d/100$ qubits communication. We have to show that there can be at most $O(S)$ output bits. At this point the following observation from [Kla03a] will be helpful.

Proposition 1. *Suppose there is an algorithm that on input x first receives S qubits of initial information depending arbitrarily on x for free. Suppose the algorithm produces some output correctly with probability p.*

Then the same algorithm with the initial information replaced by the totally mixed state has success probability at least $p/2^S$.

Suppose the circuit computes the correct output with probability $1/2$. Then each circuit slice computes its outputs correctly with probability $1/2$. Proposition 1 tells us that we may replace the initial state on S qubits by a totally mixed state, and still compute correctly with probability $(1/2) \cdot 1/2^S$. Hence it suffices to show that any protocol with communication $d/100$ that attempts to make ℓ bits of output has success probability exponentially small in ℓ. Then ℓ must be bounded by $O(S)$. What is left to do is provided by the following bipartite product result.

Theorem 4. *Suppose a quantum protocol with communication $d/100$ makes $k \leq d/(100 \log |Z|)$ outputs for function values $f(x_i, y_j)$ of $f : X \times Y \to Z$ with $mdisc(f) \leq 2^{-d}$. Then the probability that these outputs are simultaneously correct is at most $(1 + o(1)) \cdot |Z|^{-k}$.*

We establish this result in two steps. First we show that for each function with multiple outputs and small multicolor discrepancy all quantum protocols have small success probability.

Lemma 3. *If there is a quantum protocol with communication c that computes the outputs of a function $f : X^l \times Y^r \to Z^k$ so that the success probability of the protocol is $1/|Z|^k + \alpha$ (in the worst case), then $mdisc(f) \geq \alpha^2/2^{10c}$.*

Conversely, if $c \leq -\log mdisc(f)/10 - k \log |Z|$, then the success probability of quantum protocols with communication c is at most $(1 + o(1)) \cdot |Z|^{-k}$.

The next step is to derive multicolor discrepancy bounds for $f_{l,r}$ from multicolor discrepancy bounds for f.

Lemma 4. *Let $f : X \times Y \to Z$ have $mdisc(f) \leq 2^{-d}$. Let the set $O = \{(i_1, j_1), \ldots, (i_k, j_k)\}$ contain the indices of k outputs for $f_{l,r}$. Denote by f_O the function that computes these outputs. Then $mdisc(f_O) \leq O(2^{-d/4})$, if $k \leq d/5$.*

These two lemmas imply Theorem 4. Now we can conclude the following more general version of Theorem 1.

Theorem 5. *Let $f : X \times Y \to Z$ with $mdisc(f) \leq 1/2^d$. Then every quantum protocol using space S that computes $f_{l,r}$ needs communication $\Omega(dlr \log |Z|/S)$.*

Proof. Note that if $S = \Omega(d)$, we are immediately done, since communicating the outputs requires at least $lr \log |Z|$ bits. If $S \leq d/200$, we can apply Theorem 4 and Proposition 1. Consider a circuit slice with communication $d/100$ and ℓ outputs. Apply Theorem 4 to obtain that the success probability of any protocol without initial information is at most $(1+o(1)) \cdot |Z|^{-k}$ for k being the minimum of ℓ and $d/(100 \log |Z|)$. With Proposition 1 we get that this must be at least $(1/2) \cdot 2^{-S}$, and hence $k \leq (S+2)/\log |Z|$. In the case $k = d/(100 \log |Z|)$ we get the contradiction $S+2 \geq k \log |Z| = d/100$ to our assumption, otherwise we get $\ell \leq (S+2)/\log |Z|$ and hence $C/(d/100) \cdot (S+2)/\log |Z| \geq lr$ as desired.

We also get the following corollary in the same way.

Corollary 3. *Let f be a function with m output bits so that for all $k < d$ and each subset O of k output bits $mdisc(f_O) < 2^{-d}$. Then every quantum protocol with communication C and space S satisfies the tradeoff $CS = \Omega(dm)$.*

4 Applications

In this section we apply Theorem 5 and Corollary 3 to show some explicit communication-space tradeoffs. We have already stated our result regarding matrix and matrix-vector products over finite fields in the introduction (Corollary 1). The only missing piece is an upper bound on the multicolor discrepancy of IP^F for finite fields F.

Lemma 5. $mdisc(\widetilde{IP}^F) \leq |F|^{-n/4}$.

Proof. The following is proved in [MNT93].

Fact 6. *Let Y be a pairwise universal family of hash functions from X to Z. Let $A \subseteq X$, $B \subseteq Y$, and $E \subseteq Z$. Then*

$$\left| Prob_{x \in A, h \in B}(h(x) \in E) - \frac{|E|}{|Z|} \right| \leq \sqrt{\frac{|Y| \cdot |E|}{|A| \cdot |B| \cdot |Z|}}. \tag{1}$$

IP^F can be changed slightly to give a universal family, with $X = F^n$ and $Z = F$, by letting $h(x) = IP^F(x, y) + a$ for y drawn randomly from F^n and a from F. Then the set of hash functions has size $|Y| = |F|^{n+1}$.

To bound the multicolor discrepancy of evaluating the hash family we can set E to contain any single element of F. Hence for each rectangle $A \times B$ containing at least $|F|^{(3/2) \cdot n}$ entries the right hand side of inequality (1) is at most $|F|^{(n+1)/2}/(\sqrt{|F|^{(3/2) \cdot n} \cdot |F|}) = |F|^{-n/4}$. This is an upper bound on $\mu(A \times B)$ times the multicolor discrepancy, and hence also an upper bound on the latter itself. Smaller rectangles can have multicolor discrepancy at most $|F|^{-n/2-1}$, thus the multicolor discrepancy of evaluating the hash function is at most $|F|^{-n/4}$. Hence also IP^F has small discrepancy: its communication matrix is a rectangle in the communication matrix for the hash evaluation.

Proof (of Corollary 2). We again make use of Fact 6. Assume that the output is encoded in binary in some standard way using $\lceil \log |Z| \rceil$ bits. Fix an arbitrary value of k output bits to get a subset E of possible outputs in Z. We would like to have $|E|/|Z| = 2^{-k}$, but this is not quite possible, e.g. for Z being $\{0, \ldots, p-1\}$ for some prime p. If we restrict ourselves to the lower $\log(|Z|)/2$ bits of the binary encoding of elements of Z, however, then each such bit is 1 resp. 0 with probability $1/2 \pm 1/\sqrt{|Z|}$ for a uniformly random $z \in Z$, even conditioned on other bits, so that the probability of a fixed value of k of them is between $(1/2 - 1/\sqrt{|Z|})^k$ and $(1/2 + 1/\sqrt{|Z|})^k$. Then $|\,|E|/|Z| - 1/2^k\,| \le 2/\sqrt{|Z|}$.

Let $R = A \times B$ be any rectangle in the communication matrix. Assume that $|R| \ge \sqrt{|X|} \cdot |Y|$. Then the right hand side of (1) is $\le \sqrt{|Y|/(\sqrt{|X|}|Y|)} = 1/|X|^{1/4}$. If R is smaller, then its multicolor discrepancy is at most $1/\sqrt{|X|}$. So we can apply Corollary 3 with a multicolor discrepancy of at most $|X|^{-1/4} + 2|Z|^{-1/2}$. Note that the number of output bits we consider is $\log |Z|/2$, and we get $CS = \Omega(\log |X| \cdot \log |Z|)$ or $\Omega((\log |Z|)^2)$, whichever is smaller.

5   A Direct Product Result for the Rectangle Bound

Theorem 2 is an immediate consequence of the following direct product result for the rectangle bound, plus a result of Razborov [Ra92].

Lemma 7. *Let $f : X \times Y \to \{0, 1\}$ be a function and denote by f_k the problem to compute f on k distinct instances. Assume that $bound(f) \ge b$ and that this is achieved on a balanced distribution ν.*

Then there is a constant $\gamma > 0$ such that the average success probability of each classical protocol with communication $b/3$ for f_k on ν^k is at most $2^{-\gamma k}$ for any $k \le b$.

Now we state the result of Razborov [Ra92].

Fact 8. *$bound(DISJ) \ge \epsilon n$ for some constant $\epsilon > 0$.*

References

[A04]   S. Aaronson. Limitations of Quantum Advice and One-Way Communication. In *Proceedings of 19th IEEE Conference on Computational Complexity*, pages 320–332, 2004. quant-ph/0402095.

[AA03]   S. Aaronson and A. Ambainis. Quantum search of spatial regions. In *Proceedings of 44th IEEE FOCS*, pages 200–209, 2003. quant-ph/0303041.

[BHK01]   L. Babai, T. Hayes, P. Kimmel. The Cost of the Missing Bit: Communication Complexity with Help. *Combinatorica*, 21(4), pages 455-488, 2001. Earlier version in STOC'98.

[Bea91]   P. Beame. A general sequential time-space tradeoff for finding unique elements. *SIAM Journal on Computing*, 20(2) pages 270–277, 1991. Earlier version in STOC'89.

[BTY94]   P. Beame, M. Tompa, and P. Yan. Communication-space tradeoffs for unrestricted protocols. *SIAM Journal on Computing*, 23(3), pages 652–661, 1994. Earlier version in FOCS'90.

[BCW98]   H. Buhrman, R. Cleve, A. Wigderson. Quantum vs. classical communication and computation. *30th ACM Symposium on Theory of Computing*, pages 63–68, 1998. quant-ph/9802040.

[BS04]   H. Buhrman, R. Špalek. Quantum Verification of Matrix Products. quant-ph/0409035.

[Cob66]   A. Cobham. The Recognition Problem for the Set of Perfect Squares. *Conference Record of the Seventh Annual Symposium on Switching and Automata Theory ("FOCS")*, pages 78–87, 1966.

[CW90]   D. Coppersmith, S. Winograd. Matrix Multiplication via Arithmetic Progressions. *J. Symb. Comput.* 9(3), pages 251–280, 1990.

[HW02]   P. Høyer and R. de Wolf. Improved quantum communication complexity bounds for disjointness and equality. In *Proceedings of 19th STACS*, LNCS 2285, pages 299–310, 2002. quant-ph/0109068.

[KS92]   B. Kalyanasundaram and G. Schnitger. The probabilistic communication complexity of set intersection. *SIAM Journal on Discrete Mathematics*, 5(4), pages 545–557, 1992. Earlier version in Structures'87.

[Kla01]   H. Klauck. Lower Bounds for Quantum Communication Complexity. In *42nd IEEE FOCS*, pages 288–297, 2001. quant-ph/0106160.

[Kla03a]   H. Klauck. Quantum time-space tradeoffs for sorting. In *Proceedings of 35th ACM STOC*, pages 69–76, 2003. quant-ph/0211174.

[Kla03b]   H. Klauck. Rectangle Size Bounds and Threshold Covers in Communication Complexity. In *Proceedings of 18th IEEE Conference on Computational Complexity*, pages 118–134, 2003. cs.CC/0208006.

[KSW04]   H. Klauck, R. de Wolf, R. Špalek. Quantum and Classical Strong Direct Product Theorems and Optimal Time-Space Tradeoffs. To appear in *45th IEEE FOCS*, 2004. quant-ph/0402123.

[KN97]   E. Kushilevitz and N. Nisan. *Communication Complexity*. Cambridge University Press, 1997.

[Kre95]   I. Kremer. Quantum communication. Master's thesis, Hebrew University, Computer Science Department, 1995.

[LTT92]   T.W. Lam, P. Tiwari, and M. Tompa. Trade-offs between communication and space. *Journal of Computer and Systems Sciences*, 45(3), pages 296–315, 1992. Earlier version in STOC'89.

[MNT93]   Y. Mansour, N. Nisan, P. Tiwari. The Computational Complexity of Universal Hashing. *Theoretical Computer Science*, 107(1), pages 121–133, 1993. Earlier version in STOC'90.

[NC00]   M. A. Nielsen and I. L. Chuang. *Quantum Computation and Quantum Information*. Cambridge University Press, 2000.

[PR98]   J. Pagter, T. Rauhe. Optimal Time-Space Trade-Offs for Sorting. *Proceedings of 39th IEEE FOCS*, pages 264–268, 1998.

[PRW97]   I. Parnafes, R. Raz, and A. Wigderson. Direct product results and the GCD problem, in old and new communication models. In *Proceedings of 29th ACM STOC*, pages 363–372, 1997.

[Ra92]   A.A. Razborov. On the distributional complexity of disjointness. *Theoretical Computer Science*, 106(2), pages 385–390, 1992.

[Ra03]   A.A. Razborov. Quantum communication complexity of symmetric predicates. *Izvestiya of the Russian Academy of Science, Mathematics*, 67(1), pages 159–176, 2003. quant-ph/0204025.

[Sha01]   R. Shaltiel. Towards proving strong direct product theorems. In *Proceedings of 16th IEEE Conference on Computational Complexity*, pages 107–119, 2001.

[Yao93]   A. C-C. Yao. Quantum circuit complexity. In *Proceedings of 34th IEEE FOCS*, pages 352–360, 1993.

Adaptive Stabilization of Reactive Protocols

Shay Kutten[1] and Boaz Patt-Shamir[2]

[1] The Technion, Haifa 32000, Israel
kutten@ie.technion.ac.il
[2] Tel Aviv University, Tel Aviv 69978, Israel
boaz@eng.tau.ac.il

Abstract. A self-stabilizing distributed protocol can recover from any state-corrupting fault. A self-stabilizing protocol is called *adaptive* if its recovery time is proportional to the number of processors hit by the fault. General adaptive protocols are known for the special case of function computations: these are tasks that map static distributed inputs to static distributed outputs. In *reactive* distributed systems, input values at each node change on-line, and dynamic distributed outputs are to be generated in response in an on-line fashion. To date, only some specific reactive tasks have had an adaptive implementation. In this paper we outline the first proof that *all* reactive tasks admit adaptive protocols. The key ingredient of the proof is an algorithm for distributing input values in an adaptive fashion. Our algorithm is optimal, up to a constant factor, in its fault resilience, response time, and recovery time.

1 Introduction

Self-stabilizing distributed systems (sometimes abbreviated stabilizing systems) recover from a particularly devastating type of fault: state-corrupting faults. A state corrupting fault may flip arbitrarily the bits of the volatile memory in the affected nodes; such faults are tricky, since the local state of each processor may seem perfectly legal, and only a global view can indicate that the state is actually corrupted. The model of stabilizing systems, that entails the idea of state-corrupting faults, is an abstraction of *all* transient faults: if a system is self-stabilizing, then it can recover from any transient fault, so long as its code remains intact. Many systems today are implicitly designed to be stabilizing, at least in some sense. For example, one of the popular techniques used by practitioners to achieve partial stabilization is the time-out mechanism: the idea is that each piece of information is stamped with a "time to live" attribute, which says when does this particular piece of information expire. When executed properly, this approach ensures that stale state will eventually be flushed out of the system. But to ensure correctness, the duration of the timeout (and hence the stabilization time) is proportional to the worst-case cross-network latency (see, e.g., the spanning tree algorithm of Perlman [27]).

Another approach to make a system stabilizing, championed mainly in the theoretical community, is the *global reset* method (see, e.g., [11]). In this approach, the idea is that a special stabilizing mechanism monitors the system for

K. Lodaya and M. Mahajan (Eds.): FSTTCS 2004, LNCS 3328, pp. 396–407, 2004.

illegal states, and whenever an inconsistency is detected, it invokes a special stabilizing reset protocol that imposes some legal global state on the system. The
best reset protocols offer stabilization with relatively low space and communication overhead [10, 9, 11], but at a price of inherently high stabilization time—the
cross-network latency time. Still, the time complexity of reset is better than the
time-out approach for the following reason. On one hand, time-outs expire after
a fixed pre-determined amount of time, which must obviously be the *worst-case*
cross-network latency. On the other hand, the stabilization time of a reset protocol is proportional to the *actual* cross network latency when the reset is invoked,
and the actual time is typically much better than the worst-case time.

Nevertheless, the global reset approach was not widely adopted in practice.
Intuitively, the reason for that is that reset-based stabilization is too "twitchy":
the slightest disturbance to the consistency of the system may trigger a system-
wide service outage (or "hiccup") for a non-negligible amount of time, which
is clearly undesirable. In response to this shortcoming, a new approach, called
adaptive protocols, has recently taken the focus of attention in this research area
[23, 18, 22, 21, 3]. Informally, a stabilizing system is called adaptive if its recovery
time depends on the severity of the fault, measured by the number of processors
whose state was corrupted. For example, the adaptive system proposed in [21]
has the following property: if the state of f nodes is arbitrarily corrupted, then
the correct output is recovered everywhere in $O(f)$ time.

However, most previous results for adaptive systems were limited to *distributed
function computation*: in this model, it is assumed that each node has a constant
input, and the task is to output a fixed function of the inputs. For example, the
input at each node may be the (non-changing) weights of its incident edges, and
the output is a (non-changing) minimum spanning tree of the network graph.
This model, while appropriate for some types of applications, does not capture
the full generality of distributed *reactive* systems [24]. In a reactive system, the
environment injects new inputs to the system from time to time, and the system
is required to produce new output values depending on the given inputs, in an
on-line fashion. More precisely, a specification of a reactive task consists of all
possible inputs, and for each input, all possible outputs. Unfortunately, the only
known results for adaptive reactive protocols either restrict the fault model in a
significant way, or they give ad-hoc solutions for specific problems (see below).

In this paper we outline the first proof that general reactive systems can be
implemented by an adaptive protocol. More specifically, we consider the following
setting. We assume that we are given a synchronous system, where in each round,
nodes exchange messages and perform some local computations. In each step,
the environment (that models users, or other interacting applications) may input
a value to each node, and expects output values to appear at the nodes. The
reactive task specifies what value each node is required to output at each step.
The output values are typically a function of (possibly remote) input values.

If each node had all input values locally available, then it could compute its
required output at each step. Thus, the key ingredient in our general implementation is an adaptive algorithm for distributing input values, which we describe

in detail in this paper. This primitive task simply requires all nodes to eventually output a value input at a distinguished source node. Our algorithm is *adaptive* and optimal, up to a constant factor, in the following measures.

- *Response time*: the elapsed time between inputting a value and changing the relevant output values.
- *Recovery time*, which consists of the following two measures [18, 21]. *Output stabilization* is the time it takes until the outputs stabilize to correct values after a fault; and *state stabilization*, which is the time until the system completely recovers internally from a fault (meaning that it is prepared to sustain another fault).
- *Resilience*: the severity of faults from which the algorithm fully recovers.

Resilience is measured in terms of agility [12]. To explain this concept, consider the following situation. Suppose that immediately after a value is input at a node, a fault occurs, and the state of that node is corrupted. Clearly, there is no way for the system to recover the input value in that case, since all its traces may have been completely wiped out. More generally, assume that a message can traverse one link in one time unit. Now, if a value is input at a node v at time t, and at time $t_f \geq t$ all nodes in distance $t_f - t$ from v are hit by a fault, then, by the same reasoning, the input value may be irrecoverable. In this paper, we consider protocols that can recover from such faults—assuming that they occur sufficiently late in the game (so that the protocol gets the chance to replicate the input value elsewhere). The notion of agility makes this intuition concrete. Formal definition is provided in Section 2.

As mentioned above, in this paper we focus on solving the basic building block problem we call *Stabilizing Value Distribution* (abbreviated SBD). We observe that any reactive task can be reduced to SBD, and therefore, we only outline this reduction in this paper. The reduction is straightforward, albeit inefficient in terms of communication and memory overhead. In this paper we concentrate not on the algorithmic ideas of the reduction (the one we propose is rather simple), but rather in the existential proof that any implementable reactive specification has an adaptive solution.

Contributions of This paper. Our main technical contribution is the first adaptive protocol for the basic building block of SBD. Our protocol is also self-stabilizing, and has optimal agility (up to a constant factor). As a corollary, the presented protocol shows that theoretically, any reactive task admits a self-stabilizing adaptive implementation. Our protocol complements results of [22, 21] dealing with non-reactive tasks. There, it is assumed that all inputs and outputs are initially replicated at all nodes. A fault may corrupt some replicas, and the task is to recover the original values. In a way, this task is self-stabilizing, adaptive consensus. The question "how to perform the initial replication?" in a self-stabilizing and adaptive manner is answered in the current paper.

Related Work. The study of stabilizing protocols was initiated by Dijkstra [14] for the task of token passing. General algorithms started with *reset-based* approaches [20, 4, 10, 5]. In reset-based stabilization, the state is constantly monitored; if an error is detected, a special reset protocol is invoked, whose effect is to consistently establish a correct global state, from which the system can resume normal operation. (The correct state may either be some agreed upon fixed state, or a state that is in some sense "close" to the faulty state [16].) The best reset protocols in terms of time are given in [9], where the stabilization time is proportional to the diameter of the network. Logarithmic space protocols are given in [4, 10], and a randomized constant-space protocol is given in [19]. An extensive survey of self-stabilization is offered in [15].

The idea of adaptive protocols (with variants called fault-local, local stabilizing, or fault containing) is treated in [22, 23, 18, 21, 6, 7], all of them non-reactive.

In [21] it is proven that if a fault hits f nodes, then the output stabilization time is $\Omega(f)$ time units; and that the state stabilization time may be as large as the network diameter even for a small number of faults. This establishes the optimality of our algorithm in the recovery time complexity measures.

In [13], an adaptive protocol for specific task of token passing on a ring is presented. The only general solution for adaptive stabilization of reactive tasks is [3], but it uses a much weaker fault model. Specifically, in [3] it is assumed that the effect of a fault at a node is to change the local state to one chosen *uniformly at random*. This unique assumption allows the protocol to detect faults locally with high probability, by artificially "padding" local state spaces with many identifiable, unreachable local states. The assumption that faults drive the system to a uniformly chosen random state means that with high probability, each affected node is put in one of these bogus states, and hence nodes can locally detect whether their state is legal. We stress that the model of [3] is a fundamental departure from the self-stabilization model (used in the current paper): in self-stabilization, the heart of the difficulty is that faults are *not* locally detectable; in [3], the focus is on local correction.

The technique of *core*, used in this paper, was proposed in [12] for broadcast with error confinement (in error confinement, the goal is to allow only nodes that were directly hit by a fault to err). Roughly speaking, the idea of the technique of core is to perform broadcast in stages such that nodes receiving the broadcast message in a certain stage, consult with a set of the nodes that received it in a previous stage (called the current "core"). In [12], nodes joined the core using a specific rule that ensured error confinement. In this paper we use a different rule, that ensures adaptivity (the rule of [12] is not adaptive).

Another tool we use here is a technique that is becoming rather popular in adaptive protocols, namely that error recovery messages travel faster than other kinds of messages. This technique, called *regulated broadcasts*, appeared first in [21, 2] and was used also, e.g., in [7, 13].

Paper Organization. In Section 2 we formalize the model and introduce some notation. In Section 3 we present our algorithm for SBD, and in Section 4 we analyze its properties. Finally, in Section 5, we briefly discuss extensions of the basic result.

2   Preliminaries

2.1   System Model

The system topology is represented by an undirected connected graph $G = (V, E)$, where graph nodes represent processors (also termed network nodes) and edges represent communication links. The number of the nodes is denoted by $n = |V|$. The distance (in the number of edges) between nodes $u, v \in V$ is denoted by $\mathsf{dist}(u, v)$. The diameter of the graph is denoted by diam. We denote

$$\mathsf{ball}_v(d) = \{u \mid \mathsf{dist}(v, u) \le d\}$$

for $d \ge 0$ (thus $\mathsf{ball}_v(0) = \{v\}$). For $v \in V$, we define $\mathcal{N}(v) = \mathsf{ball}_v(1) - \{v\}$, called the *neighbors* of i. We assume that the network topology is fixed and known to the nodes.

   A *distributed protocol* is a specification of the space of *local states* for each node and a description of the *actions* which modify the local states. Included in each local state are distinguished *input* and *output registers*, visible to the *external environment*. The environment can take two types of actions: input injection, i.e., assign values to input registers, and fault injection, i.e., arbitrarily change the state of an arbitrary set of nodes. The nodes whose states are modified by a fault injection action are said to be *faulty*. By convention, we denote the set of faulty nodes by F, their number by $f = |F|$, and the time of the fault by t_f. To abstract the fact that fault injections are infrequent, we assume without loss of generality that there is just one fault (in fact, another fault may occur after the system has stabilized from the previous one). We say that the faulty nodes were *hit* by a fault at time t_f. If a node v was not hit by a fault in a time interval I, we say that v is *I-intact*.

   We assume that the system is synchronous, namely the execution proceeds in rounds, where in each round, each processor sends messages to its neighbors, receives messages, and does some local computation. In this paper we do not restrict message sizes, which allows us to abstract the underlying communication mechanism by assuming that actions may depend also on the state of neighboring nodes (this is justified, e.g., in [4, 17]). Thus, in each step, each node reads its own variables and the variables of its neighbors, and then changes its local state according to the actions specification. As a convention, we denote the location of variables using subscripts, and their time using parentheses; for example, $\mathsf{B}_v(t)$ refers to the value of the variable B in node v at time t. Time is measured by the number of synchronous steps.

   As is usually assumed, a state corrupting fault may change only volatile state, but not code nor constants such as the node's unique identity ID.

2.2   Tasks and Problem Statement

An *input assignment* (respectively, *output assignment*) is a mapping from node names to a given input domain (resp., output range). An *input assignment history* (resp., *output assignment history*) for time t is a set of input assignments (resp., output assignments), one for each time step $0, 1, \ldots, t$. A reactive *task* (or *problem*) is specified by a function mapping each time step to a binary relation over the input and output histories. This means that a reactive problem says what are the possible inputs, and for each input, what is the required output. A reactive problem is said to be *solved* by a given algorithm if in any execution of the algorithm, at each time step t, the sequence of values taken by the input and output registers satisfy the mapping specified by the problem for time t.

Standard techniques (based on the full-information protocol) show that one can reduce any reactive problem to the following basic building block problem.

Stabilizing Value Distribution Problem (SBD)
Each node v has a single output register denoted by out_v. A special node called *source*, denoted by s, has, in addition, an input register denoted by B_s. At time 0, the environment writes an *input value* $\mathsf{B}_s(0)$. The requirement is that eventually, out_v holds $\mathsf{B}_s(0)$ for each node v.

The requirement is to be fulfilled even though at some unknown time $t_f > 0$, some unknown subset F of the nodes is corrupted arbitrarily. We denote $f = |F|$.

2.3 Agility

Consider a fault that occurs at time t_f. We say that a value input to the system at time t_0 is ρ-*recoverable* if only a minority of the nodes in distance $\rho(t_f - t_0)$ from the origin of the value are affected by the fault, for some $0 \leq \rho \leq 1$. An environment is said to be ρ-*constrained* if all inputs are ρ-recoverable. For a given ρ, a system is said to have *agility* ρ if it eventually outputs the correct outputs when run on a ρ-constrained environment. For example, the protocol for SBD in which the source repeatedly broadcasts its input value has 0 agility: once the source is hit by a fault, it may never recover to produce correct output values. On the other hand, a system with agility 1 can recover from any fault so long as the majority of nodes that *potentially* could have heard about the input value remains intact.

3   The Algorithm

In this section we present an algorithm for the SBD problem. We first review the technique of regulated broadcast, introduced in [21].

3.1   Regulated Broadcasts

Regulated Broadcast (abbreviated RB) is an adaptive protocol to distribute and maintain a value under conditions that are more favorable than those studied in the current paper. Specifically, the problem of regulated broadcast is identical to SBD with the crucial difference that *the source is never faulty*. The value at node v of the regulated broadcast rooted at s is called the *vote* of s at v. In our implementation, the RB protocol will be initiated by many nodes and thus we will have many independent *instances* of the RB protocol running in parallel. We identify instances by their root node.

A vote x of node u at node v is called *authentic* if x was indeed communicated by u. The protocol presented in [21] ensures the following properties.

Lemma 1. *If the fault occurs at some time t_f, and it affects f nodes then:*

- *By time $t_f + 2f$, any vote received by any node is authentic.*
- *Each node u starts receiving, at time no later than $t_f + 2 \cdot \text{dist}(u, v)$, authentic votes at every time step.*

If no fault occurs, each node u starts receiving, by time $2 \cdot \text{dist}(u, v)$, authentic votes at every time step (the RB protocol is assumed to start at time 0).

Note that in the case the above Lemma, hence no faults occur during time interval $(t_f, t_f + 2 \cdot f]$, by the assumption that no additional batch of faults occur until the system stabilizes from the current batch. (Otherwise the algorithm still stabilizes, but is not required to be time adaptive).

As a consequence, the RB protocol allows every non-faulty node v to verify whether a value communicated to it by an RB protocol is authentic. We formalize this verifiability property in the following lemma for later reference. (It follows directly from the RB properties.)

Lemma 2. *Suppose that node v receives the same vote from a node u during $\text{dist}(u, v)$ consecutive steps. Then this vote is authentic.*

3.2   Algorithm for *SBD*

Overview. The algorithm presented here expands the ideas of [12], presented there for the more limited task of error confinement. At time 0, the source s gets the input value and starts a broadcast to all other nodes. The idea is to quickly, but carefully, create replicas of the original input value. The algorithm should be quick, in the sense that it should create many replicas, or otherwise it will have low agility. On the other hand, the algorithm should be careful in the sense that it should try to make sure that new replicas have the correct values, or otherwise its action would only be to amplify the effect of the original fault.

Consider a node v that receives a message that is supposed to be sent by a remote node u. There are two difficulties to be answered. First, the message may have never been sent by u: a faulty node between u and v may have altered its contents, or even fabricated it completely from scratch. And second, even if u has indeed sent the message, there is no reason for v to adopt the contents of the message blindly, as u may be faulty, or it have been fooled earlier!

The basic approach we take to overcome these difficulties is to slow the system down, so that the protocol will have enough time to make sure that its actions are sound. Specifically, the first difficulty is circumvented by using regulated broadcast, that allows each node to verify the authenticity of each message it receives (cf. Lemma 2). The second concern is addressed by a special variant of the core technique, whose main property is the following.

Definition 1 (Core Invariant). *At each time step t there exists a set of nodes* core(t) *such that the majority of the votes of nodes in* core(t) *is exactly the original input value.*

The central idea of the algorithm is that once a node v has verified the votes of a majority of the current core, then it can (1) set its output correctly, and (2) join the core itself, and start disseminating the correct value. To make the algorithm adaptive, the core-joining rule is based on time as follows.

Definition 2. *A node v joins the core at time t after verifying the authenticity of the votes of a majority of the nodes of some previous core* core(t') *where $t' = Pt$ for some constant $P < 1$.*

As we shall see, this rule leads to asymptotically optimal agility while maintaining adaptivity. Intuitively, this rule allows core to grow during the time it takes v to consult the nodes of core(Pt), thus improving the agility.

We remark that in the algorithm of [12], a different rule is used. The Core Invariant is maintained inductively by forcing each node v to verify directly that the values of all the nodes in some core were received in v before letting v join the core. Definition 2 is simpler and not operational.

Algorithm Description. The algorithm works as follows. The source node s sleeps until the environment writes the input value in B_s, and then the source initiates an RB protocol rooted at the source. We say that $t_0^s = 0$. Each other node $v \neq s$ sleeps until v receives an RB message, at a step denoted by $t_0^v > t_0^s$. Non-source nodes start their own instance of the RB protocol when a certain condition is met (see below).

To complete the specification of the algorithm, we need to explain when does a node start its RB, what is the value each node broadcasts, and what is the value it writes in its output register. We describe the algorithm for a generic node v. Lemma 1 motivates the following concepts.

Definition 3. *Node u is said to have a* stable *vote at node v at time t, denoted by* stable$_v(u,t)$, *if v receives the same value from the RB rooted at u for at least* dist(u,v) *consecutive time units in the time interval $[t - 4\text{dist}(u,v), t]$. A node set A is said to be* verified *at node v at time t, denoted by* verified$_v(A)$, *if there is a majority of nodes of A with identical stable votes at node v at time t.*

At each time step t, v does the following. We use $\alpha = 0.107$ and $\beta = 2\alpha$. We define core(t) $\equiv$ ball$_s(\alpha t)$.

Algorithm Disseminate
(1) Participate in the currently active RB instances. Each instance of the RB protocol carries the identity of its root u, the current distance from the root, and the value of B_u.
(2) Set out$_v$ to be the majority of the current votes of RBs of nodes in core(t).
(3) If verified(core(Pt)) is true, then set B_v to the majority of values in core(Pt) and start an RB of B_v.

(4) If B_v is defined, then continue the execution of the RB protocol rooted at v, disseminating the value of B_v (which may be different than the value used in the previous step).

For Steps 2 and 3, note that core(t) can be locally computed by v for any t since the topology is known to v and hence the distance to each node is known. For Step 3, note that verified can be computed by virtue of Lemma 2: this is done by locally counting the number of steps since the last change of the value arriving from the RB rooted at u.

4   Analysis

Intuitively, an execution unfolds as follows. At any given time, the core nodes execute an RB rooted in each of them. Each node that received and verified the votes from a majority of some *previous* core becomes a core member itself. The core expansion rate is α, i.e., at time t all nodes at distance αt from the source are in the core. The interesting point is that the core cannot grow too fast: to make it grow fast, nodes must learn very quickly about the previous core, which they cannot due to physical distance that forces long delays to ensure verifiability.

We start with the following lemma concerning verifiability.

Lemma 3. *Consider an* RB *protocol rooted at a node* u, *and suppose that* B_u *remains fixed during a time interval* $[t_1, t_2)$. *Then, for every node* v *with* dist$(u, v) \leq \frac{t_2 - t_1}{6}$ *such that* v *is* $[t_1, t_2)$-*intact, we have that* stable$_v(u, t_2)$.

Proof. There are two cases to consider. If no fault occurs before time $t_1 + 3 \cdot$ dist(u, v), then by Lemma 1 v receives $B_u(t_1)$ at least during the interval $[t_1 + 2 \cdot$ dist$(u, v), t_1 + 3 \cdot$ dist$(u, v)]$. Hence, stable$_v(u, t)$ holds at least in the interval $[t_1 + 3 \cdot$ dist$(u, v), t_1 + 6 \cdot$ dist$(u, v)]$, and the lemma is satisfied in this case. If a fault occurs at time $t_f < t_1 + 3 \cdot$ dist(u, v), then by Lemma 1 we have that by time $t_f + 2 \cdot$ dist(u, v), v starts receiving $B_u(t_1)$ uninterrupted, and therefore stable$_v(u, t)$ starts holding no later than time $t_f + 3 \cdot$ dist$(u, v) < t_1 + 6 \cdot$ dist(u, v), and we are done in this case too. $\square$

Intuitively, the algorithm is feasible only if the time interval from $P\tau$ to τ is large enough for the votes of all the nodes in core$(P\tau)$ become stable at nodes in core(τ) − core$(\tau − 1)$. The following technical lemma will be used to show that for a certain choice of P and α, feasibility is achievable.

Lemma 4. *Let* $t_0 > 0$, $0 < \alpha < 0.107$, $P = 2\alpha$, *and* $\tau \geq t_0/P$. *Then* $P\tau + 6(t_0/2 + \alpha P\tau) \leq \tau$.

Proof. By assumptions, we have

$$0 \geq P\tau + 6(t_0/2 + \alpha P\tau) - \tau \geq 4P\tau + 6\alpha P\tau - \tau = 8\alpha\tau + 12\alpha^2\tau - \tau .$$

Dividing by τ and solving the quadratic equation $12\alpha^2 + 8\alpha - 1 \leq 0$ for α, we get that it is satisfied for $(-\sqrt{7/36} - 1/3) \leq \alpha \leq (\sqrt{7/36} - 1/3) \approx 0.107$. $\square$

The following lemma proves the feasibility of the algorithm.

Lemma 5. *Let τ be a time and v be any node with $\mathsf{dist}(s, v) \le \tau/2$ such that v is $[\mathsf{P}\tau, \tau]$-intact. Assume that for all $u \in \mathsf{core}(\mathsf{P}t) - F$ at all times $\mathsf{P}\tau \le t < \tau$, the following holds: (1) $\mathsf{B}_u(t) = \mathsf{B}_s(0)$, and (2) node u is the root of an RB protocol disseminating $\mathsf{B}_u(t)$. Then $\mathsf{verified}(\mathsf{core}(\mathsf{P}\tau))$ is true at v at time τ.*

Proof. Consider a node v and let $u \in \mathsf{core}(\mathsf{P}\tau)) - F$. By Lemma 1, $\mathsf{dist}(s, v) \le t_0^v/2$. By definition of core, $\mathsf{dist}(s, u) \le \alpha\mathsf{P}\tau$, and hence, by the triangle inequality, $\mathsf{dist}(u, v) \le t_0^v/2 + \alpha\mathsf{P}\tau$. By assumption, u started its RB no later than time $\mathsf{P}\tau$. Therefore, by Lemma 3, we have that $\mathsf{stable}_v(u, t)$ holds for all $t \ge \mathsf{P}\tau + 6(t_0/2 + \alpha\mathsf{P}t)$. In particular, by Lemma 4, it holds for $t = \tau$. Hence, by time τ, $\mathsf{stable}_v(u, \tau)$ holds. Since this is true for all $u \in \mathsf{core}(\mathsf{P}\tau) - F$, and since $|F| < |\mathsf{core}(\mathsf{P}\tau)|$, we may conclude that $\mathsf{verified}(\mathsf{core}(\mathsf{P}\tau))$ is true at v at time τ, as required. □

We now show that if the environment is sufficiently constrained, then the values disseminated by algorithm are correct.

Lemma 6. *If $f < |\mathsf{core}(\mathsf{P}t_f)|/2$ then for all times τ and for all nodes $v \in \mathsf{core}(\tau)$ such that v is $[t_0^v, \infty]$-intact we have that $\mathsf{B}_v(\tau) = \mathsf{B}_s(0)$.*

Proof. (Sketch.) We prove that the following invariant holds for all times τ:

1. If $v \in \mathsf{core}(\tau) - \mathsf{core}(\tau - 1)$ and v is $[t_0^v, \infty]$- intact, then $\mathsf{B}_v(\tau) = \mathsf{B}_s(0)$.
2. If $v \in \mathsf{core}(\tau)$, v is $[t_0^v, \infty]$- intact, and $\mathsf{B}_v(\tau) = \mathsf{B}_s(0)$, then $\mathsf{B}_v(\tau + 1) = \mathsf{B}_s(0)$.

Clearly, the invariant implies the lemma. To prove the invariant, suppose, for contradiction, that it does not hold, and let τ be the first time the invariant is violated. First, note that $\tau > 0$ since the invariant holds trivially for $\tau = 0$. Now, if the invariant is violated at time τ, then there exists a node $v \in \mathsf{core}(\tau)$ such that v is $[t_0^v, \infty]$-intact, and such that at time τ, we have $\mathsf{B}_v(\tau) \ne \mathsf{B}_s(0)$. We first claim that $\mathsf{verified}(\mathsf{core}(\mathsf{P}\tau))$ holds at v. This follows from the fact that by the minimality of τ and the algorithm, all nodes in $\mathsf{core}(\mathsf{P}\tau)$ continuously broadcasts their value, and therefore Lemma 5 guarantees that $\mathsf{verified}(\mathsf{core}(\mathsf{P}\tau))$ holds. Moreover, by the definition of $\mathsf{verified}$, the value of the votes of these nodes at v was stable, and hence it is authentic by Lemma 2.

Finally, we note that since the invariant holds at time $\mathsf{P}\tau$, we have that the votes of each node $u \in \mathsf{core}(\mathsf{P}\tau) - F$ is correct, i.e., $\mathsf{B}_u(\tau') = \mathsf{B}_s(0)$ for all $\tau' < \tau$. It remains to show that these votes are the majority of the votes of $\mathsf{core}(\mathsf{P}\tau)$. To see that, we consider two possible cases. If there are no faulty nodes, or if $t_f > \tau$, then we are done. Otherwise, $t_f \le \tau$, and hence, by assumption,

$$|F| < \frac{|\mathsf{core}(\mathsf{P}t_f)|}{2} \le \frac{|\mathsf{core}(\mathsf{P}\tau)|}{2}.$$

□

We can now summarize the properties of our algorithm. For conciseness, we treat the case of no faults as $t_f = \infty$.

Theorem 1. *Let $\rho = 2\alpha^2$. Suppose that a fault hits a set F of f nodes at time $t_f \le \infty$. If $f < |\mathsf{ball}_s(\rho t_f)|/2$, then*

1. There exists a time $T = t_f + O(f)$ such that $\mathsf{out}_v(t) = \mathsf{B}_s(0)$ for all $t > T$ and all $v \in \mathsf{ball}_s(\alpha t)$.
2. There exists a time $T = \frac{1}{\mathsf{P}}\min\{t_f, 2\mathsf{diam}\}$ such that $\mathsf{B}_v(t) = \mathsf{B}_s(0)$ for all $t > T$ and $v \in \mathsf{ball}_s(\alpha t)$.
3. For all $t < t_f$ and $v \in \mathsf{ball}_s(\alpha t)$ we have that $\mathsf{out}_v(t) = \mathsf{B}_v(t) = \mathsf{B}_s(0)$.

Proof. Let $v \in \mathsf{ball}_s(\alpha t_f)$. To prove Part 1, first note that, by Lemma 1, there exists a time $T_1 = t_f + O(f)$, such that by time T_1, v receives only authentic votes. We claim that the votes equal to $\mathsf{B}_s(0)$ is a majority among the votes received at v. By Lemma 6 and the assumption on the number of faults, there are at most f incorrect votes from nodes in $\mathsf{core}(t) \supseteq \mathsf{ball}_s(\rho t_f)$ (for any $t \geq t_f$). On the other hand, $2f < |\mathsf{ball}_s(\rho t_f)| \leq |\mathsf{ball}_s(\alpha t)|$, and hence $|\mathsf{ball}_v(2f+1) \cap \mathsf{ball}_s(\alpha t)| \geq 2f+1$. Therefore, by Lemma 1, there exists a time $T_2 = t_f + O(f)$ such that at least $f + 1$ correct votes arrive. The claim follows for $T = \max\{T_1, T_2\}$.

We prove Part 2 of the theorem. Let $T = \frac{1}{\mathsf{P}}\min(t_f, 2 \cdot \mathsf{diam})$, and consider any $t \geq T$. By Lemma 6, this part of the theorem holds for every node $v \in \mathsf{core}(t)$ such that v is $[t_0^v, \infty]$-intact. We prove the claim for $v \in F \cap \mathsf{ball}_s(\alpha t)$ such that $t_f \geq t_0^v$. Namely, $\mathsf{dist}(s, v) \leq \frac{t_f}{2} \leq \frac{t\mathsf{P}}{2}$. By the choice of T, v is $[\mathsf{P}t, t]$-intact. Finally, by Lemma 6, for all $u \in \mathsf{core}(t) - F$ we have that $\mathsf{B}_u(t) = \mathsf{B}_s(0)$. Thus we can apply Lemma 5 and conclude that $\mathsf{verified}(\mathsf{core}(\mathsf{P}t))$ holds at v at time t. This means that v assigns to $\mathsf{B}_v(t)$ the majority vote of all the nodes of $\mathsf{core}(\mathsf{P}t)$. These votes are authentic, by Lemma 2. By the assumption on f, and since $t \geq t_f$, for a majority of these authentic votes the following holds: each comes from some node u that is $[t_0^u, t]$ intact. By Lemma 6 the votes of this majority are correct. The claim follows.

The proof of Part 3 is similar to the proof of Part 2.   □

5   Conclusion

In this paper we introduced the first protocol that implements broadcast in an adaptive way. Due to lack of space, we can only sketch here a few applications and extensions of this *SBD* protocol. First, as already mentioned, the *SBD* protocol implies the existence of an adaptive solution for any adaptive task. More details are given in [1]. Briefly, in synchronous systems, where the topology is known in a advance, the idea is as follows: in each round, the input at each node is considered to be the root of a new instance of *SBD*, and the output can be computed locally since all inputs are eventually available locally.

Second, we note that the *SBD* protocol replicates its root bit *everywhere*. It is possible to trade this maximal fault resiliency for better complexity, by parameterizing the protocol to have some prescribed amount of replications. Third, let us mention that the assumption that the network is synchronous can be lifted using known techniques (e.g., [2] gives an asynchronous RB protocol).

Finally, let us stress once again that while in this paper we demonstrated the existence of an adaptive solution, much work remains to be done in making such a solution practical in terms of computational complexity.

References

1. Longer version of this paper iew3.technion.ac.il//zipped/kp00.ps.
2. Y. Afek and A. Bremler. Self-stabilizing unidirectional network algorithms by power supply. *Chicago J. of Theoretical Computer Science*, 1998(3), Dec. 1998.
3. Y. Afek and S. Dolev. Local stabilizer. *JPDC*, 62(5):745–765, 2002.
4. Y. Afek, S. Kutten, and M. Yung. The local detection paradigm and its applications to self-stabilization. *Theor. Comput. Sci.*, 186(1-2):199–229, 1997.
5. A. Arora and M. Gouda. Distributed reset. *IEEE T. Comp.*, 43(9):1026–1038, 1994.
6. A. Arora and H. Zhang. GS^3: scalable self-configuration and self-healing in wireless networks. In *Proc. 21st PODC*, pages 58–67, July 2002.
7. A. Arora and H. Zhang. LSRP: Local stabilization in shortest path routing. In *Proc. 2003 Int. Conf. on Dependable Systems and Networks (DSN)*, 2003.
8. B. Awerbuch, I. Cidon, I. Gopal, M. Kaplan, and S. Kutten. Distributed control for PARIS. In *9th PODC*, 1990.
9. B. Awerbuch, S. Kutten, Y. Mansour, B. Patt-Shamir, and G. Varghese. Time optimal self-stabilizing synchronization. In *Proc. 25th STOC*, pages 652–661, 1993.
10. B. Awerbuch, B. Patt-Shamir, and G. Varghese. Self-stabilization by local checking and correction. In *32nd FOCS*, pages 268–277, Oct. 1991.
11. B. Awerbuch, B. Patt-Shamir, G. Varghese, and S. Dolev. Self-stabilization by local checking and global reset. In *Proc. 8th WDAG*, pages 326–339. 1994.
12. Y. Azar, S. Kutten, and B. Patt-Shamir. Distributed error confinement. In *22nd PODC*, pages 33–42, June 2003.
13. J. Beauquier, C. Genolini, and S. Kutten. Optimal reactive k-stabilization: the case of mutual exclusion. In *18th PODC*, pages 209–218, May 1999.
14. E. W. Dijkstra. Self-stabilizing systems in spite of distributed control. *Comm. ACM*, 17(11):643–644, November 1974.
15. S. Dolev. *Self-Stabilization*. MIT Press, 2000.
16. S. Dolev and T. Herman. Superstabilizing protocols for dynamic distributed systems. *Chicago J. of Theoretical Computer Science*, 1997(4), Dec. 1997.
17. S. Dolev, A. Israeli, and S. Moran. Self-stabilization of dynamic systems assuming only read/write atomicity. In *9th PODC*, 1990.
18. S. Ghosh, A. Gupta, T. Herman, and S. V. Pemmaraju. Fault-containing self-stabilizing algorithms. In *15th PODC*, May 1996.
19. G. Itkis and L. Levin. Fast and lean self-stabilizing asynchronous protocols. In *35th FOCS*, pages 226–239, Nov. 1994.
20. S. Katz and K. Perry. Self-stabilizing extensions for message-passing systems. In *10th PODC*, Quebec City, Canada, Aug. 1990.
21. S. Kutten and B. Patt-Shamir. Time-adaptive self-stabilization. In *16th PODC*, pages 149–158, 1997.
22. S. Kutten and D. Peleg. Fault-local distributed mending. In *14th PODC*, 1995.
23. S. Kutten and D. Peleg. Tight fault locality (extended abstract). In *36th FOCS*, pages 704–713, 1995.
24. Z. Manna and A. Pnueli. Models for reactivity. *Acta Informatica*, 3:609–678, 1993.
25. J. McQuillan, I. Richer, and E. Rosen. The new routing algorithm for the ARPANET. *IEEE Trans. Comm.*, 28(5):711–719, May 1980.
26. J. Moy. OSPF version 2, Apr. 1998. Internet RFC 2328.
27. R. Perlman. *Interconnections*. Addison-Wesley Publishing Co., 2nd edition, 2000.

Visibly Pushdown Games

Christof Löding[1,*], P. Madhusudan[2,**], and Olivier Serre[1,*]

[1] LIAFA, Université Paris VII, France
[2] University of Pennsylvania

Abstract. The class of visibly pushdown languages has been recently defined as a subclass of context-free languages with desirable closure properties and tractable decision problems. We study visibly pushdown games, which are games played on visibly pushdown systems where the winning condition is given by a visibly pushdown language. We establish that, unlike pushdown games with pushdown winning conditions, visibly pushdown games are decidable and are 2EXPTIME-complete. We also show that pushdown games against LTL specifications and CARET specifications are 3EXPTIME-complete. Finally, we establish the topological complexity of visibly pushdown languages by showing that they are a subclass of Boolean combinations of Σ_3 sets. This leads to an alternative proof that visibly pushdown automata are not determinizable and also shows that visibly pushdown games are determined.

1 Introduction

The theory of two-player games on graphs is a prominent area in formal verification and automata theory. The peculiar acceptance conditions used in the study of automata on infinite words and trees, result in a theory of infinite games that serves as a simple and unified framework for various proofs and constructions in automata theory. In particular, the determinacy theorem for these games and the solvability of infinite games on finite graphs are closely related to the decidability of the monadic second-order logic on trees [14, 16].

In formal verification, infinite games are useful in two contexts. First, the model-checking problem for the μ-calculus is intimately related to solving parity games [6], the precise complexity of which is still open. Second, the theory of games form a natural abstraction of the synthesis and control-synthesis problems, where the aim is to synthesize a system that satisfies a given specification [9].

While most results in model checking involve problems on finite graphs, abstraction of data from software programs with procedures results in pushdown models, where the stack is required to maintain the call-stack of the program.

* Supported by the European Community Research Training Network "Games and Automata for Synthesis and Validation" (GAMES).
** Supported partially by ARO URI award DAAD19-01-1-0473, and NSF awards ITR/SY 0121431 and CCR 0306382.

Formal verification of these models against regular specifications is however tractable since emptiness of pushdown automata is decidable. In fact, a variety of program analysis questions, static code analysis, and compiler optimization can be reduced to reachability in pushdown models [10] and contemporary software model-checking tools such as SLAM [3] implement these decision procedures.

Although checking software models against regular specifications is useful, there are important context-free requirements—specification of pre-post conditions for procedures, security properties that require stack inspection, etc. Recently, a temporal logic called CARET [1] has been defined which allows specification of such context-free properties and yet preserves decidability of pushdown model-checking.

In [2], the class of *visibly pushdown languages* (VPL) is proposed as an automata theoretic generalization of CARET. These languages are accepted by visibly pushdown automata (VPA), which are pushdown automata whose stack-operations are determined by the input. Like the class of regular languages, VPL is closed under all Boolean operations; moreover, decision problems such as inclusion, which are undecidable for context-free languages, are decidable for VPL. VPL includes the class of languages defined by CARET and forms a robust subclass of context-free languages [2].

Turning back to games, pushdown games with parity winning conditions are known to be decidable [15]. This shows that pushdown games with any external ω-regular winning condition can also be solved. However, it is easy to see that solving pushdown games against pushdown winning conditions is *undecidable*. In [5] a new winning condition for pushdown games was proposed, which declares a play winning if and only if along the play, the stack is *repeatedly bounded* (i.e. there is some stack depth n such that the stack was below depth n infinitely often). The main motivation for this winning condition was that it defined a class of plays that was in the Σ_3 level of the Borel hierarchy (ω-regular winning conditions define only sets that are in the Boolean closure of Σ_2). It was shown that solving these games was decidable. Note that for any pushdown game, if we label the push transitions, pop transitions, and internal transitions differently, then the set of repeatedly bounded plays is a visibly pushdown language.

Since visibly pushdown automata have a decidable model-checking problem and since the set of repeatedly bounded words is a VPL, a natural question arises: given a visibly pushdown game graph $\mathcal{G}$ and a VPL L describing the set of winning plays, is the game problem $(\mathcal{G}, L)$ decidable? The main result of this paper is that this problem is decidable and is 2EXPTIME-complete. Thus, the tractability of visibly pushdown languages extends to the game problem as well.

The main technical challenge in handling visibly pushdown games is that the specification automaton, which is a VPA, is not, in general, determinizable [2]. This prevents us from taking a product with the game graph to reduce it to a pushdown game with internal winning conditions. We invent a new kind of VPA, called *stair* VPA, in which the winning condition is interpreted only at certain points along the run, and the states met at other points are ignored. The i'th letter of a word belongs to this evaluation set if for no $j > i$, the stack depth at j is less than that at i. We then show that for every (nondeterministic) VPA, there exists an equivalent *deterministic* stair VPA. We take the product of the game graph with the deterministic stair VPA, and show how pushdown games with stair winning conditions can be solved.

The above result yields a 3EXPTIME decision procedure for pushdown games against CARET specifications. However, this high complexity is not due to the context-free nature of the specification, as we show the surprising result that pushdown games against LTL specifications is already 3EXPTIME-hard. We also establish that solving pushdown games against nondeterministic VPA (or even nondeterministic Büchi automata) specifications is 2EXPTIME-hard.

Finally, we show that the class VPL is contained in the Boolean closure of Σ_3, $B(\Sigma_3)$. This is one level higher than the class $B(\Sigma_2)$ which contains all regular ω-languages. As a consequence, we get an alternative proof that visibly pushdown automata cannot be determinized and also establish that visibly pushdown games are determined (i.e. from any position in the game, one of the players must have a winning strategy).

2   Preliminaries

For a finite set X we denote the set of finite words over X by X^*, the set of infinite words (ω-words) over X by X^ω, and the empty word by ε. For $\alpha \in X^* \cup X^\omega$ and $n \in \mathbb{N}$ we write $\alpha(n)$ for the nth letter in α and $\alpha\lceil_n$ for the prefix of length n of α, i.e., $\alpha\lceil_0 = \varepsilon$ and $\alpha\lceil_n = \alpha(0) \cdots \alpha(n-1)$ for $n \geq 1$.

A pushdown alphabet is a tuple $\widetilde{A} = \langle A_c, A_r, A_{\text{int}} \rangle$ that comprises three disjoint finite alphabets—A_c is a finite set of *calls*, A_r is a finite set of *returns*, and A_{int} is a finite set of *internal actions*. For any such $\widetilde{A}$, let $A = A_c \cup A_r \cup A_{\text{int}}$.

We define *visibly pushdown systems* over $\widetilde{A}$. Intuitively, the pushdown system is restricted such that it pushes onto the stack only when it reads a call, pops the stack only at returns, and does not use the stack on internal actions. The input hence controls the kind of operations permissible on the stack—however, there is no restriction on the symbols that can be pushed or popped.

Definition 1 (Visibly Pushdown System [2]). *A visibly pushdown system (VPS) over $\langle A_c, A_r, A_{\text{int}} \rangle$ is a tuple $\mathcal{S} = (Q, Q_{in}, \Gamma, \Delta)$ where Q is a finite set of states, $Q_{in} \subseteq Q$ is a set of initial states, Γ is a finite stack alphabet that contains a special bottom-of-stack symbol $\bot$ and $\Delta \subseteq (Q \times A_c \times Q \times (\Gamma \setminus \{\bot\})) \cup (Q \times A_r \times \Gamma \times Q) \cup (Q \times A_{\text{int}} \times Q)$ is the transition relation.*

A stack is a nonempty finite sequence over Γ ending in the bottom-of-stack symbol $\bot$; let us denote the set of all stacks as $St = (\Gamma \setminus \{\bot\})^* . \{\bot\}$. A transition (q, a, q', γ), where $a \in A_c$ and $\gamma \neq \bot$, is a push-transition where on reading a, γ is pushed onto the stack and the control changes from state q to q'. Similarly, (q, a, γ, q') is a pop-transition where γ is read from the top of the stack and popped (if the top of stack is $\bot$, then it is read but not popped), and the control state changes from q to q'. Note that on internal actions, there is no stack operation.

The configuration graph of a VPS $\mathcal{S}$ is the graph $G_{\mathcal{S}} = (V_{\mathcal{S}}, E_{\mathcal{S}})$, where $V_{\mathcal{S}} = \{(q, \sigma) \mid q \in Q, \sigma \in St\}$, and $E_{\mathcal{S}}$ is the set that contains all triples $((q, \sigma), a, (q', \sigma')) \in V_{\mathcal{S}} \times A \times V_{\mathcal{S}}$, that satisfy the following:

[Push] If a is a call, then $\exists \gamma \in \Gamma$ such that $(q, a, q', \gamma) \in \Delta$ and $\sigma' = \gamma.\sigma$.

[Pop] If a is a return, then $\exists \gamma \in \Gamma$ such that $(q, a, \gamma, q') \in \Delta$ and either $\gamma \neq \bot$ and $\sigma = \gamma.\sigma'$, or $\gamma = \bot$ and $\sigma = \sigma' = \bot$.

[Internal] If a is an internal action, then $(q, a, q') \in \Delta$ and $\sigma = \sigma'$.

For a word $\alpha = a_1 a_2 a_3 \cdots$ in A^ω, a run of $\mathcal{S}$ on α is a sequence $\rho = (q_0, \sigma_0)(q_1, \sigma_1)(q_2, \sigma_2) \cdots \in V_{\mathcal{S}}^\omega$ of configurations, where $q_0 \in Q_{in}$, $\sigma_0 = \bot$ and $((q_i, \sigma_i), a, (q_{i+1}, \sigma_{i+1})) \in E_{\mathcal{S}}$ for every $i \in \mathbb{N}$.

A *visibly pushdown automaton* (VPA) over $\langle A_c, A_r, A_{\text{int}} \rangle$ is a tuple $\mathcal{M} = (Q, Q_{in}, \Gamma, \Delta, \Omega)$ where $(Q, Q_{in}, \Gamma, \Delta)$ is a VPS, and Ω is an acceptance condition. In a Büchi VPA, $\Omega = F \subseteq Q$ is a set of final states, while in a parity VPA, $\Omega : Q \to \mathbb{N}$.

For a run $\rho = (q_0, \sigma_0)(q_1, \sigma_1)(q_2, \sigma_2) \cdots$, we consider the set $inf(\rho) \subseteq Q$ which is the set of all states that occur in ρ infinitely often. A word $\alpha \in A^\omega$ is accepted by a Büchi VPA if there is a run ρ over α which infinitely often visits F, i.e., if $inf(\rho) \cap F \neq \emptyset$. A word $\alpha \in A^\omega$ is accepted by a parity VPA if there is a run ρ over α such that the minimal color visited infinitely often by ρ is even, i.e., if the minimal color in $\Omega(inf(\rho)) = \{\Omega(q) \mid q \in inf(\rho)\}$ is even. The language $L(\mathcal{M})$ of a VPA $\mathcal{M}$ is the set of words accepted by $\mathcal{M}$.

A VPA is deterministic if it has a unique initial state q_{in}, and for each input letter and configuration there is at most one successor configuration. For deterministic VPAs we denote the transition relation by δ instead of Δ and write $\delta(q, a) = (q', \gamma)$ instead of $(q, a, q', \gamma) \in \delta$ if $a \in A_c$, $\delta(q, a, \gamma) = q'$ instead of $(q, a, \gamma, q') \in \delta$ if $a \in A_r$, and $\delta(q, a) = q'$ instead of $(q, a, q') \in \delta$ if $a \in A_{\text{int}}$.

Infinite Two-Player Games. Let A be a finite alphabet. A *game graph* $\mathcal{G}$ over A is a graph $\mathcal{G} = (V, V_E, V_A, E)$ where (V, E) is a deterministic graph with edges labeled with letters of A (i.e. $E \subseteq V \times A \times V$ such that if $(v, a, v_1), (v, a, v_2) \in E$, then $v_1 = v_2$), and (V_E, V_A) partitions V between two players, Eve and Adam. An infinite two-player game is a pair $\mathbb{G} = (\mathcal{G}, \Omega)$, where the winning condition Ω can be of two kinds: An *internal winning condition* Ω is a subset of V^ω and an *external winning condition* Ω is a subset of A^ω.

The players, Eve and Adam, play in $\mathbb{G}$ by moving a token between positions. A *play* from some initial node v_0 proceeds as follows: the player owning v_0 moves the token to some vertex v_1 along an edge of the form $e_0 = (v_0, a_0, v_1) \in E$. Then the player owning v_1 moves the token to v_2 along an edge $e_1 = (v_1, a_1, v_2) \in E$, and so on, forever. If one of the players cannot make a move, the other player wins. Otherwise, the play is an infinite sequence $\lambda = v_0 a_0 v_1 a_1 \cdots \in (V.A)^\omega$ in G. For internal winning conditions, Eve wins λ if $v_0 v_1 v_2 \cdots \in \Omega$, and Adam wins it otherwise. If Ω is an external winning condition, Eve wins λ if $a_0 a_1 a_2 \cdots \in \Omega$, and Adam wins it otherwise. A *partial play* is any prefix of a play.

A *strategy* for Eve is a function assigning to any partial play ending in some node in $v \in V_E$ an edge $(v, a, v') \in E$. Eve *respects* a strategy f during some play $\lambda = v_0 a_0 v_1 a_1 \cdots$ if for any $i \geq 0$ such that $v_i \in V_{\mathrm{E}}$, $(v_i, a_{i+1}, v_{i+1}) = f(v_0 a_0 v_1 a_1 \cdots v_i)$. Finally, a strategy f is said to be *winning* from some position v, if any play starting from v where Eve respects f is winning for her.

A *visibly pushdown game* $\mathcal{H} = (\mathcal{S}, Q_{\mathrm{E}}, Q_{\mathrm{A}}, \mathcal{M})$ consists of a VPS $\mathcal{S}$, a VPA $\mathcal{M}$ (both over a common pushdown alphabet $\widetilde{A}$), and a partition $\langle Q_{\mathrm{E}}, Q_{\mathrm{A}} \rangle$ of the state set Q of $\mathcal{S}$. $\mathcal{H}$ defines the game $\mathbb{G}_{\mathcal{H}} = (\mathcal{G}, \Omega)$, where $\mathcal{G} = (V, V_{\mathrm{E}}, V_{\mathrm{A}}, E)$, (V, E) is the configuration graph of $\mathcal{S}$, $V_{\mathrm{E}} = \{(q, \sigma) \mid q \in Q_{\mathrm{E}}\}$, and $V_{\mathrm{A}} = \{(q, \sigma) \mid q \in Q_{\mathrm{A}}\}$. The set Ω is the external winning condition $\Omega = L(\mathcal{M})$.

We can now state the main problem we address in this paper: Given a visibly pushdown game $\mathcal{H} = (\mathcal{S}, Q_{\mathrm{E}}, Q_{\mathrm{A}}, \mathcal{M})$ and a state p_{in} of $\mathcal{S}$, is there a strategy for Eve that is winning for her from the position $(p_{in}, \bot)$, in the game $\mathbb{G}_{\mathcal{H}}$?

3   Deterministic Stair VPAs

Visibly pushdown automata over ω-words cannot be determinized [2]. In this section, in order to obtain a determinization theorem, we propose a new mode of acceptance for VPAs. Instead of evaluating the acceptance condition on the whole run, we evaluate it only on a subsequence of the run. This subsequence is obtained by discarding those configurations for which a future configuration of smaller stack height exists. The sequence thus obtained is non-decreasing with respect to the stack height, and hence we dub VPAs using this mode of acceptance as *stair* VPAs (denoted STVPA). The main theorem of this section is that for every nondeterministic Büchi VPA, we can effectively construct an equivalent deterministic parity STVPA.

For $Y \subseteq \mathbb{N}$ and $\rho \in X^{\omega}$ (for some set X) we define the subsequence $\rho|_Y \in X^* \cup X^{\omega}$ of ρ induced by Y as follows. Let $n_0 < n_1 < n_2 < \cdots$ be an ascending enumeration of the elements in Y. Then $\rho|_Y = \rho(n_0)\rho(n_1)\rho(n_2)\cdots$.

For $w \in A^*$ we define the stack height $sh(w)$ inductively by $sh(\varepsilon) = 0$ and

$$
sh(ua) = \begin{cases} sh(u) & \text{if } a \in A_{\mathrm{int}}, \\ sh(u) + 1 & \text{if } a \in A_c, \\ \max\{sh(u) - 1, 0\} & \text{if } a \in A_r. \end{cases}
$$

For $\alpha \in A^{\omega}$ define $Steps_\alpha = \{n \in \mathbb{N} \mid \forall m \geq n : sh(\alpha\!\restriction_m) \geq sh(\alpha\!\restriction_n)\}$. Note that $Steps_\alpha$ is infinite for each $\alpha \in A^{\omega}$.

Let L_{mwm} denote the set of all *minimally well-matched words*—the words of the form $cwr \in A^*$, where the last letter $r \in A_r$ is the matching return for the first letter $c \in A_c$ (formally, $c \in A_c$, $r \in A_r$, $sh(w) = 0$ and for any prefix w' of w, $sh(cw') > 0$).

For any word $\alpha \in A^{\omega}$, we can group maximal subwords of α which are in L_{mwm}, and get a unique factorization $\alpha = w_1 w_2 \ldots$ where each $w_i \in L_{\mathrm{mwm}} \cup A$. It is easy to see that if $w_i = c$, for some $c \in A_c$, then there is no $j > i$ such that $w_j = r$, for some $r \in A_r$. In fact, the points at which the word factorizes is exactly $Steps_\alpha$, i.e. $n \in Steps_\alpha$ iff $\exists i \geq 0 : |w_1 \ldots w_i| = n$.

To define acceptance for STVPAs, we evaluate the acceptance condition at the subsequence $\rho|_{Steps_\alpha}$ for any run ρ on α, i.e. at the positions after each prefix $w_1 \ldots w_i$, where $i \in \mathbb{N}$.

Definition 2 (Stair VPA). *A (nondeterministic) stair VPA (STVPA) $\mathcal{M} = (Q, Q_{in}, \Gamma, \Delta, \Omega)$ over $\langle A_c, A_r, A_{int} \rangle$ has the same components as a VPA. A word $\alpha \in A^\omega$ is accepted by $\mathcal{M}$ if there is a run ρ of $\mathcal{M}$ on α such that $\rho|_{Steps_\alpha}$ satisfies the acceptance condition Ω of $\mathcal{M}$. The language accepted by $\mathcal{M}$ is $L(\mathcal{M}) = \{\alpha \in A^\omega \mid \mathcal{M} \text{ accepts } \alpha\}$.*

Example 1. Let $L_{\mathrm{rb}} = \{\alpha \in A^\omega \mid \exists \ell \forall m \exists n > m : sh(\alpha \lceil_n) = \ell\}$ (with $A_{int} = \emptyset$, $A_r = \{r\}$, and $A_c = \{c\}$) be the set of all repeatedly bounded words. As shown in [2] there is no deterministic VPA for this language. Now consider the parity STVPA $\mathcal{M}_{\mathrm{rb}}$ with states q_1, q_2, initial state q_1, stack alphabet $\Gamma = \{\gamma, \bot\}$, coloring function $\Omega(q_1) = 1$, $\Omega(q_2) = 2$, and transition function $\delta(q_1, c) = \delta(q_2, c) = (q_1, \gamma)$ and $\delta(q_1, r, \gamma) = \delta(q_2, r, \gamma) = \delta(q_1, r, \bot) = \delta(q_2, r, \bot) = q_2$. For a run ρ of this STVPA the sequence $\rho|_{Steps_\alpha}$ contains infinitely many q_1 iff the input contains infinitely many unmatched calls and thus $L(\mathcal{M}_{\mathrm{rb}}) = L_{\mathrm{rb}}$.

We aim at proving that for each nondeterministic Büchi VPA $\mathcal{M}$ there is an equivalent deterministic parity STVPA D. Let $\alpha \in A^\omega$ and let the factorization of α be $\alpha = w_1 w_2 \ldots$. A stair VPA reading α can refer to the states after each w_i only. In order to capture the way $\mathcal{M}$ acts on a subword w_i, we use *summary information* which, intuitively, describes all possible transformations $\mathcal{M}$ can undergo when reading the word w_i. For this purpose let $\mathcal{M} = (Q, Q_{in}, \Gamma, \Delta, F)$ and set $T_Q = 2^{Q \times \{0,1\} \times Q}$. The transformation $T_{w_i} \in T_Q$ induced by w_i is defined as follows: $(q, f, q') \in T_{w_i}$ iff there is a run of $\mathcal{M}$ on w_i leading from $(q, \bot)$ to (q', σ), for some $\sigma \in St$, with $f = 1$ iff this run meets some state in F. Note that the initial stack content does not matter if $w_i \in A_c \cup A_{int} \cup L_{\mathrm{mwm}}$, and if $w_i \in A_r$, we know that when w_i occurs in α, the stack must be empty.

Now consider the sequence $\tau_\alpha = T_{w_1} T_{w_2} \ldots \in T_Q^\omega$. $\mathcal{M}$ accepts α iff we can string together a consistent run using the summaries in τ_α such that it visits F infinitely often. Formally, a word $\tau \in T_Q^\omega$ is *good* if there exists $\rho \in Q^\omega$ such that $\rho(0) \in Q_{in}$ and for all $i \in \mathbb{N}$, $(\rho(i), f_i, \rho(i+1)) \in \tau(i)$, for some $f_i \in \{0,1\}$, where $f_i = 1$ for infinitely many $i \in \mathbb{N}$. Then it is easy to see that $\alpha \in L(\mathcal{M})$ iff τ_α is good. Note that the set of all good words over T_Q is in fact a regular ω-language over the alphabet T_Q. Hence we can build a deterministic parity automaton $S_T = (S, s_{in}, \delta, \Omega)$ which accepts the set of all good words. Moreover, S_T can be constructed such that $S = 2^{O(|Q| \cdot \log|Q|)}$ [13].

We can also show that the summary information can be generated by a deterministic VPS. Formally, there is a deterministic VPS C with output such that on reading any finite word w, if the factorization of w is $w'_1 \ldots w'_k$, C outputs the transformation $T_{w'_k}$ on its last transition. Such a VPS C is easy to construct: the state-space of C is T_Q with initial state $Id_Q = \{(q, 0, q) \mid q \in Q\}$. On reading an internal action $a \in A_{int}$ (or on reading a return when the stack is empty), C updates its state from T to $T \circ T_a$ and outputs T_a; on reading a call $c \in A_c$, it pushes c and the current state T onto the stack, updates the state to Id_Q, and outputs T_c; on reading a return $r \in A_r$ when the stack is nonempty, it pops T' and $c \in A_c$, updates its state from T to $T' \circ \bigcup_{\gamma \in \Gamma}(T_{c,\gamma} \circ T \circ T_{r,\gamma})$, and outputs $\bigcup_{\gamma \in \Gamma}(T_{c,\gamma} \circ T \circ T_{r,\gamma})$. Here, $T_1 \circ T_2$ is defined to be the set of all triples (q, f, q') such that there are some elements $(q, f_1, q_1) \in T_1$, $(q_1, f_2, q') \in T_2$ and $f = \max\{f_1, f_2\}$. The transformation $T_{c,\gamma}$ (resp. $T_{r,\gamma}$) is the one induced by the transitions pushing γ on reading c (resp. popping γ on reading r).

We are now ready to construct the deterministic parity STVPA D accepting $L(\mathcal{M})$. The state-space of D is $\mathcal{T}_Q \times S$, and we will construct D such that after reading any finite word w with factorization $w = w'_1, \dots w'_k$, the second component of D's state is the state which $S_\mathcal{T}$ would reach on the word $T_{w'_1} \dots T_{w'_k}$. D inherits the parity condition from $S_\mathcal{T}$ and it is easy to see that the above property ensures that D accepts $L(\mathcal{M})$.

D simulates the VPS C on the first component and the second component is updated using the outputs of C. In addition to the information stored on the stack by C, when reading a call symbol $c \in A_c$, D also pushes onto the stack the state it was in before the call symbol was read. When D reads a return symbol and the stack is not empty, the second component needs to be updated to $\delta(s, T)$ where s is the state $S_\mathcal{T}$ was in before it read the call corresponding to the current return, and T is the summary of the segment from the corresponding call to the current return. The state s is available on the top of the stack (since D had pushed it at the corresponding call) and T corresponds to the output of C; hence D can update the second component appropriately. We have:

Theorem 1. *For each nondeterministic Büchi* VPA $\mathcal{M}$ *over* A *there exists a deterministic parity* STVPA D *such that* $L(\mathcal{M}) = L(D)$. *Moreover, we can construct* D *such that it has* $2^{\mathcal{O}(|Q|^2)}$ *states, where* Q *is the state-space of* $\mathcal{M}$.

As Theorem 1 shows, evaluating the acceptance condition on $\rho|_{Steps_\alpha}$ instead of ρ increases the expressive power of deterministic VPAs. A nondeterministic VPA can guess the positions of $Steps_\alpha$ (and verify its correctness), and hence stair acceptance does not change the expressive power of nondeterministic VPAs.

Theorem 2. *For each nondeterministic parity* STVPA $\mathcal{M}$ *one can construct a nondeterministic Büchi* VPA $\mathcal{M}'$ *such that* $L(\mathcal{M}) = L(\mathcal{M}')$.

4   Games

In this section, our main aim is to prove that the problem of solving visibly pushdown games as stated at the end of Section 2 is in 2EXPTIME. Our first step is to internalize the winning condition $\mathcal{M}$ by transforming it to a deterministic stair VPA and then taking its product with the game graph defined by $\mathcal{H}$. This results in a game with a stair parity winning condition, which we then solve.

A *stair parity game* $ST = (S, Q_E, Q_A, col)$ consists of a VPS $S = (Q, Q_{in}, \Gamma, \Delta)$, a partition $\langle Q_E, Q_A \rangle$ of Q, and a coloring function $col : Q \to \mathbb{N}$. The game defined by ST is $\mathbb{G}_{ST} = (\mathcal{G}, \Omega)$ with $\mathcal{G} = (V, V_E, V_A, E)$, where (V, E) is the configuration graph of S, $V_E = \{(p, \sigma) \mid p \in Q_E\}$, and $V_A = \{(p, \sigma) \mid p \in Q_A\}$. The set Ω is the internal winning condition $\Omega = \{\lambda \in V^\omega \mid \min_{col}(\lambda|_{Steps_\lambda})$ is even$\}$ where $\min_{col}(\beta) = \min\{i \mid \exists^\infty n \; s.t. \; col(\beta(n)) = i\}$. Here, $Steps_\lambda$ is the natural adaption of the definition of $Steps_\alpha$ to sequences of configurations, i.e, $Steps_\lambda = \{n \in \mathbb{N} \mid \forall m \geq n \; |\lambda(m)| \geq |\lambda(n)|\}$.

Note that the labeling of the edges in a stair parity game does not matter and, in the sequel, we will ignore it.

To transform a visibly pushdown game $\mathcal{H} = (S, Q_E, Q_A, \mathcal{M})$ into a stair parity game let D be some deterministic STVPA such that $L(D) = L(\mathcal{M})$. Since S and D are over the same pushdown alphabet $\widetilde{A}$, we can take the synchronized product $S \otimes D$ to get a pushdown system S' (ignoring the acceptance condition). We then have a stair parity game $ST = (S', Q'_E, Q'_A, col)$, where the partition of the state-space is inherited from $\mathcal{H}$ and the coloring function is inherited from the coloring function of D. Since D is deterministic one can easily show the following proposition, where q_{in} denotes the initial state of D.

Proposition 1. *Let $p_{in} \in Q$. Then $(p_{in}, \bot)$ is winning for Eve in $\mathbb{G}_\mathcal{H}$ if and only if $((p_{in}, q_{in}), \bot)$ is winning for Eve in $\mathbb{G}_{ST}$.*

Now we explain how to adapt the classical techniques for pushdown parity games and its variants [15, 4, 11] in order to solve stair parity games.

Let $ST = (S, Q_E, Q_A, col)$ be a stair parity game, where $S = (Q, Q_{in}, \Gamma, \Delta)$ and let $\mathcal{G} = (V, V_E, V_A, E)$ be the associated game graph. We construct a *finite* game graph $\overline{\mathcal{G}}$ with a parity winning condition, such that Eve has a winning strategy in $\mathcal{G}$ iff she has a winning strategy in $\overline{\mathcal{G}}$. Intuitively, in $\overline{\mathcal{G}}$, we keep track of only the control state and the symbol on the top of the stack. The interesting aspect of the game is when it is in a control state p with top-of-stack γ, and the player owning p wants to push a letter γ' onto the stack. For every strategy of Eve there is a certain set of possible (finite) continuations of the play that will end with popping this γ' symbol from the stack. We require Eve to declare the set R of all states the game can be in after the popping of γ' along these plays.

Adam now has two choices—he can either continue the game by pushing γ' onto the stack and updating the state (we call this a *pursue* move), or he can pick some state $p'' \in R$ and continue from that state, leaving γ on the top of the stack (we call this a *jump* move). If he does a pursue move, then he remembers R and if there is a pop-transition on γ' later on in the play, the play stops right there and Eve is declared the winner if and only if the resulting state is in R.

The crucial point to note is that the *jump* transitions along infinite plays in $\overline{\mathcal{G}}$ (i.e. plays that never meet a pop-transition with the stack being non-empty) essentially skip words of L_{mwm}, and hence the play really corresponds to evaluating a play λ in the pushdown game at $Steps_\lambda$. Therefore the stair parity condition gets evaluated along the play and ensures correctness of the reduction.

Let us now describe the construction more precisely. The main nodes of $\overline{\mathcal{G}}$ are tuples in $Q \times \Gamma \times 2^Q$. A node (p, γ, R) has color $col(p)$ and belongs to Eve iff $p \in Q_E$. Intuitively, a node (p, γ, R) denotes that the current state of $\mathcal{S}$ is p, γ is the symbol on the top of the stack, and R is the current commitment Eve has made, i.e. Eve has claimed that if a pop-γ transition is executed, then the resulting state will be in R. The starting node is $(p_{in}, \perp, \emptyset)$.

In order to simulate an internal-transition $(p, p') \in \Delta$, we have edges of the form $(p, \gamma, R) \to (p', \gamma, R)$ in $\overline{\mathcal{G}}$. Also, if the stack is empty, pop-transitions are handled like internal transitions: if $(p, \perp, p') \in \Delta$, then there is an edge $(p, \perp, R) \to (p', \perp, R)$ in $\overline{\mathcal{G}}$.

Pop-transitions are not simulated but are represented in $\overline{\mathcal{G}}$ by edges to a vertex $t\!t$ (winning for Eve) and a vertex $f\!f$ (winning for Adam) to verify the claims made by Eve. Recall that in (p, γ, R) the set R represents the claim of Eve that on a pop-γ transition the next state will be in R. Hence, in $\overline{\mathcal{G}}$ there is an edge from (p, γ, R) to $t\!t$ if there is $p' \in R$ and a pop-transition $(p, \gamma, p') \in \Delta$. If p belongs to Eve, then this transition can be used by Eve to win the game because she was able to prove that her claim was correct. If there is a pop-transition $(p, \gamma, p') \in \Delta$ with $p' \notin R$, then there is an edge from (p, γ, R) to $f\!f$, which can be used by Adam to win (if p belongs to Adam) since Eve made a false claim.

The simulation of a push-transition takes place in several steps. For a node (p, γ, R) the player owning p first picks a particular push-transition (p, p', γ') by moving to the node $(p, \gamma, R, p', \gamma')$, which belongs to Eve. Then Eve proposes a set $R' \subseteq Q$ containing the states that she claims to be reached if γ' gets eventually popped. She does this by moving to the node $(p, \gamma, R, p', \gamma', R')$, which belongs to Adam. Now, Adam has two kinds of choices. He can do a *jump* move by picking a state $p'' \in R'$ and move to the node (p'', γ, R). Or he can do a *pursue* move by moving to the node (p', γ', R').

If $\overline{\mathbb{G}}$ denotes the parity game played on $\overline{\mathcal{G}}$, we get the following result which can be shown using similar methods as, e.g., in [15, 4, 11].

Theorem 3. *Let $p_{in} \in Q$. Eve has a winning strategy from $(p_{in}, \perp)$ in the pushdown game $\mathbb{G}_{\mathcal{ST}}$ if and only if she has a winning strategy in $\overline{\mathbb{G}}$ from $(p_{in}, \perp, \emptyset)$. In addition, one can effectively build pushdown strategies for both players in $\mathbb{G}_{\mathcal{ST}}$.*

As a corollary of Theorem 3, Proposition 1, and the fact that the transformation from Proposition 1 preserves pushdown strategies, we have the following:

Corollary 1. *The problem of deciding the winner in a visibly pushdown game is in 2EXPTIME and pushdown strategies can be effectively built for both players.*

It is a well known result that there always exists memoryless winning strategies in parity games [6, 17]. Nevertheless, it is not the case for the preceding winning conditions:

Proposition 2. *There exist a stair parity (resp. visibly) pushdown game and a configuration winning for Eve such that any winning strategy for Eve from this position requires infinite memory.*

Visibly pushdown games are solvable in 2EXPTIME, as we showed above. Let us now consider pushdown games where the alphabet A is a subset of $2^{\mathcal{P}}$ where $\mathcal{P}$ is a finite set of propositions. CARET is a temporal logic that can express a subclass of context-free languages which is contained in VPL [1, 2]. From constructions in [1], it follows that for every CARET formula φ over $2^{\mathcal{P}}$, and a partition $\widetilde{A}$ of $2^{\mathcal{P}}$ into calls, returns, and internal actions, we can construct a Büchi visibly pushdown automaton of size $2^{O(|\varphi|)}$ over $\widetilde{A}$ which accepts the precise set of strings that satisfy φ. Hence, it follows that solving visibly pushdown games against CARET specifications is in 3EXPTIME.

However, this high complexity is not due to the pushdown nature of the specification nor due to the fact that we are dealing with ω-length plays. If we consider pushdown games against an LTL specification φ, we can solve this by first constructing a nondeterministic Büchi automaton accepting the models of φ and then constructing an equivalent deterministic parity automaton for it (resulting in an automaton whose size is doubly exponential in φ). Then, we can take the product of the pushdown game and this automaton, and solve the resulting parity pushdown game in exponential time [15]. The whole procedure works in 3EXPTIME. By a reduction from the word problem for alternating doubly exponential space bounded Turing machines one can show that this is a lower bound as well:

Theorem 4. *Given a pushdown game and an LTL formula, checking whether Eve has a winning strategy is 3EXPTIME-complete.*

We also establish the exact complexity of the following pushdown game problems:

Theorem 5

- Given a pushdown game and a CARET formula, checking whether Eve has a winning strategy is 3EXPTIME-complete.
- Given a pushdown game and a nondeterministic Büchi automaton, checking whether Eve has a winning strategy is 2EXPTIME-complete.
- Given a visibly pushdown game graph and a nondeterministic Büchi VPA, checking whether Eve has a winning strategy is 2EXPTIME-complete.

5   Topological Complexity

It is well known that the class of regular ω-languages is contained in the Boolean closure of the second level of the Borel hierarchy. Our goal is to show that this topological complexity is increased only by one level when we pass to visibly pushdown languages, i.e., we show that the class of visibly pushdown languages is contained in the Boolean closure of the third level of the Borel hierarchy. For more details on the definitions and results used in this section we refer the reader to [7] for set-theory in general and to [12] for results related to ω-languages.

For a set X we consider X^ω as a topological space with the Cantor topology. The open sets of X^ω are those of the form $U \cdot X^\omega$ for $U \subseteq X^*$. A set $L \subseteq X^\omega$ is closed if its complement $L^- = X^\omega \setminus L$ is open.

To define the finite levels of the Borel hierarchy we start with the class $\mathbf{\Sigma_1}$ of open sets. For each $n \geq 1$, $\mathbf{\Pi_n}$ is the class of complements of $\mathbf{\Sigma_n}$-sets and $\mathbf{\Sigma_{n+1}}$ is the class of countable unions of $\mathbf{\Pi_n}$-sets. By $B(\mathbf{\Sigma_n})$ we denote the class of finite Boolean combinations of $\mathbf{\Sigma_n}$-sets (using union, intersection, and complement).

For $L_1 \subseteq X_1^\omega, L_2 \subseteq X_2^\omega$ we say L_1 reduces continuously to L_2 if there is a continuous mapping $\varphi : X_1^\omega \to X_2^\omega$ such that $\varphi^{-1}(L_2) = L_1$, i.e., $\alpha \in L_1$ iff $\varphi(\alpha) \in L_2$ for all $\alpha \in X_1^\omega$. A language $L \subseteq X^\omega$ is called $\mathbf{\Sigma_n}$-complete if it is in $\mathbf{\Sigma_n}$ and every $K \in \mathbf{\Sigma_n}$ continuously reduces to L. The definition of $\mathbf{\Pi_n}$-complete sets is analogous.

We show the result that any VPL L belongs to $B(\mathbf{\Sigma_3})$ by using the model of stair VPA introduced in Section 3. Let $L \subseteq A^\omega$ be a VPL and let $\mathcal{M} = (Q, q_{in}, \Gamma, \delta, \Omega)$ be a deterministic parity stair VPA with $L(\mathcal{M}) = L$. To show that L is in $B(\mathbf{\Sigma_3})$, we define for each $q \in Q$ the language L_q containing all the words α for which the run of $\mathcal{M}$ on α infinitely often visits q on positions from $Steps_\alpha$, and show that L_q belongs to $\mathbf{\Pi_3}$. The language L itself can be written as a finite Boolean combination of the sets L_q corresponding to the definition of the parity acceptance condition: $\alpha \in A^\omega$ is in L iff $\alpha \in L_q$ for some q with $\Omega(q)$ even and $\alpha \notin L_{q'}$ for all q' with $\Omega(q') < \Omega(q)$.

For the definition of L_q we will use the following sets of finite words.

- For each $q \in Q$, let $U_q \subseteq A^*$ be the set of all words w such that the run of $\mathcal{M}$ on w ends in a configuration with state q.
- Let $U_{mr} = (A_c \cup A_{int} \cup L_{mwm})^*$ be the set of all words without unmatched returns.
- Let $U_0 = (A_r \cup A_{int} \cup L_{mwm})^*$ be the set of all words of stack height 0.

We describe L_q by stating that for each position $m \in \mathbb{N}$ there is a position $n > m$ that is in $Steps_\alpha$ and the prefix of α up to position n is in U_q. The only difficulty is to express that position n is in the set $Steps_\alpha$. For this we distinguish two cases (which are not mutually exclusive). Position n is in $Steps_\alpha$ if $\alpha{\restriction}n$ has stack height 0 or if the suffix of α starting from position n does not contain any unmatched returns. Formally, for $\alpha \in A^\omega$ and $n \in \mathbb{N}$ we get that $n \in Steps_\alpha$ and the run of $\mathcal{M}$ on $\alpha{\restriction}n$ ends in a configuration with state q iff α is in the set

$$L_{q,n} = [(U_q \cap A^n).A^\omega] \cap \left[(U_0 \cap A^n).A^\omega \cup \left(\bigcap_{n'>n} (A^n.U_{mr} \cap A^{n'}).A^\omega\right)\right].$$

The basic sets involved in this definition are of the form $U.A^\omega$ for U finite (since we always intersect with the set of words up to a certain length). These sets are open as well as closed. Since the class of closed sets is closed under countable intersections and finite unions we obtain that $L_{q,n}$ is closed for each q and n.

By adding the quantifications for m and n we obtain the following definition of L_q: $L_q = \bigcap_{m \in \mathbb{N}} \bigcup_{n>m} L_{q,n}$. It directly follows from the definition that L_q is in $\mathbf{\Pi_3}$ and hence we obtain the following theorem.

Theorem 6. *The class of* ω-VPLs *is contained in* $B(\Sigma_3)$.

One should note that there are nondeterministic Büchi VPAs accepting Σ_3-complete sets. The language L_{rb} from Example 1 is shown to be Σ_3-complete in [5]. The complement of this language is Π_3-complete and is also a VPL (since visibly pushdown languages are closed under complement).

There are no complete sets for the class $B(\Sigma_3)$ but it is not difficult to see that there are VPLs that are true $B(\Sigma_3)$-sets in the sense that they are neither in Σ_3 nor in Π_3. A simple way to define such a language is to consider an alphabet A with priorities assigned to the letters, i.e., there are k calls, k internal actions, and k returns, respectively, and they are assigned numbers from 1 to k. If we define L to be the language containing all α such that $\alpha|_{Steps_\alpha}$ satisfies the parity condition w.r.t. the numbers assigned to the letters, then it is not difficult to see that L is neither in Σ_3 nor in Π_3. But obviously L can be accepted by a StVPA that moves on each letter to a state with the corresponding priority.

Furthermore, let us note that languages accepted by deterministic VPAs are in $B(\Sigma_2)$. The proof is similar to the one showing that regular ω-languages are in $B(\Sigma_2)$ [12]. From this result we obtain an alternative proof that the language L_{rb} cannot be accepted by a deterministic VPA, since L_{rb} is Σ_3-complete. Finally, the results of this section imply that games with a VPL winning condition are determined because games with Borel winning conditions are determined [8].

References

1. R. Alur, K. Etessami, and P. Madhusudan. A temporal logic of nested calls and returns. In *TACAS'04*, volume 2988 of *LNCS*, pages 467–481. Springer, 2004.
2. R. Alur and P. Madhusudan. Visibly pushdown languages. In *Proceedings of the 36th Annual ACM Symposium on Theory of Computing, STOC '04*, 2004.
3. T. Ball and S. Rajamani. Bebop: A symbolic model checker for boolean programs. In *SPIN 2000*, volume 1885 of *LNCS*, pages 113–130. Springer, 2000.
4. A. Bouquet, O. Serre, and I. Walukiewicz. Pushdown games with the unboundedness and regular conditions. In *Proceedings of FSTTCS'03*, volume 2914 of *LNCS*, pages 88–99. Springer, 2003.
5. T. Cachat, J. Duparc, and W. Thomas. Solving pushdown games with a Σ_3 winning condition. In *CSL'02*, volume 2471 of *LNCS*, pages 322–336. Springer, 2002.
6. E.A. Emerson, C.S. Jutla, and A.P. Sistla. On model-checking for fragments of μ-calculus. In *CAV '93*, volume 697 of *LNCS*, pages 385–396. Springer, 1993.
7. A.S. Kechris. *Classical Descriptive Set Theory*, volume 156 of *Graduate texts in mathematics*. Springer Verlag, 1994.
8. D. A. Martin. Borel Determinacy. *Annals of Mathematics*, 102:363–371, 1975.
9. A. Pnueli and R. Rosner. On the synthesis of a reactive module. In *Proc. 16th ACM Symposium on Principles of Programming Languages*, Austin, January 1989.
10. T. Reps, S. Horwitz, and S. Sagiv. Precise interprocedural dataflow analysis via graph reachability. In *Proc. of ACM Symp. POPL*, pages 49–61, 1995.
11. O. Serre. Games with winning conditions of high borel complexity. In *Proceedings of ICALP'04*, volume 3142 of *LNCS*, pages 1150–1162. Springer, 2004.
12. L. Staiger. *Handbook of Formal Language Theory*, volume III, chapter ω-Languages, pages 339–387. Springer, 1997.

13. W. Thomas. *Handbook of Formal Language Theory*, volume III, chapter Languages, Automata, and Logic, pages 389–455. Springer, 1997.

14. W. Thomas. A short introduction to infinite automata. In *Proceedings of DLT '01*, volume 2295 of *LNCS*, pages 130–144. Springer, 2002.

15. I. Walukiewicz. Pushdown processes: Games and model checking. *Information and Computation*, 164(2), January 2001.

16. I. Walukiewicz. A landscape with games in the background. In *Proceedings of LICS'04, Invited talk*, 2004. To appear.

17. W. Zielonka. Infinite games on finitely coloured graphs with applications to automata on infinite trees. *TCS*, 200(1-2):135–183, 1998.

Refinement and Separation Contexts

Ivana Mijajlović[1], Noah Torp-Smith[2], and Peter O'Hearn[1]

[1] Queen Mary, University of London
{ivanam, ohearn}@dcs.qmul.ac.uk
[2] IT University of Copenhagen
noah@itu.dk

Abstract. A separation context is a client program which does not dereference internals of a module with which it interacts. We use certain "precise" relations to unambiguously describe the storage of a module and prove that separation contexts preserve such relations. We also show that a *simulation* theorem holds for separation contexts, while this is not the case for arbitrary client programs.

1 Introduction

Pointers wreak havoc with data abstractions [1–4]. To see why, suppose that a data abstraction uses a linked list in its internal representation; for example, an implementation of resource manager will use a free list. If a client program dereferences or otherwise accesses a pointer into this representation, then it will be sensitive to changes to the internal representation of the module. In theoretical terms, this havoc is manifest in the failure of classical "abstraction, logical relation, simulation" theorems for data abstraction. For example, the client program will behave differently if, say, the first rather than the second field in a cons cell is used to link together elements of a free list.

Data refinement is a method where one starts with an abstract specification of a data type and derives its concrete representation. Hoare introduced a method of refinement for imperative programs [5, 6]. His treatment of refinement assumes a static-scope based separation between the abstract data type and variables of the client. Pointers break those assumptions, as described above.

Previous approaches to abstraction in the presence of pointers [1, 3, 4, 7, 8] typically work by restricting what can point across certain boundaries. These solutions are limited and complex, and have difficulty coping with situations where pointers transfer between program components or where pointers across boundaries do exist without being dereferenced at the wrong time.

Separation logic [9], on the other hand, enables us to check code of a client for safety, even if there are pointers into the internals of a module [12]. It just ensures that pointers not be dereferenced at the wrong time, without permission.

This paper takes a first step towards bringing the ideas from separation logic into refinement. We present a model, but not yet a logic, which ensures separation between a client and a module, throughout the process of refinement of

K. Lodaya and M. Mahajan (Eds.): FSTTCS 2004, LNCS 3328, pp. 421–433, 2004.

the module. Our conditions for abstraction, based on a notion of "separation context", are considerably simpler than ones developed by Banerjee et al [3] and Reddy et al [4], and can easily handle examples with dangling pointers and examples of dynamic ownership transfer. We illustrate this with the nastiest problem we know of – toy versions of `malloc` and `free`.

The paper is organized as follows: we give some basic ideas and motivation in Section 2. In Section 3, we give relevant definitions regarding the programming language and relations on states. This enables us to define *unary separation contexts* in Section 4, and to prove properties about them. A separation context is a client program that does not dereference pointers into module internals. The idea that a module owns a part of the heap is described by a *precise* relation, which is a special kind of relation that unambiguously identifies a specific portion of the heap. We show that separation contexts respect these unary relations, where arbitrary contexts do not. Finally, in Section 5, we prove a *simulation theorem* which is a cousin of a classic logical relations or abstraction theorem, and which fails when a context is not a separation context. We also give a condition which ensures that a separation context for an abstract module is automatically a separation context for all its refinements.

2   Basic Ideas

We will discuss two simple examples in which we consider two different pieces of client code. In both programs we assume that the client code interacts with the memory manager module through two provided operations, new() and dispose(), for allocating and disposing memory, respectively. Suppose the module keeps locations available for allocating to a client, in a singly linked list.

To begin with we regard the program state as being separated into two parts, one of which belongs to a client, and the other which belongs to the module. The module's part always contains the free list. The statement new(x); takes a location from the free list puts it into x; at this point we regard the boundary between the client and module states as shifting: the ownership of the cell has transferred from the module to the client, so that the separation between client and module states is dynamic rather than determined once-and-for-all before a program runs. Similarly, when a client disposes a location we regard the ownership of that location as transferring from the client to the module. The concept of "ownership" here is simple: at any program point we regard the state as being separated into two parts, and ownership is just membership in one or the other component of the separated states.

Now, some programs respect this concept of separation while others do not. Consider the following client code.

new(x); do something with x; dispose(x); dispose(x)

This simple program behaves very badly – it disposes the same location twice. This is possible because after disposing the location pointed to by x the first time, x holds the value of the location. Depending on the implementation of dispose, this code could destroy the structure of the free list, and might eventually cause a program crash. This program contradicts our assumption of separation: the second dispose(x) statement accesses a cell which the client does not own, since it was previously transferred to the module.

In fact, *any* attempt to use the location after first dispose will contradict separation, say if we replace the second dispose by a statement $[x] := 42$ that mutates x's location. And both cases contradict abstraction. For instance, if the manager uses the $[x]$ field as a pointer to the next node in the free list, then $[x] := 42$ will corrupt the free list, but if the manager uses a different representation of the free list, corruption might not occur: depends whether or not it is representation-dependent.

In contrast, the following code obeys separation: the client code reads and writes to its own part, and disposes only a location which belongs to it.

$$\mathsf{new}(x); [x] := 15; y := [x]; \mathsf{dispose}(x)$$

The issue here is not exclusive to low-level programming languages. In a garbage collected language thread and connection pools are sometimes used to avoid the overhead of creating and destroying threads and database connections (such as when in a web server). Then, a thread or connection id should not be used after it has been returned to a pool, until it has been doled out again.

In the formal development to follow a "separation contexts" will be a piece of client code together with a precondition which ensures respect for separation.

3   Preliminary Definitions

In this section, we give relevant definitions regarding the storage model and relations in it. We give a programming language and its semantics.

Storage Model. We describe our models in an abstract way, which will allow various realizations of "heaps". We assume a countably infinite set Var of variables given. Let $S : \mathsf{Var} \to \mathsf{Val}$ be the set of *stacks* (that is, finite, partial maps from variables to values), and let H be a set of *heaps*, where we just assume that we have a set with a partial commutative monoid structure $(H, *, e)$. In effect, our development is on the level of the abstract model theory of BI [10], rather than the single model used in separation logic [11, 9]. We assume that $*$ is injective in the sense that for each h, the partial function $h * - : H \rightharpoonup H$ is injective. The set of *states* is the set of stack-heap pairs.

The subheap order $\sqsubseteq$ is induced by $*$ in the following way

$$h_1 \sqsubseteq h_2 \iff \exists h_3.h_1 * h_3 h_2.$$

Two heaps h_1 and h_2 are disjoint, denoted $h_1 \# h_2$, if $h_1 * h_2$ is defined. We will often take H to be a set of finite partial functions

$$H = \mathsf{Ptr} \rightharpoonup_{fin} \mathsf{Val}, \text{ where } \mathsf{Ptr} = \{0, 1, 2, \ldots\} \quad \mathsf{Val} = \{\ldots, -1, 0, 1, \ldots\}.$$

The combination $h * h'$ of two such heaps is defined only when they have disjoint domains, in which case it is the union of the graphs of the two functions. We will not restrict ourselves to this (RAM) model, but will assume it in examples unless stated differently.

Separation Logic. Separation logic is an extension of Hoare logic, where *heaps* have been added to the storage model. The usual assertion language of Hoare logic is extended with assertions that express properties about heaps

$$A, B ::= \mathsf{emp} \mid e_1 \mapsto e_2 \mid A * B \mid \mathsf{T} \mid \forall_* p \in m.\ A \mid \cdots.$$

The first asserts that the heap is empty, the second says that the current heap has exactly one pointer in its domain, and the third is the *separating conjunction* and means that the current heap can be split into two disjoint parts for which A and B hold, respectively. The fourth is true for any state, and the last assertion form is an iterated separating conjunction over a finite set. The semantics of assertions is given by a judgement $s, h \models A$ which asserts that the assertion A holds in the state (s, h). More about separation logic can be found in [9].

Unary Relations. Certain special properties are used to identify the heap portion owned by a module [12].

Definition 1. *A relation $M \subseteq S \times H$ is* precise *if for any state s, h there is at most one subheap $h_0 \sqsubseteq h$, such that $(s, h_0) \in M$.*

We illustrate precise unary relations with an example. Let α be a sequence of integers. The predicate $\mathsf{list}(\alpha, x)$ is defined inductively on the sequence α by

$$\mathsf{list}(\varepsilon, x) \overset{\text{def}}{=} x = nil \wedge \mathsf{emp}, \qquad \mathsf{list}(a \cdot \alpha, x) \overset{\text{def}}{=} x = a \wedge \exists y.\ x \mapsto y * \mathsf{list}(\alpha, y)$$

where ε represents the empty sequence and $\cdot$ conses an element a onto the front of a sequence α. This predicate says that x points to a non-circular singly-linked list whose addresses are the sequence α (this is called a "Bornat list" in [9]). For any given s, h, there can be at most one subheap which satisfies $\mathsf{list}(\alpha, x)$, consisting of the cells in α. Generally, a precise relation gives you a way to "pick out the relevant cells".

We define the *separating conjunction of unary relations* $M, M' \subseteq S \times H$ by

$$M * M' = \{(s, h) \mid \exists h_0, h_1.h_0 \# h_1 \wedge h = h_0 * h_1 \wedge (s, h_0) \in M \wedge (s, h_1) \in M'\}.$$

Taking into account that $*$ is injective, a precise relation M induces a unique splitting of a state (s, h). We write (s, h_M) for the substate of (s, h) uniquely described by M, if it exists. Otherwise, $(s, h_M) = e$, the unit.

The Model. Our model will use a simple language with two kinds of atomic operations: the client operations and the module operations. The denotation of client commands will be given by functions $f : (S \times H) \to (S \times H) \uplus \{wrong\}$, and the denotation of module operations will be given by binary relations $t \subseteq$

$(S \times H) \times (S \times H) \uplus \{wrong\}$. The special state *wrong* results when a program illegally accesses storage beyond the current heap. We presume there is a fixed set of module variables Var_M, which are never changed by the client:

$$\forall x \in \mathsf{Var}_M. \quad \begin{aligned} f(s,h) &= wrong \Leftrightarrow \forall v. f(s\backslash\{x \mapsto v\}, h) = wrong \text{ and} \\ f(s,h) &= (s',h') \Leftrightarrow \forall v. f(s\backslash\{x \mapsto v\}, h) = (s'\backslash\{x \mapsto v\}, h'). \end{aligned}$$

For a unary relation on states M, we write M_{wrong} to denote $M \cup \{wrong\}$. We will write $(s,h)[t](s',h')$ to denote that the states (s,h) and (s',h') are in the binary relation t.

The relation $M \subseteq S \times H$ is said to be *preserved* by a function f (respectively relation t) on states, if for all $(s,h), (s',h')$, such that state (s,h) is in M and $f(s,h) = (s',h')$ (respectively $(s,h)[t](s',h')$), imply $(s',h') \in M_{wrong}$.

The reader will have recognized an asymmetry in our model: client primitive operations are required to be deterministic, while in module operations non-determinism is allowed. One effect of this is that, when frame conditions are imposed later, the client operations will not be able to do any allocation; allocation will have to be viewed as a module operation. Technically, the determinism restriction is needed for our simple simulation theorem.

Local Functions and Relations. We will consider functions and relations on states that access resources in a local way. More formally, we say that a function $f : (S \times H) \rightarrow (S \times H) \uplus \{wrong\}$ (relation $t \subseteq (S \times H) \times (S \times H) \uplus \{wrong\}$) is *local* [12] if it satisfies the following properties

- **Safety Monotonicity:** For all states (s,h) and heaps h_1 such that $h \# h_1$, if $f(s,h) \neq wrong$ (respectively $\neg(s,h)[t]wrong$), then $f(s, h * h_1) \neq wrong$ (respectively $\neg(s, h * h_1)[t]wrong$).
- **Frame Property:** For all states (s,h) and heaps h_1 with $h \# h_1$, if $f(s,h) \neq wrong$ (respectively $\neg(s,h)[t]wrong$) and $f(s, h * h_1) = (s',h')$, (respectively $(s, h*h_1)[t](s',h')$) then there is a subheap $h'_0 \sqsubseteq h'$ such that $h'_0 \# h_1$, $h'_0 * h_1 = h'$ and $f(s,h) = (s',h'_0)$ (respectively $(s,h)[t](s',h'_0)$).

The properties are the ones needed for soundness of the Frame Rule of separation logic; see [13]. We will only consider local functions and relations.

Programming Language. The programming language is an extension of the simple while-language with a finite set of atomic client operations f_j ($j \in J$) and a finite set of module operations oper_i, $i \in I$. The syntax of the *user language* is

$$c_{user} ::= \mathsf{f}_j,\ j \in J \mid \mathsf{oper}_i,\ i \in I \mid c_1; c_2 \mid \textbf{if } e \textbf{ then } c \textbf{ else } c \mid \textbf{while } e \textbf{ do } c,$$
$$e ::= int \mid var \mid e + e \mid e \times e \mid e - e, \quad int \in \mathsf{Int}, \ var \in \mathsf{Var},$$
$$\mathsf{Int} = \{\dots -1, 0, 1, \dots\}, \ \mathsf{Var} = \{x, y, \dots\}, \ I, J - \text{finite indexing sets.}$$

The expressions used in the language do not access heap storage. Commands such as $x := e$, $[e_1] := e_2$, $x := [e]$, etc. are examples of atomic operations.

The semantics of the language is parameterized by a precise relation M and a collection $(oper_i)_{i \in I}$ of binary relations that preserve $M * \mathsf{T}$. It defines a big-step transition relation $\leadsto \subseteq (c_{user} \times (S \times H)) \times ((S \times H) \uplus \{wrong, av\})$ on

Table 1. Operational semantics

$$(s,h) = (s,h_M) * (s,h_U)$$

$$\dfrac{f_j(s,h) = (s',h')}{\mathsf{f}_j, s, h \rightsquigarrow s', h'} \qquad \dfrac{f_j(s,h) \neq wrong \quad f_j(s,h_U) = wrong}{\mathsf{f}_j, s, h \rightsquigarrow av} \qquad \dfrac{f_j(s,h) = wrong}{\mathsf{f}_j, s, h \rightsquigarrow wrong}$$

$$\dfrac{(s,h)[oper_i](s',h')}{\mathsf{oper}_i, s, h \rightsquigarrow s', h'} \qquad \dfrac{(s,h)[oper_i]wrong}{\mathsf{oper}_i, s, h \rightsquigarrow wrong} \qquad \dfrac{c_1, s, h \rightsquigarrow s', h' \quad c_2, s', h' \rightsquigarrow K}{c_1; c_2, s, h \rightsquigarrow K}$$

$$\dfrac{c_1, s, h \rightsquigarrow wrong}{c_1; c_2, s, h \rightsquigarrow wrong} \qquad \dfrac{[\![e]\!]s = 0}{\textbf{while } e \textbf{ do } c, s, h \rightsquigarrow s, h} \qquad \dfrac{[\![e]\!]s \neq 0 \quad c; \textbf{while } e \textbf{ do } c, s, h \rightsquigarrow K}{\textbf{while } e \textbf{ do } c, s, h \rightsquigarrow K}$$

$$\dfrac{c_1, s, h \rightsquigarrow av}{c_1; c_2, s, h \rightsquigarrow av} \qquad \dfrac{[\![e]\!]s \neq 0 \quad c_1, s, h \rightsquigarrow K}{\textbf{if } e \textbf{ then } c_1 \textbf{ else } c_2, s, h \rightsquigarrow K} \qquad \dfrac{[\![e]\!]s = 0 \quad c_2, s, h \rightsquigarrow K}{\textbf{if } e \textbf{ then } c_1 \textbf{ else } c_2, s, h \rightsquigarrow K}$$

configurations, where av denotes a state in which client code illegally accesses the heap storage owned by the module, and will be referred to as "access violation". The operational semantics of the language is given in Table 1. State $(s, h_M) \in M$ denotes the substate of (s, h) uniquely determined by relation M in the second rule. What is left over, (s, h_U), is the client's state. K denotes an element of $(S \times H) \uplus \{av, wrong\}$.

4   Unary Separation Contexts

An essential point in the semantics in Table 1 is the way that module state is subtracted when client operations f_j are performed. If a client operation does not go wrong in a global state, but goes wrong when the module state is subtracted, we judge that this was due to an attempt to access the module's state; in the semantics this is rendered as an access violation, and a separation context is then a program (with a precondition) that does not lead to access violation.

Definition 2. *Let $M \subseteq S \times H$ be a precise unary relation, let P be a unary predicate on states, and for $i \in I$ let $oper_i \subseteq (S \times H) \times (S \times H) \uplus \{wrong\}$ preserve relation $M * \top$. A program c is a* unary separation context *for M, P and $(oper_i)_{i \in I}$ if for all executions and all $(s, h) \in M * P$ $c, s, h \not\rightsquigarrow av$.*

The idea is that M describes the heap storage owned by the module, and a separation context will never access that storage. Separation contexts preserve the resource invariant of a module because they change storage owned by the module only through the provided operations.

Theorem 1. *Let $M \subseteq S \times H$ be a precise relation, let P be a unary predicate on states, and for $(i \in I)$ let $oper_i \subseteq S \times H \times (S \times H) \uplus \{wrong\}$ preserve $M * \top$, and let c be a separation context for M, P and $(oper_i)_{i \in I}$. Then for all such P and all states (s, h) and (s', h'), if $(s, h) \in M * P$, and $c, s, h \rightsquigarrow s', h'$, then $(s', h') \in (M * \top)_{wrong}$.*

Separation Context Examples. We now revisit the ideas discussed in Section 2 in our more formal setting. In order to specify the operations of the memory manager module, we make use of the "greatest relation" for the specification $\{P\}\mathsf{oper}\{Q\}[X]$, which is the largest local relation satisfying a triple $\{P\} - \{Q\}$ and changing only the variables in the set X. It is similar to the "generic commands" introduced by Schwarz [14] and the "specification statements" studied in the refinement literature, but adapted to work with locality conditions in [12].

The predicate $\exists \alpha.\mathsf{list}(\alpha, ls)$ describes the free list, and we choose it as the M component in the definition of a separation context. The operations $\mathsf{new}(x)$ and $\mathsf{dispose}(x)$ are the greatest relations satisfying the following specifications.

$$\mathsf{new}_C(x): \quad \{\mathsf{list}(a \cdot \alpha, ls)\} - \{\mathsf{list}(\alpha, ls) * x \mapsto a\}[x, ls]$$
$$\{\mathsf{list}(\varepsilon, ls)\} - \{\mathsf{list}(\varepsilon, ls) * x \mapsto -\}[x, ls]$$
$$\mathsf{dispose}_C(x): \quad \{\mathsf{list}(\alpha, ls) * x \mapsto a\} - \{\mathsf{list}(a \cdot \alpha, ls)\}[ls]$$

For future reference, we will call this the *concrete* interpretation of the memory manager module. With these definitions we can judge whether a program (together with a precondition) is a separation context.

Consider the following three programs

$Program_1:$	$Program_2:$	$Program_3:$
$\mathsf{new}(x);$	$\mathsf{dispose}(x);$	$[81] := 42$
$[x] := 47;$	$[x] := 47;$	
$\mathsf{dispose}(x);$		

We indicate whether a program, together with a precondition, is a separation context in the following table.

Context	Separation context?
$\{\mathsf{emp}\}\ Program_1$	✓
$\{x \mapsto -\}\ Program_2$	✓
$\{\mathsf{emp}\}\ Program_2$	✗
$\{81 \mapsto -\}\ Program_3$	✓
$\{\mathsf{emp}\}\ Program_3$	✗

Most of the entries are easy to explain, and correspond to our informal discussion from earlier. The last one, though, requires some care. For, how do we know that $[81] := 42$ interferes with the free list? The answer is that we do not. It might or might not be the case that location 81 is in the free list, at any given point in time. But, the notion of separation context is fail-safe: if there is *any* possibility that 81 is in the free list, on any run, then the program is judged not to be a separation context. And we can easily construct an example state where 81 is indeed in the free list. On the other hand in the second-last entry the precondition $81 \mapsto -$ ensures that 81 cannot be in the free list. This is because of the use of $*$ to separate the module and client states.

5   Refinement and Separation

In this section we first introduce precise binary relations and the separating conjunction of binary relations. We give a definition of refinement and prove a binary relation-preservation theorem.

Let $R \subseteq (S_0 \times H_0) \times (S_1 \times H_1)$ be a binary relation. We say that R is *precise*, if each of its two projections on the corresponding set of states is precise. Formally, for any state $(s_i, h_i) \in (S_i \times H_i)$ there is at most one $h_i' \sqsubseteq h_i$ such that there exists a state $(s_{1-i}, h_{1-i}) \in (S_{1-i} \times H_{1-i})$ such that $(s_i, h_i')[R](s_{1-i}, h_{1-i})$, for i=0,1.

We illustrate precise binary relations with an example. Suppose we have two different implementations of a memory manager module. In the first implementation we assume that f is a set variable, which keeps track of all owned locations. In the second implementation, we let this information be kept in a list. We use the list predicate $list(\alpha, ls)$, defined in Section 3. Now, a precise binary relation

$$R = \left\{ ((s,h),(s',h')) \,\middle|\, \begin{array}{l} (s,h \models \forall_* p \in f.\ p \mapsto -) \wedge (s',h' \models list(\alpha, ls)) \wedge \\ set(\alpha) = s(f) \end{array} \right\},$$

where $set(\alpha)$ is defined as the set of pointers in the sequence α, relates these two implementations. Relation R relates pairs of states, such that one state can be described as a set of different pointers, while the other is determined by the list of exactly the pointers that appear in the mentioned set.

For two binary relations $R, R' \subseteq (S_1 \times H_1) \times (S_2 \times H_2)$ on states, we define their separating conjunction [4] as

$$R * R' = \left\{ ((s_1, h_1),(s_2, h_2)) \,\middle|\, \begin{array}{l} \exists h_1', h_1'', h_2', h_2''.\ h_1 = h_1' * h_1'' \wedge h_2 = h_2' * h_2'' \wedge \\ (s_1, h_1')[R](s_2, h_2') \wedge (s_1, h_1'')[R'](s_2, h_2'') \end{array} \right\}$$

Similarly to the unary case, for a binary relation on states R we will write R_{wrong} to denote $R \cup \{(wrong, wrong)\}$.

5.1   Refinement and Separation Contexts

In this section, we formally express what it means for one module to be a *refinement* (or an implementation) of another. For simplicity, we assume that there is only one operation of the module, i.e., that the index set I from the syntax of the user language is singleton. In previous work on refinement [6], our definition of refinement is called an upward simulation.

In the following, we will take H_1, H_2 and H_3 to be three (in general different, but possibly equal) heap models, assuming that $(H_1, *_1, e_1)$, $(H_2, *_2, e_2)$ and $(H_3, *_3, e_3)$ have partial commutative monoid structure.

Definition 3. *Let $Z \subseteq (S_1 \times H_1) \times (S_2 \times H_2)$ be a binary relation. We define $oper^2 \subseteq (S_2 \times H_2) \times (S_2 \times H_2) \uplus \{wrong\}$ to be a refinement of $oper^1 \subseteq (S_1 \times H_1) \times (S_1 \times H_1) \uplus \{wrong\}$ with respect to Z, if*

- *for all states $(s_1, h_1), (s_2, h_2), (s_2', h_2')$, such that $(s_1, h_1)[Z](s_2, h_2)$ and $(s_2, h_2)[oper^2](s_2', h_2')$ there exists a state (s_1', h_1'), such that $(s_1, h_1)[oper^1](s_1', h_1')$, and $(s_1', h_1')[Z](s_2', h_2')$, and*

- *for all states* $(s_1, h_1), (s_2, h_2)$, *such that* $(s_1, h_1)[Z](s_2, h_2)$ *if*
  $(s_2, h_2)[oper^2]wrong$ *then* $(s_1, h_1)[oper^1]wrong$.

In order to prove the relation preservation theorem, we need to instantiate the refinement relation to a separating conjunction of binary relations, $R, Q \subseteq (S_1 \times H_1) \times (S_2 \times H_2)$. We assume that the following properties hold:

- R is precise
- Q is such that for any two states $(s_1, h_1), (s_2, h_2)$ related by Q and a guard (condition of **if** and **while** statements) b, $s_1(b) \Leftrightarrow s_2(b)$
- $oper^2 \subseteq (S_2 \times H_2) \times (S_2 \times H_2) \uplus \{wrong\}$ is a refinement of $oper^1 \subseteq (S_1 \times H_1) \times (S_1 \times H_1) \uplus \{wrong\}$ with respect to $R * Q$
- We denote a pair (f_j^1, f_j^2) by $\mathbf{f}_j$. Pair $\mathbf{f}_j$,is such that it maps Q-related states to Q_{wrong}-related states.

The role of R is to relate abstract and concrete subheaps which belong to the module, while Q relates the clients' parts of the heaps.

Simulation Theorem (Informally): Suppose we have two instantiations of a client program, which use calls to concrete and abstract module operations respectively, related by a refinement relation. Then, provided both of these two instantiations are separation contexts with respect to the corresponding modules, the effect of the concrete computation can be tracked by the abstract.

Stating this more formally requires some notation. For a program c, let $c_i \subseteq (S_i \times H_i) \times (S_i \times H_i) \uplus \{wrong\}$ be a relation denoted by c in the operational semantics defined by R_i and $oper^i$, $i = 1, 2$, where R_i is the projection of R onto $(S_i \times H_i)$. Q_P denotes $Q \cap (P \times Q(P))$, where Q is a binary relation on states, P is a unary relation on states, and $Q(P)$ is their composition.

Theorem 2 (Simulation Theorem). *Let* $R, Q, oper^i, c, c_i$ *for* $i = 1, 2$, *be as above, and let* $P \subseteq Q_1$ *be a unary relation on states. Let* c_1 *be a separation context for* R_1, P *and* $oper^1$, *and let* c_2 *be a separation context for* $R_2, Q(P)$ *and* $oper^2$. *Then for all such* P *and all* $(s_1, h_1), (s_2, h_2), (s_2', h_2')$ *if* $(s_1, h_1) [R * Q_P] (s_2, h_2)$ *and* $(s_2, h_2)[c_2](s_2', h_2')$ *then there exists a state* (s_1', h_1') *such that* $(s_1, h_1)[c_1](s_1', h_1')$ *and* $(s_1', h_1')[R * Q](s_2', h_2')$.

The crucial assumption is that c_1 and c_2 are separation contexts for the given modules and preconditions, and without this condition the theorem fails.

One shortcoming is that we have to check whether both c_1 and c_2 are separation contexts to apply Theorem 2. From the point of view of program development it would be better if we knew that when we had a separation context for an abstract module then it would automatically remain a separation context for all its refinements. Then the check could be done once and for all. In order to realize this aim, an extra concept is needed: safety. A safe separation context is a client which does not touch any storage not in its possession.

Definition 4 (Safe Separation Context). *Let c be a separation context for the precise relation M, precondition P and family of operations $(oper^i)_{i \in I}$. Program c is a* safe separation context *for M, P, $(oper^i)_{i \in I}$ if for all executions and all states $(s, h) \in M * P$, $c, s, h \not\rightarrow wrong$.*

Theorem 3. *Let R, Q, $oper^i$, c, c_i for $i = 1, 2$ be as in Theorem 2, and let $P \subseteq Q_1$ be a unary relation on states. If c_1 is a safe separation context for R_1, P and $oper^1$, then c_2 is a safe separation context for $R_2, Q(P)$ and $oper^2$.*

Safe Separation Context Example. To see the role of the concept of safety, consider an *abstract* version of the memory manager procedures, the "magical malloc module". It is magical in that the module does not own any locations at all, producing them as if out of thin air. (In implementation terms, the thin air is like a call to a system routine such as sbrk.) Therefore, the resource invariant of the module, M in our formal setup, is the predicate emp. Now, we define the abstract operations $new_A(x)$ and $dispose_A(x)$ as the greatest relations satisfying the following specifications.

$$new_A(x) : \{emp\} - \{x \mapsto -\}[x], \quad dispose_A(x) : \{x \mapsto -\} - \{emp\}[\ ]$$

This is the meaning of allocation and disposal that is usually presumed in separation logic. Because the manager owns no storage whatsoever, there is no way for a client to trample on it. As a result, *every* client program is a separation context for this abstract module.

But, not every context is safe. Consider the context

$$\{emp\} \ [81] := 42$$

from the Separation Context Examples in Section 4. It immediately goes wrong, and so is not safe. Recall also that in the more concrete semantics, from the same section, this is not even an ordinary separation context.

This shows the import of Theorem 3. If we know that our context is safe in the abstract setting, then this ensures that module internals will not be tampered with in refinements. Put another way, module tampering in a concrete implementation can show up as going wrong in the abstract, and the concept of safe separation context protects against this.

Refinement Examples. Here, we illustrate refinement relations between different interpretations of the memory manager module with two examples.

To define the refinement relations we borrow some notation from relational separation logic [15]. Let $S_1 \times H_1$ and $S_2 \times H_2$ be two state spaces. Let $P \subseteq S_1 \times H_1$, $Q \subseteq S_2 \times H_2$ and $R \subseteq (S_1 \times H_1) \times (S_2 \times H_2)$ be predicates. We let

$$\binom{P}{Q} \wedge R \quad \text{denote} \quad \{(s_1, h_1), (s_2, h_2) \mid (s_1, h_1 \models P \ \wedge \ s_2, h_2 \models Q) \ \wedge \ R\}.$$

The first example involves refinement between the *abstract* and the *concrete* interpretations of the memory manager module. We have already specified both interpretations, the abstract – in the Safe Separation Context Example above, and the concrete – in the ordinary Separation Context Example from Section 4.

The refinement relation Z_{AC} between these two interpretations is a separating conjunction of binary relations R_{AC} and Q_{AC}. These are given by

$$R_{AI} = \begin{pmatrix} \mathsf{emp} \\ \exists \alpha. \ \mathsf{list}(\alpha, ls) \end{pmatrix} \qquad Q_{AI} = \mathbf{Id}.$$

Relation R_{AI} relates modules' states of the two interpretations and is basically the relation between their resource invariants. Relation Q_{AC} relates clients' states and is the identity relation.

In the second example, we introduce the *intermediate* version of the memory manager module. We do this for two reasons. First, this illustrates the use of two different heap models, as allowed in our formal setting. Second, considering refinement between the intermediate and the concrete interpretations requires a subtler refinement relation.

On the intermediate level, the intention is to keep locations owned by the module in a set, without committing to the representation of the set. If this set becomes empty, we call a "system routine" (like sbrk) to get a new location.

For this interpretation, we assume the following heap model. Let Loc be an infinite set of locations. A heap will be an element of the Cartesian product $\mathcal{P}_{fin}(Loc) \times H_1$, where $(H_1, *_1, e_1)$ is the partial commutative monoid of the RAM model. We say that a pair (N, h) from this product is *well-defined* if $N \cap dom(h) = \emptyset$. The intermediate heap model H consists of these well-defined elements. Two intermediate heaps (N_1, h_1) and (N_2, h_2) are disjoint, $(N_1, h_1) \#_1 (N_2, h_2)$, whenever $N_1 \cap N_2 = \emptyset$ and $N_1 \cap dom(h_2) = \emptyset$ and $N_2 \cap dom(h_1) = \emptyset$ and $dom(h_1) \cap dom(h_2) = \emptyset$. We define $*$ between two heaps by

$$(N_1, h_1) * (N_2, h_2) = \begin{cases} (N_1 \cup N_2, h_1 *_1 h_2), \ \text{if } (N_1, h_1) \#_1 (N_2, h_2) \ \text{and} \\ \qquad\qquad\qquad\qquad (N_1, h_1), (N_2, h_2) \ \text{well defined} \\ \mathsf{undefined}, \qquad\qquad\quad \text{otherwise} \end{cases}$$

We say that $s, (N, h) \models act(p)$ if and only if $p \in N$. The resource invariant can be described with $\forall_* p \in f. \ act(p)$, where f is a set variable. We now define operations $\mathsf{new}_I(x)$ and $\mathsf{dispose}_I(x)$ as the greatest relations satisfying the specifications

$\mathsf{new}_I(x) :$ $\{\forall_* p \in f. \ act(p) \wedge f = Y \neq \emptyset\} - \{(\forall_* p \in f. \ act(p) \wedge f = Y \setminus \{x\}) *$
$\qquad\qquad x \mapsto -\}[x, f]$
$\qquad\qquad \{\forall_* p \in f. \ act(p) \wedge f = \emptyset\} - \{(\forall_* p \in f. \ act(p) \wedge f = \emptyset) * x \mapsto -\}[x]$
$\mathsf{dispose}_I(x) :\{(\forall_* p \in f. \ act(p) \wedge f = Y) * x \mapsto -\} - \{\forall_* p \in f. \ act(p) \wedge$
$\qquad\qquad f = Y \cup \{x\}\}[f]$

The variable Y is used to keep track of the initial contents of f, similarly to how α was used in the concrete interpretation. Note that it is not altered because it is not in the modifies set, a set of actual locations owned by the module. We intend that $\mathsf{new}_I(x)$ is the greatest relation satisfying both stated specifications.

Now, the refinement relation Z_{IC} between intermediate and concrete relations is a separating conjunction of binary relations R_{IC} and Q_{IC} given by

$$R_{IC} = \left(\begin{matrix} f \\ \mathsf{list}(\alpha, ls) \end{matrix} \right) \wedge set(\alpha)val(f) \qquad Q_{IC} = \mathbf{Id},$$

where $val(f)$ is the value of set variable f. It can be verified that the operations preserve these relations as required in the definition of refinement.

In these two examples we have not exercised the possibility of using a non-identity relation to relate the abstract and concrete client states. A good such example compares two implementations of a buffer, one of which copies two values where the other passes a single pointer to the two values. It is omitted here for space reasons.

Directions for Future Work. There are several directions for further work. First, we have, for simplicity, considered the interaction between a client and a single module; in the future we plan on investigating independence between modules. Second, it would be worthwhile to consider multiple-instance classes (e.g. [3]); here we have, in effect, a single single-instance class. It would also be important to remove the restriction of determinism, imposed to the client operations. Finally, we would like to use the model to make the connection back to logic. Perhaps a relational version of the hypothetical frame rule, or the modular procedure rule, from [12] can be formulated, borrowing from Yang's relational separation logic [15].

Acknowledgements. We would like to thank Hongseok Yang, Josh Berdine, Richard Bornat and Cristiano Calcagno for invaluable discussions and anonymous referees for their careful comments. Torp-Smith's research was partially supported by Danish Natural Science Research Council Grant 51–00–0315 and Danish Technical Research Council Grant 56–00–0309. Mijajlović and O'Hearn were supported by the EPSRC.

References

1. Hogg, J.: Islands: Aliasing Protection In Object-Oriented Languages. *OOPSLA'91*
2. Hogg, J., Lea, D., Wills, A., deChampeaux, D., Holt, R.: The Geneva Convention On The Treatment of Object Aliasing. *OOPS Messenger* (1992)
3. Banerjee, A., Naumann, D. A.: Representation Independence, Confinement and Access Control [extended abstract]. *29th POPL.* (2002)
4. Reddy, U. S., Yang, H.: Correctness of Data Representations involving Heap Data Structures. *Proceedings of ESOP* .Springer Verlag (2003) 223–237
5. Hoare, C. A. R.: Proof of Correctness of Data Representations. *Acta Informatica.* Vol. 1. (1972) 271–281
6. He, J., Hoare, C. A. R., Sanders, J. W.: Data Refinement Refined (Resume). *Proceedings of ESOP.* LNCS. Vol. 213. Springer Verlag (1986) 187–196
7. Clarke, D. G., Noble, J., Potter, J. M.: Simple Ownership Types for Object Containment. *Proceedings of ECOOP.* (2001)

8. Boyapati, C., Liskov, B., Shrira, L.: Ownership Types for Object Encapsulation. *30th POPL.* (2003)

9. Reynolds, J. C.: Separation Logic: A Logic for Shared Mutable Data Structures. *Proceedings of 17th LICS.* (2002) 55–74

10. D. Pym, P. O'Hearn, H. Yang.: Possible Worlds and Resources: The Semantics of BI. *Theoretical Computer Science* 313(1) (2004) 257-305

11. Ishtiaq, S., O'Hearn, P. W.: BI as an Assertion Language for Mutable Data Structures. *28th POPL* (2001) 14-26

12. O'Hearn, P., Yang, H., Reynolds, J. C.: Separation and information hiding. *31st POPL.* (2004) 268–280

13. H. Yang, P. O'Hearn.: A semantic basis for local reasoning. In *Proceedings of FOSSACS'02* (2002) 402–416

14. J. Schwarz.: Generic Commands - A Tool for Partial Correctness Formalisms. *Comput. J.* 20(2) (1977) 151-155

15. Yang, H.: Relational Separation Logic. *Theoretical Computer Science* (to appear)

Decidability of MSO Theories of Tree Structures

Angelo Montanari and Gabriele Puppis

Dipartimento di Matematica e Informatica, Università di Udine
via delle Scienze 206, 33100 Udine, Italy
{montana, puppis}@dimi.uniud.it

Abstract. In this paper we provide an automaton-based solution to the decision problem for a large set of monadic second-order theories of deterministic tree structures. We achieve it in two steps: first, we reduce the considered problem to the problem of determining, for any Rabin tree automaton, whether it accepts a given tree; then, we exploit a suitable notion of tree equivalence to reduce (a number of instances of) the latter problem to the decidable case of regular trees. We prove that such a reduction works for a large class of trees, that we call residually regular trees. We conclude the paper with a short discussion of related work.

1   Introduction

The automatic verification of properties of infinite state systems is a crucial problem in computer science, which turns out to be undecidable in many cases. A natural approach to this problem is to model a transition system as a directed graph, whose vertices (resp. edges) represent system configurations (resp. transitions). The expected behavior of the system is then expressed by a logical formula, which can be satisfied or not by the corresponding graph. The verification problem consists in deciding the satisfiability (resp. truth) of a given formula (resp. sentence) over a fixed graph structure. In this paper, we address the verification problem for systems of monadic second-order (MSO) logic interpreted over deterministic tree structures.

A fundamental result in the case of finite state systems is Büchi's theorem [2], that shows the decidability of the MSO theory of the linear order $(\mathbb{N}, <)$. Such a result takes advantage of closure properties of language acceptors (Büchi automata) with respect to union, intersection, complementation, and projection. Later, Rabin extended this result to the theory of the infinite (complete) binary tree by exploiting a new class of automata, called Rabin tree automata [20]. Büchi's theorem has also been used to deal with expansions of $(\mathbb{N}, <)$ with suitable unary predicates. Given a unary predicate $P \subseteq \mathbb{N}$, the decision problem for the theory of the expanded structure $(\mathbb{N}, <, P)$ is the problem of determining, for any Büchi automaton M, whether M accepts (the infinite word that characterizes) P. Elgot and Rabin gave a positive answer to this problem for some relevant predicates, such as the factorial one [15]. Recently, Carton and Thomas generalized such a result to the class of the so-called residually ultimately periodic words (which includes the class of morphic infinite words) [7].

K. Lodaya and M. Mahajan (Eds.): FSTTCS 2004, LNCS 3328, pp. 434–446, 2004.
© Springer-Verlag Berlin Heidelberg 2004

In [19], Muller and Schupp brought the interest to MSO theories of graphs by identifying a large family of decidable graphs. Several approaches to the problem of deciding graph theories have been proposed in the literature. The transformational approach solves the problem for those graphs that are obtained by applying decidability-preserving transformations to structures which are known to be decidable, e.g., unfoldings [14], tree-graph operations [23], first-order interpretations and inverse rational mappings [10], MSO definable transductions [13]. Other approaches capture decidable graph structures through rewriting systems [8], transducers [4], or equational systems [11, 12]. As a matter of fact, different characterizations of the same family of graphs have been obtained by following different approaches. As an example, prefix-recognizable graphs [3] can be equivalently described by means of rational restrictions of inverse rational mappings of the infinite complete binary tree [10], MSO interpretations of infinite regular trees [22], and vertex-replacement equational graphs [1].

In this paper we extend Carton and Thomas' automaton-based approach [7] to cope with the decision problem for a large set of MSO theories of deterministic tree structures. First, we reduce the considered problem to the problem of determining, for any Rabin tree automaton, whether it accepts a given tree. Then, we exploit a suitable notion of tree equivalence to reduce (a number of instances of) the latter problem to the decidable case of regular trees. We prove that such a reduction works for a large class of trees, that we call residually regular trees. Successively, we show that the proposed technique can be used to decide the theories of some meaningful relational structures, including several trees in the Caucal hierarchy [9] and trees outside it [6]. We conclude the paper with a short discussion of related work.

2   Basic Notions

MSO logics. MSO logics over graph structures are defined as follows. Given a finite alphabet Λ, a Λ-labeled graph structure is a tuple $\mathcal{G} = (S, (E_l)_{l \in \Lambda})$, where S (also denoted $\mathcal{D}om(\mathcal{G})$) is a countable set of vertices (states) and $(E_l)_{l \in \Lambda}$ are binary relations defining the edge labels. A graph is said to be *deterministic* if, for each relation E_l, $(u, v) \in E_l$ and $(u, w) \in E_l$ imply $v = w$. MSO formulas are built up from atoms of the forms $x_i = x_j$, $X_k(x_j)$, and $E_l(x_i, x_j)$ by means of the Boolean connectives $\vee$ and $\neg$ and the existential quantification over first-order variables $x_i, x_j, \ldots$, interpreted as single vertices, and second-order ones $X_k, \ldots$, interpreted as sets of vertices. The semantics of an MSO formula is defined in the standard way [21]. For a given MSO formula $\varphi(x_1, \ldots, x_n, X_1, \ldots, X_m)$, with free variables $x_1, \ldots, x_n, X_1, \ldots, X_m$, we write $\mathcal{G} \vDash \varphi[v_1, \ldots, v_n, V_1, \ldots, V_m]$ whenever φ holds in the structure $\mathcal{G}$ with the interpretation v_i for x_i, for $1 \leq i \leq n$, and V_j for X_j, for $1 \leq j \leq m$. In the following, we shall adopt a simplified, but expressively equivalent, set-up where all variables are second-order and atomic formulas are of the forms $X_i \subseteq X_j$ and $E_l(X_i, X_j)$. The decision problem for a given structure $\mathcal{G}$ is the problem of establishing, for any MSO sentence φ, whether $\mathcal{G} \vDash \varphi$. We shall focus our attention on expanded graph structures $(\mathcal{G}, \bar{V})$, where

$\bar{V} = (V_1, \ldots, V_m)$, with $V_j \subseteq \mathcal{D}om(\mathcal{G})$ for $1 \leq j \leq m$. The decision problem for expanded structures $(\mathcal{G}, \bar{V})$ is the problem of establishing, for any MSO formula $\varphi(X_1, \ldots, X_m)$, whether $\mathcal{G} \vDash \varphi[\bar{V}]$. The set of all sentences (resp. formulas) that hold in a structure $\mathcal{G}$ (resp. $(\mathcal{G}, \bar{V})$) is called the *MSO theory* of $\mathcal{G}$ (resp. $(\mathcal{G}, \bar{V})$), denoted by $MTh(\mathcal{G})$ (resp. $MTh(\mathcal{G}, \bar{V})$). $MTh(\mathcal{G})$ (resp. $MTh(\mathcal{G}, \bar{V})$) is said to be decidable iff there is an effective way to test whether any MSO sentence (resp. formula) ϕ belongs to $MTh(\mathcal{G})$ (resp. $MTh(\mathcal{G}, \bar{V})$). As a matter of fact, any expanded structure $(\mathcal{G}, \bar{V})$ can be encoded into a Σ-*colored* graph $\mathcal{G}_{\bar{V}}$, with $|\Sigma| = 2^m$, called the *canonical representation* of $\bar{V}$. Each color $c \in \Sigma$ is a subset of $\{1, \ldots, m\}$: for any vertex $v \in \mathcal{D}om(\mathcal{G})$, the color of v is the set of all and only the indexes i such that $v \in V_i$.

Trees. For any $k > 0$, let $[k]$ be the set $\{1, \ldots, k\}$. A k-*ary (Σ-colored) tree* is a $[k]$-labeled Σ-colored graph whose domain is a *prefix-closed* language over $[k]$, and whose edge relations are such that $(u, v) \in E_l$ iff $v = ul$, for every $l \in [k]$. Given a tree $\mathcal{T}$, we denote by $\mathcal{T}(v)$ the color of the vertex v. The *frontier* $\mathcal{F}r(\mathcal{T})$ of $\mathcal{T}$ is the prefix-free language $\{u \in \mathcal{D}om(\mathcal{T}) : \forall l \in [k]. \; ul \notin \mathcal{D}om(\mathcal{T})\}$. In this paper, we mainly deal with *full* trees, namely, trees such that if $(u, ul) \in E_l$ for some $l \in [k]$, then $(u, ui) \in E_i$ for every $i \in [k]$. Though the standard notion of full tree includes both empty trees and singletons, it is convenient to exclude them. A *path* of $\mathcal{T}$ is a (finite or infinite) word u such that every finite prefix of u belongs to $\mathcal{D}om(\mathcal{T})$. Given a path u of $\mathcal{T}$, we denote by $\mathcal{T}|u$ the sequence of colors associated with the vertices of u (formally, the finite or infinite sequence $\mathcal{T}(u_0)\mathcal{T}(u_1)\mathcal{T}(u_2)\ldots$, where u_i denotes the i-character prefix $u[1..i]$ of u). A *branch* is a maximal path, namely, a path which is not a proper prefix of any word in $\mathcal{D}om(\mathcal{T})$. We denote the set of all (finite or infinite) branches by $\mathcal{B}ch(\mathcal{T})$.

Tree Automata. A k-*ary Rabin tree automaton* over the alphabet Σ is a quadruple $M = (S, I, E, AP)$, where S is a finite set of states, $I \subseteq S$ is a set of initial states, $E \subseteq S \times \Sigma \times S^k$ is a transition relation, and AP is a finite set of accepting pairs (L_i, U_i), with $L_i, U_i \subseteq S$ [20]. Given an infinite complete k-ary (Σ-colored) tree $\mathcal{T}$, a *run* of the automaton M on $\mathcal{T}$ is any infinite complete k-ary (S-colored) tree $\mathcal{R}$ such that $(\mathcal{R}(u), \mathcal{T}(u), \mathcal{R}(u1), \ldots, \mathcal{R}(uk)) \in E$ for every $u \in \mathcal{D}om(\mathcal{R})$. We say that $\mathcal{R}$ is *successful*, and thus $\mathcal{T}$ is *accepted* by M, if $\mathcal{R}(\varepsilon) \in I$ and, for every branch u, there exists (L_i, U_i) such that $\mathcal{I}nf(\mathcal{R}|u) \cap L_i = \emptyset$ and $\mathcal{I}nf(\mathcal{R}|u) \cap U_i \neq \emptyset$, where $\mathcal{I}nf(\alpha)$ is the set of elements that occur infinitely often in α. We further denote by $\mathcal{I}mg(\alpha)$ the set of elements that occur in α. The language $\mathscr{L}(M)$ is the set of all trees accepted by M.

3   An Automaton-Based Approach to Decidability

In this section, we develop an automaton-based method to decide MSO theories of infinite (complete) deterministic trees. It can be viewed as a generalization of Carton and Thomas' method, which exploits noticeable properties of *residually ultimately periodic words* to decide MSO theories of labeled linear orderings [7].

As a first step, we show how to reduce the decision problem for the considered MSO theories to the acceptance problem for Rabin tree automata. Rabin's Theorem [20] establishes a strong correspondence between MSO formulas satisfied by an expanded tree structure $(\mathcal{T}, \bar{V})$ and Rabin tree automata accepting its canonical representation $\mathcal{T}_{\bar{V}}$: for every formula $\varphi(\bar{X})$, we can compute a Rabin tree automaton M (and, conversely, for every Rabin tree automaton M, we can compute a formula $\varphi(\bar{X})$) such that $\mathcal{T} \vDash \varphi[\bar{V}]$ iff $\mathcal{T}_{\bar{V}} \in \mathscr{L}(M)$. Let us denote by $Acc(\mathcal{T}_{\bar{V}})$ the problem of deciding, for any given Rabin tree automaton, whether it recognizes $\mathcal{T}_{\bar{V}}$. We have that

$$MTh(\mathcal{T}, \bar{V}) \text{ is decidable} \quad \text{iff} \quad Acc(\mathcal{T}_{\bar{V}}) \text{ is decidable.}$$

By exploiting the closure under intersection and the decidability of the emptiness problem for Rabin tree automata, one can easily show that the problem $Acc(\mathcal{T}_{\bar{V}})$ is decidable for any *regular* tree $\mathcal{T}_{\bar{V}}$ (a regular tree is a tree containing only finitely many non-isomorphic subtrees). In the following, we shall extend the class of trees for which this acceptance problem turns out to be decidable. We introduce the class of *residually regular trees* and we solve their acceptance problem by reducing them to equivalent regular trees (according to a suitable notion of tree equivalence).

Let us preliminarily introduce some tools for tree manipulation [17] (for the sake of simplicity, hereafter we shall omit the subscript $\bar{V}$, thus writing $\mathcal{T}$ for $\mathcal{T}_{\bar{V}}$).

Definition 1. *Let $\mathcal{T}$ be a k-ary tree, $U \subseteq \mathcal{F}r(\mathcal{T})$, and $(\mathcal{R}_u)_{u \in U}$ be a family of k-ary trees. We denote by $\mathcal{T}[u/\mathcal{R}_u]_{u \in U}$ the tree resulting from the simultaneous substitution in $\mathcal{T}$ of each node $u \in U$ by $\mathcal{R}_u$.*

Definition 2. *For every pair of (full) k-ary Σ-colored trees $\mathcal{T}_1$ and $\mathcal{T}_2$ and every color $c \in \Sigma$, the concatenation $\mathcal{T}_1 \cdot_c \mathcal{T}_2$ is the tree resulting from the simultaneous substitution of all the c-colored leaves of $\mathcal{T}_1$ by $\mathcal{T}_2$, namely, the (full) k-ary Σ-colored tree $\mathcal{T}_1[u/\mathcal{T}_2]_{u \in U}$, where $U = \{u \in \mathcal{F}r(\mathcal{T}_1) : \mathcal{T}_1(u) = c\}$.*

It is not difficult to show that the operator $\cdot_c$ is not associative. We assume that it associates to the left. Definition 2 can be generalized to the case of *infinite* concatenations. Given an infinite sequence $(c_n)_{n \in \mathbb{N}}$ of colors in Σ and an infinite sequence $(\mathcal{T}_n)_{n \in \mathbb{N}}$ of full k-ary (Σ-colored) trees, the infinite concatenation $\mathcal{S} = \mathcal{T}_0 \cdot_{c_0} \mathcal{T}_1 \cdot_{c_1} \ldots$ is defined as follows: $\mathcal{D}om(\mathcal{S}) = \bigcup_{n \in \mathbb{N}} \mathcal{D}om(\mathcal{S}_n)$, where $\mathcal{S}_0 = \mathcal{T}_0$, $\mathcal{S}_{n+1} = \mathcal{S}_n \cdot_{c_n} \mathcal{T}_{n+1}$, and $\mathcal{S}(u) = c$ if and only if $\mathcal{S}_n(u) = c$ for all, but finitely many, n. A *factorization* is a finite or infinite concatenation $\mathcal{T}_0 \cdot_{c_0} \mathcal{T}_1 \cdot_{c_1} \ldots$ (we denote infinite concatenations by $\prod_{i \in \mathbb{N}} (\mathcal{T}_i)_{c_i}$). A factorization is *ultimately periodic* if every $\mathcal{T}_n$ is a regular full tree and there are two positive integers p and q (called respectively *prefix* and *period*) such that, for every $n \geq p$, $c_n = c_{n+q}$ (if c_{n+q} exists) and $\mathcal{T}_n = \mathcal{T}_{n+q}$ (if $\mathcal{T}_{n+q}$ exists). The following proposition links ultimately periodic factorizations to regular trees [17].

Proposition 1. *A full tree $\mathcal{T}$ is regular iff it has an ultimately periodic factorization.*

From Proposition 1, it immediately follows that $Acc(\mathcal{T})$ is decidable for any infinite (complete) deterministic tree $\mathcal{T}$ generated by an ultimately periodic factorization.

3.1   Residually Regular Trees

We now show how to reduce the acceptance problem for a large class of infinite (complete) deterministic trees to the acceptance problem for equivalent (according to a suitable notion of tree equivalence $\equiv_M$) regular trees. As a preliminary step, we introduce the notion of (finite or infinite) partial run of a Rabin tree automaton $M = (S, I, E, AP)$: a *partial run* of M on a full, finite or infinite, (Σ-colored) tree $\mathcal{T}$ is a full (S-colored) tree $\mathcal{P}$ such that (i) $Dom(\mathcal{P}) = Dom(\mathcal{T})$ and (ii) $(\mathcal{P}(v), \mathcal{T}(v), \mathcal{P}(v1), \dots, \mathcal{P}(vk)) \in E$, for every $v \in Dom(\mathcal{P}) \setminus Fr(\mathcal{P})$.

Definition 3. *Given a Rabin tree automaton $M = (S, I, E, AP)$ over Σ, and two full (Σ-colored) trees $\mathcal{T}_1$ and $\mathcal{T}_2$, $\mathcal{T}_1 \equiv_M \mathcal{T}_2$ holds iff, for every partial run $\mathcal{P}_1$ of M on $\mathcal{T}_1$, there exists a partial run $\mathcal{P}_2$ of M on $\mathcal{T}_2$ (and vice versa) such that*

1. *$\mathcal{T}_1(\varepsilon) = \mathcal{T}_2(\varepsilon)$ and $\mathcal{P}_1(\varepsilon) = \mathcal{P}_2(\varepsilon)$;*
2. *for every $v \in Fr(\mathcal{T}_1)$, there exists $u \in Fr(\mathcal{T}_2)$ such that $\mathcal{T}_1(v) = \mathcal{T}_2(u)$, $\mathcal{P}_1(v) = \mathcal{P}_2(u)$, and $Img(\mathcal{P}_1|v)) = Img(\mathcal{P}_2|u)$, and vice versa;*
3. *for any infinite branch $v \in Bch(\mathcal{T}_1)$, there exists an infinite branch $u \in Bch(\mathcal{T}_2)$ such that $Inf(\mathcal{P}_1|v) = Inf(\mathcal{P}_2|u)$, and vice versa.*

The equivalence $\equiv_M$ satisfies the following properties [17].

Theorem 1. *It holds that:*

1. *$\equiv_M$ has finite index;*
2. *for every pair of factorizations $\mathcal{T}_0 \cdot_{c_0} \mathcal{T}_1 \cdot_{c_1} \dots$ and $\mathcal{T}'_0 \cdot_{c_0} \mathcal{T}'_1 \cdot_{c_1} \dots$ such that $\mathcal{T}_i \equiv_M \mathcal{T}'_i$ for every i, we have $\mathcal{T}_0 \cdot_{c_0} \mathcal{T}_1 \cdot_{c_1} \dots \equiv_M \mathcal{T}'_0 \cdot_{c_0} \mathcal{T}'_1 \cdot_{c_1} \dots$;*
3. *for every pair of $\equiv_M$-equivalent infinite (complete) trees $\mathcal{T}_1, \mathcal{T}_2$, we have that $\mathcal{T}_1 \in \mathcal{L}(M)$ iff $\mathcal{T}_2 \in \mathcal{L}(M)$ (in such a case we say that $\mathcal{T}_1$ and $\mathcal{T}_2$ are indistinguishable by automaton M).*

It is worth pointing out that the proposed notion of equivalence can be easily tailored to different kinds of automata, such as, for instance, Muller and parity tree automata.

Taking advantage of Theorem 1, we identify a large class of deterministic trees, that we call residually regular trees, whose acceptance problem is decidable. We say that an infinite sequence $\mathcal{S} = \mathcal{T}_0 \mathcal{T}_1 \mathcal{T}_2 \dots$ of finite full trees is 1-residually ultimately periodic if, for every Rabin tree automaton M, one can compute an ultimately periodic sequence $\mathcal{S}' = \mathcal{T}'_0 \mathcal{T}'_1 \mathcal{T}'_2 \dots$ of finite trees such that $\mathcal{T}_i \equiv_M \mathcal{T}'_i$, for all i. We call 1-residually regular trees those trees that are obtained by concatenating the trees in a 1-residually ultimately periodic sequence. The notion of 1-residually ultimately periodic factorization can be extended to level n, with n being any countable ordinal, by no longer considering finite trees but level $n' < n$ residually regular trees. For every countable ordinal n, n-residually regular trees can be defined as follows, where we denote by $[i]_{p,q}$ either i or $p + ((i - p) \bmod q)$, depending on whether $i < p$ or not.

Definition 4. *Given a countable ordinal n, a factorization $\mathcal{T}_0 \cdot_{c_0} \mathcal{T}_1 \cdot_{c_1} \cdots$ is n-residually ultimately periodic iff the following two conditions hold:*

1. *for every i, either $\mathcal{T}_i$ is a finite full tree or we can provide an n'-residually ultimately periodic factorization of $\mathcal{T}_i$, with $n' < n$;*
2. *for any Rabin tree automaton M, there exist two positive integers p and q (called* prefix *and* period *of the factorization with respect to $\equiv_M$) such that $c_i = c_{[i]_{p,q}}$ and $\mathcal{T}_i \equiv_M \mathcal{T}_{[i]_{p,q}}$, for every i.*

An n-residually regular tree is a tree enjoying an n-residually ultimately periodic factorization. A residually ultimately periodic factorization is an n-residually ultimately periodic factorization, for some countable ordinal n. A residually regular tree is a tree enjoying a residually ultimately periodic factorization.

It is worth noticing that the above definition allows residually ultimately periodic factorizations to encompass residually regular factors of any arbitrary level. For instance, we can start with some factors $\mathcal{T}_0, \mathcal{T}_1, \mathcal{T}_2, \ldots$ which respectively are level $1, 2, 3, \ldots$ residually regular, and concatenate them to build an ω-residually regular tree; then, we can concatenate ω-residually regular trees to obtain an $(\omega + 1)$-residually regular tree, and so on.

In order to reduce the decision problem for (n-)residually regular trees to regular trees, we introduce the notion of $\equiv_M$-*regular form*. Such a notion is defined by transfinite induction on n, given a Rabin tree automaton M and an n-residually ultimately periodic factorization. Precisely, an $\equiv_M$-regular form of a 1-residually ultimately periodic factorization $\prod_{i \in \mathbb{N}} (\mathcal{T}_i)_{c_i}$ is a tree $\prod_{i \in \mathbb{N}} (\mathcal{T}_i')_{c_i}$, where $\mathcal{T}_i' = \mathcal{T}_{[i]_{p,q}}$ and p and q are respectively a prefix and a period of the factorization with respect to $\equiv_M$. For any countable ordinal $n > 1$, an $\equiv_M$-regular form of an n-residually ultimately periodic factorization $\prod_{i \in \mathbb{N}} (\mathcal{T}_i)_{c_i}$ is a tree $\prod_{i \in \mathbb{N}} (\mathcal{T}_i')_{c_i}$, where, depending on whether $\mathcal{T}_i$ is finite or not, $\mathcal{T}_i'$ is either $\mathcal{T}_{[i]_{p,q}}$ or an $\equiv_M$-regular form of an n'-residually ultimately periodic factorization of $\mathcal{T}_{[i]_{p,q}}$, with $n' < n$ and p and q being respectively a prefix and a period of the factorization with respect to $\equiv_M$. It is easy to verify that an $\equiv_M$-regular form of a residually ultimately periodic factorization $\prod_{i \in \mathbb{N}} (\mathcal{T}_i)_{c_i}$ is a *regular* tree which is $\equiv_M$-equivalent to the tree generated by $\prod_{i \in \mathbb{N}} (\mathcal{T}_i)_{c_i}$. Furthermore, the factorization of an $\equiv_M$-regular form is computable from a given n-residually ultimately periodic factorization $\mathcal{S}$, which can be finitely represented by a function mapping an integer $i \in \mathbb{N}$ to (an n'-residually, with $n' < n$, ultimately periodic factorization of) the i-th factor of $\mathcal{S}$. Hence, we have the following theorem [17].

Theorem 2. *Let $\mathcal{T}$ be the infinite (complete) deterministic tree resulting from an n-residually ultimately periodic factorization $\prod_{i \in \mathbb{N}} (\mathcal{T}_i)_{c_i}$, M be a Rabin tree automaton, and $\mathcal{T}'$ be an $\equiv_M$-regular form of $\prod_{i \in \mathbb{N}} (\mathcal{T}_i)_{c_i}$. We have that $\mathcal{T} \in \mathscr{L}(M)$ iff $\mathcal{T}' \in \mathscr{L}(M)$.*

The upshot of such a result is that residually regular trees enjoy a decidable acceptance problem and hence a decidable MSO theory.

3.2   Properties of Residually Ultimately Periodic Factorizations

We now identify some structural properties that allow us to easily build residually ultimately periodic factorizations. The resulting framework somehow generalizes previous results by Zhang [24] and Carton and Thomas [7]. Let $T_{k,\Sigma}^{full}$ denote the language of all full k-ary Σ-colored trees. For any Rabin tree automaton M, the equivalence $\equiv_M$ induces an homomorphism from the infinite groupoid (i.e., a set endowed with a binary operation) $(T_{k,\Sigma}^{full}, \cdot_c)$ to the finite groupoid $([T_{k,\Sigma}^{full}]_{/\equiv_M}, \cdot_c)$. Given a groupoid $(G, \cdot)$, an element $g \in G$, and a number $n \in \mathbb{N}$, we denote by g^{n+1} the n-fold iteration of $\cdot g$ applied to g, namely, $g^{n+1} = g \cdot g \cdot \ldots \cdot g$. We define ultimately periodic functions with respect to finite groupoids.

Definition 5. A function $f : \mathbb{N} \rightarrow \mathbb{N}$ is ultimately periodic with respect to finite groupoids (residually ultimately periodic for short) if, for every finite groupoid $(G, \cdot)$ and every $g \in G$, there exist $p \geq 0$ and $q > 0$ such that $g^{f(n)+1} = g^{f([n]_{p,q})+1}$, that is, $(g^{f(n)+1})_{n \in \mathbb{N}}$ is a ultimately periodic sequence.

We say that a function is *effectively* residually ultimately periodic iff, for every groupoid $(G, \cdot)$ and every $g \in G$, it is possible to compute a prefix p and a period q of the ultimately periodic sequence $(g^{f(n)+1})_{n \in \mathbb{N}}$. As a simple example, the identity function is effectively residually ultimately periodic. From now on, we restrict our attention to effectively residually ultimately periodic functions, which can be characterized as follows.

Proposition 2. A function $f : \mathbb{N} \rightarrow \mathbb{N}$ is (effectively) residually ultimately periodic iff for all $l \geq 0$ and $r > 0$, one can compute $p \geq 0$ and $q > 0$ such that $[f(n)]_{l,r} = [f([n]_{p,q})]_{l,r}$.

Definition 6. A function $f : \mathbb{N} \rightarrow \mathbb{N}$ has unbounded infimum if it holds that $\lim\inf_{n \rightarrow \infty} f(n) = \infty$. In this case, we assume that, for any k, we can compute n_0 such that $f(n) \geq k$ for all $n \geq n_0$.

The following theorem provides a number of ways to build residually ultimately periodic functions [17]. Examples of generated functions are n^2, 2^n, $2^n - n^2$, n^n, $n!$, and the exponential tower $2^{2^{\cdot^{\cdot^{2}}}}$.

Theorem 3. Let f and g be residually ultimately periodic functions. The following functions are residually ultimately periodic as well:

1. **(Sum)** $f + g$;
2. **(Difference)** $f - g$, provided that it has unbounded infimum;
3. **(Product)** $f * g$;

4. **(Quotient)** h defined by $h(n) = \lfloor \frac{f(n)}{d} \rfloor$, with $d > 0$;
5. **(Exponentiation)** f^g, provided that it has unbounded infimum;
6. **(Exponential tower)** h defined by $h(0) = 1$ and $h(n+1) = b^{h(n)}$, with $b > 0$;
7. **(Generalized sum)** h defined by $h(n) = \sum_{i=0}^{n-1} f(i)$;
8. **(Generalized product)** h defined by $h(n) = \prod_{i=0}^{n-1} f(i)$;
9. **(Substitution)** $g \circ f$.

The next theorem shows how one can combine (colored) trees to obtain residually ultimately periodic factorizations [17]. In particular, case *1.* links residually ultimately periodic functions to residually ultimately periodic trees; case *2.* states that by interleaving the factors of residually ultimately periodic factorizations we obtain again a residually ultimately periodic factorization; case *3.* gives the possibility of periodically grouping the factors of a given factorization; case *4.* is useful to recursively define the factors of a residually ultimately periodic factorization.

Theorem 4. *Given an ultimately periodic sequence of colors $c_1 c_2 c_3 \ldots$, the factorization $\prod_{i \in \mathbb{N}} (T_i)_{c_i}$ is residually ultimately periodic in each of the following cases:*

1. **(Iteration)** *if $T_i = \mathcal{U}^{(f(i)+1)_c}$, where $\mathcal{U}^{(f(i)+1)_c}$ denotes the $f(i)$-fold iteration of $\cdot_c \mathcal{U}$ applied to $\mathcal{U}$, with $\mathcal{U}$ being a residually regular tree and f being a residually ultimately periodic function;*
2. **(Interleaving)** *if there is $q > 0$ such that, for every $0 \le i < q$, $\prod_{j \in \mathbb{N}} (T_{jq+i})_c$ is a residually ultimately periodic factorization;*
3. **(Grouping)** *if there is $q > 0$ and there is a residually ultimately periodic factorization $\prod_{j \in \mathbb{N}} (\mathcal{U}_j)_c$ such that, for every $i \in \mathbb{N}$, $T_i = (\mathcal{U}_{iq} \cdot_c \mathcal{U}_{iq+1} \cdot_c \ldots \cdot_c \mathcal{U}_{iq+q-1})$;*
4. **(Recursion)** *if T_0 is a residually regular tree and there is a residually ultimately periodic factorization $\prod_{j \in \mathbb{N}} (\mathcal{U}_j)_c$ such that $T_{i+1} = \mathcal{U}_i \cdot_c (T_i \cdot_d \mathcal{U}_i) \cdot_c (T_i \cdot_d \mathcal{U}_i) \cdot_c \ldots$.*

4   Some Applications of the Proposed Method

In the following, we apply the proposed method to decide the theories of two meaningful tree structures. Futhermore, we provide an embedding of some representative graphs of the so-called Caucal hierarchy [9], namely, tree generators for MSO interpretations, into our framework. We first recall the basic notions of unfolding and MSO interpretation [22].

Definition 7. *Let $\mathcal{G} = (S, (E_l)_{l \in \Lambda})$ be a graph structure and let $v_0 \in S$ be a designated vertex of $\mathcal{G}$. The unfolding of $\mathcal{G}$ from v_0, denoted by $Unf(\mathcal{G}, v_0)$, is a tree structure $(S', (E'_l)_{l \in \Lambda})$, where S' is the set of all the finite paths of the form $v_0 l_0 v_1 \ldots l_{n-1} v_n$, and E'_l is the set of all the pairs of paths of the form $(v_0 l_0 v_1 \ldots l_{n-1} v_n, v_0 l_0 v_1 \ldots l_{n-1} v_n l v_{n+1})$.*

Notice that the unfolding of any finite graph is (isomorphic to) a regular tree. Moreover, unfoldings from MSO definable vertices preserve the decidability of the

MSO theories of graph structures [14]. Another transformation which preserves decidability is the MSO interpretation, which is defined as follows.

Definition 8. *Given a graph structure* $\mathcal{G} = (S, (E_l)_{l \in \Lambda})$ *and a finite set of labels* Γ, *an MSO interpretation of* $\mathcal{G}$ *in* Γ *is a family* $(\varphi_l)_{l \in \Gamma}$ *of MSO formulas over* $\mathcal{G}$. *It gives raise to a graph* $\mathcal{G}' = (S', (E'_l)_{l \in \Gamma})$, *where, for each* $l \in \Sigma$, $E'_l = \{(v, w) \in S \times S : \mathcal{G} \models \varphi_l[v, w]\}$, *and* $S' \subseteq S$ *is the set of all vertices occurring in the edge relations* E'_l.

As a first example of application of our approach, consider the semi-infinite line $\mathcal{L}$ with forward edges, backward edges and loops (cf. Figure 1), which belongs to the Caucal hierarchy, and its unfolding from the leftmost vertex.

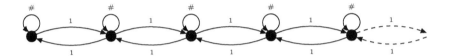

Fig. 1. The semi-infinite line $\mathcal{L}$

We provide an alternative proof of the decidability of the MSO theory of the unfolding of $\mathcal{L}$. The unfolded graph can be embedded into the infinite complete $\{w, b\}$-colored tree $\mathcal{T}$ of Figure 2. Black nodes b correspond to nodes of the original structure, while white nodes w are added to complete the tree. For the sake of readability, we adopt $\{1, \bar{1}, \#\}$ instead of $\{1, 2, 3\}$ as the set of edge labels. By adding an auxiliary third color c to manage concatenation, a factorization $\prod_{i \in \mathbb{N}}(\mathcal{T}_i)_c$ of $\mathcal{T}$ can be inductively defined as follows (see the dashed regions in Figure 2):

- $\mathcal{T}_0 = \mathcal{U} \cdot_w \mathcal{W}$;
- $\mathcal{T}_{i+1} = \mathcal{U} \cdot_w (\mathcal{T}_i \cdot_c \mathcal{U}) \cdot_w (\mathcal{T}_i \cdot_c \mathcal{U}) \cdot_w \ldots$,

where $\mathcal{U} = \prod_{j \in \mathbb{N}}(b\langle w, b, c \rangle)_b$ (we denote by $b\langle w, b, c \rangle$ the full finite ternary tree with a b-colored root and 3 leaves colored by w, b, and c, respectively) and $\mathcal{W}$ is the infinite complete ternary $\{w\}$-colored tree. From Theorem 4 (case 4.), it follows that such a factorization is residually ultimately periodic. This accounts for the decidability of $MTh(\mathcal{T})$.

As a second example, consider the infinite binary $\{w, b\}$-colored tree $\mathcal{T}_{tow}$ such that $\mathcal{T}_{tow}(u) = b$ iff $u = 1^n 0^m$, with $m < tow(n)$, where tow is the exponential tower defined by $tow(0) = 1$ and $tow(n + 1) = 2^{tow(n)}$ (cf. Figure 3). In [6], Carayol and Wöhrle show that such a tree does not belong to the Caucal hierarchy, but it enjoys a decidable MSO theory. We give an alternative proof of the decidability of $MTh(\mathcal{T}_{tow})$ by providing a residually ultimately periodic factorization of $\mathcal{T}_{tow}$. A factorization $\prod_{i \in \mathbb{N}}(\mathcal{T}_i)_c$ of $\mathcal{T}_{tow}$ can be defined as follows (see the dashed regions in Figure 3):

- $\mathcal{T}_0 = b\langle w, c \rangle \cdot_w \mathcal{W}$;
- $\mathcal{T}_i = b\langle b, c \rangle \cdot_b (b\langle b, w \rangle \cdot_w \mathcal{W})^{(tow(i)-1)_b} \cdot_b \mathcal{W}$ for $i \geq 1$,

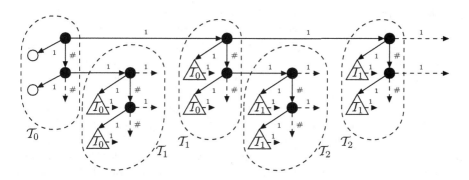

Fig. 2. The tree $\mathcal{T}$ embedding the unfolding of $\mathcal{L}$

where $\mathcal{W}$ is the infinite complete binary $\{w\}$-colored tree. From Theorem 4 (case 1.), it follows that such a factorization is residually ultimately periodic, and thus $MTh(\mathcal{T}_{tow})$ is decidable.

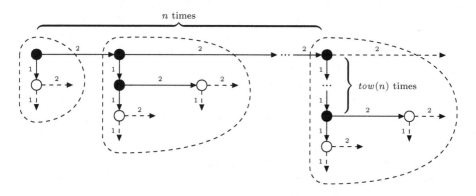

Fig. 3. The residually regular tree $\mathcal{T}_{tow}$

We conclude the section by showing that residually regular trees allow us to capture a relevant subclass of the graphs in the Caucal hierarchy [9]. The level 0 of the Caucal hierarchy consists of all the finite graphs. At level $n + 1$, we find all the graphs which are obtained from level n graphs by applying an unfolding followed by an MSO interpretation. Since both unfoldings and MSO interpretations preserve decidability, the resulting hierarchy contains only graphs with a decidable MSO theory. In [6], Carayol and Wöhrle show that, for each level of the Caucal hierarchy, there exists a representative graph, called generator, from which all the other graphs belonging to that level can be obtained by the application of the basic operations of rational marking and MSO interpretation. These generators are closely related to the 'tree generators' introduced by Cachat to simulate games on higher order pushdown systems [5]. The level 1 tree generator $\mathcal{C}_1$ is the infinite complete binary tree.

The level 2 tree generator $\mathcal{C}_2$ is the tree obtained from $\mathcal{C}_1$ by adding reverse edges and a loop for each vertex (labeled by fresh symbols, e.g., $\bar{1}, \bar{2}, \#$), and then by unfolding the resulting graph from its root. $\mathcal{C}_3$ is obtained by applying the same operation (which we shortly denote by $MSOUnf$) to $\mathcal{C}_2$, and so on. Since $MSOUnf$ is an MSO interpretation followed by an unfolding, tree generators belong to the Caucal hierarchy. Tree generators can be embedded into residually regular trees as follows. First, $\mathcal{C}_1$ can be viewed as a uniformly colored tree and thus it obviously is a residually regular tree. Then, by generalizing the construction used in the case of the semi-infinite line, one can prove that the class of residually regular trees is closed under $MSOUnf$ [17]. As matter of fact, we need to slightly modify the definition of $MSOUnf$ to operate inside the class of *full* trees; however, this is a trivial generalization which preserves all results about decidability and expressiveness of tree generators.

5   Conclusions

In this paper we devised an automaton-based method that allows us to solve the decision problem for the MSO theories of several deterministic tree structures. First, by taking advantage of well-known results from automata theory, we reduced the problem to the acceptance problem for Rabin tree automata. Then, we introduced the class of residually regular trees, which extends that of regular trees, and we showed that one can solve the acceptance problem for this family of trees by reducing it to the acceptance problem for equivalent regular trees. Finally, we applied the proposed method to some meaningful examples of tree structures.

The proposed method generalizes the one developed by Carton and Thomas to decide the theory of the linear order $(\mathbb{N}, <)$ extended with suitable unary relations, that is, those relations which are encoded by residually ultimately periodic words [7]. Since any ω-word over a finite alphabet Σ can be seen as an infinite 1-ary Σ-colored tree and string concatenation is definable in terms of tree concatenation, the notion of residually regular tree subsumes that of residually ultimately periodic word. Furthermore, some interesting binary relations over the linear order $(\mathbb{N}, <)$ turn out to be MSO definable in terms of residually regular trees. As an example, in [17, 18] we give an alternative decidability proof for the theory of the linear order $(\mathbb{N}, <)$ extended with the flip function [16, 22]. Finally, many trees in the Caucal hierarchy [9] can be embedded into residually regular trees. This last fact hints at the possibility of establishing a connection between our approach and the transformational one developed by Caucal for deciding MSO theories of infinite graphs.

We are currently trying to determine whether or not any deterministic tree in the Caucal hierarchy can be embedded into a suitable residually regular tree. We already know that the converse does not hold, since there exist some deterministic trees, such as, for instance, $\mathcal{T}_{tow}$ (cf. Section 4), which do not belong to the Caucal hierarchy, but can be handled by our method. We are also investigating the possibility of extending the proposed automaton-based framework to manage non-deterministic trees. To this end, we are looking for a more general notion of tree equivalence based on more expressive automata, such as, for instance, the automata on tree-like structures used in [23].

References

[1] K. Barthelmann. On equational simple graphs. Technical Report 9, UniversitSt Mainz, Institut fnr Informatik, 1997.

[2] J.R. Bnchi. On a decision method in restricted second order arithmetic. In *Proceedings of the International Congress on Logic, Methodology and Philosophy of Science*, pages 1–11. Stanford University Press, 1960.

[3] A. Blumensath. Prefix-recognizable graphs and monadic second-order logic. Technical Report AIB-06-2001, RWTH Aachen, 2001.

[4] A. Blumensath and E. Gradel. Automatic structures. In *Logic in Computer Science*, pages 51–62, 2000.

[5] T. Cachat. Higher order pushdown automata, the Caucal hierarchy of graphs and parity games. In *Proceedings of the 30th International Colloquium on Automata, Languages, and Programming*, volume 2719 of *LNCS*, pages 556–569, 2003.

[6] A. Carayol and S. Wöhrle. The Caucal hierarchy of infinite graphs in terms of logic and higher-order pushdown automata. In *Proceedings of the 23rd Conference on Foundations of Software Technology and Theoretical Computer Science*, volume 2914 of *LNCS*, pages 112–123. Springer, 2003.

[7] O. Carton and W. Thomas. The monadic theory of morphic infinite words and generalizations. *Information and Computation*, 176:51–65, 2002.

[8] D. Caucal. On the regular structure of prefix rewriting. *Theoretical Computer Science*, 106:61–86, 1992.

[9] D. Caucal. On infinite terms having a decidable monadic theory. In *Proceedings of the 27th International Symposium on Mathematical Foundations of Computer Science*, volume 2420 of *LNCS*, pages 165–176. Springer, 2002.

[10] D. Caucal. On infinite transition graphs having a decidable monadic theory. *Theoretical Computer Science*, 290:79–115, 2003.

[11] B. Courcelle. The monadic second-order logic of graphs II: Infinite graphs of bounded tree width. *Mathematical Systems Theory*, 21:187–221, 1989.

[12] B. Courcelle. Graph rewriting: An algebraic and logic approach. In J. Van Leeuwen, editor, *Handbook of Theoretical Computer Science*, pages 193–242. Elsevier, 1990.

[13] B. Courcelle. Monadic second-order graph transductions: a survey. *Theoretical Computer Science*, 126:53–75, 1994.

[14] B. Courcelle and I. Walukiewicz. Monadic second-order logic, graph coverings, and unfoldings of transition systems. *Annals of Pure and Applied Logic*, 92:35–62, 1998.

[15] C.C. Elgot and M.O. Rabin. Decidability and undecidability of extensions of second (first) order theory of (generalized) successor. *Journal of Symbolic Logic*, 31(2):169–181, 1966.

[16] A. Montanari, A. Peron, and A. Policriti. Extending Kamp's theorem to model time granularity. *Journal of Logic and Computation*, 12(4):641–678, 2002.

[17] A. Montanari and G. Puppis. Decidability of MSO theories of tree structures. Research Report 01, Dipartimento di Matematica e Informatica, Universita di Udine, Italy, 2004.

[18] A. Montanari and G. Puppis. Decidability of the theory of the totally unbounded ω-layered structure. In *Proceedings of the 11th International Symposium on Temporal Representation and Reasoning (TIME)*, pages 156–160, 2004.

[19] D. Muller and P. Schupp. The theory of ends, pushdown automata, and second-order logics. *Theoretical Computer Science*, 37:51–75, 1985.

[20] M.O. Rabin. Decidability of second-order theories and automata on infinite trees. *Transactions of the American Mathematical Society*, 141:1–35, 1969.

[21] W. Thomas. Languages, automata, and logic. In G. Rozemberg and A. Salomaa, editors, *Handbook of Formal Languages*, volume 3, pages 389–455. Springer, 1997.

[22] W. Thomas. Constructing infinite graphs with a decidable MSO-theory. In *Proceedings of the International Symposium on Mathematical Foundations of Computer Science*, LNCS, pages 113–124. Springer, 2003.

[23] I. Walukiewicz. Monadic second-order logic on tree-like structures. *Theoretical Computer Science*, 275:311–346, 2002.

[24] G. Zhang. Automata, boolean matrices, and ultimate periodicity. *Information and Computation*, 152(1):138–154, 1999.

Distributed Algorithms for Coloring and Domination in Wireless Ad Hoc Networks

Srinivasan Parthasarathy[1] and Rajiv Gandhi[2]

[1] Department of Computer Science, University of Maryland, College Park,
MD 20742, Research supported by NSF Award CCR-0208005
sri@cs.umd.edu

[2] Department of Computer Science, Rutgers University, Camden, NJ 08102
rajivg@camden.rutgers.edu

Abstract. We present fast distributed algorithms for coloring and (connected) dominating set construction in wireless ad hoc networks. We present our algorithms in the context of Unit Disk Graphs which are known to realistically model wireless networks. Our distributed algorithms take into account the loss of messages due to contention from simultaneous interfering transmissions in the wireless medium.

We present randomized distributed algorithms for (conflict-free) Distance-2 coloring, dominating set construction, and connected dominating set construction in Unit Disk Graphs. The coloring algorithm has a time complexity of $O(\Delta \log^2 n)$ and is guaranteed to use at most $O(1)$ times the number of colors required by the optimal algorithm. We present two distributed algorithms for constructing the (connected) dominating set; the former runs in time $O(\Delta \log^2 n)$ and the latter runs in time $O(\log^2 n)$. The two algorithms differ in the amount of local topology information available to the network nodes.

Our algorithms are geared at constructing Well Connected Dominating Sets (WCDS) which have certain powerful and useful structural properties such as low size, low stretch and low degree. In this work, we also explore the rich connections between WCDS and routing in ad hoc networks. Specifically, we combine the properties of WCDS with other ideas to obtain the following interesting applications:

- An online distributed algorithm for collision-free, low latency, low redundancy and high throughput broadcasting.
- Distributed capacity preserving backbones for unicast routing and scheduling.

1   Introduction

Wireless ad hoc networks are composed of a set of mobile nodes which communicate with one another over a shared wireless channel. Unlike wired networks,

---

[2] Part of this work was done when the author was a student at the University of Maryland and was supported by NSF Award CCR-9820965. Research also supported by Rutgers University's Research Council grant.

K. Lodaya and M. Mahajan (Eds.): FSTTCS 2004, LNCS 3328, pp. 447–459, 2004.

nodes in an ad hoc network do not rely on a pre-existing communication infrastructure. Instead, they communicate either directly with each other or with the help of intermediate nodes in the network. The distributed, wireless and self-configuring nature of ad hoc networks render them useful for several applications such as mobile battlefields, disaster relief, sensing and monitoring. However, the lack of a fixed communication infrastructure introduces several challenging and interesting research issues in the design of communication protocols for these networks. Any communication protocol for ad hoc networks should also contend with the issue of interference in the wireless medium. When two or more nodes transmit a message to a common neighbor at the same time, the common node will not receive any of these messages. In such a case, we say that a collision has occurred at the common node.

Coloring and connected domination are two fundamental primitives with several applications in the wireless context. In wireless networks, we seek a conflict-free coloring of the nodes such that two nodes which belong to the same color class may transmit simultaneously without resulting in collisions. Clearly, such a coloring has natural applications to collision-free wireless scheduling. In order to overcome the lack of a fixed routing infrastructure, several researchers have also proposed construction of a *virtual backbone* in ad hoc networks. A virtual backbone typically consists of a small subset of nodes in the network which gather and maintain information such as local topology and traffic conditions. This information can be made use of by higher level protocols for providing efficient communication services. Connected Dominating Sets (CDS) are the earliest structures proposed as candidates for virtual backbones in ad hoc networks [9, 8, 20].

Both coloring and (connected) dominating set construction are classical problems which have received tremendous attention in the literature. In general, all existing distributed algorithms for these problems can be classified into two categories. The first category of algorithms are fast sub-linear time algorithms which do *not* consider message losses due to collisions. Further, these all algorithms model the network as an arbitrary undirected graph; both these assumptions render them unsuitable for wireless ad hoc networks. The second category of algorithms are (slower) linear time algorithms. These algorithms can be implemented such that only a single node in the network transmits at any time and hence no collisions occur during the course of the algorithm. A linear time algorithm does not exploit the massive parallelism available in the ad hoc network and is unsuitable for dynamic network conditions displayed by ad hoc networks.

In this work, we focus on developing fast distributed algorithms for coloring and (connected) dominating set construction in wireless ad hoc networks. Specifically, we view the following as the main contributions of this work.

1.1 Our Contributions

- **Incorporating Wireless Interference:** We present distributed algorithms for conflict-free coloring, dominating set construction and connected dominating sets in the context of wireless networks. While several distributed algorithms exist for coloring and domination in arbitrary graphs, we use Unit Disk Graphs which realistically model wireless networks. Further, our algorithms handle wireless interference; we take into account the loss of messages at a node due to collisions from simultaneous neighboring transmissions. We are not aware of any work which study these problems under message losses due to wireless collision.

- **Distributed Coloring:** We present a distributed conflict-free (D2) coloring of nodes in the network. This primitive arises naturally in many applications such as broadcast scheduling and channel assignment in wireless networks. In general, the colors could represent time slots or frequencies assigned to the nodes. Minimizing the number of colors used in the coloring is very desirable for these applications, but is known to be NP-hard [19]. Our algorithm runs in time $O(\Delta \log^2 n)$, where Δ is the maximum degree and n is the number of network nodes and uses $O(\Delta)$ colors for the D2-coloring; this is at most $O(1)$ times the number of colors used by an optimal algorithm.

- **Distributed (Connected) Dominating Set:** We present distributed algorithms for dominating set and connected dominating set construction where require knowledge of only local topology and global network parameters such as size and the maximum degree. We present two algorithms: a D2-coloring based algorithm and a broadcast based algorithm which utilizes the work of Gandhi *et al.* [10]. The coloring based algorithm requires each node to know the maximum degree Δ and the total number of network nodes n and runs in time $O(\Delta \log^2 n)$. The broadcast based algorithm requires each node to know their three-hop topology and runs in time $O(\log^2 n)$. All these algorithms incorporate message losses due to collisions from interfering transmissions.

- **Wireless Routing Applications:** The distributed CDS algorithms presented in this paper are geared at constructing CDSs with certain powerful structural properties such as low size, low stretch and low degree (henceforth, we refer to such a CDS as a Well Connected Dominating Sets (WCDS)). The work by Alzoubi [1] deals with a linear-time distributed construction of WCDS in ad hoc networks. In this paper, we also explore the rich connections between WCDS and routing in wireless networks. Specifically, we combine the structural properties of WCDS with other ideas to obtain the following interesting applications:
  - An online distributed algorithm for collision-free, low latency, low redundancy and high throughput broadcasting.
  - Distributed capacity preserving backbones for unicast routing and scheduling.

We note that our algorithms and analysis only require that nodes know a good estimate of the values of the network parameters n and Δ instead of their exact values. Such estimates are easy to obtain in many practical scenarios. For instance, consider the scenario where n nodes with unit transmission radii are randomly placed in a square grid of area n. In this case, the maximum degree

$\Delta = \Theta(\frac{\log n}{\log \log n})$ with high probability. Due to lack of space, we omit the proofs of all the claims presented in this paper. All the proofs appear in the full version of this work[1].

2   Background

2.1   Network and Interference Model

We model the network connectivity using a unit disk graph (UDG) $G = (V, E)$: the nodes in V are embedded in the plane. Each node has a maximum transmission range and an edge $(u, v) \in E$ if u and v are within the maximum transmission range of each other. We assume that the maximum transmission range is the same for all nodes in the network (and hence w.l.o.g., equal to one unit). Time is discrete and synchronous across the network; units of time are also referred to as time slots. Since the medium of transmission is wireless, whenever a node transmits a message, all its neighbors hear the message. If two or more neighbors of a node w transmit at the same time, w will be unable to receive any of those messages. In this case we also say that w experiences collision. In any time slot, a node can either receive a message, experience collision, or transmit a message but cannot do more than one of these. We work with the above interference model for ease of exposition and analysis. However, all the results presented in this paper easily extend to the so called **protocol model** [11] of interference also.

2.2   Definitions

We now describe the definitions and notations used in the rest of the paper. All the definitions below are with respect to the undirected graph $G = (V, E)$.

Connected Dominating Set (CDS): A set $W \subseteq V$ is a dominating set if every node $u \in V$ is either in W or is adjacent to some node in W. If the induced subgraph of the nodes in W is connected, then W is a connected dominating set (CDS). A Minimum Connected Dominating Set (MCDS) is a CDS with the minimum number of nodes.

Maximal Independent Set (MIS): A set $M \subseteq V$ is an independent set if no two nodes in M are adjacent to each other. M is also a Maximal Independent Set (MIS) if there exists no set $M' \supseteq M$ such that M' is an independent set. Note that, in an undirected graph, every MIS is a dominating set.

Well Connected Dominating Set (WCDS): A CDS W is a WCDS if it satisfies the following properties:

(P1) Low Size: Let OPT be an MCDS for G. Then, $|W| \le k_1|OPT|$, where k_1 is a constant.

---

[1] Available at http://www.cs.umd.edu/~sri/distcoldom.ps

(P2) Low Degree: Let $G' = (W, E')$ be the graph induced by the nodes in W. For all $u \in W$, let $d'(u)$ denote the degree of u in G'. Then, $\forall u \in W, d'(u) \leq k_2$, where k_2 is a constant.

(P3) Low Stretch: Let $D(p, q)$ denote the length of the shortest path between p and q in G. Let $D_W(p, q)$ denote the length of the shortest path between p and q such that all the intermediate nodes in the path belong to W. Let $s_W \doteq \max_{\{p,q\} \in V} \frac{D_W(p,q)}{D(p,q)}$. Then, $s_W \leq k_3$, where k_3 is a constant.

Distance-k Neighborhood (Dk-Neighborhood): For any node u, the Dk-neighborhood of u is the set of all other nodes which are within k hops away from u.

Distance-2 Vertex Coloring (D2-Coloring): D2-coloring is an assignment of colors to the vertices of the graph such that every vertex has a color and two vertices which are D2-neighbors of each other are not assigned the same color. Vertices which are assigned the same color belong to the same *color class*. This definition is motivated by the fact that nodes belonging to the same color class can transmit messages simultaneously without any collisions.

3 Related Work

Coloring, dominating set construction and connected domination are classical problems which have been extensively studied in the literature. However, we are not aware of any distributed algorithms for these problems which incorporate the geometry and transmission characteristics of wireless networks. To the best of our knowledge, we are the first to study these problems for realistic multi-hop wireless network models (Unit Disk Graphs) and incorporate loss of messages due to collisions from interfering transmissions. In [19], it was shown that even in the case of UDGs, it is NP-hard to minimize the number of colors used in the D2-coloring. However, for many restricted graph classes such as UDGs, several *centralized* approximation algorithms exist which use within O(1) times the number of colors used by an optimal D2-coloring [19, 12, 18]. It was shown in [7] that computing an MCDS is NP-hard even for UDGs. Cheng *et al.*[6] propose a centralized polynomial time approximation scheme (PTAS) for approximating MCDS in UDGs. Several distributed approximation algorithms exist for computing MCDS in UDGs [21, 16, 2, 3, 5]. These algorithms produce a solution whose size is within O(1) times that of an MCDS. The time and message complexity of these algorithms are O(n) and O(n log n) respectively. All these algorithms have a stretch of O(n) [1]. Alzoubi *et al.*[4] proposed a distributed CDS algorithm for UDGs which has O(n) time and message complexity and which results in a CDS of size O(1) times MCDS. Alzoubi [1] showed that this CDS also has O(1) stretch. We improve upon the time complexity of all the above algorithms by proposing the first sub-linear time distributed algorithms for ad hoc networks which constructs a WCDS of size O(1) times MCDS and O(1) stretch. In particular, we note that in comparison with [1], we achieve a drastic decrease in the time complexity (from $O(n)$ to $O(\log^2 n)$) at the expense of a slight increase in the message complexity (from $O(n)$ to $O(n \log n)$). While the distributed algorithm presented in [1] holds for both synchronous and asynchronous models of communication, we restrict our focus only to the synchronous communication model and leverage in the design of our distributed algorithms.

4   Distributed D2-Coloring

In this section, we present our distributed D2-coloring algorithm for unit disk graphs. Our algorithm is modeled after Luby's distributed graph coloring algorithm [15]. The key technical difficulty in our algorithm as opposed to Luby's algorithm, lies in the the fact that simultaneous transmissions from neighboring nodes could result in collisions and hence loss of messages at a particular node. We handle this by probabilistic retransmission of the messages, and ensure that all messages are eventually received by their intended recepients with high probability. Further, while Luby's distributed coloring algorithm was a *D1-coloring of arbitrary graphs*, our algorithm is intended for *D2-coloring of unit disk graphs*. This allows us to exploit the geometric properties of UDGs to D2-color it using $O(\Delta)$ colors; this yields a $O(1)$ approximation for the number of colors.

Our algorithm is parametrized by three positive integers: c, t, and r (to be specified later). Each node u has a list of colors $L(u)$ which is initialized to $\{1, 2, \dots c\}$. Time is divided into *frames of length c time slots*. As in Luby's algorithm [15], our algorithm also proceeds in a synchronous round by round fashion. Typically, each round involves the following steps. Some of the yet-uncolored nodes choose a tentative colors for themselves. Some of these nodes will be successful, since none of their D2-neighbors would have chosen the same tentative color as themselves. In this case, the tentative color becomes the permanent color for these nodes. The unsuccessful nodes update their color list by removing the set of colors chosen by their successful D2-neighbors in this round and continue their attempts to color themselves in the future rounds. The coloring algorithm terminates after t rounds. We now present the details of a specific round.

Each round consists of four phases: **TRIAL, TRIAL-REPORT, SUCCESS** and **SUCCESS-REPORT**. The details of these phases are given below.

TRIAL: Only the yet-uncolored nodes participate in this phase. This phase consists of a single frame. At the beginning of this phase, each yet-uncolored node u *wakes up* or *goes to sleep* with probability $1/2$ respectively. If u is awake, it chooses a tentative color $color(u)$ uniformly at random from $L(u)$. Note that $L(u)$ is the list of colors available for node u in the current round and this list may change in the future rounds. Node u then transmits a TRIAL message $\{ID(u), color(u)\}$ at the time slot corresponding to $color(u)$ in this frame: for e.g., if u is awake and if $color(u) = 5$, u transmits the message $\{ID(u), 5\}$ at the fifth time slot of this frame. In general, the TRIAL message (and other types of messages below) may not reach all the neighbors of u due to collisions.

TRIAL-REPORT: This phase consists of r frames. At the beginning of this phase, *every* node u in the network prepares a TRIAL-REPORT message. This message is the concatenation of all the TRIAL messages received by u in this round. During *every* frame of this phase, u chooses a time slot independently at random within the frame, and broadcasts the TRIAL-REPORT message during this time.

SUCCESS: This phase consists of a single frame. At the beginning of this phase, every node u which is *awake*, determines if the tentative color it chose during the TRIAL phase is a safe color or not. Intuitively, $color(u)$ is safe if no node in its D2-neighborhood chose the same color as u. In our algorithm, u deems $color(u)$ to be safe if the following conditions hold:

1. u received a TRIAL-REPORT message from each of its neighbors.
2. Each TRIAL-REPORT message received by u contained the TRIAL message sent by u.

If the above conditions are met, $color(u)$ becomes the permanent color for u. In this case, u creates a SUCCESS message $\{ID(u), color(u)\}$ and broadcasts it to all its neighbors. This transmission is done at the time slot corresponding to $color(u)$ within this frame. In future rounds, u does not participate in the **TRIAL** and **SUCCESS** phases since it successfully colored itself in this round.
SUCCESS-REPORT: This phase is similar to the **TRIAL-REPORT** phase. The SUCCESS-REPORT message for *every* node u in the network is a concatenation of SUCCESS messages which were received by u in this round. This phase also consists of r frames. During *every* frame of this phase, u chooses a time slot independently at random within the frame and broadcasts its SUCCESS-REPORT message during this slot. Crucially, *at the end of this phase, any yet-uncolored node v removes from its list $L(v)$, any color found in the SUCCESS or SUCCESS-REPORT messages received by v in this round.* This ensures that, in the future rounds, v does not choose the colors of its successful D2-neighbors. This completes the description of a single round of the algorithm; the algorithm consists of t such rounds. We show that for an appropriate choice of parameters, our algorithm yields a $O(1)$-approximate D2-coloring for UDGs with high probability in $O(\Delta \log^2 n)$ time. Specifically, let the parameters have the following values: $c = k_1 \Delta$, $t = k_2 \log n$, and $r = k_3 \log n$, where k_1, k_2 and k_3 are constants. The following theorem holds.

Theorem 1. *The distributed D2-coloring algorithm computes a valid D2-coloring using $O(\Delta)$ colors in $O(\Delta \log^2 n)$ running time w.h.p. The number of colors used is at most $O(1)$ times the optimal coloring. All messages in the algorithm require at most $O(\Delta \log n)$ bits. The total number of messages transmitted by the algorithm is at most $O(n \log^2 n)$.*

5   Distributed Dominating Set Construction

In this section, we present our distributed dominating set algorithms for unit disk graphs. We note that any Maximal Independent Set (MIS) is also a dominating set in an undirected graph. Further, in the case of UDGs, it is well known that the number of nodes in *any* Maximal Independent Set (MIS) is at most five times the number of nodes in the minimum dominating set. Hence, a distributed MIS algorithm also yields a 5-approximate dominating set in UDGs. Henceforth, we focus on distributed MIS construction in UDGs.

5.1   D2-Coloring Based MIS Algorithm

We now present a simple D2-coloring based distributed MIS algorithm. Observe that if we have a D2-coloring of the nodes using c colors, we can build an MIS iteratively in c time slots as follows: during slot i, all nodes belonging to color class i attempt to join the MIS. A node joins the MIS if and only if none of its neighbors are currently part of the MIS. After joining the MIS, the node broadcasts a message to its neighbors indicating that it joined the MIS. Nodes transmitting during the same time slot belong to the same color class and hence do not share a common neighbor. For the same reason, none of the messages are lost due to collisions. Clearly, this stage requires exactly c time steps. Since the distributed D2-coloring algorithm of Section 4 colors the UDG using $O(\Delta)$ colors w.h.p. in $O(\Delta \log^2 n)$ time, we also have a distributed MIS algorithm which terminates correctly w.h.p. in $O(\Delta \log^2 n)$ time.

Theorem 2. *The D2-coloring based distributed algorithm constructs an MIS in $O(\Delta \log^2 n)$ time w.h.p and the total number of messages transmitted during the algorithm is $O(n \log^2 n)$.*

5.2   Broadcast Based MIS Construction

We now present our broadcast based distributed MIS algorithm, which makes use of knowledge of the Distance-2 topology, and constructs an MIS in $O(\log^2 n)$ time. Specifically, we assume that each node knows its D2-neighborhood and the edges between these nodes. As in Luby's distributed MIS algorithm [14], our algorithm also proceeds in a synchronous round by round fashion. The MIS is initially empty. Typically, some nodes are successful at the end of each round. A node is deemed successful if either the node joins the MIS or one of its neighbors joins the MIS. Successful nodes do not participate in the future rounds (except for forwarding messages), while remaining nodes continue their attempts to be successful in the future rounds. The MIS construction terminates after t such rounds.

During the algorithm, each node u maintains a status variable which is defined as follows: status(u)=in if u has joined the MIS; status(u)=out if any neighbor of u has joined the MIS; status(u)=$unsure$ otherwise. All nodes are initially *unsure* and become *in* or *out* of MIS during the course of the algorithm. Let V_i be the set of nodes whose status is *unsure* at the end of round $i - 1$. For any node $u \in V_i$, let $N_i(u) = N(u) \cap V_i$. Let MIS_i be the set of nodes which join MIS in round i.

There are four phases in each round of the algorithm: **TRIAL, CANDIDATE-REPORT, JOIN**, and **PREPARE**. We now present the details of these phases for a particular round i.

TRIAL: In this phase, each *unsure* node decides if it is a candidate for MIS_i. Specifically, each *unsure* node u chooses itself to be a candidate for joining MIS_i, with probability $\frac{1}{2(|N_i(u)|+1)}$. Node u will not be a candidate in this round with the complement probability. This phase does not required any message transmissions.

CANDIDATE-REPORT: This phase ensures that each node knows if there is a neighbor who is a candidate. This step consists of p time frames, each frame consisting of two slots. During *every* frame of this phase, each *candidate* node chooses one of the two slots independently at random and broadcasts a CANDIDATE message. Any node which receives a CANDIDATE message or experiences collision during this phase, knows that there is a neighboring candidate; otherwise it assumes that there is no neighboring candidate.

JOIN: This phase requires a single time slot. In this phase, some *unsure* nodes become either *in* or *out*. How should a candidate decide if it should join MIS_i (become *in*)? A candidate joins MIS_i if none of its neighbors are candidates for MIS_i, i.e., if it did not receive a CANDIDATE message during the previous phase. All nodes who joined MIS_i transmit a JOIN message. *unsure* nodes which receive a JOIN message or experience collision, change their status to *out*. Other *unsure* nodes do not change their status.

PREPARE: Each *unsure* node u computes $N_{i+1}(u)$ at the end of this phase. This phase consists of p time frames. Each frame is further subdivided into α sub-frames of length c. During *every* frame of this phase, each node in MIS_i, chooses independently at random, one of the α sub-frames. During this sub-frame, it broadcasts a PREPARE message using the algorithm in [10] to its D2-neighbors. The length of the sub-frame, c is the number of time steps required by [10] to transmit a message from a node to its D2-neighbors. The PREPARE message broadcast by a node simply consists of its ID. By the end of this phase, every *unsure* node knows all the nodes in its D2-neighborhood which joined MIS_i. Hence, it can easily compute $N_{i+1}(u)$.

The algorithm terminates after t such rounds. The theorem below claims that for an appropriate choice of parameters, the algorithm yields an MIS with high probability in time $O(\log^2 n)$. The analysis of this theorem involves a tricky charging argument which heavily relies on the geometry of UDGs.

Theorem 3. *The broadcast based distributed algorithm computes an MIS with high probability in $O(\log^2 n)$ time. Each message is at most $O(\log n)$ bits in length and the expected number of messages transmitted is $O(n \log n)$.*

6 Distributed Connected Domination

In this section, we present the results for our distributed connected dominating set algorithms for UDGs. Alzoubi [1] presented a centralized algorithm for constructing a CDS with a stretch of $O(1)$, size which is at most $O(1)$ times that of the minimum CDS, and has $O(1)$ degree. Henceforth, we will call a CDS with these properties as Well Connected Dominating Set (or WCDS). Alzoubi also presented a distributed implementation of his centralized algorithm which runs in linear time. The basic idea behind the centralized algorithm is as follows: we first compute an MIS by iteratively choosing vertices which are currently not in MIS and which do not currently have a neighbor in MIS. Since the input graph is an undirected graph, any maximal independent set is also a dominating set. Connectivity is handled as an orthogonal component as follows: every MIS node u is connected to every other MIS node v in its D3-neighborhood, using a shortest path between u and v. Nodes in the shortest paths along with the nodes in MIS constitute the CDS W.

We present two distributed implementations of this approach. Due to lack of space, the details of these implementations are presented in the full version. We note that in both the algorithms, the basic idea is for each node in the MIS to broadcast a message to its D3-neighborhood. After this step, each node in the MIS connects itself to every other node in the MIS which is at most three hops away, through a shortest path. The two implementations differ in how the MIS is computed and how this broadcasting is achieved. The first implementation uses the D2-coloring based scheme. The broadcasting is easily achieved in a collision-free manner since the D2-coloring also yields a natural collision-free schedule. The running time for this algorithm is $O(\Delta \log^2 n)$ and is dominated by the D2-coloring step. In the second implementation, the MIS is constructed via the broadcast algorithm discussed in Section 5.2. Here the broadcasting is achieved using the algorithm in [10]. This implementation has a running time of $O(\log^2 n)$ and is dominated by the MIS construction. As discussed in Section 5, these algorithms differ in extent of local topology information available to each node in the network.

7   Network-Wide Broadcasting

We now present our results pertaining to our broadcast algorithm. Due to lack of space, the details of the algorithm are presented in the full version. The basic idea behind the broadcast algorithm is to first construct a WCDS W, and obtain a valid D2-coloring of the WCDS. For ease of analysis, we assume that messages are generated only by nodes in W. Our algorithm requires that nodes in W have a valid D2-coloring using k colors. Let time be divided into frames of length k. Every node in the WCDS, retransmits a message after receiving it, in the first time slot in the following frame which corresponds to its own color. If there are multiple messages to be transmitted, the one with the lowest ID is chosen for transmission. This simple scheme guarantees that all nodes in the network receive all messages collision-free. In addition, this scheme optimizes the latency, the number of retransmissions, and the throughput of the broadcast to within a constant factor of their respective optimal values. We analyze the behavior of our broadcast algorithm under the following packet injection model.

Theorem 4. *The broadcast algorithm supports an long term rate of message generation, which is within $O(1)$ factor of the optimal rate. Further, the latency experienced by any message is at most $O(1)$ times the optimal latency for this message. All messages are received collision-free by all nodes in the network. In addition, the number of retransmissions for any message is at most $O(1)$ times the optimal number of retransmissions required to broadcast the message.*

8   Unicast Routing

In this section, we show that a WCDS is an efficient backbone for unicast routing in ad hoc networks. We derive our results in this section under the Distance-2 *edge* interference model (D2-model) [17, 18, 13]. We show that any routing algorithm could be modified to operate over a WCDS such that, the modified routing algorithm will use only the nodes in WCDS as intermediate nodes in the paths, *without incurring significant loss in the quality of the paths and schedules* when compared with the original algorithm. We formalize this intuition below.

Let $\mathcal{P} = \{p_1, \ldots p_n\}$ be a set of paths such that the maximum length of any path is d. We will refer to the elements of $\mathcal{P}$ as both paths and packets interchangeably. For any disk z, let $n(z)$ denote the number of edges in all the paths in $\mathcal{P}$ with an end point inside z. Let Z be the set of all disks on the plane with radius $1/2$. Let $c = \max_{z|z \in Z} n(z)$: i.e., c is the maximum number of edges in $\mathcal{P}$ which have an end point inside any fixed disk of radius $1/2$. We call d and c, the *dilation* and *congestion* of $\mathcal{P}$ respectively. A schedule S for $\mathcal{P}$ specifies the time at which every packet is transmitted collision-free along each edge in its path. The length of the schedule $|S|$ is the maximum latency of any packet in this schedule, i.e., the maximum time at which any packet traverses any edge. Observe that, under the D2-model, both c and d (and hence $\frac{c+d}{2}$) are lower bounds on the length of any schedule for $\mathcal{P}$. We now state the following surprising claim from [13].

Claim. Let OPT be an optimal collision-free schedule for $\mathcal{P}$ under the D2-model. Let $|OPT|$ denote the length of OPT (which is the maximum latency experienced by a packet in OPT). Then, $|OPT| = \Theta(c + d)$.

The following theorem holds.

Theorem 5. *There exists a set of paths $\mathcal{P}'$ such that each path in $\mathcal{P}$ can be replaced by an alternate path in $\mathcal{P}'$. Further, these paths are such that all their internal nodes are from the WCDS and congestion c' and dilation d' of the path system $\mathcal{P}'$ are such that $c' + d' = \Theta(c + d)$.*

Acknowledgments. We would like to thank V.S. Anil Kumar, Madhav Marathe and Aravind Srinivasan for several useful discussions.

References

1. K. M. Alzoubi. Connected dominating set and its induced position-less sparse spanner for mobile ad hoc networks. In *Proceedings of the Eighth IEEE Symposium on Computers and Communications*, June 2003.
2. K. M. Alzoubi, P.-J. Wan, and O. Frieder. Distributed heuristics for connected dominating sets in wireless ad hoc networks. *IEEE ComSoc/KICS Journal on Communication Networks*, 4:22–29, 2002.
3. K. M. Alzoubi, P.-J. Wan, and O. Frieder. Message efficient construction of non-trivial connected dominating sets in wireless ad hoc networks. *To appear in Special Issue of ACM Journal of Monet*, 2002.
4. K. M. Alzoubi, P.-J. Wan, and O. Frieder. Message-optimal connected-dominating-set construction for routing in mobile ad hoc networks. In *Proceedings of the Third ACM International Symposium on Mobile Ad Hoc Networking and Computing*, June 2002.
5. K. M. Alzoubi, P.-J. Wan, and O. Frieder. New distributed algorithm for connected dominating set in wireless ad hoc networks. *IEEE HICSS35*, 2002.
6. X. Cheng, X. Huang, D. Li, and D.-Z. Du. Polynomial-time approximation scheme for minimum connected dominating set in ad hoc wireless networks. Technical report.
7. B. Clark, C. Colbourn, and D. Johnson. Unit disk graphs. *Discrete Mathematics*, 86:165–177, 1990.
8. B. Das, R. Sivakumar, , and V. Bharghavan. Routing in ad-hoc networks using a virtual backbone. In *6th International Conference on Computer Communications and Networks (IC3N '97)*, pages 1–20, September 1997.
9. Bevan Das and Vaduvur Bharghavan. Routing in ad-hoc networks using minimum connected dominating sets. In *ICC (1)*, pages 376–380, 1997.
10. Rajiv Gandhi, Srinivasan Parthasarathy, and Arunesh Mishra. Minimizing broadcast latency and redundancy in ad hoc networks. In *Proceedings of the fourth ACM international symposium on Mobile ad hoc networking and computing*, pages 222–232. ACM Press, 2003.
11. Piyush Gupta and P. R. Kumar. The capacity of wireless networks. *IEEE Transactions on Information Theory*, 46(2):388–404, March 2000.
12. Sven O. Krumke, Madhav V. Marathe, and S. S. Ravi. Models and approximation algorithms for channel assignment in radio networks. *Wireless Networks*, 7(6):575–584, 2001.
13. V. S. Anil Kumar, Madhav V. Marathe, Srinivasan Parthasarathy, and Aravind Srinivasan. End-to-End Packet Scheduling in Ad Hoc Networks. To appear in ACM SODA 2004.
14. Michael Luby. A simple parallel algorithm for the maximal independent set problem. *SIAM Journal on Computing*, 15(4):1036–1053, November 1986.
15. Michael Luby. Removing randomness in parallel computation without a processor penalty. *Journal of Computer and System Sciences*, 47(2):250–286, 1993.
16. Madhav V. Marathe, Heinz Breu, Harry B. Hunt III, S. S. Ravi, and Daniel J. Rosenkrantz. Simple heuristics for unit disk graphs. *Networks*, 25:59–68, 1995.
17. S. Ramanathan. A unified framework and algorithm for channel assignment in wireless networks. *Wireless Networks*, 5(2):81–94, 1999.
18. Subramanian Ramanathan and Errol L. Lloyd. Scheduling algorithms for multihop radio networks. *IEEE/ACM Transactions on Networking (TON)*, 1(2):166–177, 1993.

19. Arunabha Sen and Ewa Melesinska. On approximation algorithms for radio network scheduling. In *Proceedings of the 35th Allerton Conference on Communication, Control and Computing*, pages 573–582, 1997.

20. R. Sivakumar, B. Das, and V. Bharghavan. Spine routing in ad hoc networks. *ACM/Baltzer Cluster Computing Journal (special issue on Mobile Computing)*, 1998.

21. P.-J. Wan, K. Alzoubi, and O. Frieder. Distributed construction of connnected dominating set in wireless ad hoc networks. In *IEEE INFOCOM*, 2002.

Monotone Multilinear Boolean Circuits for Bipartite Perfect Matching Require Exponential Size

Ashok Kumar Ponnuswami and H. Venkateswaran

College of Computing,
Georgia Institute of Technology,
Atlanta GA 30309, USA
{pashok, venkat}@cc.gatech.edu

Abstract. A monotone boolean circuit is said to be *multilinear* if for any AND gate in the circuit, the minimal representation of the two input functions to the gate do not have any variable in common. We show that multilinear boolean circuits for bipartite perfect matching require exponential size. In fact we prove a stronger result by characterizing the structure of the smallest multilinear boolean circuits for the problem. We also show that the upper bound on the minimum depth of monotone circuits for perfect matching in general graphs is $O(n)$.

1 Introduction

Since Razborov [7] showed a super-polynomial lower bound on the size of monotone circuits for perfect matching and established a super-polynomial gap between the power of general circuits and monotone circuits, there have been other functions in P [9] for which the gap has been shown to be exponential. But the lower bound for monotone circuits for perfect matching is still super-polynomial. It has been shown in [6] that monotone circuits for perfect matching require linear depth.

Let PM denote the problem of finding whether a graph has a perfect matching and let BPM denote the problem of finding whether a bipartite graph has a perfect matching. The upper bound on size of arithmetic circuits for permanent in [1] yields a $2^{O(n)}$ size monotone boolean circuit for BPM directly (replace the product and plus gates with AND and OR gates respectively) and can be generalized to an upper bound on size for PM also. But the depth of these circuits is $\Omega(n \log n)$. We show in Section 2 that linear depth monotone circuits can be constructed for PM.

Since attempts to show an exponential lower bound on the size of monotone circuits for BPM have not succeeded, it seems worthwhile to check if such a bound can be shown for restricted monotone circuits. In Section 3 we show that under two different restrictions on the function calculated by AND gates and OR gates, monotone circuits for BPM require exponential size. We call the circuits satisfying the restriction on the AND gates *multilinear* because of the

K. Lodaya and M. Mahajan (Eds.): FSTTCS 2004, LNCS 3328, pp. 460–468, 2004.
© Springer-Verlag Berlin Heidelberg 2004

similarity to the restriction of multilinearity in arithmetic circuits. As defined in [5], an arithmetic circuit is multilinear if at each gate the power of any variable in minimal representation of the polynomial computed is at most 1. Equivalently, for any product gate, the minimal representation of the polynomials of its two input gates have no variable in common. A recent result of Raz [5] shows a super-polynomial lower bound on multilinear arithmetic formulas for the permanent. Multilinearity for arithmetic circuits has been extensively studied for the lack of strong lower bounds for general arithmetic circuits and because they seem to be the most intuitive circuits for multilinear functions (see [4] and [5] for more references). We call a monotone boolean circuit *multilinear* if for any *AND* gate, the minimal representation of the of the two inputs to the gate do not have any variable in common. We say a monotone boolean circuit is in the *simplest form* if it satisfies the restriction on *OR* gates and a stronger restriction on *AND* gates than multilinearity. The circuits constructed in Section 2 and the circuits obtained from [1] for perfect matching are examples of circuits in the simplest form. It turns out that the smallest multilinear boolean circuits for *BPM* are also in the simplest form. The upper bound on size implied by Section 2 and the lower bound shown in Section 3 are very close showing that the analysis of the lower bound for monotone multilinear boolean circuits is quite tight. Since the circuits in the simplest form not only seem to be the most natural circuits for *PM* and *BPM*, but also attain the lower bound for multilinear boolean circuits and provide the best known upper bound on the size and depth of monotone circuits for these problems, it seems plausible to conjecture that these are the smallest monotone circuits for the perfect matching problem.

To the best of our knowledge, our lower bounds are not implied by any of the known lower bounds for arithmetic and boolean circuits. When a multilinear boolean circuit for BPM is converted to an arithmetic circuit in the natural way (by replacing the *AND* and *OR* gates by product and plus gates), it does not necessarily yield a multilinear arithmetic circuit for permanent because boolean circuits can use idempotence.

We use the notion of *minterm* defined in [2] to analyze the circuits. Our lower bounds use a direct argument for circuits computing *BPM*. One of the key lemmas (based on the idea that there are not "many" perfect matchings that do not have an edge crossing a "balanced" cut) is reminiscent of the tree separator theorem [3]. The tree separator theorem has had many applications such as small depth circuits for context-free language recognition [8] and showing the relationship between depth and size of monotone circuits (see [10]).

In what follows, we will assume that all circuits are monotone boolean circuits in which the *AND* and *OR* gates have fan-in 2. The inputs to the circuit correspond to edges of a graph G on a set $V = \{1, 2, \ldots n\}$ of n vertices, where n is even. That is, the input corresponding to pair $\{i, j\}$ is 1 if the edge is present in G and 0 otherwise.

2   Upper Bounds on Depth and Size of Monotone Boolean Circuits for PM

Let $S \subseteq V$ and S be even. A subset m of edges is said to be an S-matching if m is a matching with an edge incident on each vertex of S and no edge in m has one end point in S and the other in $V - S$ (m may contain edges that have both end-points in $V - S$). We say m is an exact S-matching if m is an S-matching and m has no edge incident on a vertex in $V - S$.

We first describe the depth upper bound for PM.

Theorem 1. PM has monotone circuits of $O(n)$ depth.

Proof. For the sake of simplicity of this construction, we assume $n = 2^k$, though the result can be proven for any even n. If $n = 2$, the construction is trivial. So assume $n > 2$. Suppose for each $S \subseteq V, |S| = n/2$, we are given a circuit C_S that evaluates to 1 iff there is a S-matching in the input graph G. If we take the AND of C_S and C_{S^c}, we get a circuit C_P that evaluates to 1 iff there is a perfect matching that does not cross the partition $P = \{S, S^c\}$. If we take the OR of all circuits corresponding to the partitions of V into two sets of $n/2$ vertices, we get a circuit C_V for perfect matching on V (see Figure 1). Since the number of partitions of V into $n/2$ vertices is $\frac{n!}{2!(n/2)!^2}$, the depth of the OR gates at the output of C_V is $\lfloor \log n! - \log 2! - 2\log(n/2)! \rfloor \le an + b$ where a and b are positive constants independent of n. Therefore the depth of C_V is $an + b + 1 + \max_S depth(C_S)$ where $depth(C_S)$ is the depth of C_S. The C_S may be recursively constructed the same way as C_V since C_S is a circuit for perfect matching on the graph induced by S. Therefore the depth of $C \le (an + b + 1) + (an/2 + b + 1) + \ldots = O(n)$. If n were not a power of 2, at each level of recursion, split the set of vertices into two sets of even sizes in the most balanced way. For example if $n = 36$, we need to consider all subsets of size 18 at the first level, all subsets of size 8 and 10 at the second level, all subsets of size 4 and 6 at the third level and so on. $\square$

The upper bound on size for PM obtained above is $n^{O(1)}2^{3n/2}$ as the level of recursion that contains the maximum number of gates is the second level with $O(\binom{n}{n/2}\binom{n/2}{n/4})$ gates. Since finding if there is a perfect matching in a bipartite graph on n vertices is the same as checking whether the permanent of the $n/2 \times n/2$ incidence matrix is not zero, we can obtain a upper bound of $n^{O(1)}2^{n/2}$ on size for BPM by replacing the product and sum gates in the arithmetic circuit for permanent given in [1]. The same approach can be generalized to obtain a better size upper bound for PM as follows. In the construction in Theorem 1, instead of considering partitions $\{S, S^c\}$ into the most balanced even sets, consider partitions such that S is a set of two vertices, one of which is the vertex of smallest index in V. Now the circuit for each S^c can be constructed recursively. At level 2, we need at most $\binom{n-1}{n-2}$ subcircuits to compute the different possible values for S^c. In general, at level i, we need at most $\binom{n-i}{n-2i}$ subcircuits. Solving for the value for i that maximizes $\binom{n-i}{n-2i}$, we get that the circuit constructed has size $O(2^{0.695n})$.

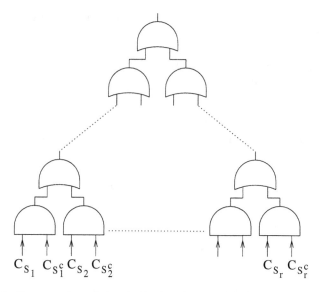

$$C_{S_1} \quad C_{S_1^c} C_{S_2} \quad C_{S_2^c} \qquad\qquad C_{S_r} \quad C_{S_r^c}$$

Fig. 1. Construction of circuit C_V for showing the depth upper bound

3   Lower Bound on Size of Restricted Monotone Circuits for *BPM*

A *minterm* of a monotone boolean function is a minimal set of variables that when set to 1, the function evaluates to 1 irrespective of the value of the variables. Let C be a circuit. Let g be a gate of C. The function computed by g is the boolean function representing the output of g in terms of the input gates. The set of minterms of g in circuit C, denoted by $minterm_C(g)$ (or $minterm(g)$ if the circuit is clear from the context) is the set of minterms of the function computed by g.

Throughout this section, we assume that the inputs to a circuit correspond to the edges of a bipartite graph G on a bipartition $\{V', V'^c\}$ of $V = \{1, 2, \ldots n\}$ into equal sets. That is, there is an input corresponding to each pair $(i, j) \in V' \times V'^c$ that is 1 if the edge between i and j is present in G and 0 otherwise. The *edge set* of gate g is the set of all edges that appear in some minterm of g. The *vertex set* of a subset m of the edges is the set of all end points of the edges in m. The *vertex set* of g is the vertex set of its edge set. The edge set and vertex set of a subcircuit of C are defined to be the respective values for the output gate of the subcircuit.

3.1   Lower Bound for Simple Circuits for BPM

A circuit is said to be *simple* if for any OR gate g in the circuit with input gates g_1 and g_2, the vertex sets of g, g_1 and g_2 are the same. It can be seen by induction that in a simple circuit, the vertex set of any minterm of a gate is the same as the vertex set of the gate. The statement is true for input gates. If it is true for the input gates g_1 and g_2 of an OR gate g, it is true for g as well since minterms of g are either minterms of g_1 or g_2. If the statement is true for the input gates g_1 and g_2 of an AND gate g, all the minterms of g have the same vertex set since any minterm of g is the union of some minterm of g_1 with some minterm of g_2 and all minterms of g_1 have the same vertex set, as do minterms of g_2.

Lemma 1. *Assume $n > 2$. Let C be a simple monotone circuit for BPM. For any perfect matching m, $\exists V_m \subseteq V$, $|V|/3 \leq |V_m| \leq 2|V|/3$ such that V_m is the vertex set of some gate g and m is a V_m-matching.*

Proof. Set $U = V$, $m' = m$ and let g be the output gate of C. At any stage later, we will ensure that (U, m', g) satisfy the following constraints:

(1) U is the vertex set of g.
(2) m' is a subset of m, m' is a minterm of g and U is the vertex set of m' (and hence m is a U-matching).

Also, let $U > 2|V|/3$, which is true initially when $U = V$. Since $|V| = n > 2$, the gate g can not be an input gate. If g is an OR gate, one of the two input gates g_1 or g_2 of g, say g_1, has m' as a minterm. Let $g \leftarrow g'$ and repeat. If g is an AND gate, let V_1 and V_2 be the vertex sets of its input gates g_1 and g_2 respectively. Without loss of generality, let $|V_1| \geq |V_2|$. There must be some minterm m_1 of g_1 and m_2 of g_2 such that $m' = m_1 \bigcup m_2$. From a remark above the lemma, we know that the vertex sets of m_1 and m_2 are V_1 and V_2 respectively, and hence $U = V_1 \bigcup V_2$. Therefore (V_1, m_1, g_1) satisfy conditions (1) and (2). If $|V|/3 \leq V_1 \leq 2|V|/3$, then V_1 is the required value for V_m. If not, $|V_1| > 2|V|/3$, since otherwise $|V_1| + |V_2| \leq 2|V|/3$, contradicting $|U| > 2|V|/3$. Since C has a finite depth, and input gates have vertex set of size 2, we will successfully find a value for V_m. □

The problem with proving the above lemma for general monotone circuits for BPM is that for a particular gate, there can be two minterms with different vertex sets. So we can not associate a "cut" with each gate such that none of its minterms crosses it.

Theorem 2. *Simple monotone circuits for BPM require exponential size.*

Proof. Let $n > 2$ and let C be a simple monotone circuit for perfect matching. Enumerate one set V_m satisfying the conditions of Lemma 1 for each possible perfect matching m on the bipartition $\{V', V'^c\}$. For each $U \subseteq V$ of size p, there are at most $(p/2)!\frac{n-p}{2}!$ perfect matchings that do not cross it (assuming G is a complete graph, this number is exactly $(p/2)!\frac{n-p}{2}!$ if U contains the same number of vertices from V' and V'^c and zero otherwise). Therefore, each $U \subseteq V, |V|/3 \leq |U| \leq 2|V|/3$ corresponds to at most $(n/6)!(n/3)!$ perfect matchings. Since the number of perfect matchings in a complete bipartite graph is $(n/2)!$, we must have enumerated

$$\frac{(n/2)!}{(n/6)!(n/3)!} = n^{\Omega(1)}2^{(n/2\log 3 - n/3)} = \Omega(2^{.459n})$$

distinct subsets of V, each of them corresponding to a different gate of C. Therefore, the number of gates in C is $\Omega(2^{.459n})$. □

3.2   Lower Bound for Multilinear Circuits for BPM

A circuit C is said to be *multilinear* if the edge set of any AND gate is the disjoint union of the edge set of its input gates. Unlike simple circuits, multilinear circuits are expressive enough to compute any monotone boolean function.

A circuit is said to be in the *simplest form* if it is simple and the vertex set of any AND gate is the disjoint union of the vertex set of its input gates. It can be seen that the circuits used to show upper bound on depth and size for PM were in the simplest form. Also note that circuits in simplest form are also multilinear.

Theorem 3. *A multilinear circuit of smallest possible size for BPM is also in the simplest form.*

Proof. Let C be a multilinear circuit for bipartite perfect matching on $\{V', V'^c\}$ of smallest possible size. We will define a *required vertex set* V_g for each gate g satisfying:

(1) If g is an AND gate with input gates g_1 and g_2, the required vertex of g is the disjoint union of the required vertex sets of g_1 and g_2.
(2) If g is an OR gate with input gates g_1 and g_2, the required vertex sets of g, g_1 and g_2 are the same.
(3) There is at least one minterm of g that is an exact V_g-matching.
(4) All minterms of g have an edge to each vertex in V_g.
(5) If the output from g is replaced by a new subcircuit that computes a function f such that any minterm m of f is the superset of some minterm m' of g, and all minterms of g that are exact V_g-matchings are also minterms of f, then C still computes the same function.

Intuitively, if an input gate g_1 to an OR gate g has no minterm that is an exact V_g-matching, we can replace the input from g_1 to g with a zero input without affecting the function calculated by the circuit. For gate g (and any other gate on the path from g to the output), the effect of this change is to increase the size of some minterms while some minterms drop out. But all minterms that are exact V_g-matchings are unaffected as they must have been minterms of the other input gate to g.

The required vertex set of the output gate is defined to be its vertex set V. It can be seen that it satisfies conditions (3)-(5). We define the required vertex set of a gate g_1 based on the required vertex set of its parents (gates to which g_1 supplies an input) in C. Each parent gate g of g_1 passes a *requirement*, a subset of V, to g_1 as defined below:

Case 1: g is an AND gate: By property (3), $\exists m \in minterm(g)$ such that m is an exact V_g-matching. Let g_2 be the other input gate to g. Therefore, $\exists m_1 \in$

$minterm(g_1)$ and $\exists m_2 \in minterm(g_2)$ such that $m = m_1 \bigcup m_2$ and $m_1 \bigcap m_2 = \emptyset$ (by multilinearity of C). The requirements passed to g_1 and g_2 are the vertex sets of m_1 and m_2, say V_1 and V_2, respectively. Hence, m_1 is an exact V_1-matching. Suppose some $m' \in minterm(g_1)$ does not have an edge to some $v \in V_1$. Then some subset m'' of $m' \bigcup m_2$ is a minterm of g. Also, m_2 does not have an edge to v since $m_1 \bigcup m_2$ was a $V_1 \bigcup V_2$-matching and m_1 has an edge to v. But then m'' does not have an edge to a vertex v in the required vertex set of g, contradicting (4) for g. Therefore, all $m' \in minterm(g_1)$ have an edge to each vertex of V_1.

This also means that any $m' \in minterm(g)$ which is an exact V_g-matching is produced by the disjoint union of $m_1' \in minterm(g_1)$ and $m_2' \in minterm(g_2)$ where m_1' and m_2' are exact V_1-matching and exact V_2-matching respectively (Since $m' = m_1' \bigcup m_2'$ is an exact V_g-matching, if m_1' is not an exact V_1-matching, then $\exists e_1 \in m_1'$ such that e_1 has an endpoint $v_2 \in V_2$. But m_2' has some edge e_2 incident on v_2. For $m_1' \bigcup m_2'$ to be a matching, e_1 and e_2 must be the same edge. But this contradicts the multilinearity of circuit C). Suppose we replace the input from g_1 to g in C with an input from a new subcircuit C_1 having output gate g_1' to get a circuit C'. Let g_1' satisfy the condition that $\forall m' \in minterm_{C'}(g_1'), \exists m \in minterm_C(g_1)$ such that $m \subseteq m'$, and if $m \in minterm_C(g_1)$ is an exact V_1-matching, then $m \in minterm_{C'}(g_1')$. Then if $m \in minterm_C(g)$ and m is an exact $V_1 \bigcup V_2$-matching, then $m \in minterm_{C'}(g)$ too. If $m \in minterm_{C'}(g)$ then $\exists m_1 \in minterm_{C'}(g_1')$ and $m_2 \in minterm_{C'}(g_2)$ such that $m = m_1 \bigcup m_2$. Since m_1 is the superset of some minterm of g_1 in C, m is the superset of some minterm in C. Therefore, by property (5) for g, C and C' compute the same function.

Case 2: g is an OR gate: Let g_2 be the other input gate to g. g passes its own required vertex set V_g as the requirement to g_1 and g_2. Suppose g_1 does not have any minterm that is an exact V_g-matching. Replace the input from g_1 to g with the zero input to get a circuit C' (This has the same affect as replacing the output from g with the output from g_2 and deleting g). If $m \in minterm_C(g)$ is an exact V_g-matching, then $m \notin minterm_C(g_1)$. Therefore $m \in minterm_C(g_2)$. This implies $m \in minterm_{C'}(g)$. If $m \in minterm_{C'}(g)$, then $m \in minterm_C(g_2)$. Therefore, $\exists m' \in minterm_C(g)$ such that $m' \subseteq m$. Therefore, by property (5) for g, C and C' are equivalent. Therefore C is not the smallest multilinear circuit for bipartite perfect matching on $\{V', V'^c\}$, a contradiction. Therefore g_1 and g_2 both have a minterm that is an exact V_g-matching.

Since minterms of g_1 are the superset of some minterm of g, all minterms of g_1 have an edge to every vertex in V_g.

Let the input from g_1 to g be replaced by an input from a new subcircuit C_1 with output gate g_1'. Also let all minterms of g_1 in C that are exact V_g-matchings be minterms of g_1', and if $m' \in minterm_{C'}(g_1')$, then $\exists m \in minterm_C(g_1)$ such that $m \subseteq m'$. Therefore if $m' \in minterm_{C'}(g)$, either $m' \in minterm_{C'}(g_1')$ or $m' \in minterm_C(g_2)$. In either case, $\exists m \in minterm_C(g)$ such that $m \subseteq m'$. Also if $m \in minterm_C(g)$ is an exact V_g-matching, then either $m \in minterm_C(g_1)$

or $m \in minterm_C(g_2)$. Therefore, $m \in minterm_{C'}(g)$. Therefore, by property (5) for g, C and C' are equivalent.

If for some gate g_1, all its parents pass the same requirement V_0, define V_0 to be the required vertex set for g_1. Conditions (3)-(5) are satisfied for g_1.

Suppose two parents g and g' of a gate g_1 pass different requirements V_1 and V_2 respectively. Without loss of generality, assume there exists vertex v satisfying $v \in V_1$, but $v \notin V_2$. Since g passed V_1 as requirement to g_1, all minterms of g_1 have an edge to v. But since g' passed V_2 as requirement to g_1, there exists a minterm m of g_1 that is an exact V_2-matching, and hence m does not have an edge to v, a contradiction. Therefore, all parents of g_1 pass the same requirement.

We will now show that the required vertex set of each gate is in fact its vertex set. Let g be a gate whose required vertex set is not the same as its vertex set. Therefore $\exists m \in minterm(g)$ with an edge e to a vertex outside its required vertex set. If g is an OR gate, one of its two input gates, say g', has m as a minterm. Since the required vertex sets of g and g' are the same, g' too has an edge to a vertex v outside its required vertex set. If g is an AND gate with inputs g_1 and g_2, then $\exists m_1 \in minterm(g_1)$ and $m_2 \in minterm(g_2)$ such that $m_1 \bigcup m_2 = m$. Let $e \in m_1$. Then g_1 has a minterm m_1 that has an edge to a vertex v outside its required vertex set (since the requirement passed by an AND gate to its input gate is a subset of its required vertex set). Since C has finite depth, we obtain a input gate whose required vertex set is not the same as its vertex set. But this is a contradiction of property (3).

Therefore, from conditions (1) and (2), multilinear circuit C was in fact in the simplest form too. $\square$

Corollary 1. *Multilinear circuits for BPM require exponential size.*

Proof. This is easily seen from Theorem 2 and Theorem 3, since circuits in simplest form are also simple. $\square$

References

1. Mark Jerrum and Marc Snir. Some exact complexity results for straight-line computations over semirings. *J. ACM*, 29:874–897, 1982.
2. Mauricio Karchmer and Avi Wigderson. Monotone circuits for connectivity require super-logarithmic depth. In *Proceedings of the twentieth annual ACM symposium on Theory of computing*, pages 539–550. ACM Press, 1988.
3. P. M. Lewis II, R. E. Stearns, and J. Hartmanis. Memory bounds for recognition of context-free and context-sensitive languages. In *Conf. Record Switching Circ. Theory and Log. Des.*, pages 191–202, 1965.
4. Noam Nisan and Avi Wigderson. Lower bounds on arithmetic circuits via partial derivatives. In *Proceedings of the 36th FOCS*, pages 16–25, 1996.
5. Ran Raz. Multi-linear formulas for permanent and determinant are of super-polynomial size. In *Electronic Colloquium on Computational Complexity*, volume 67, 2003.

6. Ran Raz and Avi Wigderson. Monotone circuits for matching require linear depth. In *ACM Symposium on Theory of Computing*, pages 287–292, 1990.

7. A. A. Razborov. Lower bounds on the monotone complexity of some boolean functions. *Doklady Akademii Nauk SSSR*, 281:798–801, 1985. In Russian. English translation in *Soviet Mathematics Doklady*, 31:354–357, 1985.

8. Walter L. Ruzzo. Tree-size bounded alternation. *Journal of Computer and System Sciences*, 21(2):218–235, 1980.

9. E. Tardos. The gap between monotone and non-monotone circuit complexity is exponential. *Combinatorica*, 8:141–142, 1988.

10. Ingo Wegener. *The complexity of Boolean functions*. John Wiley & Sons, Inc., 1987.

Testing Geometric Convexity

Luis Rademacher[**] and Santosh Vempala[**]

Mathematics Department and CSAIL, MIT
{lrademac, vempala}@math.mit.edu

Abstract. We consider the problem of determining whether a given set S in $\mathbb{R}^n$ is *approximately* convex, i.e., if there is a convex set $K \in \mathbb{R}^n$ such that the volume of their symmetric difference is at most $\epsilon \operatorname{vol}(S)$ for some given ϵ. When the set is presented only by a membership oracle and a random oracle, we show that the problem can be solved with high probability using $\operatorname{poly}(n)(c/\epsilon)^n$ oracle calls and computation time. We complement this result with an exponential lower bound for the natural algorithm that tests convexity along "random" lines. We conjecture that a simple 2-dimensional version of this algorithm has polynomial complexity.

1 Introduction

Geometric convexity has played an important role in algorithmic complexity theory. Fundamental problems (sampling, optimization, etc.) that are intractable in general can be solved efficiently with the assumption of convexity. The algorithms developed for these problems assume that the input is a convex set and are often not well-defined for arbitrary sets. Nevertheless, sampling-based approaches for optimization might be extendable to approximately convex sets, since there is hope that approximately convex sets can be sampled efficiently. This raises a basic question: How can we test if a given compact set in $\mathbb{R}^n$ is convex? Similarly, do short proofs of convexity or non-convexity of a set exist? Can one find these proofs efficiently?

To address these questions, we first need to decide how the set (called S henceforth) is specified. At the least, we need a membership oracle, i.e., a blackbox that takes as input a point $x \in \mathbb{R}^n$ and answers YES or NO to the question "Does x belong to S?" This is enough to prove that a set is not convex. We find 3 points $x, y, z \in R^n$ such that $x, z \in S$, $y \in [x, z]$ and $y \notin S$. Since a set is convex iff it is convex along every line, such a triple constitutes a proof of non-convexity.

On the other hand, how can we prove that a set *is* convex? Imagine the perverse situation where a single point is deleted from a convex set. We would have to test an uncountable number of points to detect the non-convexity. So we relax the goal to determining if a set is approximately convex. More precisely, given $0 < \epsilon \le 1$, either determine that S is not convex or that there is a convex set K such that

$$\operatorname{vol}(S \setminus K) + \operatorname{vol}(K \setminus S) \le \epsilon \operatorname{vol}(S) .$$

[**] Partially supported by NSF grant CCR-0307536

K. Lodaya and M. Mahajan (Eds.): FSTTCS 2004, LNCS 3328, pp. 469–480, 2004.

In words, the condition above says that at most an ϵ fraction of S has to be changed to make it convex. We will call this the problem of testing approximate convexity.

This formulation of the problem fits the *property testing* framework developed in the literature ([1]). In fact there has been some work on testing convexity of discrete 1-dimensional functions ([2]), but the general problem is open.

Testing approximate convexity continues to be intractable if S is specified just by a membership oracle. Consider the situation where a small part of S is very far from the rest. How do we find it? To counter this, we assume that we also have access to uniform random points in S, i.e., a random oracle[1]. (There are other alternatives, but we find this to be the cleanest). In this paper, we address the question of testing approximate convexity of a set given by a membership oracle and a random oracle. The complexity of an algorithm is measured by the number of calls to these oracles and the additional computation time.

We begin with a proof that the problem is well-defined, i.e., there exists a closest convex set. Then we give a simple algorithm with complexity $\mathsf{poly}(n)(c/\epsilon)^n$ for any set S in $\mathbb{R}^n$. The algorithm uses random sampling from a convex polytope as a subroutine. Next, we consider what is perhaps the most natural algorithm for testing approximate convexity: get a pair of random points from the set and test if the intersection of the line through them with S is convex. This is motivated by the following conjecture: If the intersection of S with "most" lines is convex, then S itself is approximately convex. Many property testing algorithms in the literature have this flavor, i.e., get a random subset and test if the subset has the required property. Surprisingly, it turns out that the number of tests needed can be *exponential* in the dimension. We construct an explicit family of sets for which the lines through most (all but an exponentially small fraction) pairs of points have convex intersections with the set (i.e., they intersect S in intervals), yet the set is far from convex. Finally, we conjecture that if "most" 2-dimensional sections of a set S are convex, then S is approximately convex.

2   Preliminaries

The following notation will be used. Let $S \subseteq \mathbb{R}^n$. If S is measurable, $\mathrm{vol}(S)$ denotes the volume of S. The convex hull of S is denoted $\mathrm{conv}(S)$. Let $\langle x, y \rangle = \sum_{i=1}^{n} x_i y_i$, the usual inner product in $\mathbb{R}^n$.

---

[1] A non-trivial example where testing approximate convexity makes sense and the oracles are naturally available is testing approximate convexity of the union of m convex bodies given by membership oracles. In this case, the individual membership oracles give a membership oracle for the union. Also, the membership oracles can simulate random oracles for every convex set (approximately, see [3]), and allow us to approximate the volumes of the convex bodies. Finally, by using a technique similar to the one used to approximate the number of satisfying assignments of a DNF formula (see [4], for example), one can simulate a random oracle for the union (approximately) by means of the individual membership and random oracles and the individual volumes, in time polynomial in m and the other parameters.

Let $A, B \subseteq \mathbb{R}^n$ be measurable sets. The *symmetric difference measure distance* (or simply, *distance*) between A and B is

$$d(A, B) = \mathrm{vol}(A \Delta B) .$$

Let $\mathcal{K}$ denote the set of all compact convex sets in $\mathbb{R}^n$ with nonempty interior, and the empty set.

Proposition 1. *Let $S \subseteq \mathbb{R}^n$ compact. Then $\inf_{C \in \mathcal{K}} d(S, C)$ is attained.*

Proof. The set $\mathcal{K}$ with distance d is a metric space. The selection theorem of Blaschke (see the appendix) implies that $\{C \in \mathcal{K}, C \subseteq \mathrm{conv}\, S\}$ is compact. Moreover, $d(S, \cdot) : \mathcal{K} \to \mathbb{R}$ is continuous. Also, it is sufficient to consider convex sets contained in $\mathrm{conv}\, S$, that is,

$$\inf_{C \in \mathcal{K}} d(S, C) = \inf_{C \in \mathcal{K}, C \subseteq \mathrm{conv}\, S} d(S, C) .$$

The last expression is the infimum of a continuous function on a compact set, thus it is attained. $\qquad\square$

Definition 2. *Given $S \subseteq \mathbb{R}^n$ compact, a set $C \in \mathrm{argmin}_{C \in \mathcal{K}} d(S, C)$ is called a closest convex set of S. S is said to be ϵ-convex iff $d(S, C) \leq \epsilon \,\mathrm{vol}(S)$.*

3   Algorithms for Testing Approximate Convexity

We are interested in the following algorithmic problem:

Let $S \subseteq \mathbb{R}^n$ be compact. We are given a *membership oracle* that given $x \in \mathbb{R}^n$ answers "YES" if $x \in S$ and "NO" if $x \notin S$; we also have access to a *random oracle* that when called gives a uniformly sampled random point from S. For any given $\epsilon > 0$, our goal is to determine either that S is ϵ-convex (output "YES") or that S is not convex (output "NO").

In this section, we will give a randomized algorithm for the problem. We will prove that the algorithm works with probability at least $3/4$. This can be easily boosted to any desired $1 - \delta$ while incurring an additional factor of $O(\ln(1/\delta))$ in the complexity.

3.1   The One-Dimensional Case

One-dimensional algorithm

INPUT: Access to membership and random oracles of $S \subseteq \mathbb{R}$.

1. Get $12/\epsilon$ points from the random oracle. Let C be their convex hull (the interval containing them).
2. Choose $12/\epsilon$ random points in C. Check if they are all in S using the membership oracle. If so, output "YES", else output "NO".

Theorem 3. *With probability at least 3/4, the one-dimensional algorithm determines that S is not convex or that S is ϵ-convex.*

Proof. Clearly, if S is convex then the algorithm answers "YES". So assume that
S is not ϵ-convex. We say that the first step succeeds if we get at least one point
in the leftmost $\epsilon/4$ fraction of S and another point in the rightmost $\epsilon/4$ fraction
of S. The first step fails with probability at most $2(1 - \epsilon/4)^{12/\epsilon} \leq 2/e^3$. Suppose
the first step succeeds. Then,

$$\mathrm{vol}(S \setminus C) \leq \mathrm{vol}(S)\frac{\epsilon}{2} \ .$$

This implies that

$$\mathrm{vol}(C \setminus S) \geq \mathrm{vol}(S)\frac{\epsilon}{2} \ .$$

From this, we get

$$\begin{aligned}
\mathrm{vol}(C \setminus S) &\geq \max\left\{\frac{\epsilon}{2}\mathrm{vol}(S), \mathrm{vol}(C) - \mathrm{vol}(S)\right\} \\
&= \mathrm{vol}(C)\max\left\{\frac{\epsilon}{2}\frac{\mathrm{vol}(S)}{\mathrm{vol}(C)}, 1 - \frac{\mathrm{vol}(S)}{\mathrm{vol}(C)}\right\} \ .
\end{aligned} \tag{1}$$

Given that $\epsilon > 0$, the expression

$$\max\left\{\frac{\epsilon}{2}\alpha, 1 - \alpha\right\}$$

is minimized as a function of α when $\frac{\epsilon}{2}\alpha = 1 - \alpha$, i.e., for $\alpha = \frac{2}{\epsilon+2}$. Thus, from
Equation (1) we get

$$\mathrm{vol}(C \setminus S) \geq \frac{\epsilon}{2 + \epsilon}\,\mathrm{vol}(C) \ .$$

That is, conditioned on the success of the first step, with probability at least
$1 - (1 - \epsilon/3)^{12/\epsilon} \geq 1 - 1/e^4$ the algorithm answers "NO". Thus, overall the
algorithm answers "NO" with probability at least $(1 - 1/e^4)(1 - 2/e^3) \geq 3/4$.
$\qquad\square$

3.2   The General Case

Here we consider the problem in $\mathbb{R}^n$. It is not evident that the time complexity
of the problem can be made independent of the given set S (that is, depending
only on ϵ and the dimension). The following algorithm shows such independence
($m = m(\epsilon, n)$ will be chosen later).

---

n-dimensional algorithm
INPUT: Access to membership and random oracles of $S \subseteq \mathbb{R}^n$.

1. Get m random points from S. Let C be their convex hull.
2. Get $4/\epsilon$ random points from S. If any of them is not in C, output "NO".
3. Get $6/\epsilon$ random points from C. If each of them is in S according to the
   membership oracle, then output "YES", else output "NO".

Checking if a point y belongs to C is the same as answering whether y can be expressed as a convex combination of the m points that define C. This can be done by solving a linear program. The third step requires random points from C, which is a convex polytope. Sampling convex bodies is a well-studied algorithmic problem and can be done using $O^*(n^3)$ calls to a membership oracle (see [3], for example).

To prove the correctness of the algorithm we will use the following lemmas (the first is from [5] and the second is paraphrased from [6]).

Lemma 4. *Let* $C = \mathrm{conv}\{X_1, \ldots, X_m\}$, *where the* X_i's *are independent uniform random samples from a convex body* K. *Then for any integer* $t > 0$, $\mathbb{E}\big((\mathrm{vol}(C)/\mathrm{vol}(K))^t\big)$ *is minimized iff* K *is an ellipsoid.*

Lemma 5. *Let* $B_n \subseteq \mathbb{R}^n$ *be the unit ball. Let* $C = \mathrm{conv}\{X_1, \ldots, X_m\}$, *where the* X_i's *are independent uniform random samples from* B_n. *There exists a constant* c *such that, for* $m = (cn/\epsilon)^n$,

$$\mathbb{E}\big(\mathrm{vol}(B_n \setminus C)\big) \leq \epsilon\,\mathrm{vol}(B_n) \ .$$

Theorem 6. *Using* $m = (224cn/\epsilon)^n$ *random points and* $\mathrm{poly}(n)/\epsilon$ *membership calls, the* n-*dimensional algorithm determines with probability at least* $3/4$ *that* S *is not convex or that* S *is* ϵ-*convex.*

Proof. First, assume that S is convex. We want to show that the algorithm outputs "YES" with probability at least $3/4$. Let $X = \mathrm{vol}(S \setminus C)/\mathrm{vol}(S)$. Then by Lemma 4, $\mathbb{E}(X)$ is maximized when K is a ball and using Lemma 5 with our choice of m, we get that

$$\mathbb{E}(X) \leq \frac{\epsilon}{224n} \ .$$

By Markov's inequality, with probability at least $6/7$,

$$\mathrm{vol}(S \setminus C) \leq \frac{\epsilon}{32}\,\mathrm{vol}(S) \ .$$

Given this, Markov's inequality implies that the algorithm will not stop at step 2 with probability at least $3/4$: in step 2, if we let Y be the number of points not in C then

$$\mathbb{E}(Y) \leq \frac{\epsilon}{32}\frac{4}{\epsilon} = \frac{1}{8} \ ,$$

and therefore, by Markov's inequality,

$$\mathbb{P}(\text{algorithm outputs ``NO'' in step 2}) = \mathbb{P}(Y \geq 1) = \mathbb{P}\big(Y \geq 8\mathbb{E}(Y)\big) \leq \frac{1}{8} \ .$$

Thus, the algorithm outputs "YES" with probability at least $\frac{6}{7}\frac{7}{8} = \frac{3}{4}$.

Next, if S is not ϵ-convex, the analysis can be divided into two cases after the first step: either $\mathrm{vol}(S \setminus C) \geq \mathrm{vol}(S)\epsilon/2$ or $\mathrm{vol}(S \setminus C) < \mathrm{vol}(S)\epsilon/2$. In the first

case, step 2 outputs "NO" with probability at least $1 - \left(1 - \frac{\epsilon}{2}\right)^{4/\epsilon} \geq 1 - \frac{1}{e^2} \geq \frac{3}{4}$.
In the second case we have

$$\mathrm{vol}(C \setminus S) \geq \frac{\epsilon}{2} \mathrm{vol}(S)$$

and by the same analysis as the one-dimensional case, $\mathrm{vol}(C \setminus S) \geq \frac{\epsilon}{3} \mathrm{vol}(C)$.
Thus, step 3 outputs "NO" with probability at least $1 - (1 - \frac{\epsilon}{3})^{6/\epsilon} \geq 3/4$.   □

Note that, unlike the one-dimensional case, this algorithm has two-sided error.
The complexity of the algorithm is independent of S and depends only on n
and ϵ. It makes an exponential number of calls to the random oracle and this
dependency is unavoidable for this algorithm. It is known for example that the
convex hull of any subset of fewer than c^n points of the ball, contains less than
half its volume [7].

The one-dimensional algorithm suggests another algorithm for the general
case: let $\ell(x, y)$ be the line through x and y,

Lines-based algorithm
INPUT: Access to membership and random oracles of $S \subseteq \mathbb{R}^n$ compact.

Generate m pairs of random points (x, y) and test if $\ell(x, y) \cap S$ is convex.

How large does m need to be? Somewhat surprisingly, we show in the next
section that this algorithm also has an exponential complexity. Testing if $\ell(x, y) \cap$
S is convex is not a trivial task (note that we have a membership oracle for
$\ell(x, y) \cap S$ from the oracle for S, but simulating a random oracle is not so
simple). However, for the purpose of showing a lower bound in m we will assume
that the one-dimensional algorithm checks *exactly* whether $\ell(x, y) \cap S$ is convex
(that is, it is an interval).

4   The Lines-Based Algorithm Is Exponential

In this section, we construct an explicit family of compact sets each of which
has the following properties: (i) the set is far from convex, and (ii) for all but an
exponentially small fraction of pairs of points from the set, the line through the
pair of points has a convex intersection with the set. This implies that the lines-
based algorithm (described at the end of Section 3.2) has exponential worst-case
complexity. Thus, although exact convexity is characterized by "convex along
every line," the corresponding reduction of approximate convexity to "convex
along most lines" is not efficient.

The proof of the lower bound is in two parts, first we show that the algorithm
needs many tests and then that the test family is far from convex (i.e., ϵ is large).

4.1   The Family of Sets: The Cross-Polytope with Peaks

The n-dimensional cross-polytope is an n-dimensional generalization of the oc-
tahedron and can be defined as the unit ball with the norm $|x|_1 = \sum_{i=1}^{n} |x_i|$. Let

T_n be the "cross-polytope with peaks", that is, the union of the cross-polytope and, for each of its facets $i \in \{1, \ldots, 2^n\}$, the convex hull of the facet and a point $v_i = \lambda d$, where d is the unit outer normal to the facet and $\lambda \geq 1/\sqrt{n}$ is a parameter (that may depend on the dimension). Informally, one adds an n-dimensional simplex on top of each facet of the cross-polytope. The volume of the cross-polytope is a $\frac{1}{\lambda\sqrt{n}}$ fraction of the volume of T_n. We will choose $\lambda = \frac{\sqrt{n}}{n-2}$. In that case, the cross-polytope as a convex set shows that T_n is $O(\frac{1}{n})$-convex. We will prove that T_n is not $\frac{1}{12n^2}$-convex, i.e., for any convex set K, we have $d(K, T_n) > \frac{1}{12n^2} \operatorname{vol} T_n$.

4.2   The Non-convexity of the Family Cannot be Detected by the Lines-Based Algorithm

Proposition 7. *If* $\lambda \leq \frac{\sqrt{n}}{n-2}$ *then the one-dimensional test has an exponentially low probability of detecting the non-convexity of the cross-polytope with peaks.*

Proof. First, we will prove the following claim:

Under the hypothesis, every peak is contained in the intersection of the half-spaces determining the n facets of the cross-polytope adjacent to the peak.

It is enough to see that the point $v_i = \lambda d$ (a vertex of the peak) is contained in that intersection. Because of the symmetry, we can concentrate on any particular pair of adjacent facets, say those having normals $d = (1, 1, \ldots, 1)/\sqrt{n}$ and $d' = (-1, 1, \ldots, 1)/\sqrt{n}$. The halfspace determining the facet with normal d is given by $\{x \in \mathbb{R}^n : \langle x, d' \rangle \leq 1/\sqrt{n}\}$. Then $v_i = \lambda d$ is contained in the halfspace associated to the facet with normal d' (which is sufficient) if

$$\langle \lambda d, d' \rangle \leq \frac{1}{\sqrt{n}} \ .$$

That is,

$$\lambda \leq \frac{\sqrt{n}}{n-2} \ .$$

This proves the claim.

It is sufficient to note that, for the algorithm to answer "NO", we need to choose a line whose intersection with T_n is not convex. Suppose that a line L shows non-convexity. Then it does not intersect the cross-polytope part of T_n a.s. (almost surely), otherwise L intersects exactly 2 facets of the cross-polytope a. s., and intersects only the peaks that are associated to those facets, because of the claim (if one follows the line after it leaves the cross-polytope through one of the facets, it enters a peak, and that peak is the only peak on that side of the facet, because of the claim), and thus $L \cap T_n$ would be convex. Now, while intersecting a peak, L intersects two of its facets at two points that are not at the same distance of the cross-polytope, a.s. The half of L that leaves the peak through the farthest point cannot intersect any other peak because of the claim (the halfspace determined by the respective facet of the cross-polytope containing this peak contains only this peak, and this half of L stays in this halfspace). The half of L that leaves the peak through the closest point will cross the hyperplane determined by one of the adjacent peaks[2] before intersecting any other peak, a.s.; after crossing that hyperplane it can intersect only one peak, namely, the peak associated to that hyperplane, because of the claim. Thus, L has to intersect exactly 2 peaks that have to be adjacent a. s., and L does not intersect the cross-polytope. In other words, the two random points that determine L are in the same peak or in adjacent peaks. The probability of this event is no more than $\frac{n+1}{2^n}$. □

4.3   The Sets in the Family Are Far from Convex

To prove that T_n is far from being convex, we will prove that a close convex set must substantially cover most peaks, and because of this, a significant volume of a close convex set must lie between pairs of adjacent substantially covered peaks, outside of T_n, adding to the symmetric difference. The following lemma will be useful for this part. For $A \subseteq \mathbb{R}^n$ and H a hyperplane and $v \in \mathbb{R}^n$ a unit normal for H, let

$$w_H(A) = \sup_{x \in A}\langle v, x\rangle - \inf_{x \in A}\langle v, x\rangle .$$

Lemma 8. *Let $A, B \subseteq \mathbb{R}^n$ compact. Let H be a separating hyperplane[3] for A, B. Let $C = H \cap \mathrm{conv}(A \cup B)$. Then*

$$V_{n-1}(C) \geq \min\left\{ \frac{\mathrm{vol}\, A}{w_H(A)}, \frac{\mathrm{vol}\, B}{w_H(B)} \right\} .$$

Proof. There exist sections, parallel to H, of A and B that have $(n-1)$-volumes at least $(\mathrm{vol}\, A)/w_H(A)$ and $(\mathrm{vol}\, B)/w_H(B)$, respectively. That is, there exist $a, b \in \mathbb{R}^n$ such that $A' = (H + a) \cap A$, $B' = (H + b) \cap B$ satisfy $V_{n-1}(A') \geq (\mathrm{vol}\, A)/w_H(A)$ and $V_{n-1}(B') \geq (\mathrm{vol}\, B)/w_H(B)$. Clearly $H \cap \mathrm{conv}(A' \cup B') \subseteq C$ and therefore

$$\begin{aligned} V_{n-1}(C) &\geq V_{n-1}(H \cap \mathrm{conv}(A' \cup B')) \\ &\geq \min\{V_{n-1}(A'), V_{n-1}(B')\} \\ &\geq \min\left\{ \frac{\mathrm{vol}\, A}{w_H(A)}, \frac{\mathrm{vol}\, B}{w_H(B)} \right\} . \end{aligned}$$

□

This bound is sharp: consider a cylinder with a missing slice in the middle, that is, consider in the plane as A a rectangle with axis-parallel sides and non-

---

[2] "The hyperplane determined by a peak" is the unique hyperplane that contains the facet of the cross-polytope associated to the peak.
[3] That is, a set of the form $H = \{x \in \mathbb{R}^n \ : \ \langle x, y\rangle = \alpha\}$ for some $y \in \mathbb{R}^n$ and $\alpha \in \mathbb{R}$, such that for all $x \in A$ we have $\langle x, y\rangle \leq \alpha$ and for all $x \in B$ we have $\langle x, y\rangle \geq \alpha$.

adjacent vertices $(1,0)$ and $(2,1)$, as B the reflection of A with respect to the y-axis and as the separating line, the y-axis.

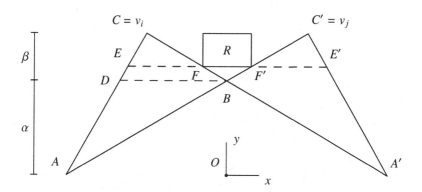

Fig. 1. Projection of the peaks (i,j) of the cross-polytope with peaks onto v_i, v_j for $n = 4$

Lemma 9. *For* $\lambda = \frac{\sqrt{n}}{n-2}$, T_n *is not* $\frac{1}{12n^2}$*-convex.*

Proof. Let C_n be a closest convex set to T_n.

Consider a pair of adjacent peaks (i,j). Figure 1 shows the projection of the pair onto the plane containing the vertices v_i, v_j and the origin. B is the projection of the intersection of the two peaks, an $(n-2)$-dimensional simplex. A and C are the other two vertices of one of the peaks, A' and C' are the respective vertices of the other peak. The plane is orthogonal to the two respective facets of the cross-polytope, the segment AB is the projection of one of them and $A'B$ is the projection of the other facet. D is such that DB is orthogonal to OB, where O is the origin.

First, we will prove that the volume of the preimage (with respect to the projection) of the triangle DBC is a $\frac{1}{n-1}$ fraction of the volume of the peak. To see this, let Q be the preimage of DB in the peak, which is a $(n-1)$-dimensional simplex. Let α be the height of the triangle ABD with respect to A, and let β be the height of the triangle DBC with respect to C. Then the volume of the peak is

$$\frac{1}{n}V_{n-1}(Q)(\alpha + \beta) .$$

Also, the volume of the preimage of DBC is

$$\frac{1}{n}V_{n-1}(Q)\beta .$$

Thus, the volume of the preimage of the triangle DBC is a $\frac{\beta}{\alpha+\beta}$ fraction of the volume of the peak. We can compute α and β. Without loss of generality we can assume that v_i is parallel to $(-1,1,\ldots,1)$ and v_j is parallel to $(1,\ldots,1)$. Then $(0, \frac{1}{n-1},\ldots,\frac{1}{n-1})$ is a vector in the preimage of B that is in the projection plane, and α is the norm of that vector, that is, $\alpha = 1/\sqrt{n-1}$. An orthonormal basis of the projection plane corresponding to the x, y axes of Figure 1 is

$$\{(1, 0, \ldots, 0), (0, 1/\sqrt{n-1}, \ldots, 1/\sqrt{n-1})\}.$$

Then, $\alpha + \beta$ is the length of the projection of v_j onto $(0, 1/\sqrt{n-1}, \ldots, 1/\sqrt{n-1})$, that is, $\alpha + \beta = \frac{\sqrt{n-1}}{n-2}$ and $\beta = \frac{1}{(n-2)\sqrt{n-1}}$. Thus, $\frac{\beta}{\alpha+\beta} = \frac{1}{n-1}$, as claimed.

EF is a segment parallel to DB and at a distance $\frac{\beta}{n+1}$ from it. That way, the volume of the preimage of the triangle EFC is a $(1 - \frac{1}{n+1})^n \geq \frac{1}{e}$ fraction of the volume of the preimage of the triangle DBC, which, as we saw, is a $\frac{1}{n-1}$ fraction of the volume of the peak. That is, the preimage of the triangle EFC is at least a $\frac{1}{e(n-1)}$ fraction of the volume of the peak.

Given a particular peak, we will say that it is *substantially covered* (by C_n) iff the volume of the intersection of C_n and the peak is at least a $1 - \frac{1}{2e(n-1)}$ fraction of the volume of the peak. Because of the choice of EF, if a peak is substantially covered, then at least a $\frac{1}{2e(n-1)}$ fraction of its volume is covered in the preimage of the triangle EFC (that is, above the segment EF).

Now we will prove that every pair of adjacent substantially covered peaks contributes to $C_n \setminus T_n$ at least with a $\frac{1}{6n^2}$ fraction of the volume of a peak, disjoint from the contribution of other pairs. To see this, let U be the subset of C_n intersected with peak i that projects onto EFC and let V be the subset of C_n intersected with peak j that projects onto $F'E'C'$. We will apply Lemma 8 to U, V and every hyperplane which is a preimage of a vertical line intersecting the rectangle R. Moreover, for any such hyperplane H we have that $w_H(U)$ and $w_H(V)$ are no more than the length of DB, which is a $\frac{\beta}{\alpha+\beta} = \frac{1}{n-1}$ fraction of the length of AA' (which is 2), i.e., $\frac{2}{n-1}$. Certainly $W = R \cap \text{conv}(U \cup V)$ is contained in C_n and disjoint from T_n. Because of the choice of EF, the width of the rectangle R is a $\frac{1}{n+1}$ fraction of the distance between C and C', that is, $\frac{2}{(n+1)(n-2)}$. Also, $\text{vol}\, U$ and $\text{vol}\, V$ are no less than a $\frac{1}{2e(n-1)}$ fraction of the volume of a peak. Lemma 8 gives that

$$\frac{\text{vol}\, W}{\text{vol(one peak)}} \geq (\text{width of } R) \min\left\{\frac{\text{vol}\, U}{\frac{2}{n-1}}, \frac{\text{vol}\, V}{\frac{2}{n-1}}\right\} \frac{1}{\text{vol(one peak)}}$$

$$\geq \frac{2}{(n+1)(n-2)} \frac{n-1}{2} \frac{1}{2e(n-1)}$$

$$\geq \frac{1}{2e(n-2)(n+1)}$$

$$\geq \frac{1}{6n^2} .$$

Let $\epsilon(n) = d(C_n, T_n)$. We claim that the number of peaks that are not substantially covered is a fraction that is at most $en^2\epsilon(n)$ of the total number of peaks. To see this, let $q(n)$ be the fraction of the volume of T_n that the peaks contain. Clearly

$$q(n) = \frac{\lambda - \frac{1}{\sqrt{n}}}{\lambda} = \frac{2}{n} .$$

Let X be the number of peaks that are not substantially covered. Then,

$$X \frac{1}{2e(n-1)} q(n) \le \epsilon(n) ,$$

that is,

$$X \le en(n-1)\epsilon(n) \le en^2\epsilon(n) . \tag{2}$$

We will see now that eventually (as n grows) the number of pairs of adjacent peaks that are substantially covered is a substantial fraction of the total number of adjacent pairs. For a contradiction, assume that, for some subsequence, $\epsilon(n) < \frac{1}{12n^2}$. For n sufficiently large, $en^2\epsilon(n) \le 1/4$. The number of peaks is 2^n; the number of (unordered) pairs of adjacent peaks is $n2^{n-1}$. A peak that is not substantially covered can participate in at most n pairs of adjacent peaks. Because of (2), there are at most $\frac{1}{4}2^n = 2^{n-2}$ peaks that are not substantially covered (for large n and a subsequence). That way, all the peaks that are not substantially covered can participate in at most $n2^{n-2} = \frac{1}{2}n2^{n-1}$ pairs of adjacent peaks. Thus, at least $1/2$ of the pairs of adjacent peaks involve only substantially covered peaks. For γ equal to the volume of the contribution to $C_n \setminus T_n$ of a pair of substantially covered peaks, this implies that

$$\epsilon(n) \ge \frac{\text{vol}(C_n \setminus T_n)}{\text{vol}\, T_n}$$

$$\ge \frac{\text{vol}(C_n \setminus T_n)}{\text{vol}(\text{all peaks})} \frac{\text{vol}(\text{all peaks})}{\text{vol}\, T_n}$$

$$\ge \frac{\frac{1}{2}n2^{n-1}\gamma}{2^n \,\text{vol}(\text{one peak})} q(n)$$

$$\ge \frac{n}{4} \frac{1}{6n^2} \frac{2}{n}$$

$$\ge \frac{1}{12n^2}$$

which is a contradiction. □

5   An Algorithm Based on Planes

In this section, we state a conjecture about approximate convexity. Let S be a compact subset of $\mathbb{R}^n$ whose center of gravity is the origin. For a pair of points $x, y \ne 0$ in $\mathbb{R}^n$ let the subspace spanned by them be $H(x,y)$ and define $P(x,y) = S \cap H(x,y)$ to be the part of S on this subspace. Our conjecture is the following:

Conjecture. Let μ be the distribution on 2-dimensional sections $P(x, y)$ obtained by picking x and y uniformly at random from S. If

$$\mathbb{P}_\mu\big(P(x, y) \text{ is convex}\big) > 1 - \epsilon \,,$$

then S is $O(n\epsilon)$-convex.

The conjecture motivates the following algorithm (here $p(\cdot)$ and $q(\cdot)$ are fixed polynomials):

Repeat $p(n, 1/\epsilon)$ times

1. Get random points x, y from S.
2. Test if $P(x, y)$ is $q(1/n, \epsilon)$-convex.

Acknowledgements

We would like to thank David Jerison, Dana Ron and Ronitt Rubinfeld for discussions on this topic. We also thank an anonymous member of the program committee for suggesting an interesting application.

References

1. Goldreich, O., Goldwasser, S., Ron, D.: Property testing and its connection to learning and approximation. J. ACM **45** (1998) 653–750
2. Parnas, M., Ron, D., Rubinfeld, R.: On testing convexity and submodularity. SIAM J. Comput. **32** (2003) 1158–1184 (electronic)
3. Lovász, L., Vempala, S.: Hit-and-run from a corner. In: STOC '04. ACM, New York (2004)
4. Motwani, R., Raghavan, P.: Randomized Algorithms. Cambridge University Press (1995)
5. Groemer, H.: On the mean value of the volume of a random polytope in a convex set. Arch. Math. (Basel) **25** (1974) 86–90
6. Bárány, I., Buchta, C.: Random polytopes in a convex polytope, independence of shape, and concentration of vertices. Math. Ann. **297** (1993) 467–497
7. Bárány, I., Füredi, Z.: Computing the volume is difficult. Discrete Comput. Geom. **2** (1987) 319–326
8. Rockafellar, R.T., Wets, R.J.: Variational Analysis. Number 317 in Grundlehren der mathematischen Wissenschaften. Springer-Verlag (1998)

Appendix

For the Hausdorff metric or the symmetric difference volume metric, we have (see [8], Theorem 4.18, for example):

Theorem 10 (Blaschke's Selection Theorem). *In $\mathbb{R}^n$, any bounded sequence $(C_k)_{k \in \mathbb{N}}$ of nonempty, convex sets has a subsequence converging to some nonempty, compact, convex set C.*

Complexity of Linear Connectivity Problems in Directed Hypergraphs[*]

Mayur Thakur[1,***] and Rahul Tripathi[2]

[1] Dept. of Computer Science, University of Missouri–Rolla, Rolla, MO 65409, USA
thakurk@umr.edu
[2] Dept. of Computer Science, University of Rochester, Rochester, NY 14627, USA
rahult@cs.rochester.edu

Abstract. We introduce a notion of linear hyperconnection (formally denoted L-hyperpath) between nodes in a directed hypergraph and relate this notion to existing notions of hyperpaths in directed hypergraphs. We observe that many interesting questions in problem domains such as secret transfer protocols, routing in packet filtered networks, and propositional satisfiability are basically questions about existence of L-hyperpaths or about cyclomatic number of directed hypergraphs w.r.t. L-hypercycles (the minimum number of hyperedges that need to be deleted to make a directed hypergraph free of L-hypercycles). We prove that the L-hyperpath existence problem, the cyclomatic number problem, the minimum cyclomatic set problem, and the minimal cyclomatic set problem are each complete for a different level (respectively, NP, Σ_2^p, Π_2^p, and DP) of the polynomial hierarchy.

1 Introduction

Roughly speaking, a directed hypergraph is a generalization of directed graphs in which each directed hyperedge is allowed to have multiple source (tail) nodes and multiple destination (head) nodes. Thus, a (simple) directed edge is a hyperedge with exactly one tail node and exactly one head node. Directed hypergraphs have been used to model a wide variety of problems in propositional logic [6, 20], relational databases [3, 11, 28], urban transportation planning [10, 18], chemical reaction mechanisms [26, 30], Petri nets [2, 23], operations research [10], and probabilistic parsing [16]. They have been introduced under different names such as "And-Or graphs" and "FD-graphs."

Ausiello, D'Atri, and Saccá [3] introduced the notion of directed hypergraphs, though they called them "FD-graphs," where FD stands for "functional dependency," and used them to represent dependencies among attributes in relational databases. They presented efficient algorithms for several problems related to transitive closure, minimization, etc., of attributes in a database. Gallo et al. [10]

---

[*] Supported in part by grants NSF-INT-9815095 and NSF-CCF-0426761.
[***] Work done in part while affiliated with the Department of Computer Science at the University of Rochester, Rochester, NY 14627, USA.

first formalized the basic notions related to directed hypergraphs like connectivity, paths, and cuts, and showed applications of directed hypergraphs to problems such as functional dependency in relational database theory and route planning in urban transport system design. More recently, a unified view of deterministic and probabilistic parsing has been obtained by showing them to be equivalent to traversals in directed hypergraphs [16].

The notion of *connection* in a directed graph is simple and can be recursively defined as follows. Each node is connected to itself and a node x is connected to another node y, if there exists a node z such that there is a connection from node x to node z and there is an edge from node z to node y. But there does not seem to be one common intuitive notion for a *hyperconnection* (i.e., connection in directed hypergraphs). In fact, different notions of hyperpaths and hypercycles in directed hypergraphs have been defined in the literature [7, 8, 10, 19, 30] based on varying intuitive notions of hyperconnection in problem domains.

In this paper, first we review these notions of hyperpaths and hypercycles in directed hypergraphs. We describe our notion of linear hyperconnection, and define L-hyperpath and L-hypercycle. We identify domains such as secret transfer protocols, packet filtered networks, and propositional satisfiability, where the notion of linear hyperconnection can be used to capture key problems. We study the complexity of basic computational problems in directed hypergraphs: finding whether hyperpaths of certain a type exist between two given nodes, finding whether hyperpaths of a certain type with a given bound on certain measure exist between two given nodes, etc.

The cyclomatic number of a (simple) graph is the minimum number of edges that need to be removed to make the graph acyclic. Intuitively speaking, the cyclomatic number of a graph measures the degree of cyclicity of a graph. We can define the cyclomatic number of a directed hypergraph analogously to that in simple graphs. That is, the cyclomatic number of a directed hypergraph w.r.t. L-hypercycles is the minimum number of hyperedges that need to be removed such that the resulting hypergraph does not contain any L-hypercycle. We study the computational complexity of problems related to cyclomatic number of directed hypergraphs w.r.t. L-hypercycles: computing the cyclomatic number of a directed hypergraph, finding whether a given set of hyperedges forms a cyclomatic set, finding whether these hyperedges form a minimal cyclomatic set, etc. We prove that many of these fundamental problems are computationally hard (under standard complexity-theoretic assumptions). We prove that these problems are each complete for a different level of the polynomial hierarchy (see Definition 7 for precise definitions of these problems): CYCLOMATIC-NUMBER is Σ_2^p-complete, MIN-CYCLOMATIC-SET is Π_2^p-complete, and MINIMAL-CYCLOMATIC-SET is DP-complete.

It is interesting to compare the complexity of connectivity problems on directed graphs and directed hypergraphs. In particular, consider the complexity of the following *path existence* problems:

- Is there a path between two given vertices in a directed graph? This problem is known to be NL-complete.

- Is there a B-hyperpath between two given vertices in a directed hypergraph? This problem is in P [10].
- Is there an L-hyperpath between two given vertices in a directed hypergraph? In this paper, we show that this problem is NP-complete.

Compare also the complexity of the following *cyclomatic number* problems:

- Is there a set of k edges whose deletion makes a directed graph free of cycles? This problem is NP-complete [14].
- Is there a set of k hyperedges whose deletion makes a directed hypergraph free of L-hypercycles? In this paper, we show that this problem is Σ_2^p-complete.

(Due to space limitations, proofs of most results have been omitted. Please see the full version [27] for omitted proofs and for details of how L-hyperpaths in directed hypergraphs can be used to model practical problems.)

2   Notions of Hyperpaths in Directed Hypergraphs

Definition 1 ([10]). *A directed hypergraph $\mathcal{H}$ is a tuple (V, E), where V is a finite set and $E \subseteq 2^V \times 2^V$ such that, for every $e = (T(e), H(e)) \in E$, $T(e) \neq \emptyset$, $H(e) \neq \emptyset$, and $T(e) \cap H(e) = \emptyset$. For every integer $k \geq 1$, a k-directed hypergraph $\mathcal{H}$ is a directed hypergraph in which, for every $e \in E(\mathcal{H})$, $|T(e)| \leq k$ and $|H(e)| \leq k$.*

A B-hyperedge (F-hyperedge) is a hyperedge $e = (T(e), H(e))$ such that $|H(e)| = 1$ (respectively, $|T(e)| = 1$). A B-hypergraph (F-hypergraph) is a hypergraph $\mathcal{H}$ such that each hyperedge in $\mathcal{H}$ is a B-hyperedge (respectively, F-hyperedge). A directed hypergraph $\mathcal{H}' = (V', E')$ is a subhypergraph of $\mathcal{H}$ if $V' \subseteq V$, $E' \subseteq E$.

Let $e = (T(e), H(e))$ be a hyperedge in some directed hypergraph $\mathcal{H}$. Then, $T(e)$ is known as the *tail* of e and $H(e)$ is known as the *head* of e. The size of representing a directed hypergraph $\mathcal{H}$ is taken to be $|V(\mathcal{H})| + |E(\mathcal{H})|$ unless another representation scheme is explicitly mentioned as in, for example, Section 6. Given a directed hypergraph $\mathcal{H} = (V, E)$, its symmetric image $\overline{\mathcal{H}}$ is a directed hypergraph defined as follows: $V(\overline{\mathcal{H}}) = V(\mathcal{H})$ and $E(\overline{\mathcal{H}}) = \{(H, T) \mid (T, H) \in E(\mathcal{H})\}$.

Definition 2 ([10]). *Let $\mathcal{H} = (V, E)$ be a directed hypergraph.*

1. *A simple path Π_{st} from $s \in V(\mathcal{H})$ to $t \in V(\mathcal{H})$ in $\mathcal{H}$ is a sequence $(v_1, e_1, v_2, e_2, \ldots, v_k, e_k, v_{k+1})$ consisting of distinct vertices and hyperedges such that $s = v_1$, $t = v_{k+1}$, and for every $1 \leq i \leq k$, $v_i \in T(e_i)$ and $v_{i+1} \in H(e_i)$. If, in addition, $t \in T(e_1)$ then Π_{st} is a simple cycle. A simple path is cycle-free if it does not contain any subpath that is a simple cycle.*
2. *A B-hyperpath from $s \in V(\mathcal{H})$ to $t \in V(\mathcal{H})$ in $\mathcal{H}$ can be defined in terms of a notion of B-connection in directed hypergraphs. The recursive definition of B-connection to a node s is as follows: (i) a node s is B-connected to itself, and (ii) if there is a hyperedge e such that all the nodes in $T(e)$ are B-connected to s, then every node in $H(e)$ is B-connected to s. A B-hyperpath*

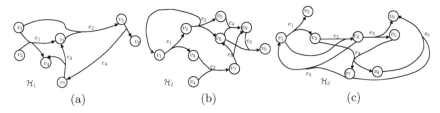

(a)   (b)   (c)

Fig. 1. (a) $\Pi_{v_1 v_4} = (v_1, e_2, v_5, e_4, v_7, e_3, v_4)$ is a simple path and $\Pi_{v_1 v_3} = (v_1, e_2, v_5, e_4, v_7, e_3, v_3)$ is a simple cycle in $\mathcal{H}_1$. (b) Directed hypergraph $\mathcal{G}_1$ with $V(\mathcal{G}_1) = \{v_1, v_2, v_3, v_5, v_6, v_8, v_9\}$ and $E(\mathcal{G}_1) = \{e_1, e_2, e_4, e_6\}$ is a B-hyperpath from v_1 to v_9 in $\mathcal{H}_2$, directed hypergraph $\mathcal{G}_2$ with $V(\mathcal{G}_2) = \{v_3, v_4, v_6, v_7, v_8, v_9\}$ and $E(\mathcal{G}_2) = \{e_3, e_5, e_6\}$ is an F-hyperpath from v_3 to v_9 in $\mathcal{H}_2$, and directed hypergraph $\mathcal{G}_3$ with $V(\mathcal{G}_3) = \{v_6, v_7, v_8, v_9\}$ and $E(\mathcal{G}_3) = \{e_5, e_6\}$ is a BF-hyperpath from v_7 to v_9 in $\mathcal{H}_2$. (c) A directed hypergraph $\mathcal{H}_3$ with an L-hypercycle. In all the figures, arrows on a hyperedge point to the vertices in the head of the hyperedge

from s to t in $\mathcal{H}$ is a minimal (with respect to deletion of vertices and hyperedges) subhypergraph of $\mathcal{H}$ where t is B-connected to s. (See also [7, 8] and [5] for equivalent, but alternative, characterizations of B-hyperpaths.)

3. An F-hyperpath Π_{st} from $s \in V(\mathcal{H})$ to $t \in V(\mathcal{H})$ in $\mathcal{H}$ is a subhypergraph of $\mathcal{H}$ such that $\overline{\Pi}_{st}$ is a B-hyperpath from t to s in $\overline{\mathcal{H}}$.

4. A BF-hyperpath is a hypergraph that is both a B-hyperpath and an F-hyperpath.

Even though the notions of B- and F-hyperpath capture problems in several different problem domains (see, e.g., [10, 12]), there are other problem domains for which these definitions do not seem to be the right one. We mention three such problem domains in Section 3.

3 L-Hyperpath

3.1   Definition and Relationship with Other Notions of Hyperpaths

The notions of hyperpaths (B-, F-, and BF-hyperpaths) defined by Gallo et al. [10] differ from the notion of a (directed) path in a (simple) directed graph in that, roughly speaking, the hyperpaths are not required to be "linear." By that we mean that while a path in a directed graph is an alternating sequence of vertices and edges, a (B-, F-, or BF-) hyperpath may not have this form. Although the definition of a simple path (Definition 2, part 1) requires linearity, that definition is too weak to capture the expressiveness of directed hypergraphs in the following sense: Given any directed hypergraph $\mathcal{H}$ and $u, v \in V(\mathcal{H})$, there is a simple path from u to v in $\mathcal{H}$ if and only if there is a simple path from u to v in a directed graph G with $V(G) = V(\mathcal{H})$ and $E(G) = \{(u, v) \mid (\exists e \in E(\mathcal{H}))[u \in T(e) \text{ and } v \in H(e)]\}$.

In this section, we introduce a notion of linear hyperpath, called L-hyperpath, and relate this notion of L-hyperpath with previously studied notions of directed hyperpaths.

Definition 3. *An L-hyperpath Π_{st} from s to t in a directed hypergraph $\mathcal{H} = (V, E)$ is a sequence $(v_1, e_1, v_2, e_2, \ldots, v_k, e_k, v_{k+1})$ consisting of distinct vertices and hyperedges such that $s = v_1$, $t = v_{k+1}$, for every $1 \leq i \leq k$, $v_i \in T(e_i)$ and $v_{i+1} \in H(e_i)$, and for every $1 \leq i \leq k$, $T(e_i) \subseteq \{s\} \cup H(e_1) \cup \ldots \cup H(e_{i-1})$. If, in addition, $t \in T(e_1)(= \{s\})$ then Π_{st} is an L-hypercycle in $\mathcal{H}$.*

L-hyperpaths inherit the linearity property from simple paths and the restricted B-connection property from B-hyperpaths. L-hyperpaths may alternatively be expressed in terms of directed hypergraphs as follows. For any L-hyperpath $\Pi = (v_1, e_1, v_2, e_2, \ldots, v_k, e_k, v_{k+1})$, let $\mathcal{H}_\Pi$ be defined as the subhypergraph of $\mathcal{H}$ such that, $V(\mathcal{H}_\Pi) = \{v_1\} \cup H(e_1) \cup H(e_2) \cup \ldots \cup H(e_k)$ and $E(\mathcal{H}_\Pi) = \{e_1, e_2, \ldots, e_k\}$. We say that $\mathcal{H}_\Pi$ is the *hypergraph representation* of Π. In Figure 1(c), $\Pi_1 = (v_1, e_1, v_3, e_2, v_4, e_3, v_5, e_4, v_7)$ is an L-hyperpath and $\Pi_2 = (v_1, e_1, v_3, e_2, v_4, e_3, v_5, e_4, v_7, e_5, v_1)$ is an L-hypercycle in $\mathcal{H}_3$. Also, note that there is no L-hyperpath from v_4 to v_1 in $\mathcal{H}_3$ and that the hypergraph representation of Π_1 is $\mathcal{H}' = (V(\mathcal{H}_3), \{e_1, e_2, e_3, e_4\})$.

Theorem 4. *Let $\mathcal{H}$ be a B-hypergraph, $\mathcal{G}$ be a subhypergraph of $\mathcal{H}$, and $s, t \in V(\mathcal{G})$. Then, the following holds: $\mathcal{G}$ is the hypergraph representation of an L-hyperpath Π_{st} from s to t if and only if $\mathcal{G}$ is a minimal (w.r.t. deletion of vertices and hyperedges) subhypergraph of $\mathcal{H}$ such that t is B-connected to s and there is a simple cycle-free path from s to t that consists of all the hyperedges of $\mathcal{G}$.*

The study of L-hyperpaths is interesting from a theoretical point of view because, as argued earlier, the notion of L-hyperpaths is a restriction of the notion of simple paths and the notion of B-hyperpaths. The study of cyclomatic number of hypergraphs is of fundamental significance (see [9, 1]) and so it is interesting to investigate the complexity of computing the cyclomatic number (in the L-hypercycle notion) of directed hypergraphs. On the practical side, we show in the full version [27] of this paper that many interesting questions in problem domains such as secret transfer protocols, routing in packet filtered networks, and propositional satisfiability can be modeled using the notion of L-hyperconnection. The linearity constraint of L-hyperpaths turns out to be crucial in correctly modeling problems in these domains.

4 Computational Problems on Directed Hyperpaths

Many applications of graphs require one to associate a cost (or, weight) on the edges of the graph. The cost of a path in a graph is then defined to be the sum of cost of edges in the path. In contrast, since the structure of a hyperpath is more complicated, a number of measures on hyperpaths in a directed hypergraph are defined and studied in the literature [4, 7, 8, 15, 17, 18, 24]. We observe that the measures defined for previously studied notions of directed hyperpaths are applicable also for L-hyperpaths if the hypergraph representation of an L-hyperpath is considered in the definition. This indicates that the notion of L-hyperpaths is robust and it suggests that L-hyperpaths may be used to model a variety of problems that require these measures on hyperpaths.

For any $X \in \{B, F, L\}$ and for any measure function μ_X on X-hyperpaths of $\mathcal{H}$, we define the following decision problems related to directed hypergraphs:

1. X-HYPERPATH $= \{\langle \mathcal{H}, s, t \rangle \mid \mathcal{H}$ is a directed hypergraph that contains an X-hyperpath Π_{st} from s to $t\}$.
2. μ_X-OPT-HYPERPATH $= \{\langle \mathcal{H}, s, t, k \rangle \mid \mathcal{H}$ is a directed weighted hypergraph that contains an X-hyperpath Π_{st} from s to t such that $\mu_X(\Pi_{st}) \leq k\}$.

Gallo et al. [10] showed that both B-HYPERPATH and F-HYPERPATH are solvable in polynomial time. Ausiello et al. [7] and Italiano and Nanni [15] proved that μ_B-OPT-HYPERPATH is NP-complete when μ_B is one of the following measure functions: (a) number of hyperedges, (b) cost, (c) size. Ausiello et al. [7] and Ausiello, Italiano, and Nanni [8] proved that μ_B-OPT-HYPERPATH is solvable in polynomial time when μ_B is the rank of a B-hyperpath (see [7, 8] for the definition of rank). Theorem 5 states our result related to L-hyperpaths.

Theorem 5. *For every $k \geq 2$, L-HYPERPATH is NP-complete when restricted to k-directed B-hypergraphs.*

It follows from the proof of Theorem 5 that, for every $k \geq 2$ and for any polynomial-time computable measure μ_L on L-hyperpaths, the problems L-HYPERCYCLE (given a directed hypergraph $\mathcal{H}$, does $\mathcal{H}$ contain an L-hypercycle?) and μ_L-OPT-HYPERPATH are NP-complete when restricted to k-directed B-hypergraphs. A simple observation shows that the problems L-HYPERPATH and μ_L-OPT-HYPERPATH are in P when restricted to F-hypergraphs. Thus, roughly speaking, the intrinsic hardness of these problems is due to the presence of B-hyperedges. In contrast, we find that the proofs of Theorems 8 and 9 seem to require both B- and F-hyperedges in the construction. It will be interesting to see whether proofs of Theorems 8 and 9 can be carried out without requiring F-hyperedges in the construction.

5   Cyclomatic Number of a Directed Hypergraph

The cyclomatic number of a hypergraph is the minimum number of hyperedges that need to be deleted so that the resulting hypergraph has no hypercycle. For a connected graph $G = (V, E)$, the cyclomatic number is given by $|E| - |V| + 1$. The cyclomatic number of any undirected hypergraph is also efficiently computable [1]. For directed hypergraphs, the notion of cyclomatic number can be defined as follows.

Definition 6. *Given a directed hypergraph $\mathcal{H} = (V, E)$, the cyclomatic number of $\mathcal{H}$ with respect to L-hypercycles is the following:* $\min\{k \in \mathbb{N} \mid (\exists B \subseteq E)[|B| = k$ *and there are no L-hypercycles in $(V, E - B)]\}$.

In this section, we study the complexity of several decision problems related to the abovementioned definition of cyclomatic number of a directed hypergraph.

Definition 7. *1.* CYCLOMATIC-SET $= \{\langle \mathcal{H}, B \rangle \mid \mathcal{H} = (V, E)$ *is a directed hypergraph and* $B \subseteq E$ *such that* $\mathcal{H}' = (V, E - B)$ *has no L-hypercycle* $\}$.
  2. CYCLOMATIC-NUMBER $= \{\langle \mathcal{H}, k \rangle \mid \mathcal{H} = (V, E)$ *is a directed hypergraph such that there exists a set* $B \subseteq E$, $|B| \leq k$ *and* $\langle \mathcal{H}, B \rangle \in$ CYCLOMATIC-SET$\}$.
  3. MIN-CYCLOMATIC-SET $= \{\langle \mathcal{H}, B \rangle \mid \langle \mathcal{H}, B \rangle \in$ CYCLOMATIC-SET *and, for each* B' *such that* $|B'| < |B|$, $\langle \mathcal{H}, B' \rangle \notin$ CYCLOMATIC-SET$\}$.
  4. MINIMAL-CYCLOMATIC-SET $= \{\langle \mathcal{H}, B \rangle \mid \langle \mathcal{H}, B \rangle \in$ CYCLOMATIC-SET *and, for each* B' *such that* $B' \subsetneq B$, $\langle \mathcal{H}, B' \rangle \notin$ CYCLOMATIC-SET$\}$.

Clearly CYCLOMATIC-SET is coNP-complete, since for any directed hypergraph $\mathcal{H}$, $\langle \mathcal{H} \rangle \in$ L-HYPERCYCLE $\iff \langle \mathcal{H}, \emptyset \rangle \notin$ CYCLOMATIC-SET. The completeness results for remaining problems is stated below.

Theorem 8. *For every* $k \geq 2$, CYCLOMATIC-NUMBER *is* Σ_2^p*-complete when restricted to* k*-directed hypergraphs.*

Proof Sketch: It is clear that CYCLOMATIC-NUMBER is in Σ_2^p. We give a polynomial-time many-one reduction σ from $\mathrm{QSAT}_2(F)$, a problem known to be Σ_2^p-complete (see [21]), to CYCLOMATIC-NUMBER. An instance $\langle X, Y, \phi \rangle$ is in $\mathrm{QSAT}_2(F)$ if and only if ϕ is a boolean formula on disjoint sets X and Y of variables and there exists a truth-value assignment α for X such that for all truth-value assignments β for Y, it holds that $\phi(\alpha, \beta) =$ False.

Let $\langle X, Y, \phi \rangle$ be an instance of $\mathrm{QSAT}_2(F)$, where $X = \{x_1, x_2, \ldots, x_m\}$ and $Y = \{y_1, y_2, \ldots, y_n\}$ are disjoint sets of variables. Without loss of generality, we assume that each variable appears in any clause at most once. Let the clauses of ϕ be $\phi_1, \phi_2, \ldots \phi_s$, and, for $i \in \{1, \ldots, s\}$, let p_i denote the number of occurrences of variables from Y in ϕ_i. Also, for each $1 \leq i \leq s$ and $1 \leq j \leq p_i$, we use $y_{v(i,j)}$ to denote the j-th variable in ϕ_i that belongs to Y. For each $i \leq n$, let n_i denote the number of occurrences of y_i (i.e., as y_i or $\overline{y_i}$) in ϕ. On input $\langle X, Y, \phi \rangle$, σ outputs $\langle \mathcal{H}, m \rangle$ where $\mathcal{H}$ is a directed hypergraph whose construction we describe below. The construction of $\mathcal{H}$ uses four kinds of gadgets. These are selector, k-divider for $k \geq 1$, k-chooser for $k \geq 0$, and switch as shown in Figures 2 and 3.

$\mathcal{H}$ consists of (1) s choosers, $C_1, C_2, \ldots, C_s$, where C_i is a p_i-chooser corresponding to clause ϕ_i, $1 \leq i \leq s$, (2) n dividers, $D_1, D_2, \ldots, D_n$, where D_i is an n_i-divider corresponding to variable y_i, $1 \leq i \leq n$, (3) m selectors, $L_1, L_2, \ldots, L_m$, where L_i corresponds to variable x_i, $1 \leq i \leq m$, and (4) $\sum_{i=1}^{s} p_i$ switches, $S_{1,1}, S_{1,2}, \ldots, S_{1,p_1}, S_{2,1}, \ldots, S_{2,p_2}, \ldots, S_{s,p_s}$ where $S_{i,j}$, $1 \leq i \leq s$ and $1 \leq j \leq p_i$, corresponds to the j-th literal in ϕ_i that belongs to Y. Note that if for some i, $p_i = 0$, i.e., if clause ϕ_i does not have any variable from Y, then there is no switch corresponding to clause ϕ_i.

We use $h(k, j)$ to denote the sum of the number of occurrences of y_j in clauses $\phi_1, \ldots, \phi_k$ with $h(0, j) = 0$ for each j. For each switch S_{ℓ_1, ℓ_2}, where $1 \leq \ell_1 \leq s$ and $1 \leq \ell_2 \leq p_{\ell_1}$, let $\mathrm{succ}(S_{\ell_1, \ell_2})$ be the switch succeeding S_{ℓ_1, ℓ_2} in the ordering $S_{1,1}, S_{1,2}, \ldots, S_{1,p_1}, S_{2,1}, \ldots, S_{2,p_2}, \ldots, S_{s,p_s}$ if $\ell_1 \neq s$ and $\ell_2 \neq p_s$, and is undefined if $\ell_1 = s$ and $\ell_2 = p_s$. For each label x and for each gadget y, we use the shorthand vertex$_\mathcal{H}(x, y)$ (edge$_\mathcal{H}(x, y)$) to denote "the vertex labeled x in gadget y in $\mathcal{H}$" (respectively, "the hyperedge labeled x in gadget y in $\mathcal{H}$").

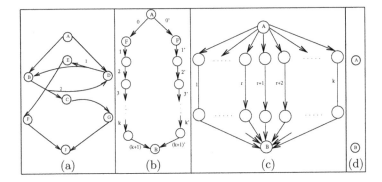

Fig. 2. Gadgets used in the reduction from $\text{QSAT}_2(F)$ to CYCLOMATIC-NUMBER. (a) A selector. (b) A k-divider, where $k \geq 1$. (c) A k-chooser, where $k \geq 1$. (d) A 0-chooser

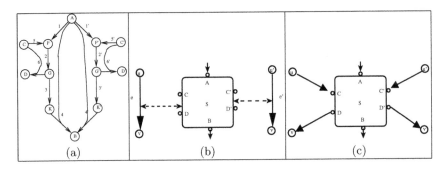

Fig. 3. (a) A switch. (b) Schematic representation of placing a switch S (shown as a rectangular box in the figure) between edges $e = (\{u\}, \{v\})$ and $e' = (\{u'\}, \{v'\})$. (c) The actual placement of a switch S between edges e and e': the edges e and e' are deleted and new edges $(\{u\}, \{C\})$, $(\{D\}, \{v\})$, $(\{u'\}, \{C'\})$ and $(\{D'\}, \{v'\})$ are added

The vertices of $\mathcal{H}$ consist exactly of the vertices of the above gadgets. The gadgets are connected by hyperedges that are described as follows.

1. (Place a switch between the edge in chooser C_i corresponding to an occurrence of a variable y_j and an edge in divider D_j.) For each $1 \leq i \leq s$, and for each $1 \leq j \leq p_i$, if $y_{v(i,j)}$ occurs as $y_{v(i,j)}$ in ϕ_i, then place switch $S_{i,j}$ between edge j of p_i-chooser C_i and edge $h(i, v(i, j))$ of divider $D_{v(i,j)}$. Otherwise, that is if $y_{v(i,j)}$ occurs as $\overline{y_{v(i,j)}}$ in ϕ_i, then place switch $S_{i,j}$ between edge j of p_i-chooser C_i and edge $h(i, v(i, j))'$ of divider $D_{v(i,j)}$.
2. (Connect the choosers in series.) For each $1 \leq i < s$, connect vertex$_{\mathcal{H}}(B, C_i)$ to vertex$_{\mathcal{H}}(A, C_{i+1})$ with a simple directed edge.
3. (Connect the dividers in series.) For each $1 \leq j < n$, connect vertex$_{\mathcal{H}}(B, D_j)$ to vertex$_{\mathcal{H}}(A, D_{j+1})$ with a simple directed edge.
4. (Connect the selectors in series.) For each $1 \leq k < m$, connect vertex$_{\mathcal{H}}(J, L_k)$ to vertex$_{\mathcal{H}}(A, L_{k+1})$ with a simple directed edge.

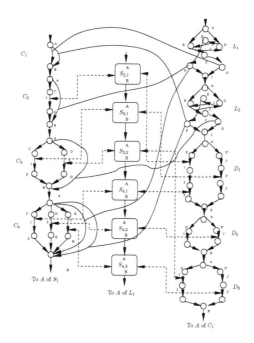

Fig. 4. Hyperedges used to connect gadgets when $\phi = (x_1 \vee \overline{x_2}) \wedge (\overline{x_1} \vee y_1) \wedge (x_2 \vee \overline{y_1} \vee y_3) \wedge (\overline{x_1} \vee \overline{x_2} \vee y_1 \vee \overline{y_2} \vee \overline{y_3})$. C_1, C_2, C_3, and C_4 are 0-chooser, 1-chooser, 2-chooser, and 3-chooser, respectively. D_1, D_2, and D_3 are 3-divider, 1-divider, and 2-divider, respectively. $S_{2,1}, \ldots, S_{4,3}$ are switches and L_1 and L_2 are selectors in $\mathcal{H}$. The hyperedges connecting selectors to choosers are bypass hyperedges

5. (Connect the switches in series.) For each ℓ_1, ℓ_2, where $1 \leq \ell_1 \leq s$ and $1 \leq \ell_2 \leq p_{\ell_1}$, if $\mathrm{succ}(S_{\ell_1, \ell_2})$ is defined then connect $\mathrm{vertex}_{\mathcal{H}}(B, S_{\ell_1, \ell_2})$ to $\mathrm{vertex}_{\mathcal{H}}(A, \mathrm{succ}(S_{\ell_1, \ell_2}))$ with a simple directed edge.

6. (Connect choosers, switches and selectors.) If ϕ does not contain any variable from Y, then connect $\mathrm{vertex}_{\mathcal{H}}(B, C_s)$ to $\mathrm{vertex}_{\mathcal{H}}(A, L_1)$ with a simple directed edge. Otherwise, i.e., if there is at least one clause ϕ_i with an occurrence of a Y variable, do the following. Let S_{ℓ_1, ℓ_2} be the first switch and $S_{\ell'_1, \ell'_2}$ be the last switch (note: switches are ordered in the lexicographic ordering of pairs (i,j) denoting switches $S_{i,j}$ such that $1 \leq \ell_1 \leq s$, $1 \leq \ell'_1 \leq s$, $1 \leq \ell_2 \leq p_{\ell_1}$ and $1 \leq \ell'_2 \leq p_{\ell'_1}$. Connect $\mathrm{vertex}_{\mathcal{H}}(B, C_s)$ to $\mathrm{vertex}_{\mathcal{H}}(A, S_{\ell_1, \ell_2})$ and connect $\mathrm{vertex}_{\mathcal{H}}(B, S_{\ell'_1, \ell'_2})$ to $\mathrm{vertex}_{\mathcal{H}}(A, L_1)$ with simple directed edges.

7. (Connect dividers and choosers.) Connect $\mathrm{vertex}_{\mathcal{H}}(B, D_n)$ to $\mathrm{vertex}_{\mathcal{H}}(A, C_1)$ with a simple directed edge.

8. (Connect selectors and dividers.) Connect $\mathrm{vertex}_{\mathcal{H}}(J, L_m)$ to $\mathrm{vertex}_{\mathcal{H}}(A, D_1)$ with a simple directed edge.

9. **Bypass hyperedges:** (Connect the selector L_i corresponding to a variable x_i with the chooser C_j.) If a variable x_i occurs as x_i in ϕ_j, then add a hyperedge $(\{\mathrm{vertex}_{\mathcal{H}}(G, L_i), \mathrm{vertex}_{\mathcal{H}}(A, C_j)\}, \{\mathrm{vertex}_{\mathcal{H}}(B, C_j)\})$. Otherwise, if x_i

occurs as $\overline{x_i}$ in ϕ_j then add a hyperedge $(\{\text{vertex}_{\mathcal{H}}(F, L_i), \text{vertex}_{\mathcal{H}}(A, C_j)\}, \{\text{vertex}_{\mathcal{H}}(B, C_j)\})$.

We show in [27] that if $\langle X, Y, \phi \rangle \in \text{QSAT}_2(F)$ then the cyclomatic number of $\mathcal{H}$ is m and if $\langle X, Y, \phi \rangle \notin \text{QSAT}_2(F)$ then the cyclomatic number of $\mathcal{H}$ is $m + 1$.   ∎

Via constructions based on the gadgets used in the proof of Theorem 8, we can show the following results.

Theorem 9. *For every* $k \geq 2$, MIN-CYCLOMATIC-SET *is* Π_2^p-*complete when restricted to* k-*directed hypergraphs.*

Theorem 10. *For every* $k \geq 2$, MINIMAL-CYCLOMATIC-SET *is* DP-*complete when restricted to* k-*directed B-hypergraphs.*

6   Succinct Representations of Directed Hypergraphs

It is to be noted that a hypergraph on n vertices may have $\Theta(3^n)$ hyperedges in the worst case. In contrast, the number of edges in a (simple) graph is $O(n^2)$. From an implementation perspective, any representation that stores information for individual hyperedges of a hypergraph is impractical for hypergraphs with a large number of hyperedges. Thus, alternative ways to represent hypergraphs must be explored. Several graphs occurring in practice, such as the graphs that model VLSI circuits, have a highly organized structure and can be described in a succinct way by a circuit or a boolean formula. Galperin and Wigderson [13] showed that trivial graph properties, (e.g., the existence of a triangle) become NP-complete, and Papadimitriou and Yannakakis [22] showed that graph properties that are ordinarily NP-complete become NEXP-complete when the graph is succinctly described by a circuit. In this section, we investigate the computational complexity of the L-hyperpath existence problem when directed hypergraphs are represented in an exponentially succinct way.

Definition 11.   *1. A succinct representation of a directed hypergraph* $\mathcal{H}(V, E)$, *where* $V = \{1, \ldots, n\}$, *is a boolean circuit* $C_{\mathcal{H}}$ *with* $2n$ *input gates and an output gate such that, for each* $e \subseteq 2^V \times 2^V$, $e \in E$ *if and only if* $C_{\mathcal{H}}(x, y)$ *outputs* 1, *where* $x = \chi_{T(e)}(1) \ldots \chi_{T(e)}(n)$ *and* $y = \chi_{H(e)}(1) \ldots \chi_{H(e)}(n)$.
   2. A succinct representation of a k-*directed hypergraph* $\mathcal{H}(V, E)$, *where* $V = \{1, \ldots, n\}$, *is a boolean circuit* $C_{\mathcal{H}}$ *with* $2k\lceil \log(n + 1) \rceil$ *input gates and an output gate, where* $0^{\lceil \log(n+1) \rceil}$ *is the encoding of a dummy node not in* $\mathcal{H}$ *and for each* $1 \leq i \leq n$, $bin(i)$—*the binary representation of integer* i *in* $\lceil \log(n+1) \rceil$ *bits*—*is the encoding of node* i *in* $\mathcal{H}$. *Furthermore, for each* $e = (\{i_1, \ldots, i_{\ell_1}\}, \{j_1, \ldots, j_{\ell_2}\}) \subseteq 2^V \times 2^V$, $i_1 < \ldots < i_{\ell_1}$ *and* $j_1 < \ldots < j_{\ell_2}$, $e \in E$ *iff* $C_{\mathcal{H}}(x, y)$ *outputs* 1, *where* $x = 0^{(n-\ell_1)\lceil \log(n+1) \rceil} bin(i_{\ell_1}) \ldots bin(i_2)bin(i_1)$ *and* $y = 0^{(n-\ell_2)\lceil \log(n+1) \rceil} bin(j_{\ell_2}) \ldots bin(j_2)bin(j_1)$.

Definition 12.   *1.* SUCCINCT-LHYPERPATH $= \{\langle C, u, v \rangle \,|\, C$ *succinctly represents a directed hypergraph* $\mathcal{H}_C$ *and* $\langle \mathcal{H}_C, u, v \rangle \in$ L-HYPERPATH$\}$.
2. k-SUCCINCT-LHYPERPATH $= \{\langle C, u, v \rangle \,|\, C$ *succinctly represents a k-directed hypergraph* $\mathcal{H}_C$ *and* $\langle \mathcal{H}_C, u, v \rangle \in$ L-HYPERPATH$\}$.

Wagner [29] (see also [22]) showed that even for simple subclasses of graphs—directed trees, directed acyclic graphs, directed forests, and undirected forests—the reachability problem for each class with succinct input representation is PSPACE-complete. Tantau [25] showed that the reachability problem for succinctly represented (strong) tournaments is Π_2^p-complete. Using the proof of Theorem 5, it can be easily shown that SUCCINCT-LHYPERPATH is NP-complete and, for every $k \geq 2$, k-SUCCINCT-LHYPERPATH is NEXP-complete.

We leave open the exact complexity of the L-hyperpath existence problem with succinct input representation for particular subclasses of directed hypergraphs.

7   Open Problems

Theorem 5 proves that L-HYPERPATH in NP-complete even when restricted to 2-directed hypergraphs with only B-hyperedges. However, Theorem 8 only shows that the CYCLOMATIC-NUMBER problem is Σ_2^p-complete for 2-directed hypergraphs. In fact, the construction uses both B- and F-hyperedges. It is interesting to analyze the complexity of the CYCLOMATIC-NUMBER problem restricted to directed hypergraphs with only B-hyperedges.

Acharya [1] showed a connection between the cyclomatic number and the planarity of an undirected hypergraph. It will be interesting to find connections between the cyclomatic number of directed hypergraphs w.r.t. L-hypercycles and notions in the theory of directed hypergraphs.

In this paper, we mentioned three problem domains where L-hyperpaths can be used to model the problem. It will be interesting to find more domains where L-hyperpaths can be used to model interesting problems.

Acknowledgment. We thank Edith Hemaspaandra, Lane Hemaspaandra, Christopher Homan, Proshanto Mukherji, Srinivasan Parathasarathy, Len Schubert, and Holger Spakowski for helpful discussions and insightful comments. We are grateful to anonymous referees for helpful comments.

References

[1] B. Acharya. On the cyclomatic number of a hypergraph. *Discrete Mathematics*, 27:111–116, 1979.

[2] P. Alimonti, E. Feuerstein, and U. Nanni. Linear time algorithms for liveness and boundedness in conflict-free Petri nets. In *Proceedings, 1st Latin American Symposium on Theoretical Informatics*, pages 1–14. Springer-Verlag *Lecture Notes in Computer Science #583*, 1992.

[3] G. Ausiello, A. D'Atri, and D. Saccá. Graph algorithms for functional dependency manipulation. *Journal of the ACM*, 30:752–766, 1983.

[4] G. Ausiello, A. D'Atri, and D. Saccá. Minimal representation of directed hypergraphs. *SIAM Journal on Computing*, 15:418–431, 1986.

[5] G. Ausiello, P. Franciosa, and D. Frigioni. Directed hypergraphs: Problems, algorithmic results, and a novel decremental approach. In *Italian Conference on TCS*, pages 312–328. Springer-Verlag *LNCS #2202*, 2001.

[6] G. Ausiello and R. Giaccio. On-line algorithms for satisfiability formulae with uncertainty. *Theoretical Computer Science*, 171:3–24, 1997.

[7] G. Ausiello, R. Giaccio, G. Italiano, and U. Nanni. Optimal traversal of directed hypergraphs. Manuscript, 1997.

[8] G. Ausiello, G. Italiano, and U. Nanni. Hypergraph traversal revisited: Cost measures and dynamic algorithms. In *Proceedings of the 23rd International Symposium on MFCS*, pages 1–16. Springer-Verlag *LNCS #1450*, 1998.

[9] C. Berge. *Graphs and Hypergraphs*. North-Holland, 1973.

[10] G. Gallo, G. Longo, S. Pallottino, and S. Nguyen. Directed hypergraphs and applications. *Discrete Applied Mathematics*, 42:177–201, 1993.

[11] G. Gallo and G. Rago. A hypergraph approach to logical inference for datalog formulae. Technical Report 28/90, Dip. di Informatica, Univ. of Pisa, Italy, 1990.

[12] G. Gallo and M. Scutella. Directed hypergraphs as a modelling paradigm. Technical Report TR-99-02, Dipartimento di Informatica, February 1999.

[13] H. Galperin and A. Wigderson. Succinct representations of graphs. *Information and Control*, 56(3):183–198, March 1983.

[14] M. Garey and D. Johnson. *Computers and Intractability: A Guide to the Theory of NP-Completeness*. W. H. Freeman and Company, 1979.

[15] G. Italiano and U. Nanni. On line maintainenance of minimal directed hypergraphs. In *3rd Italian Conf. on Theoretical Computer Science*, pages 335–349. World Scientific Co., 1989.

[16] D. Klein and C. Manning. Parsing and hypergraphs. In *Proceedings of the 7th International Workshop on Parsing Technologies (IWPT-2001)*, 2001.

[17] D. Knuth. A generalization of Dijkstra's algorithm. *Information Processing Letters*, 6(1):1–5, 1977.

[18] S. Nguyen and S. Pallottino. Hyperpaths and shortest hyperpaths. *Combinatorial Optimization*, 1403:258–271, 1989.

[19] L. Nielsen, D. Pretolani, and K. Andersen. A remark on the definition of a B-hyperpath. Technical report, Department of Operations Research, University of Aarhus, 2001.

[20] N. Nilson. *Principles of Artificial Intelligence*. Springer Verlag, 1982.

[21] C. Papadimitriou. *Computational Complexity*. Addison-Wesley, 1994.

[22] C. Papadimitriou and M. Yannakakis. A note on succinct representations of graphs. *Information and Control*, 71(3):181–185, December 1986.

[23] C. Petri. Communication with automata. Technical Report Supplement 1 to Tech. Report RADC-TR-65-377,1, Univ. of Bonn, 1962.

[24] G. Ramalingam and T. Reps. An incremental algorithm for a generalization of the Shortest Path problem. *Journal of Algorithms*, 21:267–305, 1996.

[25] T. Tantau. A note on the complexity of the reachability problem for tournaments. In *ECCCTR: Electronic Colloquium on Computational Complexity*, 2001.

[26] O. Temkin, A. Zeigarnik, and D. Bonchev. *Chemical Reaction Networks: A Graph-Theoretical Approach*. CRC Press, 1996.

[27] M. Thakur and R. Tripathi. Complexity of linear connectivity problems in directed hypergraphs. Technical Report TR814, Department of Computer Science, University of Rochester, September 2003.

[28] J. Ullman. *Principles of Database Systems*. Computer Science Press, 1982.

[29] K. Wagner. The complexity of combinatorial problems with succinct input representations. *Acta Informatica*, 23:325–356, 1986.

[30] A. Zeigarnik. On hypercycles and hypercircuits in hypergraphs. *DIMACS Series in Discrete Mathematics and Theoretical Computer Science*, 51, 2000.

Actively Learning to Verify Safety for FIFO Automata

Abhay Vardhan, Koushik Sen, Mahesh Viswanathan, and Gul Agha*

Dept. of Computer Science, Univ. of Illinois at Urbana-Champaign, USA
{vardhan, ksen, vmahesh, agha}@cs.uiuc.edu

Abstract. We apply machine learning techniques to verify *safety* properties of *finite state machines* which communicate over *unbounded FIFO channels*. Instead of attempting to iteratively compute the reachable states, we use *Angluin's L* algorithm* to learn these states symbolically as a regular language. The learnt set of reachable states is then used either to prove that the system is safe, or to produce a valid execution of the system that leads to an unsafe state (*i.e.* to produce a counterexample). Specifically, we assume that we are given a model of the system and we provide a novel procedure which answers both *membership* and *equivalence* queries for a representation of the reachable states. We define a new *encoding* scheme for representing reachable states and their witness execution; this enables the learning algorithm to analyze a larger class of FIFO systems automatically than a naive encoding would allow. We show the upper bounds on the running time and space for our method. We have implemented our approach in Java, and we demonstrate its application to a few case studies.

1   Introduction

Infinite state systems often arise as natural models for various software systems at the design and modeling stage. An interesting class of infinite state systems consists of finite state machines that communicate over unbounded first-in-first-out channels, called *FIFO automata*. FIFO automata are commonly used to model various communication protocols; languages, such as Estelle and SDL (Specification and Description Language), in which processes have infinite queue size; distributed systems and various *actor* systems. A generic task in the automated verification of safety properties of any system is to compute a representation for the set of reachable states. For finite state systems, this is typically done by an exhaustive exploration of the state-space. However, for infinite state systems, exhaustive exploration of the state space is impossible; in fact, the verification problem in general can shown to be undecidable.

* The third author was supported in part by DARPA/AFOSR MURI Award F49620-02-1-0325 and NSF 04-29639. The other three authors were supported in part by DARPA IPTO TASK Program (contract F30602-00-2-0586), ONR Grant N00014-02-1-0715, and Motorola Grant MOTOROLA RPS #23 ANT.

K. Lodaya and M. Mahajan (Eds.): FSTTCS 2004, LNCS 3328, pp. 494–505, 2004.

In the LEVER (LEarning to VERify) project, we are pursuing the goal of using *machine learning* techniques for verification of infinite state systems. The idea is as follows. Instead of computing the reachable states by iteratively applying the transition relation until a fixpoint is reached (which may not be possible in a finite number of iterations), we view the identification of the reachable states as a *language inference* problem. Naturally, in order for a learner to be able to learn the reachable region, we have to provide it with some information about the reachable states. We can easily find examples of reachable states by executing some sample sequence of transitions. Moreover, given a set of states as the supposed reachable region, we can check if this set is a fixpoint under the transition relation. If it is not a fixpoint then clearly it is not the correct reachable region. However, most learning algorithms also require either negative examples of the concept being learned or the ability to make membership and equivalence queries. To provide this information, the algorithm learns an *annotated trace language* representing reachable states as well as system executions witnessing the reachability of these states. If the learning algorithm outputs a set of traces that is closed under the transition relation of the system and does not reach any of the unsafe states then clearly the system can deemed to be correct. On the other hand, unsafe states output by the learning algorithm can be used to obtain executions (called counter-examples) leading to the unsafe state because we learn traces which provide witnesses along with the reachable states. Spurious counter-examples can be used by the learner to refine the hypothesis, and the process is repeated until either a valid counterexample is found or the system is shown to be correct. Finally, based on the practical success enjoyed by *regular model checking* [6], we assume that the set of annotated traces to be learnt is regular. Our main observation is that this learning based approach is a *complete verification* method for systems whose annotated trace language is regular (for a precise condition see Section 4). In other words, for such systems, we will eventually either find a buggy execution that violates the safety property, or we will successfully prove that no unsafe state is reachable. We have previously applied the RPNI[11] algorithm for verification of safety properties [14].

This paper presents two main new ideas. Firstly, we give a new scheme for the *annotations* on traces. With this annotation scheme, many more practical FIFO systems have regular annotated trace languages, thus enlarging the class of systems that can be provably verified by our method. Secondly and more significantly, we provide a method to devise a *knowledgeable teacher* which can answer membership (whether a string belongs to the target) as well as equivalence-queries (given a hypothesis, whether it matches the concept being learnt). In the context of learning annotated traces, equivalence queries can be answered only to a limited extent. However, we overcome our limitation to answer equivalence queries exactly and present an approach that is still able to use the powerful query-based learning framework. Our decision to use Angluin's L* algorithm [2] gives us significant benefits. First, the number of samples we need to consider is polynomial in the size of the *minimal* automaton representing the annotated traces. Second, we are guaranteed to learn the minimal automaton that represents the annotated traces. Finally, we can show that the running time is bounded by a polynomial in the size of the minimal automaton representing the annotated traces and the time taken to verify if an annotated trace is valid for the FIFO system.

We have implemented our algorithm in Java and demonstrated the feasibility of this method by running the implementation on simple examples and network protocols, such as the alternating-bit protocol and the sliding window protocol. Our approach is complementary to previously proposed algorithmic verification methods; there are examples of FIFO automata that our method successfully verifies; however other approaches, fail (see [13]). We give the requirements under which classes of infinite state systems other than FIFO automata can be verified using the learning approach. Proofs of propositions and the details of the complexity analysis are available in the full version of the paper [13].

Related Work: For automatic verification of infinite state FIFO systems, the state space has to be represented by symbolic means. Some common representations are regular sets [6,1], Queue Decision Diagrams [4], semi-linear regular expressions [7], and constrained QDDs [5]. Since an iterative approach of computing the fixpoint for reachability may not terminate, various mechanisms are used for finding the reachable set. In the approach using *meta-transitions* and *acceleration* [4,5,7], a sequence of transitions, referred to as a *meta-transition*, is selected, and the effect of its infinite iteration is calculated. Another popular method for verification of FIFO automata (and parameterized and integer systems) is *regular model checking* [6,1] where reachable states are represented as regular sets, and a transducer is used to represent the transition relation. An approach for computing the reachable region that is closely related to ours is *widening* given in [6] and extended in [12] for parametric systems. However, in addition to proving a system correct, our approach can also detect bugs, which is not possible using widening (except for certain special contexts where it can be shown to be exact).

We introduced the learning to verify approach in [14], where we used RPNI [11] to learn the regular set from positive and negative queries without active queries. Concurrently and independently of our work, Habermehl *et al.* [8] have also proposed a learning based approach for verification of systems whose transition can be represented by a length-preserving transducer. They find all strings of a certain length that can be reached from the initial state and use a state merging algorithm to learn the regular set representing the reachable region.

A more detailed description of the related work is available from the full version of this paper [13].

2   Learning Framework

We use Angluin's L* algorithm [2] which falls under the category of *active learning*. Angluin's L* algorithm requires a *Minimally Adequate Teacher*, which provides an oracle for membership (whether a given string belongs to a target regular set) and equivalence queries (whether a given hypothesis matches the target regular set). If the teacher answers *no* to an equivalence query, it also provides a string in the symmetric difference of the hypothesis and the target sets. The main idea behind Angluin's L* algorithm is to systematically explore strings in the alphabet for membership and create a DFA with minimum number of states to make a conjecture for the target set. If the conjecture is incorrect, the string returned by the teacher is used to make corrections, possibly after more membership queries. The algorithm maintains a prefix closed set S representing different possible states of the target DFA, a set SA for the transition function consisting of strings from S extended with one letter of the alphabet, and a suffix closed set E denoting *experiments* to distinguish between states. An *observation table* with rows from $(S \cup SA)$ and columns from E stores results of the membership queries for strings in $(S \cup SA).E$ and is used to create the DFA for a conjecture. Angluin's algorithm is guaranteed to terminate in polynomial time with the minimal DFA representing the target set.

3   FIFO Automata

A FIFO automaton [7] is a 6-tuple $(Q, q_0, C, M, \Theta, \delta)$ where Q is a finite set of *control states*, $q_0 \in Q$ is the initial control state, C is a finite set of *channel names*, M is a finite alphabet for contents of a channel, Θ is a finite set of transitions names, and $\delta : \Theta \to Q \times ((C \times \{?, !\} \times M) \cup \{\tau\}) \times Q$ is a function that assigns a *control transition* to each transition name. For a transition name θ, if the associated control transition $\delta(\theta)$ is of the form $(q, c?m, q')$ then it denotes a *receive* action, if it is of the form $(q, c!m, q')$ it denotes a *send* action, and if it is of the form (q, τ, q') then it denotes an *internal* action. We use the standard operational semantics of FIFO automata in which channels are considered to be perfect and messages sent by a sender are received in the order in which they were sent. For states $s_1, s_2 \in S = Q \times (M^*)^C$, we write $s_1 \xrightarrow{\theta} s_2$ if the transition θ leads from s_1 to s_2. For $\sigma = \theta_1 \theta_2 \cdots \theta_n \in \Theta^*$, we say $s \xrightarrow{\sigma} s'$ when there exist states $s_1 \ldots s_{n-1}$ such that $s \xrightarrow{\theta_1} s_1 \xrightarrow{\theta_2} \cdots s_{n-1} \xrightarrow{\theta_n} s'$. The trace language of the FIFO automaton is $L(F) = \{\sigma \in \Theta^* \mid \exists s. \; s_0 \xrightarrow{\sigma} s\}$ where $s_0 = (q_0, (\epsilon, \ldots, \epsilon))$, i.e., the initial control state with no messages in the channels.

4   Verification Procedure

We assume that we are given a model of the FIFO automata which enables us to identify the transition relation of the system. To use Angluin's L* algorithm for learning, we need to answer both membership and equivalence queries for the reachable set. However, there is no immediate way of answering a membership query (whether a certain state is actually reachable or not). Therefore, instead of learning the set of reachable states directly, we learn a language which allows us to identify both the reachable states and candidate witnesses (in terms of the transitions of the system) to these states. The validity of any witness can then be checked, allowing membership queries to be answered.

For equivalence queries, we can provide an answer in one direction. We will show that the reachable region with its witness executions can be seen as the least fixpoint of a relation derived from the transitions. Hence, an answer to the equivalence query can come from checking if the proposed language is a fixpoint under this relation. If it is not a fixpoint then it is certainly not equivalent to the target; but if it is a fixpoint, we are unable to tell if it is also the least fixed point. However, we are ultimately interested in only checking whether a given safety property holds. If the proposed language is a fixpoint but does not intersect with the unsafe region, the safety property clearly holds and we are done. On the other hand, if the fixpoint does intersect with unsafe states, we can check if such an unsafe state is indeed reachable using the membership query. If the unsafe state is reachable then we have found a valid counterexample to the safety property and are done. Otherwise the proposed language is not the right one since it contains an invalid trace.

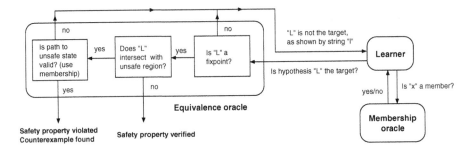

Fig. 1. Verification procedure

Figure 1 shows the high level view of the verification procedure. The main problems we have to address now are:

- What is a suitable representation for the reachable states and their witnesses?
- Given a language representation, we need to answer the following questions raised in Figure 1:
    - (Membership Query) Given a string x, is x a valid string for a reachable state and its witness?
    - (Equivalence Query(I)) Is a hypothetical language L a fixpoint under the transition relation? If not, we need a string which demonstrates that L is not a fixpoint.
    - (Equivalence Query(II)) Does any string in L witness the reachability of some "unsafe" state?

4.1   Representation of the Reachable States and Their Witnesses

Let us now consider the language which can allow us to find both reachable states and their witnesses. The first choice that comes to mind is the language of the traces, $L(F)$. Since each trace uniquely determines the final state in the trace, $L(F)$ has the information about the states that can be reached. While it is easy to compute the state s such that $s_0 \xrightarrow{\sigma} s$ for a *single* trace σ, it is not clear how to obtain the set of states reached, given a *set of traces*. In fact, even if $L(F)$ is regular, there is no known algorithm to compute the corresponding set of reachable states.[1] The main difficulty is that determining if a receive action can be executed depends non-trivially on the sequence of actions executed before the receive.

In [14], we overcame this difficulty by annotating the traces in a way that makes it possible to compute the set of reachable states. We briefly describe this annotation scheme before presenting the actual scheme used in this paper. Consider a set $\overline{\Theta}$ of *co-names* defined as follows:

$$\overline{\Theta} = \{\overline{\theta} \mid \theta \in \Theta \text{ and } \delta(\theta) \notin Q \times \{\tau\} \times Q\}$$

Thus, for every send or receive action in our FIFO automaton, there is a new transition name with a *bar*. A barred transition $\overline{\theta}$ in an annotated trace of the system denotes either a message sent that will later be consumed, or the receipt of a message that was sent earlier in the trace. Annotated traces of the automaton are obtained by marking send-receive pairs in a trace exhibited by the system.

The above annotation scheme allowed us to calculate the reachable set for any regular set of annotated traces by a simple homomorphism. However, one difficulty we encountered is that for some practical FIFO systems, the annotated trace language is not regular; the nonregularity often came from the fact that a receive transition has to be matched to a send which could have happened at an arbitrary time earlier in the past. To alleviate this problem, we use a new annotation scheme in which only the send part of the send-receive pair is kept. This gives an annotated trace language which is regular for a much larger class of FIFO systems (although we cannot hope to be able to cover all classes of FIFO systems since they are Turing expressive). We now describe this annotation in detail.

As before, we have a new set of barred names but this time only for the send transitions:

$$\overline{\Theta} = \{\overline{\theta} \mid \theta \in \Theta \text{ and } \delta(\theta) \in Q \times \{c_i!a_j\} \times Q \text{ for some } c_i, a_j\}$$

We also define another set of names $T_Q = \{t_q \mid q \in Q\}$ consisting of a symbol for each control state in the FIFO.

Now let the alphabet of *annotated traces* Σ be defined as $(\Theta - \Theta_r) \cup \overline{\Theta} \cup T_Q$ where Θ_r is the set of receive transitions $\{\theta_r \mid \delta(\theta_r) \in Q \times \{c_i?a_j\} \times Q \text{ for some } c_i, a_j\}$.

Given a sequence of transitions l in $L(F)$, let $\mathcal{A}$ be a function which produces an annotated string in Σ^*. $\mathcal{A}$ takes each receive transition θ_{r_i} in l and finds the

---

[1] This can sometimes be computed for simple loops using meta-transitions.

matching send transition θ_{s_i} which must occur earlier in l. Then, θ_{r_i} is removed and θ_{s_i} replaced by $\overline{\theta_{s_i}}$. Once all the receive transitions have been accounted for, $\mathcal{A}$ appends the symbol $t_q \in T_Q$ corresponding to the control state q which is the destination of the last transition in l. Intuitively, for a send-receive pair which cancel each other's effect on the channel contents, $\mathcal{A}$ deletes the received transition and replaces the send transition with a barred symbol. As before, a barred symbol indicates that the message sent gets consumed by a later receive. Notice that in the old annotation scheme both the send and the receive were replaced with a barred version; here the receive transition is dropped altogether. The reason we still keep the send transition with a bar is, as we will show shortly, that this allows us to decide whether any given string is a valid annotated trace. The symbol t_q is appended to the annotated trace to record the fact that the trace l leads to the control state q.

As an example, consider the FIFO automaton shown in Figure 2. For the following traces in $L(F)$: $\theta_1\theta_2\theta_3$, $\theta_1\theta_2\theta_3\theta_1\theta_2$, the strings output by $\mathcal{A}$ are respectively: $\overline{\theta_1}\theta_3 t_{q_0}$, $\overline{\theta_1}\theta_3\theta_1 t_{q_2}$.

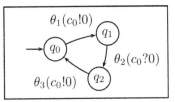

Fig. 2. A FIFO automaton

Let the language of annotated traces be $AL(F) = \{\mathcal{A}(t) \mid t \in L(F)\}$ which consists of all strings in Σ^* that denote correctly annotated traces of F. Let $AL^{old}(F)$ be the annotated trace language corresponding to the old annotation scheme described earlier (in which we keep both parts of a send-receive pair). The following proposition shows that the new annotation scheme has regular annotated trace language for more FIFO automata than the old scheme.

Proposition 1. *The set of FIFO automata for which $AL(F)$ is regular is strictly larger than the set of FIFO automata for which $AL^{old}(F)$ is regular.*

$AL(F)$ can be seen to represent both the reachable states of the FIFO system and the annotated traces which in some sense witness the reachability of these states. Thus, $AL(F)$ is a suitable candidate for the language to use in the verification procedure shown in Figure 1.

Given a string l in Σ^*, we say that l is well-formed if l ends with a symbol from T_Q and there is no other occurrence of symbols from T_Q. We say that a language L is well-formed if all strings in L are well-formed. For a well-formed string l ending in symbol t_q, let $\mathcal{T}(l)$ denote the prefix of l without t_q and let $\mathcal{C}(l)$ denote the control state q.

4.2   Answering Membership Queries

In order to answer a membership query for $AL(F)$, given a string l in Σ^* we need to verify if l is a correct annotation for some valid sequence of transitions l' in $L(F)$. Let $\mathcal{A}^{-1}(l)$ be a function which gives the set (possibly empty) of all sequences of transitions l' for which $\mathcal{A}(l') = l$. First, if l is not well-formed, $\mathcal{A}^{-1}(l) = \emptyset$ since all valid annotations are clearly well-formed. Assuming l is well-formed, if we ignore the bars in $\mathcal{T}(l)$, we get a string l'' which could potentially be in $\mathcal{A}^{-1}(l)$ except that the transitions corresponding to any receives are missing. We can identify the possible missing receive transitions by looking at the barred symbols in $\mathcal{T}(l)$; each barred send can potentially be matched by a receive transition that operates on the same channel and has the same letter. However, we do not know the exact positions where these receive transitions are to be inserted in l''. We can try all possible (finitely many) positions and simulate each resulting transition sequence on the fly on the FIFO system. Any transition sequence which is valid on the FIFO and gives back l on application of $\mathcal{A}$ is then a member of $\mathcal{A}^{-1}(l)$. If $\mathcal{A}^{-1}(l) \neq \emptyset$ then l is a valid annotated trace.

For illustration, let us consider a membership query for the string $\overline{\theta_1 \theta_3} \theta_1 t_{q_2}$ for the FIFO automata shown in Figure 2. We identify the possible missing receive transitions as two instances of θ_2. Since a receive can only occur after a send for the same channel and letter, the possible completions of the input string with receives are $\{\theta_1 \theta_2 \theta_3 \theta_2 \theta_1, \theta_1 \theta_2 \theta_3 \theta_1 \theta_2, \theta_1 \theta_3 \theta_2 \theta_2 \theta_1, \theta_1 \theta_3 \theta_2 \theta_1 \theta_2, \theta_1 \theta_3 \theta_1 \theta_2 \theta_2\}$. Of these, $\theta_1 \theta_2 \theta_3 \theta_1 \theta_2$ can be correctly simulated on the FIFO system and gives back the input string $\overline{\theta_1 \theta_3} \theta_1 t_{q_2}$ on application of $\mathcal{A}$. Therefore, the answer to the membership query is *yes*. An example for a negative answer is $\overline{\theta_1} t_{q_0}$.

4.3   Answering Equivalence Queries

For learning $AL(F)$ in the active learning framework, we need a method to verify whether a supposed language L of annotated traces is equivalent to $AL(F)$. If not, then we also need to identify a string in the symmetric difference of $AL(F)$ and L to allow the learner to make progress.

Given a string $l \in L$ and a transition θ in the FIFO, we can find if it is possible to *extend* l using θ. More precisely, we define a function $Post(l, \theta)$ as follows. If l is well-formed, let $source(\theta)$ and $target(\theta)$ be the control states which are respectively the source and the target of θ.

$$Post(l, \theta) = \begin{cases} \emptyset & \text{if } l \text{ not well-formed or if } \mathcal{C}(l) \neq source(\theta) \\ \{\mathcal{T}(l) \theta\ t_{\text{target}(\theta)}\} & \text{otherwise if } \delta(\theta) = \tau \text{ or } \delta(\theta) = c_i! a_j \\ \{deriv(\mathcal{T}(l), \theta)\ t_{\text{target}(\theta)}\} & \text{otherwise if } \delta(\theta) = c_i? a_j \end{cases}$$

$deriv(\mathcal{T}(l), \theta)$ checks the first occurrence of a send θ_s in $\mathcal{T}(l)$ for channel c_i and if the send is for the character a_j, replaces θ_s with $\overline{\theta_s}$. $deriv(\mathcal{T}(l), \theta)$ is empty if no such θ_s could be found or if θ_s outputs a character other than a_j. Intuitively, *deriv* is similar to the concept of the derivative in formal language theory, except that we look at only the channel that θ operates upon.

Let $Post(l)$ be $\bigcup_{\theta \in \Theta} Post(l, \theta)$ and $Post(L)$ be $\bigcup_{l \in L} Post(l)$.

Theorem 1. *Let* $\mathcal{F}(L) = Post(L) \cup \{t_{q_0}\}$ *where* q_0 *is the initial control state.* $\mathcal{F}(L)$ *is a monotone set operator, i.e. it preserves set-inclusion. Moreover,* $AL(F)$ *is the least fixpoint of the functional* $\mathcal{F}(L)$.

Theorem 1 gives us a method for answering equivalence queries for $AL(F)$ in one direction. If L is not a fixpoint, it cannot be equivalent to $AL(F)$. In this case, we can also find a string in $L \oplus AL(F)$ as required for Angluin's algorithm.

Here, $A \oplus B$ denotes the symmetric difference of two sets. Consider the following cases:

1. $\mathcal{F}(L) - L \neq \emptyset$. Let l be some string in this set. If l is t_{q_0} then it is in $AL(F) \oplus L$. Otherwise, we can check if l is a valid annotation using the procedure described in Section 4.2. If yes, then l is in $AL(F) \oplus L$. Otherwise, it must be true that $l \in Post(l')$ for some $l' \in L$. If l is not valid, l' cannot be valid since $Post()$ of a valid annotation is always valid. Hence $l' \notin AL(F)$ or $l' \in AL(F) \oplus L$.

2. $\mathcal{F}(L) \subsetneq L$. From standard fixpoint theory, since $AL(F)$ is the least fixed point under $\mathcal{F}$, it must be the intersection of all prefixpoints of $\mathcal{F}$ (a set Z is a prefixpoint if it *shrinks* under the functional $\mathcal{F}$, i.e. $\mathcal{F}(Z) \subseteq Z$). Now, L is clearly a prefixpoint. Applying $\mathcal{F}$ to both sides of the equation $\mathcal{F}(L) \subsetneq L$ and using monotonicity of $\mathcal{F}$, we get $\mathcal{F}(\mathcal{F}(L)) \subsetneq \mathcal{F}(L)$. Thus, $\mathcal{F}(L)$ is also a prefixpoint. Let l be some string in the set $L - \mathcal{F}(L)$. Since l is outside the intersection of two prefixpoints, it is not in the least fixpoint $AL(F)$. Hence, l is in $AL(F) \oplus L$.

3. $\mathcal{F}(L) = L$. Let $\mathcal{W}(L)$ be the set of annotated traces in L which can reach unsafe states (We will describe how $\mathcal{W}(L)$ is computed in the next section). If $\mathcal{W}(L)$ is empty, since L is a fixpoint, we can abort the learning procedure and declare that the safety property holds. For the other case, if $\mathcal{W}(L)$ is not empty then let l be some annotated trace in this set. We check if l is a valid annotation using the procedure described in Section 4.2. If it is valid, we have found a valid counterexample and can again abort the whole learning procedure since we have found an answer (in the negative) to the safety property verification. Otherwise, l is in $AL(F) \oplus L$.

A subtle point to note is that although we attempt to learn $AL(F)$, because of the limitation in the equivalence query, the final language obtained after the termination of the verification procedure may not be $AL(F)$. It might be some fixpoint which contains $AL(F)$ or it might be simply some set which contains a valid annotated trace demonstrating the reachability of some unsafe state. However, this is not a cause for concern to us since in all cases the answer for the safety property verification is correct.

4.4   Finding Annotated Traces Leading to Unsafe States

In the previous section, we referred to a set $\mathcal{W}(L)$ in L which can reach unsafe states. We now show how this can be computed.

We assume that for each control state $q \in Q$, we are given a recognizable set [3] describing the unsafe channel configurations. Equivalently, for each q, the unsafe channel contents are given by a finite union of products of regular languages: $\bigcup_{0 \leq i \leq n_q} P_{q,i}$ where $P_{q,i} = \prod_{0 \leq j \leq k} U_q(i, c_j)$ and $U_q(i, c_j)$ is a regular language for contents of channel c_j. For each $P_{q,i}$, an unsafe state s_u is some $(q, u_0, u_1, \ldots u_k)$ such that $u_j \in U_q(i, c_j)$.

For a channel c, consider a function $h_c : \Sigma \to M^*$ defined as follows:

$$h_c(t) = \begin{cases} m \text{ if } t \in \Theta \text{ and } \delta(t) = c!m \\ \epsilon \text{ otherwise} \end{cases}$$

Let h_c also denote the unique homomorphism from Σ^* to M^* that extends the above function.

Let L_q be the subset of an annotated trace set L consisting of all well-formed strings ending in t_q, i.e. $L_q = \{l \mid l \in L \text{ and } \mathcal{C}(l) = q\}$.

If an unsafe state $s_u = (q, u_0, u_1, \ldots u_k)$ is reachable, then there must exist a sequence of transitions $l_\theta \in \Theta^*$ such that $s_0 \xrightarrow{l_\theta} s_u$, where s_0 is the initial state. In l_θ, if the receives and the sends which match the receives are taken out, only the remaining transitions which are sends can contribute to the channel contents in s_u. Looking at the definition of h_c, it can be seen that for each channel content u_j in s_u, $u_j = h_{c_j}(\mathcal{A}(l_\theta))$ (recall that $\mathcal{A}$ converts a sequence of transitions into an annotated trace). Thus, for s_u to be reachable, there must be some annotated trace $l \in AL(F)$ such that $s_u = (\mathcal{C}(l), h_{c_0}(l), h_{c_1}(l), \ldots, h_{c_k}(l))$.

Let $h_{c_j}^{-1}(U_q(i, c_j))$ denote the inverse homomorphism of $U_q(i, c_j)$ under h_{c_j}. For each $P_{q,i}$, $\bigcap_{0 \le j \le k} h_{c_j}^{-1}(U_q(i, c_j))$ gives a set of annotated strings which can reach the unsafe channel configurations for control state q. Intersecting this with L_q verifies if any string in L can reach these set of unsafe states. If we perform such checks for all control states for all $P_{q,i}$, we can verify if any unsafe state is reached by L. Thus, the set of annotated traces in L that can lead to an unsafe state is given by:

$$\mathcal{W}(L) = \bigcup_{q \in Q} \left(\bigcup_{0 \le i \le n_q} \left(L_q \cap \bigcap_{0 \le j \le k} h_{c_j}^{-1}(U_q(i, c_j)) \right) \right)$$

We summarize the verification algorithm in Figure 3.

Theorem 2. *For verifying safety properties of FIFO automata, the learning to verify algorithm satisfies the following properties:*

1. *If an answer is returned by algorithm, it is always correct.*
2. *If $AL(F)$ is regular, the procedure is guaranteed to terminate.*
3. *The number of membership and equivalence queries are at most as many as needed by Angluin's algorithm. The total time taken is bounded by a polynomial in the size of the minimal automaton for $AL(F)$ and linear in the time taken for membership queries for $AL(F)$.*

5   Generalization to Other Infinite State Systems

The verification procedure described for FIFO automata can be generalized to other infinite state systems. The challenge for each class of system is to identify the alphabet Σ which provides an annotation enabling the following:

algorithm *learner*
begin
Angluin's L^* algorithm
end

algorithm *isMember*
Input: Annotated trace l
Output: is $l \in AL(F)$?
begin
  if l not well-formed return *no*
  else
    find receives matching barred symbols
    find possible positions for receives
    simulate resulting strings on FIFO
      system on the fly
    if any string reaches $C(l)$ with
      correct annotation, return *yes*
  return *no*
end

algorithm *Equivalence Check*
Input: Annotated trace set L
Output: is $L = AL(F)$?
If not, then some string in $L \oplus AL(F)$
begin
  $\mathcal{F}(L) = Post(L) \cup \{t_{q_0}\}$
  if $\exists l \in (\mathcal{F}(L) - L)$
    if *isMember(l)*
      return (no, l)
    else
      return (no, l' where $l = Post(l')$)
  else if $\mathcal{F}(L) \subsetneq L$
    return (no, $l \in (L - \mathcal{F}(L))$)
  else if $\exists l \in \mathcal{W}(L)$
    if *isMember(l)*
      Print (safety prop. does not hold, l); stop
    else
      return (no, l)
  else
    Print (safety prop. holds); stop
end

Fig. 3. Learning to verify algorithm

- membership query for the annotated trace language,
- function to compute $Post()$ for a given annotated set, and
- function to find if a string in an annotated set can reach an unsafe state

Notice that in the verification procedure we do not assume anything else about FIFO automata other than the above functions. In fact, the learning algorithm does not have to be limited to regular languages; any suitable class of languages can be used if the required decision procedures are available.

6   Implementation

We have updated the LEVER (LEarning to VERify) tool suite first introduced in [14] with the active learning based verification procedure for FIFO automata. The tool, written in Java, is available from [9]. We use a Java DFA package available from http://www.brics.dk/~amoeller/automaton/.

We have used LEVER to analyze some canonical FIFO automata verification problems: *Producer Consumer*, *Alternating bit protocol* and *Sliding window protocol* (window size and maximum sequence number 2). Table 1

	Size	T	Size$_{old}$	T_{old}	T_{rmc}
Producer Consumer	7	0.3s	20	0.4s	3.3s
Alternating Bit	33	2s	104	4.1s	24.7s
Sliding Window	133	54s	665	81.2s	78.4s

Table 1. Running time

shows the results obtained. We compare the number of states of the final automaton (Size) and the running times (T) using the verification procedure in this paper with the procedure we used earlier in [14] (columns $Size_{old}$ and T_{old}). It can be seen that there is an improvement using the new procedure (although the comparison of Size should be taken with the caveat that the annotation in the two procedures is slightly different). All executions were done on a 1594 MHz notebook computer with 512 MB of RAM using Java virtual machine version 1.4.1 from Sun Microsystems. We also report the time taken (T_{rmc}) by the regular model checking tool [10] on the same examples. Although a complete comparative analysis with all available tools remains to be done, it can be seen the running time of LEVER is slightly better than the regular model checking tool.

References

1. P. A. Abdulla, B. Jonsson, M. Nilsson, and J. d'Orso. Algorithmic improvements in regular model checking. In *Computer-Aided Verification (CAV'03)*, volume 2725 of *LNCS*, pages 236–248. Springer, 2003.
2. D. Angluin. Learning regular sets from queries and counterexamples. *Inform. Comput.*, 75(2):87–106, Nov. 1987.
3. J. Berstel. *Transductions and Context-Free-Languages*. B.G. Teubner, Stuttgart, 1979.
4. B. Boigelot. *Symbolic Methods for Exploring Infinite State Spaces*. PhD thesis, Collection des Publications de la Faculté des Sciences Appliquées de l'Université de Liége, 1999.
5. A. Bouajjani and P. Habermehl. Symbolic reachability analysis of FIFO-channel systems with nonregular sets of configurations. *Theoretical Computer Science*, 221(1–2):211–250, June 1999.
6. A. Bouajjani, B. Jonsson, M. Nilsson, and T. Touili. Regular model checking. In E. A. Emerson and A. P. Sistla, editors, *Proceedings of the 12th International Conference on Computer-Aided Verification (CAV'00)*, volume 1855 of *LNCS*, pages 403–418. Springer, 2000.
7. A. Finkel, S. Purushothaman Iyer, and G. Sutre. Well-abstracted transition systems: Application to FIFO automata. *Information and Computation*, 181(1):1–31, 2003.
8. P. Habermehl and T. Vojnar. Regular model checking using inference of regular languages. In *Proc. of Infinity'04, London, UK (to appear)*, 2004.
9. LEVER. Learning to verify tool. http://osl.cs.uiuc.edu/~{}vardhan/lever.html, 2004.
10. M. Nilsson. http://www.regularmodelchecking.com, 2004.
11. J. Oncina and P. Garcia. Inferring regular languages in polynomial update time. In *Pattern Recognition and Image Analysis*, volume 1 of *Series in Machine Perception and Artificial Intelligence*, pages 49–61. World Scientific, Singapore, 1992.
12. T. Touili. Regular model checking using widening techniques. In *ENTCS*, volume 50. Elsevier, 2001.
13. A. Vardhan, K. Sen, M. Viswanathan, and G. Agha. Actively learning to verify safety for FIFO automata (full version). http://osl.cs.uiuc.edu/docs/lever-active/activeFifo.pdf, 2004.
14. A. Vardhan, K. Sen, M. Viswanathan, and G. Agha. Learning to verify safety properties. In *Proc. of ICFEM'04, Seattle, USA (to appear)*, 2004.

Reasoning About Game Equilibria
Using Temporal Logic

G. Venkatesh

Indian Institute of Management, Bangalore - 560076, India

Abstract. We use linear time temporal logic formulas to model strategic and extensive form games. This allows us to use temporal tableau to reason about the game structure. We order the nodes of the tableau according to the players' preferences. Using this, we can derive a decision procedure for reasoning about the equilibria of these games. The main result developed in this paper is that every finite game can be converted into an equivalent bargaining game on temporal tableau, where the players negotiate the equilbrium outcome. The decision method proposed in this paper has a number of merits compared to others that can be found in the growing literature connecting games to logic - it captures a wide variety of game forms, it is easy to understand and implement, and it can be enhanced to take into account bounded rationality assumptions.

1   Introduction

There has been considerable recent interest in the connections between game theory and logic. In one direction, game theory has helped formulate better semantic models for a variety of logics [10]. In the other direction, modal logic has helped in understanding games and equilibria, specifically the epistemic issues in games of imperfect or incomplete information [4, 3, 2, 11, 6, 7, 14, 1, 9].

The idea of using a temporal logic (CTL) to model extensive games and to reason about backward induction was discussed in [2]. The key argument used here is that CTL frames have sufficient structure to represent the game trees of sequential games. In [3], a new consequence mechanism (different from the usual logical consequence relation) is defined so that propositional formulas hold in the Nash equlibrium of a strategic game iff these formulas are consequences of theories representing the players' preference orderings. By using an appropriate modal logic, this idea is extended to extensive games and subgame pefect equilibria in [4]. In [11, 6], a logic programming setting is used to capture the game structure and players' preferences, so that properties of the game equilibria can be directly computed.

In this paper, we motivate the use of a simple linear time temporal logic formulation to model and reason about both strategic form (simultaneous move) and extensive form (sequential move) games. As in [2], we argue that there is enough structure in the models of linear time temporal logic to represent a variety of game forms. Besides, we can extend the tableau based decision procedures for

K. Lodaya and M. Mahajan (Eds.): FSTTCS 2004, LNCS 3328, pp. 506–517, 2004.

temporal logic ([13, 5, 14]) to compute game theoretic consequences as defined in
[3]. This is accomplished by modeling each player's preferences using an ordering
relationship on the tableau nodes, and by converting the original game into a
negotiation game on the nodes of the tableau. A notable aspect of the ordering of
the tableau nodes is that it accomodates defeasible reasoning, which is required
to resolve some of the paradoxes arising in repeated games.

The paper is organised as follows: Section 1 introduces strategic games and
PTL, with examples showing the approach. Section 2 deals with extensive form
games. Section 3 explains the basic result showing equivalence between game
equilibria and negotiation outcomes on temporal tableau. Sections 4 and 5 conclude with possible extensions and directions for future work.

2   Strategic Form Games

Strategic game situations arise when a set of players make their moves simultaneously, and the outcome of the game is dependent on the combination of
moves selected by the players. We follow the notation in [8], where the set of
players is denoted by $N = \{1, ..., n\}$, and for each player $i \in N$, the (finite
set of) actions (also called choices or strategies) available to her is denoted by
A_i, with $A_i \cap A_j = \phi$ for $i \neq j$. The set of consequences is denoted by $\mathcal{C}$.
$\mathcal{A} = A_1 \times A_2 \times ... \times A_n$ is the set of *strategy profiles*.

A *strategic game form* is given by $\mathcal{G} = < N, \mathcal{A}, \mathcal{C}, g >$ where $g : \mathcal{A} \to \mathcal{C}$
is a map that associates with each strategy profile a consequence. The player's
preferences for the consequences is given by the complete, reflexive, transitive
ordering $\succeq_i$ on $\mathcal{C}$. A *strategic game* $<\mathcal{G}, \succeq_i>$ is a strategic game form together
with a preference ordering for each player.

To model uncertainty between action and consequence, we could consider
a set of states Ω, and write the consequence relation $g : \mathcal{A} \times \Omega \to \mathcal{C}$. It is
useful to recall [9], who considers consequences, acts and states as three ways
of partitioning a space of possible worlds. *Consequences* partition the space of
possibilities by what matters to the agent. *Acts* partition the space by what the
agent controls, or has the capacity to decide, and *States* by features of the world
on which the consequences may depend, but over which the agent has no control.

2.1   PTL

We use propositional variables P_i^r to denote that player i has chosen an action
$a_r \in A_i$. We assume that each consequence in $\mathcal{C}$ can be described using a propositional language using variables C_j, $j = 1, ..., m$. Similarly, we assume that states
in Ω can be described using a propositional language with variables $M \in Aux$.
Define PTL by the BNF grammar:

$$\phi ::= P_i^r \mid C_j \mid M \mid \neg\phi \mid \phi_1 \wedge \phi_2 \mid \phi_1 \vee \phi_2 \mid \bigcirc \phi \mid \square\phi \mid \Diamond\phi \mid \phi_1 \bigcup \phi_2$$

We abbreviate $\neg\phi_1 \vee \phi_2$ by $\phi_1 \Rightarrow \phi_2$, $(\phi_1 \Rightarrow \phi_2) \wedge (\phi_2 \Rightarrow \phi_1)$ by $\phi_1 \Leftrightarrow \phi_2$,
and $\phi_1 \Leftrightarrow \neg\phi_2$ by $\phi_1 \oplus \phi_2$.

2.2   Modeling Strategic Form Games in PTL

We take it that actions of players in this period have bearing on the consequences in the next period. Thus, the relationship between actions and consequences is captured through temporal formulas using the next operator $\bigcirc$. For example, the statement "If player 1 chooses a_1 and Player 2 chooses a_2 then the consequence is C_1" is represented by $P_1^1 \wedge P_2^2 \Rightarrow \bigcirc C_1$. To express that each player has to choose exactly one of her actions, we can use the choice formulas $P_i^r \Rightarrow \bigwedge_{r' \neq r} \neg P_i^{r'}$. We let $\Gamma(\mathcal{G})$ denote the set of all such action-consequence and choice formulas arising from the game form $\mathcal{G}$, and will abbreviate $\Gamma(\mathcal{G})$ to Γ whenever the game form is clear from the context.

We assume that for each player i, there is a complete, reflexive, transitive ordering $\succeq_i$ on $\{C_j | j = 1, ..., m\}$. We can always directly derive this ordering from the ordering of $\mathcal{C}$, if we use one variable C_j to represent an element of $\mathcal{C}$. But, as we shall see later, we could gain some modeling flexibility by considering the ordering on C_j and allowing properties of $\mathcal{C}$ to be modeled by propositional formulas over C_j.

Example 1 (Prisoner's Dilemma).
Game Description: Two suspects in a crime are put into separate cells. If they both confess, each will be sentenced to 3 years in prison. If only one of them confesses, he will be freed and used as a witness against the other, who will receive 5 years. If neither confesses, they will both be convicted for a minor offense and spend one year in prison.

We use four action propositions $P_1^c, P_1^n, P_2^c, P_2^n$, where P_i^c means i chooses to confess and P_i^n means i chooses to not confess. The four consequences are $C_{3y,3y}, C_{5y,free}, C_{free,5y}, C_{1y,1y}$, where $C_{p,q}$ represents the sentence p for Player 1 and q for Player 2. The temporal formulas representing this game are:

(F1) $P_1^c \wedge P_2^c \Rightarrow \bigcirc C_{3y,3y}$ (F2) $P_1^c \wedge P_2^n \Rightarrow \bigcirc C_{free,5y}$
(F3) $P_1^n \wedge P_2^c \Rightarrow \bigcirc C_{5y,free}$ (F4) $P_1^n \wedge P_2^n \Rightarrow \bigcirc C_{1y,1y}$
(F5) $P_1^c \oplus P_1^n$ (F6) $P_2^c \oplus P_2^n$

The obvious preference ordering is $C_{free,5y} \succeq_1 C_{1y,1y} \succeq_1 C_{3y,3y} \succeq_1 C_{5y,free}$ for Player 1, and $C_{5y,free} \succeq_2 C_{1y,1y} \succeq_2 C_{3y,3y} \succeq_2 C_{free,5y}$ for Player 2.

2.3   Tableau Construction

Let 2^{PTL} be the collection of all subsets of PTL formulas, and $\Gamma \subseteq PTL$. A tableau is a graph $< T(\Gamma), \Rightarrow^\circ, S >$, with nodes $T(\Gamma) \subseteq 2^{PTL}$, and $\Rightarrow^\circ \subseteq T(\Gamma) \times T(\Gamma)$ are arcs labeled $\bigcirc$ between nodes defined by
$\Rightarrow^\circ = \{< n_1, n_2 > \mid \phi \in n_2 \text{ iff } \bigcirc\phi \in n_1\}$
and $S \subseteq T(\Gamma)$ is the set of start states.
Whenever there is no confusion we will write $T(\Gamma)$ instead of $< T(\Gamma), \Rightarrow^\circ, S >$.

Let for any $\Delta \subseteq PTL$, $Next(\Delta) = \{\phi \mid \bigcirc\phi \in \Delta\}$.

The construction of $T(\Gamma)$ proceeds as follows:

We start with $T(\Gamma) = \{\Gamma\}$ and $S = \{\Gamma\}$.

Tableau Construction Procedure (see [12, 5])

Repeat the following operations on $T(\Gamma)$ (and S) till there are no further changes:

Replace $\neg(\phi \vee \psi)$ by $\neg\phi \wedge \neg\psi$, $\neg(\phi \wedge \psi)$ by $\neg\phi \vee \neg\psi$, $\neg \bigcirc \phi$ by $\bigcirc \neg\phi$;

Replace $\neg\Diamond\phi$ by $\Box\neg\phi$, $\neg\Box\phi$ by $\Diamond\neg\phi$, $\neg(\phi \bigcup \psi)$ by $\Box\neg\psi \vee \neg\psi \bigcup (\neg\phi \wedge \neg\psi)$;

Replace $\Diamond\phi$ by $\Diamond P \wedge \Box(P \Leftrightarrow \phi)$, where P is a new propositional variable;

Replace $\phi \bigcup \psi$ by $\phi \bigcup P \wedge \Box(P \Leftrightarrow \psi) \wedge \Diamond P$, P being a new propositional variable;

Replace $\Diamond P$ by $P \vee \bigcirc\Diamond P$ and $\phi \bigcup P$ by $P \vee \phi \wedge \neg P \wedge \bigcirc\phi \bigcup P$;

Replace $\phi \wedge \psi$ by two formulas ϕ and ψ ;

Replace $\Box\phi$ by two formulas ϕ and $\bigcirc\Box\phi$;

Replace a node $\Delta \cup \{\phi \vee \psi\}$ by two nodes $\Delta \cup \{\phi\}$ and $\Delta \cup \{\psi\}$;

Add $Next(n)$ to $T(\Gamma)$ and $< n, Next(n) >$ to $\Rightarrow°$;

Tableaus can be used to check if a set of formulas is unsatisfiable. A node in the tableau is *unsatisfiable* if it contains P and $\neg P$ for some proposition P. A *strongly connected component (SCC)* is a subset of nodes O such that $\forall n, n' \in O$, there is a path from n to n' in the tableau. An SCC is *terminal* if there are no nodes outside the SCC that are reachable from a SCC node. A terminal SCC is said to be *unsatisfiable* if all the nodes of the SCC contain both $\neg P$ and $\bigcirc\Diamond P$.

Node Deletion Procedure

Repeat deletion of nodes from the tableau as follows:

Delete unsatisfiable nodes;

Delete unsatisfiable terminal SCCs;

Delete n if $Next(n)$ is deleted

If there are no nodes left in S after this, the tableau is said to be *empty*.

Proposition 1. $\Gamma \subseteq PTL$ *is unsatisfiable iff the tableau* $T(\Gamma)$ *is empty* . *([13])*

If the tableau is not empty, we let the remaining set of nodes of the tableau be denoted by $T(\Gamma)$, and the remaining start nodes by S.

2.4   Preference Relations on Tableau Nodes

The end nodes $E \subseteq T(\Gamma)$ defined by $E = \{n \in T(\Gamma) \mid \exists j : C_j \in n\}$ are those nodes that contain consequence variables. The models of relevance to us are sequence of nodes starting with a node in S and ending at a node in E. We should note that such sequences may also contain intermediate nodes in E.

Since end nodes may contain more than one consequence variable, we extend the ordering as follows: We draw an arc labeled $\succeq_i$ from end node n_1 to end node n_2 if $\forall C \in n_2$, $\exists C' \in n_1$ such that $C' \succeq_i C$. This means that each player considers only the most preferred consequence in a node. We use this to model reversal of preferences: since it is possible that $n_2 \succeq_i n_1$ but $n_1 \cup \{C\} \succeq_i n_2$.

An end node n_2 is said to be *inferior* to another end node n_1 for player i if there is a path with arcs labeled $\succeq_i$ from node n_1 to node n_2. We will use preferences to eliminate inferior nodes from E. Now, there is another way that we can show that tableaus are *empty*: i.e. when $E = \emptyset$.

For the Prisoners' dilemma example, let $\Gamma = \{F1, F2, F3, F4, F5, F6\}$. The relevant part of $T(\Gamma)$ and ordering of end nodes is displayed below:

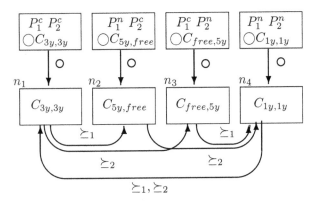

2.5   Prisoners' Dilemma as a Negotiation Game on Tableau

We now look at eliminating end nodes that are not preferred by the players. However, it is unlikely that there is a common most preferred end node - Player 1 prefers n_3 the most, while for Player 2 it is n_2. Similarly for least preferred end nodes - n_2 is the least preferred for Player 1, while for Player 2 it is n_3.

But interestingly, we can define a negotiation game on end nodes, in which the players can negotiate the nodes they would like to eliminate. The game starts with a collection of all end nodes in the tableau. A player attempts to eliminate n that is inferior to n', which is *permitted* only if she has an action that leads to n' but not to n. Another player can *defeat* this if she has an action that will prevent this selection from taking place. The player whose selection is defeated loses the game. To prevent this, a player will only select nodes that cannot be defeated. When the players make such undefeated offers of end node sets, the negotiated outcome is taken as the intersection of the selected sets.

In our example, Player 1 finds n_2 is inferior to n_1, and has a move (P_1^c) that leads to n_1 but not to n_2. Besides, Player 2 cannot defeat this (both result from the same action P_2^c of Player 2). So Player 1 can successfully offer to eliminate n_2. Similarly between n_3 and n_4, she offers to eliminate n_4. Player 1 thus offers $\{n_1, n_3\}$ in her first move. Likewise, Player 2 will offer $\{n_1, n_2\}$. Since both have to arrive at a common set, they take the intersection of these sets which has only n_1, and this is the negotiated outcome.

It can be easily observed that this line of reasoning is exactly the same as the one used for finding mutual best responses in a Nash equilibrium (see [3]).

2.6   Game Theoretic Consequence

We now explain how to prove properties of equilibria using tableaus.

To prove that both players will serve 3 years in prison, we show that $\Gamma \cup \{\neg\bigcirc C_{3y,3y}\}$ is unsatisfiable. The tableau is similar to $T(\Gamma)$ except that all end nodes contain $\neg C_{3y,3y}$ (n_1 already contains $C_{3y,3y}$). If n_1 is the result of negotiation, then this will result in the elimination of all the end nodes. Unfortunately, it is not so straightforward. Since node deletion precedes negotiation, we would find that n_1 is already eliminated before negotiation starts. Then the players will be unable to eliminate n_2 and n_3 respectively during negotiation (they need n_1 for this). The negotiated solution is $\{n_2, n_3\}$, and the tableau is not empty.

We work around this by *marking* sub-formulas originating from $\neg \bigcirc C_{3y,3y}$, so that n_1 survives the deletion procedure. Post negotiation, we remove the markings, and carry out the node deletion procedure again. This time, the only surviving end node n_1 is deleted, leaving us with an empty tableau.

Marking/Unmarking: To *mark* ϕ, replace each proposition P by a new proposition P^* to get ϕ^*. To *unmark* - replace P^* in ϕ by the original proposition P.

Example 2 (Hawk-Dove).
Game Description: Two contestants in a fight could each act like a hawk or as a dove. The best outcome is to win without a fight - which occurs when she is a hawk, while the other is a dove. The worst is when both are hawks, since both get badly hurt. Both could be doves in which case peace prevails.

We use propositions $P_1^h, P_1^d, P_2^h, P_2^d$ to denote the two players choice of hawkish or dovish behaviour, and use $C_{hurt}, C_{peace}, C_{1wins}, C_{2wins}$ to model the consequences. The consequence formulas are given by $P_1^h \wedge P_2^h \Rightarrow \bigcirc C_{hurt}$, $P_1^h \wedge P_2^d \Rightarrow \bigcirc(C_{1wins} \wedge \neg C_{hurt})$, $P_1^d \wedge P_2^h \Rightarrow \bigcirc(C_{2wins} \wedge \neg C_{hurt})$ and $P_1^d \wedge P_2^d \Rightarrow \bigcirc(C_{peace} \wedge \neg C_{hurt})$, and the preference ordering by $C_{1wins} \succeq_1 C_{peace} \succeq_1 C_{2wins} \succeq_1 C_{hurt}$ and $C_{2wins} \succeq_2 C_{peace} \succeq_2 C_{1wins} \succeq_2 C_{hurt}$. The tableau is displayed below:

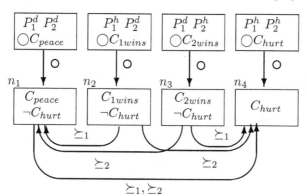

Player 1 finds n_1 inferior to n_2 and n_4 inferior to n_3, with Player 2 not being able to defeat these selections. Thus Player 1 offers the reduced set $\{n_2, n_3\}$ in the next round. Player 2 likewise offers $\{n_2, n_3\}$ based on her preferences. The negotiation stops here since neither is able to eliminate any more states.

To prove that neither player is hurt in the equilibrium, we include $\bigcirc C_{hurt}^*$ to the set of formulas and construct the tableau. C_{hurt}^* is added to $\{n_1, n_2, n_3, n_4\}$. The equilibrium negotiation produces $\{n_2, n_3\}$. Unmarking will replace C_{hurt}^* by C_{hurt} in both of these nodes, which leads to a contradiction and both of these are eliminated. We end up with an empty tableau.

Example 3 (Bertrand Pricing).
Game Description: Two profitable firms selling an identical product get into a phase of intense rivalry characterised by a price war. Each firm could choose to change their price from high to low. The firm offering a low price could capture the entire market but not make profits. A firm makes losses only if it sells nothing.

We wish to show that in equilibrium neither will make profits or losses. P_i^{Low} denotes that Player i prices low, M_i denotes that i sells in the market, and $C_{i,loss}$, $C_{i,profit}$ denotes i's consequences of making losses or profits. The preference ordering can be written as $C_{i,profit} \succeq_i \neg C_{i,loss} \succeq_i C_{i,loss}$ where we order consequence literals rather than consequence variables to avoid introduction of another consequence variable that would just represent $\neg C_{i,loss}$.

Simple Model: At least one of the firms will drop prices, i.e. $P_1^{Low} \vee P_2^{Low}$. The third statement is expressed by $P_1^{Low} \Rightarrow \bigcirc(M_1 \wedge \neg C_{1,profit})$, $\neg P_1^{Low} \wedge P_2^{Low} \Rightarrow \bigcirc \neg M_1$, $P_2^{Low} \Rightarrow \bigcirc(M_2 \wedge \neg C_{2,profit})$ and $\neg P_2^{Low} \wedge P_1^{Low} \Rightarrow \bigcirc \neg M_2$. The last statement is $\bigcirc(\neg M_1 \Leftrightarrow C_{1,loss})$, $\bigcirc(\neg M_2 \Leftrightarrow C_{2,loss})$. The choice function is $\bigcirc(C_{i,profit} \Rightarrow \neg C_{i,loss})$. The relevant part of the tableau is shown below:

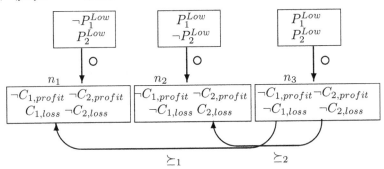

Node n_1 is inferior to node n_3 for firm 1 and firm 2 cannot defeat this selection, while node n_2 is inferior to node n_3 for player 2 and firm 1 cannot defeat the selection. n_3 is thus the negotiated equilibrium.

To prove that neither firm makes profits, we include $\bigcirc(C_{1,profit}^* \vee C_{2,profit}^*)$. n_3 contains $(C_{1,profit}^* \vee C_{2,profit}^*)$ and is the negotiated outcome. When unmarked, this contradicts with $\neg C_{1,profit}$ and $\neg C_{1,profit}$ already present in n_3.

We get the same result when we include $\bigcirc(C_{1,loss}^* \vee C_{2,loss}^*)$, and thus we are able to conclude that neither firm makes profits or losses.

Full Model: We could consider a repeated game, where at each stage the players choose to retain or drop prices. Eventually one of them drops prices, expressed by $\Diamond(P_1^{Low} \vee P_2^{Low})$. The action-consequences are $\Box(P_1^{Low} \Rightarrow \bigcirc(M_1 \wedge \neg C_{1,profit}))$, $\Box(\neg P_1^{Low} \wedge P_2^{Low} \Rightarrow \bigcirc \neg M_1)$, $\Box(P_2^{Low} \Rightarrow \bigcirc(M_2 \wedge \neg C_{2,profit}))$ and $\Box(\neg P_2^{Low} \wedge P_1^{Low} \Rightarrow \bigcirc \neg M_2)$. The remaining relations are: $\Box(\neg M_1 \Leftrightarrow C_{1,loss})$, $\Box(\neg M_2 \Leftrightarrow C_{2,loss})$, $\Box(C_{i,profit} \Rightarrow \neg C_{i,loss})$. Both firms make profits till the price war starts, which is expressed by $(C_{1,profit} \wedge C_{2,profit}) \bigcup (P_1^{Low} \vee P_2^{Low})$.

To show that one of the firms will not make losses, we use $\Box(\neg C_{1,loss}^* \vee \neg C_{2,loss}^*)$. We build the tableau with its negation $\Diamond(C_{1,loss}^* \wedge C_{2,loss}^*)$. We don't need any equilibrium arguments, though we would need to eliminate nodes with unsatisfiable eventualities using SCCs (see [5]). In our case, $\Diamond(P_1^{Low} \vee P_2^{Low})$ cannot be satisfied in the only surviving SCC with the propositions $\neg P_1^{Low}, \neg P_2^{Low}$.

To show that neither firm will make losses, we use $\Box(\neg C_{1,loss}^* \wedge \neg C_{2,loss}^*)$. To prove this, we add $\Diamond(C_{1,loss}^* \vee C_{2,loss}^*)$. We can recognise the following cases:

1. Loop containing $\neg P_1^{Low}, \neg P_2^{Low}$: The eventuality $\Diamond(P_1^{Low} \vee P_2^{Low})$ cannot be satisfied.
2. Transition from node containing $\neg P_1^{Low}, \neg P_2^{Low}$ to a node containing either P_1^{Low} or P_2^{Low}: The entire $\Diamond(C_{1,loss}^* \vee C_{2,loss}^*)$ is carried into the latter node.
3. SCC of nodes containing either P_1^{Low} or P_2^{Low}: Nodes containing $C_{1,loss}$ and $C_{2,loss}$ are considered inferior to those containing $\neg C_{1,loss}, \neg C_{2,loss}$ by Players 1 and 2 respectively (all other contents of these nodes being identical) (Note: We need a more precise definition of defeating node selections in a SCC). The eventuality fails in the SCC once these inferior nodes are removed.

3   Extensive Form Games

To define extensive form games, we use *histories* (see [8]) which are finite sequences of actions taken from the sets A_i. If $h = a_0 a_1 ... a_k$ is a history, then $a_0 a_1 ... a_l$, with $l < k$ is a called a *prefix* of h. We consider finite sets H of histories that are prefix closed i.e. if h' is a prefix of $h \in H$, then $h' \in H$. The set of terminal histories $Z \subseteq H$ are those that are not prefixes of any history in H. $\mathcal{P} : (H \backslash Z) \to N$ is defined by $\mathcal{P}(a_0 a_1 ... a_k) = i$, iff $a_k \in A_i$. A *finite extensive game form* is a tuple $\mathcal{G} =< N, A_i, H, \mathcal{P}, \mathcal{C}, g >$ where $g : Z \to \mathcal{C}$ is a map that associates with each terminal history a consequence. An *extensive game* is such a tuple together with orderings $\succeq_i$ of $\mathcal{C}$ for each player i .

3.1   Modeling Extensive Form Games in PTL

We use the $\bigcirc$ operators to represent progression of stages of the game. Hence a sequence $\bigcirc...\bigcirc$ of l applications of the $\bigcirc$ operator (represented by $\bigcirc^l$) denotes the $l + 1$-th stage of the game.

Let $a_0 a_1 ... a_k \in Z$ be a terminal history, and let $\mathcal{P}(a_0 a_1 ... a_l) = i_l$, for all $l \leq k$. To state that a consequence C_r holds in this history, we can use the PTL formula $P_{i_0}^{a_0} \wedge \bigcirc P_{i_1}^{a_1} ... \wedge \bigcirc^k P_{i_k}^{a_k} \Rightarrow \bigcirc^{(k+1)} C_r$. Let $\Gamma(\mathcal{G})$ be the collection of all such temporal formulas derived from the histories in H.

Example 4 (Chain Store Game).
Game Description: A single local competitor in each city decides whether to start a store competing with the chain store. If it does, the chain store could start a price war (when both make losses) or could accomodate the competitor (in which case they share the profits). The best situation for the chain store is if the competitor stays out, when it enjoys monopoly profits.

We use propositions $P_1^E, P_1^O, P_2^F, P_2^A$ where Player 1 is the local competitor whose actions are to enter or stay out, and Player 2 is the chain store who can fight or accomodate. We use $C_{loss}, C_{mpoly}, C_{share}$ to model consequences with the ordering being $C_{share} \succeq_1 C_{mpoly} \succeq_1 C_{loss}$ and $C_{mpoly} \succeq_2 C_{share} \succeq_2 C_{loss}$. The consequence formulas are given by:

$$\Gamma = \{P_1^O \Rightarrow \bigcirc C_{mpoly}, P_1^E \wedge \bigcirc P_2^F \Rightarrow \bigcirc\bigcirc C_{loss}, P_1^E \wedge \bigcirc P_2^A \Rightarrow \bigcirc\bigcirc C_{share}\}.$$

We can argue about the tableau nodes using the corresponding temporal formulas. The end nodes are $\{\bigcirc\bigcirc C_{share}, \bigcirc\bigcirc C_{loss}, \bigcirc C_{mpoly}\}$. Player 2 finds $\bigcirc\bigcirc C_{loss}$ inferior to $\bigcirc\bigcirc C_{share}$, with Player 1 unable to defeat the selection. Thus Player 2 offers the reduced set $\{\bigcirc\bigcirc C_{share}, \bigcirc C_{mpoly}\}$. If Player 1 makes no elimination offer, this set becomes the result of the first round. In the next round, Player 1 eliminates the inferior $\bigcirc C_{mpoly}$, with Player 2 unable to defeat this selection. The equilibrium is $\{\bigcirc\bigcirc C_{share}\}$, and we are able to prove that in equilibrium the chain store will always share profits with new entrants. This line of reasoning is just the backward induction argument, which starts from the leaves of the extensive game form and moves backward to the root.

Note that, Player 1 could eliminate $\bigcirc\bigcirc C_{loss}$ in the first round, which it finds inferior to $\bigcirc C_{mpoly}$ and Player 2 is unable to defeat this. The negotiation method thus provides for both forward and backward reasoning.

Chain Store Paradox: Backward reasoning can give rise to paradoxical situations, since it assumes that players ignore the past when making choices affecting the future. Consider a repeated game in which the chain store competes in several cities. Without loss of generality, we let Player 1 represent all the competitors. The consequence formulas can be represented through $\Box(P_1^O \Rightarrow \bigcirc C_{mpoly})$, $\Box(P_1^E \wedge \bigcirc P_2^F \Rightarrow \bigcirc\bigcirc C_{loss}), \Box(P_1^E \wedge \bigcirc P_2^A \Rightarrow \bigcirc\bigcirc C_{share})$. Since $\bigcirc\bigcirc\Diamond\neg C_{share}$ cannot be satisfied, we can show that the chain store will always share profits.

The chain store paradox arises because, while the chain store may accomodate one competitor, it is not credible that it will share profits in all cities. It may rather choose to start a price war and build a reputation as a fighter to deter competition. In other words, past does influence the future through the *reputation* of Player 2, which we model using proposition C_{image} earned by Player 2 if it **"surprises"** the opponent by fighting: $\Box(P_2^F \Rightarrow \bigcirc C_{image})$.

The preference relations are: $C_{image} \succeq_2 C_{mpoly}, C_{mpoly} \succeq_1 C_{image} \succeq_1 C_{loss}$ (Player 2 values its reputation the most, while Player 1 fears this more than a monopoly). Note that since $\{C_{image}, C_{loss}\} \succeq_2 \{C_{share}\} \succeq_2 \{C_{loss}\}$, this causes a reversal of preferences, i.e. Player 2 prefers to maintain his reputation at the cost of making losses. Knowing this, Player 1 should opt to stay out.

To show this, note that Player 2 finds $\bigcirc\bigcirc C_{share}$ inferior to $\{\bigcirc\bigcirc C_{loss}, \bigcirc\bigcirc C_{image}\}$, with Player 1 unable to defeat the selection. Player 2 thus offers end nodes $\{\bigcirc\bigcirc C_{loss}, \bigcirc\bigcirc C_{image}\}$ and $\bigcirc C_{mpoly}$. Player 1 continues to offer $\bigcirc\bigcirc C_{share}$ and $\bigcirc C_{mpoly}$ as before. The negotiated outcome is thus $\bigcirc C_{mpoly}$, which is reached when Player 1 opts to stay out.

Note that this **makes the logic non-monotonic:** $\bigcirc\bigcirc C_{share}$ was a game theoretic consequence of Γ, but is not a consequence of $\Gamma \cup \{\Box(P_2^F \Rightarrow \bigcirc C_{image})\}$.

4   Negotiation Games Over Tableau

We now formalise the negotiation game described using examples so far.

A *game form over tableau* is defined as a game $< N, 2^E >$ where the players $N = \{1, ..., n\}$ select subsets of E. For each player i, $\succeq_i \subseteq E \times E$ is defined by $\succeq_i = \{< n_1, n_2 > \mid \forall C \in n_2, \exists C' \in n_1 \; C' \succeq_i C\}$. Let $\succeq_i^*$ be the transitive closure of $\succeq_i$. Node n is *inferior* to n' for player i if $n' \succeq_i^* n$, but not $n \succeq_i^* n'$.

A *path* to end nodes E in the tableau T is a sequence of nodes $n_0, n_1, ..., n_k$ with $n_0 \in S$ and $n_k \in E$. The set of all such paths is denoted by $Paths(E)$. A *path prefix of length* l is the sub-sequence $n_0, n_1, ..., n_l$ of the path $n_0, n_1, ..., n_k$, with $l \leq k$. We write $Paths(E, l)$ to denote the set of such path prefixes. For $n \in E$, $Actions_i(l, n) = \{P_i^r \mid P_i^r \in n_l, \; n_0, ..., n_l \in Paths(\{n\}, l)\}$.

We define $Control_i(n, n', l)$ inductively as follows:

$Control_i(n, n', 0) = True$ iff $Actions_i(0, n) \neq Actions_i(0, n')$
$Control_i(n, n', l) = True$ iff $Actions_i(l, n) \neq Actions_i(l, n')$
  and $\neg Control_j(n, n', l - 1)$, for all $j \neq i$ and for $l > 0$.

Intuitively, Player i can take an action at l which would lead to n but not to n' or vice-versa, and she cannot be pre-empted in this by anyone else.
Let $Improve_i(n, l) = \{n' \mid Control_i(n, n', l) \text{ and } n \text{ is inferior to } n'\}$ be nodes that offer improvements for i.

For $n' \in Improve_i(n, l)$, we say that player $j \neq i$ can **defeat the selection** n' of i if either $Control_j(n, n', l)$, or there is an end node $n'' \in Improve_j(n', k)$ with $k > l$. Intuitively, j can defeat i's selection at l, either if i and j have to co-ordinate their actions at l, or j can later divert the game to node n'' instead. We let $Feasible_i(n) = \bigcup_{l \geq 0} \{n' \in Improve_i(n, l) \mid \forall j \neq i : j \text{ cannot defeat the selection } n' \text{ of } i\}$.

If E^k is the set of end nodes at any stage, we say $E_i \subseteq E^k$ is a *feasible subset* for player i if $\forall n \in E^k - E_i, Feasible_i(n) \cap E_i \neq \emptyset$.

The Negotiation Game
We set $E^0 = E$ as the available set for each player at the start. At each stage $k \geq 1$ of the game, player i chooses a feasible subset $E_i \subseteq E^{k-1}$. The negotiated outcome of stage k is taken as $E^k = \cap_{i \in N} E_i$. The negotiation game stops when $E^{m+1} = E^m$, i.e. when the players cannot improve on the negotiated outcome.

A terminal SCC O is now said to be *unsatisfiable* if there is some proposition P, such that $\forall n \in O - (E - E^m)$, n contains both $\neg P$ and $\bigcirc \Diamond P$.

4.1   *Tableau Based Game Consequence Decision Procedure*

To show that a formula ϕ holds in all the equilibria of a game represented by a set of formulas Γ:

Mark the formula ϕ to get ϕ^*;
Construct the tableau $T(\Gamma \cup \{\neg \phi^*\})$;
Execute the node deletion procedure;
Execute the negotiation game;

Unmark all the formulas in the tableau;
Execute the node deletion procedure (using new definition of unsatisfiable SCCs)

We let $TG(\Gamma, \phi)$ denote the tableau resulting from this procedure.
$TG(\Gamma, \phi)$ is said to be *empty* if either the set of start or end nodes is $\emptyset$.
We abbreviate $TG(\Gamma, False)$ by $TG(\Gamma)$.

Proposition 2 (Soundess and Completeness for Strategic Form Games)
If Γ is the set of temporal formulas representing the strategic game $\mathcal{G}$. Then:
(1) The game has a Nash equilibrium iff the tableau $TG(\Gamma)$ is not empty.
(2) ϕ is true in the Nash equilibria iff the tableau $TG(\Gamma, \phi)$ is empty.

Proof. Detailed proof omitted. We first show that the negotiation game corresponds to eliminating the choices that are not best responses, so that the intersection will yield the Nash equilibrium. This proves (1). For (2), we use induction on the structure of the formula ϕ and the nodes of the tableau. (Proof sketch follows the line of argument used in [3]) $\square$

Proposition 3 (Soundness and Completeness for Extensive Form Games)
Let Γ be the set of temporal formulas representing the extensive form game
$< N, A_i, H, \mathcal{P}, \succeq_i >$ *Then:*
(1) The tableau $TG(\Gamma)$ will not be empty, and
(2) ϕ holds in the sub-game perfect equilibrium iff $TG(\Gamma, \phi)$ is empty.

Proof. Detailed proof omitted. The negotiation game follows the backward induction argument (Kuhn's theorem, see [8]). This proves (1). For (2), we use induction on the structure of the formula ϕ and the nodes of the tableau. (Proof sketch follows the line of argument used in [4]) $\square$

5   Bounded Rationality

We saw in section 2.1 that the game theoretic consequence relationship defined here is non-monotonic, and hence permits defeasible reasoning. In the example, the chain store could "surprise" the competitor by choosing to fight, which causes a revision in preference orderings and changes the negotiated outcome. An agent "learns" about the game from surprise deviations from its calculated equilibrium.

Since temporal logic allows modeling of eventually periodic sequences, we can take the basic epistemic unit to be finite or eventually periodic sequences of actions and outcomes. As agents interact through game playing, they gain more such units of knowledge about the game. The agent i's knowledge accretion is thus defined by the sequence of sets $\Gamma_i^0, \Gamma_i^1, \ldots$ of temporal formulas. Then ϕ will hold in the equilibria at stage l only if it is a consequence of each Γ_i^l.

The two key computational elements we have introduced are - identifying end node improvements (which involves preference orderings), and checking if the selection can be defeated (which don't). In principle, we could plug-in more limited procedures for these two computations for each agent. The procedures can then be improved as the agent gains experience playing games.

6   Possible Extensions

Adding simultaneous moves in the extensive form does not change the decision procedure. The negotiation process can be easily extended to capture coordination, where the players mutually prefer one equilibrium over another. It is also possible to create a simple model of mixed strategies using multisets of end nodes.

The method suggested is also quite amenable to creating a logic calculator for games (see [5]).

Future work will be directed at coming up with a logic system that directly captures the preference relations, using a method similar to the one in [3].

References

1. G B Asheim and M Dufwenberg: Deductive Reasoning in Extensive Games. *The Economic Journal 113 (April 2003)*. Blackwell Publishing. 305–325.
2. G Bonanno: Branching time logic, perfect information games and backward induction. In *3rd Conference on Logic and Foundations of Game and Decision Theory*, Torino, Italy, Dec 1998. International Centre for Economic Research (ICER).
3. P Harrenstein: A Game-Theoretical Notion of Consequence. In *5th Conference on Logic and Foundations of Game and Decision Theory*, Torino, Italy, Jun 2002. International Centre for Economic Research (ICER).
4. P Harrenstein, W van der Hoek, J-J Meyer and C Witteven: A Modal Characterization of Nash Equilibrium, *Fundamenta Informaticae*, 57, pp. 281–321, 2003.
5. G L J M Janssen: Hardware verification using Temporal Logic: A Practical View. *IFIP (1990)*. L J M Claesen (ed). 159–168. Available at the TLA home page http://research.microsoft.com/users/lamport/tla/logic-calculators.html
6. Marina De Vos and Dick Vermeir: Choice Logic Programs and Nash equilibria in Strategic Games. In Jorg Flum and Mario Rodriguez-Artalejo (eds), *Computer Science Logic (CSL '99)*, *LNCS-1683*. Springer Verlag. 266–276.
7. Marina De Vos and Dick Vermeir: Dynamically Ordered Probabilistic Choice Logic Programming. *FST&TCS -20*, *LNCS*-1974, Springer Verlag, 2000.
8. Martin J Osborne and Ariel Rubinstein: *A Course in Game Theory*, The MIT Press, Cambridge, Massachusets, London, England, third edition, 1996.
9. R Stalnaker: Extensive and strategic forms: Games and models for games. *Research in Economics 53 (1999)*. 293–319. Academic Press.
10. van Benthem: Logic and Games. Lecture notes. 1999. ILLC Amsterdam & Stanford University.
11. S van Otterloo, W van der Hoek, M Woolridge: Preferences in Game Logics. In AAMAS 2004. New York. http://www.aamas2004.org/proceedings/021_otterloos_preferences.pdf
12. G Venkatesh: A decision method for temporal logic based on resolution. In *Proceedings of the 5th FST & TCS conference*. Vol. 206, LNCS, 272–289.
13. P Wolper: The tableau method for temporal logic - an overview. *Logique et Analyse 28 (1985)*. 119–152.
14. M Woolridge, C Dixon and M Fisher: A tableau based proof procedure for temporal logics of knowledge and belief. *Journal of Applied Non-Classical Logics (1998)*. Vol 8(3), 225–258.

Alternation in Equational Tree Automata Modulo XOR

Kumar Neeraj Verma

Institut für Informatik, TU München, Germany
verma@in.tum.de

Abstract. Equational tree automata accept terms modulo equational theories, and have been used to model algebraic properties of cryptographic primitives in security protocols. A serious limitation is posed by the fact that alternation leads to undecidability in case of theories like ACU and that of Abelian groups, whereas for other theories like XOR, the decidability question has remained open. In this paper, we give a positive answer to this open question by giving effective reductions of alternating general two-way XOR automata to equivalent one-way XOR automata in 3EXPTIME, which also means that they are closed under intersection but not under complementation. We also show that emptiness of these automata, which is needed for deciding secrecy, can be decided directly in 2EXPTIME, without translating them to one-way automata. A key technique we use is the study of Branching Vector Plus-Minimum Systems (BVPMS), which are a variant of VASS (Vector Addition Systems with States), and for which we prove a pumping lemma allowing us to compute their coverability set in EXPTIME.

1 Introduction

Tree automata [7, 4] are a well known tool for verifying cryptographic protocols [14, 8, 3]. Most approaches to verifying cryptographic protocols are based on the assumption of *perfect cryptography* which ignores the algebraic properties of encryption. Such an analysis is often unrealistic. For example an attack [17] was found against Bull's recursive authentication protocol which uses XOR for encryption, although the protocol was shown to be secure [16] assuming perfect cryptography. To deal with such algebraic properties, we have introduced *equational tree automata* [20, 22, 21] which accept terms modulo equational theories. While related, but not identical, notions of automata have independently been introduced by others [15, 13], the distinguishing feature of our approach is the description of automata transitions using Horn clauses, which provide a uniform framework for expressing variants of *general two-wayness* and *alternation* [18] (see also [4], Chapter 7), as well as for dealing with arbitrary equational theories.

Protocol insecurity is NP-complete [2, 1] for several theories including XOR, assuming bounded number of sessions. This may help in detecting attacks which require very small number of sessions. But for *certifying* protocols we need some *safe* abstraction, which does not miss any attacks. A common safe abstraction is to let a bounded number of nonces be used in infinitely many sessions, although security still remains undecidable [3], even with perfect cryptography. With this abstraction, any protocol can easily be modeled using Horn clauses, following e.g. the approach of [5]. The idea is to define an unary predicate I such that $I(m)$ holds exactly for messages m known to the

K. Lodaya and M. Mahajan (Eds.): FSTTCS 2004, LNCS 3328, pp. 518–530, 2004.

intruder. Then to obtain clauses of alternating general two-way automata we use some safe abstraction, as in [10], or [9]. The secrecy problem then reduces to the intersection-emptiness problem of these automata: we check that $I(m)$ is false for certain set of m's.

In our previous work, we have dealt with equational tree automata [22, 21] for the theory ACU (consisting of the axioms $x + (y + z) = (x + y) + z$, $x + y = y + x$ and $x + 0 = x$) of an associative-commutative symbol $+$ with unit 0, and its variants, since these are the ones which occur most frequently in cryptographic protocols. These variants are obtained by adding certain axioms to the theory ACU. The variants studied include the theory AG of Abelian groups obtained by adding the axiom $x + (-x) = 0$, the theory XOR obtained by adding the axiom $x + x = 0$, and the theory ACUI obtained by adding the axiom $x + x = x$ of idempotence. We have used the theories ACU and AG to model [20] the IKA.1 group key agreement protocol [19] using decidable fragments of our equational tree automata. More efficient approximate verification techniques for the same modeling are used in [10] to obtain a fully automated proof of security of this protocol in the so-called pure eavesdropper model. Unfortunately alternation leads to undecidability in case of theories ACU and AG. Similarly general two-wayness encodes alternation and leads to undecidability.

While alternation and general two-wayness lead to undecidability for theories ACU and AG, the question was left open for the theories XOR and ACUI. Surprisingly, we show in this paper that XOR automata are decidable even with alternation and general two-wayness. We show that these automata can actually be reduced to equivalent one-way XOR automata in 3EXPTIME, hence they are closed under intersection but not under complementation, and their emptiness is decidable. We also show the latter problem to be decidable in 2EXPTIME, without constructing the equivalent one-way automata. Recall also that emptiness of alternating tree automata is EXPTIME-hard already in the non-equational case [4]. Our results imply that secrecy of cryptographic protocols with XOR modeled using alternating general two-way XOR automata is decidable in 2EXPTIME.

While our techniques used to deal with non-alternating equational tree automata relied heavily on semilinear, or Presburger-definable, sets, the techniques required in this paper to deal with the alternating case are remarkably different, based on studying Branching Vector Plus-Minimum Systems (BVPMS), which are a variant of VASS [11], similar to Branching VASS (BVASS) [23]. Unlike VASS and BVASS, BVPMS have a minimum operation but no subtraction. We show an interesting and natural connection between BVPMS and alternating XOR automata. A key result of the paper is a pumping lemma for BVPMS, allowing us to compute their *coverability sets*, which are approximations of the set of reachable configurations, in EXPTIME. In contrast, coverability sets of VASS and BVASS are computed using the Karp-Miller construction [12] which however only gives a non-primitive recursive algorithm. Our techniques also yield similar decidability results for the theory ACUI which was the other open case.

Note that alternation is crucial for precise analysis $A \rightarrow B : \{Na\}_{K_{ab}^1}, \{Na\}_{K_{ab}^2}$
of protocols. Consider the following example protocol $B \rightarrow A : Na$
in standard notation, where K_{ab}^i are private keys between $A \rightarrow B : \{Nb\}_{K_{ab}^1}$

A and B. Following [5], and knowing that an intruder knows (m_1, m_2) iff it knows both m_1 and m_2, we get clauses of the form $I(\text{enc}(Na, K_{ab}^1))$, $I(\text{enc}(Na, K_{ab}^2))$, $I(x) \Leftarrow$

$I(\mathtt{enc}(x, K_{ab}^1)) \wedge I(\mathtt{enc}(x, K_{ab}^2)), I(\mathtt{enc}(Nb, K_{ab}^1))$ (enc represents encryption) and also clauses for deductive abilities of the intruder, e.g. $I(\mathtt{pair}(x, y)) \Leftarrow I(x) \wedge I(y)$, $I(y) \Leftarrow I(\mathtt{pair}(x, y))$. These clauses are translatable to alternating general two-way automata clauses. E.g. the third clause above is translated as $P(K_{ab}^1), Q(K_{ab}^2), R(x) \Leftarrow I(\mathtt{enc}(x, y)) \wedge Q(y), I(x) \Leftarrow I(\mathtt{enc}(x, y)) \wedge R(x) \wedge P(y)$ for fresh predicates P, Q, R. Nb is secret, and $I(Nb)$ is not deducible. Note however that the variable x on the left side of the third clause appears twice on the right. Such clauses violate the restrictions imposed to obtain decidability in [22] and can easily encode alternation [22]. We may abstract this as the clause $I(x) \Leftarrow I(\mathtt{enc}(x, K_{ab}^1)) \wedge I(\mathtt{enc}(y, K_{ab}^2))$, (note distinct variables x and y). But now $I(Nb)$ becomes true, producing a false attack. The point we are making here is that disallowing alternation may force us to abstract away too much information from the protocols.

To our knowledge the only other work which presents decidability results for unbounded number of sessions in presence of some equational theory is [5, 6], which presents a decidable class $\mathcal{C}^\oplus$ of Horn clauses with XOR. This is incomparable to ours: they don't allow $+$-pop clauses (see Section 2) unless $P = P_1 = P_2$ but allow more general clauses involving other symbols. The clauses required for the example protocol modeled using $\mathcal{C}^\oplus$ in [5, 6] belong to our class. We give a 2EXPTIME algorithm for deciding secrecy whereas the complexity upper bound known for $\mathcal{C}^\oplus$ is non-elementary, as remarked in [6]. In this work we are also interested in the expressiveness and closure properties of our automata, besides the secrecy problem.

The paper is organized as follows. We start in the next section by introducing equational tree automata and examining the structure of derivations in alternating XOR automata. We then introduce BVPMS in Section 3 and show how to decide emptiness of alternating XOR automata by using their connections with BVPMS. In Section 4 we prove a pumping lemma for BVPMS which allows us to compute their coverability sets. This is then used in Section 5 to eliminate alternation from XOR automata. These results are used to treat general two-wayness in Section 6.

2   Equational Tree Automata

Consider a signature which includes the special symbols $+$ and 0. Symbols other than $+, 0$ are called *free*. *Functional terms* are terms of the form $f(t_1, \ldots, t_n)$ where f is free. We use unary predicates to represent states of automata. Read an atom $P(t)$ as 'term t is accepted at state P'. An *(equational) tree automaton* is a finite set of definite clauses $P(t) \Leftarrow P_1(t_1) \wedge \ldots \wedge P_n(t_n)$ (t, t_i's may contain variables). Read this clause as 'if t_i is accepted at P_i for $1 \leq i \leq n$ then t is accepted at P'. $P(t)$ is the *head*, and the remaining part the *tail* of the clause. Given an equational theory $\mathcal{E}$ modulo which an automaton $\mathcal{A}$ is considered, *derivations* of ground atoms are defined using the rules:

$$\frac{P_1(t_1\sigma)\ldots P_n(t_n\sigma)}{P(t\sigma)} (P(t) \Leftarrow P_1(t_1) \wedge \ldots \wedge P_n(t_n) \in \mathcal{A}) \qquad \frac{P(s)}{P(t)} (s =_\mathcal{E} t)$$

where σ is a ground substitution, and $=_\mathcal{E}$ is the congruence on terms induced by the theory $\mathcal{E}$. Hence the derivable atoms are the elements of the least Herbrand model modulo $\mathcal{E}$. If S is a set of states then we also say that $S(t)$ is derivable to mean that $P(t)$ is derivable for all $P \in S$. We write $\mathcal{A}/\mathcal{E}$ to indicate the equational theory modulo which the automaton $\mathcal{A}$ is considered. We define the language $L_P(\mathcal{A}/\mathcal{E}) = \{t \mid P(t) \text{ is derivable}\}$. If in addition some state P is designated as *final* then the language accepted by the automaton is $L_P(\mathcal{A}/\mathcal{E})$. A state is *empty* if it accepts no term.

We are in particular interested in the following kinds of clauses, called *zero clauses*, +-pop clauses, alternation clauses, free pop clauses and general push clauses respectively, where $x_1, \ldots, x_n$ are mutually distinct in clauses (4) and (5),

$$P(0) \quad (1) \qquad\qquad P(x+y) \Leftarrow P_1(x) \wedge P_2(y) \qquad (2)$$

$$P(x) \Leftarrow P_1(x) \wedge \ldots \wedge P_n(x) \quad (n \geq 1)(3)$$

$$P(f(x_1, \ldots, x_n)) \Leftarrow P_1(x_1) \wedge \ldots \wedge P_n(x_n) \quad (f \text{ is free})(4)$$

$$P(x_i) \Leftarrow Q(f(x_1, \ldots, x_n)) \wedge P_1(x_{i_1}) \wedge \ldots \wedge P_k(x_{i_k})(5)$$

$$(f \text{ is free}, 1 \leq i, i_1, \ldots, i_k \leq n)$$

x, y are distinct in clause (2), and P, Q, P_i's are states. See [10] for an example modeling of cryptographic protocols using these clauses. *Alternating automata* contain clauses (1-4). *Alternating general two-way automata* contain clauses (1- 5). Alternation clauses (3) in which $n = 1$ are called ϵ *clauses*. *One-way automata* are alternating automata in which all alternation clauses are ϵ clauses. In the non-equational case, one-way automata are exactly the classical tree automata usually described in the literature: clause (4) is usually written as the rewrite rule $f(P_1, \ldots, P_n) \rightarrow P$, and ϵ clauses are written as $P_1 \rightarrow P$. For an automaton $\mathcal{A}$, we denote by $\mathcal{A}_{free}$ the set of clauses (4) in $\mathcal{A}$, and by $\mathcal{A}_{eq}$ the set of clauses (1-3) in $\mathcal{A}$. The (emptiness of) *intersection* of a set S of states is the (emptiness of) the set of terms t such that $S(t)$ is derivable. In presence of alternation clauses, deciding intersection-emptiness of S is the same as deciding emptiness of a fresh state P by adding the clause $P(x) \Leftarrow \bigwedge_{Q \in S} Q(x)$.

XOR Derivations. We examine the structure of derivations in alternating XOR automata and relate them to BVPMS. Recall that modulo XOR, any term can be converted to a *normal* form by repeatedly replacing subterms $t + t$ by 0. If $s =_{XOR} t$ then s and t have the same normal form (upto $=_{ACU}$ congruence). As our interest is in the theory XOR, throughout this paper, if $s =_{ACU} t$ then we treat s and t as the same object. This will not cause any confusion. We think of derivations in equational tree automata as trees. At each node we either apply a clause or rewrite using the equational theory. Let $\mathcal{A}/\mathcal{E}$ be an alternating automaton on a finite set of states $\mathbb{P}$. Then any derivation δ of an atom $P(t)$ in $\mathcal{A}/\mathcal{E}$ is uniquely described as $C[\delta_1, \ldots, \delta_n]$ (the ordering of the δ_i's being ignored) such that each subtree δ_i uses an application of a free pop clauses at the root node, and the nodes in C contain only applications of clauses from $\mathcal{A}_{eq}$ and rewritings using $\mathcal{E}$. If the conclusion of each δ_i is $P_i(t_i)$ then we call the (unordered) list $P_1(t_1), \ldots, P_n(t_n)$ as the *functional support* of δ. (Clearly each t_i is functional.) This definition generalizes that of [22] for one-way automata.

Let $\mathcal{Z}_{\mathbb{P}} = \{S \mid \emptyset \neq S \subseteq \mathbb{P}\}$. Introduce a new set of constants: $A = \{a_S \mid S \in \mathcal{Z}_{\mathbb{P}}\}$. We use a_S as abstraction for functional terms accepted at each state in S, in order to analyze derivations. Let $p = |\mathcal{Z}_{\mathbb{P}}| = 2^{|\mathbb{P}|} - 1$. We name the elements of $\mathcal{Z}_{\mathbb{P}}$ as $\mathbb{S}_1, \ldots, \mathbb{S}_p$. Modulo ACU, any term on the signature $A \cup \{0, +\}$ is of the form $\sum_{i=1}^{p} n_i a_{\mathbb{S}_i}$, equivalently p-tuples $(n_1, \ldots, n_p) \in \mathbb{N}^p$. In this paper we consider them interchangeably as terms or p-tuples. For $\nu \in \mathbb{N}^p$ the ith component of ν is $\nu[i]$. If $I = \{i_1, \ldots, i_k\}$ where $1 \le i_1 < \ldots < i_k \le p$ then $\nu[I]$ denotes $(\nu[i_1], \ldots, \nu[i_k]) \in \mathbb{N}^k$. The tuple $(n, \ldots, n)$ is also written as n. For $n \in \mathbb{N}$ define the *characteristic* $n^* \in \{0, 1\}$ as: $n^* = 0$ if n is even, and $n^* = 1$ otherwise. For $\nu \in \mathbb{N}^p$ define $\nu^* = (\nu[1]^*, \ldots, \nu[p]^*) \in \{0, 1\}^p$. Define partial order $\le_{xor}$ (on $\mathbb{N}$ and on $\mathbb{N}^p$) as: $x \le_{xor} y$ iff $x \le y$ and $x^* = y^*$. For $Z \subseteq \mathbb{Z}_\mathbb{P}$, define $\mathcal{X}_{\mathcal{A},Z}$ to consist of atoms modulo ACU which can be deduced by the following rules.

1. $\dfrac{}{P_{(a_S)}}$ $(P \in S \in Z)$	**2.** $\dfrac{P(t+a_S+a_S)}{P(t)}$	**3.** $\dfrac{P_1(t_1) \quad P_2(t_2)}{P(t_1+t_2)}$ $(P(x+y) \Leftarrow P_1(x) \wedge P_2(y) \in \mathcal{A})$
4. $\dfrac{}{P(0)}$ $(P(0) \in \mathcal{A})$	**5.** $\dfrac{P_1(t) \ldots P_n(t)}{P(t)}$ $(P(x) \Leftarrow P_1(x) \wedge \ldots \wedge P_n(x) \in \mathcal{A})$	

Rule 2 is another way of saying that if $P(t) \in \mathcal{X}_{\mathcal{A},Z}$ and $t' \le_{xor} t$ then $P(t') \in \mathcal{X}_{\mathcal{A},Z}$. An atom in $\mathcal{X}_{\mathcal{A},Z}$ summarizes the effect of an arbitrarily large derivation in $\mathcal{A}/XOR$ using clauses of $\mathcal{A}_{eq}$. The constants a_S represent the effect of applying the clauses of $\mathcal{A}_{free}$. The sets in Z account for the terms which are canceled using the XOR axiom during the derivation. This is formally stated by Lemmas 1 and 2, and illustrated by Example 1. Let $(X_j)_{1 \le j \le k}$ denote an unordered list $X_1, \ldots, X_k$.

Lemma 1. *Let $t_1 + \ldots + t_n$ be the normal form of t where each t_i is functional. Then every derivation δ of $P(t)$ in $\mathcal{A}/XOR$ has a functional support of the form $(P_i^j(t_i))_{1 \le i \le n, 1 \le j \le k_i}, (Q_i^j(u_i))_{1 \le i \le m, 1 \le j \le l_i}$ with $k_i \ge 1$ for $1 \le i \le n$, $m \ge 0$ and $l_i \ge 1$ for $1 \le i \le m$, such that, letting $S_i = \{P_i^j \mid 1 \le j \le k_i\}$ for $1 \le i \le n$ and letting $T_i = \{Q_i^j \mid 1 \le j \le l_i\}$ for $1 \le i \le m$, for all $U_1 \supseteq S_1, \ldots, U_n \supseteq S_n, V_1 \supseteq T_1, \ldots, V_m \supseteq T_m, Z \supseteq \{U_1, \ldots, U_n, V_1, \ldots, V_m\}$ we have $P(a_{U_1} + \ldots + a_{U_n}) \in \mathcal{X}_{\mathcal{A},Z}$.*

Lemma 2. *Let $P(a_{S_1} + \ldots + a_{S_n}) \in \mathcal{X}_{\mathcal{A},Z}$. Then $S_i \in Z$ for $1 \le i \le n$. If there are terms $t_1, \ldots, t_n$ such that $S_1(t_1), \ldots, S_n(t_n)$ are derivable in $\mathcal{A}/XOR$, and if for each $S \in Z$ there is some term t_S such that $S(t_S)$ is derivable in $\mathcal{A}/XOR$, then $P(t_1 + \ldots + t_n)$ is derivable in $\mathcal{A}/XOR$.*

Example 1. Let automaton $\mathcal{A}$ have following clauses:

$P_1(g(x)) \Leftarrow P_5(x)$	$P(x+y) \Leftarrow P_1(x) \wedge P_2(y)$	$P_5(f(x)) \Leftarrow P_6(x)$
$P_2(x+y) \Leftarrow P_3(x) \wedge P_4(y)$	$P_3(x) \Leftarrow P_7(x) \wedge P_8(x)$	$P_9(0)$
$P_4(x+y) \Leftarrow P_6(x) \wedge P_9(y)$	$P_6(a)$	$P_7(a)$	$P_8(a)$

$$\dfrac{\dfrac{\dfrac{P_6(a)}{P_5(f(a))}}{P_1(g(f(a)))} \quad \dfrac{\dfrac{P_7(a) \quad P_8(a)}{P_3(a)} \quad \dfrac{P_6(a) \quad P_9(0)}{P_4(a)}}{P_2(a+a)}}{\dfrac{P(g(f(a)) + a + a)}{P(g(f(a)))}}$$

Here is a possible derivation in $\mathcal{A}/XOR$. Its functional support is $P_1(g(f(a)))$, $P_7(a), P_8(a), P_6(a)$. Also $P(a_{\{P_1\}}) \in \mathcal{X}_{\mathcal{A},\{\{P_1\},\{P_7,P_8,P_6\}\}}$.

3   Branching Vector Plus-Minimum Systems

We will see that alternating XOR automata are naturally related to Branching Vector Plus-Minimum System (BVPMS). Fix some $1 \leq r \in \mathbb{N}$. We will be dealing with non-negative r-tuples (i.e. elements of $\mathbb{N}^r$). A *BVPMS* on some finite set $\mathbb{Q}$ of states is defined to be a finite set of clauses of the following form, called *constant clauses*, *addition clauses* and *minimum clauses* respectively, where P, P_i's are from $\mathbb{Q}$, x, y are distinct variables, and $x_1, \ldots, x_n$ are mutually distinct variables.

$$P(\nu) \qquad\qquad (\nu \in \{0,1\}^r) \qquad (6) \qquad P(x+y) \Leftarrow P_1(x) \wedge P_2(y) \quad (7)$$

$$P(x_1 \sqcap \ldots \sqcap x_n) \Leftarrow P_1(x_1) \wedge \ldots \wedge P_n(x_n)(n \geq 1) \qquad\qquad (8)$$

A *configuration* is of the form $P(\nu)$ for $P \in \mathbb{Q}$ and $\nu \in \mathbb{N}^r$. As for tree automata, we can read it as 'ν is accepted at P'. *Derivations* of configurations in BVPMS are inductively defined in a similar way as derivations of atoms in equational tree automata. We interpret $+$ as componentwise addition of r-tuples, and $\sqcap$ as componentwise minimum. Then by instantiating all the variables in a clause by r-tuples, if the resulting configurations in the tail are derivable then the resulting configuration in the head is said to be derivable. The restriction $\nu \in \{0,1\}^r$ in clause (6) is for the complexity results. Using clauses (6) and (7), we can clearly express clauses $P'(\nu')$ for arbitrary $\nu' \in \mathbb{N}^r$.

Lemma 3. *The emptiness problem for BVPMS, i.e. the question whether some state accepts no tuple, is decidable in polynomial time.*

From XOR Automata to BVPMS. The minimum clauses allow us to model the alternation clauses of automata in presence of the cancellation axiom of XOR. Let $\mathcal{A}$ be an alternating XOR automaton on a finite set of states $\mathbb{P}$. Let $\mathcal{Z}_\mathbb{P}$ and p be as in Section 2. We use a BVPMS $\mathcal{V}$ on p-tuples to compute the sets $\mathcal{X}_{\mathcal{A},Z}$. (The parameter r above is instantiated to p). The set of states of $\mathcal{V}$ is $\mathbb{Q} = \mathbb{P} \times \{0,1\}^p \times 2^{\mathcal{Z}_\mathbb{P}}$. The configuration $(P, \nu', Z)(\nu)$ represents the fact that $P(\nu) \in \mathcal{X}_{\mathcal{A},Z}$ and $\nu' = \nu^*$. The intuition is that Rules 2 and 5 in the definition of sets $\mathcal{X}_{\mathcal{A},Z}$ can be represented by minimum clauses. However we should not take the minimum of an even number with an odd number. This is controlled by ν' in the state (P, ν', Z). The clauses of $\mathcal{V}$ are as listed below. Note that by the conventions of Section 2, $a_S \in \{0,1\}^p$ in item (iii). We use the parameter c_1 to denote the maximum size of any clause in $\mathcal{A}$, the size of a clause being the number of atoms in it, and c_2 to denote the number of clauses in $\mathcal{A}$. The corresponding parameters for BVPMS are v_1 and v_2. Without loss of generality we assume that in clause (3), $P_1, \ldots, P_n$ are mutually distinct. We have $|\mathbb{Q}| = 2^{2^{O(|\mathbb{P}|)}}$, $v_1 = O(|\mathbb{P}|)$, and $v_2 = c_2 \cdot 2^{2^{O(|\mathbb{P}|)}}$. $\mathcal{V}$ is computable in time $c_2 \cdot 2^{2^{O(|\mathbb{P}|)}}$.

(i) $(P, 0, Z)(0)$ for each $Z \subseteq \mathcal{Z}_\mathbb{P}$ and clause $P(0) \in \mathcal{A}$	**(iii)** $(P, a_S, Z)(a_S)$ for each $P \in S \in Z \subseteq \mathcal{Z}_\mathbb{P}$.
(ii) $(P, (\nu_1 + \nu_2)^*, Z)(x + y) \Leftarrow (P_1, \nu_1, Z)(x) \wedge (P_2, \nu_2, Z)(y)$ for each $\nu_1, \nu_2 \in \{0,1\}^p$, $Z \subseteq \mathcal{Z}_\mathbb{P}$ and clause $P(x+y) \Leftarrow P_1(x) \wedge P_2(y) \in \mathcal{A}$.	**(iv)** $(P, \nu, Z)(x_1 \sqcap \ldots \sqcap x_n) \Leftarrow (P_1, \nu, Z)(x_1) \wedge \ldots \wedge (P_n, \nu, Z)(x_n)$ for each $\nu \in \{0,1\}^p, Z \subseteq \mathcal{Z}_\mathbb{P}$ and clause $P(x) \Leftarrow P_1(x) \wedge \ldots \wedge P_n(x) \in \mathcal{A}$.

Lemma 4. *We have the following results:*
(i) If $P(\nu) \in \mathcal{X}_{A,Z}$ then for some ν', $(P, \nu^*, Z)(\nu')$ is derivable in $\mathcal{V}$ and $\nu \leq_{xor} \nu'$.
(ii) If $(P, \nu', Z)(\nu)$ is derivable in $\mathcal{V}$ then $P(\nu) \in \mathcal{X}_{A,Z}$ and $\nu' = \nu^*$.

This relation between BVPMS and sets $\mathcal{X}_{A,Z}$, together with the relation between sets $\mathcal{X}_{A,Z}$ and derivations in $\mathcal{A}$ as stated by Lemmas 1 and 2, are the basis of all results about alternating XOR automata in this paper. First we show how to decide emptiness of the latter. Recall that *propositional Horn clauses* are of the form $X \Leftarrow X_1 \wedge \ldots \wedge X_n$ where X, X_i's are *propositions*. Derivations of propositions using a set of propositional Horn clauses are inductively defined as usual. Let $\mathcal{A}$ and $\mathcal{V}$ be as above. Introduce proposition X_S for $S \in \mathcal{Z}_{\mathbb{P}}$, and define a set H of propositional Horn clause to contain:

(i) clause $X_S \Leftarrow X_{S_1} \wedge \ldots \wedge X_{S_n}$, where $S = \{P^1, \ldots, P^k\}$, $S_i = \{P_i^1, \ldots, P_i^k\}$ for $1 \leq i \leq n$, and $P^j(f(x_1, \ldots, x_n)) \Leftarrow P_1^j(x_1) \wedge \ldots \wedge P_n^j(x_n) \in \mathcal{A}_{free}$ for $1 \leq j \leq k$
(ii) clause $X_S \Leftarrow \bigwedge_{T \in Z} X_T$, where for some $\nu' \in \{0, 1\}^p$, for all $P \in Z$, the state (P, ν', Z) is non-empty in $\mathcal{V}$.

Then X_S is derivable from H iff S has non-empty intersection. Clauses (i) are standard. Clauses (ii) take care of permutations and cancellations using the XOR axioms.

Theorem 1. *Emptiness of alternating XOR automata is decidable in 2EXPTIME.*

Eliminating alternation requires more work. The *coverability set* of BVPMS is (some finite representation of) the downward closure of the set of derivable configurations, for the following ordering on configurations: $P(\nu) \leq P'(\nu')$ iff $P = P'$ and $\nu \leq \nu'$, where $\leq$ also denotes the component-wise ordering on tuples. Since the sets $\mathcal{X}_{A,Z}$ are downward closed (for an ordering on configurations based on $\leq_{xor}$), our main interest is in the coverability set of $\mathcal{V}$. For this we use a pumping lemma.

4   A Pumping Lemma for BVPMS

Fix a BVPMS $\mathcal{V}$ on r-tuples on a finite set of states $\mathcal{Q}$. We will show that if a certain component in a derivable configuration exceeds $2^{|\mathcal{Q}|}$ then it can become arbitrarily large. We use a pumping argument which iterates certain portions of the derivation. Compared to usual pumping arguments, the main difficulty here is that we need to do simultaneous pumping on several (possibly overlapping) parts of the derivation. For example in clauses (8), in order to *strictly* increase $x_1 \sqcap \ldots \sqcap x_n$ in some lth component, we have to ensure that *each* x_i strictly increases in the lth component. At the same time we have to take care that the other components do not decrease while pumping. Also note that because of the minimum clauses, the values of configurations need not increase and might even decrease if an observer goes from a node in a derivation towards the root.

An *Add-Min Tree (AMT)* in $\mathcal{V}$ is a finite tree $\mathcal{T}$, each of whose nodes is labeled with an element of $\mathcal{Q}$, and each of whose edges is labeled with some $\nu \in \mathbb{N}^r$. Instead of pumping directly on the derivations in $\mathcal{V}$, we will compute AMTs which pick out those paths on which we will pump. The values from other paths will label the edges. AMTs are what we will pump on. As usual, positions (or nodes) in an AMT are described using strings of positive integers. The empty string λ is the root node. The k children of a node

α are $\alpha \cdot 1, \ldots, \alpha \cdot k$. The state labeling the node α is denoted $\theta_T(\alpha)$. For all notations we define, we omit the AMTs in subscripts if there is no confusion. If β is a descendant of some node α then the *distance* from α to β, denoted $d_T(\alpha, \beta)$ is the sum of the labels of all the edges on the path from α to β. An AMT T is *feasible* if for every non-leaf node α with k children, if $(\theta(\alpha \cdot i))(\nu_i)$ is derivable in V for some ν_i for $1 \le i \le k$, then $(\theta(\alpha))(\bigsqcap_{1 \le i \le k}(\nu_i + d(\alpha, \alpha \cdot i)))$ is derivable in V. A *valued AMT* is an AMT T together with a label $\omega_T(\alpha) \in \mathbb{N}^r$ for every node α of T, such that, if α is a non-leaf node with k children then $\omega(\alpha) = \bigsqcap_{1 \le i \le k}(\omega(\alpha \cdot i) + d(\alpha, \alpha \cdot i))$, and if α is a leaf node then $(\theta(\alpha))(\omega(\alpha))$ is derivable in V. From definitions:

Lemma 5. *For a node α in a valued feasible AMT T, $(\theta(\alpha))(\omega(\alpha))$ is derivable in V.*

As addition distributes over minimum, we have:

Lemma 6. *In a valued AMT T, for every node α we have*
$$\omega(\alpha) = \bigsqcap_{\beta \text{ is a leaf in the subtree rooted at } \alpha}(\omega(\beta) + d(\alpha, \beta)).$$

For $1 \le l \le r$, we say $\nu_1 <_l \nu_2$ to mean that $\nu_1 \le \nu_2$ and $\nu_1[l] < \nu_2[l]$. Given two (possibly valued) AMTs T_1 and T_2, we say $T_1 <_l T_2$ to mean that $\theta_{T_1}(\lambda) = \theta_{T_2}(\lambda)$, and for every leaf node α of T_2, there is a leaf node β of T_1, such that $\theta_{T_1}(\beta) = \theta_{T_2}(\alpha)$ and $d_{T_1}(\lambda, \beta) <_l d_{T_2}(\lambda, \alpha)$.

Lemma 7. *Let T_1 be a valued AMT and T_2 a feasible AMT such that $T_1 <_l T_2$. Then $(\theta_{T_2}(\lambda))(\nu)$ is derivable in V for some ν such that $\omega_{T_1}(\lambda) <_l \nu$.*

Proof. (Sketch:) For each leaf node α of T_2 let β_α be a leaf node of T_1 such that $\theta_{T_1}(\beta_\alpha) = \theta_{T_2}(\alpha)$ and $d_{T_1}(\lambda, \beta_\alpha) <_l d_{T_2}(\lambda, \alpha)$. We transform T_2 into a valued AMT by defining $\omega_{T_2}(\alpha)$ for each node α of T_2. We do this by induction on the height of α. If α is a leaf, we define $\omega_{T_2}(\alpha) = \omega_{T_1}(\beta_\alpha)$. If α is a non-leaf node with k children, we define $\omega_{T_2}(\alpha) = \bigsqcap_{1 \le i \le k}(\omega_{T_2}(\alpha.i) + d_{T_2}(\alpha, \alpha.i))$. Clearly this makes T_2 a valued AMT. From Lemma 5, $(\theta_{T_2}(\lambda))\omega_{T_2}(\lambda)$ is derivable. We now use Lemma 6 and arithmetic properties of minimum to show that $\omega_{T_1}(\lambda) <_l \omega_{T_2}(\lambda)$.   □

We call a node α of an AMT T an *l-major node* if every edge out of α has a label ν with $0 <_l \nu$. Otherwise α is an *l-minor node*. Trivially a leaf node is always l-major. We use l-major nodes for pumping in AMTs:

Lemma 8. *Let T be a feasible AMT such that every leaf node α has a strict ancestor (call it β_α) which is l-major, such that $\theta_T(\beta_\alpha) = \theta_T(\alpha)$. Then there is a feasible AMT T' with $T <_l T'$.*

Proof. Let AMT T' be obtained from T by replacing each leaf node α by the subtree of T at position β_α. T' is feasible since T is feasible and $\theta_T(\beta_\alpha) = \theta_T(\alpha)$. To show that $T <_l T'$, pick any leaf node γ of T'. We have to find a leaf node β of T such that $\theta_T(\beta) = \theta_{T'}(\alpha)$

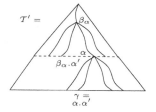

and $d_T(\lambda, \beta) <_l d_{T'}(\lambda, \alpha)$. By construction, there is a leaf node α of T and a string α' such that $\gamma = \alpha \cdot \alpha'$, $d_T(\beta_\alpha, \beta_\alpha \cdot \alpha') = d_{T'}(\alpha, \gamma)$ and $\theta_T(\beta_\alpha \cdot \alpha') = \theta_{T'}(\gamma)$. We show that the required β is $\beta_\alpha \cdot \alpha'$. As β_α is a strict major ancestor of α we have $0 <_l d_T(\beta_\alpha, \alpha)$. Hence $d_T(\lambda, \beta_\alpha \cdot \alpha') <_l d_T(\lambda, \beta_\alpha \cdot \alpha') + d_T(\beta_\alpha, \alpha) = d_T(\lambda, \beta_\alpha) + d_T(\beta_\alpha, \beta_\alpha \cdot \alpha') + d_T(\beta_\alpha, \alpha) = d_{T'}(\lambda, \beta_\alpha) + d_{T'}(\alpha, \gamma) + d_{T'}(\beta_\alpha, \alpha) = d_{T'}(\lambda, \gamma)$.   □

Observe that in the above proof we pump on every path of T. The pumping lemma is now proved below. Given a derivation of a configuration in which the lth component is large enough, we compute a suitable AMT in which every path has large enough number of l-major nodes, allowing us to do pumping.

Lemma 9. *If $P(\nu)$ is derivable in V and $\nu[l] \geq 2^{|\mathbb{Q}|}$ then $P(\nu')$ is derivable in V for some $\nu <_l \nu'$.*

Proof. Given some derivation δ of some atom $Q(\mu)$ in V, we define a valued feasible AMT T_δ by recursion on δ. T looks almost the same as δ except that when a node of δ uses an addition clause, then in T_δ we selectively forget one of the children, and the corresponding tuple is used as an edge label. The construction is such that the root of T_δ is labeled with Q and μ. The construction is as follows:

(i) If δ is the derivation of $Q(\mu)$ by applying the clause $Q(\mu)$, then T_δ is a leaf labeled Q and μ.

(ii) If δ is the derivation of $Q(\mu_1 \sqcap \ldots \sqcap \mu_k)$, using a minimum clause, from the derivations δ_i of $Q_i(\mu_i)$ for $1 \leq i \leq k$, then T_δ has the root node λ labeled with Q and $\mu_1 \sqcap \ldots \sqcap \mu_k$, has k children $T_{\delta_1}, \ldots, T_{\delta_k}$, and each edge out of λ is labeled 0.

(iii) If δ is the derivation of $Q(\mu_1 + \mu_2)$ using an addition clause, from the derivations δ_1 and δ_2 of $Q_1(\mu_1)$ and $Q_2(\mu_1)$ respectively, then assume $\mu_1[l] \leq \mu_2[l]$. (The case $\mu_2[l] \leq \mu_1[l]$ is treated similarly.) Then T_δ has the root node λ labeled with Q and $\mu_1 + \mu_2$, has one child T_{δ_2}, and the edge out of λ is labeled μ_1.

Clearly T_δ is valued and feasible. The first step produces an l-major (leaf) node. The second step creates an l-minor node. The third step creates an l-major node iff $\mu_1[l] > 0$. Thus T_δ has the property that if β is a child of α then:

(i) If α is l-minor then $\omega(\beta)[l] \geq \omega(\alpha)[l]$.   (ii) If α is l-major then $2\omega(\beta)[l] \geq \omega(\alpha)[l]$.

Hence for any $i \geq 1$, if α is the ith l-major node on any path from the root, then $2^{i-1} \cdot \omega(\alpha)[l] \geq \omega(\lambda)[l]$. Now let δ' be a derivation in V of the atom $P(\nu)$. Let $T = T_{\delta'}$. Since $\nu[l] \geq 2^{|\mathbb{Q}|}$, and since by construction $\omega_T(\alpha) \leq 1$ for any leaf node α, hence every maximal path ξ in T contains at least $|\mathbb{Q}| + 1$ distinct l-major nodes. Hence at least two of them should be labeled with the same state. Let them be at the (distinct) positions α_ξ and $\alpha_\xi \cdot \beta_\xi$. Let T_1 be the AMT obtained from T by chopping off the subtree below position $\alpha_\xi \cdot \beta_\xi$ for each maximal path ξ of T. Since T is valued and feasible, by Lemma 5, T_1 is also valued and feasible. For every leaf position γ of T_1, there is some maximal path ξ of T such that $\gamma = \alpha_\xi \cdot \beta_\xi$. Hence every γ has a strict major ancestor labeled with the same state. By Lemma 8 there is a feasible AMT T_2 such that $T_1 <_l T_2$. The result then follows from Lemma 7.   □

Repeated applications of Lemma 9 allows us to show:

Theorem 2. *If $P(\nu)$ is derivable in $\mathcal{V}$ and $\nu[I] \geq 2^{|Q|}$, where $I \subseteq \{1,\ldots,r\}$, then for any number K there is some $\nu' \geq \nu$ such that $P(\nu')$ is derivable in $\mathcal{V}$ and $\nu'[I] \geq K$.*

Computing the Coverability Set. The pumping lemma allows us to compute the coverability set for BVPMS. Define $\nu^\sharp \in (\mathbb{N} \cup \{\infty\})^r$ for $\nu \in \mathbb{N}^r$ as: $\nu^\sharp[i] = \infty$ if $\nu[i] \geq 2^{|Q|}$ and $\nu^\sharp[i] = \nu[i]$ otherwise. We extend $+, \sqcap$ and $\leq$ by letting $n + \infty = \infty + \infty = \infty$, $n \sqcap \infty = n$, $\infty \sqcap \infty = \infty$, $n \leq \infty$ and $\infty \leq \infty$ for $n \in \mathbb{N}$. They are extended to r-tuples as usual. Define set $C_\mathcal{V} = \{P(\nu^\sharp) \mid P(\nu) \text{ is derivable in } \mathcal{V}\}$.

Lemma 10. *$C_\mathcal{V}$ is the coverability set of $\mathcal{V}$, in the sense that*
(i) If $P(\nu) \in C_\mathcal{V}$ and $\nu \geq \nu' \in \mathbb{N}^r$ then there is some $\nu'' \geq \nu'$ such that $P(\nu'')$ is derivable in $\mathcal{V}$.
(ii) If $P(\nu)$ is derivable in $\mathcal{V}$ then $\nu \leq \nu'$ for some $P(\nu') \in C_\mathcal{V}$.

Theorem 3. *The coverability set of BVPMS can be computed in EXPTIME.*

5   Eliminating Alternation

Let $\mathcal{A}$ be an alternating XOR automaton on a finite set of states $\mathbb{P}$. We define a corresponding BVPMS $\mathcal{V}$ on set of states $\mathbb{Q}$ as in Section 3. Let $\mathcal{Z}_\mathbb{P} = \{\mathbb{S}_1,\ldots,\mathbb{S}_p\}$ as in Section 2. We now define an equivalent one-way XOR automaton $\mathcal{B}$. We will need clauses of the form $P(x_1 + \ldots + x_n) \Leftarrow P_1(x_1) \wedge \ldots \wedge P_n(x_n)$ which are translatable in linear time to clauses of one-way automata by using some auxiliary states. We also need *extended ϵ-clauses* of the form $P(x) \Leftarrow P_1(x) \wedge Q_1(y_1) \wedge \ldots \wedge Q_n(y_n)$ where $x, y_1, \ldots, y_n$ are mutually distinct variables. This can be thought of as the ϵ clause $P(x) \Leftarrow P_1(x)$ together with emptiness tests on states $Q_1, \ldots, Q_n$. As emptiness for one-way equational tree automata is decidable in polynomial time [22, 20], these clauses do not increase the expressiveness of one-way equational tree automata and can be eliminated in polynomial time [22, 20]. The states of $\mathcal{B}$ are of the form $(S, \nu', Z, (\nu_P)_{P \in S})$ and $\overline{S}$ for $S \in \mathcal{Z}_\mathbb{P}$, $\nu' \in \{0,1\}^p$, $Z \subseteq \mathcal{Z}_\mathbb{P}$ and tuples $\nu_P \in (\mathbb{N} \cup \{\infty\})^p$ such that $(P, \nu', Z)(\nu_P) \in C_\mathcal{V}$ for each $P \in S$. State $\overline{S}$ is supposed to accept the terms accepted at each state in S. The clauses added to $\mathcal{B}$ are as follows. We would have liked $\mathcal{B}$ to contain the clause $\overline{S}(x_1 + \ldots + x_n) \Leftarrow \overline{S}_1(x_1) \wedge \ldots \wedge \overline{S}_n(x_n) \wedge \bigwedge_{T \in Z} \overline{T}(y_T)$ if $P(a_{S_1} + \ldots + a_{S_n}) \in \mathcal{X}_{\mathcal{A},Z}$ for each $P \in S$. However $\mathcal{X}_{\mathcal{A},Z}$ may be infinite. Hence we use states $(S, \nu', Z, (\nu_P)_{P \in S})$, and clauses (1a) and (1c), together with the loops in clauses (1b) to achieve this effect. Clauses (2) are standard.

(1) For each state $(S, \nu', Z, (\nu_P)_{P \in S})$ (call it $\mathcal{S}$) of $\mathcal{B}$, let $\nu = \bigsqcap_{P \in S} \nu_P$. Let $I = \{i \mid \nu[i] = \infty\}$ and $J = \{1,\ldots,p\} \setminus I$. We add to $\mathcal{B}$ the clauses

   (a) $\mathcal{S}(\sum_{i \in I, \nu'[i]=1} x_i + \sum_{i \in J} \sum_{j=1}^{n_i} x_i^j) \Leftarrow \bigwedge_{i \in I, \nu'[i]=1} \overline{\mathbb{S}}_i(x_i) \wedge \bigwedge_{i \in J} \bigwedge_{j=1}^{n_i} \overline{\mathbb{S}}_i(x_i^j)$
   for n_i's such that $n_i \leq_{xor} \nu[i]$.
   (b) $\mathcal{S}(x + y + z) \Leftarrow \mathcal{S}(x) \wedge \overline{\mathbb{S}}_i(y) \wedge \overline{\mathbb{S}}_i(z)$ for each $i \in I$,
   (c) the extended ϵ-clause $\overline{S}(x) \Leftarrow \mathcal{S}(x) \wedge \bigwedge_{T \in Z} \overline{T}(y_T)$.

(2) For each free f and clauses $P^i(f(x_1,\ldots,x_n)) \Leftarrow P_1^i(x_1) \wedge \ldots \wedge P_n^i(x_n) \in \mathcal{A}$ for $1 \leq i \leq k$, we add to $\mathcal{B}$ the clause $\overline{S}(f(x_1,\ldots,x_n)) \Leftarrow \overline{S}_1(x_1) \wedge \ldots \wedge \overline{S}_n(x_n)$ where $S = \{P^1,\ldots,P^k\}$ and for $1 \leq i \leq n$, $S_i = \{P_i^1,\ldots,P_i^k\}$.

The purpose of the clauses (1a) and (1b) is to accept at S a summation of terms accepted at the $\overline{S}_i$'s. For $i \in I$, the number of summands from $\overline{S}_i$ is an arbitrarily large even or odd number with characteristic $\nu'[i]$. For $i \in J$ the number of summands from $\overline{S}_i$ is some $n_i \leq_{xor} \nu[i]$. We do so because the elements of $C_{\mathcal{V}}$ can be considered as 'limits' of elements of $\mathcal{X}_{A,Z}$'s. If P_f is the final state of $\mathcal{A}$ then $\overline{\{P_f\}}$ is the final state of $\mathcal{B}$. Now since alternating automata are trivially closed under intersection, and one-way XOR automata are not closed under complementation [21]:

Theorem 4. *Alternating XOR automata can be converted to equivalent one-way XOR automata in 3EXPTIME. The class of languages accepted by them is same as that accepted by one-way XOR automata, is closed under intersection, but not closed under complementation.*

6   Eliminating General Two-Wayness

Let $\mathcal{A}$ be an alternating general two-way XOR automaton on a finite set of states $\mathbb{P}$. Define BVPMS $\mathcal{V}$ as in Section 3. In the absence of alternation clauses, and with restriction $i \notin \{i_1, \dots, i_k\}$ in clauses (5), these automata have been shown to be equivalent to one-way XOR automata in [22]. The case of alternation clauses was open. Also clauses (5) without restriction can encode alternation [22] and the question of its decidability was open. We now show decidability in presence of all these clauses. The standard 'saturation' procedure in the non-equational case 'short-cuts' pop and general push clauses to get new alternation clauses, till the general push clauses become redundant. The problematic $+$-pop clauses are now dealt with using BVPMS. For example, given clauses $R(x) \Leftarrow Q(f(x,y)) \wedge P^1(x) \wedge P^2(y)$, $Q(x+y) \Leftarrow P_1(x) \wedge Q'(y)$, $Q'(x+y) \Leftarrow P_2(x) \wedge P_3(y)$ and $P_1(f(x,y)) \Leftarrow Q_1(x) \wedge Q_2(y)$, we can infer the clause $R(x) \Leftarrow Q_1(x) \wedge P^1(x)$, provided that $\{P^2, Q_2\}$ has non-empty intersection, and $\{P_2, P_3\}$ has non-empty intersection. Formally for any alternating general two-way automaton $\mathcal{A}'$, let automaton $\mathcal{A}'_{alt}$ consist of clauses (1-4) of $\mathcal{A}'$. If

(i) $\mathcal{A}$ contains a general push clause $R(x_l) \Leftarrow Q(f(x_1, \dots, x_n)) \wedge \bigwedge_{i=1}^{n} \bigwedge_{j=1}^{k_i} P_i^j(x_i)$,
(ii) (Q, a_S, Z) is non-empty in $\mathcal{V}$ for some S, Z,
(iii) $P(f(x_1, \dots, x_n)) \Leftarrow Q_1^P(x_1) \wedge \dots \wedge Q_n^P(x_n) \in \mathcal{A}$ for some Q_i^P's for each $P \in S$
(iv) the set $\{P_i^j \mid 1 \leq j \leq k_i\} \cup \{Q_i^P \mid P \in S\}$ has non-empty intersection in $\mathcal{A}_{alt}/XOR$ for $i \in \{1, \dots, n\} \setminus \{l\}$
(v) each $T \in Z$ has non empty intersection in $\mathcal{A}_{alt}/XOR$

then consider the clause $C = R(x_l) \Leftarrow \bigwedge_{j=1}^{k_l} P_l^j(x_l) \wedge \bigwedge_{P \in S} Q_l^P(x_l)$. If $C \notin \mathcal{A}$ then we write $\mathcal{A} \rhd \mathcal{A} \cup \{C\}$, which we take to constitute one step of our saturation procedure. Arbitrarily many applications of clauses (1-3) may occur in between the applications of the free pop clauses and the general push clause. However after cancellations using the XOR axiom, only a functional term should be left. This is checked by condition (ii). Conditions (iv) and (v) can be effectively checked by Theorem 1.

Given any alternating general two-way automaton $\mathcal{A}$ our saturation procedure now consists of (don't care non-deterministically) generating a sequence $(\mathcal{A} =)\mathcal{A}_0 \rhd \mathcal{A}_1 \rhd \mathcal{A}_2 \dots$ until no new clauses can be added. This terminates because only finitely many alternation clauses are possible. Let the final saturated automaton be $\mathcal{C}$. We remove all general push clauses to get alternating automaton $\mathcal{C}_{alt}$ equivalent to $\mathcal{A}$.

Theorem 5. *Alternating general two-way XOR automata can be converted to equivalent one-way XOR automata in 3EXPTIME. The class of languages accepted by them is same as that accepted by one-way XOR automata, is closed under intersection, but not closed under complementation.*

7   Conclusion

We have given a positive answer to the open question of the decidability of alternating general two-way XOR automata, in contrast to previous negative answers in case of other theories. We have given 3EXPTIME reduction of these automata to one-way XOR automata, thus also settling the expressiveness and closure properties of these automata. We have shown that emptiness of these automata is decidable in 2EXPTIME, meaning that secrecy of protocols modeled using these automata is decidable in 2EXPTIME. Emptiness test for alternating general two-way XOR automata is trivially EXPTIME-hard, but a more precise characterization of its complexity remains to be done. A key technique of independent interest is a pumping lemma for Branching Vector Plus Minimum Systems, allowing us to compute their coverability sets in EXPTIME.

Acknowledgments. I thank Helmut Seidl for many discussions and suggestions, and Jean Goubault-Larrecq as well as the anonymous referees for valuable comments.

References

1. Y. Chevalier, R. Küsters, M. Rusinowitch, and M. Turuani. Deciding the security of protocols with Diffie-Hellman exponentiation and products in exponents. In *FSTTCS'03*, pages 124–135. Springer-Verlag LNCS 2914, 2003.
2. Y. Chevalier, R. Küsters, M. Rusinowitch, and M. Turuani. An NP decision procedure for protocol insecurity with XOR. In *LICS'03*, pages 261–270, 2003.
3. H. Comon and V. Cortier. Tree automata with one memory, set constraints and cryptographic protocols. *Theoretical Computer Science*, 2004. To appear.
4. H. Comon, M. Dauchet, R. Gilleron, F. Jacquemard, D. Lugiez, S. Tison, and M. Tommasi. Tree automata techniques and applications. http://www.grappa.univ-lille3.fr/tata, 1997.
5. H. Comon-Lundh and V. Cortier. New decidability results for fragments of first-order logic and application to cryptographic protocols. In *RTA'03*, pages 148–164. Springer-Verlag LNCS 2706, 2003.
6. V. Cortier. *Vérification Automatique des Protocoles Cryptographiques*. Ph.D. thesis, ENS Cachan, France, 2003.
7. F. Gécseg and M. Steinby. Tree languages. In G. Rozenberg and A. Salomaa, editors, *Handbook of Formal Languages*, volume 3, chapter 1, pages 1–68. Springer-Verlag, 1997.
8. J. Goubault-Larrecq. A method for automatic cryptographic protocol verification. In *FMPPTA'00*, pages 977–984. Springer-Verlag LNCS 1800, 2000.

9. J. Goubault-Larrecq. Une fois qu'on n'a pas trouvé de preuve, comment le faire comprendre à un assistant de preuve? In V. Ménissier-Morain, editor, *Actes des 12èmes Journées Francophones des Langages Applicatifs (JFLA'04)*. INRIA, collection didactique, 2004.

10. J. Goubault-Larrecq, M. Roger, and K. N. Verma. Abstraction and resolution modulo AC: How to verify Diffie-Hellman-like protocols automatically. *Journal of Logic and Algebraic Programming*, 2004. To Appear. Available as Research Report LSV-04-7, LSV, ENS Cachan.

11. J. Hopcroft and J. J. Pansiot. On the reachability problem for 5-dimensional vector addition systems. *Theoretical Computer Science*, 8:135–159, 1979.

12. R. M. Karp and R. E. Miller. Parallel program schemata. *J. Computer and System Sciences*, 3(2):147–195, 1969.

13. D. Lugiez. Counting and equality constraints for multitree automata. In *FOSSACS'03*, pages 328–342. Springer-Verlag LNCS 2620, 2003.

14. D. Monniaux. Abstracting cryptographic protocols with tree automata. In *SAS'99*, pages 149–163. Springer-Verlag LNCS 1694, 1999.

15. H. Ohsaki. Beyond regularity: Equational tree automata for associative and commutative theories. In *CSL'01*, pages 539–553. Springer-Verlag LNCS 2142, 2001.

16. L. C. Paulson. Mechanized proofs for a recursive authentication protocol. In *CSFW'97*, pages 84–95. IEEE Computer Society Press, 1997.

17. P. Ryan and S. Schneider. An attack on a recursive authentication protocol: A cautionary tale. *Information Processing Letters*, 65(1):7–10, 1998.

18. G. Slutzki. Alternating tree automata. *Theoretical Computer science*, 41:305–318, 1985.

19. M. Steiner, G. Tsudik, and M. Waidner. Key agreement in dynamic peer groups. *IEEE Transactions on Parallel and Distributed Systems*, 11(8):769–780, 2000.

20. K. N. Verma. *Automates d'arbres bidirectionnels modulo théories équationnelles*. Ph.D. thesis, ENS Cachan, 2003.

21. K. N. Verma. On closure under complementation of equational tree automata for theories extending AC. In *LPAR'03*, pages 183–197. Springer-Verlag LNCS 2850, 2003.

22. K. N. Verma. Two-way equational tree automata for AC-like theories: Decidability and closure properties. In *RTA'03*, pages 180–196. Springer-Verlag LNCS 2706, 2003.

23. K. N. Verma and J. Goubault-Larrecq. Karp-Miller trees for a branching extension of VASS. Research Report LSV-04-3, LSV, ENS Cachan, France, January 2004.

Author Index

Lecture Notes in Computer Science

For information about Vols. 1–3242

please contact your bookseller or Springer